THE CRICKET WHO'S WHO 2004

Introduction by
MARTYN BALL

Edited by
CHRIS MARSHALL

Statistics by
RICHARD LOCKWOOD

Photographs by
GETTY IMAGES
and
BILL SMITH

Queen Anne Press

QUEEN ANNE PRESS
a division of Lennard Associates Limited
Mackerye End, Harpenden, Herts AL5 5DR

Published in association with
The Cricketers' Who's Who Limited

First published in Great Britain 2004

British Library Cataloguing in Publication is available

ISBN 1 85291 656 7

Typeset in Times and Univers Condensed
Editor (for Queen Anne Press): Kirsty Ennever
Quiz compiled by Peter Brierley
Cover design by Paul Cooper

Printed and bound by
The Bath Press

ACKNOWLEDGEMENTS

Cover photographs by Getty Images
Some of the long-serving players with Benefits or Testimonials in 2004
Front cover: Jon Lewis, Chris Silverwood, Glen Chapple
Back: Adam Hollioake

The publishers would also like to thank the county clubs, the players
and their families for their assistance in helping to assemble
the information and photographs in this book.

Extra information has also been gathered from the pages of *The Cricketer*, *The Wisden
Cricketer*, *The Times*, *The Sunday Times,* CricInfo.com and CricketArchive.com

County photocall photographers for Getty Images:
Derbyshire/Ross Kinnaird; Durham/Laurence Griffiths; Essex/Clive Rose;
Glamorgan/Stu Forster; Gloucestershire/Shaun Botterill; Hampshire/Julian Herbert;
Kent/Mike Hewitt; Leicestershire/David Rogers; Northamptonshire/Mark Thompson;
Nottinghamshire/Ross Kinnaird; Somerset/Stu Forster; Surrey/Clive Rose;
Sussex/Mike Hewitt; Warwickshire/Gary M. Prior; Worcestershire/Ben Radford

Thanks also to the following for providing additional photographs:
Bucks Free Press, John Dawson Cricket Images, Derby Evening Telegraph,
Empics, Ken Grime, Harborough Mail, Vic Isaacs, Kent Messenger Group,
Greg Lansdowne, Middlesbrough Evening Gazette, Pete Norton,
Nottingham Evening Post, Portsmouth News, Nigel Stockley, Stoke Sentinel,
Mike Vimpany, Michael Waldron, Simon Wilkinson

CONTENTS

PCA Events

MAY 2nd
PCA Masters v New Zealand
Shenley Cricket Centre, Hertfordshire Ⓢ

MAY 19th
Marriott Eve of Test Dinner
including Celebrity Q&A
In association with the PCA and The Prince's Trust
Marriott Hotel Regents Park

JUNE 7th
CBI/PCA Sporting Gala Dinner
including Celebrity Q&A
The Royal Lancaster Hotel Ⓢ

JUNE 10th
PCA Corporate 6-a-side Cricket Day
The Lord's Nursery Ground Ⓢ

JULY 22nd & 23rd
PCA Business Partners
England v West Indies Test Match
Hospitality *including Carribean Party*
Marriott Hotel Regents Park & Lord's Cricket Ground Ⓢ

AUGUST 18th
PCA Corporate 6-a-side Challenge
J.P. Getty's Cricket Ground, Wormsley, Oxfordshire Ⓢ

SEPTEMBER 21st
PCA Players' Awards Evening
Royal Albert Hall - *the most prestigious
event in the cricketing calendar* Ⓢ

NOV 2004
PCA Masters
London v Bridgetown
Bridgetown Oval, Barbados Ⓢ

Ⓢ = Sponsorship information and opportunities

FOR EVENT HOSPITALITY AND SPONSORSHIP ENQUIRIES
**Fiona Holdsworth - 0207 544 8668
Lee Atkins - 0207 544 8670**

✳ cricnet.com
The Official Website Of The Professional Cricketers' Association

INTRODUCTION

Every journalist, TV pundit, radio presenter and even the tea lady at Wantage Road seems to have voiced their concerns during the past twelve months about the state of English cricket – none of them with anything very positive to say.

Without doubt, there are areas within cricket that need to be addressed. However, I firmly believe that the game I have passionately purveyed is not in dire straits but merely at a crossroads. It was after all only a couple of years ago that people were commenting on how rugby had got things wrong in its new professional era; how the domestic structure and the lack of detailed attention in preparing our national side were leaving England trailing behind the southern hemisphere. Need I say more?

Cricket has much to look forward to in 2004. Sussex defend the much prized crown of County Champions, Gloucestershire try to retain yet another one-day title in the Cheltenham & Gloucester Trophy, and Surrey have the enviable task of trying to keep their hands on the National League and Twenty20.

Internationally, Michael Vaughan's England team have fascinating challenges with home series against New Zealand and West Indies. Both visiting teams have world-class players with great experience of English conditions. And at the end of a gruelling summer, the eyes of the whole cricketing world will be on this country when we host the ICC Champions Trophy for the first time. Let's hope that the weather holds until the end of September, allowing the competition to be the spectacle it deserves to be.

A successful summer will hold us in good stead for the really testing period that follows, in which our national side will pit their skills against the two top-ranked teams in the world – against South Africa during winter 2004-05 and then against Australia in the Ashes series in summer 2005. Both these teams epitomise what

Duncan Fletcher, Nasser Hussain and now Michael Vaughan are trying to achieve, and if England have a successful eighteen months, we could emulate our rugby counterparts and stand top of the world rankings.

One thing is for sure – it will be a period of reviewing and decision-making on many cricketing issues. For that reason it is imperative that the stakeholders of the game communicate professionally and all work together. Communication lines between the ECB, the first-class counties and the game's main stakeholders, the players, have improved considerably. There is now a real sense of unity in trying to create a product that is the envy of the rest of the world.

As players we are very lucky to have a body that represents us so professionally in all aspects – the Professional Cricketers' Association (PCA). Our association and the services it is now able to offer the membership have grown enormously due to the dedication and commitment of past and present officers, and it is with great honour and responsibility that I now chair this association in aiming to fulfil the following objectives:

- To act as the collective and representative voice of the first-class cricketers in England
- To safeguard the rights of both present, past and future first-class cricketers
- To provide and improve the welfare of its members in key areas – insurance/education/legal/financial/benevolent/cricket representation
- To provide advice, services or assistance where deemed appropriate
- To pursue initiatives that will ultimately benefit the membership
- To promote the sport of cricket

The coming months will see many debates, various review groups and numerous journalistic panels recommending change to our domestic structure. All avenues must be explored and all opinions and proposals listened to and considered. The game needs to study all aspects of its finances and move ahead with well-constructed business plans. Decision-makers must communicate and respect all stakeholders of the game without allowing personal agendas to affect the outcome. It is vital that all parties work together.

It is the joint responsibility of all the stakeholders to ensure that the England team is supported and given every opportunity to become the strongest nation in world cricket. Along with the obvious financial support required, it is imperative that the National Academy, Regional Centres of Excellence and the County Championship regularly produce enough cricketers of quality for England to excel on the world stage.

This in no way means that county cricket is just a breeding ground or development vehicle. It should still be able to stand independently as a valued, competitive and exciting form of entertainment for all sport viewers and supporters throughout this country. Last year's success of the Twenty20 Cup shows that with careful consideration and planning, direct marketing to specific audiences and quality player participation we can produce a product with great credibility. So much so that other nations are now following our lead in this initiative – rather than the other way round, which until recently had always been the tendency.

One constant in all opinions is that we must have a domestic structure that allows the best players to play against the best. With such a high percentage of teams either promoted or relegated in both formats of the game it presently does not allow the concentration of talent to be maximised to the full. Whatever changes to our beloved game are recommended, the issue of concentrating talent must be the foremost objective. We have seen other countries and other sports where structural change has led to subsequent success, and addressing this issue has been fundamental in bringing about their improvement.

I am sure the ECB, the first-class counties and the PCA will continue to talk to each other and work closely together throughout this period of change.

Finally, I would like to take this opportunity to wish all my fellow cricketers, cricket supporters and everyone else involved in the game an enjoyable and successful 2004 season. If the decisions that are being called for are made diligently and professionally between all stakeholders of the game, there will be no need for pessimism and concern. Instead we will have a vibrant, exciting and financially viable product of which all involved in English cricket can be proud.

Martyn Ball
Chairman
The Professional Cricketers' Association
March 2004

PCA County Representatives:

Derbys	Kevin Dean	Middx	Simon Cook
Durham	Neil Killeen	Northants	Toby Bailey
Essex	Paul Grayson	Notts	Darren Bicknell
Glamorgan	Mark Wallace	Somerset	Keith Dutch
Glos	James Averis	Surrey	Ian Salisbury
Hants	James Hamblin	Sussex	Richard Montgomerie
Kent	Martin Saggers	Warwicks	Dougie Brown
Lancs	Mark Chilton	Worcs	Steve Rhodes
Leics	Paul Nixon	Yorks	Richard Dawson

BENEFITS AND TESTIMONIALS 2004

Durham
Jon Lewis Benefit
Brambledown
Brandon Village
Durham DH7 8SU
Secretary: Ian Johnson
0191 378 2288/07718 970758
ianjohnson@brambledown.com
www.jj2004.co.uk

Gloucestershire
Jack Russell Testimonial
41 High Street
Chipping Sodbury
BS37 6BA
Secretary: Jane Gardiner
07751 042914
jrtestimonial@hotmail.com

Kent
Min Patel Benefit
6 Doubleday Drive
Bapchild
Kent ME9 9PJ
Secretary: Carol Buck
01795 422165/07931 594221
carolwilsonbuck@aol.com

Lancashire
Glen Chapple Benefit
Chairman: Paul Beck
0161 929 5799
paulb@lbm.co.uk
www.glenchapplebenefit.co.uk

Leicestershire
Phillip DeFreitas Benefit
3 Freemans Lane
Burbage
Hinckley LE10 2HZ
Secretary: Cathy Bown
01455 632606/07733 136847
daffy.de-freitas@ntlworld.com

Nottinghamshire
Paul Johnson Testimonial
c/o Nottinghamshire CCC
Trent Bridge
Nottingham NG2 6AG
07932 680655
johno2004@hotmail.com
www.johnotestimonial.com

Somerset
Keith Parsons Benefit
c/o The County Ground
Taunton TA1 1JF
Secretary: Brian Daw
01823 442707
kparsonsbenefit@aol.com
www.kparsonsbenefit2004.com

Surrey
Adam Hollioake Benefit
12 Fawe Park Road, SW15 2EA
Secretary: Tawny Hazelwood
020 8874 9599
tawny@adamhollioake.com
www.adamhollioake.com

Sussex
Keith Greenfield Testimonial
81 Church Road
Hove BN3 2BB
Secretary: Ian Poysden
07774 623450/01273 208813
ian.poysden@allfieldfinancial.com
www.allfieldfinancial.com

Warwickshire
Nick Knight Benefit
66 Parkfield Road
Stourbridge DY8 1EY
Secretary: Sarah Guthrie
01384 396171
benefit@nickknight.eclipse.co.uk
www.nickknight.org

Worcestershire
Tom Moody Benefit
Sixways, Pershore Lane
Hindlip, Worcester WR3 8ZE
Secretary: Louise Brook
01905 459300
louise@wrfc.co.uk
www.tommoody.com

Yorkshire
Chris Silverwood Benefit
c/o 11 Knowl Road
Mirfield,West Yorks WF14 8DQ
Secretary: Victoria Mallalieu
07961 080758
victoria@chris-silverwood.co.uk
www.chris-silverwood.co.uk

Editor's Notes

The cricketers listed in this volume include all those who played 1st XI cricket for a first-class county at least once last season, in any form of cricket, and all those registered (at the time of going to press at the end of February) to play for the 18 first-class counties in 2004, even those who have yet to make a first-team appearance. All statistics are complete to the end of the last English season (the Stop press sections for individual players cover subsequent highlights). Figures about 1000 runs, 50 wickets and 50 dismissals in a season refer to matches in England only. All first-class figures include figures for Test matches, which are also extracted and listed separately. One-Day 100s and One-Day five wickets in an innings are for the English domestic competitions (including the now discontinued Benson and Hedges Cup) and all One-Day Internationals, home and abroad. Career records include 'rebel' tours to South Africa. In the interests of space 2003 statistics are not given for those whose appearances in first-class cricket or one-day competitions were only for teams other than the county for which they are now registered – i.e. universities, Board XIs, minor counties etc (excluding international cricketers on tours to England). These appearances are, however, reflected in their career statistics and reference is made in the Extras section to the team for which they played.

The figures for batting and bowling averages refer to the full first-class English list for 2003, followed in brackets by the 2002 figures. Inclusion in the batting averages depends on a minimum of six completed innings; a bowler has to have taken at least ten wickets and bowled in a minimum of six innings. Strike rate refers to a bowler's record of balls bowled per wicket taken.

The following abbreviations apply: ODI means One-Day International; * means not out. In statistics tables All First means all first-class matches; 1-day Int – One-Day Internationals; C&G – C&G Trophy (including NatWest); NCL – National Cricket League (including previous one-day and Sunday leagues); Twenty20 – Twenty20 Cup.

This year we have included a new category – Favourite band. We also welcome the Scottish Saltires, pen portraits of the 2004 squad appearing on pages 785-788. Please also note that Worcestershire ceased awarding caps in 2001 and now present 'colours' to each player who appears for the county in the Championship.

A book of this complexity and detail has to be prepared several months in advance of the cricket season, and occasionally there are recent changes in a player's circumstances or the structure of the game which cannot be included in time. Many examples of facts, statistics and even opinions which can quickly become outdated in the period between the compilation of the book and its publication, months later, will spring to the reader's mind, and I ask him or her to make the necessary commonsense allowance and adjustments.

Chris Marshall, March 2004

THE PLAYERS

ABDUL RAZZAQ — Middlesex

Name: Abdul Razzaq
Role: Right-hand bat, right-arm
fast-medium bowler
Born: 2 December 1979, Lahore
Height: 5ft 11in
County debut: 2002
Test debut: 1999-2000
Tests: 24
One-Day Internationals: 140
1st-Class 50s: 16
1st-Class 100s: 6
1st-Class 200s: 1
1st-Class 5 w. in innings: 8
1st-Class 10 w. in match: 2
1st-Class catches: 18
One-Day 100s: 1
One-Day 5 w. in innings: 3
Place in batting averages: 145th av. 29.81
(2002 17th av. 60.66)
Place in bowling averages: 138th av. 47.56 (2002 61st av. 29.11)
Strike rate: 76.00 (career 52.45)
Education: Furqan Model Secondary School, Lahore
Overseas tours: Pakistan to Sri Lanka 1996-97, to India (one-day series) 1996-97,
to South Africa 1997-98 (one-day series), to India (one-day series) 1998-99, to UK,
Ireland and Holland (World Cup) 1999, to Australia 1999-2000, to West Indies
1999-2000, to Sri Lanka 1999-2000, to Kenya (ICC Knockout Trophy) 2000-01, to
New Zealand 2000-01 (one-day series), to England 2001, to Sharjah (v West Indies)
2001-02, to Morocco (Morocco Cup) 2002, to Kenya (Nairobi Triangular) 2002,
to Sri Lanka (ICC Champions Trophy) 2002-03, to South Africa 2002-03, to Africa
(World Cup) 2002-03, to England 2003 (NatWest Challenge), to New Zealand 2003-
04, plus other one-day tournaments
Overseas teams played for: Lahore City; Khan Research Labs; Lahore Blues;
Pakistan International Airlines; Zarai Taraqiati Bank
Extras: Took 7-51 on first-class debut, for Lahore City v Karachi Whites 1996-97.
Scored 87 v West Indies at Georgetown 1999-2000, in the process sharing with

Inzamam-ul-Haq (135) in a record sixth-wicket partnership for Pakistan in Tests v West Indies (206). Took Test hat-trick (Kaluwitharana, Herath, Pushpakumara) v Sri Lanka at Galle in June 2000, becoming the youngest player – and the second Pakistan bowler, after Wasim Akram (twice) – to take a hat-trick in Tests. FICA Young Player of the Year 2001. His Test awards include Man of the Match for his century (134) and match figures of 4-71 in first Test v Bangladesh at Dhaka 2001-02. His ODI awards include Man of the Match for his 84-ball 86 v New Zealand in the second ODI at Rawalpindi 2002. Joined Middlesex as overseas player in 2002. Scored 43-ball 59 v Australia in the final of the Nairobi Triangular tournament 2002. Scored maiden ODI century (112) in second ODI v South Africa at Port Elizabeth 2002-03, in the process sharing with Salim Elahi (135) in a second-wicket stand of 267. Left Middlesex at the end of the 2003 season

Best batting: 203* Middlesex v Glamorgan, Cardiff 2002
Best bowling: 7-51 Lahore City v Karachi Whites, Thatta 1996-97

2003 Season

	M	Inns	NO	Runs	HS	Avge	100s	50s	Ct	St	O	M	Runs	Wkts	Avge	Best	5wI	10wM
Test																	-	-
All First	8	11	0	328	81	29.81	-	3	2	-	202.4	28	761	16	47.56	3-69	-	-
1-day Int	3	3	1	93	64	46.50	-	1	-	-	18	1	83	2	41.50	1-22	-	
C & G	2	2	0	48	30	24.00	-	-	1	-	20	1	100	4	25.00	2-49	-	
NCL	5	5	2	190	79	63.33	-	2	1	-	43	0	235	8	29.37	3-45	-	
Twenty20	3	2	0	50	33	25.00	-	-	-	-	12	0	93	3	31.00	1-25	-	-

Career Performances

	M	Inns	NO	Runs	HS	Avge	100s	50s	Ct	St	Balls	Runs	Wkts	Avge	Best	5wI	10wM
Test	24	38	4	1002	134	29.47	3	4	7	-	3367	1584	48	33.00	4-24	-	-
All First	76	114	16	3151	203 *	32.15	7	16	18	-	12171	7181	232	30.95	7-51	8	2
1-day Int	140	119	27	2563	112	27.85	1	14	20	-	6077	4444	170	26.14	6-35	3	
C & G	3	3	0	56	30	18.66	-	-	1	-	180	158	5	31.60	2-49	-	
NCL	13	11	2	239	79	26.55	-	2	2	-	589	471	19	24.78	3-19	-	
Twenty20	3	2	0	50	33	25.00	-	-	-	-	72	93	3	31.00	1-25	-	

ADAMS, C. J.   Sussex

Name: Christopher (Chris) John Adams
Role: Right-hand bat, right-arm medium bowler, slip fielder, county captain
Born: 6 May 1970, Whitwell, Derbyshire
Height: 6ft **Weight:** 13st 7lbs
Nickname: Grizzly, Grizwold
County debut: 1988 (Derbyshire), 1998 (Sussex)
County cap: 1992 (Derbyshire), 1998 (Sussex)

Benefit: 2003 (Sussex)
Test debut: 1999-2000
Tests: 5
One-Day Internationals: 5
1000 runs in a season: 5
1st-Class 50s: 70
1st-Class 100s: 34
1st-Class 200s: 3
1st-Class catches: 299
One-Day 100s: 18
One-Day 5 w. in innings: 1
Place in batting averages: 102nd av. 35.77
(2002 54th av. 44.63)
Strike rate: (career 76.85)
Parents: John and Eluned (Lyn)
Wife and date of marriage: Samantha
Claire, 26 September 1992
Children: Georgia Louise, 4 October 1993;
Sophie Victoria, 13 October 1998

Family links with cricket: Brother David played 2nd XI cricket for Derbyshire and Gloucestershire. Father played for Yorkshire Schools and uncle played for Essex 2nd XI
Education: Chesterfield Boys Grammar School; Repton School
Qualifications: 6 O-levels, NCA coaching awards, Executive Development Certificate in Coaching and Management Skills
Overseas tours: Repton School to Barbados 1987; England NCA North to Northern Ireland 1987; England XI to New Zealand (Cricket Max) 1997; England to South Africa and Zimbabwe 1999-2000; Sussex to Grenada 2001, 2002; Blade to Barbados 2001
Overseas teams played for: Takapuna, New Zealand 1987-88; Te Puke, New Zealand 1989-90; Primrose, Cape Town, South Africa 1991-92; Canberra Comets, Australia 1998-99; University of NSW, Australia 2000-01
Career highlights to date: 'Lifting the County Championship trophy for the first time in Sussex's history. It was an unbelievable moment and it was great to do it at Hove in front of our fans. Unforgettable.'
Cricket moments to forget: 'Pre-season tour to Grenada in 2002 when Umer Rashid died.'
Cricketers particularly admired: Ian Botham
Young players to look out for: Matt Prior, Tim Ambrose, 'Georgia Adams!'
Other sports played: Golf, football, 'dabbled a bit with ice hockey'
Other sports followed: Football ('Arsenal!')
Favourite band: Celine Dion
Relaxations: 'Speed walking, philately, time with my family'
Extras: Represented English Schools U15 and U19, MCC Schools U19 and, in 1989, England YC. Took two catches as 12th man for England v India at Old Trafford in 1990. Set Derbyshire record for the highest score in the Sunday League (141*) v Kent

at Chesterfield 1992 and record for the fastest century by a Derbyshire batsman (57 minutes, finishing on 140*) v Worcestershire at Worcester 1992. Set record for the highest score by a Derbyshire No. 3, 239 v Hampshire at Southampton 1996. Released by Derbyshire at the end of the 1997 season and joined Sussex for 1998 as captain. Scored 135 and 105 v Essex at Chelmsford 1998, becoming the third player to score centuries in each innings of a match for two counties; he had also done so for Derbyshire. Sussex Player of the Year 1998 and 1999. Set individual one-day record score for Sussex of 163 (off 107 balls) v Middlesex in the National League at Arundel 1999; the innings included nine sixes, a Sussex Sunday/National League record. Sussex 1st XI Fielder of the Season 2000. BBC South Cricketer of the Year 2001. Scored a century in each innings (140/190) v Lancashire at Hove 2003. Scored century (115*) v Middlesex at Hove in the NCL 2003, sharing with Murray Goodwin (118*) in a new record third-wicket partnership for the one-day league and a competition record for any wicket for Sussex (228*). 'Winner of the 2004 Sussex team "Most Stylish Hairdo" award – just beat Matt Prior'

Opinions on cricket: 'It's still the greatest game on earth and it's up to the current players and administrators to ensure it remains so. We've got to evolve to survive, but we must never forget the truth of the game.'

Best batting: 239 Derbyshire v Hampshire, Southampton 1996

Best bowling: 4-28 Sussex v Durham, Riverside 2001

2003 Season

	M	Inns	NO	Runs	HS	Avge	100s	50s	Ct	St	O	M	Runs	Wkts	Avge	Best	5wI	10wM
Test																		
All First	16	27	0	966	190	35.77	4	2	18	-	1	0	1	0	-	-	-	-
1-day Int																		
C & G	2	2	1	119	80 *	119.00	-	1	1	-								
NCL	12	11	4	450	115 *	64.28	2	2	7	-								
Twenty20	5	5	0	113	36	22.60	-	-	3	-								

Career Performances

	M	Inns	NO	Runs	HS	Avge	100s	50s	Ct	St	Balls	Runs	Wkts	Avge	Best	5wI	10wM
Test	5	8	0	104	31	13.00	-	-	6	-	120	59	1	59.00	1-42	-	-
All First	257	422	29	14750	239	37.53	37	70	299	-	3151	1855	41	45.24	4-28	-	-
1-day Int	5	4	0	71	42	17.75	-	-	3	-							
C & G	28	27	7	1263	129 *	63.15	4	8	11	-	114	91	1	91.00	1-15	-	
NCL	197	188	32	6200	163	39.74	11	39	105	-	884	814	27	30.14	5-16	1	
Twenty20	5	5	0	113	36	22.60	-	-	3	-							

1. Name the trophy for which England and West Indies compete in their Test series against one another.

ADAMS, J. H. K.   Hampshire

Name: <u>James</u> Henry Kenneth Adams
Role: Left-hand bat, left-arm medium bowler
Born: 23 September 1980, Winchester
Height: 6ft 1in **Weight:** 14st
Nickname: Jimmy, Bison, Nugget
County debut: 2002
1st-Class 50s: 3
1st-Class 100s: 1
1st-Class catches: 9
Place in batting averages: 169th av. 26.44
Strike rate: 39.00 (career 51.00)
Parents: Jenny and Mike
Marital status: Single
Family links with cricket: 'Dad played a bit
for Kent Schoolboys. Brothers Ben and Tom
played/play for Hampshire age groups'
Education: Sherborne School;
Loughborough University
Qualifications: 9 GCSEs, 3 A-levels, Level 1 coaching
Career outside cricket: Student
Off-season: 'University'
Overseas tours: England U19 to Sri Lanka (U19 World Cup) 1999-2000; West of
England to West Indies 1995; Sherborne School to Pakistan
Overseas teams played for: Woodville, Adelaide 1999-2000; Melville, Perth 2000-01
Career highlights to date: 'County debut. First first-class 100 v Somerset for
Loughborough'
Cricket moments to forget: 'Kidderminster, June 2000'
Cricketers particularly admired: 'M. Parker, R. Smith, B. Lara …'
Young players to look out for: 'J. Francis, J. Tomlinson, K. Latouf, C. Benham …'
Other sports played: Hockey (Dorset age group when 14); 'fair interest in most
sports'
Other sports followed: Football (Aston Villa); 'follow most ball sports'
Injuries: 'Sconed by most; sustained minor fracture after being hit above eye
by A. Nel'
Favourite band: Led Zeppelin, The Who, Blind Melon
Relaxations: Music, PlayStation, 'kick about with mates'
Extras: Played in U15 World Cup 1996. Hampshire Young Player of the Year 1998.
Represented England U19 v Sri Lanka U19 in 'Test' series 2000. Part of Hampshire's
2nd XI Championship winning side 2001. Played for Loughborough University CCE
2002, scoring a century in each innings (103/113) v Kent at Canterbury; captain of
LUCCE 2003, scoring maiden first-class century (107) v Somerset at Taunton.

Represented British Universities 2002 and was captain v India A and
v Zimbabweans 2003
Opinions on cricket: 'Twenty20 seemed to work well and bodes well for future.'
Best batting: 107 LUCCE v Somerset, Taunton 2003
Best bowling: 2-24 LUCCE v Surrey, The Oval 2003

2003 Season

	M	Inns	NO	Runs	HS	Avge	100s	50s	Ct	St	O	M	Runs	Wkts	Avge	Best	5wI	10wM
Test																		
All First	13	26	1	661	107	26.44	1	3	6	-	13	1	44	2	22.00	2-24	-	-
1-day Int																		
C & G																			
NCL																			
Twenty20																			

Career Performances

	M	Inns	NO	Runs	HS	Avge	100s	50s	Ct	St	Balls	Runs	Wkts	Avge	Best	5wI	10wM
Test																	
All First	16	31	2	749	107	25.82	1	3	9	-	204	146	4	36.50	2-24	-	-
1-day Int																	
C & G																		
NCL	3	3	0	28	17	9.33	-	-	2	-	1	6	0	-	-	-	-
Twenty20																	

ADSHEAD, S. J.   Gloucestershire

Name: <u>Stephen</u> John Adshead
Role: Right-hand bat, wicket-keeper
Born: 29 January 1980, Worcester
Height: 5ft 8in **Weight:** 13st
Nickname: Adzo, Shed
County debut: 2000 (Leicestershire), 2003 (Worcestershire)
County colours: 2003 (Worcestershire)
1st-Class 50s: 1
1st-Class catches: 7
1st-Class stumpings: 2
Parents: David and Julie
Marital status: Engaged to Becky
Family links with cricket: 'Dad and brother play local club cricket'
Education: Bridley Moor HS, Redditch
Qualifications: 10 GCSEs, 2 A-levels, ECB Level 2 coaching
Career outside cricket: Coaching

Overseas tours: Leicestershire to Potchefstroom, South Africa 2001; ECB XI to Ireland 2003
Overseas teams played for: Fish Hoek, Cape Town 1998-99; Witwatersrand Technical, Johannesburg 1999-2000; Central Hawke's Bay, New Zealand 2000-01
Career highlights to date: 'Winning AON Trophy 2000; Man of Match in final' (*Top-scored for Leicestershire 2nd XI with 58*)
Cricket moments to forget: 'The entire 2002 season was a pretty miserable time'
Cricketers particularly admired: Alec Stewart, Steve Waugh
Favourite band: U2
Relaxations: 'TV, eating out, spending as much time as possible with Becky'

Extras: Released by Leicestershire at the end of the 2002 season. Played two Championship and two Twenty20 matches for Worcestershire in 2003 as an uncontracted player; also played for Shropshire (including C&G) and ECB XI in 2003. Has joined Gloucestershire for 2004
Opinions on cricket: 'Too many players forget to enjoy the game, which is why we all got good at it in the first place.'
Best batting: 63 Worcestershire v Glamorgan, Cardiff 2003

2003 Season

	M	Inns	NO	Runs	HS	Avge	100s	50s	Ct	St	O	M	Runs	Wkts	Avge	Best	5wI	10wM
Test																		
All First	2	4	1	102	63	34.00	-	1	7	1								
1-day Int																		
C & G	1	1	1	77	77 *	-	-	1	2	-								
NCL																		
Twenty20	2	2	1	2	1 *	2.00	-	-	1	-								

Career Performances

	M	Inns	NO	Runs	HS	Avge	100s	50s	Ct	St	Balls	Runs	Wkts	Avge	Best	5wI	10wM
Test																	
All First	3	5	1	102	63	25.50	-	1	7	2							
1-day Int																	
C & G	4	4	1	147	77 *	49.00	-	1	5	2							
NCL																	
Twenty20	2	2	1	2	1 *	2.00	-	-	1	-							

AFZAAL, U.   Northamptonshire

Name: Usman Afzaal
Role: Left-hand bat, slow left-arm bowler
Born: 9 June 1977, Rawalpindi, Pakistan
Height: 6ft **Weight:** 12st 7lbs
Nickname: Saeed, Gulfraz, Usy Bhai, Trevor
County debut: 1995 (Nottinghamshire)
County cap: 2000 (Nottinghamshire)
Test debut: 2001
Tests: 3
1000 runs in a season: 3
1st-Class 50s: 37
1st-Class 100s: 13
1st-Class catches: 63
One-Day 100s: 1
Place in batting averages: 107th av. 34.07
(2002 52nd av. 45.53)
Strike rate: (career 95.46)
Parents: Firdous and Shafi Mahmood
Marital status: Single
Family links with cricket: Older brother Kamran played for NAYC and for
Nottinghamshire U15-U19 ('top player'); younger brother Aqib played for Notts and
England U15; 'Uncle Mac and Uncle Raja great players'
Education: Manvers Pierrepont School; South Notts College
Qualifications: Coaching certificates
Career outside cricket: Printing company
Overseas tours: Nottinghamshire to South Africa; England U19 to West Indies 1994-
95, to Zimbabwe 1995-96; 'the great ZRK tour to Lahore, Pakistan' 2000; England A
to West Indies 2000-01; England to India and New Zealand 2001-02
Overseas teams played for: Victoria Park, Perth
Career highlights to date: 'Playing for England in the Ashes'
Cricket moments to forget: 'Every time I get out'
Cricketers particularly admired: David Gower, Saeed Anwar, Ian Botham, Clive
Rice, Uncle Raja and Uncle Mac
Young players to look out for: Bilal Shafayat, Aqib Afzaal, Nadeem Malik
Other sports played: Indoor football
Other sports followed: Football ('a bit of Man U')
Relaxations: 'Praying; spending time with friends and family; listening to
Indian music'
Extras: Played for England U15 against South Africa and, in 1994, for England U17
against India. Broke the U16 bowling record in the Texaco Trophy. Won Denis
Compton Award 1996. Took wicket (Adam Gilchrist) with third ball in Test cricket

v Australia at The Oval 2001. C&G Man of the Match award for his 3-8 (from four overs) and 64* v Ireland at Clontarf 2002. Left Nottinghamshire at the end of the 2003 season and has joined Northamptonshire for 2004

Best batting: 161* Nottinghamshire v India A, Trent Bridge 2003
Best bowling: 4-101 Nottinghamshire v Gloucestershire, Trent Bridge 1998

2003 Season

	M	Inns	NO	Runs	HS	Avge	100s	50s	Ct	St	O	M	Runs	Wkts	Avge	Best	5wI	10wM
Test																		
All First	9	15	1	477	161 *	34.07	1	2	3	-	4	2	14	0	-		-	-	-
1-day Int																		
C & G	2	2	0	85	71	42.50	-	1	-	-	9	0	33	2	16.50	2-33	-
NCL	12	12	0	338	105	28.16	1	2	6	-								
Twenty20	4	4	0	44	17	11.00	-	-	-	-								

Career Performances

	M	Inns	NO	Runs	HS	Avge	100s	50s	Ct	St	Balls	Runs	Wkts	Avge	Best	5wI	10wM
Test	3	6	1	83	54	16.60	-	1	-	-	54	49	1	49.00	1-49	-	-
All First	130	226	20	6692	161 *	32.48	13	37	63	-	6301	3347	66	50.71	4-101	-	-
1-day Int																	
C & G	10	8	2	310	71	51.66	-	2	2	-	144	98	5	19.60	3-8	-
NCL	65	58	8	1679	105	33.58	1	13	20	-	596	569	21	27.09	3-48	-
Twenty20	4	4	0	44	17	11.00	-	-	-	-							

2. Who was the 'Big Bird' from Somerset who took 5-4 in 11 balls in the Prudential World Cup final in 1979?

ALI, K.   Worcestershire

Name: Kabir Ali
Role: Right-hand bat, right-arm
medium-fast bowler
Born: 24 November 1980, Birmingham
Height: 6ft **Weight:** 12st 7lbs
Nickname: Kabby, Taxi
County debut: 1999
County colours: 2002
Test debut: 2003
Tests: 1
One-Day Internationals: 1
50 wickets in a season: 2
1st-Class 50s: 5
1st-Class 5 w. in innings: 9
1st-Class 10 w. in match: 2
1st-Class catches: 10
One-Day 5 w. in innings: 1
Place in batting averages: 196th av. 23.81
(2002 259th av. 15.94)
Place in bowling averages: 16th av. 23.16 (2002 26th av. 25.08)
Strike rate: 37.19 (career 44.85)
Parents: Shabir Ali and M. Begum
Marital status: Single
Family links with cricket: 'Father played club cricket. Cousin Kadeer also plays with
me [at Worcestershire]. Cousin Moeen Ali plays at Warwickshire'
Education: Moseley School; Wolverhampton University
Qualifications: GNVQ Leisure and Tourism, coaching
Career outside cricket: Student
Overseas tours: Warwickshire U19 to Cape Town 1998; ECB National Academy to
Australia and Sri Lanka 2002-03; England to Australia 2002-03 (VB Series); England
VI to Hong Kong 2003
Overseas teams played for: Midland-Guildford, Perth
Career highlights to date: 'Playing for England'
Cricketers particularly admired: Wasim Akram, Glenn McGrath
Young players to look out for: Moeen Ali, Omer Ali, Aatif Ali
Other sports played: Football, snooker
Other sports followed: Football, snooker
Relaxations: 'Playing snooker and spending time with family and friends'
Extras: Warwickshire Youth Young Player of the Year award. Won Gold Award on
B&H debut for his 4-29 v Glamorgan 2000. Represented England U19 v Sri Lanka
U19 2000. NBC Denis Compton Award for the most promising young Worcestershire

player 2000. Junior Royals Player of the Year 2001. Professional Cricketers' Association Young Player of the Year 2002. Worcestershire Player of the Year 2002. Called up from the ECB National Academy squad at Adelaide to the England one-day squad in Australia 2002-03 and played for England XI v Australia A at Sydney. Took 5-48 in the Zimbabweans' second innings of the tied match at Worcester 2003, including the final two wickets with the scores level. His 8-53 v Yorkshire 2003 was the best return at Scarborough since Bill Bowes' 9-112 v Essex in 1932. Made ODI debut in the rained-off match v Zimbabwe at Headingley in the NatWest Series 2003. Made Test debut in the fourth Test v South Africa at Headingley 2003, taking a wicket (Neil McKenzie) with his fifth ball. Worcestershire Young Player of the Year 2003. Don Kenyon Award 2003 for the best Championship match-winning performance by a Worcestershire player (8-58 v Derbyshire, following 68 in Worcestershire's only innings). PCA Young Player of the Year 2003, for the second year running

Opinions on cricket: 'Should play more day/night games.'

Best batting: 84* Worcestershire v Durham, Stockton 2003

Best bowling: 8-53 Worcestershire v Yorkshire, Scarborough 2003

2003 Season

	M	Inns	NO	Runs	HS	Avge	100s	50s	Ct	St	O	M	Runs	Wkts	Avge	Best	5wl	10wM
Test	1	2	0	10	9	5.00	-	-	-	-	36	5	136	5	27.20	3-80	-	-
All First	14	20	4	381	84 *	23.81	-	2	2	-	415.2	72	1552	67	23.16	8-53	3	-
1-day Int	1	0	0	0	0	-	-	-	-	-								
C & G	5	4	3	43	23 *	43.00	-	-	1	-	36	3	158	2	79.00	1-25	-	
NCL	12	7	1	139	92	23.16	-	1	3	-	85.1	10	472	22	21.45	4-30	-	
Twenty20																		

Career Performances

	M	Inns	NO	Runs	HS	Avge	100s	50s	Ct	St	Balls	Runs	Wkts	Avge	Best	5wl	10wM
Test	1	2	0	10	9	5.00	-	-	-	-	216	136	5	27.20	3-80	-	-
All First	48	66	14	1085	84 *	20.86	-	5	10	-	7967	4643	177	26.23	8-53	9	2
1-day Int	1	0	0	0	0	-	-	-	-	-							
C & G	14	9	4	74	23 *	14.80	-	-	3	-	608	455	17	26.76	4-2	-	
NCL	46	25	7	249	92	13.83	-	1	9	-	1821	1557	69	22.56	5-36	1	
Twenty20																		

3. Which Staffordshire-born bowler's hat-trick contained Richardson, Murray and Hooper at Old Trafford in 1995?

ALI, K.   Worcestershire

Name: Kadeer Ali
Role: Right-hand bat, right-arm
medium bowler
Born: 7 March 1983, Birmingham
Height: 6ft 2in **Weight:** 13st
Nickname: Kaddy
County debut: 2000
County colours: 2002
1st-Class 50s: 3
1st-Class catches: 5
Place in batting averages: 139th av. 30.42
Parents: Munir Ali and Maqsood Begum
Marital status: Single
Family links with cricket: 'Cousin Kabir
also plays for Worcestershire. Brother Moeen
Ali plays for Warwickshire CCC. Father is
cricket coach'
Education: Handsworth Grammar;
Moseley Sixth Form College
Qualifications: 5 GCSEs, Level 1 coach
Career outside cricket: Student
Off-season: 'Playing in Australia'
Overseas tours: England U19 to India 2000-01, to Australia and (U19 World Cup)
New Zealand 2001-02; ECB National Academy (England A) to Malaysia and India
2003-04
Overseas teams played for: WA University, Perth 2002-03
Career highlights to date: 'Scoring a hundred against England in Perth when I played
a game for National Academy. Playing against Australia'
Cricket moments to forget: 'First-class debut – got a pair against Glamorgan'
Cricket superstitions: 'None'
Cricketers particularly admired: Rahul Dravid, Graeme Hick
Young players to look out for: Moeen Ali ('little brother'), Stephen Moore
Other sports followed: Football (Birmingham City FC)
Relaxations: 'Watching movies, spending time with mates, listening to music'
Extras: Young Player awards at Warwickshire CCC. Played for Worcestershire Board
XI in the NatWest 1999 and in the second round of the C&G 2003, which was played
in September 2002. Represented England U19 v Sri Lanka U19 2000 and v West
Indies U19 2001, scoring century (155) in the second 'Test' at Trent Bridge 2001.
NBC Denis Compton Award for the most promising young Worcestershire player
2001, 2002. Represented England U19 v India U19 2002; scored 97 and 111 in the
third 'Test' at Northampton, in the process sharing with Bilal Shafayat (118 and 201*)

in partnerships of 212 and 256; also scored a 122-ball 125 in the third 'ODI' at Taunton. Represented ECB National Academy v England XI at Perth 2002-03, scoring a century (100). Contributed century (182, as captain) to Worcestershire 2nd XI record total (686), v Warwickshire 2nd XI at Barnt Green 2003

Opinions on cricket: 'Twenty20 was a huge success, and I think it's the way forward.'

Best batting: 99 Worcestershire v Yorkshire, Worcester 2003

2003 Season

	M	Inns	NO	Runs	HS	Avge	100s	50s	Ct	St	O	M	Runs	Wkts	Avge	Best	5wI	10wM
Test																		
All First	8	14	0	426	99	30.42	-	3	2	-								
1-day Int																		
C & G	2	2	0	50	30	25.00	-	-	-	-	1	0	4	1	4.00	1-4	-	
NCL	6	6	1	105	52	21.00	-	1	-	-								
Twenty20	5	5	0	122	53	24.40	-	1	2	-								

Career Performances

	M	Inns	NO	Runs	HS	Avge	100s	50s	Ct	St	Balls	Runs	Wkts	Avge	Best	5wI	10wM
Test																	
All First	17	29	0	504	99	17.37	-	3	5	-	102	57	0	-	-	-	-
1-day Int																	
C & G	4	4	0	140	66	35.00	-	1	-	-	27	25	1	25.00	1-4	-	
NCL	8	8	1	182	57	26.00	-	2	-	-							
Twenty20	5	5	0	122	53	24.40	-	1	2	-							

4. Scorer of the fastest century ever against a side touring England (44 minutes v 1975 Australians), which Essex leg-spinner featured in England's successful 1967-68 tour of West Indies?

ALI, M. M. Warwickshire

Name: <u>Moeen</u> Munir Ali
Role: Left-hand bat, right-arm
off-spin bowler; 'batter who bowls'
Born: 18 June 1987, Birmingham
Height: 6ft **Weight:** 10st 7lbs
Nickname: Moe, Eddy, Bart, Elvis
County debut: No first-team appearance
Parents: Munir Ali and Maqsood Begum
Marital status: Single
Family links with cricket: 'Dad cricket
coach; Kabir Ali (cousin) plays for
Worcestershire and England; brother Kadeer
Ali plays for Worcestershire and is with
National Academy; younger brother plays
youth cricket'
Education: Moseley School
Qualifications: GCSEs and Leisure and
Tourism
Career outside cricket: Student
Off-season: 'Playing and training in Australia (Perth) for eight weeks'
Overseas tours: 'Streets to Arena' to Pakistan 2002
Career highlights to date: 'Becoming one of the youngest professional cricketers at 15 years old. Hitting 195* in 20 overs'
Cricket moments to forget: 'None'
Cricket superstitions: 'None'
Cricketers particularly admired: Nick Knight, Sanath Jayasuriya, Saeed Anwar, Wasim Akram, Kabir Ali, Kadeer Ali, Mohammed Sheikh
Young players to look out for: Omar Munir Ali, Atif Ali, Behram Ali
Other sports played: Football
Other sports followed: Football (Birmingham City)
Favourite band: B21
Relaxations: 'Playing snooker at Premier in Balsall Heath and listening to music (chilling out)'
Extras: Represented England U15 2002. Has won five Warwickshire youth awards since age of 11
Opinions on cricket: 'Youngsters should be given more chances at international standard and first-class.'

ALLEN, A. P. W. Warwickshire

Name: Alexander (<u>Sandy</u>) Phillip
Wortley Allen
Role: Right-hand bat, wicket-keeper
Born: 13 October 1984, Solihull
Height: 5ft 10in **Weight:** 12st 9lbs
Nickname: Fonz, Sand, Bags
County debut: 2002
Parents: Martyn and Lynne
Marital status: Single
Family links with cricket: Grandfather
(Esmond Lewis) kept wicket for
Warwickshire CCC; father played club
cricket for local side
Education: Arden School, Knowle, Solihull;
Solihull Sixth Form College
Qualifications: 8 GCSEs, BTEC in Sports
Science, Level 1 ECB coaching
Off-season: 'Playing golf'

Career highlights to date: 'Debut for Warwickshire 2002 against West Indies A. ECB
38-County final against Devon [2002]. 2nd XI Trophy final at the Rose Bowl [2003]'
Cricket moments to forget: 'Any loss'
Cricket superstitions: 'Left pad on first'
Cricketers particularly admired: Andrew Flintoff
Young players to look out for: James Ord
Other sports played: Golf, football (district and Birmingham City), rugby (county;
'played at Twickenham'), athletics (county)
Other sports followed: Football (Birmingham City FC)
Favourite band: Daniel Bedingfield
Relaxations: 'Snooker, golf'
Extras: Played for the Warwickshire Board side that won the last ECB 38-County
competition 2002. Played for Warwickshire Board XI in the first round of the C&G
2003, which was played in August 2002
Opinions on cricket: 'More day/night cricket to bring the crowds in. More
Twenty20 cricket.'
Best batting: 18* Warwickshire v West Indies A, Edgbaston 2002

2003 Season (did not make any first-class or one-day appearances)

Career Performances

	M	Inns	NO	Runs	HS	Avge	100s	50s	Ct	St	Balls	Runs	Wkts	Avge	Best	5wI	10wM
Test																	
All First	1	1	1	18	18 *	-	-	-	-	-							
1-day Int																	
C & G	1	1	0	10	10	10.00	-	-	1	-							
NCL																	
Twenty20																	

ALLEYNE, D.   Nottinghamshire

Name: David Alleyne
Role: Right-hand bat, wicket-keeper
Born: 17 April 1976, York
Height: 5ft 11in **Weight:** 13st 7lbs
Nickname: Bones, Gears
County debut: 1999 (one-day, Middlesex),
2001 (first-class, Middlesex)
1st-Class catches: 12
Parents: Darcy and Jo
Marital status: Engaged to Dawn
Family links with cricket: Father played for
local club Northampton Exiles
Education: Enfield Grammar; Hertford
Regional College, Ware; City and Islington
College
Qualifications: 6 GCSEs, City and Guilds,
BTEC Diploma in Leisure Studies, Level 3
coaching award
Career outside cricket: Coaching; teaching
Overseas tours: Middlesex to Johannesburg 2000-01
Overseas teams played for: Stratford, New Zealand; Inglewood, New Zealand
1997-98; Sturt, Adelaide 1999-2000; Midland-Guildford, Perth 2000-01; Karori CC,
Wellington, New Zealand 2001-02
Career highlights to date: 'Gaining promotion [in Championship] in last game of
[2002] season!'
Cricketers particularly admired: Viv Richards, Desmond Haynes, Carl Hooper, Jack
Russell, Alec Stewart, Keith Piper
Young players to look out for: 'All those who are putting in 110 per cent; they know
who they are'

Other sports played: Judo, football (Middlesex U15, U16; Enfield Borough U16)
Other sports followed: Football (Liverpool FC)
Relaxations: 'Relaxing with Dawn and family'
Extras: Represented Middlesex U11 to U17. London Cricket College (three years). Represented Middlesex Cricket Board. Middlesex 2nd XI Player of the Year 1999, 2000, 2002. Left Middlesex at the end of the 2003 season and has joined Nottinghamshire for 2004
Opinions on cricket: 'Pitches need to be a consistent standard at the start of play. Away teams should get the choice at the toss.'
Best batting: 49* Middlesex v Derbyshire, Derby 2002

2003 Season

	M	Inns	NO	Runs	HS	Avge	100s	50s	Ct	St	O	M	Runs	Wkts	Avge	Best	5wI	10wM
Test																		
All First																		
1-day Int																		
C & G	3	3	0	22	19	7.33	-	-	1	-								
NCL	5	1	1	0	0 *	-	-	-	2	-								
Twenty20	5	2	1	11	6 *	11.00	-	-	3	-								

Career Performances

	M	Inns	NO	Runs	HS	Avge	100s	50s	Ct	St	Balls	Runs	Wkts	Avge	Best	5wI	10wM
Test																	
All First	5	7	1	148	49 *	24.66	-	-	12	-							
1-day Int																	
C & G	5	5	0	30	19	6.00	-	-	3	-							
NCL	25	20	2	226	58	12.55	-	1	19	6							
Twenty20	5	2	1	11	6 *	11.00	-	-	3	-							

5. What was the then record individual Test score made by
Brian Lara at St. John's, Antigua, in 1994?

ALLEYNE, M. W.   Gloucestershire

Name: <u>Mark</u> Wayne Alleyne
Role: Right-hand bat, right-arm medium
bowler, occasional wicket-keeper,
county one-day captain
Born: 23 May 1968, Tottenham, London
Height: 5ft 10in **Weight:** 14st
Nickname: Boo-Boo
County debut: 1986
County cap: 1990
Benefit: 1999
One-Day Internationals: 10
1000 runs in a season: 6
50 wickets in a season: 1
1st-Class 50s: 69
1st-Class 100s: 21
1st-Class 200s: 1
1st-Class 5 w. in innings: 8
1st-Class catches: 268
1st-Class stumpings: 3
One-Day 100s: 4
One-Day 5 w. in innings: 3
Place in batting averages: 228th av. 19.30 (2002 177th av. 25.22)
Place in bowling averages: (2002 149th av. 51.52)
Strike rate: 88.66 (career 65.01)
Parents: Euclid (deceased) and Hyacinth
Wife and date of marriage: Louise Maria, 9 October 1998
Family links with cricket: Brother played for Gloucestershire 2nd XI and Middlesex
YC. Father played club cricket in Barbados and England
Education: Harrison College, Barbados; Cardinal Pole School, East London
Qualifications: 6 O-levels, NCA Senior Coaching Award, volleyball coaching
certificate
Career outside cricket: 'Business and lifestyle management'
Overseas tours: England YC to Sri Lanka 1986-87, to Australia 1987-88; England XI
to New Zealand (Cricket Max) 1997; England A to Bangladesh and New Zealand
1999-2000 (captain), to West Indies 2000-01 (captain); England to Australia 1998-99
(CUB Series), to South Africa and Zimbabwe 1999-2000 (one-day series), to Kenya
(ICC Knockout Trophy) 2000-01, to Pakistan and Sri Lanka 2000-01 (one-day series)
Career highlights to date: '1) England debut in Brisbane 2) England Man of the
Match in East London, South Africa 3) Each one of our five consecutive trophies'
Cricket moments to forget: 'Missing promotion in the Championship and being
relegated in the Norwich Union League in the same week [2001]'

Cricketers particularly admired: Gordon Greenidge, Viv Richards, Jack Russell, Steve Waugh

Other sports played: Basketball, football

Other sports followed: 'Still follow Tottenham religiously but support our local football and rugby teams'

Relaxations: 'Sport crazy but also an avid gardener. Keen historian'

Extras: Graduate of Haringey Cricket College. In 1986 became (at 18 years 54 days) the youngest player to score a century for Gloucestershire, with his 116* v Sussex at Bristol. In 1990 also became the youngest to score a double hundred for the county, with his 256 v Northamptonshire at Northampton. In 1992 struck then highest Sunday League score for Gloucestershire (134*). Cricket Select Sunday League Player of the Year 1992. Scored 112 in the B&H Super Cup final v Yorkshire at Lord's 1999, winning the Man of the Match award. Leading all-rounder in the single-division four-day era of the County Championship with 6409 runs (av. 32.53) and 216 wickets (av. 31.18) 1993-99. Captain of Gloucestershire's one-day double-winning side (NatWest and B&H Super Cup) 1999 and of treble-winning side (NatWest, B&H and Norwich Union National League) 2000. Man of the Match in ODI v South Africa at East London February 2000 (53, 3-55 and a catch to dismiss Jonty Rhodes). Played 393 consecutive competitive games, a Gloucestershire record, between 28 July 1990 and 24 June 2000. One of *Wisden*'s Five Cricketers of the Year 2001. Honorary fellowship from University of Gloucestershire, October 2001. Gloucestershire captain 1997-2003; appointed Gloucestershire player/coach and one-day captain for 2004

Best batting: 256 Gloucestershire v Northamptonshire, Northampton 1990

Best bowling: 6-49 Gloucestershire v Middlesex, Lord's 2000

Stop press: Awarded MBE in the New Year honours list 2004

2003 Season

	M	Inns	NO	Runs	HS	Avge	100s	50s	Ct	St	O	M	Runs	Wkts	Avge	Best	5wI	10wM
Test																		
All First	8	13	3	193	32 *	19.30	-	-	9	-	133	32	460	9	51.11	3-77	-	-
1-day Int																		
C & G	4	2	1	29	27	29.00	-	-	1	-	34	2	118	2	59.00	2-33	-	
NCL	10	8	3	111	35	22.20	-	-	6	-	79.2	4	371	12	30.91	4-26	-	
Twenty20	5	3	3	40	21 *	-	-	-	5	-	18	1	137	5	27.40	2-33	-	

Career Performances

	M	Inns	NO	Runs	HS	Avge	100s	50s	Ct	St	Balls	Runs	Wkts	Avge	Best	5wI	10wM
Test																	
All First	322	529	51	14705	256	30.76	22	69	268	3	26200	13348	403	33.12	6-49	8	-
1-day Int	10	8	1	151	53	21.57	-	1	3	-	366	280	10	28.00	3-27	-	
C & G	47	36	6	663	73	22.10	-	1	16	-	1995	1249	50	24.98	5-30	1	
NCL	259	236	50	5354	134 *	28.78	3	23	107	-	8875	7122	232	30.69	5-28	1	
Twenty20	5	3	3	40	21 *	-	-	-	5	-	108	137	5	27.40	2-33	-	

AMBROSE, T. R. Sussex

Name: Timothy (<u>Tim</u>) Raymond Ambrose
Role: Right-hand bat, wicket-keeper
Born: 1 December 1982, Newcastle,
New South Wales, Australia
Height: 5ft 7in
Nickname: Shambrose
County debut: 2001
County cap: 2003
1st-Class 50s: 12
1st-Class 100s: 2
1st-Class catches: 41
1st-Class stumpings: 7
Place in batting averages: 72nd av. 40.47
(2002 89th av. 38.00)
Parents: Raymond and Sally
Marital status: Single
Family links with cricket: 'Cousin played
Sydney first grade; father is captain of local
grade D4 team'
Education: Merewether Selective High, NSW
Career outside cricket: Greenkeeping
Off-season: 'Training in South Africa'
Overseas tours: Sussex to Grenada 2001, 2002
Overseas teams played for: Wallsend, NSW 2000; Nelson Bay, NSW 2001;
Newcastle, NSW 2002
Career highlights to date: 'Winning the Championship 2003. Maiden first-class
century, 149 v Yorkshire'
Cricketers particularly admired: Alec Stewart, Ian Healy, Steve Waugh,
Mushtaq Ahmed
Young players to look out for: Andrew Hodd, Matt Prior
Other sports played: Football, squash, golf, rugby league, rugby union, AFL,
'I'll have a go at anything'
Other sports followed: Rugby league (Newcastle Knights), Australian Rules (Sydney
Swans), football (Tottenham Hotspur)
Favourite band: Jeff Buckley, Ben Harper
Relaxations: Guitar, music
Extras: Captained Newcastle (NSW) U16 1999 Bradman Cup winning side. 'Scored
138 in first ever game.' Played for New South Wales U17. Won NSW Junior Cricketer
of the Year three years running. Scored 87 and took two catches and a stumping in his
second one-day match, in the Norwich Union League v Lancashire at Hove 2001.
Scored 52 on first-class debut v Warwickshire at Edgbaston 2001. C&G Man of the

Match award for his 95 v Buckinghamshire at Beaconsfield 2002. Awarded Sussex cap 2003. Holds a British passport and is not considered an overseas player
Opinions on cricket: 'Great game. Love it.'
Best batting: 149 Sussex v Yorkshire, Headingley 2002

2003 Season

	M	Inns	NO	Runs	HS	Avge	100s	50s	Ct	St	O	M	Runs	Wkts	Avge	Best	5wI	10wM
Test																		
All First	15	26	3	931	93 *	40.47	-	9	29	7								
1-day Int																		
C & G	2	2	0	48	43	24.00	-	-	1	-								
NCL	11	11	0	235	44	21.36	-	-	14	-								
Twenty20	5	5	2	108	54 *	36.00	-	1	5	3								

Career Performances

	M	Inns	NO	Runs	HS	Avge	100s	50s	Ct	St	Balls	Runs	Wkts	Avge	Best	5wI	10wM
Test																	
All First	30	51	4	1821	149	38.74	2	12	41	7	6	1	0	-	-	-	-
1-day Int																	
C & G	5	5	0	159	95	31.80	-	1	2	-							
NCL	27	25	1	512	87	21.33	-	1	26	3							
Twenty20	5	5	2	108	54 *	36.00	-	1	5	3							

AMIN, R. M.   Leicestershire

Name: <u>Rupesh</u> Mahesh Amin
Role: Right-hand bat, left-arm orthodox spin bowler
Born: 20 August 1977, Clapham, London
Height: 5ft 11in **Weight:** 10st 7lbs
Nickname: Idi, Plug, Rups
County debut: 1997 (Surrey), 2003 (Leicestershire)
1st-Class catches: 6
Strike rate: 109.62 (career 100.74)
Parents: Mahesh and Aruna
Marital status: Single
Family links with cricket: Father played club cricket
Education: Riddlesdown High School; John Ruskin Sixth Form
Qualifications: 8 GCSEs, 3 A-levels, ECB Level 1 cricket coaching

Overseas tours: Bishen Bedi Academy to Sharjah 1999
Overseas teams played for: Manly-Warringah District CC, Sydney 1997-98;
University of New South Wales 1999-2000
Career highlights to date: 'Winning County Championship in 1999'
Cricket moments to forget: 'Being hit out of ground by Mal Loye at Whitgift School in NUL'
Cricketers particularly admired: Saqlain Mushtaq, Anil Kumble, Sachin Tendulkar
Young players to look out for: Rikki Clarke, Ravi Bopara
Other sports played: Football
Other sports followed: Football (Liverpool), snooker (Ronnie O'Sullivan), baseball
Relaxations: Going to cinema, eating good food, going out and seeing places
Extras: Played for Croydon District U15 side that won Hobbs Trophy against London Schools. Left Surrey at the end of the 2002 season and joined Leicestershire for 2003; retired at the end of the 2003 season
Opinions on cricket: 'Not enough rest periods during season to regroup yourself mentally and physically. Too much cricket to be played during a season.'
Best batting: 12 Surrey v Leicestershire, The Oval 1998
Best bowling: 4-87 Surrey v Somerset, The Oval 1999

2003 Season

	M	Inns	NO	Runs	HS	Avge	100s	50s	Ct	St	O	M	Runs	Wkts	Avge	Best	5wI	10wM
Test																		
All First	5	7	2	30	11	6.00	-	-	-	-	146.1	24	601	8	75.12	2-41	-	-
1-day Int																		
C & G																		
NCL																		
Twenty20																		

Career Performances

	M	Inns	NO	Runs	HS	Avge	100s	50s	Ct	St	Balls	Runs	Wkts	Avge	Best	5wI	10wM
Test																	
All First	20	25	10	65	12	4.33	-	-	6	-	3526	1709	35	48.82	4-87	-	-
1-day Int																	
C & G																	
NCL	4	1	1	0	0*	-	-	-	1	-	84	97	2	48.50	2-43	-	
Twenty20																	

> 6. Which Warwickshire opener retired hurt after 33 minutes
> of his Test debut in 1984 and never played another Test?

ANDERSON, J. M.   Lancashire

Name: <u>James</u> Michael Anderson
Role: Left-hand bat, right-arm
fast-medium bowler
Born: 30 July 1982, Burnley
Height: 6ft 2in **Weight:** 12st 7lbs
Nickname: Jimmy
County debut: 2001 (one-day),
2002 (first-class)
County cap: 2003
Test debut: 2003
Tests: 7
One-Day Internationals: 23
50 wickets in a season: 1
1st-Class 5 w. in innings: 6
1st-Class catches: 7
Place in batting averages: (2002 306th
av. 7.25)
Place in bowling averages: 60th av. 30.04
(2002 12th av. 22.28)

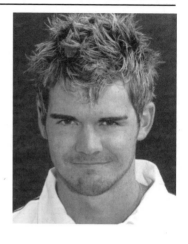

Strike rate: 48.70 (career 43.48)
Parents: Michael and Catherine
Marital status: Single
Family links with cricket: Father and uncle played for Burnley
Education: St Theodore's RC High School; St Theodore's RC Sixth Form Centre –
both Burnley
Qualifications: 10 GCSEs, 1 A-level, 1 GNVQ, Level 2 coaching award
Off-season: Touring with England
Overseas tours: Lancashire to Cape Town 2002; ECB National Academy to Australia
2002-03; England to Australia 2002-03 (VB Series), to Africa (World Cup) 2002-03, to
Bangladesh and Sri Lanka 2003-04, to West Indies 2003-04
Cricketers particularly admired: Michael Atherton, Darren Gough, Courtney Walsh,
Shaun Pollock, Ian Botham
Young players to look out for: David Brown, Jonathan Clare (both Burnley CC)
Other sports played: Golf (15 handicap), football, 'most active sports'
Other sports followed: Football (Burnley FC), golf
Relaxations: 'Television, music, all sports'
Extras: Played for Lancashire Board XI in the NatWest 2000. Represented England
U19 v West Indies U19 2001, taking 5-45 in the first 'Test' at Leicester. Took 50 first-
class wickets in his first full season 2002. NBC Denis Compton Award for the most
promising young Lancashire player 2002. Called up from ECB National Academy
squad at Adelaide to England one-day squad for the VB Series in Australia 2002-03 as

cover for Andrew Caddick. Took 1-12 from ten overs (including five successive maidens) v Australia at Adelaide in the VB Series 2002-03. England's leading wicket-taker in the 2002-03 World Cup (10 wickets; av. 22.50), winning two Man of the Match awards. Became youngest bowler to take a hat-trick for Lancashire (aged 20 years 9½ months), v Essex (Robinson, Hussain, Jefferson) at Old Trafford 2003. Became youngest bowler to record a five-wicket innings return on England Test debut (5-73, including 4-5 in 14 balls) in the first Test v Zimbabwe at Lord's 2003. Became the first England bowler to take an ODI hat-trick (Abdul Razzaq, Shoaib Akhtar, Mohammad Sami) v Pakistan at The Oval in the NatWest Challenge 2003, having also dismissed Imran Nazir with the first ball of the match. Awarded Lancashire cap 2003. Cricket Writers' Club Young Player of the Year 2003. ECB central contract 2003-04
Best batting: 21* England v South Africa, Lord's 2003
Best bowling: 6-23 Lancashire v Hampshire, West End 2002
Stop press: Withdrawn from first-class portion of England tour to Bangladesh 2003-04 with knee injury (replaced by Richard Johnson) and sidelined for part of the Sri Lanka tour with ankle injury

2003 Season

	M	Inns	NO	Runs	HS	Avge	100s	50s	Ct	St	O	M	Runs	Wkts	Avge	Best	5wI	10wM
Test	7	10	9	43	21 *	43.00	-	-	2	-	225.5	53	821	26	31.57	5-73	2	-
All First	11	13	12	55	21 *	55.00	-	-	5	-	332.5	72	1232	41	30.04	5-61	3	-
1-day Int	9	1	1	6	6 *	-	-	-	-	-	71	6	332	19	17.47	4-27	-	
C & G	3	2	2	7	7 *	-	-	-	2	-	24	2	95	6	15.83	3-14	-	
NCL	1	1	1	1	1 *	-	-	-	-	-	6	0	30	0	-	-	-	
Twenty20																		

Career Performances

	M	Inns	NO	Runs	HS	Avge	100s	50s	Ct	St	Balls	Runs	Wkts	Avge	Best	5wI	10wM
Test	7	10	9	43	21 *	43.00	-	-	2	-	1355	821	26	31.57	5-73	2	-
All First	24	29	20	113	21 *	12.55	-	-	7	-	3957	2346	91	25.78	6-23	6	-
1-day Int	23	10	3	24	8	3.42	-	-	2	-	1148	930	42	22.14	4-25	-	
C & G	5	3	3	12	7 *	-	-	-	2	-	264	193	9	21.44	3-14	-	
NCL	4	1	1	1	1 *	-	-	-	1	-	168	146	6	24.33	3-42	-	
Twenty20																	

7. Which Leytonstone-born opener scored 154*
(61.11 per cent of the total) in England's second innings
of the first Test at Headingley in 1991?

ANDERSON, R. S. G. Northamptonshire

Name: Ricaldo (<u>Ricky</u>) Sherman Glenroy Anderson
Role: Right-hand bat, right-arm medium-fast bowler
Born: 22 September 1976, Hammersmith, London
Height: 5ft 10in **Weight:** 11st 11lbs
County debut: 1999 (Essex), 2002 (Northamptonshire)
50 wickets in a season: 1
1st-Class 50s: 2
1st-Class 5 w. in innings: 8
1st-Class 10 w. in match: 1
1st-Class catches: 7
Place in batting averages: (2002 251st av. 16.60)
Strike rate: 90.00 (career 50.85)
Parents: Heather and Junior
Marital status: Single
Education: Alperton High School; Barnet College; NWL College; London Cricket College
Qualifications: 6 GCSEs, BTEC National in Engineering
Overseas tours: Middlesex U16 to Jersey; BWIA to Trinidad and Tobago 1998, 1999, 2000
Overseas teams played for: Coronation CC, South Africa 1996-97
Cricketers particularly admired: Malcolm Marshall, Stuart Law, Carl Hooper
Other sports followed: Football (Liverpool)
Relaxations: Music
Extras: Took 50 first-class wickets in his first season 1999. Left Essex in the 2001-02 off-season and joined Northamptonshire for 2002
Best batting: 67* Essex v Sussex, Chelmsford 2000
Best bowling: 6-34 Essex v Northamptonshire, Ilford 2000

2003 Season

	M	Inns	NO	Runs	HS	Avge	100s	50s	Ct	St	O	M	Runs	Wkts	Avge	Best	5wI	10wM
Test																		
All First	2	2	0	13	13	6.50	-	-	-	-	30	4	147	2	73.50	2-33	-	-
1-day Int																		
C & G																		
NCL	2	1	0	17	17	17.00	-	-	-	-	18	0	98	4	24.50	3-42	-	
Twenty20	1	1	1	0	0*	-	-	-	1	-	4	0	29	4	7.25	4-29	-	

Career Performances

	M	Inns	NO	Runs	HS	Avge	100s	50s	Ct	St	Balls	Runs	Wkts	Avge	Best	5wl	10wM
Test																	
All First	39	51	5	650	67 *	14.13	-	2	7	-	6103	3398	120	28.31	6-34	8	1
1-day Int																	
C & G	1	1	0	4	4	4.00	-	-	-	-	42	53	1	53.00	1-53	-	
NCL	19	15	2	102	22	7.84	-	-	-	-	780	678	15	45.20	3-30	-	
Twenty20	1	1	1	0	0 *	-	-	-	1	-	24	29	4	7.25	4-29	-	

ANDREW, G. M. — Somerset

Name: Gareth Mark Andrew
Role: Left-hand bat, right-arm fast-medium bowler; all-rounder
Born: 27 December 1983, Yeovil
Height: 6ft **Weight:** 13st 7lbs
Nickname: Brad, Gaz, Sobers
County debut: 2003
1st-Class catches: 2
Place in bowling averages: 64th av. 31.00
Strike rate: 46.80 (career 46.80)
Parents: Peter and Susan
Marital status: Single
Family links with cricket: 'Dad played club cricket'
Education: Ansford Community School; Richard Huish College, Taunton
Qualifications: 10 GCSEs, 3 A-levels, Level 1 coach
Career outside cricket: 'In second gap year and undecided about university'
Off-season: 'Training in Taunton'
Overseas tours: West of England U15 to West Indies 1999; England U17 to Australia 2001; Somerset Academy to Western Australia 2002; Aus Academy to Perth 2003
Overseas teams played for: Swanbourne CC, Perth 2002-03
Career highlights to date: 'Debuts in both forms of cricket'
Cricket moments to forget: 'Whenever bowling in the Twenty20'
Cricket superstitions: 'None'
Cricketers particularly admired: Andrew Flintoff, Ian Botham
Young players to look out for: James Hildreth, Neil Edwards, Mark Mitchell
Other sports played: Football (Bruton Town FC, Yeovil District U11-U16, Castle Cary AFC)
Other sports followed: Football (Yeovil Town, Man Utd)

Injuries: Out for four weeks with an ankle and shin problem
Favourite band: Red Hot Chili Peppers ('anything really')
Relaxations: 'Going home; watching DVDs; and people-watching from Starbucks with Dewsy'
Extras: Played for Somerset Board XI in the NatWest 2000 and the C&G 2002. Represented England U19 v South Africa U19 2003
Opinions on cricket: 'Too much cricket. Longer game should be shortened by a day to get more competitive, resultful cricket.'
Best batting: 11 Somerset v Yorkshire, Headingley 2003
Best bowling: 3-14 Somerset v Derbyshire, Taunton 2003

2003 Season

	M	Inns	NO	Runs	HS	Avge	100s	50s	Ct	St	O	M	Runs	Wkts	Avge	Best	5wI	10wM
Test																		
All First	4	5	0	36	11	7.20	-	-	2	-	78	13	310	10	31.00	3-14	-	-
1-day Int																		
C & G																		
NCL	9	6	1	51	23	10.20	-	-	4	-	38.2	4	222	11	20.18	3-38	-	
Twenty20	3	2	0	2	2	1.00	-	-	-	-	6	0	53	2	26.50	2-36	-	

Career Performances

	M	Inns	NO	Runs	HS	Avge	100s	50s	Ct	St	Balls	Runs	Wkts	Avge	Best	5wI	10wM
Test																	
All First	4	5	0	36	11	7.20	-	-	2	-	468	310	10	31.00	3-14	-	-
1-day Int																	
C & G	2	1	0	1	1	1.00	-	-	1	-	53	35	0	-		-	-
NCL	9	6	1	51	23	10.20	-	-	4	-	230	222	11	20.18	3-38	-	
Twenty20	3	2	0	2	2	1.00	-	-	-	-	36	53	2	26.50	2-36	-	

8. What was unusual about the Test side that West Indies fielded in Antigua in April 1994?

ATRI, V.   Nottinghamshire

Name: Vikram Atri
Role: Right-hand bat, leg-spin bowler
Born: 9 March 1983, Hull
Height: 5ft 7in   **Weight:** 9st 6lbs
Nickname: Speedy, Big Dave, Bouffant
County debut: 2002
1st-Class 50s: 3
1st-Class catches: 5
Place in batting averages: 142nd av. 30.00
Parents: Gulshan and Kuldip
Marital status: Single
Family links with cricket: Father played
club cricket for a number of years, including
in the Yorkshire and Bradford leagues
Education: Fernwood Comprehensive
School; Bilborough College and
Loughborough University
Qualifications: 11 GCSEs, 3½ A-levels,
Level 1 cricket coach
Career highlights to date: 'Making my first-class debut for Notts against West Indies
A and scoring 98 in debut innings'
Cricket moments to forget: 'Getting out for 98 on first-class debut!'
Cricket superstitions: 'Always put my left pad on first'
Cricketers particularly admired: Sachin Tendulkar, Rahul Dravid, Michael Vaughan,
Shane Warne
Young players to look out for: Bilal Shafayat, John Francis, James Adams
Other sports played: Hockey (Nottinghamshire U13-U18)
Other sports followed: Football ('mad Liverpool supporter'), 'all sports really'
Relaxations: 'Sleeping and generally chilling'
Extras: Played for Nottinghamshire Board XI in the C&G 2001. Played for
Loughborough University CCE 2002, helping them to a clean sweep of all trophies;
also played for LUCCE 2003. Scored 98 on first-class debut v West Indies A at Trent
Bridge 2002
Opinions on cricket: 'The game should be more batsman-friendly! Haven't played
long enough to form a valued opinion.'
Best batting: 98 Nottinghamshire v West Indies A, Trent Bridge 2002

2003 Season

	M	Inns	NO	Runs	HS	Avge	100s	50s	Ct	St	O	M	Runs	Wkts	Avge	Best	5wI	10wM
Test																		
All First	5	10	2	240	82 *	30.00	-	2	3	-								
1-day Int																		
C & G																		
NCL																		
Twenty20																		

Career Performances

	M	Inns	NO	Runs	HS	Avge	100s	50s	Ct	St	Balls	Runs	Wkts	Avge	Best	5wI	10wM
Test																	
All First	6	11	2	338	98	37.55	-	3	5	-							
1-day Int																	
C & G	1	1	0	0	0	0.00	-	-	-	-							
NCL																	
Twenty20																	

AVERIS, J. M. M.   Gloucestershire

Name: <u>James</u> Maxwell Michael Averis
Role: Right-hand bat, right-arm
fast-medium bowler
Born: 28 May 1974, Bristol
Height: 5ft 11in **Weight:** 13st 7lbs
Nickname: Avo, Fish, Goat
County debut: 1994 (one-day),
1997 (first-class)
County cap: 2001
1st-Class 5 w. in innings: 3
1st-Class catches: 10
One-Day 5 w. in innings: 4
Place in batting averages: (2002 288th
av. 10.37)
Place in bowling averages: (2002 88th
av. 33.23)
Strike rate: 71.55 (career 74.82)
Parents: Mike and Carol
Wife and date of marriage: Anna, 26 October 2002
Family links with cricket: 'Father and grandfather played and have lots of advice'
Education: Bristol Cathedral School; Portsmouth University; St Cross College,
Oxford University

Qualifications: 10 GCSEs, 3 A-levels, BSc (Hons) Geographical Science, Diploma in Social Studies (Oxon), FPC I and II

Overseas tours: Bristol Schools to Australia 1990-91; Gloucestershire to Zimbabwe 1997, to South Africa 1999, to Cape Town 2000, to Kimberley 2001, to Stellenbosch 2002; Bristol RFC to South Africa 1996; Oxford University RFC to Japan and Australia 1997

Overseas teams played for: Union CC, Port Elizabeth, South Africa; Kraifontaine, Boland, South Africa 2001

Career highlights to date: 'Winning treble in 2000'

Cricket moments to forget: 'Dropping the biggest dolly in 2000 NatWest final'

Cricket superstitions: 'Must eat on way to ground. Always use same toilet'

Cricketers particularly admired: Viv Richards, Malcolm Marshall, Ian Botham

Other sports played: Football (Bristol North West), rugby (played for Bristol RFC, captain of South West U21 1995, Oxford Blue 1996)

Other sports followed: Rugby (Bristol RFC), football (Liverpool FC)

Relaxations: 'Reading, surfing, eating out'

Extras: Double Oxford Blue in 1996-97. Played in every one-day game in Gloucestershire's treble-winning season 2000. Gloucestershire Player of the Year 2001

Opinions on cricket: 'Each side should include eight England eligible players. Two up/two down. More non-Test grounds used for international games.'

Best batting: 43 Gloucestershire v Nottinghamshire, Bristol 2002

Best bowling: 5-51 Gloucestershire v Nottinghamshire, Bristol 2002

2003 Season

	M	Inns	NO	Runs	HS	Avge	100s	50s	Ct	St	O	M	Runs	Wkts	Avge	Best	5wI	10wM
Test																		
All First	4	3	1	12	8	6.00	-	-	1	-	107.2	30	298	9	33.11	3-84	-	-
1-day Int																		
C & G	4	1	1	4	4*	-	-	-	1	-	32.5	2	142	10	14.20	6-23	1	
NCL	13	6	4	22	11*	11.00	-	-	-	-	100	7	560	17	32.94	4-50	-	
Twenty20	2	0	0	0	0	-	-	-	1	-	7	0	59	2	29.50	2-25	-	

Career Performances

	M	Inns	NO	Runs	HS	Avge	100s	50s	Ct	St	Balls	Runs	Wkts	Avge	Best	5wI	10wM
Test																	
All First	43	59	12	512	43	10.89	-	-	10	-	7333	4309	98	43.96	5-51	3	-
1-day Int																	
C & G	15	6	5	33	12*	33.00	-	-	2	-	715	537	28	19.17	6-23	1	
NCL	69	39	18	180	23*	8.57	-	-	8	-	3095	2475	102	24.26	5-20	3	
Twenty20	2	0	0	0	0	-	-	-	1	-	42	59	2	29.50	2-25	-	

AZHAR MAHMOOD   Surrey

Name: Azhar Mahmood Sagar
Role: Right-hand bat, right-arm
fast-medium bowler; all-rounder
Born: 28 February 1975, Rawalpindi,
Pakistan
Height: 6ft **Weight:** 13st 5lbs
Nickname: Aju
County debut: 2002
Test debut: 1997-98
Tests: 21
One-Day Internationals: 127
1st-Class 50s: 19
1st-Class 100s: 4
1st-Class 5 w. in innings: 13
1st-Class 10 w. in match: 3
1st-Class catches: 74
One-Day 5 w. in innings: 4
Place in batting averages: 96th av. 37.08
Place in bowling averages: 65th av. 31.34 (2002 1st av. 17.25)
Strike rate: 48.65 (career 48.65)
Parents: Mohammed Aslam Sagar and Nusrat Perveen
Wife and date of marriage: Ebba Azhar, 13 April 2003
Education: FG No. 1 High School, Islamabad
Qualifications: 'A-level equivalent'
Career outside cricket: 'Property'
Off-season: Playing for Pakistan and South African province
Overseas tours: Pakistan Youth to New Zealand 1994-95; Pakistan A to Bangladesh
1996, to England 1997; Pakistan to India (Pepsi Independence Cup) 1997, to South
Africa and Zimbabwe 1997-98, to Bangladesh (Wills International Cup) 1998-99, to
India 1998-99, to UK, Ireland and Holland (World Cup) 1999, to Australia 1999-2000,
to Sri Lanka 2000, to Kenya (ICC Knockout) 2000-01, to New Zealand 2000-01, to
England 2001, to Bangladesh 2001-02, to Australia (Super Challenge II) 2002, to
Morocco (Morocco Cup) 2002, to Zimbabwe 2002-03, to Africa (World Cup) 2002-03,
to New Zealand 2003-04, plus other one-day tournaments in Toronto, Kenya, Sharjah,
Bangladesh and Singapore
Overseas teams played for: Islamabad; United Bank; Rawalpindi; Pakistan
International Airlines
Career highlights to date: 'First Test match (debut) against South Africa in 1997 in
Pakistan (Rawalpindi). I scored 128* in the first innings and 50* in the second, plus
two wickets – Man of the Match'
Cricket moments to forget: 'World Cup 1999 – final against Australia (which we
lost)'

Cricket superstitions: 'None'
Cricketers particularly admired: Imran Khan, Wasim Akram, Steve Waugh
Young players to look out for: Bilal Asad, Rikki Clarke
Other sports played: Snooker, basketball, kite flying
Other sports followed: Football (Man U)
Injuries: Out for two weeks with a hamstring injury; also suffered broken nose
Relaxations: 'Listening to music, training, spending time with my family'
Extras: Made first-class debut for Islamabad 1993-94. Scored 379 runs (av. 31.58) and topped bowling averages with 40 wickets at 20.72 on Pakistan A tour of England 1997. Scored 128* and 50* on Test debut in the first Test v South Africa at Rawalpindi 1997-98; during first innings shared with Mushtaq Ahmed (59) in a tenth-wicket stand of 151, equalling the world tenth-wicket record in Tests set by Brian Hastings and Richard Collinge for New Zealand v Pakistan at Auckland 1972-73. Scored century (136) in the first Test v South Africa at Johannesburg 1997-98, becoming the first Pakistan player to score a Test century in South Africa. Took 6-18 v West Indies in the Coca-Cola Champions Trophy in Sharjah 1999-2000 and 5-28 v Sri Lanka in the final of the same competition, winning the Man of the Match award on both occasions. Was Surrey's overseas player at the start of the 2002 season, pending the arrival of Saqlain Mushtaq, absent on international duty; returned as an overseas player for 2003. Topped English first-class bowling averages 2002 with 20 wickets at 17.25. Represented Pakistan in the 2002-03 World Cup. Scored 98 v Essex at Chelmsford 2003, in the process sharing with Adam Hollioake (77) in a new record seventh-wicket partnership for Surrey in the one-day league (154)
Opinions on cricket: 'State of sport now – there's a lot more cricket now than when I started. Hardly any off time. Cricketing standards have improved through fielding, third umpiring, and cricket is a lot faster, hence viewed by a wider audience. Because of the fast pace, we are able to get results in Test matches; before, most Test matches were drawn. Having overseas players in county [cricket] is very good because it's become more competitive and helps groom younger players. There have also been a lot more spectators this year with two overseas players in each team. Twenty20 Cup was very exciting and is another form of fast cricket – was great! There are no central contracts for Pakistani players. It's essential that players have such contracts as it adds stability and security, improving our performance.'
Best batting: 136 Pakistan v South Africa, Johannesburg 1997-98
Best bowling: 8-61 Surrey v Lancashire, The Oval 2002

2003 Season

	M	Inns	NO	Runs	HS	Avge	100s	50s	Ct	St	O	M	Runs	Wkts	Avge	Best	5wl	10wM
Test																		
All First	11	14	2	445	98	37.08	-	4	17	-	283.5	52	1097	35	31.34	5-78	1	-
1-day Int	3	3	1	66	30	33.00	-	-	-	-	16.3	0	100	1	100.00	1-41	-	
C & G	3	3	0	36	20	12.00	-	-	2	-	26	5	112	6	18.66	4-49	-	
NCL	12	11	2	277	98	30.77	-	2	2	-	89	4	466	18	25.88	6-37	1	
Twenty20	5	4	1	114	57 *	38.00	-	1	1	-	18.5	0	123	12	10.25	4-20	-	

Career Performances

	M	Inns	NO	Runs	HS	Avge	100s	50s	Ct	St	Balls	Runs	Wkts	Avge	Best	5wI	10wM
Test	21	34	4	900	136	30.00	3	1	14	-	3015	1402	39	35.94	4-50	-	-
All First	94	146	19	3579	136	28.18	4	19	74	-	16110	8080	331	24.41	8-61	13	3
1-day Int	127	97	21	1375	67	18.09	-	3	37	-	5616	4281	113	37.88	6-18	3	
C & G	3	3	0	36	20	12.00	-	-	2	-	156	112	6	18.66	4-49	-	
NCL	13	11	2	277	98	30.77	-	2	2	-	544	476	19	25.05	6-37	1	
Twenty20	5	4	1	114	57 *	38.00	-	1	1	-	113	123	12	10.25	4-20	-	

BAILEY, T. M. B.   Northamptonshire

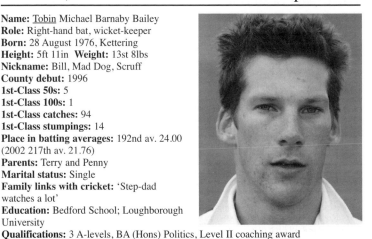

Name: Tobin Michael Barnaby Bailey
Role: Right-hand bat, wicket-keeper
Born: 28 August 1976, Kettering
Height: 5ft 11in **Weight:** 13st 8lbs
Nickname: Bill, Mad Dog, Scruff
County debut: 1996
1st-Class 50s: 5
1st-Class 100s: 1
1st-Class catches: 94
1st-Class stumpings: 14
Place in batting averages: 192nd av. 24.00
(2002 217th av. 21.76)
Parents: Terry and Penny
Marital status: Single
Family links with cricket: 'Step-dad
watches a lot'
Education: Bedford School; Loughborough
University
Qualifications: 3 A-levels, BA (Hons) Politics, Level II coaching award
Career outside cricket: Coaching
Overseas tours: Bedford to South Africa 1994, to Bermuda; Northamptonshire to
Grenada 2000, 2001
Cricketers particularly admired: Jack Russell, Mike Atherton, Alan Knott
Young players to look out for: Mark Powell
Other sports played: Hockey and tennis (both for Beds at youth level), golf ('badly')
Other sports followed: Rugby (Bedford RFC), football (Leicester City FC)
Relaxations: Watching videos, playing golf and eating out
Extras: Bedfordshire Young Player of the Year and Northants County League Young
Player of the Year in 1995. Holmwoods Schools Cricketer of the Year. Played for
England Schools U19 and was a reserve for the England U19 tour to Zimbabwe
1995-96. Won the BUSA Championship with Loughborough University in 1996 and

captained the university to BUSA Championship shared win with Durham University in 1998 (final washed out by rain). Represented British Universities 1997 and 1998. Northamptonshire Young Player of the Year 2000. NBC Denis Compton Award for the most promising young Northamptonshire player 2000. Scored maiden first-class century (101*) v Somerset at Taunton 2003

Best batting: 101* Northamptonshire v Somerset, Taunton 2003

2003 Season

	M	Inns	NO	Runs	HS	Avge	100s	50s	Ct	St	O	M	Runs	Wkts	Avge	Best	5wI	10wM
Test																		
All First	14	19	3	384	101 *	24.00	1	-	29	6	1	0	3	0	-		-	-
1-day Int																		
C & G	1	1	0	19	19	19.00	-	-	1	2								
NCL	12	9	7	156	31 *	78.00	-	-	13	5								
Twenty20	3	2	2	1	1 *	-	-	-	-	3								

Career Performances

	M	Inns	NO	Runs	HS	Avge	100s	50s	Ct	St	Balls	Runs	Wkts	Avge	Best	5wI	10wM
Test																	
All First	49	66	10	1235	101 *	22.05	1	5	94	14	6	3	0	-		-	-
1-day Int																	
C & G	4	4	0	37	19	9.25	-	-	2	4							
NCL	40	25	13	432	44 *	36.00	-	-	43	13							
Twenty20	3	2	2	1	1 *	-	-	-	-	3							

BALL, M. C. J.   Gloucestershire

Name: Martyn Charles John Ball
Role: Right-hand bat, off-spin bowler, slip fielder
Born: 26 April 1970, Bristol
Height: 5ft 9in **Weight:** 12st 10lbs
Nickname: Benny, Barfo
County debut: 1988
County cap: 1996
Benefit: 2002
1st-Class 50s: 15
1st-Class 5 w. in innings: 12
1st-Class 10 w. in match: 1
1st-Class catches: 205
One-Day 5 w. in innings: 2
Place in batting averages: 181st av. 25.33 (2002 247th av. 16.71)
Place in bowling averages: 96th av. 36.00 (2002 117th av. 38.08)

Strike rate: 81.10 (career 78.85)
Parents: Kenneth Charles and Pamela Wendy
Wife and date of marriage: Mona,
28 September 1991
Children: Kristina, 9 May 1990; Alexandra,
2 August 1993; Harrison, 5 June 1997
Education: King Edmund Secondary School,
Yate; Bath College of Further Education
Qualifications: 6 O-levels, 2 A-levels,
advanced cricket coach
Career outside cricket: Sports marketing
Overseas tours: Gloucestershire to Namibia
1991, to Kenya 1992, to Sri Lanka 1993, to
Zimbabwe 1996, 1997, to South Africa 1999;
MCC to New Zealand 1998-99; England to
India 2001-02

Overseas teams played for: North
Melbourne, Australia 1988-89; Old Hararians,
Zimbabwe 1990-91
Cricketers particularly admired: Ian Botham, Vic Marks, John Emburey,
Jack Russell
Other sports played: Rugby, football (both to county schoolboys level), 'enjoy golf
and skiing'
Other sports followed: 'All sport – massive Man City fan'
Relaxations: 'Spending some quality time at home with family'
Extras: Represented county schools. Played for Young England against Young New
Zealand in 1989. Produced best match bowling figures for the Britannic County
Championship 1993 season – 14-169 against Somerset at Taunton. Called up for
England Test tour of India 2001-02 after withdrawal of Robert Croft
Best batting: 75 Gloucestershire v Somerset, Taunton 2003
Best bowling: 8-46 Gloucestershire v Somerset, Taunton 1993

2003 Season

	M	Inns	NO	Runs	HS	Avge	100s	50s	Ct	St	O	M	Runs	Wkts	Avge	Best	5wI	10wM
Test																		
All First	10	15	3	304	75	25.33	-	2	12	-	378.3	99	1008	28	36.00	5-104	1	-
1-day Int																		
C & G	4	1	0	7	7	7.00	-	-	8	-	36.3	0	152	7	21.71	2-21	-	
NCL	14	8	4	40	10	10.00	-	-	6	-	102	1	522	21	24.85	5-33	1	
Twenty20	6	2	1	13	11 *	13.00	-	-	1	-	24	0	136	8	17.00	2-21	-	

Career Performances

	M	Inns	NO	Runs	HS	Avge	100s	50s	Ct	St	Balls	Runs	Wkts	Avge	Best	5wl	10wM
Test																	
All First	172	264	49	4253	75	19.78	-	15	205	-	27204	12740	345	36.92	8-46	12	1
1-day Int																	
C & G	32	19	6	169	31	13.00	-	-	27	-	1529	1013	36	28.13	3-39	-	
NCL	160	113	41	948	45	13.16	-	-	61	-	5892	4798	152	31.56	5-33	2	
Twenty20	6	2	1	13	11 *	13.00	-	-	1	-	144	136	8	17.00	2-21	-	

BANES, M. J. Kent

Name: Matthew (<u>Matt</u>) John Banes
Role: Right-hand bat, right-arm medium bowler
Born: 10 December 1979, Pembury
Height: 5ft 9in **Weight:** 12st 7lbs
Nickname: Bano
County debut: 1999
1st-Class 50s: 3
1st-Class catches: 4
Strike rate: (career 98.00)
Parents: Chris and Jane Ann
Marital status: Single
Education: Tonbridge School; Durham University
Qualifications: 10 GCSEs, 4 A-levels
Overseas tours: Tonbridge School to Australia 1996-97; Durham University CC to Cape Town 2000; Yellowhammers to Cape Town 2001-02
Career highlights to date: 'A fifty [53] on debut for Kent v New Zealanders on TV'
Cricketers particularly admired: Mike Atherton, Steve Waugh
Young players to look out for: Rob Ferley
Other sports played: Hockey (Durham University 1st XI)
Other sports followed: Football (Arsenal)
Relaxations: Reading, films
Extras: Set record for most centuries (11 in three years) for Tonbridge School 1st XI. Played in Old Tonbridgians side that won *The Cricketer* Cup 1999. Scored 53 on first-class debut v New Zealanders at Canterbury 1999. Represented British Universities 2000, 2001 and 2002. Captain of Durham University CCE 2001 and 2002. Played for Kent Board XI in the C&G 2002 and 2003. Released by Kent at the end of the 2003 season

Best batting: 69 DUCCE v Lancashire, Durham 2002
Best bowling: 3-65 DUCCE v Lancashire, Durham 2001

2003 Season

	M	Inns	NO	Runs	HS	Avge	100s	50s	Ct	St	O	M	Runs	Wkts	Avge	Best	5wI	10wM
Test																		
All First	1	2	0	39	24	19.50	-	-	1	-								
1-day Int																		
C & G	1	1	0	4	4	4.00	-	-	-	-								
NCL	1	1	0	0	0	0.00	-	-	-	-								
Twenty20																		

Career Performances

	M	Inns	NO	Runs	HS	Avge	100s	50s	Ct	St	Balls	Runs	Wkts	Avge	Best	5wI	10wM
Test																		
All First	11	18	1	388	69	22.82	-	3	4	-	294	175	3	58.33	3-65	-	-
1-day Int																		
C & G	3	3	0	110	82	36.66	-	1	2	-	12	11	1	11.00	1-11	-	
NCL	1	1	0	0	0	0.00	-	-	-	-							
Twenty20																		

BASSANO, C. W. G.   Derbyshire

Name: <u>Christopher</u> Warwick Godfrey Bassano
Role: Right-hand bat, leg-spin bowler
Born: 11 September 1975, East London, South Africa
Height: 6ft 2in **Weight:** 13st 7lbs
Nickname: Bass, Bassy
County debut: 2001
County cap: 2002
1000 runs in a season: 1
1st-Class 50s: 12
1st-Class 100s: 3
1st-Class catches: 26
One-Day 100s: 4
Place in batting averages: 254th av. 14.57 (2002 67th av. 42.52)
Parents: Brian and Allison
Marital status: Single
Family links with cricket: 'Father played throughout his life, was a radio

commentator, provincial manager, and held development positions in South Africa; also wrote books on cricket etc.'

Education: Grey School, Port Elizabeth; Launceston Church Grammar School, Tasmania; University of Tasmania, Hobart

Qualifications: Bachelor of Applied Science (Horticulture)

Career outside cricket: Trout fishing guide

Career highlights to date: 'Being selected to play representative cricket or to play at a higher level is always a highlight'

Cricket moments to forget: 'Losing'

Cricketers particularly admired: Graeme Pollock, Steve Waugh

Other sports played: Hockey

Other sports followed: Rugby union

Relaxations: Fly fishing

Extras: Captained Eastern Province U13 1987-88. Played for Tasmania U16, U17, U19 (captain), U23 (captain) and 2nd XI. Became the first player to score a century in each innings of his Championship debut, 186* and 106 v Gloucestershire at Derby 2001; his first innings lasted 8¾ hours and also produced the highest score by a Derbyshire batsman on Championship debut. Scored 100-ball 121 v Glamorgan at Cardiff in the C&G 2003, winning Man of the Match award and sharing with Andrew Gait (87*) in a new competition record third-wicket partnership for Derbyshire (191). Is diabetic. His ancestry includes a set of brothers from Venice who were musicians at the court of Henry VIII. Is not considered an overseas player

Best batting: 186* Derbyshire v Gloucestershire, Derby 2001

2003 Season

	M	Inns	NO	Runs	HS	Avge	100s	50s	Ct	St	O	M	Runs	Wkts	Avge	Best	5wI	10wM
Test																		
All First	12	22	3	277	53*	14.57	-	2	7	-								
1-day Int																		
C & G	4	4	0	265	121	66.25	2	-	-	-								
NCL	16	15	3	559	126*	46.58	2	3	3	-								
Twenty20	5	3	0	76	43	25.33	-	-	3	-								

Career Performances

	M	Inns	NO	Runs	HS	Avge	100s	50s	Ct	St	Balls	Runs	Wkts	Avge	Best	5wI	10wM
Test																	
All First	36	65	6	1889	186*	32.01	3	12	26	-	12	11	0	-	-	-	-
1-day Int																	
C & G	4	4	0	265	121	66.25	2	-	-	-							
NCL	35	34	4	972	126*	32.40	2	5	7	-							
Twenty20	5	3	0	76	43	25.33	-	-	3	-							

BATTY, G. J.   Worcestershire

Name: <u>Gareth</u> Jon Batty
Role: Right-hand bat, off-spin bowler
Born: 13 October 1977, Bradford, Yorkshire
Height: 5ft 11in **Weight:** 12st 4lbs
Nickname: Bats, Ging, Rohnan
County debut: 1997 (Yorkshire), 1998 (one-day, Surrey), 1999 (first-class, Surrey), 2002 (Worcestershire)
County colours: 2002 (Worcestershire)
One-Day Internationals: 2
50 wickets in a season: 2
1st-Class 50s: 6
1st-Class 5 w. in innings: 4
1st-Class catches: 29
Place in batting averages: 211th av. 22.04 (2002 219th av. 21.34)
Place in bowling averages: 35th av. 26.25 (2002 71st av. 30.94)
Strike rate: 57.46 (career 60.09)
Parents: David and Rosemary
Marital status: Single
Family links with cricket: 'Dad is Yorkshire Academy coach and U17 manager; brother played for Yorkshire and Somerset'
Education: Bingley Grammar
Qualifications: 9 GCSEs, BTEC Art and Design, coaching certificate
Off-season: England tour to Bangladesh and Sri Lanka
Overseas tours: England U15 to South Africa 1993; England U19 to Zimbabwe 1995-96, to Pakistan 1996-97; ECB National Academy to Australia and Sri Lanka 2002-03; England to Bangladesh and Sri Lanka 2003-04, to West Indies 2003-04
Overseas teams played for: Marist Newman, Australia
Career highlights to date: 'Playing for England'
Cricket moments to forget: 'Every time I lose'
Cricketers particularly admired: Alec Stewart
Other sports played: Rugby
Other sports followed: Rugby league (Leeds Rhinos)
Favourite band: Coldplay
Relaxations: Going to the gym
Extras: National U15 bowling award. *Daily Telegraph* Young Player of the Year 1993. Surrey Supporters' Club Most Improved Player Award and Young Player of the Year Award 2001. Surrey CCC Young Player of the Year Award 2001. ECB 2nd XI Player of the Year 2001. Released by Surrey at the end of the 2001 season and joined

Worcestershire for 2002, taking 56 first-class wickets. Called up from the ECB National Academy squad in Adelaide to the England one-day squad for the VB Series in Australia 2002-03 as cover for the injured Jeremy Snape. Made ODI debut v Australia at Sydney in the VB Series 2002-03. Leading all-rounder in the inaugural Twenty20 Cup 2003

Best batting: 74 Worcestershire v Derbyshire, Worcester 2002

Best bowling: 6-71 Worcestershire v Essex, Southend 2002

Stop press: Made Test debut in the first Test v Bangladesh at Dhaka 2003-04, taking a wicket (Alok Kapali) with his third ball

2003 Season

	M	Inns	NO	Runs	HS	Avge	100s	50s	Ct	St	O	M	Runs	Wkts	Avge	Best	5wI	10wM
Test																		
All First	18	28	4	529	60	22.04	-	3	14	-	574.4	142	1575	60	26.25	6-88	1	-
1-day Int																		
C & G	5	4	1	44	20	14.66	-	-	2	-	35.3	4	136	5	27.20	2-25	-	
NCL	13	11	3	119	31	14.87	-	-	3	-	87	7	336	12	28.00	3-51	-	
Twenty20	5	5	0	150	87	30.00	-	1	1	-	20	0	172	9	19.11	3-45	-	

Career Performances

	M	Inns	NO	Runs	HS	Avge	100s	50s	Ct	St	Balls	Runs	Wkts	Avge	Best	5wI	10wM
Test																	
All First	42	67	10	1207	74	21.17	-	6	29	-	8012	3738	133	28.10	6-71	4	-
1-day Int	2	2	0	3	3	1.50	-	-	2	-	120	120	1	120.00	1-65	-	
C & G	9	7	1	54	20	9.00	-	-	6	-	359	247	8	30.87	2-25	-	
NCL	51	45	11	775	83 *	22.79	-	4	14	-	1707	1341	40	33.52	4-36	-	
Twenty20	5	5	0	150	87	30.00	-	1	1	-	120	172	9	19.11	3-45	-	

BATTY, J. N.   Surrey

Name: Jonathan (<u>Jon</u>) Neil Batty

Role: Right-hand bat, wicket-keeper, county captain

Born: 18 April 1974, Chesterfield

Height: 5ft 10in **Weight:** 11st 6lbs

Nickname: JB

County debut: 1997

County cap: 2001

50 dismissals in a season: 1

1st-Class 50s: 13

1st-Class 100s: 6

1st-Class catches: 234

1st-Class stumpings: 32

Place in batting averages: 18th av. 56.94
(2002 107th av. 35.33)
Strike rate: (career 78.00)
Parents: Roger and Jill
Marital status: Single
Family links with cricket: Father played to a
high standard of club cricket
Education: Wheatley Park; Repton; Durham
University (St Chad's); Keble College,
Oxford
Qualifications: 10 GCSEs, 4 A-levels,
BSc (Hons) in Natural Sciences, Diploma in
Social Studies (Oxon)
Overseas tours: Repton School to Holland
1991; MCC to Bangladesh 1996; Surrey to
South Africa 1997, 2001
Overseas teams played for: Mount Lawley
CC, Perth 1997-2002
Career highlights to date: 'Winning three County Championships'
Cricket moments to forget: 'None!'
Cricketers particularly admired: David Gower, Alec Stewart, Jack Russell
Other sports played: Golf, squash
Other sports followed: Football (Nottingham Forest)
Relaxations: Reading, listening to music, movies
Extras: Oxford Blue 1996. Has also played for Oxfordshire and represented Minor
Counties. Carried his bat for 154* v Lancashire 2003, becoming the first Surrey
batsman to achieve the feat at Old Trafford since Harry Jupp in 1870. Appointed
captain of Surrey for 2004
Opinions on cricket: 'Influx of EU cricketers is complete rubbish and will destroy the
English game if allowed to continue. Where is the need for two overseas players? If
people think they will increase crowds, they are sadly mistaken. Combined with the
EU situation it will be terrible for the game!'
Best batting: 168* Surrey v Essex, Chelmsford 2003
Best bowling: 1-21 Surrey v Lancashire, Old Trafford 2000

2003 Season

	M	Inns	NO	Runs	HS	Avge	100s	50s	Ct	St	O	M	Runs	Wkts	Avge	Best	5wl	10wM
Test																		
All First	12	22	5	968	168 *	56.94	3	4	32	2								
1-day Int																		
C & G	3	3	1	102	55 *	51.00	-	1	3	-								
NCL	15	11	3	113	28	14.12	-	-	19	4								
Twenty20	7	6	3	64	19 *	21.33	-	-	8	-								

Career Performances

	M	Inns	NO	Runs	HS	Avge	100s	50s	Ct	St	Balls	Runs	Wkts	Avge	Best	5wI	10wM
Test																	
All First	94	135	22	3351	168 *	29.65	6	13	234	32	78	61	1	61.00	1-21	-	-
1-day Int																	
C & G	7	5	2	109	55 *	36.33	-	1	5	-							
NCL	78	55	13	584	40	13.90	-	-	84	15							
Twenty20	7	6	3	64	19 *	21.33	-	-	8	-							

BELL, I. R.   Warwickshire

Name: <u>Ian</u> Ronald Bell
Role: Right-hand bat, right-arm medium bowler
Born: 11 April 1982, Coventry
Height: 5ft 10in **Weight:** 11st
Nickname: Belly
County debut: 1999
County cap: 2001
1st-Class 50s: 15
1st-Class 100s: 4
1st-Class catches: 25
One-Day 100s: 1
One-Day 5 w. in innings: 1
Place in batting averages: 138th av. 30.50 (2002 186th av. 24.37)
Strike rate: 64.33 (career 74.07)
Parents: Terry and Barbara
Marital status: Single
Family links with cricket: Brother Keith has played for England U18
Education: Princethorpe College, Rugby
Overseas tours: Warwickshire U19 to Cape Town 1998-99; England U19 to New Zealand 1998-99, to Malaysia and (U19 World Cup) Sri Lanka 1999-2000, to India 2000-01 (captain); England A to West Indies 2000-01; ECB National Academy to Australia 2001-02, to Sri Lanka 2002-03
Career highlights to date: 'Selection for ECB Academy and as replacement for England A tour to West Indies. Captaining England U19. Receiving my county cap and scoring my first County Championship century'
Cricket moments to forget: 'Being bowled for a duck when making county debut'
Cricketers particularly admired: Michael Atherton, Steve Waugh, Alec Stewart, Nick Knight
Young players to look out for: Keith Bell

Other sports played: Football (was at Coventry City School of Excellence), rugby, golf
Other sports followed: Football (Aston Villa), rugby union (Northampton Saints)
Relaxations: Golf, listening to music
Extras: Played for England U14, U15, U16, U17; captained England U19. NBC Denis Compton Award for the most promising young Warwickshire player 1999, 2000, 2001. Gray-Nicolls Trophy for Best Young Schools Cricketer 2000. Scored maiden first-class century (130) v Oxford University CCE at The Parks 2001, becoming (at 19 years 56 days) the youngest player to score a first-class century for Warwickshire. Scored maiden Championship century (103) v Nottinghamshire at Edgbaston 2001, becoming (at 19 years 115 days) the youngest Warwickshire batsman to score a Championship 100. Cricket Society's Most Promising Young Cricketer of the Year Award 2001. Scored century (104) in ECB National Academy's innings victory over Commonwealth Bank [Australian] Cricket Academy in Adelaide 2001-02. Called up to the England Test squad in New Zealand 2001-02 as batting cover after Mark Butcher suffered a fractured thumb. B&H Gold Award for his 65* in the last B&H final, v Essex at Lord's 2002. Recorded maiden one-day century (125) and maiden one-day five-wicket return (5-41) v Essex at Chelmsford in the NCL 2003
Best batting: 135 Warwickshire v Derbyshire, Derby 2001
Best bowling: 4-12 Warwickshire v India A, Edgbaston 2003

2003 Season

	M	Inns	NO	Runs	HS	Avge	100s	50s	Ct	St	O	M	Runs	Wkts	Avge	Best	5wI	10wM
Test																		
All First	17	30	2	854	107	30.50	1	5	5	-	96.3	15	407	9	45.22	4-12	-	-
1-day Int																		
C & G	3	3	0	50	41	16.66	-	-	2	-	5	0	31	0	-		-	-
NCL	16	16	3	560	125	43.07	1	4	1	-	40.5	1	247	9	27.44	5-41	1	
Twenty20	5	5	0	51	20	10.20	-	-	-	-	5	0	44	1	44.00	1-29	-	

Career Performances

	M	Inns	NO	Runs	HS	Avge	100s	50s	Ct	St	Balls	Runs	Wkts	Avge	Best	5wI	10wM
Test																	
All First	50	85	6	2628	135	33.26	4	15	25	-	963	561	13	43.15	4-12	-	-
1-day Int																	
C & G	6	6	0	135	50	22.50	-	1	3	-	33	33	0	-		-	-
NCL	31	30	4	977	125	37.57	1	7	2	-	245	247	9	27.44	5-41	1	
Twenty20	5	5	0	51	20	10.20	-	-	-	-	30	44	1	44.00	1-29	-	

> 9. Which Kent bowler whose father and grandfather also played Test cricket represented England in the 1997-98 Test series?

BENHAM, C. C.   Hampshire

Name: Christopher (<u>Chris</u>) Charles Benham
Role: Right-hand bat, right-arm
off-spin bowler
Born: 24 March 1983, Frimley, Surrey
Height: 6ft 2in **Weight:** 13st
Nickname: Benny, Beano, Benoit
County debut: No first-team appearance
Parents: Frank and Sandie
Marital status: Single
Family links with cricket: 'Both older
brothers, Nick and Andy, played local
club cricket'
Education: Yateley Comprehensive School;
Yateley Sixth Form College; Loughborough
University
Qualifications: 10 GCSEs, 3 A-levels
Career outside cricket: Studying for Sports
Science and Physical Education degree at
Loughborough University

Off-season: 'Training with Loughborough UCCE squad'
Overseas tours: West of England U15 to West Indies 1998
Career highlights to date: 'Being part of Hampshire 2nd XI squad that won the 2nd
XI Championship in 2001'
Cricketers particularly admired: Ricky Ponting, V.V.S. Laxman, Sachin Tendulkar,
Michael Vaughan
Young players to look out for: Andrew Hodd, David Wigley, Nick Ferraby
Other sports played: Football (school, district and county sides; trials with Swindon
and Crystal Palace), tennis, golf
Other sports followed: Football (Reading FC)
Injuries: Out for half of the 2003 season with a lower back disc problem and a torn
hamstring
Favourite band: Kings of Leon
Relaxations: 'Listening to music; watching DVDs; spending time with my girlfriend;
going to the gym'
Extras: Played for ESCA U15 v Scotland. Represented England U16 v Denmark.
Played for Hampshire Board XI in the C&G 2001. Played for Loughborough
University CCE 2002

2003 Season (did not make any first-class or one-day appearances)

Career Performances

	M	Inns	NO	Runs	HS	Avge	100s	50s	Ct	St	Balls	Runs	Wkts	Avge	Best	5wI	10wM
Test																	
All First																	
1-day Int																	
C & G	1	1	0	0	0	0.00	-	-	-	-							
NCL																	
Twenty20																	

BENNING, J. G. E.   Surrey

Name: <u>James</u> Graham Edward Benning
Role: Right-hand bat, right-arm medium bowler; batting all-rounder
Born: 4 May 1983, Mill Hill, London
Height: 5ft 11in **Weight:** 13st
Nickname: Benno
County debut: 2002 (one-day), 2003 (first-class)
Strike rate: 78.00 (career 78.00)
Parents: Sandy and David
Marital status: Single
Family links with cricket: 'Dad played for Middlesex'
Education: Caterham School
Qualifications: 12 GCSEs, 3 AS-levels
Off-season: 'Perth, Australia/club cricket'
Overseas tours: Surrey YC to Barbados 1999-2000, to Sri Lanka 2002
Overseas teams played for: North Dandenong, Australia 2001-02
Career highlights to date: 'Making County Championship debut'
Cricket moments to forget: 'Dropping two catches in front of a lively crowd at Canterbury, live on Sky'
Cricket superstitions: 'Order in which I put my kit on'
Cricketers particularly admired: Alec Stewart, Adam Hollioake
Young players to look out for: Neil Saker, Scott Newman, Ben Scott
Other sports played: Rugby, football
Other sports followed: Football (Watford)
Favourite band: 'Listen to almost all music apart from thrash metal'
Relaxations: 'Going to the gym, music, spending time around friends'

Extras: Played for Buckinghamshire in the C&G 2001. Played for England U15-U19, including representing England U19 v India U19 2002. First recipient of Ben Holpioake Scholarship
Best batting: 47 Surrey v Essex, The Oval 2003
Best bowling: 1-39 Surrey v Essex, The Oval 2003

2003 Season

	M	Inns	NO	Runs	HS	Avge	100s	50s	Ct	St	O	M	Runs	Wkts	Avge	Best	5wI	10wM
Test																		
All First	2	3	0	87	47	29.00	-	-	-	-	13	1	81	1	81.00	1-39	-	-
1-day Int																		
C & G																		
NCL	2	2	0	31	25	15.50	-	-	2	-	9	1	43	4	10.75	4-43	-	
Twenty20	5	5	0	73	27	14.60	-	-	-	-	2	0	12	0	-		-	-

Career Performances

	M	Inns	NO	Runs	HS	Avge	100s	50s	Ct	St	Balls	Runs	Wkts	Avge	Best	5wI	10wM
Test																	
All First	2	3	0	87	47	29.00	-	-	-	-	78	81	1	81.00	1-39	-	-
1-day Int																	
C & G	2	2	0	43	23	21.50	-	-	1	-	18	26	1	26.00	1-26	-	
NCL	3	3	0	41	25	13.66	-	-	2	-	96	101	6	16.83	4-43	-	
Twenty20	5	5	0	73	27	14.60	-	-	-	-	12	12	0	-		-	-

BETTS, M. M.   Middlesex

Name: <u>Melvyn</u> Morris Betts
Role: Right-hand bat, right-arm fast-medium bowler
Born: 26 March 1975, Durham
Height: 5ft 11in **Weight:** 12st
Nickname: Betsy
County debut: 1993 (Durham), 2001 (Warwickshire)
County cap: 1998 (Durham), 2001 (Warwickshire)
1st-Class 50s: 5
1st-Class 5 w. in innings: 13
1st-Class 10 w. in match: 2
1st-Class catches: 34
Place in batting averages: 155th av. 29.00 (2002 199th av. 23.54)
Place in bowling averages: 104th av. 37.30 (2002 148th av. 51.15)
Strike rate: 55.46 (career 51.19)
Parents: Melvyn and Shirley
Wife and date of marriage: Angela, 3 October 1998

Children: Chloe, 16 July 1999; Meghan, 14 May 2002
Family links with cricket: 'Dad and uncle play for local team Sacriston'
Education: Fyndoune Community College
Qualifications: 9 GCSEs, plus qualifications in engineering and sports and recreational studies
Off-season: 'Spending time with family'
Overseas tours: England U19 to Sri Lanka 1993-94; England A to Zimbabwe and South Africa 1998-99; Durham CCC to South Africa 1996
Career highlights to date: '9-64 v Northamptonshire'
Cricketers particularly admired: David Boon
Other sports played: Football, golf
Other sports followed: Football (Newcastle United FC), darts
Favourite band: U2
Relaxations: 'Local pub with friends outside cricket'
Extras: Played for England U19 v India U19 1994. Left Durham at the end of the 2000 season and joined Warwickshire for 2001. Took 5-22 on his Championship debut for Warwickshire against his old county, Durham, at Edgbaston 2001. Left Warwickshire at the end of the 2003 season and has joined Middlesex for 2004
Best batting: 73 Warwickshire v Lancashire, Edgbaston 2003
Best bowling: 9-64 Durham v Northamptonshire, Northampton 1997

2003 Season

	M	Inns	NO	Runs	HS	Avge	100s	50s	Ct	St	O	M	Runs	Wkts	Avge	Best	5wl	10wM
Test																		
All First	10	14	2	348	73	29.00	-	2	2	-	240.2	30	970	26	37.30	5-43	1	-
1-day Int																		
C & G																		
NCL	1	1	1	1	1 *	-	-	-	-	-	4	0	25	0	-	-	-	
Twenty20																		

Career Performances

	M	Inns	NO	Runs	HS	Avge	100s	50s	Ct	St	Balls	Runs	Wkts	Avge	Best	5wl	10wM
Test																	
All First	99	146	33	1656	73	14.65	-	5	34	-	15767	9220	308	29.93	9-64	13	2
1-day Int																	
C & G	9	7	1	40	14	6.66	-	-	2	-	552	427	15	28.46	4-34	-	
NCL	50	35	17	196	21	10.88	-	-	9	-	2113	1747	53	32.96	4-39	-	
Twenty20																	

BICHEL, A. J. Worcestershire

Name: Andrew (<u>Andy</u>) John Bichel
Role: Right-hand bat, right-arm
fast-medium bowler
Born: 27 August 1970, Laidley, Queensland
Height: 5ft 11in **Weight:** 13st 9lbs
Nickname: Bic, Andre
County debut: 2001
County cap: 2001; colours 2002
Test debut: 1996-97
Tests: 15
One-Day Internationals: 54
50 wickets in a season: 1
1st-Class 50s: 11
1st-Class 100s: 1
1st-Class 5 w. in innings: 22
1st-Class 10 w. in match: 4
1st-Class catches: 65
One-Day 100s: 1
One-Day 5 w. in innings: 3

Place in batting averages: (2002 135th av. 30.44)
Place in bowling averages: (2002 24th av. 25.05)
Strike rate: (career 48.20)
Parents: Trevor and Shirley
Wife: Dionn
Children: Keegan
Family links with cricket: 'Uncle Don played for Queensland. Cricket is a huge part of our family in Southeast Queensland'
Education: Laidley High; Ipswich TAFE College
Qualifications: Carpenter and joiner
Career outside cricket: Project management
Off-season: Playing for Queensland
Overseas tours: Queensland Academy to South Africa 1994; Australian Academy to South Africa 1996; Australia A to Scotland and Ireland 1998; Australia to South Africa 1996-97, to England 1997, to New Zealand (one-day series) 1997-98, to Malaysia (Commonwealth Games) 1998, to West Indies 1998-99, to South Africa 2001-02, to Kenya (PSO Tri-Nation Tournament) 2002, to Sri Lanka (ICC Champions Trophy) 2002-03, to Sri Lanka and Sharjah (v Pakistan) 2002-03, to Africa (World Cup) 2002-03, to West Indies 2002-03, to India (TVS Cup) 2003-04
Overseas teams played for: Queensland 1992-93 –
Cricket moments to forget: 'Any game that is close that you lose – always makes it hard to forget. But in sport you have to learn from your mistakes'

Cricketers particularly admired: Allan Border, Sachin Tendulkar, Glenn McGrath, Dennis Lillee
Other sports played: Rugby league (first grade TRL); tennis (first grade LTA)
Other sports followed: Rugby league (Brisbane Broncos), AFL (Brisbane Lions)
Relaxations: 'Fishing in my boat on Moreton Bay; going to the beach; golf'
Extras: Sheffield Shield Player of the Year 1996-97. Queensland Player of the Year 1998-99. Took 60 first-class wickets at 20.11 in the 1999-2000 Australian season, including 6-47 in Victoria's first innings in the Pura Milk Cup final. Was Worcestershire's overseas player 2001-02. Won the Dick Lygon Award 2001 as Worcestershire's Player of the Year; was also the Worcestershire Supporters' Association Player of the Year 2001 and the winner of the inaugural Don Kenyon Award for the season's best first-class match-winning performance (113 runs and seven wickets v Glamorgan). Man of the Match v South Africa at Sydney in the VB Series 2001-02 (5-19). His 9-93 v Gloucestershire at Worcester 2002 was the best innings return by a Worcestershire bowler since Neal Radford took 9-70 v Somerset at Worcester in 1986 and the best innings return in April in Championship history. Man of the Match v England at Port Elizabeth in the World Cup 2002-03 (34* following 7-20, the third best bowling return in ODI history). Has same birthday as the late Sir Donald Bradman. ACB contract 2003-04. Has returned to Worcestershire as an overseas player for 2004
Best batting: 110 Queensland v Victoria, Brisbane 1997-98
Best bowling: 9-93 Worcestershire v Gloucestershire, Worcester 2002

2003 Season (did not make any first-class or one-day appearances)

Career Performances

	M	Inns	NO	Runs	HS	Avge	100s	50s	Ct	St	Balls	Runs	Wkts	Avge	Best	5wI	10wM
Test	15	18	1	319	71	18.76	-	1	12	-	2357	1320	42	31.42	5-60	1	-
All First	110	142	13	2738	110	21.22	1	11	65	-	21885	11040	454	24.31	9-93	22	4
1-day Int	54	27	9	397	64	22.05	-	1	14	-	2717	1991	70	28.44	7-20	2	
C & G	5	4	0	42	27	10.50	-	-	-	-	234	145	10	14.50	3-9	-	
NCL	20	15	1	161	36 *	11.50	-	-	9	-	920	580	34	17.05	5-21	1	
Twenty20																	

10. Who captained England in the 1997-98 ODI series in the West Indies?

BICKNELL, D. J.   Nottinghamshire

Name: <u>Darren</u> John Bicknell
Role: Left-hand opening bat, occasional
slow left-arm bowler
Born: 24 June 1967, Guildford
Height: 6ft 4½in **Weight:** 14st 7lbs
Nickname: Denz, Bickers
County debut: 1987 (Surrey), 2000 (Notts)
County cap: 1990 (Surrey), 2000 (Notts)
Benefit: 1999 (Surrey)
1000 runs in a season: 7
1st-Class 50s: 76
1st-Class 100s: 37
1st-Class 200s: 2
1st-Class catches: 98
One-Day 100s: 10
Place in batting averages: 117th av. 33.42
(2002 126th av. 31.91)
Strike rate: (career 53.95)
Parents: Vic and Valerie
Wife and date of marriage: Rebecca, 21 September 1992
Children: Lauren Elizabeth, 21 September 1993; Sam, 9 November 1995;
Emily, 16 December 1997
Family links with cricket: Brother Martin plays for Surrey
Education: Robert Haining County Secondary; Guildford County College
of Technology
Qualifications: 8 O-levels, 2 A-levels, senior coaching award
Career outside cricket: Scottish Courage brewery account manager
Overseas tours: Surrey to Sharjah 1988, 1989, to Dubai 1990, to Perth 1995;
Nottinghamshire to Johannesburg 2000, 2001, 2002; England A to Zimbabwe and
Kenya 1989-90, to Pakistan 1990-91, to Bermuda and West Indies 1991-92
Overseas teams played for: Coburg, Melbourne 1986-87
Career highlights to date: 'England A call-up. Debut for Surrey. Being capped by
Notts and Surrey. And every time I reach a hundred'
Cricket moments to forget: 'My first-ball dismissal in my debut A 'Test' match v
Zimbabwe, and brother Martin getting me out twice'
Cricket superstitions: 'Try and wear same clothes if successful previously'
Cricketers particularly admired: Mark Taylor, David Gower, Angus Fraser,
Martin Bicknell
Young players to look out for: Bilal Shafayat, Rikki Clarke, Kevin Pietersen
Other sports played: Golf (11 handicap)
Other sports followed: Football (West Ham United, Nottingham Forest)

Relaxations: Family, golf and TV

Extras: Shared Surrey record third-wicket stand of 413 with David Ward v Kent at Canterbury in 1990 – both made career bests. Surrey Batsman of the Year four times. Left Surrey and joined Nottinghamshire for 2000. Became first English cricketer to take part in more than one partnership of 400-plus when he scored 180* in a first-wicket stand of 406* with Guy Welton (200*) v Warwickshire at Edgbaston 2000; the stand broke several records, including that for the highest Nottinghamshire partnership for any wicket, formerly 398 by Arthur Shrewsbury and William Gunn v Sussex at Trent Bridge 1890, and that for the highest unbeaten first-wicket partnership in Championship history. Was acting captain of Nottinghamshire in 2001 during the absence through injury of Jason Gallian. Scored 108 v Middlesex at Trent Bridge 2002, in the process sharing with Kevin Pietersen (254*) in a record partnership for any wicket in matches between Nottinghamshire and Middlesex (316)

Opinions on cricket: 'Am enjoying watching England improve – central contracts being a big part of it. English net facilities appalling – general. Teams should socialise more!'

Best batting: 235* Surrey v Nottinghamshire, Trent Bridge 1994

Best bowling: 3-7 Surrey v Sussex, Guildford 1996

2003 Season

	M	Inns	NO	Runs	HS	Avge	100s	50s	Ct	St	O	M	Runs	Wkts	Avge	Best	5wI	10wM
Test																		
All First	16	29	1	936	81	33.42	-	9	4	-	0.3	0	4	0	-	-	-	-
1-day Int																		
C & G	1	1	0	33	33	33.00	-	-	-	-								
NCL	5	5	0	44	15	8.80	-	-	-	-								
Twenty20																		

Career Performances

	M	Inns	NO	Runs	HS	Avge	100s	50s	Ct	St	Balls	Runs	Wkts	Avge	Best	5wI	10wM
Test																	
All First	272	478	39	16778	235 *	38.21	39	76	98	-	1241	793	23	34.47	3-7	-	-
1-day Int																	
C & G	25	25	5	939	135 *	46.95	1	5	1	-							
NCL	147	141	16	4433	125	35.46	6	31	35	-	42	45	2	22.50	1-11	-
Twenty20																	

11. Which former Middlesex batsman became Courtney Walsh's 450th Test wicket at Edgbaston in 2000?

BICKNELL, M. P.   Surrey

Name: <u>Martin</u> Paul Bicknell
Role: Right-hand bat, right-arm
fast-medium bowler
Born: 14 January 1969, Guildford
Height: 6ft 4in **Weight:** 15st
Nickname: Bickers
County debut: 1986
County cap: 1989
Benefit: 1997
Test debut: 1993
Tests: 4
One-Day Internationals: 7
50 wickets in a season: 11
1st-Class 50s: 22
1st-Class 100s: 3
1st-Class 5 w. in innings: 40
1st-Class 10 w. in match: 4
1st-Class catches: 93
One-Day 5 w. in innings: 3
Place in batting averages: 74th av. 40.00 (2002 151st av. 28.66)
Place in bowling averages: 47th av. 27.82 (2002 73rd av. 31.38)
Strike rate: 53.36 (career 51.94)
Parents: Vic and Val
Wife and date of marriage: Loraine, 29 September 1995
Children: Eleanor, 31 March 1995; Charlotte, 22 July 1996
Family links with cricket: 'Brother plays, but with no luck'
Education: Robert Haining County Secondary
Qualifications: 2 O-levels, NCA coach
Career outside cricket: 'Running "Martin Bicknell Golf"'
Overseas tours: England YC to Sri Lanka 1986-87, to Australia 1987-88; England A
to Zimbabwe and Kenya 1989-90, to Bermuda and West Indies 1991-92, to South
Africa 1993-94; England to Australia 1990-91
Career highlights to date: 'A *Wisden* Cricketer of the Year 2001'
Cricket moments to forget: 'It's all been an experience!!'
Cricketers particularly admired: 'All honest county trundlers'
Young players to look out for: Tim Murtagh
Other sports played: Golf
Other sports followed: Football (Leeds United), golf
Relaxations: 'Playing golf, reading; spending time with my children'
Extras: His figures of 9 for 45 v Cambridge University at Fenner's in 1988 were the
best for the county for 30 years. Took 7-30 in National League v Glamorgan at The

Oval 1999, the best Sunday/National League return by a Surrey bowler. His 16-119 (including 9-47 in the second innings) v Leicestershire at Guildford in 2000 equalled the Surrey record for wickets taken in a match and is the second best match return in Surrey history behind Tony Lock's 16-83 v Kent at Blackheath in 1956. One of *Wisden*'s Five Cricketers of the Year 2001. Scored maiden first-class century (110*) v Kent at Canterbury 2001 out of a total of 193-8. Wetherell Award for the Cricket Society's leading all-rounder in English first-class cricket 2000 and 2001. Surrey Supporters' Player of the Year 1993, 1997, 1999, 2000, 2001. Surrey Players' Player of the Year 1997, 1998, 1999, 2000, 2001. Surrey CCC Bowler of the Season Award 2001. Took 6-42 v Kent at The Oval 2002, in the process achieving the feat of having recorded a five-wicket innings return against all 17 counties besides his own. Scored a career best 141 v Essex at Chelmsford 2003, following up with 4-67 in Essex's first innings. Recalled to the England side for the fourth Test v South Africa at Headingley 2003, 10 years (and a world record 114 Test matches having passed) after his last appearance, taking a wicket (Herschelle Gibbs) with his second ball. Took Test best 4-84 (6-155 the match) in South Africa's second innings of the fifth Test at his home ground of The Oval 2003

Best batting: 141 Surrey v Essex, Chelmsford 2003
Best bowling: 9-45 Surrey v Cambridge University, The Oval 1988

2003 Season

	M	Inns	NO	Runs	HS	Avge	100s	50s	Ct	St	O	M	Runs	Wkts	Avge	Best	5wI	10wM
Test	2	3	0	19	15	6.33	-	-	2	-	93	22	280	10	28.00	4-84	-	-
All First	14	15	4	440	141	40.00	2	-	4	-	444.4	110	1391	50	27.82	5-42	3	-
1-day Int																		
C & G	2	1	1	3	3 *	-	-	-	-	-	18	5	46	1	46.00	1-23	-	
NCL	11	5	3	44	14 *	22.00	-	-	4	-	91	9	436	11	39.63	2-30	-	
Twenty20	3	2	2	11	10 *	-	-	-	1	-	11	1	61	4	15.25	2-11	-	

Career Performances

	M	Inns	NO	Runs	HS	Avge	100s	50s	Ct	St	Balls	Runs	Wkts	Avge	Best	5wI	10wM
Test	4	7	0	45	15	6.42	-	-	2	-	1080	543	14	38.78	4-84	-	-
All First	267	322	80	5790	141	23.92	3	22	93	-	51011	24139	982	24.58	9-45	40	4
1-day Int	7	6	2	96	31 *	24.00	-	-	2	-	413	347	13	26.69	3-55	-	
C & G	43	20	9	216	66 *	19.63	-	1	17	-	2631	1504	59	25.49	4-35	-	
NCL	198	101	46	786	57 *	14.29	-	1	43	-	8600	6021	241	24.98	7-30	3	
Twenty20	3	2	2	11	10 *	-	-	-	1	-	66	61	4	15.25	2-11	-	

BISHOP, J. E.   Essex

Name: <u>Justin</u> Edward Bishop
Role: Left-hand lower middle order bat,
left-arm fast-medium opening bowler
Born: 4 January 1982, Bury St Edmunds
Height: 6ft **Weight:** 13st 8lbs
Nickname: Bish, Bash, Basher, Tractor Boy
County debut: 1999
1st-Class 50s: 2
1st-Class 5 w. in innings: 1
1st-Class catches: 3
Place in batting averages: 220th av. 20.83
(2002 293rd av. 9.85)
Place in bowling averages: 82nd av. 33.54
(2002 133rd av. 42.72)
Strike rate: 47.54 (career 58.06)
Parents: Keith and Anne
Marital status: Single
Family links with cricket: 'Dad played
for Bury St Edmunds and Suffolk; Mum does teas!'
Education: County Upper School, Bury St Edmunds; Durham University
Qualifications: GCSEs, 1 A-level (PE), GNVQ (Advanced) Science, Level 1
coaching awards in cricket and athletics
Overseas tours: England U19 to Malaysia and (U19 World Cup) Sri Lanka
1999-2000, to India 2000-01; British Universities to South Africa 2002
Career highlights to date: 'Taking seven wickets in an U19 "One-Day International"
for England v West Indies'
Cricketers particularly admired: Mark Ilott ('ability to swing ball back into
right-handers')
Young players to look out for: Ravinder Bopara
Other sports played: Football (Suffolk U15)
Other sports followed: Football (Ipswich Town FC)
Extras: Played for England U15 1997. Represented England U17 at the ECC Colts
Festival in Northern Ireland 1999. Played for Suffolk in the NatWest 2000. Took 7-42
for England U19 v Sri Lanka U19 in third 'Test' at Worcester 2000. Took 7-41 for
England U19 v West Indies U19 at Chelmsford 2001, the best England U19 figures in
an 'ODI'. Played for Durham University CCE in 2002 and 2003. Scored 50 for
DUCCE v Nottinghamshire at Trent Bridge 2003 and also took 4-111 in the county's
only innings. Represented British Universities v Zimbabweans and v India A 2003
Best batting: 50 DUCCE v Nottinghamshire, Trent Bridge 2003
　　　　　　　50 DUCCE v Lancashire, Durham 2003
Best bowling: 5-148 Essex v Leicestershire, Chelmsford 2001

2003 Season

	M	Inns	NO	Runs	HS	Avge	100s	50s	Ct	St	O	M	Runs	Wkts	Avge	Best	5wI	10wM
Test																		
All First	5	6	0	125	50	20.83	-	2	1	-	87.1	10	369	11	33.54	4-111	-	-
1-day Int																		
C & G																		
NCL	2	1	0	1	1	1.00	-	-	1	-	8.5	0	68	2	34.00	1-21	-	
Twenty20																		

Career Performances

	M	Inns	NO	Runs	HS	Avge	100s	50s	Ct	St	Balls	Runs	Wkts	Avge	Best	5wI	10wM
Test																	
All First	21	28	4	285	50	11.87	-	2	3	-	2845	1934	49	39.46	5-148	1	-
1-day Int																	
C & G	3	3	0	3	3	1.00	-	-	-	-	127	78	3	26.00	2-34	-	
NCL	20	13	6	55	16 *	7.85	-	-	4	-	701	666	23	28.95	3-33	-	
Twenty20																	

BLACKWELL, I. D.   Somerset

Name: Ian David Blackwell
Role: Left-hand bat, slow left-arm bowler
Born: 10 June 1978, Chesterfield
Height: 6ft 2in   **Weight:** 16st 7lbs
Nickname: Blacko, Blackie, Albert, Pip, Yuf
County debut: 1997 (Derbyshire), 2000 (Somerset)
County cap: 2001 (Somerset)
One-Day Internationals: 14
1000 runs in a season: 1
1st-Class 50s: 14
1st-Class 100s: 10
1st-Class 200s: 1
1st-Class 5 w. in innings: 5
1st-Class catches: 34
One-Day 100s: 1
Place in batting averages: 28th av. 50.43 (2002 87th av. 38.21)
Place in bowling averages: 102nd av. 37.11 (2002 115th av. 37.72)
Strike rate: 77.77 (career 90.28)
Parents: John and Marilyn
Family links with cricket: Father played for Derbyshire Over 50s and is also involved at Chesterfield CC

Education: Manor Community School (GCSEs); Brookfield Community School (A-levels)

Qualifications: 9 GCSEs, 1 A-level, NCA senior coaching award

Off-season: Touring with England

Overseas tours: Somerset to Cape Town 2000, 2001; England VI to Hong Kong 2001; England to Sri Lanka (ICC Champions Trophy) 2002-03, to Australia 2002-03 (VB Series), to Africa (World Cup) 2002-03, to Bangladesh and Sri Lanka 2003-04 (one-day series), to West Indies 2003-04 (one-day series); ECB National Academy to Australia 2002-03

Overseas teams played for: Delacombe Park CC, Melbourne, Australia 1997, 1999

Cricket moments to forget: 'Scoring 0 and 5 against Lancashire in the Championship 1998; in the same game Graham Lloyd hit me for 28 in an over – the Kellogg's factory was in danger!!!'

Cricketers particularly admired: Phillip DeFreitas, Ian Botham, Brian Lara, Glenn McGrath, Jamie Cox, Marcus Trescothick

Young players to look out for: Matt Wood, Arul Suppiah, Ian Bell

Other sports followed: Golf, football (Chesterfield FC)

Relaxations: Golf ('but it's not that relaxing!!')

Extras: Played for Derbyshire from the age of eight through to the 1st XI. Set record for number of balls lost (seven) in a score of 213* off 156 balls at Bolsover, which included 21 fours and 15 sixes and equalled the Bassetlaw League 1A record. Left Derbyshire at end of 1999 season and joined Somerset for 2000. Became first batsman in Championship history to score two centuries (103/122) in a match batting at No. 7, v Northants at Northampton 2001. C&G Man of the Match award for his 53-ball 86 in the semi-final v Kent at Taunton 2002. Called up to the England one-day squad for the ICC Champions Trophy in Sri Lanka 2002-03 as a replacement for the injured Andrew Flintoff, scoring a 68-ball 82 v India at Colombo in his second ODI. Scored 134-ball double century (the fastest by an Englishman in terms of balls received) v Derbyshire at Taunton 2003, finishing with 247*; in the process passed 1000 first-class runs in a season for the first time and shared with Nixon McLean (39) in a new record tenth-wicket partnership for Somerset (163). Struck a 56-ball 111 v Sussex at Hove in the NCL 2003

Best batting: 247* Somerset v Derbyshire, Taunton 2003

Best bowling: 5-49 Somerset v Hampshire, West End 2002

2003 Season

	M	Inns	NO	Runs	HS	Avge	100s	50s	Ct	St	O	M	Runs	Wkts	Avge	Best	5wI	10wM
Test																		
All First	15	26	3	1160	247 *	50.43	3	2	7	-	466.4	111	1336	36	37.11	5-65	2	-
1-day Int																		
C & G	2	1	0	39	39	39.00	-	-	-	-	7	1	17	1	17.00	1-17	-	
NCL	17	16	1	566	111	37.73	1	3	5	-	108	5	594	18	33.00	3-27	-	
Twenty20	5	5	0	74	29	14.80	-	-	2	-	15.2	0	116	0	-		-	-

Career Performances

	M	Inns	NO	Runs	HS	Avge	100s	50s	Ct	St	Balls	Runs	Wkts	Avge	Best	5wI	10wM
Test																	
All First	83	128	7	4112	247 *	33.98	11	14	34	-	11647	5418	129	42.00	5-49	5	-
1-day Int	14	14	1	252	82	19.38	-	1	5	-	570	415	14	29.64	3-26	-	
C & G	17	15	2	342	86	26.30	-	2	5	-	576	436	9	48.44	2-34	-	
NCL	82	77	6	2035	111	28.66	1	14	21	-	2618	2163	71	30.46	4-24	-	
Twenty20	5	5	0	74	29	14.80	-	-	2	-	92	116	0	-	-	-	-

BLAIN, J. A. R. Northamptonshire

Name: <u>John</u> Angus Rae Blain
Role: Right-hand bat, right-arm
fast-medium bowler
Born: 4 January 1979, Edinburgh
Height: 6ft 2in **Weight:** 13st 7lbs
Nickname: Blainy, Haggis, Hag
County debut: 1997
One-Day Internationals: 5
1st-Class 5 w. in innings: 2
1st-Class catches: 5
One-Day 5 w. in innings: 2
Place in batting averages: (2002 308th
av. 6.71)
Place in bowling averages: 85th av. 34.53
(2002 154th av. 56.81)
Strike rate: 40.23 (career 62.06)
Parents: John and Elma
Marital status: Single

Education: Penicuik HS; Jewel and Esk Valley College
Qualifications: 8 GCSEs, 1 A-level, HNC Leisure and Recreation, Level 1
coaching award
Off-season: 'Scotland tour to Dubai in February'
Overseas tours: Northants CCC to Zimbabwe 1997, to Grenada 2001, 2002; Scotland
U19 to Holland (International Youth Tournament) 1994-95, to Bermuda (International
Youth Tournament) 1997, to South Africa (U19 World Cup) 1997-98 (captain);
Scotland to Denmark (European Championships) 1996, to Malaysia (ICC Trophy)
1997, to Malaysia (Commonwealth Games) 1998, to Sharjah 1999, to Canada (ICC
Trophy) 2001, to Dubai (ICC Six Nations Challenge) 2003-04
Overseas teams played for: New Plymouth Old Boys, New Zealand 1998-99;
Taranaki Cricket Association, New Zealand 1998-99
Career highlights to date: 'World Cup 1999, England'

Cricket moments to forget: 'Not qualifying for the 2003 World Cup, failing in the last match by six runs in Canada 2001'

Cricket superstitions: 'Keep a tidy kitbag'

Cricketers particularly admired: Devon Malcolm, Michael Kasprowicz

Young players to look out for: Richard King

Other sports played: Football (schoolboy forms with Hibernian FC and Falkirk FC, making youth and reserve team appearances), golf

Other sports followed: Rugby

Favourite band: Counting Crows

Relaxations: 'Listening to music and going out for a beer; going home to Scotland to spend time with family; watching football, going to gym and sleeping!'

Extras: Was youngest ever player to play for Scotland national side, at 17 years and 114 days. Played for Scotland in the B&H and NatWest competitions. Made his first-class debut for Scotland against Ireland in 1996. Took 5-24 on Sunday League debut for Northamptonshire v Derbyshire at Derby 1997. Represented Scotland in the 1999 World Cup, taking 10 wickets and finishing top of the strike rate chart for the tournament. Played two matches for Scottish Saltires in the NCL 2003. Released by Northamptonshire at the end of the 2003 season

Opinions on cricket: 'Too many so-called British- or English-qualified imports coming into the game.'

Best batting: 34 Northamptonshire v Surrey, Northampton 2001

Best bowling: 6-42 Northamptonshire v Kent, Canterbury 2001

2003 Season

	M	Inns	NO	Runs	HS	Avge	100s	50s	Ct	St	O	M	Runs	Wkts	Avge	Best	5wI	10wM
Test																		
All First	4	2	1	6	5	6.00	-	-	-	-	87.1	7	449	13	34.53	5-84	1	-
1-day Int																		
C & G																		
NCL	2	2	2	6	5 *	-	-	-	-	-	13.4	0	70	1	70.00	1-25	-	
Twenty20																		

Career Performances

	M	Inns	NO	Runs	HS	Avge	100s	50s	Ct	St	Balls	Runs	Wkts	Avge	Best	5wI	10wM
Test																	
All First	20	22	8	150	34	10.71	-	-	5	-	3041	2313	49	47.20	6-42	2	-
1-day Int	5	5	1	15	9	3.75	-	-	1	-	223	210	10	21.00	4-37	-	
C & G	2	1	0	6	6	6.00	-	-	1	-	126	103	4	25.75	2-47	-	
NCL	9	4	4	9	5 *	-	-	-	3	-	388	344	12	28.66	5-24	1	
Twenty20																	

BLAKEY, R. J. Yorkshire

Name: <u>Richard</u> John Blakey
Role: Right-hand bat, wicket-keeper
Born: 15 January 1967, Huddersfield
Height: 5ft 10in **Weight:** 11st 4lbs
Nickname: Dick
County debut: 1985
County cap: 1987
Benefit: 1998
Test debut: 1992-93
Tests: 2
One-Day Internationals: 3
1000 runs in a season: 5
50 dismissals in a season: 6
1st-Class 50s: 86
1st-Class 100s: 10
1st-Class 200s: 3
1st-Class catches: 778
1st-Class stumpings: 57
One-Day 100s: 3

Place in batting averages: 160th av. 27.52 (2002 44th av. 47.31)
Strike rate: (career 63.00)
Parents: Brian and Pauline
Wife and date of marriage: Michelle, 28 September 1991
Children: Harrison Brad, 22 September 1993
Family links with cricket: Father played local cricket
Education: Rastrick Grammar School
Qualifications: 4 O-levels, Senior NCA Coach
Career outside cricket: Started own leisure company
Overseas tours: England YC to West Indies 1984-85; Yorkshire to Barbados 1986-87, to Cape Town 1990-91; England A to Zimbabwe and Kenya 1989-90, to Pakistan 1990-91; England to India and Sri Lanka 1992-93
Overseas teams played for: Waverley, Sydney 1985-87; Mt Waverley, Sydney 1987-88; Bionics, Zimbabwe 1989-90
Cricketers particularly admired: Martyn Moxon, Dermot Reeve, Ian Botham, Alan Knott
Other sports followed: All
Relaxations: All sports, particularly golf and squash, eating out, drawing, photography
Extras: Made record individual score for Yorkshire 2nd XI (273*) v Northamptonshire 2nd XI 1986. Yorkshire's Young Player of the Year 1989. Was awarded a citation by the International Committee for Fair Play in 1995, the only cricketer among the 25 winners worldwide. Scored 60 v Leicestershire at Scarborough in the NUL 2002, in the process

sharing with Richard Dawson (41) in a new record eighth-wicket partnership for Yorkshire in the one-day league (89). Vice-captain of Yorkshire 2002. Yorkshire Players' Player of the Year and Club Player of the Year 2002. Scored 206-ball 223* v Northamptonshire at Headingley 2003

Best batting: 223* Yorkshire v Northamptonshire, Headingley 2003
Best bowling: 1-68 Yorkshire v Nottinghamshire, Sheffield 1986

2003 Season

	M	Inns	NO	Runs	HS	Avge	100s	50s	Ct	St	O	M	Runs	Wkts	Avge	Best	5wI	10wM
Test																		
All First	13	19	2	468	223 *	27.52	1	-	32	1								
1-day Int																		
C & G	2	2	0	34	23	17.00	-	-	-	2								
NCL	15	13	1	190	41	15.83	-	-	15	2								
Twenty20	5	4	1	101	32	33.66	-	-	5	-								

Career Performances

	M	Inns	NO	Runs	HS	Avge	100s	50s	Ct	St	Balls	Runs	Wkts	Avge	Best	5wI	10wM
Test	2	4	0	7	6	1.75	-	-	2	-							
All First	348	554	87	14674	223 *	31.42	13	86	778	57	63	68	1	68.00	1-68	-	-
1-day Int	3	2	0	25	25	12.50	-	-	2	1							
C & G	45	32	11	495	75	23.57	-	2	51	5							
NCL	245	216	51	5482	130 *	33.22	3	27	239	46							
Twenty20	5	4	1	101	32	33.66	-	-	5	-							

BLEWETT, G. S.   Kent

Name: Gregory (<u>Greg</u>) Scott Blewett
Role: Right-hand bat, right-arm medium bowler
Born: 28 October 1971, Adelaide, Australia
Height: 6ft **Weight:** 11st
Nickname: Blewy
County debut: 1999 (Yorkshire), 2001 (Nottinghamshire), 2003 (Kent)
County cap: 1999 (Yorkshire), 2001 (Nottinghamshire)
Test debut: 1994-95
Tests: 46
One-Day Internationals: 32
1000 runs in a season: 1
1st-Class 50s: 78

1st-Class 100s: 37
1st-Class 200s: 5
1st-Class 5 w. in innings: 1
1st-Class catches: 167
Place in batting averages: 129th av. 31.41
Strike rate: 129.00 (career 81.04)
Parents: Bob and Shirley
Wife and date of marriage: Jodie,
26 June 1998
Family links with cricket: Father played for
South Australia
Education: Prince Alfred College, Adelaide
Overseas tours: Australian Institute of Sport
to Sri Lanka 1990-91; Australia YC to
England 1991; Australia A to South Africa
(one-day series) 2002-03; Australia to New
Zealand (Bank of New Zealand Centenary
Series) 1994-95, to West Indies 1994-95, to
South Africa 1996-97, to England 1997, to India 1997-98, to West Indies 1998-99, to
Sri Lanka 1999-2000, to Zimbabwe 1999-2000, to New Zealand 1999-2000
Overseas teams played for: South Australia 1991-92 –
Cricketers particularly admired: Greg Chappell, Gordon Greenidge, Viv Richards
Other sports played: Golf
Other sports followed: Australian Football League (Adelaide Crows)
Relaxations: Golf, films, socialising
Extras: Scored centuries (102* and 115) in his first two Test matches, v England at
Adelaide and Perth in 1994-95. Scored 214 at Johannesburg 1996-97, sharing in record
fifth-wicket partnership for Australia in Tests v South Africa, 385 with Steve Waugh.
Was due to play for Middlesex in 1997 but was selected for Ashes tour. Was the only
Australian to make 1000 Test runs in 1997 calendar year. Holds the unenviable record
of being the first Australian to be out for 99 twice in Test cricket. In 1998-99, made
1175 first-class runs (av. 146.86 and including five 100s and a 200) before Christmas
in the Australian season, breaking David Hookes' record of 1163 set in 1982-83 and
becoming only the sixth Australian to score four consecutive first-class 100s. Averaged
118.70 in full Australian first-class season 1998-99. Was Yorkshire's overseas player in
1999. Leading run-scorer in the Pura Cup 2000-01 with 1162 runs (av. 68.35),
including a match-saving 260* v Queensland at Brisbane. Was Nottinghamshire's
overseas player in 2001. Scored 133 v Durham at Trent Bridge 2001, becoming only
the second player to score a century on Championship debut for Notts. Has a share in
record South Australian Sheffield Shield/Pura Cup partnerships for the second wicket
(386 with Darren Lehmann v Tasmania at Hobart 2001-02) and the third wicket (286
with Darren Lehmann v Tasmania at Adelaide 1993-94). Leading run-scorer in the
Pura Cup (843; av. 49.58) and the ING Cup (486; av. 54.00) 2002-03. Was an overseas
player for Kent April to June 2003, deputising first for Andrew Symonds and then for
Mohammad Sami

Best batting: 268 South Australia v Victoria, Melbourne 1993-94
Best bowling: 5-29 Australian XI v West Indies, Hobart 1996-97

2003 Season

	M	Inns	NO	Runs	HS	Avge	100s	50s	Ct	St	O	M	Runs	Wkts	Avge	Best	5wI	10wM
Test																		
All First	7	12	0	377	71	31.41	-	3	7	-	43	10	150	2	75.00	1-6	-	-
1-day Int																		
C & G	2	2	0	67	50	33.50	-	1	1	-	1	0	11	0	-		-	-
NCL	7	7	0	168	46	24.00	-	-	-	-	18	0	120	0	-		-	-
Twenty20	3	3	1	20	15	10.00	-	-	1	-	1	0	10	0	-		-	-

Career Performances

	M	Inns	NO	Runs	HS	Avge	100s	50s	Ct	St	Balls	Runs	Wkts	Avge	Best	5wI	10wM
Test	46	79	4	2552	214	34.02	4	15	45	-	1436	720	14	51.42	2-9	-	-
All First	207	370	25	15878	268	46.02	42	78	167	-	10536	5480	130	42.15	5-29	1	-
1-day Int	32	30	3	551	57 *	20.40	-	2	7	-	749	647	14	46.21	2-6	-	
C & G	7	7	1	178	77	29.66	-	2	3	-	196	110	7	15.71	4-18	-	
NCL	34	34	0	847	89	24.91	-	3	12	-	505	508	7	72.57	1-14	-	
Twenty20	3	3	1	20	15	10.00	-	-	1	-	6	10	0	-		-	

BLOOMFIELD, T. F.   Middlesex

Name: Timothy (<u>Tim</u>) Francis Bloomfield
Role: Right-hand bat, right-arm
fast-medium bowler
Born: 31 May 1973, Ashford, Middlesex
Height: 6ft 2in **Weight:** 14st
Nickname: Bloomers, Boof, Frank
County debut: 1997
County cap: 2001
50 wickets in a season: 1
1st-Class 5 w. in innings: 6
1st-Class catches: 8
Strike rate: 80.75 (career 54.74)
Parents: Richard and Pauline
Marital status: Engaged to Emma
Education: Halliford Independent School
Qualifications: 8 GCSEs, NCA coaching
award
Overseas tours: Berkshire U25 to Barbados
1996; Middlesex to South Africa 2000; MCC to Sri Lanka 2001, to Kenya 2002

Career highlights to date: 'Getting capped by Middlesex at Lord's'
Cricket moments to forget: 'All of the 2002 season, having not played due to injury'
Cricketers particularly admired: Ian Botham, Viv Richards, Angus Fraser
Young players to look out for: Nick Compton
Other sports played: Football, golf, tennis, snooker
Other sports followed: Football (Liverpool)
Relaxations: Sport, music
Extras: Has also played for Berkshire. Took 4-17 v Somerset at Southgate in the NatWest 2000, winning the Man of the Match award
Best batting: 31* Middlesex v Northamptonshire, Northampton 2002
Best bowling: 5-36 Middlesex v Glamorgan, Cardiff 1999

2003 Season

	M	Inns	NO	Runs	HS	Avge	100s	50s	Ct	St	O	M	Runs	Wkts	Avge	Best	5wl	10wM
Test																		
All First	5	4	1	19	9 *	6.33	-	-	2	-	107.4	14	428	8	53.50	4-57	-	-
1-day Int																		
C & G																			
NCL	9	2	1	18	15	18.00	-	-	1	-	67	4	362	13	27.84	4-25	-	
Twenty20	4	1	0	0	0	0.00	-	-	1	-	14	0	122	4	30.50	2-44	-	

Career Performances

	M	Inns	NO	Runs	HS	Avge	100s	50s	Ct	St	Balls	Runs	Wkts	Avge	Best	5wl	10wM
Test																	
All First	57	61	25	298	31 *	8.27	-	-	8	-	8540	5236	156	33.56	5-36	6	-
1-day Int																	
C & G	6	2	1	7	7 *	7.00	-	-	-	-	259	191	6	31.83	4-17	-	
NCL	46	16	6	71	15	7.10	-	-	10	-	1986	1505	47	32.02	4-25	-	
Twenty20	4	1	0	0	0	0.00	-	-	1	-	84	122	4	30.50	2-44	-	

12. Which rugby union international captained England
against West Indies at Old Trafford in June 1966?

BOPARA, R. S.   Essex

Name: Ravinder (<u>Ravi</u>) Singh Bopara
Role: Right-hand top-order bat, right-arm
medium bowler
Born: 4 May 1985, Newham, London
Height: 5ft 10in **Weight:** 12st
Nickname: Puppy
County debut: 2002
1st-Class catches: 9
Place in batting averages: (2002 159th
av. 27.50)
Strike rate: 90.00 (career 92.00)
Parents: Baldish and Charanjit
Marital status: Single
Education: Brampton Manor School;
Barking Abbey Sports College
Qualifications: 7 GCSEs, ECB Level 1
coaching
Off-season: U19 World Cup; 'playing
overseas'
Overseas tours: England U19 to Australia 2002-03, to Bangladesh (U19 World Cup)
2003-04
Career highlights to date: 'Playing against India and Pakistan overseas teams.
Meeting Sachin Tendulkar; facing Shoaib Akhtar and Mohammad Sami'
Cricket moments to forget: 'I went out to bat once and didn't realise I didn't have a
box on until I got hit there'
Cricketers particularly admired: Sachin Tendulkar, Viv Richards, Carl Hooper
Young players to look out for: Bilal Shafayat, 'Zobie' Sharif, 'and any players who
are hungry for success'
Other sports followed: Football (Arsenal)
Favourite band: Tupac and the Outlawz
Relaxations: 'Chillin' with my boys in the 'hood'
Extras: Played for Development of Excellence XI (South) v West Indies U19 at
Arundel 2001. Played for Essex Board XI in the C&G 2002. Represented England
U19 v South Africa U19 2003
Opinions on cricket: 'Too much time and money is spent on looking for young
players in private schools. We should be looking at youngsters in the inner cities and
state schools. Players to be as natural as they can'
Best batting: 48 Essex v Durham, Colchester 2002
                48 Essex v Middlesex, Lord's 2003
Best bowling: 1-23 Essex v Surrey, The Oval 2003

2003 Season

	M	Inns	NO	Runs	HS	Avge	100s	50s	Ct	St	O	M	Runs	Wkts	Avge	Best	5wl	10wM
Test																		
All First	4	7	3	163	48	40.75	-	-	3	-	30	3	122	2	61.00	1-23	-	-
1-day Int																		
C & G																			
NCL	7	7	2	82	32 *	16.40	-	-	1	-	14.1	0	97	1	97.00	1-34	-	
Twenty20	5	3	1	30	22	15.00	-	-	1	-								

Career Performances

	M	Inns	NO	Runs	HS	Avge	100s	50s	Ct	St	Balls	Runs	Wkts	Avge	Best	5wl	10wM
Test																	
All First	8	14	4	328	48	32.80	-	-	9	-	276	196	3	65.33	1-23	-	-
1-day Int																	
C & G	1	1	0	1	1	1.00	-	-	-	-							
NCL	9	9	2	82	32 *	11.71	-	-	1	-	85	97	1	97.00	1-34	-	
Twenty20	5	3	1	30	22	15.00	-	-	1	-							

BOTHA, A. G.   Derbyshire

Name: Anthony (<u>Ant</u>) Greyvensteyn Botha
Role: Left-hand bat, slow left-arm bowler
Born: 17 November 1976, Pretoria, South Africa
County debut: No first-team appearance
1st-Class 50s: 5
1st-Class 5 w. in innings: 2
1st-Class 10 w. in match: 1
1st-Class catches: 36
Strike rate: (career 68.48)
Education: Maritzburg College; Maritzburg Technikon
Overseas tours: South Africa U19 to India 1995-96
Overseas teams played for:
Natal/KwaZulu-Natal 1995-96 – 1998-99; Easterns 1999-2000 – 2002-03
Extras: Represented South African Schools 1995. Made first-class debut for Natal B v Free State B at Durban 1995-96. Played for South African Academy v New Zealand Academy in home series 1997. Man of the Match v Boland at Paarl in the SuperSport Series 2000-01. Man of the Match v Eastern Province at Benoni in the Standard Bank Cup 2001-02. Played for Derbyshire

Premier League and Premier Cup double winners Clifton 2003, scoring 200* v Denby.
Is not considered an overseas player
Best batting: 94 KwaZulu-Natal B v Eastern Province B, Port Elizabeth 1997-98
Best bowling: 8-53 KwaZulu-Natal B v Northerns B, Centurion 1997-98

2003 Season (did not make any first-class or one-day appearances)

Career Performances

	M	Inns	NO	Runs	HS	Avge	100s	50s	Ct	St	Balls	Runs	Wkts	Avge	Best	5wl	10wM
Test																	
All First	44	70	10	1205	94	20.08	-	5	36	-	8013	3516	117	30.05	8-53	2	1
1-day Int																	
C & G																		
NCL																		
Twenty20																		

BOWLER, P. D. Somerset

Name: <u>Peter</u> Duncan Bowler
Role: Right-hand opening bat, occasional
off-spin bowler, occasional wicket-keeper
Born: 30 July 1963, Plymouth
Height: 6ft 2in **Weight:** 13st 10lbs
Nickname: Tom
County debut: 1986 (Leicestershire),
1988 (Derbyshire), 1995 (Somerset)
County cap: 1989 (Derbyshire),
1995 (Somerset)
Benefit: 2000 (Somerset)
1000 runs in a season: 9
1st-Class 50s: 98
1st-Class 100s: 39
1st-Class 200s: 3
1st-Class catches: 221
1st-Class stumpings: 1
One-Day 100s: 7
Place in batting averages: 106th av. 34.07 (2002 118th av. 33.30)
Strike rate: (career 96.76)
Parents: Peter and Etta
Wife and date of marriage: Joanne, 10 October 1992
Children: Peter Robert, 21 September 1993; Rebekah, 25 August 1995
Education: Scots College, Sydney, Australia; Daramalan College, Canberra, Australia;
Nottingham Trent University

Qualifications: Australian Year 12 certificate, LLB
Cricketers particularly admired: Gus Valence, Rob Jeffery, Bill Carracher, Phil Russell
Other sports followed: Rugby union
Relaxations: Family and reading
Extras: First Leicestershire player to score a first-class century on debut (100* v Hampshire at Leicester 1986). Moved to Derbyshire at the end of the 1987 season and scored a hundred (155*) on debut v Cambridge University at Fenner's 1988, becoming the first player to score hundreds on debut for two counties. His 241* v Hampshire at Portsmouth 1992 is the highest score by a Derbyshire No. 1. First batsman to 2000 runs in 1992, finishing equal leading run-scorer (2044) with Mike Roseberry of Middlesex. Derbyshire Player of the Year 1992. Joined Somerset for 1995. Took over the Somerset captaincy mid-season 1997; relinquished captaincy after 1998 season. Passed 5000 runs in Sunday/National League, v Durham 1999. Top-scoring English batsman in first-class cricket in his benefit season (2000) with 1305 runs (av. 62.14). Scored 164 v Glamorgan at Taunton 2001, in the process sharing with Ian Blackwell in a record fifth-wicket stand for Somerset in matches v Glamorgan (163)
Best batting: 241* Derbyshire v Hampshire, Portsmouth 1992
Best bowling: 3-25 Somerset v Northamptonshire, Taunton 1998

2003 Season

	M	Inns	NO	Runs	HS	Avge	100s	50s	Ct	St	O	M	Runs	Wkts	Avge	Best	5wI	10wM
Test																		
All First	9	15	1	477	92	34.07	-	5	11	-	4	0	8	0	-	-	-	-
1-day Int																		
C & G																		
NCL	2	2	0	11	10	5.50	-	-	-	-								
Twenty20																		

Career Performances

	M	Inns	NO	Runs	HS	Avge	100s	50s	Ct	St	Balls	Runs	Wkts	Avge	Best	5wI	10wM
Test																	
All First	302	515	53	18533	241 *	40.11	42	98	221	1	3290	2049	34	60.26	3-25	-	-
1-day Int																	
C & G	36	36	0	1108	111	30.77	2	5	13	-	36	26	0	-	-	-	-
NCL	220	213	19	6336	138 *	32.65	3	51	80	1	308	323	8	40.37	3-31	-	
Twenty20																	

BRANDY, D. G.   Leicestershire

Name: <u>Damian</u> Gareth Brandy
Role: Right-hand bat, right-arm fast-medium
bowler; all-rounder
Born: 14 September 1981, Highgate, London
Height: 6ft 1in **Weight:** 14st 2lbs
Nickname: Damo, Brandytime
County debut: 2002
1st-Class 50s: 1
1st-Class catches: 3
Place in batting averages: 217th av. 21.14
Strike rate: 25.50 (career 38.25)
Parents: Judy-May and Winston
Marital status: Single (long-term girlfriend)
Family links with cricket: 'Dad was very
good club cricketer, playing for Essex and
London league clubs'
Education: St John's C of E Secondary,

Epping; Harlow College
Qualifications: 11 GCSEs, 3 A-levels, Level 1 coaching
Off-season: 'Working hard on my game at home'
Overseas teams played for: Bankstown, Sydney 2000-01; Potchefstroom Boys High,
South Africa 2002-03
Career highlights to date: 'First-team debut v Somerset under lights in
September 2002'
Cricket moments to forget: 'Being left out of Twenty20 squad for finals 2003'
Cricketers particularly admired: Viv Richards, Sachin Tendulkar, Rahul Dravid,
Devon Malcolm
Young players to look out for: Tom New, Luke Wright
Other sports played: Golf, football (West Ham Youth)
Other sports followed: Football (Arsenal, Leicester City)
Favourite band: Maxwell, Eric Benet
Relaxations: 'Reading autobiographies; holidays; eating nice food; spending time
with girlfriend and family'
Extras: Played for Essex from U11 to 2nd XI. Scored century in first 2nd XI game for
Leicestershire, v Durham 2001
Opinions on cricket: 'Not sure county cricket should panic or be forced to change its
entire structure. We have a unique game in our country, with conditions and amount
played different to the rest of the world. We also have a lot of very talented players
and need all 18 counties to give maximum opportunity. No EU players! Young players
to be given more guidance.'
Best batting: 52 Leicestershire v Kent, Canterbury 2003
Best bowling: 2-11 Leicestershire v LUCCE, Leicester 2003

2003 Season

	M	Inns	NO	Runs	HS	Avge	100s	50s	Ct	St	O	M	Runs	Wkts	Avge	Best	5wI	10wM
Test																		
All First	6	9	2	148	52	21.14	-	1	2	-	8.3	1	58	2	29.00	2-11	-	-
1-day Int																		
C & G																		
NCL	1	1	1	0	0*	-	-	-	-	-								
Twenty20	3	3	2	27	13	27.00	-	-	2	-								

Career Performances

	M	Inns	NO	Runs	HS	Avge	100s	50s	Ct	St	Balls	Runs	Wkts	Avge	Best	5wI	10wM
Test																	
All First	8	12	2	176	52	17.60	-	1	3	-	153	172	4	43.00	2-11	-	-
1-day Int																	
C & G																	
NCL	3	3	1	50	35	25.00	-	-	-	-							
Twenty20	3	3	2	27	13	27.00	-	-	2	-							

BRANT, S. A. Essex

Name: <u>Scott</u> Andrew Brant
Role: Right-hand bat, left-arm
fast-medium bowler
Born: 26 January 1983, Harare, Zimbabwe
Nickname: Woody
County debut: 2003
County cap: 2003
1st-Class 5 w. in innings: 1
1st-Class catches: 7
Place in batting averages: 294th av. 4.62
Place in bowling averages: 61st av. 30.18
Strike rate: 55.91 (career 54.47)
Education: Nudgee College, Brisbane;
Bond University, Queensland
Overseas teams played for:
Norths (Northern Suburbs), Brisbane;
Queensland 2001-02 –
Other sports played: Hockey, swimming,
triathlon, athletics (all at Zimbabwe Youth level; pole vault gold medallist at South
African junior championships)
Extras: Born in Zimbabwe and moved to Australia with his family in 1999. Played for
Queensland U19 2000-01. Took 3-34 from ten overs as Norths beat Valley in the final

of the 2001-02 Brisbane limited overs competition at Allan Border Field. Had match figures of 6-54 (3-23 and 3-31) v Victoria at Brisbane 2001-02 in his second first-class game, winning the Man of the Match award. Joined Essex as an overseas player in 2003. Recorded maiden first-class five-wicket return (6-45) v Nottinghamshire at Trent Bridge 2003. Awarded Essex cap 2003

Best batting: 23 Essex v Lancashire, Old Trafford 2003
Best bowling: 6-45 Essex v Nottinghamshire, Trent Bridge 2003

2003 Season

	M	Inns	NO	Runs	HS	Avge	100s	50s	Ct	St	O	M	Runs	Wkts	Avge	Best	5wI	10wM
Test																		
All First	11	14	6	37	23	4.62	-	-	3	-	344.5	77	1117	37	30.18	6-45	1	-
1-day Int																		
C & G	2	0	0	0	0	-	-	-	-	-	19	2	99	5	19.80	3-54	-	
NCL	7	3	2	20	14 *	20.00	-	-	4	-	53.4	2	294	13	22.61	4-25	-	
Twenty20	5	2	1	1	1 *	1.00	-	-	2	-	20	0	182	6	30.33	2-34	-	

Career Performances

	M	Inns	NO	Runs	HS	Avge	100s	50s	Ct	St	Balls	Runs	Wkts	Avge	Best	5wI	10wM
Test																	
All First	16	18	8	72	23	7.20	-	-	7	-	2615	1342	48	27.95	6-45	1	-
1-day Int																	
C & G	2	0	0	0	0	-	-	-	-	-	114	99	5	19.80	3-54	-	
NCL	7	3	2	20	14 *	20.00	-	-	4	-	322	294	13	22.61	4-25	-	
Twenty20	5	2	1	1	1 *	1.00	-	-	2	-	120	182	6	30.33	2-34	-	

13. Which Essex all-rounder opened the batting after opening the bowling and taking 7-34 at Kingston, Jamaica, in 1954?

BREESE, G. R.   Durham

Name: <u>Gareth</u> Rohan Breese
Role: Right-hand bat, right-arm
off-spin bowler
Born: 9 January 1976, Montego Bay,
Jamaica
County debut: No first-team appearance
Test debut: 2002-03
Tests: 1
1st-Class 50s: 12
1st-Class 100s: 1
1st-Class 5 w. in innings: 7
1st-Class 10 w. in match: 2
1st-Class catches: 29
Strike rate: (career 59.74)
Overseas tours: West Indies U19 to
Pakistan 1995-96; Jamaica to Malaysia
(Commonwealth Games) 1998-99; West
Indies A to England 2002; West Indies to
India 2002-03
Overseas teams played for: Jamaica 1995-96 –
Extras: Represented West Indies U19 in home series v England U19 1994-95. Second-
highest wicket-taker in the Busta Cup 2000-01 with 36 av. 15.11 and in 2001-02 with
44 av. 20.18. Appointed captain of Jamaica for 2004. Is a British passport holder and is
not considered an overseas player
Best batting: 124 Jamaica v Lancashire, Kingston 1995-96
Best bowling: 7-60 Jamaica v Barbados, Bridgetown 2000-01

2003 Season (did not make any first-class or one-day appearances)

Career Performances

	M	Inns	NO	Runs	HS	Avge	100s	50s	Ct	St	Balls	Runs	Wkts	Avge	Best	5wI	10wM
Test	1	2	0	5	5	2.50	-	-	1	-	188	135	2	67.50	2-108	-	-
All First	42	65	11	1553	124	28.75	1	12	29	-	7826	2994	131	22.85	7-60	7	2
1-day Int																	
C & G																	
NCL																	
Twenty20																	

BRESNAN, T. T. Yorkshire

Name: Timothy (Tim) Thomas Bresnan
Role: Right-hand bat, right-arm
fast-medium bowler
Born: 28 February 1985, Pontefract
Height: 6ft **Weight:** 13st
Nickname: Brezy Lad, Brez
County debut: 2001 (one-day),
2003 (first-class)
1st-Class 50s: 1
1st-Class catches: 1
Strike rate: 67.85 (career 67.85)
Parents: Julie and Ray
Marital status: Single
Family links with cricket: 'Dad played local
league cricket'
Education: Castleford High School;
Pontefract New College
Qualifications: 8 GCSEs
Off-season: England U19 tour to Bangladesh
Overseas tours: Yorkshire U16 to Cape Town 2001; England U17 to Australia
2000-01; England U19 to Australia and (U19 World Cup) New Zealand 2001-02,
to Australia 2002-03, to Bangladesh (U19 World Cup) 2003-04
Career highlights to date: 'Winning [U19] "Test" series against India [2002]'
Cricket moments to forget: 'Eight ducks in a row in 2000 season, for various teams'
Cricket superstitions: 'None'
Cricketers particularly admired: Ian Botham
Young players to look out for: Joseph Sayers, Chris Gilbert, David Stiff
Other sports played: Golf, football
Other sports followed: Football (Leeds United)
Favourite band: Girls Aloud
Relaxations: Golf, PlayStation
Extras: Bunbury Festival Best All-rounder and Most Outstanding Player. Made one-
day debut v Kent at Headingley 2001 aged 16 years 102 days, making him the
youngest player to represent Yorkshire since Paul Jarvis in 1981. NBC Denis Compton
Award for the most promising young Yorkshire player 2002. Represented England U19
v India U19 2002 and v South Africa U19 2003, taking 5-81 in first 'Test' at
Headingley. Scored maiden first-class fifty (52) v India A at Headingley 2003
Opinions on cricket: 'Local league cricket should be publicised better, drawing better
crowds and should all play 50 overs with circles and fielding restrictions.'
Best batting: 52 Yorkshire v India A, Headingley 2003
Best bowling: 3-88 Yorkshire v India A, Headingley 2003

2003 Season

	M	Inns	NO	Runs	HS	Avge	100s	50s	Ct	St	O	M	Runs	Wkts	Avge	Best	5wI	10wM
Test																		
All First	4	4	0	81	52	20.25	-	1	1	-	79.1	16	259	7	37.00	3-88	-	-
1-day Int																		
C & G	2	1	0	14	14	14.00	-	-	1	-	14	0	73	3	24.33	2-53	-	
NCL	11	8	1	204	61	29.14	-	1	7	-	79.5	5	374	15	24.93	3-29	-	
Twenty20	5	2	1	18	13 *	18.00	-	-	2	-	18	0	116	7	16.57	3-31	-	

Career Performances

	M	Inns	NO	Runs	HS	Avge	100s	50s	Ct	St	Balls	Runs	Wkts	Avge	Best	5wI	10wM
Test																	
All First	4	4	0	81	52	20.25	-	1	1	-	475	259	7	37.00	3-88	-	-
1-day Int																	
C & G	3	1	0	14	14	14.00	-	-	1	-	126	91	4	22.75	2-53	-	
NCL	28	18	6	269	61	22.41	-	1	10	-	1090	849	29	29.27	3-29	-	
Twenty20	5	2	1	18	13 *	18.00	-	-	2	-	108	116	7	16.57	3-31	-	

BRESSINGTON, A. N.   Gloucestershire

Name: <u>Alastair</u> Nigel Bressington
Role: Left-hand bat, right-arm fast-medium bowler; all-rounder
Born: 28 November 1979, Bristol
Height: 6ft 1in **Weight:** 14st
Nickname: Magic, Bressy
County debut: 2000
1st-Class catches: 3
Strike rate: (career 52.75)
Parents: Adrian and Marjorie
Marital status: Single
Family links with cricket: Brother Nathan plays for Gloucestershire 2nd XI
Education: Marling Grammar School, Stroud; UWIC
Qualifications: 12 GCSEs, 4 A-levels
Cricketers particularly admired: Jack Russell, Ian Botham
Other sports played: Rugby (Gloucestershire Colts; Gloucester RFC U21; Newbury)
Other sports followed: Rugby (Bristol RFC), football (Liverpool FC)
Relaxations: Music, reading
Extras: Played for Gloucestershire Board XI in the NatWest 1999 and 2000. Took

wicket with third ball in first-class cricket v Glamorgan at Bristol 2000 and took five wickets in debut match, including that of Matthew Maynard. Captain of Cardiff University CCE 2001 and 2002. Played for Gloucestershire v India A in a 50-over match at Cheltenham 2003

Best batting: 17* Gloucestershire v Hampshire, Cheltenham 2001
Best bowling: 4-36 Gloucestershire v Glamorgan, Bristol 2000

2003 Season (did not make any first-class or one-day appearances)

Career Performances

	M	Inns	NO	Runs	HS	Avge	100s	50s	Ct	St	Balls	Runs	Wkts	Avge	Best	5wI	10wM
Test																	
All First	6	6	3	42	17 *	14.00	-	-	3	-	844	446	16	27.87	4-36	-	-
1-day Int																	
C & G	3	2	0	98	54	49.00	-	1	2	-	150	86	5	17.20	3-21	-	
NCL	4	3	0	42	22	14.00	-	-	2	-	150	118	1	118.00	1-31	-	
Twenty20																	

BRIDGE, G. D.   Durham

Name: <u>Graeme</u> David Bridge
Role: Right-hand bat, slow left-arm bowler
Born: 4 September 1980, Sunderland
Height: 5ft 7in **Weight:** 12st 9lbs
Nickname: Moot, Bridgey
County debut: 1999
1st-Class 50s: 1
1st-Class 5 w. in innings: 1
1st-Class catches: 17
Place in batting averages: 193rd av. 24.00 (2002 269th av. 14.15)
Place in bowling averages: 116th av. 39.84 (2002 108th av. 35.85)
Strike rate: 69.36 (career 69.49)
Parents: Anne and John
Marital status: Engaged to Leanne
Children: Olivia Molly, 13 September 2003
Family links with cricket: 'Dad and brother played club cricket badly!'
Education: Southmoor School
Qualifications: 5 GCSEs
Career outside cricket: 'Admin'

Off-season: 'Spending time with family'
Overseas tours: England U19 to New Zealand 1998-99, to Malaysia and (U19 World Cup) Sri Lanka 1999-2000; Durham to Cape Town 2002
Career highlights to date: 'First-class debut; getting promoted in NCL; U19 tour of New Zealand; two Gold Awards'
Cricket moments to forget: 'Twisting ankle on Sky. Breaking a finger in warm-up'
Cricketers particularly admired: Martin Love, David Boon, Paul Collingwood, Steve Harmison
Young players to look out for: Liam Plunkett, Nigel Kent
Other sports played: Football (5-a-side)
Other sports followed: Football (Sunderland AFC)
Relaxations: 'Reading, watching SAFC home or away, beating Peng on PlayStation'
Extras: Played in U15 World Cup 1996. Represented England U19 v Australia U19 1999. Played for Durham Board XI in the NatWest 1999 and in the second round of the C&G 2003, which was played in September 2002. C&G Man of the Match award on county one-day debut for his 3-44 v Gloucestershire at Bristol 2001
Opinions on cricket: 'Enjoy.'
Best batting: 50 Durham v Yorkshire, Riverside 2003
Best bowling: 6-84 Durham v Hampshire, Riverside 2001

2003 Season

	M	Inns	NO	Runs	HS	Avge	100s	50s	Ct	St	O	M	Runs	Wkts	Avge	Best	5wI	10wM
Test																		
All First	8	13	3	240	50	24.00	-	1	7	-	289	59	996	25	39.84	4-47	-	-
1-day Int																		
C & G																		
NCL	9	7	2	44	16	8.80	-	-	-	-	71.2	6	286	14	20.42	4-20	-	
Twenty20																		

Career Performances

	M	Inns	NO	Runs	HS	Avge	100s	50s	Ct	St	Balls	Runs	Wkts	Avge	Best	5wI	10wM
Test																	
All First	26	43	7	560	50	15.55	-	1	17	-	4517	2272	65	34.95	6-84	1	-
1-day Int																	
C & G	8	6	2	63	19	15.75	-	-	1	-	368	276	7	39.42	3-44	-	
NCL	23	18	6	123	24	10.25	-	-	3	-	1052	709	29	24.44	4-20	-	
Twenty20																	

14. Which Nottinghamshire all-rounder averaged over 50 in Test cricket but scored a 'duck' in his only ODI?

BRIGNULL, D. S.   Leicestershire

Name: David (<u>Dave</u>) Stephen Brignull
Role: Right-hand bat, right-arm
fast-medium bowler
Born: 27 November 1981, Forest Gate,
London
Height: 6ft 4in   **Weight:** 15st 10lbs
Nickname: Briggers, Brig-Dog
County debut: 2002 (one-day),
2003 (first-class)
Strike rate: 58.85 (career 58.85)
Parents: Sharon Penfold and
Stephen Brignull
Marital status: Single
Family links with cricket: 'Uncles on both
sides of family played for Essex Schools'
Education: Lancaster Boys School;
Wyggeston and Queen Elizabeth I College
Qualifications: 11 GCSEs, 3 A-levels,
Level 1 coaching

Off-season: 'I'm staying here training with Leicester City youth team and Tigers physiologist. Maybe holidaying at Christmas with girlfriend Sarah'
Overseas tours: Leicestershire U19 to South Africa 2000-01
Overseas teams played for: Lafarge CC, Lichtenburg, South Africa 2000-01
Career highlights to date: '3-48 on Sky against Glamorgan in the National League – a game we won off the last ball'
Cricket moments to forget: 'Being hit for 26 in one over in club cricket'
Cricketers particularly admired: Robin Smith, Darren Gough
Young players to look out for: Tom New, Luke Wright
Other sports played: Rugby (Wigston RFC), volleyball (for college team that came fourth in nationals)
Other sports followed: Rugby (Leicester Tigers), football (West Ham), American football (Oakland Raiders)
Injuries: Out for one week with a strained oblique muscle; for one week with a chest infection
Favourite band: Eminem
Relaxations: 'Music, socialising'
Extras: Represented England U17 at the ECC Colts Festival in Northern Ireland 1999. Leicestershire Youth Bowler of the Year and U19 Player of the Season 2001. Hat-trick against Derbyshire U19. Played for Leicestershire Board XI in the NatWest 1999 and C&G 2001
Opinions on cricket: 'I think that the Twenty20 Cup was a great idea and really took

off, both with players and the supporters. It is exactly what is needed for cricket in this country.'
Best batting: 46 Leicestershire v Middlesex, Leicester 2003
Best bowling: 2-30 Leicestershire v Kent, Canterbury 2003

2003 Season

	M	Inns	NO	Runs	HS	Avge	100s	50s	Ct	St	O	M	Runs	Wkts	Avge	Best	5wI	10wM
Test																		
All First	3	4	0	58	46	14.50	-	-	-	-	68.4	14	235	7	33.57	2-30	-	-
1-day Int																		
C & G	1	1	0	5	5	5.00	-	-	2	-	7	0	44	0	-		-	-
NCL	7	4	3	10	4 *	10.00	-	-	2	-	33.2	0	180	8	22.50	3-40	-	
Twenty20																		

Career Performances

	M	Inns	NO	Runs	HS	Avge	100s	50s	Ct	St	Balls	Runs	Wkts	Avge	Best	5wI	10wM
Test																	
All First	3	4	0	58	46	14.50	-	-	-	-	412	235	7	33.57	2-30	-	-
1-day Int																	
C & G	3	3	1	20	9 *	10.00	-	-	3	-	154	129	4	32.25	2-35	-	
NCL	8	5	3	11	4 *	5.50	-	-	2	-	254	232	10	23.20	3-40	-	
Twenty20																	

BROPHY, G. L.   Northamptonshire

Name: Gerard Louis Brophy
Role: Right-hand bat, wicket-keeper
Born: 26 November 1975, Welkom, South Africa
Height: 5ft 11in **Weight:** 12st
Nickname: Scuba, Broph
County debut: 2002
1st-Class 50s: 7
1st-Class 100s: 4
1st-Class catches: 92
1st-Class stumpings: 5
Place in batting averages: 9th av. 62.28
Parents: Gerard and Trish
Wife and date of marriage: Alison, 3 January 2004
Education: Christian Brothers College, Boksburg; Wits Technikon (both South Africa)

Qualifications: Marketing Diploma, Level 2 coach
Off-season: 'Working up to Christmas; South Africa for three months'
Overseas tours: South Africa U17 to England 1993; South African Academy to Zimbabwe, Kenya
Overseas teams played for: Gauteng; Free State
Career highlights to date: 'Captaincy of Free State 2000-01. First dismissal [in collaboration] with Allan Donald'
Cricket moments to forget: 'Messing up a live TV interview'
Cricket superstitions: 'Right pad on first and right glove on first'
Cricketers particularly admired: Ray Jennings, Ian Healy, Allan Donald, Hansie Cronje
Young players to look out for: Jacques Rudolph
Other sports played: Golf, rugby
Other sports followed: Golf, rugby
Injuries: Out for about ten weeks with twice-broken left thumb
Favourite band: Coldplay
Relaxations: 'Fishing, travelling, braais, scuba diving'
Extras: Captained South Africa U17. Played for Ireland in the NatWest 2000. Parents live in Brisbane, Australia. Holds a British passport and is not considered an overseas player
Best batting: 185 South African Academy v President's XI, Harare 1999-2000

2003 Season

	M	Inns	NO	Runs	HS	Avge	100s	50s	Ct	St	O	M	Runs	Wkts	Avge	Best	5wl	10wM
Test																		
All First	7	12	5	436	152*	62.28	2	1	14	-								
1-day Int																		
C & G	1	1	0	13	13	13.00	-	-	-	-								
NCL	9	8	1	134	35*	19.14	-	-	9	3								
Twenty20	2	2	1	20	16*	20.00	-	-	1	1								

Career Performances

	M	Inns	NO	Runs	HS	Avge	100s	50s	Ct	St	Balls	Runs	Wkts	Avge	Best	5wl	10wM
Test																	
All First	34	58	11	1712	185	36.42	4	7	92	5							
1-day Int																	
C & G	2	2	0	28	15	14.00	-	-	-	-							
NCL	13	12	1	195	54	17.72	-	1	11	3							
Twenty20	2	2	1	20	16*	20.00	-	-	1	1							

BROWN, A. D.   Surrey

Name: <u>Alistair</u> Duncan Brown
Role: Right-hand bat, off-spin bowler, occasional wicket-keeper
Born: 11 February 1970, Beckenham
Height: 5ft 10in **Weight:** 12st 8lbs
Nickname: Lordy
County debut: 1992
County cap: 1994
Benefit: 2002
One-Day Internationals: 16
1000 runs in a season: 6
1st-Class 50s: 45
1st-Class 100s: 30
1st-Class 200s: 2
1st-Class catches: 192
1st-Class stumpings: 1
One-Day 100s: 14
One-Day 200s: 2
Place in batting averages: 180th av. 25.47 (2002 34th av. 50.45)
Strike rate: 70.00 (career 443.00)
Parents: Robert and Ann
Wife and date of marriage: Sarah, 10 October 1998
Children: Max Charles, 9 March 2001; Joe Robert, 11 March 2003
Family links with cricket: Father played for Surrey Young Amateurs in the 1950s
Education: Caterham School
Qualifications: 5 O-levels, NCA Senior Coach
Overseas tours: England VI to Singapore 1993, 1994, 1995, to Hong Kong 1997; England to Sharjah (Champions Trophy) 1997-98, to Bangladesh (Wills International Cup) 1998-99
Overseas teams played for: North Perth, Western Australia 1989-90
Cricketers particularly admired: Ian Botham, Viv Richards
Other sports played: Golf, football, snooker, 'winner of the Lanzarote Open Pool Championship 1990'
Other sports followed: Football (West Ham United), rugby league (London Broncos)
Extras: Scored three of the eight fastest centuries of the 1992 season (71, 78 & 79 balls). Awarded Man of the Match for his 118 against India in the third One-Day International at Old Trafford 1996. Recorded the highest-ever score in the Sunday League with 203 off 119 balls against Hampshire at Guildford in 1997 and received an individual award at the PCA Dinner for that achievement. Scored 72-ball century v Northamptonshire at The Oval to become joint winner (with Carl Hooper) of the EDS Walter Lawrence Trophy for the fastest first-class 100 of the 1998 season. Scored

31-ball 50 v South Africa in the Texaco Trophy match at Headingley 1998, the fastest 50 in the history of the Texaco Trophy. Surrey CCC Batsman of the Season Award 2001. Scored century (177) v Sussex at The Oval 2002, in the process sharing with Nadeem Shahid (150) in a record fifth-wicket partnership for Surrey v Sussex (262). C&G Man of the Match award for his 160-ball 268 out of 438-5 v Glamorgan at The Oval 2002; it set a new record for the highest individual score in professional one-day cricket worldwide (overtaking Graeme Pollock's 222 for Eastern Province v Border in 1974) and Brown also became the first batsman to have scored two double centuries in one-day cricket. Scored 107 v Leicestershire at The Oval 2002, in the process sharing with Adam Hollioake (208) in a new record fifth-wicket partnership for Surrey in matches against Leicestershire (282)

Best batting: 295* Surrey v Leicestershire, Oakham School 2000
Best bowling: 1-11 Surrey v Warwickshire, The Oval 2003

2003 Season

	M	Inns	NO	Runs	HS	Avge	100s	50s	Ct	St	O	M	Runs	Wkts	Avge	Best	5wI	10wM
Test																		
All First	14	21	2	484	74	25.47	-	5	12	-	11.4	3	29	1	29.00	1-11	-	-
1-day Int																		
C & G	3	3	0	5	5	1.66	-	-	2	-	2	0	17	0	-		-	-
NCL	15	15	0	491	89	32.73	-	4	8	-	2.4	0	26	1	26.00	1-9	-	
Twenty20	7	7	1	151	55 *	25.16	-	1	6	-								

Career Performances

	M	Inns	NO	Runs	HS	Avge	100s	50s	Ct	St	Balls	Runs	Wkts	Avge	Best	5wI	10wM
Test																	
All First	184	288	28	11051	295 *	42.50	32	45	192	1	886	461	2	230.50	1-11	-	-
1-day Int	16	16	0	354	118	22.12	1	1	6	-	6	5	0	-		-	-
C & G	34	30	2	870	268	31.07	1	3	11	-	18	26	0	-		-	-
NCL	194	189	5	5809	203	31.57	12	25	67	-	285	278	9	30.88	3-39	-	
Twenty20	7	7	1	151	55 *	25.16	-	1	6	-							

15. Which spinner became the eleventh Middlesex player to captain England, in the second Test at Lord's in 1988?

BROWN, D. R.   Warwickshire

Name: Douglas (<u>Dougie</u>) Robert Brown
Role: Right-hand bat, right-arm
fast-medium bowler
Born: 29 October 1969, Stirling, Scotland
Height: 6ft 2in **Weight:** 14st 7lbs
Nickname: Hoots
County debut: 1992
County cap: 1995
One-Day Internationals: 9
1000 runs in a season: 1
50 wickets in a season: 3
1st-Class 50s: 38
1st-Class 100s: 5
1st-Class 200s: 1
1st-Class 5 w. in innings: 17
1st-Class 10 w. in match: 4
1st-Class catches: 103
One-Day 100s: 1
One-Day 5 w. in innings: 1

Place in batting averages: 40th av. 46.72 (2002 156th av. 27.95)
Place in bowling averages: 89th av. 35.38 (2002 86th av. 33.00)
Strike rate: 62.97 (career 52.99)
Parents: Alastair and Janette
Wife and date of marriage: Brenda, 2 October 1993
Children: Lauren, 14 September 1998
Family links with cricket: 'Both grandads played a bit'
Education: Alloa Academy; West London Institute of Higher Education (Borough
Road College)
Qualifications: 9 O-Grades, 5 Higher Grades, BEd (Hons) Physical Education,
ECB Level III coach
Career outside cricket: PE teacher
Overseas tours: Scotland XI to Pakistan 1988-89; England VI to Hong Kong 1997,
2001, 2003; England A to Kenya and Sri Lanka 1997-98; England to Sharjah
(Champions Trophy) 1997-98, to West Indies 1997-98 (one-day series), to Bangladesh
(Wills International Cup) 1998-99; Scotland to Dubai (ICC Six Nations Challenge)
2003-04
Overseas teams played for: Primrose, Cape Town 1992-93; Vredenburg Saldhana,
Cape Town 1993-94; Eastern Suburbs, Wellington 1995-96; Wellington, New Zealand
1995-96
Career highlights to date: 'Playing in a Lord's final for the first time, in 1995
v Northants'

Cricketers particularly admired: Dermot Reeve, 'and as I play more, the likes of Phillip DeFreitas, who keep running in each day'
Young players to look out for: Ian Bell 'who looks the genuine article'
Other sports played: Golf
Other sports followed: Football (Alloa Athletic), 'most sports'
Relaxations: Sport, music
Extras: Played football at Hampden Park for Scotland U18. Has played first-class and B&H cricket for Scotland. Scored 1118 runs and took 109 wickets in all first-team county cricket 1997. Set record for the earliest Championship 100 in an English season with his maiden first-class century (142) v Northamptonshire at Edgbaston on 15 April 1999. Scored maiden first-class double century v Sussex at Hove 2000 (203; the highest score recorded by a Warwickshire No. 7), during which he shared in a record Warwickshire partnership for the seventh wicket (289 with Ashley Giles). Vice-captain of Warwickshire 2002-03. Warwickshire All-rounder of the Year 2002. Scored 108 v Essex at Edgbaston in the C&G 2003, winning Man of the Match award and sharing with Ashley Giles (71*) in a competition record seventh-wicket partnership (170). Scored century (112) v Lancashire 2003, sharing with Jonathan Trott (126) in a new record sixth-wicket partnership for Warwickshire at Edgbaston (216). Scored 1000 first-class runs in a season for the first time 2003
Best batting: 203 Warwickshire v Sussex, Hove 2000
Best bowling: 8-89 First-Class Counties XI v Pakistan A, Chelmsford 1997

2003 Season

	M	Inns	NO	Runs	HS	Avge	100s	50s	Ct	St	O	M	Runs	Wkts	Avge	Best	5wl	10wM
Test																		
All First	16	26	4	1028	140 *	46.72	3	7	10	-	377.5	81	1274	36	35.38	5-72	2	-
1-day Int																		
C & G	3	3	0	148	108	49.33	1	-	3	-	18	3	71	4	17.75	2-34	-	
NCL	13	10	3	223	49	31.85	-	-	2	-	86.3	6	490	15	32.66	4-37	-	
Twenty20	5	4	0	5	3	1.25	-	-	2	-	13	0	131	2	65.50	1-26	-	

Career Performances

	M	Inns	NO	Runs	HS	Avge	100s	50s	Ct	St	Balls	Runs	Wkts	Avge	Best	5wl	10wM
Test																	
All First	162	248	33	6510	203	30.27	6	38	103	-	23160	12326	437	28.20	8-89	17	4
1-day Int	9	8	4	99	21	24.75	-	-	1	-	324	305	7	43.57	2-28	-	
C & G	27	26	3	585	108	25.43	1	4	7	-	1262	876	27	32.44	2-18	-	
NCL	146	119	18	2242	82 *	22.19	-	11	37	-	5325	4130	167	24.73	4-37	-	
Twenty20	5	4	0	5	3	1.25	-	-	2	-	78	131	2	65.50	1-26	-	

BROWN, J. F.   Northamptonshire

Name: <u>Jason</u> Fred Brown
Role: Right-hand bat, off-spin bowler
Born: 10 October 1974,
Newcastle-under-Lyme
Height: 6ft **Weight:** 13st
Nickname: Cheese, Fish, Brownie
County debut: 1996
County cap: 2000
50 wickets in a season: 2
1st-Class 5 w. in innings: 13
1st-Class 10 w. in match: 3
1st-Class catches: 13
One-Day 5 w. in innings: 1
Place in batting averages: 250th av. 15.16
(2002 285th av. 10.66)
Place in bowling averages: 22nd av. 23.71
(2002 126th av. 40.64)
Strike rate: 58.81 (career 64.02)

Parents: Peter and Cynthia
Wife and date of marriage: Sam, 26 September 1998
Children: Millie
Education: St Margaret Ward RC School, Stoke-on-Trent
Qualifications: 9 GCSEs, Level 1 coaching qualification
Overseas tours: Kidsgrove League U18 to Australia 1990; Northants CCC to Zimbabwe 1998, to Grenada 2000; England A to West Indies 2000-01; England to Sri Lanka 2000-01
Overseas teams played for: North East Valley, Dunedin, New Zealand 1996-97
Cricketers particularly admired: John Emburey, Carl Hooper
Young players to look out for: Mark Powell
Other sports played: Golf
Other sports followed: Football (Port Vale)
Relaxations: 'Reading, listening to music'
Extras: Represented Staffordshire at all junior levels, in Minor Counties, and in the NatWest 1995. Once took 10-16 in a Kidsgrove League game against Haslington U18 playing for Sandyford U18. Took 100th first-class wicket in 23rd match, v Sussex at Northampton 2000, going on to take his 50th wicket of the season in the same game, only his seventh of the summer. Took 5-27 v Somerset at Northampton in the Twenty20 2003
Best batting: 38 Northamptonshire v Hampshire, Northampton 2003
Best bowling: 7-69 Northamptonshire v Durham, Riverside 2003

2003 Season

	M	Inns	NO	Runs	HS	Avge	100s	50s	Ct	St	O	M	Runs	Wkts	Avge	Best	5wI	10wM
Test																		
All First	14	12	6	91	38	15.16	-	-	2	-	647	188	1565	66	23.71	7-69	4	-
1-day Int																		
C & G	1	1	1	2	2 *	-	-	-	-	-	8	0	37	0	-		-	-
NCL	18	4	3	7	4 *	7.00	-	-	9	-	132	4	543	15	36.20	3-28	-	
Twenty20	5	0	0	0	0	-	-	-	2	-	17.5	0	122	11	11.09	5-27	1	

Career Performances

	M	Inns	NO	Runs	HS	Avge	100s	50s	Ct	St	Balls	Runs	Wkts	Avge	Best	5wI	10wM
Test																	
All First	62	73	33	294	38	7.35	-	-	13	-	15878	7136	248	28.77	7-69	13	3
1-day Int																	
C & G	9	6	5	8	3	8.00	-	-	-	-	540	402	9	44.66	3-35	-	
NCL	59	20	11	46	16	5.11	-	-	17	-	2627	1814	58	31.27	4-26	-	
Twenty20	5	0	0	0	0	-	-	-	2	-	107	122	11	11.09	5-27	1	

BROWN, M. J.   Hampshire

Name: <u>Michael</u> James Brown
Role: Right-hand bat, occasional wicket-keeper
Born: 9 February 1980, Burnley
Height: 6ft **Weight:** 12st
Nickname: Weasel, Vin, Crime, Browny, Gollum
County debut: 1999 (Middlesex)
1st-Class 50s: 4
1st-Class catches: 12
Place in batting averages: (2002 191st av. 24.16)
Parents: Peter and Valerie
Marital status: Single
Family links with cricket: 'Father played league cricket for 30 years. Mum makes great tuna sandwiches. Brother David plays for DUCCE'
Education: Queen Elizabeth's Grammar School, Blackburn; Durham University
Qualifications: 10 GCSEs, 4 A-levels, 2.1 Economics/Politics
Off-season: 'Fremantle Cricket Club'
Overseas teams played for: Western Province CC, Cape Town 1998-99; Fremantle CC 2002-04

Career highlights to date: '98 v Zimbabwe. British Universities v Pakistan 2001: facing Wasim and Waqar – great experience'

Cricket moments to forget: 'Every time I leave straight balls'

Cricket superstitions: 'Always tap non-striker's end four times at end of over when at that end'

Cricketers particularly admired: Dale Benkenstein, Gary Kirsten, Wasim Akram, Mike Atherton, James Foster

Young players to look out for: David Brown, Ravi Bopara, Jacques Rudolph

Other sports played: Football ('town team')

Other sports followed: Football (Burnley FC)

Injuries: Out for six weeks with split webbing

Favourite band: Counting Crows 'and all "cheese"'

Relaxations: 'Sleeping; prowling round Perth'

Extras: Represented ECB U19 A v Pakistan U19 in two one-day games 1998. Played for Durham University CCE 2001 and 2002, scoring two fifties (55 and 60*) for DUCCE v Worcestershire at Worcester 2001. Represented British Universities 2001 and 2002. 'Was at non-striker's end as five wickets fell in one over, Middlesex 2nd XI v Glamorgan 2nd XI, July 2001.' 'Kept wicket for Middlesex v Zimbabwe [at Shenley 2003] after both wicket-keepers were injured before and on morning of game', also scoring 98 in Middlesex's first innings. Left Middlesex at the end of the 2003 season and has joined Hampshire for 2004

Opinions on cricket: 'Nine players in every side should be eligible to play for England. Two overseas players only, regardless of injuries and Test calls. Too many EU players. Counties are too short-sighted with regard to winning the next game regardless of the long-term development of players.'

Best batting: 98 Middlesex v Zimbabweans, Shenley 2003

2003 Season

	M	Inns	NO	Runs	HS	Avge	100s	50s	Ct	St	O	M	Runs	Wkts	Avge	Best	5wI	10wM
Test																		
All First	1	1	0	98	98	98.00	-	1	2	-								
1-day Int																		
C & G																		
NCL																		
Twenty20																		

Career Performances

	M	Inns	NO	Runs	HS	Avge	100s	50s	Ct	St	Balls	Runs	Wkts	Avge	Best	5wI	10wM
Test																	
All First	12	19	3	488	98	30.50	-	4	12	-							
1-day Int																	
C & G																	
NCL	1	1	0	18	18	18.00	-	-	-	-							
Twenty20																	

BRUCE, J. T. A. Hampshire

Name: <u>James</u> Thomas Anthony Bruce
Role: Right-hand bat, right-arm
medium-fast bowler
Born: 17 December 1979, Hammersmith,
London
Height: 6ft 1in **Weight:** 13st 10lbs
Nickname: Brucey, Bula, Bear, Eugene
County debut: 2003
1st-Class catches: 4
Place in batting averages: 282nd av. 8.50
Place in bowling averages: 131st av. 43.63
Strike rate: 61.89 (career 73.00)
Parents: Andrew and Claire
Marital status: Single
Family links with cricket: 'All three of my
brothers have played youth cricket for
Hampshire'
Education: Eton College, Durham University

Qualifications: BA (Hons) Geography, Level 1 coaching
Off-season: 'In Australia'
Overseas tours: West of England U15 to West Indies 1995; Eton College to South
Africa 1998-99; Yellowhammers to South Africa 2001-02; Durham University to
South Africa 2001
Overseas teams played for: Balmain Tigers, Sydney 2002-03; South Perth CC, Perth
2003-04
Career highlights to date: 'Making my Championship debut against Somerset.
Making my NCL debut in a day/night game on Sky v Notts at Trent Bridge'
Cricket moments to forget: 'Having my box split in two by Mike Kasprowicz'
Cricket superstitions: 'Too many to mention'
Cricketers particularly admired: Robin Smith, Shaun Udal, Wasim Akram,
Brett Lee
Young players to look out for: Kevin Latouf, Mitchell Stokes, Edward Bruce
Other sports played: Rugby, golf
Injuries: 'A few niggles but nothing serious thankfully'
Favourite band: Linkin Park
Relaxations: 'I like spending time on the beach, watching TV and sleeping'
Extras: Played for DUCCE in 2001 and 2002. Played for Cumberland in the
C&G 2002
Opinions on cricket: 'I think the introduction of Twenty20 has helped improve the
popularity of county cricket to the general public and helped players to develop new
aspects to their game. I also strongly believe that too many EU passport qualified

players can only hinder the development of local young players and their transition from youth to first-class cricket.'

Best batting: 21* Hampshire v Glamorgan, West End 2003
Best bowling: 3-42 Hampshire v Glamorgan, West End 2003

2003 Season

	M	Inns	NO	Runs	HS	Avge	100s	50s	Ct	St	O	M	Runs	Wkts	Avge	Best	5wI	10wM
Test																		
All First	8	11	3	68	21*	8.50	-	-	3	-	196	39	829	19	43.63	3-42	-	-
1-day Int																		
C & G																			
NCL	3	1	1	6	6*	-	-	-	-	-	20	1	100	4	25.00	3-45	-	
Twenty20																			

Career Performances

	M	Inns	NO	Runs	HS	Avge	100s	50s	Ct	St	Balls	Runs	Wkts	Avge	Best	5wI	10wM
Test																	
All First	14	17	6	95	21*	8.63	-	-	4	-	1752	1218	24	50.75	3-42	-	-
1-day Int																	
C & G	1	1	0	0	0	0.00	-	-	-	-							
NCL	3	1	1	6	6*	-	-	-	-	-	120	100	4	25.00	3-45	-	
Twenty20																		

BRUNNSCHWEILER, I.   Hampshire

Name: Iain Brunnschweiler
Role: Right-hand bat, wicket-keeper
Born: 10 December 1979, Southampton
Height: 6ft **Weight:** 12st 7lbs
Nickname: Bruno, Brown, Brunchy
County debut: 2000
1st-Class catches: 20
Parents: Arthur and Joan
Marital status: Single
Family links with cricket: 'They mostly dislike it!'
Education: King Edward VI School, Southampton
Qualifications: 9 GCSEs, 3 A-levels, ECB Level 1 cricket coaching award, UEFA Part B football coaching award
Career outside cricket: Journalism
Overseas tours: England U17 to Bermuda

1997; King Edward VI School to South Africa 1998; Hampshire CCC to Cape
Town 2001

Overseas teams played for: Belmont DCC, Newcastle, NSW 1998-99; Nullamara,
Perth 2000-01; Perth CC 2001-02

Career highlights to date: 'Hitting the winning runs for Hampshire against Australia
in 2001'

Cricket moments to forget: 'Losing the U17 Texaco Trophy final against Northants
in 1997 (and getting a golden duck)'

Cricketers particularly admired: Robin Smith, Adi Aymes, Jack Russell, Ian Healy

Young players to look out for: James Tomlinson, Ben Adams, Chris Marlow,
Fergus Haycock

Other sports played: Football (Southampton Youth), hockey, rugby

Other sports followed: Football (Southampton FC)

Relaxations: 'Music; going out with my friends and enjoying good food and liquid'

Extras: Played for Hampshire Board XI in the second round of the C&G 2003, which
was played in September 2002. 'Longest surname in English county cricket?' Released
by Hampshire at the end of the 2003 season

Opinions on cricket: 'People are too opinionated.'

Best batting: 34 Hampshire v Yorkshire, Scarborough 2003

2003 Season

	M	Inns	NO	Runs	HS	Avge	100s	50s	Ct	St	O	M	Runs	Wkts	Avge	Best	5wI	10wM
Test																		
All First	4	4	0	58	34	14.50	-	-	11	-								
1-day Int																		
C & G																		
NCL																		
Twenty20																		

Career Performances

	M	Inns	NO	Runs	HS	Avge	100s	50s	Ct	St	Balls	Runs	Wkts	Avge	Best	5wI	10wM
Test																	
All First	6	8	1	91	34	13.00	-	-	20	-							
1-day Int																	
C & G	1	1	0	37	37	37.00	-	-	2	-							
NCL	2	1	0	0	0	0.00	-	-	3	-							
Twenty20																	

16. Which Nottinghamshire player,
Cricket Writers' Club Young Cricketer of the Year 2000,
made his ODI debut at Trent Bridge in 2000?

BRYANT, J. D. C. Derbyshire

Name: <u>James</u> Douglas Campbell Bryant
Role: Right-hand bat, right-arm medium bowler
Born: 4 February 1976, Durban, South Africa
Height: 6ft **Weight:** 11st 10lbs
Nickname: Ginga
County debut: 2003 (Somerset)
1st-Class 50s: 17
1st-Class 100s: 6
1st-Class 200s: 1
1st-Class catches: 48
Place in batting averages: 144th av. 29.90
Strike rate: (career 38.00)
Parents: Nick and Helen
Marital status: Single
Education: Maritzburg College; University of Port Elizabeth
Qualifications: BComm (Hons) Business Management, Level 2 coach
Career outside cricket: Entrepreneur
Overseas tours: South African Academy to Ireland and Scotland 1999; South Africa A to West Indies 2000-01
Overseas teams played for: Eastern Province 1996-97 – 2002-03
Career highlights to date: '234* v North West and achieving South African highest first-class batting partnership – 441'
Other sports played: Golf, tennis, squash
Other sports followed: Rugby (Natal Sharks)
Relaxations: 'Reading, watersports, golf'
Extras: Scored career-best 234* v North West at Potchefstroom in the SuperSport Series 2002-03, in the process sharing with Carl Bradfield (196) in a new record partnership for any wicket in South African domestic first-class cricket (441). Is a British passport holder and is not considered an overseas player. Left Somerset in the 2003-04 off-season and has joined Derbyshire for 2004
Best batting: 234* Eastern Province v North West, Potchefstroom 2002-03
Best bowling: 1-22 Eastern Province B v North West, Fochville 1998-99

	M	Inns	NO	Runs	HS	Avge	100s	50s	Ct	St	O	M	Runs	Wkts	Avge	Best	5wI	10wM
Test																		
All First	14	24	2	658	109 *	29.90	1	2	8	-	1	0	8	0	-		-	-	-
1-day Int																		
C & G	2	1	0	9	9	9.00	-	-	-	-								
NCL	6	6	1	84	56 *	16.80	-	1	-	-								
Twenty20	1	1	0	0	0	0.00	-	-	-	-								

Career Performances

	M	Inns	NO	Runs	HS	Avge	100s	50s	Ct	St	Balls	Runs	Wkts	Avge	Best	5wI	10wM
Test																	
All First	62	113	14	3596	234 *	36.32	7	17	48	-	38	37	1	37.00	1-22	-	-
1-day Int																	
C & G	2	1	0	9	9	9.00	-	-	-	-							
NCL	6	6	1	84	56 *	16.80	-	1	-	-							
Twenty20	1	1	0	0	0	0.00	-	-	-	-							

BURNS, M.   Somerset

Name: Michael Burns
Role: Right-hand bat, right-arm medium bowler, county captain
Born: 6 February 1969, Barrow-in-Furness
Height: 6ft **Weight:** 14st
Nickname: George, Ashley, Butch, Onslow
County debut: 1991 (Warwickshire), 1997 (Somerset)
County cap: 1999 (Somerset)
1000 runs in a season: 2
1st-Class 50s: 45
1st-Class 100s: 6
1st-Class 200s: 1
1st-Class 5 w. in innings: 1
1st-Class catches: 121
1st-Class stumpings: 7
One-Day 100s: 2
Place in batting averages: 82nd av. 39.06 (2002 95th av. 37.39)
Place in bowling averages: 113th av. 39.53 (2002 125th av. 40.36)
Strike rate: 71.00 (career 68.38)
Parents: Robert and Linda, stepfather Stan

Wife and date of marriage: Carolyn, 9 October 1994
Children: Elizabeth, 12 January 1997; Adam, 3 August 2000
Family links with cricket: 'Grandfather was a great back-garden bowler'
Education: Walney Comprehensive; Barrow College of Further Education
Qualifications: 'Few CSEs, couple of GCEs', qualified fitter at VSEL in Barrow, coaching award
Career outside cricket: 'Open to offers'
Overseas teams played for: Gill College, South Africa 1991-92; Motueka, Nelson, New Zealand 1992-93; Alex Sports Club, Harare 1993-94; Lindisfarne, Tasmania 1999-2000
Career highlights to date: '2001 Cheltenham & Gloucester final'
Cricket moments to forget: 'Losing the 1999 NatWest final to Gloucestershire'
Cricket superstitions: 'None'
Cricketers particularly admired: Marcus Trescothick
Young players to look out for: Adam Burns ('if he's no good at golf'), Arul Suppiah
Other sports played: Rugby league ('had trials for Barrow RLFC and Carlisle RLFC'), golf
Other sports followed: Football (Liverpool FC), rugby league (Walney Central ARLFC)
Relaxations: TV, family, cinema, Indian food
Extras: Played for Cumberland 1989-90. Player of the Tournament at Benson and Hedges Thailand International Cricket Sixes in 1989. Left Warwickshire and joined Somerset for the 1997 season. Scored club record of 217 for Lindisfarne in 1999-2000 season. Scored 160 v Oxford Universities at Taunton on 7 April 2000, setting new record for the earliest ever 100 in a first-class cricket season in this country. His 221 v Yorkshire at Bath in 2001 set a new record for the highest score by a Somerset player at the ground (overtaking Mark Lathwell's 206 v Surrey in 1994) and for the highest score by a Somerset player against Yorkshire (overtaking Viv Richards' 217 at Harrogate in 1975). C&G Man of the Match award for his 83-ball 71 in the quarter-final v Kent at Canterbury 2001. Captain of Somerset since 2003
Best batting: 221 Somerset v Yorkshire, Bath 2001
Best bowling: 6-54 Somerset v Leicestershire, Taunton 2001

2003 Season

	M	Inns	NO	Runs	HS	Avge	100s	50s	Ct	St	O	M	Runs	Wkts	Avge	Best	5wI	10wM
Test																		
All First	18	32	3	1133	118*	39.06	2	8	15	-	153.5	29	514	13	39.53	3-35	-	-
1-day Int																		
C & G	2	1	0	47	47	47.00	-	-	-	-	13	0	64	3	21.33	2-13	-	
NCL	17	16	3	279	91	21.46	-	1	9	2	25.3	2	199	3	66.33	2-26	-	
Twenty20	4	3	0	47	33	15.66	-	-	1	-	6	0	55	2	27.50	1-15	-	

Career Performances

	M	Inns	NO	Runs	HS	Avge	100s	50s	Ct	St	Balls	Runs	Wkts	Avge	Best	5wI	10wM
Test																	
All First	129	209	11	6431	221	32.47	7	45	121	7	4240	2588	62	41.74	6-54	1	-
1-day Int																	
C & G	25	24	3	639	84 *	30.42	-	4	8	-	378	337	10	33.70	2-13	-	
NCL	137	128	15	2653	115 *	23.47	2	15	66	11	1188	1162	37	31.40	4-39	-	
Twenty20	4	3	0	47	33	15.66	-	-	1	-	36	55	2	27.50	1-15	-	

BURROWS, T. G. Hampshire

Name: Thomas (<u>Tom</u>) George Burrows
Role: Right-hand middle-order bat,
wicket-keeper
Born: 5 May 1985, Reading
Height: 5ft 8in **Weight:** 10st 10lbs
Nickname: T
County debut: No first-team appearance
(*see* **Extras**)
Parents: Anthony and Victoria
Marital status: Single
Family links with cricket: 'My father was
briefly on Gloucestershire ground staff and
played club cricket'
Education: Reading School
Qualifications: 12 GCSEs, 4 AS-levels,
3 A-levels, Level 1 cricket coach
Off-season: 'In Perth playing for Melville
Cricket Club'

Overseas teams played for: Melville CC, Perth 2003-04
Career highlights to date: 'Keeping wicket in second innings v Yorkshire 2002'
Cricket moments to forget: 'The entire game against Somerset 2nd XI 2003'
Cricket superstitions: 'Never wear a jumper to bat'
Cricketers particularly admired: Steve Waugh, Jack Russell
Young players to look out for: David Wheeler, Kevin Latouf
Other sports played: Rugby, football
Other sports followed: Rugby (London Irish RFC), football (Chelsea FC)
Injuries: Out for two weeks with damaged ligaments in a thumb
Favourite band: R Kelly
Relaxations: 'Listening to music; watching rugby'
Extras: Appeared as substitute wicket-keeper for Hampshire v Yorkshire at West End
2002 but has yet to make full debut. Played for Berkshire in the C&G 2003

Opinions on cricket: 'Too many overs are played per day. I believe that 90 overs in a day would allow players to concentrate on how to get batsmen out and set plans rather than rushing to get the overs through.'

2003 Season (did not make any first-class or one-day appearances for his county)

Career Performances

	M	Inns	NO	Runs	HS	Avge	100s	50s	Ct	St	Balls	Runs	Wkts	Avge	Best	5wI	10wM
Test																	
All First																	
1-day Int																	
C & G	1	1	0	1	1	1.00	-	-	1	-							
NCL																	
Twenty20																	

BUTCHER, M. A.   Surrey

Name: <u>Mark</u> Alan Butcher
Role: Left-hand bat, right-arm medium bowler
Born: 23 August 1972, Croydon
Height: 5ft 11in   **Weight:** 13st
Nickname: Butch, Baz
County debut: 1991
County cap: 1996
Test debut: 1997
Tests: 57
1000 runs in a season: 7
1st-Class 50s: 72
1st-Class 100s: 25
1st-Class 200s: 2
1st-Class 5 w. in innings: 1
1st-Class catches: 203
One-Day 100s: 1
Place in batting averages: 10th av. 61.15
(2002 46th av. 46.80)
Strike rate: 33.62 (career 61.41)
Parents: Alan and Elaine
Wife and date of marriage: Judy, 4 October 1997
Children: Alita, 1999
Family links with cricket: Father Alan played for Glamorgan, Surrey and England and is now coach with Surrey; brother Gary played for Glamorgan and Surrey; uncle Ian played for Gloucestershire and Leicestershire; uncle Martin played for Surrey
Education: Trinity School; Archbishop Tenison's, Croydon

Qualifications: 5 O-levels, senior coaching award
Career outside cricket: Singer, guitar player
Off-season: Touring with England
Overseas tours: England YC to New Zealand 1990-91; Surrey to Dubai 1990, 1993, to Perth 1995; England A to Australia 1996-97; England to West Indies 1997-98, to Australia 1998-99, to South Africa 1999-2000, to India and New Zealand 2001-02, to Australia 2002-03, to Bangladesh and Sri Lanka 2003-04, to West Indies 2003-04
Overseas teams played for: South Melbourne, Australia 1993-94; North Perth 1994-95
Cricketers particularly admired: Ian Botham, David Gower, Viv Richards, Larry Gomes, Graham Thorpe, Alec Stewart, Michael Holding
Other sports followed: Football (Crystal Palace)
Relaxations: Music, playing the guitar, novels, wine
Extras: Played his first game for Surrey in 1991 against his father's Glamorgan in the Refuge Assurance League at The Oval, the first-ever match of any sort between first-class counties in which a father and son have been in opposition. His 259 v Leicestershire 1999 was the highest score by a left-hander at Grace Road and the fourth highest individual score recorded there overall. Captained England in third Test v New Zealand at Old Trafford 1999, deputising for the injured Nasser Hussain. His 4-42 in the first Test v Australia at Edgbaston 2001 included four wickets in 14 balls. Scored 145* v Glamorgan 2001, becoming the first Surrey batsman to carry his bat at The Oval since Grahame Clinton did so in 1984. Man of the Match in the fourth Test v Australia at Headingley 2001 for his match-winning 173*, having also scored 47 in the first innings; England's Man of the Series v Australia 2001 with 456 runs (more than any other batsman on either side) at an average of 50.66. Slazenger Sheer Instinct Award 2001 for the cricketer who has impressed the most in the recent season. Captained Surrey in Adam Hollioake's absence during the first part of the 2002 season. His other Test awards include England's Man of the Series v Sri Lanka 2002 and Man of the Match in the first Test v Zimbabwe at Lord's 2003 (137 in England's only innings and match figures of 5-68). Scored century (106) in the third Test v South Africa 2003, sharing with Nasser Hussain (116) in a record partnership for any wicket for England in Tests v South Africa at Trent Bridge (189). ECB central contract 2003-04. Recorded song 'You're Never Gone' in memory of the late Ben Hollioake
Best batting: 259 Surrey v Leicestershire, Leicester 1999
Best bowling: 5-86 Surrey v Lancashire, Old Trafford 2000

2003 Season

	M	Inns	NO	Runs	HS	Avge	100s	50s	Ct	St	O	M	Runs	Wkts	Avge	Best	5wI	10wM
Test	7	11	1	590	137	59.00	2	3	7	-	30.5	3	129	5	25.80	4-60	-	-
All First	14	20	1	1162	144	61.15	4	5	17	-	44.5	4	175	8	21.87	4-60	-	-
1-day Int																		
C & G	1	1	0	14	14	14.00	-	-	1	-	2	0	15	0	-		-	-
NCL	3	3	0	116	104	38.66	1	-	-	-								
Twenty20																		

Career Performances

	M	Inns	NO	Runs	HS	Avge	100s	50s	Ct	St	Balls	Runs	Wkts	Avge	Best	5wl	10wM
Test	57	104	4	3559	173 *	35.59	8	15	52	-	901	541	15	36.06	4-42	-	-
All First	212	363	26	13400	259	39.76	27	72	203	-	7616	4190	124	33.79	5-86	1	-
1-day Int																	
C & G	20	20	5	673	91	44.86	-	6	10	-	318	231	5	46.20	2-57	-	
NCL	94	81	14	1522	104	22.71	1	5	27	-	1717	1571	37	42.45	3-23	-	
Twenty20																	

BUTLER, I. G.   Gloucestershire

Name: <u>Ian</u> Gareth Butler
Role: Right-hand bat, right-arm fast bowler
Born: 24 November 1981, Middlemore, Auckland
County debut: 2003
Test debut: 2001-02
Tests: 4
One-Day Internationals: 9
1st-Class 5 w. in innings: 1
1st-Class catches: 5
Place in bowling averages: 52nd av. 28.11
Strike rate: 43.76 (career 46.26)
Overseas tours: New Zealand U19 to Sri Lanka (U19 World Cup) 1999-2000; New Zealand to Sharjah (Sharjah Cup) 2001-02, to Pakistan 2001-02, to West Indies 2001-02, to Sri Lanka 2003, to India 2003-04
Overseas teams played for: Northern Districts 2001-02 –
Extras: Represented New Zealand U19 v South Africa U19 2000-01. Took 4-60 v England at Wellington 2001-02 in his second Test match. Was an overseas player with Gloucestershire in May and early June 2003, deputising for Ian Harvey, absent on international duty
Best batting: 26 New Zealand v West Indies, Bridgetown 2001-02
Best bowling: 5-44 Northern Districts v Central Districts, Napier 2002-03
Stop press: Recorded maiden Test five-wicket return (6-46) in the second Test v Pakistan at Wellington 2003-04

2003 Season

	M	Inns	NO	Runs	HS	Avge	100s	50s	Ct	St	O	M	Runs	Wkts	Avge	Best	5wI	10wM
Test																		
All First	4	5	0	20	13	4.00	-	-	-	-	124	24	478	17	28.11	4-74	-	-
1-day Int																		
C & G	1	0	0	0	0	-	-	-	-	-	9	0	40	0	-		-	-
NCL	2	1	0	0	0	0.00	-	-	-	-	13.2	0	88	1	88.00	1-54	-
Twenty20																		

Career Performances

	M	Inns	NO	Runs	HS	Avge	100s	50s	Ct	St	Balls	Runs	Wkts	Avge	Best	5wI	10wM
Test	4	6	1	50	26	10.00	-	-	3	-	657	455	14	32.50	4-60	-	-
All First	19	24	7	161	26	9.47	-	-	5	-	3377	1948	73	26.68	5-44	1	-
1-day Int	9	5	3	6	3	3.00	-	-	4	-	339	328	6	54.66	2-32	-
C & G	1	0	0	0	0	-	-	-	-	-	54	40	0	-		-	-
NCL	2	1	0	0	0	0.00	-	-	-	-	80	88	1	88.00	1-54	-
Twenty20																		

CADDICK, A. R.   Somerset

Name: <u>Andrew</u> Richard Caddick
Role: Right-hand bat, right-arm
fast-medium bowler
Born: 21 November 1968, Christchurch,
New Zealand
Height: 6ft 5in   **Weight:** 14st 13lbs
Nickname: Des, Shack
County debut: 1991
County cap: 1992
Benefit: 1999
Test debut: 1993
Tests: 62
One-Day Internationals: 54
50 wickets in a season: 7
100 wickets in a season: 1
1st-Class 50s: 5
1st-Class 5 w. in innings: 61
1st-Class 10 w. in match: 15
1st-Class catches: 70
One-Day 5 w. in innings: 3
Place in batting averages: (2002 305th av. 7.41)
Place in bowling averages: (2002 42nd av. 27.35)

Strike rate: 32.57 (career 49.22)

Parents: Christopher and Audrey

Wife and date of marriage: Sarah, 27 January 1995

Children: Ashton Faye, 24 August 1998; Fraser Michael, 12 October 2001

Education: Papanui High School, Christchurch, New Zealand

Qualifications: Qualified plasterer and tiler

Career outside cricket: Plasterer and tiler

Overseas tours: New Zealand YC to Australia (U19 World Cup) 1987-88, to England 1988; England A to Australia 1992-93; England to West Indies 1993-94, to Zimbabwe and New Zealand 1996-97, to West Indies 1997-98, to South Africa and Zimbabwe 1999-2000, to Kenya (ICC Knockout Trophy) 2000-01, to Pakistan and Sri Lanka 2000-01, to India (one-day series) and New Zealand 2001-02, to Sri Lanka (ICC Champions Trophy) 2002-03, to Australia 2002-03, to Africa (World Cup) 2002-03

Career highlights to date: 'Bowling West Indies out at Lord's [2000] and thus getting my name up on the board'

Cricketers particularly admired: Dennis Lillee, Richard Hadlee, Robin Smith, Jimmy Cook

Other sports followed: 'Mostly all'

Injuries: Out for most of the 2003 season with a foot injury and a prolapsed disc

Relaxations: Golf

Extras: Rapid Cricketline 2nd XI Championship Player of the Year 1991. Whyte and Mackay Bowler of the Year 1997. Took 105 first-class wickets in 1998 season. Leading wicket-taker in the single-division four-day era of the County Championship with 422 wickets (av. 22.48) 1993-99. Cornhill England Player of the Year 1999-2000. Took 5-16 from 13 overs as West Indies were bowled out for 54 in their second innings in the second Test at Lord's 2000. Took 5-14 in fourth Test v West Indies at Headingley 2000, becoming the fifth England bowler to take four wickets in an over in a Test match. One of *Wisden*'s Five Cricketers of the Year 2001. Scored a 40-ball 49* v Australia at Edgbaston 2001, in the process sharing with Alec Stewart in the first century stand for the last wicket (103) since 1903-04 for England in Tests v Australia. Had then Test best match figures of 9-172 in the first Test v New Zealand 2001-02, which took place in his birthplace, Christchurch. Took 200th Test wicket (Craig McMillan) in the third Test v New Zealand at Auckland 2001-02. Recorded maiden Test ten-wicket match return (3-121 and 7-94) in England victory in fifth Test v Australia at Sydney 2002-03, in the process passing Darren Gough's then total of 228 wickets to move into seventh place in the list of England Test wicket-takers. His international awards include England's Man of the Series v New Zealand 1999 and joint Man of the Match (with Gary Kirsten) in the third Test at Durban 1999-2000, having returned 7-46 in South Africa's first innings. Retired from ODI cricket in March 2003

Best batting: 92 Somerset v Worcestershire, Worcester 1995

Best bowling: 9-32 Somerset v Lancashire, Taunton 1993

2003 Season

	M	Inns	NO	Runs	HS	Avge	100s	50s	Ct	St	O	M	Runs	Wkts	Avge	Best	5wI	10wM
Test																		
All First	1	1	0	1	1	1.00	-	-	-	-	38	8	110	7	15.71	4-66	-	-
1-day Int																		
C & G																		
NCL	1	1	1	0	0 *	-	-	-	-	-	8	2	27	2	13.50	2-27	-	
Twenty20																		

Career Performances

	M	Inns	NO	Runs	HS	Avge	100s	50s	Ct	St	Balls	Runs	Wkts	Avge	Best	5wI	10wM
Test	62	95	12	861	49 *	10.37	-	-	21	-	13558	6999	234	29.91	7-46	13	1
All First	203	273	51	3156	92	14.21	-	5	70	-	44162	22296	897	24.85	9-32	61	15
1-day Int	54	38	18	249	36	12.45	-	-	9	-	2937	1965	69	28.47	4-19	-	
C & G	28	14	6	29	8	3.62	-	-	5	-	1694	940	45	20.88	6-30	2	
NCL	96	39	12	292	39	10.81	-	-	14	-	4187	3016	118	25.55	4-18	-	
Twenty20																	

CAIRNS, C. L.　　　Nottinghamshire

Name: Christopher (Chris) Lance Cairns
Role: Right-hand bat, right-arm
fast-medium bowler
Born: 13 June 1970, Picton, New Zealand
Height: 6ft 2in **Weight:** 14st
County debut: 1988
County cap: 1993
Test debut: 1989-90
Tests: 55
One-Day Internationals: 167
1000 runs in a season: 1
50 wickets in a season: 3
1st-Class 50s: 66
1st-Class 100s: 12
1st-Class 5 w. in innings: 29
1st-Class 10 w. in match: 6
1st-Class catches: 79
One-Day 100s: 6
One-Day 5 w. in innings: 3
Place in batting averages: 133rd av. 30.71
Place in bowling averages: 143rd av. 50.33
Strike rate: 73.60 (career 52.77)

Parents: Lance and Sue

Family links with cricket: Father played for New Zealand; uncle played first-class cricket in New Zealand

Education: Christchurch Boys' High School, New Zealand

Qualifications: 5th and 6th form certificates

Overseas tours: New Zealand YC to Australia (U19 World Cup) 1987-88; New Zealand to Australia 1989-90, 1993-94, 1997-98, 2001-02, to India 1995-96, 1999-2000, to India and Pakistan (World Cup) 1995-96, to West Indies 1995-96, to Pakistan 1996-97, (one-day series) 2003-04, to Zimbabwe 1997-98, 2000-01, to Sri Lanka 1997-98, to UK, Ireland and Holland (World Cup) 1999, to England 1999, to Kenya (ICC Knockout Trophy) 2000-01, to Africa (World Cup) 2002-03, plus other one-day tours and tournaments

Overseas teams played for: Northern Districts 1988-89; Canterbury 1990-91 –

Cricketers particularly admired: Mick Newell, Richard Hadlee, Dennis Lillee

Other sports followed: Most sports

Extras: Represented New Zealand in the 1991-92 World Cup. Hit the fastest first-class hundred of the 1995 season (65 balls for Nottinghamshire v Cambridge University at Fenner's). One of the *New Zealand Cricket Almanack* two Players of the Year 1998, 1999, 2000. Took 7-27 v West Indies at Hamilton 1999-2000, returning 10-100 in the match to make himself and his father Lance the only father and son to have taken ten wickets in a Test match; also won Man of the Match award. National Bank Player of the Year 1999-2000 in New Zealand and won the Redpath Cup for batting and the Winsor Cup for bowling (only the second player, after John Reid in 1954-55, to win the batting and bowling trophies in one year). Canterbury of New Zealand Sportsperson of the Year 2000. One of *Wisden*'s Five Cricketers of the Year 2000. Had first innings figures of 5-146 and scored 61 and 43 in the first Test v Australia at Brisbane 2001-02, his first international match after a year out with a knee injury. Took his 150th ODI wicket (Nasser Hussain) v England at Auckland 2001-02 in his 150th ODI. His other Test and ODI awards include New Zealand's Man of the Series v England 1999 and Man of the Match for his 102* in the ICC Knockout Trophy final v India in Kenya 2000-01. Was prevented by injury from rejoining Notts as overseas player for 2002 but returned for 2003. Scored 91* v Sussex at Trent Bridge in the NCL 2003, sharing with Chris Read (79*) in a new record sixth-wicket partnership for the one-day league (167*). One-day captain of Notts 2003 (*see entry on Jason Gallian*). Left Nottinghamshire during the 2003-04 off-season

Opinions on cricket: 'Great game.'

Best batting: 126 New Zealand v India, Hamilton 1998-99

Best bowling: 8-47 Nottinghamshire v Sussex, Arundel 1995

17. Who marked his 100th Test with a century against West Indies at Old Trafford in 2000?

2003 Season

	M	Inns	NO	Runs	HS	Avge	100s	50s	Ct	St	O	M	Runs	Wkts	Avge	Best	5wI	10wM
Test																		
All First	13	23	2	645	104	30.71	1	4	7	-	184	31	755	15	50.33	3-59	-	-
1-day Int																		
C & G	1	1	0	67	67	67.00	-	1	2	-								
NCL	14	14	6	510	91 *	63.75	-	6	4	-	97	3	504	13	38.76	3-48	-	
Twenty20																		

Career Performances

	M	Inns	NO	Runs	HS	Avge	100s	50s	Ct	St	Balls	Runs	Wkts	Avge	Best	5wI	10wM
Test	55	92	5	2852	126	32.78	4	20	15	-	10445	5675	197	28.80	7-27	12	1
All First	205	322	38	9996	126	35.19	12	66	79	-	32401	17248	614	28.09	8-47	29	6
1-day Int	167	153	16	3973	115	29.00	4	20	54	-	6326	4968	156	31.84	5-42	1	
C & G	8	8	1	373	77	53.28	-	4	4	-	482	279	14	19.92	4-18	-	
NCL	74	64	16	2165	126 *	45.10	2	15	21	-	2945	2362	99	23.85	6-52	2	
Twenty20																	

CARBERRY, M. A.   Kent

Name: <u>Michael</u> Alexander Carberry
Role: Left-hand bat, right-arm off-spin bowler
Born: 29 September 1980, Croydon
Height: 6ft **Weight:** 12st 7lbs
Nickname: Carbs
County debut: 2001 (Surrey), 2003 (Kent)
1st-Class 50s: 7
1st-Class 100s: 2
1st-Class catches: 10
Place in batting averages: 101st av. 35.82
Strike rate: 138.00 (career 138.00)
Parents: Maria and Neville
Marital status: Single
Family links with cricket: 'My dad played club cricket'
Education: St John Rigby RC College
Qualifications: 10 GCSEs
Overseas tours: Surrey U17 to South Africa 1997; England U19 to New Zealand 1998-99, to Malaysia and (U19 World Cup) Sri Lanka 1999-2000
Overseas teams played for: Portland CC, Melbourne
Career highlights to date: 'Getting chance to play first-class cricket'

Cricketers particularly admired: Brian Lara, Steve Waugh, Mark Butcher, Graham Thorpe
Young players to look out for: Tim Murtagh, Carl Greenidge, Scott Newman
Other sports played: Basketball, football
Other sports followed: Football (Tottenham Hotspur)
Relaxations: 'Nightclubbing, weights, DJ-ing'
Extras: Second schoolboy to score a century for Croydon U13 since Ali Brown. Scored century (126*) for ECB U18 v Pakistan U19 at Abergavenny 1998. Represented England U19 v Australia U19 1999 (scoring 50 in the third 'Test' at Chester-le-Street) and v Sri Lanka U19 2000. Played for Surrey Board XI in 1999 NatWest. NBC Denis Compton Award for the most promising young Surrey player 1999, 2000. Left Surrey during the 2002-03 off-season and joined Kent for 2003. Scored century (137) on Kent debut v Cambridge UCCE at Fenner's 2003
Best batting: 153* Surrey v CUCCE, Fenner's 2002
Best bowling: 1-45 Kent v Surrey, The Oval 2003

2003 Season

	M	Inns	NO	Runs	HS	Avge	100s	50s	Ct	St	O	M	Runs	Wkts	Avge	Best	5wI	10wM
Test																		
All First	14	24	1	824	137	35.82	1	6	2	-	23	2	94	1	94.00	1-45	-	-
1-day Int																		
C & G																		
NCL	8	7	0	145	79	20.71	-	1	-	-	4	0	21	1	21.00	1-21	-	
Twenty20	5	4	1	29	10	9.66	-	-	3	-								

Career Performances

	M	Inns	NO	Runs	HS	Avge	100s	50s	Ct	St	Balls	Runs	Wkts	Avge	Best	5wI	10wM
Test																	
All First	22	38	2	1358	153*	37.72	2	7	10	-	138	94	1	94.00	1-45	-	-
1-day Int																	
C & G	3	2	0	23	19	11.50	-	-	-	-							
NCL	16	15	1	206	79	14.71	-	1	3	-	24	21	1	21.00	1-21	-	
Twenty20	5	4	1	29	10	9.66	-	-	3	-							

CARTER, N. M. Warwickshire

Name: <u>Neil</u> Miller Carter
Role: Left-hand bat, left-arm
fast bowler
Born: 29 January 1975, Cape Town,
South Africa
Height: 6ft 2in **Weight:** 14st 4lbs
Nickname: Carts
County debut: 2001
1st-Class 50s: 1
1st-Class 100s: 1
1st-Class 5 w. in innings: 4
1st-Class catches: 9
One-Day 5 w. in innings: 1
Place in batting averages: 238th av. 16.85
(2002 59th av. 43.57)
Place in bowling averages: (2002 144th
av. 47.85)
Strike rate: 94.50 (career 60.61)

Parents: John and Heather
Marital status: Single
Education: Hottentots Holland High School; Cape Technikon
Qualifications: Diploma in Financial Information Systems, Certified Novell Engineer,
Level 2 coaching
Career outside cricket: Computers, accounting
Overseas tours: SA Country Schools U15 to England 1992; Warwickshire to Cape
Town 2001, 2002
Overseas teams played for: Boland 1998-99 – 2001-02
Career highlights to date: 'Winning last B&H Cup in 2002. Winning Standard Bank
Cup for Boland 1999-2000'
Cricket moments to forget: 'Any performance under par'
Cricketers particularly admired: Jacques Kallis, Shaun Pollock, Allan Donald
Other sports played: Golf, swimming
Other sports followed: Rugby union (Stormers, Springboks), football (Sheffield
Wednesday)
Relaxations: Steam train photography ('gricing')
Extras: Made first-class debut for Boland during the 1999-2000 season. Won Man of
the Match award in first one-day match for Warwickshire (4-21 and a 43-ball 40), in
C&G Trophy v Essex at Edgbaston 2001. Recorded maiden one-day five-wicket return
(5-31) v Durham in the NUL at Edgbaston 2002; also struck 24 from nine balls as
opener in the same match. Swept his first ball (the last of the game) for a match-
winning four in the B&H semi-final v Lancashire at Old Trafford 2002. Scored maiden

first-class century (103) v Sussex at Hove 2002; his 67-ball hundred was the second fastest for Warwickshire since centuries began to be recorded in terms of balls received. Struck a 37-ball 75 v Leicestershire at Edgbaston in the NCL 2003. Is not considered an overseas player

Best batting: 103 Warwickshire v Sussex, Hove 2002
Best bowling: 6-63 Boland v Griqualand West, Kimberley 2000-01

2003 Season

	M	Inns	NO	Runs	HS	Avge	100s	50s	Ct	St	O	M	Runs	Wkts	Avge	Best	5wI	10wM
Test																		
All First	5	7	0	118	38	16.85	-	-	1	-	126	20	522	8	65.25	5-75	1	-
1-day Int																		
C & G																		
NCL	14	13	1	228	75	19.00	-	1	-	-	105.3	4	512	14	36.57	2-19	-	
Twenty20	7	7	0	145	47	20.71	-	-	2	-	23	0	165	7	23.57	3-19	-	

Career Performances

	M	Inns	NO	Runs	HS	Avge	100s	50s	Ct	St	Balls	Runs	Wkts	Avge	Best	5wI	10wM
Test																	
All First	29	38	8	567	103	18.90	1	1	9	-	4667	2885	77	37.46	6-63	4	-
1-day Int																	
C & G	4	2	0	46	40	23.00	-	-	1	-	201	142	8	17.75	4-21	-	
NCL	29	26	5	327	75	15.57	-	1	3	-	1309	1071	38	28.18	5-31	1	
Twenty20	7	7	0	145	47	20.71	-	-	2	-	138	165	7	23.57	3-19	-	

CAWDRON, M. J.   Northamptonshire

Name: Michael (<u>Mike</u>) John Cawdron
Role: Left-hand bat, right-arm
medium-fast bowler
Born: 7 October 1974, Luton
Height: 6ft 3in **Weight:** 13st 7lbs
Nickname: Muscles
County debut: 1995 (one-day,
Gloucestershire), 1999 (first-class,
Gloucestershire), 2002 (Northamptonshire)
1st-Class 5 w. in innings: 6
1st-Class 10 w. in match: 1
1st-Class catches: 4
Place in batting averages: 272nd av. 10.50
Place in bowling averages: 30th av. 25.20
Strike rate: 42.75 (career 50.31)
Parents: William and Mandy
Marital status: Single
Family links with cricket: Father and
brother played local village cricket
Education: Cheltenham College

Qualifications: 10 GCSEs, 3 A-levels, NCA coaching award
Overseas tours: West of England U14 to Holland; Cheltenham College to Zimbabwe
1992; Gloucestershire YC to Sri Lanka 1993-94; Gloucestershire Gypsies to
Zimbabwe 1994-95, to Cape Town 1997; Christians in Sport to Zimbabwe 1998,
to South Africa 2000; Gloucestershire to Kimberley and Cape Town 2001
Career highlights to date: 'Playing in 1999 NatWest final v Somerset'
Cricketers particularly admired: Jack Russell, Jeremy Snape, Kim Barnett ('they are
all very tough players who have made the most of their talents')
Other sports followed: Rugby, hockey, rackets, clay-pigeon shooting, golf
Relaxations: Cinema, videos, eating and going out with friends
Extras: Winner of the *Daily Telegraph* Regional Bowling Award 1993. Captain of
MCC Schools and ESCA U19 1993. 'Made 50 off 32 balls on Sunday League debut
against Essex at my old school' (Cheltenham College). Scored 42 and took 5-35 on
first-class debut, v Hampshire at Bristol 1999; went on to take two more five-wicket
hauls in his next two Championship games. Released by Gloucestershire at the end of
the 2001 season and joined Northamptonshire for 2002
Best batting: 42 Gloucestershire v Hampshire, Bristol 1999
Best bowling: 6-25 First-Class Counties XI v New Zealand A, Milton Keynes 2000

2003 Season

	M	Inns	NO	Runs	HS	Avge	100s	50s	Ct	St	O	M	Runs	Wkts	Avge	Best	5wI	10wM
Test																		
All First	6	6	0	63	24	10.50	-	-	1	-	142.3	31	504	20	25.20	6-87	1	-
1-day Int																		
C & G	1	1	0	8	8	8.00	-	-	-	-	10	2	26	2	13.00	2-26	-	
NCL	15	6	3	68	37 *	22.66	-	-	2	-	115	11	550	26	21.15	4-31	-	
Twenty20	5	1	0	1	1	1.00	-	-	1	-	18	0	157	7	22.42	3-24	-	

Career Performances

	M	Inns	NO	Runs	HS	Avge	100s	50s	Ct	St	Balls	Runs	Wkts	Avge	Best	5wI	10wM
Test																	
All First	24	32	4	396	42	14.14	-	-	4	-	3673	1802	73	24.68	6-25	6	1
1-day Int																	
C & G	10	7	3	34	17	8.50	-	-	1	-	480	333	14	23.78	4-34	-	
NCL	50	30	11	319	50	16.78	-	1	6	-	1976	1616	53	30.49	4-17	-	
Twenty20	5	1	0	1	1	1.00	-	-	1	-	108	157	7	22.42	3-24	-	

CHAPPLE, G.   Lancashire

Name: Glen Chapple
Role: Right-hand bat, right-arm medium-fast bowler
Born: 23 January 1974, Skipton, Yorkshire
Height: 6ft 2in **Weight:** 12st 7lbs
Nickname: Chappy, Boris, Boomor, Cheeky
County debut: 1992
County cap: 1994
50 wickets in a season: 4
1st-Class 50s: 15
1st-Class 100s: 4
1st-Class 5 w. in innings: 20
1st-Class 10 w. in match: 1
1st-Class catches: 54
One-Day 5 w. in innings: 4
Place in batting averages: 88th av. 37.72
(2002 211th av. 22.40)
Place in bowling averages: 91st av. 35.59
(2002 63rd av. 29.51)
Strike rate: 60.53 (career 55.91)
Parents: Eileen and Michael
Marital status: Single

Family links with cricket: Father played in Lancashire League for Nelson and was a professional for Darwen and Earby
Education: West Craven High School; Nelson and Colne College
Qualifications: 8 GCSEs, 2 A-levels
Overseas tours: England U18 to Canada (International Youth Tournament) 1991; England YC to New Zealand 1990-91, to Pakistan 1991-92, to India 1992-93; England A to India 1994-95, to Australia 1996-97; England VI to Hong Kong 2002, 2003
Cricketers particularly admired: Dennis Lillee, Robin Smith
Other sports followed: Football (Liverpool), golf
Relaxations: 'Watching films, music, socialising'
Extras: Set record for fastest century in first-class cricket (21 minutes; against declaration bowling) v Glamorgan at Old Trafford 1993. Man of the Match in the 1996 NatWest final against Essex at Lord's for his 6-18. Shared in a record eighth-wicket partnership for Lancashire in matches against Northamptonshire (136*) with Warren Hegg at Northampton 2001, scoring 72*; also scored 31 in the first innings and took nine wickets in the match. Scored 155 v Somerset at Old Trafford 2001, equalling Wasim Akram's record, set in 1998 v Nottinghamshire, for the highest score by a Lancashire No. 8. Lancashire Player of the Year 2002. Scored century (132) v Warwickshire at Old Trafford 2003, following up with 4-82 in Warwickshire's first innings. Called up to England squad for the third Test v South Africa at Trent Bridge 2003. Granted a benefit for 2004
Best batting: 155 Lancashire v Somerset, Old Trafford 2001
Best bowling: 6-30 Lancashire v Somerset, Blackpool 2002

2003 Season

	M	Inns	NO	Runs	HS	Avge	100s	50s	Ct	St	O	M	Runs	Wkts	Avge	Best	5wI	10wM
Test																		
All First	16	21	3	679	132 *	37.72	2	3	8	-	494.2	90	1744	49	35.59	6-98	2	-
1-day Int																		
C & G	4	3	1	95	45 *	47.50	-	-	-	-	35	2	145	3	48.33	1-25	-	
NCL	16	10	3	236	77 *	33.71	-	2	4	-	111.5	11	539	25	21.56	4-37	-	
Twenty20	5	5	1	71	55 *	17.75	-	1	1	-	19	1	101	9	11.22	2-13	-	

Career Performances

	M	Inns	NO	Runs	HS	Avge	100s	50s	Ct	St	Balls	Runs	Wkts	Avge	Best	5wI	10wM
Test																	
All First	162	220	51	3957	155	23.41	4	15	54	-	27232	14063	487	28.87	6-30	20	1
1-day Int																	
C & G	27	17	3	239	81 *	17.07	-	1	6	-	1400	1013	30	33.76	6-18	2	
NCL	134	68	19	806	77 *	16.44	-	4	24	-	5362	4162	151	27.56	6-25	1	
Twenty20	5	5	1	71	55 *	17.75	-	1	1	-	114	101	9	11.22	2-13	-	

CHERRY, D. D.   Glamorgan

Name: <u>Daniel</u> David Cherry
Role: Left-hand bat, right-arm
off-cutter bowler
Born: 7 February 1980, Newport, Gwent
Height: 5ft 9in **Weight:** 12st 9lbs
Nickname: Rhino, Banners, DC, Kiwi
County debut: 1998
1st-Class catches: 4
Place in batting averages: (2002 256th
av. 16.12)
Parents: David and Elizabeth
Marital status: Single
Family links with cricket: Father is a
qualified coach and played club cricket
Education: Tonbridge School, Kent;
University of Wales, Swansea
Qualifications: 10 GCSEs, 3 A-levels,
BA History, Level 1 coach
Off-season: 'Coaching, fitness work'
Overseas tours: Tonbridge School to Australia 1996-97; Glamorgan to Cape
Town 2002
Overseas teams played for: Doutta Stars, Melbourne 2002-03
Career highlights to date: 'First-class debut'
Cricket moments to forget: 'Bagging a pair on 2nd XI Championship debut'
Cricketers particularly admired: Michael Atherton, Graham Thorpe,
Steve James
Young players to look out for: Adam Harrison
Other sports played: Rugby, rackets (Public Schools doubles champion)
Other sports followed: Rugby (Neath), football (Everton)
Favourite band: Super Furry Animals
Relaxations: Reading true crime books, listening to music; 'socialising with the
high-quality clientele that frequents Pembrokeshire's premier nightspot – "The Sands
Discotheque Deluxe"'
Extras: Played for ECB U19 XI v Pakistan U19 1998. Played in Old Tonbridgians
Cricketer Cup winning side 1998. Awarded Glamorgan 2nd XI cap 2002
Opinions on cricket: 'Surely the development of youngsters has to be the way
forward; not bringing in more overseas and EU-qualified players. Australia are the best
team in the world, yet I see their game employing hardly any overseas players.'
Best batting: 47 Glamorgan v Gloucestershire, Cheltenham 2002

2003 Season

	M	Inns	NO	Runs	HS	Avge	100s	50s	Ct	St	O	M	Runs	Wkts	Avge	Best	5wI	10wM
Test																		
All First	1	1	0	9	9	9.00	-	-	-	-								
1-day Int																		
C & G																		
NCL																		
Twenty20	2	2	0	12	11	6.00	-	-	1	-	1	0	6	2	3.00	2-6	-	

Career Performances

	M	Inns	NO	Runs	HS	Avge	100s	50s	Ct	St	Balls	Runs	Wkts	Avge	Best	5wI	10wM
Test																	
All First	7	10	0	149	47	14.90	-	-	4	-	18	0	0	-	-	-	-
1-day Int																	
C & G																	
NCL																	
Twenty20	2	2	0	12	11	6.00	-	-	1	-	6	6	2	3.00	2-6	-	

CHILTON, M. J.   Lancashire

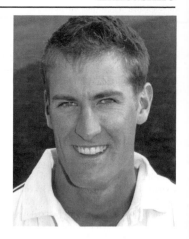

Name: <u>Mark</u> James Chilton
Role: Right-hand bat, right-arm medium bowler
Born: 2 October 1976, Sheffield
Height: 6ft 2in **Weight:** 12st 10lbs
Nickname: Dip, Chill
County debut: 1997
County cap: 2002
1000 runs in a season: 1
1st-Class 50s: 15
1st-Class 100s: 10
1st-Class catches: 71
One-Day 100s: 3
One-Day 5 w. in innings: 1
Place in batting averages: 29th av. 50.17 (2002 163rd av. 27.17)
Strike rate: 258.00 (career 167.00)
Parents: Jim and Sue
Marital status: Single
Family links with cricket: Father played local cricket
Education: Manchester Grammar School; Durham University
Qualifications: 10 GCSEs, 3 A-levels, BA (Hons) Business Economics, senior coaching award

Off-season: 'Rest, then training and playing in Perth'
Overseas tours: Manchester Grammar School to Barbados 1993-94, to South Africa 1995-96; Durham University to Zimbabwe 1997-98
Overseas teams played for: East Torrens, Adelaide 2000-01; North Sydney CC, Sydney 2002-03
Career highlights to date: 'Lancashire cap'
Cricket moments to forget: 'Losing two semi-finals in last over'
Cricket superstitions: 'None'
Cricketers particularly admired: Michael Atherton, David Gower
Young players to look out for: Kyle Hogg, Steven Crook
Other sports played: Football, golf
Other sports followed: 'Interest in most sports', football (Manchester United)
Favourite band: Oasis
Relaxations: 'Music, guitar, relaxing with friends and family'
Extras: Represented England U14, U15, U17. Awarded England U15 Batsman of the Year in 1992. Played for North of England v New Zealand U19 in 1996. Played for British Universities in 1997 Benson and Hedges Cup, winning the Gold Award against Sussex. C&G Man of the Match award for his 76* v Derbyshire at Old Trafford 2002. Scored 1000 first-class runs in a season (including six centuries) for the first time 2003
Opinions on cricket: 'The increase in overseas and EU players is a worry. The money should be spent on grass-roots cricket and academies. There must be a minimum of six or seven players in each team eligible to play for England. We need to look at restructuring club cricket and creating a pyramid system where the best players are concentrated into one league and play with and against each other every week. This will raise standards and help identify talent.'
Best batting: 125 Lancashire v Middlesex, Old Trafford 2003
Best bowling: 1-1 Lancashire v Sri Lanka A, Old Trafford 1999

2003 Season

	M	Inns	NO	Runs	HS	Avge	100s	50s	Ct	St	O	M	Runs	Wkts	Avge	Best	5wI	10wM
Test																		
All First	17	25	2	1154	125	50.17	6	3	15	-	43	9	109	1	109.00	1-2	-	-
1-day Int																		
C & G	4	4	0	113	51	28.25	-	1	3	-	2	0	9	0	-		-	-
NCL	17	15	2	426	103	32.76	1	1	3	-	13	0	81	5	16.20	3-20	-	
Twenty20	1	1	0	23	23	23.00	-	-	-	-								

Career Performances

	M	Inns	NO	Runs	HS	Avge	100s	50s	Ct	St	Balls	Runs	Wkts	Avge	Best	5wI	10wM
Test																	
All First	80	129	8	3879	125	32.05	10	15	71	-	1002	506	6	84.33	1-1	-	-
1-day Int																	
C & G	9	9	1	343	76 *	42.87	-	3	5	-	54	51	2	25.50	1-20	-	
NCL	61	56	5	1250	103	24.50	1	5	11	-	412	384	15	25.60	3-20	-	
Twenty20	1	1	0	23	23	23.00	-	-	-	-							

CLAPP, D. A.   Hampshire

Name: <u>Dominic</u> Adrian Clapp
Role: Right-hand bat, right-arm
medium bowler
Born: 25 May 1980, Southport, Merseyside
Height: 6ft 0½ **Weight:** 13st 7lbs
Nickname: Hans, Poppa, Gruber, Rhino,
Link, Cornelius
County debut: 2002 (Sussex),
2003 (Hampshire)
Parents: Adrian and Sarah
Marital status: Single
Family links with cricket: Brother plays for
his local club side, Broadwater
Education: Lancing College; Worthing Sixth
Form College
Qualifications: 6 GCSEs, 1 A-level,
Level 1 and 2 cricket coach

Overseas tours: Sussex U14 to Jersey 1994;
Lancing College to Australia 1996; Sussex U19 to Barbados 1997; Sussex Martlets to
Australia 2000; Sussex to Grenada 2001
Overseas teams played for: St Bernhards CC, Melbourne
Cricketers particularly admired: Murray Goodwin, Steve Waugh, Jacques Kallis,
Damien Martyn, Mike Atherton, Tony Cottey, Ray Beiber, John Kaye
Young players to look out for: Matt Prior, Ian Bell, Nicky Peng, Lawrence Prittipaul,
Jimmy Adams
Other sports played: Tennis (Sussex U10, U11, U12), golf, two-touch football
Other sports followed: Football (Tottenham Hotspur), rugby, golf, tennis,
athletics, boxing
Relaxations: 'Reading newspapers, magazines, books; spending time with my friends;
playing cards'
Extras: Sussex U14 Player of the Year 1994. Set record for highest score in Sussex
Youth cricket, 189 v Middlesex 1998. Played two Development of Excellence games
v Australia U19 1999. Sussex Young Cricketer of the Year 1999. Played for Sussex
Board XI in the NatWest 2000. Released by Sussex at the end of the 2002 season;
played one first-class match for Hampshire in 2003 and is registered for 2004
Best batting: 6 Sussex v Leicestershire, Horsham 2002

2003 Season

	M	Inns	NO	Runs	HS	Avge	100s	50s	Ct	St	O	M	Runs	Wkts	Avge	Best	5wI	10wM
Test																		
All First	1	1	0	4	4	4.00	-	-	-	-								
1-day Int																		
C & G																		
NCL																		
Twenty20																		

Career Performances

	M	Inns	NO	Runs	HS	Avge	100s	50s	Ct	St	Balls	Runs	Wkts	Avge	Best	5wI	10wM
Test																	
All First	2	2	0	10	6	5.00	-	-	-	-							
1-day Int																	
C & G	2	2	0	14	10	7.00	-	-	-	-	36	46	3	15.33	3-46	-	
NCL																	
Twenty20																	

CLARK, M. W. — Warwickshire

Name: <u>Michael</u> Wayne Clark
Role: Right-hand bat, left-arm medium-fast bowler
Born: 31 March 1978, Mount Lawley, Western Australia
Height: 6ft 4in **Weight:** 14st 2lbs
Nickname: Potty, Spike
County debut: 2003
1st-Class 5 w. in innings: 1
1st-Class catches: 9
Strike rate: 66.00 (career 56.00)
Family links with cricket: Father Wayne played for Western Australia and Australia, coached Yorkshire to the 2001 County Championship and was appointed coach of Western Australia for 2003-04
Overseas teams played for: Subiaco; Western Australia 2001-02 –
Extras: Played AFL for Fremantle and Collingwood. Opened bowling with his father for ACB Chairman's XI v England XI at Lilac Hill 2002-03. Set new tenth-wicket partnership record for Western Australia in domestic one-day competition (43) with Peter Worthington v New South Wales in the ING Cup final at Perth 2002-03. Western

Australia's leading wicket-taker in the Pura Cup 2002-03 with 38 at 23.13. Was an overseas player with Warwickshire at the start of the 2003 season, deputising for Shane Bond, absent on international duty, but was released after sustaining a back injury

Best batting: 26 Western Australia v Tasmania, Perth 2002-03
Best bowling: 5-47 Western Australia v South Australia, Perth 2002-03

2003 Season

	M	Inns	NO	Runs	HS	Avge	100s	50s	Ct	St	O	M	Runs	Wkts	Avge	Best	5wl	10wM
Test																		
All First	1	2	1	4	2*	4.00	-	-	-	-	33	7	110	3	36.66	2-71	-	-
1-day Int																		
C & G																		
NCL																		
Twenty20																		

Career Performances

	M	Inns	NO	Runs	HS	Avge	100s	50s	Ct	St	Balls	Runs	Wkts	Avge	Best	5wl	10wM
Test																	
All First	16	22	10	138	26	11.50	-	-	9	-	2688	1313	48	27.35	5-47	1	-
1-day Int																	
C & G																	
NCL																	
Twenty20																	

18. Which knight shared a 399-run partnership
with Sir Garfield Sobers at Bridgetown in 1960?

CLARKE, A. J.   Essex

Name: Andrew (<u>Andy</u>) John Clarke
Role: Left-hand bat, right-arm
fast-medium bowler
Born: 9 November 1975, Harold Wood,
Essex
Height: 6ft 2in **Weight:** 12st 8lbs
Nickname: Vicram, Nobby, Ken
County debut: 2001 (one-day),
2002 (first-class)
1st-Class 5 w. in innings: 1
1st-Class catches: 2
Strike rate: 50.57 (career 40.92)
Parents: Mary and John (both deceased)
Marital status: Single
Family links with cricket: 'Dad played club
cricket'
Education: St Martins School, Hutton;
Brentwood College of Higher Education
Qualifications: 7 GCSEs, 1 AS-level, 2 A-levels, Level 2 coaching
Career outside cricket: 'Property'
Overseas tours: MCC to Amsterdam 1998
Cricketers particularly admired: 'My dad'
Other sports played: Football, squash
Other sports followed: Football (West Ham)
Relaxations: 'Listening to music; time with family and friends'
Extras: MCC Young Cricketers cap and Player of the Year 1998. Played for Essex
Board XI and Essex in the C&G 2001. Recorded maiden first-class five-wicket return
on first-class debut v Glamorgan at Swansea 2002; his 5-54 included three wickets in
his first six overs
Best batting: 41 Essex v Warwickshire, Chelmsford 2003
Best bowling: 5-54 Essex v Glamorgan, Swansea 2002

2003 Season

	M	Inns	NO	Runs	HS	Avge	100s	50s	Ct	St	O	M	Runs	Wkts	Avge	Best	5wI	10wM
Test																		
All First	3	4	1	87	41	29.00	-	-	1	-	59	13	205	7	29.28	4-34	-	-
1-day Int																		
C & G	1	0	0	0	0	-	-	-	-	-	5	0	38	0	-		-	-
NCL	8	4	2	11	6	5.50	-	-	2	-	58.5	4	314	13	24.15	4-28	-	
Twenty20																		

Career Performances

	M	Inns	NO	Runs	HS	Avge	100s	50s	Ct	St	Balls	Runs	Wkts	Avge	Best	5wI	10wM
Test																	
All First	5	8	2	129	41	21.50	-	-	2	-	573	318	14	22.71	5-54	1	-
1-day Int																	
C & G	5	2	0	9	9	4.50	-	-	2	-	204	155	2	77.50	1-19	-	
NCL	22	11	4	21	6	3.00	-	-	5	-	872	722	30	24.06	4-28	-	
Twenty20																	

CLARKE, M. J. Hampshire

Name: <u>Michael</u> John Clarke
Role: Right-hand bat, slow left-arm bowler
Born: 2 April 1981, Liverpool,
New South Wales
Height: 5ft 10in **Weight:** 11st
County debut: No first-team appearance
One-Day Internationals: 5
1st-Class 50s: 9
1st-Class 100s: 7
1st-Class catches: 27
Strike rate: (career 117.00)
Overseas tours: Australia U19 to England
1999 (vice-captain), to Sri Lanka (U19 World
Cup) 1999-2000 (captain); Australia A to
South Africa (one-day series) 2002-03;
Australia to West Indies 2002-03, to India
(TVS Cup) 2003-04
Overseas teams played for:
New South Wales 1999-2000 –
Other sports followed: Rugby league
Cricketers admired: Mark Waugh
Favourite band: Bon Jovi
Relaxations: Beach, watching rugby
Extras: Attended Commonwealth Bank [Australian] Cricket Academy 2000. Has
represented Australia A in home matches. Scored 75* and took three catches in the
third ODI v West Indies at Gros Islet 2002-03, winning Man of the Match award. Has
been professional for Ramsbottom in the Lancashire League. ACB contract 2003-04.
Has joined Hampshire as an overseas player for 2004
Best batting: 134 New South Wales v Queensland, Brisbane 2002-03
Best bowling: 2-25 New South Wales v Tasmania, Hobart 2001-02
Stop press: Scored 44* and took 2-36 in the final of the TVS Cup v India at Kolkata
(Calcutta) 2003-04, winning Man of the Match award

2003 Season (did not make any first-class or one-day appearances)

Career Performances

	M	Inns	NO	Runs	HS	Avge	100s	50s	Ct	St	Balls	Runs	Wkts	Avge	Best	5wI	10wM
Test																	
All First	33	60	3	2113	134	37.07	7	9	27	-	468	231	4	57.75	2-25	-	-
1-day Int	5	5	3	209	75*	104.50	-	2	3	-	66	49	1	49.00	1-24	-	
C & G																	
NCL																	
Twenty20																	

CLARKE, R.   Surrey

Name: Rikki Clarke
Role: Right-hand bat, right-arm fast-medium bowler; all-rounder
Born: 29 September 1981, Orsett, Essex
Height: 6ft 4½in **Weight:** 14st
Nickname: Clarkey, Monkey Boy ('ask Nad Shahid; he made it up')
County debut: 2001 (one-day), 2002 (first-class)
One-Day Internationals: 7
1st-Class 50s: 7
1st-Class 100s: 4
1st-Class catches: 25
Place in batting averages: 78th av. 39.35 (2002 33rd av. 50.78)
Place in bowling averages: 121st av. 41.70 (2002 128th av. 41.00)
Strike rate: 57.94 (career 59.62)
Parents: Bob and Janet
Marital status: 'Girlfriend Beks'
Family links with cricket: 'Dad bowled one ball before pulling hamstring last year in a Wales village game'
Education: Broadwater; Godalming College
Qualifications: 5 GCSEs, GNVQ Leisure and Tourism
Career outside cricket: 'Footballer in the park'
Off-season: 'England tour'
Overseas tours: Surrey U19 to Barbados; MCC Young Cricketers to Cape Town; England to Sri Lanka (ICC Champions Trophy) 2002-03, to Bangladesh and Sri Lanka 2003-04, to West Indies 2003-04; ECB National Academy to Australia and Sri Lanka 2002-03

Career highlights to date: 'Being picked for England in the Test and one-day squads'
Cricket superstitions: 'Left pad on first'
Cricketers particularly admired: Andrew Flintoff, Ian Botham, Darren Gough
Young players to look out for: Jimmy Anderson, Scott Newman, Tim Murtagh, Jim Troughton
Other sports played: Football, golf, snooker
Other sports followed: Football (Tottenham Hotspur)
Favourite band: B2K, Fabolous, Jagged Edge, R Kelly
Relaxations: 'Sleeping, watching films, snooker'
Extras: Named after former Tottenham Hotspur and Argentina footballer Ricky Villa. Represented England U17 at the ECC Colts Festival in Northern Ireland 1999. Scored maiden first-class century (107*) on first-class debut v Cambridge University CCE at Fenner's 2002. NBC Denis Compton Award for the most promising young Surrey player 2002. Cricket Writers' Club Young Player of the Year 2002. Surrey Supporters' Young Player of the Year 2002. Surrey Sponsors' Young Player of the Year 2002. Made ODI debut v Pakistan at Old Trafford in the NatWest Challenge 2003, taking the wicket of Imran Nazir with his first ball in international cricket. Scored century (139) v Leicestershire at Leicester 2003, following up with 4-21 in Leicestershire's first innings
Opinions on cricket: 'One or no overseas players. They are stopping the young English talent progressing.'
Best batting: 153* Surrey v Somerset, Taunton 2002
Best bowling: 4-21 Surrey v Leicestershire, Leicester 2003
Stop press: Made Test debut in the first Test v Bangladesh at Dhaka 2003-04

2003 Season

	M	Inns	NO	Runs	HS	Avge	100s	50s	Ct	St	O	M	Runs	Wkts	Avge	Best	5wI	10wM
Test																		
All First	11	16	2	551	139	39.35	2	1	10	-	164.1	22	709	17	41.70	4-21	-	-
1-day Int	7	4	0	64	37	16.00	-	-	9	-	21.2	0	113	3	37.66	1-29	-	
C & G	3	3	0	57	47	19.00	-	-	-	-	14	0	102	1	102.00	1-51	-	
NCL	13	13	3	213	46 *	21.30	-	-	4	-	64	1	396	12	33.00	3-48	-	
Twenty20	2	1	0	15	15	15.00	-	-	1	-	4	0	20	0	-	-	-	

Career Performances

	M	Inns	NO	Runs	HS	Avge	100s	50s	Ct	St	Balls	Runs	Wkts	Avge	Best	5wI	10wM
Test																	
All First	24	37	4	1390	153 *	42.12	4	7	25	-	1908	1382	32	43.18	4-21	-	-
1-day Int	7	4	0	64	37	16.00	-	-	9	-	128	113	3	37.66	1-29	-	
C & G	8	7	0	122	55	17.42	-	1	1	-	205	231	4	57.75	2-56	-	
NCL	26	26	5	536	98 *	25.52	-	3	10	-	740	702	19	36.94	3-48	-	
Twenty20	2	1	0	15	15	15.00	-	-	1	-	24	20	0	-	-	-	

CLIFFORD, I. J. — Warwickshire

Name: <u>Ian</u> Jeffrey Clifford
Role: Right-hand bat, wicket-keeper
Born: 12 October 1982, Birmingham
Height: 5ft 6in **Weight:** 9st 12lbs
Nickname: Cliffy
County debut: 2002
1st-Class catches: 15
1st-Class stumpings: 1
Place in batting averages: (2002 317th
av. 3.33)
Parents: Michael and Sheila
Marital status: Single
Education: Park Hall Secondary School
Qualifications: Level 1 coaching
Overseas tours: Warwickshire Development
squad to West Indies 1999-2000
Career highlights to date: 'Taking four

catches and a stumping as a substitute fielder'
Cricket moments to forget: 'Coming 317th (bottom) in the County Championship
batting averages 2002'
Cricket superstitions: 'Always walk on the pitch left foot first'
Cricketers particularly admired: Keith Piper, Jack Russell, Ian Healy
Young players to look out for: Naqaash Tahir, Moeen Munir, Huw Jones
Other sports played: Cycling
Other sports followed: Football (Aston Villa)
Extras: Played for Warwickshire Board XI in the C&G 2001 and 2002. Appeared in
Championship match v Leicestershire at Edgbaston 2002 as substitute wicket-keeper
after Tony Frost suffered a broken finger, later making full debut v Somerset, also at
Edgbaston
Opinions on cricket: 'I think that the set-up of the two-divisional system has
improved competitiveness right across the county circuit.'
Best batting: 7 Warwickshire v Kent, Edgbaston 2002

2003 Season (did not make any first-class or one-day appearances)

Career Performances

	M	Inns	NO	Runs	HS	Avge	100s	50s	Ct	St	Balls	Runs	Wkts	Avge	Best	5wI	10wM
Test																	
All First	4	6	0	20	7	3.33	-	-	15	1							
1-day Int																	
C & G	2	2	1	8	5 *	8.00	-	-	2	1							
NCL	3	1	0	1	1	1.00	-	-	5	-							
Twenty20																	

CLOUGH, G. D. Nottinghamshire

Name: <u>Gareth</u> David Clough
Role: Right-hand bat, right-arm medium bowler; all-rounder
Born: 23 May 1978, Leeds
Height: 6ft **Weight:** 12st 7lbs
Nickname: Banga, Cloughie
County debut: 1998 (Yorkshire), 2001 (Nottinghamshire)
1st-Class 50s: 1
1st-Class catches: 3
Strike rate: 150.00 (career 93.33)
Parents: David and Gillian
Marital status: Engaged to Fiona
Education: Pudsey Grangefield
Qualifications: 9 GCSEs, 3 A-levels, Level 1 cricket coach
Off-season: Coaching
Overseas tours: Yorkshire to Durban and Cape Town 1999; Nottinghamshire to Johannesburg 2001-03
Overseas teams played for: Somerset West, Cape Town 1996-97; Deepdene Bears, Melbourne 1999-2000, 2001-02
Career highlights to date: 'Making my first-class debut – Yorkshire v Glamorgan 1998, Sophia Gardens'
Cricket moments to forget: 'B&H semi-final v Surrey at The Oval 2001' (*Nottinghamshire conceded 361 runs, more than any other first-class county in B&H history, and were then dismissed for 187*)
Cricket superstitions: 'None'
Cricketers particularly admired: Steve Waugh, Ian Botham
Young players to look out for: Mark Footit, Andrew Parkin-Coates

Other sports played: Golf, football (A.J. Harris' Derby Rejects and Paul Franks' Marlboro Lights)
Other sports followed: Football (Everton FC), rugby league (Leeds Rhinos)
Injuries: Out for four weeks with a 'dodgy heel'
Favourite band: Little Me
Relaxations: 'Socialising with friends; watching films; eating good food and drinking good wine'
Extras: Formerly with Yorkshire. Played for Nottinghamshire 2nd XI in 2000, topping the bowling averages with 37 wickets at 19.05 and scoring 400 runs
Opinions on cricket: 'The introduction of a two-divisional structure in the domestic game has made the game more competitive throughout the season, and floodlit games have made cricket more of a spectator sport – which are both big positives.'
Best batting: 55 Nottinghamshire v India A, Trent Bridge 2003
Best bowling: 3-69 Nottinghamshire v Gloucestershire, Trent Bridge 2001

2003 Season

	M	Inns	NO	Runs	HS	Avge	100s	50s	Ct	St	O	M	Runs	Wkts	Avge	Best	5wI	10wM
Test																		
All First	3	4	1	72	55	24.00	-	1	1	-	25	0	119	1	119.00	1-76	-	-
1-day Int																		
C & G	2	2	1	38	27 *	38.00	-	-	1	-	13	1	75	3	25.00	3-47	-	
NCL	13	9	4	181	42 *	36.20	-	-	7	-	97	1	518	16	32.37	4-32	-	
Twenty20	5	3	0	41	29	13.66	-	-	-	-	18	0	147	5	29.40	2-30	-	

Career Performances

	M	Inns	NO	Runs	HS	Avge	100s	50s	Ct	St	Balls	Runs	Wkts	Avge	Best	5wI	10wM
Test																	
All First	9	13	1	133	55	11.08	-	1	3	-	840	544	9	60.44	3-69	-	-
1-day Int																	
C & G	3	2	1	38	27 *	38.00	-	-	1	-	114	113	3	37.66	3-47	-	
NCL	27	18	6	276	42 *	23.00	-	-	9	-	1117	975	29	33.62	4-32	-	
Twenty20	5	3	0	41	29	13.66	-	-	-	-	108	147	5	29.40	2-30	-	

19. What was significant about Brian Lara's first Test as captain at Sabina Park, Jamaica, in 1998?

COLLINGWOOD, P. D. Durham

Name: <u>Paul</u> David Collingwood
Role: Right-hand bat, right-arm
medium bowler
Born: 26 May 1976, Shotley Bridge,
Tyneside
Height: 5ft 11in **Weight:** 12st
Nickname: Colly
County debut: 1995 (one-day),
1996 (first-class)
County cap: 1998
One-Day Internationals: 38
1000 runs in a season: 1
1st-Class 50s: 28
1st-Class 100s: 8
1st-Class catches: 96
One-Day 100s: 2
Place in batting averages: 157th av. 28.16
(2002 26th av. 53.00)

Place in bowling averages: (2002 33rd av. 25.80)
Strike rate: 91.75 (career 86.01)
Parents: David and Janet
Marital status: Single
Family links with cricket: Father and brother play in the Tyneside Senior League for Shotley Bridge CC
Education: Blackfyne Comprehensive School; Derwentside College
Qualifications: 9 GCSEs and 2 A-levels
Overseas tours: Durham Cricket Academy to Sri Lanka 1996 (captain); England VI to Hong Kong 2001, 2002; England to Zimbabwe (one-day series) 2001-02, to India and New Zealand 2001-02 (one-day series), to Australia 2002-03, to Africa (World Cup) 2002-03, to Bangladesh and Sri Lanka 2003-04, to West Indies 2003-04
Overseas teams played for: Bulleen CC, Melbourne 1995-96, 1996-97 ('won flag on both occasions'); Cornwall CC, Auckland 1997-98; Alberton CC, Johannesburg 1998-99; Richmond CC, Melbourne 2000-01
Cricket moments to forget: 'Being Matthew Walker's (Kent) first first-class wicket'
Cricket superstitions: 'Left pad on first, and wearing them on the wrong legs'
Cricketers particularly admired: Steve Waugh, Jacques Kallis, Glenn McGrath, Shane Warne
Young players to look out for: Gordon Muchall
Other sports played: Golf (9 handicap)
Other sports followed: Football ('The Red and Whites' – Sunderland)
Injuries: Out for most of the 2003 season with a dislocated collarbone

Extras: Took wicket (David Capel) with first ball on first-class debut against Northants, then scored 91 in Durham's first innings. Durham Player of the Year 2000. Awarded the Ron Brierley Scholarship 2000 through the ECB in conjunction with the Victorian Cricket Association, Australia; joint winner of the Jack Ryder Medal, awarded by the umpires, for his performances in Victorian Premier Cricket 2000-01. His ODI awards include Man of the Match v India at Cuttack 2001-02 for his all-round performance, including 71*; v New Zealand at Napier 2001-02 (4-38); and v Sri Lanka in the VB Series at Perth 2002-03 (100; his maiden ODI century). Recorded then highest score by a Durham player at the Riverside ground, 190 v Sri Lankans 2002. ECB central contract 2003-04

Best batting: 190 Durham v Sri Lanka, Riverside 2002
Best bowling: 4-31 Durham v Derbyshire, Derby 2002
Stop press: Made Test debut in the first Test v Sri Lanka at Galle 2003-04

2003 Season

	M	Inns	NO	Runs	HS	Avge	100s	50s	Ct	St	O	M	Runs	Wkts	Avge	Best	5wI	10wM
Test																		
All First	4	7	1	169	68	28.16	-	2	4	-	61.1	7	228	4	57.00	3-38	-	-
1-day Int																		
C & G																		
NCL	5	4	0	190	54	47.50	-	1	2	-	38	6	156	2	78.00	1-17	-	
Twenty20																		

Career Performances

	M	Inns	NO	Runs	HS	Avge	100s	50s	Ct	St	Balls	Runs	Wkts	Avge	Best	5wI	10wM
Test																	
All First	95	164	11	4899	190	32.01	8	28	96	-	5591	2629	65	40.44	4-31	-	-
1-day Int	38	37	10	874	100	32.37	1	5	18	-	667	665	16	41.56	4-38	-	
C & G	11	10	1	262	60	29.11	-	2	1	-	246	196	4	49.00	2-7	-	
NCL	89	85	7	2296	118 *	29.43	1	15	48	-	1970	1542	50	30.84	3-20	-	
Twenty20																	

COLLYMORE, C. D. Warwickshire

Name: <u>Corey</u> Dalanelo Collymore
Role: Right-hand bat, right-arm
fast-medium bowler
Born: 21 December 1977, Boscobelle,
St Peter, Barbados
County debut: 2003
Test debut: 1998-99
Tests: 3
One-Day Internationals: 42
1st-Class 5 w. in innings: 7
1st-Class catches: 17
One-Day 5 w. in innings: 1
Strike rate: 103.50 (career 50.08)
Overseas tours: West Indies to Toronto
(DMC Cup) 1999, to England 2000,
to Zimbabwe 2001, to Kenya 2001, to Sri
Lanka (LG Abans Triangular Series) 2001-02,
to Sharjah (v Pakistan) 2001-02, to Sri Lanka

(ICC Champions Trophy) 2002-03, to India 2002-03 (one-day series), to Bangladesh
2002-03, to Africa (World Cup) 2002-03, to Zimbabwe 2003-04, to South Africa
2003-04
Overseas teams played for: Barbados 1998-99 –
Extras: Represented West Indies U19 in home series v Pakistan U19 1996-97. Took
4-49 in the final of the Coca-Cola Cup v India at Harare 2001, winning the Man of the
Match award. Took 5-51 v Sri Lanka at Colombo in the LG Abans Triangular Series
2001-02, winning the Man of the Match award. Player of the [Test] Series v Sri Lanka
2002-03, performances including 7-57 in the second Test at Kingston. Was an overseas
player with Warwickshire in August and September 2003, replacing the injured Collins
Obuya
Best batting: 20 Barbados v West Indies B, Bridgetown 2002-03
Best bowling: 7-57 West Indies v Sri Lanka, Kingston 2002-03

2003 Season

	M	Inns	NO	Runs	HS	Avge	100s	50s	Ct	St	O	M	Runs	Wkts	Avge	Best	5wI	10wM
Test																		
All First	5	8	3	25	11 *	5.00	-	-	2	-	138	24	475	8	59.37	3-42	-	-
1-day Int																		
C & G																		
NCL	3	0	0	0	0	-	-	-	-	-	26	2	122	5	24.40	3-26	-	
Twenty20																		

	M	Inns	NO	Runs	HS	Avge	100s	50s	Ct	St	Balls	Runs	Wkts	Avge	Best	5wI	10wM
Test	3	4	1	30	13	10.00	-	-	-	-	624	268	15	17.86	7-57	2	-
All First	38	47	19	212	20	7.57	-	-	17	-	6260	2993	125	23.94	7-57	7	-
1-day Int	42	17	8	55	13*	6.11	-	-	7	-	2137	1536	49	31.34	5-51	1	
C & G																	
NCL	3	0	0	0	0	-	-	-	-	-	156	122	5	24.40	3-26	-	
Twenty20																	

COMPTON, N. R. D.   Middlesex

Name: Nicholas (<u>Nick</u>) Richard Denis Compton
Role: Right-hand bat, right-arm off-spin bowler; batting all-rounder
Born: 26 June 1983, Durban, South Africa
Height: 6ft 2in **Weight:** 13st 10lbs
Nickname: Compo, Ledge, Cheser
County debut: 2001 (one-day)
Parents: Richard and Glynis
Marital status: Single
Family links with cricket: Grandfather Denis Compton played football and cricket for England
Education: Hilton College, South Africa/Harrow School; Durham University
Qualifications: AAC (A-levels), ECB coach Level 1
Career outside cricket: Student
Overseas tours: England U19 to Australia and (U19 World Cup) New Zealand 2001-02
Overseas teams played for: DHS Old Boys, Durban 1997-98; University of Western Australia, Perth 2001
Career highlights to date: '86 not out for Middlesex XI against Lancashire at Denis Compton Oval, Shenley'
Cricket moments to forget: 'Dropping three catches against Australia 2002'
Sportsmen particularly admired: Jacques Kallis, Rahul Dravid, Muhammad Ali (boxer)
Young players to look out for: Hasim Amla (South African), Shaun Marsh (Australian), Brett Jones (Australian), Bilal Shafayat, Chris Whelan
Other sports played: Golf (6 handicap), represented Natal at junior level at tennis, football and hockey

Other sports followed: Football (Arsenal), golf, rugby union (Natal Sharks)
Injuries: Out for entire 2003 season with osteitis pubis ('16 months so far ...')
Relaxations: 'Chilling with a few boys on a beach; music and girls'
Extras: Played for Natal U13 and U15. Natal Academy award 1997. Represented Harrow v Eton in 1999 (match abandoned), 2000, and 2001 (captain). Middlesex U17 Batsman of the Season 1999. Middlesex U19 Player of the Season 2000. NBC Denis Compton Award for the most promising young Middlesex player 2001 and 2002. Represented England U19 v India U19 2002
Opinions on cricket: 'A lack of passion and character in the English game to date.'

2003 Season (did not make any first-class or one-day appearances)

Career Performances

	M	Inns	NO	Runs	HS	Avge	100s	50s	Ct	St	Balls	Runs	Wkts	Avge	Best	5wI	10wM
Test																	
All First																	
1-day Int																	
C & G																	
NCL	5	5	3	129	86 *	64.50	-	1	-	-	30	20	0	-	-	-	-
Twenty20																	

COOK, A. N. Essex

Name: Alastair (<u>Ali</u>) Nathan Cook
Role: Left-hand top-order bat, right-arm off-spin bowler, wicket-keeper
Born: 25 December 1984, Gloucester
Height: 6ft 2in **Weight:** 11st 9lbs
Nickname: Cooky, Johnson, Jimmy, Chef, Biscuit
County debut: 2003
1st-Class 50s: 3
1st-Class catches: 3
Parents: Graham and Stephanie
Marital status: Single
Family links with cricket: 'Dad scored bucketload of runs for village; brothers play for Maldon CC'
Education: Bedford School
Qualifications: 9 GCSEs, 3 A-levels
Off-season: 'Fitness; England U19 tour'

Overseas tours: England U19 to Bangladesh (U19 World Cup) 2003-04 (captain)
Career highlights to date: 'Making my first-team debut. Scoring a hundred in both innings against Surrey 2nd XI'

Cricket moments to forget: 'Running myself out in the U15 World Cup first match, first ball'

Cricketers particularly admired: Graham Gooch, Andy Flower, Graham Thorpe

Young players to look out for: Mark Pettini, Ravi Bopara, Will Jefferson, James Foster

Other sports played: Squash, tennis, football, golf

Other sports followed: Rugby

Relaxations: 'Sleeping, seeing friends'

Extras: Holds Bedford School season record and career record with 19 hundreds. Scored century in each innings (137/143) for Essex 2nd XI v Surrey 2nd XI at The Oval 2003. Played for England U19 v South Africa U19 ('Tests' and 'ODIs') 2003. Played for Essex Board XI in the C&G 2003. Scored 69* on first-class debut v Nottinghamshire at Chelmsford 2003 and a further two half-centuries in his next two Championship matches

Opinions on cricket: 'Great game, although tea should be half an hour.'

Best batting: 84 Essex v Surrey, The Oval 2003

Stop press: Had consecutive scores of 108*, 108* and 87 in the U19 World Cup 2003-04 in Bangladesh

2003 Season

	M	Inns	NO	Runs	HS	Avge	100s	50s	Ct	St	O	M	Runs	Wkts	Avge	Best	5wI	10wM
Test																		
All First	3	6	1	239	84	47.80	-	3	3	-	2	0	11	0	-		-	-	-
1-day Int																		
C & G	1	1	0	27	27	27.00	-	-	1	-								
NCL	1	1	0	25	25	25.00	-	-	1	-								
Twenty20																		

Career Performances

	M	Inns	NO	Runs	HS	Avge	100s	50s	Ct	St	Balls	Runs	Wkts	Avge	Best	5wI	10wM
Test																	
All First	3	6	1	239	84	47.80	-	3	3	-	12	11	0	-		-	-	-
1-day Int																	
C & G	1	1	0	27	27	27.00	-	-	1	-							
NCL	1	1	0	25	25	25.00	-	-	1	-							
Twenty20																	

20. Which Keynsham-born opener made his Test debut v West Indies at Old Trafford in 2000, scoring 66 and 38*?

COOK, J. W.   Northamptonshire

Name: <u>Jeffrey</u> William Cook
Role: Left-hand bat, right-arm
medium bowler
Born: 2 February 1972, Sydney, Australia
Height: 6ft 4in **Weight:** 14st
Nickname: Cookie
County debut: 2000
1st-Class 50s: 12
1st-Class 100s: 2
1st-Class 5 w. in innings: 1
1st-Class catches: 16
One-Day 100s: 2
Place in batting averages: 176th av. 25.85
(2002 105th av. 35.52)
Place in bowling averages: 31st av. 25.21
Strike rate: 51.31 (career 70.86)
Parents: Roma and Les
Wife and date of marriage: Fiona,
10 October 1998
Children: Alexander, 21 April 2000
Family links with cricket: Mother represented New South Wales
Education: James Cook High School, Kogarah, NSW
Qualifications: NCA Level 2 coaching award, ACB Level 1 coaching award
Overseas tours: Northamptonshire to Grenada 2000, 2001
Overseas teams played for: St George DCC, Sydney 1987-93;
Easts CC, Sydney 1999-2002
Career highlights to date: 'First [first-class] century (137) v Glos in my second
game. Winning second division of Championship in 2000 with Northants. Fielding for
England v Pakistan at Lord's 2001'
Cricket moments to forget: 'First ever pair – v Yorkshire at Headingley 2001'
Cricketers particularly admired: David Gower, Mark Taylor, Mark Waugh,
Steve Waugh
Other sports played: Football, tennis
Other sports followed: Football (Liverpool), rugby league (Parramatta)
Relaxations: 'Time with family'
Extras: Represented NSW at U17, U19 and Colts levels. Represented New South
Wales and Australia at indoor cricket. Played for Northants Board XI in 1999 NatWest,
scoring 130 v Wiltshire at Northampton and winning the Man of the Match award.
Shared in record second-wicket stand for Northants in matches v Surrey (172) with
Mike Hussey at Northampton 2001. Recorded maiden first-class five-wicket return
(5-31) v Durham at Northampton 2003. Is not considered an overseas player, having
qualified by residency

Best batting: 137 Northamptonshire v Gloucestershire, Cheltenham 2000
Best bowling: 5-31 Northamptonshire v Durham, Northampton 2003

2003 Season

	M	Inns	NO	Runs	HS	Avge	100s	50s	Ct	St	O	M	Runs	Wkts	Avge	Best	5wI	10wM
Test																		
All First	14	22	2	517	85	25.85	-	3	3	-	162.3	46	479	19	25.21	5-31	1	-
1-day Int																		
C & G	1	1	0	57	57	57.00	-	1	-	-	7	0	33	1	33.00	1-33	-	
NCL	16	13	3	190	49	19.00	-	-	3	-	81.4	7	416	15	27.73	3-69	-	
Twenty20	5	5	0	35	18	7.00	-	-	2	-	6	0	60	1	60.00	1-24	-	

Career Performances

	M	Inns	NO	Runs	HS	Avge	100s	50s	Ct	St	Balls	Runs	Wkts	Avge	Best	5wI	10wM
Test																	
All First	49	79	7	2156	137	29.94	2	12	16	-	2055	1084	29	37.37	5-31	1	-
1-day Int																	
C & G	7	7	0	362	130	51.71	1	2	-	-	138	108	2	54.00	1-5	-	
NCL	53	48	4	861	102	19.56	1	2	16	-	1071	882	40	22.05	4-35	-	
Twenty20	5	5	0	35	18	7.00	-	-	2	-	36	60	1	60.00	1-24	-	

COOK, S. J.   Middlesex

Name: <u>Simon</u> James Cook
Role: Right-hand bat, right-arm medium-fast bowler
Born: 15 January 1977, Oxford
Height: 6ft 4in **Weight:** 13st
Nickname: Donk, Cookie
County debut: 1997 (one-day), 1999 (first-class)
County cap: 2003
1st-Class 50s: 3
1st-Class 5 w. in innings: 2
1st-Class catches: 17
Place in batting averages: 251st av. 15.07 (2002 249th av. 16.68)
Place in bowling averages: 109th av. 38.81 (2002 40th av. 27.18)
Strike rate: 73.85 (career 60.06)
Parents: Phil and Sue
Marital status: Single

Education: Matthew Arnold School
Qualifications: GCSEs, NVQ Business Administration II
Career outside cricket: Coaching Middlesex youth squads
Off-season: Coaching
Overseas tours: Middlesex to South Africa 2000
Overseas teams played for: Rockingham, Perth 2000-01
Cricketers particularly admired: Angus Fraser, Mark Waugh, Glenn McGrath
Young players to look out for: Jamie Dalrymple, Ed Joyce, Nick Compton, John Maunders
Other sports followed: Football (Liverpool), 'any other ball sport'
Relaxations: 'Sleeping, playing any sport, watching television and videos'
Extras: Scored career best 93* v Nottinghamshire at Lord's 2001, helping Middlesex to avoid the follow-on, then took a wicket with the first ball of his opening spell. Awarded Middlesex cap 2003
Best batting: 93* Middlesex v Nottinghamshire, Lord's 2001
Best bowling: 8-63 Middlesex v Northamptonshire, Northampton 2002

2003 Season

	M	Inns	NO	Runs	HS	Avge	100s	50s	Ct	St	O	M	Runs	Wkts	Avge	Best	5wI	10wM
Test																		
All First	12	17	3	211	65	15.07	-	1	5	-	332.2	78	1048	27	38.81	4-42	-	-
1-day Int																		
C & G	3	3	1	57	33*	28.50	-	-	1	-	27	0	126	5	25.20	3-37	-	
NCL	17	10	5	170	67*	34.00	-	1	1	-	124	6	667	14	47.64	4-30	-	
Twenty20	5	3	1	28	19*	14.00	-	-	1	-	18.2	0	124	9	13.77	3-14	-	

Career Performances

	M	Inns	NO	Runs	HS	Avge	100s	50s	Ct	St	Balls	Runs	Wkts	Avge	Best	5wI	10wM
Test																	
All First	54	72	11	1096	93*	17.96	-	3	17	-	7989	4338	133	32.61	8-63	2	-
1-day Int																	
C & G	7	7	3	110	39*	27.50	-	-	1	-	342	253	9	28.11	3-37	-	
NCL	69	49	11	564	67*	14.84	-	2	10	-	2926	2291	72	31.81	4-30	-	
Twenty20	5	3	1	28	19*	14.00	-	-	1	-	110	124	9	13.77	3-14	-	

CORK, D. G.   Lancashire

Name: <u>Dominic</u> Gerald Cork
Role: Right-hand bat, right-arm
fast-medium bowler
Born: 7 August 1971, Newcastle-under-
Lyme, Staffordshire
Height: 6ft 2½in   **Weight:** 14st
Nickname: Corky
County debut: 1990 (Derbyshire)
County cap: 1993 (Derbyshire)
Benefit: 2001 (Derbyshire)
Test debut: 1995
Tests: 37
One-Day Internationals: 32
50 wickets in a season: 7
1st-Class 50s: 42
1st-Class 100s: 4
1st-Class 200s: 1
1st-Class 5 w. in innings: 28
1st-Class 10 w. in match: 5
1st-Class catches: 156
One-Day 5 w. in innings: 4
Place in batting averages: 204th av. 22.80 (2002 136th av. 30.43)
Place in bowling averages: 43rd av. 27.26 (2002 4th av. 18.90)
Strike rate: 53.42 (career 53.18)
Parents: Gerald and Mary
Wife and date of marriage: Donna, 28 August 2000
Children: Ashleigh, 28 April 1990; Gregory, 29 September 1994
Family links with cricket: 'Father and two brothers played in the same side at Betley
CC in Staffordshire'
Education: St Joseph's College, Trent Vale, Stoke-on-Trent; Newcastle College
Qualifications: 2 O-levels, Level 2 coach
Career outside cricket: 'None at the moment, but once I retire I would like to go into
the media side'
Off-season: 'Getting fit for the new season'
Overseas tours: England YC to Australia 1989-90; England A to Bermuda and West
Indies 1991-92, to Australia 1992-93, to South Africa 1993-94, to India 1994-95;
England to South Africa 1995-96, to India and Pakistan (World Cup) 1995-96,
to New Zealand 1996-97, to Australia 1998-99, to Pakistan and Sri Lanka 2000-01, to
Sri Lanka (ICC Champions Trophy) 2002-03
Overseas teams played for: East Shirley, Christchurch, New Zealand 1990-91
Career highlights to date: 'Making my debut for England'

Cricket moments to forget: 'Every time the team loses'
Cricket superstitions: 'None'
Cricketers particularly admired: Kim Barnett, Mike Atherton, Ian Botham, Malcolm Marshall
Young players to look out for: Kyle Hogg, Luke Sutton
Other sports played: Golf, football
Other sports followed: Football (Stoke City)
Injuries: Stress fracture, hernia, broken ankle
Favourite band: 'Anything R&B'
Relaxations: 'Listening to music'
Extras: Played Minor Counties cricket for Staffordshire 1989 and 1990. In 1990 he took a wicket in his first over in first-class cricket, v New Zealanders at Derby, and scored a century as nightwatchman for England U19 v Pakistan at Taunton. Took 8-53 before lunch on his 20th birthday, v Essex at Derby 1991. Selected for England A in 1991 – his first full season of first-class cricket. PCA Young Player of the Year 1991. Achieved first-class hat-trick against Kent 1994. Took 7-43 on Test debut against West Indies at Lord's 1995, the best innings figures by an England debutant. Achieved hat-trick against the West Indies at Old Trafford in the fourth Test 1995 – the first by an Englishman in Test cricket for 38 years. PCA Player of the Year 1995. Finished at the top of the Whyte and Mackay ratings for bowling in 1995. Cornhill England Player of the Year 1995-96. One of *Wisden*'s Five Cricketers of the Year 1996. Man of the Match in the second Test v West Indies at Lord's 2000; on his recall to the Test side he recorded match figures of 7-52 followed by a match-winning 33* in England's second innings. Scored maiden first-class 200 (200*, the highest score by a Derbyshire No. 8) v Durham at Derby 2000, sharing in the process in a new record seventh-wicket partnership for Derbyshire (258) with Mathew Dowman. Took 700th first-class wicket (Jon Lewis) v Durham at Derby 2003. Derbyshire captain 1998-2003. Left Derbyshire at the end of the 2003 season and has joined Lancashire for 2004
Best batting: 200* Derbyshire v Durham, Derby 2000
Best bowling: 9-43 Derbyshire v Northamptonshire, Derby 1995

2003 Season

	M	Inns	NO	Runs	HS	Avge	100s	50s	Ct	St	O	M	Runs	Wkts	Avge	Best	5wI	10wM
Test																		
All First	16	29	3	593	92	22.80	-	3	11	-	445.1	100	1363	50	27.26	6-28	3	2
1-day Int																		
C & G	4	3	0	75	59	25.00	-	1	4	-	33.2	2	134	6	22.33	2-17	-	
NCL	16	14	1	279	49	21.46	-	-	7	-	128	11	537	23	23.34	3-15	-	
Twenty20	5	5	0	45	25	9.00	-	-	-	-	8	1	39	1	39.00	1-24	-	

Career Performances

	M	Inns	NO	Runs	HS	Avge	100s	50s	Ct	St	Balls	Runs	Wkts	Avge	Best	5wI	10wM
Test	37	56	8	864	59	18.00	-	3	18	-	7678	3906	131	29.81	7-43	5	-
All First	222	334	44	7305	200*	25.18	5	42	156	-	38400	18933	722	26.22	9-43	28	5
1-day Int	32	21	3	180	31*	10.00	-	-	6	-	1772	1368	41	33.36	3-27	-	
C & G	25	22	4	618	93	34.33	-	7	12	-	1517	931	48	19.39	5-18	2	
NCL	123	105	12	1859	83*	19.98	-	7	56	-	5429	3989	150	26.59	6-21	1	
Twenty20	5	5	0	45	25	9.00	-	-	-	-	48	39	1	39.00	1-24	-	

COSKER, D. A.   Glamorgan

Name: <u>Dean</u> Andrew Cosker
Role: Right-hand bat, left-arm
spin bowler, point fielder
Born: 7 January 1978, Weymouth, Dorset
Height: 5ft 11in **Weight:** 12st 7lbs
Nickname: Lurks
County debut: 1996
County cap: 2000
1st-Class 5 w. in innings: 2
1st-Class catches: 70
One-Day 5 w. in innings: 1
Place in batting averages: 265th av. 13.33
(2002 287th av. 10.45)
Place in bowling averages: 120th av. 40.88
(2002 147th av. 50.60)
Strike rate: 93.47 (career 79.33)
Parents: Des and Carol
Marital status: Living with partner Katie
Education: Millfield School
Qualifications: 10 GCSEs, 4 A-levels
Career outside cricket: 'A lurker. Many business proposals!'
Off-season: 'Team-building in Usk!'
Overseas tours: West of England U15 to West Indies 1993-94; Millfield School to Sri Lanka 1994-95; England U17 to Holland 1995; England U19 to Pakistan 1996-97; England A to Kenya and Sri Lanka 1997-98, to Zimbabwe and South Africa 1998-99; Glamorgan CCC to Cape Town and Jersey
Overseas teams played for: Gordon CC, Sydney 1996-97; Crusaders, Durban 2001-02
Career highlights to date: 'County cap 2000. My England A tours. Championship with Glamorgan 1997. One-day [league] champs 2002'
Cricket moments to forget: 'Losing Benson and Hedges final 2001. And most Twenty20 games!'

Cricket superstitions: 'Just to consume vast amounts of crisps during the day's play'
Cricketers particularly admired: 'All the veterans of Glamorgan!'
Young players to look out for: Adam Harrison
Other sports played: Football
Other sports followed: Football (Spurs)
Favourite band: Nickelback
Relaxations: 'Lurking, golf'
Extras: *Daily Telegraph* Regional Bowling Award. England U15 and U17. Played for U19 TCCB Development of Excellence XI v South Africa U19 1995. Played for England U19 v Zimbabwe U19 1997. Leading wicket-taker on England A tour of Zimbabwe and South Africa 1998-99. Third youngest Glamorgan player to receive county cap. Shared with Robert Croft in a new record tenth-wicket partnership for Glamorgan in matches against Derbyshire (81) at Swansea 2003. Recorded maiden one-day five-wicket return (5-54) v Essex at Chelmsford in the NCL 2003
Opinions on cricket: 'Enjoy.'
Best batting: 49 Glamorgan v Sussex, Cardiff 1999
Best bowling: 6-140 Glamorgan v Lancashire, Colwyn Bay 1998

2003 Season

	M	Inns	NO	Runs	HS	Avge	100s	50s	Ct	St	O	M	Runs	Wkts	Avge	Best	5wl	10wM
Test																		
All First	9	12	6	80	42	13.33	-	-	7	-	264.5	67	695	17	40.88	3-49	-	-
1-day Int																		
C & G	2	1	1	2	2 *	-	-	-	-	-	12	0	74	0	-		-	-
NCL	14	7	4	24	7 *	8.00	-	-	3	-	95	1	506	17	29.76	5-54	1	
Twenty20	5	2	2	7	7 *	-	-	-	1	-	17	0	128	5	25.60	2-24	-	

Career Performances

	M	Inns	NO	Runs	HS	Avge	100s	50s	Ct	St	Balls	Runs	Wkts	Avge	Best	5wl	10wM
Test																	
All First	102	121	35	947	49	11.01	-	-	70	-	19040	8898	240	37.07	6-140	2	-
1-day Int																	
C & G	10	6	4	18	5	9.00	-	-	1	-	482	365	8	45.62	3-26	-	
NCL	80	37	15	204	27 *	9.27	-	-	26	-	3383	2742	89	30.80	5-54	1	
Twenty20	5	2	2	7	7 *	-	-	-	1	-	102	128	5	25.60	2-24	-	

21. First selected for England aged 18, this Yorkshireman captained in one Test against the West Indies and won. Who was he?

COTTEY, P. A. Sussex

Name: Phillip Anthony (<u>Tony</u>) Cottey
Role: Right-hand bat
Born: 2 June 1966, Swansea
Height: 5ft 5in **Weight:** 10st 7lbs
Nickname: Cotts, TC
County debut: 1986 (Glamorgan),
1999 (Sussex)
County cap: 1992 (Glamorgan),
1999 (Sussex)
1000 runs in a season: 8
1st-Class 50s: 73
1st-Class 100s: 29
1st-Class 200s: 1
1st-Class catches: 175
Place in batting averages: 43rd av. 45.96
(2002 128th av. 31.77)
Strike rate: (career 95.87)
Parents: Bernard John and Ruth

Wife and date of marriage: Gail, 5 October 1992
Children: Lowri Rhiannon, 16 October 1993; Seren Nia, 6 August 1997
Family links with cricket: Father played club cricket for Swansea CC
Education: Bishopston Comprehensive, Swansea; Coleg Sir Gar, Llanelli
Qualifications: 9 O-levels, HND Sports Science, Level 3 cricket coach, Certificate of
Professional Competence
Career outside cricket: 'New business, Ysbryd Ltd – Welsh leisurewear'
Off-season: 'Promoting Ysbryd'
Overseas tours: Glamorgan to La Manga, Barbados, Trinidad, Zimbabwe and
Cape Town 1987-96, to Jersey 1998; Sussex to Grenada 2002
Overseas teams played for: Penrith, Sydney 1986-88; Benoni, Johannesburg
1990-93; Eastern Transvaal 1991-92
Career highlights to date: 'Winning Championship in 1997 with Glamorgan and in
2003 with Sussex'
Cricket moments to forget: 'Any of the four semi-final losses at Glamorgan and the
semi-final loss at Gloucestershire 1999 in Super Cup with Sussex'
Cricketers particularly admired: Ian Botham, Matthew Maynard, Sachin Tendulkar,
Mark Robinson
Young players to look out for: Tim Ambrose, Matt Prior
Other sports played: Football ('pro player with Swansea City 1982-85')
Other sports followed: Rugby (Dunvant RFC), football (Swansea City AFC)
Injuries: Out for two weeks with a back spasm
Favourite band: Rolling Stones

143

Relaxations: 'Golf, road running; spending time with family; following all sports'
Extras: Three Welsh Youth caps (one as captain). Glamorgan Player of the Year in 1994. Ran the New York Marathon in 1995 and the Athens Marathon in 1996. Left Glamorgan at the end of the 1998 season and joined Sussex. Sussex Clubman of the Year 1999. Scored 703 runs (three centuries; four fifties) in seven Championship innings June/July 2003. In 2003 joined select band of players who have won the Championship with two counties (Glamorgan 1997; Sussex 2003 – 'the only Welshman to achieve this'). Sussex Team Man of the Year 2003
Opinions on cricket: 'A bit concerned about the influx of dual-passport-holding cricketers from around the world flooding into the domestic game.'
Best batting: 203 Glamorgan v Leicestershire, Swansea 1996
Best bowling: 4-49 Glamorgan v Leicestershire, Swansea 1996

2003 Season

	M	Inns	NO	Runs	HS	Avge	100s	50s	Ct	St	O	M	Runs	Wkts	Avge	Best	5wI	10wM
Test																		
All First	15	25	0	1149	188	45.96	3	7	8	-	13	1	59	0	-	-	-	-
1-day Int																		
C & G																			
NCL	13	13	1	236	41	19.66	-	-	5	-	1	0	13	0	-		-	-
Twenty20																			

Career Performances

	M	Inns	NO	Runs	HS	Avge	100s	50s	Ct	St	Balls	Runs	Wkts	Avge	Best	5wI	10wM
Test																	
All First	266	431	51	14057	203	36.99	30	73	175	-	1534	954	16	59.62	4-49	-	-
1-day Int																	
C & G	31	30	7	610	68	26.52	-	4	8	-	186	135	3	45.00	1-9	-	
NCL	182	157	28	3127	92 *	24.24	-	16	61	-	587	586	15	39.06	4-56	-	
Twenty20																	

COVERDALE, P. S.   Northamptonshire

Name: <u>Paul</u> Stephen Coverdale
Role: Right-hand bat, right-arm medium bowler
Born: 24 July 1983, Harrogate
Height: 5ft 10in **Weight:** 11st 8lbs
Nickname: Covers, Flaps, Drill Sergeant, Incredible Hulk
County debut: No first-team appearance
Parents: Stephen and Jane
Marital status: Single
Family links with cricket: Father played for Yorkshire CCC and Cambridge University and was Chief Executive of Northamptonshire

Education: Wellingborough School; Loughborough University
Qualifications: 9 GCSEs, 3 A-levels, ECB Level I coaching
Career outside cricket: Student
Off-season: 'Studying at Loughborough University; training hard, and the odd bit of drinking!'
Overseas tours: Northamptonshire U19 to South Africa 2000
Overseas teams played for: Swanbourne, Perth 2002
Cricket moments to forget: 'Leaving a straight one first ball in a 2nd XI match last year and then breaking my hand on the changing room wall in anger. Was too embarrassed to announce it immediately and so attempted to field through it!'

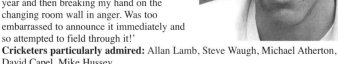

Cricketers particularly admired: Allan Lamb, Steve Waugh, Michael Atherton, David Capel, Mike Hussey
Young players to look out for: David Paynter, Adam Shantry, Monty Panesar, Chris Munns
Other sports played: Rugby, golf
Other sports followed: Rugby (Northampton Saints), football
Injuries: Out for two weeks with split webbing in right hand
Favourite band: Dire Straits
Relaxations: 'Socialising and going out with friends; having a few down the Student Union; ruining a great classic on the karaoke; watching and playing sports'
Extras: Played county age groups, captaining at U14, U15, U17 and U19. Represented East England Schools U18. Played for Northamptonshire Board XI in the C&G 2001, C&G 2002 and in the first round of the C&G 2003, which was played in August 2002. Joined the Northants Academy in 2000. Joined Loughborough UCCE Academy in 2002. Represented English Universities in the Home Nations Tournament 2003
Opinions on cricket: 'In general it seems that county 2nd XIs are getting younger and there are a lot of young players involved in first-class cricket now. This can only be good for the future of the game, and is a tribute to the investment made by the ECB and the counties in the academy set-ups.'

2003 Season (did not make any first-class or one-day appearances)

Career Performances

	M	Inns	NO	Runs	HS	Avge	100s	50s	Ct	St	Balls	Runs	Wkts	Avge	Best	5wI	10wM
Test																	
All First																	
1-day Int																	
C & G	3	3	0	33	19	11.00	-	-	2	-	96	48	1	48.00	1-21	-	
NCL																	
Twenty20																	

COWAN, A. P. Essex

Name: <u>Ashley</u> Preston Cowan
Role: Right-hand bat, right-arm fast-medium bowler, 'benefit-only wicket-keeper'
Born: 7 May 1975, Hitchin, Hertfordshire
Height: 6ft 5in **Weight:** 15st
Nickname: Dic Dic, Wallace, Vic
County debut: 1995
County cap: 1997
50 wickets in a season: 1
1st-Class 50s: 9
1st-Class 5 w. in innings: 8
1st-Class catches: 48
One-Day 5 w. in innings: 2
Place in batting averages: (2002 200th av. 23.46)
Place in bowling averages: (2002 41st av. 27.19)
Strike rate: (career 59.88)
Parents: Jeff and Pam
Wife and date of marriage: Cath, 14 October 2001
Family links with cricket: 'Father played village cricket. Mother made the teas'
Education: Framlingham College
Qualifications: 8 GCSEs, 3 A-levels
Career outside cricket: Business
Overseas tours: England to West Indies 1997-98
Overseas teams played for: Zingari CC, Durban 1995-97
Career highlights to date: 'Getting England blazer. Winning finals at Lord's'
Cricket moments to forget: 'Any time I get smashed around the park. Losing [NatWest] final at Lord's 1996'

Cricketers particularly admired: Ian Botham, Allan Donald, Curtly Ambrose, Glenn McGrath
Young players to look out for: Mark Pettini, Justin Bishop
Other sports played: Rugby, hockey (Chelmsford), golf (single-figure handicap), squash
Other sports followed: Rugby (Saracens), golf, football ('anybody who plays Man U')
Injuries: Out for the entire 2003 season after knee surgery
Relaxations: Sports, sleeping, reading
Extras: Played rugby and hockey for East of England U18. Was the youngest person to play for Cambridgeshire. Became first Essex player to take a first-class hat-trick at Castle Park, Colchester, v Gloucestershire in 1996. Took three wickets in four balls in the final over of National League match at Southend 2000 to prevent Glamorgan scoring the six runs needed for victory; the over also contained a run-out
Opinions on cricket: 'More day/night cricket.'
Best batting: 94 Essex v Leicestershire, Leicester 1998
Best bowling: 6-47 Essex v Glamorgan, Cardiff 1999

2003 Season (did not make any first-class or one-day appearances)

Career Performances

	M	Inns	NO	Runs	HS	Avge	100s	50s	Ct	St	Balls	Runs	Wkts	Avge	Best	5wI	10wM
Test																	
All First	100	149	28	2178	94	18.00	-	9	48	-	16168	8777	270	32.50	6-47	8	-
1-day Int																	
C & G	17	12	4	67	17 *	8.37	-	-	5	-	983	643	23	27.95	4-27	-	
NCL	90	69	16	652	40 *	12.30	-	-	36	-	3932	2892	114	25.36	5-14	1	
Twenty20																	

22. Which former Sussex and Kent batsman joined his brother Colin as an England ODI when he appeared at Lord's in June 1995?

COX, J.   Somerset

Name: Jamie Cox
Role: Right-hand bat, off-spin bowler
Born: 15 October 1969, Burnie, Tasmania
Height: 6ft **Weight:** 12st 7lbs
Nickname: Buzz, Skippy
County debut: 1999
County cap: 1999
1000 runs in a season: 3
1st-Class 50s: 73
1st-Class 100s: 44
1st-Class 200s: 3
1st-Class catches: 106
One-Day 100s: 5
Place in batting averages: 49th av. 45.29
(2002 130th av. 31.47)
Strike rate: (career 132.75)
Parents: David and Kaye
Wife: Helen

Children: Lachlan William Joseph, November 2001
Family links with cricket: Father played State Colts and is life member of local club
Education: Wynyard High; Deakin University
Qualifications: School Certificate, Diploma of Management, Bachelor of Business
degree; currently studying for Diploma of Drafting
Off-season: Playing for Tasmania
Overseas tours: Australia U19 to West Indies 1988; Australia A to Zimbabwe 1989,
to Malaysia (Super 8s) 1997; Australia XI to Zimbabwe 1991-92; Tasmania
to Zimbabwe 1995-96
Overseas teams played for: Tasmania 1987-88 –
Cricketers particularly admired: Ian Botham, Geoff Marsh, David Boon,
Steve Waugh
Other sports played: Golf, soccer ('poorly')
Other sports followed: Australian Rules football (Western Bulldogs)
Relaxations: Music, home design
Extras: First Tasmania player to attend the Australian Cricket Academy, in 1988.
Scored 1349 runs in the 1996-97 season, with five 100s, including two in one match v
New South Wales. Players' Player of the Year 1996-97. Tasmanian Cricket Player of
the Year 1996-97. Scored 115* in the first innings of the 1997-98 Sheffield Shield final
v Western Australia, becoming the first player to carry his bat in a Shield final. Joined
Somerset as overseas player and captain in 1999 (captain 1999-2002). Became the first
Somerset player to score a 200 (216) and a 100 (129*) in a match, v Hampshire at
Southampton 1999. Scored 1070 runs (av. 66.88) in the Pura Cup 2000-01, passing

during the season David Boon's record of 9096 career first-class runs for Tasmania to become the state's leading run-scorer. *Wisden Australia* Pura Cup Cricketer of the Year 2000-01; also Pura Cup Player of the Year 2000-01 (voted on by the umpires). Captain of Tasmania 1999-2001. Played in his 140th first-class match for Tasmania against Western Australia at Hobart 2001-02, overtaking David Boon's record of 139 matches to become Tasmania's most-capped first-class player. Became the third player to pass 10,000 first-class runs in Australian domestic cricket, v South Australia 2002-03. Has returned to Somerset for 2004 as cover for Ricky Ponting while on international duty
Opinions on cricket: 'In good shape. Must be careful not to overprotect centrally contracted players. Bonus points to be removed. Points for wins only.'
Best batting: 245 Tasmania v New South Wales, Hobart 1999-2000
Best bowling: 3-46 Somerset v Middlesex, Taunton 1999

2003 Season

	M	Inns	NO	Runs	HS	Avge	100s	50s	Ct	St	O	M	Runs	Wkts	Avge	Best	5wI	10wM
Test																		
All First	15	27	3	1087	160	45.29	3	5	10	-	2	0	15	0	-	-	-	-
1-day Int																		
C & G	2	2	1	46	39 *	46.00	-	-	-	-								
NCL	16	14	0	479	130	34.21	2	1	5	-								
Twenty20	4	4	0	128	53	32.00	-	1	2	-								

Career Performances

	M	Inns	NO	Runs	HS	Avge	100s	50s	Ct	St	Balls	Runs	Wkts	Avge	Best	5wI	10wM
Test																	
All First	234	414	29	16824	245	43.69	47	73	106	-	531	338	4	84.50	3-46	-	-
1-day Int																	
C & G	17	17	2	620	114	41.33	1	3	6	-	42	33	1	33.00	1-33	-	
NCL	68	66	1	2186	130	33.63	4	12	28	-	96	82	3	27.33	3-28	-	
Twenty20	4	4	0	128	53	32.00	-	1	2	-							

23. Which artist kept wicket for England in the 1997-98 series,
taking 12 catches and a stumping?

CRAVEN, V. J.   Yorkshire

Name: <u>Victor</u> John Craven
Role: Left-hand middle/top-order bat, right-arm medium bowler
Born: 31 July 1980, Harrogate
Height: 6ft **Weight:** 13st 8lbs
Nickname: Cow, Magoo
County debut: 2000
1st-Class 50s: 5
1st-Class catches: 16
Place in batting averages: 159th av. 28.10 (2002 201st av. 23.10)
Strike rate: 56.25 (career 74.00)
Parents: Vic and Sue
Marital status: Single
Family links with cricket: 'Father played local cricket and introduced me to the game'
Education: Harrogate Grammar School
Qualifications: 10 GCSEs, GNVQ (Advanced) Business, Level 2 cricket coaching

Career outside cricket: Gym instructor
Overseas tours: Yorkshire to South Africa
Overseas teams played for: Tatura CC, Victoria 1998-99; Deepdene Bears, Melbourne 2000-01
Career highlights to date: 'Playing against West Indies and scoring 53 [for Yorkshire in 2000]'
Cricket moments to forget: 'All bad drops and misfields'
Cricketers particularly admired: Michael Atherton, Graham Thorpe
Young players to look out for: John Sadler, Michael Lumb
Other sports played: Soccer, golf, snooker
Other sports followed: Football (Leeds United), rugby league (Leeds Rhinos)
Relaxations: 'Cinema, gym, socialising with pals'
Extras: Has Yorkshire 2nd XI cap
Best batting: 72 Yorkshire v Hampshire, West End 2002
Best bowling: 2-25 Yorkshire v Hampshire, Scarborough 2003

2003 Season

	M	Inns	NO	Runs	HS	Avge	100s	50s	Ct	St	O	M	Runs	Wkts	Avge	Best	5wI	10wM
Test																		
All First	6	11	1	281	47	28.10	-	-	-	-	75	18	253	8	31.62	2-25	-	-
1-day Int																		
C & G	2	2	1	12	11 *	12.00	-	-	1	-	3.3	0	21	0	-		-	-
NCL	11	11	2	181	47	20.11	-	-	2	-	36.1	2	170	8	21.25	4-22	-	
Twenty20	2	2	2	17	17 *	-	-	-	1	-	1	0	5	0	-		-	-

Career Performances

	M	Inns	NO	Runs	HS	Avge	100s	50s	Ct	St	Balls	Runs	Wkts	Avge	Best	5wI	10wM
Test																	
All First	27	47	5	1004	72	23.90	-	5	16	-	666	393	9	43.66	2-25	-	-
1-day Int																	
C & G	3	3	1	38	26	19.00	-	-	1	-	21	21	0	-		-	-
NCL	25	25	2	429	59	18.65	-	2	8	-	229	191	9	21.22	4-22	-	
Twenty20	2	2	2	17	17 *	-	-	-	1	-	6	5	0	-		-	-

CRAWLEY, J. P.   Hampshire

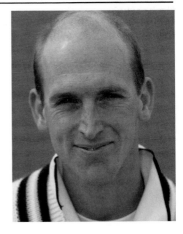

Name: <u>John</u> Paul Crawley
Role: Right-hand bat, occasional wicket-keeper
Born: 21 September 1971, Maldon, Essex
Height: 6ft 2in **Weight:** 13st 7lbs
Nickname: Creepy, Jonty, JC
County debut: 1990 (Lancashire), 2002 (Hampshire)
County cap: 1994 (Lancashire), 2002 (Hampshire)
Test debut: 1994
Tests: 37
One-Day Internationals: 13
1000 runs in a season: 8
1st-Class 50s: 107
1st-Class 100s: 36
1st-Class 200s: 6
1st-Class catches: 181
One-Day 100s: 6
Place in batting averages: 110th av. 33.76 (2002 23rd av. 53.80)
Strike rate: (career 132.00)
Parents: Frank and Jean (deceased)

Marital status: Married

Family links with cricket: Father played in Manchester Association; brother Mark played for Lancashire and Nottinghamshire; brother Peter plays for Warrington CC and has played for Scottish Universities and Cambridge University; uncle was excellent fast bowler; godfather umpires in Manchester Association

Education: Manchester Grammar School; Trinity College, Cambridge; Open University Business School

Qualifications: 10 O-levels, 2 AO-Levels, 3 A-levels, 2 S-levels, BA in History, MA (Cantab), Professional Certificate in Management

Career outside cricket: 'Currently sales and marketing at the Rose Bowl plc'

Overseas tours: England YC to Australia 1989-90, to New Zealand 1990-91 (captain); England A to South Africa 1993-94, to West Indies 2000-01; England to Australia 1994-95, 1998-99, 2002-03, to South Africa 1995-96, to Zimbabwe and New Zealand 1996-97, to West Indies 1997-98

Overseas teams played for: Midland-Guildford, Perth 1990

Cricketers particularly admired: Michael Atherton, Neil Fairbrother, Graham Gooch, Alec Stewart, David Gower, Allan Donald, Ian Salisbury

Other sports followed: Football (Manchester United), golf

Relaxations: 'Playing or trying to play the guitar'

Extras: Sir John Hobbs Silver Jubilee Memorial Prize 1987. Played for England YC v New Zealand 1989, v Pakistan 1990 and v Australia (as captain) 1991. First to score 1000 runs in U19 'Tests'. Scored 286 for England A against Eastern Province at Port Elizabeth in 1994, the highest score by an Englishman on an England or England A tour for almost 30 years. Finished top of the first-class batting averages on England's tour to South Africa in 1995-96 with 336 runs at 67.20. Lancashire vice-captain 1998. Scored century in each innings (124/136) v Glamorgan at Colwyn Bay 1998. Topped English first-class batting averages for 1998 season (1851 runs; av. 74.04). Lancashire Player of the Year 1998. Lancashire captain 1999-2001. Left Lancashire during the 2001-02 off-season and joined Hampshire for 2002. Scored 272 on debut for Hampshire v Kent at Canterbury 2002, passing Denis Baldry's Hampshire debut record of 151 set in 1959 v Glamorgan and F. E. Lacey's 1884 record for the highest individual score for Hampshire v Kent (211); also became one of only five English batsmen to have made five first-class scores of 250 or above. Recalled to Test side in 2002 for first time since 1998-99 and scored 64 and 100* in second Test after recall, v India at Lord's. Captain of Hampshire 2003

Best batting: 286 England A v Eastern Province, Port Elizabeth 1993-94

Best bowling: 1-90 Lancashire v Sussex, Hove 1992

2003 Season

	M	Inns	NO	Runs	HS	Avge	100s	50s	Ct	St	O	M	Runs	Wkts	Avge	Best	5wI	10wM
Test																		
All First	16	27	1	878	93	33.76	-	8	5	-								
1-day Int																		
C & G	1	1	0	4	4	4.00	-	-	-	-								
NCL	18	18	3	692	102	46.13	1	6	8	-								
Twenty20	4	4	1	46	23	15.33	-	-	1	-								

Career Performances

	M	Inns	NO	Runs	HS	Avge	100s	50s	Ct	St	Balls	Runs	Wkts	Avge	Best	5wI	10wM
Test	37	61	9	1800	156	34.61	4	9	29	-							
All First	274	450	45	18850	286	46.54	42	107	181	-	132	201	1	201.00	1-90	-	-
1-day Int	13	12	1	235	73	21.36	-	2	1	1							
C & G	28	27	4	931	113 *	40.47	2	5	9	-	6	4	0	-		-	-
NCL	138	135	12	3669	102	29.82	2	25	41	3							
Twenty20	4	4	1	46	23	15.33	-	-	1	-							

CROFT, R. D. B.   Glamorgan

Name: <u>Robert</u> Damien Bale Croft
Role: Right-hand bat, off-spin bowler, county captain
Born: 25 May 1970, Morriston, Swansea
Height: 5ft 11in **Weight:** 13st 7lbs
Nickname: Crofty
County debut: 1989
County cap: 1992
Benefit: 2000
Test debut: 1996
Tests: 21
One-Day Internationals: 50
50 wickets in a season: 6
1st-Class 50s: 41
1st-Class 100s: 4
1st-Class 5 w. in innings: 36
1st-Class 10 w. in match: 6
1st-Class catches: 143
One-Day 100s: 2
One-Day 5 w. in innings: 1
Place in batting averages: 147th av. 29.56 (2002 104th av. 35.57)
Place in bowling averages: 59th av. 29.66 (2002 132nd av. 42.52)

Strike rate: 67.55 (career 79.00)
Parents: Malcolm and Susan
Wife: Marie
Children: Callum James Bale Croft
Family links with cricket: Father and grandfather played league cricket
Education: St John Lloyd Catholic School, Llanelli; Neath Tertiary College; West Glamorgan Institute of Higher Education
Qualifications: 6 O-levels, OND Business Studies, HND Business Studies, NCA senior coaching certificate
Overseas tours: England A to Bermuda and West Indies 1991-92, to South Africa 1993-94; England to Zimbabwe and New Zealand 1996-97, to West Indies 1997-98, to Australia 1998-99, to Sharjah (Coca-Cola Cup) 1998-99, to Sri Lanka 2000-01, to Sri Lanka 2003-04; England VI to Hong Kong 2003
Career highlights to date: 'Playing for England and winning the Championship with Glamorgan in 1997'
Cricket moments to forget: 'None. This career is too short to forget any of it'
Cricketers particularly admired: Ian Botham, Viv Richards, Shane Warne
Young players to look out for: 'Everyone at Glamorgan'
Other sports played: 'Give anything a go'
Other sports followed: Football (Liverpool FC), rugby (Llanelli and Wales)
Interests/relaxations: 'Everything'
Extras: Captained England South to victory in International Youth Tournament 1989 and was voted Player of the Tournament. Glamorgan Young Player of the Year 1992. Scored Test-best 37* at Old Trafford 1998, resisting for 190 minutes to deny South Africa victory. Represented England in the 1999 World Cup. Made his 16th England Test appearance v West Indies at Edgbaston 2000, passing Jeff Jones's total of 15 Tests to become the most capped Welshman. Honorary fellow of West Glamorgan Institute of Higher Education. Scored 69-ball 119 v Surrey at The Oval in the C&G 2002, striking each of Martin Bicknell's first five balls for four as Glamorgan made 429 in reply to Surrey's 438-5. Scored century (122) in his 400th first-class innings, v Somerset at Cardiff 2003. Scored 64 v Essex at Cardiff 2003, sharing with Jimmy Maher (142) in a new record opening partnership for Glamorgan in the one-day league. Glamorgan Player of the Year 2003 (jointly with Michael Kasprowicz). Glamorgan vice-captain 2002-03; appointed captain of Glamorgan during 2003, taking over from the injured Steve James
Best batting: 143 Glamorgan v Somerset, Taunton 1995
Best bowling: 8-66 Glamorgan v Warwickshire, Swansea 1992
Stop press: Man of the Match in England's victory v Pakistan in the final of the Hong Kong Sixes 2003. Called up to the England Test tour to Sri Lanka 2003-04. Retired from international cricket in January 2004

2003 Season

	M	Inns	NO	Runs	HS	Avge	100s	50s	Ct	St	O	M	Runs	Wkts	Avge	Best	5wl	10wM
Test																		
All First	17	29	4	739	122	29.56	1	4	9	-	731.5	192	1928	65	29.66	6-71	5	1
1-day Int																		
C & G	2	2	0	43	22	21.50	-	-	-	-	18	0	96	3	32.00	3-54	-	
NCL	16	16	1	445	70	29.66	-	4	4	-	112	0	577	18	32.05	3-33	-	
Twenty20	5	4	0	105	53	26.25	-	1	2	-	20	0	180	8	22.50	3-32	-	

Career Performances

	M	Inns	NO	Runs	HS	Avge	100s	50s	Ct	St	Balls	Runs	Wkts	Avge	Best	5wl	10wM
Test	21	34	8	421	37 *	16.19	-	-	10	-	4619	1825	49	37.24	5-95	1	-
All First	283	415	79	8666	143	25.79	4	41	143	-	61702	28031	781	35.89	8-66	36	6
1-day Int	50	36	12	344	32	14.33	-	-	11	-	2466	1743	45	38.73	3-51	-	
C & G	36	30	6	611	119	25.45	1	3	5	-	2140	1365	43	31.74	4-47	-	
NCL	184	157	29	3058	114 *	23.89	1	15	51	-	7716	5719	193	29.63	6-20	1	
Twenty20	5	4	0	105	53	26.25	-	1	2	-	120	180	8	22.50	3-32	-	

CROOK, S. P. Lancashire

Name: Steven Paul Crook
Role: Right-hand bat, right-arm fast-medium bowler
Born: 28 May 1983, Adelaide, Australia
Height: 5ft 11in **Weight:** 13st
Nickname: Crooky, Hairdo
County debut: 2003
1st-Class catches: 1
Strike rate: 111.50 (career 111.50)
Parents: Martyn Crook (father), Sue Carey (mother), Doug Carey (stepfather)
Marital status: Single
Family links with cricket: 'Brother Andrew'
Education: Rostrevor College; Magill University
Qualifications: Matriculation
Overseas tours: Australia U19 to New Zealand (U19 World Cup) 2001-02
Overseas teams played for: South Australia Redbacks
Career highlights to date: 'Signing two-year contract with Lancashire'
Cricket moments to forget: 'Getting the yips!'
Cricket superstitions: 'None'

Cricketers particularly admired: Brett Lee, Shoaib Akhtar
Young players to look out for: Paul Horton
Other sports played: Football (Australia U17 trials)
Other sports followed: Football (Tottenham Hotspur FC)
Relaxations: Playing golf
Extras: Attended Australian Institute of Sport Cricket Academy. Represented South Australia U13-U19. Member of Australia U19 World Cup squad 2001-02. Is not considered an overseas player
Opinions on cricket: 'Cricket has reached an exciting time, with so many opportunities for young players who show great potential.'
Best batting: 27 Lancashire v Warwickshire, Edgbaston 2003
Best bowling: 1-6 Lancashire v Warwickshire, Edgbaston 2003

2003 Season

	M	Inns	NO	Runs	HS	Avge	100s	50s	Ct	St	O	M	Runs	Wkts	Avge	Best	5wI	10wM
Test																		
All First	2	1	0	27	27	27.00	-	-	1	-	37.1	4	155	2	77.50	1-6	-	-
1-day Int																		
C & G																		
NCL	3	1	0	1	1	1.00	-	-	1	-	11	0	83	1	83.00	1-27	-	
Twenty20																		

Career Performances

	M	Inns	NO	Runs	HS	Avge	100s	50s	Ct	St	Balls	Runs	Wkts	Avge	Best	5wI	10wM
Test																	
All First	2	1	0	27	27	27.00	-	-	1	-	223	155	2	77.50	1-6	-	-
1-day Int																	
C & G																	
NCL	3	1	0	1	1	1.00	-	-	1	-	66	83	1	83.00	1-27	-	
Twenty20																	

24. Who captained West Indies on their 2000 tour to England?

CUNLIFFE, R. J.   Leicestershire

Name: <u>Robert</u> John Cunliffe
Role: Right-hand bat
Born: 8 November 1973, Oxford
Height: 5ft 10in **Weight:** 13st
County debut: 1993 (one-day, Glos),
1994 (first-class, Glos), 2002 (Leics)
1st-Class 50s: 10
1st-Class 100s: 3
1st-Class catches: 53
One-Day 100s: 3
Place in batting averages: (2002 271st
av. 13.44)
Parents: Barry and Janet
Wife and date of marriage: Claire Louise,
25 November 2000
Children: One son; one daughter
Family links with cricket: 'Dad played in
his younger days for his wife's village team
and was groundsman for nine years at Banbury Twenty CC'
Education: Banbury School; Banbury Technical College
Qualifications: Carpentry course, coaching award
Overseas tours: England U19 to India 1992-93
Overseas teams played for: Richmond City CC, Melbourne 1995-97
Cricketers particularly admired: Robin Smith
Other sports played: Football
Extras: Played in England U19 home series v West Indies U19 1993. B&H Gold
Award for his 143-ball 137 v Surrey at The Oval 1996; scored 116* in following round
v Ireland, sharing in a Gloucestershire record B&H partnership (221) with A. J. Wright
(123). Scored 61 in the B&H Super Cup final at Lord's 1999, in the process sharing in
a third-wicket partnership of 157 from 156 balls with Mark Alleyne (112). Left
Gloucestershire during the 2001-02 off-season and joined Leicestershire for 2002;
released by Leicestershire at the end of the 2003 season
Best batting: 190* Gloucestershire v Oxford University, Bristol 1995

2003 Season

	M	Inns	NO	Runs	HS	Avge	100s	50s	Ct	St	O	M	Runs	Wkts	Avge	Best	5wl	10wM
Test																		
All First	1	1	0	0	0	0.00	-	-	-	-								
1-day Int																		
C & G																		
NCL	1	1	1	1	1*	-	-	-	-	-								
Twenty20																		

	M	Inns	NO	Runs	HS	Avge	100s	50s	Ct	St	Balls	Runs	Wkts	Avge	Best	5wI	10wM
Test																	
All First	68	114	7	2542	190 *	23.75	3	10	53	-	7	3	0	-	-	-	-
1-day Int																	
C & G	12	10	0	234	69	23.40	-	1	2	-							
NCL	48	43	6	780	66	21.08	-	5	12	-							
Twenty20																	

CURRIE, M. R. Lancashire

Name: <u>Mark</u> Robert Currie
Role: Right-hand bat, right-arm
off-spin bowler
Born: 22 September 1979, Manchester
Height: 6ft **Weight:** 12st 7lbs
Nickname: Ruby, Cuz
County debut: 2002
1st-Class 50s: 2
1st-Class catches: 3
Parents: Martin and Jennifer
Marital status: Single
Family links with cricket: Father and
brothers played local club cricket
Education: Poynton County High School;
City of Westminster College
Qualifications: 9 GCSEs, GNVQ Leisure
and Tourism and Sports Leader award,
Level II coaching
Career outside cricket: Coaching
Off-season: 'End of season tour to Grenada; training, golf'
Overseas tours: Cheshire U17 to Sydney 1997; MCC Young Professionals to South
Africa 2000; Lancashire to Cape Town 2003
Overseas teams played for: Hammersley Carine, Perth 2000-02
Career highlights to date: 'Getting a contract, first-team debut and Championship
debut'
Cricket moments to forget: 'Breaking my index finger – twice'
Cricket superstitions: 'None'
Cricketers particularly admired: Mark Waugh, Damien Martyn, Sachin Tendulkar
Young players to look out for: Ryan Bradshaw, Paul Sawyer
Other sports played: Football, golf
Other sports followed: Football (Manchester City FC)

Favourite band: For Tomorrows
Relaxations: 'Listening to music, going out with friends, golf'
Extras: Four years with MCC Young Professionals. Played for Cheshire 1997-2002, including the C&G 2001, C&G 2002 and the second round of the C&G 2003, which was played in September 2002. Leading run-scorer in league from which Hammersley Carine (Perth) were promoted 2001-02
Best batting: 97 Lancashire v DUCCE, Durham 2003

2003 Season

	M	Inns	NO	Runs	HS	Avge	100s	50s	Ct	St	O	M	Runs	Wkts	Avge	Best	5wI	10wM
Test																		
All First	2	3	0	166	97	55.33	-	2	3	-								
1-day Int																		
C & G																		
NCL	2	1	0	16	16	16.00	-	-	-	-								
Twenty20																		

Career Performances

	M	Inns	NO	Runs	HS	Avge	100s	50s	Ct	St	Balls	Runs	Wkts	Avge	Best	5wI	10wM
Test																	
All First	3	5	1	216	97	54.00	-	2	3	-							
1-day Int																	
C & G	3	3	0	118	94	39.33	-	1	1	-							
NCL	2	1	0	16	16	16.00	-	-	-	-							
Twenty20																	

CUSDEN, S. M. J.   Kent

Name: <u>Simon</u> Mark James Cusden
Role: Right-hand bat, right-arm fast-medium bowler; all-rounder
Born: 21 February 1985
Height: 6ft 5in **Weight:** 15st
Nickname: Cussy, Cus, Ronnie, Freak
County debut: No first-team appearance
Parents: Mark and Michaela
Marital status: Single
Family links with cricket: 'Dad's a village legend'
Education: Simon Langton Grammar School for Boys
Qualifications: 9 GCSEs, 4 AS-levels
Off-season: 'Reserve for England U19 World Cup to Bangladesh'
Overseas tours: Simon Langton GS to Barbados 2001; England U19 to Australia 2002-03; ECB U18 to Holland 2003
Career highlights to date: 'England U19 tour. Getting a contract at Kent. 7-80 v Surrey for Kent 2nd XI'
Cricket moments to forget: 'One over for 29 v Old Stacians in a Sunday game'
Cricket superstitions: 'None'
Cricketers particularly admired: Dennis Lillee, Allan Donald, Steve Waugh, Ian Botham
Young players to look out for: Daniel Wenham, Michael Burt, Amadu Ainscough
Other sports followed: Football (Chelsea FC)
Favourite band: Foo Fighters
Relaxations: 'Listening to music; going to gym; spending time with girlfriend'
Extras: Part of St Lawrence and Highland Court's Kent League Premier Division winning side in first season with the club
Opinions on cricket: 'Television replays for lbws and caught behind. More day/night cricket. More 2nd XI games.'

---

25. Who were the three England bowlers who dismissed West Indies for 54 at Lord's and 61 at Headingley in 2000?

DAGNALL, C. E.   Leicestershire

Name: <u>Charles</u> Edward Dagnall
Role: Right-hand bat, right-arm
medium-fast bowler
Born: 10 July 1976, Bury, Lancashire
Height: 6ft 3in **Weight:** '14st on a
bowling day; 17st on a batting day'
Nickname: Daggers
County debut: 1999 (Warwickshire),
2002 (Leicestershire)
1st-Class 5 w. in innings: 2
1st-Class catches: 1
Place in batting averages: 236th av. 17.16
Place in bowling averages: 94th av. 35.89
Strike rate: 63.39 (career 57.03)
Parents: Mike and Jackie
Marital status: Single
Family links with cricket: 'Dad ran
town team'

Education: Bridgewater School, Worsley; UMIST
Qualifications: 9 GCSEs, 4 A-levels, BSc (Hons) Chemistry
Career outside cricket: Singer and radio presenter
Overseas tours: Warwickshire to Bloemfontein 2000, to Cape Town 2001
Overseas teams played for: Newtown and Chilwell, Geelong, Australia 1994-95;
St Josephs, Geelong 1998-99
Career highlights to date: 'Winning B&H Gold Award v Worcestershire
[at Worcester] in 2001. And also getting my full quota of bouncers in for one over
v Worcestershire at Kidderminster'
Cricket moments to forget: 'Alan Richardson getting 91 v Hampshire'
Cricket superstitions: 'Stop bowling filthy half-volleys'
Young players to look out for: Jamie Spires, Luke Wright
Other sports played: Golf, football, tennis, Scrabble
Other sports followed: Football (Burnley FC, 'still hate Stoke'); NFL (Tampa Bay
Buccaneers)
Relaxations: 'Educating the masses about music; meeting new people; talking;
playing the bass guitar with the world famous band Two Tone Deaf'
Extras: Played for Cumberland. Man of the Match in the Board XI final 1999
(Warwickshire v Essex). Topped Warwickshire 2nd XI batting averages 1998 and was
third in bowling averages. Awarded Warwickshire 2nd XI cap 1999. Took a wicket
with his fourth ball in first-class cricket v Oxford University at The Parks 1999. B&H
Gold Award for his 21* batting at No. 11 (following 2-18) v Worcestershire at
Worcester 2001. Left Warwickshire at the end of the 2001 season and joined
Leicestershire for 2002

Opinions on cricket: 'The loan system, which at the moment is useless, could be a huge success. Ask me for details. Also, is two overseas players the answer? Somehow I doubt it. Let's plunge that money into youth systems.'
Best batting: 23* Leicestershire v Surrey, The Oval 2003
Best bowling: 6-50 Warwickshire v Derbyshire, Derby 2001

2003 Season

	M	Inns	NO	Runs	HS	Avge	100s	50s	Ct	St	O	M	Runs	Wkts	Avge	Best	5wI	10wM
Test																		
All First	10	11	5	103	23 *	17.16	-	-	-	-	295.5	70	1005	28	35.89	5-66	1	-
1-day Int																		
C & G	3	3	2	28	24 *	28.00	-	-	-	-	25.2	4	91	6	15.16	3-39	-	
NCL	15	10	2	50	10	6.25	-	-	3	-	94.5	8	533	18	29.61	4-41	-	
Twenty20	2	1	0	2	2	2.00	-	-	-	-	5	0	51	1	51.00	1-40	-	

Career Performances

	M	Inns	NO	Runs	HS	Avge	100s	50s	Ct	St	Balls	Runs	Wkts	Avge	Best	5wI	10wM
Test																	
All First	20	20	8	148	23	* 12.33	-	-	1	-	3308	1823	58	31.43	6-50	2	-
1-day Int																	
C & G	4	4	2	32	24	* 16.00	-	-	-	-	206	128	7	18.28	3-39	-	
NCL	37	16	3	114	28	8.76	-	-	4	-	1600	1155	49	23.57	4-34	-	
Twenty20	2	1	0	2	2	2.00	-	-	-	-	30	51	1	51.00	1-40	-	

DAKIN, J. M.   Leicestershire

Name: <u>Jonathan</u> Michael Dakin
Role: Left-hand bat, right-arm medium-fast bowler
Born: 28 February 1973, Hitchin, Herts
Height: 6ft 6in **Weight:** 16st
Nickname: Deuce
County debut: 1993 (Leicestershire), 2002 (Essex)
County cap: 2000 (Leicestershire), 2003 (Essex)
1st-Class 50s: 13
1st-Class 100s: 5
1st-Class 5 w. in innings: 1
1st-Class catches: 21
One-Day 100s: 2
One-Day 5 w. in innings: 1
Place in batting averages: 190th av. 24.17 (2002 221st av. 21.11)
Place in bowling averages: 46th av. 27.47 (2002 68th av. 30.82)
Strike rate: 52.87 (career 63.12)

Parents: Fred John and Gloria May
Marital status: Single
Family links with cricket: 'Brother keeps winning titles for Leicester Ivanhoe'
Education: King Edward VII School, Johannesburg, South Africa
Qualifications: Matriculation
Career outside cricket: 'Bottle store worker'
Off-season: 'North Hobart Demons (Tasmania)'
Overseas tours: Rutland Tourists to Jersey 1992; Leicestershire CCC to South Africa 1996, 1997, to Barbados, to Sri Lanka, to Anguilla
Overseas teams played for: Wanderers, South Africa 1986-92; Alberts, South Africa 1993; Kaponga CC, New Zealand 1995-96; North Hobart, Tasmania 2001-04

Career highlights to date: 'Two Championship titles (Leicestershire); second division champions [2002]'
Cricket moments to forget: 'Lord's finals (lost three)'
Cricketers particularly admired: Darren Maddy, Phil DeFreitas
Young players to look out for: Ali Cook, Mark Pettini
Other sports played: Golf
Other sports followed: Rugby union (Leicester Tigers)
Injuries: Out for four weeks with an impingement in an ankle
Favourite band: U2
Relaxations: Eating out
Extras: Won three Bain Hogg trophies in four years; scored 193 against Middlesex in the Bain Hogg in 1996. C&G Man of the Match award for his 179 v Wales at Swansea 2001; at the time it was the fourth highest individual score in Gillette/NatWest/C&G history and the highest in the 50-over format of the competition. Left Leicestershire at the end of the 2001 season and joined Essex for 2002. Recorded maiden first-class five-wicket return (5-86) v Middlesex at Lord's 2003. Awarded Essex cap 2003. Left Essex at the end of the 2003 season and has rejoined Leicestershire for 2004
Opinions on cricket: 'Great idea Twenty20. Sunday league should be 40 overs. Pitch panel abolished as only certain grounds seem to get done. Get rid of toss – opposing captains get choice; this will stop bad pitches.'
Best batting: 190 Leicestershire v Northamptonshire, Northampton 1997
Best bowling: 5-86 Essex v Middlesex, Lord's 2003

2003 Season

	M	Inns	NO	Runs	HS	Avge	100s	50s	Ct	St	O	M	Runs	Wkts	Avge	Best	5wI	10wM
Test																		
All First	11	19	2	411	59	24.17	-	2	2	-	352.3	79	1099	40	27.47	5-86	1	-
1-day Int																		
C & G	2	1	1	11	11 *	-	-	-	-	-	16.1	1	64	4	16.00	3-30	-	
NCL	7	7	1	98	40 *	16.33	-	-	-	-	50	2	273	9	30.33	3-51	-	
Twenty20	5	4	1	23	9	7.66	-	-	2	-	20	0	160	6	26.66	2-31	-	

Career Performances

	M	Inns	NO	Runs	HS	Avge	100s	50s	Ct	St	Balls	Runs	Wkts	Avge	Best	5wI	10wM
Test																	
All First	74	110	11	2727	190	27.54	5	13	21	-	9721	5082	154	33.00	5-86	1	-
1-day Int																	
C & G	15	13	1	307	179	25.58	1	-	1	-	588	411	14	29.35	3-30	-	
NCL	123	107	17	1672	68 *	18.57	-	2	23	-	3483	2935	105	27.95	5-30	1	
Twenty20	5	4	1	23	9	7.66	-	-	2	-	120	160	6	26.66	2-31	-	

DALE, A.   Glamorgan

Name: Adrian Dale
Role: Right-hand bat, right-arm
medium bowler
Born: 24 October 1968, Johannesburg,
South Africa
Height: 5ft 11in **Weight:** 12st
Nickname: Arthur
County debut: 1989
County cap: 1992
Benefit: 2002 (£110,983)
1000 runs in a season: 4
1st-Class 50s: 58
1st-Class 100s: 21
1st-Class 200s: 2
1st-Class 5 w. in innings: 4
1st-Class catches: 104
One-Day 100s: 2
One-Day 5 w. in innings: 2
Place in batting averages: 183rd av. 25.26 (2002 96th av. 37.34)
Strike rate: 96.00 (career 70.96)
Parents: John and Maureen
Wife and date of marriage: Ruth, 9 January 1999

Children: Jessica, 12 January 2001; Luke, December 2002
Family links with cricket: Father played occasionally for Glamorgan 2nd XI
Education: Chepstow Comprehensive; Swansea University
Qualifications: 9 O-levels, 3 A-levels, BA (Hons) Economics
Career outside cricket: Estate agency. Glamorgan marketing department
Overseas tours: Welsh Schools U16 to Australia 1986-87; Combined Universities to Barbados 1988-89; Glamorgan to Trinidad 1989-90, 1991-92, to Zimbabwe 1990-91, to Cape Town 1992-93, 1999, 2002; England A to South Africa 1993-94
Overseas teams played for: Bionics, Zimbabwe 1990-91; Cornwall, New Zealand 1991-93, 1995-97
Career highlights to date: '1997 County Championship win'
Cricket moments to forget: 'Losing the 2000 B&H Cup final at Lord's'
Cricket superstitions: 'None'
Cricketers particularly admired: Ian Botham, Michael Holding, Mike Gatting
Young players to look out for: 'There's good young talent at Glamorgan'
Other sports followed: Football (Arsenal), rugby union (Wales)
Relaxations: Travelling, eating out
Extras: Played in successful Combined Universities sides of 1989 and 1990. Only batsman to score two half-centuries against the West Indies tourists in the same match in 1991. Took a wicket with his first delivery at Lord's. Recorded Glamorgan's then best one-day bowling figures, 6-22, against Durham 1993. Shared in Glamorgan's highest ever partnership, 425*, with Viv Richards against Middlesex 1993. Scored two centuries in a match (108/113) v Gloucestershire at Cardiff 1999. Glamorgan CCC Player of the Year 2000, 2001. Vice-captain of Glamorgan in 2001. Glamorgan Supporters' Player of the Year 2001
Best batting: 214* Glamorgan v Middlesex, Cardiff 1993
Best bowling: 6-18 Glamorgan v Warwickshire, Cardiff 1993

2003 Season

	M	Inns	NO	Runs	HS	Avge	100s	50s	Ct	St	O	M	Runs	Wkts	Avge	Best	5wI	10wM
Test																		
All First	15	27	1	657	123	25.26	1	2	12	-	48	9	159	3	53.00	3-29	-	-
1-day Int																		
C & G	2	2	0	22	13	11.00	-	-	1	-	14.1	0	55	2	27.50	2-30	-	
NCL	16	12	1	241	60	21.90	-	1	6	-	85.5	1	435	13	33.46	4-35	-	
Twenty20	5	5	0	29	18	5.80	-	-	1	-	15	0	139	5	27.80	2-15	-	

Career Performances

	M	Inns	NO	Runs	HS	Avge	100s	50s	Ct	St	Balls	Runs	Wkts	Avge	Best	5wI	10wM
Test																	
All First	244	400	32	12345	214 *	33.54	23	58	104	-	15399	8232	217	37.93	6-18	4	-
1-day Int																	
C & G	38	35	4	919	110	29.64	1	3	7	-	1485	1077	31	34.74	3-15	-	
NCL	208	177	23	4322	82	28.06	-	25	46	-	6388	5409	174	31.08	6-22	1	
Twenty20	5	5	0	29	18	5.80	-	-	1	-	90	139	5	27.80	2-15	-	

DALRYMPLE, J. W. M.   Middlesex

Name: James (<u>Jamie</u>) William
Murray Dalrymple
Role: Right-hand bat, off-spin bowler
Born: 21 January 1981, Nairobi, Kenya
Height: 6ft **Weight:** 13st 7lbs
Nickname: JD, Pest
County debut: 2000 (one-day),
2001 (first-class)
1st-Class 50s: 2
1st-Class 100s: 2
1st-Class 200s: 1
1st-Class 5 w. in innings: 1
1st-Class catches: 16
Place in batting averages: 76th av. 39.66
(2002 79th av. 41.15)
Place in bowling averages: 132nd av. 44.08
Strike rate: 86.08 (career 106.78)
Parents: Douglas and Patricia
Marital status: Single
Family links with cricket: 'Dad played lots of club cricket.' Brother Simon played for
Oxford University in 2002
Education: Radley College, Abingdon; St Peter's College, Oxford University
Qualifications: 10 GCSEs, 5 A-levels, degree in History
Off-season: 'Resting, training with MCC in UAE and a Middlesex group in India'
Overseas tours: Middlesex to South Africa 2000
Career highlights to date: 'Varsity Match 2003 – a personal and team success'
Cricket moments to forget: 'Middlesex v Warwickshire at Edgbaston 2003 – being
part of the loss of eight wickets in a session, and the match'
Cricketers particularly admired: David Gower, Carl Hooper, Ian Botham,
Mark Waugh
Young players to look out for: Tom Mees
Other sports played: Rugby (college), hockey (university)
Other sports followed: Rugby (Northampton RUFC)
Favourite band: 'Don't have a favourite'
Relaxations: Reading, golf
Extras: Represented England U19 v Sri Lanka U19 in 2000. Played for Oxford
University CCE 2001 and 2002 (captain 2002); made first-class debut for OUCCE
against his county club, Middlesex, at The Parks 2001. Represented British
Universities 2001 and captained British Universities v Sri Lankans and v West Indies
A 2002. Oxford Blue 2001, 2002 (captain) and 2003 (captain). Took 4-152 and scored
137 in the four-day Varsity Match at The Parks and scored 78 and took 4-42 in the

50-over match at Lord's 2002. Became third ever Oxford University batsman to score a double century in the Varsity Match (236*) at Fenner's 2003, in the process sharing with Neil Millar (108) in a record third-wicket partnership for the match (263); also took 5-49 in the Cambridge first innings and scored 105* in the 50-over Varsity Match at Lord's

Opinions on cricket: 'How about some turning wickets?'
Best batting: 236* Oxford University v Cambridge University, Fenner's 2003
Best bowling: 5-49 Oxford University v Cambridge University, Fenner's 2003

2003 Season

	M	Inns	NO	Runs	HS	Avge	100s	50s	Ct	St	O	M	Runs	Wkts	Avge	Best	5wI	10wM
Test																		
All First	7	11	2	357	236 *	39.66	1	-	6	-	172.1	27	529	12	44.08	5-49	1	-
1-day Int																		
C & G																		
NCL	11	11	5	128	38	21.33	-	-	3	-	66	0	339	10	33.90	3-55	-	
Twenty20																		

Career Performances

	M	Inns	NO	Runs	HS	Avge	100s	50s	Ct	St	Balls	Runs	Wkts	Avge	Best	5wI	10wM
Test																	
All First	20	35	4	1095	236 *	35.32	3	2	16	-	2990	1574	28	56.21	5-49	1	-
1-day Int																	
C & G																	
NCL	32	29	9	469	52	23.45	-	1	13	-	1017	839	28	29.96	4-14	-	
Twenty20																	

26. Which Norfolk-born Surrey opener made his debut against West Indies in 1963, 13 years after his cousin appeared against the same opposition?

DANISH KANERIA   Essex

Name: Danish Parabha Shanker Kaneria
Role: Right-hand bat, right-arm
leg-spin bowler
Born: 16 December 1980, Karachi, Pakistan
Nickname: Nani-Danny
County debut: No first-team appearance
Test debut: 2000-01
Tests: 12
One-Day Internationals: 6
1st-Class 5 w. in innings: 18
1st-Class 10 w. in match: 2
1st-Class catches: 13
Strike rate: (career 47.99)
Family links with cricket: Cousin, wicket-
keeper Anil Dalpat, played nine Tests for
Pakistan 1983-84
Overseas tours: Pakistan U19 to Sri Lanka
(U19 World Cup) 1999-2000; Pakistan A to
Kenya 2000, to Sri Lanka 2001; Pakistan to Bangladesh 2001-02, to Sharjah (v West
Indies) 2001-02, to Sharjah (v Australia) 2002-03, to England (NatWest Challenge)
2003, to New Zealand 2003-04, plus other one-day tournaments
Overseas teams played for: Pakistan National Shipping Corporation 1998-99;
Karachi Whites 1998-99, 2000-01, 2001-02; Pakistan Reserves 1999-2000; Habib
Bank 1999-2000, 2000-01, 2001-02, 2002-03
Extras: Represented Pakistan U19 in home series v South Africa U19 1998-99. Only
the second Hindu to play in Tests for Pakistan, after his cousin Anil Dalpat. Had match
figures of 12-94 (6-42/6-52) v Bangladesh at Multan in the first match of the Asian
Test Championship 2001-02. Man of the [Test] Series, Pakistan in Bangladesh 2001-02.
Has joined Essex as an overseas player for 2004
Best batting: 42 Habib Bank v Allied Bank, Sheikhupura 2001-02
Best bowling: 7-39 Karachi Whites v Gujranwala, Karachi 2000-01
Stop press: Had match figures of 7-111 (2-65/5-46) in the first Test v South Africa at
Lahore 2003-04, winning Man of the Match award

---

27. Which Italian-born batsman captained England in the 1963
home series against West Indies then stood down from captaincy to fight James
Callaghan for the Cardiff South-East seat in Parliament?

2003 Season (did not make any first-class or one-day appearances)

Career Performances

	M	Inns	NO	Runs	HS	Avge	100s	50s	Ct	St	Balls	Runs	Wkts	Avge	Best	5wI	10wM
Test	12	14	7	53	15	7.570	-	-	3	-	2788	1338	51	26.23	7-77	4	1
All First	45	52	26	220	42	8.46	-	-	13	-	10607	4728	221	21.39	7-39	18	2
1-day Int	6	4	3	3	3 *	3.00	-	-	-	-	312	195	7	27.85	3-31	-	
C & G																	
NCL																	
Twenty20																	

DAVIES, A. P.   Glamorgan

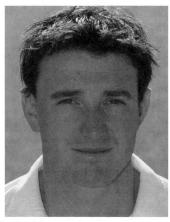

Name: <u>Andrew</u> Philip Davies
Role: Left-hand bat, right-arm medium-fast bowler
Born: 7 November 1976, Neath
Height: 6ft **Weight:** 12st
Nickname: Diver
County debut: 1995
1st-Class 5 w. in innings: 1
1st-Class catches: 4
One-Day 5 w. in innings: 2
Place in batting averages: (2002 295th av. 9.66)
Place in bowling averages: (2002 51st av. 28.00)
Strike rate: 138.00 (career 62.02)
Parents: Anne and Phil
Wife and date of marriage: Nerys, 1 February 2003
Family links with cricket: 'Dad and brother play local league'
Education: Dwr-y-Felin Comprehensive School; Christ College, Brecon
Qualifications: 7 GCSEs, 1 A-level, Level 2 coach
Career outside cricket: 'Petrol pump attendant'
Off-season: 'Went to New Zealand for nine days'
Overseas tours: Wales MC to Barbados; Glamorgan to Pretoria, to Cape Town (twice)
Overseas teams played for: Marist CC, Whangarei, New Zealand 1995-96
Career highlights to date: 'Getting Steve Waugh out and winning Sunday League'
Cricket moments to forget: 'Going to Napier (New Zealand)'
Cricket superstitions: 'None'
Cricketers particularly admired: 'Too many!'

Other sports played: 'Try and play golf now and again'
Other sports followed: Football (Swansea City)
Injuries: Out for eight weeks with a broken right thumb
Favourite band: Robbie Williams
Relaxations: 'Listening to music'
Extras: Wales U19 Player of the Year 1995. Wales Player of the Year 1996. 2nd XI cap 1998. 2nd XI Player of the Year 1998, 1999. 1st XI Player of the Month August-September 1998. Glamorgan's leading wicket-taker (21) in the NUL 2001
Best batting: 40 Glamorgan v Essex, Cardiff 2001
Best bowling: 5-79 Glamorgan v Worcestershire, Cardiff 2002

2003 Season

	M	Inns	NO	Runs	HS	Avge	100s	50s	Ct	St	O	M	Runs	Wkts	Avge	Best	5wI	10wM
Test																		
All First	3	3	1	32	19*	16.00	-	-	1	-	46	8	225	2	112.50	1-22	-	-
1-day Int																		
C & G	2	2	2	9	5*	-	-	-	-	-	8	0	60	1	60.00	1-22	-	
NCL	9	3	2	6	3	6.00	-	-	2	-	59.5	3	338	14	24.14	3-31	-	
Twenty20																		

Career Performances

	M	Inns	NO	Runs	HS	Avge	100s	50s	Ct	St	Balls	Runs	Wkts	Avge	Best	5wI	10wM
Test																	
All First	21	25	4	254	40	12.09	-	-	4	-	2605	1589	42	37.83	5-79	1	-
1-day Int																	
C & G	4	3	2	10	5*	10.00	-	-	-	-	150	167	6	27.83	5-19	1	
NCL	44	18	10	83	24	10.37	-	-	8	-	1804	1438	68	21.14	5-39	1	
Twenty20																	

DAVIES, M. A.   Durham

Name: <u>Mark</u> Anthony Davies
Role: Right-hand bat, right-arm fast-medium bowler
Born: 4 October 1980, Stockton-on-Tees
Height: 6ft 3in **Weight:** 13st
Nickname: Davo
County debut: 1998 (one-day), 2002 (first-class)
1st-Class 5 w. in innings: 1
1st-Class catches: 3
Place in batting averages: (2002 284th av. 10.82)
Place in bowling averages: 134th av. 46.27 (2002 34th av. 26.16)
Strike rate: 81.27 (career 64.70)

Parents: Howard and Mandy
Marital status: Single
Education: Northfield School, Billingham;
Stockton Sixth Form College
Qualifications: 5 GCSEs, NVQ Level 3
Sport and Recreation
Overseas tours: Durham to South Africa
2002
Overseas teams played for: North
Kalgoorlie CC, Western Australia
Career highlights to date: 'Gaining
promotion in the NUL 2001'
Cricketers particularly admired:
Glenn McGrath
Other sports played: Football, golf, boxing
Other sports followed: Football
(Middlesbrough)
Relaxations: Socialising, golf
Extras: Represented England U19 v Sri Lanka U19 2000. Played for Durham Board
XI in the NatWest 2000 and for Durham Board XI and Durham in the C&G 2001.
Attended Durham Academy
Best batting: 33 Durham v Derbyshire, Darlington 2002
Best bowling: 5-61 Durham v Glamorgan, Riverside 2002

2003 Season

	M	Inns	NO	Runs	HS	Avge	100s	50s	Ct	St	O	M	Runs	Wkts	Avge	Best	5wI	10wM
Test																		
All First	5	8	3	64	21	12.80	-	-	-	-	149	35	509	11	46.27	2-34	-	-
1-day Int																		
C & G																			
NCL	12	5	4	31	19 *	31.00	-	-	-	-	96	10	374	13	28.76	2-15	-	
Twenty20	4	1	1	3	3 *	-	-	-	2	-	16	0	144	2	72.00	1-32	-	

Career Performances

	M	Inns	NO	Runs	HS	Avge	100s	50s	Ct	St	Balls	Runs	Wkts	Avge	Best	5wI	10wM
Test																	
All First	19	32	10	248	33	11.27	-	-	3	-	3041	1451	47	30.87	5-61	1	-
1-day Int																	
C & G	8	5	1	8	6	2.00	-	-	-	-	342	220	5	44.00	1-11	-	
NCL	35	20	7	122	31 *	9.38	-	-	7	-	1536	1031	41	25.14	4-13	-	
Twenty20	4	1	1	3	3 *	-	-	-	2	-	96	144	2	72.00	1-32	-	

DAVIS, M. J. G. Sussex

Name: <u>Mark</u> Jeffrey Gronow Davis
Role: Right-hand bat, right-arm
off-spin bowler
Born: 10 October 1971, Port Elizabeth,
South Africa
Height: 6ft 2in **Weight:** 12st 8lbs
Nickname: Davo, Doxy, Sparky
County debut: 2001
County cap: 2002
1st-Class 50s: 7
1st-Class 100s: 2
1st-Class 5 w. in innings: 5
1st-Class 10 w. in match: 1
1st-Class catches: 61
Place in batting averages: 175th av. 25.90
(2002 170th av. 26.33)
Place in bowling averages: 144th av. 50.73
(2002 118th av. 38.60)
Strike rate: 94.80 (career 79.88)
Parents: Jeremy and Marilyn
Wife and date of marriage: Candice, 8 April 2000
Family links with cricket: 'Father supports Sussex. My brothers, William and
Patrick, play league cricket in Sussex'
Education: Grey High School; University of Pretoria
Qualifications: BA Psychology and English
Career outside cricket: Head coach of UPE International Cricket Academy in Port
Elizabeth
Overseas tours: South Africa U24 to Sri Lanka 1995; Northern Transvaal to
Zimbabwe 1992-93, to Kenya 1994-95, 1995-96
Overseas teams played for: Northern Transvaal/Northerns 1991-92 – 2000-01
Career highlights to date: 'Winning the County Championship last year. It was
second to none, unbelievable! That and my 168 v Middlesex the same season'
Cricket superstitions: 'None'
Cricketers particularly admired: 'All my team-mates', Tim May, Shane Warne
Young players to look out for: Matt Prior, Tim Ambrose
Other sports played: Golf, tennis
Other sports followed: Rugby ('support the Springboks'), football (Middlesbrough)
Favourite band: 'Very eclectic tastes – no real favourite'
Relaxations: 'Golf, music, going out with friends, watching good movies'
Extras: Made first-class debut for Northern Transvaal B 1990-91. Captain of Northern
Transvaal/Northerns 1997-2000, during which time the province won the first two

trophies in its history. Represented South Africa A v Zimbabwe 1995. Member of MCC. Scored maiden first-class century (111) v Somerset at Taunton 2002, in the process sharing with Robin Martin-Jenkins (205*) in a record eighth-wicket partnership for Sussex (291); the stand fell one run short of the record eighth-wicket partnership in English first-class cricket, set by Bobby Peel and Lord Hawke for Yorkshire v Warwickshire at Birmingham in 1896. Scored career best 168 v Middlesex at Hove 2003, sharing with Matt Prior (148) in a record seventh-wicket partnership for Sussex in matches against Middlesex (195) and with Billy Taylor (35*) in a record tenth-wicket partnership for Sussex in matches against Middlesex (106). Is not considered an overseas player

Best batting: 168 Sussex v Middlesex, Hove 2003
Best bowling: 8-37 Northerns B v North West, Potchefstroom 1994-95

2003 Season

	M	Inns	NO	Runs	HS	Avge	100s	50s	Ct	St	O	M	Runs	Wkts	Avge	Best	5wI	10wM
Test																		
All First	11	12	2	259	168	25.90	1	-	4	-	237	46	761	15	50.73	3-44	-	-
1-day Int																		
C & G	2	2	2	53	32 *	-	-	-	-	-	18	0	81	0	-		-	-
NCL	18	13	5	185	37	23.12	-	-	4	-	133.5	6	621	20	31.05	4-14	-	
Twenty20	5	4	3	35	18 *	35.00	-	-	2	-	19	0	128	6	21.33	3-13	-	

Career Performances

	M	Inns	NO	Runs	HS	Avge	100s	50s	Ct	St	Balls	Runs	Wkts	Avge	Best	5wI	10wM
Test																	
All First	111	167	27	2686	168	19.18	2	7	61	-	16616	7529	208	36.19	8-37	5	1
1-day Int																	
C & G	7	5	5	95	32 *	-	-	-	-	-	408	267	4	66.75	2-37	-	
NCL	47	31	9	388	37	17.63	-	-	10	-	2066	1567	49	31.97	4-14	-	
Twenty20	5	4	3	35	18 *	35.00	-	-	2	-	114	128	6	21.33	3-13	-	

28. Which former fiery cricket pundit had match figures of 12-119 against West Indies at Edgbaston in 1963?

DAWES, J. H. Middlesex

Name: Joseph (Joe) Henry Dawes
Role: Right-hand bat, right-arm
fast-medium bowler
Born: 29 August 1970, Herston, Brisbane,
Queensland
Nickname: Wallops
County debut: 2003
County cap: 2003
1st-Class 5 w. in innings: 8
1st-Class 10 w. in match: 2
1st-Class catches: 10
Place in batting averages: 260th av. 13.85
Place in bowling averages: 67th av. 31.50
Strike rate: 58.52 (career 49.73)
Career outside cricket: Former police
officer. Was also community relations and
media manager for Peter Dutton, Member of
Australian Parliament

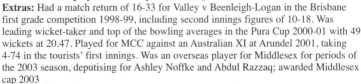

Overseas tours: MCC to Singapore and Malaysia 2002
Overseas teams played for: Valley, Brisbane; Queensland 1997-98 –
Extras: Had a match return of 16-33 for Valley v Beenleigh-Logan in the Brisbane
first grade competition 1998-99, including second innings figures of 10-18. Was
leading wicket-taker and top of the bowling averages in the Pura Cup 2000-01 with 49
wickets at 20.47. Played for MCC against an Australian XI at Arundel 2001, taking
4-74 in the tourists' first innings. Was an overseas player for Middlesex for periods of
the 2003 season, deputising for Ashley Noffke and Abdul Razzaq; awarded Middlesex
cap 2003
Best batting: 32* Middlesex v Essex, Chelmsford 2003
Best bowling: 7-67 Queensland v South Australia, Brisbane 2002-03

2003 Season

	M	Inns	NO	Runs	HS	Avge	100s	50s	Ct	St	O	M	Runs	Wkts	Avge	Best	5wI	10wM
Test																		
All First	10	12	5	97	32 *	13.85	-	-	3	-	331.4	58	1071	34	31.50	5-46	1	-
1-day Int																		
C & G	1	0	0	0	0	-	-	-	-	-	10	1	30	2	15.00	2-30	-	
NCL	12	5	2	5	2	1.66	-	-	3	-	77	1	451	4	112.75	1-22	-	
Twenty20	1	1	0	0	0	0.00	-	-	-	-	3	0	33	0	-		-	-

Career Performances

	M	Inns	NO	Runs	HS	Avge	100s	50s	Ct	St	Balls	Runs	Wkts	Avge	Best	5wl	10wM
Test																	
All First	54	67	24	410	32 *	9.53	-	-	10	-	10395	5058	209	24.20	7-67	8	2
1-day Int																	
C & G	1	0	0	0	0	-	-	-	-	-	60	30	2	15.00	2-30	-	
NCL	12	5	2	5	2	1.66	-	-	3	-	462	451	4	112.75	1-22	-	
Twenty20	1	1	0	0	0	0.00	-	-	-	-	18	33	0	-		-	-

DAWSON, R. K. J. Yorkshire

Name: <u>Richard</u> Kevin James Dawson
Role: Right-hand bat, right-arm
off-spin bowler
Born: 4 August 1980, Doncaster
Height: 6ft 4in **Weight:** 11st 4lbs
Nickname: Billy Dog
County debut: 2001
Test debut: 2001-02
Tests: 7
1st-Class 50s: 4
1st-Class 5 w. in innings: 4
1st-Class catches: 24
Place in batting averages: 152nd av. 29.18
(2002 215th av. 22.21)
Place in bowling averages: 140th av. 49.41
(2002 120th av. 38.77)
Strike rate: 85.35 (career 77.43)
Parents: Kevin and Pat
Marital status: Single
Family links with cricket: Brother Gareth plays for Doncaster Town CC
Education: Batley GS; Exeter University
Qualifications: 10 GCSEs, 4 A-levels, degree in Exercise and Sports Science
Overseas tours: England U18 to Bermuda 1997; England U19 to New Zealand
1998-99; England to India and New Zealand 2001-02, to Australia 2002-03; ECB
National Academy to Sri Lanka 2002-03
Cricketers particularly admired: Steve Waugh, Graeme Swann
Other sports played: Football
Other sports followed: Football (Doncaster Rovers FC)
Relaxations: Sleeping, listening to music
Extras: Captained England U15. Sir John Hobbs Silver Jubilee Memorial Prize 1995.
Played for Devon 1999 and 2000. Represented England U19 v Australia U19 in 1999.

Has Yorkshire 2nd XI cap. Captained British Universities 2000. NBC Denis Compton Award for the most promising young Yorkshire player 2001. Made Test debut in first Test v India at Mohali 2001-02, taking 4-134 in India's first innings. Scored 41 v Leicestershire at Scarborough in the NUL 2002, in the process sharing with Richard Blakey (60) in a new record eighth-wicket partnership for Yorkshire in the one-day league (89)

Best batting: 87 Yorkshire v Kent, Canterbury 2002
Best bowling: 6-82 Yorkshire v Glamorgan, Scarborough 2001

2003 Season

	M	Inns	NO	Runs	HS	Avge	100s	50s	Ct	St	O	M	Runs	Wkts	Avge	Best	5wI	10wM
Test																		
All First	12	18	2	467	77	29.18	-	2	11	-	241.5	47	840	17	49.41	3-119	-	-
1-day Int																		
C & G																		
NCL	7	6	1	29	14	5.80	-	-	4	-	49.2	1	219	8	27.37	3-26	-	
Twenty20																		

Career Performances

	M	Inns	NO	Runs	HS	Avge	100s	50s	Ct	St	Balls	Runs	Wkts	Avge	Best	5wI	10wM
Test	7	13	3	114	19 *	11.40	-	-	3	-	1116	677	11	61.54	4-134	-	-
All First	51	78	12	1448	87	21.93	-	4	24	-	8440	4668	109	42.82	6-82	4	-
1-day Int																	
C & G	9	3	0	14	7	4.66	-	-	2	-	435	339	9	37.66	4-34	-	
NCL	30	23	2	154	41	7.33	-	-	9	-	1034	818	30	27.26	4-37	-	
Twenty20																	

DEAN, K. J.   Derbyshire

Name: <u>Kevin</u> James Dean
Role: Left-hand bat, left-arm medium bowler ('might get wind now Corky has gone')
Born: 16 October 1975, Derby
Height: 6ft 5in   **Weight:** 14st
Nickname: Deany, Red Face, The Wall, George
County debut: 1996
County cap: 1998
50 wickets in a season: 2
1st-Class 50s: 2
1st-Class 5 w. in innings: 14
1st-Class 10 w. in match: 4
1st-Class catches: 17
One-Day 5 w. in innings: 1

Place in batting averages: 288th av. 7.04
(2002 226th av. 20.41)
Place in bowling averages: 110th av. 38.85
(2002 17th av. 23.50)
Strike rate: 65.04 (career 44.13)
Parents: Ken and Dorothy
Marital status: Single
Education: Leek High School; Leek College
of Further Education
Qualifications: 8 GCSEs, 1 AS-level,
3 A-levels
Career outside cricket: Working for
Ladbrokes
Off-season: 'Being a member of the
ATR crew'
Overseas tours: MCC to Australia 2002-03
Overseas teams played for: Sturt CC,
Adelaide 1996-97
Career highlights to date: 'Can't split – 1) Hitting the winning runs against Australia
for Derbyshire in 1997; 2) Getting either hat-trick'
Cricket moments to forget: 'Losing in the NatWest final [1998]'
Cricket superstitions: 'Last person out of changing room for first session of fielding'
Cricketers particularly admired: Dominic Cork, Wasim Akram, Michael Holding
Young players to look out for: Tom Lungley, Mark Davies, Jacob Harris
Other sports played: Football, golf, tennis, snooker
Other sports followed: Football (Derby County), horse racing
Relaxations: 'Going horse racing. Talking with Sutts and trying to keep it vaguely
interesting. Fleecing fruit machines with Tetley, but not casinos, yet!'
Extras: A member of the Staffordshire U16 Texaco winning team. Achieved first-class
hat-trick (E. Smith, Hooper, Llong) against Kent at Derby 1998. Took second first-
class hat-trick (Habib, Kumble, Ormond) v Leicestershire at Leicester 2000. Joint
leading wicket-taker in English first-class cricket 2002 (with Martin Saggers) with 83
wickets (av. 23.50). Derbyshire Player of the Year 2002 (jointly with Michael
DiVenuto)
Best batting: 54* Derbyshire v Worcestershire, Derby 2002
Best bowling: 8-52 Derbyshire v Kent, Canterbury 2000

2003 Season

	M	Inns	NO	Runs	HS	Avge	100s	50s	Ct	St	O	M	Runs	Wkts	Avge	Best	5wI	10wM
Test																		
All First	16	24	3	148	30 *	7.04	-	-	4	-	444.3	107	1593	41	38.85	4-39	-	-
1-day Int																		
C & G	4	2	0	4	2	2.00	-	-	2	-	32	5	125	8	15.62	3-6	-	
NCL	15	7	4	30	12	10.00	-	-	1	-	119	16	508	13	39.07	2-17	-	
Twenty20																		

Career Performances

	M	Inns	NO	Runs	HS	Avge	100s	50s	Ct	St	Balls	Runs	Wkts	Avge	Best	5wI	10wM
Test																	
All First	89	120	37	942	54 *	11.34	-	2	17	-	14654	8269	332	24.90	8-52	14	4
1-day Int																	
C & G	15	5	2	12	8	4.00	-	-	6	-	822	546	28	19.50	3-6	-	
NCL	83	39	22	188	16 *	11.05	-	-	14	-	3614	2780	91	30.54	5-32	1	
Twenty20																	

DEFREITAS, P. A. J.   Leicestershire

Name: <u>Phillip</u> Anthony Jason DeFreitas
Role: Right-hand bat, right-arm
fast-medium bowler, county captain
Born: 18 February 1966, Scotts Head,
Dominica
Height: 6ft **Weight:** 13st 7lbs
Nickname: Padge, Daffy, Linchy
County debut: 1985 (Leics),
1989 (Lancs), 1994 (Derbys)
County cap: 1986 (Leics),
1989 (Lancs), 1994 (Derbys)
Test debut: 1986-87
Tests: 44
One-Day Internationals: 103
50 wickets in a season: 14
1st-Class 50s: 53
1st-Class 100s: 10
1st-Class 5 w. in innings: 61
1st-Class 10 w. in match: 6
1st-Class catches: 126
One-Day 5 w. in innings: 7
Place in batting averages: 214th av. 21.43 (2002 147th av. 29.00)
Place in bowling averages: 23rd av. 24.05 (2002 72nd av. 31.25)
Strike rate: 54.05 (career 57.53)
Parents: Sybil and Martin
Marital status: Divorced
Children: Alexandra Elizabeth Jane, 5 August 1991
Family links with cricket: Father played in Windward Islands. All six brothers play
Education: Willesden High School
Qualifications: 2 O-levels
Overseas tours: England YC to West Indies 1984-85; England to Australia 1986-87,

to Pakistan, Australia and New Zealand 1987-88, to India (Nehru Cup) and West Indies 1989-90, to Australia 1990-91, to New Zealand 1991-92, to India and Sri Lanka 1992-93, to Australia 1994-95, to South Africa 1995-96, to India and Pakistan (World Cup) 1995-96; England XI to New Zealand (Cricket Max) 1997
Overseas teams played for: Port Adelaide, South Australia 1985; Mosman, Sydney 1988; Boland, South Africa 1993-94, 1995-96
Cricketers particularly admired: Ian Botham, Geoff Boycott, Mike Gatting, Viv Richards, Malcolm Marshall, David Hughes, Neil Fairbrother
Other sports followed: Football (Manchester City)
Extras: Left Leicestershire and joined Lancashire at end of 1988 season. Man of the Match in 1990 NatWest Trophy final. One of *Wisden*'s Five Cricketers of the Year 1992. Man of the Tournament in the Hong Kong Sixes 1993. Left Lancashire at the end of the 1993 season and joined Derbyshire. Player of the Series against New Zealand 1994. Captained Derbyshire for part of 1997 season after the departure of Dean Jones. Is the only playing English cricketer to have appeared in two World Cup finals. Took 1000th first-class wicket (Usman Afzaal caught by Karl Krikken) v Notts at Trent Bridge 1999. Left Derbyshire at end of 1999 season and rejoined Leicestershire for 2000. Scored 97 and 123* v Lancashire at Leicester 2000 (also bowled 47 overs in Lancashire's only innings). Shared in a Leicestershire record eighth-wicket partnership for the one-day league (116) with Neil Burns v Northamptonshire at Leicester in the NUL 2001. Took 6-65 v Glamorgan at Cardiff 2001, in the process achieving the feat of having recorded a five-wicket innings return against all 18 counties. Passed 10,000 runs in first-class cricket v Somerset at Leicester 2002 to achieve the career double of 10,000 runs and 1000 wickets. Scored 103 v Sussex at Leicester 2003, following up with 5-55 in Sussex's first innings. Captain of Leicestershire since 2003. Granted a benefit for 2004
Opinions on cricket: '1. First division players should get paid more than second division players. 2. Prize money should be paid only to first division; the reward for second division teams is to get promoted to play for prize money. 3. Championship games should never follow day/night games.'
Best batting: 123* Leicestershire v Lancashire, Leicester 2000
Best bowling: 7-21 Lancashire v Middlesex, Lord's 1989

2003 Season

	M	Inns	NO	Runs	HS	Avge	100s	50s	Ct	St	O	M	Runs	Wkts	Avge	Best	5wI	10wM
Test																		
All First	16	25	2	493	103	21.43	1	2	6	-	540.3	154	1443	60	24.05	7-51	4	1
1-day Int																		
C & G	3	3	0	64	30	21.33	-	-	1	-	27	7	60	5	12.00	3-20	-	
NCL	16	16	1	315	90	21.00	-	2	6	-	111	5	480	19	25.26	5-40	1	
Twenty20	6	6	0	49	18	8.16	-	-	-	-	17	0	148	6	24.66	3-39	-	

Career Performances

	M	Inns	NO	Runs	HS	Avge	100s	50s	Ct	St	Balls	Runs	Wkts	Avge	Best	5wI	10wM
Test	44	68	5	934	88	14.82	-	4	14	-	9838	4700	140	33.57	7-70	4	-
All First	355	506	47	10535	123 *	22.95	10	53	126	-	69335	33339	1205	27.66	7-21	61	6
1-day Int	103	66	23	690	67	16.04	-	1	26	-	5712	3775	115	32.82	4-35	-	
C & G	48	32	4	526	69	18.78	-	1	9	-	2877	1479	62	23.85	5-13	4	
NCL	227	178	29	2903	90	19.48	-	8	43	-	9359	6738	245	27.50	5-26	2	
Twenty20	6	6	0	49	18	8.16	-	-	-	-	102	148	6	24.66	3-39	-	

DENLY, J. L.   Kent

Name: Joseph (Joe) Liam Denly
Role: Right-hand bat, leg-spin bowler
Born: 16 March 1986, Canterbury
Height: 6ft **Weight:** 11st 8lbs
Nickname: Denners
County debut: No first-team appearance
Parents: Jayne and Nick
Marital status: Single
Education: Chaucer Technology School
Qualifications: 10 GCSEs
Off-season: 'Going to Australia to train for eight weeks'
Overseas tours: ECB U18 to Holland 2003
Overseas teams played for: Hammersley Carine, Perth 2003
Career highlights to date: 'Scoring 164* for Kent 2nd XI v Sussex'
Cricket superstitions: 'Left pad on first'
Cricketers particularly admired: Sachin Tendulkar, Steve Waugh
Young players to look out for: Charlie Hemphrey
Other sports played: Football (Charlton Athletic U14, U15)
Other sports followed: Football (Arsenal)
Injuries: Broken arm
Favourite band: Big Brova
Relaxations: 'Sleeping'
Extras: Has represented England U17 and U18

DENNING, N. A.   Essex

Name: Nicholas (<u>Nick</u>) Alexander Denning
Role: Right-hand bat, right-arm
fast-medium bowler
Born: 3 October 1978, Ascot
Height: 5ft 11in **Weight:** 11st 7lbs
Nickname: Denzil, Nudger
County debut: 2003 (one-day)
Parents: John Philip and Jill Patricia
Marital status: Single
Family links with cricket: Father played and
brother played up to Berkshire U19
Education: Bradfield College, Berkshire;
Cheltenham and Gloucester College of
Higher Education
Qualifications: 9 GCSEs, 3 A-levels, degree
in Sports and Exercise Sciences, Sports
Massage Therapy, ECB Level 2 coaching
Career outside cricket: Fitness training

Overseas tours: Bradfield College to Barbados 1997; MCC YC to Cape Town 2000
Overseas teams played for: CBC Old Boys 2000-01
Career highlights to date: 'Signing for Essex and being capped by Berkshire'
Cricket moments to forget: 'Bagging a pair while on trial'
Cricket superstitions: 'Always turn the same direction when I reach my bowling
mark'
Cricketers particularly admired: Darren Gough, Mike Atherton, Allan Donald
Young players to look out for: James Morris (Berkshire)
Other sports played: 'Most sports but nothing too competitive'
Other sports followed: 'Follow most sports', football (Arsenal)
Relaxations: 'Relaxing with friends and family and going on holiday'
Extras: Played for Berkshire, including the C&G 2002, and the first and second
rounds of the C&G 2003, which were played in August and September 2002. Took
6-42 from 19.5 overs, including a spell of 6-4, v Cornwall at Wash Common in the
Minor Counties Championship 2002. Took wicket (Younis Khan) with his first ball for
Essex, v Pakistanis at Chelmsford in a 50-over match 2003. Released by Essex at the
end of the 2003 season
Opinions on cricket: 'Introduction of two-division cricket is good for the game as it
encourages competition throughout the whole of the season.'

2003 Season

	M	Inns	NO	Runs	HS	Avge	100s	50s	Ct	St	O	M	Runs	Wkts	Avge	Best	5wI	10wM
Test																		
All First																			
1-day Int																			
C & G																			
NCL	1	0	0	0	0	-	-	-	-	-	4	0	48	0	-	-	-	-
Twenty20																			

Career Performances

	M	Inns	NO	Runs	HS	Avge	100s	50s	Ct	St	Balls	Runs	Wkts	Avge	Best	5wI	10wM
Test																	
All First																		
1-day Int																		
C & G	3	1	1	1	1*	-	-	-	-	-	162	119	4	29.75	3-22	-	
NCL	1	0	0	0	0	-	-	-	-	-	24	48	0	-	-	-	
Twenty20																	

DENNINGTON, M. J.   Kent

Name: Matthew (Matt) John Dennington
Role: Right-hand bat, right-arm medium-fast bowler
Born: 16 October 1982, Durban, South Africa
Height: 6ft 1in **Weight:** 12st 10lbs
Nickname: Denners
County debut: 2003 (one-day)
Parents: John and Yvonne
Marital status: Single
Education: Northwood Boys, Durban; Varsity College and University of South Africa (UNISA)
Qualifications: 'Matric; currently studying for degree in marketing'
Career outside cricket: Student
Off-season: 'Playing cricket in Durban, South Africa'
Overseas teams played for: Crusaders CC, Durban 1998-2002; KwaZulu-Natal B 2002-03
Career highlights to date: 'Making my debut for Kent 1st XI 2003'
Cricket moments to forget: 'Colliding with team-mate going for a catch on the boundary and breaking my kneecap'

Cricket superstitions: 'Not a superstitious cricketer'
Cricketers particularly admired: Paddy Clift, Allan Donald
Young players to look out for: James Tredwell, Michael Carberry, Chad Keegan
Other sports played: Rugby, golf
Other sports followed: Rugby (Natal Sharks)
Injuries: Out for two to three weeks with a broken finger
Favourite band: Red Hot Chili Peppers
Relaxations: 'Going to gym; surfing and other watersports; playing golf'
Extras: Natal Schools 1999-2000. Natal Academy 2001-02. Natal B 2002. Played for Kent Board XI in the C&G 2003. Took 4-28 v Kent at Chelmsford in the Twenty20 2003, winning Man of the Match award
Opinions on cricket: 'The game is quicker in modern times – bowlers are bowling faster, batsmen are hitting the ball further. Twenty20 has exploited this. It has brought crowds in because of its exciting nature.'

2003 Season

	M	Inns	NO	Runs	HS	Avge	100s	50s	Ct	St	O	M	Runs	Wkts	Avge	Best	5wI	10wM
Test																		
All First																		
1-day Int																		
C & G	1	1	0	1	1	1.00	-	-	-	-	8	2	51	1	51.00	1-51	-	
NCL	2	2	2	28	18 *	-	-	-	-	-	8	0	51	0	-	-	-	
Twenty20	4	2	0	16	12	8.00	-	-	-	-	15	0	120	8	15.00	4-28	-	

Career Performances

	M	Inns	NO	Runs	HS	Avge	100s	50s	Ct	St	Balls	Runs	Wkts	Avge	Best	5wI	10wM
Test																	
All First																	
1-day Int																	
C & G	1	1	0	1	1	1.00	-	-	-	-	48	51	1	51.00	1-51	-	
NCL	2	2	2	28	18 *	-	-	-	-	-	48	51	0	-	-	-	
Twenty20	4	2	0	16	12	8.00	-	-	-	-	90	120	8	15.00	4-28	-	

29. Which West Indies spinner, grandfather of Lancashire's Kyle Hogg, took 26 wickets in the 1950 four-Test series in England?

DERNBACH, J.   Surrey

Name: Jade Dernbach
Role: Right-hand bat, right-arm fast bowler
Born: 3 March 1986, South Africa
Height: 6ft 2in **Weight:** 13st
County debut: 2003
Strike rate: 78.00 (career 78.00)
Parents: Carmen and Graeme
Marital status: Single
Education: St John the Baptist
Overseas tours: La Manga tournament,
Spain 2003
Career highlights to date: 'Making my first-
team debut for Surrey against India A'
Cricket moments to forget: 'Going out first
ball in the ECB U17 final in 2003'
Cricketers particularly admired:
Jacques Kallis, Jonty Rhodes, James
Anderson, Rikki Clarke
Other sports played: Rugby (Surrey U16)
Other sports followed: Football (Arsenal)
Favourite band: Usher
Relaxations: 'Going out with friends; swimming, playing football and rugby; listening
to music'
Extras: Sir Jack Hobbs Fair Play Award. Surrey U19 Player of the Year. Made first-
class debut v India A at The Oval 2003 aged 17, becoming the youngest player for 30
years to play first-class cricket for Surrey. Surrey Academy 2003, 2004
Best batting: 3 Surrey v India A, The Oval 2003
Best bowling: 1-74 Surrey v India A, The Oval 2003

2003 Season

	M	Inns	NO	Runs	HS	Avge	100s	50s	Ct	St	O	M	Runs	Wkts	Avge	Best	5wI	10wM
Test																		
All First	1	1	0	3	3	3.00	-	-	-	-	13	3	74	1	74.00	1-74	-	-
1-day Int																		
C & G																			
NCL																			
Twenty20																			

Career Performances

	M	Inns	NO	Runs	HS	Avge	100s	50s	Ct	St	Balls	Runs	Wkts	Avge	Best	5wI	10wM
Test																	
All First	1	1	0	3	3	3.00	-	-	-	-	78	74	1	74.00	1-74	-	-
1-day Int																	
C & G																		
NCL																		
Twenty20																		

DIVENUTO, M. J.   Derbyshire

Name: <u>Michael</u> James DiVenuto
Role: Left-hand bat, right-arm medium/
leg-break bowler, county captain
Born: 12 December 1973, Hobart, Tasmania
Height: 5ft 11in **Weight:** 12st 12lbs
Nickname: Diva
County debut: 1999 (Sussex),
2000 (Derbyshire)
County cap: 1999 (Sussex),
2000 (Derbyshire)
One-Day Internationals: 9
1000 runs in a season: 4
1st-Class 50s: 79
1st-Class 100s: 26
1st-Class 200s: 1
1st-Class catches: 196
One-Day 100s: 5
Place in batting averages: 32nd av. 49.03
(2002 15th av. 61.52)
Strike rate: (career 153.00)
Parents: Enrico and Elizabeth
Wife and date of marriage: Renae, 31 December 2003
Family links with cricket: 'Dad and older brother Peter both played grade cricket in Tasmania.' Brother Peter also plays for Italy
Education: St Virgil's College, Hobart
Qualifications: HSC (5 x Level III subjects), Level 3 cricket coach
Career outside cricket: Part-time sports journalist with Southern Cross TV, Hobart
Off-season: Playing for Tasmania
Overseas tours: Australian Cricket Academy to India and Sri Lanka 1993, to South Africa 1996; Australia A to Malaysia (Super 8s) 1997 (captain), to Scotland and Ireland 1998 (captain), to Los Angeles 1999; Australia to South Africa 1996-97

(one-day series), to Hong Kong (Super 6s) 1997, to Malaysia (Super 8s) 1998; Tasmania to Zimbabwe 1995-96

Overseas teams played for: North Hobart CC, Tasmania; Kingborough, Tasmania; Tasmania 1991-92 –

Career highlights to date: 'Playing for Australia. Man of the Match award v South Africa at Johannesburg 1997. Dismissing Jamie Cox at Taunton in 1999, my first wicket in first-class cricket'

Cricket moments to forget: 'Being dismissed by Jamie Cox at Taunton in 1999, *his* first wicket in first-class cricket'

Cricketers particularly admired: David Boon, Dean Jones, Kepler Wessels, Mark and Steve Waugh

Young players to look out for: 'My nephew Jack DiVenuto'

Other sports played: Australian Rules (Tasmanian U15, U16 and Sandy Bay FC)

Other sports followed: Australian Rules football (Geelong Cats)

Injuries: Out for three one-day games with a hip flexor strain

Favourite band: U2

Relaxations: Golf, sleeping and eating

Extras: Man of the Match for his 89 in fifth ODI v South Africa at Johannesburg 1997. Scored then career-best 189 v Western Australia in 1997-98 Sheffield Shield final, contributing more than 50 per cent of Tasmania's total in their second innings. Joined Sussex as overseas player for 1999. Joined Derbyshire as overseas player for 2000. Scored 173* v Derbyshire Board XI at Derby in NatWest 2000, a record for Derbyshire in one-day cricket. Took five slip catches in an innings v Durham at Riverside 2001, later scoring 111 in victory chase. Scored maiden first-class double hundred (230) v Northamptonshire at Derby 2002, in the process setting a new record for the highest individual innings for Derbyshire v Northamptonshire. Carried his bat for 192* v Middlesex at Lord's 2002; also scored 113 in the second innings. Derbyshire Player of the Year 2002 (jointly with Kevin Dean). First batsman to 1000 Championship runs 2003. Vice-captain of Derbyshire 2002-03. Appointed captain of Derbyshire for 2004

Opinions on cricket: 'The game is in good shape and moving forward as it should be. Twenty20 cricket has been a breath of fresh air. Big crowds, great atmospheres and some brilliant cricket have been a winner with the players and supporters.'

Best batting: 230 Derbyshire v Northamptonshire, Derby 2002

Best bowling: 1-0 Tasmania v Queensland, Brisbane 1999-2000

2003 Season

	M	Inns	NO	Runs	HS	Avge	100s	50s	Ct	St	O	M	Runs	Wkts	Avge	Best	5wI	10wM
Test																		
All First	16	31	0	1520	150	49.03	5	8	25	-	6	0	23	0	-	-	-	-
1-day Int																		
C & G	3	3	0	76	51	25.33	-	1	2	-								
NCL	15	14	0	655	130	46.78	3	3	5	-								
Twenty20	5	5	2	198	67	66.00	-	2	-	-	13	0	88	5	17.60	3-19	-	

Career Performances

	M	Inns	NO	Runs	HS	Avge	100s	50s	Ct	St	Balls	Runs	Wkts	Avge	Best	5wl	10wM
Test																	
All First	180	316	15	12682	230	42.13	27	79	196	-	765	430	5	86.00	1-0	-	-
1-day Int	9	9	0	241	89	26.77	-	2	1	-							
C & G	9	9	1	434	173 *	54.25	1	3	6	-							
NCL	70	69	4	2290	130	35.23	3	14	20	-	30	30	0	-		-	-
Twenty20	5	5	2	198	67	66.00	-	2	-	-	78	88	5	17.60	3-19	-	

DRAKES, V. C. Leicestershire

Name: <u>Vasbert</u> Conniel Drakes
Role: Right-hand bat, right-arm fast bowler
Born: 5 August 1969, St Michael's, Barbados
Height: 6ft 2in **Weight:** 12st
County debut: 1996 (Sussex),
1999 (Nottinghamshire), 2001
(Warwickshire), 2003 (Leicestershire)
County cap: 1996 (Sussex),
1999 (Nottinghamshire), 2001
(Warwickshire)
Test debut: 2002-03
Tests: 7
One-Day Internationals: 30
50 wickets in a season: 1
1st-Class 50s: 16
1st-Class 100s: 4
1st-Class 5 w. innings: 27
1st-Class 10 w. in match: 3
1st-Class catches: 52
One-Day 5 w. in innings: 4
Place in batting averages: 276th av. 9.50
Place in bowling averages: 123rd av. 42.09
Strike rate: 78.09 (career 50.65)
Parents: Leon and Caroline
Education: St Lucy Secondary and College School, Barbados
Qualifications: NCA coach
Career outside cricket: Electrician
Overseas tours: Barbados U19 to UK 1987; Barbados U21 to UK 1990; Barbados to South Africa 1993-94, to Malaysia (Commonwealth Games) 1998-99; West Indies to England 1995, to Sri Lanka (ICC Champions Trophy) 2002-03, to India 2002-03 (one-day series), to Bangladesh 2002-03, to Africa (World Cup) 2002-03, to Zimbabwe 2003-04, to South Africa 2003-04

Overseas teams played for: Barbados 1991-92 – 1995-96, 2002-03 –; Border, South Africa 1996-97 – 2002-03
Cricketers particularly admired: Desmond Haynes, Malcolm Marshall
Other sports followed: Tennis, golf, basketball, football (Arsenal) and volleyball
Relaxations: Listening to music
Extras: Once took 9-2 for Lamhey CC. Was Sussex overseas player in 1996 and 1997. Took 56 wickets for Border 1998-99, two short of the South African record shared by Peter Pollock and Sylvester Clarke. Was Nottinghamshire's overseas player in 1999. Took nine wickets on Championship debut for Nottinghamshire, v Worcestershire at Trent Bridge 1999. Took four wickets in four balls for Nottinghamshire in the final over of their National League victory v Derbyshire at Trent Bridge 1999; Derbyshire started the over needing ten runs with five wickets in hand. Took 60 first-class wickets (av. 16.31) for Border in the SuperSport Series 1999-2000 to set a new competition record and become Man of the Series. One of *South African Cricket Annual*'s five Cricketers of the Year 2000. Was Warwickshire's overseas player in 2001; awarded Warwickshire cap 2001, becoming the first overseas player to be capped by three counties. Took 5-33 v Kenya at Kimberley in the World Cup 2002-03, winning Man of the Match award. Struck winning runs as West Indies successfully chased 418 to win v Australia in the fourth Test in Antigua 2002-03. Man of the [ODI] Series in Bangladesh 2002-03. Joined Leicestershire for the latter part of the 2003 season as a replacement for the injured Virender Sehwag, becoming the first overseas player to play for four counties
Best batting: 180* Barbados v Leeward Islands, The Valley 1994-95
Best bowling: 8-59 Border v KwaZulu-Natal, Durban 1996-97

2003 Season

	M	Inns	NO	Runs	HS	Avge	100s	50s	Ct	St	O	M	Runs	Wkts	Avge	Best	5wI	10wM
Test																		
All First	5	7	1	57	18	9.50	-	-	1	-	143.1	33	463	11	42.09	3-58	-	-
1-day Int																		
C & G																		
NCL	7	6	2	74	43*	18.50	-	-	2	-	52	3	244	4	61.00	1-22	-	
Twenty20																		

Career Performances

	M	Inns	NO	Runs	HS	Avge	100s	50s	Ct	St	Balls	Runs	Wkts	Avge	Best	5wI	10wM
Test	7	11	2	194	30	21.55	-	-	1	-	1405	751	23	32.65	5-93	1	-
All First	156	243	29	4486	180*	20.96	4	16	52	-	29936	15291	591	25.87	8-59	27	3
1-day Int	30	14	5	82	25	9.11	-	-	5	-	1454	1158	47	24.63	5-33	2	
C & G	12	6	1	118	35	23.60	-	-	1	-	732	442	21	21.04	4-62	-	
NCL	53	42	10	532	43*	16.62	-	-	9	-	2374	1896	61	31.08	5-31	1	
Twenty20																		

DUMELOW, N. R. C.   Derbyshire

Name: <u>Nathan</u> Robert Charles Dumelow
Role: Right-hand bat, right-arm
off-spin bowler
Born: 30 April 1981, Derby
Height: 5ft 10in **Weight:** 12st 2lbs
Nickname: Pig
County debut: 2001
1st-Class 50s: 6
1st-Class 5 w. in innings: 2
1st-Class 10 w. in match: 1
1st-Class catches: 5
Place in batting averages: 186th av. 24.78
Place in bowling averages: 129th av. 43.11
Strike rate: 71.61 (career 80.75)
Parents: Kate and Robert
Marital status: Single
Family links with cricket: 'Dad plays for
Derbyshire Over 50s'
Education: Denstone College

Qualifications: 7 GCSEs
Career outside cricket: Farmer
Overseas tours: Derbyshire U16 to Barbados; Derbyshire U17 to South Africa
Overseas teams played for: Schoeman Park CC, Bloemfontein 2000-01
Career highlights to date: 'Taking four wickets against Pakistan [2001]'
Cricket moments to forget: 'Day/night game v Worcestershire' (*Took 2-59 from five
overs as Worcs posted 288-6 and beat Derbys by 138 runs at Derby in the NUL 2001*)
Cricketers particularly admired: Viv Richards
Young players to look out for: Chris Bassano, Tom Lungley
Other sports played: Golf, snooker
Other sports followed: Football (Derby County FC)
Relaxations: Fishing, shooting
Extras: Won all Derbyshire age-group awards. Played for Derbyshire Board XI in the
NatWest 1999 and 2000. Took 4-81 on first-class debut v Pakistanis at Derby 2001,
including the wickets of Yousuf Youhana, Inzamam-ul-Haq and Abdul Razzaq. Scored
50* on Championship debut v Hampshire at Derby 2001. Derbyshire's Most Improved
Player 2001. Won eight awards while playing club cricket in Tasmania 2001-02,
including those for best batting and bowling averages and for fair play. Recorded
maiden first-class five-wicket return (5-82) v Northamptonshire at Northampton 2003
and took 5-78 in the second innings for a maiden ten-wicket match
Best batting: 75 Derbyshire v Hampshire, West End 2003
Best bowling: 5-78 Derbyshire v Northamptonshire, Northampton 2003

2003 Season

	M	Inns	NO	Runs	HS	Avge	100s	50s	Ct	St	O	M	Runs	Wkts	Avge	Best	5wI	10wM
Test																		
All First	10	17	3	347	75	24.78	-	3	2	-	214.5	43	776	18	43.11	5-78	2	1
1-day Int																		
C & G	2	2	0	25	15	12.50	-	-	-	-	10	0	47	0	-		-	-
NCL	13	11	3	86	28 *	10.75	-	-	-	-	95.2	3	486	15	32.40	3-26	-	
Twenty20	5	4	0	17	12	4.25	-	-	-	-	8.5	0	69	7	9.85	3-8	-	

Career Performances

	M	Inns	NO	Runs	HS	Avge	100s	50s	Ct	St	Balls	Runs	Wkts	Avge	Best	5wI	10wM
Test																	
All First	21	35	4	731	75	23.58	-	6	5	-	2584	1644	32	51.37	5-78	2	1
1-day Int																	
C & G	5	5	0	81	32	16.20	-	-	-	-	192	137	2	68.50	2-21	-	
NCL	28	25	5	356	52	17.80	-	1	1	-	1134	960	31	30.96	3-24	-	
Twenty20	5	4	0	17	12	4.25	-	-	-	-	53	69	7	9.85	3-8	-	

DURSTON, W. J. Somerset

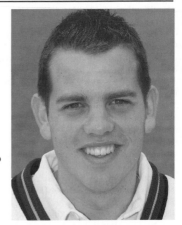

Name: Wesley (<u>Wes</u>) John Durston
Role: Right-hand bat, right-arm off-spin
bowler; all-rounder
Born: 6 October 1980, Taunton
Height: 5ft 10in **Weight:** 12st
Nickname: Fred, Ace
County debut: 2002
1st-Class 50s: 1
1st-Class catches: 5
Strike rate: 80.00 (career 81.00)
Parents: Gillian and Steven
Wife: Christina
Family links with cricket: 'Dad and my two
brothers, Dan and Greg, all play. On
occasions all four played in same local team
(Compton Dundon)'
Education: Millfield School; University
College, Worcester
Qualifications: 10 GCSEs, 2 A-levels, BSc Sports Studies, ECB Level 1
cricket coaching
Career outside cricket: Coaching
Overseas tours: West of England to West Indies 1996

Career highlights to date: 'Three centuries (106, 162*, 126) in three days at Tonbridge Festival for Millfield School 1999. First-class debut v West Indies A 2002, scoring 26 and 55, and the match tied chasing 453 to win'

Cricket moments to forget: 'Scoring 0 v Kent, being lbw and breaking left big toe in NUL 2002'

Cricket superstitions: 'Right foot on and off field first. Placing my right inner glove in my pocket while I bat'

Cricketers particularly admired: Brian Lara, Graham Gooch, Muttiah Muralitharan

Young players to look out for: James Hildreth, Richard Timms, Judd Doughty, Tom Goodey

Other sports played: Hockey (Shrewsbury HC and Shropshire; also West of England U21), golf ('occasionally')

Other sports followed: Football 'passionately' (Man Utd), 'any sport that's on TV'

Relaxations: 'Spending time with wife; computers (Internet); watching sport'

Extras: Captained winning Lord's Taverners team v Shrewsbury School at Trent Bridge 1996. Wetherell Schools All-rounder Award 1999; scored 956 runs and took 35 wickets. Played for Somerset Board XI in the NatWest 2000 and in the first round of the C&G 2003, which was played in August 2002. Captained Somerset 2nd XI on occasion in 2002. Scored 44-ball 55 on first-class debut at Taunton 2002 as Somerset, chasing 454 to win, tied with West Indies A

Opinions on cricket: 'As there is so much one-day cricket in the county game, more attention should be given to this in the 2nd XI. The AON Trophy does not provide enough practice of this format for cricketers in the 2nd XI. And this should be where new structures are trialled, such as the new 20-over format.'

Best batting: 55 Somerset v West Indies A, Taunton 2002
Best bowling: 1-16 Somerset v Durham, Riverside 2003

2003 Season

	M	Inns	NO	Runs	HS	Avge	100s	50s	Ct	St	O	M	Runs	Wkts	Avge	Best	5wI	10wM
Test																		
All First	2	4	1	48	30 *	16.00	-	-	4	-	40	8	125	3	41.66	1-16	-	-
1-day Int																		
C & G																		
NCL	7	6	2	145	51 *	36.25	-	1	1	-	13	0	73	0	-		-	-
Twenty20	5	4	0	85	34	21.25	-	-	1	-	6	0	65	3	21.66	3-31	-	

Career Performances

	M	Inns	NO	Runs	HS	Avge	100s	50s	Ct	St	Balls	Runs	Wkts	Avge	Best	5wI	10wM
Test																	
All First	3	6	1	129	55	25.80	-	1	5	-	324	190	4	47.50	1-16	-	-
1-day Int																	
C & G	2	2	0	75	50	37.50	-	1	-	-	84	75	2	37.50	1-32	-	
NCL	9	8	2	145	51 *	24.16	-	1	1	-	90	92	0	-		-	-
Twenty20	5	4	0	85	34	21.25	-	-	1	-	36	65	3	21.66	3-31	-	

DUTCH, K. P.   Somerset

Name: <u>Keith</u> Philip Dutch
Role: Right-hand bat, off-spin bowler
Born: 21 March 1973, Harrow, Middlesex
Height: 5ft 9in **Weight:** 11st 4lbs
Nickname: Dutchy, Oik
County debut: 1993 (Middlesex),
2001 (Somerset)
County cap: 2001 (Somerset)
1st-Class 50s: 9
1st-Class 100s: 1
1st-Class 5 w. in innings: 1
1st-Class catches: 70
One-Day 5 w. in innings: 2
Place in batting averages: 244th av. 16.10
(2002 240th av. 18.00)
Place in bowling averages: (2002 153rd
av. 56.80)
Strike rate: 94.62 (career 73.21)
Parents: Alan and Ann

Wife and date of marriage: Emma, 11 November 2000
Children: Lauren Beth Amy, 15 January 1999
Family links with cricket: Father coached
Education: Nower Hill High School, Pinner; Weald College, Harrow
Qualifications: 5 GCSEs, 1 AS-level, staff tutor coach
Off-season: Coaching
Overseas tours: MCC to Central and East Africa 1997, to Canada 2000-01
Overseas teams played for: Worcester United, South Africa 1992-93; Geelong City, Australia, 1994; Rygersdal CC, Cape Town 1997-98
Career highlights to date: 'Man of the Match award in C&G semi-final and winning C&G final 2001'
Cricketers particularly admired: Mark Ramprakash, John Emburey
Young players to look out for: Owais Shah, David Nash, Stephen Peters, Ed Joyce
Other sports followed: Football (Arsenal FC)
Relaxations: Music, TV and shopping for clothes
Extras: Middlesex 2nd XI Player of the Year 1995. In 1996 scored over 1,000 2nd XI Championship runs and took 63 wickets, setting in the process a record for the highest-ever batting total (261 v Somerset) and best bowling figures (15 for 157 v Leicestershire) by a Middlesex player in the history of the 2nd XI Championship. 2nd XI Championship Player of the Year in 1993, 1996 and 1999. Took five catches in Cambridge University's first innings at Fenner's 2000. Scored 91 and took 6-62 (both then career bests) in a single day v Essex at Chelmsford 2000. Released by Middlesex

at the end of the 2000 season and joined Somerset for 2001. C&G Man of the Match award for his 54-ball 61 in the semi-final v Warwickshire at Taunton 2001
Best batting: 118 Somerset v Essex, Taunton 2001
Best bowling: 6-62 Middlesex v Essex, Chelmsford 2000

2003 Season

	M	Inns	NO	Runs	HS	Avge	100s	50s	Ct	St	O	M	Runs	Wkts	Avge	Best	5wl	10wM
Test																		
All First	7	10	0	161	61	16.10	-	1	9	-	126.1	25	428	8	53.50	3-56	-	-
1-day Int																		
C & G	2	1	0	14	14	14.00	-	-	1	-								
NCL	18	16	0	392	65	24.50	-	2	7	-	90	0	542	13	41.69	4-34	-	
Twenty20	5	5	1	133	70	33.25	-	1	1	-	10	0	83	3	27.66	2-14	-	

Career Performances

	M	Inns	NO	Runs	HS	Avge	100s	50s	Ct	St	Balls	Runs	Wkts	Avge	Best	5wl	10wM
Test																	
All First	66	94	9	1620	118	19.05	1	9	70	-	7029	3739	96	38.94	6-62	1	-
1-day Int																	
C & G	21	16	8	282	61 *	35.25	-	1	16	-	816	568	16	35.50	3-26	-	
NCL	110	96	20	1456	65	19.15	-	5	40	-	3737	3032	109	27.81	6-40	2	
Twenty20	5	5	1	133	70	33.25	-	1	1	-	60	83	3	27.66	2-14	-	

EALHAM, M. A.   Nottinghamshire

Name: <u>Mark</u> Alan Ealham
Role: Right-hand bat, right-arm medium bowler; all-rounder
Born: 27 August 1969, Ashford, Kent
Height: 5ft 10in **Weight:** 14st
Nickname: Ealy, Border, Skater
County debut: 1989 (Kent)
County cap: 1992 (Kent)
Benefit: 2003 (Kent)
Test debut: 1996
Tests: 8
One-Day Internationals: 64
1000 runs in a season: 1
1st-Class 50s: 52
1st-Class 100s: 7
1st-Class 5 w. in innings: 19
1st-Class 10 w. in match: 1
1st-Class catches: 96

One-Day 100s: 1
One-Day 5 w. in innings: 4
Place in batting averages: 98th av. 36.44 (2002 109th av. 34.94)
Place in bowling averages: 40th av. 26.65 (2002 98th av. 34.07)
Strike rate: 56.50 (career 60.18)
Parents: Alan and Sue
Wife and date of marriage: Kirsty, 24 February 1996
Children: George, 8 March 2002
Family links with cricket: Father played for Kent
Education: Stour Valley Secondary School
Qualifications: 9 CSEs
Career outside cricket: Plumber
Overseas tours: England A to Australia 1996-97, to Kenya and Sri Lanka 1997-98;
England VI to Hong Kong 1997, 2001; England to Sharjah (Champions Trophy)
1997-98, to Bangladesh (Wills International Cup) 1998-99, to Australia 1998-99
(CUB Series), to Sharjah (Coca-Cola Cup) 1998-99, to South Africa and Zimbabwe
1999-2000 (one-day series), to Kenya (ICC Knockout Trophy) 2000-01, to Pakistan
and Sri Lanka 2000-01 (one-day series)
Overseas teams played for: South Perth, Australia 1992-93; University, Perth
1993-94
Cricketers particularly admired: Ian Botham, Viv Richards, Robin Smith,
Steve Waugh, Paul Blackmore and Albert 'for his F and G'
Other sports followed: Football (Manchester United), 'and most other sports'
Relaxations: Playing golf and snooker, watching films
Extras: Set then record for fastest Sunday League century (44 balls), v Derbyshire at
Maidstone 1995. Represented England in the 1999 World Cup. Returned a new
England best ODI bowling analysis with his 5-15 v Zimbabwe at Kimberley in
January 2000; all five were lbw. Vice-captain of Kent 2001. Scored 83* v Sussex at
Tunbridge Wells 2002, in the process sharing with Ben Trott (26) in a ground record
tenth-wicket partnership for Kent (77). Left Kent at the end of the 2003 season and has
joined Nottinghamshire for 2004
Opinions on cricket: 'Two-divisional cricket is a success, but only two teams from
each division to go up and down.'
Best batting: 153* Kent v Northamptonshire, Canterbury 2001
Best bowling: 8-36 Kent v Warwickshire, Edgbaston 1996

2003 Season

	M	Inns	NO	Runs	HS	Avge	100s	50s	Ct	St	O	M	Runs	Wkts	Avge	Best	5wl	10wM
Test																		
All First	17	25	0	911	101	36.44	1	7	18	-	357.5	106	1013	38	26.65	6-35	3	-
1-day Int																		
C & G	2	1	0	15	15	15.00	-	-	1	-	16	4	29	2	14.50	1-12	-	
NCL	16	14	1	301	73	23.15	-	2	5	-	115.3	7	505	13	38.84	4-19	-	
Twenty20	5	5	0	69	22	13.80	-	-	-	-	17.4	0	116	5	23.20	2-31	-	

Career Performances

	M	Inns	NO	Runs	HS	Avge	100s	50s	Ct	St	Balls	Runs	Wkts	Avge	Best	5wI	10wM
Test	8	13	3	210	53 *	21.00	-	2	4	-	1060	488	17	28.70	4-21	-	-
All First	192	304	47	8141	153 *	31.67	7	52	96	-	25577	12133	425	28.54	8-36	19	1
1-day Int	64	45	4	716	45	17.46	-	-	9	-	3222	2193	67	32.73	5-15	2	
C & G	30	26	7	554	58 *	29.15	-	2	8	-	1601	819	36	22.75	4-10	-	
NCL	180	152	37	2926	112	25.44	1	13	48	-	7263	5350	180	29.72	6-53	2	
Twenty20	5	5	0	69	22	13.80	-	-	-	-	106	116	5	23.20	2-31	-	

EDWARDS, N. J. Somerset

Name: Neil James Edwards
Role: Left-hand bat, occasional right-arm medium bowler
Born: 14 October 1983, Truro, Cornwall
Height: 6ft 3in **Weight:** 14st
Nickname: Toastie, Shanksy
County debut: 2002
1st-Class 50s: 1
1st-Class 100s: 1
1st-Class catches: 2
Place in batting averages: 75th av. 40.00
Parents: Lynn and John
Marital status: Single
Family links with cricket: 'Cousin played first-class cricket for Worcestershire'
Education: Cape Cornwall School; Richard Huish College
Qualifications: 11 GCSEs, 3 A-levels, Level 1 coach
Off-season: 'Training hard'
Overseas tours: Cornwall U13 to South Africa 1997; West of England to West Indies 1999; Somerset Academy to Australia 2002; England U19 to Australia 2002-03
Career highlights to date: '160 for Somerset v Hampshire in County Championship 2003'
Cricket moments to forget: 'Duck on debut for Cornwall'
Cricket superstitions: 'Never change batting gloves when batting'
Cricketers particularly admired: Marcus Trescothick, Matthew Hayden
Young players to look out for: Ryan Edwards, Tom Edwards, Kerry Matthew, Nicole Richards
Other sports played: Football
Other sports followed: Football (Stoke City FC)

Favourite band: 'I listen to any music'
Relaxations: 'Spending time at home in Cornwall with girlfriend, family and friends; playing on my Xbox'
Extras: Scored 213 for Cornwall U19 v Dorset U19 at 16 years old. Scored a second innings 97 in England U19's victory over Australia U19 in the first 'Test' at Adelaide 2002-03. Represented England U19 v South Africa U19 2003. Somerset Wyverns Award for Best Performance by an Uncapped Player 2003 (160 v Hampshire)
Opinions on cricket: 'More one-day cricket with the use of floodlights. Twenty20 introduced into 2nd XI cricket, as well as more one-day cricket.'
Best batting: 160 Somerset v Hampshire, Taunton 2003

2003 Season

	M	Inns	NO	Runs	HS	Avge	100s	50s	Ct	St	O	M	Runs	Wkts	Avge	Best	5wl	10wM
Test																		
All First	5	9	0	360	160	40.00	1	1	1	-	18.5	1	71	0	-	-	-	-
1-day Int																		
C & G																		
NCL																		
Twenty20	1	1	0	1	1	1.00	-	-	-	-								

Career Performances

	M	Inns	NO	Runs	HS	Avge	100s	50s	Ct	St	Balls	Runs	Wkts	Avge	Best	5wl	10wM
Test																	
All First	6	11	0	418	160	38.00	1	1	2	-	113	71	0	-	-	-	-
1-day Int																	
C & G																	
NCL																	
Twenty20	1	1	0	1	1	1.00	-	-	-	-							

ELWORTHY, S.   Nottinghamshire

Name: Steven Elworthy
Role: Right-hand bat, right-arm fast-medium bowler
Born: 23 February 1965, Bulawayo, Zimbabwe
Height: 6ft 4in   **Weight:** 13st 9lbs
County debut: 1996 (Lancashire), 2003 (Nottinghamshire)
County cap: 2003 (Nottinghamshire)
Test debut: 1998
Tests: 4
One-Day Internationals: 39
1st-Class 50s: 9
1st-Class 5 w. in innings: 18
1st-Class 10 w. in match: 4

1st-Class catches: 48
Place in batting averages: 206th av. 22.37
Place in bowling averages: 66th av. 31.35
Strike rate: 48.05 (career 52.03)
Education: Chaplin HS/Sandown HS; Wits University, South Africa
Qualifications: Degree in Electrical Engineering
Overseas tours: South Africa A to Zimbabwe 1994-95, (one-day series) 2002-03; Lancashire to Jamaica 1995-96; South Africa to England 1998, to Malaysia (Commonwealth Games) 1998-99, to Bangladesh (Wills International Cup) 1998-99, to New Zealand 1998-99, to UK, Ireland and Holland (World Cup) 1999, to Kenya (LG Cup) 1999-2000, to India 1999-2000 (one-day series), to Sharjah (Coca-Cola Sharjah Cup) 1999-2000, to Australia 2001-02

Overseas teams played for: Transvaal 1987-88; Northern Transvaal/Northerns 1988-89 – 2002-03
Extras: Represented Zimbabwe at cricket, tennis, swimming, rugby, football at junior level before leaving to complete his education in South Africa. Made first-class debut for Transvaal B v Natal B, Johannesburg 1987-88. Northern Transvaal Player of the Year 1993-94 and 1994-95. Was Lancashire's overseas player in 1996. Took 4-66 and 4-93 in the third Test v New Zealand at Wellington 1998-99, winning Man of the Match award. Took 3-17 from 10 overs v India in the Coca-Cola Cup in Sharjah 1999-2000, winning Man of the Match award. Leading wicket-taker in SuperSport Series 2001-02 with 52 (av. 18.11) and one of *South African Cricket Annual*'s five Cricketers of the Year 2002. Northerns all-time leading wicket-taker in first-class cricket. Was an overseas player with Nottinghamshire April to May 2003, deputising for Stuart MacGill and Chris Cairns, absent on international duty; awarded Nottinghamshire cap 2003
Best batting: 89 Northerns v Boland, Centurion 1997-98
Best bowling: 7-65 Northern Transvaal v Natal, Durban 1994-95

2003 Season

	M	Inns	NO	Runs	HS	Avge	100s	50s	Ct	St	O	M	Runs	Wkts	Avge	Best	5wI	10wM
Test																		
All First	5	8	0	179	52	22.37	-	1	3	-	160.1	22	627	20	31.35	5-71	1	-
1-day Int																		
C & G	1	0	0	0	0	-	-	-	-	-	10	0	42	1	42.00	1-42	-	
NCL	3	3	0	10	5	3.33	-	-	-	-	23.3	0	134	7	19.14	4-41	-	
Twenty20																		

Career Performances

	M	Inns	NO	Runs	HS	Avge	100s	50s	Ct	St	Balls	Runs	Wkts	Avge	Best	5wI	10wM
Test	4	5	1	72	48	18.00	-	-	1	-	867	444	13	34.15	4-66	-	-
All First	134	196	27	3439	89	20.34	-	9	48	-	25018	13296	476	27.93	7-65	18	4
1-day Int	39	16	8	100	23	12.50	-	-	9	-	1702	1235	44	28.06	3-17	-	
C & G	3	2	1	13	8	13.00	-	-	-	-	168	92	6	15.33	4-40	-	
NCL	17	12	2	69	15	6.90	-	-	4	-	705	611	18	33.94	4-41	-	
Twenty20																	

FARROW, J. C.   Worcestershire

Name: <u>Jonathan</u> Colin Farrow
Role: Right-hand bat, right-arm fast bowler
Born: 22 February 1984, Stockport
Nickname: Faz, Jonny
County debut: No first-team appearance
Parents: Colin and Susan
Marital status: Single
Family links with cricket: 'Dad plays for Cheshire Over-50s'
Education: Kingsway High, Stockport/Wilmslow High, Cheshire; University College, Worcester
Qualifications: 9 GCSEs, 3 A-levels
Off-season: 'At university'
Career highlights to date: 'Signing for Worcestershire'
Cricket superstitions: 'None'
Cricketers particularly admired: Glenn McGrath
Other sports played: Football, badminton
Other sports followed: Football (Manchester United)
Extras: Played for Cheshire in the first and second rounds of the C&G 2003, which were played in August and September 2002

30. Now Lancashire's cricket manager, which all-rounder took five wickets and scored 37 runs at his home ground on Test debut v West Indies in July 1995?

2003 Season (did not make any first-class or one-day appearances)

Career Performances

	M	Inns	NO	Runs	HS	Avge	100s	50s	Ct	St	Balls	Runs	Wkts	Avge	Best	5wI	10wM
Test																	
All First																	
1-day Int																	
C & G	2	0	0	0	0	-	-	-	-	-	90	109	2	54.50	2-81	-	
NCL																	
Twenty20																	

FELLOWS, G. M. *Yorkshire*

Name: <u>Gary</u> Matthew Fellows
Role: Right-hand bat, right-arm medium bowler
Born: 30 July 1978, Halifax
Height: 5ft 9in **Weight:** 11st 2lbs
Nickname: Mousey
County debut: 1998
1st-Class 50s: 6
1st-Class 100s: 1
1st-Class catches: 23
Place in batting averages: 233rd av. 17.75 (2002 160th av. 27.38)
Strike rate: 57.00 (career 74.78)
Parents: Eric and Tina
Marital status: Single
Family links with cricket: 'Dad played; brothers still do'
Education: North Halifax Grammar School, Illingworth, Halifax
Qualifications: 10 GCSEs, 1 A-level, Level 1 coaching award
Career outside cricket: Fitness training
Overseas teams played for: Bulawayo Athletic Club, Zimbabwe 1996-97
Career highlights to date: 'Winning the Championship and the C&G Trophy'
Cricket moments to forget: 'Relegation!'
Cricket superstitions: 'Left pad on first'
Cricketers particularly admired: Craig White, Mark Waugh
Other sports played: Football (on Bradford City books for one season)
Other sports followed: Football (Halifax Town)
Relaxations: Most sports 'and a laugh with the lads after the game'. Golf

Extras: Awarded Yorkshire 2nd XI cap 1998. C&G Man of the Match award for his 89-ball 80* v Surrey at Headingley 2001. Scored 50 and took 4-19 v Durham at Headingley in the NUL 2002. Scored 109 v Lancashire at Old Trafford 2002, becoming the seventh Yorkshire batsman to record his maiden first-class century in a Roses match. Scored 88 v Warwickshire at Edgbaston 2002, in the process sharing with Richard Blakey (103) in a new record sixth-wicket partnership for Yorkshire in matches v Warwickshire (175). Released by Yorkshire at the end of the 2003 season
Best batting: 109 Yorkshire v Lancashire, Old Trafford 2002
Best bowling: 3-23 Yorkshire v Essex, Chelmsford 2001

2003 Season

	M	Inns	NO	Runs	HS	Avge	100s	50s	Ct	St	O	M	Runs	Wkts	Avge	Best	5wI	10wM
Test																		
All First	6	8	0	142	53	17.75	-	1	1	-	19	2	48	2	24.00	1-20	-	-
1-day Int																		
C & G																		
NCL	3	3	1	9	5 *	4.50	-	-	3	-	8.5	0	51	0	-		-	-
Twenty20																		

Career Performances

	M	Inns	NO	Runs	HS	Avge	100s	50s	Ct	St	Balls	Runs	Wkts	Avge	Best	5wI	10wM
Test																	
All First	48	74	6	1592	109	23.41	1	6	23	-	2393	1228	32	38.37	3-23	-	-
1-day Int																	
C & G	12	8	3	230	80 *	46.00	-	2	3	-	72	55	0	-		-	-
NCL	62	52	8	893	67	20.29	-	4	21	-	619	589	13	45.30	4-19	-	
Twenty20																	

FERLEY, R. S.   Kent

Name: <u>Robert</u> Steven Ferley
Role: Right-hand bat, left-arm spin bowler
Born: 4 February 1982, Norwich
Height: 5ft 8in **Weight:** 12st 4lbs
Nickname: Mr Shaky Shake, Billy Bob, Bob Turkey
County debut: 2003
1st-Class 50s: 2
1st-Class catches: 7
Place in batting averages: 173rd av. 26.20
Place in bowling averages: 128th av. 43.00
Strike rate: 64.75 (career 68.61)
Parents: Pam and Tim (divorced)
Marital status: Single

Education: King Edward VII High School; Sutton Valence School (A-levels); Grey College, Durham University
Qualifications: 10 GCSEs, 3 A-levels
Overseas tours: England U19 to India 2000-01; British Universities to South Africa 2002
Career highlights to date: 'Dismissing Charles Clarke for a golden duck. Dismissing Charles Clarke to all parts of the boundary'
Cricketers particularly admired: Steve Waugh, Steve Marsh, Min Patel, Charles Clarke
Young players to look out for: James Tredwell
Other sports played: Rugby, hockey, tennis, football
Other sports followed: Football (Liverpool)
Relaxations: 'Films, interior design, keeping fit'

Extras: Represented England U17 at the ECC Colts Festival in Northern Ireland 1999. Took 4-32 (including 3-2 in nine balls) on his 19th birthday v India U19 in the second 'ODI' at Vijayawada 2000-01. Played for Durham University CCE 2001, 2002 and 2003. Represented British Universities 2001, 2002 and v Zimbabweans and India A 2003. Represented England U19 v West Indies U19 2001. Played for Kent Board XI in the C&G 2002, and in the second round of the C&G 2003, which was played in September 2002. Took 4-76 on Championship debut v Surrey at The Oval 2003
Best batting: 78* DUCCE v Durham, Durham 2003
Best bowling: 4-76 Kent v Surrey, The Oval 2003

2003 Season

	M	Inns	NO	Runs	HS	Avge	100s	50s	Ct	St	O	M	Runs	Wkts	Avge	Best	5wI	10wM
Test																		
All First	10	14	4	262	78 *	26.20	-	2	5	-	259	44	1032	24	43.00	4-76	-	-
1-day Int																		
C & G																			
NCL	1	0	0	0	0	-	-	-	-	-	9	0	59	3	19.66	3-59	-	
Twenty20																			

31. Which current batsman became the first teenager to represent West Indies since E.T. Willett in 1973 when he made his debut at his home ground, Georgetown, Guyana, in March 1994?

Career Performances

	M	Inns	NO	Runs	HS	Avge	100s	50s	Ct	St	Balls	Runs	Wkts	Avge	Best	5wI	10wM
Test																	
All First	18	24	7	399	78 *	23.47	-	2	7	-	2676	1672	39	42.87	4-76	-	-
1-day Int																	
C & G	2	1	0	6	6	6.00	-	-	-	-	82	43	3	14.33	2-30	-	
NCL	1	0	0	0	0	-	-	-	-	-	54	59	3	19.66	3-59	-	
Twenty20																	

FERRABY, N. J.   Leicestershire

Name: Nicholas (Nick) John Ferraby
Role: Right-hand bat, right-arm
medium bowler
Born: 31 May 1983, Market Harborough,
Leicestershire
Height: 6ft **Weight:** 11st 5lbs
Nickname: Furbs, Ferrers
County debut: No first-team appearance
Parents: Paul and Jill
Marital status: Single
Family links with cricket: 'My grandmother
played for Oxfordshire! Both my older
brothers, Robin and Alex, played at school
but didn't carry it on'
Education: Oakham School; Loughborough
University
Qualifications: 9 GCSEs, 2 A-levels, 'and a
2.1 in my degree hopefully!'
Overseas tours: Leicestershire U19 to Johannesburg 2000-01
Career highlights to date: 'Being signed by Leicestershire'
Cricket moments to forget: 'Any time I get out!'
Cricket superstitions: 'Don't believe in superstition'
Cricketers particularly admired: Michael Vaughan, Ricky Ponting
Young players to look for: Chris Benham
Other sports played: Hockey (England U16, U18 – 'gold medal in European
competition' – and U21; Loughborough Students – 'National Prem'); 'like most sports
but play just recreationally'
Other sports followed: Rugby (Leicester Tigers), ice hockey (Nottingham Panthers)
Injuries: Out for the first month of the season with an ankle injury
Favourite band: Red Hot Chili Peppers, Delirious
Relaxations: 'Working out in the gym; watching films; listening to music (all sorts);
and most importantly spending time with friends'

Extras: Leicestershire Young Batsman of the Year 2000. Played for Leicestershire Board XI in the first and second rounds of the C&G 2003, which were played in August/September 2002

2003 Season (did not make any first-class or one-day appearances)

Career Performances

	M	Inns	NO	Runs	HS	Avge	100s	50s	Ct	St	Balls	Runs	Wkts	Avge	Best	5wI	10wM
Test																	
All First																	
1-day Int																	
C & G	2	2	0	1	1	0.50	-	-	-	-	42	31	0	-		-	-
NCL																	
Twenty20																	

FISHER, I. D. Gloucestershire

Name: Ian Douglas Fisher
Role: Left-hand bat, left-arm spin bowler
Born: 31 March 1976, Bradford
Height: 5ft 11in **Weight:** 13st 6lbs
Nickname: Fish, Flash, Fishy
County debut: 1995-96 (Yorkshire),
2002 (Gloucestershire)
1st-Class 50s: 7
1st-Class 100s: 1
1st-Class 5 w. in innings: 6
1st-Class 10 w. in match: 1
1st-Class catches: 13
Place in batting averages: 188th av. 24.33
(2002 183rd av. 24.69)
Place in bowling averages: 44th av. 27.39
(2002 151st av. 53.90)
Strike rate: 48.25 (career 71.78)
Parents: Geoff and Linda
Marital status: Single
Family links with cricket: Father played club cricket
Education: Beckfoot Grammar School
Qualifications: 9 GCSEs, NCA coaching award, sports leader's award, lifesaver
(bronze), YMCA gym instructor
Overseas tours: Yorkshire to Zimbabwe 1996, to South Africa 1998, 1999, 2001,
to Perth 2000; MCC to Sri Lanka 2001
Overseas teams played for: Somerset West, Cape Town 1994-95; Petone Riverside,
Wellington, New Zealand 1997-98

Career highlights to date: 'Winning the Championship with Yorkshire [2001]'
Cricket moments to forget: 'My pair'
Cricketers particularly admired: Darren Lehmann, Shane Warne
Young players to look out for: Tim Bresnan
Other sports played: Football (Westbrook)
Other sports followed: Football (Leeds United)
Relaxations: Music, movies, catching up with friends, shopping, eating out
Extras: Played England U17 and Yorkshire Schools U15, U16 and Yorkshire U19. Yorkshire 2nd XI cap. Bowled the last first-class ball delivered at the Northlands Road ground, Southampton, September 2000. Released by Yorkshire at the end of the 2001 season and joined Gloucestershire for 2002. Scored maiden first-class century (103*) v Essex at Gloucester 2002, in the process sharing with Jack Russell (107) in a record seventh-wicket partnership for Gloucestershire in matches v Essex (207). Recorded three Championship five-wicket returns in successive innings 2003, including maiden ten-wicket match (5-30/5-93) v Durham at Bristol
Best batting: 103* Gloucestershire v Essex, Gloucester 2002
Best bowling: 5-30 Gloucestershire v Durham, Bristol 2003

2003 Season

	M	Inns	NO	Runs	HS	Avge	100s	50s	Ct	St	O	M	Runs	Wkts	Avge	Best	5wI	10wM
Test																		
All First	10	12	3	219	71	24.33	-	1	4	-	225.1	50	767	28	27.39	5-30	3	1
1-day Int																		
C & G																		
NCL																		
Twenty20																		

Career Performances

	M	Inns	NO	Runs	HS	Avge	100s	50s	Ct	St	Balls	Runs	Wkts	Avge	Best	5wI	10wM
Test																	
All First	50	70	15	1332	103 *	24.21	1	7	13	-	7394	3876	103	37.63	5-30	6	1
1-day Int																	
C & G	3	1	0	5	5	5.00	-	-	2	-	150	87	3	29.00	1-21	-	
NCL	27	14	4	73	20	7.30	-	-	3	-	970	706	28	25.21	3-20	-	
Twenty20																	

32. Which 'Celebrity' bowler took 6-25 at The Oval to ensure an England victory over West Indies in August 1991?

FLEMING, S. P. Yorkshire

Name: <u>Stephen</u> Paul Fleming
Role: Left-hand bat, occasional right-arm
slow-medium bowler
Born: 1 April 1973, Christchurch,
New Zealand
Height: 6ft 3in
County debut: 2001 (Middlesex),
2003 (Yorkshire)
County cap: 2001 (Middlesex)
Test debut: 1993-94
Tests: 75
One-Day Internationals: 202
1000 runs in a season: 1
1st-Class 50s: 64
1st-Class 100s: 19
1st-Class 200s: 1
1st-Class catches: 219
One-Day 100s: 5

Place in batting averages: 81st av. 39.08
Education: Cashmere High School; Christchurch College of Education
Overseas tours: New Zealand U19 to India 1991-92; New Zealand to England 1994, to South Africa 1994-95, to India 1995-96, to India and Pakistan (World Cup) 1995-96, to West Indies 1995-96, to Pakistan 1996-97, to Zimbabwe 1997-98 (captain), to Australia 1997-98 (captain), to Sri Lanka 1997-98 (captain), to UK, Ireland and Holland (World Cup) 1999 (captain), to England 1999 (captain), to India 1999-2000 (captain), to Zimbabwe 2000-01 (captain), to Kenya (ICC Knockout Trophy) 2000-01 (captain), to South Africa 2000-01 (captain), to Australia 2001-02 (captain), to Pakistan 2002 (captain), to West Indies 2002 (captain), to Sri Lanka (ICC Champions Trophy) 2002-03 (captain), to Africa (World Cup) 2002-03 (captain), to Sri Lanka 2003 (captain), plus other one-day tournaments
Overseas teams played for: Canterbury 1991-92 – 1999-2000; Wellington 2001-02 –
Extras: Captain of New Zealand since 1996-97. Scored then career best 174* at Colombo 1997-98, in the process sharing with Craig McMillan in a record fourth-wicket partnership for New Zealand in Tests against Sri Lanka (240). One of the *New Zealand Cricket Almanack* two Players of the Year 1998 and 2003. Led his country to series victory in England in 1999, which included New Zealand's first wins at Lord's and The Oval. Led New Zealand to victory in the ICC Knockout Trophy in Kenya 2000-01. Scored 60 v Pakistan at Dunedin 2000-01, in the process sharing with Nathan Astle in a record partnership for any wicket for New Zealand in ODIs (193). Was Middlesex overseas player in 2001. Scored 130 in the first Test v West Indies at Bridgetown 2002, winning Man of the Match award. Scored 274* and 69* in the first

Test v Sri Lanka at Colombo 2003. Has won numerous ODI awards, including Man of the Match for his 134* v South Africa at Johannesburg in the 2002-03 World Cup. Joined Yorkshire as an overseas player for 2003; left Yorkshire at the end of the 2003 season

Best batting: 274* New Zealand v Sri Lanka, Colombo 2002-03
Stop press: Scored 192 in the first Test v Pakistan at Hamilton 2003-04, winning Man of the Match award

2003 Season

	M	Inns	NO	Runs	HS	Avge	100s	50s	Ct	St	O	M	Runs	Wkts	Avge	Best	5wl	10wM
Test																		
All First	7	14	2	469	98	39.08	-	3	13	-								
1-day Int																		
C & G																		
NCL	7	7	1	285	139 *	47.50	1	1	3	-								
Twenty20	4	4	0	62	58	15.50	-	1	1	-								

Career Performances

	M	Inns	NO	Runs	HS	Avge	100s	50s	Ct	St	Balls	Runs	Wkts	Avge	Best	5wl	10wM
Test	75	130	9	4671	274 *	38.60	5	34	114	-							
All First	164	274	26	10416	274 *	42.00	20	64	219	-	102	129	0	-	-	-	-
1-day Int	202	195	17	5523	134 *	31.02	4	34	99	-	29	28	1	28.00	1-8	-	
C & G																	
NCL	17	16	1	392	139 *	26.13	1	1	5	-							
Twenty20	4	4	0	62	58	15.50	-	1	1	-							

FLINTOFF, A.   Lancashire

Name: Andrew Flintoff
Role: Right-hand bat, right-arm fast-medium bowler
Born: 6 December 1977, Preston
Height: 6ft 4in
County debut: 1995
County cap: 1998
Test debut: 1998
Tests: 26
One-Day Internationals: 62
1st-Class 50s: 27
1st-Class 100s: 12
1st-Class 5 w. in innings: 1
1st-Class catches: 122
One-Day 100s: 2
Place in batting averages: 5th av. 72.46 (2002 152nd av. 28.40)

Place in bowling averages: 139th av. 48.46 (2002 152nd av. 54.85)
Strike rate: 92.80 (career 79.75)
Parents: Colin and Susan
Family links with cricket: Brother Chris and father both play local league cricket
Education: Ribbleton Hall High School
Qualifications: 9 GCSEs
Off-season: Touring with England
Overseas tours: England Schools U15 to South Africa 1993; England U19 to West Indies 1994-95, to Zimbabwe 1995-96, to Pakistan 1996-97 (captain); England A to Kenya and Sri Lanka 1997-98, to Zimbabwe and South Africa 1998-99; England to Sharjah (Coca-Cola Cup) 1998-99, to South Africa and Zimbabwe 1999-2000, to Kenya (ICC Knockout Trophy)

2000-01, to Pakistan and (one-day series) Sri Lanka 2000-01, to Zimbabwe (one-day series) 2001-02, to India and New Zealand 2001-02, to Australia 2002-03, to Africa (World Cup) 2002-03, to Bangladesh and Sri Lanka 2003-04, to West Indies 2003-04; ECB National Academy to Australia 2001-02; England VI to Hong Kong 2001
Cricketers particularly admired: Jason Gallian, John Crawley, Stephen Titchard, Warren Hegg
Other sports followed: Football (Preston North End and Liverpool FC)
Relaxations: Listening to music and sleeping
Extras: Represented England U14 to U19. Captained England U19 in the series v Zimbabwe U19 1997. Scored 61 off 24 balls in Championship match v Surrey at Old Trafford 1998, including 34 from one over by Alex Tudor. Became the 50th recipient of the Cricket Writers' Club Young Player of the Year award 1998. PCA Young Player of the Year 1998. Struck 50 (including four sixes) on ODI debut, v Pakistan in Sharjah 1998-99. Scored 143 off 66 balls, including nine sixes, in National League v Essex at Chelmsford 1999. His 160 v Yorkshire at Old Trafford 1999 included 111 runs before lunch, the first century before lunch by a Lancashire batsman in a Roses match. Won the EDS Walter Lawrence Trophy 1999 (for the fastest first-class century of the season) for his hundred off 61 balls (before lunch) for Lancashire v Gloucestershire at Bristol. Represented England in the 1999 World Cup. NatWest Man of the Match award for his 111-ball 135* in the quarter-final v Surrey at The Oval 2000. Lancashire Player of the Year 2000. Vice-captain of Lancashire 2002. Scored maiden Test century (137) v New Zealand in the first Test at Christchurch 2001-02, in the process sharing with Graham Thorpe in a stand of 281 that set several new records, including that for the highest sixth-wicket partnership for England in Tests; he struck five fours and a six from the first 12 deliveries he received. His Test awards are [England's] Man of the Series v South Africa 2003 and Man of the Match in the third Test v India at Bangalore 2001-02. His ODI awards include Man of the NatWest Series v Zimbabwe

and South Africa 2003 and Man of the Match for his 60-ball 84 in the first ODI v Pakistan at Karachi 2000-01 and for his 28-ball 50* (the fastest ODI fifty by an England player) and 3-49 v Sri Lanka at Trent Bridge in the NatWest Series 2002. ECB central contract 2003-04

Best batting: 160 Lancashire v Yorkshire, Old Trafford 1999
Best bowling: 5-24 Lancashire v Hampshire, Southampton 1999
Stop press: Withdrawn from Bangladesh Test series 2003-04 after failing to recover from a groin injury (replaced by Martin Saggers). Won all three ODI Man of the Match awards and the Man of the Series award v Bangladesh 2003-04, in the process passing Ian Botham's England record of 44 sixes in ODIs. BBC North West Sports Personality of the Year 2003

2003 Season

	M	Inns	NO	Runs	HS	Avge	100s	50s	Ct	St	O	M	Runs	Wkts	Avge	Best	5wl	10wM
Test	5	8	0	423	142	52.87	1	3	-	-	182	44	592	10	59.20	2-55	-	-
All First	10	14	1	942	154	72.46	3	5	7	-	232	57	727	15	48.46	2-47	-	-
1-day Int	10	10	3	279	54	39.85	-	2	5	-	75.3	11	272	15	18.13	4-32	-	
C & G	4	3	0	59	31	19.66	-	-	5	-	24.1	1	109	7	15.57	3-54	-	
NCL	3	3	1	92	43 *	46.00	-	-	3	-	16	1	83	3	27.66	3-46	-	
Twenty20																		

Career Performances

	M	Inns	NO	Runs	HS	Avge	100s	50s	Ct	St	Balls	Runs	Wkts	Avge	Best	5wl	10wM
Test	26	41	0	1066	142	26.00	2	5	14	-	4343	2148	43	49.95	4-50	-	-
All First	108	167	11	5512	160	35.33	12	27	122	-	9890	4725	124	38.10	5-24	1	-
1-day Int	62	54	6	1298	84	27.04	-	8	24	-	2117	1535	59	26.01	4-17	-	
C & G	23	19	4	671	135 *	44.73	1	3	16	-	714	473	17	27.82	3-54	-	
NCL	59	58	3	1378	143	25.05	1	6	17	-	1391	1043	47	22.19	4-24	-	
Twenty20																	

FLOWER, A. Essex

Name: Andrew (Andy) Flower
Role: Left-hand bat, wicket-keeper, occasional right-arm medium/off-spin bowler
Born: 28 April 1968, Cape Town, South Africa
Height: 5ft 10in
Nickname: Petals
County debut: 2002
County cap: 2002
Test debut: 1992-93
Tests: 63
One-Day Internationals: 213
1000 runs in a season: 2

1st-Class 50s: 60
1st-Class 100s: 31
1st-Class 200s: 3
1st-Class catches: 309
1st-Class stumpings: 21
One-Day 100s: 6
Place in batting averages: 34th av. 47.84
(2002 36th av. 50.04)
Strike rate: 31.50 (career 96.83)
Family links with cricket: Younger brother
Grant plays for Zimbabwe
Education: Vainona High School
Off-season: Playing for South Australia
Overseas tours: Zimbabwe to Australia and
New Zealand (World Cup) 1991-92,
to India 1992-93, to Pakistan 1993-94
(captain), to Australia 1994-95 (captain), to
New Zealand 1995-96 (captain), to India and

Pakistan (World Cup) 1995-96 (captain), to Sri Lanka and Pakistan 1996-97, to Sri
Lanka and New Zealand 1997-98, to Bangladesh (Wills International Cup) 1998-99, to
Pakistan 1998-99, to UK, Ireland and Holland (World Cup) 1999, to South Africa
1999-2000, to West Indies 1999-2000 (captain), to England 2000 (captain), to Kenya
(ICC Knockout Trophy) 2000-01, to India 2000-01, to New Zealand and Australia
2000-01, to Bangladesh, Sri Lanka and India 2001-02, to Sri Lanka (ICC Champions
Trophy) 2002-03, plus other one-day tournaments
Overseas teams played for: Mashonaland 1993-94 – 2002-03; South Australia
2003-04 –
Other sports played: Tennis, squash; rugby, hockey (at school)
Extras: Captained Zimbabwe Schools. Made first-class debut for ZCU President's XI
v Young West Indies at Harare 1986. First represented Zimbabwe 1988-89. Scored
century (115*) on ODI debut v Sri Lanka at New Plymouth in the 1992 World Cup,
batting right through the Zimbabwe innings. Appeared in Zimbabwe's inaugural Test,
v India at Harare 1992-93, scoring 59. Scored 156 v Pakistan at Harare 1994-95 in
Zimbabwe's first Test win, in the process sharing with Grant Flower (201*) in a
fourth-wicket stand of 269, the highest partnership between brothers in Test cricket
and at the time the highest partnership for Zimbabwe for any wicket in Tests. Scored
100* v Pakistan at Bulawayo 1997-98, in the process sharing with Murray Goodwin in
a new record partnership for Zimbabwe for any wicket in Tests (277*). Scored maiden
Test double century (232*) v India at Nagpur 2000-01 to help save the match after
Zimbabwe had followed on; was Man of the Series, having scored 183*, 70 and 55 in
his other three innings for a series average of 270.00. Scored 73 v Bangladesh at
Bulawayo 2000-01, in the process equalling Everton Weekes's world record, set 1947-49,
of seven consecutive Test half-centuries. FICA International Player of the Year 2001.
Scored 142 and 199* v South Africa in the first Test at Harare 2001, becoming the first
wicket-keeper to score a century in each innings of a Test match and the first

Zimbabwe player to reach 4000 Test runs; his performance took him to the top of the PricewaterhouseCoopers ratings for Test batsmen, making him the first wicket-keeper/batsman to achieve the feat. Equalled Zimbabwe's then highest individual score in ODIs with his 142* v England at Harare 2001-02, in the process sharing with Heath Streak in a new world record seventh-wicket partnership for ODIs (130). Scored century in each innings (114/156*) for Mashonaland in the Logan Cup 2001-02 v Mashonaland A, for whom brother Grant scored 235* in the first innings. One of *Wisden's* Five Cricketers of the Year 2002. Joined Essex as overseas player for 2002, finishing the season with an average of more than 50 in each of the four domestic competitions. A former captain of Zimbabwe. Represented Zimbabwe in the 2002-03 World Cup, retiring from international cricket after the competition. Is no longer considered an overseas player

Best batting: 232* Zimbabwe v India, Nagpur 2000-01
Best bowling: 1-1 Mashonaland v Mashonaland CD, Harare South 1993-94

2003 Season

	M	Inns	NO	Runs	HS	Avge	100s	50s	Ct	St	O	M	Runs	Wkts	Avge	Best	5wI	10wM
Test																		
All First	17	29	3	1244	201 *	47.84	2	7	17	-	10.3	0	29	2	14.50	1-5	-	-
1-day Int																		
C & G	1	1	0	82	82	82.00	-	1	-	-								
NCL	15	15	1	531	103	37.92	2	2	8	2								
Twenty20	5	5	0	266	83	53.20	-	2	3	-								

Career Performances

	M	Inns	NO	Runs	HS	Avge	100s	50s	Ct	St	Balls	Runs	Wkts	Avge	Best	5wI	10wM
Test	63	112	19	4794	232 *	51.54	12	27	150	9	3	4	0	-	-	-	-
All First	166	277	54	12032	232 *	53.95	34	60	309	21	581	250	6	41.66	1-1	-	-
1-day Int	213	208	16	6785	145	35.33	4	55	141	32	30	23	0	-	-	-	
C & G	4	3	0	202	82	67.33	-	2	4	-							
NCL	29	29	5	1037	103	43.20	2	8	24	6							
Twenty20	5	5	0	266	83	53.20	-	2	3	-							

FOSTER, J. S.   Essex

Name: <u>James</u> Savin Foster
Role: Right-hand bat, wicket-keeper
Born: 15 April 1980, Whipps Cross, London
Height: 6ft **Weight:** 12st
Nickname: Fozzy, Chief
County debut: 2000
County cap: 2001
Test debut: 2001-02

Tests: 7
50 dismissals in a season: 1
1st-Class 50s: 10
1st-Class 100s: 1
1st-Class catches: 131
1st-Class stumpings: 13
Place in batting averages: 168th av. 26.50
Parents: Martin and Diana
Marital status: Single
Family links with cricket: 'Dad played for
Essex Amateurs'
Education: Forest School; Durham
University
Qualifications: 10 GCSEs, 3 A-levels,
hockey and cricket Level 1 coaching awards
Overseas tours: BUSA to South Africa 1999;
Durham University to South Africa 1999, to
Vienna (European Indoor Championships)

1999; England A to West Indies 2000-01; England to Zimbabwe
(one-day series) 2001-02, to India and New Zealand 2001-02, to Australia 2002-03
Career highlights to date: 'Playing for my country'
Cricket moments to forget: 'None yet'
Cricketers particularly admired: Nasser Hussain, Stuart Law, Robert Rollins,
Ian Healy, Jack Russell, Alec Stewart, Adam Gilchrist
Young players to look out for: John Chambers, Adnan Akram, Arfan Akram,
Tony Palladino, Ravi Bopara, Michael Brown, Steven Miel
Other sports played: Hockey (Essex U21), tennis (played for GB U14 v Sweden
U14; national training squad)
Other sports followed: Football (Wimbledon FC)
Relaxations: Socialising
Extras: Essex U17 Player of the Year 1997. Represented ECB U19 v Pakistan U19
1998. Represented England U19 v Australia U19 1999. Represented BUSA 1999, 2000
and 2001. Scored 52 on Championship debut v Glamorgan at Southend 2000. Voted
Essex Cricket Society 2nd XI Player of the Year 2000. Scored 53 on England A debut
v Guyana in Grenada 2000-01. Played for Durham University CCE 2001. NBC Denis
Compton Award for the most promising young Essex player 2001. Scored 40 in second
Test v India at Ahmedabad 2001-02, in the process sharing with Craig White in a
record seventh-wicket partnership for England in Tests in India (105). Made 50 first-
class dismissals in a season for the first time 2003
Best batting: 103 DUCCE v Worcestershire, Worcester 2001

2003 Season

	M	Inns	NO	Runs	HS	Avge	100s	50s	Ct	St	O	M	Runs	Wkts	Avge	Best	5wI	10wM
Test																		
All First	17	26	0	689	85	26.50	-	4	49	2								
1-day Int																		
C & G	2	2	0	32	22	16.00	-	-	3	-								
NCL	9	9	1	146	41	18.25	-	-	11	2								
Twenty20	4	3	0	1	1	0.33	-	-	1	-								

Career Performances

	M	Inns	NO	Runs	HS	Avge	100s	50s	Ct	St	Balls	Runs	Wkts	Avge	Best	5wI	10wM
Test	7	12	3	226	48	25.11	-	-	17	1							
All First	55	83	8	1958	103	26.10	1	10	131	13	12	6	0	-	-	-	-
1-day Int																	
C & G	3	3	0	65	33	21.66	-	-	5	-							
NCL	32	31	9	454	56 *	20.63	-	1	39	5							
Twenty20	4	3	0	1	1	0.33	-	-	1	-							

FRANCIS, J. D.   Somerset

Name: <u>John</u> Daniel Francis
Role: Left-hand bat, slow left-arm bowler
Born: 13 November 1980, Bromley, Kent
Height: 5ft 11in **Weight:** 13st
Nickname: Long John, Franky, Junior
County debut: 2001 (Hampshire)
1st-Class 50s: 6
1st-Class catches: 13
One-Day 100s: 1
Place in batting averages: 227th av. 19.42
(2002 204th av. 23.00)
Strike rate: (career 24.00)
Parents: Linda and Daniel
Marital status: Single
Family links with cricket: Brother Simon
played for Hampshire 1997-2001; now plays
for Somerset. Father played club cricket.
Grandfather played in the services
Education: King Edward VI, Southampton; Durham and Loughborough Universities
Qualifications: 10 GCSEs, 3 A-levels, BSc Sports Science, ECB Level 1
coaching award
Off-season: 'Training and working hard at my game at Taunton'

Overseas tours: Twyford School to Barbados 1993; West of England U15 to West Indies 1995; King Edward VI, Southampton to South Africa 1998; Durham University to South Africa 2000; British Universities to South Africa 2002
Career highlights to date: 'Scoring maiden century for Hampshire in NUL match v Northamptonshire at the Rose Bowl 2002 in 83 balls'
Cricket moments to forget: 'Getting first ever pair, in a match v Yorkshire'
Cricket superstitions: 'Too many to say'
Cricketers particularly admired: Graham Thorpe, Adam Hollioake, Mike Hussey, Simon Francis
Young players to look out for: Kevin Pietersen, Mark Powell, James Adams, Neil Wood
Other sports played: Hockey (England U18), golf, squash
Favourite band: David Gray
Relaxations: Drawing and painting, socialising
Extras: Hampshire Young Sportsman of the Year 1995. Sir John Hobbs Silver Jubilee Memorial Prize for outstanding U16 player of the year 1996. Leading run-scorer in U15 World Cup 1996. Played for Loughborough University CCE in 2001, 2002 and 2003; scored a century (107) v Leicestershire at Leicester 2001. Scored 189* for British Universities v South Africa Universities in South Africa 2002. NBC Denis Compton Award for the most promising young Hampshire player 2002. Represented British Universities 2002 and v Zimbabweans and India A 2003. Left Hampshire at the end of the 2003 season and has joined Somerset for 2004
Best batting: 82 Hampshire v Leicestershire, Leicester 2002
Best bowling: 1-1 Hampshire v Leicestershire, Leicester 2002

2003 Season

	M	Inns	NO	Runs	HS	Avge	100s	50s	Ct	St	O	M	Runs	Wkts	Avge	Best	5wI	10wM
Test																		
All First	10	19	0	369	65	19.42	-	2	6	-								
1-day Int																		
C & G																		
NCL	11	11	2	290	62 *	32.22	-	2	1	-								
Twenty20																		

Career Performances

	M	Inns	NO	Runs	HS	Avge	100s	50s	Ct	St	Balls	Runs	Wkts	Avge	Best	5wI	10wM
Test																	
All First	22	40	2	891	82	23.44	-	6	13	-	48	35	2	17.50	1-1	-	-
1-day Int																	
C & G																	
NCL	27	27	7	818	103 *	40.90	1	6	4	-							
Twenty20																	

FRANCIS, S. R. G.   Somerset

Name: <u>Simon</u> Richard George Francis
Role: Right-hand bat, right-arm
medium-fast bowler
Born: 15 August 1978, Bromley, Kent
Height: 6ft 1in **Weight:** 14st
Nickname: Franco, Guru
County debut: 1997 (Hampshire),
2002 (Somerset)
1st-Class 5 w. in innings: 1
1st-Class catches: 3
Place in batting averages: 267th av. 12.09
(2002 300th av. 8.37)
Place in bowling averages: 83rd av. 33.68
(2002 94th av. 33.82)
Strike rate: 56.25 (career 61.43)
Parents: Daniel and Linda
Marital status: Single
Family links with cricket: Brother John

plays at Somerset. Father played club cricket. Grandfather played for the Navy
Education: King Edward VI, Southampton; Durham University
Qualifications: 9 GCSEs, 1 AS-Level, 3 A-levels, BA (Hons) Sport in the
Community, Level 1 coaching in hockey, Level III coaching in cricket
Career outside cricket: Cricket and hockey coaching
Off-season: 'At the National Academy'
Overseas tours: England U17 to Holland (International Youth Tournament) 1995;
England U19 to Pakistan 1996-97; Durham University to Zimbabwe 1997-98;
Hampshire to Boland 2001; ECB National Academy (England A) to Malaysia and
India 2003-04
Overseas teams played for: Maties (Stellenbosch University), South Africa 2000;
Melville CC, Perth 2001
Career highlights to date: 'Run out in semi-final of C&G v Kent and five wickets v
Warwickshire [both 2002]' (*His run out of Kent's James Golding with a direct hit from
the prone position was described as the 'turning point of the match' by his coach
Kevin Shine*)
Cricket moments to forget: 'Whole of the B&H competition 2002'
Cricketers particularly admired: Malcolm Marshall, Richard Hadlee, Allan Donald,
Graham Dilley
Young players to look out for: John Francis
Other sports played: Golf, hockey (England U18 1995)
Injuries: Out for two months with a torn oblique
Relaxations: 'Films, sleeping, reading, listening to music'

Extras: *Daily Telegraph* West Region Bowling Award U15. Played in Durham University's BUSA Championship-winning side 1999. Put on 90 for the tenth wicket with Dimitri Mascarenhas v Surrey at The Oval 2000, the pair falling just two runs short of pulling off a remarkable Championship victory. Released by Hampshire at the end of the 2001 season and joined Somerset for 2002. Took hat-trick v Loughborough UCCE at Taunton 2003

Best batting: 44 Somerset v Yorkshire, Taunton 2003
Best bowling: 5-73 Somerset v Warwickshire, Taunton 2002

2003 Season

	M	Inns	NO	Runs	HS	Avge	100s	50s	Ct	St	O	M	Runs	Wkts	Avge	Best	5wI	10wM
Test																		
All First	10	13	2	133	44	12.09	-	-	2	-	328.1	72	1179	35	33.68	4-47	-	-
1-day Int																		
C & G	1	0	0	0	0	-	-	-	-	-	10	1	19	1	19.00	1-19	-	
NCL	9	7	3	58	33 *	14.50	-	-	4	-	60.5	0	418	9	46.44	3-50	-	
Twenty20	5	4	2	19	9 *	9.50	-	-	3	-	17	0	146	4	36.50	2-22	-	

Career Performances

	M	Inns	NO	Runs	HS	Avge	100s	50s	Ct	St	Balls	Runs	Wkts	Avge	Best	5wI	10wM
Test																	
All First	36	51	20	291	44	9.38	-	-	3	-	5406	3358	88	38.15	5-73	1	-
1-day Int																	
C & G	2	0	0	0	0	-	-	-	-	-	96	29	1	29.00	1-19	-	
NCL	29	18	9	140	33 *	15.55	-	-	9	-	1133	1044	28	37.28	4-60	-	
Twenty20	5	4	2	19	9 *	9.50	-	-	3	-	102	146	4	36.50	2-22	-	

---

33. Which former Leicestershire, Nottinghamshire and Surrey all-rounder was Man of the Match for his 3-24 v West Indies in a 1992 World Cup game in Melbourne?

FRANKS, P. J. — Nottinghamshire

Name: <u>Paul</u> John Franks
Role: Left-hand bat, right-arm fast-medium bowler, county vice-captain
Born: 3 February 1979, Sutton-in-Ashfield
Height: 6ft 1½in **Weight:** 13st 10lbs
Nickname: Pike, Franno, The General
County debut: 1996
County cap: 1999
One-Day Internationals: 1
50 wickets in a season: 2
1st-Class 50s: 12
1st-Class 100s: 2
1st-Class 5 w. in innings: 9
1st-Class catches: 41
One-Day 5 w. in innings: 2
Place in batting averages: 71st av. 40.50 (2002 179th av. 25.08)
Place in bowling averages: 122nd av. 42.03 (2002 28th av. 25.40)
Strike rate: 63.42 (career 55.22)
Parents: Pat and John
Marital status: Single
Family links with cricket: 'Dad was a local league legend'
Education: Minster School, Southwell; West Notts College
Qualifications: 7 GCSEs, GNVQ (Advanced) Leisure Management, coaching Level 1
Overseas tours: England U19 to Pakistan 1996-97, to South Africa (including U19 World Cup) 1997-98; England A to Zimbabwe and South Africa 1998-99, to Bangladesh and New Zealand 1999-2000, to West Indies 2000-01; Notts CCC to South Africa 1998, 1999
Career highlights to date: 'England [one-day] debut v West Indies on home ground in 2000'
Cricket moments to forget: 'Any time I get my poles removed or go the distance'
Cricketers particularly admired: Glenn McGrath, Mike Atherton, Allan Donald, Phil 'bowls like me' DeFreitas
Young players to look out for: Kyle Hogg, Nadeem Malik, Bilal Shafayat, Matt Prior, Richard Hodgkinson
Other sports played: Golf
Other sports followed: Football (Mansfield Town)
Relaxations: 'Taking it generally steady'
Extras: Became youngest ever Notts player (and third-youngest player ever in English first-class cricket, aged 18 years 163 days) to take a hat-trick, v Warwickshire at Trent

Bridge 1997. Won U19 World Cup winner's medal in Johannesburg 1998. Attended Dennis Lillee coaching school, Chennai (Madras), March 1997, February 1998 and March 1999. NBC Denis Compton Award 1999. Cricket Writers' Young Player of the Year 2000. Vice-captain of Nottinghamshire since 2003. Scored maiden first-class century (123*) v Leicestershire at Leicester 2003

Best batting: 123* Nottinghamshire v Leicestershire, Leicester 2003
Best bowling: 7-56 Nottinghamshire v Middlesex, Lord's 2000

2003 Season

	M	Inns	NO	Runs	HS	Avge	100s	50s	Ct	St	O	M	Runs	Wkts	Avge	Best	5wI	10wM
Test																		
All First	16	26	8	729	123 *	40.50	2	1	9	-	296	49	1177	28	42.03	4-62	-	-
1-day Int																		
C & G	2	2	1	88	84 *	88.00	-	1	1	-	8	0	38	2	19.00	1-19	-	
NCL	15	15	1	330	55	23.57	-	1	5	-	83.1	3	468	14	33.42	4-12	-	
Twenty20	5	4	2	62	29 *	31.00	-	-	3	-	6.3	0	51	3	17.00	2-31	-	

Career Performances

	M	Inns	NO	Runs	HS	Avge	100s	50s	Ct	St	Balls	Runs	Wkts	Avge	Best	5wI	10wM
Test																	
All First	98	147	29	2943	123 *	24.94	2	12	41	-	16180	8545	293	29.16	7-56	9	-
1-day Int	1	1	0	4	4	4.00	-	-	1	-	54	48	0	-	-	-	
C & G	13	9	4	198	84 *	39.60	-	1	4	-	612	474	18	26.33	3-7	-	
NCL	74	60	19	834	60	20.34	-	2	12	-	3099	2531	94	26.92	6-27	2	
Twenty20	5	4	2	62	29 *	31.00	-	-	3	-	39	51	3	17.00	2-31	-	

34. Which Durban-born batsman provided the tenth instance of brothers having played for England when he made his Test debut v West Indies at Headingley in 1988?

FROST, T. Warwickshire

Name: Tony Frost
Role: Right-hand bat, wicket-keeper
Born: 17 November 1975, Stoke-on-Trent
Height: 5ft 10in **Weight:** 10st 6lbs
County debut: 1997
County cap: 1999
1st-Class 50s: 8
1st-Class 100s: 2
1st-Class catches: 115
1st-Class stumpings: 9
Place in batting averages: 195th av. 23.85
(2002 132nd av. 30.80)
Parents: Ivan and Christine
Marital status: Single
Family links with cricket: Father played for
Staffordshire
Education: James Brinkley High School;
Stoke-on-Trent College

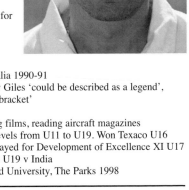

Qualifications: 5 GCSEs
Overseas tours: Kidsgrove U18 to Australia 1990-91
Cricketers particularly admired: Ashley Giles 'could be described as a legend',
'Pop' Welch and George Burns 'in the JT bracket'
Other sports followed: Football, golf
Relaxations: Listening to music, watching films, reading aircraft magazines
Extras: Represented Staffordshire at all levels from U11 to U19. Won Texaco U16
competition with Staffordshire in 1992. Played for Development of Excellence XI U17
v South Africa and U18 v West Indies and U19 v India
Best batting: 111* Warwickshire v Oxford University, The Parks 1998

2003 Season

	M	Inns	NO	Runs	HS	Avge	100s	50s	Ct	St	O	M	Runs	Wkts	Avge	Best	5wI	10wM
Test																		
All First	13	21	1	477	84	23.85	-	4	33	2								
1-day Int																		
C & G	1	1	0	47	47	47.00	-	-	-	-								
NCL	3	3	0	31	12	10.33	-	-	1	3								
Twenty20	1	1	0	31	31	31.00	-	-	-	-								

	M	Inns	NO	Runs	HS	Avge	100s	50s	Ct	St		Balls	Runs	Wkts	Avge	Best	5wI	10wM
Test																		
All First	51	77	8	1697	111 *	24.59	2	8	115	9		12	15	0	-		-	-	-
1-day Int																		
C & G	4	4	0	61	47	15.25	-	-	5	1								
NCL	32	15	5	148	22 *	14.80	-	-	23	6								
Twenty20	1	1	0	31	31	31.00	-	-	-	-								

FULTON, D. P. Kent

Name: David (<u>Dave</u>) Paul Fulton
Role: Right-hand top-order bat, left-arm
spin bowler, occasional wicket-keeper,
county captain
Born: 15 November 1971, Lewisham
Height: 6ft 2in **Weight:** 12st 7lbs
Nickname: Tav, Rave
County debut: 1992
County cap: 1998
1000 runs in a season: 2
1st-Class 50s: 39
1st-Class 100s: 18
1st-Class 200s: 2
1st-Class catches: 222
Place in batting averages: 91st av. 37.44
(2002 57th av. 43.80)
Strike rate: (career 175.00)
Parents: John and Ann
Wife and date of marriage: Claudine Kay Tomlin, 19 December 2003
Family links with cricket: Father played for village
Education: The Judd School, Tonbridge; University of Kent at Canterbury
Qualifications: 10 GCSEs, 3 A-levels, BA (Hons) Politics and International Relations,
advanced cricket coach, rugby coach, gym instructor qualification
Career outside cricket: Journalist
Off-season: 'Writing, training, rebuilding the body!'
Overseas tours: Kent SCA U17 to Singapore and New Zealand 1987-88; Kent to
France 1998, to Port Elizabeth 2001
Overseas teams played for: Avendale CC, Cape Town 1993-94; Victoria CC,
Cape Town 1994-95; University of WA, Perth 1995-96; Petersham-Marrickville CC,
Sydney 1998-99, 1999-2000
Career highlights to date: 'Will Kendall caught and bowled Fulton (first and only
first-class victim). PCA Player of the Year 2001'

Cricket moments to forget: 'Already forgotten'
Cricketers particularly admired: Gordon Greenidge, Graham Gooch, Courtney Walsh, Steve Waugh
Young players to look out for: Joe Denly
Other sports played: Chess (England junior), table tennis ('top 10 in UK as a junior'; played for South England juniors); rugby, football, tennis, golf, squash
Other sports followed: Football (Nottingham Forest), rugby (Harlequins)
Injuries: Out for seven weeks after 'blow to right eye in nets resulting in partial loss of vision'; for two weeks with a broken finger
Relaxations: 'Reading, music, fitness; walking Poppy, our dog'
Extras: Was the last person to catch Viv Richards in a first-class match, in 1993. Set record for the longest innings ever played by a Kent batsman in scoring his 207 against Yorkshire at Maidstone in 1998. Has best catching strike rate in Kent fielding history. Scored double century (208*) and century (104*) v Somerset at Canterbury 2001, also taking seven catches in the match; followed up with 197 v Northamptonshire at Northampton in next Championship innings. Scored 196 v Northamptonshire at Canterbury 2001, in the process equalling Arthur Fagg's 1938 season tally of nine centuries for Kent, one behind Frank Woolley's Kent record of ten, set in 1928 and 1934. First batsman to 1000 first-class runs in 2001 and the season's leading English batsman in terms of runs scored (second overall) and average (fifth overall) with 1892 runs (av. 75.68). Kent Batsman of the Year (Denness Award) 2001. PCA Player of the Year 2001. Captain of Kent in County Championship 2002; overall captain of Kent since 2003. Carried his bat for 94* v Essex at Canterbury 2003, after James Middlebrook finished off the Kent second innings with a hat-trick
Opinions on cricket: 'I'm concerned about EU-qualified players flooding into our game. Counties while trying to run their businesses successfully must not lose sight of the bigger picture.'
Best batting: 208* Kent v Somerset, Canterbury 2001
Best bowling: 1-37 Kent v Oxford University, Canterbury 1996

2003 Season

	M	Inns	NO	Runs	HS	Avge	100s	50s	Ct	St	O	M	Runs	Wkts	Avge	Best	5wI	10wM
Test																		
All First	11	19	1	674	94 *	37.44	-	5	4	-								
1-day Int																		
C & G	1	1	0	0	0	0.00	-	-	-	-								
NCL	9	6	1	83	48	16.60	-	-	5	-								
Twenty20	5	4	2	40	15	20.00	-	-	1	-								

Career Performances

	M	Inns	NO	Runs	HS	Avge	100s	50s	Ct	St	Balls	Runs	Wkts	Avge	Best	5wI	10wM
Test																	
All First	153	269	17	9217	208 *	36.57	20	39	222	-	175	112	1	112.00	1-37	-	-
1-day Int																	
C & G	16	16	1	351	63	23.40	-	2	9	-	6	9	0	-		-	-
NCL	52	49	2	813	82	17.29	-	2	25	-							
Twenty20	5	4	2	40	15	20.00	-	-	1	-							

GAIT, A. I. Derbyshire

Name: Andrew Ian Gait
Role: Right-hand opening bat
Born: 19 December 1978, Bulawayo, Zimbabwe
Height: 6ft 1in **Weight:** 13st 7lbs
Nickname: Bob, Gaitor
County debut: 2002
1st-Class 50s: 17
1st-Class 100s: 4
1st-Class catches: 43
Place in batting averages: 166th av. 26.56 (2002 133rd av. 30.71)
Parents: Roger and Hazel
Marital status: Single
Education: Kearsney College, KwaZulu-Natal; 'studying through Open University in the UK'
Qualifications: Level 2 coaching
Career outside cricket: 'Studying, visiting family, coaching and keeping fit'
Off-season: 'Studying in UK and holiday back in South Africa'
Overseas tours: South African National Academy to Kenya and Zimbabwe 1998
Overseas teams played for: Free State 1998-2001
Career highlights to date: 'Chasing 400-plus in fourth innings and winning v Natal 1999-2000; scored 101'
Cricket moments to forget: '2003 cricket season'
Cricketers particularly admired: Allan Donald, Steve Waugh, Jacques Kallis
Young players to look out for: Kevin Pietersen, Jim Troughton, Graeme Smith
Other sports played: Running, cycling, keeping fit, surfing
Other sports followed: Rugby (Natal Sharks)
Injuries: Out for four weeks with a torn hand ligament
Favourite band: U2, Goo Goo Dolls, Matchbox Twenty

Relaxations: Gym, running; beach, outdoors; music

Extras: Represented South Africa U19 in U19 World Cup 1997-98. Set Free State record for highest individual score in one-day cricket (138*). Scored 101 in the highest successful fourth-innings run chase by a South African province – 443 by Free State v KwaZulu-Natal at Durban 1999-2000. Scored 87* v Glamorgan at Cardiff in the C&G 2003, sharing with Chris Bassano (121) in a new competition record third-wicket partnership for Derbyshire (191). Holds a British passport and is not considered an overseas player

Opinions on cricket: 'I still believe that the English season is too long and the standard of the pitches needs to improve.'

Best batting: 175 Derbyshire v Northamptonshire, Northampton 2002

2003 Season

	M	Inns	NO	Runs	HS	Avge	100s	50s	Ct	St	O	M	Runs	Wkts	Avge	Best	5wI	10wM
Test																		
All First	13	25	0	664	110	26.56	1		4	10	-							
1-day Int																		
C & G	3	3	1	96	87 *	48.00	-	1	-	-								
NCL	7	7	1	112	37	18.66	-	-	4	-								
Twenty20	2	1	0	2	2	2.00	-	-	-	-								

Career Performances

	M	Inns	NO	Runs	HS	Avge	100s	50s	Ct	St	Balls	Runs	Wkts	Avge	Best	5wI	10wM
Test																	
All First	49	93	1	2584	175	28.08	4	17	43	-							
1-day Int																	
C & G	4	4	1	96	87 *	32.00	-	1	-	-							
NCL	15	15	1	214	37	15.28	-	-	7	-							
Twenty20	2	1	0	2	2	2.00	-	-	-	-							

GALE, A. W.   Yorkshire

Name: <u>Andrew</u> William Gale

Role: Left-hand bat

Born: 28 November 1983, Dewsbury

Height: 6ft 2in **Weight:** 13st 5lbs

Nickname: Galey

County debut: No first-team appearance

Parents: Denise and Alan

Marital status: 'Attached'

Family links with cricket: Grandfather keen cricketer

Education: Heckmondwike Grammar

Qualifications: 10 GCSEs, 3 A-levels, Level 2 cricket coaching

Off-season: 'Training, seeing girlfriend, and playing football'
Overseas tours: England U17 to Australia 2001; England U19 to Australia 2002-03; Yorkshire to Grenada 2002
Career highlights to date: '164 for Yorkshire 2nd XI v Leicestershire 2nd XI 2002. Being on Yorkshire staff. Captaining England U19'
Cricket superstitions: 'Don't like odd numbers'
Cricketers particularly admired: Marcus Trescothick, Mark Butcher, Graeme Smith
Young players to look out for: Tim Bresnan, Joe Sayers, Chris Taylor, Richard Pyrah
Other sports played: Football, golf
Other sports followed: Football (Huddersfield Town)

Relaxations: 'Golf and listening to music; spending time with girlfriend; playing PlayStation'
Extras: Has played for England since U15 level. Played for Yorkshire Board XI in the C&G 2002 and in the second round of the C&G 2003, which was played in September 2002. Yorkshire League Young Batsman of the Year 2002
Opinions on cricket: 'Should have just one overseas player; if we have two it could take the places of youngsters who may have the potential to be as good as the overseas.'

2003 Season (did not make any first-class or one-day appearances)

Career Performances

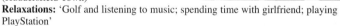

	M	Inns	NO	Runs	HS	Avge	100s	50s	Ct	St	Balls	Runs	Wkts	Avge	Best	5wl	10wM
Test																	
All First																		
1-day Int																		
C & G	3	3	0	35	17	11.66	-	-	1	-							
NCL																		
Twenty20																		

GALLIAN, J. E. R.   Nottinghamshire

Name: <u>Jason</u> Edward Riche Gallian
Role: Right-hand bat, right-arm
medium bowler, county captain
Born: 25 June 1971, Manly, NSW, Australia
Height: 6ft **Weight:** 14st
Nickname: Gal
County debut: 1990 (Lancashire),
1998 (Nottinghamshire)
County cap: 1994 (Lancashire),
1998 (Nottinghamshire)
Test debut: 1995
Tests: 3
1000 runs in a season: 4
1st-Class 50s: 47
1st-Class 100s: 25
1st-Class 300s: 1
1st-Class 5 w. in innings: 1
1st-Class catches: 144
One-Day 100s: 7
One-Day 5 w. in innings: 1

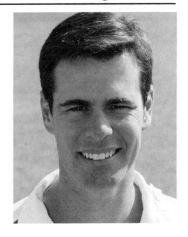

Place in batting averages: 37th av. 47.71 (2002 74th av. 41.80)
Strike rate: 186.00 (career 72.61)
Parents: Ray and Marilyn
Wife and date of marriage: Charlotte, 2 October 1999
Children: Tom, 12 April 2001; Harry, 9 September 2003
Family links with cricket: Father played for Stockport
Education: The Pittwater House Schools, Australia; Oxford University
Qualifications: Higher School Certificate, Diploma in Social Studies
(Keble College, Oxford)
Off-season: 'Looking after my new son Harry'
Overseas tours: Australia U20 to West Indies 1989-90; England A to India 1994-95,
to Pakistan 1995-96, to Australia 1996-97; England to South Africa 1995-96;
Nottinghamshire to Johannesburg 2000, to South Africa 2001
Overseas teams played for: NSW U19 1988-89; NSW Colts and NSW 2nd XI
1990-91; Manly 1993-94
Career highlights to date: 'Playing Test cricket'
Cricket moments to forget: 'Breaking a finger in my first Test match'
Cricket superstitions: 'None'
Cricketers particularly admired: Desmond Haynes, Mike Gatting
Young players to look out for: Samit Patel
Other sports followed: Rugby league and union, football

Injuries: Out for five weeks with a broken right thumb
Favourite band: INXS
Relaxations: Listening to music, playing golf
Extras: Represented Australia YC 1988-90; was captain v England YC 1989-90. Represented Australia U20 and U21 1991-92. Took wicket of D. A. Hagan of Oxford University with his first ball in first-class cricket 1990. Played for Oxford University in 1992 and for Combined Universities in the B&H Cup 1992. Captained Oxford University 1993. Recorded highest individual score in history of Old Trafford with his 312 v Derbyshire in 1996. Left Lancashire during the 1997-98 off-season and joined Nottinghamshire for 1998. Scored 91 v Leicestershire at Trent Bridge in the NUL 2002, in the process sharing with Nicky Boje (86) in a record fourth-wicket partnership for Nottinghamshire in the one-day league (190). Scored 111* opening the innings as Nottinghamshire reached 323-9 to beat Derbyshire in the Championship at Derby 2002; his stand of 46* with Greg Smith was a Nottinghamshire record for the last wicket to win a match. Carried his bat for 112* (out of 211) v Surrey at Trent Bridge 2003. Captain of Nottinghamshire from part-way through the 1998 season to 2002; Nottinghamshire club captain and captain in first-class cricket 2003 (*see entry on Chris Cairns*); has been reappointed overall captain for 2004
Opinions on cricket: 'Two divisions is very good. Four-day cricket needs to be more intense.'
Best batting: 312 Lancashire v Derbyshire, Old Trafford 1996
Best bowling: 6-115 Lancashire v Surrey, Southport 1996

2003 Season

	M	Inns	NO	Runs	HS	Avge	100s	50s	Ct	St	O	M	Runs	Wkts	Avge	Best	5wI	10wM
Test																		
All First	13	24	3	1002	126 *	47.71	4	5	16	-	31	6	94	1	94.00	1-7	-	-
1-day Int																		
C & G	2	2	0	17	16	8.50	-	-	-	-	8	0	42	1	42.00	1-33	-	
NCL	14	14	1	367	69	28.23	-	2	2	-	10	1	63	2	31.50	1-13	-	
Twenty20	5	5	0	143	62	28.60	-	1	1	-								

Career Performances

	M	Inns	NO	Runs	HS	Avge	100s	50s	Ct	St	Balls	Runs	Wkts	Avge	Best	5wI	10wM
Test	3	6	0	74	28	12.33	-	-	1	-	84	62	0	-	-	-	-
All First	170	298	29	10213	312	37.96	26	47	144	-	6898	3919	95	41.25	6-115	1	-
1-day Int																	
C & G	18	18	1	533	101 *	31.35	1	4	10	-	210	164	2	82.00	1-11	-	
NCL	116	114	11	3330	130	32.33	4	18	36	-	904	888	30	29.60	2-10	-	
Twenty20	5	5	0	143	62	28.60	-	1	1	-							

GANNON, B. W. Middlesex

Name: <u>Benjamin</u> Ward Gannon
Role: Right-hand bat, right-arm
medium bowler
Born: 5 September 1975, Oxford
Height: 6ft 3in **Weight:** 13st 7lbs
Nickname: Louis, Ganja
County debut: 1999 (Gloucestershire),
2003 (Middlesex)
1st-Class 5 w. in innings: 3
1st-Class catches: 8
Place in bowling averages: (2002 129th
av. 41.73)
Strike rate: (career 52.47)
Parents: Martin and Jane
Marital status: Single
Education: Abingdon School; Cheltenham
and Gloucester College of Higher Education

Qualifications: 3 A-levels, BSc (Hons)
Sports Science and Physical Geography, coaching awards in football, rugby and
cricket, fitness qualifications
Overseas tours: Gloucestershire to Zimbabwe 1997, to South Africa 2000, 2001;
Forest Nomads to Zimbabwe 1998
Overseas teams played for: Waverley, Sydney 1993-94; Union CC, Port Elizabeth
2000; Easterns CC, Cape Town 2001
Career highlights to date: 'Making debut against Glamorgan'
Cricketers particularly admired: Courtney Walsh, Curtly Ambrose, Glenn McGrath,
'Syd' Lawrence
Other sports played: 'I'll have a go at most sports'
Other sports followed: Boxing, rugby, tennis, athletics, climbing
Relaxations: Listening to music, keeping fit, travelling, photography
Extras: NBC Denis Compton Award 1999. Released by Gloucestershire at the end of
the 2002 season and joined Middlesex for 2003. Released by Middlesex at the end of
the 2003 season
Best batting: 28 Gloucestershire v Essex, Colchester 2000
Best bowling: 6-80 Gloucestershire v Glamorgan, Cardiff 1999

2003 Season

	M	Inns	NO	Runs	HS	Avge	100s	50s	Ct	St	O	M	Runs	Wkts	Avge	Best	5wl	10wM
Test																		
All First	1	1	1	1	1*	-	-	-	-	-	23	4	102	0	-		-	-
1-day Int																		
C & G																		
NCL	2	0	0	0	0	-	-	-	1	-	6	0	53	0	-		-	-
Twenty20																		

Career Performances

	M	Inns	NO	Runs	HS	Avge	100s	50s	Ct	St	Balls	Runs	Wkts	Avge	Best	5wl	10wM
Test																	
All First	32	37	17	188	28	9.40	-	-	8	-	4460	2832	85	33.31	6-80	3	-
1-day Int																	
C & G																	
NCL	2	0	0	0	0	-	-	-	1	-	36	53	0	-		-	-
Twenty20																	

GAZZARD, C. M.   Somerset

Name: Carl Matthew Gazzard
Role: Right-hand bat, wicket-keeper
Born: 15 April 1982, Penzance
Height: 6ft **Weight:** 13st
Nickname: Gazza, Sling Boy
County debut: 2002
1st-Class catches: 8
1st-Class stumpings: 1
Parents: Paul and Alison
Marital status: Single
Family links with cricket: Father and brother both played for Cornwall Schools; mother's a keen follower
Education: Mounts Bay Comprehensive; Richard Huish College, Taunton
Qualifications: 10 GCSEs, 2 A-levels, Level 1 and 2 coaching
Off-season: 'Training hard'
Overseas tours: Cornwall Schools U13 to Johannesburg; West of England U15 to West Indies; Somerset Academy to Durban 1999
Overseas teams played for: Subiaco-Floreat, Perth 2000-01; Scarborough, Perth 2002-03

Career highlights to date: 'England U19 v Sri Lanka U19 2000 – 3-0 victory in ODIs and 1st "Test" victory. First-class debut v West Indies A'
Cricket moments to forget: 'Dislocating my shoulder in Perth – kept me out for 2001 season'
Cricket superstitions: 'None'
Cricketers particularly admired: Marcus Trescothick, Graham Rose
Other sports played: Football (played through the age groups for Cornwall)
Other sports followed: Football (West Ham United)
Relaxations: 'Any sport, watching TV, socialising'
Extras: Played for England U13, U14, U15, U19. Won the Graham Kersey Award for Best Wicket-keeper at Bunbury Festival. Played for Cornwall in Minor Counties aged 16 and in the NatWest Trophy 1999. Scored 58 on NCL debut v Nottinghamshire at Taunton 2003
Best batting: 41 Somerset v Northamptonshire, Taunton 2003

2003 Season

	M	Inns	NO	Runs	HS	Avge	100s	50s	Ct	St	O	M	Runs	Wkts	Avge	Best	5wl	10wM
Test																		
All First	3	5	1	109	41	27.25	-	-	5	-								
1-day Int																		
C & G																		
NCL	14	13	0	358	81	27.53	-	3	16	1								
Twenty20	5	5	0	105	39	21.00	-	-	3	-								

Career Performances

	M	Inns	NO	Runs	HS	Avge	100s	50s	Ct	St	Balls	Runs	Wkts	Avge	Best	5wl	10wM
Test																	
All First	4	7	1	140	41	23.33	-	-	8	1							
1-day Int																	
C & G	1	1	0	16	16	16.00	-	-	2	-							
NCL	14	13	0	358	81	27.53	-	3	16	1							
Twenty20	5	5	0	105	39	21.00	-	-	3	-							

35. Which West Indies captain scored a Test century on his adopted home ground, Old Trafford, in July 1980?

GIBBS, H. H. Durham

Name: <u>Herschelle</u> Herman Gibbs
Role: Right-hand opening bat, right-arm leg-break or fast-medium bowler
Born: 23 February 1974, Cape Town, South Africa
Height: 5ft 10in
Nickname: Scooter, Gibbsy
County debut: No first-team appearance
Test debut: 1996-97
Tests: 50
One-Day Internationals: 135
1st-Class 50s: 41
1st-Class 100s: 21
1st-Class 200s: 4
1st-Class catches: 99
One-Day 100s: 12
Place in batting averages: 67th av. 42.14
Strike rate: (career 44.00)
Education: Diocesan College
Overseas tours: Western Province to Zimbabwe 1993-94, to Australia 1995-96; South Africa A to England 1996, to Sri Lanka 1998; South Africa to India 1996-97, to Australia 1997-98, to Malaysia (Commonwealth Games) 1998-99, to New Zealand 1998-99, to UK, Ireland and Holland (World Cup) 1999, to India 1999-2000, to West Indies 2000-01, to Zimbabwe 2001-02, to Australia 2001-02, to Sri Lanka (ICC Champions Trophy) 2002-03, to Bangladesh 2003, to England 2003, to Pakistan 2003-04, plus other one-day tournaments in Kenya, India, Sharjah, Morocco and Bangladesh
Overseas teams played for: Western Province 1990-91 –
Cricket superstitions: Left shoe and left pad on first
Cricketers particularly admired: Peter Kirsten, Viv Richards, Glenn McGrath, Brian Lara, Adam Gilchrist, Sachin Tendulkar, Shane Warne, Daryll Cullinan, Steve Waugh; Herman Gibbs (father), Duncan Fletcher – as coaches
Young players to look out for: Graeme Smith
Other sports followed: Football (Manchester United), golf (Tiger Woods)
Favourite band: Bob Marley, Michael Jackson, Mariah Carey, Celine Dion, Kool and the Gang, Barry White, Whitney Houston, Luther Vandross
Relaxations: Golf, time with family and friends, cinema, shopping
Extras: Made first-class debut for Western Province B v Transvaal B at Cape Town 1990-91. One of *South African Cricket Annual*'s five Cricketers of the Year 1999 and 2003. Man of the Match for his 67* in the 2002-03 Standard Bank Cup final v Griqualand West at Cape Town. Represented South Africa in the 2002-03 World Cup. Shared with Jacques Kallis in a South African record second-wicket partnership in

Tests (315*), v New Zealand at Christchurch 1998-99. Shared with Graeme Smith in a South African record opening partnership in Tests (368), v Pakistan at Cape Town 2002-03. Shared with Graeme Smith (277) in a record opening partnership for South Africa in Tests against England (338) at Edgbaston 2003, scoring 179. Has won several Test awards, including Man of the Series v India 2001-02 and Man of the Match for his 211* in the second Test v New Zealand at Christchurch 1998-99, his 104 in the third Test v Australia at Durban 2001-02, and his 228 in the second Test v Pakistan at Cape Town 2002-03. Has also won numerous ODI awards, including Man of the Match for his 93* v Zimbabwe at Cardiff in the NatWest Series 2003. Has joined Durham as an overseas player for 2004

Best batting: 228 South Africa v Pakistan, Cape Town 2002-03
Best bowling: 2-14 South Africa A v Somerset, Taunton 1996
Stop press: Man of the Match award for his 192 in the fourth Test v West Indies at Centurion 2003-04

2003 Season

	M	Inns	NO	Runs	HS	Avge	100s	50s	Ct	St	O	M	Runs	Wkts	Avge	Best	5wl	10wM
Test	5	9	0	478	183	53.11	2	-	5	-								
All First	8	14	0	590	183	42.14	2	1	6	-								
1-day Int	7	7	1	117	93 *	19.50	-	1	1	-								
C & G																		
NCL																		
Twenty20																		

Career Performances

	M	Inns	NO	Runs	HS	Avge	100s	50s	Ct	St	Balls	Runs	Wkts	Avge	Best	5wl	10wM
Test	50	83	3	3585	228	44.81	10	11	34	-							
All First	135	228	9	9725	228	44.40	25	41	99	-	132	74	3	24.66	2-14	-	-
1-day Int	135	134	10	4443	153	35.83	12	18	55	-							
C & G																	
NCL																	
Twenty20																	

GIDDINS, E. S. H.   Hampshire

Name: Edward (Ed) Simon Hunter Giddins
Role: Right-hand bat, right-arm medium-fast swing bowler
Born: 20 July 1971, Eastbourne
Height: 6ft 4in **Weight:** 14st
Nickname: Chief
County debut: 1991 (Sussex), 1998 (Warwickshire), 2001 (Surrey), 2003 (Hampshire)
County cap: 1994 (Sussex), 1998 (Warwickshire)

Test debut: 1999
Tests: 4
50 wickets in a season: 4
1st-Class 5 w. in innings: 22
1st-Class 10 w. in match: 2
1st-Class catches: 22
One-Day 5 w. in innings: 2
Place in bowling averages: 34th av. 25.84
(2002 91st av. 33.45)
Strike rate: 45.61 (career 53.09)
Parents: Simon and Pauline
Marital status: 'Attached to Claire'
Children: Isabella, 28 May 2002
Education: Eastbourne College
Qualifications: 8 O-levels, 2 A-levels,
Level 1 coaching certificate
Career outside cricket: 'Property developer
and hen-party transporter'

Overseas tours: England A to Pakistan
1995-96
Overseas teams played for: Mosman, Sydney 1994-95
Career highlights to date: '5-15 and Man of the Match at Lord's 2000. B&H Cup
win with Surrey 2001'
Cricket superstitions: 'Left first'
Cricketers particularly admired: Ian Gould, Eddie Hemmings
Other sports played: Golf
Other sports followed: Football (Fulham FC)
Relaxations: Travel
Extras: Joined Warwickshire for the 1998 season. Recorded maiden Test five-wicket
return (5-15; 7-42 in match) in the first Test v Zimbabwe at Lord's 2000, winning the
Man of the Match award. Left Warwickshire during the 2000-01 off-season and joined
Surrey for 2001. C&G Man of the Match award v Surrey Board XI at Guildford 2001.
Left Surrey at the end of the 2002 season and joined Hampshire for 2003. Retired
from county cricket during the 2003 season
Best batting: 34 Sussex v Essex, Hove 1995
Best bowling: 6-47 Sussex v Yorkshire, Eastbourne 1996

2003 Season

	M	Inns	NO	Runs	HS	Avge	100s	50s	Ct	St	O	M	Runs	Wkts	Avge	Best	5wI	10wM
Test																		
All First	3	4	1	10	10	3.33	-	-	-	-	98.5	18	336	13	25.84	4-88	-	-
1-day Int																		
C & G																		
NCL	4	0	0	0	0	-	-	-	1	-	30	3	174	2	87.00	2-32	-	
Twenty20	5	2	0	1	1	0.50	-	-	-	-	11	0	109	2	54.50	1-19	-	

Career Performances

	M	Inns	NO	Runs	HS	Avge	100s	50s	Ct	St	Balls	Runs	Wkts	Avge	Best	5wI	10wM
Test	4	7	3	10	7	2.50	-	-	-	-	444	240	12	20.00	5-15	1	-
All First	147	175	74	534	34	5.28	-	-	22	-	25380	13562	478	28.37	6-47	22	2
1-day Int																	
C & G	23	7	4	27	13	9.00	-	-	5	-	1337	878	25	35.12	3-24	-	
NCL	128	50	22	67	13 *	2.39	-	-	23	-	5471	4286	150	28.57	5-20	1	
Twenty20	5	2	0	1	1	0.50	-	-	-	-	66	109	2	54.50	1-19	-	

GIDMAN, A. P. R. Gloucestershire

Name: Alexander (<u>Alex</u>) Peter Richard Gidman
Role: Right-hand bat, right-arm medium bowler; batting all-rounder
Born: 22 June 1981, High Wycombe
Height: 6ft 2in **Weight:** 13st 7lbs
Nickname: Giddo, Gids
County debut: 2001 (one-day), 2002 (first-class)
1st-Class 50s: 6
1st-Class 100s: 1
1st-Class catches: 12
Place in batting averages: 153rd av. 29.07 (2002 110th av. 34.87)
Place in bowling averages: (2002 136th av. 44.20)
Strike rate: 124.80 (career 81.20)
Parents: Alistair and Jane
Marital status: Single
Family links with cricket: 'Brother an MCC Young Cricketer'
Education: Wycliffe College
Qualifications: 7 GCSEs, 1 A-level, GNVQ in Leisure and Tourism
Off-season: 'National Academy'
Overseas tours: MCC Young Cricketers to Cape Town 1999; Gloucestershire to South Africa; ECB National Academy (England A) to Malaysia and India 2003-04 (captain)
Overseas teams played for: Albion CC, New Zealand 2001
Career highlights to date: 'C&G [final] victory v Worcestershire 2003'
Cricket moments to forget: 'C&G quarter-final loss to Kent 2002'
Cricket superstitions: 'None'
Cricketers particularly admired: Steve Waugh, Jonty Rhodes, Damien Martyn
Young players to look out for: Stephen Pope

Other sports played: Golf
Other sports followed: 'Follow all sports; any national teams'
Favourite band: Counting Crows
Relaxations: 'Reading papers in local coffee shops'
Extras: Played for Gloucestershire Board XI in the C&G 2001 and 2002. Scored 67 on first-class debut v Derbyshire at Derby 2002. Gloucestershire Young Player of the Year 2002 and 2003. NBC Denis Compton Award for the most promising young Gloucestershire player 2002
Opinions on cricket: 'I fear that young players may find a boredom factor coming into game due to load of cricket. Points system must be looked at – draws are too rewarding.'
Best batting: 117 Gloucestershire v Northamptonshire, Bristol 2002
Best bowling: 3-33 Gloucestershire v Middlesex, Cheltenham 2002
Stop press: Forced to return home early from England A tour to India 2003-04 with a hand injury

2003 Season

	M	Inns	NO	Runs	HS	Avge	100s	50s	Ct	St	O	M	Runs	Wkts	Avge	Best	5wI	10wM
Test																		
All First	8	16	2	407	68	29.07	-	2	7	-	104	20	441	5	88.20	2-46	-	-
1-day Int																		
C & G	4	4	2	102	41	51.00	-	-	-	-	14.1	1	47	4	11.75	2-12	-	
NCL	12	11	2	372	73	41.33	-	2	9	-	43	1	200	4	50.00	3-26	-	
Twenty20	6	4	1	122	61	40.66	-	1	4	-	2	0	25	1	25.00	1-25	-	

Career Performances

	M	Inns	NO	Runs	HS	Avge	100s	50s	Ct	St	Balls	Runs	Wkts	Avge	Best	5wI	10wM
Test																	
All First	18	33	3	965	117	32.16	1	6	12	-	1218	883	15	58.86	3-33	-	-
1-day Int																	
C & G	8	8	2	163	41	27.16	-	-	1	-	214	153	5	30.60	2-12	-	
NCL	23	20	3	516	73	30.35	-	2	13	-	300	246	7	35.14	3-26	-	
Twenty20	6	4	1	122	61	40.66	-	1	4	-	12	25	1	25.00	1-25	-	

> 36. Which current umpire scored his second Test century, the first ever Test 100 at Antigua, in the fourth Test v West Indies 1980-81?

GILDER, G. M.   Somerset

Name: <u>Gary</u> Michael Gilder
Role: Right-hand bat, left-arm
fast-medium bowler
Born: 6 July 1974, Harare, Zimbabwe
County debut: 2003
1st-Class 5 w. in innings: 6
1st-Class 10 w. in match: 2
1st-Class catches: 19
Strike rate: 174.00 (career 54.66)
Overseas tours: South Africa A to England
1996, to Sri Lanka 1998
Overseas teams played for: Natal/
KwaZulu-Natal 1994-95 – 2001-02
Extras: Made first-class debut for Natal B v
Eastern Transvaal at Potchefstroom 1994-95.
Took 8-22 from 10 overs (10-65 in match) for
South Africa A v Worcestershire at Worcester
1996. Played for Natal President's XI v West
Indies A at Durban 1997-98. Took 4-26 for

South Africa A v Sri Lanka A at Colombo 1998, winning Man of the Match award.
Played for Boldon CC in the Durham Senior League 2002-03. Recruited by Somerset
during the 2003 season as cover in the pace bowling department; released at the end of
the season. Is not considered an overseas player
Best batting: 39 KwaZulu-Natal v Gauteng, Johannesburg 1998-99
Best bowling: 8-22 South Africa A v Worcestershire, Worcester 1996

2003 Season

	M	Inns	NO	Runs	HS	Avge	100s	50s	Ct	St	O	M	Runs	Wkts	Avge	Best	5wl	10wM
Test																		
All First	3	3	2	19	12	19.00	-	-	1	-	29	2	133	1	133.00	1-56	-	-
1-day Int																		
C & G																		
NCL	3	2	2	9	8 *	-	-	-	1	-	24	1	145	5	29.00	2-31	-	
Twenty20																		

	M	Inns	NO	Runs	HS	Avge	100s	50s	Ct	St	Balls	Runs	Wkts	Avge	Best	5wI	10wM
Test																	
All First	51	51	13	408	39	10.73	-	-	19	-	8254	4032	151	26.70	8-22	6	2
1-day Int																	
C & G																	
NCL	3	2	2	9	8*	-	-	-	1	-	144	145	5	29.00	2-31	-	
Twenty20																	

GILES, A. F. — Warwickshire

Name: Ashley Fraser Giles
Role: Right-hand bat, slow left-arm bowler
Born: 19 March 1973, Chertsey
Height: 6ft 4in **Weight:** 15st 7lbs
Nickname: Splash, Skinny
County debut: 1993
County cap: 1996
Test debut: 1998
Tests: 25
One-Day Internationals: 32
50 wickets in a season: 2
1st-Class 50s: 18
1st-Class 100s: 3
1st-Class 5 w. in innings: 20
1st-Class 10 w. in match: 3
1st-Class catches: 59
One-Day 100s: 1
One-Day 5 w. in innings: 3
Place in batting averages: 121st av. 32.70 (2002 216th av. 22.00)
Place in bowling averages: 146th av. 52.09 (2002 95th av. 33.94)
Strike rate: 102.22 (career 70.50)
Parents: Michael and Paula
Wife and date of marriage: Stine, 9 October 1999
Children: Anders Fraser, 29 May 2000; Matilde, February 2002
Family links with cricket: 'Dad played and brother Andrew still plays club cricket at Ripley, Surrey'
Education: George Abbott County Secondary, Burpham, Guildford
Qualifications: 9 GCSEs, 2 A-levels, coaching certificate
Off-season: Touring with England
Overseas tours: Surrey U19 to Barbados 1990-91; Warwickshire to Cape Town 1996, 1997, to Bloemfontein 1998; England A to Australia 1996-97, to Kenya and Sri Lanka

1997-98; England to Sharjah (Champions Trophy) 1997-98, to Bangladesh (Wills International Cup) 1998-99, to Australia 1998-99 (CUB Series), to South Africa and Zimbabwe 1999-2000 (one-day series), to Kenya (ICC Knockout Trophy) 2000-01, to Pakistan and Sri Lanka 2000-01, to India and New Zealand 2001-02, to Sri Lanka (ICC Champions Trophy) 2002-03, to Australia 2002-03, to Africa (World Cup) 2002-03, to Bangladesh and Sri Lanka 2003-04, to West Indies 2003-04

Overseas teams played for: Vredenburg/Saldanha, Cape Town 1992-95; Avendale CC, Cape Town 1995-96

Cricketers particularly admired: Dermot Reeve, Tim Munton, Dougie Brown, Ian Botham

Young players to look out for: Ian Bell

Other sports played: Golf (14 handicap), football

Other sports followed: Football (QPR)

Relaxations: 'Cinema, music, spending lots of time with my family'

Extras: Surrey Young Cricketer of the Year 1991. NBC Denis Compton Award for Warwickshire in 1996. Warwickshire Player of the Year in 1996 and 2000. Warwickshire Most Improved Player 1996. Cricket Society's Leading Young All-rounder 1996. Scored hundred (123*) and took five wickets in an innings (5-28) in same match (v Oxford University at The Parks) in 1999, the first time this feat had been performed by a Warwickshire player since Tom Cartwright achieved it v Lancashire at Edgbaston in 1961. Scored 128*, the best by a Warwickshire No. 8, v Sussex at Hove 2000, in the process sharing with Dougie Brown in a new record seventh-wicket partnership for Warwickshire (289). Took 23 wickets (12-135 and 11-196) in two games v Northamptonshire 2000. Took 17 Test wickets in series v Pakistan 2000-01, the highest total by an England bowler in a series in Pakistan. Man of the Match for his 5-57 (including spell of 5-10 in 19 balls) in ODI v India at Delhi 2001-02. Scored 71* v Essex at Edgbaston in the C&G 2003, sharing with Dougie Brown (108) in a competition record seventh-wicket partnership (170). ECB central contract 2003-04

Best batting: 128* Warwickshire v Sussex, Hove 2000

Best bowling: 8-90 Warwickshire v Northamptonshire, Northampton 2000

Stop press: Had match figures of 8-132 and scored a 107-ball match-saving 17* in the first Test v Sri Lanka at Galle 2003-04

2003 Season

	M	Inns	NO	Runs	HS	Avge	100s	50s	Ct	St	O	M	Runs	Wkts	Avge	Best	5wI	10wM
Test	6	8	0	218	52	27.25	-	2	2	-	176	26	569	9	63.22	2-45	-	-
All First	12	18	1	556	96	32.70	-	4	2	-	374.5	62	1146	22	52.09	5-115	1	-
1-day Int	8	4	3	24	20 *	24.00	-	-	1	-	63	2	257	3	85.66	2-3	-	
C & G	3	3	2	123	71 *	123.00	-	1	-	-	30	2	136	5	27.20	2-35	-	
NCL	5	4	2	76	61 *	38.00	-	1	2	-	40	0	168	8	21.00	2-27	-	
Twenty20																		

Career Performances

	M	Inns	NO	Runs	HS	Avge	100s	50s	Ct	St	Balls	Runs	Wkts	Avge	Best	5wl	10wM
Test	25	36	5	542	52	17.48	-	2	15	-	6033	2671	64	41.73	5-67	2	-
All First	139	190	36	4126	128 *	26.79	3	18	59	-	29190	11985	414	28.94	8-90	20	3
1-day Int	32	19	8	138	21 *	12.54	-	-	9	-	1446	1123	27	41.59	5-57	1	
C & G	23	17	6	496	107	45.09	1	3	3	-	1247	839	36	23.30	5-21	1	
NCL	90	59	14	845	61 *	18.77	-	2	29	-	3408	2466	119	20.72	5-36	1	
Twenty20																	

GOODE, C. M.   Northamptonshire

Name: Christopher (<u>Chris</u>) Martin Goode
Role: Right-hand bat, right-arm medium-fast bowler; all-rounder
Born: 12 October 1984, Kettering
Height: 6ft 2in **Weight:** 12st 5lbs
Nickname: Goodey
County debut: No first-team appearance
Parents: Martin and Carla
Marital status: Single
Family links with cricket: 'Dad played locally'
Education: Huxlow Comprehensive, Irthlingborough; Tresham College, Kettering
Qualifications: 9 GCSEs, AS-level Sports Studies, 2 A-levels, Level 2 coach
Career outside cricket: 'University'
Off-season: 'Working hard; getting fitter'
Overseas tours: Northamptonshire U19 to South Africa 2000, 2002
Career highlights to date: 'Playing in Costcutter U15 World Cup 2000'
Cricket moments to forget: 'Being beaten by Pakistan in the semi-final of the U15 World Cup'
Cricket superstitions: 'None'
Cricketers particularly admired: Mike Hussey, Mal Loye, Glenn McGrath
Young players to look out for: 'Me'
Other sports played: Football (Northampton Town U10-U16)
Other sports followed: Football (Man Utd, Rushden & Diamonds)
Injuries: Out for six weeks with a torn muscle in side
Favourite band: 'Don't have one; listen to anything'
Relaxations: Music

Extras: Represented England U15 in Costcutter U15 World Challenge 2000, taking 4-22 v India in opening game
Opinions on cricket: 'Play hard; enjoy it!'

GOODWIN, M. W.   Sussex

Name: <u>Murray</u> William Goodwin
Role: Right-hand bat, right-arm medium/
leg-spin bowler
Born: 11 December 1972, Harare, Zimbabwe
Height: 5ft 9in **Weight:** 11st 2lbs
Nickname: Muzza, Fuzz, Goodie
County debut: 2001
County cap: 2001
Test debut: 1997-98
Tests: 19
One-Day Internationals: 71
1000 runs in a season: 3
1st-Class 50s: 37
1st-Class 100s: 24
1st-Class 200s: 2
1st-Class 300s: 1
1st-Class catches: 84
One-Day 100s: 8

Place in batting averages: 13th av. 59.42 (2002 68th av. 42.10)
Strike rate: (career 98.42)
Parents: Penny and George
Wife and date of marriage: Tarsha, 13 December 1997
Children: Jayden William
Family links with cricket: 'Dad is a coach. Eldest brother played for Zimbabwe'
Education: St John's, Harare, Zimbabwe; Newtonmoore Senior High, Bunbury, Western Australia
Qualifications: Level II coach
Career outside cricket: Coaching, commentating; business
Off-season: Playing for Western Australia
Overseas tours: Australian Cricket Academy to South Africa 1992, to Sri Lanka and India 1993; Zimbabwe to Sri Lanka and New Zealand 1997-98, to Bangladesh (Wills International Cup) 1998-99, to Pakistan 1998-99, to UK, Ireland and Holland (World Cup) 1999, to South Africa 1999-2000, to West Indies 1999-2000, to England 2000
Overseas teams played for: Excelsior, Holland 1997; Mashonaland 1997-98 – 1998-99; Western Australia 1994-95 – 1996-97, 2000-01 –

Career highlights to date: 'Becoming the highest individual scorer in Sussex's history – 335* v Leicestershire, September 2003 at Hove. Broke Duleepsinhji's record of 333 in 1930'

Cricket moments to forget: 'Test against Sri Lanka – we felt the umpiring to be very dubious' (*In the second Test v Zimbabwe 1997-98 at Colombo, chasing 326 to win, Sri Lanka won by five wickets having been 137 for five*)

Cricketers particularly admired: Allan Border, Steve Waugh, Curtly Ambrose, Sachin Tendulkar

Young players to look out for: Shaun Marsh

Other sports played: Hockey (WA Country), golf, tennis

Other sports followed: 'All'

Injuries: 'Ball cut above right eye during Old Trafford County Championship match; did not have to leave field, batted on, stitches done whilst being interviewed by Phil Tufnell on his [Radio] Five Live show!'

Favourite band: 'No real favourites; I have a very eclectic collection'

Relaxations: 'Socialising with friends'

Extras: Emigrated to Australia aged 13. Attended Australian Cricket Academy. Made first-class debut for Western Australia v England, Perth 1994-95, scoring 91 and 77. Scored century (111) in only his second ODI, v Sri Lanka at Colombo 1997-98, winning Man of the Match award. Scored 166* v Pakistan at Bulawayo 1997-98, in the process sharing with Andy Flower (100*) in the highest partnership for Zimbabwe for any wicket in Tests (277*). Scored 148* for Zimbabwe v England in second Test at Trent Bridge 2000, winning Man of the Match award. Scored 112* v West Indies in NatWest Triangular Series at Riverside 2000, winning Man of the Match award. Retired from international cricket in 2000. Scored 167 for Western Australia v New South Wales at Perth in the Mercantile Mutual Cup 2000-01, setting a new record for the highest individual score in Australian domestic one-day cricket. Joined Sussex as overseas player for 2001. Scored maiden first-class double century (203*) v Nottinghamshire at Trent Bridge 2001, having already scored a century (115) in the first innings; in the process of scoring his 203* he shared with Richard Montgomerie in a record partnership for any wicket for Sussex in matches against Notts (372*). Scored 87 v Essex at Hove in the Norwich Union League 2001, in the process sharing with Richard Montgomerie in a Sussex record opening partnership in the one-day league (176). Joint Sussex Player of the Year (with Richard Montgomerie) 2001. Scored century (118*) v Middlesex at Hove in the NCL 2003, sharing with Chris Adams (115*) in a new record third-wicket partnership for the one-day league and a competition record for any wicket for Sussex (228*). Carried his bat for 118* v Lancashire at Old Trafford 2003. Scored maiden first-class triple century (335*) v Leicestershire at Hove 2003, surpassing K. S. Duleepsinhji's 333 in 1930 to set a new record for the highest individual score for Sussex (and winning the Sussex Outstanding Performance of the Year Award 2003)

Opinions on cricket: 'Play long hours and lots of practice for little financial gain.'

Best batting: 335* Sussex v Leicestershire, Hove 2003

Best bowling: 2-23 Zimbabweans v Lahore Division, Lahore 1998-99

2003 Season

	M	Inns	NO	Runs	HS	Avge	100s	50s	Ct	St		O	M	Runs	Wkts	Avge	Best	5wl	10wM
Test																			
All First	17	29	3	1545	335 *	59.42	4	5	12	-		3	0	17	0	-		-	-
1-day Int																			
C & G	2	2	0	53	32	26.50	-	-	-	-									
NCL	18	18	3	731	129 *	48.73	4	2	5	-									
Twenty20	5	5	0	66	38	13.20	-	-	2	-									

Career Performances

	M	Inns	NO	Runs	HS	Avge	100s	50s	Ct	St		Balls	Runs	Wkts	Avge	Best	5wl	10wM
Test	19	37	4	1414	166 *	42.84	3	8	10	-		119	69	0	-	-	-	-
All First	122	214	16	9154	335 *	46.23	27	37	84	-		690	355	7	50.71	2-23	-	-
1-day Int	71	70	3	1818	112 *	27.13	2	8	20	-		248	210	4	52.50	1-12	-	
C & G	8	8	1	320	110 *	45.71	1	1	-	-		42	56	1	56.00	1-28	-	
NCL	49	48	8	1565	129 *	39.12	4	10	15	-								
Twenty20	5	5	0	66	38	13.20	-	-	2	-								

GOUGH, D.   Essex

Name: Darren Gough
Role: Right-hand bat, right-arm fast bowler
Born: 18 September 1970, Barnsley
Height: 5ft 11in **Weight:** 13st 9lbs
Nickname: Rhino, Dazzler
County debut: 1989 (Yorkshire)
County cap: 1993 (Yorkshire)
Benefit: 2001 (Yorkshire)
Test debut: 1994
Tests: 58
One-Day Internationals: 121
50 wickets in a season: 4
1st-Class 50s: 14
1st-Class 100s: 1
1st-Class 5 w. in innings: 27
1st-Class 10 w. in match: 3
1st-Class catches: 44
One-Day 5 w. in innings: 6
Place in batting averages: 222nd av. 20.66
Place in bowling averages: 130th av. 43.30
Strike rate: 81.35 (career 50.75)
Parents: Trevor and Christine

Children: Liam James, 24 November 1994; Brennan Kyle, 9 December 1997
Education: Priory Comprehensive; Airedale and Wharfdale College (part-time)
Qualifications: 2 O-levels, 5 CSEs, BTEC Leisure, NCA coaching award
Overseas tours: England YC to Australia 1989-90; Yorkshire to Barbados 1989-90, to South Africa 1991-92, 1992-93; England A to South Africa 1993-94; England to Australia 1994-95, 1998-99, 2002-03, to South Africa 1995-96, to India and Pakistan (World Cup) 1995-96, to Zimbabwe and New Zealand 1996-97, to Sharjah (Coca-Cola Cup) 1998-99, to South Africa and Zimbabwe 1999-2000, to Kenya (ICC Knockout Trophy) 2000-01, to Pakistan and Sri Lanka 2000-01, to India and New Zealand 2001-02 (one-day series), to Australia 2002-03
Overseas teams played for: East Shirley, Christchurch, New Zealand 1991-92
Cricketers particularly admired: Shane Warne, Steve Waugh, Ian Botham, Michael Atherton, Malcolm Marshall
Young players to look out for: Michael Lumb
Other sports played: Golf, football
Other sports followed: Football (Barnsley and Tottenham Hotspur)
Relaxations: Golf, cinema
Extras: Scored 65 in his first Test innings, v New Zealand at Old Trafford 1994, batting at No. 9. Yorkshire Sports Personality of the Year 1994. Cornhill England Player of the Year 1994-95 and 1998-99. Took hat-trick against Kent at Headingley in 1995. Whyte and Mackay Bowler of the Year 1996. Took Test hat-trick (Healy, MacGill, Miller) v Australia at Sydney 1998-99, the first Ashes hat-trick by an England bowler since J. Hearne's at Leeds in 1899. Was third English cricketer to reach 100 ODI wickets. *Sheffield Star* Sports Personality of the Year. One of *Wisden*'s Five Cricketers of the Year 1999. Represented England in the 1999 World Cup. Won Freeserve Fast Ball award 2000 (for the fastest recorded ball bowled in a televised match) for a delivery timed at 93.1 mph at Lord's on 20 May during the first Test v Zimbabwe. Vodafone England Cricketer of the Year 2000-01. *GQ* Sportsman of the Year 2001. Took 200th Test wicket (Rashid Latif) v Pakistan at Lord's 2001 in his 50th Test, in the same match passing John Snow's total of 202 wickets to move into seventh place in the list of England Test wicket-takers (*see entry on Andrew Caddick*); his 5-61 in Pakistan's first innings was also his first Test five-wicket return at Lord's. Became first England bowler to take 150 ODI wickets, v India at Cuttack 2001-02. Forced to return home early from England tour of Australia 2002-03 after failing to recover from an injury to his right knee but did recover to take the first wicket by any bowler in the 2003 County Championship, v Northamptonshire at Headingley. Man of the Match in the NatWest Series final v South Africa at Lord's 2003. His other international awards include England Player of the Series in the Texaco one-day rubber v South Africa 1998, England's Man of the [Test] Series v West Indies 2000 and Man of the [Test] Series v Sri Lanka 2000-01. Retired from Test cricket after the second Test v South Africa at Lord's 2003. Left Yorkshire during the 2003-04 off-season and has joined Essex for 2004
Best batting: 121 Yorkshire v Warwickshire, Headingley 1996
Best bowling: 7-28 Yorkshire v Lancashire, Headingley 1995

2003 Season

	M	Inns	NO	Runs	HS	Avge	100s	50s	Ct	St	O	M	Runs	Wkts	Avge	Best	5wI	10wM
Test	2	3	0	49	34	16.33	-	-	1	-	53	9	215	1	215.00	1-88	-	-
All First	9	13	1	248	83	20.66	-	2	3	-	271.1	55	866	20	43.30	3-40	-	-
1-day Int	10	1	1	14	14 *	-	-	-	-	-	83	12	314	14	22.42	4-26	-	
C & G	1	1	0	0	0	0.00	-	-	-	-	10	2	43	2	21.50	2-43	-	
NCL	8	5	1	76	33	19.00	-	-	1	-	63.1	7	235	8	29.37	2-26	-	
Twenty20																		

Career Performances

	M	Inns	NO	Runs	HS	Avge	100s	50s	Ct	St	Balls	Runs	Wkts	Avge	Best	5wI	10wM
Test	58	86	18	855	65	12.57	-	2	13	-	11821	6503	229	28.39	6-42	9	-
All First	202	273	51	3627	121	16.33	1	14	44	-	36899	19578	727	26.92	7-28	27	3
1-day Int	121	72	30	469	45	11.16	-	-	17	-	6594	4698	188	24.98	5-44	2	
C & G	28	15	1	234	46	16.71	-	-	3	-	1763	1034	58	17.82	7-27	2	
NCL	114	75	21	749	72 *	13.87	-	1	20	-	4942	3526	143	24.65	5-13	2	
Twenty20																	

GOUGH, M. A. Durham

Name: <u>Michael</u> Andrew Gough
Role: Right-hand bat, off-spin bowler,
specialist gully fielder
Born: 18 December 1979, Hartlepool
Height: 6ft 5in **Weight:** 14st
Nickname: Besty
County debut: 1998
1st-Class 50s: 15
1st-Class 100s: 2
1st-Class 5 w. in innings: 1
1st-Class catches: 57
One-Day 100s: 1
Place in batting averages: 202nd av. 23.36
(2002 31st av. 51.33)
Strike rate: 57.33 (career 82.86)
Parents: Michael and Jean
Marital status: Engaged
Family links with cricket: 'Dad played

Minor Counties cricket for Durham. Cousin Paul played for Durham U19. Uncle John
was a good opening bat'
Education: English Martyrs School and Sixth Form College, Hartlepool
Qualifications: 10 GCSEs, cricket coaching award

Overseas tours: Durham U21 to Sri Lanka November 1996; Durham to Sri Lanka 2001, to South Africa 2002; England U17 to Bermuda (International Youth Tournament) 1997; England U19 to South Africa (including U19 World Cup) 1997-98, to New Zealand 1998-99 (captain); England A to Bangladesh and New Zealand 1999-2000

Overseas teams played for: Claremont-Nedlands, Perth 2001

Cricket superstitions: 'Left pad first, and left foot on and off pitch first'

Cricketers particularly admired: Brad Hodge, Jacques Kallis, Sachin Tendulkar, Rahul Dravid, Ronnie Irani

Young players to look out for: Gordon Muchall, Liam Plunkett, Gary Scott

Other sports played: Football (had trials with Arsenal, Sheffield United and Hartlepool, and attended Middlesbrough FC School of Excellence)

Other sports followed: Football (Hartlepool United season-ticket holder)

Relaxations: 'Cinema, TV, socialising, eating out, football, music'

Extras: Captained North of England and England U15. Part of winning England U17 team at the International Youth Tournament in Bermuda 1997. Durham CCC Young Player of the Year 1997. Scored 62 on first-class debut, v Essex at Riverside 1998. Became youngest player to score a first-class century for Durham, 123 against Cambridge University at Fenner's 1998, aged 18 years 151 days. Captained England U19 v Australia U19 1999. C&G Man of the Match award for his 132 (his maiden one-day century) v Wales at Cardiff 2002. Carried his bat for 75* v Essex at Riverside 2002

Opinions on cricket: 'Far too much cricket played; not enough time for rest and preparation. Reduce amount of overs in a day. Extend tea break by ten minutes. Need to improve pitches and practice facilities.'

Best batting: 123 Durham v Cambridge University, Fenner's 1998

Best bowling: 5-66 Durham v Middlesex, Riverside 2001

2003 Season

	M	Inns	NO	Runs	HS	Avge	100s	50s	Ct	St	O	M	Runs	Wkts	Avge	Best	5wI	10wM
Test																		
All First	13	25	0	584	73	23.36	-	4	8	-	28.4	5	109	3	36.33	2-23	-	-
1-day Int																		
C & G	1	1	0	5	5	5.00	-	-	-	-								
NCL	3	3	0	47	22	15.66	-	-	2	-	26	1	139	2	69.50	1-38	-	
Twenty20																		

Career Performances

	M	Inns	NO	Runs	HS	Avge	100s	50s	Ct	St	Balls	Runs	Wkts	Avge	Best	5wI	10wM
Test																	
All First	67	119	3	2952	123	25.44	2	15	57	-	2486	1350	30	45.00	5-66	1	-
1-day Int																	
C & G	6	5	0	200	132	40.00	1	-	2	-	84	71	0	-	-	-	-
NCL	30	27	3	496	57	20.66	-	2	9	-	853	724	15	48.26	3-26	-	
Twenty20																	

GRANT, J. B.   Essex

Name: Joseph (Joe) Benjamin Grant
Role: Right-hand bat, right-arm
fast-medium bowler
Born: 17 December 1967, White House,
St James, Jamaica
County debut: 2001
1st-Class 5 w. in innings: 1
1st-Class catches: 7
Place in batting averages: (2002 302nd
av. 8.00)
Place in bowling averages: (2002 85th
av. 32.90)
Strike rate: 33.71 (career 53.68)
Overseas teams played for: Jamaica
1990-91 – 1995-96
Extras: Opened the bowling for Jamaica with
Courtney Walsh. Has played in the Yorkshire
leagues. Played for Cambridgeshire in the
Minor Counties Championship in 2001, taking 21 wickets (av. 12.38) in three matches.
Is not considered an overseas player. Released by Essex at the end of the 2003 season
Best batting: 36* Jamaica v Guyana, Albion 1994-95
Best bowling: 5-38 Essex v CUCCE, Fenner's 2002

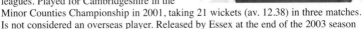

2003 Season

	M	Inns	NO	Runs	HS	Avge	100s	50s	Ct	St	O	M	Runs	Wkts	Avge	Best	5wI	10wM
Test																		
All First	3	4	1	11	4	3.66	-	-	1	-	39.2	3	181	7	25.85	3-61	-	-
1-day Int																		
C & G	1	0	0	0	0	-	-	-	1	-	5	0	40	0	-		-	-
NCL	3	0	0	0	0	-	-	-	-	-	12.2	0	56	3	18.66	2-41	-	
Twenty20																		

Career Performances

	M	Inns	NO	Runs	HS	Avge	100s	50s	Ct	St	Balls	Runs	Wkts	Avge	Best	5wI	10wM
Test																	
All First	29	35	14	165	36 *	7.85	-	-	7	-	3382	2247	63	35.66	5-38	1	-
1-day Int																	
C & G	1	0	0	0	0	-	-	-	1	-	30	40	0	-		-	-
NCL	9	2	0	2	2	1.00	-	-	3	-	296	183	11	16.63	3-13	-	
Twenty20																	

GRAY, A. K. D.   Yorkshire

Name: Andrew (<u>Andy</u>) Kenneth
Donovan Gray
Role: Right-hand bat, right-arm
off-spin bowler
Born: 19 May 1974, Armadale,
Western Australia
Nickname: Graysie
County debut: 2001
1st-Class 50s: 2
1st-Class 100s: 1
1st-Class catches: 14
Place in batting averages: 87th av. 37.72
Place in bowling averages: 148th av. 53.23
Strike rate: 107.69 (career 90.50)
Overseas teams played for: Willetton,
Western Australia
Extras: Played for Wilberfoss in division one
of the York Senior League. Played for

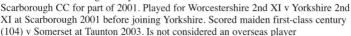

Scarborough CC for part of 2001. Played for Worcestershire 2nd XI v Yorkshire 2nd
XI at Scarborough 2001 before joining Yorkshire. Scored maiden first-class century
(104) v Somerset at Taunton 2003. Is not considered an overseas player
Best batting: 104 Yorkshire v Somerset, Taunton 2003
Best bowling: 4-128 Yorkshire v Surrey, The Oval 2001

2003 Season

	M	Inns	NO	Runs	HS	Avge	100s	50s	Ct	St	O	M	Runs	Wkts	Avge	Best	5wI	10wM
Test																		
All First	9	13	2	415	104	37.72	1	1	12	-	233.2	51	692	13	53.23	3-43	-	-
1-day Int																		
C & G	2	1	0	0	0	0.00	-	-	2	-	20	1	74	4	18.50	3-37	-	
NCL	11	9	5	81	30*	20.25	-	-	1	-	68	0	331	7	47.28	2-28	-	
Twenty20	5	2	0	17	13	8.50	-	-	3	-	14.2	0	140	4	35.00	1-11	-	

Career Performances

	M	Inns	NO	Runs	HS	Avge	100s	50s	Ct	St	Balls	Runs	Wkts	Avge	Best	5wI	10wM
Test																	
All First	16	23	3	612	104	30.60	1	2	14	-	2534	1270	28	45.35	4-128	-	-
1-day Int																	
C & G	2	1	0	0	0	0.00	-	-	2	-	120	74	4	18.50	3-37	-	
NCL	18	13	6	109	30*	15.57	-	-	2	-	613	511	15	34.06	4-34	-	
Twenty20	5	2	0	17	13	8.50	-	-	3	-	86	140	4	35.00	1-11	-	

GRAYSON, A. P.   Essex

Name: Adrian <u>Paul</u> Grayson
Role: Right-hand opening bat, left-arm spin
bowler, county vice-captain
Born: 31 March 1971, Ripon
Height: 6ft 1in **Weight:** 12st
Nickname: Larry
County debut: 1990 (Yorkshire),
1996 (Essex)
County cap: 1996 (Essex)
One-Day Internationals: 2
1000 runs in a season: 4
1st-Class 50s: 41
1st-Class 100s: 15
1st-Class 5 w. in innings: 1
1st-Class catches: 121
Place in batting averages: 189th av. 24.25
(2002 115th av. 34.33)
Strike rate: 98.00 (career 91.96)
Parents: Adrian and Carol
Wife and date of marriage: Alison, 30 September 1994
Children: Oliver, 30 January 1997; Beth, 3 February 1999
Family links with cricket: 'Father is a staff coach; brother Simon plays when free
from football commitments'
Education: Bedale Comprehensive School
Qualifications: 8 CSEs, BTEC in Leisure Studies, Level 2 cricket coach
Off-season: 'Working for Ridley's Brewery. Football coach at Felsted School'
Overseas tours: England YC to Australia 1989-90; England to Kenya (ICC Knockout
Trophy) 2000-01, to Pakistan 2000-01 (one-day series), to Zimbabwe (one-day series)
2001-02; Yorkshire to Barbados 1989-90, to Cape Town 1991, 1992, 1993, to Leeward
Islands 1994
Overseas teams played for: Petone, Wellington 1991-92, 1995-96
Career highlights to date: 'Playing for England. All the trophies won with Essex'
Cricket moments to forget: 'Being bowled out for 57 in NatWest final 1996'
Cricket superstitions: 'Have a lucky vest. Left pad on first'
Cricketers particularly admired: Graham Gooch, Martyn Moxon, Darren Gough
Young players to look out for: Oliver Grayson, Ravi Bopara
Other sports played: Golf (16 handicap), football (Essex CCC charity side; was
offered apprentice forms with Middlesbrough FC at 16 but signed for Yorkshire)
Other sports followed: Football (Leeds United)
Relaxations: 'Spending time with my wife and children; playing golf; watching
football'

Extras: Played for England YC v New Zealand YC 1989 and v Pakistan YC 1990. Yorkshire Player of the Year 1994. Released by Yorkshire at end of 1995 and joined Essex for 1996. Essex Player of the Year 1997, 2001. Scored two centuries (173/149) in match v Northamptonshire at Northampton 2001. Vice-captain of Essex since 2002 **Opinions on cricket:** 'Three sides promoted and relegated is one too many. No heavy roller should be used after the start of the match. Better one-day pitches.'
Best batting: 189 Essex v Glamorgan, Chelmsford 2001
Best bowling: 5-20 Essex v Yorkshire, Scarborough 2001

2003 Season

	M	Inns	NO	Runs	HS	Avge	100s	50s	Ct	St	O	M	Runs	Wkts	Avge	Best	5wI	10wM
Test																		
All First	10	18	2	388	90	24.25	-	3	5	-	147	29	453	9	50.33	4-47	-	-
1-day Int																		
C & G	2	2	2	48	41 *	-	-	-	1	-	19	1	101	0	-		-	-
NCL	7	6	0	115	40	19.16	-	-	2	-	39	0	189	5	37.80	2-13	-	
Twenty20	5	5	3	86	34 *	43.00	-	-	1	-	18	0	149	5	29.80	2-36	-	

Career Performances

	M	Inns	NO	Runs	HS	Avge	100s	50s	Ct	St	Balls	Runs	Wkts	Avge	Best	5wI	10wM
Test																	
All First	175	288	25	8290	189	31.52	15	41	121	-	12507	5871	136	43.16	5-20	1	-
1-day Int	2	2	0	6	6	3.00	-	-	1	-	90	60	3	20.00	3-40	-	
C & G	28	22	3	494	82 *	26.00	-	3	9	-	1151	891	25	35.64	3-24	-	
NCL	157	129	18	2133	69 *	19.21	-	6	44	-	5297	4476	143	31.30	4-25	-	
Twenty20	5	5	3	86	34 *	43.00	-	-	1	-	108	149	5	29.80	2-36	-	

37. Which Sussex fast bowler put on a record 128 for the last wicket in partnership with Ken Higgs against West Indies at The Oval in 1966?

GREENIDGE, C. G.   Northamptonshire

Name: <u>Carl</u> Gary Greenidge
Role: Right-hand bat, right-arm
fast-medium bowler
Born: 20 April 1978, Basingstoke
Height: 5ft 10in **Weight:** 12st 8lbs
Nickname: Carlos, Gs, Jackal
County debut: 1998 (one-day, Surrey),
1999 (first-class, Surrey),
2002 (Northamptonshire)
50 wickets in a season: 1
1st-Class 5 w. in innings: 4
1st-Class catches: 12
Place in batting averages: (2002 298th
av. 9.41)
Place in bowling averages: 137th av. 47.22
(2002 76th av. 31.71)

Strike rate: 62.90 (career 53.33)
Parents: Gordon and Anita
Marital status: 'Long-term girlfriend Luisa'
Family links with cricket: Father Gordon played for Hampshire and West Indies, as
did cousin (on mother's side) Andy Roberts
Education: St Michael's, Barbados; Heathcote School, Chingford; City of
Westminster College
Qualifications: GNVQ Leisure and Tourism, NCA senior coaching award
Off-season: 'Playing district cricket in Melbourne'
Cricket moments to forget: 'Yorkshire v Northants, April 2003, first game of the
season – easily my worst ever game' (*Northants conceded 673 runs and lost by an
innings*)
Cricket superstitions: 'None'
Cricketers particularly admired: Malcolm Marshall, Michael Holding, Viv Richards
Young players to look out for: Scott Newman, Mark Powell, Michael Carberry
Other sports played: Football ('PlayStation!')
Other sports followed: Football (Arsenal), basketball (LA Lakers)
Injuries: Injuries to both ankles
Favourite band: Bob Marley and the Wailers
Relaxations: 'PlayStation, movies, reading, music'
Extras: Spent a year on Lord's groundstaff. Took 5-60 (8-124 the match) on
Championship debut for Surrey, v Yorkshire at The Oval 1999. Released by Surrey at
the end of the 2001 season and joined Northamptonshire for 2002
Opinions on cricket: 'The game is slowly moving forward, what with the
introduction and success of the Twenty20 Cup, which can only be good for English

cricket. I think that 2nd XI matches should be played in the same conditions as 1st XI – it would go a long way towards creating a more competitive atmosphere. Also, let's have shorter sessions in the Championship; one hour for lunch and half an hour for tea!'

Best batting: 46 Northamptonshire v Derbyshire, Derby 2002
Best bowling: 6-40 Northamptonshire v Durham, Riverside 2002

2003 Season

	M	Inns	NO	Runs	HS	Avge	100s	50s	Ct	St	O	M	Runs	Wkts	Avge	Best	5wl	10wM
Test																		
All First	8	6	2	32	13	8.00	-	-	2	-	230.4	25	1039	22	47.22	3-33	-	-
1-day Int																		
C & G																			
NCL	7	0	0	0	0	-	-	-	2	-	53	6	322	11	29.27	3-24	-	
Twenty20																		

Career Performances

	M	Inns	NO	Runs	HS	Avge	100s	50s	Ct	St	Balls	Runs	Wkts	Avge	Best	5wl	10wM
Test																	
All First	28	30	4	221	46	8.50	-	-	12	-	4640	3057	87	35.13	6-40	4	-
1-day Int																	
C & G	3	1	0	12	12	12.00	-	-	1	-	144	160	1	160.00	1-73	-	
NCL	32	12	3	51	20	5.66	-	-	12	-	1295	1173	37	31.70	3-22	-	
Twenty20																	

38. An Old Blundellian, which Glamorgan opener made his Test debut against West Indies at Edgbaston in July 1991?

GROVE, J. O.   Leicestershire

Name: <u>Jamie</u> Oliver Grove
Role: Right-hand bat, right-arm
fast-medium bowler
Born: 3 July 1979, Bury St Edmunds
Height: 6ft 2in **Weight:** 12st 6lbs
Nickname: Groover, Grover
County debut: 1998 (Essex),
2000 (Somerset), 2002 (Leicestershire)
1st-Class 5 w. in innings: 1
1st-Class catches: 2
Strike rate: 120.00 (career 67.58)
Parents: Chris and Pat
Marital status: Single
Family links with cricket: 'Dad played
Minor Counties and brother plays local
cricket. Mum is a keen fan!'
Education: County Upper School, Bury St
Edmunds; Saxon Training College
Qualifications: 9 GCSEs, Modern Apprenticeship in Precision Engineering
Career outside cricket: Engineer
Overseas tours: England U19 to South Africa (including U19 World Cup) 1997-98
Career highlights to date: 'Taking five wickets on debut for Somerset'
Cricket moments to forget: 'Anything that involved me being hit out of the park'
Cricketers particularly admired: Ian Botham
Other sports played: 'All sports'
Other sports followed: Football (West Ham United)
Relaxations: 'Listening to music, chillin' with mates'
Extras: Played for England at U15, U17 and U19 level. Was part of the successful
England U19 World Cup winning squad in South Africa in 1997-98. Released by
Essex at the end of the 1999 season and joined Somerset for 2000. Recorded maiden
first-class five-wicket return (5-90) v Leicestershire at Leicester 2000 on debut for
Somerset. Member of Somerset's 2nd XI Trophy runners-up side 2001. Member of
Somerset's C&G Trophy winning squad 2001. Left Somerset at the end of the 2001
season and joined Leicestershire for 2002. Released by Leicestershire at the end of the
2003 season
Best batting: 33 Essex v Surrey, Chelmsford 1998
Best bowling: 5-90 Somerset v Leicestershire, Leicester 2000

2003 Season

	M	Inns	NO	Runs	HS	Avge	100s	50s	Ct	St	O	M	Runs	Wkts	Avge	Best	5wI	10wM
Test																		
All First	1	0	0	0	0	-	-	-	-	-	20	3	64	1	64.00	1-21	-	-
1-day Int																		
C & G	3	3	2	5	2 *	5.00	-	-	-	-	16	0	68	5	13.60	3-43	-	
NCL	5	2	2	3	3 *	-	-	-	2	-	26.4	0	159	3	53.00	1-38	-	
Twenty20	6	2	2	6	6 *	-	-	-	2	-	15	0	137	3	45.66	3-23	-	

Career Performances

	M	Inns	NO	Runs	HS	Avge	100s	50s	Ct	St	Balls	Runs	Wkts	Avge	Best	5wI	10wM
Test																	
All First	25	31	9	204	33	9.27	-	-	2	-	2906	2089	43	48.58	5-90	1	-
1-day Int																	
C & G	5	3	2	5	2 *	5.00	-	-	-	-	180	118	9	13.11	4-36	-	
NCL	31	11	4	34	13	4.85	-	-	9	-	1264	1078	29	37.17	3-24	-	
Twenty20	6	2	2	6	6 *	-	-	-	2	-	90	137	3	45.66	3-23	-	

GUNTER, N. E. L. Derbyshire

Name: <u>Neil</u> Edward Lloyd Gunter
Role: Left-hand bat, right-arm medium-fast bowler
Born: 12 May 1981, Basingstoke
Height: 6ft
Nickname: Gunts, Wolfman
County debut: 2002
1st-Class catches: 3
Strike rate: 67.75 (career 48.16)
Parents: Tim and Caroline
Marital status: Single
Family links with cricket: 'Dad played cricket for The Mote, Maidstone'
Education: The Clere School; Newbury College
Qualifications: GCSEs and A-levels
Off-season: 'In Oz – Melbourne'
Overseas teams played for: Port Adelaide, South Australia 2002-03
Career highlights to date: 'Signing for Derbyshire'
Cricket moments to forget: 'NUL debut' (*Had figures of 0-80 from nine overs and was out first ball v Gloucestershire at Bristol 2002*)

Cricketers particularly admired: Dominic Cork, Michael DiVenuto
Young players to look out for: Nathan Dumelow ('if he wants it')
Other sports played: Snooker
Other sports followed: 'Passing interest in most sports'
Favourite band: Embrace, The Music, Richard Ashcroft
Relaxations: 'Watching movies; music; sofas'
Extras: Berkshire Young Player of the Year 2000. Played for Berkshire in the C&G 2001. MCC groundstaff 2001. Took 4-14 from eight overs (plus 2-39 in the first innings) on first-class debut v West Indies A at Derby 2002
Best batting: 20* Derbyshire v Hampshire, West End 2003
Best bowling: 4-14 Derbyshire v West Indies A, Derby 2002

2003 Season

	M	Inns	NO	Runs	HS	Avge	100s	50s	Ct	St	O	M	Runs	Wkts	Avge	Best	5wI	10wM
Test																		
All First	3	2	2	29	20 *	-	-	-	-	-	45.1	5	234	4	58.50	2-48	-	-
1-day Int																		
C & G																			
NCL	3	1	0	5	5	5.00	-	-	2	-	12	0	86	0	-		-	-
Twenty20	3	2	2	11	9 *	-	-	-	-	-	12	0	61	1	61.00	1-12	-	

Career Performances

	M	Inns	NO	Runs	HS	Avge	100s	50s	Ct	St	Balls	Runs	Wkts	Avge	Best	5wI	10wM
Test																	
All First	5	5	2	47	20 *	15.66	-	-	3	-	578	387	12	32.25	4-14	-	-
1-day Int																	
C & G	1	1	0	5	5	5.00	-	-	-	-	24	25	0	-		-	-
NCL	5	2	0	5	5	2.50	-	-	2	-	144	177	0	-		-	-
Twenty20	3	2	2	11	9 *	-	-	-	-	-	72	61	1	61.00	1-12	-	

GUY, S. M.   Yorkshire

Name: Simon Mark Guy
Role: Right-hand bat, wicket-keeper
Born: 17 November 1978, Rotherham
Height: 5ft 7in **Weight:** 10st 7lbs
Nickname: Rat
County debut: 2000
1st-Class catches: 37
1st-Class stumpings: 4
Place in batting averages: 279th av. 9.12
Parents: Darrell and Denise
Wife and date of marriage: Suzanne, 13 October 2001

Family links with cricket: 'Father played for Notts and Worcs 2nd XI and for Rotherham Town CC. Brothers play local cricket for Treeton CC'
Education: Wickersley Comprehensive School
Qualifications: GNVQ in Leisure and Recreation, qualified cricket coach, 'two years at the Yorkshire Cricket School under Ralph Middlebrook'
Overseas tours: Yorkshire to South Africa 1999, 2001, to Grenada 2002
Overseas teams played for: Orange Cyrus, NSW 1999-2000
Career highlights to date: 'Playing the last ever County Championship game at Southampton and winning off the last ball with 13 Yorkshire and past Yorkshire men on the pitch at the same time'

Cricket moments to forget: 'On my debut against the Zimbabweans, smashing a door after getting out – but I still say it was an accident'
Cricket superstitions: 'This book is not big enough'
Cricketers particularly admired: Darren Lehmann, Jack Russell
Young players to look out for: Joe Sayers
Other sports played: 'I like to play all sports', rugby (currently Darlington RUFC; also played for South Yorkshire and Yorkshire)
Other sports followed: Rugby (Rotherham RUFC), 'Treeton Welfare CC, where all my family play'
Relaxations: 'Playing all sports, socialising with friends, watching cartoons, and eating a lot'
Extras: Set fifth-wicket partnership record in Yorkshire League (199 unbroken). Topped Yorkshire 2nd XI batting averages 1998 (106.00). Awarded 2nd XI cap 2000. Took five catches in an innings for first time for Yorkshire 1st XI 2000
Best batting: 42 Yorkshire v Somerset, Taunton 2000

2003 Season

	M	Inns	NO	Runs	HS	Avge	100s	50s	Ct	St	O	M	Runs	Wkts	Avge	Best	5wI	10wM
Test																		
All First	6	8	0	73	26	9.12	-	-	16	2								
1-day Int																		
C & G																			
NCL	2	1	0	1	1	1.00	-	-	3	-								
Twenty20																			

Career Performances

	M	Inns	NO	Runs	HS	Avge	100s	50s	Ct	St	Balls	Runs	Wkts	Avge	Best	5wI	10wM
Test																	
All First	13	19	3	221	42	13.81	-	-	37	4	24	8	0	-	-	-	-
1-day Int																	
C & G																	
NCL	2	1	0	1	1	1.00	-	-	3	-							
Twenty20																	

HABIB, A. Essex

Name: Aftab Habib
Role: Right-hand bat, 'very, very
slow bowler'
Born: 7 February 1972, Reading
Height: 5ft 9in **Weight:** 13st
Nickname: Afie, Tabby, Inzy, Habiby
County debut: 1992 (Middlesex),
1995 (Leicestershire), 2002 (Essex)
County cap: 1998 (Leicestershire),
2002 (Essex)
Test debut: 1999
Tests: 2
1000 runs in a season: 2
1st-Class 50s: 38
1st-Class 100s: 18
1st-Class 200s: 1
1st-Class catches: 68
One-Day 100s: 1

Place in batting averages: 103rd av. 35.14 (2002 56th av. 43.81)
Strike rate: 16.00 (career 64.00)
Parents: Tahira (deceased) and Hussain
Marital status: Single
Family links with cricket: Cousin of Zahid Sadiq (ex-Surrey and Derbyshire)
Education: Taunton School
Qualifications: 7 GCSEs, Level 2 coaching
Career outside cricket: Property management
Off-season: 'Travelling; relaxing at home'
Overseas tours: Berkshire CCC to South Africa 1996; England YC to Australia
1989-90, to New Zealand 1990-91; England A to Bangladesh and New Zealand 1999-
2000, to West Indies 2000-01
Overseas teams played for: Globe Wakatu, Nelson, New Zealand 1992-93,

1996-97; Riccarton CC, Christchurch, New Zealand 1997-98; Kingborough CC, Hobart
Career highlights to date: 'Playing for England in 1999'
Cricket moments to forget: 'Losing three one-day finals and a Test match at Lord's'
Cricketers particularly admired: Sachin Tendulkar, Mark Waugh, Ricky Ponting
Young players to look out for: Ravi Bopara, Mark Pettini, Alastair Cook, 'cousin Fuhraz Amjad'
Other sports played: 'Enjoy most sports', football (Reading Schools)
Other sports followed: Football (Reading FC, Liverpool), rugby (Leicester Tigers, New Zealand All Blacks)
Injuries: Out for three to four weeks with an intercostal muscle injury
Favourite band: Adnan Sami
Relaxations: 'Music, reading, golf, cinema'
Extras: Played for England U15-U19. Middlesex 2nd XI Seaxe Player of the Year 1992. Released by Middlesex at end of 1994 season. Played for Berkshire. Leicestershire 2nd XI Player of the Year in 1995. With James Whitaker, set then record partnership for Leicestershire for fifth wicket (320), v Worcestershire at Leicester in 1996. Championship medals with Leicestershire in 1996 and 1998. Scored 101* for England A v New Zealand A to help save the first 'Test' at Lincoln 1999-2000. Left Leicestershire during the 2001-02 off-season and joined Essex for 2002
Opinions on cricket: 'Less matches would improve level of quality of games.'
Best batting: 215 Leicestershire v Worcestershire, Leicester 1996
Best bowling: 1-10 Essex v Kent, Chelmsford 2003

2003 Season

	M	Inns	NO	Runs	HS	Avge	100s	50s	Ct	St	O	M	Runs	Wkts	Avge	Best	5wI	10wM
Test																		
All First	13	22	1	738	151	35.14	2	4	9	-	2.4	0	10	1	10.00	1-10	-	-
1-day Int																		
C & G																		
NCL	8	8	1	193	50	27.57	-	1	1	-	1	0	10	0	-		-	-
Twenty20	2	2	1	26	16 *	26.00	-	-	1	-								

Career Performances

	M	Inns	NO	Runs	HS	Avge	100s	50s	Ct	St	Balls	Runs	Wkts	Avge	Best	5wI	10wM
Test	2	3	0	26	19	8.66	-	-	-	-							
All First	131	197	27	7388	215	43.45	19	38	68	-	64	62	1	62.00	1-10	-	-
1-day Int																	
C & G	18	14	2	326	67	27.16	-	2	6	-	10	11	2	5.50	2-5	-	
NCL	88	78	17	1702	99 *	27.90	-	8	28	-	7	14	0	-		-	
Twenty20	2	2	1	26	16 *	26.00	-	-	1	-							

HALL, A. J. Worcestershire

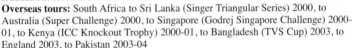

Name: <u>Andrew</u> James Hall
Role: Right-hand bat, right-arm fast-medium
bowler; all-rounder
Born: 31 July 1975, Johannesburg,
South Africa
County debut: 2003
County colours: 2003
Test debut: 2001-02
Tests: 8
One-Day Internationals: 39
1st-Class 50s: 19
1st-Class 100s: 3
1st-Class 5 w. in innings: 9
1st-Class 10 w. in match: 1
1st-Class catches: 43
Place in batting averages: 125th av. 31.78
Place in bowling averages: 19th av. 23.51
Strike rate: 50.34 (career 52.49)
Wife: Leanie
Education: Hoërskool Alberton
Overseas tours: South Africa to Sri Lanka (Singer Triangular Series) 2000, to
Australia (Super Challenge) 2000, to Singapore (Godrej Singapore Challenge) 2000-
01, to Kenya (ICC Knockout Trophy) 2000-01, to Bangladesh (TVS Cup) 2003, to
England 2003, to Pakistan 2003-04
Overseas teams played for: Transvaal/Gauteng 1994-95 – 2000-01;
Easterns 2001-02 –
Extras: Played indoor cricket for South Africa. Made first-class debut for Transvaal
v Zimbabwe A at Johannesburg 1995-96. Played for South Africa Academy in series v
New Zealand Academy 1997. Was shot in the hand and face by a mugger in
Johannesburg in 1999 and was car-jacked in 2002. Played for Durham Board XI in the
NatWest 1999 and for Suffolk in the C&G 2002. Man of the Match in the 1999-2000
SuperSport Series final v Border at Johannesburg. Man of the Match in tied indoor
ODI v Australia at Melbourne 2000. Made Test debut in the second Test v Australia at
Cape Town 2001-02, scoring 70 batting at No. 8. One of *South African Cricket
Annual*'s five Cricketers of the Year 2002. Had match figures of 5-20 from 13 overs in
the first Test v Sri Lanka at Johannesburg 2002-03, including a second innings analysis
of 3-1 from two overs. Had match figures of 11-99 (6-77/5-22) in the SuperSport
Series final 2002-03, winning the Man of the Match award; was also Man of the
Series. Represented South Africa in the 2002-03 World Cup. Joined Worcestershire as
an overseas player for 2003. Called up to South Africa Test squad in England 2003 as
replacement for Jacques Kallis, absent on compassionate grounds. Man of the Match

v Lancashire in the C&G semi-final at Worcester 2003 (20-ball 26 and 4-36, including double wicket maiden in final over of game). Became only the fifth player in Test history to run out of partners on 99*, in the fourth Test v England at Headingley 2003
Best batting: 153 Easterns v North West, Benoni 2001-02
Best bowling: 6-77 Easterns v Western Province, Benoni 2002-03

2003 Season

	M	Inns	NO	Runs	HS	Avge	100s	50s	Ct	St	O	M	Runs	Wkts	Avge	Best	5wI	10wM
Test	4	7	2	121	99 *	24.20	-	1	7	-	144.4	29	430	16	26.87	3-18	-	-
All First	11	16	2	445	104	31.78	1	3	11	-	293.4	70	823	35	23.51	3-10	-	-
1-day Int	7	5	1	111	56	27.75	-	1	3	-	50.1	4	216	8	27.00	3-38	-	
C & G	4	4	0	49	26	12.25	-	-	2	-	26.1	6	111	7	15.85	4-36	-	
NCL	5	5	1	115	47 *	28.75	-	-	-	-	33	1	160	1	160.00	1-13	-	
Twenty20	2	2	0	48	46	24.00	-	-	-	-	8	0	34	2	17.00	2-17	-	

Career Performances

	M	Inns	NO	Runs	HS	Avge	100s	50s	Ct	St	Balls	Runs	Wkts	Avge	Best	5wI	10wM
Test	8	13	3	265	99 *	26.50	-	2	9	-	1241	621	23	27.00	3-1	-	-
All First	63	92	15	2630	153	34.15	3	19	43	-	10499	4634	200	23.17	6-77	9	1
1-day Int	39	29	5	568	81	23.66	-	2	16	-	1008	728	25	29.12	3-32	-	
C & G	8	8	0	221	78	27.62	-	2	4	-	361	249	13	19.15	4-33	-	
NCL	5	5	1	115	47 *	28.75	-	-	-	-	198	160	1	160.00	1-13	-	
Twenty20	2	2	0	48	46	24.00	-	-	-	-	48	34	2	17.00	2-17	-	

39. What did Graeme Hick suffer for the first time in the Edgbaston Test v West Indies in June 2000?

HAMBLIN, J. R. C.   Hampshire

Name: <u>James</u> Rupert Christopher Hamblin
Role: Right-hand bat, right-arm
fast-medium bowler; all-rounder
Born: 16 August 1978, Pembury, Kent
Height: 6ft **Weight:** 14st
Nickname: Hambo
County debut: 2001
1st-Class 50s: 3
1st-Class 5 w. in innings: 1
1st-Class catches: 5
Place in batting averages: 46th av. 45.50
(2002 241st av. 18.00)
Strike rate: 58.28 (career 71.57)
Parents: Bryan and Amanda
Marital status: Single
Family links with cricket: 'Father (C.B.
Hamblin) played for Oxford University
1971-73 and scored a first-class hundred'

Education: Charterhouse School; University of the West of England, Bristol
Qualifications: 9 GCSEs, 2 A-levels, BA (Hons) Social Science
Career outside cricket: Retailing
Off-season: 'Working in retail'
Overseas tours: BUSA to South Africa 2000; Hampshire to Cape Town 2000
Overseas teams played for: Harare Sports Club, Zimbabwe 1996-97; Old
Edwardians, Johannesburg 2000-01; Melville, Perth 2001-03
Career highlights to date: 'First Twenty20 match – Man of the Match. [Also] 6-93
and 96 v Derbyshire 2003'
Cricket moments to forget: 'Any time I don't get selected'
Cricket superstitions: 'None'
Cricketers particularly admired: James Kirtley
Young players to look out for: James Tomlinson
Other sports played: Rackets, golf, tennis
Other sports followed: 'All sports'
Favourite band: Matchbox Twenty
Relaxations: Playing golf and snooker
Extras: 2nd XI Player of the Month for August/September 1999 and for
August/September 2001. Played in Charterhouse Friars' *Cricketer* Cup winning side
2000; scored 174 for Charterhouse Friars v Old Whitgiftians in the first round of the
2002 *Cricketer* Cup. Took 3-23 and scored a 42-ball 61 (50 from 28 balls) v Sussex at
Hove in the Norwich Union League 2001. Recorded maiden first-class five-wicket
return (6-93) v Derbyshire at Derby 2003, following up with a career best 96 in
Hampshire's first innings

Opinions on cricket: 'I think that we play too much cricket. Twenty20 is a fantastic innovation – need to get people watching more live cricket at county level.'
Best batting: 96 Hampshire v Derbyshire, Derby 2003
Best bowling: 6-93 Hampshire v Derbyshire, Derby 2003

2003 Season

	M	Inns	NO	Runs	HS	Avge	100s	50s	Ct	St	O	M	Runs	Wkts	Avge	Best	5wI	10wM
Test																		
All First	5	8	2	273	96	45.50	-	2	1	-	68	13	262	7	37.42	6-93	1	-
1-day Int																		
C & G	1	1	0	4	4	4.00	-	-	-	-								
NCL	13	13	0	278	53	21.38	-	1	4	-	23	1	112	6	18.66	3-20	-	
Twenty20	5	5	0	124	38	24.80	-	-	1	-	8	0	71	7	10.14	3-31	-	

Career Performances

	M	Inns	NO	Runs	HS	Avge	100s	50s	Ct	St	Balls	Runs	Wkts	Avge	Best	5wI	10wM
Test																	
All First	11	18	2	440	96	27.50	-	3	5	-	1002	723	14	51.64	6-93	1	-
1-day Int																	
C & G	1	1	0	4	4	4.00	-	-	-	-							
NCL	33	27	2	441	61	17.64	-	2	11	-	756	650	25	26.00	4-29	-	
Twenty20	5	5	0	124	38	24.80	-	-	1	-	48	71	7	10.14	3-31	-	

HAMILTON, G. M.   Durham

Name: <u>Gavin</u> Mark Hamilton
Role: Left-hand bat, right-arm medium-fast bowler
Born: 16 September 1974, Broxburn
Height: 6ft 3in   **Weight:** 13st
Nickname: Hammy, Jock, Dits, 'anything Scottish'
County debut: 1994 (Yorkshire)
County cap: 1998 (Yorkshire)
Test debut: 1999-2000
Tests: 1
One-Day Internationals: 5
50 wickets in a season: 1
1st-Class 50s: 15
1st-Class 100s: 1
1st-Class 5 w. in innings: 9
1st-Class 10 w. in match: 2
1st-Class catches: 28

One-Day 5 w. in innings: 2
Strike rate: (career 49.05)
Parents: Gavin and Wendy
Marital status: Single
Family links with cricket: Father 'long-term fast bowler at club level' (Sidcup, Kent; West Lothian, Scotland). Brother opening bat for Sidcup CC and has opened batting for Scotland
Education: Hurstmere School, Sidcup
Qualifications: 10 GCSEs and two coaching awards
Overseas tours: England to South Africa and Zimbabwe 1999-2000; Yorkshire pre-season tours to South Africa, Zimbabwe and West Indies; Scotland to Dubai (ICC Six Nations Challenge) 2003-04
Overseas teams played for: Welling, Municipals, and Stellenbosch University – all South Africa; Spotswood, Melbourne
Cricketers particularly admired: Craig White, Mark Robinson, Chris Adams
Other sports played: Golf ('a lot of it'), football (Arsenal YTS)
Other sports followed: Football (Falkirk FC)
Relaxations: Listening to music and reading the paper
Extras: Took ten wickets (5-69/5-43) and scored 149 runs (79/70) v Glamorgan at Cardiff in 1998, the second best all-round contribution in Yorkshire history. Wetherell Award for the Cricket Society's leading all-rounder in English first-class cricket 1998; Yorkshire Players' Player of the Year 1998; Yorkshire Supporters' Player of the Year 1998. Scored 76 for Scotland v Pakistan at Chester-le-Street in the 1999 World Cup, the first 50 scored by a Scotland player in World Cup cricket. Scored 217 runs (av. 54.25) in the 1999 World Cup, more than any England batsman. Finished in top 15 of first-class batting and bowling averages 1999. Scored 57* and took 5-34 v Sussex in the National League at Scarborough 2000. Released by Yorkshire at the end of the 2003 season and has joined Durham for 2004
Best batting: 125 Yorkshire v Hampshire, Headingley 2000
Best bowling: 7-50 Yorkshire v Surrey, Headingley 1998

2003 Season

	M	Inns	NO	Runs	HS	Avge	100s	50s	Ct	St	O	M	Runs	Wkts	Avge	Best	5wI	10wM
Test																		
All First	1	1	0	68	68	68.00	-	1	1	-								
1-day Int																		
C & G																		
NCL	3	2	0	31	20	15.50	-	-	1	-								
Twenty20	3	3	1	41	41 *	20.50	-	-	1	-								

Career Performances

	M	Inns	NO	Runs	HS	Avge	100s	50s	Ct	St	Balls	Runs	Wkts	Avge	Best	5wI	10wM
Test	1	2	0	0	0	0.00	-	-	-	-	90	63	0	-	-	-	-
All First	81	108	20	2321	125	26.37	1	15	28	-	11724	6067	239	25.38	7-50	9	2
1-day Int	5	5	1	217	76	54.25	-	2	1	-	214	149	3	49.66	2-36	-	
C & G	11	9	3	148	39	24.66	-	-	3	-	504	340	19	17.89	3-27	-	
NCL	74	52	12	743	57 *	18.57	-	2	12	-	2435	2033	81	25.09	5-16	2	
Twenty20	3	3	1	41	41 *	20.50	-	-	1	-							

HANCOCK, T. H. C. Gloucestershire

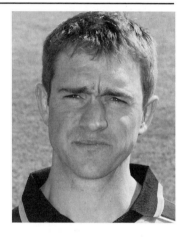

Name: Timothy (Tim) Harold Coulter Hancock
Role: Right-hand bat, right-arm medium bowler
Born: 20 April 1972, Reading
Height: 5ft 11in **Weight:** 12st 7lbs
Nickname: Herbie
County debut: 1991
County cap: 1998
1000 runs in a season: 1
1st-Class 50s: 47
1st-Class 100s: 6
1st-Class 200s: 1
1st-Class catches: 109
One-Day 100s: 2
One-Day 5 w. in innings: 1
Place in batting averages: 104th av. 34.28
(2002 148th av. 29.00)
Strike rate: (career 66.06)
Parents: John and Jennifer
Wife and date of marriage: Rachael, 26 September 1998
Children: George, 30 January 2000; Annabel Rachael, 28 August 2001
Family links with cricket: 'Dad and brother very keen players'
Education: St Edward's, Oxford; Henley College
Qualifications: 8 GCSEs, senior coaching award
Overseas tours: Gloucestershire to Kenya 1991, to Sri Lanka 1992-93, to Zimbabwe (two visits)
Overseas teams played for: CBC Old Boys, Bloemfontein 1991-92; Wynnum Manley, Brisbane 1992-93; Harlequins, Durban 1994-95
Career highlights to date: 'Winning at Lord's four times and doing the treble in one-day competitions in 2000'

Cricket moments to forget: 'Breaking my hand in fielding practice days before the 2001 B&H final'
Cricketers particularly admired: Viv Richards, Gordon Greenidge, Ian Botham
Other sports played: Hockey, golf
Other sports followed: 'I like to play and watch rugby, but don't do either enough'
Relaxations: 'Family life and a round of golf'
Extras: Played hockey for Oxfordshire U19. Vice-captain of Gloucestershire 2000-02. Scored maiden one-day century (110) to win Man of the Match award in the NatWest quarter-final v Northamptonshire at Bristol 2000
Best batting: 220* Gloucestershire v Nottinghamshire, Trent Bridge 1998
Best bowling: 3-5 Gloucestershire v Essex, Colchester 1998

2003 Season

	M	Inns	NO	Runs	HS	Avge	100s	50s	Ct	St	O	M	Runs	Wkts	Avge	Best	5wI	10wM
Test																		
All First	12	21	0	720	97	34.28	-	5	13	-	5	0	22	0	-	-	-	-
1-day Int																		
C & G	2	2	0	144	135	72.00	1	-	1	-								
NCL	7	6	0	162	82	27.00	-	1	2	-								
Twenty20																		

Career Performances

	M	Inns	NO	Runs	HS	Avge	100s	50s	Ct	St	Balls	Runs	Wkts	Avge	Best	5wI	10wM
Test																	
All First	171	300	19	7863	220 *	27.98	7	47	109	-	2907	1680	44	38.18	3-5	-	-
1-day Int																	
C & G	20	19	0	803	135	42.26	2	5	7	-	233	178	13	13.69	6-58	1	
NCL	137	125	2	2279	82	18.52	-	9	49	-	696	654	22	29.72	3-18	-	
Twenty20																	

HARDINGES, M. A.   Gloucestershire

Name: <u>Mark</u> Andrew Hardinges
Role: Right-hand bat, right-arm medium-fast bowler
Born: 5 February 1978, Gloucester
Height: 6ft 1in **Weight:** 13st 7lbs
Nickname: Dinges
County debut: 1999
1st-Class 100s: 1
1st-Class catches: 3
Strike rate: 54.00 (career 88.15)
Parents: David and Jean
Marital status: Single

Family links with cricket: Brother and father played club cricket
Education: Malvern College; Bath University
Qualifications: 10 GCSEs, 3 A-levels, BSc (Hons) Economics and Politics
Overseas tours: Malvern College to South Africa 1996; Gloucestershire to South Africa 1999, 2000
Overseas teams played for: Newtown and Chilwell, Geelong, Australia 1997
Career highlights to date: 'Norwich Union debut v Notts 2001 – scored 65 and set domestic one-day seventh-wicket partnership record (164) with J. Snape. Also Lord's final v Surrey'
Cricket moments to forget: 'Glos v Somerset [Norwich Union 2001] – bowled three overs for 30 and was run out for 0 on Sky TV'
Cricketers particularly admired: Kim Barnett, Steve Waugh, Mark Alleyne
Young players to look out for: James Pearson, Neil Stovold, David Nash
Other sports played: Golf, tennis (Gloucester U14), football (university first team)
Other sports followed: Football (Tottenham)
Relaxations: Golf
Extras: Represented British Universities 2000. Scored 65 v Nottinghamshire at Trent Bridge on NUL debut 2001, in the process sharing in a then record seventh-wicket partnership for domestic one-day competitions (164) with Jeremy Snape. Scored maiden first-class century (172) on his only first-class appearance of 2002, v Oxford University CCE at The Parks. C&G Man of the Match award for his 4-19 v Shropshire at Shrewsbury School 2002
Best batting: 172 Gloucestershire v OUCCE, The Parks 2002
Best bowling: 2-16 Gloucestershire v Essex, Bristol 2000

2003 Season

	M	Inns	NO	Runs	HS	Avge	100s	50s	Ct	St	O	M	Runs	Wkts	Avge	Best	5wl	10wM
Test																		
All First	2	3	1	27	17	13.50	-	-	1	-	27	9	118	3	39.33	1-28	-	-
1-day Int																		
C & G	1	1	0	1	1	1.00	-	-	-	-	5	1	24	0	-		-	-
NCL	6	4	0	29	19	7.25	-	-	3	-	38	1	218	6	36.33	3-40	-	
Twenty20	4	3	1	44	24	22.00	-	-	-	-	4	0	37	3	12.33	3-37	-	

Career Performances

	M	Inns	NO	Runs	HS	Avge	100s	50s	Ct	St	Balls	Runs	Wkts	Avge	Best	5wl	10wM
Test																	
All First	10	11	1	259	172	25.90	1	-	3	-	1146	617	13	47.46	2-16	-	-
1-day Int																	
C & G	5	4	0	14	12	3.50	-	-	2	-	120	73	6	12.16	4-19	-	
NCL	20	18	4	194	65	13.85	-	1	7	-	690	589	14	42.07	3-40	-	
Twenty20	4	3	1	44	24	22.00	-	-	-	-	24	37	3	12.33	3-37	-	

HARMISON, S. J.   Durham

Name: Stephen James Harmison
Role: Right-hand bat, right-arm
fast bowler
Born: 23 October 1978, Ashington,
Northumberland
Height: 6ft 4in **Weight:** 14st
Nickname: Harmy
County debut: 1996
County cap: 1999
Test debut: 2002
Tests: 11
One-Day Internationals: 6
50 wickets in a season: 2
1st-Class 5 w. in innings: 5
1st-Class catches: 16
Place in batting averages: 281st av. 8.66
(2002 310th av. 5.86)
Place in bowling averages: 42nd av. 27.08
(2002 66th av. 30.33)

Strike rate: 56.64 (career 61.54)
Parents: Jimmy and Margaret
Wife and date of marriage: Hayley, 8 October 1999
Children: Emily Alice, 1 June 1999; Abbie
Family links with cricket: Brother James has played for Northumberland; brother
Ben has also played for Northumberland and was called up to the England U19 squad
at the U19 World Cup 2003-04 in Bangladesh
Education: Ashington High School
Off-season: Touring with England
Overseas tours: England U19 to Pakistan 1996-97; England A to Zimbabwe and
South Africa 1998-99; ECB National Academy to Australia 2001-02; England to
Australia 2002-03, to Africa (World Cup) 2002-03, to Bangladesh 2003-04, to West
Indies 2003-04

Cricketers particularly admired: David Boon, Courtney Walsh
Young players to look out for: Gordon Muchall, Kyle Hogg, James Anderson
Other sports played: Football (played for Ashington in Northern League), golf, snooker
Other sports followed: Football ('Newcastle United season-ticket holder')
Relaxations: Spending time with family
Extras: Represented Northumberland U17. Returned match figures of 7-120 (4-78 and 3-42) in ECB National Academy's innings victory over Commonwealth Bank [Australian] Cricket Academy at Adelaide 2001-02. Returned then Test best figures of 4-55 (6-77 in match) in the second Test v Zimbabwe 2003, the inaugural Test at Riverside, his home ground. Shared with Andrew Flintoff in record tenth-wicket partnership for England in Tests v South Africa (99) in the fifth Test at The Oval 2003 and improved on his Test best bowling figures with 4-33 in South Africa's second innings. Awarded six-month ECB central contract 2003
Best batting: 36 Durham v Kent, Canterbury 1998
                  36 Durham v Worcestershire, Worcester 1998
Best bowling: 6-111 Durham v Sussex, Riverside 2001
Stop press: Had match figures of 9-79 (5-35/4-44) in the first Test v Bangladesh at Dhaka 2003-04, winning Man of the Match award. Missed the second Test v Bangladesh at Chittagong 2003-04 with a back problem and was ruled out of the subsequent Test series in Sri Lanka (replaced by Richard Johnson)

2003 Season

	M	Inns	NO	Runs	HS	Avge	100s	50s	Ct	St	O	M	Runs	Wkts	Avge	Best	5wI	10wM
Test	6	8	2	40	14	6.66	-	-	-	-	188.1	42	561	18	31.16	4-33	-	-
All First	11	14	5	78	14 *	8.66	-	-	2	-	349.2	97	1002	37	27.08	4-33	-	-
1-day Int	1	0	0	0	0	-	-	-	-	-	3	0	18	0	-	-	-	-
C & G	2	1	1	0	0 *	-	-	-	2	-	20	2	62	2	31.00	2-37	-	
NCL	7	1	0	0	0	0.00	-	-	-	-	57.5	2	289	14	20.64	4-43	-	
Twenty20																		

Career Performances

	M	Inns	NO	Runs	HS	Avge	100s	50s	Ct	St	Balls	Runs	Wkts	Avge	Best	5wI	10wM
Test	11	17	4	90	20 *	6.92	-	-	1	-	2218	1136	32	35.50	4-33	-	-
All First	86	123	32	760	36	8.35	-	-	16	-	16247	8323	264	31.52	6-111	5	-
1-day Int	6	2	1	9	7	9.00	-	-	3	-	250	246	5	49.20	2-39	-	
C & G	5	4	2	4	2 *	2.00	-	-	3	-	252	184	4	46.00	2-37	-	
NCL	31	11	5	27	11 *	4.50	-	-	3	-	1408	1192	38	31.36	4-43	-	
Twenty20																	

HARRIS, A. J.   Nottinghamshire

Name: <u>Andrew</u> James Harris
Role: Right-hand bat, right-arm
fast-medium bowler
Born: 26 June 1973, Ashton-under-Lyne,
Lancashire
Height: 6ft **Weight:** 11st 9lbs
Nickname: AJ, Honest
County debut: 1994 (Derbyshire),
2000 (Nottinghamshire)
County cap: 1996 (Derbyshire),
2000 (Nottinghamshire)
50 wickets in a season: 1
1st-Class 5 w. in innings: 12
1st-Class 10 w. in match: 3
1st-Class catches: 28
One Day 5 w. in innings: 1
Place in batting averages: 296th av. 3.36

(2002 281st av. 11.61)
Place in bowling averages: 150th av. 56.66 (2002 10th av. 22.01)
Strike rate: 83.53 (career 53.45)
Parents: Norman (deceased) and Joyce
Wife and date of marriage: Kate, 7 October 2000
Children: Jacob Alexander, 28 August 2002
Education: Hadfield Comprehensive School; Glossopdale Community College
Qualifications: 6 GCSEs, 1 A-level
Overseas tours: England A to Australia 1996-97
Overseas teams played for: Ginninderra West Belconnen, Australian Capital Territory
1992-93; Victoria University of Wellington CC, New Zealand 1997-98
Career highlights to date: 'Helping Nottinghamshire achieve first-division status in
the Frizzell Championship for 2003'
Cricket moments to forget: 'Having forgotten my shirt I had to walk out to field in
the last Norwich Union game of the 2001 season (which happened to be on TV)
wearing the diminutive Guy Welton's shirt'
Cricket superstitions: 'None'
Cricketers particularly admired: Merv Hughes, Allan Donald
Young players to look out for: Bilal Shafayat
Other sports played: Golf, snooker, football
Other sports followed: Football (Man City)
Relaxations: 'Good food, good wine and the odd game of golf'
Extras: Left Derbyshire at end of the 1999 season and joined Nottinghamshire for
2000. Scored 41* v Northamptonshire at Northampton 2002, in the process sharing

with Paul McMahon in a record last-wicket stand for Nottinghamshire in matches v
Northamptonshire (68). Nottinghamshire Player of the Year 2002. Had the misfortune
to be 'timed out' v Durham UCCE at Trent Bridge 2003 (was suffering from groin
injury)
Best batting: 41* Nottinghamshire v Northamptonshire, Northampton 2002
Best bowling: 7-54 Nottinghamshire v Northamptonshire, Trent Bridge 2002

2003 Season

	M	Inns	NO	Runs	HS	Avge	100s	50s	Ct	St	O	M	Runs	Wkts	Avge	Best	5wI	10wM
Test																		
All First	10	12	1	37	16 *	3.36	-	-	2	-	208.5	31	850	15	56.66	4-23	-	-
1-day Int																		
C & G																		
NCL	5	0	0	0	0	-		-	3	-	33	1	178	5	35.60	2-18	-	
Twenty20	1	0	0	0	0	-	-	-	-	-	4	0	32	1	32.00	1-32	-	

Career Performances

	M	Inns	NO	Runs	HS	Avge	100s	50s	Ct	St	Balls	Runs	Wkts	Avge	Best	5wI	10wM
Test																	
All First	90	126	32	812	41 *	8.63	-	-	28	-	15556	9315	291	32.01	7-54	12	3
1-day Int																	
C & G	11	5	3	21	11 *	10.50	-	-	1	-	601	402	11	36.54	3-10	-	
NCL	79	28	13	109	16 *	7.26	-	-	20	-	3377	2994	97	30.86	5-35	1	
Twenty20	1	0	0	0	0	-	-	-	-	-	24	32	1	32.00	1-32	-	

40. A former captain of Gloucestershire, which bowler took 34 wickets
in the 2000 England v West Indies series?

HARRIS, C. Z.   Derbyshire

Name: <u>Chris</u> Zinzan Harris
Role: Left-hand bat, right-arm
medium bowler
Born: 20 November 1969, Christchurch,
New Zealand
County debut: 2003 (one-day; *see Extras*)
Test debut: 1992-93
Tests: 23
One-Day Internationals: 230
1st-Class 50s: 31
1st-Class 100s: 9
1st-Class 200s: 2
1st-Class catches: 76
One-Day 100s: 1
One-Day 5 w. in innings: 1
Strike rate: (career 103.03)
Family links with cricket: Father, P. G. Z.
(Zin) Harris, played for Canterbury and New
Zealand 1949-50 – 1964-65; older brother Ben Harris played for Canterbury
1988-89 – 1994-95
Overseas tours: Canterbury to South Africa 1993-94; New Zealand to Australia (B&H
World Series) 1990-91, to Sri Lanka 1992-93, to Australia 1993-94, to South Africa
1994-95, to India and Pakistan (World Cup) 1995-96, to West Indies 1995-96, to
Pakistan 1996-97, to Zimbabwe 1997-98, to Australia 1997-98, to Sri Lanka 1998, to
Malaysia (Commonwealth Games) 1998-99, to Bangladesh (Wills International Cup)
1998-99, to UK, Ireland and Holland (World Cup) 1999, to England 1999, to India
1999-2000, to Kenya (ICC Knockout Trophy) 2000-01, to Pakistan 2002, to West
Indies 2002, to Sri Lanka (ICC Champions Trophy) 2002-03, to Africa (World Cup)
2002-03, plus numerous other one-day series and tournaments
Overseas teams played for: Canterbury 1989-90 –
Extras: Represented New Zealand in the 1991-92 World Cup. One of *New Zealand
Cricket Almanack*'s two Players of the Year 1997. Has won several ODI awards,
including Man of the Series in Zimbabwe 1997-98 and Man of the Match v Australia
at Melbourne (63*/1-17) and at Sydney (42*/3-37) in the VB Series 2001-02. Leading
wicket-taker for New Zealand in ODIs. Was an overseas player with Derbyshire
towards the end of the 2003 season, replacing Mohammad Kaif; also played for
Gloucestershire v India A in a 50-over match at Cheltenham July 2003
Best batting: 251* Canterbury v Central Districts, Rangiora 1996-97
Best bowling: 4-22 Canterbury v Wellington, Christchurch 1996-97

	M	Inns	NO	Runs	HS	Avge	100s	50s	Ct	St	O	M	Runs	Wkts	Avge	Best	5wI	10wM
Test																		
All First																		
1-day Int																		
C & G																		
NCL	4	4	1	30	23 *	10.00	-	-	-	-	36	4	141	4	35.25	2-27	-	
Twenty20																		

Career Performances

	M	Inns	NO	Runs	HS	Avge	100s	50s	Ct	St	Balls	Runs	Wkts	Avge	Best	5wI	10wM
Test	23	42	4	779	71	20.50	-	5	14	-	2560	1170	16	73.12	2-16	-	-
All First	101	158	34	5639	251 *	45.47	11	31	76	-	10818	4357	105	41.49	4-22	-	-
1-day Int	230	198	61	4125	130	30.10	1	15	91	-	10174	7258	197	36.84	5-42	1	
C & G																	
NCL	4	4	1	30	23 *	10.00	-	-	-	-	216	141	4	35.25	2-27	-	
Twenty20																	

HARRISON, D. S.   Glamorgan

Name: <u>David</u> Stuart Harrison
Role: Right-hand bat, right-arm medium-fast bowler, occasional wicket-keeper; all-rounder
Born: 31 July 1981, Newport
Height: 6ft 4in **Weight:** 15st
Nickname: Harry, Hazza, Sunroof, Moorhead, Butter
County debut: 1999
1st-Class 50s: 1
1st-Class 5 w. in innings: 1
1st-Class catches: 3
One-Day 5 w. in innings: 1
Place in batting averages: 263rd av. 13.55
Place in bowling averages: 70th av. 32.10
Strike rate: 54.90 (career 59.59)
Parents: Stuart and Susan
Marital status: Single
Family links with cricket: 'Dad played for Glamorgan in early 1970s (bowling his old school seamers!)' Brother Adam in England squad to U19 World Cup in Bangladesh 2003-04
Education: West Monmouth Comprehensive, Pontypool; Pontypool College
Qualifications: 8 GCSEs, 2 A-levels, Levels 1 and 2 coaching awards

Overseas tours: Gwent U15 to Cape Town 1996; Wales U16 to Jersey 1996, 1997; England U19 to Malaysia and (U19 World Cup) Sri Lanka 1999-2000; Glamorgan to Cape Town 2002

Overseas teams played for: Claremont, Cape Town 2002 (during Glamorgan tour)

Career highlights to date: 'Winning NUL division one title at Canterbury [2002]. Making my Glamorgan debut April 1999 – fifth youngest ever to play for Glamorgan in County Championship!'

Cricket moments to forget: 'Being abused by Dave Houghton on Sky TV for my poor throwing from the boundary (can't hide on TV!)'

Cricketers particularly admired: Matthew Maynard, Craig White

Young players to look out for: Mark Powell, 'little brother Adam'

Other sports played: Squash (Wales U13-U15), 'handy golfer', five-a-side football (Super Dragon Rovers)

Other sports followed: Football (Cardiff City)

Relaxations: 'Sleeping, Sky Digital, JD and Coke, socialising'

Extras: Represented Glamorgan U12-U19. Represented England at U17, U18 and U19 levels. Represented England U19 v Sri Lanka U19 2000. Recorded maiden one-day five-wicket return (5-26), then struck a career-best 37* from 35 balls v Yorkshire at Headingley in the NUL 2002. Recorded maiden first-class five-wicket return (5-80) then scored maiden first-class fifty (66) v Gloucestershire at Cardiff 2003. Glamorgan Young Player of the Year 2003

Opinions on cricket: 'It's a great thing to get paid for something you love doing. Make the most of it because you never know what's around the corner.'

Best batting: 66 Glamorgan v Gloucestershire, Cardiff 2003

Best bowling: 5-80 Glamorgan v Gloucestershire, Cardiff 2003

2003 Season

	M	Inns	NO	Runs	HS	Avge	100s	50s	Ct	St	O	M	Runs	Wkts	Avge	Best	5wI	10wM
Test																		
All First	16	25	5	271	66	13.55	-	1	3	-	366	84	1284	40	32.10	5-80	1	-
1-day Int																		
C & G																		
NCL	9	7	2	72	20	14.40	-	-	1	-	59	1	291	7	41.57	4-44	-	
Twenty20	2	1	0	4	4	4.00	-	-	-	-	5	0	61	1	61.00	1-43	-	

Career Performances

	M	Inns	NO	Runs	HS	Avge	100s	50s	Ct	St	Balls	Runs	Wkts	Avge	Best	5wI	10wM
Test																	
All First	20	30	5	327	66	13.08	-	1	3	-	2622	1525	44	34.65	5-80	1	-
1-day Int																	
C & G																	
NCL	17	14	6	138	37 *	17.25	-	-	3	-	660	572	16	35.75	5-26	1	
Twenty20	2	1	0	4	4	4.00	-	-	-	-	30	61	1	61.00	1-43	-	

HARRITY, M. A. Worcestershire

Name: <u>Mark</u> Andrew Harrity
Role: Right-hand bat, left-arm fast bowler
Born: 9 March 1974, Adelaide, Australia
Height: 6ft 4in **Weight:** 13st 9lbs
Nickname: Hags
County debut: 2003
County colours: 2003
1st-Class 5 w. in innings: 2
1st-Class catches: 26
Place in bowling averages: 141st av. 49.90
Strike rate: 91.00 (career 71.15)
Parents: Judith and Stuart
Marital status: Engaged to Laura
Children: Lachlan, 1 August 2000
Education: Taperoo High School
Career outside cricket: 'Coaching at
Adelaide Oval; raising my son'
Off-season: 'Club cricket in South Australia'

Overseas tours: Young Australia (Australia A) to England and Netherlands 1995
Overseas teams played for: South Australia 1993-94 – 2002-03; West Torrens, South Australia 2001-02 –
Career highlights to date: 'Winning the Sheffield Shield with South Australia in 1995-96'
Cricket moments to forget: 'Bringing up Dean Jones's 100 after kicking the ball into the boundary for four runs in 1994'
Cricket superstitions: 'Always wear sweatband'
Cricketers particularly admired: Dean Jones, Jason Gillespie
Young players to look out for: Michael Clarke (NSW), Kadeer Ali
Other sports played: Australian Rules football ('past player')
Other sports followed: Australian Rules football (Port Power, Port Magpies)
Injuires: Out for four weeks with tendonitis of the shoulder
Favourite band: Bon Jovi, U2
Relaxations: 'Play guitar, piano'
Extras: Selected for Prime Minister's XI v West Indians at Canberra 1995-96 and for Prime Minister's XI v England tourists at Canberra 1998-99, taking 3-46. Played for Australian XI v West Indians at Brisbane 1995-96. One of South Australia's leading wicket-takers for several seasons (one-day and four-day), topping the state's wicket-taking list in the ING Cup 2001-02 with 17 wickets (av. 19.76). Has name on Adelaide Oval locker for ten years' service (locker was previously that of Sir Donald Bradman and Les Favell). Is not considered an overseas player
Opnions on cricket: 'Lots of exciting young talent coming through. Twenty20 good concept!'

271

Best batting: 19 South Australia v Victoria, Melbourne 2001-02
Best bowling: 5-65 South Australia v Tasmania, Hobart 2001-02

2003 Season

	M	Inns	NO	Runs	HS	Avge	100s	50s	Ct	St	O	M	Runs	Wkts	Avge	Best	5wl	10wM
Test																		
All First	7	9	6	30	16	10.00	-	-	-	-	166.5	37	549	11	49.90	4-39	-	-
1-day Int																		
C & G	1	0	0	0	0	-	-	-	1	-	7.5	0	23	3	7.66	3-23	-	
NCL	7	3	1	17	15	8.50	-	-	1	-	40	2	260	9	28.88	3-27	-	
Twenty20	5	3	1	0	0*	0.00	-	-	2	-	17.4	0	143	7	20.42	2-20	-	

Career Performances

	M	Inns	NO	Runs	HS	Avge	100s	50s	Ct	St	Balls	Runs	Wkts	Avge	Best	5wl	10wM
Test																	
All First	90	100	52	251	19	5.22	-	-	26	-	14854	8109	208	38.98	5-65	2	-
1-day Int																	
C & G	1	0	0	0	0	-	-	-	1	-	47	23	3	7.66	3-23	-	
NCL	7	3	1	17	15	8.50	-	-	1	-	240	260	9	28.88	3-27	-	
Twenty20	5	3	1	0	0*	0.00	-	-	2	-	106	143	7	20.42	2-20	-	

41. Who were the spin twins who had match figures of 5-77 and 11-48 respectively against West Indies at The Oval in 1957?

HARVEY, I. J.   Yorkshire

Name: <u>Ian</u> Joseph Harvey
Role: Right-hand bat, right-arm
fast-medium bowler
Born: 10 April 1972, Wonthaggi,
Victoria, Australia
Height: 5ft 9in **Weight:** 12st 8lbs
Nickname: Freak
County debut: 1999 (Gloucestershire)
County cap: 1999 (Gloucestershire)
One-Day Internationals: 55
1st-Class 50s: 33
1st-Class 100s: 9
1st-Class 5 w. in innings: 14
1st-Class 10 w. in match: 2
1st-Class catches: 86
One-Day 100s: 1
One-Day 5 w. in innings: 8
Place in batting averages: 52nd av. 44.88

(2002 60th av. 43.33)
Place in bowling averages: 15th av. 23.14 (2002 5th av. 19.03)
Strike rate: 43.40 (career 54.84)
Family links with cricket: Brothers play club cricket in Australia
Education: Wonthaggi Technical College
Overseas tours: Australian Academy to New Zealand 1994-95; Australia to Sharjah
(Coca-Cola Cup) 1997-98, to New Zealand 1999-2000 (one-day series), to Kenya
(ICC Knockout Trophy) 2000-01, to India 2000-01 (one-day series), to England 2001
(one-day series), to South Africa 2001-02 (one-day series), to Africa (World Cup)
2002-03, to West Indies 2002-03 (one-day series), to India (TVS Cup) 2003-04;
Australia A to South Africa 2002-03
Overseas teams played for: Dandenong, Victoria; Fitzroy-Doncaster, Victoria;
Victoria 1993-94 –
Extras: The nickname 'Freak' is a reference to his brilliant fielding and was
reportedly coined by Shane Warne. Attended Commonwealth Bank [Australian]
Cricket Academy 1994. Took a wicket (Jonty Rhodes) with his second ball in ODI
cricket 1997-98. Top scorer (57) for Victoria in their Mercantile Mutual Cup final
victory over New South Wales 1998-99. Joined Gloucestershire in 1999 as overseas
player. Top wicket-taker in the 1999 National League competition with 30 wickets at
15.80. Had match figures of 10-32 from 25 overs (and scored 60 in Gloucestershire's
only innings) v Sussex at Hove 2000. Man of the Match in the Carlton Series first
final v West Indies at Sydney 2000-01 (47* at No. 8/2-5 from six overs). Won the
Walter Lawrence Trophy for the season's fastest first-class hundred with his 61-ball

273

century v Derbyshire at Bristol 2001; also took 5-89 in Derbyshire's second innings. Took hat-trick (Knight, N. Smith, Bell) v Warwickshire at Bristol in the B&H 2002. Has won numerous Australian and English domestic awards, including C&G Man of the Match in the quarter-final v Warwickshire at Edgbaston 2003 (5-23 and a run out) and in the final v Worcestershire at Lord's 2003 (2-37 and a 36-ball 61). Scored the first ever century in the Twenty20 (100* from 50 balls), v Warwickshire at Edgbaston 2003. ACB contract 2003-04. Left Gloucestershire at the end of the 2003 season and has joined Yorkshire for 2004

Best batting: 136 Victoria v South Australia, Melbourne 1995-96
Best bowling: 8-101 Australia A v South Africa A, Adelaide 2002-03

2003 Season

	M	Inns	NO	Runs	HS	Avge	100s	50s	Ct	St	O	M	Runs	Wkts	Avge	Best	5wI	10wM
Test																		
All First	6	12	3	404	128 *	44.88	1	1	4	-	195.2	54	625	27	23.14	4-43	-	-
1-day Int																		
C & G	2	2	0	73	61	36.50	-	1	-	-	19	1	60	7	8.57	5-23	1	
NCL	7	7	0	264	96	37.71	-	1	1	-	60.2	2	311	17	18.29	5-38	1	
Twenty20	6	6	2	248	100 *	62.00	1	1	-	-	23.5	0	153	10	15.30	3-28	-	

Career Performances

	M	Inns	NO	Runs	HS	Avge	100s	50s	Ct	St	Balls	Runs	Wkts	Avge	Best	5wI	10wM
Test																	
All First	116	196	18	5816	136	32.67	9	33	86	-	18539	9053	338	26.78	8-101	14	2
1-day Int	55	41	11	554	48 *	18.46	-	-	13	-	2560	1992	65	30.64	4-16	-	
C & G	16	15	0	290	61	19.33	-	1	6	-	840	518	35	14.80	5-23	1	
NCL	54	53	3	1534	96	30.68	-	9	14	-	2479	1707	108	15.80	5-19	4	
Twenty20	6	6	2	248	100 *	62.00	1	1	-	-	143	153	10	15.30	3-28	-	

42. Which player was in Leicestershire's 1998 County Championship winning side and was also West Indies' leading wicket-taker in the 1997-98 ODI series against England?

HASAN ADNAN   Derbyshire

Name: Mohammad Hasan Adnan
Role: Right-hand bat, right-arm
off-spin bowler
Born: 15 May 1975, Lahore, Punjab
County debut: 2003
1st-Class 50s: 24
1st-Class 100s: 4
1st-Class catches: 26
Overseas teams played for: Islamabad
1994-95, 2000-01; Gujranwala 1997-98 –
1998-99; Water and Power Development
Authority (WAPDA) 1997-98 –
Extras: Man of the Match for WAPDA v
National Bank at Sheikhupura in the Tissot
Cup 1998-99. Man of the Match for WAPDA
v Lahore City at Faisalabad in the Tissot Cup
1999-2000 (101*). Made two appearances as
professional for Todmorden in the Lancashire
League 2003. Is not considered an overseas player
Best batting: 130 WAPDA v Bahawalpur, Bahawalpur 1999-2000

2003 Season

	M	Inns	NO	Runs	HS	Avge	100s	50s	Ct	St	O	M	Runs	Wkts	Avge	Best	5wI	10wM
Test																		
All First	2	4	1	189	84	63.00	-	2	1	-								
1-day Int																		
C & G																		
NCL	1	1	0	29	29	29.00	-	-	2	-								
Twenty20																		

Career Performances

	M	Inns	NO	Runs	HS	Avge	100s	50s	Ct	St	Balls	Runs	Wkts	Avge	Best	5wI	10wM
Test																	
All First	51	81	14	3095	130	46.19	4	24	26	-	18	20	0	-	-	-	-
1-day Int																	
C & G																	
NCL	1	1	0	29	29	29.00	-	-	2	-							
Twenty20																	

HATCH, N. G. Durham

Name: <u>Nicholas</u> Guy Hatch
Role: Right-hand bat, right-arm
medium-fast bowler
Born: 21 April 1979, Darlington
Height: 6ft 7in **Weight:** 14st 10lbs
Nickname: Tony
County debut: 2001
1st-Class catches: 4
Place in bowling averages: 103rd av. 37.23
Strike rate: 69.07 (career 65.27)
Parents: Mike and Paula
Marital status: Single
Family links with cricket: Father played
club cricket with Darlington CC for over 20
years. Brother plays club cricket in London
Education: Barnard Castle School;
Hull University
Qualifications: 11 GCSEs, 5 A-levels,
BA History and Politics

Overseas teams played for: Claremont-Nedlands CC, Perth 2000-01, 2001-02
Career highlights to date: 'First-class debut'
Cricketers particularly admired: Courtney Walsh, Steve Waugh, Curtly Ambrose
Young players to look out for: Nicky Peng, Gordon Muchall
Other sports played: Rugby union (played for North of England U19)
Other sports followed: All sports
Relaxations: Reading, socialising with friends
Extras: Represented British Universities v New Zealand A 2000. Released by Durham
at the end of the 2003 season
Best batting: 24 Durham v Sussex, Riverside 2001
Best bowling: 4-61 Durham v Worcestershire, Riverside 2002

2003 Season

	M	Inns	NO	Runs	HS	Avge	100s	50s	Ct	St	O	M	Runs	Wkts	Avge	Best	5wl	10wM
Test																		
All First	5	5	2	16	5	5.33	-	-	1	-	149.4	28	484	13	37.23	3-66	-	-
1-day Int																		
C & G																		
NCL	2	1	0	6	6	6.00	-	-	-	-	18	3	80	1	80.00	1-36	-	
Twenty20																		

Career Performances

	M	Inns	NO	Runs	HS	Avge	100s	50s	Ct	St	Balls	Runs	Wkts	Avge	Best	5wI	10wM
Test																	
All First	18	25	12	157	24	12.07	-	-	4	-	3133	1795	48	37.39	4-61	-	-
1-day Int																	
C & G	2	0	0	0	0	-	-	-	-	-	102	65	3	21.66	2-51	-	
NCL	10	5	2	44	20 *	14.66	-	-	-	-	420	358	10	35.80	3-26	-	
Twenty20																	

HAVELL, P. M. R.   Derbyshire

Name: <u>Paul</u> Matthew Roger Havell
Role: Left-hand bat, right-arm fast-medium bowler
Born: 4 July 1980, Melbourne, Australia
Height: 6ft 3in **Weight:** 14st 2lbs
Nickname: Trigger, Two-Tone Malone, Hauler
County debut: 2001 (Sussex), 2003 (Derbyshire)
1st-Class catches: 2
Place in bowling averages: 90th av. 35.57
Strike rate: 45.71 (career 48.71)
Parents: Roger and Caroline
Marital status: Single
Family links with cricket: 'Brother Mark played up to Sussex U19 until back problems ended any hope of going any further'
Education: Warden Park School
Qualifications: 9 GCSEs, 1 A-level, Level 2 coach
Off-season: 'Going to Mel to see Dad'
Overseas tours: Sussex U19 to Barbados 1997-98; Sussex to Grenada 2000-01
Overseas teams played for: East Doncaster CC, Australia 1998-99; Carlton CC, Melbourne 2000-01; Fairfield-Liverpool, Sydney 2002-03
Career highlights to date: 'Making my first-class debut [for Derbyshire] against South Africa, and first first-class wicket – Graeme Smith lbw'
Cricket moments to forget: 'Don't have any … yet!'
Cricket superstitions: 'None'
Cricketers particularly admired: James Kirtley
Young players to look out for: Matthew 'Big Cheese' Prior, 'all players at DCCC'
Favourite band: Matchbox Twenty
Relaxations: 'Watching movies and chilling at home'
Extras: Sussex Young Cricketer of the Year 1995. Released by Sussex at the end of

the 2002 season; joined Derbyshire during 2003, taking 4-129 on debut v South
Africans at Derby

Opinions on cricket: 'It's getting harder and harder to keep your place on a county
staff. I lost mine at Sussex in 2002 and I'm not gonna let it happen again. So when
you have something, keep hold of it!'

Best batting: 7* Derbyshire v Somerset, Taunton 2003

Best bowling: 4-129 Derbyshire v South Africans, Derby 2003

2003 Season

	M	Inns	NO	Runs	HS	Avge	100s	50s	Ct	St	O	M	Runs	Wkts	Avge	Best	5wI	10wM
Test																		
All First	4	6	5	10	7 *	10.00	-	-	2	-	106.4	18	498	14	35.57	4-129	-	-
1-day Int																		
C & G																			
NCL	1	0	0	0	0	-	-	-	-	-	2	0	17	0	-		-	-
Twenty20																			

Career Performances

	M	Inns	NO	Runs	HS	Avge	100s	50s	Ct	St	Balls	Runs	Wkts	Avge	Best	5wI	10wM
Test																	
All First	5	6	5	10	7 *	10.00	-	-	2	-	682	514	14	36.71	4-129	-	-
1-day Int																	
C & G																		
NCL	2	0	0	0	0	-	-	-	-	-	36	37	0	-		-	-
Twenty20																		

HAYNES, J. J.   Lancashire

Name: <u>Jamie</u> Jonathan Haynes
Role: Right-hand bat, wicket-keeper
Born: 5 July 1974, Bristol
Height: 5ft 10½in **Weight:** 13st
Nickname: JJ, Wolf, Monkey
County debut: 1996
1st-Class 50s: 3
1st-Class catches: 35
1st-Class stumpings: 2
Parents: Steve Haynes and Moiya Ford
Wife and date of marriage: Michelle, 20 December 2003
Family links with cricket: 'Dad and uncle played for Gloucestershire. [American]
uncle number one cricket authority in New York'
Education: St Edmunds College, Canberra; University of Canberra

Qualifications: Year 12 Certificate, coaching certificate, 'partially complete BA Journalism'
Career outside cricket: 'Sniffing around our sponsor'
Off-season: Training with Lancashire
Overseas tours: Lancashire pre-season tours
Overseas teams played for: Weston Creek CC, Canberra; Queanbeyan CC, Canberra; Tuggeranong Valley CC, Canberra 1995-96; South Canberra CC 1996-97
Career highlights to date: 'Winning any trophies'
Cricket moments to forget: 'Losing four front teeth while keeping wicket'
Cricket superstitions: 'Don't cross on stairs unless fingers crossed'
Cricketers particularly admired: Warren Hegg, 'Cool' Carl Hooper, Jack Russell, Carl Butrum
Young players to look out for: Kyle Hogg, Steven Crook
Other sports played: Australian Rules football (Queanbeyan Tigers), golf, rugby
Other sports followed: Football (Manchester United), rugby (Sale Sharks), Australian Rules (Carlton)
Favourite band: Counting Crows, REM
Relaxations: 'Cooking, golf; tennis ball drills with "Mad Mal Loye"'
Extras: Top scorer with 80 as nightwatchman in Lancashire's first innings v Sri Lanka A at Old Trafford 1999
Opinions on cricket: 'I think it would be nice if people stopped bagging the system that they made a lot of money out of.'
Best batting: 80 Lancashire v Sri Lanka A, Old Trafford 1999

2003 Season

	M	Inns	NO	Runs	HS	Avge	100s	50s	Ct	St	O	M	Runs	Wkts	Avge	Best	5wI	10wM
Test																		
All First	2	3	0	25	13	8.33	-	-	3	-								
1-day Int																		
C & G																		
NCL																		
Twenty20	1	1	0	9	9	9.00	-	-	-	-								

Career Performances

	M	Inns	NO	Runs	HS	Avge	100s	50s	Ct	St	Balls	Runs	Wkts	Avge	Best	5wl	10wM
Test																	
All First	16	24	4	443	80	22.15	-	3	35	2							
1-day Int																	
C & G	1	1	1	59	59 *	-		-	1	1	-						
NCL	10	5	1	32	12	8.00	-	-	13	3							
Twenty20	1	1	0	9	9	9.00	-	-	-	-							

HAYWARD, M. Middlesex

Name: Mornantau (<u>Nantie</u>) Hayward
Role: Right-hand bat, right-arm fast bowler
Born: 6 March 1977, Uitenhage,
South Africa
County debut: 2003 (Worcestershire)
County colours: 2003 (Worcestershire)
Test debut: 1999-2000
Tests: 14
One-Day Internationals: 21
50 wickets in a season: 1
1st-Class 50s: 1
1st-Class 5 w. in innings: 9
1st-Class 10 w. in match: 2
1st-Class catches: 24
One-Day 5 w. in innings: 1
Place in batting averages: 286th av. 7.68
Place in bowling averages: 13th av. 22.88
Strike rate: 38.28 (career 50.72)
Education: Daniel Pienaar Technical High
Overseas tours: South Africa U19 to India 1995-96; South Africa to England 1998, to India 1999-2000, to Sharjah (Coca-Cola Sharjah Cup) 1999-2000, to Sri Lanka 2000, to Australia (Super Challenge) 2000, to Australia 2001-02
Overseas teams played for: Eastern Province 1995-96 –
Extras: Represented South Africa Schools 1995. Made first-class debut for Eastern Province B v Zimbabwe Board XI at Harare 1995-96. Represented South Africa Academy in home series v New Zealand Academy 1997. Has represented South Africa A against various touring sides. Made Test debut in second Test v England at Port Elizabeth 1999-2000, taking 4-75 in England's first innings. Man of the Match award for his 4-31 in fifth Coca-Cola Cup match v India at Sharjah 1999-2000. One of *South African Cricket Annual*'s five Cricketers of the Year 2000. Recorded maiden Test five-wicket return (5-56) in the first Test v Pakistan at Durban 2002-03. Joined

Worcestershire as an overseas player for 2003, taking 5-70 (9-165 in match) on Championship debut v Hampshire at Worcester. Has joined Middlesex as an overseas player for 2004

Best batting: 55* Eastern Province v Boland, Port Elizabeth 1997-98
Best bowling: 6-31 Eastern Province v Easterns, Port Elizabeth 1999-2000

2003 Season

	M	Inns	NO	Runs	HS	Avge	100s	50s	Ct	St	O	M	Runs	Wkts	Avge	Best	5wI	10wM
Test																		
All First	16	21	5	123	28	7.68	-	-	5	-	427.3	83	1533	67	22.88	5-46	2	-
1-day Int																		
C & G	4	1	0	4	4	4.00	-	-	1	-	29	2	143	8	17.87	5-49	1	
NCL	8	3	2	14	11	14.00	-	-	-	-	58	2	289	12	24.08	3-32	-	
Twenty20	2	1	0	2	2	2.00	-	-	-	-	7.2	0	53	3	17.66	3-21	-	

Career Performances

	M	Inns	NO	Runs	HS	Avge	100s	50s	Ct	St	Balls	Runs	Wkts	Avge	Best	5wI	10wM
Test	14	14	6	69	14	8.62	-	-	1	-	2565	1417	50	28.34	5-56	1	-
All First	83	85	29	727	55 *	12.98	-	1	24	-	15420	8334	304	27.41	6-31	9	2
1-day Int	21	5	1	12	4	3.00	-	-	4	-	993	858	21	40.85	4-31	-	
C & G	4	1	0	4	4	4.00	-	-	1	-	174	143	8	17.87	5-49	1	
NCL	8	3	2	14	11	14.00	-	-	-	-	348	289	12	24.08	3-32	-	
Twenty20	2	1	0	2	2	2.00	-	-	-	-	44	53	3	17.66	3-21	-	

43. Which former Cambridge University captain averaged 70.89
in 11 ODIs against West Indies?

HEGG, W. K.   Lancashire

Name: <u>Warren</u> Kevin Hegg
Role: Right-hand bat, wicket-keeper,
county captain
Born: 23 February 1968, Manchester
Height: 5ft 9in **Weight:** 12st 10lbs
Nickname: Chucky
County debut: 1986
County cap: 1989
Benefit: 1999 (£178,000)
Test debut: 1998-99
Tests: 2
50 dismissals in a season: 6
1st-Class 50s: 51
1st-Class 100s: 7
1st-Class catches: 793
1st-Class stumpings: 84
Place in batting averages: 130th av. 31.07
(2002 228th av. 19.80)

Parents: Kevin (deceased) and Glenda
Wife and date of marriage: Joanne, 29 October 1994
Children: Chloe Louise, 13 November 1998
Family links with cricket: Brother Martin plays in local leagues
Education: Unsworth High School; Stand College, Whitefield
Qualifications: 5 O-levels, 7 CSEs, qualified coach
Career outside cricket: Runs Parkfield Inn at Whitefield, near Manchester
Overseas tours: NCA North U19 to Bermuda 1985; England YC to Sri Lanka 1986-87,
to Australia (U19 World Cup) 1987-88; England A to Pakistan and Sri Lanka 1990-91,
to Australia 1996-97; England to Australia 1998-99, to India and New Zealand 2001-02
Overseas teams played for: Sheffield, Tasmania 1988-90, 1992-93
Cricketers particularly admired: Ian Botham, Alan Knott, Bob Taylor,
Gehan Mendis, Ian Healy
Other sports played: Football (Old Standians)
Other sports followed: Rugby league (Salford City Reds), football (Man United)
Relaxations: 'Golf, golf, golf'
Extras: Became youngest player for 30 years to score a century for Lancashire with
his 130 v Northamptonshire at Northampton in 1987 aged 19 (in his fourth first-class
game). Took 11 catches in match v Derbyshire at Chesterfield 1989, equalling world
first-class record. Wombwell Cricket Lovers' Society joint Wicket-keeper of the Year
1993. Vice-captain of Lancashire 1999 and 2001. Lancashire Player of the Year 2001.
Lancashire captain since 2002, the first wicket-keeper to hold the post in an official
capacity
Best batting: 134 Lancashire v Leicestershire, Old Trafford 1996

2003 Season

	M	Inns	NO	Runs	HS	Avge	100s	50s	Ct	St	O	M	Runs	Wkts	Avge	Best	5wI	10wM
Test																		
All First	16	20	7	404	61 *	31.07	-	1	46	3								
1-day Int																		
C & G	4	3	0	12	7	4.00	-	-	8	-								
NCL	18	10	3	132	39	18.85	-	-	26	3								
Twenty20	5	4	0	54	45	13.50	-	-	4	2								

Career Performances

	M	Inns	NO	Runs	HS	Avge	100s	50s	Ct	St	Balls	Runs	Wkts	Avge	Best	5wI	10wM
Test	2	4	0	30	15	7.50	-	-	8	-							
All First	321	466	90	10388	134	27.62	7	51	793	84	6	7	0	-	-	-	-
1-day Int																	
C & G	47	25	1	423	60	17.62	-	1	57	7							
NCL	241	148	54	1877	54	19.96	-	2	255	42							
Twenty20	5	4	0	54	45	13.50	-	-	4	2							

HEMP, D. L.   Glamorgan

Name: <u>David</u> Lloyd Hemp
Role: Left-hand bat
Born: 15 November 1970,
Hamilton, Bermuda
Height: 6ft 1in **Weight:** 12st 10lbs
Nickname: Hempy, Mad Dog
County debut: 1991 (Glamorgan),
1997 (Warwickshire)
County cap: 1994 (Glamorgan),
1997 (Warwickshire)
1000 runs in a season: 3
1st-Class 50s: 51
1st-Class 100s: 18
1st-Class catches: 118
One-Day 100s: 5
Place in batting averages: 112th av. 33.72
(2002 155th av. 28.05)
Strike rate: (career 60.70)
Parents: Clive and Elisabeth
Wife and date of marriage: Angela, 16 March 1996
Children: Cameron, January 2002
Family links with cricket: Father and brother both played for Swansea CC

Education: Olchfa Comprehensive School; Millfield School; Birmingham University
Qualifications: 5 O-levels, 2 A-levels, MBA, Level III coaching award
Career outside cricket: PR/marketing; coaching
Off-season: Working for PR/marketing company
Overseas tours: Welsh Cricket Association U18 to Barbados 1986; Welsh Schools U19 to Australia 1987-88; Glamorgan to Trinidad 1990; South Wales Cricket Association to New Zealand and Australia 1991-92; England A to India 1994-95
Overseas teams played for: Crusaders, Durban 1992-98
Career highlights to date: '99* England A v India A, Calcutta "Test" match 1994-95'
Cricket moments to forget: 'None'
Cricket superstitions: 'None'
Cricketers particularly admired: David Gower, Viv Richards
Young players to look out for: Mark Wallace, Jon Hughes, Moeen Ali
Other sports played: Football
Other sports followed: Football (Swansea City, West Ham United)
Injuries: Out for three and a half weeks with a broken finger
Favourite band: Nickelback
Relaxations: 'Golf, reading'
Extras: In 1989 scored 104* and 101* for Welsh Schools U19 v Scottish Schools U19 and 120 and 102* v Irish Schools U19. Scored 258* for Wales v MCC 1991. Left Glamorgan at the end of the 1996 season and joined Warwickshire. Scored two 100s (138/114*) v Hampshire at Southampton 1997. Vice-captain of Warwickshire 2001. Left Warwickshire in the 2001-02 off-season and rejoined Glamorgan for 2002. Scored 88-ball 102 v Surrey at The Oval in the C&G 2002 as Glamorgan made 429 in reply to Surrey's 438-5
Opinions on cricket: 'Reduce amount of cricket played, which would allow for more quality practice in between games. Bowlers would remain fairly fresh all season. Batters should become more disciplined because of less innings, which would hopefully raise standard and competitiveness of cricket played. Away captain should have choice of whether to bat or bowl. Cricketers are only as good as the surface they play on. Improve the wickets, which will improve the standard of players. Pitch inspectors less tolerant; more points deducted for poor surfaces. Keep two divisions with three up/three down as majority of games will remain competitive up till end of season. Twelve-month contracts for all players – therefore under control of county all year which, if done properly, will/should lead to better/quicker development of players.'
Best batting: 186* Warwickshire v Worcestershire, Edgbaston 2001
Best bowling: 3-23 Glamorgan v South Africa A, Cardiff 1996

	M	Inns	NO	Runs	HS	Avge	100s	50s	Ct	St	O	M	Runs	Wkts	Avge	Best	5wI	10wM
Test																		
All First	12	21	3	607	85 *	33.72	-	5	5	-								
1-day Int																		
C & G	1	1	0	16	16	16.00	-	-	1	-								
NCL	14	12	3	355	83 *	39.44	-	2	5	-								
Twenty20	5	5	1	75	49 *	18.75	-	-	2	-								

Career Performances

	M	Inns	NO	Runs	HS	Avge	100s	50s	Ct	St	Balls	Runs	Wkts	Avge	Best	5wI	10wM
Test																	
All First	185	309	29	9577	186 *	34.20	18	51	118	-	1032	778	17	45.76	3-23	-	-
1-day Int																	
C & G	24	23	2	880	112	41.90	4	3	6	-	48	43	1	43.00	1-40	-	
NCL	135	117	15	2214	83 *	21.70	-	10	56	-	74	86	3	28.66	2-43	-	
Twenty20	5	5	1	75	49 *	18.75	-	-	2	-							

HEWITT, J. P.   Kent

Name: James Peter Hewitt
Role: Left-hand bat, right-arm medium-fast bowler
Born: 26 February 1976, Southwark, London
Height: 6ft 3in   **Weight:** 14st 7lbs
Nickname: Hewie, Shoes, Dog, Carlo, Duke B ('ask Rob Ferley')
County debut: 1995 (one-day, Middlesex), 1996 (first-class, Middlesex), 2002 (Kent)
County cap: 1998 (Middlesex)
50 wickets in a season: 1
1st-Class 50s: 3
1st-Class 5 w. in innings: 5
1st-Class catches: 23
Strike rate: (career 49.91)
Parents: Gill and Terry
Wife and date of marriage: Joanne, 4 October 2003
Family links with cricket: 'Father and grandfather both played; Mum watches'
Education: Teddington School, Middlesex; Richmond College; City of Westminster College
Qualifications: GCSEs; City and Guilds Parts I, II and III in Recreation and Leisure; GNVQ Leisure and Tourism; coaching Levels I, II, III and advanced staff coach

Career outside cricket: Coaching
Overseas teams played for: University, Perth 1997-98; Shenton Park 2000-02
Career highlights to date: 'Beating Australians at Lord's for Middlesex [2001]'
Cricket moments to forget: 'Every time not picked (quite a lot over past couple of years!)'
Cricket superstitions: 'Same routine every time go out to bat'
Cricketers particularly admired: Richard Hadlee, Jacques Kallis, Sachin Tendulkar, Damien Martyn, Adam Hollioake ('not just for cricket')
Young players to look out for: Joe Denly, Scott Newman, Simon Cusden, Charlie Hemphrey
Other sports played: Athletics ('represented South of England at cross-country'), football ('played for Chelsea Youth'); 'I will play all sports'
Other sports followed: Football (Chelsea)
Relaxations: 'Spending time with family and friends'
Extras: First Middlesex bowler since J. H. S. Hunt in 1902 to take a wicket with first ball in first-class cricket (R. I. Dawson of Gloucestershire at Lord's 1996). Released by Middlesex at the end of the 2001 season and joined Kent for 2002. Released by Kent during the 2003 season
Opinions on cricket: 'Too many back-door cricketers. Second-team pitches outside first-class grounds are poor. Tea should be half an hour.'
Best batting: 75 Middlesex v Essex, Chelmsford 1997
Best bowling: 6-14 Middlesex v Glamorgan, Cardiff 1997

2003 Season

	M	Inns	NO	Runs	HS	Avge	100s	50s	Ct	St	O	M	Runs	Wkts	Avge	Best	5wI	10wM
Test																		
All First																		
1-day Int																		
C & G	2	1	0	2	2	2.00	-	-	-	-	18	3	75	3	25.00	3-26	-	
NCL	1	1	0	7	7	7.00	-	-	-	-	6	0	34	0	-	-	-	
Twenty20																		

Career Performances

	M	Inns	NO	Runs	HS	Avge	100s	50s	Ct	St	Balls	Runs	Wkts	Avge	Best	5wI	10wM
Test																		
All First	61	82	13	1264	75	18.31	-	3	23	-	8485	4948	170	29.10	6-14	5	-
1-day Int																		
C & G	8	4	2	25	14 *	12.50	-	-	2	-	396	324	7	46.28	3-26	-	
NCL	60	35	13	275	32 *	12.50	-	-	19	-	2103	1580	56	28.21	4-24	-	
Twenty20																		

HEWSON, D. R.   Derbyshire

Name: Dominic (<u>Dom</u>) Robert Hewson
Role: Right-hand bat, right-arm
medium bowler
Born: 3 October 1974, Cheltenham
Height: 5ft 9in **Weight:** 13st
Nickname: Chopper
County debut: 1996 (Gloucestershire),
2002 (Derbyshire)
1st-Class 50s: 15
1st-Class 100s: 3
1st-Class catches: 34
Place in batting averages: 259th av. 13.87
(2002 224th av. 20.68)
Strike rate: (career 174.00)
Parents: Robert and Julie
Wife and date of marriage:
Amy, 14 October 2000
Education: Cheltenham College; University
of West of England

Qualifications: 10 GCSEs, 3 A-levels, City and Guilds in Tree Surgery
Career outside cricket: Tree surgeon
Overseas teams played for: Constantia, Cape Town 1995-96; Central Hawke's Bay,
New Zealand 1998-99
Career highlights to date: 'Playing at Gloucestershire CCC during their successes of
1999 and 2000'
Cricketers particularly admired: Courtney Walsh
Other sports followed: Rugby (Gloucester RFC)
Relaxations: Seeing friends, fishing, and watching sport
Extras: Made debut for Gloucestershire 2nd XI in July 1993. Left Gloucestershire in
the 2001-02 off-season and joined Derbyshire for 2002. Scored century (102*) on
debut for Derbyshire v Glamorgan at Cardiff 2002
Best batting: 168 Gloucestershire v Derbyshire, Bristol 2001
Best bowling: 1-7 Gloucestershire v Kent, Bristol 1998

---

44. Which Barnsley-born Essex bowler was England's Man of the Series
with 24 wickets against West Indies in 2000?

2003 Season

	M	Inns	NO	Runs	HS	Avge	100s	50s	Ct	St	O	M	Runs	Wkts	Avge	Best	5wI	10wM
Test																		
All First	9	16	0	222	57	13.87	-	1	4	-	4	0	14	0	-		-	-
1-day Int																		
C & G	4	3	0	140	69	46.66	-	1	3	-	13	0	50	2	25.00	1-18	-	
NCL	16	14	1	274	50	21.07	-	1	5	-	63.1	1	349	15	23.26	4-25	-	
Twenty20	5	3	0	42	36	14.00	-	-	1	-	19	0	109	10	10.90	4-18	-	

Career Performances

	M	Inns	NO	Runs	HS	Avge	100s	50s	Ct	St	Balls	Runs	Wkts	Avge	Best	5wI	10wM
Test																	
All First	71	130	8	2787	168	22.84	3	15	34	-	174	91	1	91.00	1-7	-	-
1-day Int																	
C & G	10	9	0	344	69	38.22	-	2	4	-	78	50	2	25.00	1-18	-	
NCL	41	35	1	564	52	16.58	-	2	10	-	379	349	15	23.26	4-25	-	
Twenty20	5	3	0	42	36	14.00	-	-	1	-	114	109	10	10.90	4-18	-	

HICK, G. A.   Worcestershire

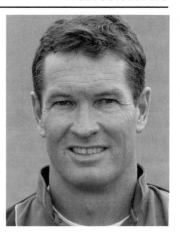

Name: <u>Graeme</u> Ashley Hick
Role: Right-hand bat, off-spin bowler
Born: 23 May 1966, Harare, Zimbabwe
Height: 6ft 3in **Weight:** 14st 4lbs
Nickname: Hicky, Ash
County debut: 1984
County cap: 1986; colours 2002
Benefit: 1999
Test debut: 1991
Tests: 65
One-Day Internationals: 120
1000 runs in a season: 17
1st-Class 50s: 136
1st-Class 100s: 108
1st-Class 200s: 11
1st-Class 300s: 2
1st-Class 400s: 1
1st-Class 5 w. in innings: 5
1st-Class 10 w. in match: 1
1st-Class catches: 572
One-Day 100s: 32
One-Day 5 w. in innings: 1

Place in batting averages: 114th av. 33.50 (2002 19th av. 55.88)
Strike rate: (career 90.19)
Parents: John and Eve
Wife and date of marriage: Jackie, 5 October 1991
Children: Lauren Amy, 12 September 1992; Jordan Ashley, 5 September 1995
Family links with cricket: Father has served on Zimbabwe Cricket Union Board of Control and played representative cricket in Zimbabwe
Education: Prince Edward Boys' High School, Zimbabwe
Qualifications: 4 O-levels, NCA coaching award
Overseas tours: Zimbabwe to England (World Cup) 1983, to Sri Lanka 1983-84, to England 1985; England to Australia and New Zealand (World Cup) 1991-92, to India and Sri Lanka 1992-93, to West Indies 1993-94, to Australia 1994-95, to South Africa 1995-96, to India and Pakistan (World Cup) 1995-96, to Sharjah (Akai Singer Champions Trophy) 1997-98, to West Indies 1997-98 (one-day series), to Bangladesh (Wills International Cup) 1998-99, to Australia 1998-99, to Sharjah (Coca-Cola Cup) 1998-99, to South Africa and Zimbabwe 1999-2000 (one-day series), to Kenya (ICC Knockout Trophy) 2000-01, to Pakistan and Sri Lanka 2000-01
Overseas teams played for: Old Hararians, Zimbabwe 1982-90; Northern Districts, New Zealand 1987-89; Queensland 1990-91; Auckland 1997-98
Cricketers particularly admired: Steve Waugh, Glenn McGrath
Other sports played: Golf ('relaxation'), hockey (played for Zimbabwe)
Other sports followed: Football (Liverpool FC), golf, tennis, squash, hockey
Relaxations: 'Leaning against Steve Rhodes at first slip'
Extras: Youngest player participating in 1983 World Cup (aged 17). In 1986, at age 20, he became the youngest player to score 2000 runs in an English season. One of *Wisden*'s Five Cricketers of the Year 1987. In 1988 he made 405* v Somerset at Taunton, the highest individual first-class score in England since A. C. MacLaren's 424 for Lancashire v Somerset at Taunton in 1895, and scored 1000 first-class runs by end of May, hitting a record 410 runs in April. In 1990 became youngest batsman ever to make 50 first-class centuries and scored 645 runs without being dismissed – a record for English cricket. Also in 1990 became the fastest to 10,000 runs in county cricket (179 innings). Qualified to play for England 1991. Finished top of the first-class batting averages 1997. Scored hundredth first-class 100 (132) v Sussex at Worcester 1998 with his second 100 of the match; at the age of 32, he became the second youngest player after Wally Hammond to score one hundred 100s; received an Individual Performance Award from the PCA in recognition of his achievement. Represented England in the 1999 World Cup. Scored two centuries in a match (101/150) for the fourth time, v Essex at Chelmsford 1999. Won ODI Man of the Match awards v Zimbabwe, the country of his birth, for his match-winning 87* at Bulawayo and his 80 and 5-33 at Harare, February 2000. Scored 101 in England's only innings in his first Test v Zimbabwe at Lord's 2000; it was his first Test century at Lord's. Scored 40 in match-winning 91-run partnership with Graham Thorpe in third Test v Pakistan at Karachi 2000-01. Scored 200* v Durham at Riverside 2001, in the process achieving the feat of having recorded centuries against each of the other 17 counties, both home and away. Passed Allan Lamb's career total of 32,502 runs during

the 2001 season, becoming the highest scoring African-born cricketer. Scored 315* v Durham at Worcester 2002 to become only the fifth batsman to have scored three triple hundreds; it was also the highest individual score by a Worcestershire batsman at the ground, overtaking Glenn Turner's 311 in 1982. Scored 77* v Kent at Worcester in the NUL 2002, in the process becoming only the third player to record 8000 runs in the one-day league. Captain of Worcestershire 2000-02. Scored his 122nd first-class century (155) v Derbyshire at Derby 2003 to move into equal twelfth spot in the all-time century-makers' list alongside Tom Graveney

Opinions on cricket: 'Wickets still need to improve!'
Best batting: 405* Worcestershire v Somerset, Taunton 1988
Best bowling: 5-18 Worcestershire v Leicestershire, Worcester 1995

2003 Season

	M	Inns	NO	Runs	HS	Avge	100s	50s	Ct	St	O	M	Runs	Wkts	Avge	Best	5wI	10wM
Test																		
All First	13	23	3	670	155	33.50	1	3	19	-	21	5	63	0	-		-	-	-
1-day Int																		
C & G	4	4	0	135	97	33.75	-	1	-	-	6	1	26	1	26.00	1-26	-	
NCL	13	13	1	349	108	29.08	1	3	2	-	15	0	69	0	-		-	-
Twenty20																		

Career Performances

	M	Inns	NO	Runs	HS	Avge	100s	50s	Ct	St	Balls	Runs	Wkts	Avge	Best	5wI	10wM
Test	65	114	6	3383	178	31.32	6	18	90	-	3057	1306	23	56.78	4-126	-	-
All First	453	748	72	35916	405 *	53.13	122	136	572	-	20835	10268	231	44.45	5-18	5	1
1-day Int	120	118	15	3846	126 *	37.33	5	27	64	-	1236	1026	30	34.20	5-33	1	
C & G	50	50	8	2277	172 *	54.21	7	10	25	-	1283	817	24	34.04	4-54	-	
NCL	243	232	37	8420	141 *	43.17	13	60	80	-	2942	2546	88	28.93	4-21	-	
Twenty20																	

HILDRETH, J. C.   Somerset

Name: James Charles Hildreth
Role: Right-hand bat, right-arm medium bowler; all-rounder
Born: 9 September 1984, Milton Keynes
Height: 5ft 9in   **Weight:** 12st 7lbs
Nickname: Hildy, Hildz
County debut: 2003
Parents: David and Judy
Marital status: Single
Education: Millfield School; Loughborough University
Qualifications: 10 GCSEs, 3 A-levels, ECB Level 1 coaching
Off-season: 'Uni or travelling'

Overseas tours: 'West' to West Indies 1999, 2000; Millfield to Sri Lanka 2001; England U19 to Bangladesh (U19 World Cup) 2003-04
Career highlights to date: '116* on U19 "Test" debut against South Africa'
Cricket moments to forget: 'Being bowled first ball by Shoaib Akhtar'
Cricket superstitions: 'Left pad before right when getting padded up'
Other sports played: Hockey (West of England), squash (South of England), tennis (South of England), football (England Independent Schools, Luton Town), rugby (Millfield)
Other sports followed: Football (Charlton Athletic)
Favourite band: Jack Johnson
Relaxations: Travelling, snowboarding, music
Extras: Member of Stony Stratford CC. Played for Somerset Board XI in the first round of the C&G 2003, which was played in August 2002. Represented England U19 v South Africa U19 2003, becoming the third batsman to score a century (116*) on England U19 debut, in the third 'Test' at Chelmsford
Best batting: 9 Somerset v Derbyshire, Taunton 2003

2003 Season

	M	Inns	NO	Runs	HS	Avge	100s	50s	Ct	St	O	M	Runs	Wkts	Avge	Best	5wI	10wM
Test																		
All First	1	2	0	9	9	4.50	-	-	-	-								
1-day Int																		
C & G																		
NCL	9	8	0	120	30	15.00	-	-	3	-								
Twenty20																		

Career Performances

	M	Inns	NO	Runs	HS	Avge	100s	50s	Ct	St	Balls	Runs	Wkts	Avge	Best	5wI	10wM
Test																	
All First	1	2	0	9	9	4.50	-	-	-	-							
1-day Int																	
C & G	1	1	0	4	4	4.00	-	-	1	-	36	44	1	44.00	1-44	-	
NCL	9	8	0	120	30	15.00	-	-	3	-							
Twenty20																	

HINDLEY, R. J. E.   Hampshire

Name: <u>Richard</u> James Edward Hindley
Role: Left-hand bat, right-arm
off-spin bowler
Born: 25 April 1975, Portsmouth
Height: 6ft 3in **Weight:** 14st 2lbs
Nickname: Richie
County debut: 2003
1st-Class 50s: 1
Parents: William and Julie
Marital status: Single
Education: Havant College; New College
of Southampton
Qualifications: BSc (Hons) Sports Studies,
ECB Level III coach
Off-season: 'Playing cricket in Newcastle,
NSW, for Cardiff Boolaroo District CC'
Overseas teams played for: Cardiff
Boolaroo DCC, New South Wales 1999-2001,
2002-04
Career highlights to date: 'Hampshire first-team debut v Glamorgan, July 2003'
Cricket moments to forget: 'Any time I get out cheaply, which happens a lot'
Cricket superstitions: 'None'
Cricketers particularly admired: David Gower, Viv Richards, Ian Botham,
Shane Warne
Other sports played: Golf, football, tennis – 'not talented enough to have achieved
anything'
Other sports followed: Australian rugby league (Newcastle Knights), football
(Aston Villa FC)
Injuries: Out for six weeks with two broken fingers
Relaxations: 'Reading books (autobiographies); playing golf, football, tennis etc;
travelling to see friends'
Extras: Has taken hat-trick and four wickets in four balls in club cricket. Played for
Hampshire Board XI in the C&G 2001, C&G 2002 and in the first and second rounds
of the C&G 2003, which took place in August/September 2002. Scored 70-ball 68* on
first-class debut v Glamorgan at West End 2003, after being called up from club
cricket to replace the injured Shaun Udal; is registered for 2004
Best batting: 68* Hampshire v Glamorgan, West End 2003

2003 Season

	M	Inns	NO	Runs	HS	Avge	100s	50s	Ct	St	O	M	Runs	Wkts	Avge	Best	5wl	10wM
Test																		
All First	1	2	1	76	68 *	76.00	-	1	-	-	9	0	46	0	-		-	-	-
1-day Int																		
C & G																		
NCL																		
Twenty20																		

Career Performances

	M	Inns	NO	Runs	HS	Avge	100s	50s	Ct	St	Balls	Runs	Wkts	Avge	Best	5wl	10wM
Test																	
All First	1	2	1	76	68 *	76.00	-	1	-	-	54	46	0	-		-	-	-
1-day Int																	
C & G	4	4	2	50	38	25.00	-	-	2	-	124	92	3	30.66	2-27	-
NCL																	
Twenty20																	

HODD, A. J.   Surrey

Name: <u>Andrew</u> John Hodd
Role: Right-hand bat, wicket-keeper
Born: 12 January 1984, Chichester
Height: 5ft 9in **Weight:** 10st 6lbs
Nickname: Hoddy, General, Hoddmeister
County debut: 2003 (Sussex; *see Extras*)
1st-Class catches: 2
Parents: Karen and Adrian
Marital status: Single
Family links with cricket: 'Long line of enthusiastic club cricketers'
Education: Bexhill High School; Loughborough University
Qualifications: 9 GCSEs, 4 A-levels, ECB Level 1 coach
Career outside cricket: Student
Off-season: 'At Loughborough Uni'
Overseas tours: South of England U14 to West Indies 1998; Sussex Academy to South Africa 1999, to Sri Lanka 2001; England U17 to Australia 2000-01; England U19 to Australia 2002-03
Career highlights to date: 'Winning the first four-day U19 "Test" against Australia in Adelaide, January 2003'

293

Cricket moments to forget: 'Scoring a duck on my first appearance at the Melbourne Cricket Ground'

Cricket superstitions: 'Never shave morning of a game and must have coffee before a game'

Cricketers particularly admired: Adam Gilchrist, Ryan Campbell, Murray Goodwin

Young players to look out for: Luke Wright, Ravinder Bopara, Krishna Singh (Sussex)

Other sports played: Football ('county at Youth level'), tennis, golf

Other sports followed: Football (Liverpool), tennis (Andy Roddick)

Injuries: Out for three and a half weeks with a strained medial knee ligament

Favourite band: Jackson Five

Relaxations: 'Music, friends, beach, going out'

Extras: Played for England U14, U15, U17 and U19, including England U19 v South Africa U19 2003. Graham Kersey Trophy, Bunbury 1999. Several junior Player of the Year awards at Sussex. Played for Sussex Board XI in the second round of the C&G 2003, which was played in September 2002. Sussex County League Young Player of the Year 2002. Attended Sussex Academy. Played for Sussex v West Indies A in a limited overs fixture at Hove 2002. Sussex 2nd XI Player of the Year 2003. Left Sussex during the 2003-04 off-season and has joined Surrey for 2004

Opinions on cricket: 'Too much cricket. Too many contracted players (squads are too big), and wickets are not up to scratch. Less time for playing and more time for practice.'

2003 Season

	M	Inns	NO	Runs	HS	Avge	100s	50s	Ct	St	O	M	Runs	Wkts	Avge	Best	5wI	10wM
Test																		
All First	1	0	0	0	0	-	-	-	2	-								
1-day Int																		
C & G																		
NCL																		
Twenty20																		

Career Performances

	M	Inns	NO	Runs	HS	Avge	100s	50s	Ct	St	Balls	Runs	Wkts	Avge	Best	5wI	10wM
Test																	
All First	1	0	0	0	0	-	-	-	2	-							
1-day Int																	
C & G	1	1	0	1	1	1.00	-	-	1	-							
NCL																	
Twenty20																	

HODGE, B. J. Leicestershire

Name: Bradley (<u>Brad</u>) John Hodge
Role: Right-hand bat, right-arm
off-spin bowler, county vice-captain
Born: 29 December 1974, Sandringham,
Melbourne, Australia
Height: 5ft 7½in **Weight:** 12st 8lbs
Nickname: Bunk
County debut: 2002 (Durham),
2003 (Leicestershire)
1000 runs in a season: 1
1st-Class 50s: 32
1st-Class 100s: 21
1st-Class 200s: 1
1st-Class 300s: 1
1st-Class catches: 67
One-Day 100s: 1
Place in batting averages: 8th av. 62.29
(2002 106th av. 35.50)
Strike rate: 58.28 (career 74.00)
Parents: John and Val
Marital status: Engaged to Megan
Education: St Bede's College, Mentone; Deakin University
Off-season: 'Going back home'
Overseas tours: Australia U19 to New Zealand 1992-93; Commonwealth Bank
[Australian] Cricket Academy to Zimbabwe 1998-99; Australia A to Los Angeles
(Moov America Challenge) 1999
Overseas teams played for: Victoria 1993-94 –
Career highlights to date: First game for Victoria. Century in each innings v South
Australia, Adelaide 2001-02
Cricketers particularly admired: Allan Border, Dennis Lillee, Dean Jones,
Sachin Tendulkar
Other sports played/followed: Australian Rules football (Melbourne), golf, tennis,
soccer, skiing
Extras: Attended Commonwealth Bank [Australian] Cricket Academy 1993. Leading
run-scorer for Victoria in the Sheffield Shield in his first season (1993-94) with 903
runs (av. 50.16), including one century and seven 50s. Has represented Australia A
against various touring sides since 1998-99. Victoria's Pura Cup Player of the Year
2000-01 (973 runs; av. 54.06); also Victoria's leading run-scorer in the Mercantile
Mutual Cup 2000-01 (374 runs; av. 46.75). Scored two centuries in match (140/110*),
v South Australia at Adelaide 2001-02. Victoria's Pura Cup Player of the Year for the
second successive season 2001-02 (858 runs; av. 57.20) and winner of the national

Pura Cup Player of the Season Award 2001-02 (jointly with Jimmy Maher of Queensland). Was Durham's overseas player from late July 2002, replacing the injured Martin Love; joined Leicestershire as an overseas player for 2003. Scored 202* v Loughborough UCCE at Leicester 2003, in the process sharing with Darren Maddy (229*) in a record partnership for any wicket for Leicestershire and the second highest partnership for the third wicket in English first-class cricket (436*). Scored 61-ball 97 and took 3-6 v Yorkshire at Leicester in the Twenty20 2003 and finished up as leading run-scorer in the inaugural competition (301). His maiden triple century (302* from 280 balls) v Nottinghamshire 2003 is the highest individual first-class score by a Leicestershire player and the highest individual Championship score recorded at Trent Bridge. Appointed vice-captain of Leicestershire for 2004

Best batting: 302* Leicestershire v Nottinghamshire, Trent Bridge 2003
Best bowling: 4-17 Australia A v West Indians, Hobart 2000-01

2003 Season

	M	Inns	NO	Runs	HS	Avge	100s	50s	Ct	St	O	M	Runs	Wkts	Avge	Best	5wI	10wM
Test																		
All First	16	26	2	1495	302 *	62.29	5	3	12	-	68	12	274	7	39.14	3-35	-	-
1-day Int																		
C & G	3	3	0	5	4	1.66	-	-	1	-								
NCL	16	16	0	475	104	29.68	1	2	6	-	48	0	256	6	42.66	3-34	-	
Twenty20	6	6	0	301	97	50.16	-	3	3	-	13	0	89	6	14.83	3-6	-	

Career Performances

	M	Inns	NO	Runs	HS	Avge	100s	50s	Ct	St	Balls	Runs	Wkts	Avge	Best	5wI	10wM
Test																	
All First	118	212	20	8147	302 *	42.43	23	32	67	-	3478	1956	47	41.61	4-17	-	-
1-day Int																	
C & G	3	3	0	5	4	1.66	-	-	1	-							
NCL	19	19	1	670	104	37.22	1	4	9	-	330	285	7	40.71	3-34	-	
Twenty20	6	6	0	301	97	50.16	-	3	3	-	78	89	6	14.83	3-6	-	

45. This West Indian off-spinner spent six years at Edgbaston, a spell at Burnley in the Lancashire League and had match figures of 11-157 at Old Trafford in June 1963. Who is he?

HOGG, G. B. Warwickshire

Name: George Bradley (<u>Brad</u>) Hogg
Role: Left-hand bat, left-arm
wrist-spin bowler
Born: 6 February 1971, Narrogin,
Western Australia
Height: 6ft 1in **Weight:** 12st 9lbs
Nickname: Hoggy
County debut: No first-team appearance
Test debut: 1996-97
Tests: 3
One-Day Internationals: 34
1st-Class 50s: 15
1st-Class 100s: 2
1st-Class 5 w. in innings: 4
1st-Class catches: 38
Strike rate: (career 77.19)
Overseas tours: Australia to Sri Lanka
(Singer World Series) 1996, to India 1996-97,
to Africa (World Cup) 2002-03, to West Indies 2002-03, to India (TVS Cup) 2003-04;
Australia A to South Africa (one-day series) 2002-03
Overseas teams played for: Willetton; Western Australia 1993-94 –
Extras: Played for Australian XI v West Indians 1995-96 and 1996-97. Shared in a
Mercantile Cup competition record sixth-wicket partnership of 173 with Mike Hussey
v Victoria at Melbourne 1999-2000. Won Man of the Match award for Australia A v
South Africa A at Centurion 2002-03 (3-38). ACB contract 2003-04. Has joined
Warwickshire as an overseas player for 2004
Best batting: 111* Western Australia v New South Wales, Sydney 1995-96
Best bowling: 5-53 Western Australia v New South Wales, Sydney 1999-2000

2003 Season (did not make any first-class or one-day appearances)

Career Performances

	M	Inns	NO	Runs	HS	Avge	100s	50s	Ct	St	Balls	Runs	Wkts	Avge	Best	5wI	10wM
Test	3	4	1	25	17*	8.33	-	-	-	-	450	333	6	55.50	2-40	-	-
All First	69	104	23	2474	111*	30.54	2	15	38	-	7874	4358	102	42.72	5-53	4	-
1-day Int	34	19	8	226	71*	20.54	-	2	11	-	1655	1174	34	34.52	3-31	-	
C & G																	
NCL																	
Twenty20																	

HOGG, K. W. Lancashire

Name: Kyle William Hogg
Role: Left-hand bat, right-arm
fast-medium bowler; all-rounder
Born: 2 July 1983, Birmingham
Height: 6ft 4in **Weight:** 13st
Nickname: Boss, Hoggy
County debut: 2001
1st-Class 50s: 3
1st-Class 5 w. in innings: 2
1st-Class catches: 8
Place in batting averages: (2002 278th
av. 12.11)
Place in bowling averages: (2002 83rd
av. 32.68)
Strike rate: 83.14 (career 57.62)
Parents: Sharon and William
Marital status: Single
Family links with cricket: Father played for
Lancashire and Warwickshire; grandfather Sonny Ramadhin played for Lancashire
and West Indies
Education: Saddleworth High School
Qualifications: GCSEs
Off-season: 'Training (12-month contract)'
Overseas tours: England U19 to India 2000-01, to Australia and (U19 World Cup)
New Zealand 2001-02; Lancashire to South Africa, to Grenada; ECB National
Academy to Australia and Sri Lanka 2002-03
Career highlights to date: 'Winning second division of one-day league'
Cricket moments to forget: '[B&H 2002] semi-final v Warwickshire'
Cricket superstitions: 'None'
Cricketers particularly admired: Andrew Flintoff, David Byas, Stuart Law,
Carl Hooper
Young players to look out for: 'All Lancs 2nd XI'
Other sports played: Football
Other sports followed: Football (Man Utd)
Injuries: Out for five weeks with a torn calf; for five weeks with illness
Favourite band: Stone Roses, Red Hot Chili Peppers, Bob Marley
Relaxations: 'Relaxing with friends'
Extras: Represented England U19 v West Indies U19 2001, taking 5-88 (including
three wickets in four balls) in the second 'Test' at Trent Bridge; and v India U19 2002,
scoring century (103) in second 'ODI' at Taunton. NBC Denis Compton Award for the
most promising young Lancashire player 2001. Recorded maiden first-class five-

wicket return (5-48) on Championship debut v Leicestershire at Old Trafford 2002. Included in provisional England squad of 30 for the 2002-03 World Cup

Opinions on cricket: 'Too much cricket. Not enough time to prepare for games, which leads to some games not played at full intensity.'

Best batting: 53 Lancashire v Nottinghamshire, Trent Bridge 2003

Best bowling: 5-48 Lancashire v Leicestershire, Old Trafford 2002

2003 Season

	M	Inns	NO	Runs	HS	Avge	100s	50s	Ct	St	O	M	Runs	Wkts	Avge	Best	5wI	10wM
Test																		
All First	5	5	0	158	53	31.60	-	1	1	-	97	22	370	7	52.85	2-66	-	-
1-day Int																		
C & G	1	1	1	0	0*	-	-	-	-	-	7	0	34	0	-		-	-
NCL	13	6	2	39	22	9.75	-	-	1	-	75	4	391	17	23.00	4-24	-	
Twenty20	2	2	0	9	7	4.50	-	-	-	-	4.1	0	47	1	47.00	1-16	-	

Career Performances

	M	Inns	NO	Runs	HS	Avge	100s	50s	Ct	St	Balls	Runs	Wkts	Avge	Best	5wI	10wM
Test																	
All First	16	19	1	362	53	20.11	-	3	8	-	2065	1238	36	34.38	5-48	2	-
1-day Int																	
C & G	3	2	1	0	0*	0.00	-	-	-	-	96	78	2	39.00	2-27	-	
NCL	27	14	5	142	24	15.77	-	-	5	-	983	770	33	23.33	4-20	-	
Twenty20	2	2	0	9	7	4.50	-	-	-	-	25	47	1	47.00	1-16	-	

---

46. Which Yorkshireman – the oldest man to play Test cricket – was aged 52 years 165 days on the last day of the fourth Test v West Indies at Kingston in 1929-30?

HOGGARD, M. J.   Yorkshire

Name: <u>Matthew</u> James Hoggard
Role: Right-hand bat, right-arm
fast-medium bowler
Born: 31 December 1976, Leeds
Height: 6ft 2in **Weight:** 14st
Nickname: Oggie
County debut: 1996
County cap: 2000
Test debut: 2000
Tests: 19
One-Day Internationals: 20
50 wickets in a season: 1
1st-Class 5 w. in innings: 11
1st-Class catches: 18
One-Day 5 w. in innings: 4
Place in batting averages: (2002 261st
av. 15.83)

Place in bowling averages: 55th av. 28.85
(2002 104th av. 34.72)
Strike rate: 64.42 (career 53.75)
Parents: Margaret and John
Marital status: Living with girlfriend Sarah
Family links with cricket: 'Dad is a cricket badger'
Education: Pudsey Grangefield
Qualifications: GCSEs and A-levels
Off-season: Touring with England
Overseas tours: Yorkshire CCC to South Africa; England U19 to Zimbabwe 1995-96;
England to Kenya (ICC Knockout Trophy) 2000-01, to Pakistan and Sri Lanka
2000-01, to Zimbabwe (one-day series) 2001-02, to India and New Zealand 2001-02,
to Sri Lanka (ICC Champions Trophy) 2002-03, to Australia 2002-03, to Africa (World
Cup) 2002-03, to Bangladesh and Sri Lanka 2003-04, to West Indies 2003-04
Overseas teams played for: Pirates, Johannesburg 1995-97; Free State 1998-2000
Career highlights to date: 'Taking my first Test wicket (Younis Khan)'
Cricketers particularly admired: Allan Donald, Courtney Walsh
Young players to look out for: Joe Sayers, Michael Lumb, Tim Bresnan
Other sports played: Rugby
Other sports followed: Rugby league (Leeds Rhinos)
Injuries: Out for much of the 2003 season with a knee injury
Relaxations: Dog walking
Extras: Was top wicket-taker in the 2000 National League competition with 37
wickets at 12.37, in the process surpassing Howard Cooper's Yorkshire one-day league

season record of 29 wickets set in 1975. PCA Young Player of the Year 2000. Returned match figures of 8-30 (4-13/4-17) from 22.3 overs v Pakistan Board XI at Lahore 2000-01 and took 17 wickets in total in his two matches in Pakistan. Man of the Match in the second ODI v Zimbabwe at Harare 2001-02 (3-37). Took 7-63 v New Zealand in the first Test at Christchurch 2001-02, the best innings return by an England opening bowler in Tests v New Zealand. Had match figures of 7-147 (2-55/5-92) to win the Man of the Match award in the second Test v Sri Lanka at Edgbaston 2002; also scored 17* in England's innings, sharing in a record tenth-wicket stand for England in Tests v Sri Lanka (91) with Graham Thorpe. Took career best 7-49 v Somerset at Headingley 2003 in his first Championship match back after knee surgery
Best batting: 32 England v India, Trent Bridge 2002
Best bowling: 7-49 Yorkshire v Somerset, Headingley 2003
Stop press: Man of the [Test] Series v Bangladesh 2003-04

2003 Season

	M	Inns	NO	Runs	HS	Avge	100s	50s	Ct	St	O	M	Runs	Wkts	Avge	Best	5wI	10wM
Test	1	1	0	19	19	19.00	-	-	1	-	33	13	59	3	19.66	3-24	-	-
All First	7	8	5	68	21 *	22.66	-	-	3	-	225.3	57	606	21	28.85	7-49	1	-
1-day Int																		
C & G	1	1	1	7	7 *	-	-	-	-	-	0.3	0	0	1	0.00	1-0	-	
NCL	4	2	2	1	1 *	-	-	-	1	-	36	2	153	7	21.85	3-29	-	
Twenty20																		

Career Performances

	M	Inns	NO	Runs	HS	Avge	100s	50s	Ct	St	Balls	Runs	Wkts	Avge	Best	5wI	10wM
Test	19	27	10	125	32	7.35	-	-	6	-	4270	2320	69	33.62	7-63	2	-
All First	81	100	35	465	32	7.15	-	-	18	-	15490	7633	290	26.32	7-49	11	-
1-day Int	20	5	2	10	5	3.33	-	-	3	-	976	817	27	30.25	5-49	1	
C & G	6	1	1	7	7 *	-	-	-	1	-	257	174	11	15.81	5-65	1	
NCL	38	16	9	16	5 *	2.28	-	-	5	-	1746	1190	66	18.03	5-28	2	
Twenty20																		

47. Which Jamaican took 14-149 at the Oval in 1976,
93 wickets in all against England and was known
in Derbyshire as 'Whispering Death'?

HOLLIOAKE, A. J. Surrey

Name: <u>Adam</u> John Hollioake
Role: Right-hand bat, right-arm
medium bowler
Born: 5 September 1971,
Melbourne, Australia
Height: 5ft 11in **Weight:** 14st
Nickname: Smokey
County debut: 1992 (one-day),
1993 (first-class)
County cap: 1995
Test debut: 1997
Tests: 4
One-Day Internationals: 35
1000 runs in a season: 2
1st-Class 50s: 53
1st-Class 100s: 16
1st-Class 200s: 1
1st-Class 5 w. in innings: 1
1st-Class catches: 151
One-Day 100s: 2
One-Day 5 w. in innings: 8

Place in batting averages: 84th av. 38.22 (2002 9th av. 67.09)
Strike rate: 96.40 (career 73.83)
Parents: John and Daria
Wife: Sherryn
Children: Bennaya, 25 May 2002
Education: St Joseph's College, Sydney; St Patrick's College, Ballarat (Australia);
St George's College, Weybridge; Surrey Tutorial College, Guildford
Qualifications: GCSEs, A-levels
Career outside cricket: Property developer
Overseas tours: School trip to Zimbabwe; Surrey YC to Australia; England YC to
New Zealand 1990-91; England A to Australia 1996-97 (captain); England VI to Hong
Kong 1997 (captain), 2002; England to Sharjah (Champions Trophy) 1997-98
(captain), to West Indies 1997-98 (captain in one-day series), to Bangladesh (Wills
International Cup) 1998-99 (captain), to Australia 1998-99 (CUB Series), to Sharjah
(Coca-Cola Cup) 1998-99, to Australia 2002-03 (VB Series)
Overseas teams played for: Fremantle, Western Australia 1990-91; North Shore,
Sydney 1992-93; Geelong, Victoria; North Perth, Western Australia 1995-97
Career highlights to date: 'Getting my first wicket bowling leg spin'
Cricket moments to forget: 'Getting hit on my helmet by Glen Chapple'
Cricket superstitions: 'None'

Cricketers particularly admired: 'Every cricketer who gives their best and takes up the challenge to compete'
Young players to look out for: Rikki Clarke, Tim Murtagh, Scott Newman
Other sports played: Rugby (played for London Counties, Middlesex and South of England; England U18 trialist)
Extras: Scored a century (123) on first-class debut v Derbyshire at Ilkeston 1993. Surrey Young Player of the Year 1993. Scored fastest ever one-day 50 – 15 balls v Yorkshire in the Sunday League at Scarborough 1994. Scored two centuries in match (128/117*) v Somerset at Taunton 1996. His 39 wickets in the Sunday League 1996 is a season record for the domestic one-day league. Surrey Supporters' Player of the Year and Surrey Players' Player of the Year 1996. Man of the Match in the first ODI against Australia at Headingley 1997. Captained England in the Texaco Trophy one-day series v South Africa 1998. Represented England in the 1999 World Cup. Coached Hong Kong in the Asian Cricket Council Trophy in Sharjah 2000. Took 5-77 and made two run-outs v Glamorgan at The Oval in the C&G 2002 as Surrey bowled Glamorgan out for 429 in reply to their own 438-5. C&G Man of the Match award for his 59-ball 117* (century from 52 balls) in the quarter-final v Sussex at Hove 2002. Scored a 103-ball 122* (out of 225) as Surrey avoided the follow-on v Kent at Canterbury 2002; the innings contained 98 in boundaries, one six striking an elderly woman spectator, to whom Hollioake later presented the ball, signed. Scored maiden first-class double century (208) v Leicestershire at The Oval 2002, in the process sharing with Alistair Brown (107) in a new record fifth-wicket partnership for Surrey in matches against Leicestershire (282). One of *Wisden*'s Five Cricketers of the Year 2003. Scored 77 v Essex at Chelmsford 2003, in the process sharing with Azhar Mahmood (98) in a new record seventh-wicket partnership for Surrey in the one-day league (154). Took 6-17 (Surrey's third best one-day figures) from 4.4 overs v Kent at Canterbury in the NCL 2003. Captain of Surrey 1997-2003. Granted a benefit for 2004. Has announced that he will retire at the end of the 2004 season
Best batting: 208 Surrey v Leicestershire, The Oval 2002
Best bowling: 5-62 Surrey v Glamorgan, Swansea 1998
Stop press: Completed a 2000-mile walk/cycle/sail from Edinburgh to Tangiers during autumn 2003 to raise money for the Ben Hollioake Memorial Fund

2003 Season

	M	Inns	NO	Runs	HS	Avge	100s	50s	Ct	St	O	M	Runs	Wkts	Avge	Best	5wI	10wM
Test																		
All First	14	19	1	688	122	38.22	2	3	11	-	80.2	11	300	5	60.00	2-32	-	-
1-day Int																		
C & G	3	3	0	86	33	28.66	-	-	1	-	13	0	103	5	20.60	3-19	-	
NCL	15	15	0	377	77	25.13	-	2	4	-	82.5	1	443	23	19.26	6-17	1	
Twenty20	7	6	0	74	24	12.33	-	-	-	-	25.1	0	197	16	12.31	5-21	1	

Career Performances

	M	Inns	NO	Runs	HS	Avge	100s	50s	Ct	St	Balls	Runs	Wkts	Avge	Best	5wI	10wM
Test	4	6	0	65	45	10.83	-	-	4	-	144	67	2	33.50	2-31	-	-
All First	162	244	20	8964	208	40.01	17	53	151	-	8343	4641	113	41.07	5-62	1	-
1-day Int	35	30	6	606	83 *	25.25	-	3	13	-	1208	1019	32	31.84	4-23	-	
C & G	30	24	4	703	117 *	35.15	1	3	11	-	951	848	35	24.22	5-77	1	
NCL	154	141	18	3292	111	26.76	1	14	45	-	4915	4510	223	20.22	6-17	6	
Twenty20	7	6	0	74	24	12.33	-	-	-	-	151	197	16	12.31	5-21	1	

HOLLOWAY, P. C. L. Somerset

Name: <u>Piran</u> Christopher Laity Holloway
Role: Left-hand bat, off-spin bowler, wicket-keeper
Born: 1 October 1970, Helston, Cornwall
Height: 5ft 8in **Weight:** 11st 5lbs
Nickname: Oggy, Leg, Piras
County debut: 1988 (Warwickshire), 1994 (Somerset)
County cap: 1997 (Somerset)
1st-Class 50s: 32
1st-Class 100s: 9
1st-Class catches: 86
1st-Class stumpings: 1
One-Day 100s: 3
Place in batting averages: (2002 120th av. 32.92)
Parents: Chris and Mary
Family links with cricket: 'Mum and Dad are keen'
Education: Millfield School; Taunton School; Loughborough University
Qualifications: 7 O-levels, 2 A-levels, BSc (Hons) Sports Science
Career outside cricket: Coaching
Overseas tours: Millfield School to Barbados 1986; England YC to Australia 1989-90; Warwickshire CCC to Cape Town 1992, 1993; Somerset CCC to Holland 1994
Overseas teams played for: North Perth, 1993-94; Nedlands, Perth 1994-96; Claremont-Nedlands, Perth 1996-98
Cricketers particularly admired: Ian Botham, David Gower
Other sports followed: Squash, football, rugby, tennis, surfing
Relaxations: Music, surfing, travel
Extras: Sir John Hobbs Silver Jubilee Memorial Prize 1986. Played Young England for three years. Was fourth in the county averages in 1991 (av. 65.75). Somerset Young

Player of the Year 1995. Scored the most runs in A-grade cricket in Perth in 1997-98 season, in which Claremont-Nedlands won the Bank West Cup. Scored 78 v Glamorgan at Cardiff 2001, in the process sharing with Marcus Trescothick (147) in a record opening partnership for Somerset in matches against Glamorgan (240).
Released by Somerset at the end of the 2003 season
Best batting: 168 Somerset v Middlesex, Uxbridge 1996

2003 Season

	M	Inns	NO	Runs	HS	Avge	100s	50s	Ct	St	O	M	Runs	Wkts	Avge	Best	5wI	10wM
Test																		
All First	2	3	0	137	96	45.66	-	1	-	-								
1-day Int																		
C & G																		
NCL																		
Twenty20																		

Career Performances

	M	Inns	NO	Runs	HS	Avge	100s	50s	Ct	St	Balls	Runs	Wkts	Avge	Best	5wI	10wM
Test																	
All First	128	216	28	5923	168	31.50	9	32	86	1	76	69	0	-	-	-	-
1-day Int																	
C & G	16	15	3	549	90	45.75	-	4	8	1							
NCL	102	92	17	1905	117	25.40	3	10	36	7							
Twenty20																		

48. This Jamaican scored seven centuries in Tests, including 302 against England at Barbados in 1974, but none during his one season at Derbyshire. Who is he?

HOOPER, C. L.   Lancashire

Name: <u>Carl</u> Llewellyn Hooper
Role: Right-hand bat, off-spin bowler
Born: 15 December 1966, Georgetown,
Guyana
Height: 6ft **Weight:** 13st
County debut: 1992 (Kent),
2003 (Lancashire)
County cap: 1992 (Kent), 2003 (Lancashire)
Test debut: 1987-88
Tests: 102
One-Day Internationals: 227
1000 runs in a season: 8
1st-Class 50s: 100
1st-Class 100s: 62
1st-Class 200s: 5
1st-Class 5 w. in innings: 18
1st-Class catches: 376
One-Day 100s: 13
One-Day 5 w. in innings: 1

Place in batting averages: 7th av. 67.72
Place in bowling averages: 62nd av. 30.40
Strike rate: 73.26 (career 83.59)
Overseas tours: West Indies B to Zimbabwe 1986-87; Young West Indies to Zimbabwe 1989-90; West Indies to New Zealand 1986-87, to India and Pakistan (World Cup) 1987-88, to India 1987-88, to England 1988, to Australia 1988-89, to Pakistan 1990-91, to England 1991, to Australia and New Zealand (World Cup) 1991-92, to Australia 1992-93, to South Africa (Total International Series) 1992-93, to Sri Lanka 1993-94, to India 1994-95, to England 1995, to Australia 1995-96, 1996-97, to Pakistan 1997-98, to Sharjah (Singer-Akai Champions Trophy) 1997-98, to South Africa 1998-99, to Bangladesh (Wills International Cup) 1998-99, to Zimbabwe and Kenya 2001 (captain), to Sri Lanka 2001-02 (captain), to Sharjah (v Pakistan) 2001-02 (captain), to Sri Lanka (ICC Champions Trophy) 2002-03 (captain), to India 2002-03 (captain), to Africa (World Cup) 2002-03 (captain), plus other one-day series and tournaments
Overseas teams played for: Guyana 1984-85 –
Extras: Made first-class debut for Demerara v Berbice at Georgetown in the final of the Jones Cup 1983-84. Represented West Indies U23 v New Zealanders 1984-85. Represented West Indies YC v England YC in home series 1984-85. Made maiden Test century (100*) in his second Test, v India at Calcutta 1987-88. Was Kent's overseas player 1992-94, 1996, 1998. One of India's Cricketers of the Year 1995. Retired from international cricket in 1999 but returned in 2001 as captain of West Indies until

replaced after the 2002-03 World Cup. Man of the Match v England A in the semi-final of the Busta International Shield 2000-01 at Georgetown (match figures of 7-117 plus 91 in Guyana's first innings). Scored 149* for Guyana in the final of the Busta International Shield v Jamaica at Kingston 2001-02, winning the Man of the Match award. Has won several Test awards, including Man of the Match for his match-winning 94* v England in the second Test at Port of Spain 1997-98 and for his 233 in the first Test v India at his home ground of Georgetown 2001-02. Has also won numerous ODI awards, including Man of the Series in the Singer-Akai Champions Trophy 1997-98 and Man of the Match for his 112* v Pakistan in Sharjah 2001-02. Captain of West Indies 2001 – 2002-03. Joined Lancashire as an overseas player for 2003, originally to deputise for the injured Harbhajan Singh. Scored 201 v Middlesex at Old Trafford 2003, in the process becoming the second batsman (after Mark Ramprakash) to score a century against all 18 counties. Scored century (177) v Warwickshire at Edgbaston 2003, sharing with Stuart Law (168) in a Lancashire record fifth-wicket partnership of 360 as the county scored 781. Awarded Lancashire cap 2003

Best batting: 236* Kent v Glamorgan, Canterbury 1993
Best bowling: 7-93 Kent v Surrey, The Oval 1998

2003 Season

	M	Inns	NO	Runs	HS	Avge	100s	50s	Ct	St	O	M	Runs	Wkts	Avge	Best	5wI	10wM
Test																		
All First	14	20	2	1219	201	67.72	6	3	15	-	366.2	86	912	30	30.40	6-51	2	-
1-day Int																		
C & G	3	3	0	73	61	24.33	-	1	2	-	20	0	82	2	41.00	2-29	-	
NCL	16	14	6	597	88*	74.62	-	7	13	-	90.1	2	379	14	27.07	3-18	-	
Twenty20	5	5	1	56	22*	14.00	-	-	4	-	18	0	95	5	19.00	4-18	-	

Career Performances

	M	Inns	NO	Runs	HS	Avge	100s	50s	Ct	St	Balls	Runs	Wkts	Avge	Best	5wI	10wM
Test	102	173	15	5762	233	36.46	13	27	115	-	13794	5635	113	49.86	5-26	4	-
All First	326	514	49	22341	236*	48.04	67	100	376	-	45060	18999	539	35.24	7-93	18	-
1-day Int	227	206	43	5762	113*	35.34	7	29	120	-	9573	6957	193	36.04	4-34	-	
C & G	16	15	1	534	136*	38.14	1	2	10	-	897	554	9	61.55	2-12	-	
NCL	98	90	16	3662	145	49.48	5	30	56	-	3866	2723	82	33.20	5-41	1	
Twenty20	5	5	1	56	22*	14.00	-	-	4	-	108	95	5	19.00	4-18	-	

HOPKINSON, C. D. — Sussex

Name: <u>Carl</u> Daniel Hopkinson
Role: Right-hand bat, right-arm medium-fast bowler; 'batter that bowls'
Born: 14 September 1981, Brighton
Height: 5ft 11in
Nickname: Hoppo
County debut: 2001 (one-day), 2002 (first-class)
1st-Class catches: 2
Strike rate: (career 54.00)
Parents: Jane and Jerry
Marital status: Single
Family links with cricket: 'Dad played in the local team, which got me interested, and coached me from a young age'
Education: Chailey; Brighton College
Qualifications: 7 GCSEs, 3 A-levels, Level 1 coaching
Overseas tours: Tours to India 1997-98, to South Africa 1999
Overseas teams played for: Rockingham-Mandurah, Western Australia 2000-01
Career highlights to date: 'Playing in my first day/night game on TV; also my debut'
Cricket moments to forget: 'Playing on my debut and taking guard before the incoming batsman was announced; in other words, they didn't know who I was!'
Cricketers particularly admired: Dennis Lillee, Ian Botham, Viv Richards, Graham Thorpe
Young players to look out for: Krishna Singh
Other sports played: Rugby ('won Rosslyn Park National Sevens'), squash, football
Other sports followed: Football (Leeds United and Brighton & Hove Albion)
Favourite band: 50 Cent
Relaxations: 'Going out in Brighton with my mates, cinema etc.'
Extras: South of England and England squads until U17. Sussex Young Player of the Year 2000. Sussex 2nd XI Fielder of the Year 2001, 2003. Played for Sussex Board XI in the C&G 2001 and 2002. Took wicket (John Wood) with his third ball on county debut, in the Norwich Union League v Lancashire at Hove 2001. Took four catches and achieved a run out v Glamorgan at Hove in the Norwich Union League 2001. Took 3-19 and scored a match-winning 67* v Scotland at Edinburgh in the NCL 2003
Best batting: 33 Sussex v Warwickshire, Hove 2002
Best bowling: 1-35 Sussex v Warwickshire, Hove 2002

2003 Season

	M	Inns	NO	Runs	HS	Avge	100s	50s	Ct	St	O	M	Runs	Wkts	Avge	Best	5wI	10wM
Test																		
All First	1	1	1	7	7 *	-	-	-	-	-	2	0	8	0	-		-	-
1-day Int																		
C & G																			
NCL	13	10	1	152	67 *	16.88	-	1	6	-	43	0	250	6	41.66	3-19	-	
Twenty20	1	1	0	4	4	4.00	-	-	-	-								

Career Performances

	M	Inns	NO	Runs	HS	Avge	100s	50s	Ct	St	Balls	Runs	Wkts	Avge	Best	5wI	10wM
Test																	
All First	2	3	1	49	33	24.50	-	-	2	-	54	43	1	43.00	1-35	-	-
1-day Int																	
C & G	2	2	0	58	43	29.00	-	-	1	-	90	88	0	-		-	-
NCL	17	13	2	176	67 *	16.00	-	1	12	-	282	268	8	33.50	3-19	-	
Twenty20	1	1	0	4	4	4.00	-	-	-	-							

HORTON, P. J. Lancashire

Name: Paul James Horton
Role: Right-hand bat, right-arm medium/
off-spin bowler
Born: 20 September 1982, Sydney, Australia
Height: 5ft 10in **Weight:** 11st 3lbs
Nickname: Horts, Ozzy
County debut: 2003
1st-Class catches: 1
Parents: Donald William and Norma
Marital status: Single
Education: Colo High School,
Sydney/Broadgreen Comprehensive,
Liverpool; St Margaret's High School
Qualifications: 11 GCSEs, 3 A-levels,
Level 2 ECB coach
Overseas tours: Hawkesbury U15 to New
Zealand 1997; Lancashire to Cape Town
2002-03, to Grenada 2003
Overseas teams played for: Hawkesbury, Sydney 1992-93 – 1997-98;
Penrith, NSW 2002-03
Career highlights to date: 'First-class debut v Durham UCCE 2003'
Cricket moments to forget: 'First 2nd XI game for Lancashire at Old Trafford – out
for 0'

Cricket superstitions: 'None'
Cricketers particularly admired: Dean Jones, Sachin Tendulkar, Mark Waugh
Young players to look out for: Steven Crook, Chris Whelan, Kyle Hogg
Other sports played: Football, golf, squash, tennis, badminton
Other sports followed: Football (Liverpool)
Favourite band: Red Hot Chili Peppers
Relaxations: 'Golf, socialising with friends, watching sport'
Extras: Captained Lancashire U17 and U19. Captained Lancashire Board XI in the first and second rounds of the C&G 2003, which were played in August/September 2002. Lancashire Young Player of the Year Award 2001, 2002. Played for Lancashire side that won the inaugural ECB 38-County U21 Competition 2003. Leading run-scorer for Lancashire 2nd XI in the 2nd XI Championship 2003 (861 runs; av. 50.65)
Best batting: 2* Lancashire v DUCCE, Durham 2003

2003 Season

	M	Inns	NO	Runs	HS	Avge	100s	50s	Ct	St	O	M	Runs	Wkts	Avge	Best	5wl	10wM
Test																		
All First	1	1	1	2	2*	-	-	-	1	-								
1-day Int																		
C & G																		
NCL																		
Twenty20																		

Career Performances

	M	Inns	NO	Runs	HS	Avge	100s	50s	Ct	St	Balls	Runs	Wkts	Avge	Best	5wl	10wM
Test																	
All First	1	1	1	2	2*	-	-	-	1	-							
1-day Int																	
C & G	2	2	0	49	26	24.50	-	-	-	-							
NCL																	
Twenty20																	

HUGGINS, T. B.   Northamptonshire

Name: Thomas (Tom) Benjamin Huggins
Role: Right-hand opening bat, right-arm occasional off-spin bowler
Born: 8 March 1983, Peterborough
Height: 6ft 3in **Weight:** 15st ('ish')
Nickname: Huggo, Sheep's Head, The Viking
County debut: 2003
Parents: John and Elizabeth
Marital status: Single
Family links with cricket: 'Dad's a coach; brother plays a bit'

Education: Kimbolton School; De Montfort University, Bedford
Qualifications: 9 GCSEs, 3 A-levels, Level 3 coach
Off-season: 'Uni; coaching'
Overseas tours: Huntingdon Cricket 2000 to Zimbabwe 1999
Career highlights to date: 'First-class debut; getting a double hundred against Worcestershire 2nd XI at Kidderminster 2003; any time I get a wicket'
Cricket moments to forget: 'First first-class innings' (*Was out third ball v Cambridge University CCE at Fenner's 2003*)
Cricket superstitions: 'Loads'
Cricketers particularly admired:
Graham Thorpe, Mike Hussey
Young players to look out for:
Adam Shantry, Mark Powell, Tim Roberts
Other sports played: Football, hockey
Other sports followed: 'Most sports that are on TV'
Favourite band: Oasis, Red Hot Chili Peppers, Athlete
Relaxations: 'Listening to music; playing snooker; going out with friends'
Extras: Huntingdonshire Young Player of the Year 1997, 1998, 2000. Recorded highest individual score in Huntingdonshire Youth cricket (185* v Norfolk U19 2000). Set three records for Kimbolton School 1st XI in 2001. Played for Cambridgeshire in the C&G 2002. Scored double century (210) v Worcestershire 2nd XI at Kidderminster 2003
Opinions on cricket: 'Standards are improving, but there needs to be more practice time. Second-team cricket should mirror first-class cricket so as to better prepare players.'
Best batting: 40 Northamptonshire v CUCCE, Fenner's 2003

2003 Season

	M	Inns	NO	Runs	HS	Avge	100s	50s	Ct	St	O	M	Runs	Wkts	Avge	Best	5wI	10wM
Test																		
All First	1	2	0	40	40	20.00	-	-	-	-								
1-day Int																		
C & G																		
NCL																		
Twenty20																		

Career Performances

	M	Inns	NO	Runs	HS	Avge	100s	50s	Ct	St	Balls	Runs	Wkts	Avge	Best	5wI	10wM
Test																	
All First	1	2	0	40	40	20.00	-	-	-	-							
1-day Int																	
C & G	1	1	0	2	2	2.00	-	-	-	-							
NCL																	
Twenty20																	

HUGHES, J.   Glamorgan

Name: Jonathan Hughes
Role: Right-hand bat, right-arm medium bowler
Born: 30 June 1981, Pontypridd
Height: 5ft 11in
Nickname: Jonny, Tuck Box, Hughesy
County debut: 2001
1st-Class 50s: 3
1st-Class catches: 12
Place in batting averages: 212th av. 21.88 (2002 182nd av. 25.00)
Parents: Steve and Anne
Marital status: Single
Family links with cricket: 'Dad and brothers Matthew (18) and Gareth (24) play for Hopkinstown'
Education: Coed y Lan Comprehensive, Pontypridd
Qualifications: MCC coaching badges
Overseas tours: Hopkinstown to Barbados 1998
Overseas teams played for: Easts-Redlands, Brisbane 2000, 2001
Career highlights to date: 'Debut v Surrey for Glamorgan in County Championship'
Cricketers particularly admired: Matthew Maynard, Ian Botham
Young players to look out for: Mark Wallace
Other sports played: Football (Hopkinstown)
Other sports followed: Rugby (Pontypridd), football (Everton)
Relaxations: Going to the pub
Extras: Captained Welsh Schools. Was on Lord's groundstaff 1998-99. Glamorgan 2nd XI Player of the Year 2001. Glamorgan Young Player of the Year 2001. Scored 74, including 14 fours, v Worcestershire at Worcester 2002 in his second first-class match. NBC Denis Compton Award for the most promising young Glamorgan player 2002
Best batting: 74 Glamorgan v Worcestershire, Worcester 2002

2003 Season

	M	Inns	NO	Runs	HS	Avge	100s	50s	Ct	St	O	M	Runs	Wkts	Avge	Best	5wI	10wM
Test																		
All First	10	17	0	372	73	21.88	-	2	10	-								
1-day Int																		
C & G	1	1	0	51	51	51.00	-	1	-	-								
NCL	2	2	0	31	30	15.50	-	-	1	-								
Twenty20	1	1	0	1	1	1.00	-	-	-	-								

Career Performances

	M	Inns	NO	Runs	HS	Avge	100s	50s	Ct	St	Balls	Runs	Wkts	Avge	Best	5wI	10wM
Test																	
All First	18	29	1	684	74	24.42	-	3	12	-							
1-day Int																	
C & G	1	1	0	51	51	51.00	-	1	-	-							
NCL	3	3	0	40	30	13.33	-	-	1	-							
Twenty20	1	1	0	1	1	1.00	-	-	-	-							

HUNT, T. A.   Middlesex

Name: Thomas (<u>Thos</u>) Aaron Hunt
Role: Left-hand bat, right-arm medium-fast bowler
Born: 19 January 1982, Melbourne, Australia
Height: 6ft 3in **Weight:** 13st 4lbs
Nickname: Hopalong, Peg-leg
County debut: 2002 (*see Extras*)
Strike rate: 44.00 (career 51.14)
Parents: Jennifer Hunt and Tim Woodbridge
Marital status: Single
Education: Acton High; St Clement Danes
Qualifications: 9 GCSEs, 1 A-level, Level 1 coaching award
Cricket moments to forget: '1st XI debut at Lord's [v Australians 2001]'
Cricketers particularly admired: Curtly Ambrose, Waqar Younis
Young players to look out for: Ian Bell
Other sports played: 'Keen skier, also played school and Sunday league football'
Other sports followed: Football (Man Utd)
Relaxations: 'Music; spending time with girlfriend'
Extras: Made 1st XI debut for Middlesex v Australians in a one-day fixture at Lord's

2001 but did not appear for the county in first-class cricket or domestic competition until 2002. Released by Middlesex at the end of the 2003 season
Best batting: 3 Middlesex v Sri Lankans, Shenley 2002
Best bowling: 3-43 Middlesex v CUCCE, Fenner's 2002

2003 Season

	M	Inns	NO	Runs	HS	Avge	100s	50s	Ct	St	O	M	Runs	Wkts	Avge	Best	5wl	10wM
Test																		
All First	1	0	0	0	0	-	-	-	-	-	22	4	96	3	32.00	2-28	-	-
1-day Int																		
C & G																			
NCL																			
Twenty20																			

Career Performances

	M	Inns	NO	Runs	HS	Avge	100s	50s	Ct	St	Balls	Runs	Wkts	Avge	Best	5wl	10wM
Test																	
All First	3	1	0	3	3	3.00	-	-	-	-	358	285	7	40.71	3-43	-	-
1-day Int																	
C & G																		
NCL	3	1	0	0	0	0.00	-	-	1	-	90	80	1	80.00	1-24	-	
Twenty20																	

HUNTER, I. D.   Durham

Name: <u>Ian</u> David Hunter
Role: Right-hand bat, right-arm fast-medium bowler
Born: 11 September 1979, Durham City
Height: 6ft 2in **Weight:** 12st 7lbs
Nickname: Sticks, Hunts
County debut: 1999 (one-day), 2000 (first-class)
1st-Class 50s: 2
1st-Class catches: 6
Place in batting averages: (2002 237th av. 18.54)
Place in bowling averages: (2002 119th av. 38.75)
Strike rate: 102.00 (career 67.73)
Parents: Ken and Linda
Marital status: Single

Family links with cricket: Brother plays for local village side
Education: Fyndoune Community College, Sacriston; New College, Durham
Qualifications: 9 GCSEs, 1 A-level (PE), BTEC National Diploma in Sports Science, Level I and II cricket coaching awards
Overseas tours: Durham U21 to Sri Lanka 1996; Durham to Cape Town 2002
Career highlights to date: 'Scoring 63 on first-class debut' (*v Leicestershire at Riverside 2000 as nightwatchman*)
Cricket superstitions: 'Always put my left pad on first'
Cricketers particularly admired: Allan Donald, Steve Waugh
Other sports played: Football, golf
Other sports followed: Football (Durham City AFC)
Relaxations: Socialising with friends; keeping fit, golf, football
Extras: Set a new Durham best analysis for the 2nd XI Championship with his 11-155 v Lancashire 2nd XI 1999. Represented England U19 v Australia U19 1999. Played for Durham Board XI in the C&G 2001, 2002 and 2003. Released by Durham at the end of the 2003 season
Opinions on cricket: 'Pitches are becoming increasingly flat! More day/night cricket – "it's a right laugh".'
Best batting: 65 Durham v Northamptonshire, Northampton 2002
Best bowling: 4-55 Durham v Warwickshire, Edgbaston 2001

2003 Season

	M	Inns	NO	Runs	HS	Avge	100s	50s	Ct	St	O	M	Runs	Wkts	Avge	Best	5wI	10wM
Test																		
All First	2	2	0	91	47	45.50	-	-	-	-	51	6	191	3	63.66	2-55	-	-
1-day Int																		
C & G	1	1	0	2	2	2.00	-	-	1	-	10	1	45	2	22.50	2-45	-	
NCL	2	2	0	4	4	2.00	-	-	1	-	18	0	77	5	15.40	3-34	-	
Twenty20	3	2	1	27	25*	27.00	-	-	-	-	10	1	92	2	46.00	1-21	-	

Career Performances

	M	Inns	NO	Runs	HS	Avge	100s	50s	Ct	St	Balls	Runs	Wkts	Avge	Best	5wI	10wM
Test																	
All First	21	32	4	577	65	20.60	-	2	6	-	3048	1894	45	42.08	4-55	-	-
1-day Int																	
C & G	3	3	0	16	13	5.33	-	-	1	-	138	92	3	30.66	2-45	-	
NCL	36	21	4	131	21	7.70	-	-	8	-	1518	1212	41	29.56	4-29	-	
Twenty20	3	2	1	27	25*	27.00	-	-	-	-	60	92	2	46.00	1-21	-	

HUSSAIN, N.   Essex

Name: Nasser Hussain
Role: Right-hand bat, leg-break bowler,
county club captain
Born: 28 March 1968, Madras, India
Height: 6ft **Weight:** 12st 7lbs
Nickname: Nashwan
County debut: 1987
County cap: 1989
Benefit: 1999 (£271,500)
Test debut: 1989-90
Tests: 87
One-Day Internationals: 88
1000 runs in a season: 5
1st-Class 50s: 101
1st-Class 100s: 48
1st-Class 200s: 2
1st-Class catches: 336
One-Day 100s: 9
Place in batting averages: 42nd av. 46.05 (2002 81st av. 40.25)
Strike rate: (career 156.00)
Parents: Joe and Shireen
Wife and date of marriage: Karen, 24 September 1993
Children: Jacob, 8 June 2001; Joel, 18 November 2002
Family links with cricket: Father played zonal cricket in India. Played for Madras in Ranji Trophy 1966-67. Brother Mel played for Hampshire. Brother Abbas played for Essex 2nd XI
Education: Forest School, Snaresbrook; Durham University
Qualifications: 10 O-levels, 3 A-levels, BSc (Hons) in Natural Sciences, NCA cricket coaching award
Off-season: Touring with England
Overseas tours: England YC to Sri Lanka 1986-87, to Australia (U19 World Cup) 1987-88; England A to Pakistan and Sri Lanka 1990-91, to Bermuda and West Indies 1991-92, to Pakistan 1995-96 (captain); England to India (Nehru Cup) 1989-90, to West Indies 1989-90, 1993-94, 1997-98, to Zimbabwe and New Zealand 1996-97, to Australia 1998-99, 2002-03 (captain), to South Africa and Zimbabwe 1999-2000 (captain), to Kenya (ICC Knockout Trophy) 2000-01 (captain), to Pakistan and Sri Lanka 2000-01 (captain), to Zimbabwe (one-day series) 2001-02 (captain), to India and New Zealand 2001-02 (captain), to Sri Lanka (ICC Champions Trophy) 2002-03 (captain), to Australia 2002-03 (captain), to Africa (World Cup) 2002-03 (captain), to Bangladesh and Sri Lanka 2003-04, to West Indies 2003-04
Overseas teams played for: Madras 1986-87; Adelaide University 1990; Petersham, Sydney 1992-93; Stellenbosch University, South Africa 1994-95; Primrose, Cape Town

Cricketers particularly admired: Mark Waugh, Graham Gooch, Sachin Tendulkar
Other sports played: Golf (10 handicap), football
Other sports followed: Football (Leeds United)
Relaxations: Listening to music; watching television
Extras: Cricket Writers' Club Young Cricketer of the Year 1989. Set records for third (347* v Lancashire at Ilford 1992), fourth (314 v Surrey at The Oval 1991) and fifth (316 v Leicestershire at Leicester 1991) wicket partnerships for Essex (with Mark Waugh, Salim Malik and Mike Garnham respectively). Essex Player of the Year 1993. Finished 2nd in the Whyte and Mackay batting ratings 1995. Appointed Essex vice-captain 1996. Appointed England vice-captain 1996-97. Scored 207 in the first Test v Australia at Edgbaston 1997, in the process sharing with Graham Thorpe (138) in record fourth-wicket partnership for England in Tests v Australia (288) and winning Man of the Match award. Represented England in the 1999 World Cup. Appointed England captain after 1999 World Cup. Topped England batting averages in the 1999-2000 Test series v South Africa with 370 runs at 61.66; during the series he became the first player to bat for 1000 minutes in Test cricket without being out. In 2000 led England to victory in the NatWest triangular one-day series, to a Test series win over Zimbabwe, and to a first Test series win over West Indies for 31 years; followed up with series wins in Pakistan and Sri Lanka in the winter of 2000-01, which made England only the second touring side to win two Test rubbers on the sub-continent in the same season. npower Contribution to Cricket Award 2001. Awarded OBE in New Year honours list 2001-02. Scored 106 in first innings of the first Test v New Zealand at Christchurch 2001-02, coming to the wicket with England at 0-2 and being last out with the score on 228; was England's top run-scorer in the three-match series with 280 (av. 56.00). Vodafone England Cricketer of the Year 2001-02. One of *Wisden*'s Five Cricketers of the Year 2003. Other Test awards include [England's] Man of the Series v India 1996 and Man of the Match in the first Test v India at Lord's 2002. Resigned as England one-day captain and retired from ODI cricket after the 2002-03 World Cup and stood down as England Test captain after the first Test v South Africa at Edgbaston 2003. Scored his 50th first-class century (116) in the third Test v South Africa 2003, sharing with Mark Butcher (106) in a record partnership for any wicket for England in Tests v South Africa at Trent Bridge (189). Essex captain 1999; handed over 1st XI captaincy to Ronnie Irani at the start of the 2000 season but remains club captain. ECB central contract 2003-04
Best batting: 207 England v Australia, Edgbaston 1997
Best bowling: 1-38 Essex v Worcestershire, Kidderminster 1992

2003 Season

	M	Inns	NO	Runs	HS	Avge	100s	50s	Ct	St	O	M	Runs	Wkts	Avge	Best	5wI	10wM
Test	6	10	1	330	116	36.66	1	1	1	-								
All First	11	19	2	783	206	46.05	2	3	3	-								
1-day Int																		
C & G	2	2	0	6	6	3.00	-	-	1	-								
NCL	5	5	2	431	161 *	143.66	2	1	1	-								
Twenty20																		

Career Performances

	M	Inns	NO	Runs	HS	Avge	100s	50s	Ct	St	Balls	Runs	Wkts	Avge	Best	5wl	10wM
Test	87	154	14	5196	207	37.11	13	28	57	-	30	15	0	-	-	-	-
All First	321	523	51	19872	207	42.10	50	101	336	-	312	323	2	161.50	1-38	-	-
1-day Int	88	87	10	2332	115	30.28	1	16	40	-							
C & G	33	31	4	1105	108	40.92	2	6	23	-							
NCL	150	139	20	4123	161 *	34.64	3	26	64	-							
Twenty20																	

HUSSEY, D. J. Nottinghamshire

Name: David (<u>Dave</u>) John Hussey
Role: Right-hand bat, right-arm
off-spin bowler
Born: 15 July 1977, Morley,
Western Australia
County debut: No first-team appearance
1st-Class 50s: 1
1st-Class catches: 2
One-Day 100s: 1
Strike rate: (career 54.00)
Parents: Helen and Ted
Family links with cricket: Elder brother
Mike plays for Western Australia and played
for Northamptonshire 2001-03
Overseas teams played for: Victoria
2002-03 –
Cricketers particularly admired: Damien
Martyn, Mark Waugh, Brendon Julian; Greg
Shipperd, Rod Marsh, Ian Kevan (as coaches)
Young cricketers to look out for: Matthew Harrison, Aaron Finch, Cameron Huckett
Other sports followed: Australian Rules, squash
Favourite band: Red Hot Chili Peppers, Blink 182, Counting Crows
Relaxations: Movies, shopping
Extras: Played for Western Australia U19 and 2nd XI. Represented Australia U19 v
New Zealand U19 1995-96. Played for Sussex Board XI in the C&G 2001 and 2002,
scoring 118* v Essex Board XI at Chelmsford in the 2002 competition, winning Man
of the Match award. Scored 27-ball 35* on ING Cup debut in Victoria's last-over win
v Queensland at Brisbane 2002-03. Has joined Nottinghamshire as an overseas player
for 2004 as cover for Damien Martyn while on international duty
Best batting: 62 Victoria v Queensland, Brisbane 2002-03
Best bowling: 1-6 Victoria v Western Australia, Melbourne 2002-03

Stop press: Man of the Match v New South Wales at Melbourne in the Pura Cup 2003-04 (120/50). Scored 212* and won Man of the Match award as Victoria scored 455-7 to beat New South Wales at Newcastle in the Pura Cup 2003-04; it was the second highest successful fourth innings run chase in Australian domestic cricket history after South Australia's 506-6 v Queensland at Adelaide 1991-92. Man of the Match v South Australia at Adelaide in the ING Cup 2003-04 (113)

2003 Season (did not make any first-class or one-day appearances)

Career Performances

	M	Inns	NO	Runs	HS	Avge	100s	50s	Ct	St	Balls	Runs	Wkts	Avge	Best	5wI	10wM
Test																	
All First	3	4	0	88	62	22.00	-	1	2	-	54	6	1	6.00	1-6	-	-
1-day Int																	
C & G	3	3	1	164	118*	82.00	1	-	4	-	161	161	6	26.83	3-48	-	
NCL																	
Twenty20																	

HUSSEY, M. E. K.   Northamptonshire

Name: Michael (<u>Mike</u>) Edward Killeen Hussey
Role: Left-hand bat, right-arm medium bowler
Born: 27 May 1975, Perth, Western Australia
Height: 6ft **Weight:** 12st 7lbs
Nickname: Huss
County debut: 2001
County cap: 2001
1000 runs in a season: 3
1st-Class 50s: 49
1st-Class 100s: 25
1st-Class 200s: 3
1st-Class 300s: 3
1st-Class catches: 137
One-Day 100s: 5
Place in batting averages: 2nd av. 89.31 (2002 8th av. 68.66)
Strike rate: 84.00 (career 93.66)
Parents: Helen and Ted
Wife: Amy
Family links with cricket: Younger brother Dave was formerly with Western Australia and now plays for Victoria and has joined Nottinghamshire for 2004

Education: Prendiville; Curtin
Career outside cricket: Teacher
Overseas tours: Australia U19 to India 1993-94; Australian Cricket Academy to Pakistan 1995; Australia A to Scotland and Ireland 1998, to South Africa (one-day series) 2002-03
Overseas teams played for: Wanneroo, Western Australia; Western Australia 1994-95 –
Cricketers particularly admired: Steve Waugh, Mark Taylor, Sachin Tendulkar, Dennis Lillee
Young players to look out for: Shaun Marsh
Other sports played: Golf, squash, tennis
Other sports followed: Australian Rules (West Coast Eagles), football (Man Utd)
Relaxations: Movies, beach
Extras: Attended Commonwealth Bank [Australian] Cricket Academy 1995. Finished third in the Sheffield Shield Player of the Year award in his first full season 1995-96. Sir Donald Bradman Young Cricketer of the Year 1998. Excalibur Award (Western Australia) 1998-2000. Scored maiden Mercantile Cup century (100*) v Victoria at Melbourne 1999-2000, sharing in a competition record sixth-wicket partnership of 173 with Brad Hogg. Carried his bat for 172* v South Australia in the Pura Milk Cup 1999-2000. Joined Northamptonshire as overseas player for 2001. Scored maiden first-class triple century (329*) v Essex at Northampton 2001, in the process overtaking Mal Loye's record for the highest individual score by a Northants player (322*); followed up with a 33-ball 70* in the second innings and was on the field for the entire match. Scored 208 v Somerset at Taunton 2001, in the process sharing with Russell Warren (144) in a record third-wicket partnership for Northants in matches against Somerset (287). Leading run-scorer in English first-class cricket 2001 with 2055 runs (all in the Championship) at 79.03, at the same time becoming the first Northants batsman to score 2000 Championship runs in a season since Allan Lamb did so in 1981. Northamptonshire Player of the Year 2001 and 2002, the first player to win the award twice in succession. Leading run-scorer in Australia's one-day ING Cup 2001-02 with 440 runs (av. 55.00); in the match v New South Wales at Perth, struck sponsor's sign at square leg with a sweep shot, winning a $200,000 prize. Was first batsman to reach 1000 first-class runs in the 2002 season. Scored 310* v Gloucestershire at Bristol 2002, in the process sharing with Graeme Swann (183) in a stand of 318; was once again on the field for the entire match; scored 264 v Gloucestershire at Gloucester 2003. Scored third triple century in successive seasons (331*), v Somerset at Taunton 2003, breaking his own record for the highest individual score by a Northamptonshire player. Captain of Northamptonshire 2002-03. Has not returned to Northamptonshire for the 2004 season. Appointed vice-captain of Western Australia for 2003-04
Best batting: 331* Northamptonshire v Somerset, Taunton 2003
Best bowling: 2-21 Western Australia v Queensland, Perth 1998-99
Stop press: Made ODI debut v India in the VB Series 2003-04 at Perth

2003 Season

	M	Inns	NO	Runs	HS	Avge	100s	50s	Ct	St	O	M	Runs	Wkts	Avge	Best	5wI	10wM
Test																		
All First	14	21	2	1697	331*	89.31	6	5	17	-	14	2	52	1	52.00	1-5	-	-
1-day Int																		
C & G	1	1	0	5	5	5.00	-	-	1	-								
NCL	18	18	3	820	123	54.66	3	6	8	-	5	0	44	1	44.00	1-12	-	
Twenty20	5	5	1	279	88	69.75	-	3	5	-								

Career Performances

	M	Inns	NO	Runs	HS	Avge	100s	50s	Ct	St	Balls	Runs	Wkts	Avge	Best	5wI	10wM
Test																	
All First	136	241	18	11807	331*	52.94	31	49	137	-	562	321	6	53.50	2-21	-	-
1-day Int																	
C & G	5	5	0	99	59	19.80	-	1	2	-	30	30	1	30.00	1-20	-	
NCL	43	43	6	1724	123	46.59	4	13	18	-	30	44	1	44.00	1-12	-	
Twenty20	5	5	1	279	88	69.75	-	3	5	-							

HUTCHISON, P. M.   Middlesex

Name: Paul Michael Hutchison
Role: Left-hand bat, left-arm seamer
Born: 9 June 1977, Leeds
Height: 6ft 4in **Weight:** 13st
Nickname: Hutch, Hooch
County debut: 1995-96 (Yorkshire), 2002 (Sussex)
County cap: 1998 (Yorkshire)
50 wickets in a season: 1
1st-Class 5 w. in innings: 7
1st-Class 10 w. in match: 1
1st-Class catches: 10
Strike rate: 85.57 (career 45.49)
Parents: David Hutchison and Rita Laycock (deceased)
Wife and date of marriage: Emma, 18 October 2003
Family links with cricket: Brother Richard plays for Pudsey St Lawrence CC in the Bradford League
Education: Pudsey Crawshaw; 'just listening to Richard Montgomerie and Robin Martin-Jenkins!'
Qualifications: 8 GCSEs, GNVQ Leisure and Tourism, qualified cricket coach, basic IT ('thanks to PCA')

Off-season: 'In New Zealand playing for Stokes Valley, Wellington'
Overseas tours: England U19 to Zimbabwe 1995-96; England A to Kenya and Sri Lanka 1997-98, to Zimbabwe and South Africa 1998-99; Yorkshire to Zimbabwe and Botswana 1996, to South Africa 1998, 1999, 2001; Sussex to Grenada 2002
Overseas teams played for: Stokes Valley, Wellington, New Zealand 2003-04
Career highlights to date: 'My Championship debut 7-50. My two England A tours. My two Championship winner's medals'
Cricket superstitions: 'Batting – left pad on first; bowling – always turn right at end of run-up'
Cricketers particularly admired: Matt Maynard, Neil Fairbrother, Courtney Walsh, Craig White, Darren Gough, Graham Dilley, Malcolm Marshall, Mark Robinson, Jason Lewry, Murray Goodwin
Young players to look out for: Michael Lumb, Tim Ambrose, Matt Prior, John Sadler
Other sports played: Golf, football
Other sports followed: 'Most sports; anything on Sky Sports; any team from my area (Leeds/Bradford)'
Favourite band: U2, Red Hot Chili Peppers, Foo Fighters, Justin Timberlake, Robbie Williams
Relaxations: Golf, cinema, socialising with friends
Extras: Represented England at U17, U18 and U19 levels. Played for Pudsey St Lawrence in the Bradford League. Had a place at the Yorkshire Academy. Took 7-38 on first first-class appearance of 1997, against Pakistan A. Took 7-50 against Hampshire at Portsmouth 1997, the best Championship debut figures for Yorkshire since Wilfred Rhodes took 7-24 v Somerset in 1898. Voted Wombwell Cricket Lovers' Young Player of the Year for 1997. Released by Yorkshire at the end of the 2001 season and joined Sussex for 2002. Left Sussex at the end of the 2003 season and has joined Middlesex for 2004
Opinions on cricket: 'Too much emphasis on not losing at first-class level. Sussex won four more matches than Lancs, who were second, and only secured the title during the last match. To be successful at county and Test level we need to learn to play to win. Twenty20 was a success and needs to be built upon.'
Best batting: 30 Yorkshire v Essex, Scarborough 1998
Best bowling: 7-31 Yorkshire v Sussex, Hove 1998

2003 Season

	M	Inns	NO	Runs	HS	Avge	100s	50s	Ct	St	O	M	Runs	Wkts	Avge	Best	5wl	10wM
Test																		
All First	5	3	0	23	18	7.66	-	-	1	-	99.5	17	405	7	57.85	4-94	-	-
1-day Int																		
C & G																		
NCL	11	7	2	65	20	13.00	-	-	-	-	86	7	398	16	24.87	4-29	-	
Twenty20	3	1	1	0	0*	-	-	-	1	-	10	0	72	3	24.00	2-22	-	

Career Performances

	M	Inns	NO	Runs	HS	Avge	100s	50s	Ct	St	Balls	Runs	Wkts	Avge	Best	5wI	10wM
Test																	
All First	52	53	27	252	30	9.69	-	-	10	-	7673	4356	168	25.92	7-31	7	1
1-day Int																	
C & G	3	1	1	4	4 *	-	-	-	-	-	132	62	5	12.40	3-18	-	
NCL	36	17	7	86	20	8.60	-	-	5	-	1526	1144	47	24.34	4-29	-	
Twenty20	3	1	1	0	0 *	-	-	-	1	-	60	72	3	24.00	2-22	-	

HUTTON, B. L.   Middlesex

Name: Benjamin (<u>Ben</u>) Leonard Hutton
Role: Left-hand bat, right-arm
medium bowler
Born: 29 January 1977, Johannesburg,
South Africa
Height: 6ft 2in **Weight:** 12st
Nickname: Gibbo, The Gibbonian
County debut: 1999
County cap: 2003
1st-Class 50s: 10
1st-Class 100s: 8
1st-Class catches: 70
One-Day 5 w. in innings: 1
Place in batting averages: 73rd av. 40.04
(2002 150th av. 28.77)
Strike rate: 99.60 (career 83.56)
Parents: Charmaine and Richard
Marital status: Single
Family links with cricket: Sir Leonard Hutton (grandfather) Yorkshire and England;
Richard Hutton (father) Yorkshire and England; Ben Brocklehurst (grandfather)
Somerset
Education: Radley College; Durham University
Qualifications: 10 GCSEs, 3 A-levels, BA (Hons) Social Sciences, NCA
coaching award
Career outside cricket: 'Apprentice insurance broker'
Off-season: 'Working for RP Hodson Insurance Brokers'
Overseas tours: Durham University to Zimbabwe 1997-98; Middlesex to Portugal
1996, 1997, 1998, to South Africa 1999, to Malta 2001, to Bombay 2003;
MCC to Italy
Overseas teams played for: Pirates CC, Johannesburg 1996; Wanderers CC,
Johannesburg 1997; Gosnells, Perth 2001-02

Career highlights to date: 'Scoring 73 v Aussies in 2001. Being capped by Middlesex 2003'

Cricket moments to forget: 'Breaking my hand v Gloucestershire 2001. First pair in first-class cricket. Being run out backing up twice in two games'

Cricket superstitions: 'None'

Cricketers particularly admired: 'Both my grandfathers, my father, Justin Langer, Andy Flower, Mark Ramprakash, Angus Fraser'

Young players to look out for: Matt Prior, Bilal Shafayat, Chad Keegan

Other sports played: Golf, rackets

Other sports followed: 'All sport, except motor racing'

Injuries: Out for two months overall with a broken hand and a side strain

Favourite band: 'Too many to mention'

Relaxations: 'Reading; debating with David Nash about him standing too far back to seam bowlers!'

Extras: Played in Durham University's BUSA Championship winning side 1997, 1998 (shared) and 1999. Opened for Middlesex v Essex at Southend 1999 with Andrew Strauss, his former opening partner at Radley. His maiden first-class century, 133 v Oxford University CCE at The Parks, was the first first-class century of the 2001 season. Awarded Middlesex cap 2003

Opinions on cricket: 'We should increase the length of the tea break to half an hour. Twenty20 great success that has really improved the profile of the game. Individuals should stop criticising the game's structure in this country and be more pro-active in trying to ensure that our system produces cricketers who can compete with the best in the world.'

Best batting: 139 Middlesex v Derbyshire, Southgate 2001
Best bowling: 4-37 Middlesex v Sri Lankans, Shenley 2002

2003 Season

	M	Inns	NO	Runs	HS	Avge	100s	50s	Ct	St	O	M	Runs	Wkts	Avge	Best	5wI	10wM
Test																		
All First	18	30	6	961	107	40.04	4	1	17	-	83	14	363	5	72.60	2-43	-	-
1-day Int																		
C & G	3	3	0	28	27	9.33	-	-	3	-	5	0	30	1	30.00	1-14	-	
NCL	18	14	8	131	43 *	21.83	-	-	5	-	12.4	0	72	0	-		-	-
Twenty20	5	3	1	15	9 *	7.50	-	-	2	-	2	0	25	1	25.00	1-14	-	

Career Performances

	M	Inns	NO	Runs	HS	Avge	100s	50s	Ct	St	Balls	Runs	Wkts	Avge	Best	5wI	10wM
Test																	
All First	62	102	11	2794	139	30.70	8	10	70	-	1922	1201	23	52.21	4-37	-	-
1-day Int																	
C & G	5	4	0	42	27	10.50	-	-	4	-	78	88	3	29.33	2-42	-	
NCL	50	40	11	667	77	23.00	-	3	19	-	754	682	20	34.10	5-45	1	
Twenty20	5	3	1	15	9 *	7.50	-	-	2	-	12	25	1	25.00	1-14	-	

IMRAN TAHIR   Middlesex

Name: Mohammad Imran Tahir
Role: Right-hand bat, right-arm
leg-spin bowler
Born: 27 March 1979, Lahore, Punjab
County debut: 2003
1st-Class 5 w. in innings: 6
1st-Class 10 w. in match: 2
1st-Class catches: 17
Strike rate: 354.00 (career 53.74)
Overseas tours: Pakistan U19 to South
Africa 1996-97, to Australia 1997-98, to
South Africa (U19 World Cup) 1997-98
Overseas teams played for:
Lahore City 1996-97 – 1997-98; Water and
Power Development Authority (WAPDA)
1997-98 – 1998-99; REDCO Pakistan Ltd
1999-2000; Lahore Whites 2000-01; Sui Gas
Corporation of Pakistan 2001-02, 2003-04;
Sialkot 2002-03
Extras: Represented Pakistan U19 in home series v England U19 and Australia U19
1996-97. Played for Norton-in-Hales in the North Staffordshire & South Cheshire
League; in 2002 took 104 wickets, equalling the league record for the number of
wickets in a season and breaking the club's season record of 97 held by Garry Sobers.
Was an overseas player with Middlesex during May 2003, deputising for Abdul
Razzaq, absent on international duty
Best batting: 48 REDCO v KRL, Rawalpindi 1999-2000
Best bowling: 8-76 REDCO v Karachi Blues, Lahore 1999-2000

2003 Season

	M	Inns	NO	Runs	HS	Avge	100s	50s	Ct	St	O	M	Runs	Wkts	Avge	Best	5wI	10wM
Test																		
All First	3	3	1	30	29	15.00	-	-	-	-	59	13	196	1	196.00	1-128	-	-
1-day Int																		
C & G	1	0	0	0	0	-	-	-	1	-	10	2	41	0	-	-	-	-
NCL	2	0	0	0	0	-	-	-	-	-	6	0	28	0	-	-	-	-
Twenty20																		

	M	Inns	NO	Runs	HS	Avge	100s	50s	Ct	St	Balls	Runs	Wkts	Avge	Best	5wI	10wM
Test																	
All First	30	34	9	338	48	13.52	-	-	17	-	5428	2791	101	27.63	8-76	6	2
1-day Int																	
C & G	1	0	0	0	0	-	-	-	1	-	60	41	0	-		-	-
NCL	2	0	0	0	0	-	-	-	-	-	36	28	0	-		-	-
Twenty20																	

INNES, K. J. Sussex

Name: <u>Kevin</u> John Innes
Role: Right-hand bat, right-arm
medium bowler
Born: 24 September 1975, Wellingborough
Height: 5ft 10in **Weight:** 11st 5lbs
Nickname: KJ, Squirrel, Ernie
County debut: 1994 (Northamptonshire),
2002 (Sussex)
1st-Class 50s: 3
1st-Class 100s: 1
1st-Class catches: 14
One-Day 5 w. in innings: 1
Place in batting averages: 199th av. 23.50
(2002 127th av. 31.86)
Place in bowling averages: (2002 57th
av. 28.75)
Strike rate: 65.33 (career 55.14)
Parents: Peter and Jane
Wife and date of marriage: Caroline, 2001

Education: Weston Favell Upper School, Northampton
Qualifications: 10 GCSEs, Level 3 Staff 1 coach
Overseas tours: England U18 to South Africa 1992-93, to Denmark 1993; England
U19 to Sri Lanka 1993-94
Overseas teams played for: Karori, New Zealand 1995-97
Cricketers particularly admired: Glenn McGrath, Steve Waugh
Young players to look out for: Mark Powell
Other sports played: Golf, snooker, fishing
Relaxations: 'Spending time with my wife; sleeping and eating out; music, reading
books/magazines'
Extras: Won the MCC Lord's Taverners Award U13 and U15. Became youngest
player to play for Northants 2nd XI, aged 14 years 9 months. Played for England U19

v India U19 1994. 2nd XI Championship Player of the Year 1998. Left Northamptonshire during the 2001-02 off-season and joined Sussex for 2002. Scored maiden first-class century (103*) v Nottinghamshire at Horsham 2003 before being replaced in the Sussex side by James Kirtley (released by England), thus becoming the first 12th man to score a first-class hundred

Best batting: 103* Sussex v Nottinghamshire, Horsham 2003
Best bowling: 4-41 Sussex v Surrey, Hove 2002

2003 Season

	M	Inns	NO	Runs	HS	Avge	100s	50s	Ct	St	O	M	Runs	Wkts	Avge	Best	5wI	10wM
Test																		
All First	8	12	4	188	103 *	23.50	1	-	1	-	98	18	354	9	39.33	2-18	-	-
1-day Int																		
C & G	1	1	0	4	4	4.00	-	-	2	-	8	0	53	0	-		-	-
NCL	7	6	1	65	21	13.00	-	-	4	-	41.2	1	226	10	22.60	5-41	1	
Twenty20	5	5	1	22	10	5.50	-	-	-	-	8.3	0	72	1	72.00	1-28	-	

Career Performances

	M	Inns	NO	Runs	HS	Avge	100s	50s	Ct	St	Balls	Runs	Wkts	Avge	Best	5wI	10wM
Test																	
All First	42	66	17	1188	103 *	24.24	1	3	14	-	4191	2305	76	30.32	4-41	-	-
1-day Int																	
C & G	8	5	2	38	25	12.66	-	-	5	-	249	250	5	50.00	3-26	-	
NCL	61	42	14	638	55	22.78	-	2	19	-	1949	1726	62	27.83	5-41	1	
Twenty20	5	5	1	22	10	5.50	-	-	-	-	51	72	1	72.00	1-28	-	

---

49. A Devonian who was 36 years old on Test debut
and played only two Tests, both against the West Indies – name this
former Gloucestershire and Essex left-arm bowler.

IRANI, R. C. Essex

Name: Ronald (<u>Ronnie</u>) Charles Irani
Role: Right-hand bat, right-arm
medium-fast bowler, county 1st XI captain
Born: 26 October 1971, Leigh, Lancashire
Height: 6ft 4in **Weight:** 14st 8lbs
Nickname: Reggie
County debut: 1990 (Lancashire),
1994 (Essex)
County cap: 1994 (Essex)
Benefit: 2003 (Essex)
Test debut: 1996
Tests: 3
One-Day Internationals: 31
1000 runs in a season: 5
50 wickets in a season: 1
1st-Class 50s: 54
1st-Class 100s: 18
1st-Class 200s: 1
1st-Class 5 w. in innings: 9
1st-Class catches: 68
One-Day 100s: 3
One-Day 5 w. in innings: 4
Place in batting averages: 128th av. 31.42 (2002 16th av. 61.06)
Place in bowling averages: (2002 6th av. 20.37)
Strike rate: 66.66 (career 60.15)
Parents: Jimmy and Anne
Wife's name: Lorraine
Children: Simone, 25 September 2000; Maria, 6 January 2002
Family links with cricket: 'Father played league cricket for over 30 years. Mum did teas for years as well'
Education: Smithills Comprehensive School
Qualifications: 9 GCSEs
Off-season: 'Recovering from micro-fracture surgery in right knee'
Overseas tours: England YC to Australia 1989-90; England A to Pakistan 1995-96, to Bangladesh and New Zealand 1999-2000; England to Zimbabwe and New Zealand 1996-97, to Sri Lanka (ICC Champions Trophy) 2002-03, to Australia 2002-03 (VB Series), to Africa (World Cup) 2002-03; England VI to Hong Kong 2002
Overseas teams played for: Technicol Natal, Durban 1992-93; Eden-Roskill, Auckland 1993-94
Career highlights to date: 'Playing for England. Winning one-day trophies with Essex'

Cricket moments to forget: 'Admiring lady streaker and getting caught on TV cameras doing it!'
Cricketers particularly admired: Graham Gooch, Javed Miandad, Viv Richards, Wasim Akram
Young players to look out for: Will Jefferson, Justin Bishop
Other sports played: Golf, pool
Other sports followed: Football (Manchester United), Muay Thai boxing
Injuries: Right knee
Favourite band: Manic Street Preachers, Travis, Joyce Simms, Alexander O'Neal
Relaxations: Fly fishing
Extras: Played for England YC in home series v Australian YC 1991, scoring a century and three 50s in six innings and being named Bull Man of the Series. Appointed vice-captain of Essex in 1999. Achieved double of 1000 first-class runs and 50 first-class wickets in 1999. His then career best innings of 168* v Glamorgan at Cardiff 2000 lasted nine hours and 20 minutes, during which time he received 479 balls. Scored a 55-ball century (ending up 108*) v Glamorgan at Chelmsford in the Norwich Union League 2001. Recorded a five-wicket innings return (5-58) and scored a century (119) for Essex v Surrey at Ilford 2001, following up with a wicket with the first ball of his opening spell in Surrey's second innings. C&G Man of the Match award for his 86* plus 2-47 v Middlesex at Chelmsford 2002. Took a season record 20 wickets in the 2002 B&H. Man of the Match award v India at The Oval in the NatWest Series 2002 for his 53 (his maiden ODI fifty) and 5-26 (his maiden ODI five-wicket return and the best ODI analysis recorded at The Oval); also named 'Fans' Player of the Series'. Took 4-37 v Zimbabwe at Colombo in the ICC Champions Trophy 2002-03. Captained England XI v Sir Donald Bradman XI at Bowral 2002-03. Granted Freedom of the City of London in April 2003. Took over 1st XI captaincy of Essex at the start of the 2000 season, Nasser Hussain remaining as club captain. Has weekly radio show on Dream 107.7FM
Opinions on cricket: 'Three-day cricket to return to allow for a Twenty20 league. "The trend is my friend!"'
Best batting: 207* Essex v Northamptonshire, Ilford 2002
Best bowling: 6-71 Essex v Nottinghamshire, Trent Bridge 2002

2003 Season

	M	Inns	NO	Runs	HS	Avge	100s	50s	Ct	St	O	M	Runs	Wkts	Avge	Best	5wl	10wM
Test																		
All First	13	20	1	597	102 *	31.42	1	4	4	-	100	33	245	9	27.22	4-59	-	-
1-day Int																		
C & G	2	2	0	49	38	24.50	-	-	1	-	19	3	93	3	31.00	2-42	-	
NCL	13	13	1	332	64	27.66	-	3	4	-	22	3	81	5	16.20	3-21	-	
Twenty20	5	5	0	118	39	23.60	-	-	1	-								

Career Performances

	M	Inns	NO	Runs	HS	Avge	100s	50s	Ct	St	Balls	Runs	Wkts	Avge	Best	5wI	10wM
Test	3	5	0	86	41	17.20	-	-	2	-	192	112	3	37.33	1-22	-	-
All First	186	305	36	10035	207 *	37.30	19	54	68	-	20389	10007	339	29.51	6-71	9	-
1-day Int	31	30	5	360	53	14.40	-	1	6	-	1283	989	24	41.20	5-26	1	
C & G	26	23	3	879	124	43.95	1	7	8	-	1526	1042	37	28.16	4-41	-	
NCL	152	145	22	3355	108 *	27.27	2	19	36	-	5210	3912	165	23.70	5-33	1	
Twenty20	5	5	0	118	39	23.60	-	-	1	-							

JAMES, S. P. Glamorgan

Name: <u>Stephen</u> Peter James
Role: Right-hand opening bat
Born: 7 September 1967, Lydney, Glos
Height: 6ft **Weight:** 13st
Nickname: Sid, Jamo
County debut: 1985
County cap: 1992
Benefit: 2001
Test debut: 1998
Tests: 2
1000 runs in a season: 9
1st-Class 50s: 58
1st-Class 100s: 41
1st-Class 200s: 5
1st-Class 300s: 1
1st-Class catches: 173
One-Day 100s: 7
Place in batting averages: (2002 27th
av. 52.90)
Parents: Peter and Margaret
Wife and date of marriage: Jane Louise, 26 September 1997
Children: Bethan Amy, 28 August 1998 ('during Test match!')
Family links with cricket: Father played for Gloucestershire 2nd XI. Distant relative
of Dominic Ostler
Education: Monmouth School; University College, Swansea; Cambridge University
Qualifications: BA (Hons) Wales – Classics; BA (Hons) Cantab – Land Economy
Off-season: 'Rehabilitation; writing for *Sunday Telegraph*, *South Wales Argus*,
Western Mail, *The Citizen* (Gloucester)'
Overseas tours: Welsh Schools to Barbados 1984; Monmouth Schools to Sri Lanka
1985; Combined Universities to Barbados 1989; Glamorgan to Trinidad 1989-90, to
Zimbabwe 1990-91, to Cape Town 1993-94, to Pretoria 1995-96; England A to Kenya
and Sri Lanka 1997-98 (vice-captain)

Overseas teams played for: Bionics, Zimbabwe 1990-92; Universals Sports Club, Zimbabwe 1992-96

Career highlights to date: 'Hitting winning runs to win the Championship in 1997'

Cricket moments to forget: 'Pair in a day, Luton 1992'

Cricketers particularly admired: Michael Atherton, Graham Burgess

Young players to look out for: 'All our youngsters at Glamorgan', Rob White

Other sports played/followed: Rugby union (Cardiff RFC and Lydney RFC; 'played for Lydney, Gloucestershire and Cambridge University and was on bench for Varsity Match'), football (West Ham United)

Injuries: 'Required major knee surgery after just one game [2003]; given 50 per cent chance of playing again'

Favourite band: Deacon Blue

Relaxations: Reading, *Telegraph* crosswords, videos, weight-training

Extras: Scored maiden century (106) in only second first-class innings, v Oxford University at The Parks 1987. In 1995 broke Matthew Maynard's club record for number of one-day runs in a season with 1263; in same season, also broke Hugh Morris's club record for number of Sunday League runs in a season with 815. First player to reach 1000 runs in 1997 and was voted the Cricketer of the Year by both the Wombwell Cricket Lovers' Society and the PCA. Appointed vice-captain of Glamorgan in 1999. Set record for highest post-war score by a Glamorgan batsman, with 259* v Nottinghamshire at Colwyn Bay 1999 (his fifth successive century v Nottinghamshire and still the highest score by a Glamorgan No. 1), beating Matthew Maynard's 243 in 1991. Set record (batting at No. 2) for highest individual score ever by a Glamorgan batsman, with 309* v Sussex at Colwyn Bay in 2000, setting in the process a new record first-wicket partnership for Glamorgan of 374 with Matthew Elliott (177); during his innings he also became the first Glamorgan batsman to record five scores of 200-plus. Captained Wales to victory over an England XI in a one-day warm-up match at Cardiff 2002, top-scoring with 83*. Scored 184 v Nottinghamshire at Colwyn Bay 2002, in the process sharing with Adrian Dale (109) in a record fourth-wicket partnership for Glamorgan in matches against Nottinghamshire (217) and bringing his Championship total at the ground in his three innings since 1999 (did not play there in 2001) to 752 for once out. Captain of Glamorgan 2001-03; relinquished captaincy part-way through 2003 after being ruled out for the remainder of the season with a knee injury

Opinions on cricket: 'Don't the counties realise that by signing all these EU players they are signing their own death warrant? They are saying that there are not enough home-grown players to fill the inflated number of positions available – the only solution being less counties.'

Best batting: 309* Glamorgan v Sussex, Colwyn Bay 2000

Stop press: Retired during the 2003-04 off-season due to knee injury

2003 Season

	M	Inns	NO	Runs	HS	Avge	100s	50s	Ct	St	O	M	Runs	Wkts	Avge	Best	5wl	10wM
Test																		
All First	1	2	0	15	14	7.50	-	-	1	-								
1-day Int																		
C & G																		
NCL																		
Twenty20																		

Career Performances

	M	Inns	NO	Runs	HS	Avge	100s	50s	Ct	St	Balls	Runs	Wkts	Avge	Best	5wl	10wM
Test	2	4	0	71	36	17.75	-	-	-	-							
All First	245	424	33	15891	309 *	40.64	47	58	173	-	2	3	0	-	-	-	-
1-day Int																	
C & G	30	29	3	1144	123	44.00	3	6	9	-							
NCL	152	146	20	4292	107	34.06	2	32	35	-							
Twenty20																	

JAQUES, P. A.   Northamptonshire

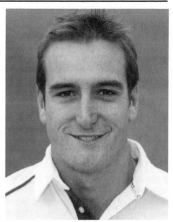

Name: Philip Anthony Jaques
Role: Left-hand bat, left-arm spin bowler
Born: 3 May 1979, Sydney, Australia
Height: 6ft 1in
Nickname: Jakesy, Donk
County debut: 2003
County cap: 2003
1000 runs in a season: 1
1st-Class 50s: 6
1st-Class 100s: 4
1st-Class 200s: 1
1st-Class catches: 11
One-Day 100s: 2
Place in batting averages: 16th av. 58.70
Parents: Mary and Stuart
Marital status: Single
Family links with cricket: 'Dad played
league cricket in South Lancashire League'
Education: Figtree High School; 'currently studying PE at uni'
Qualifications: Fitness trainer
Career outside cricket: Coaching, PE teacher
Off-season: Sydney grade cricket

Overseas teams played for: Sutherland CC, Sydney; New South Wales Blues
Extras: Attended Australian Cricket Academy 2000. Made first-class debut for New South Wales v Queensland at Brisbane 2000-01. Scored maiden first-class century (149*) v Worcestershire at Worcester 2003 on his 24th birthday and maiden first-class double century (222) in his next Championship innings v Yorkshire at Northampton 2003. Scored 1409 first-class runs in his first season of county cricket 2003. Awarded Northamptonshire cap 2003. Holds a British passport
Best batting: 222 Northamptonshire v Yorkshire, Northampton 2003

2003 Season

	M	Inns	NO	Runs	HS	Avge	100s	50s	Ct	St	O	M	Runs	Wkts	Avge	Best	5wI	10wM
Test																		
All First	16	25	1	1409	222	58.70	5	6	9	-	4	0	25	0	-	-	-	-
1-day Int																		
C & G	1	1	0	5	5	5.00	-	-	-	-								
NCL	18	18	1	803	117	47.23	2	6	4	-								
Twenty20	5	5	0	97	33	19.40	-	-	1	-								

Career Performances

	M	Inns	NO	Runs	HS	Avge	100s	50s	Ct	St	Balls	Runs	Wkts	Avge	Best	5wI	10wM
Test																	
All First	18	29	1	1495	222	53.39	5	6	11	-	24	25	0	-	-	-	-
1-day Int																	
C & G	1	1	0	5	5	5.00	-	-	-	-							
NCL	18	18	1	803	117	47.23	2	6	4	-							
Twenty20	5	5	0	97	33	19.40	-	-	1	-							

50. Which England captain and Surrey batsman
took part in the world record fourth-wicket partnership in Tests
(411 v West Indies in 1957) with Colin Cowdrey?

JEFFERSON, W. I. Essex

Name: William (Will) Ingleby Jefferson
Role: Right-hand bat, right-arm medium bowler
Born: 25 October 1979, Derby ('but native of Norfolk')
Height: 6ft 10½in **Weight:** 15st 2lbs
Nickname: Jeffo
County debut: 2000
County cap: 2002
1st-Class 50s: 8
1st-Class 100s: 3
1st-Class catches: 32
One-Day 100s: 3
Place in batting averages: 108th av. 33.95 (2002 124th av. 32.60)
Parents: Richard and Pauline
Marital status: Single
Family links with cricket: Grandfather Jefferson played for the Army and Combined Services in the 1920s. Father, R. I. Jefferson, played for Cambridge University 1961 and Surrey 1961-66
Education: Oundle School, Northants; Durham University
Qualifications: 9 GCSEs, 3 A-levels, BA (Hons) Sport in the Community, Levels 1 and 2 cricket coaching awards
Overseas tours: Oundle School to South Africa 1995
Overseas teams played for: Young People's Club, Paarl, South Africa 1998-99; South Perth, Western Australia 2002-03
Career highlights to date: 'Being awarded county cap on final day of the 2002 season. Scoring 165* to help beat Notts and secure 2002 second division Championship'
Cricket moments to forget: 'Losing to Loughborough in the final of the BUSA Championships in 2000 off the last ball of the match'
Cricketers particularly admired: Mark Waugh, Shaun Pollock, Jacques Kallis, Steve Waugh, Nasser Hussain
Young players to look out for: Jamie Dalrymple, Justin Ontong (South African)
Other sports played: Golf (12 handicap), tennis, swimming
Other sports followed: 'Follow most sports'
Relaxations: 'Spending time with my girlfriend; listening to music; catching up with family and friends'
Extras: Aged 15, received a letter handwritten by Sir Colin Cowdrey congratulating him on scoring 83 and 106* in his two games in the Sun Life of Canada U15 Club Championships. Holmwoods School Cricketer of the Year 1998. Represented British

Universities 2000, 2001 and 2002. Played for Durham University CCE 2001 and 2002. Scored century before lunch on the opening day for Essex v Cambridge UCCE at Fenner's 2003. NBC Denis Compton Award for the most promising young Essex player 2002

Opinions on cricket: 'How can you expect fitness and performance levels to be maintained and players to remain physically and mentally fresh with such a congested fixture list?'

Best batting: 165* Essex v Nottinghamshire, Chelmsford 2002

2003 Season

	M	Inns	NO	Runs	HS	Avge	100s	50s	Ct	St	O	M	Runs	Wkts	Avge	Best	5wI	10wM
Test																		
All First	14	27	4	781	125 *	33.95	1	5	12	-								
1-day Int																		
C & G	2	2	0	132	132	66.00	1	-	2	-								
NCL	14	14	0	472	74	33.71	-	5	8	-								
Twenty20	3	3	0	32	19	10.66	-	-	-	-								

Career Performances

	M	Inns	NO	Runs	HS	Avge	100s	50s	Ct	St	Balls	Runs	Wkts	Avge	Best	5wI	10wM
Test																	
All First	34	64	8	1802	165 *	32.17	3	8	32	-							
1-day Int																	
C & G	2	2	0	132	132	66.00	1	-	2	-							
NCL	31	31	1	1012	111 *	33.73	2	7	17	-							
Twenty20	3	3	0	32	19	10.66	-	-	-	-							

51. Australian born, which Nottinghamshire captain made his debut for England in the two-and-a-half-day Test at Edgbaston in July 1995?

JOHNSON, R. L. Somerset

Name: <u>Richard</u> Leonard Johnson
Role: Right-hand bat, right-arm
fast-medium bowler
Born: 29 December 1974, Chertsey, Surrey
Height: 6ft 2in **Weight:** 14st 3lbs
Nickname: Jono, Lenny, The Greek
County debut: 1992 (Middlesex),
2001 (Somerset)
County cap: 1995 (Middlesex),
2001 (Somerset)
Test debut: 2003
Tests: 1
One-Day Internationals: 7
50 wickets in a season: 4
1st-Class 50s: 6
1st-Class 100s: 1
1st-Class 5 w. in innings: 16
1st-Class 10 w. in match: 3
1st-Class catches: 52
One-Day 5 w. in innings: 1
Place in batting averages: 174th av. 26.16 (2002 212th av. 22.30)
Place in bowling averages: 33rd av. 25.64 (2002 8th av. 21.25)
Strike rate: 52.02 (career 50.06)
Parents: Roger and Mary Anne
Wife and date of marriage: Nicky, 4 October 2003
Family links with cricket: Father and grandfather played club cricket
Education: Sunbury Manor School; Spelthorne College
Qualifications: 9 GCSEs, A-level in Physical Education, NCA senior coaching award
Overseas tours: England U18 to South Africa 1992-93; England U19 to Sri Lanka
1993-94; England A to India 1994-95; MCC to Bangladesh 1999-2000, to Canada
2000-01; England to India 2001-02, to Bangladesh and Sri Lanka 2003-04
Cricket moments to forget: 'Losing C&G final [2002]'
Cricketers particularly admired: Ian Botham, Richard Hadlee and Angus Fraser 'for
his quality bowling and his dedication to moaning'
Young players to look out for: Matthew Wood, Ed Joyce
Other sports followed: Football (Tottenham), rugby (London Irish)
Relaxations: 'Eating out with wife and friends; having a few beers with Nashy'
Extras: Represented Middlesex at all levels from U11. Took 10 for 45 v Derbyshire in
July 1994, becoming the first person to take ten wickets in an English first-class innings
since Ian Thomson (Sussex) in 1964; also most economical ten-wicket haul since Hedley
Verity's 10 for 10 in 1932. Left Middlesex at the end of the 2000 season and joined

Somerset for 2001. Took five wickets in an innings in his first two Championship matches for Somerset – 5-107 v Lancashire and 5-106 v Glamorgan. Scored maiden first-class century (106 from 84 balls) v Gloucestershire at Bristol 2003. Took 6-33 on Test debut in the second Test v Zimbabwe at Riverside 2003, including wickets with his third and fourth balls in Test cricket; it was the fourth best first Test innings analysis by an England bowler and won him the Man of the Match award. Made ODI debut v Zimbabwe at Trent Bridge in the NatWest Series 2003

Opinions on cricket: 'Overseas players are vital to keep the standard of domestic cricket high, but the situation with EU-qualified players has to be looked at.'

Best batting: 118 Somerset v Gloucestershire, Bristol 2003

Best bowling: 10-45 Middlesex v Derbyshire, Derby 1994

Stop press: Originally selected for one-day portions of the England tours to Bangladesh and Sri Lanka 2003-04 but was called up to replace the injured James Anderson for the Bangladesh first-class portion and was retained for the Sri Lanka Test series as a replacement for the injured Steve Harmison. Had match figures of 9-93 (5-49/4-44) in the second Test v Bangladesh at Chittagong 2003-04, winning second Man of the Match award in his second Test

2003 Season

	M	Inns	NO	Runs	HS	Avge	100s	50s	Ct	St	O	M	Runs	Wkts	Avge	Best	5wI	10wM
Test	1	1	0	24	24	24.00	-	-	-	-	34	11	100	6	16.66	6-33	1	-
All First	11	15	3	314	118	26.16	1	-	5	-	364.1	85	1077	42	25.64	6-33	2	-
1-day Int	7	3	1	10	10	5.00	-	-	-	-	46	4	177	8	22.12	3-32	-	
C & G	2	1	0	3	3	3.00	-	-	-	-	20	2	87	2	43.50	2-58	-	
NCL	6	5	1	113	53	28.25	-	1	1	-	48	2	266	7	38.00	3-41	-	
Twenty20																		

Career Performances

	M	Inns	NO	Runs	HS	Avge	100s	50s	Ct	St	Balls	Runs	Wkts	Avge	Best	5wI	10wM
Test	1	1	0	24	24	24.00	-	-	-	-	204	100	6	16.66	6-33	1	-
All First	126	179	25	2736	118	17.76	1	6	52	-	21328	11258	426	26.42	10-45	16	3
1-day Int	7	3	1	10	10	5.00	-	-	-	-	276	177	8	22.12	3-32	-	
C & G	26	15	3	181	45 *	15.08	-	-	4	-	1380	1014	38	26.68	5-50	1	
NCL	96	66	17	642	53	13.10	-	1	10	-	3992	3403	104	32.72	4-45	-	
Twenty20																	

JONES, G. O.   Kent

Name: <u>Geraint</u> Owen Jones
Role: Right-hand bat, wicket-keeper
Born: 14 July 1976, Kundiawa,
Papua New Guinea
Height: 5ft 10in **Weight:** 11st
Nickname: Jonesy
County debut: 2001
County cap: 2003
50 dismissals in a season: 1
1st-Class 50s: 8
1st-Class 100s: 2
1st-Class catches: 60
1st-Class stumpings: 5
Place in batting averages: 54th av. 44.77
Parents: Emrys, Carol (deceased),
Maureen (stepmother)
Marital status: Single
Family links with cricket: 'Father was
star off-spinner in local school side'
Education: Harristown State High School, Toowoomba, Queensland;
MacGregor SHS, Brisbane
Qualifications: Level 1 coach
Off-season: 'In as much air con as poss'
Overseas tours: Beenleigh-Logan U19 to New Zealand 1995; Kent to Port Elizabeth
2001-02; England to Bangladesh and Sri Lanka 2003-04, to West Indies 2003-04
Overseas teams played for: Beenleigh-Logan, Brisbane 1995-98; Valleys, Brisbane
2001-02
Career highlights to date: 'Maiden first-class hundred against Leicestershire 2003'
Cricket moments to forget: 'Third-ball nought in last innings this year [2003] against
Warwickshire'
Cricket superstitions: 'Left pad first'
Cricketers particularly admired: Jack Russell, Alec Stewart
Young players to look out for: James Tredwell, Rob Ferley
Other sports played: Golf
Other sports followed: Rugby (Crickhowell RFC)
Favourite band: Matchbox Twenty
Extras: Scored a 39-ball 39 on Norwich Union League debut v Surrey at The Oval
2001, having arrived at the crease with his side on 59 for 5. Scored maiden first-class
50 (76*) v Sri Lankans at Canterbury 2002 in only his second first-class match. Scored
maiden first-class century (104) v Leicestershire at Canterbury 2003, reaching his
hundred with a six. Set new record for a season's tally of wicket-keeping dismissals in

NCL (33; 27/6) 2003; also equalled record for number of wicket-keeping catches in one match, six v Leicestershire at Canterbury 2003. Made 59 first-class dismissals plus 985 first-class runs in his first full season of county cricket 2003. Awarded Kent cap 2003

Opinions on cricket: 'Great game; love playing it. Definitely play too much; needs to be looked at and evaluated.'

Best batting: 108* Kent v Essex, Chelmsford 2003

2003 Season

	M	Inns	NO	Runs	HS	Avge	100s	50s	Ct	St	O	M	Runs	Wkts	Avge	Best	5wI	10wM
Test																		
All First	18	27	5	985	108 *	44.77	2	7	54	5								
1-day Int																		
C & G	2	2	1	64	34	64.00	-	-	1	1								
NCL	16	13	1	300	74 *	25.00	-	2	27	6								
Twenty20	5	4	1	41	20 *	13.66	-	-	5	-								

Career Performances

	M	Inns	NO	Runs	HS	Avge	100s	50s	Ct	St	Balls	Runs	Wkts	Avge	Best	5wI	10wM
Test																	
All First	23	32	6	1152	108 *	44.30	2	8	60	5	6	4	0	-	-	-	-
1-day Int																	
C & G	3	2	1	64	34	64.00	-	-	2	1							
NCL	27	24	3	455	74 *	21.66	-	2	28	6							
Twenty20	5	4	1	41	20 *	13.66	-	-	5	-							

52. Who achieved the best innings return v West Indies by an England bowler at Trinidad in 1998? This recently retired seamer took 8-53.

JONES, H. R.   Warwickshire

Name: <u>Huw</u> Rhys Jones
Role: Right-hand bat, leg-spin bowler
Born: 23 November 1980, Oxford
Height: 6ft **Weight:** 13st 3lbs
Nickname: Jonah, Bones
County debut: 2002 (one-day)
1st-Class 50s: 2
1st-Class catches: 6
Place in batting averages: (2002 218th
av. 21.66)
Parents: John and Elizabeth
Marital status: Single
Family links with cricket: 'Dad played club
cricket for Leamington'
Education: Trinity School; Warwick Sixth
Form; Oxford Brookes University
Qualifications: 8 GCSEs, 3 A-levels
Overseas tours: Warwickshire U19 to Cape
Town 1998

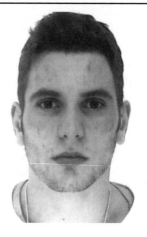

Overseas teams played for: Karori CC, Wellington, New Zealand; Hams Tech CC,
Border, South Africa
Career highlights to date: 'Scoring 97 against Worcestershire in first-class game for
OUCCE. Making my debut for Warwickshire 1st XI against Glamorgan'
Cricket moments to forget: 'Being lbw on 97 against Worcestershire and missing
chance to get maiden first-class hundred'
Cricketers particularly admired: Michael Vaughan, Matthew Hayden,
Sachin Tendulkar
Young players to look out for: Graham Charlesworth, Stewart Reeve, Patrick Wolf
Other sports played: Basketball, football, golf, snooker
Other sports followed: Football (Arsenal FC)
Relaxations: 'Going out with mates; spending time with girlfriend'
Extras: Played in U15 World Cup 1996. Played for Oxford University CCE 2001,
2002 and 2003; scored 97 v Worcestershire at The Parks 2002 and 114 v
Loughborough in the UCCE final at Lord's 2002. Represented British Universities
2002. Played for Warwickshire Board XI in the C&G 2002, winning Man of the Match
award for his 72 v Leicestershire at Coventry. Played for the Warwickshire Board XI
side that won the final ECB 38-County competition 2002
Opinions on cricket: 'More floodlit cricket – it attracts crowds. Tighten up
qualifications on British-qualified players.'
Best batting: 97 OUCCE v Worcestershire, The Parks 2002

Career Performances

	M	Inns	NO	Runs	HS	Avge	100s	50s	Ct	St	Balls	Runs	Wkts	Avge	Best	5wl	10wM
Test																	
All First	8	14	1	304	97	23.38	-	2	6	-							
1-day Int																	
C & G	2	2	0	82	72	41.00	-	1	-	-							
NCL	1	1	0	6	6	6.00	-	-	-	-							
Twenty20																	

JONES, P. S.   Northamptonshire

Name: Philip Steffan Jones
Role: Right-hand bat, right-arm
fast-medium bowler
Born: 9 February 1974, Llanelli
Height: 6ft 1in   **Weight:** 15st
Nickname: Jona
County debut: 1997 (Somerset)
50 wickets in a season: 1
1st-Class 50s: 3
1st-Class 100s: 1
1st-Class 5 w. in innings: 5
1st-Class 10 w. in match: 1
1st-Class catches: 16
One-Day 5 w. in innings: 1
Place in batting averages: 161st av. 27.30
Place in bowling averages: 124th av. 42.27
(2002 137th av. 44.47)
Strike rate: 55.77 (career 62.09)
Parents: Lyndon and Ann
Wife and date of marriage: Alex, 12 October 2002
Family links with cricket: Father played at a high standard and played first-class
rugby
Education: Ysgol Gyfun y Strade, Llanelli; Loughborough University; Homerton
College, Cambridge University
Qualifications: BSc Sports Science, PGCE in Physical Education
Career outside cricket: Personal fitness trainer
Off-season: 'Training very hard again!'
Overseas tours: Wales Minor Counties to Barbados 1996; Somerset CCC to South
Africa 1999, 2000

Career highlights to date: 'Winning C&G Trophy with Somerset CCC'
Cricket moments to forget: 'Whole of last season – especially not being selected for the first NCL game when my record is far better than those selected in the competition'
Cricket superstitions: 'Always give 110 per cent effort'
Young players to look out for: Aaron Laraman
Other sports played: Rugby union (Wales Schools, U18, Youth; Swansea, Bristol, Exeter and Moseley)
Other sports followed: Baseball, rugby union, athletics
Favourite band: Will Young
Relaxations: 'Spending time with my wife and close friends; going back to Wales to see my family'
Extras: Represented Wales Minor Counties. Played first-class cricket and first-class rugby for two years. Took nine wickets (6-67 and 3-81) in the Varsity Match at Lord's 1997. Took 59 first-class wickets in 2001, 'Somerset's most successful season'. Left Somerset at the end of the 2003 season and has joined Northamptonshire for 2004
Opinions on cricket: 'There should be a minimum fitness level for county players to reach before playing for England. Too many unathletic, overweight, unco-ordinated players represent England in a sport where I dedicate 100 per cent of my time, effort and money. One-off performances are not good enough. To be consistent you have to be fit and athletic and dedicated.'
Best batting: 105 Somerset v New Zealanders, Taunton 1999
Best bowling: 6-67 Cambridge University v Oxford University, Lord's 1997

2003 Season

	M	Inns	NO	Runs	HS	Avge	100s	50s	Ct	St	O	M	Runs	Wkts	Avge	Best	5wl	10wM
Test																		
All First	8	12	2	273	63	27.30	-	2	2	-	204.3	27	930	22	42.27	5-42	1	-
1-day Int																		
C & G	1	1	1	8	8 *	-	-	-	-	-	10	1	80	1	80.00	1-80	-	
NCL	14	11	5	110	19 *	18.33	-	-	4	-	106.1	2	658	14	47.00	3-27	-	
Twenty20	5	4	2	26	24 *	13.00	-	-	-	-	16	0	159	5	31.80	2-24	-	

Career Performances

	M	Inns	NO	Runs	HS	Avge	100s	50s	Ct	St	Balls	Runs	Wkts	Avge	Best	5wl	10wM
Test																	
All First	69	84	23	1105	105	18.11	1	3	16	-	11673	6913	188	36.77	6-67	5	1
1-day Int																	
C & G	19	5	4	55	26 *	55.00	-	-	2	-	962	846	25	33.84	4-25	-	
NCL	85	50	26	276	27	11.50	-	-	17	-	3761	3397	130	26.13	5-23	1	
Twenty20	5	4	2	26	24 *	13.00	-	-	-	-	96	159	5	31.80	2-24	-	

JONES, S. P. Glamorgan

Name: <u>Simon</u> Philip Jones
Role: Left-hand bat, right-arm fast bowler
Born: 25 December 1978, Morriston, Swansea
Height: 6ft 3in **Weight:** 14st 7lbs
Nickname: Racehorse, Horse
County debut: 1998
County cap: 2002
Test debut: 2002
Tests: 2
1st-Class 5 w. in innings: 4
1st-Class catches: 8
Place in batting averages: (2002 239th av. 18.16)
Place in bowling averages: (2002 44th av. 27.52)
Strike rate: (career 58.58)
Parents: Irene and Jeff
Marital status: Single

Family links with cricket: 'Dad played for Glamorgan and England (15 Tests)'
Education: Coedcae Comprehensive School; Millfield School
Qualifications: 12 GCSEs, 1 A-level, basic and senior coaching awards
Career outside cricket: Fitness instructor
Off-season: 'England academy (boot camp)'
Overseas tours: Dyfed Schools to Zimbabwe 1994; Glamorgan to South Africa 1998; ECB National Academy to Australia 2001-02; England to Australia 2002-03; ECB National Academy (England A) to Malaysia and India 2003-04
Career highlights to date: 'Test debut v India at Lord's 2002. Selection for Ashes tour'
Cricket moments to forget: 'Injuring my right knee in Australia'
Cricketers particularly admired: Allan Donald, 'my dad', Michael Holding
Young players to look out for: Ian Bell, Nicky Peng, 'Erj Mustafa'
Injuries: Out for ten months with cruciate ligament damage to right knee
Relaxations: 'Eating out with friends, drinking, cinemas'
Extras: Struck a 14-ball 46 (including six sixes and two fours) v Yorkshire at Scarborough 2001. NBC Denis Compton Award for the most promising young Glamorgan player 2001. Made Test debut in the first Test v India at Lord's 2002, striking a 43-ball 44 (more runs than his father scored in his Test career); the Joneses are the eleventh father and son to have played in Tests for England. Took 5-78 for England XI v Western Australia at Perth 2002-03. Forced to return home early from England tour of Australia 2002-03 after rupturing the anterior cruciate ligament of his right knee while fielding during the first Test at Brisbane

Opinions on cricket: 'Too many games. More rest in between games.'
Best batting: 46 Glamorgan v Yorkshire, Scarborough 2001
Best bowling: 6-45 Glamorgan v Derbyshire, Cardiff 2002
Stop press: Had match figures of 10-88 (5-57/5-31) for England A v Tamil Nadu at Chennai 2003-04. Selected for England tour to West Indies 2003-04

2003 Season (did not make any first-class or one-day appearances)

Career Performances

	M	Inns	NO	Runs	HS	Avge	100s	50s	Ct	St	Balls	Runs	Wkts	Avge	Best	5wI	10wM
Test	2	1	0	44	44	44.00	-	-	-	-	270	161	5	32.20	2-61	-	-
All First	42	49	13	397	46	11.02	-	-	8	-	5917	3738	101	37.00	6-45	4	-
1-day Int																	
C & G	1	0	0	0	0	-	-	-	-	-	30	30	0	-	-	-	-
NCL	1	1	1	12	12*	-	-	-	-	-	42	39	1	39.00	1-39	-	-
Twenty20																	

JOYCE, E. C.   Middlesex

Name: Edmund (Ed) Christopher Joyce
Role: Left-hand middle-order bat, occasional right-arm medium bowler
Born: 22 September 1978, Dublin
Height: 5ft 10in **Weight:** 12st 3lbs
Nickname: Joycey, Spud
County debut: 1999
County cap: 2002
1000 runs in a season: 2
1st-Class 50s: 11
1st-Class 100s: 9
1st-Class catches: 37
Place in batting averages: 79th av. 39.34 (2002 29th av. 52.79)
Strike rate: 168.00 (career 186.00)
Parents: Maureen and Jim
Marital status: Single
Family links with cricket: 'Two of my four brothers have played for Ireland and two of my four sisters (twins) have played for Ireland's ladies'
Education: Presentation College, Bray, County Wicklow; Trinity College, Dublin
Qualifications: Irish Leaving Certificate, BA (Hons) Economics and Geography
Off-season: 'Buying a house; doing coaching courses; visiting home'

Overseas tours: Ireland U19 to Bermuda (International Youth Tournament) 1997, to South Africa (U19 World Cup) 1997-98; Ireland to Canada (ICC Trophy) 2001
Overseas teams played for: Coburg CC, Melbourne 1996-97; University CC, Perth 2001-02
Career highlights to date: 'Making hundred at Lord's in 2001'
Cricket moments to forget: 'All the dropped catches at the start of last season'
Cricket superstitions: 'None'
Cricketers particularly admired: Larry Gomes, Brian Lara
Young players to look out for: Eoin Morgan, Nick Compton
Other sports played: Golf, rugby, soccer, snooker
Other sports followed: Rugby (Leinster), football (Manchester United)
Favourite band: The Mars Volta
Relaxations: Cinema, eating out, listening to music
Extras: Leinster U19 to Oxford Festival. Was only player to score a century (105 v Denmark Colts) at the International Youth Tournament, Bermuda 1997. Represented Ireland senior side from 1997, including appearances in the Triple Crown tournament and the NatWest. NBC Denis Compton Award for the most promising young Middlesex player 2000. Scored maiden first-class century (104) v Warwickshire at Lord's 2001, becoming the first Irish-born-and-bred player to record a 100 in the County Championship. C&G Man of the Match award for his 72 v Northamptonshire at Northampton 2003. Is not considered an overseas player
Opinions on cricket: 'Twenty20 cricket is great and will be around for a while. Still too much National League cricket.'
Best batting: 129 Middlesex v Derbyshire, Lord's 2002
Best bowling: 1-20 Middlesex v CUCCE, Fenner's 2002

2003 Season

	M	Inns	NO	Runs	HS	Avge	100s	50s	Ct	St	O	M	Runs	Wkts	Avge	Best	5wI	10wM
Test																		
All First	18	30	4	1023	117	39.34	3	4	7	-	56	7	219	2	109.50	1-23	-	-
1-day Int																		
C & G	3	3	0	84	72	28.00	-	1	-	-								
NCL	18	17	3	561	77	40.07	-	5	10	-	9	0	62	2	31.00	2-10	-	
Twenty20	4	4	1	53	31	17.66	-	-	1	-	1	0	12	0	-		-	-

Career Performances

	M	Inns	NO	Runs	HS	Avge	100s	50s	Ct	St	Balls	Runs	Wkts	Avge	Best	5wI	10wM
Test																	
All First	48	76	9	2810	129	41.94	9	11	37	-	558	395	3	131.66	1-20	-	-
1-day Int																	
C & G	9	9	2	290	73	41.42	-	2	1	-							
NCL	44	41	6	978	77	27.94	-	6	19	-	54	62	2	31.00	2-10	-	
Twenty20	4	4	1	53	31	17.66	-	-	1	-	6	12	0	-		-	-

KAIF, M. — Derbyshire

Name: Mohammad Kaif
Role: Right-hand bat, right-arm
off-spin bowler
Born: 1 December 1980, Allahabad, India
County debut: 2002 (Leicestershire),
2003 (Derbyshire)
Test debut: 1999-2000
Tests: 4
One-Day Internationals: 54
1st-Class 50s: 17
1st-Class 100s: 5
1st-Class catches: 30
One-Day 100s: 1
Place in batting averages: 209th av. 22.13
Strike rate: 24.00 (career 68.58)
Family links with cricket: Father,
Mohammad Tarif, played first-class cricket in
India; brother Mohammad Saif plays first-
class cricket in India for Uttar Pradesh

Overseas tours: India U15 to England (U15 World Cup) 1996; India U19 to South
Africa (U19 World Cup) 1997-98, to Sri Lanka (U19 World Cup) 1999-2000 (captain);
India A to Los Angeles (Moov America Challenge) 1999, to West Indies 1999-2000, to
South Africa 2001-02; India to Sri Lanka 2001, to West Indies 2001-02 (one-day
series), to England 2002, to Sri Lanka (ICC Champions Trophy) 2002-03, to New
Zealand 2002-03, to Africa (World Cup) 2002-03, to Bangladesh (TVS Cup) 2003
Overseas teams played for: Uttar Pradesh 1997-98 –
Extras: A member of the India U15 side that won the U15 World Cup (Lombard
Challenge) 1996. Represented India U19 v Sri Lanka U19 1998-99. Captained India
U19 to victory in the U19 World Cup in Sri Lanka 1999-2000. Player of the
Tournament in the 1999-2000 Challenger Trophy (India v India A v India B). Attended
Indian National Cricket Academy. Scored 75-ball 87* in India's victory in the NatWest
Series final v England at Lord's 2002, sharing in a stand of 121 from 106 balls with
Yuvraj Singh and winning the Man of the Match award. Was Leicestershire's overseas
player during August 2002, replacing Michael Bevan, absent on international duty.
Scored 111* v Zimbabwe at Colombo in the ICC Champions Trophy 2002-03, setting
a new world record for the highest score by a No. 7 in ODIs. Joined Derbyshire as an
overseas player for 2003; left Derbyshire at the end of the 2003 season. C&G Man of
the Match award in his second match for Derbyshire for his 81 v Surrey in the quarter-
final at Derby 2003
Best batting: 136 India A v South Africa A, Kimberley 2001-02
Best bowling: 3-4 Uttar Pradesh v Vidarbha, Kanpur 2001-02

2003 Season

	M	Inns	NO	Runs	HS	Avge	100s	50s	Ct	St	O	M	Runs	Wkts	Avge	Best	5wl	10wM
Test																		
All First	8	15	0	332	87	22.13	-	1	5	-	4	1	21	1	21.00	1-21	-	-
1-day Int																		
C & G	2	2	0	153	81	76.50	-	2	1	-								
NCL	8	8	1	225	70	32.14	-	2	4	-								
Twenty20	5	5	1	75	53	18.75	-	1	2	-								

Career Performances

	M	Inns	NO	Runs	HS	Avge	100s	50s	Ct	St	Balls	Runs	Wkts	Avge	Best	5wl	10wM
Test	4	8	1	141	37	20.14	-	-	1	-	18	4	0	-	-	-	-
All First	53	85	9	2931	136	38.56	5	17	30	-	1166	524	17	30.82	3-4	-	-
1-day Int	54	44	9	1072	111 *	30.62	1	5	25	-							
C & G	2	2	0	153	81	76.50	-	2	1	-							
NCL	9	9	2	285	70	40.71	-	3	5	-							
Twenty20	5	5	1	75	53	18.75	-	1	2	-							

KASPROWICZ, M. S.   Glamorgan

Name: <u>Michael</u> Scott Kasprowicz
Role: Right-hand bat, right-arm fast bowler
Born: 10 February 1972, Brisbane, Australia
Height: 6ft 4in   **Weight:** 15st 5lbs
Nickname: Kasper
County debut: 1994 (Essex), 1999 (Leicestershire), 2002 (Glamorgan)
County cap: 1994 (Essex), 1999 (Leicestershire), 2002 (Glamorgan)
Test debut: 1996-97
Tests: 17
One-Day Internationals: 16
50 wickets in a season: 4
1st-Class 50s: 11
1st-Class 5 w. in innings: 44
1st-Class 10 w. in match: 6
1st-Class catches: 74
One-Day 5 w. in innings: 1
Place in batting averages: 182nd av. 25.27 (2002 144th av. 29.33)
Place in bowling averages: 6th av. 21.15 (2002 37th av. 26.66)
Strike rate: 44.61 (career 50.67)
Parents: Wally and Joan

Wife and date of marriage: Lindsay, 5 December 2002
Family links with cricket/rugby: 'Brother Adam represented Queensland U17 and U19. Brother Simon plays for NSW Waratahs in Super 12 rugby competition'
Education: Brisbane State High School
Qualifications: Level 2 cricket coaching
Off-season: 'Playing for Queensland Bulls'
Overseas tours: Australia YC to England 1991; Young Australia (Australia A) to England and Netherlands 1995; Australia to England 1997, to India 1997-98, to Sharjah (Coca-Cola Cup) 1997-98, to Malaysia (Commonwealth Games) 1998-99, to Pakistan 1998-99, to Bangladesh (Wills International Cup) 1998-99, to New Zealand 1999-2000, to India 2000-01, to India (TVS Cup) 2003-04
Overseas teams played for: Queensland 1989-90 –
Career highlights to date: 'Representing Australia and receiving baggy green cap. Glamorgan 2002 NUL title win'
Cricketers particularly admired: Dennis Lillee, Steve Waugh
Young players to look out for: Mark Wallace, David Harrison
Other sports played: Rugby (Australian Schoolboys 1989, including tour of New Zealand)
Other sports followed: Rugby league (Brisbane Broncos), Australian Rules football (Brisbane Lions)
Relaxations: 'Fishing, beach, music'
Extras: Played for Queensland U17 and U19 and made his Queensland debut aged 17. Played for Australia U17. Took nine wickets in the first 'Test' at Leicester on Australia YC tour to England 1991. Attended Australian Cricket Academy 1991. Was Essex's overseas player in 1994. Took 7-36 in the second innings of the sixth Test v England at The Oval 1997. Took 5-28 from 18 overs in the second innings of the third Test v India at Bangalore 1997-98. Was Leicestershire's overseas player in 1999. Was leading wicket-taker in the Pura Cup 2001-02 with 49 wickets at 22.08, including match figures of 9-163 in the final v Tasmania at Brisbane. Joined Glamorgan as overseas player for 2002. Took wickets (Robinson, Middlebrook) with the first two balls of Essex's second innings at Swansea 2002. Took his 400th first-class wicket for Queensland during the 2002-03 season. His 9-36 in Durham's second innings at Cardiff 2003 included a spell of 9-22 from 64 balls; took 9-45 in Durham's second innings in the return match at Riverside 2003. Glamorgan Player of the Year 2003 (jointly with Robert Croft)
Opinions on cricket: 'By giving the "benefit of the doubt" to the bowler we will have a fun, quick game. Instead of the ball just missing leg stump, it will just hit it.'
Best batting: 92 Australians v India A, Nagpur 2000-01
Best bowling: 9-36 Glamorgan v Durham, Cardiff 2003
Stop press: Selected for Australia's tour to Sri Lanka 2003-04

2003 Season

	M	Inns	NO	Runs	HS	Avge	100s	50s	Ct	St	O	M	Runs	Wkts	Avge	Best	5wI	10wM
Test																		
All First	15	26	4	556	78	25.27	-	2	7	-	572.3	140	1629	77	21.15	9-36	4	2
1-day Int																		
C & G	2	2	0	37	19	18.50	-	-	1	-	20	2	103	4	25.75	3-43	-	
NCL	16	11	5	146	35 *	24.33	-	-	4	-	125.5	14	584	20	29.20	3-20	-	
Twenty20	5	5	1	63	31	15.75	-	-	1	-	18	1	129	4	32.25	2-25	-	

Career Performances

	M	Inns	NO	Runs	HS	Avge	100s	50s	Ct	St	Balls	Runs	Wkts	Avge	Best	5wI	10wM
Test	17	23	5	234	25	13.00	-	-	6	-	3338	1739	47	37.00	7-36	2	-
All First	192	258	54	3739	92	18.32	-	11	74	-	39479	20259	779	26.00	9-36	44	6
1-day Int	16	8	6	60	28 *	30.00	-	-	3	-	817	709	22	32.22	3-50	-	
C & G	6	5	0	90	25	18.00	-	-	1	-	365	271	14	19.35	5-60	1	
NCL	55	39	10	398	38	13.72	-	-	10	-	2460	1836	65	28.24	4-28	-	
Twenty20	5	5	1	63	31	15.75	-	-	1	-	108	129	4	32.25	2-25	-	

KATICH, S. M.   Hampshire

Name: Simon Mathew Katich
Role: Left-hand bat, left-arm
wrist-spin bowler
Born: 21 August 1975, Midland,
Western Australia
Height: 6ft **Weight:** 12st 8lbs
Nickname: Kat
County debut: 2000 (Durham),
2002 (Yorkshire), 2003 (Hampshire)
County cap: 2000 (Durham),
2003 (Hampshire)
Test debut: 2001
Tests: 1
One-Day Internationals: 1
1000 runs in a season: 2
1st-Class 50s: 36
1st-Class 100s: 20
1st-Class 200s: 1
1st-Class 5 w. in innings: 2
1st-Class catches: 104
One-Day 100s: 2
Place in batting averages: 11th av. 60.15

Place in bowling averages: 86th av. 34.76
Strike rate: 56.70 (career 63.98)
Parents: Vince and Kerry
Marital status: Single
Education: Trinity College, Perth; University of Western Australia
Qualifications: Bachelor of Commerce degree
Off-season: Playing in Australia
Overseas tours: Australian Cricket Academy to South Africa 1996; Australia to Sri Lanka and Zimbabwe 1999-2000, to England 2001; Australia A to South Africa (one-day series) 2002-03 (vice-captain)
Overseas teams played for: Western Australia 1996-97 – 2001-02; New South Wales 2002-03 –
Career highlights to date: 'Test debut at Leeds'
Cricket moments to forget: 'None'
Cricket superstitions: 'Like to wear old gear'
Cricketers particularly admired: Viv Richards, David Gower
Young players to look out for: Michael Clarke
Other sports played: Australian Rules, hockey, golf
Other sports followed: Australian Rules (Richmond), football (Newcastle United)
Relaxations: 'Movies, beach'
Extras: Attended Commonwealth Bank [Australian] Cricket Academy 1996. Scored century (106) for Western Australia v England XI at Perth 1998-99. Captained ACB Chairman's XI v England XI 1998-99. Scored 115 in Western Australia's first innings in their 1998-99 Sheffield Shield final victory. *Wisden Australia*'s Sheffield Shield Cricketer of the Year 1998-99. Was Durham's overseas player in 2000. Took over as captain of Western Australia during 2000-01 season after retirement of Tom Moody. Finished the 2000-01 season with a Western Australian record 1145 Pura Cup runs (av. 71.56), having become the first WA batsman to score a century against each of the other states (two v Queensland, home and away) in a single season. Was Yorkshire's overseas player during June 2002, replacing Darren Lehmann, absent on international duty. Joined New South Wales for 2002-03. Man of the Match in the Pura Cup final v Queensland at Brisbane 2002-03. Joined Hampshire as an overseas player for 2003; awarded Hampshire cap 2003; has not returned for 2004. Scored 117 and 79* and had first innings figures of 4-21 v Northamptonshire at West End 2003. Hampshire Cricket Society Player of the Year 2003
Opinions on cricket: 'The game needs less of the third umpire!'
Best batting: 228* Western Australia v South Australia, Perth 2000-01
Best bowling: 7-130 New South Wales v Victoria, Melbourne 2002-03
Stop press: Recorded maiden Test five-wicket return (6-65) in the second Test v Zimbabwe at Sydney 2003-04. Scored maiden Test century (125) in the fourth Test v India at Sydney 2003-04, following up with 77* in the second innings. Selected for Australia's tour to Sri Lanka 2003-04. Named State Player of the Year at the 2004 Allan Border Medal awards

2003 Season

	M	Inns	NO	Runs	HS	Avge	100s	50s	Ct	St	O	M	Runs	Wkts	Avge	Best	5wI	10wM
Test																		
All First	13	22	3	1143	143 *	60.15	4	6	15	-	160.4	29	591	17	34.76	4-21	-	-
1-day Int																		
C & G	1	1	1	82	82 *	-	-	1	1	-								
NCL	18	18	1	728	106	42.82	2	6	13	-	31.2	1	184	6	30.66	2-25	-	
Twenty20	5	5	2	179	59 *	59.66	-	2	1	-								

Career Performances

	M	Inns	NO	Runs	HS	Avge	100s	50s	Ct	St	Balls	Runs	Wkts	Avge	Best	5wI	10wM
Test	1	2	1	15	15	15.00	-	-	1	-							
All First	100	175	26	7304	228 *	49.02	21	36	104	-	3583	2098	56	37.46	7-130	2	-
1-day Int	1	0	0	0	-	-	-	-	-	-							
C & G	4	4	2	166	82 *	83.00	-	1	2	-							
NCL	36	36	5	1365	106	44.03	2	12	23	-	290	278	8	34.75	2-25	-	
Twenty20	5	5	2	179	59 *	59.66	-	2	1	-							

KEEDY, G.   Lancashire

Name: Gary Keedy
Role: Left-hand bat, slow left-arm bowler
Born: 27 November 1974, Wakefield
Height: 5ft 11in **Weight:** 12st 6lbs
Nickname: Keeds
County debut: 1994 (Yorkshire),
1995 (Lancashire)
County cap: 2000 (Lancashire)
50 wickets in a season: 1
1st-Class 50s: 1
1st-Class 5 w. in innings: 12
1st-Class 10 w. in match: 3
1st-Class catches: 29
One-Day 5 w. in innings: 1
Place in batting averages: (2002 262nd
av. 15.64)
Place in bowling averages: 38th av. 26.55
(2002 122nd av. 39.78)
Strike rate: 55.58 (career 74.38)
Parents: Roy and Pat
Wife and date of marriage: Andrea, 12 October 2002
Family links with cricket: Twin brother plays for Castleford in the Yorkshire League

Education: Garforth Comprehensive
Qualifications: 8 GCSEs, Level 2 coaching award
Off-season: 12-month contract
Overseas tours: England U18 to South Africa 1992-93, to Denmark 1993; England U19 to Sri Lanka 1993-94; Lancashire to Portugal 1995, to Jamaica 1996, to South Africa 1997
Overseas teams played for: Frankston, Melbourne 1995-96
Career highlights to date: 'Probably bowling Yorkshire out at Headingley. My involvement with Lancashire in general; receiving my county cap was a proud moment'
Cricketers particularly admired: Shane Warne, Graham Gooch
Young players to look out for: Kyle Hogg, James Anderson
Other sports played: Football, snooker
Other sports followed: Football (Leeds United), rugby league (Leeds Rhinos)
Injuries: Out for two weeks with a broken hand; for six weeks with appendicitis
Relaxations: PlayStation
Extras: Player of the Series for England U19 v West Indies U19 in 1993. Graduate of the Yorkshire Cricket Academy. Played for England U19 in the home series against India U19 in 1994. His match return of 10-155 v Durham at Old Trafford 2000 included second innings figures of 6-56 from 50 overs. Scored 25* v Sussex at Old Trafford 2002, in the process sharing with Stuart Law (218) in a tenth-wicket stand of 145 that avoided the follow-on. Took 50 first-class wickets in a season for the first time 2003
Opinions on cricket: 'Too many Italian-looking, Greek-speaking Dutchmen who were educated in South Africa and live in Australia who have played for New Zealand but aren't considered to be overseas players in the English domestic game!'
Best batting: 57 Lancashire v Yorkshire, Headingley 2002
Best bowling: 6-56 Lancashire v Durham, Old Trafford 2000

2003 Season

	M	Inns	NO	Runs	HS	Avge	100s	50s	Ct	St	O	M	Runs	Wkts	Avge	Best	5wI	10wM
Test																		
All First	13	10	6	16	6	4.00	-	-	4	-	555.5	126	1593	60	26.55	6-68	5	1
1-day Int																		
C & G																			
NCL	1	0	0	0	0	-	-	-	-	-	9	0	57	1	57.00	1-57	-	
Twenty20																			

Career Performances

	M	Inns	NO	Runs	HS	Avge	100s	50s	Ct	St	Balls	Runs	Wkts	Avge	Best	5wl	10wM
Test																	
All First	107	121	63	679	57	11.70	-	1	29	-	21646	10038	291	34.49	6-56	12	3
1-day Int																	
C & G	1	0	0	0	0	-	-	-	-	-	60	40	1	40.00	1-40	-	
NCL	15	4	2	13	10 *	6.50	-	-	1	-	538	496	15	33.06	5-30	1	
Twenty20																	

KEEGAN, C. B.   Middlesex

Name: <u>Chad</u> Blake Keegan
Role: Right-hand bat, right-arm
fast-medium bowler
Born: 30 July 1979, Sandton, Johannesburg,
South Africa
Height: 6ft 1in **Weight:** 12st
Nickname: Wick
County debut: 2001
County cap: 2003
50 wickets in a season: 1
1st-Class 5 w. in innings: 3
1st-Class catches: 9
One-Day 5 w. in innings: 2
Place in batting averages: 246th av. 15.88
(2002 313th av. 5.80)
Place in bowling averages: 63rd av. 30.55
(2002 138th av. 45.00)

Strike rate: 55.77 (career 58.05)
Parents: Sharon and Blake
Marital status: Single
Education: Durban High School
Qualifications: YMCA fitness instructor
Off-season: 'Searching for the perfect wave'
Overseas tours: MCC to Argentina and Chile 2001
Overseas teams played for: Durban High School Old Boys 1994-97; Crusaders,
Durban 1998-99
Career highlights to date: 'Being awarded Player of the Year for Middlesex 2003'
Cricket moments to forget: 'Losing my pants diving for a ball at Lord's'
Cricket superstitions: 'Tapping the bat either side of the crease three times'
Cricketers particularly admired: Malcolm Marshall, Neil Johnson
Other sports played: 'Any extreme sports, golf'

Other sports followed: Football (Liverpool)
Injuries: Out for one game with sore feet
Favourite band: Jack Johnson
Relaxations: 'Making and listening to music (guitar); sketching'
Extras: Represented KwaZulu-Natal U13, KwaZulu-Natal Schools, KwaZulu-Natal U19, KwaZulu-Natal Academy. MCC Young Cricketer. Recorded maiden first-class five-wicket return (5-61) v Leicestershire at Leicester 2003. Took 50 first-class wickets in a season for the first time 2003. Awarded Middlesex cap 2003. Middlesex Player of the Year 2003. Is not considered an overseas player
Opinions on cricket: 'More floodlit games.'
Best batting: 36* Middlesex v Kent, Lord's 2003
Best bowling: 6-114 Middlesex v Leicestershire, Southgate 2003

2003 Season

	M	Inns	NO	Runs	HS	Avge	100s	50s	Ct	St	O	M	Runs	Wkts	Avge	Best	5wI	10wM
Test																		
All First	17	20	3	270	36 *	15.88	-	-	5	-	585.4	121	1925	63	30.55	6-114	3	-
1-day Int																		
C & G	3	3	3	45	29 *	-	-	-	1	-	29.4	4	112	6	18.66	4-35	-	
NCL	17	11	0	225	50	20.45	-	1	2	-	135.3	13	635	23	27.60	5-48	1	
Twenty20	5	5	1	80	31 *	20.00	-	-	1	-	19	0	151	5	30.20	3-34	-	

Career Performances

	M	Inns	NO	Runs	HS	Avge	100s	50s	Ct	St	Balls	Runs	Wkts	Avge	Best	5wI	10wM
Test																	
All First	33	40	5	373	36 *	10.65	-	-	9	-	5805	3368	100	33.68	6-114	3	-
1-day Int																	
C & G	3	3	3	45	29 *	-	-	-	1	-	178	112	6	18.66	4-35	-	
NCL	42	27	7	317	50	15.85	-	1	7	-	1978	1512	62	24.38	5-17	2	
Twenty20	5	5	1	80	31 *	20.00	-	-	1	-	114	151	5	30.20	3-34	-	

KEMP, J. M.   Worcestershire

Name: Justin Miles Kemp
Role: Right-hand bat, right-arm fast-medium bowler
Born: 2 October 1977, Queenstown, Cape Province, South Africa
Nickname: Kempie
County debut: 2003
County colours: 2003
Test debut: 2000-01
Tests: 3
One-Day Internationals: 14
1st-Class 50s: 12

1st-Class 100s: 3
1st-Class 5 w. in innings: 4
1st-Class catches: 54
Place in batting averages: 171st av. 26.36
Place in bowling averages: 12th av. 22.78
Strike rate: 43.78 (career 54.83)
Family links with cricket: Grandfather
(J. M. Kemp) played for Border 1947-48;
father (J. W. Kemp) played for Border 1975-
76 – 1976-77; cousin of former South Africa
ODI player Dave Callaghan
Education: Queens College; University of
Port Elizabeth
Overseas tours: South Africa U19 to India
1995-96; South African Academy to
Zimbabwe 1998-99; South Africa A to West
Indies 2000, to Australia 2002-03; South
Africa to West Indies 2000-01, to Zimbabwe
2001-02, to Australia 2001-02 (VB Series)

Overseas teams played for: Eastern Province 1996-97 – 2002-03; Northerns
2003-04 –
Extras: Made first-class debut for Eastern Province B v North West, Potchefstroom
1996-97. Has represented South Africa A at home against numerous touring sides since
1998-99. Has won numerous match awards in South African domestic cricket, and was
Man of the Match for Eastern Province v Sri Lankans at Korsten 2000
(93/1-29). Played for Worcestershire Board XI in the C&G 2003. Was an overseas
player with Worcestershire for periods of the 2003 season, deputising for Andrew Hall,
absent on international duty
Best batting: 188 Eastern Province v North West, Port Elizabeth 2000-01
Best bowling: 6-56 Eastern Province v Border, Port Elizabeth 2000-01

2003 Season

	M	Inns	NO	Runs	HS	Avge	100s	50s	Ct	St	O	M	Runs	Wkts	Avge	Best	5wI	10wM
Test																		
All First	6	11	0	290	90	26.36	-	1	9	-	102.1	17	319	14	22.78	5-48	1	-
1-day Int																		
C & G	1	1	0	13	13	13.00	-	-	-	-	10	0	54	0	-	-	-	-
NCL	7	7	2	182	50	36.40	-	1	4	-	29.2	0	177	2	88.50	2-13	-	
Twenty20																		

Career Performances

	M	Inns	NO	Runs	HS	Avge	100s	50s	Ct	St	Balls	Runs	Wkts	Avge	Best	5wI	10wM
Test	3	4	0	18	16	4.50	-	-	3	-	395	151	8	18.87	3-33	-	-
All First	53	87	9	2493	188	31.96	3	12	54	-	6964	3173	127	24.98	6-56	4	-
1-day Int	14	6	2	70	46	17.50	-	-	6	-	546	418	17	24.58	3-20	-	
C & G	1	1	0	13	13	13.00	-	-	-	-	60	54	0	-		-	-
NCL	7	7	2	182	50	36.40	-	1	4	-	176	177	2	88.50	2-13	-	
Twenty20																	

KENDALL, W. S. Hampshire

Name: William (<u>Will</u>) Salwey Kendall
Role: Right-hand bat, right-arm
medium bowler
Born: 18 December 1973, Wimbledon,
London
Height: 5ft 10in **Weight:** 12st 7lbs
Nickname: Villy, Wilbur, Baldy, Fish
County debut: 1996
County cap: 1999
1000 runs in a season: 3
1st-Class 50s: 32
1st-Class 100s: 9
1st-Class 200s: 1
1st-Class catches: 111
One-Day 100s: 1
Place in batting averages: 140th av. 30.07
(2002 187th av. 24.31)
Strike rate: (career 94.15)
Parents: Tom and Sue

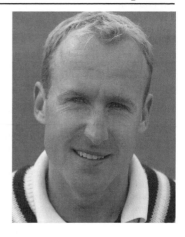

Wife and date of marriage: Emily, 27 September 2002
Family links with cricket: Father played club cricket with East Horsley, Hampshire
Hogs and MCC. Older brother James played for Durham University. Younger brother,
Ed, took new ball for Nottingham University
Education: Bradfield College, Berkshire; Keble College, Oxford University
Qualifications: 10 GCSEs, 3 A-levels, 1 AS-level, BA (Hons) Modern History
Career outside cricket: 'Bit of journalism – still trying to find the right option for the
long term'
Off-season: 'Travelling in South America, New Zealand, Australia and Southeast Asia
for a while, then coaching and training back home'
Overseas tours: Bradfield College to Barbados 1991; Troubadours to Argentina 1997;
Hampshire CCC to Anguilla 1997, to Cape Town 2001; MCC to Kenya 2001-02, to
West Africa 2003

Overseas teams played for: Frankston Peninsula CC, Melbourne 1997-98; Alma Marist CC, Cape Town 2003

Career highlights to date: 'Being part of the Hampshire side that beat the Aussies in 2001 – an unforgettable three days. Receiving my county cap on the same day I made my career best score v Sussex 1999'

Cricket moments to forget: 'Any very short innings'

Cricket superstitions: 'None'

Cricketers particularly admired: Robin Smith, Graham Thorpe, Mark Ramprakash, Shane Warne, 'and anyone playing over 36'

Young players to look out for: Jimmy Adams, James Tomlinson, Kevin Latouf, Tom Burrows

Other sports played: Hockey (Oxford Blue), football (Independent Schools 1992, Old Bradfieldians, Corinthian Casuals; offered terms by Reading), squash, golf

Other sports followed: 'All sports; an interest in Tottenham Hotspur FC'

Favourite band: Rolling Stones, Coldplay

Relaxations: 'Playing or watching sport; spending time with friends and family; hacking up golf courses; travelling; and quiet days with wife, Emily'

Extras: Surrey Young Cricketer of the Year 1992. Awarded Gray-Nicolls Trophy for Schoolboy Cricketer of the Year in memory of Len Newbery 1992. Made first-class debut for Oxford University in 1994. Hampshire Exiles Player of the Year for 1996. Hampshire Cricket Society Player of the Year 2000. Vice-captain of Hampshire 2001-02. Carried his bat for 53* v Leicestershire at West End 2002

Opinions on cricket: 'We clearly need to up the standard, but regional cricket is not the answer. Why not restrict full-time county staffs to 17-18, abandon registration and allow all players outside of this core to be free agents? Counties could receive less central funding and be allowed to sink or swim – the cream will soon rise. And bring back an "A" side for summer and winter matches. They should truly be England's 2nd XI. [Also] every county should be compelled to field at least eight current English-qualified players in every team. How they fill the three remaining places is up to them.'

Best batting: 201 Hampshire v Sussex, Southampton 1999

Best bowling: 3-37 Oxford University v Derbyshire, The Parks 1995

2003 Season

	M	Inns	NO	Runs	HS	Avge	100s	50s	Ct	St	O	M	Runs	Wkts	Avge	Best	5wI	10wM
Test																		
All First	9	13	0	391	114	30.07	1	1	6	-	9.3	2	53	0	-	-	-	-
1-day Int																		
C & G	1	1	0	21	21	21.00	-	-	3	-								
NCL	8	5	1	44	26	11.00	-	-	5	-	3	0	19	0	-	-	-	
Twenty20	4	3	0	13	12	4.33	-	-	1	-								

Career Performances

	M	Inns	NO	Runs	HS	Avge	100s	50s	Ct	St	Balls	Runs	Wkts	Avge	Best	5wI	10wM
Test																	
All First	132	216	24	6584	201	34.29	10	32	111	-	1224	692	13	53.23	3-37	-	-
1-day Int																	
C & G	12	9	2	148	39	21.14	-	-	8	-	42	26	1	26.00	1-8	-	
NCL	87	76	11	1481	110 *	22.78	1	5	43	-	84	98	1	98.00	1-32	-	
Twenty20	4	3	0	13	12	4.33	-	-	1	-							

KENWAY, D. A. Hampshire

Name: <u>Derek</u> Anthony Kenway
Role: Right-hand bat, right-arm off-spin
bowler, part-time wicket-keeper
Born: 12 June 1978, Fareham
Height: 5ft 11in **Weight:** 14st
Nickname: Kenners
County debut: 1997
County cap: 2001
1000 runs in a season: 1
1st-Class 50s: 19
1st-Class 100s: 6
1st-Class catches: 73
1st-Class stumpings: 1
One-Day 100s: 1
Place in batting averages: 158th av. 28.14
(2002 238th av. 18.30)
Strike rate: 12.00 (career 34.50)
Parents: Keith and Geraldine
Marital status: Single

Family links with cricket: 'Brother Richard plays local cricket and has played some
2nd XI'
Education: St George's, Southampton; Barton Peveril College
Qualifications: 6 GCSEs, Level 2 coaching
Career outside cricket: 'Family own roofing company'
Off-season: 'At home working for the family company'
Overseas tours: West of England U15 to West Indies 1993; ECB National Academy
to Australia 2001-02
Overseas teams played for: Beaumaris CC, Melbourne 1997-98
Career highlights to date: 'The win against Australia for Hants [2001]'
Cricket moments to forget: 'Leaving a straight one from Welchy on debut'
Cricketers particularly admired: Robin Smith

Young players to look out for: Dave Adams, Jon Doe
Other sports played: Golf, football ('locally')
Other sports followed: Football (Southampton FC)
Favourite band: U2
Relaxations: 'Quiet pint down the local; spending time with my girlfriend'
Extras: *Daily Telegraph* Batting Award (West) 1994. Southern League Young Player of the Year 1996. NBC Denis Compton Award 1999. Hampshire Cricket Society Player of the Year 2001. Scored half-century (60) in ECB National Academy's innings victory over Commonwealth Bank [Australian] Cricket Academy at Adelaide 2001-02. Scored maiden one-day century (115) v Somerset at West End in the NCL 2003. Scored century (120*) v Zimbabweans in a 50-over match at West End 2003
Opinions on cricket: 'Standard has improved with two overseas players. Things should be left alone for a while as too many changes can't be good for the English game.'
Best batting: 166 Hampshire v Nottinghamshire, West End 2001
Best bowling: 1-5 Hampshire v Warwickshire, Southampton 1997

2003 Season

	M	Inns	NO	Runs	HS	Avge	100s	50s	Ct	St	O	M	Runs	Wkts	Avge	Best	5wl	10wM
Test																		
All First	16	28	1	760	115	28.14	2	3	14	-	2	0	9	1	9.00	1-9	-	-
1-day Int																		
C & G																		
NCL	17	17	0	464	115	27.29	1	3	11	1								
Twenty20	5	5	0	115	40	23.00	-	-	2	-								

Career Performances

	M	Inns	NO	Runs	HS	Avge	100s	50s	Ct	St	Balls	Runs	Wkts	Avge	Best	5wl	10wM
Test																	
All First	78	138	14	3810	166	30.72	6	19	73	1	138	159	4	39.75	1-5	-	-
1-day Int																	
C & G	5	5	0	232	76	46.40	-	2	1	1							
NCL	70	66	2	1708	115	26.68	1	12	39	5							
Twenty20	5	5	0	115	40	23.00	-	-	2	-							

KEY, R. W. T. Kent

Name: <u>Robert</u> William Trevor Key
Role: Right-hand bat, off-spin bowler
Born: 12 May 1979, Dulwich, London
Height: 6ft 1in **Weight:** 12st 7lbs
Nickname: Keysy
County debut: 1998
County cap: 2001
Test debut: 2002
Tests: 2
One-Day Internationals: 2
1000 runs in a season: 2
1st-Class 50s: 28
1st-Class 100s: 15
1st-Class catches: 76
One-Day 100s: 1
Place in batting averages: 90th av. 37.70
(2002 71st av. 41.83)
Parents: Trevor and Lynn
Marital status: Single
Family links with cricket: Mother played for Kent Ladies. Father played club cricket in Derby. Sister Elizabeth played for her junior school side
Education: Langley Park Boys' School
Qualifications: 10 GCSEs, NCA coaching award, GNVQ Business Studies
Career outside cricket: 'Work in the futures market'
Overseas tours: Kent U13 to Holland; England U17 to Bermuda (International Youth Tournament) 1997 (captain); England U19 to South Africa (including U19 World Cup) 1997-98; England A to Zimbabwe and South Africa 1998-99; ECB National Academy to Australia 2001-02, to Sri Lanka 2002-03; England to Australia 2002-03
Overseas teams played for: Greenpoint CC, Cape Town 1996-97
Cricket moments to forget: 'Any time I have lost to Min at cards'
Cricketers particularly admired: Min Patel, Neil Taylor, Alan Wells, Mark Ealham 'for his enthusiasm'
Other sports played: Hockey, football, snooker, tennis (played for county)
Other sports followed: Football (Chelsea), basketball (Chicago Bulls)
Extras: Played for England U17 and England U19 Development XI. Also played for South England U14 and U19. Played for England U19 against Zimbabwe U19 in 1997 and captained the England U17 side to victory in the International Youth Tournament in Bermuda in July. Played for the victorious England side in the U19 World Cup in South Africa 1997-98. Shared England U19 Man of the Series award with Graeme Swann v Pakistan U19 1998. Scored century (119) v Pakistanis at Canterbury 2001 on his 22nd birthday. Scored a 33-ball 50 in title-clinching Norwich Union League

victory v Warwickshire at Edgbaston 2001. NBC Denis Compton Award for the most promising young Kent player 2001. Scored century (177) in ECB National Academy's innings victory over Commonwealth Bank [Australian] Cricket Academy at Adelaide 2001-02. Scored 174* for England XI v Australia A at Hobart 2002-03. Made ODI debut v Zimbabwe at Trent Bridge in the NatWest Series 2003

Best batting: 174* England XI v Australia A, Hobart 2002-03

2003 Season

	M	Inns	NO	Runs	HS	Avge	100s	50s	Ct	St	O	M	Runs	Wkts	Avge	Best	5wI	10wM
Test	2	2	0	22	18	11.00	-	-	3	-								
All First	14	22	2	754	140	37.70	2	1	13	-	0.4	0	4	0	-		-	-
1-day Int	2	2	0	11	11	5.50	-	-	-	-								
C & G	2	2	0	59	32	29.50	-	-	-	-								
NCL	14	14	1	381	68	29.30	-	1	4	-								
Twenty20																		

Career Performances

	M	Inns	NO	Runs	HS	Avge	100s	50s	Ct	St	Balls	Runs	Wkts	Avge	Best	5wI	10wM
Test	8	13	0	244	52	18.76	-	1	6	-							
All First	111	190	8	6165	174 *	33.87	15	28	76	-	74	44	0	-		-	-
1-day Int	2	2	0	11	11	5.50	-	-	-	-							
C & G	13	13	1	505	77	42.08	-	5	2	-							
NCL	63	59	6	1661	114	31.33	1	11	9	-							
Twenty20																	

---

53. Who became only the second player (Javed Miandad was the first) to score a century in both his first and 100th Tests, the latter at Antigua in 1990?

KHALID, S. A.   Worcestershire

Name: <u>Shaftab</u> Ahmad Khalid
Role: Right-hand bat, right-arm
off-spin bowler
Born: 6 October 1982, Pakistan
Height: 5ft 11in **Weight:** 10st 6lbs
Nickname: Shafi
County debut: 2003
County colours: 2003
1st-Class catches: 1
Place in bowling averages: 80th av. 33.40
Strike rate: 54.50 (career 54.50)
Parents: Dr Khalid Mahmood and
Mrs Nuzhat Bano
Marital status: Single
Education: Dormers Wells High School;
West Thames College
Qualifications: 11 GCSEs, 3 A-levels,
studying for LLB degree

Off-season: ECB National Academy (England A) tour
Overseas tours: ECB National Academy (England A) to Malaysia and India 2003-04
Best batting: 13 Worcestershire v Glamorgan, Cardiff 2003
Best bowling: 4-131 Worcestershire v Northamptonshire, Northampton 2003

2003 Season

	M	Inns	NO	Runs	HS	Avge	100s	50s	Ct	St	O	M	Runs	Wkts	Avge	Best	5wl	10wM
Test																		
All First	5	2	0	21	13	10.50	-	-	1	-	90.5	14	334	10	33.40	4-131	-	-
1-day Int																		
C & G																		
NCL	3	2	2	4	3*	-	-	-	-	-	16	0	92	2	46.00	2-40	-	
Twenty20	1	0	0	0	0	-	-	-	-	-	1	0	13	0	-	-	-	

Career Performances

	M	Inns	NO	Runs	HS	Avge	100s	50s	Ct	St	Balls	Runs	Wkts	Avge	Best	5wl	10wM
Test																	
All First	5	2	0	21	13	10.50	-	-	1	-	545	334	10	33.40	4-131	-	-
1-day Int																	
C & G																	
NCL	3	2	2	4	3*	-	-	-	-	-	96	92	2	46.00	2-40	-	
Twenty20	1	0	0	0	0	-	-	-	-	-	6	13	0	-	-	-	

KHAN, A. Kent

Name: Amjad Khan
Role: Right-hand bat, right-arm fast bowler
Born: 14 October 1980, Copenhagen, Denmark
Height: 6ft **Weight:** 11st 7lbs
Nickname: Ammy
County debut: 2001
50 wickets in a season: 1
1st-Class 50s: 2
1st-Class 5 w. in innings: 4
1st-Class catches: 6
Place in batting averages: 198th av. 23.60 (2002 263rd av. 15.21)
Place in bowling averages: 136th av. 46.88 (2002 77th av. 31.80)
Strike rate: 58.23 (career 48.76)
Parents: Aslam and Raisa
Marital status: Single
Education: Skolen på Duevej, Denmark; Falkonĕrgårdens Gymnasium
Off-season: 'Perth'
Overseas tours: Denmark U19 to Canada 1996, to Bermuda 1997, to South Africa and Wales 1998, to Ireland 1999; Denmark to Holland 1998, to Zimbabwe 1999, to Canada (ICC Trophy) 2001
Overseas teams played for: Kjøbenhavns Boldklub, Denmark
Cricketers particularly admired: Wasim Akram, Dennis Lillee
Young players to look out for: Kashif Qureshi
Other sports followed: Football (Denmark)
Injuries: Out for two months with a stress fracture of the shin
Favourite band: Danser med Drenge ('Danish!')
Relaxations: Working out, listening to music, sleeping
Extras: Youngest Danish international ever, at age of 17. Played for Denmark in the NatWest Trophy 1999 and 2000. Recorded maiden first-class five-wicket return (6-52) v Yorkshire at Canterbury 2002 in his third Championship match. Took 6-56 and then scored maiden first-class fifty (58) v Sussex at Hove 2002. Took 50 first-class wickets (63) in his first full season 2002. NBC Denis Compton Award for the most promising young Kent player 2002. Is not considered an overseas player
Best batting: 78 Kent v Middlesex, Lord's 2003
Best bowling: 6-52 Kent v Yorkshire, Canterbury 2002

2003 Season

	M	Inns	NO	Runs	HS	Avge	100s	50s	Ct	St	O	M	Runs	Wkts	Avge	Best	5wI	10wM
Test																		
All First	8	10	0	236	78	23.60	-	1	1	-	165	16	797	17	46.88	4-65	-	-
1-day Int																		
C & G																			
NCL	7	6	2	21	11 *	5.25	-	-	1	-	47	4	231	10	23.10	4-26	-	
Twenty20																			

Career Performances

	M	Inns	NO	Runs	HS	Avge	100s	50s	Ct	St	Balls	Runs	Wkts	Avge	Best	5wI	10wM
Test																	
All First	25	29	5	449	78	18.70	-	2	6	-	3950	2847	81	35.14	6-52	4	-
1-day Int																	
C & G	5	3	0	15	13	5.00	-	-	2	-	225	198	5	39.60	2-38	-	
NCL	10	8	2	48	21	8.00	-	-	1	-	402	331	13	25.46	4-26	-	
Twenty20																		

KHAN, R. M.   Derbyshire

Name: <u>Rawait</u> Mahmood Khan
Role: Right-hand bat
Born: 5 March 1982, Birmingham
Height: 5ft 9in **Weight:** 9st 7lbs
Nickname: Ray
County debut: 2001
1st-Class 50s: 3
1st-Class catches: 5
Place in batting averages: 219th av. 21.00
Parents: Hashim Khan and Barish Begum
Marital status: Single
Family links with cricket: Father played for
Warwickshire 2nd XI. Brother Zubair was
also with Derbyshire
Education: Moseley School; Solihull College
Cricketers particularly admired:
Steve Waugh
Other sports played: Football, badminton
Relaxations: 'Socialising with friends'
Extras: Played for Derbyshire Board XI in the NatWest 2000. Scored 91 v Indians at
Derby 2002 in his second first-class match
Best batting: 91 Derbyshire v Indians, Derby 2002

2003 Season

	M	Inns	NO	Runs	HS	Avge	100s	50s	Ct	St	O	M	Runs	Wkts	Avge	Best	5wI	10wM
Test																		
All First	9	16	0	336	76	21.00	-	2	3	-	3	1	13	0	-	-	-	-
1-day Int																		
C & G																			
NCL	2	2	0	7	5	3.50	-	-	1	-								
Twenty20																			

Career Performances

	M	Inns	NO	Runs	HS	Avge	100s	50s	Ct	St	Balls	Runs	Wkts	Avge	Best	5wI	10wM
Test																	
All First	15	25	1	510	91	21.25	-	3	5	-	36	28	0	-	-	-	-
1-day Int																	
C & G	1	1	0	29	29	29.00	-	-	-	-							
NCL	2	2	0	7	5	3.50	-	-	1	-							
Twenty20																	

KILLEEN, N.   Durham

Name: Neil Killeen
Role: Right-hand bat, right-arm medium-fast bowler
Born: 17 October 1975, Shotley Bridge
Height: 6ft 1in **Weight:** 15st
Nickname: Killer, Bully, Quinny, Squeaky, Bull
County debut: 1995
County cap: 1999
50 wickets in a season: 1
1st-Class 5 w. in innings: 7
1st-Class catches: 19
One-Day 5 w. in innings: 4
Place in batting averages: 285th av. 7.85 (2002 286th av. 10.47)
Place in bowling averages: 98th av. 36.38 (2002 75th av. 31.48)
Strike rate: 66.92 (career 58.48)
Parents: Glen and Thora
Wife and date of marriage: Clare Louise, 5 February 2000
Children: Jonathan David
Family links with cricket: 'Dad best armchair player in the game'

Education: Greencroft Comprehensive School; Derwentside College, University of Teesside

Qualifications: 8 GCSEs, 2 A-levels, first year Sports Science, Level III coaching award, Level I staff coach

Career outside cricket: Cricket coaching

Overseas tours: Durham CCC to Zimbabwe 1992; England U19 to West Indies 1994-95; MCC to Bangladesh 1999-2000

Career highlights to date: 'My county cap and first-class debut'

Cricket moments to forget: 'Injury causing me to miss most of 2001 season'

Cricketers particularly admired: Ian Botham, Curtly Ambrose, Courtney Walsh, David Boon

Young players to look out for: Nicky Peng

Other sports played: Athletics (English Schools javelin)

Sports followed: Football (Sunderland AFC), cricket (Anfield Plain CC)

Relaxations: 'Good food, good wine; golf; spending time with wife and family'

Extras: Was first Durham bowler to take five wickets in a Sunday League game (5-26 v Northamptonshire at Northampton 1995). Took three wickets in final over of National League game at Derby 2000, preventing Derbyshire scoring the six runs required for victory

Best batting: 48 Durham v Somerset, Riverside 1995

Best bowling: 7-70 Durham v Hampshire, Riverside 2003

2003 Season

	M	Inns	NO	Runs	HS	Avge	100s	50s	Ct	St	O	M	Runs	Wkts	Avge	Best	5wI	10wM
Test																		
All First	11	18	4	110	26	7.85	-	-	2	-	290	70	946	26	36.38	7-70	1	-
1-day Int																		
C & G	2	1	0	18	18	18.00	-	-	-	-	18	1	51	3	17.00	2-42	-	
NCL	16	8	4	49	13 *	12.25	-	-	2	-	130.2	17	505	25	20.20	5-22	2	
Twenty20	5	3	2	20	17 *	20.00	-	-	1	-	18.5	0	150	9	16.66	4-32	-	

Career Performances

	M	Inns	NO	Runs	HS	Avge	100s	50s	Ct	St	Balls	Runs	Wkts	Avge	Best	5wI	10wM
Test																	
All First	71	104	21	917	48	11.04	-	-	19	-	11813	5949	202	29.45	7-70	7	-
1-day Int																	
C & G	10	6	1	23	18	4.60	-	-	1	-	528	319	13	24.53	2-15	-	
NCL	102	60	24	384	32	10.66	-	-	17	-	4633	3462	148	23.39	6-31	4	
Twenty20	5	3	2	20	17 *	20.00	-	-	1	-	113	150	9	16.66	4-32	-	

KING, R. E. Northamptonshire

Name: <u>Richard</u> Eric King
Role: Right-hand bat, left-arm
medium-fast bowler; all-rounder
Born: 3 January 1984, Hitchin
Height: 6ft **Weight:** 13st
Nickname: Kingy
County debut: No first-team appearance
Strike rate: 351.00 (career 351.00)
Parents: Roger and Rosemary
Marital status: Single
Education: Bedford Modern School;
Loughborough University
Qualifications: 10 GCSEs, 3 A-levels,
Level 2 ECB coach
Career outside cricket: 'Student'
Off-season: 'Playing cricket in Melbourne,
Australia'
Overseas tours: Bedford Modern to
Barbados 1999; Northamptonshire YC to South Africa 2002
Career highlights to date: 'Playing alongside Adam Shantry'
Cricket moments to forget: 'Playing alongside Tom Huggins'
Cricket superstitions: 'Right pad on before left'
Cricketers particularly admired: Ian Botham, Shane Warne, Viv Richards,
Chris Park
Young players to look out for: Jono Shantry, Matt Hooke, Emily Kortlang
Other sports played: Rugby (East Midlands), golf
Other sports followed: Football (Arsenal)
Favourite band: Lifehouse
Relaxations: 'Listening to music, socialising, extra training'
Extras: MCC Taverners U15 Young Cricketer of the Year. Broke school record with
200* (from 140 balls) in 2001, then scored 185* a week later. Played for
Northamptonshire Board XI in the C&G 2002 and in the first round of the C&G 2003,
which was played in August 2002. Northamptonshire Academy 2002. Captained ECB
Schools XI v India U19 at Wellington College 2002. Played for Loughborough
University CCE 2003
Opinions on cricket: 'Too much cricket played in summer means players often not
performing at full capacity. Two overseas players per team is hindering progression of
young home-grown cricketers, especially when the ECB are pumping funds into
county academies.'
Best batting: 17 LUCCE v Somerset, Taunton 2003
Best bowling: 1-108 LUCCE v Surrey, The Oval 2003

2003 Season (did not make any first-class or one-day appearances for his county)

Career Performances

	M	Inns	NO	Runs	HS	Avge	100s	50s	Ct	St	Balls	Runs	Wkts	Avge	Best	5wI	10wM
Test																	
All First	3	5	0	19	17	3.80	-	-	-	-	351	313	1	313.00	1-108	-	-
1-day Int																	
C & G	2	2	0	2	2	1.00	-	-	1	-	90	66	2	33.00	2-39	-	
NCL																	
Twenty20																	

KIRBY, S. P. *Yorkshire*

Name: <u>Steven</u> Paul Kirby
Role: Right-hand bat, right-arm fast bowler
Born: 4 October 1977, Bury, Lancashire
Height: 6ft 3in **Weight:** 13st 5lbs
Nickname: Tango
County debut: 2001
County cap: 2003
50 wickets in a season: 1
1st-Class 50s: 1
1st-Class 5 w. in innings: 9
1st-Class 10 w. in match: 3
1st-Class catches: 9
Place in batting averages: 284th av. 8.07 (2002 291st av. 10.07)
Place in bowling averages: 36th av. 26.40 (2002 100th av. 34.10)
Strike rate: 41.46 (career 43.94)
Parents: Paul and Alison
Wife and date of marriage: Sasha, 11 October 2003
Education: Elton High School, Walshaw, Bury, Lancs; Bury College
Qualifications: 10 GCSEs, BTEC/GNVQ Advanced Leisure and Tourism
Off-season: 'ECB National Academy; part-time – coaching award Level 3'
Overseas tours: Yorkshire to Grenada 2001; ECB National Academy to Australia 2001-02
Overseas teams played for: Egmont Plains, New Zealand 1997-98
Career highlights to date: 'Getting Yorkshire county cap; Australia tour with England academy'
Cricket moments to forget: 'Being knocked out by Nixon McLean trying to take a return catch'

Cricketers particularly admired: Steve Waugh, Richard Hadlee, Glenn McGrath, Michael Atherton, Curtly Ambrose, Sachin Tendulkar
Young players to look out for: Tim Bresnan, John Sadler, Joe Sayers, Liam Plunkett
Other sports played: Basketball, table tennis, squash, golf – 'anything sporty and competitive'
Other sports followed: Football (Manchester United), rugby (Leicester Tigers)
Relaxations: 'Walking the dog; shooting; spending time with family; socialising with friends'
Extras: Formerly with Leicestershire but did not appear for first team. Took 14 wickets (41-18-47-14) in one day for Egmont Plains v Hawera in a New Zealand club match 1997-98. Took 7-50 in Kent's second innings at Headingley 2001, the best bowling figures by a Yorkshire player on first-class debut (Paul Hutchison's similar figures were on his Championship debut only); Kirby had replaced Matthew Hoggard (called up for England) halfway through the match. Took 12-72 against Leicestershire, his former club, at Headingley 2001. Awarded Yorkshire 2nd XI cap 2001. Returned first innings figures of 4-100 in ECB National Academy's victory over Commonwealth Bank [Australian] Cricket Academy in Adelaide 2001-02. Took 13-154 (5-74/8-80) v Somerset at Taunton 2003, the best match return by a Yorkshire bowler for 36 years. Took 50 first-class wickets in a season for the first time 2003. Awarded Yorkshire cap 2003
Opinions on cricket: '1. We play too much cricket, which reduces a) intensity; b) recovery; c) preparation. 2. Pitches are too inconsistent, which contributes to a) bad techniques; b) lack of hungry, Test-quality bowlers. 3. Too many EU overseas players with no intentions of playing for England. Reduces opportunity for true English players to improve.'
Best batting: 57 Yorkshire v Hampshire, Headingley 2002
Best bowling: 8-80 Yorkshire v Somerset, Taunton 2003
Stop press: Called up to the England A tour to India 2003-04, replacing Simon Jones

2003 Season

	M	Inns	NO	Runs	HS	Avge	100s	50s	Ct	St	O	M	Runs	Wkts	Avge	Best	5wl	10wM
Test																		
All First	14	18	4	113	33	8.07	-	-	5	-	463	80	1769	67	26.40	8-80	5	2
1-day Int																		
C & G	1	0	0	0	0	-	-	-	-	-	7	0	21	1	21.00	1-21	-	
NCL	9	6	1	29	15	5.80	-	-	3	-	65	6	358	8	44.75	3-27	-	
Twenty20																		

---

54. Who, when he dismissed Phil Simmons at Trent Bridge in 1991, became the eleventh bowler to take a wicket with his first ball in Test match cricket?

Career Performances

	M	Inns	NO	Runs	HS	Avge	100s	50s	Ct	St	Balls	Runs	Wkts	Avge	Best	5wI	10wM
Test																	
All First	34	45	9	303	57	8.41	-	1	9	-	6448	4011	151	26.56	8-80	9	3
1-day Int																	
C & G	2	1	0	0	0	0.00	-	-	-	-	102	74	2	37.00	1-21	-	
NCL	17	9	2	35	15	5.00	-	-	4	-	754	713	17	41.94	3-27	-	
Twenty20																	

KIRTLEY, R. J. Sussex

Name: Robert <u>James</u> Kirtley
Role: Right-hand bat, right-arm
fast-medium bowler, county vice-captain
Born: 10 January 1975, Eastbourne
Height: 6ft **Weight:** 12st
Nickname: Ambi
County debut: 1995
County cap: 1998
Test debut: 2003
Tests: 2
One-Day Internationals: 9
50 wickets in a season: 6
1st-Class 50s: 2
1st-Class 5 w. in innings: 27
1st-Class 10 w. in match: 4
1st-Class catches: 38
One-Day 5 w. in innings: 3
Place in batting averages: 208th av. 22.30
(2002 277th av. 12.16)
Place in bowling averages: 41st av. 26.80 (2002 15th av. 22.62)
Strike rate: 51.20 (career 48.07)
Parents: Bob and Pip
Wife and date of marriage: Jenny, 26 October 2002
Family links with cricket: Brother plays league cricket
Education: St Andrews School, Eastbourne; Clifton College, Bristol
Qualifications: 9 GCSEs, 2 A-levels, NCA coaching first level
Career outside cricket: 'Teaching?'
Off-season: Touring with England
Overseas tours: Sussex YC to Barbados 1993, to Sri Lanka 1995; Sussex to Grenada
2001; England A to Bangladesh and New Zealand 1999-2000; England to Zimbabwe
(one-day series) 2001-02, to Sri Lanka (ICC Champions Trophy) 2002-03, to Australia

2002-03 (VB Series), to Bangladesh and Sri Lanka 2003-04, to West Indies 2003-04 (one-day series)

Overseas teams played for: Mashonaland, Zimbabwe 1996-97; Namibian Cricket Board/Wanderers, Windhoek, Namibia 1998-99

Career highlights to date: 'My Test debut at Trent Bridge'

Cricket moments to forget: 'The three times I've bagged a pair'

Cricket superstitions: 'Put my left boot on first!'

Cricketers particularly admired: Curtly Ambrose, Jim Andrew, Darren Gough

Young players to look out for: Tim Ambrose, Matt Prior

Other sports followed: Rugby (England), football (Brighton & Hove Albion)

Relaxations: 'Inviting friends round for a braai (barbeque) and enjoying a cold beer with them'

Extras: Played in the Mashonaland side which defeated England on their 1996-97 tour of Zimbabwe, taking seven wickets in the match. Winner of an NBC Denis Compton Award for promising cricketers 1997. Took hat-trick (A. Morris, Z. Morris, Aymes) in the B&H v Hampshire at West End 2001. Leading wicket-taker in English first-class cricket 2001 with 75 wickets (av. 23.32); took 102 wickets in all county cricket 2001. Sussex Player of the Year 2002. Has taken 50 wickets in a season for six consecutive years. Made Test debut in the third Test v South Africa at Trent Bridge 2003, taking 6-34 in South Africa's second innings and winning Man of the Match award. Vice-captain of Sussex since 2001

Opinions on cricket: 'Pitches, particularly one-day pitches, need to be of the highest quality. It would provide entertainment and develop skills that are required for playing at international level, where pitches on the whole are superb.'

Best batting: 59 Sussex v Durham, Eastbourne 1998

Best bowling: 7-21 Sussex v Hampshire, Southampton 1999

Stop press: Originally selected for the one-day portions of the England tours to Bangladesh and Sri Lanka 2003-04 but was retained for the Test series in Sri Lanka as cover in the pace bowling department with both James Anderson and Steve Harmison injured

2003 Season

	M	Inns	NO	Runs	HS	Avge	100s	50s	Ct	St	O	M	Runs	Wkts	Avge	Best	5wI	10wM
Test	2	4	0	16	11	4.00	-	-	2	-	98.5	32	259	13	19.92	6-34	1	-
All First	13	17	7	223	40 *	22.30	-	-	5	-	529.1	127	1662	62	26.80	6-26	3	-
1-day Int																		
C & G	2	1	1	30	30 *	-	-	-	-	-	20	2	79	6	13.16	5-41	1	
NCL	8	3	0	22	18	7.33	-	-	2	-	62	9	317	10	31.70	3-33	-	
Twenty20	2	0	0	0	0	-	-	-	1	-	6.4	0	39	2	19.50	1-17	-	

Career Performances

	M	Inns	NO	Runs	HS	Avge	100s	50s	Ct	St	Balls	Runs	Wkts	Avge	Best	5wl	10wM
Test	2	4	0	16	11	4.00	-	-	2	-	0	593	259	13	19.92	6-34	1	-
All First	117	163	48	1339	59	11.64	-	2	38	-	22325	11698	465	25.15	7-21	27	4
1-day Int	9	2	0	2	1	1.00	-	-	5	-	458	420	7	60.00	2-33	-	
C & G	12	4	2	43	30 *	21.50	-	-	1	-	685	481	26	18.50	5-39	2	
NCL	92	41	21	223	19 *	11.15	-	-	24	-	3809	2965	129	22.98	4-21	-	
Twenty20	2	0	0	0	0	-	-	-	1	-	40	39	2	19.50	1-17	-	

KLUSENER, L.   Middlesex

Name: Lance Klusener
Role: Left-hand bat, right-arm
medium-fast bowler
Born: 4 September 1971, Durban,
South Africa
Height: 6ft **Weight:** 12st 10lbs
Nickname: Zulu
County debut: 2002 (Nottinghamshire)
Test debut: 1996-97
Tests: 48
One-Day Internationals: 154
1st-Class 50s: 22
1st-Class 100s: 6
1st-Class 5 w. in innings: 11
1st-Class 10 w. in match: 3
1st-Class catches: 65
One-Day 100s: 2
One-Day 5 w. in innings: 6
Strike rate: (career 56.29)
Parents: Peter and Dawn
Wife and date of marriage: Isabelle, 13 May 2000
Children: Matthew, 17 February 2002
Education: Durban High School; Durban Technikon
Overseas tours: South Africa U24 to Sri Lanka 1995; South Africa A to England
1996; South Africa to India 1996-97, to Pakistan 1997-98, to Australia 1997-98, to
England 1998, to New Zealand 1998-99, to UK, Ireland and Holland (World Cup)
1999, to Kenya (LG Cup) 1999-2000, to Zimbabwe 1999-2000, to India 1999-2000, to
Sharjah (Coca-Cola Sharjah Cup) 1999-2000, to Sri Lanka 2000, to Australia (Super
Challenge) 2000, to Singapore (Singapore Challenge) 2000, to Kenya (ICC Knockout
Trophy) 2000-01, to West Indies 2000-01, to Zimbabwe 2001-02, to Australia 2001-02,
to Morocco (Morocco Cup) 2002, to Sri Lanka (ICC Champions Trophy) 2002-03, to
New Zealand 2003-04 (one-day series)

Overseas teams played for: Natal/KwaZulu-Natal 1993-94 –
Career highlights to date: 'World Cup Man of the Tournament [1999]'
Cricketers particularly admired: Malcolm Marshall
Young players to look out for: Kevin Pietersen, Hashim Amla
Other sports played: Golf
Other sports followed: Rugby (Sharks)
Extras: Returned the best analysis by a South African on Test debut – 8-64 in India's second innings of the second Test at Kolkata (Calcutta) 1996-97. Struck his maiden Test century off an even 100 balls (102*) in the second Test v India at Cape Town 1996-97, setting record for the quickest Test hundred by a South African in terms of balls faced and sharing with Brian McMillan in a record eighth-wicket partnership for South Africa in Tests v India (147*). One of *South African Cricket Annual*'s five Cricketers of the Year 1997 and 1999. Scored 174 in the second Test v England at Port Elizabeth 1999-2000, setting a then record for the highest individual Test score at the ground, sharing with Mark Boucher in a then record eighth-wicket stand for South Africa in Tests v England (119), and winning Man of the Match award. One of *Wisden*'s Five Cricketers of the Year 2000. Topped South Africa's Test batting averages on tour of Sri Lanka 2000 (275 runs; av. 68.75) and was Man of the Series. Has won numerous ODI awards, including Player of the Tournament in the World Cup 1999 and Man of the Match v Kenya at Potchefstroom in the World Cup 2002-03 (4-16). Was Nottinghamshire's overseas player at the start of the 2002 season, pending the arrival of Nicky Boje. Has joined Middlesex as an overseas player for 2004
Best batting: 174 South Africa v England, Port Elizabeth 1999-2000
Best bowling: 8-34 Natal v Western Province, Durban 1995-96

2003 Season (did not make any first-class or one-day appearances)

Career Performances

	M	Inns	NO	Runs	HS	Avge	100s	50s	Ct	St	Balls	Runs	Wkts	Avge	Best	5wI	10wM
Test	48	68	11	1904	174	33.40	4	8	33	-	6683	2924	78	37.48	8-64	1	-
All First	111	154	32	4214	174	34.54	6	22	65	-	17283	8224	307	26.78	8-34	11	3
1-day Int	154	124	46	3381	103 *	43.34	2	19	32	-	6572	5139	175	29.36	6-49	6	
C & G																	
NCL																	
Twenty20																	

55. Which Northants stalwart became only the second player to record a century in his first match as England captain (A.C. McLaren was the first) in Barbados in 1990?

KNIGHT, N. V. — Warwickshire

Name: Nicholas Verity Knight
Role: Left-hand bat, right-arm medium-fast
bowler, close fielder, county captain
Born: 28 November 1969, Watford
Height: 6ft 1in **Weight:** 13st
Nickname: Stitch, Fungus
County debut: 1991 (Essex),
1995 (Warwickshire)
County cap: 1994 (Essex),
1995 (Warwickshire)
Test debut: 1995
Tests: 17
One-Day Internationals: 100
1000 runs in a season: 4
1st-Class 50s: 58
1st-Class 100s: 29
1st-Class 200s: 3
1st-Class catches: 253
One-Day 100s: 20
Place in batting averages: 56th av. 44.00 (2002 2nd av. 95.00)
Strike rate: (career 195.00)
Parents: John and Rosemary
Wife and date of marriage: Trudie, 3 October 1998
Family links with cricket: Father played for Cambridgeshire. Brother Andy plays
club cricket in local Cambridge leagues
Education: Felsted School; Loughborough University
Qualifications: 9 O-levels, 3 A-levels, BSc (Hons) Sociology, coaching qualification
Overseas tours: Felsted School to Australia 1986-87; England A to India 1994-95, to
Pakistan 1995-96, to Kenya and Sri Lanka 1997-98; England to Zimbabwe and New
Zealand 1996-97, to Sharjah (Champions Trophy) 1997-98, to West Indies 1997-98
(one-day series), to Bangladesh (Wills International Cup) 1998-99, to Australia 1998-99
(CUB Series), to Sharjah (Coca-Cola Cup) 1998-99, to South Africa and Zimbabwe
1999-2000 (one-day series), to Sri Lanka 2000-01 (one-day series), to Zimbabwe
(one-day series) 2001-02, to India and New Zealand 2001-02 (one-day series), to Sri
Lanka (ICC Champions Trophy) 2002-03, to Australia 2002-03 (VB Series), to Africa
(World Cup) 2002-03
Overseas teams played for: Northern Districts, Sydney 1991-92; East Torrens,
Adelaide 1992-94
Cricketers particularly admired: David Gower, Graham Gooch
Other sports played: Rugby (Eastern Counties), hockey (Essex and Young England)
Relaxations: Eating good food, painting

Extras: Captained English Schools 1987 and 1988, England YC v New Zealand 1989 and Combined Universities 1991. Won *Daily Telegraph* award 1988; voted Gray-Nicolls Cricketer of the Year 1988, Cricket Society Most Promising Young Cricketer of the Year 1989, Essex Young Player of the Year 1991 and Essex U19 Player of the Year. Left Essex at the end of the 1994 season to join Warwickshire. Scored successive centuries (113 and 125*) in the Texaco Trophy v Pakistan 1996. Warwickshire vice-captain 1999. Member of England's 1999 World Cup squad. With Anurag Singh, shared in record NatWest first-wicket stand for Warwickshire (185), v Hampshire at Edgbaston 2000. Scored century (126*) v Somerset at Edgbaston in the B&H 2002, in the process passing Alvin Kallicharran's record of 12 one-day centuries for Warwickshire. Carried his bat for 255* v Hampshire at Edgbaston 2002, in the process sharing with Alan Richardson (91) in a tenth-wicket stand of 214, which was a county best for the last wicket and the fifth highest tenth-wicket partnership in Championship history overall. Carried his bat for 245* v Sussex at Edgbaston 2002, becoming the first batsman to score two double centuries in a season for Warwickshire since Alvin Kallicharran did so in 1982. Leading English player (second overall) in the 2002 first-class batting averages with 1520 runs at 95.00. Warwickshire Batsman of the Year 2002. Leading run-scorer in the VB Series 2002-03 with 461 runs (av. 51.22). His international awards include Man of the Match in the first Test v Zimbabwe at Bulawayo 1996-97, Man of the [ODI] Series v Zimbabwe 2001-02 (302 runs; av. 100.67), and successive ODI Man of the Match awards v West Indies 1997-98. Retired from international cricket in April 2003. Scored century (122) v Worcestershire at Edgbaston in the NCL 2003, in the process passing 4000 runs in the one-day league. Appointed captain of Warwickshire for 2004. Granted a benefit for 2004

Best batting: 255* Warwickshire v Hampshire, Edgbaston 2002
Best bowling: 1-61 Essex v Middlesex, Uxbridge 1994

2003 Season

	M	Inns	NO	Runs	HS	Avge	100s	50s	Ct	St	O	M	Runs	Wkts	Avge	Best	5wI	10wM
Test																		
All First	14	26	3	1012	146	44.00	3	5	11	-	6	3	39	0	-		-	-	-
1-day Int																		
C & G	3	3	0	91	88	30.33	-	1	3	-								
NCL	15	15	0	684	122	45.60	2	5	10	-								
Twenty20	7	7	1	275	89	45.83	-	3	3	-	0.5	0	4	0	-		-	-

Career Performances

	M	Inns	NO	Runs	HS	Avge	100s	50s	Ct	St	Balls	Runs	Wkts	Avge	Best	5wI	10wM
Test	17	30	0	719	113	23.96	1	4	26	-							
All First	190	319	33	12556	255 *	43.90	32	58	253	-	195	230	1	230.00	1-61	-	-
1-day Int	100	100	10	3637	125 *	40.41	5	25	44	-							
C & G	30	30	2	1145	151	40.89	4	5	15	-							
NCL	149	137	16	4075	134	33.67	6	20	65	-	84	85	2	42.50	1-14	-	
Twenty20	7	7	1	275	89	45.83	-	3	3	-	5	4	0	-		-	-

KOENIG, S. G.   Middlesex

Name: <u>Sven</u> Gaëtan Koenig
Role: Left-hand bat
Born: 9 December 1973, Durban,
South Africa
Height: 5ft 9in **Weight:** 12st 2lbs
Nickname: Blackie, Kuala
County debut: 2002
County cap: 2002
1000 runs in a season: 2
1st-Class 50s: 39
1st-Class 100s: 12
1st-Class catches: 55
One-Day 100s: 1
Place in batting averages: 38th av. 47.50
(2002 48th av. 46.33)
Strike rate: 30.00 (career 76.00)
Parents: Gaëtan and Barbara
Wife and date of marriage:
Catherine, 27 December 2002
Education: Highbury; Hilton College; University of Cape Town
Qualifications: Law degree, Economics degree, Level 2 coach
Career outside cricket: Business
Off-season: Playing provincial cricket for Easterns in South Africa
Overseas tours: Western Province to Australia 1995; South Africa A to England 1996;
Transvaal to Australia 1997
Overseas teams played for: Western Province 1993-96; Transvaal/Gauteng
1997-2000; Easterns 2003-04
Career highlights to date: 'Playing at Lord's – debut at Lord's v Notts'
Cricket moments to forget: 'First-ball duck – lbw Malcolm Marshall – on Currie
Cup debut, Western Province v Natal'
Cricket superstitions: 'None'
Cricketers particularly admired: Desmond Haynes, Steve Waugh, Gary Kirsten
Players to look out for: David Nash, Joe Dawes
Other sports played: Golf, surfing
Other sports followed: Rugby (Springboks), football (Newcastle United)
Injuries: Out for one week with a split finger
Interests/relaxations: Surfing, fishing, business
Extras: South African Young Player of the Year 1994. Leading run-scorer in South
African domestic first-class cricket 2000-01 with 789 runs (av. 60.69). Gauteng Player
of the Year 2000-01. Scored century (141*) on first-class debut for Middlesex v
Cambridge University CCE at Fenner's and another (100) on Championship debut for

the county v Durham at Riverside 2002. Scored 1000 Championship runs in his debut season for Middlesex 2002. Holds an Italian passport and is not considered an overseas player

Opinions on cricket: 'A little less cricket would be good for the game. Twenty20 fantastic. Only need one one-day competition in county cricket.'

Best batting: 166* Middlesex v OUCCE, The Parks 2003

Best bowling: 1-0 Gauteng/Northerns v Sri Lanka A, Johannesburg 1999-2000

2003 Season

	M	Inns	NO	Runs	HS	Avge	100s	50s	Ct	St	O	M	Runs	Wkts	Avge	Best	5wI	10wM
Test																		
All First	16	27	3	1140	166 *	47.50	1	7	3	-	5	0	19	1	19.00	1-19	-	-
1-day Int																		
C & G																		
NCL																		
Twenty20																		

Career Performances

	M	Inns	NO	Runs	HS	Avge	100s	50s	Ct	St	Balls	Runs	Wkts	Avge	Best	5wI	10wM
Test																	
All First	109	187	10	7033	166 *	39.73	12	39	55	-	152	86	2	43.00	1-0	-	-
1-day Int																	
C & G	1	1	0	116	116	116.00	1	-	-	-							
NCL	12	11	1	104	43 *	10.40	-	-	3	-							
Twenty20																	

56. Which knighted Yorkshireman scored the first double century by an England captain in an overseas Test in Jamaica in 1954?

KRIKKEN, K. M. Derbyshire

Name: <u>Karl</u> Matthew Krikken
Role: Right-hand bat, wicket-keeper
Born: 9 April 1969, Bolton
Height: 5ft 10in **Weight:** 14st
Nickname: Krikk
County debut: 1987 (one-day),
1989 (first-class)
County cap: 1992
Benefit: 2002
50 dismissals in a season: 5
1st-Class 50s: 25
1st-Class 100s: 1
1st-Class catches: 527
1st-Class stumpings: 31
Place in batting averages: (2002 283rd
av. 11.26)

Strike rate: (career 134.00)
Parents: Brian and Irene
Wife and date of marriage: Leesha, 3 October 1998
Children: Harry, Chester and Millie
Family links with cricket: Father played for Lancashire and Worcestershire
Education: Rivington and Blackrod High School and Sixth Form College
Qualifications: 6 O-levels, 3 A-levels, Level 4 coach
Overseas tours: Derbyshire to Bermuda 1993, to Malaga 1997, to Portugal 2000
Overseas teams played for: CBC Old Boys, Kimberley, South Africa 1988-89;
Green Island, Dunedin, New Zealand 1990-91; United CC, Cape Town 1991-93;
Rivertonians, Cape Town 1993-94; Longford CC, Victoria, Australia 2000-01
Career highlights to date: 'Winning B&H in 1993'
Cricketers particularly admired: Bob Taylor, Alan Hill
Young players to look out for: 'Derbyshire will come of age in a few years'
Other sports followed: Football (Wigan Athletic FC, Bolton Wanderers FC)
Relaxations: 'The kids'
Extras: Derbyshire Supporters' Player of the Year 1991 and 1996; Derbyshire
Clubman of the Year 1993. In 1993 conceded no byes during a sequence of 1865 runs
scored against the county, a Derbyshire record. Derbyshire vice-captain 1998-2000.
Made 500th first-class dismissal when he caught Will Kendall off Nathan Dumelow v
Hampshire at Derby 2001. 2nd XI coach since 2003. Appointed Director of Derbyshire
Academy in November 2003
Best batting: 104 Derbyshire v Lancashire, Old Trafford 1996
Best bowling: 1-54 Derbyshire v Hampshire, Derby 1999

2003 Season

	M	Inns	NO	Runs	HS	Avge	100s	50s	Ct	St	O	M	Runs	Wkts	Avge	Best	5wl	10wM
Test																		
All First	1	2	0	15	14	7.50	-	-	1	-								
1-day Int																		
C & G																		
NCL	1	0	0	0	0	-	-	-	1	-								
Twenty20	1	1	1	3	3 *	-	-	-	1	-								

Career Performances

	M	Inns	NO	Runs	HS	Avge	100s	50s	Ct	St	Balls	Runs	Wkts	Avge	Best	5wl	10wM
Test																	
All First	214	323	60	5725	104	21.76	1	25	527	31	134	121	1	121.00	1-54	-	-
1-day Int																	
C & G	20	12	5	201	55	28.71	-	1	15	1							
NCL	138	99	33	1137	44 *	17.22	-	-	146	34							
Twenty20	1	1	1	3	3 *	-	-	-	1	-							

KRUGER, G. J-P.   Leicestershire

Name: Garnett John-Peter Kruger
Role: Right-hand bat, right-arm medium-fast bowler
Born: 5 January 1977, Cape Town, South Africa
Height: 6ft 3in **Weight:** 12st 8lbs
Nickname: Cruiser
County debut: No first-team appearance
1st-Class 50s: 1
1st-Class 5 w. in innings: 2
1st-Class 10 w. in match: 1
1st-Class catches: 9
Strike rate: (career 57.17)
Parents: Arthur and Penny
Marital status: Single
Family links with cricket: Father played cricket in Eastern Province
Education: Gelvan High School; Russell Road College
Qualifications: Fitting and machinery, architecture
Off-season: Playing cricket in South Africa
Overseas tours: South Africa A to West Indies 2000-01; South Africa VI to Hong Kong Sixes 2003

Overseas teams played for: Eastern Province 1997-98 – 2002-03; Gauteng 2003-04 –
Career highlights to date: 'Playing for Highveld Strikers (Gauteng)'
Cricket superstitions: 'None'
Cricketers particularly admired: Glenn McGrath
Other sports played: Basketball
Other sports followed: Football (Arsenal)
Favourite band: 'Most Rap music'
Relaxations: 'Sony PlayStation and sleep!'
Extras: Made first-class debut for Eastern Province B v Easterns at Benoni 1997-98. Awards include Man of the Match v North West at Port Elizabeth in the Standard Bank Cup 1999-2000 (6-23), v Gauteng at Johannesburg in the Standard Bank Cup 2000-01 (5-28), and v Gauteng at Port Elizabeth in the Standard Bank Cup 2001-02 (5-29). Has joined Leicestershire as an overseas player for 2004
Opinions on cricket: 'You need mental toughness to succeed in the game.'
Best batting: 58 South Africa A v Windward Islands, Kingstown 2000-01
Best bowling: 7-64 Eastern Province v Border, East London 1999-2000
Stop press: Represented South Africa A v Sri Lanka A and v West Indians 2003-04. Called up to South Africa squad for the first Test v West Indies 2003-04

2003 Season (did not make any first-class or one-day appearances)

Career Performances

	M	Inns	NO	Runs	HS	Avge	100s	50s	Ct	St	Balls	Runs	Wkts	Avge	Best	5wI	10wM
Test																	
All First	38	51	15	412	58	11.44	-	1	9	-	6747	3509	118	29.73	7-64	2	1
1-day Int																	
C & G																		
NCL																		
Twenty20																		

LAMB, G. A.   Hampshire

Name: Gregory (Greg) Arthur Lamb
Role: Right-hand bat, right-arm off-spin or medium bowler; all-rounder
Born: 4 March 1981, Harare, Zimbabwe
Height: 6ft **Weight:** 12st
Nickname: Lamby
County debut: No first-team appearance
1st-Class 50s: 2
1st-Class 100s: 1
1st-Class 5 w. in innings: 1
1st-Class catches: 9
Strike rate: (career 38.69)

Parents: Terry and Jackie
Marital status: Single
Children: Isabella Grace Saskia Lamb
Education: Lomagundi College; Guildford College (both Zimbabwe)
Qualifications: School and coaching qualifications
Career outside cricket: Farming
Off-season: 'Fishing and training'
Overseas tours: Zimbabwe U19 to South Africa (U19 World Cup) 1997-98, to Sri Lanka (U19 World Cup) 1999-2000; Zimbabwe A to Sri Lanka 1999-2000
Overseas teams played for: CFX [Zimbabwe] Academy 1999-2000; Mashonaland A 2000-01
Career highlights to date: 'Playing against Australia. Making my first first-class hundred'

Cricket superstitions: 'Every time I hit a four I have to touch the other side of the pitch'
Cricketers particularly admired: Aravinda de Silva
Other sports played: 'All sports'
Favourite band: Matchbox Twenty
Relaxations: 'Fishing, playing sport'
Extras: Played for Zimbabwe U12, U15 and U19. Represented CFX [Zimbabwe] Academy, Zimbabwe Cricket Union President's XI and Zimbabwe A against various touring sides. Played in Hampshire's 2nd XI Trophy winning side 2003
Best batting: 100* CFX Academy v Manicaland, Mutare 1999-2000
Best bowling: 7-73 CFX Academy v Midlands, Kwekwe 1999-2000

2003 Season (did not make any first-class or one-day appearances)

Career Performances

	M	Inns	NO	Runs	HS	Avge	100s	50s	Ct	St	Balls	Runs	Wkts	Avge	Best	5wI	10wM
Test																	
All First	16	23	3	491	100*	24.55	1	2	9	-	1006	559	26	21.50	7-73	1	-
1-day Int																	
C & G																	
NCL																	
Twenty20																	

LARAMAN, A. W.   Somerset

Name: <u>Aaron</u> William Laraman
Role: Right-hand bat, right-arm
medium-fast bowler
Born: 10 January 1979, London
Height: 6ft 5in **Weight:** 14st 7lbs
Nickname: Az, Lazza, Shanky, Long
County debut: 1998 (Middlesex),
2003 (Somerset)
1st-Class 50s: 4
1st-Class 100s: 1
1st-Class catches: 10
One-Day 5 w. in innings: 2
Place in batting averages: 44th av. 45.92
(2002 119th av. 33.00)
Place in bowling averages: 119th av. 40.79
(2002 99th av. 34.07)
Strike rate: 69.95 (career 59.82)
Parents: William and Lynda
Marital status: Single
Education: Enfield Grammar School
Qualifications: 8 GCSEs

Career outside cricket: Cricket coaching in winter
Overseas tours: England U17 to Holland 1995; England U19 to South Africa 1997-98
Overseas teams played for: Burnside CC, Christchurch, New Zealand 1999-2000;
Willetton CC, Perth 2000-01
Career highlights to date: 'Making my debut at Lord's in 1998'
Cricketers particularly admired: Steve Waugh, Glenn McGrath, Michael Atherton
Other sports followed: Football (Arsenal)
Relaxations: Working out at the gym, football, golf
Extras: Enfield Grammar School cap at the age of 13. Middlesex Colts cap. Seaxe
2nd XI Player of the Year 1997. Took 4-39 on NatWest debut v Nottinghamshire at
Lord's 2000. Scored 95-ball 82* as Middlesex successfully chased 240 to win County
Championship match v Gloucestershire at Southgate 2002. Left Middlesex at the end
of the 2002 season and joined Somerset for 2003. Scored maiden first-class century
(148*, having arrived at 136 for 5) v Gloucestershire at Taunton 2003
Best batting: 148* Somerset v Gloucestershire, Taunton 2003
Best bowling: 4-33 Middlesex v Cambridge University, Fenner's 2000

2003 Season

	M	Inns	NO	Runs	HS	Avge	100s	50s	Ct	St	O	M	Runs	Wkts	Avge	Best	5wI	10wM
Test																		
All First	13	18	5	597	148 *	45.92	1	3	5	-	279.5	58	979	24	40.79	3-20	-	-
1-day Int																		
C & G																		
NCL	4	4	0	44	33	11.00	-	-	1	-	25	0	186	1	186.00	1-53	-	
Twenty20	2	2	1	28	28 *	28.00	-	-	-	-	6	0	46	2	23.00	1-16	-	

Career Performances

	M	Inns	NO	Runs	HS	Avge	100s	50s	Ct	St	Balls	Runs	Wkts	Avge	Best	5wI	10wM
Test																	
All First	27	32	8	956	148 *	39.83	1	4	10	-	3410	1974	57	34.63	4-33	-	-
1-day Int																	
C & G	5	2	1	18	16 *	18.00	-	-	2	-	201	125	9	13.88	4-39	-	
NCL	22	19	5	159	33	11.35	-	-	5	-	850	736	25	29.44	6-42	2	
Twenty20	2	2	1	28	28 *	28.00	-	-	-	-	36	46	2	23.00	1-16	-	

LATOUF, K. J.   Hampshire

Name: Kevin John Latouf
Role: Right-hand bat, right-arm
medium bowler
Born: 7 September 1985, Pretoria,
South Africa
Height: 5ft 10in **Weight:** 12st
Nickname: Poindexter, Mushy, Latsy, Kev
County debut: No first-team appearance
Parents: Colin and Josephine
Marital status: Single
Family links with cricket: 'Uncle Brian
Venables was a batsman who played in
Dublin and now plays cricket in Kent'
Education: Millfield School; Barton Peveril
Sixth Form College
Qualifications: 11 GCSEs, 4 AS-Levels,
'currently studying for A2s'
Career outside cricket: Student
Off-season: 'Finishing A2s; training hard for April'
Overseas tours: West of England U15 to West Indies 2000, 2001
Overseas teams played for: Melville CC, Perth ('briefly')
Career highlights to date: '68 v Glamorgan 2nd XI which included Simon Jones. 80*
on 2nd XI debut – both 2003'

Cricket moments to forget: 'Golden duck in England U15 trial match'
Cricket superstitions: 'Don't believe in superstition'
Cricketers particularly admired: Ricky Ponting, Jonty Rhodes, Allan Donald
Young players to look out for: Anthony Latouf, James Hildreth, Tom Burrows, Chris Benham, Tom Cledwyn
Other sports played: Tennis (county trials), rugby (Bristol and Somerset trials), golf ('fun'), surfing, snowboarding
Other sports followed: Rugby (Natal Sharks), football (Arsenal), AFL (Collingwood)
Favourite band: Coldplay
Relaxations: 'Prefer listening to R&B and Hip Hop; going out with mates from cricket, Millfield and BP'
Extras: Played for West of England U13, U14 and U15. Played for ECB U17 and ECB U19 v India U19 2002. Played for ECB U19 v South Africa U19 2003. Played in Hampshire's 2nd XI Trophy winning side 2003
Opinions on cricket: 'People are too opinionated.'

LAW, D. R. Durham

Name: <u>Danny</u> Richard Law
Role: Right-hand bat, right-arm medium-fast bowler; all-rounder
Born: 13 July 1975, Lambeth, London
Height: 6ft 5in **Weight:** 15st
Nickname: Decas
County debut: 1993 (Sussex), 1997 (Essex), 2001 (Durham)
County cap: 1996 (Sussex), 2001 (Durham)
1st-Class 50s: 15
1st-Class 100s: 2
1st-Class 5 w. in innings: 8
1st-Class catches: 56
Place in batting averages: 257th av. 14.11 (2002 153rd av. 28.11)
Place in bowling averages: 56th av. 29.41
Strike rate: 51.75 (career 53.75)
Parents: Richard and Claudette
Marital status: Engaged to Kate
Children: Sade
Family links with cricket: Cousins play in Northampton
Education: Wolverstone Hall/Steyning Grammar School
Qualifications: Coach
Overseas tours: Sussex Schools U16 to Jersey 1991; England U18 to South Africa

1992-93, to Denmark 1993; England U19 to Sri Lanka 1993-94; Dulwich CC to Kenya and Uganda 2000-01
Overseas teams played for: Ashburton CC, Melbourne 1992-94; Essendon, Melbourne 1995-96
Career highlights to date: 'Being capped at Sussex '96 and at Durham in 2001'
Cricket superstitions: 'Left pad on first'
Cricketers particularly admired: Ian Botham, Viv Richards
Young players to look out for: Gary Pratt, Stephen Felton, David Felton, Liam Plunkett
Other sports played: Golf, football ('for the Moor House on Sundays')
Other sports followed: Football (Newcastle Utd)
Favourite band: Neptunes, 50 Cent, DMX, Wayne Wonder
Relaxations: Golf, cinema
Extras: Winner of Denis Compton Award 1996. Left Sussex during the 1996-97 off-season and joined Essex for 1997. Took Championship hat-trick v Durham at Riverside 1998. Left Essex at the end of the 2000 season and joined Durham for 2001. Scored maiden Championship century (103) v Hampshire at Riverside 2001, in the process sharing with James Brinkley in a record seventh-wicket partnership for Durham (127). Released by Durham at the end of the 2003 season
Best batting: 115 Sussex v Young Australia, Hove 1995
Best bowling: 6-53 Durham v Hampshire, West End 2001

2003 Season

	M	Inns	NO	Runs	HS	Avge	100s	50s	Ct	St	O	M	Runs	Wkts	Avge	Best	5wI	10wM
Test																		
All First	6	10	1	127	74	14.11	-	1	1	-	103.3	15	353	12	29.41	4-30	-	-
1-day Int																		
C & G																		
NCL	4	3	0	14	9	4.66	-	-	2	-	13	1	76	2	38.00	1-25	-	
Twenty20																		

Career Performances

	M	Inns	NO	Runs	HS	Avge	100s	50s	Ct	St	Balls	Runs	Wkts	Avge	Best	5wI	10wM
Test																	
All First	108	170	8	3298	115	20.35	2	15	56	-	11450	7000	213	32.86	6-53	8	-
1-day Int																	
C & G	18	14	1	251	47	19.30	-	-	4	-	355	322	10	32.20	3-51	-	
NCL	114	98	14	1746	82	20.78	-	5	23	-	2368	2158	67	32.20	3-26	-	
Twenty20																	

LAW, S. G. Lancashire

Name: <u>Stuart</u> Grant Law
Role: Right-hand bat, right-arm
leg-spin bowler
Born: 18 October 1968, Brisbane, Australia
Height: 6ft 1in **Weight:** 13st
Nickname: Lawry, Judge, LA
County debut: 1996 (Essex),
2002 (Lancashire)
County cap: 1996 (Essex),
2002 (Lancashire)
Test debut: 1995-96
Tests: 1

One-Day Internationals: 54
1000 runs in a season: 8
1st-Class 50s: 100
1st-Class 100s: 59
1st-Class 200s: 4
1st-Class 5 w. in innings: 1
1st-Class catches: 317
One-Day 100s: 13
Place in batting averages: 1st av. 91.00 (2002 28th av. 52.86)
Strike rate: (career 100.14)
Parents: Grant and Pam
Wife and date of marriage: Debbie-Lee, 31 December 1998
Children: Max, 9 January 2002
Family links with cricket: 'Cricket has always been in the family'
Education: Craigslea State High School; Brisbane State High School
Qualifications: Level 2 cricket coach
Off-season: 'Playing for Queensland in Pura Cup'
Overseas tours: Australia B to Zimbabwe 1991-92; Young Australia (Australia A) to England and Netherlands 1995 (captain); Australia to India and Pakistan (World Cup) 1995-96, to Sri Lanka (Singer World Series) 1996, to India (Titan World Series) 1996-97, to South Africa 1996-97 (one-day series), to New Zealand (one-day series) 1997-98
Overseas teams played for: Queensland Bulls 1988-89 –
Career highlights to date: 'Playing for Australia. Captaining Queensland to their first Sheffield Shield [title] win'
Cricket superstitions: 'None'
Cricketers particularly admired: Viv Richards, Greg Chappell
Other sports played: Golf, tennis
Other sports followed: Rugby league (Brisbane Broncos)

Relaxations: 'Spending time with family, friends; going to the beach'
Extras: Made his first-class debut for Queensland as a 19-year-old, scoring 179 on only his second appearance. Sheffield Shield Player of the Year 1990-91. Shared with Martin Love in record third-wicket partnership for Queensland (326), v Tasmania at Brisbane 1994-95. Is the most successful captain in Australian domestic cricket history, having captained Queensland to their first Sheffield Shield title in 1994-95, to their second in 1996-97, to the title in the first three Pura Cup competitions in 1999-2000 (Man of the Match in final), 2000-01 and 2001-02 (to equal Richie Benaud's feat of captaining his state to five titles) and to three one-day titles. Man of the Match for his 71-ball 80* in the 1997 NatWest final v Warwickshire at Lord's. One of *Wisden*'s Five Cricketers of the Year 1998. Set record for the fastest century in Australian domestic one-day cricket – 74 balls for Queensland v Tasmania at Brisbane 1998-99. Topped the English first-class batting averages for 1999 (1833 runs at 73.32). PCA Player of the Year 1999. Scored 116* and 123* v Lancashire at Old Trafford 2001, becoming the first player since Glamorgan's Hugh Morris in 1995 to score unbeaten centuries in each innings of a Championship match; followed up with a 90-ball century v Lancashire in the ensuing Norwich Union League match at the same ground. Left Essex at the end of the 2001 season and joined Lancashire as overseas player for 2002. Became Queensland's most-capped player when he passed Sam Trimble's record of 133 first-class appearances for the state, v Tasmania at Brisbane 2001-02. Stood down as captain of Queensland at the end of the 2001-02 Australian season. Scored century (168) v Warwickshire at Edgbaston 2003, sharing with Carl Hooper (177) in a Lancashire record fifth-wicket partnership of 360 as the county scored 781. Topped the English first-class batting averages for 2003 (1820 runs at 91.00). Lancashire Player of the Year 2003
Best batting: 263 Essex v Somerset, Chelmsford 1999
Best bowling: 5-39 Queensland v Tasmania, Brisbane 1995-96
Stop press: Scored 69-ball century v Tasmania at Hobart in the ING Cup 2003-04, breaking his own record for the fastest century in Australian domestic one-day cricket. Scored century (146*) v New South Wales at Brisbane 2003-04, in the process passing Sam Trimble's career aggregate for Queensland to become the state's all-time leading run-scorer in first-class cricket

2003 Season

	M	Inns	NO	Runs	HS	Avge	100s	50s	Ct	St	O	M	Runs	Wkts	Avge	Best	5wI	10wM
Test																		
All First	16	24	4	1820	236 *	91.00	7	6	17	-	7	0	29	0	-	-	-	-
1-day Int																		
C & G	4	3	0	92	59	30.66	-	1	2	-								
NCL	18	17	2	586	98	39.06	-	4	4	-								
Twenty20	5	5	0	59	29	11.80	-	-	1	-	1	0	10	0	-	-	-	

Career Performances

	M	Inns	NO	Runs	HS	Avge	100s	50s	Ct	St	Balls	Runs	Wkts	Avge	Best	5wl	10wM
Test	1	1	1	54	54 *	-	-	1	1	-	18	9	0	-	-	-	-
All First	284	469	51	21179	263	50.66	63	100	317	-	8212	4092	82	49.90	5-39	1	-
1-day Int	54	51	5	1237	110	26.89	1	7	12	-	807	635	12	52.91	2-22	-	
C & G	22	19	1	802	107	44.55	3	4	17	-	439	366	8	45.75	2-36	-	
NCL	112	109	7	3818	133	37.43	8	17	40	-	954	832	25	33.28	4-37	-	
Twenty20	5	5	0	59	29	11.80	-	-	1	-	6	10	0	-	-	-	-

LAWSON, M. A. K. Yorkshire

Name: <u>Mark</u> Anthony Kenneth Lawson
Role: Right-hand bat, right-arm
leg-spin bowler
Born: 24 November 1985, Leeds
Height: 5ft 8in **Weight:** 12st ('approx')
Nickname: Sauce
County debut: No first-team appearance
Parents: Anthony and Dawn
Marital status: Single
Family links with cricket: 'Father played
local league cricket and encouraged me to
take up the game'
Education: Castle Hall Language College,
Mirfield, West Yorkshire
Qualifications: 11 GCSEs
Off-season: U19 World Cup, Bangladesh
Overseas tours: England U19 to Australia
2002-03, to Bangladesh (U19 World Cup)
2003-04
Career highlights to date: 'Taking the catch that secured the 2nd XI Championship
for Yorkshire 2003. Making my debut for England U19 in the third "Test" against
Australia U19 at Bankstown 2002-03. Being part of the U19 World Cup squad'
Cricketers particularly admired: Shane Warne, Gareth Batty
Young players to look out for: Christopher Batchelor, Phillip Holdsworth
Other sports played: Football (school), rugby union (school, Cleckheaton 'in early
teens'), rugby league (Dewsbury Moor ARLFC 'in early teens')
Other sports followed: Rugby league (Bradford Bulls)
Relaxations: Music, dining out, cinema
Extras: Played for Yorkshire Schools U11-U16 (captain U13-U15); ESCA North of
England U14 and U15; North of England Development of Excellence U17 and U19.
Represented England U15, U17 and U19, including v South Africa U19 2003.

Awarded Brian Johnston Scholarship. Part of Terry Jenner Elite Wrist Spin Program. Made debut for Yorkshire 2nd XI 2003. Voted Yorkshire Supporters' Young Player of the Year 2003

LEATHERDALE, D. A. Worcestershire

Name: <u>David</u> Anthony Leatherdale
Role: Right-hand bat, right-arm medium bowler, cover fielder
Born: 26 November 1967, Bradford
Height: 5ft 10in **Weight:** 11st
Nickname: Lugsy, Spock
County debut: 1988
County cap: 1994; colours 2002
Benefit: 2003
1000 runs in a season: 1
1st-Class 50s: 54
1st-Class 100s: 14
1st-Class 5 w. in innings: 2
1st-Class catches: 151
One-Day 5 w. in innings: 2
Place in batting averages: 200th av. 23.42 (2002 61st av. 43.31)
Place in bowling averages: (2002 89th av. 33.43)
Strike rate: 58.50 (career 53.51)
Parents: Paul and Rosalyn
Wife: Vanessa
Children: Callum Edward, 6 July 1990; Christian Ellis, 21 March 1995
Family links with cricket: Father played local cricket; brother-in-law played for England YC in 1979
Education: Pudsey Grangefield Secondary School
Qualifications: 8 O-levels, 3 A-levels, NCA coaching award (stage 1)
Overseas tours: England Indoor to Australia and New Zealand 1994-95
Overseas teams played for: Pretoria Police, South Africa 1987-88
Career highlights to date: '5-10 v Australia 1997' (*In one-day match against the Australian tourists at Worcester*)
Cricketers particularly admired: Mark Scott, George Batty, Peter Kippax
Other sports followed: Football, American football
Injuries: Out for two weeks with a side strain
Relaxations: Golf
Extras: Scored century (147*) v Northamptonshire at Northampton 2002, in the process sharing with Stephen Peters (146) in a record fourth-wicket partnership for

Worcestershire in matches against Northamptonshire (239). Scored century (120) v Nottinghamshire at Trent Bridge 2002, in the process sharing with Steve Rhodes (124) in a new record seventh-wicket partnership for Worcestershire (256). Recorded career best C&G/NatWest score (80) v Yorkshire at Worcester 2003, winning Man of the Match award. Worcestershire One-Day Player of the Year 2003

Opinions on cricket: 'Two overseas players will only work and improve county cricket if they are of the highest quality and committed to the county they are playing for!'

Best batting: 157 Worcestershire v Somerset, Worcester 1991

Best bowling: 5-20 Worcestershire v Gloucestershire, Worcester 1998

2003 Season

	M	Inns	NO	Runs	HS	Avge	100s	50s	Ct	St	O	M	Runs	Wkts	Avge	Best	5wI	10wM
Test																		
All First	4	7	0	164	61	23.42	-	2	2	-	39	6	142	4	35.50	2-18	-	-
1-day Int																		
C & G	5	4	1	148	80	49.33	-	2	4	-	21	2	103	4	25.75	2-42	-	
NCL	16	13	1	205	32	17.08	-	-	3	-	80.2	3	375	17	22.05	5-36	1	
Twenty20	5	5	2	56	16 *	18.66	-	-	2	-	12	0	89	4	22.25	2-14	-	

Career Performances

	M	Inns	NO	Runs	HS	Avge	100s	50s	Ct	St	Balls	Runs	Wkts	Avge	Best	5wI	10wM
Test																	
All First	214	346	41	10003	157	32.79	14	54	151	-	7011	4111	131	31.38	5-20	2	-
1-day Int																	
C & G	35	30	3	628	80	23.25	-	3	17	-	538	456	14	32.57	3-14	-	
NCL	204	171	25	3016	70 *	20.65	-	12	87	-	2804	2273	108	21.04	5-9	2	
Twenty20	5	5	2	56	16 *	18.66	-	-	2	-	72	89	4	22.25	2-14	-	

LEHMANN, D. S.   Yorkshire

Name: <u>Darren</u> Scott Lehmann
Role: Left-hand bat, slow left-arm bowler
Born: 5 February 1970, Gawler, South Australia
Nickname: Boof
Height: 5ft 11in   **Weight:** 14st 2lbs
County debut: 1997
County cap: 1997
Test debut: 1997-98
Tests: 14
One-Day Internationals: 100
1000 runs in a season: 4
1st-Class 50s: 89

1st-Class 100s: 56
1st-Class 200s: 8
1st-Class catches: 117
One-Day 100s: 11
Place in batting averages: (2002 10th av. 66.82)
Strike rate: (career 84.43)
Marital status: Married (to Craig White's sister)
Off-season: Playing for South Australia and Australia
Overseas tours: Australia to Sri Lanka (Singer World Series) 1996-97, to New Zealand (one-day series) 1997-98, to Sharjah (Coca-Cola Cup) 1997-98, to India 1997-98, to Pakistan 1998-99, to Bangladesh (Wills International Cup) 1998-99, to West Indies 1998-99 (one-day series), to UK, Ireland and

Holland (World Cup) 1999, to Sri Lanka 1999-2000 (one-day series), to Zimbabwe 1999-2000 (one-day series), to India 2000-01 (one-day series), to South Africa 2001-02, to Sri Lanka (ICC Champions Trophy) 2002-03, to Africa (World Cup) 2002-03, to West Indies 2002-03
Overseas teams played for: Salisbury District CC (now Northern Districts), Adelaide; South Australia 1987-88 – 1989-90; Victoria 1990-91 – 1992-93; South Australia 1993-94 –
Other sports followed: Australian Football League (Adelaide Crows)
Relaxations: Golf, watching sport
Extras: Represented South Australia at all age groups. Scored 1128 runs (av. 57.50) in his first full Sheffield Shield season. Played in Australia's 1999 World Cup winning side, striking the winning runs in the final v Pakistan at Lord's. Scored 1142 runs at 63.44 (including seven centuries) in the 1999-2000 Australian season and was Pura Milk Cup Player of the Year. Was voted Interstate Cricketer of the Year 1999-2000 at the inaugural Allan Border Medal awards January 2000, also winning the award in 2000-01 and 2001-02. Won the EDS Walter Lawrence Trophy for the fastest first-class century of the 2000 season – 89 balls for Yorkshire v Kent at Canterbury. Top run-scorer in English first-class cricket 2000 with 1477 runs at 67.13. Scored a 44-ball 63 for South Australia v Western Australia at Adelaide 2000-01, in the process overtaking Dean Jones's total of 2122 runs to become the highest scoring batsman in Australian domestic one-day cricket. One of *Wisden*'s Five Cricketers of the Year 2001. Won three B&H Gold Awards in eight days 2001. Became only the fourth player to score a Roses match double century with his 288-ball 252 v Lancashire at Headingley 2001. His 103-ball 191, including 11 sixes, v Nottinghamshire at Scarborough in the Norwich Union League 2001 is the second highest score in the domestic one-day league, behind Alistair Brown's 203 for Surrey v Hampshire in 1997. Yorkshire Player of the Year 2001. Became the highest scoring batsman in Sheffield Shield/Pura Cup

history when he passed Jamie Siddons's career competition total of 10,643 runs v Victoria 2001-02. Scored 187 v Lancashire at Headingley 2002, in the process sharing with Anthony McGrath (165) in a record third-wicket partnership for Yorkshire at Headingley (317). Scored maiden Test century (160) in the second Test v West Indies at Port of Spain 2003. His international awards include Man of the Match in the CUB second final v England at Melbourne 1998-99 and in the VB Series v Sri Lanka at Perth 2002-03. ACB contract 2003-04. Vice-captain of Yorkshire 2001; captain of Yorkshire 2002, the first overseas player to be appointed to the office. Did not play for Yorkshire in 2003 but has returned for 2004. Captain of South Australia since 1998-99

Best batting: 255 South Australia v Queensland, Adelaide 1996-97

Best bowling: 4-42 Yorkshire v Kent, Maidstone 1998

Stop press: Selected for Australia's tour to Sri Lanka 2003-04

2003 Season (did not make any first-class or one-day appearances)

Career Performances

	M	Inns	NO	Runs	HS	Avge	100s	50s	Ct	St	Balls	Runs	Wkts	Avge	Best	5wI	10wM
Test	14	21	2	965	177	50.78	3	4	7	-	276	116	4	29.00	1-6	-	-
All First	221	375	26	19891	255	56.99	64	89	117	-	5573	2671	66	40.46	4-42	-	-
1-day Int	100	88	19	2714	119	39.33	4	14	20	-	1301	1041	37	28.13	3-16	-	
C & G	13	11	2	350	105	38.88	1	2	2	-	300	184	14	13.14	4-26	-	
NCL	65	65	8	2769	191	48.57	3	21	23	-	1267	930	36	25.83	3-31	-	
Twenty20																	

57. Born in Antigua, which Northants bowler
recorded his best Test bowling figures, 8-45, against England
at Bridgetown in April 1990?

LEWIS, J.   Gloucestershire

Name: Jonathan (<u>Jon</u>) Lewis
Role: Right-hand bat, right-arm
fast-medium bowler
Born: 26 August 1975, Aylesbury
Height: 6ft 3in   **Weight:** 14st
Nickname: Lewy, JJ, King Black
County debut: 1995
County cap: 1998
50 wickets in a season: 4
1st-Class 50s: 3
1st-Class 5 w. in innings: 20
1st-Class 10 w. in match: 3
1st-Class catches: 28
Place in batting averages: 234th av. 17.71
(2002 267th av. 14.36)
Place in bowling averages: 25th av. 24.32
(2002 116th av. 37.77)
Strike rate: 44.70 (career 53.07)
Parents: John and Jane
Marital status: Engaged
Education: Churchfields School, Swindon; Swindon College
Qualifications: 9 GCSEs, BTEC in Leisure and Hospitality, Level III coach
Off-season: 'Coaching and playing (Randwick-Petersham, Sydney)'
Overseas tours: Bath Schools to New South Wales 1993; England A to West Indies 2000-01
Overseas teams played for: Marist, Christchurch, New Zealand 1994-95; Richmond City, Melbourne 1995-96; Wanderers, Johannesburg 1996-98; Techs CC, Cape Town 1998-99; Randwick-Petersham, Sydney 2003-04
Career highlights to date: 'C&G Trophy win v Worcestershire 2003; England A tour to West Indies'
Cricket moments to forget: 'Any injury'
Cricket superstitions: 'I always get a haircut if I go for a gallon'
Cricketers particularly admired: Courtney Walsh, Jack Russell, Jonty Rhodes
Young players to look out for: Alex Gidman
Other sports played: Golf (7 handicap), football (Bristol North West FC)
Other sports followed: Football (Swindon Town FC)
Favourite band: Brand New Heavies
Relaxations: Movies
Extras: Was on Northamptonshire staff in 1994 but made no first-team appearance.
His 62 v Worcestershire at Cheltenham 1999 is the highest score by a Gloucestershire
No. 11. Took Championship hat-trick (Gallian, Afzaal and Morris) v Nottinghamshire

at Trent Bridge 2000. Leading first-class wicket-taker among English bowlers in 2000 with 72 wickets (av. 20.91). Gloucestershire Player of the Year 2000

Opinions on cricket: 'County cricket is hard work – we need a few less games. But most of all we need better practice facilities and playing surfaces. More time to prepare will make English cricketers better players. County cricket is not to blame for poor England performances!'

Best batting: 62 Gloucestershire v Worcestershire, Cheltenham 1999
Best bowling: 8-95 Gloucestershire v Zimbabweans, Gloucester 2000

2003 Season

	M	Inns	NO	Runs	HS	Avge	100s	50s	Ct	St	O	M	Runs	Wkts	Avge	Best	5wI	10wM
Test																		
All First	14	18	4	248	47	17.71	-	-	3	-	551.2	142	1800	74	24.32	7-117	5	1
1-day Int																		
C & G	2	1	1	9	9 *	-	-	-	-	-	16	4	40	2	20.00	2-28	-	
NCL	8	2	0	5	5	2.50	-	-	3	-	65	1	338	7	48.28	2-46	-	
Twenty20	4	0	0	0	0	-	-	-	-	-	16	0	126	7	18.00	2-25	-	

Career Performances

	M	Inns	NO	Runs	HS	Avge	100s	50s	Ct	St	Balls	Runs	Wkts	Avge	Best	5wI	10wM
Test																	
All First	116	170	35	1727	62	12.79	-	3	28	-	21868	11087	412	26.91	8-95	20	3
1-day Int																	
C & G	10	6	4	23	9 *	11.50	-	-	6	-	526	301	11	27.36	3-27	-	
NCL	70	42	16	277	27 *	10.65	-	-	12	-	2950	2395	74	32.36	4-22	-	
Twenty20	4	0	0	0	0	-	-	-	-	-	96	126	7	18.00	2-25	-	

LEWIS, J. J. B.   Durham

Name: Jonathan (Jon) James Benjamin Lewis
Role: Right-hand bat, county captain
Born: 21 May 1970, Isleworth, Middlesex
Height: 5ft 9in **Weight:** 12st
Nickname: Judge, JJ
County debut: 1990 (Essex), 1997 (Durham)
County cap: 1994 (Essex), 1998 (Durham)
1000 runs in a season: 4
1st-Class 50s: 57
1st-Class 100s: 14
1st-Class 200s: 1
1st-Class catches: 97
One-Day 100s: 1
Place in batting averages: 95th av. 37.12 (2002 198th av. 23.64)

Strike rate: (career 120.00)
Parents: Ted and Nina
Wife and date of marriage: Fiona,
6 July 1999
Family links with cricket: Father played
county schools. Uncle is a lifelong Somerset
supporter. Sister is right-arm medium-fast
bowler for Cisco
Education: King Edward VI School,
Chelmsford; Roehampton Institute of
Higher Education
Qualifications: 5 O-levels, 3 A-levels, BSc
(Hons) Sports Science, NCA Senior Coach
Off-season: 'In South Africa and moving into
new house'
Overseas tours: Durham to Cape Town 2002
Overseas teams played for: Old Hararians,
Zimbabwe 1991-92; Taita District, New

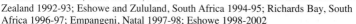

Zealand 1992-93; Eshowe and Zululand, South Africa 1994-95; Richards Bay, South
Africa 1996-97; Empangeni, Natal 1997-98; Eshowe 1998-2002
Cricketers particularly admired: John Childs, Greg Matthews, Alan Walker,
Shane Warne
Young players to look out for: 'Plenty of talent about. We'll see who wants it most'
Other sports followed: Soccer (West Ham United), rugby (Newcastle Falcons), 'most
sports really'
Relaxations: Sleep
Extras: Hit century (116*) on first-class debut in Essex's final Championship match
of the 1990 season, v Surrey at The Oval. Joined Durham for the 1997 season. Scored
a double century on his debut for Durham (210* v Oxford University at The Parks
1997), placing him in a small club, alongside Peter Bowler and Neil Taylor, of players
who have scored centuries on debut for two different counties. Scored 112 v
Nottinghamshire at Riverside 2001, in the process sharing in Durham's highest
Championship partnership for any wicket (258) with Martin Love. Became Durham's
leading first-class run-scorer when he passed John Morris's record of 5670 runs during
his 124 v Yorkshire at Headingley 2003. Durham Player of the Year and Batsman of
the Year 2003. Captain of Durham since the latter stages of the 2000 season. Granted a
benefit for 2004
Opinions on cricket: 'Central contracts appear to be working well, but I thought the
emphasis was going to be on young fast bowlers.'
Best batting: 210* Durham v Oxford University, The Parks 1997
Best bowling: 1-73 Durham v Surrey, Riverside 1998

2003 Season

	M	Inns	NO	Runs	HS	Avge	100s	50s	Ct	St	O	M	Runs	Wkts	Avge	Best	5wI	10wM
Test																		
All First	18	34	2	1188	124	37.12	1	11	5	-								
1-day Int																		
C & G	2	1	0	0	0	0.00	-	-	-	-								
NCL	17	15	4	226	43	20.54	-	-	4	-								
Twenty20	5	5	2	41	24 *	13.66	-	-	5	-								

Career Performances

	M	Inns	NO	Runs	HS	Avge	100s	50s	Ct	St	Balls	Runs	Wkts	Avge	Best	5wI	10wM
Test																	
All First	169	301	24	9214	210 *	33.26	15	57	97	-	120	121	1	121.00	1-73	-	-
1-day Int																	
C & G	19	18	4	297	65 *	21.21	-	1	1	-							
NCL	146	129	30	2820	102	28.48	1	15	25	-	8	35	0	-	-	-	
Twenty20	5	5	2	41	24 *	13.66	-	-	5	-							

LEWRY, J. D. Sussex

Name: <u>Jason</u> David Lewry
Role: Left-hand bat, left-arm
fast-medium bowler
Born: 2 April 1971, Worthing
Height: 6ft 3in **Weight:** 14st 7lbs
('depending on time of year!')
Nickname: Lewie, Urco
County debut: 1994
County cap: 1996
Benefit: 2002
50 wickets in a season: 4
1st-Class 50s: 1
1st-Class 5 w. in innings: 24
1st-Class 10 w. in match: 4
1st-Class catches: 26
Place in batting averages: 232nd av. 17.91
(2002 299th av. 9.10)
Place in bowling averages: 39th av. 26.61
(2002 113th av. 37.18)
Strike rate: 48.19 (career 49.14)
Parents: David and Veronica
Wife and date of marriage: Naomi Madeleine, 18 August 1997

Children: William, 14 February 1998; Louis, 20 November 2000
Family links with cricket: Father coaches
Education: Durrington High School, Worthing; Worthing Sixth Form College
Qualifications: 6 O-levels, 3 GCSEs, City and Guilds, NCA Award
Career outside cricket: 'Still looking, but with more urgency with each passing year!'
Overseas tours: Goring CC to Isle of Wight 1992, 1993; England A to Zimbabwe and South Africa 1998-99
Career highlights to date: 'Seven wickets in 14 balls v Hampshire at Hove 2001. The second most (most by a seamer) outstanding spell of wicket-taking in first-class cricket' (*After Pat Pocock's seven in 11 for Surrey v Sussex at Eastbourne in 1972*)
Cricket moments to forget: 'King pair, Eastbourne 1995'
Cricketers particularly admired: David Gower, Martin Andrews
Other sports played: Golf, squash; darts, pool ('anything you can do in a pub')
Other sports followed: Football (West Ham United)
Relaxations: Golf, pub games, films
Extras: His 8-106 v Leicestershire at Hove 2003 included a spell of 5-6 in 25 balls
Opinions on cricket: 'A return to "English county cricket" would be good.'
Best batting: 70 Sussex v Essex, Colchester 2003
Best bowling: 8-106 Sussex v Leicestershire, Hove 2003

2003 Season

	M	Inns	NO	Runs	HS	Avge	100s	50s	Ct	St	O	M	Runs	Wkts	Avge	Best	5wI	10wM
Test																		
All First	12	15	3	215	70	17.91	-	1	4	-	337.2	73	1118	42	26.61	8-106	3	1
1-day Int																		
C & G																		
NCL	5	3	0	21	11	7.00	-	-	2	-	39	4	182	6	30.33	2-27	-	
Twenty20	5	1	0	1	1	1.00	-	-	-	-	16.5	0	139	9	15.44	3-34	-	

Career Performances

	M	Inns	NO	Runs	HS	Avge	100s	50s	Ct	St	Balls	Runs	Wkts	Avge	Best	5wI	10wM
Test																	
All First	113	156	35	1271	70	10.50	-	1	26	-	19902	10834	405	26.75	8-106	24	4
1-day Int																	
C & G	8	5	3	35	16	17.50	-	-	-	-	504	330	15	22.00	4-42	-	
NCL	39	22	7	65	11	4.33	-	-	9	-	1644	1320	51	25.88	4-29	-	
Twenty20	5	1	0	1	1	1.00	-	-	-	-	101	139	9	15.44	3-34	-	

LIDDLE, C. J.   Leicestershire

Name: Christopher (<u>Chris</u>) John Liddle
Role: Right-hand bat, left-arm fast bowler
Born: 1 February 1984, Middlesbrough
Weight: 6ft 5in **Weight:** 12st 7lbs
Nickname: Lidz
County debut: No first-team appearance
Parents: Patricia and John
Marital status: Single
Education: Nunthorpe School; Teesside Tertiary College
Qualifications: 9 GCSEs, trained instrumentation engineer, Level 1 coaching
Career outside cricket: Apprentice instrument engineer
Off-season: 'Training or hopefully playing abroad'
Career highlights to date: 'Signing professional for Leicestershire'
Cricket superstitions: 'Right bowling boot on first for bowling; left batting pad on first for batting'
Cricketers particularly admired: Brett Lee
Young players to look out for: Brenton Parchment
Other sports played: Football
Other sports followed: Football ('whoever is winning')
Relaxations: 'Socialising; going to the gym'
Extras: Yorkshire area Bowler of the Year 2001-02

LIPTROT, C. G.   Worcestershire

Name: <u>Christopher</u> George Liptrot
Role: Left-hand bat, right-arm fast-medium bowler
Born: 13 February 1980, Wigan
Height: 6ft 3in **Weight:** 13st 9lbs
Nickname: Lippy
County debut: 1999
County colours: 2002
1st-Class 50s: 1
1st-Class 5 w. in innings: 2
1st-Class catches: 11
Strike rate: 40.00 (career 56.50)

Parents: Brian and Susan
Marital status: Single
Family links with cricket: 'My father and brother played local league cricket in Wigan'
Education: The Deanery High School, Wigan
Qualifications: 9 GCSEs
Overseas tours: Northwest Select XI to South Africa 1998; Forest Nomads to Thailand 2000
Overseas teams played for: Sunshine Coast, Brisbane 1999-2000
Career highlights to date: 'Taking five wickets [5-51] on home debut against Surrey 1999'
Cricketers particularly admired: Glenn McGrath, Graeme Hick
Young players to look out for: Kabir Ali
Other sports played: Football, rugby
Other sports followed: Football (Everton FC), rugby league (Wigan Warriors)
Relaxations: Music, spending time with friends
Extras: Represented England U19 v Australia U19 1999. NBC Denis Compton Award 1999. Worcestershire scholarship to Perth 2001. Worcestershire Supporters' Association Uncapped Player of the Year 2001. Retired at the end of the 2003 season because of a persistent back problem
Best batting: 61 Worcestershire v Warwickshire, Edgbaston 1999
Best bowling: 6-44 Worcestershire v Warwickshire, Worcester 2000

2003 Season

	M	Inns	NO	Runs	HS	Avge	100s	50s	Ct	St	O	M	Runs	Wkts	Avge	Best	5wI	10wM
Test																		
All First	1	0	0	0	0	-	-	-	2	-	20	8	47	3	15.66	3-47	-	-
1-day Int																		
C & G																		
NCL	1	0	0	0	0	-	-	-	-	-	7	0	39	0	-	-	-	-
Twenty20	4	3	0	4	4	1.33	-	-	-	-	16	0	114	5	22.80	3-32	-	

Career Performances

	M	Inns	NO	Runs	HS	Avge	100s	50s	Ct	St	Balls	Runs	Wkts	Avge	Best	5wI	10wM
Test																	
All First	30	36	11	303	61	12.12	-	1	11	-	3899	2212	69	32.05	6-44	2	-
1-day Int																	
C & G	1	1	1	2	2 *	-	-	-	-	-	30	12	2	6.00	2-12	-	
NCL	7	3	3	18	15 *	-	-	-	1	-	205	215	6	35.83	3-44	-	
Twenty20	4	3	0	4	4	1.33	-	-	-	-	96	114	5	22.80	3-32	-	

LOGAN, R. J.   Nottinghamshire

Name: <u>Richard</u> James Logan
Role: Right-hand bat, right-arm fast bowler
Born: 28 January 1980, Cannock
Height: 6ft 1in   **Weight:** 14st
Nickname: Bungle
County debut: 1999 (Northants),
2001 (Notts)
1st-Class 5 w. in innings: 4
1st-Class catches: 11
One-Day 5 w. in innings: 2
Place in batting averages: (2002 297th
av. 9.53)
Place in bowling averages: (2002 96th
av. 34.02)
Strike rate: (career 53.68)
Parents: Margaret and Robert
Marital status: Single
Family links with cricket: 'Dad played local
cricket for Cannock'
Education: Wolverhampton Grammar School
Qualifications: 11 GCSEs, 1 A-level
Off-season: 'Playing hockey and cricket abroad'
Overseas tours: England U17 to Bermuda (International Youth Tournament) 1997;
England U19 to South Africa (including U19 World Cup) 1997-98, to New Zealand
1998-99
Overseas teams played for: St George, Sydney 1999-2000; Lancaster Park, New
Zealand; Rovers, Durban; Northerns Goodwood, Cape Town
Career highlights to date: 'Winning junior World Cup'
Cricketers particularly admired: Malcolm Marshall, Dennis Lillee
Young players to look out for: Kevin Pietersen
Other sports played: Hockey
Other sports followed: Football (Wolverhampton Wanderers)
Injuries: Out for three weeks at start of 2003 season with a bruised bone in foot
Relaxations: 'Spending time with my mates. Training'
Extras: Played for Staffordshire at every level from U11 to U19, and as captain from
U13 to U17. Played for Midlands U14 and U15 (both as captain) and HMC Schools
U15. 1995 *Daily Telegraph*/Lombard U15 Midlands Bowler and Batsman of the Year.
Played for Northamptonshire U17 and U19 national champions in 1997. Has played
for England U15, U17 and U19, including v Australia U19 1999. Left
Northamptonshire in the 2000-01 off-season and joined Nottinghamshire for 2001.
C&G Man of the Match award for his 5-24 v Suffolk at Mildenhall 2001; it was his

maiden one-day five-wicket return. Took 5-26 v Lancashire at Trent Bridge in the Twenty20 2003

Opinions on cricket: 'I still believe we play too much cricket – therefore recovery is limited and quality suffers. The Twenty20 competition is fantastic. It's great to play in and by the looks of the crowds it's great to watch.'

Best batting: 37* Nottinghamshire v Hampshire, Trent Bridge 2001

Best bowling: 6-93 Nottinghamshire v Derbyshire, Trent Bridge 2001

2003 Season

	M	Inns	NO	Runs	HS		Avge	100s	50s	Ct	St	O	M	Runs	Wkts	Avge	Best	5wI	10wM
Test																			
All First	3	4	2	23	13	*	11.50	-	-	-	-	28	2	173	0	-		-	-
1-day Int																			
C & G	1	1	0	9	9		9.00	-	-	-	-	10	1	56	1	56.00	1-56	-	
NCL	12	4	1	27	13		9.00	-	-	4	-	81	7	436	18	24.22	4-32	-	
Twenty20	5	3	1	9	9		4.50	-	-	-	-	18.1	0	111	7	15.85	5-26	1	

Career Performances

	M	Inns	NO	Runs	HS		Avge	100s	50s	Ct	St	Balls	Runs	Wkts	Avge	Best	5wI	10wM
Test																		
All First	34	48	9	380	37	*	9.74	-	-	11	-	5207	3370	97	34.74	6-93	4	-
1-day Int																		
C & G	3	2	0	9	9		4.50	-	-	1	-	180	109	7	15.57	5-24	1	
NCL	35	18	5	134	24		10.30	-	-	12	-	1363	1398	37	37.78	4-32	-	
Twenty20	5	3	1	9	9		4.50	-	-	-	-	109	111	7	15.85	5-26	1	

58. Born in Oldham, who became Glamorgan's youngest capped player in 1987, a year before he made his Test debut against West Indies?

LOUDON, A. G. R.　　　　　　　　　　Kent

Name: <u>Alexander</u> Guy Rushworth Loudon
Role: Right-hand bat, right-arm
off-spin bowler
Born: 6 September 1980, London
Height: 6ft 3in **Weight:** 14st 8lbs
Nickname: Noisy, Minor, A-Lo, Minotaur
County debut: 2002 (one-day),
2003 (first-class)
1st-Class 50s: 1
1st-Class 100s: 1
1st-Class catches: 10
Place in batting averages: 62nd av. 42.70
Strike rate: 144.50 (career 80.22)
Parents: Jane and James
Marital status: Single
Family links with cricket: Brother and
father played for Hampshire 2nd XI
Education: Eton College; Durham University
Qualifications: 9 GCSEs, 1 AO-level, 3 A-levels, 2.1 degree, ECB Level 1 coaching
Career outside cricket: 'Under negotiation!'
Off-season: 'In LA, Mumbai and Sydney'
Overseas tours: Kent U11 to Holland 1990; Eton College to South Africa 1995;
England U19 to Malaysia and (U19 World Cup) Sri Lanka 1999-2000 (captain); Kent
to South Africa 2002
Career highlights to date: '172 v Durham at Racecourse'
Cricket moments to forget: 'Running out my brother at school'
Cricket superstitions: 'Try to avoid them!'
Cricketers particularly admired: Steve Waugh, Michael Atherton, Muttiah
Muralitharan
Young players to look out for: James Loudon ('aka J-Lo')
Other sports played: Golf, squash, rackets, tennis
Other sports followed: Rugby (England), football (Man Utd)
Favourite band: U2
Relaxations: 'Eating, sleeping, Sky Sports and MTV'
Extras: Captained England U15 in U15 World Cup 1996 and England U19 in U19
World Cup 1999-2000. Len Newbery Award for Best Schools Cricketer 1999. NBC
Denis Compton Award for the most promising young Kent player 1999. Silk Trophy
batting award 1999. Played for Durham University CCE 2001, 2002 and 2003, and
was captain of Durham's BUSA winning side 2003. Played for the Eton Ramblers
Cricketer Cup winning side 2001, scoring 64 in the final. Played for Kent Board XI in
the C&G 2002. Scored maiden first-class century (172) for DUCCE v Durham at

Durham 2003. Represented British Universities v India A 2003. Scored 63 v South Africans at Canterbury 2003

Opinions on cricket: 'The marketing drive in 2003 has been very successful in my humble opinion! More of the same, plus more, as long as it doesn't affect onfield performances in a negative way.'

Best batting: 172 DUCCE v Durham, Durham 2003

Best bowling: 3-86 DUCCE v Worcestershire, Worcester 2001

2003 Season

	M	Inns	NO	Runs	HS	Avge	100s	50s	Ct	St	O	M	Runs	Wkts	Avge	Best	5wI	10wM
Test																		
All First	6	11	1	427	172	42.70	1	1	4	-	48.1	2	276	2	138.00	1-52	-	-
1-day Int																		
C & G																			
NCL	1	1	0	0	0	0.00	-	-	-	-								
Twenty20																			

Career Performances

	M	Inns	NO	Runs	HS	Avge	100s	50s	Ct	St	Balls	Runs	Wkts	Avge	Best	5wI	10wM
Test																	
All First	11	18	1	523	172	30.76	1	1	10	-	722	552	9	61.33	3-86	-	-
1-day Int																	
C & G	1	1	0	53	53	53.00	-	1	-	-	6	4	0	-	-	-	
NCL	3	3	0	32	21	10.66	-	-	-	-							
Twenty20																		

---

59. F.T. and F.C. Mann were the first, but who became the second father-and-son England captaincy double at Headingley in 1988?

LOUW, J. Northamptonshire

Name: Johann Louw
Role: Right-hand bat, right-arm medium-fast bowler
Born: 12 April 1979, Cape Town, South Africa
County debut: No first-team appearance
1st-Class 50s: 3
1st-Class 5 w. in innings: 1
1st-Class catches: 12
Strike rate: (career 57.93)
Overseas teams played for:
Griqualand West 2000-01 – 2002-03; Eastern Province 2003-04 –
Extras: Played as professional for Heywood in the Central Lancashire League 2001, scoring 1026 runs (av. 42.75) and taking 75 wickets (av. 19.30). Man of the Match for Griqualand West v Northerns at Kimberley in the Standard Bank Cup 2002-03 (4-25). Played as professional for the East Lancs side that won the Lancashire League 2003, scoring 1127 league runs (av. 51.20), taking 61 league wickets (av. 17.00) and striking 76 sixes in all matches for the club. Has joined Northamptonshire as an overseas player for 2004
Best batting: 86* Griqualand West v KwaZulu-Natal, Kimberley 2001-02
Best bowling: 6-108 Griqualand West v Border, East London 2002-03
Stop press: Scored maiden first-class century (124) and had match figures of 5-131 v Boland at Port Elizabeth in the SuperSport Series 2003-04, winning Man of the Match award. Man of the Match v North West at Potchefstroom in the Standard Bank Cup 2003-04

2003 Season (did not make any first-class or one-day appearances)

Career Performances

	M	Inns	NO	Runs	HS	Avge	100s	50s	Ct	St	Balls	Runs	Wkts	Avge	Best	5wI	10wM
Test																	
All First	16	28	3	531	86*	21.24	-	3	12	-	2723	1436	47	30.55	6-108	1	-
1-day Int																	
C & G																		
NCL																		
Twenty20																		

LOVE, M. L.   Durham

Name: <u>Martin</u> Lloyd Love
Role: Right-hand bat
Born: 30 March 1974, Mundubbera, Queensland, Australia
Height: 6ft **Weight:** 13st
Nickname: Handles
County debut: 2001
County cap: 2001
Test debut: 2002-03
Tests: 5
1000 runs in a season: 1
1st-Class 50s: 54
1st-Class 100s: 20
1st-Class 200s: 7
1st-Class catches: 176
Place in batting averages: 12th av. 59.84
(2002 4th av. 82.28)
Strike rate: (career 6.00)
Parents: Ormond and Evelyn
Wife: Deborah

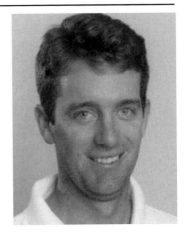

Education: Toowoomba Grammar School; University of Queensland
Qualifications: Bachelor of Physiotherapy, Level 2 coach
Career outside cricket: Physiotherapist
Off-season: Playing for Queensland Bulls
Overseas tours: Australia U19 to New Zealand 1992-93; Young Australia (Australia A) to England and Netherlands 1995; Australia to West Indies 2002-03
Overseas teams played for: Queensland Bulls 1992-93 –
Career highlights to date: 'Member of Queensland's first ever Sheffield Shield winning team 1994-95'
Cricket moments to forget: 'Any duck'
Cricket superstitions: 'Left pad on first'
Cricketers particularly admired: Allan Border
Young players to look out for: Gordon Muchall
Other sports played: Golf
Other sports followed: AFL (Brisbane Lions), rugby union (Queensland Reds)
Relaxations: 'Home renovation'
Extras: Represented Queensland U17 (1990-91) and U19 (1991-93). Made debut for Queensland in 1992-93 Sheffield Shield final v New South Wales. Shared with Stuart Law in record third-wicket partnership for Queensland (326), v Tasmania at Brisbane 1994-95. Scored century (146) in 1994-95 Sheffield Shield final v South Australia at Brisbane. Shared with Matthew Hayden in record second-wicket partnership for

Queensland (368*), v Tasmania at Hobart 1995-96. Scored century (100) in 1999-2000 Pura Milk Cup final v Victoria at Albion. Won the Ian Healy Trophy for Queensland Player of the Year 2000-01. Joined Durham as overseas player in 2001. Scored his first century for Durham (149*) v Nottinghamshire at Riverside 2001, in the process sharing in Durham's highest Championship partnership for any wicket (258) with Jon Lewis. Leading run-scorer in the Pura Cup 2001-02 with 1108 (av. 65.18). Made the highest ever individual score by a Durham batsman (251) v Middlesex at Lord's 2002. Scored two double centuries against the England touring side 2002-03 – 250 for Queensland at Brisbane and 201* for Australia A at Hobart. Made Test debut in the fourth Test v England at Melbourne 2002-03, scoring 62* in Australia's first innings. Named State Player of the Year at the 2003 Allan Border Medal awards. Scored maiden Test century (100*) in the second Test v Bangladesh at Cairns 2003. Set a new record for the highest individual score made at the Riverside ground (273), v Hampshire 2003, breaking his own record for the highest score made by a Durham batsman. ACB contract 2003-04. Left Durham at the end of the 2003 season
Opinions on cricket: 'Young players need to be given more responsibility earlier in their careers to fully develop their potential.'
Best batting: 273 Durham v Hampshire, Riverside 2003
Best bowling: 1-5 Queensland v Western Australia, Brisbane 1997-98
Stop press: Scored 300* v Victoria at Melbourne 2003-04, becoming the first player to score a first-class triple century for Queensland

2003 Season

	M	Inns	NO	Runs	HS	Avge	100s	50s	Ct	St	O	M	Runs	Wkts	Avge	Best	5wI	10wM
Test																		
All First	7	13	0	778	273	59.84	1	4	8	-								
1-day Int																		
C & G	1	0	0	0	0	-	-	-	-	-								
NCL	10	10	0	288	55	28.80	-	2	2	-								
Twenty20	3	3	0	62	51	20.66	-	1	2	-								

Career Performances

	M	Inns	NO	Runs	HS	Avge	100s	50s	Ct	St	Balls	Runs	Wkts	Avge	Best	5wI	10wM
Test	5	8	3	233	100 *	46.60	1	1	7	-							
All First	148	255	23	11588	273	49.94	27	54	176	-	6	5	1	5.00	1-5	-	-
1-day Int																	
C & G	5	4	0	132	51	33.00	-	1	1	-							
NCL	26	26	1	769	89	30.76	-	4	12	-	12	7	0	-		-	-
Twenty20	3	3	0	62	51	20.66	-	1	2	-							

LOWE, J. A.   Durham

Name: <u>James</u> Adam Lowe
Role: Right-hand bat, right-arm
off-spin bowler
Born: 4 November 1982, Bury St Edmunds
Height: 6ft 2in **Weight:** 14st 10lbs
Nickname: Lowey, J-Lo
County debut: 2003
1st-Class 50s: 1
Parents: Jim and Pat
Marital status: Single
Family links with cricket: 'Dad played for
Northallerton CC and is a qualified coach'
Education: Northallerton College
Qualifications: Coaching Level 2
Career outside cricket: 'Worked in local
leisure centre. Qualified lifeguard'
Off-season: 'In Perth with Paul Terry'
Career highlights to date: '80 on my first-
class debut v Hampshire'

Cricketers particularly admired: Ritchie Storr, Paul Collingwood, Danny Law
Young players to look out for: Liam Plunkett, Graham Onions
Other sports played: Football ('played for school and town as a youngster')
Other sports followed: Football (Middlesbrough)
Favourite band: Stone Roses
Relaxations: Eating out; watching Middlesbrough
Extras: Scored 80 on first-class debut v Hampshire at West End 2003
Opinions on cricket: 'Too many EU players.'
Best batting: 80 Durham v Hampshire, West End 2003

2003 Season

	M	Inns	NO	Runs	HS	Avge	100s	50s	Ct	St	O	M	Runs	Wkts	Avge	Best	5wI	10wM
Test																		
All First	1	2	0	80	80	40.00	-	1	-	-								
1-day Int																		
C & G																		
NCL																		
Twenty20																		

Career Performances

	M	Inns	NO	Runs	HS	Avge	100s	50s	Ct	St	Balls	Runs	Wkts	Avge	Best	5wI	10wM
Test																	
All First	1	2	0	80	80	40.00	-	1	-	-							
1-day Int																	
C & G																	
NCL																	
Twenty20																	

LOYE, M. B. Lancashire

Name: <u>Malachy</u> Bernard Loye
Role: Right-hand bat, off-spin bowler,
occasional wicket-keeper
Born: 27 September 1972, Northampton
Height: 6ft 3in **Weight:** 14st
Nickname: Mal, Chairman, Jacko,
Shermenator
County debut: 1991 (Northamptonshire),
2003 (Lancashire)
County cap: 1994 (Northamptonshire),
2003 (Lancashire)
1000 runs in a season: 3
1st-Class 50s: 37
1st-Class 100s: 24
1st-Class 200s: 1
1st-Class 300s: 1
1st-Class catches: 79
One-Day 100s: 6
Place in batting averages: 27th av. 50.57 (2002 102nd av. 36.57)
Strike rate: 24.00 (career 49.00)
Parents: Patrick and Anne
Marital status: Single
Family links with cricket: Father and brother played for Cogenhoe CC
in Northampton
Education: Moulton Comprehensive School
Qualifications: GCSEs, 'numerous coaching certificates'
Overseas tours: England U18 to Canada (International Youth Tournament) 1991;
England U19 to Pakistan 1991-92; England A to South Africa 1993-94, to Zimbabwe
and South Africa 1998-99; Northamptonshire to Cape Town 1993, to Zimbabwe 1995,
1998, to Johannesburg 1996, to Grenada 2001, 2002
Overseas teams played for: Riccarton, Christchurch, New Zealand 1992-95; Onslow,

Wellington, New Zealand 1995-96; North Perth, Australia 1997-98; Claremont, Perth 2001

Career highlights to date: 'PCA Player of the Year 1998'

Cricket moments to forget: 'Not being picked for 1995 and 1996 cup finals'

Cricket superstitions: 'None'

Cricketers particularly admired: Wayne Larkins, Gordon Greenidge, Curtly Ambrose, Devon Malcolm, Peter Carlstein, David Capel

Young players to look out for: Monty Panesar

Other sports followed: Football (Liverpool, Northampton Town), rugby union (Ireland), boxing

Relaxations: 'Playing the guitar, swimming, singing, reading. Having the odd large night out!'

Extras: Played for England YC v Australia YC 1991 and for England U19 v Sri Lanka U19 1992. PCA Young Player of the Year and Whittingdale Young Player of the Year 1993. Shared in a county then record opening stand of 372 with Richard Montgomerie as Northamptonshire followed on v Yorkshire at Northampton 1996. His 322* v Glamorgan at Northampton 1998 was the highest individual first-class score for the county until surpassed in 2001 by Mike Hussey's 329*; during his innings, Loye put on 401 with David Ripley, setting a new fifth-wicket record for first-class cricket in England. PCA Player of the Year 1998. Scored century in each innings (105/104*) v Nottinghamshire at Northampton 2002. Left Northamptonshire at the end of the 2002 season and joined Lancashire for 2003. Scored century (126) on Championship debut for Lancashire v Surrey at The Oval 2003 and another (113) in the next match v Nottinghamshire at Old Trafford to become the first batsman to score centuries in his first two matches for the county. C&G Man of the Match award for his 74 v Middlesex in the quarter-final at Old Trafford 2003

Opinions on cricket: 'Divisional system should be two up/two down, otherwise teams can have an ordinary season yet still get promoted.'

Best batting: 322* Northamptonshire v Glamorgan, Northampton 1998

Best bowling: 1-8 Lancashire v Kent, Blackpool 2003

2003 Season

	M	Inns	NO	Runs	HS	Avge	100s	50s	Ct	St	O	M	Runs	Wkts	Avge	Best	5wI	10wM
Test																		
All First	15	22	1	1062	144	50.57	5	2	4	-	4	0	16	1	16.00	1-8	-	-
1-day Int																		
C & G	4	4	2	197	116 *	98.50	1	1	1	-								
NCL	18	18	3	619	104 *	41.26	1	5	12	-								
Twenty20	5	5	0	75	45	15.00	-	-	1	-								

Career Performances

	M	Inns	NO	Runs	HS	Avge	100s	50s	Ct	St	Balls	Runs	Wkts	Avge	Best	5wl	10wM
Test																	
All First	166	265	24	9411	322 *	39.04	26	37	79	-	49	60	1	60.00	1-8	-	-
1-day Int																	
C & G	25	24	6	724	124 *	40.22	2	2	6	-							
NCL	138	134	14	3998	122	33.31	4	27	35	-							
Twenty20	5	5	0	75	45	15.00	-	-	1	-							

LUCAS, D. S. Nottinghamshire

Name: David Scott Lucas
Role: Right-hand bat, left-arm
medium-fast bowler
Born: 19 August 1978, Nottingham
Height: 6ft 3in **Weight:** 13st 3lbs
Nickname: Muke, Lukey
County debut: 1999
1st-Class 5 w. in innings: 1
1st-Class catches: 3
Strike rate: (career 60.30)
Parents: Mary and Terry
Marital status: With partner
Education: Djanogly City Technology
College, Nottingham
Qualifications: 6 GCSEs, pass in Computer-
Aided Design
Overseas tours: England (Indoor) to
Australia (Indoor Cricket World Cup) 1998
Overseas teams played for: Bankstown-Canterbury Bulldogs, Sydney 1996-97;
Wanneroo, Perth 2001-02
Career highlights to date: 'Getting Man of the Match against Derbyshire in a
close fixture'
Cricket superstitions: 'Always walk back to the left of my mark when bowling.
Always put left pad on first'
Cricketers particularly admired: Wasim Akram, Glenn McGrath, Steve Waugh,
Damien Martyn
Young players to look out for: Kevin Pietersen, Bilal Shafayat
Other sports played: Indoor cricket, football
Other sports followed: Football (Arsenal FC)
Relaxations: 'Food, cars, PS2, movies'
Extras: Won Yorkshire League with Rotherham in 1996. NBC Denis Compton Award
for the most promising young Nottinghamshire player 2000

Best batting: 49 Nottinghamshire v DUCCE, Trent Bridge 2002
Best bowling: 5-104 Nottinghamshire v Essex, Trent Bridge 1999

2003 Season

	M	Inns	NO	Runs	HS	Avge	100s	50s	Ct	St	O	M	Runs	Wkts	Avge	Best	5wI	10wM
Test																		
All First																		
1-day Int																		
C & G																		
NCL	3	1	0	16	16	16.00	-	-	-	-	27	1	155	8	19.37	3-52	-	
Twenty20																		

Career Performances

	M	Inns	NO	Runs	HS	Avge	100s	50s	Ct	St	Balls	Runs	Wkts	Avge	Best	5wI	10wM
Test																	
All First	22	28	8	436	49	21.80	-	-	3	-	3136	1909	52	36.71	5-104	1	-
1-day Int																	
C & G	1	1	1	14	14 *	-	-	-	-	-	36	40	0	-	-	-	-
NCL	26	9	2	52	19 *	7.42	-	-	3	-	1113	1036	39	26.56	4-27	-	
Twenty20																	

LUMB, M. J.   Yorkshire

Name: <u>Michael</u> John Lumb
Role: Left-hand bat, right-arm medium bowler
Born: 12 February 1980, Johannesburg, South Africa
Height: 6ft **Weight:** 13st
Nickname: China, Joe
County debut: 2000
County cap: 2003
1000 runs in a season: 1
1st-Class 50s: 13
1st-Class 100s: 4
1st-Class catches: 15
Place in batting averages: 69th av. 41.52 (2002 167th av. 26.79)
Strike rate: 78.00 (career 40.00)
Parents: Richard and Sue
Marital status: Single
Family links with cricket: Father played for Yorkshire. Uncle played for Natal
Education: St Stithians College

Qualifications: Matriculation
Off-season: 'In South Africa playing cricket'
Overseas tours: Transvaal U19 to Barbados; Yorkshire to Cape Town 2001, to Grenada 2002; ECB National Academy (England A) to Malaysia and India 2003-04
Overseas teams played for: Pirates CC, Johannesburg; Wanderers CC, Johannesburg
Career highlights to date: 'Getting my Yorkshire cap'
Cricket moments to forget: 'Relegation in 2002'
Cricket superstitions: 'None'
Cricketers particularly admired: Graham Thorpe, Darren Lehmann, Craig White, Stephen Fleming
Young players to look out for: Grant Elliott, Matthew Prior
Other sports played: Golf
Other sports followed: Rugby union (Sharks in Super 12, Leeds Tykes)
Favourite band: Oasis
Relaxations: 'Golf, socialising with friends'
Extras: Scored 66* on first-class debut v Zimbabweans at Headingley 2000. Scored maiden first-class century (122) v Leicestershire at Headingley 2001; the Lumbs thus became only the fourth father and son to have scored centuries for Yorkshire. Yorkshire Young Player of the Year 2002, 2003. Scored 1000 first-class runs in a season for the first time 2003. Awarded Yorkshire cap 2003
Opinions on cricket: 'Twenty20 was a good change. It was good for the crowds, so don't change anything yet. Maybe cheerleaders like the rugby.'
Best batting: 124 Yorkshire v Surrey, Guildford, 2002
Best bowling: 2-10 Yorkshire v Kent, Canterbury 2001

2003 Season

	M	Inns	NO	Runs	HS	Avge	100s	50s	Ct	St	O	M	Runs	Wkts	Avge	Best	5wl	10wM
Test																		
All First	17	27	2	1038	115*	41.52	2	7	7	-	13	0	73	1	73.00	1-29	-	-
1-day Int																		
C & G	2	2	0	82	82	41.00	-	1	1	-								
NCL	15	15	1	441	92	31.50	-	4	3	-								
Twenty20	5	5	0	147	55	29.40	-	2	-	-	6	0	65	3	21.66	3-32	-	

Career Performances

	M	Inns	NO	Runs	HS	Avge	100s	50s	Ct	St	Balls	Runs	Wkts	Avge	Best	5wl	10wM
Test																	
All First	38	66	5	2101	124	34.44	4	13	15	-	120	99	3	33.00	2-10	-	-
1-day Int																	
C & G	6	5	0	146	82	29.20	-	1	2	-							
NCL	33	32	3	840	92	28.96	-	6	10	-							
Twenty20	5	5	0	147	55	29.40	-	2	-	-	36	65	3	21.66	3-32	-	

LUNGLEY, T.   Derbyshire

Name: Tom Lungley
Role: Left-hand bat, right-arm
medium bowler
Born: 25 July 1979, Derby
Height: 6ft 2in **Weight:** 13st
Nickname: Lungfish, Monkfish, Sweaty,
Full Moon, Half Moon, Lungo
County debut: 2000
1st-Class catches: 6
Place in batting averages: 268th av. 11.42
(2002 275th av. 12.92)
Place in bowling averages: (2002 19th
av. 24.47)
Strike rate: 56.85 (career 46.14)
Parents: Richard and Christina
Marital status: 'Taken'
Family links with cricket: 'Dad was captain
of Derby Road CC. Grandad was bat maker
in younger days'

Education: Saint John Houghton School; South East Derbyshire College
Qualifications: 9 GCSEs, Sport and Recreation Levels 1 and 2, pool lifeguard
qualification, coaching qualifications in cricket, tennis, basketball, football and
volleyball
Career outside cricket: Painter and decorator
Overseas teams played for: Delacombe Park, Melbourne 1999-2000
Cricket moments to forget: 'Unable to speak when interviewed by Sybil Ruscoe on
Channel 4 Cricket Roadshow (live)'
Cricket superstitions: 'Always eat Jaffa Cake before play'
Cricketers particularly admired: Ian Botham, Dennis Lillee, Courtney Walsh, Curtly
Ambrose, Brian Lara, Richard Hadlee, Glenn McGrath
Other sports played: 'Enjoy playing most sports, mainly football and basketball'
Other sports followed: Football (Derby County), basketball (Derby Storm)
Extras: First homegrown cricketer to become professional from Ockbrook and
Borrowash CC. Scored 109 in Derbyshire Cup final 2000, winning Man of the Match
award. Took 4-13 v Nottinghamshire at Derby in the Twenty20 2003
Best batting: 47 Derbyshire v Warwickshire, Derby 2001
Best bowling: 4-101 Derbyshire v Glamorgan, Swansea 2003

	M	Inns	NO	Runs	HS	Avge	100s	50s	Ct	St	O	M	Runs	Wkts	Avge	Best	5wl	10wM
Test																		
All First	5	8	1	80	29	11.42	-	-	2	-	66.2	6	350	7	50.00	4-101	-	-
1-day Int																		
C & G	3	2	1	1	1 *	1.00	-	-	2	-	22.4	1	93	4	23.25	2-18	-	
NCL	7	5	1	56	30	14.00	-	-	2	-	44.5	0	290	8	36.25	3-47	-	
Twenty20	5	3	1	37	18 *	18.50	-	-	1	-	17	0	126	6	21.00	4-13	-	

Career Performances

	M	Inns	NO	Runs	HS	Avge	100s	50s	Ct	St	Balls	Runs	Wkts	Avge	Best	5wl	10wM
Test																	
All First	19	32	5	356	47	13.18	-	-	6	-	1938	1334	42	31.76	4-101	-	-
1-day Int																	
C & G	5	4	1	7	3	2.33	-	-	2	-	179	145	4	36.25	2-18	-	
NCL	25	16	5	198	45	18.00	-	-	4	-	1077	884	37	23.89	4-28	-	
Twenty20	5	3	1	37	18 *	18.50	-	-	1	-	102	126	6	21.00	4-13	-	

MacGILL, S. C. G.   Nottinghamshire

Name: <u>Stuart</u> Charles Glyndwr MacGill
Role: Right-hand bat, right-arm
leg-spin bowler
Born: 25 February 1971, Perth, Australia
Height: 6ft   **Weight:** 14st 2lbs
Nickname: Gorilla
County debut: 1997 (Somerset),
2002 (Nottinghamshire)
County cap: 2002 (Nottinghamshire)
Test debut: 1997-98
Tests: 25
One-Day Internationals: 3
1st-Class 50s: 1
1st-Class 5 w. in innings: 30
1st-Class 10 w. in match: 5
1st-Class catches: 56
Place in batting averages: 277th av. 9.33
(2002 301st av. 8.00)
Place in bowling averages: 81st av. 33.52 (2002 16th av. 23.25)
Strike rate: 58.90 (career 51.80)
Parents: Terry and Jenny
Wife: Rachel

Children: Alexander
Family links with cricket: Father (T. M. D. MacGill) played for Western Australia 1968-69 – 1972-73; grandfather (C. W. T. MacGill) played for Western Australia 1938-39 – 1950-51
Education: Christ Church GS, Perth
Off-season: 'Cricket in Oz'
Overseas tours: Australia to India 1997-98, to Pakistan 1998-99, to West Indies 1998-99, to Sri Lanka and Zimbabwe 1999-2000, to South Africa 2001-02, to West Indies 2002-03
Overseas teams played for: Sydney University; Western Australia 1993-94; New South Wales 1996-97 –
Career highlights to date: 'Mick Newell fielding at bat-pad ten years after he retired'
Cricket moments to forget: '2003 for Notts'
Cricket superstitions: 'None'
Cricketers particularly admired: Mick Newell
Young players to look out for: Paul McMahon, Ed Joyce
Other sports followed: Australian Rugby League (Newcastle), football (Newcastle United)
Favourite band: Coldplay
Relaxations: 'Reading, drinking, eating; listening to quality tunes'
Extras: Attended Commonwealth Bank [Australian] Cricket Academy 1991. Played for Devon in the NatWest 1997, 1998. Played one first-class match for Somerset 1997, v Pakistan A at Taunton. Was leading wicket-taker in Test series v England 1998-99 with 27 wickets (av. 17.70), including match figures of 12-107 in the fifth Test at Sydney. Took 4-19 on ODI debut v Pakistan at Sydney in the Carlton and United Series 1999-2000, winning Man of the Match award. Took 7-104 in the West Indies first innings in the fifth Test at Sydney 2000-01. Was leading wicket-taker in Australia's one-day ING Cup 2001-02 with 21 at 18.14. Was Nottinghamshire's overseas player for two periods during the 2002 season, replacing Nicky Boje, absent on international duty; returned to Nottinghamshire as an overseas player for 2003. Took 5-63 v Worcestershire at Kidderminster 2002, becoming the first bowler since Garfield Sobers in 1968 to record a five-wicket innings return on Championship debut for Nottinghamshire; followed up with figures of 14-165 in next match, v Middlesex at Trent Bridge; took 40 wickets (av. 23.25) overall in his six Championship matches for Nottinghamshire 2002. Bowled 84 overs for his match figures of 7-260 (2-108 and 5-152) in the fourth Test v England at Melbourne 2002-03. Had match figures of 8-59 (5-16/3-43) in the Pura Cup final v Queensland at Brisbane 2002-03. Took 100th Test wicket (Carlton Baugh) in the second Test v West Indies at Port of Spain 2003 and was Man of the Match in the third Test at Bridgetown (4-107/5-75). Man of the Series v Bangladesh 2003 (17 wickets; av. 12.88). ACB central contract 2003-04
Best batting: 53 New South Wales v South Australia, Sydney 2001-02
Best bowling: 8-111 Nottinghamshire v Middlesex, Trent Bridge 2002
Stop press: Selected for Australia's tour to Sri Lanka 2003-04

2003 Season

	M	Inns	NO	Runs	HS	Avge	100s	50s	Ct	St	O	M	Runs	Wkts	Avge	Best	5wI	10wM
Test																		
All First	11	18	6	112	27	9.33	-	-	2	-	412.2	73	1408	42	33.52	6-117	2	-
1-day Int																		
C & G	1	1	0	0	0	0.00	-	-	1	-	10	0	38	0	-		-	-
NCL	12	4	2	12	5 *	6.00	-	-	2	-	84.1	6	419	17	24.64	3-26	-	
Twenty20	5	2	1	13	8 *	13.00	-	-	1	-	17.2	0	144	6	24.00	3-42	-	

Career Performances

	M	Inns	NO	Runs	HS	Avge	100s	50s	Ct	St	Balls	Runs	Wkts	Avge	Best	5wI	10wM
Test	25	29	3	237	43	9.11	-	-	14	-	6799	3434	131	26.21	7-50	9	2
All First	106	139	33	994	53	9.37	-	1	56	-	24762	13631	478	28.51	8-111	30	5
1-day Int	3	2	1	1	1	1.00	-	-	2	-	180	105	6	17.50	4-19	-	
C & G	3	3	0	4	4	1.33	-	-	1	-	180	97	2	48.50	1-29	-	
NCL	16	7	3	24	6	6.00	-	-	5	-	679	544	20	27.20	3-26	-	
Twenty20	5	2	1	13	8 *	13.00	-	-	1	-	104	144	6	24.00	3-42	-	

MADDY, D. L. Leicestershire

Name: <u>Darren</u> Lee Maddy
Role: Right-hand opening bat, right-arm medium bowler
Born: 23 May 1974, Leicester
Height: 5ft 9in **Weight:** 12st 7lbs
Nickname: Roaster, Dazza, Fire Starter
County debut: 1993 (one-day), 1994 (first-class)
County cap: 1996
Test debut: 1999
Tests: 3
One-Day Internationals: 8
1000 runs in a season: 4
1st-Class 50s: 41
1st-Class 100s: 15
1st-Class 200s: 2
1st-Class 5 w. in innings: 4
1st-Class catches: 171
One-Day 100s: 5
Place in batting averages: 63rd av. 42.69 (2002 42nd av. 47.48)
Place in bowling averages: 48th av. 27.83 (2002 18th av. 23.83)
Strike rate: 49.52 (career 54.50)

Parents: William Arthur and Hilary Jean

Wife and date of marriage: Justine Marie, 7 October 2000

Family links with cricket: Father and younger brother, Greg, play club cricket

Education: Roundhill, Thurmaston; Wreake Valley, Syston

Qualifications: 8 GCSEs, Level 1 coach

Career outside cricket: 'Still undecided, although working on a few ideas'

Off-season: 'Playing grade cricket in Perth'

Overseas tours: Leicestershire to Bloemfontein 1995, to Western Transvaal 1996, to Durban 1997, to Barbados 1998, to Anguilla 2000, to Potchefstroom 2001; England A to Kenya and Sri Lanka 1997-98, to Zimbabwe and South Africa 1998-99; England to South Africa and Zimbabwe 1999-2000; England VI to Hong Kong 2003

Overseas teams played for: Wanderers, Johannesburg 1992-93; Northern Free State, South Africa 1993-95; Rhodes University, South Africa 1995-97; Sunshine CC, Grenada 2002; Perth CC, 2002-04

Career highlights to date: 'Winning two Championship medals. Playing for England'

Cricket moments to forget: 'Too many to mention. I hate losing a cricket match and I hate getting out – losing two Lord's finals, finishing second in the Norwich Union League, and being relegated [in Championship 2003]'

Cricket superstitions: 'Always put my left pad on first'

Cricketers particularly admired: Graham Gooch, Michael Atherton, Ian Botham, Viv Richards, Richard Hadlee

Young players to look out for: John Maunders, John Sadler, Luke Wright

Other sports played: Touch rugby, golf, squash, 5-a-side football

Other sports followed: Rugby (Leicester Tigers), football (Leicester City), baseball, golf, boxing – 'most sports really except for horse racing and motor racing'

Favourite band: 'Too many to mention – Two Tone Deaf, Bon Jovi, Def Leppard, Stereophonics, Aerosmith'

Relaxations: 'Going to the gym, playing sport, spending time with my wife, Justine; listening to music, watching TV, going on holiday, scuba diving, bungee jumping, playing the drums'

Extras: In 1994, set a new 2nd XI Championship run aggregate record (1498), the previous best having stood since 1961, and won the Rapid Cricketline 2nd XI Championship Player of the Year award. Was leading run-scorer on England A's 1997-98 tour with 687 runs at 68.7. In 1998, broke the record for the number of runs scored in the B&H competition in one season (629), previously held by Graham Gooch (591), also setting a record for the most B&H Gold Awards won in one season (five). Scored 110 for First Class Counties Select XI in one-day match v Sri Lanka A at Riverside 1999. Scored 133 for England XI in one-day match v Combined Border/Eastern Province Invitation XI at Alice 1999-2000. Had first innings figures of 5-104 and then scored 81 and 94 v Surrey at Leicester 2002. Scored 229* v Loughborough UCCE at Leicester 2003, in the process sharing with Brad Hodge (202*) in a record partnership for any wicket for Leicestershire and the second highest partnership for the third wicket in English first-class cricket (436*). Scored 56 v Worcestershire at Worcester in the NCL 2003, in the process passing 3000 runs in the one-day league

Opinions on cricket: 'Twenty20 proved to be a great success in bringing the crowds back through the gates and was great fun to play in. We still need a day off in between playing a day/night game and starting a Championship game. The gap between first-class and Test cricket is ever increasing, despite two divisional cricket. We need to bridge the gap by either playing regional teams or an England A team against the tourists. This will help players (and selectors) see if they can play at a higher level, and it also stops the touring teams getting easy practice against weakened county teams and [they will] therefore go into a match with less confidence.'

Best batting: 229* Leicestershire v LUCCE, Leicester 2003
Best bowling: 5-37 Leicestershire v Hampshire, West End 2002

2003 Season

	M	Inns	NO	Runs	HS	Avge	100s	50s	Ct	St	O	M	Runs	Wkts	Avge	Best	5wI	10wM
Test																		
All First	17	29	3	1110	229 *	42.69	1	6	15	-	297.1	59	1002	36	27.83	5-49	1	-
1-day Int																		
C & G	3	3	0	50	35	16.66	-	-	2	-	18	3	74	5	14.80	3-44	-	
NCL	16	16	1	474	80	31.60	-	5	7	-	82.4	3	460	7	65.71	2-35	-	
Twenty20	6	6	0	176	53	29.33	-	1	1	-	17.2	0	124	4	31.00	2-23	-	

Career Performances

	M	Inns	NO	Runs	HS	Avge	100s	50s	Ct	St	Balls	Runs	Wkts	Avge	Best	5wI	10wM
Test	3	4	0	46	24	11.50	-	-	4	-	84	40	0	-	-	-	-
All First	171	276	18	8575	229 *	33.23	17	41	171	-	7303	3916	134	29.22	5-37	4	-
1-day Int	8	6	0	113	53	18.83	-	1	1	-							
C & G	23	21	2	452	89	23.78	-	2	10	-	515	419	15	27.93	3-44	-	
NCL	150	137	19	3267	106 *	27.68	1	22	51	-	2822	2522	81	31.13	4-16	-	
Twenty20	6	6	0	176	53	29.33	-	1	1	-	104	124	4	31.00	2-23	-	

MAHER, J. P. Glamorgan

Name: James (Jimmy) Patrick Maher
Role: Left-hand bat, right-arm medium bowler
Born: 27 February 1974, Innisfail, Queensland, Australia
Height: 6ft **Weight:** 13st 5lbs
Nickname: Rock, Mahbo
County debut: 2001
County cap: 2001
One-Day Internationals: 25
1000 runs in a season: 1
1st-Class 50s: 41
1st-Class 100s: 15
1st Class 200s: 3
1st-Class catches: 135

1st-Class stumpings: 2
One-Day 100s: 1
Place in batting averages: 135th av. 30.68
Strike rate: (career 85.20)
Parents: Marie Ann and Warren George
Wife and date of marriage: Debbie,
6 April 2001
Children: Lily Matilda, 2002
Family links with cricket: Father and uncle
played for Queensland Country
Education: St Augustine's College, Cairns;
Nudgee College, Brisbane
Career outside cricket: Part-time radio show
Overseas tours: Australia U19 to New
Zealand 1992-93; Queensland Academy to
South Africa 1993; Australia to South Africa
2001-02 (one-day series), to Kenya (PSO Tri-
Nation Tournament) 2002, to Sri Lanka (ICC

Champions Trophy) 2002-03, to Africa (World Cup) 2002-03, to West Indies 2002-03
(one-day series), to India (TVS Cup) 2003-04
Overseas teams played for: Queensland 1993-94 –
Career highlights to date: 'Playing for Australia. Being part of Queensland's first
ever Sheffield Shield title win at The Gabba [1994-95]'
Cricket moments to forget: 'Running out Allan Border on my debut'
Cricketers particularly admired: Allan Border, Matt Hayden, Shane Warne,
Glenn McGrath
Young players to look out for: Mark Wallace, Mitchell Johnson
Other sports played: Squash ('played State titles U12-U16'), tennis ('ranked in top
ten in Queensland at U14')
Other sports followed: Rugby union (Queensland Reds), rugby league
(Canterbury Bulldogs)
Relaxations: 'Golf, dinner with friends, couple of lagers with mates'
Extras: Represented Australia U17 and U19. Attended Australian Cricket Academy
1993. Struck a six at the Gabba that broke the glass in the press box, v Tasmania
1993-94. Scored a century (100*) aged 20 for Queensland against England tourists
1994-95, sharing in an unbroken fifth-wicket partnership of 205 with Andrew
Symonds. Scored 102 v Western Australia in the final of the Mercantile Mutual Cup
1999-2000 at Perth. Scored 150 for Australia A v West Indians at Hobart 2000-01.
Scored 1142 first-class runs at 63.44 for Queensland and Australia A 2000-01. Was
Glamorgan's overseas player in 2001, returning in 2003. Topped Pura Cup batting
averages 2001-02 (1085 runs; av. 67.81) and was Pura Cup Player of the Year (jointly
with Brad Hodge of Victoria). *Wisden Australia*'s Pura Cup Cricketer of the Year
2001-02. Recalled to Australia's one-day squad for tour of South Africa 2001-02 and
was Man of the Match in his first two ODIs since 1997-98 (95 and 43*). Scored
maiden NCL century (142) v Essex at Cardiff 2003, sharing with Robert Croft (64) in

a new record opening partnership for Glamorgan in the one-day league. Captain of Queensland since 2002-03 and has captained Australia A. Has kept wicket in ODIs. Can throw both left and right handed. ACB contract 2003-04

Opinions on cricket: 'Don't fiddle around with it too much. We have a great game and all cricketers owe cricket a lot.'

Best batting: 217 Glamorgan v Essex, Cardiff 2001

Best bowling: 3-11 Queensland v Western Australia, Perth 1995-96

2003 Season

	M	Inns	NO	Runs	HS	Avge	100s	50s	Ct	St	O	M	Runs	Wkts	Avge	Best	5wI	10wM
Test																		
All First	8	16	0	491	95	30.68	-	4	7	-	1	0	2	0	-		-	-
1-day Int																		
C & G																			
NCL	10	10	0	295	142	29.50	1	1	5	-	3	0	29	3	9.66	3-29	-	
Twenty20																		

Career Performances

	M	Inns	NO	Runs	HS	Avge	100s	50s	Ct	St	Balls	Runs	Wkts	Avge	Best	5wI	10wM
Test																	
All First	131	231	27	8633	217	42.31	18	41	135	2	852	504	10	50.40	3-11	-	-
1-day Int	25	19	3	435	95	27.18	-	1	15	-							
C & G	1	1	0	30	30	30.00	-	-	1	-							
NCL	25	25	1	748	142	31.16	1	4	12	-	18	29	3	9.66	3-29	-	
Twenty20																	

MAHMOOD, S. I.   Lancashire

Name: Sajid Iqbal Mahmood
Role: Right-hand bat, right-arm fast-medium bowler
Born: 21 December 1981, Bolton
Height: 6ft 4in **Weight:** 12st 7lbs
Nickname: Saj, King
County debut: 2002
1st-Class 5 w. in innings: 1
1st-Class catches: 1
Place in bowling averages: 57th av. 29.60
Strike rate: 43.60 (career 44.40)
Parents: Shahid and Femida
Marital status: Single
Family links with cricket: Father played in Bolton League; younger brother plays in Bolton League
Education: Smithills School; North College, Bolton (sixth form)

Qualifications: 9 GCSEs, 3 A-levels
Off-season: 'England academy 2003-04'
Overseas tours: Lancashire to South Africa
2003; ECB National Academy (England A) to
Malaysia and India 2003-04
Overseas teams played for: Napier,
New Zealand 2002-03
Career highlights to date: 'Making first-
team debut and selection for academy'
Cricket moments to forget: 'None'
Cricket superstitions: 'None'
Cricketers particularly admired: Brett Lee,
Shoaib Akhtar
Injuries: Out for three weeks and for two
weeks with ankle sprains
Favourite band: Nelly, Eminem
Relaxations: 'Music and chillin' with mates'
Extras: Scored fastest hundred in Bolton
League U15 (42 balls). Played for Lancashire Board XI in the C&G 2002. His second
over in first-class cricket v Hampshire at Old Trafford 2002 lasted in excess of 67
hours, having been interrupted by bad light and rain. Recorded maiden first-class five-
wicket return (5-37) v Durham University CCE at Durham 2003
Opinions on cricket: 'Too much cricket played.'
Best batting: 34 Lancashire v Kent, Canterbury 2003
Best bowling: 5-37 Lancashire v DUCCE, Durham 2003
Stop press: Took 5-62 for England A v East Zone at Amritsar 2003-04

2003 Season

	M	Inns	NO	Runs	HS	Avge	100s	50s	Ct	St	O	M	Runs	Wkts	Avge	Best	5wI	10wM
Test																		
All First	5	5	1	62	34	15.50	-	-	1	-	109	16	444	15	29.60	5-37	1	-
1-day Int																		
C & G	1	1	1	5	5 *	-	-	-	-	-	2.3	0	8	2	4.00	2-8	-	
NCL	7	1	0	3	3	3.00	-	-	1	-	43	1	258	9	28.66	3-41	-	
Twenty20	4	3	0	21	21	7.00	-	-	-	-	15	0	115	2	57.50	1-22	-	

Career Performances

	M	Inns	NO	Runs	HS	Avge	100s	50s	Ct	St	Balls	Runs	Wkts	Avge	Best	5wI	10wM
Test																	
All First	6	6	1	80	34	16.00	-	-	1	-	666	450	15	30.00	5-37	1	-
1-day Int																	
C & G	2	2	1	16	11	16.00	-	-	-	-	39	45	2	22.50	2-8	-	
NCL	8	1	0	3	3	3.00	-	-	1	-	306	289	9	32.11	3-41	-	
Twenty20	4	3	0	21	21	7.00	-	-	-	-	90	115	2	57.50	1-22	-	

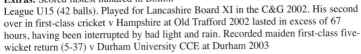

MAIDEN, G. I. Lancashire

Name: <u>Gregor</u> Ian Maiden
Role: Right-hand bat, right-arm
off-spin bowler
Born: 22 July 1979, Glasgow
Height: 6ft **Weight:** 10st 7lbs
Nickname: Rusty
County debut: 2003 (one-day)
1st-Class catches: 1
Strike rate: (career 47.00)
Parents: Martin and Lynne
Marital status: Single
Education: Hutchesons Grammar School,
Glasgow; Loughborough University
Qualifications: BSc PE and Sports Science
Career outside cricket: Coach
Overseas tours: Scotland U19 to South
Africa (U19 World Cup) 1997-98; Scotland to
Zimbabwe 2000, to Namibia 2001, to Canada
(ICC Trophy) 2001, to Dubai (ICC Six Nations Challenge) 2003-04

Overseas teams played for: South Perth 1997; Richmond, Victoria 1998; Randwick-Petersham, Sydney 2001; New Town, Tasmania 2001
Career highlights to date: 'Winning back-to-back BUSA titles with Loughborough University'
Cricket moments to forget: 'Failing to qualify for the 2003 World Cup'
Cricketers particularly admired: Curtly Ambrose, Damien Martyn
Other sports played: Hockey, golf, football
Other sports followed: Football (Aberdeen FC)
Relaxations: Films
Extras: Played for Loughborough University CCE 2001. Played first-class cricket for Scotland v South Africa Academy 1999 and v Ireland at Ayr 2000. Represented Scotland in the ICC Trophy 2001, winning the Man of the Match award v Denmark (40*/3-29). Has also played for Scotland in the NatWest 1999 and 2000, the C&G 2002, and in the NCL 2003 (Scottish Saltires). Played for Lancashire v India A at Blackpool in a 50-over match 2003, scoring 62 (at No. 10) and taking 2-36. Two uncles and grandfather played professional football
Best batting: 23* Scotland v South Africa Academy, Linlithgow 1999
Best bowling: 2-11 Scotland v South Africa Academy, Linlithgow 1999

2003 Season

	M	Inns	NO	Runs	HS	Avge	100s	50s	Ct	St	O	M	Runs	Wkts	Avge	Best	5wl	10wM
Test																		
All First																		
1-day Int																		
C & G																		
NCL	5	2	0	33	33	16.50	-	-	1	-	26	0	167	1	167.00	1-31	-	
Twenty20	1	1	1	2	2 *	-	-	-	1	-	4	0	29	2	14.50	2-29	-	

Career Performances

	M	Inns	NO	Runs	HS	Avge	100s	50s	Ct	St	Balls	Runs	Wkts	Avge	Best	5wl	10wM
Test																	
All First	3	3	1	32	23*	16.00	-	-	1	-	282	139	6	23.16	2-11	-	-
1-day Int																	
C & G	5	2	0	3	3	1.50	-	-	2	-	210	130	4	32.50	2-27	-	
NCL	5	2	0	33	33	16.50	-	-	1	-	156	167	1	167.00	1-31	-	
Twenty20	1	1	1	2	2 *	-	-	-	1	-	24	29	2	14.50	2-29	-	

MALCOLM, D. E.   Leicestershire

Name: <u>Devon</u> Eugene Malcolm
Role: Right-hand bat, right-arm fast bowler
Born: 22 February 1963, Kingston, Jamaica
Height: 6ft 2½in **Weight:** 16st 2lbs
Nickname: Dude
County debut: 1984 (Derbyshire),
1998 (Northamptonshire), 2001
(Leicestershire)
County cap: 1989 (Derbyshire),
1999 (Northamptonshire), 2001
(Leicestershire)
Benefit: 1997 (Derbyshire)
Test debut: 1989
Tests: 40
One-Day Internationals: 10
50 wickets in a season: 9
1st-Class 50s: 2
1st-Class 5 w. in innings: 46
1st-Class 10 w. in match: 9
1st-Class catches: 45
One-Day 5 w. in innings: 2
Place in batting averages: (2002 292nd av. 9.85)

Place in bowling averages: 32nd av. 25.57 (2002 67th av. 30.43)
Strike rate: 40.28 (career 50.55)
Parents: Albert and Brendalee (deceased)
Wife and date of marriage: Jennifer, 15 October 1989
Children: Erica, 11 June 1991; Natalie, 25 June 1993; Stephany, 11 July 1995
Education: St Elizabeth Technical High School, Jamaica; Richmond College, Sheffield; Derby College of Higher Education
Qualifications: O-levels, HND Business Studies, Level II coaching certificate
Overseas tours: England to West Indies 1989-90, to Australia 1990-91, to India and Sri Lanka 1992-93, to West Indies 1993-94, to Australia 1994-95, to South Africa 1995-96; England A to Bermuda and West Indies 1991-92; Christians in Sport to South Africa 2000
Overseas teams played for: Ellerslie, Auckland 1985-87
Career highlights: '9-57, England v South Africa, The Oval 1994'
Cricket moments to forget: 'South Africa tour 1996'
Cricket superstitions: 'Left boot on first'
Cricketers particularly admired: Sir Richard Hadlee, Michael Holding, Viv Richards, Steve Waugh
Young players to look out for: Steve Harmison, Simon Jones, Andrew Strauss
Other sports played: Table tennis
Other sports followed: Football (Man United), boxing
Injuries: Out for most of the season with a meniscus trim and clean-out (right knee)
Relaxations: 'Cooking, listening to music'
Extras: Played league cricket for Sheffield Works and Sheffield United; he once took six wickets for no runs off 15 deliveries. Became eligible to play for England in 1987. Had match figures of 10 for 137 v West Indies in Port-of-Spain Test 1989-90. Took 9-57 v South Africa at The Oval in 1994; received the 'Century of Bottles' Award for this best performance against the touring South Africans. Was one of *Wisden's* Five Cricketers of the Year 1995. Joined Northamptonshire for 1998. Left Northants at the end of the 2000 season and joined Leicestershire for 2001, taking 5-78 v Lancashire at Leicester in his second Championship match for the county. First bowler to reach 50 first-class wickets in the 2001 season. His 6-72 v Yorkshire at Leicester 2002 included his 1000th first-class wicket (Victor Craven). Retired at the end of the 2003 season
Opinions on cricket: 'Totally against two overseas players. Top overseas players are already centrally contracted, therefore not available.'
Best batting: 51 Derbyshire v Surrey, Derby 1989
Best bowling: 9-57 England v South Africa, The Oval 1994

---

60. Which wicket-keeper made his only appearance as
England captain in an ODI v West Indies at Scarborough in 1976?

2003 Season

	M	Inns	NO	Runs	HS	Avge	100s	50s	Ct	St	O	M	Runs	Wkts	Avge	Best	5wl	10wM
Test																		
All First	4	4	0	27	14	6.75	-	-	-	-	94	22	358	14	25.57	5-40	1	-
1-day Int																		
C & G																		
NCL																		
Twenty20																		

Career Performances

	M	Inns	NO	Runs	HS	Avge	100s	50s	Ct	St	Balls	Runs	Wkts	Avge	Best	5wl	10wM
Test	40	58	19	236	29	6.05	-	-	7	-	8480	4748	128	37.09	9-57	5	2
All First	304	366	113	1985	51	7.84	-	2	45	-	53289	31977	1054	30.33	9-57	46	9
1-day Int	10	5	2	9	4	3.00	-	-	1	-	526	404	16	25.25	3-40	-	
C & G	30	14	1	31	10 *	2.38	-	-	4	-	1757	1117	43	25.97	7-35	1	
NCL	94	38	13	155	42	6.20	-	-	10	-	4003	3369	119	28.31	4-21	-	
Twenty20																		

MALIK, M. N.   Worcestershire

Name: Muhammad Nadeem Malik
Role: Right-hand bat, right-arm
fast-medium bowler
Born: 6 October 1982, Nottingham
Height: 6ft 5in **Weight:** 14st
Nickname: Nigel, Nige, Gerz
County debut: 2001 (Nottinghamshire)
1st-Class 5 w. in innings: 2
1st-Class catches: 1
Place in batting averages: (2002 315th
av. 5.50)
Place in bowling averages: (2002 30th
av. 25.54)
Strike rate: 114.00 (career 52.74)
Parents: Abdul and Arshad
Marital status: Single
Education: Wilford Meadows Secondary
School; Bilborough College
Qualifications: 9 GCSEs
Overseas tours: ZRK to Pakistan 2000; Nottinghamshire to South Africa 2001;
England U19 to India 2000-01, to Australia and (U19 World Cup) New Zealand
2001-02

Career highlights to date: '5-57 against Derbyshire 2001'
Cricket moments to forget: 'Norwich Union match v Yorkshire at Scarborough 2001 – Lehmann 191'
Cricketers particularly admired: Glenn McGrath, Wasim Akram, Curtly Ambrose
Young players to look out for: Bilal Shafayat, Gordon Muchall
Other sports played: Football
Other sports followed: Football
Relaxations: Music, games consoles
Extras: Made Nottinghamshire 2nd XI debut in 1999, aged 16, and took 15 wickets at an average of 19.40 for the 2nd XI 2000. Played for Nottinghamshire Board XI in the NatWest 2000. Represented England U19 v West Indies U19 2001 and v India U19 2002. Left Nottinghamshire in the 2003-04 off-season and has joined Worcestershire for 2004
Best batting: 30* Nottinghamshire v Essex, Trent Bridge 2003
Best bowling: 5-57 Nottinghamshire v Derbyshire, Trent Bridge 2001

2003 Season

	M	Inns	NO	Runs	HS	Avge	100s	50s	Ct	St	O	M	Runs	Wkts	Avge	Best	5wl	10wM
Test																		
All First	2	3	1	55	30*	27.50	-	-	-	-	57	7	227	3	75.66	2-58	-	-
1-day Int																		
C & G																		
NCL																		
Twenty20																		

Career Performances

	M	Inns	NO	Runs	HS	Avge	100s	50s	Ct	St	Balls	Runs	Wkts	Avge	Best	5wl	10wM
Test																	
All First	14	16	7	100	30*	11.11	-	-	1	-	1846	1203	35	34.37	5-57	2	-
1-day Int																	
C & G	2	1	1	1	1*	-	-	-	-	-	48	32	0	-		-	-
NCL	11	6	4	21	11	10.50	-	-	3	-	462	434	6	72.33	2-34	-	
Twenty20																	

61. Which captain of two southern counties was
Man of the Match on ODI debut v West Indies
at Headingley in 1980, scoring 82*.

MARTIN, P. J. Lancashire

Name: <u>Peter</u> James Martin
Role: Right-hand bat, right-arm
fast-medium bowler
Born: 15 November 1968, Accrington
Height: 6ft 5in **Weight:** 15st 10lbs
Nickname: Digger
County debut: 1989
County cap: 1994
Benefit: 2002
Test debut: 1995
Tests: 8
One-Day Internationals: 20
50 wickets in a season: 3
1st-Class 50s: 7
1st-Class 100s: 2
1st-Class 5 w. in innings: 17
1st-Class 10 w. in match: 1
1st-Class catches: 54
One-Day 5 w. in innings: 6
Place in batting averages: 274th av. 10.00 (2002 86th av. 38.36)
Place in bowling averages: 68th av. 31.58 (2002 7th av. 21.24)
Strike rate: 63.24 (career 60.41)
Parents: Keith and Catherine
Wife and date of marriage: Bethan, 3 October 1998
Children: Oliver, 14 August 2001
Education: Danum School, Doncaster; University of Central Lancashire, Preston
Qualifications: 6 O-levels, 2 A-levels, PGCM (UCLAN), Advanced Certificate
(WSET), Levels 1 and 2 coaching certificates
Career outside cricket: 'Wine trade and painting'
Off-season: 'Working for Define Food & Wine, Sandiway, and painting'
Overseas tours: England YC to Australia (U19 World Cup) 1987-88, 'and various
other tours with English Schools and NAYC'; England to South Africa 1995-96, to
India and Pakistan (World Cup) 1995-96, to Sharjah (Champions Trophy) 1997-98,
to Bangladesh (Wills International Cup) 1998-99
Overseas teams played for: Southern Districts, Beerwah, Queensland 1988-89; South
Launceston, Tasmania 1989-90; South Canberra, ACT 1990-92
Career highlights to date: 'Playing for this long. Playing for England. Playing for the
most part in a very successful Lancashire side all my career'
Cricket moments to forget: 'Can't remember'
Cricket superstitions: 'None'
Cricketers particularly admired: 'Far too many to mention'

Young players to look out for: 'Anybody with a European passport, it seems'
Other sports played: Golf, soccer
Other sports followed: Football (Man Utd)
Relaxations: 'Painting, cooking, family, wine, outdoor stuff'
Extras: Played for England A v Sri Lankans 1991. His 78* v Durham at Old Trafford 1997 is the equal highest score by a Lancashire No. 11 (although Paul Allott was dismissed v Gloucestershire at Bristol in 1985). Scored 80* v Kent at Liverpool 2002, in the process sharing with Glen Chapple (55) in a record ninth-wicket partnership for Lancashire v Kent (109). Scored 117* v Warwickshire at Old Trafford 2002, setting a new record for the highest score by a Lancashire No. 10
Opinions on cricket: 'The laws regarding the European work permit situation are terrible. Anybody with an Irish dog seems to be able to play in England as a non-overseas player and [they] aren't eligible for England! Many coaches encourage this. For the good of encouraging lads in England, this has to change.'
Best batting: 133 Lancashire v Durham, Gateshead Fell 1992
Best bowling: 8-32 Lancashire v Middlesex, Uxbridge 1997

2003 Season

	M	Inns	NO	Runs	HS	Avge	100s	50s	Ct	St	O	M	Runs	Wkts	Avge	Best	5wI	10wM
Test																		
All First	14	12	0	120	23	10.00	-	-	8	-	432.1	99	1295	41	31.58	5-54	1	-
1-day Int																		
C & G	4	2	0	1	1	0.50	-	-	-	-	36	8	125	9	13.88	4-34	-	
NCL	16	5	4	46	29 *	46.00	-	-	5	-	117	12	460	24	19.16	3-18	-	
Twenty20	4	3	2	18	10 *	18.00	-	-	-	-	15	2	85	7	12.14	3-20	-	

Career Performances

	M	Inns	NO	Runs	HS	Avge	100s	50s	Ct	St	Balls	Runs	Wkts	Avge	Best	5wI	10wM
Test	8	13	0	115	29	8.84	-	-	6	-	1452	580	17	34.11	4-60	-	-
All First	206	239	59	3535	133	19.63	2	7	54	-	36005	16358	596	27.44	8-32	17	1
1-day Int	20	13	7	38	6	6.33	-	-	1	-	1048	806	27	29.85	4-44	-	
C & G	33	13	8	107	31 *	21.40	-	-	1	-	1886	1072	64	16.75	5-16	2	
NCL	147	47	25	284	35 *	12.90	-	-	30	-	6007	4177	192	21.75	5-21	4	
Twenty20	4	3	2	18	10 *	18.00	-	-	-	-	90	85	7	12.14	3-20	-	

62. In 1981 Colin Croft became only the second bowler
to take six wickets in an ODI (6-15 v England in St Vincent).
For which English county did he play?

MARTIN-JENKINS, R. S. C.   Sussex

Name: <u>Robin</u> Simon Christopher
Martin-Jenkins
Role: Right-hand bat, right-arm
fast-medium bowler
Born: 28 October 1975, Guildford
Height: 6ft 5in   **Weight:** 14st
Nickname: Tucker
County debut: 1995
County cap: 2000
1000 runs in a season: 1
1st-Class 50s: 20
1st-Class 100s: 2
1st-Class 200s: 1
1st-Class 5 w. in innings: 4
1st-Class catches: 23
Place in batting averages: 97th av. 36.86
(2002 69th av. 42.00)
Place in bowling averages: 118th av. 40.58
(2002 109th av. 36.02)
Strike rate: 70.45 (career 62.49)
Parents: Christopher and Judy
Wife and date of marriage: Flora, 19 February 2000
Family links with cricket: Father is *The Times* chief cricket correspondent and *TMS*
commentator. Brother captains the Radley Rangers
Education: Radley College, Oxon; Durham University
Qualifications: 10 GCSEs, 3 A-levels, 1 AS-level, Grade 3 bassoon (with merit),
BA (Hons) Social Sciences, Don Mackenzie School of Professional Photography
Certificate, SWPP (Society of Wedding and Portrait Photographers), BPPA (British
Professional Photographers Associates)
Career outside cricket: 'Weekly columnist for *Brighton Argus*. Photographer for
"Goodnightie Company"'
Off-season: 'Gym; maybe a few weeks in India; bit of writing'
Overseas tours: Radley College to Barbados 1992; Sussex U19 to Sri Lanka 1995;
Durham University to Vienna 1995; MCC to Kenya 1999; Sussex to Grenada 2001,
2002
Overseas teams played for: Lima CC, Peru 1994; Bellville CC, Cape Town 2000-01
Career highlights to date: 'Winning National League Division Two in 1999. Scoring
maiden first-class century in same match that Sussex won to take second division
Championship 2001. Scoring maiden first-class 200 v Somerset at Taunton 2002.
Winning first division Championship 2003'
Cricket moments to forget: 'Pick from any of our National League games from the
past two seasons'

Cricket superstitions: 'Never bowl first at Colwyn Bay'
Cricketers particularly admired: Angus Fraser, Robin Smith, Umer Rashid, Ben Hollioake, Adam Hollioake
Young players to look out for: Andrew Hodd
Other sports played: Golf, tennis, Rugby fives
Other sports followed: Rugby, football (Liverpool)
Relaxations: Photography, guitar, reading, TV, films
Extras: Played for ESCA from U15 to U19. *Daily Telegraph* Bowling Award 1994. European Player of the Year, Vienna 1995. Best Performance Award for Sussex 1998. NBC Denis Compton Award for the most promising young Sussex player 1998, 1999, 2000. Scored maiden first-class century (113) v Gloucestershire at Hove 2001, including 109 between lunch and tea on the first day. Scored 80* out of 246 and followed up with 5-37 v Hampshire in Championship match at West End 2002. Scored maiden first-class double century (205*) v Somerset at Taunton 2002, in the process sharing with Mark Davis (111) in a record eighth-wicket partnership for Sussex (291); the stand fell one run short of the record eighth-wicket partnership in English first-class cricket, set by Bobby Peel and Lord Hawke for Yorkshire v Warwickshire at Birmingham in 1896. BBC South Cricketer of the Year 2002
Opinions on cricket: 'Keep Twenty20 as before. Scrap National League and C&G Trophy – they're getting stale, and why are we still the only country that plays 45 overs? In their place have a one-day mini-league in regions, followed by quarters/semis/final knockout. Like old Benson and Hedges except the best Minor Counties and Scotland could be included. Keep Championship as it is with two divisions (but only two up/two down) except everyone to play each other only once and include a regional tournament in early season – best against the best.'
Best batting: 205* Sussex v Somerset, Taunton 2002
Best bowling: 7-51 Sussex v Leicestershire, Horsham 2002

2003 Season

	M	Inns	NO	Runs	HS	Avge	100s	50s	Ct	St	O	M	Runs	Wkts	Avge	Best	5wI	10wM
Test																		
All First	16	25	3	811	121 *	36.86	1	5	7	-	364	82	1258	31	40.58	3-9	-	-
1-day Int																		
C & G	2	2	0	46	38	23.00	-	-	1	-	12	3	48	1	48.00	1-28	-	
NCL	17	15	1	222	68 *	15.85	-	1	4	-	126.2	8	584	26	22.46	4-46	-	
Twenty20	5	5	2	133	56 *	44.33	-	1	-	-	19.1	0	156	8	19.50	4-20	-	

Career Performances

	M	Inns	NO	Runs	HS	Avge	100s	50s	Ct	St	Balls	Runs	Wkts	Avge	Best	5wI	10wM
Test																	
All First	85	137	17	3755	205 *	31.29	3	20	23	-	12436	6565	199	32.98	7-51	4	-
1-day Int																	
C & G	7	6	2	91	38	22.75	-	-	2	-	360	211	8	26.37	2-24	-	
NCL	87	63	5	760	68 *	13.10	-	2	24	-	3643	2502	84	29.78	4-46	-	
Twenty20	5	5	2	133	56 *	44.33	-	1	-	-	115	156	8	19.50	4-20	-	

MARTYN, D. R.   Nottinghamshire

Name: <u>Damien</u> Richard Martyn
Role: Right-hand bat, right-arm
medium bowler
Born: 21 October 1971, Darwin,
Northern Territory, Australia
Height: 5ft 11in **Weight:** 11st 9lbs
Nickname: Marto
County debut: 2003 (Yorkshire; *see Extras*)
Test debut: 1992-93
Tests: 33
One-Day Internationals: 126
1st-Class 50s: 61
1st-Class 100s: 33
1st-Class 200s: 2
1st-Class catches: 134
1st-Class stumpings: 2
One-Day 100s: 4
Strike rate: (career 87.13)

Overseas tours: Australia YC to West Indies 1990, to England 1991 (captain);
Australia A to Scotland and Ireland 1998, to Los Angeles (Moov America Challenge)
1999; Australia to Sri Lanka 1992, to New Zealand 1992-93, to England 1993, to India
(Pepsi Triangular Series) 1997-98, to Bangladesh (Wills International Cup) 1998-99, to
UK, Ireland and Holland (World Cup) 1999, to New Zealand 1999-2000, to South
Africa (one-day series) 1999-2000, to Kenya (ICC Knockout Trophy) 2000-01, to
India 2000-01, to England 2001, to South Africa 2001-02, to Sri Lanka (ICC
Champions Trophy) 2002-03, to Sri Lanka and Sharjah (v Pakistan) 2002-03, to Africa
(World Cup) 2002-03, plus other one-day series and tournaments
Overseas teams played for: South Perth; Western Australia 1990-91 –
Extras: Represented Australia YC v England YC in home series 1989-90. Attended
Commonwealth Bank [Australian] Cricket Academy 1990. Played one first-class
match for Leicestershire 1991, v West Indians at Leicester. Man of the Match in the
Sheffield Shield final v Queensland at Brisbane 1998-99. Carried his bat for 116* in
the sixth ODI v New Zealand at Auckland 1999-2000. Topped Australian batting
averages v New Zealand 1999-2000 (241 runs; av. 60.25) in his first Test series since
1993-94. One of *Wisden*'s Five Cricketers of the Year 2002. ODI Man of the Match
awards v South Africa at Cape Town 1999-2000 (50) and v Bangladesh at Cairns 2003
(92*). Test Man of the Match award in the third Test v England at Perth 2002-03.
Scored 88* in the final of the World Cup 2002-03, sharing with Ricky Ponting (140*)
in a new Australian record partnership for any wicket in ODIs and a new world record
partnership for the third wicket in ODIs (234*). ACB contract 2003-04. Was an
overseas player with Yorkshire towards the end of the 2003 season, replacing Stephen

Fleming and Yuvraj Singh. Scored 128-ball double century (including the season's fastest hundred – 65 balls) v Gloucestershire at Headingley 2003, finishing with 238 and sharing with Matthew Wood (116) in the highest Championship stand for any wicket at Headingley (330). Has joined Notts as an overseas player for 2004

Best batting: 238 Yorkshire v Gloucestershire, Headingley 2003
Best bowling: 4-30 Western Australia v Queensland, Brisbane 1998-99
Stop press: Selected for Australia's tour to Sri Lanka 2003-04

2003 Season

	M	Inns	NO	Runs	HS	Avge	100s	50s	Ct	St	O	M	Runs	Wkts	Avge	Best	5wI	10wM
Test																		
All First	2	3	1	342	238	171.00	1	1	1	-								
1-day Int																		
C & G																		
NCL																		
Twenty20																		

Career Performances

	M	Inns	NO	Runs	HS	Avge	100s	50s	Ct	St	Balls	Runs	Wkts	Avge	Best	5wI	10wM
Test	33	52	9	2000	133	46.51	5	13	15	-	198	98	2	49.00	1-0	-	-
All First	164	276	39	11794	238	49.76	35	61	134	2	3137	1465	36	40.69	4-30	-	-
1-day Int	126	106	35	3027	144 *	42.63	4	17	49	-	794	704	12	58.66	2-21	-	
C & G																	
NCL																	
Twenty20																	

MASCARENHAS, A. D.   Hampshire

Name: Adrian <u>Dimitri</u> Mascarenhas
Role: Right-hand bat, right-arm medium bowler
Born: 30 October 1977, Chiswick, London
Height: 6ft 1in **Weight:** 12st 2lbs
Nickname: Dimi, D-Train
County debut: 1996
County cap: 1998
1st-Class 50s: 15
1st-Class 100s: 3
1st-Class 5 w. in innings: 6
1st-Class catches: 41
One-Day 5 w. in innings: 1
Place in batting averages: 184th av. 25.00 (2002 194th av. 23.91)
Place in bowling averages: 72nd av. 32.17 (2002 69th av. 30.83)
Strike rate: 73.37 (career 67.52)

Parents: Malik and Pauline
Marital status: Single
Family links with cricket: Uncle played in Sri Lanka and brothers both play for Melville CC in Perth, Western Australia
Education: Trinity College, Perth
Qualifications: Level 2 coaching
Career outside cricket: Personal trainer
Overseas teams played for: Melville CC, Perth 1991-2003
Career highlights to date: 'Debut for Hampshire 1996 – 6-88 v Glamorgan'
Cricketers particularly admired: Viv Richards, Malcolm Marshall, the Waugh twins
Young players to look out for: John Francis, Jimmy Adams
Other sports followed: Australian Rules (Collingwood)
Favourite band: Red Hot Chili Peppers
Relaxations: Tennis, golf, Australian Rules

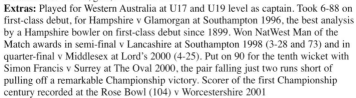

Extras: Played for Western Australia at U17 and U19 level as captain. Took 6-88 on first-class debut, for Hampshire v Glamorgan at Southampton 1996, the best analysis by a Hampshire bowler on first-class debut since 1899. Won NatWest Man of the Match awards in semi-final v Lancashire at Southampton 1998 (3-28 and 73) and in quarter-final v Middlesex at Lord's 2000 (4-25). Put on 90 for the tenth wicket with Simon Francis v Surrey at The Oval 2000, the pair falling just two runs short of pulling off a remarkable Championship victory. Scorer of the first Championship century recorded at the Rose Bowl (104) v Worcestershire 2001
Best batting: 104 Hampshire v Worcestershire, West End 2001
Best bowling: 6-26 Hampshire v Middlesex, West End 2001

2003 Season

	M	Inns	NO	Runs	HS	Avge	100s	50s	Ct	St	O	M	Runs	Wkts	Avge	Best	5wI	10wM
Test																		
All First	17	26	2	600	100 *	25.00	1	2	7	-	489.1	150	1287	40	32.17	6-55	1	-
1-day Int																		
C & G	1	1	0	1	1	1.00	-	-	-	-	10	2	31	3	10.33	3-31	-	
NCL	17	16	5	237	37	21.54	-	-	5	-	138.5	19	585	34	17.20	4-22	-	
Twenty20	5	5	1	62	39	15.50	-	-	3	-	12	0	131	3	43.66	2-51	-	

Career Performances

	M	Inns	NO	Runs	HS	Avge	100s	50s	Ct	St	Balls	Runs	Wkts	Avge	Best	5wI	10wM
Test																	
All First	103	154	15	3278	104	23.58	3	15	41	-	14585	6821	216	31.57	6-26	6	-
1-day Int																	
C & G	14	12	4	308	73	38.50	-	2	2	-	714	416	23	18.08	4-25	-	
NCL	100	88	14	1329	79	17.95	-	6	29	-	4170	2992	136	22.00	5-27	1	
Twenty20	5	5	1	62	39	15.50	-	-	3	-	72	131	3	43.66	2-51	-	

MASON, M. S.   Worcestershire

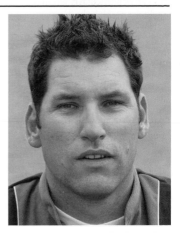

Name: Matthew (<u>Matt</u>) Sean Mason
Role: Right-hand bat, right-arm
fast-medium bowler
Born: 20 March 1974, Claremont,
Perth, Western Australia
Height: 6ft 5in **Weight:** 16st
Nickname: Mase, Alvin, Chipmunk
County debut: 2002
County colours: 2002
50 wickets in a season: 1
1st-Class 50s: 2
1st-Class 5 w. in innings: 3
1st-Class catches: 4
Place in batting averages: 247th av. 15.62
(2002 243rd av. 17.83)
Place in bowling averages: 7th av. 21.58
(2002 50th av. 27.86)
Strike rate: 49.75 (career 57.20)
Parents: Bill and Sue
Marital status: Single
Family links with cricket: Brother Simon plays for Wanneroo District CC
Education: Mazenod College, Perth
Qualifications: Level 1 ACB coach
Career outside cricket: Sales consultant with Nissan Motor Company
Off-season: 'Playing cricket in Western Australia'
Overseas teams played for: Western Australia 1996-1998
Career highlights to date: 'C&G final v Gloucestershire at Lord's 2003'
Cricket moments to forget: 'Losing the C&G final 2003'
Cricketers particularly admired: Justin Langer, Damien Martyn
Young players to look out for: James Pipe, Kabir Ali
Other sports played: Golf, tennis, Australian Rules football

Other sports followed: Rugby league (Bradford Bulls), rugby union (Wallabies)
Favourite band: U2
Relaxations: 'Listening to music; going to the movies; the beach'
Extras: Made first-class debut for Western Australia v Queensland at Perth 1996-97. Scored maiden first-class fifty (50) from 27 balls v Derbyshire at Worcester 2002. Took 50 first-class wickets in a season for the first time 2003. Dick Lygon Award to the [Worcestershire] Clubman of the Year 2003. Holds an Irish passport and is not considered an overseas player
Opinions on cricket: 'Fully support the two overseas player rule. Anything that makes the game more competitive and challenges us more as players should be welcomed.'
Best batting: 52 Worcestershire v Glamorgan, Cardiff 2003
Best bowling: 6-68 Worcestershire v Durham, Worcester 2003

2003 Season

	M	Inns	NO	Runs	HS	Avge	100s	50s	Ct	St	O	M	Runs	Wkts	Avge	Best	5wI	10wM
Test																		
All First	15	20	4	250	52	15.62	-	1	2	-	439.3	128	1144	53	21.58	6-68	2	-
1-day Int																		
C & G	5	3	2	4	3 *	4.00	-	-	-	-	42	8	124	7	17.71	3-28	-	
NCL	16	8	2	78	20 *	13.00	-	-	3	-	125	18	524	19	27.57	4-34	-	
Twenty20	4	2	0	3	3	1.50	-	-	1	-	15.1	0	103	3	34.33	1-22	-	

Career Performances

	M	Inns	NO	Runs	HS	Avge	100s	50s	Ct	St	Balls	Runs	Wkts	Avge	Best	5wI	10wM
Test																	
All First	25	33	7	367	52	14.11	-	2	4	-	4519	2006	79	25.39	6-68	3	-
1-day Int																	
C & G	7	4	2	5	3 *	2.50	-	-	-	-	363	243	10	24.30	3-28	-	
NCL	25	11	3	89	20 *	11.12	-	-	4	-	1103	774	30	25.80	4-34	-	
Twenty20	4	2	0	3	3	1.50	-	-	1	-	91	103	3	34.33	1-22	-	

63. Of the England team that beat West Indies
in the third ODI in 1988, six were born overseas.
Who was the Kenyan-born member of this sextet?

Name: <u>David</u> Daniel Masters
Role: Right-hand bat, right-arm medium-fast bowler
Born: 22 April 1978, Chatham
Height: 6ft 4ins **Weight:** 12st 5lbs
Nickname: Hod, Race Horse, Hoddy
County debut: 2000 (Kent), 2003 (Leicestershire)
1st-Class 50s: 1
1st-Class 100s: 1
1st-Class 5 w. in innings: 4
1st-Class catches: 13
One-Day 5 w. in innings: 1
Place in batting averages: 264th av. 13.45 (2002 248th av. 16.71)
Place in bowling averages: 126th av. 42.72 (2002 114th av. 37.56)
Strike rate: 69.00 (career 62.19)

Parents: Kevin and Tracey
Marital status: Single
Family links with cricket: 'Dad was on staff at Kent 1983-86'
Education: Fort Luton High School; Mid-Kent College
Qualifications: 8 GCSEs, GNVQ in Leisure and Tourism, qualified coach in cricket, football and athletics, bricklayer and plasterer
Career outside cricket: Builder
Overseas teams played for: Double View, Perth 1998-99
Cricketers particularly admired: Ian Botham
Young players to look out for: 'My brother Daniel Masters'
Other sports played: Football, boxing 'and most other sports'
Other sports followed: Football (Manchester United)
Relaxations: 'Going out with mates'
Extras: His 6-27 v Durham at Tunbridge Wells 2000 included a final spell of 4-9 from 10.2 overs. Joint Kent Player of the Year 2000 (with Martin Saggers). NBC Denis Compton Award for the most promising young Kent player 2000. Left Kent at the end of the 2002 season and joined Leicestershire for 2003. Scored maiden first-class century (119) v Sussex at Hove 2003
Best batting: 119 Leicestershire v Sussex, Hove 2003
Best bowling: 6-27 Kent v Durham, Tunbridge Wells 2000

2003 Season

	M	Inns	NO	Runs	HS	Avge	100s	50s	Ct	St	O	M	Runs	Wkts	Avge	Best	5wI	10wM
Test																		
All First	17	23	3	269	119	13.45	1	-	4	-	425.3	85	1581	37	42.72	5-53	1	-
1-day Int																		
C & G	1	1	1	24	24 *	-	-	-	-	-	5.4	2	15	4	3.75	4-15	-	
NCL	13	11	5	86	27	14.33	-	-	1	-	73.3	2	458	10	45.80	3-33	-	
Twenty20	6	3	1	1	1	0.50	-	-	1	-	18	0	135	7	19.28	2-19	-	

Career Performances

	M	Inns	NO	Runs	HS	Avge	100s	50s	Ct	St	Balls	Runs	Wkts	Avge	Best	5wI	10wM
Test																	
All First	45	53	12	465	119	11.34	1	1	13	-	7152	3885	115	33.78	6-27	4	-
1-day Int																	
C & G	4	3	1	25	24 *	12.50	-	-	-	-	185	132	5	26.40	4-15	-	
NCL	35	25	10	149	27	9.93	-	-	3	-	1342	1173	25	46.92	5-20	1	
Twenty20	6	3	1	1	1	0.50	-	-	1	-	108	135	7	19.28	2-19	-	

MAUNDERS, J. K.　　　　Leicestershire

Name: <u>John</u> Kenneth Maunders
Role: Left-hand opening bat, right-arm
medium bowler
Born: 4 April 1981, Ashford, Middlesex
Height: 5ft 10in **Weight:** 13st
Nickname: Rod, Weaz
County debut: 1999 (Middlesex),
2003 (Leicestershire)
1st-Class 50s: 3
1st-Class 100s: 2
1st-Class catches: 4
Place in batting averages: 83rd av. 38.85
Parents: Lynn and Kenneth
Marital status: Single
Family links with cricket: 'Grandfather and
two uncles play club cricket for Thames
Valley Ramblers'
Education: Ashford High School;
Spelthorne College
Qualifications: 10 GCSEs, coaching certificates
Career outside cricket: Cricket coach
Off-season: 'Plenty of coaching; working at Pacemaker Distribution; working on
game'

Overseas tours: England U19 to New Zealand 1998-99, to Malaysia and (U19 World Cup) Sri Lanka 1999-2000
Overseas teams played for: University CC, Perth 2001-02
Career highlights to date: 'Scoring maiden first-class hundred v Surrey at Grace Road'
Cricket moments to forget: 'Not any one in particular; getting 0 and dropping catches are not great moments!'
Cricket superstitions: 'Just a few small ones'
Cricketers particularly admired: Brad Hodge, Justin Langer
Other sports played: 'Played football, hockey and squash (consistently wiping the floor with Spencer Collins)'
Other sports followed: Horse racing
Relaxations: 'Spending time with Lauren; eating out; socialising with friends and family; spending time with little Rosie!; horse racing'
Extras: Awarded junior county cap at the age of 12. Has been Seaxe Player of Year. Represented England U17 and U19. NBC Denis Compton Award 1999. Played for Middlesex Board XI in the C&G 2001. Released by Middlesex at the end of the 2002 season and joined Leicestershire for 2003. Scored maiden first-class century (171) v Surrey at Leicester 2003
Opinions on cricket: 'Twenty20 cricket has been a great success, and it will continue to be, and can only be positive for cricket in general. The amount of EU players should be assessed, as it seems they take the place of promising young English cricketers, who could possibly do just as good a job. Not against two overseas players, as it does improve standards of our game, which can only be good for English players looking to play at the highest level.'
Best batting: 171 Leicestershire v Surrey, Leicester 2003

2003 Season

	M	Inns	NO	Runs	HS	Avge	100s	50s	Ct	St	O	M	Runs	Wkts	Avge	Best	5wI	10wM
Test																		
All First	12	22	2	777	171	38.85	2	3	3	-	9	1	38	0	-	-	-	-
1-day Int																		
C & G	2	2	0	25	14	12.50	-	-	-	-								
NCL	5	5	0	29	18	5.80	-	-	-	-								
Twenty20																		

Career Performances

	M	Inns	NO	Runs	HS	Avge	100s	50s	Ct	St	Balls	Runs	Wkts	Avge	Best	5wI	10wM
Test																	
All First	13	24	2	790	171	35.90	2	3	4	-	54	38	0	-	-	-	-
1-day Int																	
C & G	3	3	0	36	14	12.00	-	-	-	-	13	18	0	-	-	-	
NCL	7	7	0	84	49	12.00	-	-	1	-							
Twenty20																	

MAYNARD, M. P. — Glamorgan

Name: <u>Matthew</u> Peter Maynard
Role: Right-hand middle-order bat, right-arm medium bowler, occasional wicket-keeper
Born: 21 March 1966, Oldham, Lancashire
Height: 5ft 11in **Weight:** 13st
Nickname: Ollie, Wilf
County debut: 1985
County cap: 1987
Benefit: 1996
Test debut: 1988
Tests: 4
One-Day Internationals: 14
1000 runs in a season: 12
1st-Class 50s: 127
1st-Class 100s: 53
1st-Class 200s: 3
1st-Class catches: 357
1st-Class stumpings: 7
One-Day 100s: 14
Place in batting averages: 41st av. 46.32 (2002 20th av. 55.68)

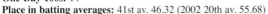

Strike rate: (career 188.16)
Parents: Ken (deceased) and Pat
Wife and date of marriage: Susan, 27 September 1986
Children: Tom, 25 March 1989; Ceri Lloyd, 5 August 1993
Family links with cricket: Father played for many years for Duckinfield. Brother Charles plays for St Fagans. Son Tom plays
Education: Ysgol David Hughes, Menai Bridge, Anglesey
Qualifications: Level 3 coach
Off-season: Commercial property broking for Thomas Carroll Group; England VI to Hong Kong; England Classics to Grenada
Overseas tours: North Wales XI to Barbados 1982; Glamorgan to Barbados 1982, to South Africa 1993; unofficial England XI to South Africa 1989-90; HKCC (Australia) to Bangkok and Hong Kong 1990; England VI to Hong Kong 1992, 1994, 2001 (captain), 2002 (captain), 2003 (captain); England to West Indies 1993-94; England XI to New Zealand (Cricket Max) 1997 (captain); England Classics to Grenada (Grenada Classics) 2003-04
Overseas teams played for: St Joseph's, Whakatane, New Zealand 1986-88; Gosnells, Perth, Western Australia 1988-89; Papakura and Northern Districts, New Zealand 1990-91; Morrinsville College and Northern Districts, New Zealand 1991-92; Otago, New Zealand 1996-97
Career highlights to date: 'Leading Glamorgan to the County Championship in 1997. Playing for England'

Cricket moments to forget: 'Playing unsuccessfully for England'
Cricketers particularly admired: Ian Botham, Viv Richards, David Gower
Young players to look out for: Tom Maynard
Other sports played: Golf, football
Other sports followed: Rugby, football
Relaxations: 'Spending time with my wife and family and relaxing'
Extras: Scored century (102) on first-class debut v Yorkshire at Swansea in 1985, reaching his 100 with three successive straight sixes and becoming the youngest centurion for Glamorgan and the first Glamorgan debutant to score a century since F. B. Pinch did so in 1921; he scored 1000 runs in his first full season. In 1987 set record for fastest 50 for Glamorgan (14 mins) v Yorkshire at Cardiff, and became youngest player to be awarded Glamorgan cap. Voted Young Cricketer of the Year 1988 by the Cricket Writers' Club. Scored 987 runs in July 1991, including a century in each innings (129/126) v Gloucestershire at Cheltenham. His 243 v Hampshire at Southampton 1991 is the highest score by a Glamorgan No. 4. Captained Glamorgan for most of 1992 in Alan Butcher's absence; Glamorgan captain 1996-2000. Voted Wombwell Cricket Lovers' Society captain of the year for 1997. Was one of *Wisden*'s Five Cricketers of the Year 1998. Appointed honorary fellow of University of Wales, Bangor. Shared in Glamorgan one-day record stand for third wicket (204) with Jacques Kallis in National League match v Surrey at Pontypridd 1999. Passed 20,000 first-class runs during his 186 in Glamorgan's first innings v Yorkshire at Headingley 1999. Published *On the Attack: the Batsman's Story* (with Paul Rees) 2001. Scored a century in each innings (140/118*) v Gloucestershire at Cheltenham 2002 (as he also did in 1991), in the process passing 20,000 runs in first-class cricket for Glamorgan. Scored 150-ball 151 v Northamptonshire at Cardiff 2002, in the process sharing with David Hemp (108) in a new record second-wicket partnership for Glamorgan in matches against Northamptonshire (252). Glamorgan Player of the Year 2002
Best batting: 243 Glamorgan v Hampshire, Southampton 1991
Best bowling: 3-21 Glamorgan v Oxford University, The Parks 1987

2003 Season

	M	Inns	NO	Runs	HS	Avge	100s	50s	Ct	St	O	M	Runs	Wkts	Avge	Best	5wI	10wM
Test																		
All First	16	28	0	1297	142	46.32	5	4	11	-	2	0	2	0	-	-	-	-
1-day Int																		
C & G	2	2	0	142	115	71.00	1	-	-	-								
NCL	15	14	3	465	72	42.27	-	2	5	-								
Twenty20	5	5	0	242	72	48.40	-	3	5	-								

Career Performances

	M	Inns	NO	Runs	HS	Avge	100s	50s	Ct	St	Balls	Runs	Wkts	Avge	Best	5wI	10wM
Test	4	8	0	87	35	10.87	-	-	3	-							
All First	379	617	57	23873	243	42.63	56	127	357	7	1129	868	6	144.66	3-21	-	-
1-day Int	14	12	1	156	41	14.18	-	-	3	-							
C & G	47	45	4	1832	151 *	44.68	3	13	23	1	18	8	0	-		-	-
NCL	256	246	27	7415	132	33.85	5	48	114	4	64	64	1	64.00	1-13	-	
Twenty20	5	5	0	242	72	48.40	-	3	5	-							

McCOUBREY, A. G. A. M. Essex

Name: <u>Adrian</u> George Agustus Mathew McCoubrey
Role: Right-hand bat, right-arm fast-medium bowler
Born: 3 April 1980, Ballymena, Northern Ireland
Height: 5ft 10in **Weight:** 11st
Nickname: Scoobie, Coubs, Coubsy
County debut: 2003
Strike rate: 48.33 (career 52.37)
Parents: Ronald and Josephine
Marital status: Single
Family links with cricket: Father played town cricket
Education: Cambridge House Boys' Grammar School; Queen's University of Belfast
Qualifications: 9 GCSEs, 3 A-levels, BEng (Hons) Aeronautical Engineering (2.1)
Career outside cricket: Engineer
Overseas tours: Ireland to Canada (ICC Trophy) 2001
Career highlights to date: 'First Irish senior cap 1999. Playing against Australia at Ormeau, Belfast 2001. Signing professional contract with Essex'
Cricket moments to forget: 'Not qualifying for 2003 World Cup'
Cricket superstitions: 'Will not play any match without wearing the Star of David around my neck'
Cricketers particularly admired: Darren Gough, Glenn McGrath
Other sports played: Football, hockey
Other sports followed: Football (Liverpool FC)
Relaxations: 'Swimming, reading, surfing the Net'
Extras: Has 23 senior Ireland caps; represented Ireland in the C&G 2002 and in the

first round of the C&G 2003, which was played in August 2002. Ballymena Adult Sportsperson of the Year 2001

Best batting: 1* Ireland v Scotland, Belfast 1999
Best bowling: 3-38 Ireland v Scotland, Belfast 1999

2003 Season

	M	Inns	NO	Runs	HS	Avge	100s	50s	Ct	St	O	M	Runs	Wkts	Avge	Best	5wI	10wM
Test																		
All First	2	3	1	1	1	0.50	-	-	-	-	24.1	3	142	3	47.33	1-7	-	-
1-day Int																		
C & G																		
NCL	2	0	0	0	0	-	-	-	-	-	8	2	41	0	-		-	-
Twenty20																		

Career Performances

	M	Inns	NO	Runs	HS	Avge	100s	50s	Ct	St	Balls	Runs	Wkts	Avge	Best	5wI	10wM
Test																	
All First	4	5	2	2	1*	0.66	-	-	-	-	419	279	8	34.87	3-38	-	-
1-day Int																	
C & G	4	3	0	13	11	4.33	-	-	-	-	162	85	3	28.33	2-20	-	
NCL	2	0	0	0	0	-	-	-	-	-	48	41	0	-		-	-
Twenty20																	

64. Which player, who ended his first-class career at Durham, won a Test cap in Jamaica in 1989, England having played 85 Test matches since his previous appearance?

McGARRY, A. C. Essex

Name: <u>Andrew</u> Charles McGarry
Role: Right-hand bat, right-arm
fast-medium bowler
Born: 8 November 1981, Basildon
Height: 6ft 5in **Weight:** 12st 7lbs
Nickname: Rodders
County debut: 1999
1st-Class 5 w. in innings: 1
1st-Class catches: 3
Strike rate: 64.20 (career 78.96)
Parents: Christine and George
Marital status: Single
Family links with cricket: Father played,
and eldest brother plays recreational cricket
Education: King Edward VI GS,
Chelmsford; South East Essex College of
Arts and Technology, Southend
Qualifications: 9 GCSEs, Level 1 and 2
ECB coaching awards

Overseas tours: England U19 to India 2000-01
Cricketers particularly admired: Ian Botham, Allan Donald
Young players to look out for: Justin Bishop, Monty Panesar, Mark Pettini
Other sports played: Basketball, volleyball, football
Other sports followed: Football (Aston Villa)
Relaxations: Going out, listening to music
Extras: First Brian Johnston Scholarship winner 1996. NBC Denis Compton Award
for the most promising young Essex player 2000. Represented England U19 v West
Indies U19 2001. Recorded maiden first-class five-wicket return (5-27) v Cambridge
UCCE at Fenner's 2003. Released by Essex at the end of the 2003 season
Best batting: 11* Essex v CUCCE, Fenner's 2002
Best bowling: 5-27 Essex v CUCCE, Fenner's 2003

2003 Season

	M	Inns	NO	Runs	HS	Avge	100s	50s	Ct	St	O	M	Runs	Wkts	Avge	Best	5wI	10wM
Test																		
All First	2	2	2	6	4 *	-	-	-	-	-	53.3	14	145	5	29.00	5-27	1	-
1-day Int																		
C & G																		
NCL																		
Twenty20																		

Career Performances

	M	Inns	NO	Runs	HS	Avge	100s	50s	Ct	St	Balls	Runs	Wkts	Avge	Best	5wI	10wM
Test																	
All First	15	18	13	28	11 *	5.60	-	-	3	-	2132	1386	27	51.33	5-27	1	-
1-day Int																	
C & G																	
NCL	12	3	1	2	1	1.00	-	-	1	-	279	259	6	43.16	2-20	-	
Twenty20																	

McGRATH, A. Yorkshire

Name: Anthony McGrath
Role: Right-hand bat, right-arm medium bowler
Born: 6 October 1975, Bradford
Height: 6ft 2in **Weight:** 14st 7lbs
Nickname: Gripper, Mags, Terry
County debut: 1995
County cap: 1999
Test debut: 2003
Tests: 4
One-Day Internationals: 10
1st-Class 50s: 31
1st-Class 100s: 10
1st-Class catches: 78
One-Day 100s: 2
Place in batting averages: 65th av. 42.50 (2002 125th av. 32.12)
Place in bowling averages: 21st av. 23.70 (2002 48th av. 27.66)
Strike rate: 47.35 (career 56.35)
Parents: Terry and Kath
Marital status: Single
Education: Yorkshire Martyrs Collegiate School
Qualifications: 9 GCSEs, BTEC National Diploma in Leisure Studies, senior coaching award
Overseas tours: England U19 to West Indies 1994-95; England A to Pakistan 1995-96, to Australia 1996-97; MCC to Bangladesh 1999-2000; England to Bangladesh and Sri Lanka 2003-04 (one-day series), to West Indies 2003-04 (one-day series)
Overseas teams played for: Deep Dene, Melbourne 1998-99; Wanneroo, Perth 1999-2001
Cricket moments to forget: 'Losing semi-final to Lancashire 1996. Relegation to Division Two 2002'

Cricketers particularly admired: Darren Lehmann, Robin Smith
Young players to look out for: Michael Lumb, John Sadler
Other sports followed: 'Most sports', football (Manchester United)
Relaxations: 'Music; spending time with friends; eating out'
Extras: Captained Yorkshire Schools U13, U14, U15 and U16; captained English Schools U17. Bradford League Young Cricketer of the Year 1992 and 1993. Played for England U17, and for England U19 in home series against India U19 1994. C&G Man of the Match for his 72* in the quarter-final v Essex at Chelmsford 2002. Scored 165 v Lancashire at Headingley 2002, in the process sharing with Darren Lehmann (187) in a record third-wicket partnership for Yorkshire at Headingley (317). Captain of Yorkshire 2003. Made Test debut in the first Test v Zimbabwe at Lord's 2003, scoring 69 in England's only innings and taking 3-16 in Zimbabwe's second innings. Made ODI debut v Pakistan at Old Trafford in the NatWest Challenge 2003
Opinions on cricket: 'I still think there is too much cricket crammed into the season. Fewer Championship games in the season would allow for more preparation and planning, enabling more quality cricket to be played.'
Best batting: 165 Yorkshire v Lancashire, Headingley 2002
Best bowling: 4-49 Yorkshire v Hampshire, West End 2002

2003 Season

	M	Inns	NO	Runs	HS	Avge	100s	50s	Ct	St	O	M	Runs	Wkts	Avge	Best	5wI	10wM
Test	4	5	0	201	81	40.20	-	2	3	-	17	1	56	4	14.00	3-16	-	-
All First	14	23	3	850	127*	42.50	1	7	8	-	134.1	21	403	17	23.70	3-16	-	-
1-day Int	10	9	2	143	52	20.42	-	1	4	-	26	1	126	2	63.00	1-15	-	
C & G	1	1	0	56	56	56.00	-	1	-	-	3	0	15	0	-		-	-
NCL	9	9	1	112	41	14.00	-	-	4	-	49	1	244	9	27.11	4-41	-	
Twenty20																		

Career Performances

	M	Inns	NO	Runs	HS	Avge	100s	50s	Ct	St	Balls	Runs	Wkts	Avge	Best	5wI	10wM
Test	4	5	0	201	81	40.20	-	2	3	-	102	56	4	14.00	3-16	-	-
All First	130	222	16	6370	165	30.92	10	31	78	-	2987	1482	53	27.96	4-49	-	-
1-day Int	10	9	2	143	52	20.42	-	1	4	-	156	126	2	63.00	1-15	-	
C & G	21	18	3	700	84	46.66	-	7	8	-	168	148	2	74.00	1-33	-	
NCL	102	94	16	2396	102	30.71	1	15	31	-	903	691	24	28.79	4-41	-	
Twenty20																	

McLEAN, N. A. M. Somerset

Name: <u>Nixon</u> Alexei McNamara McLean
Role: Left-hand bat, right-arm fast bowler
Born: 20 July 1973, Stubbs, St Vincent
Height: 6ft 5in
Nickname: Nicko
County debut: 1998 (Hampshire),
2003 (Somerset)
County cap: 1998 (Hampshire)
Test debut: 1997-98
Tests: 19
One-Day Internationals: 45
50 wickets in a season: 2
1st-Class 50s: 3
1st-Class 5 w. in innings: 14
1st-Class 10 w. in match: 1
1st-Class catches: 36
Place in batting averages: 239th av. 16.73
Place in bowling averages: 54th av. 28.80
Strike rate: 50.90 (career 52.09)
Marital status: Single
Education: Carapan SS, St Vincent
Overseas tours: West Indies to Australia 1996-97, to Bangladesh (Wills International Cup) 1998-99, to South Africa 1998-99, to Singapore (Coca-Cola Singapore Challenge) 1999, to Bangladesh (Biman Millennium Cup) 1999-2000, to Sharjah (Coca-Cola Champions' Trophy) 1999-2000, to England 2000, to Kenya (ICC Knockout Trophy) 2000-01, to Australia 2000-01, to Africa (World Cup) 2002-03; West Indies A to South Africa 1997-98
Overseas teams played for: Windward Islands 1992-93 – 2000-01; St Vincent and the Grenadines 2002-03; KwaZulu-Natal 2001-02 –
Extras: Was Hampshire's overseas player 1998-99, taking 62 first-class wickets (av. 25.40) in 1998. Took 44 wickets (av. 16.27) in KwaZulu-Natal's Supersport Series title win 2001-02, including 6-84 in the Northerns first innings in the final at Durban; also took 15 wickets at 15.33 in KwaZulu-Natal's successful Standard Bank Cup campaign 2001-02. Joined Somerset as an overseas player for 2003, taking 5-87 on debut for the county v Gloucestershire at Bristol. Scored 39 v Derbyshire at Taunton 2003, in the process sharing with Ian Blackwell (247*) in a new record tenth-wicket partnership for Somerset (163)
Best batting: 76 Somerset v Gloucestershire, Taunton 2003
Best bowling: 7-28 West Indians v Free State, Bloemfontein 1998-99

2003 Season

	M	Inns	NO	Runs	HS	Avge	100s	50s	Ct	St	O	M	Runs	Wkts	Avge	Best	5wI	10wM
Test																		
All First	17	23	4	318	76	16.73	-	1	2	-	551.3	115	1872	65	28.80	5-43	3	-
1-day Int																		
C & G	2	1	0	6	6	6.00	-	-	-	-	20	3	57	2	28.50	1-28	-	
NCL	12	9	4	133	28	26.60	-	-	2	-	87.3	3	468	21	22.28	3-51	-	
Twenty20																		

Career Performances

	M	Inns	NO	Runs	HS	Avge	100s	50s	Ct	St	Balls	Runs	Wkts	Avge	Best	5wI	10wM
Test	19	32	2	368	46	12.26	-	-	5	-	3299	1873	44	42.56	3-53	-	-
All First	121	189	27	2228	76	13.75	-	3	36	-	21412	11274	411	27.43	7-28	14	1
1-day Int	45	34	8	314	50 *	12.07	-	1	8	-	2120	1729	46	37.58	3-21	-	
C & G	8	7	3	118	36	29.50	-	-	-	-	427	234	11	21.27	3-27	-	
NCL	43	33	7	413	32	15.88	-	-	5	-	1767	1484	61	24.32	3-27	-	
Twenty20																		

McMAHON, P. J.   Nottinghamshire

Name: <u>Paul</u> Joseph McMahon
Role: Right-hand bat, off-spin bowler
Born: 12 March 1983, Wigan
Height: 6ft 1in **Weight:** 11st 8lbs
Nickname: Vince, Macca, Boffin
County debut: 2002
1st-Class catches: 3
Place in batting averages: 273rd av. 10.33
Place in bowling averages: 75th av. 33.05
Strike rate: 67.88 (career 67.95)
Parents: Gerry and Teresa
Marital status: Single
Family links with cricket: 'Dad was club professional in Lancashire and Cheshire leagues; now plays for Notts Over 50s and for Wollaton in Notts Premier League. Mum makes teas and has managed to learn how to find scores on Ceefax'
Education: Trinity RC Comprehensive, Nottingham; Wadham College, Oxford University
Qualifications: 11 GCSEs, 4 A-levels
Career outside cricket: Student

Off-season: 'Second year of law degree at Oxford University'

Overseas tours: England U19 to Australia and (U19 World Cup) New Zealand 2001-02; Nottinghamshire to South Africa 2002, 2003

Career highlights to date: 'Captaining England U19 against India U19, and taking eight wickets [4-47 and 4-58] in the victory at Northampton in the deciding final "Test"'

Cricketers particularly admired: Mike Atherton, Steve Waugh, Nasser Hussain

Young players to look out for: 'All the many young players at Notts'; Joe Sayers, Michael Munday, Tom Mees, Jamie Dalrymple

Other sports played: Football (Nottingham Schools U15, Wadham College FC), darts (Wadham College 2nd VIII)

Other sports followed: Football (AFC Wimbledon)

Favourite band: Oasis

Relaxations: Music, reading, current affairs, 'doing the Wheelhouse quiz'

Extras: Has played for Notts at every level from U11 to 1st XI. Second graduate of Nottinghamshire CCC Academy. Man of the Match in England's opening game of the 2001-02 U19 World Cup, taking 5-25 against Nepal. Took 45 wickets at an average of 18.82 in 2nd XI Championship 2002. Captain of England U19 against India U19 2002; leading wicket-taker in 'Test' series with ten wickets (av. 22.20). Shared with Andrew Harris (41*) in a record last-wicket stand for Nottinghamshire in matches v Northamptonshire (68), at Northampton 2002. Played for OUCCE 2003 and awarded Oxford Blue 2003. Nottinghamshire Young Player of the Year 2003. Appointed captain of Oxford University for 2004

Opinions on cricket: 'I feel very lucky to be part of this great game.'

Best batting: 30 Nottinghamshire v Middlesex, Lord's 2003

Best bowling: 4-59 Nottinghamshire v Essex, Chelmsford 2003

2003 Season

	M	Inns	NO	Runs	HS	Avge	100s	50s	Ct	St	O	M	Runs	Wkts	Avge	Best	5wI	10wM
Test																		
All First	6	9	0	93	30	10.33	-	-	3	-	203.4	51	595	18	33.05	4-59	-	-
1-day Int																		
C & G																		
NCL	1	1	0	0	0	0.00	-	-	-	-	5	0	33	0	-		-	-
Twenty20																		

Career Performances

	M	Inns	NO	Runs	HS	Avge	100s	50s	Ct	St	Balls	Runs	Wkts	Avge	Best	5wI	10wM
Test																	
All First	8	12	0	108	30	9.00	-	-	3	-	1359	698	20	34.90	4-59	-	-
1-day Int																	
C & G																	
NCL	1	1	0	0	0	0.00	-	-	-	-	30	33	0	-		-	-
Twenty20																	

MEES, T.   Warwickshire

Name: Thomas (Tom) Mees
Role: Right-hand bat, right-arm
fast-medium bowler
Born: 8 June 1981, Wolverhampton
Height: 6ft 3in **Weight:** 13st
Nickname: Meesy, Meesdog
County debut: No first-team appearance
1st-Class 5 w. in innings: 1
1st-Class catches: 1
Strike rate: 128.40 (career 71.55)
Parents: Mark and Christina
Marital status: Single
Family links with cricket: 'Cousin Simon
played for Worcestershire Youth. Dad played
for Cosely and umpires'
Education: Worcester Royal Grammar
School; King Edward VI College,
Stourbridge; Oxford Brookes University
Qualifications: 9 GCSEs, 3 A-levels, ECB Level 1 coaching award
Overseas tours: British Universities to South Africa 2002
Overseas teams played for: Railways, Albany, Western Australia 1999-2000
Career highlights to date: 'Taking 6-64 v Middlesex on first-class debut for
Oxford UCCE 2001'
Cricket moments to forget: 'Playing in a Birmingham League match for Old Hill v
Walsall, mistaking the umpire for the wicket-keeper and throwing the ball over the
umpire's head for four overthrows off the last ball of the game with the opposition
needing two to win!'
Cricketers particularly admired: Ian Botham, Andrew Flintoff
Young players to look out for: Jamie Dalrymple, Matt Stillwell, Patrick Wolff,
Ian Bell, Graham Wagg
Other sports played: Golf, football, tennis
Other sports followed: Football (Liverpool FC)
Relaxations: Playing golf, spending time with friends, shopping, going out
Extras: Played for Worcestershire Board XI in the NatWest 1999. Has played for
Warwickshire 2nd XI. Played for Oxford University CCE in 2001, 2002 and 2003.
Played for Warwickshire Board XI in the C&G 2001 and 2002, taking 3-19 v
Cambridgeshire at March in the 2002 competition and winning the Man of the Match
award. Recorded maiden first-class five-wicket return (6-64) for OUCCE on first-class
debut v Middlesex at The Parks 2001. Represented British Universities 2002 and v
Zimbabweans 2003
Best batting: 36* OUCCE v Hampshire, The Parks 2003
Best bowling: 6-64 OUCCE v Middlesex, The Parks 2001

2003 Season (did not make any first-class or one-day appearances for his county)

Career Performances

	M	Inns	NO	Runs	HS	Avge	100s	50s	Ct	St	Balls	Runs	Wkts	Avge	Best	5wl	10wM
Test																	
All First	8	12	2	110	36 *	11.00	-	-	1	-	1431	917	20	45.85	6-64	1	-
1-day Int																	
C & G	4	2	1	4	4 *	4.00	-	-	-	-	198	144	3	48.00	3-19	-	
NCL																	
Twenty20																	

MIDDLEBROOK, J. D.   Essex

Name: James Daniel Middlebrook
Role: Right-hand bat, off-spin bowler
Born: 13 May 1977, Leeds
Height: 6ft 1in **Weight:** 13st
Nickname: Brooky, Midi, Midders, Midhouse, Dog
County debut: 1998 (Yorkshire), 2002 (Essex)
County cap: 2003 (Essex)
50 wickets in a season: 1
1st-Class 50s: 4
1st-Class 5 w. in innings: 4
1st-Class 10 w. in match: 1
1st-Class catches: 28
Place in batting averages: 224th av. 20.16 (2002 244th av. 17.37)
Place in bowling averages: 87th av. 35.33 (2002 139th av. 45.68)
Strike rate: 63.53 (career 70.30)
Parents: Ralph and Mavis
Marital status: Single
Family links with cricket: 'Dad is a senior staff coach'
Education: Crawshaw, Pudsey ('at this school with Paul Hutchison')
Qualifications: NVQ Level 2 in Coaching Sport and Recreation, ECB senior coach
Off-season: 'Perth, at the Paul Terry academy'
Overseas tours: Yorkshire CCC to Guernsey
Overseas teams played for: Stokes Valley CC, New Zealand; Gold Coast Dolphins, Brisbane; Surfers Paradise CC, Brisbane
Career highlights to date: 'Beating Yorkshire in the NCL this year [2003] so we stayed up'

Cricket superstitions: 'Always put my batting gear on the same way'
Cricketers particularly admired: John Emburey, Ian Botham
Young players to look out for: Alastair Cook, Ravinder Bopara
Other sports played: Golf, tennis, squash, badminton
Other sports followed: Football (Leeds United), athletics
Relaxations: 'Any music – MTV – sleeping, socialising, catching up with old friends'
Extras: Played for Pudsey Congs from age of seven. Played for Yorkshire at all age levels U11 to 1st XI. Awarded Yorkshire 2nd XI cap 1998. His maiden first-class five-wicket return (6-82) v Hampshire at Southampton 2000 included a spell of four wickets in five balls. Released by Yorkshire at the end of the 2001 season and joined Essex for 2002. Took Championship hat-trick (Saggers, Muralitharan, Sheriyar) v Kent at Canterbury 2003. Took 50 first-class wickets in a season for the first time 2003. Awarded Essex cap 2003
Best batting: 84 Yorkshire v Essex, Chelmsford 2001
Best bowling: 6-82 Yorkshire v Hampshire, Southampton 2000

2003 Season

	M	Inns	NO	Runs	HS	Avge	100s	50s	Ct	St	O	M	Runs	Wkts	Avge	Best	5wI	10wM
Test																		
All First	16	25	1	484	82 *	20.16	-	2	7	-	593	87	1979	56	35.33	6-123	3	-
1-day Int																		
C & G																		
NCL	15	11	5	123	46 *	20.50	-	-	7	-	97	2	553	10	55.30	2-19	-	
Twenty20																		

Career Performances

	M	Inns	NO	Runs	HS	Avge	100s	50s	Ct	St	Balls	Runs	Wkts	Avge	Best	5wI	10wM
Test																	
All First	57	84	8	1386	84	18.23	-	4	28	-	10054	5173	143	36.17	6-82	4	1
1-day Int																	
C & G	4	2	2	12	6 *	-	-	-	3	-	126	111	1	111.00	1-46	-	
NCL	43	29	9	240	46 *	12.00	-	-	12	-	1632	1290	42	30.71	4-33	-	
Twenty20																	

> 65. Who took 134 Championship wickets in 1982
> and then 35 Test wickets in the 1988 West Indies/England series?

MILLER, D. J.   Surrey

Name: <u>Daniel</u> James Miller
Role: Left-hand bat, right-arm fast bowler
Born: 12 June 1983, Hammersmith, London
Height: 6ft 4in **Weight:** 14st 4lbs
Nickname: Windy, Funky
County debut: 2002 (one-day)
Parents: Gillian and Keith
Marital status: Single
Family links with cricket: 'My dad's got the
name but no ability'
Education: Ewell Castle Senior School;
Kingston College
Qualifications: 9 GCSEs, 4 A-levels
Overseas tours: Surrey Cricket Board to
Barbados 1999
Career highlights to date: 'Making first-
team debut at Surrey in NUL'
Cricket superstitions: 'Copying the
preparation of a good day'
Cricketers particularly admired: David Morgan, Ian Botham, Alec Stewart, Graham
Thorpe, Glenn McGrath
Young players to look out for: Neil Saker, Chris Murtagh, Simon Day
Other sports played: Football (Kingstonian Youth)
Other sports followed: Football (Tottenham Hotspur), 'all rugby union'
Relaxations: 'Going to Cheam Sports Club (Rome)'
Extras: Appeared in one NUL match in 2002. Attended Surrey Academy
Opinions on cricket: 'It's tough being a bowler; it's certainly a batsman's game!'

2003 Season (did not make any first-class or one-day appearances)

Career Performances

	M	Inns	NO	Runs	HS	Avge	100s	50s	Ct	St	Balls	Runs	Wkts	Avge	Best	5wI	10wM
Test																	
All First																	
1-day Int																	
C & G																	
NCL	1	1	0	1	1	1.00	-	-	-	-	42	32	0	-		-	-
Twenty20																	

MOHAMMAD AKRAM Sussex

Name: Mohammad Akram Awan
Role: Right-hand bat, right-arm fast bowler
Born: 10 September 1974, Islamabad, Pakistan
Height: 6ft 2in **Weight:** 13st 7lbs
Nickname: Haji
County debut: 1997 (Northamptonshire), 2003 (Essex)
Test debut: 1995-96
Tests: 9
One-Day Internationals: 23
1st-Class 5 w. in innings: 14
1st-Class 10 w. in match: 1
1st-Class catches: 25
Place in bowling averages: 51st av. 28.00
Strike rate: 43.50 (career 45.69)
Parents: Mohammad Akbar
Marital status: Married, May 1999
Children: Imaan Akram, 2002
Education: Gordon College, Rawalpindi
Career outside cricket: Business
Off-season: 'Playing abroad'
Overseas tours: Pakistan to Australia 1995-96, to England 1996, to South Africa and Zimbabwe 1997-98, to Australia 1999-2000, to West Indies 1999-2000, to New Zealand 2000-01, plus one-day tournaments in Sharjah, Singapore, Toronto, Bangladesh and Sri Lanka
Overseas teams played for: Rawalpindi Cricket Association 1992-93 – 2002-03; Allied Bank 1996-97 – 2000-01
Cricket superstitions: 'None'
Cricketers particularly admired: Wasim, Waqar
Other sports played: Tennis, swimming
Other sports followed: Football
Relaxations: 'Friends, going to different countries, pool'
Extras: Was Northamptonshire's overseas player in 1997. Recorded maiden Test five-wicket innings return (5-138) in third Test v Australia at Perth 1999-2000. Was an overseas player with Essex for the latter part of the 2003 season, replacing the injured Scott Brant. Took 5-98 on Championship debut for Essex v Sussex at Colchester. Took career best 8-49 v Surrey at The Oval 2003, including the first four wickets without conceding a run. Has joined Sussex for 2004; is no longer classed as an overseas player, having qualified by residency
Best batting: 28 Northamptonshire v Durham, Northampton 1997
Best bowling: 8-49 Essex v Surrey, The Oval 2003

2003 Season

	M	Inns	NO	Runs	HS	Avge	100s	50s	Ct	St	O	M	Runs	Wkts	Avge	Best	5wl	10wM
Test																		
All First	4	6	1	19	10	3.80	-	-	-	-	145	31	560	20	28.00	8-49	2	1
1-day Int																		
C & G																		
NCL	6	3	2	8	8 *	8.00	-	-	2	-	43	1	189	3	63.00	1-36	-	
Twenty20																		

Career Performances

	M	Inns	NO	Runs	HS	Avge	100s	50s	Ct	St	Balls	Runs	Wkts	Avge	Best	5wl	10wM
Test	9	15	6	24	10 *	2.66	-	-	4	-	1477	859	17	50.52	5-138	1	-
All First	82	109	26	596	28	7.18	-	-	25	-	12748	7310	279	26.20	8-49	14	1
1-day Int	23	9	7	14	7 *	7.00	-	-	8	-	989	790	19	41.57	2-28	-	
C & G	1	1	1	0	0 *	-	-	-	-	-	72	42	1	42.00	1-42	-	
NCL	11	6	5	11	8 *	11.00	-	-	3	-	462	330	9	36.66	4-19	-	
Twenty20																		

MOHAMMAD ALI   Derbyshire

Name: Syed Mohammad Ali Bukhari
Role: Right-hand bat, left-arm
fast-medium bowler
Born: 8 November 1973, Bahawalpur, Punjab
County debut: 2002
1st-Class 50s: 4
1st-Class 5 w. in innings: 11
1st-Class 10 w. in match: 2
1st-Class catches: 25
Place in batting averages: 287th av. 7.21
(2002 264th av. 15.13)
Place in bowling averages: 105th av. 37.85
(2002 110th av. 36.34)
Strike rate: 47.35 (career 51.13)
Overseas teams played for: Numerous,
including Bahawalpur, Islamabad Cricket
Association, Lahore Cricket Association,
Railways and United Bank
Extras: Nephew of Taslim Arif who played for Pakistan 1979-80. Played for
Glamorgan 2nd XI 2000 and 2001. Struck a 38-ball 53 on debut for Derbyshire v
Durham at Derby 2002, batting at No. 9. Is not considered an overseas player
Best batting: 92 Bahawalpur v Lahore City, Rahimyarkhan 1998-99
Best bowling: 6-37 Railways v National Bank, Faisalabad 1993-94

	M	Inns	NO	Runs	HS	Avge	100s	50s	Ct	St	O	M	Runs	Wkts	Avge	Best	5wI	10wM
Test																		
All First	10	17	3	101	31	7.21	-	-	1	-	221	36	1060	28	37.85	4-79	-	-
1-day Int																		
C & G	1	0	0	0	0	-	-	-	-	-	10	0	28	1	28.00	1-28	-	
NCL	4	3	3	13	8 *	-	-	-	-	-	29.3	1	178	4	44.50	2-23	-	
Twenty20																		

Career Performances

	M	Inns	NO	Runs	HS	Avge	100s	50s	Ct	St	Balls	Runs	Wkts	Avge	Best	5wI	10wM
Test																	
All First	80	106	25	1137	92	14.03	-	4	25	-	12988	8121	254	31.97	6-37	11	2
1-day Int																	
C & G	2	1	0	19	19	19.00	-	-	-	-	78	50	1	50.00	1-28	-	
NCL	6	5	4	25	10 *	25.00	-	-	-	-	261	244	8	30.50	3-42	-	
Twenty20																	

MOHAMMAD SAMI   Kent

Name: Mohammad Sami
Role: Right-hand bat, right-arm fast bowler
Born: 24 February 1981, Karachi, Pakistan
County debut: 2003
Test debut: 2000-01
Tests: 9
One-Day Internationals: 33
1st-Class 5 w. in innings: 7
1st-Class 10 w. in match: 1
1st-Class catches: 10
Strike rate: 29.72 (career 47.60)
Overseas tours: Pakistan U19 to Sri Lanka
(U19 World Cup) 1999-2000; Pakistan to
New Zealand 2000-01, to England 2001,
to Bangladesh 2001-02, to Sharjah
(v West Indies) 2001-02, to Sri Lanka
(ICC Champions Trophy) 2002-03, to Sri
Lanka and Sharjah (v Australia) 2002-03, to

Zimbabwe 2002-03, to South Africa 2002-03, to Africa (World Cup) 2002-03, to
England (NatWest Challenge) 2003, to New Zealand 2003-04, plus other one-day
tournaments in Sharjah, Australia, Morocco, Kenya and Sri Lanka
Overseas teams played for: Pakistan Customs 1999-2000; Karachi Whites 2000-01;
National Bank of Pakistan 2000-01 – 2002-03

Extras: Had match figures of 8-106 (3-70/5-36) on Test debut in the first Test v New Zealand at Auckland 2000-01, winning Man of the Match award. Took hat-trick (T. C. B. Fernando, Zoysa, Muralitharan) v Sri Lanka in the final of the Asian Test Championship at Lahore 2001-02. Was an overseas player with Kent in late June and early July 2003 before injuring an ankle; has returned for 2004. Took 15-114 (8-64/ 7-50) v Nottinghamshire at Maidstone 2003, the best match figures by a Kent bowler since 1939
Best batting: 41* National Bank v Sui Gas, Faisalabad 2001-02
Best bowling: 8-64 Kent v Nottinghamshire, Maidstone 2003
Stop press: ODI Man of the Match awards v South Africa at Lahore 2003-04 (3-20) and v New Zealand at Lahore 2003-04 (5-10)

2003 Season

	M	Inns	NO	Runs	HS	Avge	100s	50s	Ct	St	O	M	Runs	Wkts	Avge	Best	5wl	10wM
Test																		
All First	3	4	0	19	16	4.75	-	-	-	-	89.1	17	357	18	19.83	8-64	2	1
1-day Int	3	2	1	7	7 *	7.00	-	-	2	-	22	2	127	2	63.50	1-50	-	
C & G																		
NCL	1	0	0	0	0	-	-	-	1	-	9	1	30	3	10.00	3-30	-	
Twenty20	2	2	1	13	8	13.00	-	-	-	-	7.5	0	54	2	27.00	1-23	-	

Career Performances

	M	Inns	NO	Runs	HS	Avge	100s	50s	Ct	St	Balls	Runs	Wkts	Avge	Best	5wl	10wM
Test	9	14	9	66	22	13.20	-	-	-	-	1887	1007	25	40.28	5-36	1	-
All First	34	45	27	230	41 *	12.77	-	-	10	-	6189	3527	130	27.13	8-64	7	1
1-day Int	33	17	11	69	12 *	11.50	-	-	9	-	1575	1246	50	24.92	4-25	-	
C & G																	
NCL	1	0	0	0	0	-	-	-	1	-	54	30	3	10.00	3-30	-	
Twenty20	2	2	1	13	8	13.00	-	-	-	-	47	54	2	27.00	1-23	-	

MONTGOMERIE, R. R.   Sussex

Name: Richard Robert Montgomerie
Role: Right-hand opening bat, occasional right-arm slow bowler
Born: 3 July 1971, Rugby
Height: 5ft 10in **Weight:** 13st
Nickname: Monty
County debut: 1991 (Northamptonshire), 1999 (Sussex)
County cap: 1995 (Northamptonshire), 1999 (Sussex)
1000 runs in a season: 4
1st-Class 50s: 53
1st-Class 100s: 24
1st-Class catches: 177

One-Day 100s: 3
Place in batting averages: 113th av. 33.62
(2002 88th av. 38.00)
Strike rate: 18.00 (career 99.00)
Parents: Robert and Gillian
Marital status: Single
Family links with cricket: Father captained
Oxfordshire
Education: Rugby School; Worcester
College, Oxford University
Qualifications: 12 O-levels, 4 A-levels,
BA (Hons) Chemistry, Level II coaching
Off-season: 'Gaining experience in sports
admin; keen to get involved with London
2012, the Olympic bid'
Overseas tours: Oxford University to
Namibia 1991; Northamptonshire to
Zimbabwe and Johannesburg; Christians in
Sport to South Africa 2000; Sussex to Grenada 2001, 2002
Overseas teams played for: Sydney University CC 1995-96
Career highlights to date: 'Two Lord's finals. Winning second division of National
League in 1999 and second division of County Championship in 2001. A hundred
[157] v Australians [at Hove 2001]. Winning Championship 2003'
Cricket moments to forget: 'Running [Northants] captain Allan Lamb out on my
Championship debut … as his runner'
Cricketers particularly admired: Steve Waugh, Mark Robinson
Young players to look out for: Matt Prior, Tim Ambrose
Other sports followed: Golf, rackets, real tennis 'and many others'
Favourite band: The Police
Relaxations: Any sport, good television, reading and 'occasionally testing my brain'
Extras: Oxford rackets Blue 1990. Scored unbeaten 50 in each innings of 1991
Varsity match. Faced first ball delivered by Durham in first-class cricket, for Oxford
University at The Parks 1992. Captained Oxford University and Combined
Universities 1994. Released by Northants at the end of the 1998 season and joined
Sussex for 1999. Scored his first 100 for Sussex (113*) against his former county at
Hove 1999. Scored 160* v Nottinghamshire at Trent Bridge 2001; in the process he
shared with Murray Goodwin in a record partnership for any wicket for Sussex in
matches against Notts (372*), superseding his own record (292) set with Michael
Bevan at Hove in 2000. Scored 108 v Essex at Hove in the Norwich Union League
2001, in the process sharing with Murray Goodwin in a Sussex record opening
partnership in the one-day league (176). Man of the Match award for his 157 in the
Vodafone Challenge match against the Australians at Hove 2001. Joint Sussex Player
of the Year (with Murray Goodwin) 2001. Carried his bat for 122* v Leicestershire at
Horsham 2002. C&G Man of the Match award for his 126* v Leicestershire at
Leicester 2002. Sussex 1st XI Fielder of the Year 2003. 'Two first-class wickets!'

Opinions on cricket: 'Four-day cricket in two divisions is having the desired effect of keeping the intensity and standard high to the end of the season. Twenty20 was a success – I am sure it will continue to be so next year [2004]. I wish people would extol the virtues of county cricket instead of berating it when England lose!'

Best batting: 196 Sussex v Hampshire, Hove 2002
Best bowling: 1-0 Sussex v Middlesex, Lord's 2001

2003 Season

	M	Inns	NO	Runs	HS	Avge	100s	50s	Ct	St	O	M	Runs	Wkts	Avge	Best	5wl	10wM
Test																		
All First	17	29	2	908	105	33.62	1	7	24	-	3	0	9	1	9.00	1-9	-	-
1-day Int																		
C & G	2	2	0	44	36	22.00	-	-	-	-								
NCL	11	10	1	172	66 *	19.11	-	1	6	-								
Twenty20																		

Career Performances

	M	Inns	NO	Runs	HS	Avge	100s	50s	Ct	St	Balls	Runs	Wkts	Avge	Best	5wl	10wM
Test																	
All First	181	317	29	10442	196	36.25	24	53	177	-	198	108	2	54.00	1-0	-	-
1-day Int																	
C & G	17	17	4	799	126 *	61.46	2	6	5	-							
NCL	105	103	8	2893	108	30.45	1	21	29	-							
Twenty20																	

66. In 1955 which Surrey man dismissed Goddard, Ramadhin and Gilchrist to complete the first hat-trick for England in a home Test since 1899?

MOORE, S. C. Worcestershire

Name: <u>Stephen</u> Colin Moore
Role: Right-hand top-order bat, right-arm medium bowler
Born: 4 November 1980, Johannesburg, South Africa
Height: 6ft 1in **Weight:** 13st
Nickname: Circles, Mandy
County debut: 2003
County colours: 2003
1st-Class catches: 2
Parents: Shane and Carrol
Marital status: Single
Education: St Stithians College, Johannesburg; Exeter University
Career outside cricket: 'Studying for an MEng in electronic engineering'
Overseas tours: Wanderers Colts U19 to England 1996
Overseas teams played for: Wanderers, Johannesburg 1995-99
Cricketers particularly admired: Steve Waugh ('for ability to score runs when team in trouble'), Daryll Cullinan ('for elegant strokeplay all around the wicket')
Other sports played: Tennis (university 1st team; ranked in top 15 South African juniors), hockey (university 1st XI)
Other sports followed: Rugby (Springboks)
Relaxations: 'Wildlife; inflatable boating and other watersports; music (saxophone and guitar)'
Extras: Is not considered an overseas player
Best batting: 28* Worcestershire v Glamorgan, Cardiff 2003

2003 Season

	M	Inns	NO	Runs	HS	Avge	100s	50s	Ct	St	O	M	Runs	Wkts	Avge	Best	5wl	10wM
Test																		
All First	2	4	1	97	28 *	32.33	-	-	2	-								
1-day Int																		
C & G																		
NCL	1	1	0	12	12	12.00	-	-	-	-	1	0	10	0	-		-	-
Twenty20	5	5	3	116	39 *	58.00	-	-	2	-								

Career Performances

	M	Inns	NO	Runs	HS	Avge	100s	50s	Ct	St	Balls	Runs	Wkts	Avge	Best	5wl	10wM
Test																	
All First	2	4	1	97	28 *	32.33	-	-	2	-							
1-day Int																	
C & G																	
NCL	1	1	0	12	12	12.00	-	-	-	-	6	10	0	-		-	-
Twenty20	5	5	3	116	39 *	58.00	-	-	2	-							

MORRIS, A. C.   Hampshire

Name: Alexander (<u>Alex</u>) Corfield Morris
Role: Left-hand bat, right-arm
medium-fast bowler
Born: 4 October 1976, Barnsley
Height: 6ft 4in **Weight:** 14st
Nickname: Almo
County debut: 1995 (Yorkshire),
1998 (Hampshire)
County cap: 2001 (Hampshire)
50 wickets in a season: 2
1st-Class 50s: 7
1st-Class 5 w. in innings: 5
1st-Class 10 w. in match: 1
1st-Class catches: 34
Strike rate: (career 50.42)
Parents: Janet and Chris
Marital status: Single
Family links with cricket: Brother Zac
played for Hampshire and Yorkshire
Education: Holgate School, Barnsley; Barnsley College
Qualifications: 4 GCSEs, BTEC National Diploma in Sports Science,
senior cricket coach
Overseas tours: England U19 to West Indies 1994-95, to Zimbabwe 1995-96;
England VI to Hong Kong 1996; Michael Vaughan XI to Tenerife 1996; Craig Dudley
XI to Cyprus 1997; Anthony McGrath XI to Gran Canaria 1998; Alex Morris XI to
Cyprus 1999
Overseas teams played for: South Sydney 2002
Cricket moments to forget: 'Out off the last ball of the last game at Northlands Road,
v Yorkshire 2000'
Other sports played: Football (junior with Barnsley and Rotherham; trials for
Nottingham Forest and Leeds)

Other sports followed: Football (Barnsley FC)
Relaxations: 'Bondi Beach'
Extras: Played for Yorkshire U11-U19; made debut for 2nd XI at age 16. Played for England U15 against Barbados and in 1994 for both England U17 and U19 against India U19. Left Yorkshire and signed for Hampshire along with his brother Zac for the 1998 season. NBC Denis Compton Award 1998. Released by Hampshire at the end of the 2003 season
Best batting: 65 Hampshire v Sussex, West End 2001
Best bowling: 5-39 Hampshire v Durham, Riverside 2001

2003 Season

	M	Inns	NO	Runs	HS	Avge	100s	50s	Ct	St	O	M	Runs	Wkts	Avge	Best	5wI	10wM
Test																		
All First	2	3	0	67	46	22.33	-	-	2	-								
1-day Int																		
C & G																		
NCL																		
Twenty20																		

Career Performances

	M	Inns	NO	Runs	HS	Avge	100s	50s	Ct	St	Balls	Runs	Wkts	Avge	Best	5wI	10wM
Test																	
All First	62	81	12	1392	65	20.17	-	7	34	-	7867	4119	156	26.40	5-39	5	1
1-day Int																	
C & G	3	2	2	4	3 *	-	-	-	1	-	132	125	2	62.50	1-43	-	
NCL	32	19	5	232	48 *	16.57	-	-	6	-	792	708	26	27.23	4-49	-	
Twenty20																	

67. Which current first-class umpire became the first
England batsman to score a 100 on Test debut at Lord's,
against the West Indies?

MUCHALL, G. J.   Durham

Name: <u>Gordon</u> James Muchall
Role: Right-hand bat, right-arm
medium-fast bowler
Born: 2 November 1982,
Newcastle upon Tyne
Height: 6ft **Weight:** 13st 5lbs
Nickname: Manson, West, Cannon,
Melon, Lecter
County debut: 2002
1st-Class 50s: 8
1st-Class 100s: 4
1st-Class catches: 21
Place in batting averages: 177th av. 25.83
(2002 185th av. 24.52)
Strike rate: 62.80 (career 63.55)
Parents: Mary and Arthur
Marital status: Single
Family links with cricket: Grandfather
played for Northumberland. Younger brother (Paul) was in England U15 squad
Education: Durham School
Qualifications: 8 GCSEs, 2 A-levels
Overseas tours: England U19 to India 2000-01, to Australia and (U19 World Cup)
New Zealand 2001-02; ECB National Academy to Australia and Sri Lanka 2002-03
Overseas teams played for: Fremantle 2001-02
Career highlights to date: '127 at Lord's for Durham. 253 for England U19 v India
U19'
Cricket moments to forget: 'With the opposition needing four off the last ball to win,
going into the long barrier position and the ball bouncing over my head for four'
Cricketers particularly admired: Jacques Kallis, Ian Botham, Steve Waugh,
Darren Gough
Young players to look out for: Paul Muchall, Kyle Hogg, Kadeer Ali,
Nadeem Malik
Other sports played: Rugby (at school)
Other sports followed: Football (Newcastle United), rugby (Newcastle Falcons
and England)
Relaxations: Listening to music, socialising with friends
Extras: Represented England U19 v West Indies U19 2001 and v India U19 2002,
scoring 254 in the first 'Test' at Cardiff 2002; it was the third highest individual score
in the history of U19 international cricket. Played for Durham Board XI in the C&G
2002. Cricket Society's Most Promising Young Cricketer of the Year Award 2002.
NBC Denis Compton Award for the most promising young Durham player 2002

462

Best batting: 127 Durham v Middlesex, Lord's 2002
Best bowling: 3-26 Durham v Yorkshire, Headingley 2003

2003 Season

	M	Inns	NO	Runs	HS	Avge	100s	50s	Ct	St	O	M	Runs	Wkts	Avge	Best	5wI	10wM
Test																		
All First	13	25	1	620	121	25.83	2	3	5	-	52.2	8	216	5	43.20	3-26	-	-
1-day Int																		
C & G	2	1	0	4	4	4.00	-	-	-	-	7	0	34	0	-		-	-
NCL	12	12	0	383	87	31.91	-	2	4	-	8	0	41	1	41.00	1-15	-	
Twenty20	3	2	0	27	17	13.50	-	-	-	-	2	0	8	1	8.00	1-8	-	

Career Performances

	M	Inns	NO	Runs	HS	Avge	100s	50s	Ct	St	Balls	Runs	Wkts	Avge	Best	5wI	10wM
Test																	
All First	32	57	1	1598	127	28.53	4	8	21	-	572	410	9	45.55	3-26	-	-
1-day Int																	
C & G	4	3	0	26	19	8.66	-	-	2	-	54	45	0	-		-	-
NCL	21	21	1	611	87	30.55	-	3	7	-	48	41	1	41.00	1-15	-	
Twenty20	3	2	0	27	17	13.50	-	-	-	-	12	8	1	8.00	1-8	-	

MULLALLY, A. D.   Hampshire

Name: <u>Alan</u> David Mullally
Role: Right-hand bat, left-arm fast bowler
Born: 12 July 1969, Southend
Height: 6ft 4in **Weight:** 14st
Nickname: Spider
County debut: 1988 (Hampshire),
1990 (Leicestershire)
County cap: 1993 (Leicestershire),
2000 (Hampshire; *see* **Extras**)
Test debut: 1996
Tests: 19
One-Day Internationals: 50
50 wickets in a season: 5
1st-Class 50s: 2
1st-Class 5 w. in innings: 30
1st-Class 10 w. in match: 4
1st-Class catches: 43
One-Day 5 w. in innings: 2

Place in batting averages: 293rd av. 5.42 (2002 316th av. 4.90)
Place in bowling averages: 112th av. 39.05 (2002 27th av. 25.13)

Strike rate: 80.88 (career 61.11)
Parents: Mick and Ann
Wife and date of marriage: Chelsey, 1997
Family links with cricket: 'Younger brother is better'
Education: Cannington High School, Perth, Australia; Wembley and Carlisle Technical College
Overseas tours: Western Australia to India; Leicestershire to Jamaica 1992-93; England to Zimbabwe and New Zealand 1996-97, to Australia 1998-99, to Sharjah (Coca-Cola Cup) 1998-99, to South Africa and Zimbabwe 1999-2000, to Sri Lanka 2000-01 (one-day series)
Overseas teams played for: Western Australia 1987-90; Victoria 1990-91
Career highlights to date: 'Career best 9-93 v Derbyshire. Man of the Match in World Cup [v Zimbabwe 1999] and CUB Series v Australia [1998-99]'
Cricket moments to forget: 'Sunday League v Middlesex' (*At the Rose Bowl in 2001, Middlesex took 35 runs off the last 13 deliveries of the game to win*)
Cricketers particularly admired: Robin Smith
Other sports followed: Australian Rules football, basketball, most sports
Relaxations: Fishing, music
Extras: English-qualified as he was born in Southend. Made first-class debut for Western Australia in the 1987-88 Sheffield Shield final v Queensland at Perth. Represented Australia YC v West Indies YC and in the U19 World Cup 1987-88. Played one match for Hampshire in 1988 before joining Leicestershire. Represented England in the 1999 World Cup. Left Leicestershire at end of 1999 season and rejoined Hampshire for 2000. Took 5-18 as Hampshire bowled out the Australians for 97 at West End 2001
Best batting: 75 Leicestershire v Middlesex, Leicester 1996
Best bowling: 9-93 Hampshire v Derbyshire, Derby 2000

2003 Season

	M	Inns	NO	Runs	HS	Avge	100s	50s	Ct	St	O	M	Runs	Wkts	Avge	Best	5wl	10wM
Test																		
All First	8	10	3	38	14	5.42	-	-	2	-	229.1	55	664	17	39.05	3-31	-	-
1-day Int																		
C & G	1	0	0	0	0	-	-	-	-	-	10	1	44	2	22.00	2-44	-	
NCL	14	4	1	24	10 *	8.00	-	-	5	-	103	7	446	9	49.55	2-27	-	
Twenty20	5	2	0	0	0	0.00	-	-	1	-	15	0	104	2	52.00	1-16	-	

Career Performances

	M	Inns	NO	Runs	HS	Avge	100s	50s	Ct	St	Balls	Runs	Wkts	Avge	Best	5wl	10wM
Test	19	27	4	127	24	5.52	-	-	6	-	4525	1812	58	31.24	5-105	1	-
All First	220	248	65	1548	75	8.45	-	2	43	-	42171	19242	690	27.88	9-93	30	4
1-day Int	50	25	10	86	20	5.73	-	-	8	-	2698	1728	63	27.42	4-18	-	
C & G	28	10	5	58	19 *	11.60	-	-	3	-	1716	979	46	21.28	5-18	1	
NCL	138	61	27	270	38	7.94	-	-	26	-	6196	4301	146	29.45	5-15	1	
Twenty20	5	2	0	0	0	0.00	-	-	1	-	90	104	2	52.00	1-16	-	

MUNDAY, M. K.   Somerset

Name: <u>Michael</u> Kenneth Munday
Role: Right-hand bat, leg-spin bowler
Born: 22 October 1984, Nottingham
Height: 5ft 8in **Weight:** 12st
County debut: No first-team appearance
1st-Class 5 w. in innings: 1
1st-Class catches: 2
Place in bowling averages: 8th av. 21.78
Strike rate: 34.28 (career 34.28)
Parents: John and Maureen
Marital status: Single
Family links with cricket: 'Dad, brother and
sister have played league cricket in Cornwall'
Education: Truro School; Corpus Christi
College, Oxford University
Qualifications: 10 GCSEs, 3 A-levels
Career outside cricket: Student
Off-season: Studying chemistry at Oxford
University

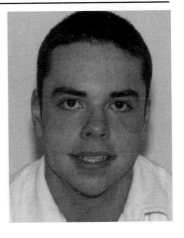

Overseas tours: Cornwall Schools U13 to South Africa 1998; ESCA West U15 to
West Indies 2000
Career highlights to date: 'Playing in the Oxford University side that beat
Cambridge by an innings at Fenner's 2003'
Cricket moments to forget: 'Being part of a Cornwall Minor Counties team that
dropped 17 catches against Dorset'
Cricket superstitions: 'None'
Cricketers particularly admired: Shane Warne, Graham Gooch
Young players to look out for: Jamie Dalrymple, Carl Gazzard
Other sports played: Chess ('Yes, it is a sport')
Other sports followed: Football (Liverpool)
Favourite band: 'None in particular'
Relaxations: Swimming, reading
Extras: Played for Cornwall in the C&G 2001. Played for Oxford University CCE
2003. Oxford Blue 2003, recording maiden first-class five-wicket return (5-83) v
Cambridge University in the Varsity Match at Fenner's
Opinions on cricket: 'The theory that the current lack of top-class English spinners is
due to the non-conduciveness of English wickets seems extraordinary, given the
success enjoyed by a number of overseas spinners in England.'
Best bowling: 5-83 Oxford University v Cambridge University, Fenner's 2003

2003 Season (did not make any first-class or one-day appearances for his county)

Career Performances

	M	Inns	NO	Runs	HS	Avge	100s	50s	Ct	St	Balls	Runs	Wkts	Avge	Best	5wI	10wM
Test																	
All First	4	3	2	0	0*	0.00	-	-	2	-	480	305	14	21.78	5-83	1	-
1-day Int																	
C & G	1	0	0	0	0	-	-	-	-	-	30	39	1	39.00	1-39	-	
NCL																	
Twenty20																	

MURALITHARAN, M. Kent

Name: Muttiah Muralitharan
Role: Right-hand bat, off-spin bowler
Born: 17 April 1972, Kandy, Sri Lanka
Height: 5ft 5in
Nickname: Murali
County debut: 1999 (Lancashire),
2003 (Kent)
County cap: 1999 (Lancashire), 2003 (Kent)
Test debut: 1992-93
Tests: 82
One-Day Internationals: 223
50 wickets in a season: 2
1st-Class 50s: 1
1st-Class 5 w. in innings: 79
1st-Class 10 w. in match: 23
1st-Class catches: 83
One-Day 5 w. in innings: 8
Place in batting averages: 289th av. 7.00
Place in bowling averages: 1st av. 13.54
Strike rate: 32.36 (career 50.31)
Marital status: Single
Education: St Anthony's College, Kandy

Overseas tours: Sri Lanka U24 to South Africa 1992-93; Sri Lanka to England 1991, to India 1993-94, to Zimbabwe 1994-95, to South Africa 1994-95, to New Zealand 1994-95, to Pakistan 1995-96, to Australia 1995-96, to India and Pakistan (World Cup) 1995-96, to New Zealand 1996-97, to West Indies 1996-97, to India 1997-98, to South Africa 1997-98, to England 1998, to Bangladesh (Wills International Cup) 1998-99, to UK, Ireland and Holland (World Cup) 1999, to Zimbabwe 1999-2000, to Pakistan 1999-2000, to Kenya (ICC Knockout Trophy) 2000-01, to South Africa 2000-01, to England 2002, to South Africa 2002-03, to Africa (World Cup) 2002-03, to West Indies 2003, plus numerous other one-day series and tournaments in Sharjah, India, Singapore, West Indies, Kenya, Pakistan, Australia, Bangladesh, New Zealand and Morocco

Overseas teams played for: Central Province, Sri Lanka 1990-1992; Tamil Union Cricket and Athletic Club 1991-92 –

Extras: Took part with Hashan Tillekeratne in record ninth-wicket partnership for Sri Lanka in Tests (83) v England at Colombo 1992-93. Took 16-220 from 113.5 overs v England at The Oval 1998, the fifth best bowling analysis in Test cricket; it included 9-65 in England's second innings, in which he took his 200th Test victim (Dominic Cork) in 42 Tests. One of *Wisden's* Five Cricketers of the Year 1999. Was Lancashire's overseas player in 1999, taking an astonishing 66 wickets in the 12 Championship innings in which he bowled; his haul included eight returns of five or more wickets in an innings (including five returns of seven) and he had five match returns of ten or more wickets. Lancashire Player of the Year 1999. Took 13-171 at Galle in 2000, winning the Man of the Match award in Sri Lanka's first Test win over South Africa. Took 7-30 v India in the Champions Trophy in Sharjah 2000, at the time the best return in ODI history. Took 300th Test wicket (Shaun Pollock) v South Africa 2000-01 in his 58th Test; only Dennis Lillee (55 Tests) has reached this mark in fewer matches. Highest wicket-taker in Test cricket for the calendar year 2000 with 75 wickets in ten matches. Returned as Lancashire's overseas player for 2001. Had figures of 1-4 from 10 overs v Derbyshire at Liverpool in the B&H 2001. Took 50 Championship wickets (av. 19.42 and including five five-wicket innings) in only seven matches in 2001; in taking his 100th Championship wicket in only his 12th match overall, he became the quickest to this milestone for any county. Man of the Series v India 2001, taking 23 wickets (av. 19.30) in the three-match rubber, including 8-87 (11-196 the match) in the third Test at Colombo. Highest wicket-taker in Test cricket for the calendar year 2001 with 80 wickets in 12 matches. Took 9-51 in Zimbabwe's first innings in the second Test at Kandy January 2002, in the process passing Ian Botham's tally of 383 Test wickets in his 71st match; reached 400 Test wickets in a record 72 matches when he dismissed Henry Olonga v Zimbabwe in the third Test at Galle, January 2002 (took 30 wickets in the three-match series at an average of 9.80). Has won numerous other series and match awards, including Man of the Match in the first Test v Bangladesh at Colombo 2002 (5-39/5-59) and in the Bank Alfalah Cup [ODI] v Pakistan at Dambulla 2003 (5-23). Was an overseas player with Kent July to September 2003, first deputising for Andrew Symonds, absent on international duty, and then replacing the injured Mohammad Sami. Took 33 wickets at 13.54 in the five Championship matches he played for Kent 2003. Awarded Kent cap 2003

Best batting: 67 Sri Lanka v India, Kandy 2001-02
Best bowling: 9-51 Sri Lanka v Zimbabwe, Kandy 2001-02
Stop press: Took 11-93 (7-46/4-47) in the first Test v England at Galle 2003-04, winning Man of the Match award

2003 Season

	M	Inns	NO	Runs	HS	Avge	100s	50s	Ct	St	O	M	Runs	Wkts	Avge	Best	5wI	10wM
Test																		
All First	5	7	0	49	15	7.00	-	-	1	-	178	41	447	33	13.54	6-36	4	-
1-day Int																		
C & G																		
NCL	8	4	2	26	11 *	13.00	-	-	1	-	68	9	269	13	20.69	5-34	1	
Twenty20																		

Career Performances

	M	Inns	NO	Runs	HS	Avge	100s	50s	Ct	St	Balls	Runs	Wkts	Avge	Best	5wI	10wM
Test	82	104	39	768	67	11.81	-	1	39	-	27578	10810	459	23.55	9-51	38	11
All First	161	193	57	1472	67	10.82	-	1	83	-	45284	17619	900	19.57	9-51	79	23
1-day Int	223	105	42	374	19	5.93	-	-	92	-	12063	7631	342	22.31	7-30	7	
C & G	5	2	0	15	15	7.50	-	-	-	-	288	186	5	37.20	3-21	-	
NCL	20	6	3	40	13 *	13.33	-	-	5	-	986	549	28	19.60	5-34	1	
Twenty20																		

MURTAGH, T. J. Surrey

Name: Timothy (Tim) James Murtagh
Role: Left-hand bat, right-arm
fast-medium bowler
Born: 2 August 1981, Lambeth, London
Height: 6ft 2in **Weight:** 12st
Nickname: Hairy Faced Dingo
County debut: 2000 (one-day),
2001 (first-class)
1st-Class 5 w. in innings: 2
1st-Class catches: 3
Place in batting averages: 261st av. 13.57
Place in bowling averages: 145th av. 51.25
(2002 22nd av. 24.94)
Strike rate: 73.41 (career 49.43)
Parents: Dominic and Elizabeth
Marital status: Single
Family links with cricket: 'Chris, younger
brother, plays in Surrey age-group cricket and

is in their Development of Excellence Programme; Uncle Andy (A. J. Murtagh) played
for Hampshire'
Education: John Fisher, Purley, Surrey; St Mary's University, Twickenham
Qualifications: 10 GCSEs, 2 A-levels

Career outside cricket: Student (Sports Science and Media Studies)
Overseas tours: Surrey U17 to South Africa 1997; England U19 to Malaysia and (U19 World Cup) Sri Lanka 1999-2000; British Universities to South Africa 2002
Cricketers particularly admired: Darren Gough, Glenn McGrath
Young players to look out for: Neil Saker, Chris Murtagh, Danny Miller
Other sports played: Rugby (was captain of John Fisher 2nd XV), skiing ('in the past')
Other sports followed: Football (Liverpool FC), rugby
Favourite band: 'The Hairy Faced Dingos'
Relaxations: Playing golf, watching sport, films, reading
Extras: Represented British Universities 2000, 2001, 2002 and v Zimbabweans 2003. Represented England U19 v Sri Lanka U19 2000; named Player of the Series. Played for Surrey Board XI and Surrey in the C&G 2001. NBC Denis Compton Award for the most promising young Surrey player 2001
Best batting: 22* British Universities v Pakistanis, Trent Bridge 2001
Best bowling: 6-86 British Universities v Pakistanis, Trent Bridge 2001

2003 Season

	M	Inns	NO	Runs	HS	Avge	100s	50s	Ct	St	O	M	Runs	Wkts	Avge	Best	5wI	10wM
Test																		
All First	7	11	4	95	21	13.57	-	-	-	-	146.5	17	615	12	51.25	4-130	-	-
1-day Int																		
C & G																		
NCL	4	3	1	8	6	4.00	-	-	-	-	34	2	200	6	33.33	3-44	-	
Twenty20	4	1	0	0	0	0.00	-	-	1	-	16	0	128	6	21.33	3-37	-	

Career Performances

	M	Inns	NO	Runs	HS	Avge	100s	50s	Ct	St	Balls	Runs	Wkts	Avge	Best	5wI	10wM
Test																	
All First	15	22	9	181	22 *	13.92	-	-	3	-	1829	1159	37	31.32	6-86	2	-
1-day Int																	
C & G	2	2	0	13	11	6.50	-	-	1	-	108	86	2	43.00	1-40	-	
NCL	22	15	7	52	14 *	6.50	-	-	4	-	1088	917	30	30.56	4-31	-	
Twenty20	4	1	0	0	0	0.00	-	-	1	-	96	128	6	21.33	3-37	-	

> 68. Which rotund North East-born opener
> was run out for 0 on Test debut against the 1966 West Indians?

MUSHTAQ AHMED   Sussex

Name: Mushtaq Ahmed
Role: Right-hand bat, leg-spin bowler
Born: 28 June 1970, Sahiwal, Pakistan
Height: 5ft 4in
Nickname: Mushie
County debut: 1993 (Somerset),
2002 (Surrey), 2003 (Sussex)
County cap: 1993 (Somerset), 2003 (Sussex)
Test debut: 1991-92
Tests: 50
One-Day Internationals: 143
50 wickets in a season: 3
100 wickets in a season: 1
1st-Class 50s: 15
1st-Class 5w. in innings: 70
1st-Class 10w. in match: 21
1st-Class catches: 98
One-Day 5 w. in innings: 3
Place in batting averages: 165th av. 26.82
Place in bowling averages: 27th av. 24.65
Strike rate: 48.72 (career 52.20)
Wife and date of marriage: Uzma, 18 December 1994
Children: Bazal, Nawal, Habiba
Career outside cricket: 'Panellist for Sky Sports cricket coverage (ad hoc)'
Off-season: Playing cricket in Pakistan (National Bank)
Overseas tours: Pakistan YC to Australia (U19 World Cup) 1987-88; Pakistan to Sharjah (Sharjah Cup) 1988-89, to Australia 1989-90, 1995-96, 1999-2000, to New Zealand and Australia (World Cup) 1991-92, to England 1992, 1996, 2001, to New Zealand 1992-93, 1993-94, 1995-96, 2000-01, to West Indies 1992-93, 1999-2000, to Sri Lanka 1994-95, 1996-97, 2000, to South Africa 1997-98, to Zimbabwe 1997-98, to India 1998-99, to UK, Ireland and Holland (World Cup) 1999, plus numerous other one-day tours and tournaments in India, Sharjah, Australia, South Africa, Zimbabwe, Singapore, Toronto and Bangladesh
Overseas teams played for: Numerous, including Multan, United Bank, and National Bank 2001-02 –
Career highlights to date: 'Winning the 1992 cricket World Cup final'
Cricket moments to forget: 'Losing the 1996 World Cup quarter-final to India at Bangalore'
Cricket superstitions: 'None'
Cricketers particularly admired: Imran Khan
Young players to look out for: Tim Ambrose, Matt Prior

Other sports followed: Hockey, football (Brazil)

Relaxations: 'Spending time with family, prayer'

Extras: Made first-class debut for Multan v Hyderabad 1986-87. Had first innings figures of 6-81 for Punjab Chief Minister's XI against England tourists at Sahiwal 1987-88. Took 16 wickets in the 1991-92 World Cup, finishing as second highest wicket-taker for Pakistan after Wasim Akram. Somerset's overseas player 1993-95 and 1997-98; Player of the Year 1993. Had match figures of 9-198 and 9-186 in successive Tests on Pakistan's tour of Australia 1995-96, following up with 10-171 (including 7-56) in next Test v New Zealand eight days later. Represented Pakistan in 1995-96 World Cup. Man of the Test series v England 1996 (17 wickets; av. 26.29) and v South Africa 1997-98 (14; 27.57). One of *Wisden*'s Five Cricketers of the Year 1997. Released by Somerset at end of 1998 season. Played for Little Stoke in the North Staffordshire/ South Cheshire League 2002. Was Surrey's overseas player during August 2002, replacing Saqlain Mushtaq, absent on international duty. Joined Sussex as an overseas player for 2003, taking 103 Championship wickets (av. 24.65). Awarded Sussex cap 2003. Sussex Player of the Year 2003. PCA Player of the Year 2003

Opinions on cricket: 'Credit should be given for first innings leads in the Championship. Fewer overs in a day's play in the Championship (say 90 not 104).'

Best batting: 90 Somerset v Sussex, Taunton 1993

Best bowling: 9-93 Multan v Peshawar, Sahiwal 1990-91

2003 Season

	M	Inns	NO	Runs	HS	Avge	100s	50s	Ct	St	O	M	Runs	Wkts	Avge	Best	5wI	10wM
Test																		
All First	16	19	2	456	60	26.82	-	3	3	-	836.3	163	2539	103	24.65	7-85	10	5
1-day Int																		
C & G	2	1	0	11	11	11.00	-	-	-	-	20	1	79	1	79.00	1-46	-	
NCL	9	4	0	37	17	9.25	-	-	1	-	76.5	6	289	7	41.28	2-16	-	
Twenty20	4	2	0	17	16	8.50	-	-	-	-	16	0	94	5	18.80	2-12	-	

Career Performances

	M	Inns	NO	Runs	HS	Avge	100s	50s	Ct	St	Balls	Runs	Wkts	Avge	Best	5wI	10wM
Test	50	70	15	636	59	11.56	-	2	22	-	12225	5901	183	32.24	7-56	10	3
All First	227	285	36	3829	90	15.37	-	15	98	-	51632	25605	991	25.83	9-93	70	21
1-day Int	143	76	34	399	34 *	9.50	-	-	30	-	7483	5296	161	32.89	5-36	1	
C & G	13	8	3	111	35	22.20	-	-	4	-	874	441	23	19.17	5-26	1	
NCL	66	47	12	398	41	11.37	-	-	6	-	2881	1962	63	31.14	3-17	-	
Twenty20	4	2	0	17	16	8.50	-	-	-	-	96	94	5	18.80	2-12	-	

MUSTARD, P.   Durham

Name: Philip Mustard
Role: Left-hand bat, wicket-keeper
Born: 8 October 1982, Sunderland
Nickname: Colonel
County debut: 2002
1st-Class 50s: 2
1st-Class catches: 44
1st-Class stumpings: 3
Place in batting averages: 210th av. 22.09
Parents: Maureen
Marital status: Single
Education: Usworth Comprehensive
Career outside cricket: Landscaping
Cricket moments to forget: 'The first game
I played I went out to bat and got a first-ball
duck, then went out to keep wicket and
dropped catches'
Cricketers particularly admired:
Mike Atherton ('professionalism')
Young players to look out for: Nicky Peng
Other sports followed: Football (Middlesbrough)
Relaxations: 'Socialising with friends down the pub'

Extras: Played for Durham Board XI in the NatWest 2000, in the C&G 2001, 2002
and 2003; also played for Durham in the C&G 2003. Scored 77-ball 75 on first-class
debut v Sri Lankans at Riverside 2002. Represented England U19 v India U19 2002
Best batting: 75 Durham v Sri Lankans, Riverside 2002

2003 Season

	M	Inns	NO	Runs	HS	Avge	100s	50s	Ct	St	O	M	Runs	Wkts	Avge	Best	5wI	10wM
Test																		
All First	13	23	1	486	70 *	22.09	-	1	42	3								
1-day Int																		
C & G	2	2	0	33	33	16.50	-	-	2	-								
NCL	13	12	0	165	41	13.75	-	-	14	1								
Twenty20	5	5	0	103	61	20.60	-	1	-	3								

Career Performances

	M	Inns	NO	Runs	HS	Avge	100s	50s	Ct	St	Balls	Runs	Wkts	Avge	Best	5wI	10wM
Test																	
All First	14	24	1	561	75	24.39	-	2	44	3							
1-day Int																	
C & G	7	6	1	47	33	9.40	-	-	9	3							
NCL	13	12	0	165	41	13.75	-	-	14	1							
Twenty20	5	5	0	103	61	20.60	-	1	-	3							

NAPIER, G. R.   Essex

Name: <u>Graham</u> Richard Napier
Role: Right-hand bat, right-arm
medium bowler
Born: 6 January 1980, Colchester
Height: 5ft 10in **Weight:** 12st 7lbs
Nickname: Plank, Napes
County debut: 1997
1st-Class 50s: 5
1st-Class 100s: 1
1st-Class 5 w. in innings: 1
1st-Class catches: 19
One-Day 5 w. in innings: 1
Place in batting averages: 141st av. 30.00
(2002 222nd av. 20.90)
Place in bowling averages: 133rd av. 45.63
(2002 78th av. 31.95)
Strike rate: 69.00 (career 60.14)
Parents: Roger and Carol
Marital status: Single
Family links with cricket: Father played for Palmers Boys School 1st XI (1965-68),
Essex Police divisional teams, and Harwich Immigration CC. 'Now makes guest
appearances on Walton beach'
Education: Gilberd School, Colchester
Qualifications: NCA coaching award
Overseas tours: England U17 to Bermuda (International Youth Tournament) 1997;
England U19 to South Africa (including U19 World Cup) 1997-98; ECB National
Academy (England A) to Malaysia and India 2003-04
Overseas teams played for: Campbelltown CC, Sydney 2000-01; North Perth,
Western Australia 2001-02
Career highlights to date: 'Testing myself against the world's best and scoring
some runs'

Cricket moments to forget: 'Being 12th man at Lord's and after a drinks break dropping the empties on a tray, towels, jumpers and anything else thrown at me in front of the MCC members'

Young players to look out for: Will Jefferson, Mark Pettini

Other sports followed: Football ('The Tractor Boys' – Ipswich Town FC)

Extras: Represented England U19 v Australia U19 1999. Man of the Match award for Essex Board XI v Lancashire Board XI in the NatWest 2000. Scored 73 (losing three cricket balls in the process) and recorded maiden one-day five-wicket return (6-29) v Worcestershire at Chelmsford in the Norwich Union League 2001. Recorded maiden first-class five-wicket return (5-66) v Nottinghamshire at Trent Bridge 2003

Best batting: 104 Essex v CUCCE, Fenner's 2001

Best bowling: 5-66 Essex v Nottinghamshire, Trent Bridge 2003

2003 Season

	M	Inns	NO	Runs	HS	Avge	100s	50s	Ct	St	O	M	Runs	Wkts	Avge	Best	5wl	10wM
Test																		
All First	15	24	8	480	89 *	30.00	-	2	3	-	379.3	60	1506	33	45.63	5-66	1	-
1-day Int																		
C & G	2	1	0	16	16	16.00	-	-	1	-	15.3	1	88	4	22.00	3-47	-	
NCL	16	14	5	182	52	20.22	-	1	3	-	108	11	536	33	16.24	4-18	-	
Twenty20	5	3	0	33	19	11.00	-	-	1	-	20	1	155	7	22.14	3-20	-	

Career Performances

	M	Inns	NO	Runs	HS	Avge	100s	50s	Ct	St	Balls	Runs	Wkts	Avge	Best	5wl	10wM
Test																	
All First	40	61	12	1323	104	27.00	1	5	19	-	4204	2783	70	39.75	5-66	1	-
1-day Int																	
C & G	7	6	1	128	79	25.60	-	1	1	-	237	206	9	22.88	3-47	-	
NCL	67	55	7	806	78	16.79	-	5	17	-	1592	1319	65	20.29	6-29	1	
Twenty20	5	3	0	33	19	11.00	-	-	1	-	120	155	7	22.14	3-20	-	

---

69. West Indies captain in the 1973 Test series,
who shared in a Warwickshire second-wicket record stand of 465
with John Jameson a year later?

Name: <u>David</u> Charles Nash
Role: Right-hand bat, wicket-keeper
Born: 19 January 1978, Chertsey
Height: 5ft 7in **Weight:** 11st 5lbs
Nickname: Nashy, Knocker
County debut: 1995 (one-day), 1997 (first-class)
County cap: 1999
50 dismissals in a season: 1
1st-Class 50s: 17
1st-Class 100s: 6
1st-Class catches: 213
1st-Class stumpings: 17
Place in batting averages: 77th av. 39.57
(2002 49th av. 46.14)
Strike rate: (career 49.00)
Parents: David and Christine
Marital status: Single
Family links with cricket: 'Father played
club cricket; brother plays now and again for Ashford CC; mother is avid watcher and
tea lady'
Education: Sunbury Manor; Malvern College, Worcs
Qualifications: 9 O-levels, 1 A-level, Levels 1 and 2 cricket coaching, qualified
football referee
Career outside cricket: Qualified cricket coach
Overseas tours: England U15 to South Africa 1993; British Airways Youth Team to
West Indies 1993-94; England U19 to Zimbabwe 1995-96, to Pakistan 1996-97;
England A to Kenya and Sri Lanka 1997-98
Overseas teams played for: Fremantle, Perth 2000-01, 2002-03
Career highlights to date: 'Touring with England A and scoring first hundred for
Middlesex at Lord's v Somerset'
Cricket moments to forget: 'All golden ducks'
Cricket superstitions: 'Too many to mention'
Cricketers particularly admired: Angus Fraser, and Andrew Strauss 'for his amazing
ability to keep going in all fitness runs when he's knackered after the first 50 yards'
Young players to look out for: Ed Joyce
Other sports played: Rugby, football ('played for Millwall U15 and my district
side'), 'and most other sports'
Other sports followed: Rugby (London Irish), football (Chelsea), cricket ('closely
watching Richard Johnson's figures on Teletext')
Relaxations: 'Listening to music, watching sport and socialising with friends'
Extras: Represented Middlesex at all ages. Played for England U14, U15, U17 and

U19. Once took six wickets in six balls when aged 11 – 'when I could bowl!' *Daily Telegraph* Southern England Batting Award 1993. Seaxe Young Player of the Year 1993. Scored 67 in the B&H v Sussex at Lord's 2002, in the process sharing with Ashley Noffke (58) in a record eighth-wicket partnership for the competition
Best batting: 114 Middlesex v Somerset, Lord's 1998
Best bowling: 1-8 Middlesex v Essex, Chelmsford 1997

2003 Season

	M	Inns	NO	Runs	HS	Avge	100s	50s	Ct	St	O	M	Runs	Wkts	Avge	Best	5wI	10wM
Test																		
All First	17	26	7	752	113	39.57	2	2	42	3	5	0	25	0	-		-	-	-
1-day Int																		
C & G	3	3	1	34	16	17.00	-	-	2	-								
NCL	17	13	2	252	62	22.90	-	2	8	-								
Twenty20																		

Career Performances

	M	Inns	NO	Runs	HS	Avge	100s	50s	Ct	St	Balls	Runs	Wkts	Avge	Best	5wI	10wM
Test																	
All First	103	145	29	3754	114	32.36	6	17	213	17	49	44	1	44.00	1-8	-	-
1-day Int																	
C & G	7	5	1	95	58	23.75	-	1	4	-							
NCL	78	59	13	976	62	21.21	-	3	59	11							
Twenty20																	

NEL, A.   Northamptonshire

Name: Andre Nel
Role: Right-hand bat, right-arm fast-medium bowler
Born: 15 July 1977, Germiston, Gauteng, South Africa
County debut: 2003
County cap: 2003
Test debut: 2001-02
Tests: 3
One-Day Internationals: 10
1st-Class 5 w. in innings: 8
1st-Class catches: 18
Place in batting averages: 178th av. 25.80
Place in bowling averages: 93rd av. 35.88
Strike rate: 70.41 (career 55.50)
Education: Hoërskool Dr E.G. Jansen, Boksburg
Overseas tours: South African Academy to Ireland and Scotland 1999; South Africa to West Indies 2000-01, to Zimbabwe 2001-02, to England 2003 (NatWest Series),

to Pakistan 2003-04; South Africa A to Zimbabwe (one-day series) 2002-03, to Australia 2002-03

Overseas teams played for: Easterns 1996-97 –

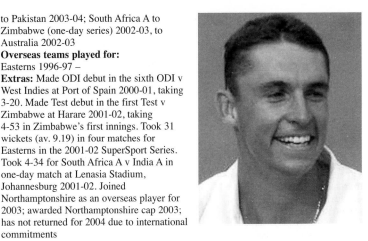

Extras: Made ODI debut in the sixth ODI v West Indies at Port of Spain 2000-01, taking 3-20. Made Test debut in the first Test v Zimbabwe at Harare 2001-02, taking 4-53 in Zimbabwe's first innings. Took 31 wickets (av. 9.19) in four matches for Easterns in the 2001-02 SuperSport Series. Took 4-34 for South Africa A v India A in one-day match at Lenasia Stadium, Johannesburg 2001-02. Joined Northamptonshire as an overseas player for 2003; awarded Northamptonshire cap 2003; has not returned for 2004 due to international commitments

Best batting: 44 Easterns v Free State, Benoni 2000-01

Best bowling: 6-25 Easterns v Gauteng, Johannesburg 2001-02

Stop press: ODI Man of the Match award v Pakistan at Rawalpindi 2003-04 (4-39). Recorded maiden Test five-wicket return (5-87) in the third Test v West Indies at Cape Town 2003-04

2003 Season

	M	Inns	NO	Runs	HS	Avge	100s	50s	Ct	St	O	M	Runs	Wkts	Avge	Best	5wI	10wM
Test																		
All First	13	13	3	258	42	25.80	-	-	4	-	422.3	99	1292	36	35.88	5-47	1	-
1-day Int	3	2	0	2	1	1.00	-	-	1	-	23	4	93	3	31.00	2-33	-	
C & G	1	1	0	14	14	14.00	-	-	-	-	10	2	36	0	-		-	-
NCL	15	7	3	33	15 *	8.25	-	-	4	-	115.3	14	410	22	18.63	3-20	-	
Twenty20	5	2	0	22	12	11.00	-	-	-	-	19	0	126	6	21.00	2-29	-	

Career Performances

	M	Inns	NO	Runs	HS	Avge	100s	50s	Ct	St	Balls	Runs	Wkts	Avge	Best	5wI	10wM
Test	3	2	0	7	7	3.50	-	-	-	-	513	289	8	36.12	4-53	-	-
All First	53	58	24	606	44	17.82	-	-	18	-	10212	4403	184	23.92	6-25	8	-
1-day Int	10	4	2	5	3 *	2.50	-	-	3	-	497	334	13	25.69	3-20	-	
C & G	1	1	0	14	14	14.00	-	-	-	-	60	36	0	-		-	
NCL	15	7	3	33	15 *	8.25	-	-	4	-	693	410	22	18.63	3-20	-	
Twenty20	5	2	0	22	12	11.00	-	-	-	-	114	126	6	21.00	2-29	-	

NEW, T. J. — Leicestershire

Name: Thomas (<u>Tom</u>) James New
Role: Left-hand bat, wicket-keeper
Born: 18 January 1985, Sutton-in-Ashfield
Height: 5ft 10in **Weight:** 9st 8lbs
Nickname: Newy
County debut: No first-team appearance
Parents: Martin and Louise
Marital status: Single
Education: Quarrydale Comprehensive
Qualifications: GCSEs
Off-season: U19 World Cup with England
Overseas tours: England U19 to Bangladesh (U19 World Cup) 2003-04
Overseas teams played for: Geelong Cement, Victoria 2001-02
Career highlights to date: 'Captaining England U15 in Costcutter World Challenge 2000'

Cricket moments to forget: 'Losing semi-final of Costcutter World Challenge 2000 to Pakistan'
Cricket superstitions: 'None'
Cricketers particularly admired: Ian Healy, Jack Russell
Young players to look out for: Luke Wright
Other sports played: Rugby (County U14/U15), football
Other sports followed: Football (Mansfield Town FC)
Relaxations: 'Golf, music'
Extras: Played for Notts U12, U13, U15, U16 and Midlands U13, U14, U15. Captained England U15 in Costcutter World Challenge [U15 World Cup] 2000. Sir John Hobbs Silver Jubilee Memorial Prize 2000. England U17-U19 squads 2000-03; reserve for U19 tour to Australia 2002-03 and represented England U19 v South Africa U19 2003. Played for Leicestershire Board XI in the C&G 2001 and in the first round of the C&G 2003, which was played in August 2002. Played for Leicestershire v India A in a 50-over match at Leicester 2003

Career Performances

	M	Inns	NO	Runs	HS	Avge	100s	50s	Ct	St	Balls	Runs	Wkts	Avge	Best	5wI	10wM
Test																	
All First																	
1-day Int																	
C & G	2	2	0	9	6	4.50	-	-	-	-							
NCL																	
Twenty20																	

NEWBY, O. J. Lancashire

Name: Oliver James Newby
Role: Right-hand bat, right-arm
fast-medium bowler
Born: 26 August 1984, Blackburn
Height: 6ft 5in **Weight:** 13st
Nickname: Newbz, Uncle, Flipper
County debut: 2003
Strike rate: 174.00 (career 174.00)
Parents: Frank and Carol
Marital status: Single
Family links with cricket: 'Dad played
league cricket for Read CC'
Education: Ribblesdale High School;
Myerscough College
Qualifications: 10 GCSEs, ND Sports
Science, Level 1 coaching
Off-season: 'Training'
Career highlights to date: 'First-class debut'

Other sports played: Golf
Favourite band: Eminem, Counting Crows
Relaxations: Music
Extras: Played for Lancashire Board XI in the first and second rounds of the C&G
2003, which were played in August/September 2002. Played for Lancashire v India A
in a 50-over match at Blackpool 2003, taking a wicket in each of his first two overs
Best bowling: 1-41 Lancashire v DUCCE, Durham 2003

	M	Inns	NO	Runs	HS	Avge	100s	50s	Ct	St	O	M	Runs	Wkts	Avge	Best	5wI	10wM
Test																		
All First	1	0	0	0	0	-	-	-	-	-	29	7	82	1	82.00	1-41	-	-
1-day Int																		
C & G																		
NCL																		
Twenty20	1	0	0	0	0	-	-	-	-	-	1	0	12	0	-		-	-

Career Performances

	M	Inns	NO	Runs	HS	Avge	100s	50s	Ct	St	Balls	Runs	Wkts	Avge	Best	5wI	10wM
Test																	
All First	1	0	0	0	0	-	-	-	-	-	174	82	1	82.00	1-41	-	-
1-day Int																	
C & G	2	1	1	3	3*	-	-	-	1	-	110	104	1	104.00	1-45	-	
NCL																	
Twenty20	1	0	0	0	0	-	-	-	-	-	6	12	0	-		-	-

NEWMAN, S. A.   Surrey

Name: Scott Alexander Newman
Role: Left-hand bat
Born: 3 November 1979, Epsom
Height: 6ft 1in **Weight:** 13st 7lbs
Nickname: Ronaldo
County debut: 2001 (one-day),
2002 (first-class)
1st-Class 50s: 1
1st-Class 100s: 1
1st-Class catches: 5
Parents: Ken and Sandy
Marital status: Engaged
Children: Lemoy, 1985;
Brandon, 8 September 2002
Family links with cricket: 'Dad and brother
both played'
Education: Trinity School, Croydon;
Brighton University

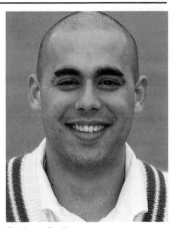

Qualifications: 10 GCSEs, GNVQ (Advanced) Business Studies
Career outside cricket: 'Father'
Off-season: 'ECB Academy'
Overseas tours: SCB to Barbados; ECB National Academy (England A) to Malaysia
and India 2003-04

Overseas teams played for: Mount Lawley CC, Perth
Career highlights to date: 'Partnership of 552 v Derbyshire II with N. Shahid (Shahid 266; Newman 284)'
Cricket moments to forget: 'Any time I fail'
Cricket superstitions: 'None'
Cricketers particularly admired: 'All of Surrey CCC'
Young players to look out for: Alastair Cook, Neil Saker, Brandon Newman, Ben Scott
Other sports played: 'Most sports'
Other sports followed: Football (Man Utd)
Favourite band: Nas
Relaxations: 'Music, relaxing with family'
Extras: Played for Surrey Board XI in the C&G 2001 and 2002. Scored 99 on first-class debut v Hampshire at The Oval 2002. Scored maiden first-class century (183) v Leicestershire at The Oval 2002, in the process sharing with Ian Ward (118) in a new record opening partnership for Surrey in matches v Leicestershire (227). Scored 284 v Derbyshire 2nd XI at The Oval 2003, in the process sharing with Nadeem Shahid (266) in an opening partnership of 552, just three runs short of the English all-cricket record first-wicket stand of 555 set by Percy Holmes and Herbert Sutcliffe for Yorkshire v Essex at Leyton 1932
Opinions on cricket: 'Less EU players.'
Best batting: 183 Surrey v Leicestershire, The Oval 2002

2003 Season

	M	Inns	NO	Runs	HS	Avge	100s	50s	Ct	St	O	M	Runs	Wkts	Avge	Best	5wI	10wM
Test																		
All First	2	4	1	42	27	14.00	-	-	2	-	1	0	5	0	-	-	-	-
1-day Int																		
C & G																		
NCL	3	3	0	33	15	11.00	-	-	1	-								
Twenty20	2	2	0	78	59	39.00	-	1	2	-								

Career Performances

	M	Inns	NO	Runs	HS	Avge	100s	50s	Ct	St	Balls	Runs	Wkts	Avge	Best	5wI	10wM
Test																	
All First	5	9	1	364	183	45.50	1	1	5	-	6	5	0	-	-	-	-
1-day Int																	
C & G	3	3	0	100	49	33.33	-	-	1	-							
NCL	8	8	0	114	37	14.25	-	-	1	-							
Twenty20	2	2	0	78	59	39.00	-	1	2	-							

NIXON, P. A.   Leicestershire

Name: <u>Paul</u> Andrew Nixon
Role: Left-hand bat, wicket-keeper
Born: 21 October 1970, Carlisle
Height: 6ft **Weight:** 12st 10lbs
Nickname: Badger, Nico, Nobby
County debut: 1989 (Leicestershire),
2000 (Kent)
County cap: 1994 (Leicestershire),
2000 (Kent)
1000 runs in a season: 1
50 dismissals in a season: 7
1st-Class 50s: 39
1st-Class 100s: 14
1st-Class catches: 669
1st-Class stumpings: 52
Place in batting averages: 151st av. 29.39
(2002 90th av. 37.60)

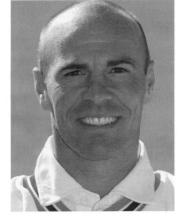

Parents: Brian and Sylvia
Wife and date of marriage: Jen, 9 October 1999
Family links with cricket: 'Grandad and father played local league cricket. Mum made the teas for Edenhall CC, Penrith'
Education: Ullswater High
Qualifications: 2 O-levels, 6 GCSEs, coaching certificates
Career outside cricket: 'Sports agent with Stellar Promotions; property in Spain – working for Ocean View Properties'
Off-season: 'Cape Town – wedding of Mr and Mrs J. Snape; holiday to Mauritius'
Overseas tours: Cumbria Schools U15 to Denmark 1985; Leicestershire to Barbados, to Jamaica, to Holland, to Johannesburg, to Bloemfontein; MCC to Bangladesh 1999-2000; England A to India and Bangladesh 1994-95; England to Pakistan and Sri Lanka 2000-01
Overseas teams played for: Melville, Western Australia; North Fremantle, Western Australia; Mitchells Plain, Cape Town 1993; Primrose CC, Cape Town 1995-96
Career highlights to date: 'Winning the Championship in 1996 with Leicestershire. Receiving phone call from David Graveney advising me of England [tour] selection'
Cricket moments to forget: 'Losing Lord's one-day finals'
Cricketers particularly admired: David Gower, Ian Botham, Ian Healy, Viv Richards
Young players to look out for: Rob Key, James Troughton
Other sports played: Golf, training with Leicester Tigers rugby team
Other sports followed: Football (Leicester City, Carlisle United, Liverpool), rugby (Leicester Tigers)
Injuries: Tennis elbow ('too much squash with Mark Ealham winter 2000')

Relaxations: Watching England rugby

Extras: County captain of Cumbria at football, cricket and rugby. Youngest person to score a century against Yorkshire (at U15). Played for England U15. Played in Minor Counties Championship for Cumberland at 16. MCC Young Pro in 1988. Took eight catches in debut match v Warwickshire at Hinckley in 1989. Played for Carlisle United. Leicestershire Young Player of the Year two years running. In 1994 became only second Leicestershire wicket-keeper to score 1000 runs in a season (1046). Voted Cumbria Sports Personality of the Year 1994-95. Was part of Leicestershire's County Championship winning side in 1996 and 1998. Left Leicestershire at end of 1999 season and joined Kent for 2000. Captained First-Class Counties Select XI v New Zealand A at Milton Keynes 2000. Scored 60 v Worcestershire at Canterbury in the NUL 2002, in the process sharing with Matthew Walker (94) in a record sixth-wicket partnership for Kent in the one-day league (116). Released by Kent at the end of the 2002 season and rejoined Leicestershire for 2003, scoring century (113*) against his former county at Canterbury in the first Championship round of the season. Played 300 first-class games in succession and has missed only four Championship matches since debut in 1989

Opinions on cricket: '1. Too many people running the game with their own personal agendas – the big picture is what matters. 2. No more ideas from me regarding the marketing of English cricket until the ECB pay me a fee for using all my previous ideas!'

Best batting: 134* Kent v Hampshire, Canterbury 2000

2003 Season

	M	Inns	NO	Runs	HS	Avge	100s	50s	Ct	St	O	M	Runs	Wkts	Avge	Best	5wI	10wM
Test																		
All First	17	27	4	676	113 *	29.39	1	3	50	2								
1-day Int																		
C & G	3	3	0	100	57	33.33	-	1	7	-								
NCL	16	16	2	292	67 *	20.85	-	2	12	4								
Twenty20	6	6	0	109	43	18.16	-	-	2	3								

Career Performances

	M	Inns	NO	Runs	HS	Avge	100s	50s	Ct	St	Balls	Runs	Wkts	Avge	Best	5wI	10wM
Test																		
All First	253	366	81	9158	134 *	32.13	14	39	669	52	33	22	0	-		-	-	-
1-day Int																		
C & G	34	28	10	565	57	31.38	-	2	45	10								
NCL	200	177	31	3209	96 *	21.97	-	14	192	45								
Twenty20	6	6	0	109	43	18.16	-	-	2	3								

NOFFKE, A. A.   Middlesex

Name: <u>Ashley</u> Allan Noffke
Role: Right-hand bat, right-arm fast bowler;
all-rounder
Born: 30 April 1977, Sunshine Coast,
Queensland, Australia
Height: 6ft 3in **Weight:** 14st
Nickname: Noffers, Wombat
County debut: 2002
County cap: 2003
1st-Class 50s: 3
1st-Class 5 w. in innings: 9
1st-Class 10 w. in match: 1
1st-Class catches: 19
Place in batting averages: 207th av. 22.33
(2002 207th av. 22.55)
Place in bowling averages: 95th av. 35.90
(2002 25th av. 25.06)
Strike rate: 70.19 (career 53.38)
Parents: Rob & Lesley Simpson, and Allan Noffke
Wife and date of marriage: Michelle, 8 April 2000
Family links with cricket: Father played club cricket
Education: Immanuel Lutheran College; Sunshine Coast University
Qualifications: Bachelor of Business, ACB Level 2 coaching certificate
Off-season: Playing cricket for Queensland
Overseas tours: Commonwealth Bank [Australian] Cricket Academy to Zimbabwe
1998-99; Australia to England 2001, to West Indies 2002-03
Overseas teams played for: Queensland 1998 –
Career highlights to date: 'Man of the Match in a winning Pura Cup final for
Queensland. Being selected for Australia for 2001 Ashes tour'
Cricket moments to forget: 'Rolling my ankle playing for Australia v Sussex, forcing
me home from the Ashes tour'
Cricket superstitions: 'None'
Cricketers particularly admired: Steve Waugh
Young players to look out for: Ed Joyce, Lee Carseldine
Other sports played: Golf
Other sports followed: Rugby league, rugby union, 'enjoy all sports'
Injuries: Out for three months with a lower back injury
Favourite band: Powderfinger
Relaxations: Fishing
Extras: Leading wicket-taker in Brisbane first-grade cricket competition 1997-98 and
1998-99. Made first-class debut for Commonwealth Bank [Australian] Cricket

Academy v Zimbabwe Cricket Academy XI 1998-99. Queensland Academy of Sport Player of the Year 1998-99. Man of the Match in the Pura Cup final v Victoria 2000-01 for his 7-120 and 43 runs batting as nightwatchman. Awarded an ACB contract 2001-02 on his 24th birthday, after just six first-class matches. Sunshine Coast Sportstar of the Year 2001. Was Middlesex's overseas player for two periods during the 2002 season, replacing Abdul Razzaq, absent on international duty; returned as an overseas player for 2003. Scored 58 in the B&H v Sussex at Lord's 2002, in the process sharing with David Nash (67) in a record eighth-wicket partnership for the competition. Took a career-best 8-24 from 15 overs v Derbyshire at Derby 2002, including a spell of 7-6 from 35 balls. Represented Australia A v England and Sri Lanka tourists 2002-03. Awarded Middlesex cap 2003; has not returned to Middlesex for 2004 due to back problem. ACB contract 2003-04

Best batting: 76 Middlesex v Worcestershire, Worcester 2002
Best bowling: 8-24 Middlesex v Derbyshire, Derby 2002

2003 Season

	M	Inns	NO	Runs	HS	Avge	100s	50s	Ct	St	O	M	Runs	Wkts	Avge	Best	5wI	10wM
Test																		
All First	7	7	1	134	40	22.33	-	-	2	-	245.4	52	754	21	35.90	5-52	1	-
1-day Int																		
C & G	2	1	0	19	19	19.00	-	-	3	-	20	2	84	1	84.00	1-47	-	
NCL	7	4	2	13	4 *	6.50	-	-	-	-	48.4	7	189	6	31.50	2-24	-	
Twenty20	3	1	0	7	7	7.00	-	-	2	-	12	0	97	8	12.12	3-22	-	

Career Performances

	M	Inns	NO	Runs	HS	Avge	100s	50s	Ct	St	Balls	Runs	Wkts	Avge	Best	5wI	10wM
Test																	
All First	47	51	9	967	76	23.02	-	3	19	-	9395	5000	176	28.40	8-24	9	1
1-day Int																	
C & G	2	1	0	19	19	19.00	-	-	3	-	120	84	1	84.00	1-47	-	
NCL	7	4	2	13	4 *	6.50	-	-	-	-	292	189	6	31.50	2-24	-	
Twenty20	3	1	0	7	7	7.00	-	-	2	-	72	97	8	12.12	3-22	-	

70. A cousin of Garfield Sobers, who scored 105*
in his second Test match at Lord's in 1966?

NOON, W. M.   Nottinghamshire

Name: <u>Wayne</u> Michael Noon
Role: Right-hand bat, wicket-keeper
Born: 5 February 1971, Grimsby
Height: 5ft 9in **Weight:** 11st 7lbs
Nickname: Noonie, Spain Boon
County debut: 1988 (one-day, Northants),
1989 (first-class, Northants), 1994 (Notts)
County cap: 1995 (Notts)
Benefit: 2003 (Notts)
1st-Class 50s: 12
1st-Class catches: 195
1st-Class stumpings: 20
Parents: Trafford and Rosemary
Marital status: Married
Education: Caistor Grammar School
Qualifications: 5 O-levels
Career outside cricket: Manager of
G. Atkins (bookmakers)
Overseas tours: Lincolnshire U15 to Pakistan 1984; Rutland tourists to South Africa
1988; England YC to Australia 1989-90 (captain); Northamptonshire to Durban 1992,
to Cape Town 1993
Overseas teams played for: Burnside West, Christchurch, New Zealand 1989-90,
1995-96; Rivertonians, Cape Town 1993-94; Canterbury, Christchurch 1994-95
Cricketers particularly admired: Ian Botham
Other sports followed: Football (Lincoln City), horse racing (flat)
Relaxations: 'Having a bet. Eating out and having a pint'
Extras: Played for England YC v New Zealand YC 1989; captain v Pakistan YC 1990.
Was the 1000th player to appear in the Sunday League competition. Broke the Northants
record for most 2nd XI hundreds in one season in 1993. Took seven catches for Notts in
Kent's first innings at Trent Bridge 1999, breaking Bruce French's county record of six.
Notts 2nd XI captain since 2003
Best batting: 83 Nottinghamshire v Northamptonshire, Northampton 1997

2003 Season

	M	Inns	NO	Runs	HS	Avge	100s	50s	Ct	St	O	M	Runs	Wkts	Avge	Best	5wI	10wM
Test																		
All First	2	4	1	38	25	12.66	-	-	7	-								
1-day Int																		
C & G	1	1	0	9	9	9.00	-	-	-	-								
NCL	2	1	0	18	18	18.00	-	-	-	1								
Twenty20	4	2	0	13	12	6.50	-	-	-	3								

Career Performances

	M	Inns	NO	Runs	HS	Avge	100s	50s	Ct	St	Balls	Runs	Wkts	Avge	Best	5wI	10wM
Test																	
All First	92	145	23	2527	83	20.71	-	12	195	20	30	34	0	-	-	-	-
1-day Int																	
C & G	8	5	1	82	34	20.50	-	-	4	2							
NCL	83	53	14	495	38	12.69	-	-	62	16							
Twenty20	4	2	0	13	12	6.50	-	-	-	3							

O'BRIEN, N. J.   Kent

Name: Niall John O'Brien
Role: Left-hand top-order bat, wicket-keeper
Born: 8 November 1981, Dublin
Height: 5ft 6in **Weight:** 10st
Nickname: Nobby
County debut: No first-team appearance
Parents: Brendan and Camilla
Marital status: Single
Family links with cricket: Father a past captain of Ireland; brother Kevin a current U19 international and an MCC Young Cricketer
Education: Marian College, Ballsbridge, Dublin
Qualifications: Cricket coach
Career outside cricket: Has coached schools cricket and hockey in Dublin
Overseas tours: Ireland U19 to Sri Lanka (U19 World Cup) 1999-2000
Overseas teams played for: Railway Union CC, Dublin; Mosman CC, Sydney 2000, 2001; University of Port Elizabeth, South Africa 2002; North Sydney CC 2003
Career highlights to date: 'Getting first senior international cap and scoring 111 v MCC. Playing Grade 1 for North Sydney CC'
Cricketers particularly admired: Steve Waugh, Brett Lee
Young players to look out for: Kevin O'Brien ('brother'), Michael Clarke
Other sports played: Hockey ('senior club in Dublin')
Other sports followed: Football (Everton)
Favourite band: Oasis
Relaxations: 'Music; walking dog Sandy when in Dublin'
Extras: Made Ireland senior debut v Denmark 2002. Scored 111 for Ireland v MCC at Cork 2002. Played for Ireland in the first round of the C&G 2003, which was played in August 2002. Irish Cricketer of the Year 2002

Career Performances

	M	Inns	NO	Runs	HS	Avge	100s	50s	Ct	St	Balls	Runs	Wkts	Avge	Best	5wl	10wM
Test																	
All First																	
1-day Int																	
C & G	1	1	0	13	13	13.00	-	-	-	-							
NCL																	
Twenty20																	

OBUYA, C. O.   Warwickshire

Name: <u>Collins</u> Omondi Obuya
Role: Right-hand bat, right-arm
leg-spin bowler
Born: 27 July 1981, Nairobi, Kenya
County debut: 2003
One-Day Internationals: 28
1st-Class 50s: 1
1st-Class 5 w. in innings: 1
1st-Class catches: 5
One-Day 5 w. in innings: 2
Strike rate: 81.00 (career 56.70)
Family links with cricket: Brothers
Kennedy Otieno Obuya and David Oluoch
Obuya also play for Kenya
Overseas tours: Kenya U19 to South Africa
(U19 World Cup) 1997-98, to Sri Lanka (U19
World Cup) 1999-2000; Kenya to South
Africa (Standard Bank Triangular

Tournament) 2001-02, to Sri Lanka 2001-02, to Namibia (ICC Six Nations Challenge)
2001-02, to Sri Lanka (ICC Champions Trophy) 2002-03, to Zimbabwe (one-day
series) 2002-03, to Sharjah (Cherry Blossom Sharjah Cup) 2002-03
Extras: Sometimes known as Collins Omondi. Made first-class debut for Kenya v
Pakistan A in Nairobi 2000. Took 5-24 (a Kenyan best in ODIs) v Sri Lanka in Nairobi
in the 2002-03 World Cup, winning Man of the Match award. Played for University of
West Indies Vice-Chancellor's XI v Australian tourists at Bridgetown 2002-03. Joined
Warwickshire as an overseas player for 2003, scoring career best 55 on Championship
debut v Nottinghamshire at Edgbaston. Took 5-24 v Glamorgan at Edgbaston in the
Twenty20 2003, winning Man of the Match award. Left Warwickshire at the end of the
2003 season

Best batting: 55 Warwickshire v Nottinghamshire, Edgbaston 2003
Best bowling: 5-97 Kenya v Zimbabwe A, Nairobi 2001-02
Stop press: Played for Kenya in the 2003-04 Carib Beer Cup domestic competition in the West Indies

2003 Season

	M	Inns	NO	Runs	HS	Avge	100s	50s	Ct	St	O	M	Runs	Wkts	Avge	Best	5wl	10wM
Test																		
All First	3	5	3	131	55	65.50	-	1	2	-	54	2	276	4	69.00	3-91	-	-
1-day Int																		
C & G																		
NCL	4	2	1	3	2*	3.00	-	-	1	-	31	2	174	5	34.80	3-65	-	
Twenty20	7	5	1	84	34*	21.00	-	-	5	-	20	0	177	10	17.70	5-24	1	

Career Performances

	M	Inns	NO	Runs	HS	Avge	100s	50s	Ct	St	Balls	Runs	Wkts	Avge	Best	5wl	10wM
Test																	
All First	14	22	4	405	55	22.50	-	1	5	-	1928	1253	34	36.85	5-97	1	-
1-day Int	28	22	3	246	29	12.94	-	-	8	-	1332	1125	25	45.00	5-24	1	
C & G																	
NCL	4	2	1	3	2*	3.00	-	-	1	-	186	174	5	34.80	3-65	-	
Twenty20	7	5	1	84	34*	21.00	-	-	5	-	120	177	10	17.70	5-24	1	

71. Which former Middlesex batsman made his Test debut in 1981,
14 miles from his birthplace in Barbados,
and was the first black West Indian to play for England?

ONIONS, G.   Durham

Name: Graham Onions
Role: Right-hand bat, right-arm medium bowler
Born: 9 September 1982, Gateshead
Height: 6ft 1in   **Weight:** 11st 2lbs
Nickname: Bunny, Onions
County debut: No first-team appearance
Parents: Maureen and Richard
Marital status: Single
Education: St Thomas More RC School, Blaydon
Qualifications: 10 GCSEs, GNVQ Advanced Science (Distinction), Level 1 coach
Career outside cricket: 'Clerical work for a major building society'
Off-season: 'Working and preparing for next season'
Career highlights to date: 'Signing a two-year professional contract with Durham'
Cricket moments to forget: 'Double stress fracture of my shin – missing end of 2000 season'
Cricket superstitions: 'Licking index and middle finger before running in to bowl – in case the ball slips out of my hand'
Cricketers particularly admired: Darren Gough, Paul Collingwood, Andy Bichel
Young players to look out for: Tim Ambrose, Mark Turner, Liam Plunkett
Other sports played: Badminton (England U17, Durham County first team)
Other sports followed: Football ('the one and only Newcastle')
Injuries: Out for six weeks with a torn oblique
Favourite band: 'No favourite, prefer Rap and R&B – Snoop Dogg, DMX'
Relaxations: 'Music, socialising with mates, cinema'
Extras: 'Voted player of the tour when training in South Africa 2002.' Played for Durham Board XI in the C&G 2003
Opinions on cricket: 'Twenty20 was a massive success – exciting to watch. In Championship or three-day games each session should be shorter (two hours each). More drinks breaks.'

Career Performances

	M	Inns	NO	Runs	HS	Avge	100s	50s	Ct	St	Balls	Runs	Wkts	Avge	Best	5wI	10wM
Test																	
All First																		
1-day Int																		
C & G	1	1	0	5	5	5.00	-	-	-	-	60	59	2	29.50	2-59	-	
NCL																		
Twenty20																		

ORMOND, J. Surrey

Name: James Ormond
Role: Right-hand bat, right-arm fast-'ish'
bowler, can also bowl off spin
Born: 20 August 1977, Walsgrave, Coventry
Height: 6ft 3in **Weight:** 15st
Nickname: Jimmy, Horse
County debut: 1995 (Leicestershire),
2002 (Surrey)
County cap: 1999 (Leicestershire),
2003 (Surrey)
Test debut: 2001
Tests: 2
50 wickets in a season: 3
1st-Class 50s: 1
1st-Class 5 w. in innings: 18
1st-Class 10 w. in match: 1
1st-Class catches: 20
One-Day 5 w. in innings: 1
Place in batting averages: 205th av. 22.60 (2002 257th av. 16.00)
Place in bowling averages: 50th av. 28.00 (2002 105th av. 34.90)
Strike rate: 46.13 (career 51.45)
Parents: Richard and Margaret
Marital status: Single
Family links with cricket: 'Dad played years of cricket in Warwickshire'
Education: St Thomas More, Nuneaton; North Warwickshire College of Further
Education
Qualifications: 6 GCSEs
Overseas tours: England U19 to Zimbabwe 1995-96; England A to Kenya and Sri
Lanka 1997-98; England to India and New Zealand 2001-02

Overseas teams played for: Sydney University CC 1996, 1998, 1999
Cricketers particularly admired: Curtly Ambrose, Courtney Walsh, Allan Donald, Sachin Tendulkar, Brian Lara, Steve Griffin
Other sports played: Football, mountain biking, 'anything'
Other sports followed: Football (Coventry City)
Relaxations: Spending time with friends and family
Extras: Played for the Development of Excellence side and England U19 against South Africa U19 1995 and for England U19 against New Zealand U19 1996. Won Leicestershire's 2nd XI bowling award. NBC Denis Compton Award for the most promising young Leicestershire player 1998, 1999, 2000. Left Leicestershire in the 2001-02 off-season and joined Surrey for 2002. Took 300th first-class wicket (Will Jefferson) v Essex at Chelmsford 2003. Took 5-26 v Middlesex at The Oval in the Twenty20 2003 and was Man of the Match (4-11) at Trent Bridge in the final of the inaugural competition. Took four wickets in an over, including hat-trick (Hutton, Joyce, Weekes), v Middlesex at Guildford 2003. Awarded Surrey cap 2003
Best batting: 50* Leicestershire v Warwickshire, Leicester 1999
Best bowling: 6-33 Leicestershire v Somerset, Leicester 1998

2003 Season

	M	Inns	NO	Runs	HS	Avge	100s	50s	Ct	St	O	M	Runs	Wkts	Avge	Best	5wl	10wM
Test																		
All First	13	15	5	226	47	22.60	-	-	2	-	392.1	74	1428	51	28.00	6-34	3	-
1-day Int																		
C & G	3	2	0	4	2	2.00	-	-	-	-	28	3	139	5	27.80	3-53	-	
NCL	10	3	1	16	6	8.00	-	-	2	-	86	6	410	13	31.53	3-46	-	
Twenty20	5	1	0	3	3	3.00	-	-	1	-	20	0	111	11	10.09	5-26	1	

Career Performances

	M	Inns	NO	Runs	HS	Avge	100s	50s	Ct	St	Balls	Runs	Wkts	Avge	Best	5wl	10wM
Test	2	4	1	38	18	12.66	-	-	-	-	372	185	2	92.50	1-70	-	-
All First	93	109	27	1223	50 *	14.91	-	1	20	-	16930	9135	329	27.76	6-33	18	1
1-day Int																	
C & G	15	8	4	38	18 *	9.50	-	-	3	-	775	595	15	39.66	3-53	-	
NCL	63	35	19	189	18	11.81	-	-	13	-	2775	1929	81	23.81	4-12	-	
Twenty20	5	1	0	3	3	3.00	-	-	1	-	120	111	11	10.09	5-26	1	

OSTLER, D. P.   Warwickshire

Name: <u>Dominic</u> Piers Ostler
Role: Right-hand bat, right-arm
medium bowler
Born: 15 July 1970, Solihull
Height: 6ft 2in **Weight:** 14st
Nickname: Ossie
County debut: 1990
County cap: 1991
Benefit: 2000
1000 runs in a season: 6
1st-Class 50s: 67
1st-Class 100s: 14
1st-Class 200s: 2
1st-Class catches: 259
One-Day 100s: 3
Place in batting averages: 252nd av. 14.87
(2002 62nd av. 43.29)
Strike rate: (career 251.00)
Parents: Mike and Ann
Wife and date of marriage: Karen, 14 October 2000
Family links with cricket: Brother used to play for Knowle and Dorridge CC
Education: Princethorpe College; Solihull College of Technology
Qualifications: 4 O-levels, A-levels, City and Guilds Recreation Course
Career outside cricket: 'In business'
Overseas tours: Gladstone Small's Benefit Tour to Barbados 1991; England A to
Pakistan 1995-96; England XI to New Zealand (Cricket Max) 1997; Andy Moles'
Benefit Tour to Barbados 1997
Overseas teams played for: Avendale CC, Cape Town 1991-92
Career highlights to date: 'Winning eight trophies'
Cricket moments to forget: 'Dropping a slip catch in final at Lord's'
Cricket superstitions: 'None'
Cricketers particularly admired: Jason Ratcliffe, Simon Millington, Graeme Welch
Young players to look out for: Ian Bell, Nick Warren
Other sports played: Golf, snooker
Other sports followed: Football (Birmingham City FC)
Relaxations: 'Spending time with wife, Karen; snooker and golf'
Extras: Was a member of the Warwickshire U19 side that won the Esso U19 County
Festivals in 1988 and 1989. Has collected winner's medals for the B&H Cup, County
Championship, NatWest Trophy and Sunday League. Scored 134* off 114 balls v
Gloucestershire at Edgbaston in the NUL 2001, equalling Nick Knight's Warwickshire
record for the highest individual score in the one-day league (although Knight was

dismissed). Scored 175 v Somerset at Edgbaston 2002, in the process passing 10,000 runs in first-class cricket. Scored 240-ball 225 v Yorkshire at Edgbaston 2002
Opinions on cricket: 'Got to improve wickets. Longer tea interval – 20 minutes is no good to anyone!'
Best batting: 225 Warwickshire v Yorkshire, Edgbaston 2002
Best bowling: 1-46 Warwickshire v Middlesex, Edgbaston 2000

2003 Season

	M	Inns	NO	Runs	HS	Avge	100s	50s	Ct	St	O	M	Runs	Wkts	Avge	Best	5wl	10wM
Test																		
All First	5	8	0	119	58	14.87	-	1	3	-	2	0	33	0	-		-	-
1-day Int																		
C & G	3	3	0	22	18	7.33	-	-	1	-								
NCL	5	5	0	52	18	10.40	-	-	1	-								
Twenty20	4	4	0	43	23	10.75	-	-	3	-								

Career Performances

	M	Inns	NO	Runs	HS	Avge	100s	50s	Ct	St	Balls	Runs	Wkts	Avge	Best	5wl	10wM
Test																	
All First	205	336	25	10856	225	34.90	16	67	259	-	251	295	1	295.00	1-46	-	-
1-day Int																	
C & G	45	44	4	1156	104	28.90	1	8	21	-	15	10	1	10.00	1-4	-	
NCL	177	167	24	4617	134 *	32.28	2	31	54	-	6	4	0	-		-	-
Twenty20	4	4	0	43	23	10.75	-	-	3	-							

PALLADINO, A. P.   Essex

Name: Antonio (Tony) Paul Palladino
Role: Right-hand lower-order bat, right-arm fast-medium bowler
Born: 29 June 1983, Whitechapel, London
Height: 6ft **Weight:** 11st 3lbs
Nickname: TP, Dino, Italian Stallion
County debut: 2003
1st-Class 5 w. in innings: 1
1st-Class catches: 2
Place in bowling averages: 149th av. 54.00
Strike rate: 88.36 (career 88.36)
Parents: Antonio and Kathleen
Marital status: Single
Family links with cricket: 'Dad played cricket in the Kent League'
Education: Cardinal Pole Secondary School; Anglia Polytechnic University
Qualifications: 9 GCSEs, Advanced GNVQ Leisure and Tourism
Career outside cricket: Student

Off-season: 'Tours with British Universities and Cambridge UCCE'

Career highlights to date: 'Taking 6-41 against Kent in my second Championship match for Essex'

Cricket moments to forget: 'Dislocating my shoulder against Sussex in my third match'

Cricket superstitions: 'Paint three dots as my run-up mark'

Cricketers particularly admired:
Ian Botham

Young players to look out for: Alastair Cook, Ravinder Bopara, Mark Pettini, Zoheb Sharif, Tom Webley, Matt Kay, Chris Peacock

Other sports played: Football, golf, snooker

Other sports followed: Football (Chelsea)

Injuries: Out for last month and a half of 2003 season with a dislocated shoulder

Favourite band: Foo Fighters, Red Hot Chili Peppers, Nirvana

Relaxations: Playing computer games; watching films

Extras: Hackney Young Sportsman of the Year. London Schools Bowler of the Year five years running. Represented England U17 v Yorkshire Academy. Represented ECB U19 v Sri Lanka U19 2000 and West Indies U19 2001. Played for Essex Board XI in the C&G 2003, including the second round, which was played in September 2002. Played for Cambridge University CCE 2003. Recorded maiden first-class five-wicket return (6-41) v Kent at Canterbury 2003

Opinions on cricket: 'All domestic one-day cricket should be in coloured clothing and be normal ODI rules, apart from Twenty20.'

Best batting: 8 Essex v Kent, Canterbury 2003

Best bowling: 6-41 Essex v Kent, Canterbury 2003

2003 Season

	M	Inns	NO	Runs	HS	Avge	100s	50s	Ct	St	O	M	Runs	Wkts	Avge	Best	5wI	10wM
Test																		
All First	6	5	3	24	8	12.00	-	-	2	-	162	31	594	11	54.00	6-41	1	-
1-day Int																		
C & G	1	1	0	16	16	16.00	-	-	1	-	10	3	34	0	-		-	-
NCL	5	2	1	1	1 *	1.00	-	-	-	-	34.1	3	156	7	22.28	3-32	-	
Twenty20																		

Career Performances

	M	Inns	NO	Runs	HS	Avge	100s	50s	Ct	St	Balls	Runs	Wkts	Avge	Best	5wI	10wM
Test																	
All First	6	5	3	24	8	12.00	-	-	2	-	972	594	11	54.00	6-41	1	-
1-day Int																	
C & G	2	1	0	16	16	16.00	-	-	1	-	113	90	3	30.00	3-56	-	
NCL	5	2	1	1	1*	1.00	-	-	-	-	205	156	7	22.28	3-32	-	
Twenty20																	

PANESAR, M. S.   Northamptonshire

Name: <u>Mudhsuden</u> Singh Panesar
Role: Left-hand bat, slow left-arm bowler
Born: 25 April 1982, Luton
Height: 6ft 1in **Weight:** 12st 7lbs
Nickname: Monty
County debut: 2001
1st-Class 5 w. in innings: 1
1st-Class catches: 7
Place in bowling averages: 127th av. 42.84
(2002 82nd av. 32.58)
Strike rate: 74.46 (career 63.94)
Parents: Paramjit and Gursharan
Marital status: Single
Family links with cricket: 'Dad played local cricket'
Education: Stopsley High School; Bedford Modern School; Loughborough University
Qualifications: 10 GCSEs, 3 A-levels
Overseas tours: Bedford Modern School to Barbados 1999; England U19 to India 2000-01; Northamptonshire to Grenada 2001-02; British Universities to South Africa 2002; ECB National Academy to Australia and Sri Lanka 2002-03
Cricketers particularly admired: Sachin Tendulkar, Steve Waugh, Matthew Hayden, Rahul Dravid
Other sports played: Badminton, tennis, snooker
Other sports followed: Football (Arsenal)
Relaxations: Music, cars, wildlife
Extras: Represented England U19 v Sri Lanka U19 2000 and v West Indies U19 2001. Had match figures of 8-131 on first-class debut v Leicestershire at Northampton 2001, including 4-11 in the second innings. NBC Denis Compton Award for the most promising young Northamptonshire player 2001. Played for Loughborough University CCE 2002. Represented British Universities 2002. Recorded maiden first-class five-

wicket return (5-77) for ECB National Academy v Sri Lanka Academy XI at Colombo 2002-03

Best batting: 28 Northamptonshire v CUCCE, Fenner's 2003
Best bowling: 5-77 ECB Academy v Sri Lanka Academy XI, Colombo 2002-03

2003 Season

	M	Inns	NO	Runs	HS	Avge	100s	50s	Ct	St	O	M	Runs	Wkts	Avge	Best	5wI	10wM
Test																		
All First	6	7	3	43	28	10.75	-	-	3	-	161.2	30	557	13	42.84	3-92	-	-
1-day Int																		
C & G																		
NCL	1	1	1	6	6 *	-	-	-	-	-	6	0	36	1	36.00	1-36	-	
Twenty20																		

Career Performances

	M	Inns	NO	Runs	HS	Avge	100s	50s	Ct	St	Balls	Runs	Wkts	Avge	Best	5wI	10wM
Test																	
All First	17	19	9	69	28	6.90	-	-	7	-	3453	1835	54	33.98	5-77	1	-
1-day Int																	
C & G																	
NCL	2	2	2	22	16 *	-	-	-	-	-	90	62	1	62.00	1-36	-	
Twenty20																	

72. Which Scunthorpe footballer took 8-103 at Lord's
in 1984 but still lost to West Indies?

PARKIN, O. T.   Glamorgan

Name: <u>Owen</u> Thomas Parkin
Role: Right-hand bat, right-arm medium-fast
swing bowler
Born: 24 September 1972, Coventry
Height: 6ft 3in **Weight:** 13st
Nickname: Parky, Cala, Long-term, Off-road
County debut: 1994
1st-Class 5 w. in innings: 2
1st-Class catches: 12
One-Day 5 w. in innings: 1
Strike rate: 72.00 (career 56.47)
Parents: Vernon Cyrus and Sarah Patricia
Wife and date of marriage: Diane Margaret,
29 September 2001
Children: Benjamin Lewis, January 2003
Family links with cricket: 'None – but
enjoyed by all family'
Education: Bournemouth School;
Bath University

Qualifications: 9 GCSEs, 4 A-levels, 1 S-level, BSc (Hons) Mathematics
Overseas tours: Dorset Youth to Denmark
Overseas teams played for: Kew, Melbourne 1992-93; North Balwyn, Melbourne
1994-95; Balmain, Sydney 1997-99; ATW Clubites, Bundaberg, Queensland
1999-2000
Career highlights: 'Lord's final, and hitting winning runs against Derby in 2000'
(*The latter batting at No. 11 in NUL after 10 required off 14 balls*)
Cricket moments to forget: 'Dropping Chris Adams at Hove 2000'
Cricket superstitions: 'Never cross on the stairs (Sophia Gardens)'
Cricketers particularly admired: Malcolm Marshall, Richard Hadlee
Young players to look out for: Adam Harrison
Other sports played: 'Most sports socially'
Other sports followed: Rugby, football (Nottingham Forest), golf
Relaxations: '*Telegraph* crossword'
Extras: Played for Dorset in the NatWest Trophy 1992 and 1993. ASW Young Player
of the Month July 1994. Took 5 for 28 v Sussex on debut in Sunday League at Hove
1996 – a Glamorgan record. Retired at the end of the 2003 season
Opinions on cricket: 'Not overly pleased with the advent of two overseas players and
the influx of "Euro" players. We keep hearing "invest in academies – bring the young
players on" and yet close the door on them to another place in the team. Seems
hypocritical to me! I like the idea of the 20-over game – the more self-financing
cricket we play the better. Why not change Championship cricket to three six-sided
leagues (ten games – perfect both from a player's perspective and commercially)?'

Best batting: 24* Glamorgan v Essex, Chelmsford 1998
Best bowling: 5-24 Glamorgan v Somerset, Cardiff, 1998

2003 Season

	M	Inns	NO	Runs	HS	Avge	100s	50s	Ct	St	O	M	Runs	Wkts	Avge	Best	5wl	10wM
Test																		
All First	1	1	0	2	2	2.00	-	-	1	-	12	5	22	1	22.00	1-19	-	-
1-day Int																		
C & G																			
NCL	1	0	0	0	0	-	-	-	-	-	4	0	39	0	-		-	-
Twenty20	3	1	0	0	0	0.00	-	-	-	-	11	0	90	3	30.00	2-9	-	

Career Performances

	M	Inns	NO	Runs	HS	Avge	100s	50s	Ct	St	Balls	Runs	Wkts	Avge	Best	5wl	10wM
Test																	
All First	41	48	20	228	24 *	8.14	-	-	12	-	6099	3014	108	27.90	5-24	2	-
1-day Int																	
C & G	11	5	2	3	2	1.00	-	-	5	-	520	361	10	36.10	3-23	-	
NCL	74	26	11	57	14 *	3.80	-	-	14	-	3125	2491	97	25.68	5-28	1	
Twenty20	3	1	0	0	0	0.00	-	-	-	-	66	90	3	30.00	2-9	-	

PARSONS, K. A.   Somerset

Name: Keith Alan Parsons
Role: Right-hand bat, right-arm medium bowler
Born: 2 May 1973, Taunton
Height: 6ft 1in **Weight:** 14st 7lbs
Nickname: Pilot, Pars, Orv
County debut: 1992
County cap: 1999
1st-Class 50s: 23
1st-Class 100s: 5
1st-Class 5 w. in innings: 2
1st-Class catches: 99
One-day 100s: 1
Place in batting averages: (2002 189th av. 24.20)
Place in bowling averages: (2002 121st av. 39.52)
Strike rate: 49.00 (career 74.13)
Parents: Alan and Lynne
Wife and date of marriage: Sharon, 12 January 2002

Children: Joseph Luke, 17 October 2002
Family links with cricket: Identical twin brother, Kevin, was on the Somerset staff 1992-94 and then captained the Somerset Board XI. Father played six seasons for Somerset 2nd XI and captained National Civil Service XI
Education: The Castle School, Taunton; Richard Huish Sixth Form College, Taunton
Qualifications: 8 GCSEs, 3 A-levels, NCA senior coach
Off-season: 'Working for Set Square Recruitment Agency in Taunton'
Overseas tours: Castle School to Barbados 1989; Somerset CCC to Cape Town 1999, 2000, 2001
Overseas teams played for: Kapiti Old Boys, Horowhenua, New Zealand 1992-93; Taita District, Wellington, New Zealand 1993-96; Wembley Downs CC, Perth 1998
Career highlights to date: 'C&G final 2001 v Leicestershire – great to win a trophy, and Man of the Match capped a dream day'
Cricket moments to forget: 'Any bad days at Taunton'
Cricket superstitions: 'None'
Cricketers particularly admired: Andy Caddick, Marcus Trescothick, Glenn McGrath, Saqlain Mushtaq
Other sports followed: Rugby union (Bath RFC), football (Nottingham Forest FC), golf, horse racing
Relaxations: Playing golf, watching movies, listening to music 'and the odd social pint of beer'
Extras: Captained two National Cup winning sides – Taunton St Andrews in National U15 Club Championship and Richard Huish College in National U17 School Championship. Represented English Schools at U15 and U19 level. Somerset Young Player of the Year 1993. C&G Man of the Match award for his 52-ball 60* (including sixes from the last two balls of the innings) and 2-40 in the final v Leicestershire at Lord's 2001. C&G Man of the Match award for his 100-ball 121 (his maiden one-day century) in the quarter-final v Worcestershire at Taunton 2002 (also took 2-37, two catches and completed a run out). Granted a benefit for 2004
Opinions on cricket: 'With the increasing number of EU-qualified players becoming available, I am worried about opportunities for youngsters to play first-team cricket, especially as we are also having two overseas players.'
Best batting: 193* Somerset v West Indians, Taunton 2000
Best bowling: 5-13 Somerset v Lancashire, Taunton 2000

2003 Season

	M	Inns	NO	Runs	HS	Avge	100s	50s	Ct	St	O	M	Runs	Wkts	Avge	Best	5wI	10wM
Test																		
All First	2	4	0	13	6	3.25	-	-	1	-	32.4	5	123	4	30.75	2-63	-	-
1-day Int																		
C & G	2	1	0	83	83	83.00	-	1	1	-	20	0	78	4	19.50	3-29	-	
NCL	18	15	0	478	90	31.86	-	2	3	-	42	0	291	6	48.50	2-32	-	
Twenty20	5	5	1	36	28 *	9.00	-	-	2	-	8	0	83	2	41.50	2-26	-	

Career Performances

	M	Inns	NO	Runs	HS	Avge	100s	50s	Ct	St	Balls	Runs	Wkts	Avge	Best	5wI	10wM
Test																	
All First	109	178	17	4298	193 *	26.69	5	23	99	-	6524	3675	88	41.76	5-13	2	-
1-day Int																	
C & G	29	26	8	813	121	45.16	1	3	8	-	1256	936	36	26.00	4-43	-	
NCL	133	112	16	2577	90	26.84	-	13	49	-	2928	2475	63	39.28	3-21	-	
Twenty20	5	5	1	36	28 *	9.00	-	-	2	-	48	83	2	41.50	2-26	-	

PARSONS, M. Somerset

Name: Michael Parsons
Role: Right-hand bat, right-arm medium-fast bowler
Born: 26 November 1984, Taunton
Height: 5ft 11in **Weight:** 11st 11lbs
Nickname: Pars
County debut: 2002 (one-day)
Parents: Dave and Hilary
Marital status: Single
Education: Ladymead; Richard Huish College
Qualifications: 10 GCSEs, 1 A-level, Level 1 ECB coach
Overseas tours: ESCA West Region U15 to West Indies 2000; Somerset U19 Cricket Academy to Australia 2002
Career highlights to date: '1st XI debut – Somerset Sabres v Leicestershire Foxes in NUL 2002, aged 17 (live on Sky TV). England U19 (debut) "Test" match v South Africa 2003'
Cricket moments to forget: 'Dropped catch in above [NUL] match, live on Sky TV'
Cricket superstitions: 'None'
Cricketers particularly admired: Allan Donald, Glenn McGrath
Young players to look out for: James Hildreth
Other sports followed: Football (Man United)
Injuries: 'Lower ab strain'
Relaxations: 'Music, PlayStation'
Extras: England U15 and U17. Bowler of ESCA West Region U15 tour to West Indies 2000. Played for Somerset Board XI in the first round of the C&G 2003, which was played in August 2002. Represented England U19 v South Africa U19 2003
Opinions on cricket: 'More day/night matches.'

2003 Season

	M	Inns	NO	Runs	HS	Avge	100s	50s	Ct	St	O	M	Runs	Wkts	Avge	Best	5wl	10wM
Test																		
All First																		
1-day Int																		
C & G																		
NCL	2	2	0	0	0	0.00	-	-	-	-	13.3	0	75	1	75.00	1-52	-	
Twenty20																		

Career Performances

	M	Inns	NO	Runs	HS	Avge	100s	50s	Ct	St	Balls	Runs	Wkts	Avge	Best	5wl	10wM
Test																	
All First																	
1-day Int																	
C & G	1	1	0	0	0	0.00	-	-	-	-	60	70	3	23.33	3-70	-	
NCL	3	2	0	0	0	0.00	-	-	-	-	111	101	1	101.00	1-52	-	
Twenty20																	

PATEL, M. M.   Kent

Name: Minal (<u>Min</u>) Mahesh Patel
Role: Right-hand bat, slow left-arm
orthodox bowler
Born: 7 July 1970, Mumbai, India
Height: 5ft 7in **Weight:** 10st
Nickname: Ho Chi, Diamond, Geez
County debut: 1989
County cap: 1994
Test debut: 1996
Tests: 2
50 wickets in a season: 3
1st-Class 50s: 11
1st-Class 5 w. in innings: 23
1st-Class 10 w. in match: 9
1st-Class catches: 88
Place in batting averages: (2002 82nd
av. 40.07)
Place in bowling averages: (2002 92nd
av. 33.50)
Strike rate: (career 73.66)
Parents: Mahesh and Aruna
Wife and date of marriage: Karuna, 8 October 1995

Family links with cricket: Father played good club cricket in India, Africa and England
Education: Dartford Grammar School; Manchester Polytechnic
Qualifications: 6 O-levels, 3 A-levels, BA (Hons) Economics
Off-season: 'Getting fit'
Overseas tours: Dartford GS to Barbados 1988; England A to India and Bangladesh 1994-95; MCC to Malta 1997, 1999, to Fiji, Sydney and Hong Kong 1998, to East and Central Africa 1999, to Bangladesh 1999-2000 (captain), to Argentina and Chile 2001; Kent to Port Elizabeth 2001; Club Cricket Conference to Australia 2002
Overseas teams played for: St Augustine's, Cape Town 1993-94; Alberton, Johannesburg 1997-98
Career highlights to date: 'Winning 2001 Norwich Union League at Edgbaston. First Test cap. Any match-winning performance for Kent'
Cricket moments to forget: 'Being left out of the final XI for the Lord's Test v India 1996'
Cricketers particularly admired: Derek Underwood, Aravinda de Silva
Other sports played: Golf, snooker
Other sports followed: Football (Tottenham Hotspur), 'most sports that you can name'
Injuries: Out for the whole of the 2003 season with a prolapsed disc
Favourite band: 'A lot of 1970s/80s soul – Phyllis Hyman, Loose Ends, Keni Burke etc.'
Extras: Played for English Schools 1988, 1989 and NCA England South 1989. Was voted Kent League Young Player of the Year 1987 while playing for Blackheath. First six overs in NatWest Trophy were all maidens. Whittingdale Young Player of the Year 1994. Granted a benefit for 2004
Best batting: 82 Kent v Leicestershire, Canterbury 2002
Best bowling: 8-96 Kent v Lancashire, Canterbury 1994

2003 Season (did not make any first-class or one-day appearances)

Career Performances

	M	Inns	NO	Runs	HS	Avge	100s	50s	Ct	St	Balls	Runs	Wkts	Avge	Best	5wI	10wM
Test	2	2	0	45	27	22.50	-	-	2	-	276	180	1	180.00	1-101	-	-
All First	160	214	44	2925	82	17.20	-	11	88	-	34621	14484	470	30.81	8-96	23	9
1-day Int																	
C & G	14	5	2	45	27 *	15.00	-	-	5	-	662	399	11	36.27	2-29	-	
NCL	41	24	7	122	15	7.17	-	-	13	-	1714	1283	50	25.66	3-22	-	
Twenty20																	

PATEL, S. R.   Nottinghamshire

Name: <u>Samit</u> Rohit Patel
Role: Right-hand bat, left-arm orthodox spin bowler; all-rounder
Born: 30 November 1984, Leicester
Height: 5ft 8in **Weight:** 12st
Nickname: Pilchy Patel
County debut: 2002
1st-Class 50s: 1
1st-Class catches: 1
Parents: Rohit and Sejal
Marital status: Single
Family links with cricket: 'Dad plays in the local league and brother plays for Notts U15'
Education: Worksop College
Qualifications: 7 GCSEs, 2 A-levels
Career outside cricket: 'Want to be a coach'
Off-season: 'U19 World Cup in Bangladesh'
Overseas tours: England U17 to Australia 2001; England U19 to Australia and (U19 World Cup) New Zealand 2001-02, to Australia 2002-03, to Bangladesh (U19 World Cup) 2003-04
Career highlights to date: 'Scoring 122 against South Africa U19 at Arundel, because we were 90-6 at the time'
Cricket moments to forget: 'Playing at Headingley in the Twenty20 Cup against Yorkshire, where I got hit for 28 in an over by Michael Lumb'
Cricket superstitions: 'Put my right pad on first'
Cricketers particularly admired: Sachin Tendulkar, Brian Lara
Young players to look out for: Akhil Patel, Bilal Shafayat, Ravinder Bopara
Other sports played: Rugby, hockey (both for Worksop College 1st XI)
Other sports followed: Football (Nottingham Forest)
Favourite band: G-Unit
Relaxations: 'Listening to music; playing snooker; just generally relaxing'
Extras: Made Nottinghamshire 2nd XI debut in 1999, aged 14. Winner of inaugural BBC *Test Match Special* U15 Young Cricketer of the Year Award 2000. Represented England U19 v India U19 2002 and v South Africa U19 2003; captained England U19 in the one-day series v South Africa U19, scoring 122 in the first match at Arundel. Christopher Martin-Jenkins's promising young cricketer of the year 2003
Opinions on cricket: 'Lunch and tea should be longer, and batters should get second chances, especially off the first ball.'
Best batting: 55 Nottinghamshire v Lancashire, Trent Bridge 2003
Stop press: Scored 102* in England U19 victory over New Zealand U19 at Dhaka in the U19 World Cup 2003-04

2003 Season

	M	Inns	NO	Runs	HS	Avge	100s	50s	Ct	St	O	M	Runs	Wkts	Avge	Best	5wI	10wM
Test																		
All First	1	2	0	64	55	32.00	-	1	1	-	8	5	10	0	-	-	-	-
1-day Int																		
C & G																			
NCL	5	4	1	90	44	30.00	-	-	1	-	11	0	56	1	56.00	1-26	-	
Twenty20	2	2	1	11	10 *	11.00	-	-	1	-	1	0	28	0	-	-	-	

Career Performances

	M	Inns	NO	Runs	HS	Avge	100s	50s	Ct	St	Balls	Runs	Wkts	Avge	Best	5wI	10wM
Test																	
All First	2	3	0	99	55	33.00	-	1	1	-	48	10	0	-	-	-	-
1-day Int																	
C & G																		
NCL	8	5	1	108	44	27.00	-	-	1	-	114	100	4	25.00	2-14	-	
Twenty20	2	2	1	11	10 *	11.00	-	-	1	-	6	28	0	-	-	-	

PATTISON, I.   Durham

Name: Ian Pattison
Role: Right-hand bat, right-arm
medium bowler
Born: 5 May 1982, Sunderland
Height: 5ft 11in   **Weight:** 13st 5lbs ('-ish')
Nickname: Patta, Patto, Mr C
County debut: 2002
1st-Class 50s: 1
1st-Class catches: 2
Place in batting averages: (2002 290th
av. 10.16)
Strike rate: 34.00 (career 50.00)
Parents: Stewart and Janice
Marital status: Single; girlfriend Anna
Family links with cricket: 'Brother plays in
local premier league'
Education: Seaham Comprehensive
Qualifications: 6 GCSEs, Level 1 coaching
award
Off-season: 'Perth after Christmas; working before'
Overseas tours: England U19 to Malaysia and (U19 World Cup) Sri Lanka 1999-
2000, to India 2000-01

Overseas teams played for: Bayswater-Morley, Perth 2002-03
Career highlights to date: 'Scoring 50 at Headingley'
Cricket moments to forget: 'Dislocating shoulder day after getting 50, whilst bowling'
Cricketers particularly admired: Darren Gough, Craig White, Damien Martyn, Steve Waugh, Graeme Smith, Jacques Kallis
Young players to look out for: Liam Plunkett, John Sadler
Other sports played: Golf
Other sports followed: Football (Sunderland AFC)
Injuries: Out for four months after dislocating a shoulder in May
Relaxations: Horse racing
Extras: Played for Durham Board XI in the NatWest 2000 and in the C&G 2002 and 2003; also played for Durham in the C&G 2003
Opinions on cricket: 'More day/night cricket.'
Best batting: 62 Durham v Yorkshire, Headingley 2003
Best bowling: 3-41 Durham v Essex, Riverside 2002

2003 Season

	M	Inns	NO	Runs	HS	Avge	100s	50s	Ct	St	O	M	Runs	Wkts	Avge	Best	5wI	10wM
Test																		
All First	1	1	0	62	62	62.00	-	1	-	-	5.4	3	7	1	7.00	1-7	-	-
1-day Int																		
C & G	2	2	0	16	11	8.00	-	-	1	-	12	0	80	0	-		-	-
NCL																		
Twenty20																		

Career Performances

	M	Inns	NO	Runs	HS	Avge	100s	50s	Ct	St	Balls	Runs	Wkts	Avge	Best	5wI	10wM
Test																	
All First	4	7	0	123	62	17.57	-	1	2	-	250	174	5	34.80	3-41	-	-
1-day Int																	
C & G	6	6	2	73	48 *	18.25	-	-	3	-	186	168	3	56.00	1-25	-	
NCL	1	1	0	0	0	0.00	-	-	-	-	24	29	0	-		-	
Twenty20																	

73. Which commentator and former Test captain had
match figures of 13-156 at Trinidad in 1974?

PAYNTER, D. E.　　　　　　Northamptonshire

Name: <u>David</u> Edward Paynter
Role: Right-hand bat, right-arm
off-spin bowler
Born: 25 January 1981, Truro
Height: 6ft 2½in **Weight:** 12st 7lbs
Nickname: Paints
County debut: 2002
1st-Class 50s: 1
1st-Class 100s: 1
1st-Class catches: 2
One-Day 100s: 1
Parents: Mark and Carole
Marital status: Single
Family links with cricket: Great-grandfather
(Eddie Paynter) played for Lancashire
(1926-1945) and England and was on the
Bodyline tour
Education: Clayton Middle School
Qualifications: 9 GCSEs, Level I, II and III coaching awards
Overseas tours: Yorkshire U19 to India 1998-99
Overseas teams played for: Grafton, Auckland 1999-2001
Cricketers particularly admired: Mark Waugh, Ricky Ponting
Other sports played: Table tennis (Yorkshire U14), rugby (Queensbury RFC)
Other sports followed: Football (Bradford City), rugby league (Bradford Bulls)
Relaxations: Gym work, listening to music, socialising with friends
Extras: Bradford League Young Player of the Year 2000. Has attended Yorkshire and
Northamptonshire academies. Played for Worcestershire 2nd XI in 2000. Played for
Northamptonshire Board XI in the C&G 2001, scoring 104 on competition debut v
Northamptonshire at Northampton. Scored maiden first-class century (146) v
Cambridge UCCE at Fenner's 2003. Released by Northamptonshire at the end of the
2003 season
Best batting: 146 Northamptonshire v CUCCE, Fenner's 2003

2003 Season

	M	Inns	NO	Runs	HS	Avge	100s	50s	Ct	St	O	M	Runs	Wkts	Avge	Best	5wI	10wM
Test																		
All First	3	5	1	236	146	59.00	1	1	-	-	6	1	26	0	-	-	-	-
1-day Int																		
C & G																		
NCL	1	1	1	4	4 *	-	-	-	-	-	7	0	56	2	28.00	2-56	-	
Twenty20																		

Career Performances

	M	Inns	NO	Runs	HS	Avge	100s	50s	Ct	St	Balls	Runs	Wkts	Avge	Best	5wI	10wM
Test																	
All First	5	9	2	268	146	38.28	1	1	2	-	36	26	0	-	-	-	-
1-day Int																	
C & G	1	1	0	104	104	104.00	1	-	-	-	36	46	0	-	-	-	
NCL	3	3	1	33	18	16.50	-	-	-	-	54	83	3	27.66	2-56	-	
Twenty20																	

PEARSON, J. A.   Gloucestershire

Name: <u>James</u> Alexander Pearson
Role: Left-hand bat
Born: 11 September 1983, Bristol
Height: 5ft 10in **Weight:** 12st 7lbs
Nickname: JP
County debut: 2002
1st-Class 50s: 1
1st-Class catches: 2
Parents: Milverton and Faith
Marital status: Single
Family links with cricket: 'Dad played club cricket'
Education: Clifton College
Qualifications: 5 GCSEs, 3 A-levels, GNVQ
Overseas tours: England U19 to Australia 2002-03
Career highlights to date: 'Making 51 opening the batting on debut v Northamptonshire'

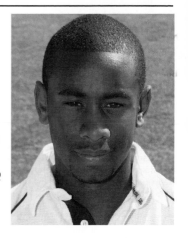

Cricketers particularly admired: Brian Lara, Courtney Walsh, Ricky Ponting
Young players to look out for: Alex Gidman, Liam Plunkett
Other sports played: 'A bit of footy now and then'
Other sports followed: Football (Arsenal)
Relaxations: 'Listening to music and going clubbing'
Extras: Played for Gloucestershire Board XI in the C&G 2001 and 2002. Scored 51 on debut v Northamptonshire at Bristol 2002. Represented England U19 v India U19 2002
Best batting: 51 Gloucestershire v Northamptonshire, Bristol 2002

2003 Season (did not make any first-class or one-day appearances)

Career Performances

	M	Inns	NO	Runs	HS	Avge	100s	50s	Ct	St	Balls	Runs	Wkts	Avge	Best	5wI	10wM
Test																	
All First	3	6	1	114	51	22.80	-	1	2	-							
1-day Int																	
C & G	2	2	0	7	7	3.50	-	-	-	-	18	29	1	29.00	1-29	-	
NCL																	
Twenty20																	

PENBERTHY, A. L. Northamptonshire

Name: Anthony (<u>Tony</u>) Leonard Penberthy
Role: Left-hand bat, right-arm
medium bowler
Born: 1 September 1969, Troon, Cornwall
Height: 6ft 1in **Weight:** 12st 7lbs
Nickname: Berth, Penbers, Sir Leonard,
Denzil
County debut: 1989
County cap: 1994
Benefit: 2002
1st-Class 50s: 40
1st-Class 100s: 10
1st-Class 5 w. in innings: 4
1st-Class catches: 108
One-Day 5 w. in innings: 4
Place in batting averages: (2002 76th
av. 41.31)
Place in bowling averages: (2002 145th
av. 49.00)
Strike rate: (career 74.43)
Parents: Gerald (deceased) and Wendy
Wife and date of marriage: Rebecca, 9 November 1996
Children: Georgia Lily, 4 March 1998; Harry Jake, 5 October 2000
Family links with cricket: Father played in local leagues in Cornwall and became a
qualified umpire instructor
Education: Camborne Comprehensive
Qualifications: 3 O-levels, 3 CSEs, Levels 1 and 2 coaching certificates
Career outside cricket: Coaching
Overseas tours: Druids to Zimbabwe 1988; Northants to Durban 1992, to Cape Town
1993, to Zimbabwe 1995, 1998, to Johannesburg 1996, to Grenada 2000, 2001

Career highlights to date: 'Wicket of Mark Taylor with first ball in first-class cricket' (*Caught behind, June 1989*)
Cricket moments to forget: 'A pair in the same game'
Cricketers particularly admired: Ian Botham, David Gower, Dennis Lillee, Viv Richards, Eldine Baptiste
Young players to look out for: Mark Powell, Monty Panesar
Other sports played: Football (trials for Plymouth Argyle), golf
Other sports followed: Football (West Ham United), rugby (Northampton Saints)
Relaxations: Listening to music, watching films and comedy programmes
Extras: Played for England YC v New Zealand YC 1989. Took only the second Sunday/National League hat-trick in Northants history v Somerset at Northampton in 1999. Scored 132* v Glamorgan at Northampton 2001, in the process sharing with Russell Warren in a record sixth-wicket partnership for Northants in matches against Glamorgan (250). Took his 158th one-day league wicket (Trevor Ward) v Leicestershire at Northampton 2001 to pass Peter Willey's county record in the competition. Scored 80 v Somerset at Northampton 2001, in the process sharing with David Ripley in a record eighth-wicket partnership for Northants in matches against Somerset (161); also shared with Curtly Ambrose in the previous record stand – 145 at Taunton in 1994. Vice-captain of Northamptonshire 2001-03. Released by Northamptonshire at the end of the 2003 season
Best batting: 132* Northamptonshire v Glamorgan, Northampton 2001
Best bowling: 5-37 Northamptonshire v Glamorgan, Swansea 1993

2003 Season

	M	Inns	NO	Runs	HS	Avge	100s	50s	Ct	St	O	M	Runs	Wkts	Avge	Best	5wI	10wM
Test																		
All First	2	3	1	93	45	46.50	-	-	-	-	17	5	54	0	-		-	-
1-day Int																		
C & G																		
NCL	2	1	0	28	28	28.00	-	-	-	-	9	1	49	0	-		-	-
Twenty20																		

Career Performances

	M	Inns	NO	Runs	HS	Avge	100s	50s	Ct	St	Balls	Runs	Wkts	Avge	Best	5wI	10wM
Test																	
All First	181	270	30	7212	132*	30.05	10	40	108	-	17194	9051	231	39.18	5-37	4	-
1-day Int																	
C & G	30	21	2	462	79	24.31	-	4	10	-	1393	1005	25	40.20	5-56	1	
NCL	168	139	28	2700	81*	24.32	-	15	42	-	6186	4954	174	28.47	5-29	3	
Twenty20																	

PENG, N.   Durham

Name: Nicky Peng
Role: Right-hand bat
Born: 18 September 1982,
Newcastle upon Tyne
Height: 6ft 3in **Weight:** 12st
Nickname: Pengy, King
County debut: 2000
County cap: 2001
1st-Class 50s: 8
1st-Class 100s: 4
1st-Class catches: 29
One-Day 100s: 3
Place in batting averages: 146th av. 29.72
(2002 190th av. 24.19)
Parents: Linda and Wilf
Marital status: Single
Education: Royal Grammar School,
Newcastle upon Tyne
Qualifications: 10 GCSEs
Overseas tours: England U19 to India 2000-01, to Australia and (U19 World Cup)
New Zealand 2001-02 (captain); ECB National Academy to Australia 2001-02;
Durham to South Africa 2002
Cricket moments to forget: 'Every time I get out!'
Cricketers particularly admired: Mike Atherton, Steve Waugh
Young players to look out for: Gordon Muchall, Ian Bell, Mark Wallace
Other sports followed: Football, rugby (Newcastle, and especially England)
Relaxations: Socialising with friends; music and films
Extras: Full name Nicky Peng Gillender. Has represented England at U14, U15, U17
and U19 levels. Represented Minor Counties at age 15. Sir John Hobbs Silver Jubilee
Memorial Prize 1998. Scored 98 on Championship debut, v Surrey at Riverside 2000.
Represented England U19 v Sri Lanka U19 2000 and v West Indies U19 2001 (captain
in first 'Test'). NBC Denis Compton Award for the most promising young Durham
player 2000, 2001. C&G Man of the Match award for his 119 v Hampshire at
Riverside 2001. Durham CCC Young Player of the Year 2001. PCA Young Player of
the Year 2001. Scored century before lunch on the opening day v Durham UCCE at
Durham 2003. Scored 99 v Derbyshire at Derby 2003, in the process sharing with
Vince Wells (106) in a new record fifth-wicket partnership for Durham (197)
Best batting: 158 Durham v DUCCE, Durham 2003

2003 Season

	M	Inns	NO	Runs	HS	Avge	100s	50s	Ct	St	O	M	Runs	Wkts	Avge	Best	5wI	10wM
Test																		
All First	15	25	0	743	158	29.72	2	2	12	-								
1-day Int																		
C & G	2	2	0	70	44	35.00	-	-	-	-								
NCL	15	15	2	466	92	35.84	-	3	2	-								
Twenty20	5	5	0	110	49	22.00	-	-	6	-								

Career Performances

	M	Inns	NO	Runs	HS	Avge	100s	50s	Ct	St	Balls	Runs	Wkts	Avge	Best	5wI	10wM
Test																		
All First	48	83	2	2033	158	25.09	4	8	29	-	6	2	0	-	-	-	-
1-day Int																		
C & G	7	7	0	243	119	34.71	1	-	1	-								
NCL	46	46	4	1185	121	28.21	2	5	12	-								
Twenty20	5	5	0	110	49	22.00	-	-	6	-								

PENNEY, T. L.   Warwickshire

Name: <u>Trevor</u> Lionel Penney
Role: Right-hand bat, leg-break bowler, occasional wicket-keeper
Born: 12 June 1968, Harare, Zimbabwe
Height: 6ft **Weight:** 11st 2lbs
Nickname: TP, Blondie
County debut: 1992
County cap: 1994
Benefit: 2003
1000 runs in a season: 2
1st-Class 50s: 36
1st-Class 100s: 15
1st-Class catches: 94
1st-Class stumpings: 2
Strike rate: (career 43.16)
Parents: George and Bets
Wife and date of marriage: Deborah-Anne, 19 December 1992
Children: Samantha Anne, 20 August 1995; Kevin, 7 June 1998
Family links with cricket: Father played club cricket. Brother Stephen captained Zimbabwe Schools
Education: Prince Edward Boys High School, Zimbabwe

Qualifications: 3 O-levels
Overseas tours: Zimbabwe U24 to England 1984; Zimbabwe to Sri Lanka 1987; ICC Associates to Australia (U19 World Cup) 1987-88 (captain)
Overseas teams played for: Old Hararians, Zimbabwe 1983-89, 1992-98; Scarborough, Perth 1989-90; Avendale, South Africa 1990-91; Boland, South Africa 1991-92; Mashonaland, Zimbabwe 1993-94, 1997-98 – 2000-01
Cricketers particularly admired: Colin Bland, Ian Botham, Allan Donald, Steve Waugh
Other sports played: Hockey (Zimbabwe and Africa), squash, tennis, golf and white water rafting
Other sports followed: Basketball (Chicago Bulls), American football (San Francisco 49ers), Formula One motor racing
Relaxations: 'Spending time with my family'
Extras: Played for Zimbabwe v Sri Lanka 1987. Played hockey for Zimbabwe 1984-87 and also made the African team who played Asia in 1987. Scored century (102*) on first-class debut for Warwickshire, v Cambridge University at Fenner's 1992. Qualified to play for England in 1992. Captained Old Hararians to victory in three Zimbabwe domestic trophies 1998-99. C&G Man of the Match award for his 58* in the quarter-final v Yorkshire at Headingley 2001. Warwickshire 2nd XI captain in 2002 and 2003; took part in a third-wicket stand of 397 with Jonathan Trott v Somerset 2nd XI at Knowle & Dorridge 2002. Has coached Zimbabwe Board XI and Zimbabwe A
Best batting: 151 Warwickshire v Middlesex, Lord's 1992
Best bowling: 3-18 Mashonaland v Mashonaland U24, Harare 1993-94

2003 Season

	M	Inns	NO	Runs	HS	Avge	100s	50s	Ct	St	O	M	Runs	Wkts	Avge	Best	5wI	10wM
Test																		
All First	1	2	0	21	19	10.50	-	-	1	-								
1-day Int																		
C & G																		
NCL	11	8	5	273	88 *	91.00	-	2	5	1								
Twenty20	7	7	1	200	52	33.33	-	1	2	-								

Career Performances

	M	Inns	NO	Runs	HS	Avge	100s	50s	Ct	St	Balls	Runs	Wkts	Avge	Best	5wI	10wM
Test																	
All First	158	248	45	7975	151	39.28	15	36	94	2	259	184	6	30.66	3-18	-	-
1-day Int																	
C & G	39	36	10	837	90	32.19	-	3	22	-	13	16	1	16.00	1-8	-	
NCL	163	138	47	2740	88 *	30.10	-	12	59	1	6	2	0	-	-	-	
Twenty20	7	7	1	200	52	33.33	-	1	2	-							

Name: Christopher (<u>Chris</u>) Thomas Peploe
Role: Left-hand lower-order bat,
slow-left arm bowler
Born: 26 April 1981, Hammersmith, London
Height: 6ft 4in **Weight:** 13st 7lbs
Nickname: Peps, Pepsy
County debut: 2003
1st-Class catches: 2
Strike rate: 195.00 (career 195.00)
Parents: Trevor and Margaret
Marital status: Single
Education: Twyford C of E High School;
University of Surrey, Roehampton
Qualifications: 9 GCSEs, 3 A-levels, Sports
Science degree, ECB Level 2 coach, qualified
gym instructor
Off-season: 'Paying off student debts;
training'
Overseas tours: MCC Young Cricketers to South Africa 2002
Career highlights to date: 'First-class debut for Middlesex v Sussex at Hove and
taking five wickets at Lord's for MCC Young Cricketers v MCC'
Cricket moments to forget: 'Getting smashed by the Aussies in the nets when bowled
at them at Lord's last time they toured'
Cricket superstitions: 'None'
Cricketers particularly admired: Graham Thorpe, Marcus Trescothick,
Matthew Hayden, Phil Tufnell
Young players to look out for: Andrew Strauss, Kevin Pietersen
Other sports played: Golf, hockey
Other sports followed: English rugby
Favourite band: Linkin Park
Relaxations: Music
Extras: MCC Young Cricketer 2002-03
Opinions on cricket: 'Test cricket is the true test of any player. One-day game is very
exciting and intense.'
Best batting: 13 Middlesex v Sussex, Hove 2003
Best bowling: 1-58 Middlesex v Zimbabweans, Shenley 2003

2003 Season

	M	Inns	NO	Runs	HS	Avge	100s	50s	Ct	St	O	M	Runs	Wkts	Avge	Best	5wI	10wM
Test																		
All First	2	2	1	13	13	13.00	-	-	2	-	65	9	239	2	119.50	1-58	-	-
1-day Int																		
C & G																		
NCL																		
Twenty20																		

Career Performances

	M	Inns	NO	Runs	HS	Avge	100s	50s	Ct	St	Balls	Runs	Wkts	Avge	Best	5wI	10wM
Test																		
All First	2	2	1	13	13	13.00	-	-	2	-	390	239	2	119.50	1-58	-	-
1-day Int																		
C & G																		
NCL																		
Twenty20																		

PETERS, S. D.   Worcestershire

Name: <u>Stephen</u> David Peters
Role: Right-hand bat, leg-break bowler
Born: 10 December 1978, Harold Wood, Essex
Height: 5ft 11in **Weight:** 11st
Nickname: Pedro, Geezer
County debut: 1996 (Essex), 2002 (Worcestershire)
County colours: 2002 (Worcestershire)
1000 runs in a season: 1
1st-Class 50s: 22
1st-Class 100s: 6
1st-Class catches: 67
Place in batting averages: 70th av. 40.58 (2002 75th av. 41.68)
Strike rate: (career 23.00)
Parents: Lesley and Brian
Marital status: Single
Family links with cricket: 'All family is linked with Upminster CC'
Education: Coopers Company and Coborn School
Qualifications: 9 GCSEs, Level 2 coaching
Off-season: 'Coaching, gym, netting'

Overseas tours: Essex U14 to Barbados; Essex U15 to Hong Kong; England U19 to Pakistan 1996-97, to South Africa (including U19 World Cup) 1997-98
Overseas teams played for: Cornwall CC, Auckland 2001-02; Willetton CC, Perth 2002-03
Career highlights to date: 'Winning B&H Cup in 1998 with Essex'
Cricket moments to forget: 'Running myself out for a pair against Durham in 2003'
Cricket superstitions: 'Binned most in 2002'
Cricketers particularly admired: 'Anyone who has played at the top level'
Young players to look out for: James Tomlinson, Mark Davis (Worcestershire)
Other sports played: Football, golf
Other sports followed: Football (West Ham United)
Relaxations: 'My sofa'
Extras: Sir John Hobbs Silver Jubilee Memorial Prize 1994; a *Daily Telegraph* Regional Batting Award 1994. Represented England at U14, U15, U17 and U19. Scored century (110) on county debut v Cambridge University at Fenner's 1996, in the process becoming (at 17 years 194 days) the youngest player to score a first-class century for Essex. Essex Young Player of the Year 1996. Scored a century (107) and was Man of the Match in the U19 World Cup final in South Africa 1997-98. Left Essex during the 2001-02 off-season and joined Worcestershire for 2002. Scored maiden Championship century (146) v Northamptonshire at Northampton 2002, in the process sharing with David Leatherdale (147*) in a record fourth-wicket partnership for Worcestershire in matches against Northamptonshire (239). Scored 1000 first-class runs in a season for the first time 2003
Opinions on cricket: 'Twenty20 good for new crowds.'
Best batting: 165 Worcestershire v Somerset, Bath 2003
Best bowling: 1-19 Essex v Oxford University, Chelmsford 1999

2003 Season

	M	Inns	NO	Runs	HS	Avge	100s	50s	Ct	St	O	M	Runs	Wkts	Avge	Best	5wI	10wM
Test																		
All First	18	30	1	1177	165	40.58	2	9	15	-								
1-day Int																		
C & G	2	2	0	9	5	4.50	-	-	1	-								
NCL	9	8	0	265	82	33.12	-	2	2	-								
Twenty20	3	3	0	28	23	9.33	-	-	3	-								

Career Performances

	M	Inns	NO	Runs	HS	Avge	100s	50s	Ct	St	Balls	Runs	Wkts	Avge	Best	5wI	10wM
Test																	
All First	90	148	16	4089	165	30.97	6	22	67	-	23	19	1	19.00	1-19	-	-
1-day Int																	
C & G	8	8	0	111	58	13.87	-	1	4	-							
NCL	74	65	3	1179	82	19.01	-	6	17	-							
Twenty20	3	3	0	28	23	9.33	-	-	3	-							

PETTINI, M. L. Essex

Name: <u>Mark</u> Lewis Pettini
Role: Right-hand bat, occasional wicket-keeper
Born: 7 August 1983, Brighton
Height: 5ft 11in **Weight:** 11st 7lbs
Nickname: Swampy, Michelle
County debut: 2001
1st-Class 50s: 4
1st-Class catches: 6
Place in batting averages: (2002 172nd av. 26.16)
Parents: Pauline and Max
Marital status: Single
Family links with cricket: 'Brother Tom plays. Mum and Dad watch'
Education: Comberton Village College and Hills Road Sixth Form College, Cambridge; Cardiff University
Qualifications: 10 GCSEs, 3 A-levels, Level 1 cricket coaching award
Off-season: 'Studying at Cardiff University'
Overseas tours: England U19 to Australia and (U19 World Cup) New Zealand 2001-02; MCC to Sierra Leone and Nigeria; Essex to Cape Town
Career highlights to date: 'Any first-team cricket played'
Cricket moments to forget: 'Losing three U19 One-Day Internationals to India [2002]'
Cricket superstitions: 'Drive round the car park twice before parking before a game. Never cut toenails during season'
Cricketers particularly admired: 'All the Essex 1st team', Graham Gooch, Damien West
Young players to look out for: Ryan Bradshaw, Ravi Bopara, Ali Cook, 'brother Tom'
Extras: Captained Cambridgeshire county sides U11-U16. Took hat-trick against Bedfordshire U12. Highest score of 173* v Hampshire U16 1999. Played for Development of Excellence XI (South) v West Indies U19 at Arundel 2001. Represented England U19 v India U19 in 'Test' series (2/3) and one-day series (3/3) 2002. Essex 2nd XI Player of the Year 2002. Scored an 81-ball 92* v Warwickshire at Edgbaston in the C&G 2003. Represented British Universities v India A 2003
Opinions on cricket: 'Tea should be half an hour.'
Best batting: 78 Essex v Warwickshire, Chelmsford 2003

2003 Season

	M	Inns	NO	Runs	HS	Avge	100s	50s	Ct	St	O	M	Runs	Wkts	Avge	Best	5wI	10wM
Test																		
All First	3	5	1	172	78	43.00	-	2	3	-								
1-day Int																		
C & G	1	1	1	92	92*	-	-	1	1	-								
NCL	14	13	1	229	59	19.08	-	1	1	-								
Twenty20	4	4	1	68	32*	22.66	-	-	3	-								

Career Performances

	M	Inns	NO	Runs	HS	Avge	100s	50s	Ct	St	Balls	Runs	Wkts	Avge	Best	5wI	10wM
Test																	
All First	7	13	1	371	78	30.91	-	4	6	-							
1-day Int																	
C & G	2	2	1	95	92*	95.00	-	1	2	-							
NCL	25	22	1	422	75	20.09	-	3	4	-							
Twenty20	4	4	1	68	32*	22.66	-	-	3	-							

PHILLIPS, B. J.   Northamptonshire

Name: <u>Ben</u> James Phillips
Role: Right-hand bat, right-arm fast-medium bowler
Born: 30 September 1975, Lewisham, London
Height: 6ft 6in **Weight:** 15st
Nickname: Bennyphil, Bus
County debut: 1996 (Kent), 2002 (Northamptonshire)
1st-Class 50s: 2
1st-Class 100s: 1
1st-Class 5 w. in innings: 2
1st-Class catches: 9
Place in batting averages: 225th av. 19.83
Place in bowling averages: 3rd av. 19.04
Strike rate: 42.57 (career 52.14)
Parents: Glynis and Trevor
Wife and date of marriage: Sarah Jane, 20 January 2003
Family links with cricket: Father and brother both keen club cricketers for Hayes CC (Kent)
Education: Langley Park School for Boys, Beckenham; Langley Park Sixth Form
Qualifications: 9 GCSEs, 3 A-levels

Career outside cricket: Personal training
Overseas tours: Northamptonshire to Grenada 2002
Overseas teams played for: University of Queensland, Australia 1993-94; Cape Technikon Greenpoint, Cape Town 1994-95, 1996-98; University of Western Australia, Perth 1998-99; Valley, Brisbane 2001-02
Career highlights to date: '100* v Lancashire, Old Trafford 1997'
Cricket moments to forget: 'Having to leave the field in a televised game against Worcestershire with a shoulder injury that kept me out for most of [2002] season – that would be up there'
Cricket superstitions: 'Arrive at the ground early – hate rushing!'
Cricketers particularly admired: Glenn McGrath, Jason Gillespie
Young players to look out for: Jake Phillips, Monty Panesar
Other sports followed: Football (West Ham United), rugby (Northampton Saints)
Relaxations: 'Enjoy swimming, watching a good movie, and just generally like spending time with family and friends'
Extras: Represented England U19 Schools in 1993-94. Set Langley Park School record for the fastest half-century, off 11 balls. Released by Kent at the end of the 2001 season and joined Northamptonshire for 2002
Best batting: 100* Kent v Lancashire, Old Trafford 1997
Best bowling: 5-47 Kent v Sussex, Horsham 1997

2003 Season

	M	Inns	NO	Runs	HS	Avge	100s	50s	Ct	St	O	M	Runs	Wkts	Avge	Best	5wI	10wM
Test																		
All First	7	8	2	119	48 *	19.83	-	-	1	-	149	47	400	21	19.04	4-45	-	-
1-day Int																		
C & G	1	1	0	19	19	19.00	-	-	1	-	7	0	38	0	-	-	-	-
NCL	12	8	1	95	25	13.57	-	-	2	-	83	5	412	8	51.50	3-25	-	
Twenty20	4	4	2	72	29 *	36.00	-	-	2	-	16	0	157	1	157.00	1-29	-	

Career Performances

	M	Inns	NO	Runs	HS	Avge	100s	50s	Ct	St	Balls	Runs	Wkts	Avge	Best	5wI	10wM
Test																	
All First	35	48	6	720	100 *	17.14	1	2	9	-	4693	2355	90	26.16	5-47	2	-
1-day Int																	
C & G	3	2	1	28	19	28.00	-	-	2	-	132	105	3	35.00	3-14	-	
NCL	30	16	3	144	29	11.07	-	-	9	-	1060	855	28	30.53	4-25	-	
Twenty20	4	4	2	72	29 *	36.00	-	-	2	-	96	157	1	157.00	1-29	-	

PHILLIPS, N. C.   Durham

Name: <u>Nicholas</u> Charles Phillips
Role: Right-hand bat, off-spin bowler
Born: 10 May 1974, Pembury, Kent
Height: 6ft **Weight:** 12st 5lbs
Nickname: Captain Chaos
County debut: 1994 (Sussex),
1998 (Durham)
County cap: 2001 (Durham)
1st-Class 50s: 4
1st-Class 5 w. in innings: 5
1st-Class 10 w. in match: 1
1st-Class catches: 44
Place in batting averages: 258th av. 14.05
(2002 205th av. 22.60)
Place in bowling averages: 114th av. 39.81
(2002 79th av. 31.95)
Strike rate: 64.52 (career 80.84)
Parents: Robert and Joan
Marital status: Single

Family links with cricket: Father plays club cricket for Hastings. Represents Sussex Over 50s and has represented Kent 2nd XI, Kent League XI and has scored over 100 club 100s
Education: William Parker School, Hastings
Qualifications: 8 GCSEs, Level 2 coaching award
Career outside cricket: Physiotherapy assistant
Overseas tours: Sussex U18 to India 1990-91; Durham to Cape Town 2002
Overseas teams played for: Marist CC, Auckland 1996-97; Taita Districts, Wellington, New Zealand 1998-99
Career highlights to date: 'Taking over captaincy for the last six weeks of the [2002] season. Promotion to Division One of NUL 2001'
Cricket superstitions: 'Make sure I put my glasses on before the start of play'
Cricketers particularly admired: Eddie Hemmings, Brad Hodge
Young players to look out for: 'Fred' Muchall
Other sports played: Hockey (Sussex U14 and U16)
Other sports followed: Football (West Ham)
Relaxations: 'Spending time with friends and girlfriend. Listening to music. Eating out and socialising with fellow players'
Extras: Represented England U19 v West Indies U19 1993. Released by Sussex at the end of the 1997 season and joined Durham. Returned the best figures for a Durham spinner since the county attained first-class status with his 12-268 v Glamorgan at Cardiff 1999. Took 3-0 from four overs as Durham bowled out Derbyshire to win

Championship match at Darlington 2002. Captained Durham during the latter part of the 2002 season in the absence, injured, of Jon Lewis. Released by Durham at the end of the 2003 season

Best batting: 58* Durham v Essex, Colchester 2002
Best bowling: 6-97 Durham v Glamorgan, Cardiff 1999

2003 Season

	M	Inns	NO	Runs	HS	Avge	100s	50s	Ct	St	O	M	Runs	Wkts	Avge	Best	5wI	10wM
Test																		
All First	13	22	5	239	39	14.05	-	-	9	-	408.4	63	1513	38	39.81	5-144	1	-
1-day Int																		
C & G	2	1	0	1	1	1.00	-	-	-	-	16.2	2	66	3	22.00	2-16	-	
NCL	5	4	2	31	24	15.50	-	-	3	-	41	1	183	6	30.50	3-41	-	
Twenty20	5	3	1	32	26 *	16.00	-	-	-	-	20	0	152	6	25.33	2-22	-	

Career Performances

	M	Inns	NO	Runs	HS	Avge	100s	50s	Ct	St	Balls	Runs	Wkts	Avge	Best	5wI	10wM
Test																	
All First	77	118	27	1410	58 *	15.49	-	4	44	-	13097	7074	162	43.66	6-97	5	1
1-day Int																	
C & G	9	6	0	53	21	8.83	-	-	-	-	385	238	7	34.00	2-16	-	
NCL	85	58	14	460	38 *	10.45	-	-	25	-	3515	2825	98	28.82	4-13	-	
Twenty20	5	3	1	32	26 *	16.00	-	-	-	-	120	152	6	25.33	2-22	-	

74. Who is the Warwickshire chief executive
who followed his 174 in Trinidad with his Test best 262*
in Jamaica in February 1974?

PHILLIPS, T. J.   Essex

Name: Timothy (<u>Tim</u>) James Phillips
Role: Left-hand bat, slow left-arm bowler
Born: 13 March 1981, Cambridge
Height: 6ft 1in **Weight:** 12st 11lbs
Nickname: Pips
County debut: 1999
1st-Class 50s: 1
1st-Class catches: 7
Place in batting averages: (2002 154th
av. 28.10)
Place in bowling averages: (2002 143rd
av. 46.88)
Strike rate: (career 80.59)
Parents: Martin (deceased) and Carolyn
Marital status: Single
Family links with cricket: 'Father played in
Lancashire League and then local village
cricket in Essex. Nick (brother) played for
Essex Schools to U15, and now plays for the mighty Lindsell'
Education: Felsted School; Durham University
Qualifications: 10 GCSEs, 3 A-levels, BA (Hons) Sport in the Community
Overseas tours: Felsted School to Australia 1995-96; England U19 to Malaysia and
(U19 World Cup) Sri Lanka 1999-2000
Career highlights to date: 'Four wickets on first-class debut v Sri Lanka A'
Cricket moments to forget: 'Pre-season tour to Cape Town – injured knee'
Cricketers particularly admired: Phil Tufnell, Graham Thorpe
Young players to look out for: Alastair Cook, Mark Pettini
Other sports played: Hockey (Essex Schools U14, U15; East of England U21 trials),
golf
Other sports followed: Rugby union
Injuries: Out for the whole of the 2003 season with cartilage and ligament damage to
a knee
Favourite band: Coldplay
Relaxations: 'Music gigs, socialising, travelling'
Extras: Winner of *Daily Telegraph* U14 National Bowling Award 1995. Holmwoods
School Cricketer of the Year runner-up 1997 and 1998. Broke Nick Knight's and
Elliott Wilson's record for runs in a season for Felsted School, scoring 1200. NBC
Denis Compton Award 1999. Played for Durham University CCE 2001 and 2002,
scoring 75 v Durham at Riverside 2002
Best batting: 75 DUCCE v Durham, Riverside 2002
Best bowling: 4-42 Essex v Sri Lanka A, Chelmsford 1999

2003 Season (did not make any first-class or one-day appearances)

Career Performances

	M	Inns	NO	Runs	HS	Avge	100s	50s	Ct	St	Balls	Runs	Wkts	Avge	Best	5wI	10wM
Test																	
All First	17	25	3	388	75	17.63	-	1	7	-	2579	1704	32	53.25	4-42	-	-
1-day Int																	
C & G	1	1	1	4	4*	-	-	-	-	-	30	27	0	-		-	-
NCL	6	6	2	16	6	4.00	-	-	2	-	210	182	6	30.33	2-36	-	
Twenty20																	

PIETERSEN, K. P.   Nottinghamshire

Name: Kevin Peter Pietersen
Role: Right-hand bat, right-arm
off-spin bowler
Born: 27 June 1980, Pietermaritzburg,
South Africa
Height: 6ft 4in **Weight:** 14st 9lbs
Nickname: KP, Kelv, Kapes
County debut: 2001
County cap: 2002
1000 runs in a season: 2
1st-Class 50s: 19
1st-Class 100s: 9
1st-Class 200s: 3
1st-Class catches: 53
One-Day 100s: 4
Place in batting averages: 25th av. 51.53
(2002 14th av. 62.21)
Place in bowling averages: 111th av. 38.90
Strike rate: 59.27 (career 85.72)
Parents: Jannie and Penny
Marital status: Single
Education: Maritzburg College; University of South Africa
Qualifications: 3 A-levels
Off-season: ECB National Academy
Overseas tours: Natal to Zimbabwe 1999-2000, to Australia 2000-01;
Nottinghamshire to South Africa 2001, 2002; ECB National Academy (England A) to
Malaysia and India 2003-04
Overseas teams played for: Berea Rovers, Durban 1997 – 2001-02; KwaZulu-Natal
1997-98 – 2000-01; Sydney University 2002-03

Career highlights to date: 'Making four consecutive 100s for Notts in August 2002'
Cricket moments to forget: 'Breaking my leg against Glamorgan in August 2002 in an NUL game'
Cricket superstitions: 'Left pad first'
Cricketers particularly admired: Shaun Pollock, Errol Stewart
Young players to look out for: Ed Joyce, Jamie Troughton, Rich Logan
Other sports played: Golf, swimming ('represented my state in 1992-93'), running
Other sports followed: Formula One (Ferrari), rugby (Natal Sharks)
Injuries: Out for three weeks with water on the knee
Relaxations: 'Spending time with family and girlfriend and travelling with girlfriend abroad'
Extras: Played for South African Schools B 1997. Merit award for cricket from Natal 1997. Scored 61* and had figures of 4-141 in 56 overs for KwaZulu-Natal v England on their 1999-2000 tour of South Africa. Scored maiden first-class century (165*) v Middlesex at Lord's 2001, in the process sharing in a record seventh-wicket stand for Notts in matches against Middlesex (199) with Paul Franks. Youngest Notts player to score a 200 in a first-class match (218* v Derbyshire at Derby 2001). Scored 1275 runs in first season of county cricket 2001. Scored 254* v Middlesex at Trent Bridge 2002 (the highest post-war Championship score by a Nottinghamshire batsman), in the process sharing with Darren Bicknell (108) in a record partnership for any wicket in matches between Nottinghamshire and Middlesex (316). Three days later, scored maiden one-day century (122 from 100 balls) v Somerset at Trent Bridge in the NUL; next day scored another century (147 from 101 balls), also v Somerset, at Taunton in the NUL; followed up with a further century (116) in next Championship match, v Gloucestershire at Trent Bridge. NUL Player of the Month August 2002; PCA Player of the Month August 2002. Scored 221 at Edgbaston 2003 to equal Joe Hardstaff Jr's record score by a Nottinghamshire batsman in matches against Warwickshire. Became first batsman to hit a ball over the pavilion at Riverside, v Durham in the NCL 2003. Is not considered an overseas player
Best batting: 254* Nottinghamshire v Middlesex, Trent Bridge 2002
Best bowling: 4-31 Nottinghamshire v DUCCE, Trent Bridge 2003
Stop press: Scored 131 for England A v India A in second 'ODI' at Bangalore 2003-04. Scored century in each innings (104/115) for England A v South Zone at Gurgaon in the Duleep Trophy 2003-04

2003 Season

	M	Inns	NO	Runs	HS	Avge	100s	50s	Ct	St	O	M	Runs	Wkts	Avge	Best	5wI	10wM
Test																		
All First	16	30	0	1546	221	51.53	4	11	17	-	108.4	18	428	11	38.90	4-31	-	-
1-day Int																		
C & G	1	1	0	5	5	5.00	-	-	1									
NCL	18	18	2	776	141 *	48.50	2	5	9	-	36.3	0	220	2	110.00	2-11	-	
Twenty20	5	5	0	150	58	30.00	-	1	-	-	11	0	80	2	40.00	2-28	-	

Career Performances

	M	Inns	NO	Runs	HS	Avge	100s	50s	Ct	St	Balls	Runs	Wkts	Avge	Best	5wI	10wM
Test																	
All First	53	86	9	3945	254 *	51.23	12	19	53	-	4115	2183	48	45.47	4-31	-	-
1-day Int																	
C & G	5	3	0	44	24	14.66	-	-	3	-	84	62	0	-		-	-
NCL	45	44	8	1677	147	46.58	4	9	22	-	832	806	15	53.73	3-39	-	
Twenty20	5	5	0	150	58	30.00	-	1	-	-	66	80	2	40.00	2-28	-	

PIPE, D. J.   Worcestershire

Name: David <u>James</u> Pipe
Role: Right-hand bat, wicket-keeper
Born: 16 December 1977, Bradford
Height: 5ft 11in **Weight:** 12st
Nickname: Pipey
County debut: 1998
County colours: 2002
1st-Class 50s: 1
1st-Class 100s: 1
1st-Class catches: 38
1st-Class stumpings: 5
Place in batting averages: 136th av. 30.66
Parents: David and Dorothy
Marital status: 'Girlfriend Emma'
Family links with cricket: 'My dad and
uncle played in the local league'
Education: Queensbury Upper School; BICC
Qualifications: 8 GCSEs, BTEC National in
Business and Finance, HND Leisure Management, senior coaching award, Diploma in
Personal Training, Diploma in Sports Therapy
Off-season: 'Personal training and preparing for the season'
Overseas teams played for: Leeming Spartans CC/South Metropolitan Cricket
Association, Perth 1998-99; Manly CC, Australia 1999-2004
Career highlights to date: 'Getting first hundred'
Cricket moments to forget: 'Any game we lose'
Cricketers particularly admired: Adam Gilchrist, Ian Healy
Other sports followed: Rugby league (Bradford Bulls, Manly Sea Eagles), boxing
('all British fighters'), AFL (West Coast Eagles)
Injuries: Out for 14 weeks with an eye injury
Relaxations: Training
Extras: MCC School of Merit Wilf Slack Memorial Trophy winner 1995. Awarded

2nd XI cap 1999. Scored 54 on Championship debut v Warwickshire at Worcester 2000. Took eight catches v Hertfordshire at Hertford in the C&G 2001 to set a new NatWest/C&G record for most catches in a match by a wicket-keeper, beating Alec Stewart's seven v Glamorgan in the NatWest 1994. Dick Lygon Award 2002 (Worcestershire Club Man of the Year). Scored maiden first-class century (104*) v Hampshire at West End 2003

Best batting: 104* Worcestershire v Hampshire, West End 2003

2003 Season

	M	Inns	NO	Runs	HS	Avge	100s	50s	Ct	St	O	M	Runs	Wkts	Avge	Best	5wl	10wM
Test																		
All First	5	9	3	184	104 *	30.66	1	-	20	2								
1-day Int																		
C & G																		
NCL	3	3	2	19	12	19.00	-	-	3	-								
Twenty20																		

Career Performances

	M	Inns	NO	Runs	HS	Avge	100s	50s	Ct	St	Balls	Runs	Wkts	Avge	Best	5wl	10wM
Test																	
All First	16	25	3	435	104 *	19.77	1	1	38	5							
1-day Int																	
C & G	3	2	0	60	56	30.00	-	1	11	-							
NCL	14	13	3	187	45	18.70	-	-	6	5							
Twenty20																	

PIPER, K. J.   Warwickshire

Name: <u>Keith</u> John Piper
Role: Right-hand bat, wicket-keeper
Born: 18 December 1969, Leicester
Height: 5ft 7in **Weight:** 10st 8lbs
Nickname: Tubbsy, Garden Boy
County debut: 1989
County cap: 1992
Benefit: 2001
50 dismissals in a season: 2
1st-Class 50s: 14
1st-Class 100s: 2
1st-Class catches: 502
1st-Class stumpings: 34
Place in batting averages: 226th av. 19.57 (2002 253rd av. 16.30)

Strike rate: (career 34.00)
Parents: John and Charlotte
Marital status: Single
Family links with cricket: Father plays club cricket in Leicester
Education: Somerset Senior
Qualifications: Senior coaching award, basketball coaching award, volleyball coaching award
Overseas tours: Haringey Cricket College to Barbados 1986, to Trinidad 1987, to Jamaica 1988; Warwickshire to La Manga 1989, to St Lucia 1990; England A to India 1994-95, to Pakistan 1995-96
Overseas teams played for: Desmond Haynes's XI, Barbados v Haringey Cricket College
Cricketers particularly admired:
Jack Russell, Alec Stewart, Dermot Reeve, Colin Metson
Other sports followed: Snooker, football, tennis
Relaxations: Music, eating
Extras: London Young Cricketer of the Year 1989 and in the last five 1992. Played for England YC 1989. Was batting partner (116*) to Brian Lara when he reached his 501*, v Durham at Edgbaston 1994. Took six catches v Leicestershire at Edgbaston in the NCL 2003, equalling the record for the one-day league. Took 500th first-class catch during the 2003 season
Best batting: 116* Warwickshire v Durham, Edgbaston 1994
Best bowling: 1-57 Warwickshire v Nottinghamshire, Edgbaston 1992

2003 Season

	M	Inns	NO	Runs	HS	Avge	100s	50s	Ct	St	O	M	Runs	Wkts	Avge	Best	5wl	10wM
Test																		
All First	4	7	0	137	42	19.57	-	-	12	1								
1-day Int																		
C & G	2	1	0	0	0	0.00	-	-	-	-								
NCL	11	5	1	27	8	6.75	-	-	15	-								
Twenty20	5	2	2	1	1*	-	-	-	3	-								

Career Performances

	M	Inns	NO	Runs	HS	Avge	100s	50s	Ct	St	Balls	Runs	Wkts	Avge	Best	5wI	10wM
Test																	
All First	199	275	44	4618	116 *	19.99	2	14	502	34	34	60	1	60.00	1-57	-	-
1-day Int																	
C & G	41	21	10	181	19	16.45	-	-	47	7							
NCL	140	71	35	548	38 *	15.22	-	-	143	35							
Twenty20	5	2	2	1	1 *	-	-	-	3	-							

PLUNKETT, L. E.   Durham

Name: <u>Liam</u> Edward Plunkett
Role: Right-hand bat, right-arm fast bowler
Born: 6 April 1985, Middlesbrough
Height: 6ft 3in **Weight:** 13st
Nickname: Pudsey
County debut: 2003
1st-Class 5 w. in innings: 1
1st-Class catches: 2
Place in batting averages: 201st av. 23.42
Place in bowling averages: 88th av. 35.36
Strike rate: 51.78 (career 51.78)
Parents: Alan and Marie
Marital status: Single ('girlfriend Lisa')
Education: Nunthorpe Comprehensive;
Teesside Tertiary
Qualifications: 9 GCSEs, volleyball
coaching badge
Off-season: England U19 World Cup tour to
Bangladesh
Overseas tours: England U19 to Australia 2002-03, to Bangladesh (U19 World Cup)
2003-04
Career highlights to date: 'Taking five wickets on debut against Yorkshire in
Championship game'
Cricket moments to forget: 'Bowling too many wides first game on the TV'
Cricket superstitions: 'None'
Cricketers particularly admired: Jacques Kallis, Allan Donald, Curtly Ambrose
Young players to look out for: Ravinder Bopara
Other sports played: Football, swimming
Other sports followed: Football (Arsenal, Middlesbrough)
Injuries: Out for three weeks with a bruised patella; for two weeks with a pulled
hamstring

Favourite band: 'Any R&B'
Relaxations: Swimming, cinema
Extras: Played for Durham Board XI in the C&G 2003, including the second round, which was played in September 2002. Became only the second bowler to record a five-wicket innings return on Championship debut for Durham, 5-53 v Yorkshire at Headingley 2003. Represented England U19 v South Africa U19 2003
Opinions on cricket: 'Getting more exciting since the Twenty20 Cup was introduced. Also getting to play against more world-class players since two overseas [rule] was introduced.'
Best batting: 40* Durham v Gloucestershire, Bristol 2003
Best bowling: 5-53 Durham v Yorkshire, Headingley 2003

2003 Season

	M	Inns	NO	Runs	HS	Avge	100s	50s	Ct	St	O	M	Runs	Wkts	Avge	Best	5wI	10wM
Test																		
All First	7	12	5	164	40 *	23.42	-	-	2	-	164	34	672	19	35.36	5-53	1	-
1-day Int																		
C & G	1	1	0	3	3	3.00	-	-	-	-	10	0	63	3	21.00	3-63	-	
NCL	2	1	1	1	1 *	-	-	-	-	-	18	0	74	5	14.80	3-38	-	
Twenty20	2	1	0	2	2	2.00	-	-	2	-	8	0	50	4	12.50	2-18	-	

Career Performances

	M	Inns	NO	Runs	HS	Avge	100s	50s	Ct	St	Balls	Runs	Wkts	Avge	Best	5wI	10wM
Test																	
All First	7	12	5	164	40 *	23.42	-	-	2	-	984	672	19	35.36	5-53	1	-
1-day Int																	
C & G	2	1	0	3	3	3.00	-	-	1	-	84	87	4	21.75	3-63	-	
NCL	2	1	1	1	1 *	-	-	-	-	-	108	74	5	14.80	3-38	-	
Twenty20	2	1	0	2	2	2.00	-	-	2	-	48	50	4	12.50	2-18	-	

75. A regular for Lancashire in the 1970s, who scored 106* against West Indies on Test debut at The Oval in 1973?

PONTING, R. T.   Somerset

Name: <u>Ricky</u> Thomas Ponting
Role: Right-hand bat, right-arm medium or off-spin bowler
Born: 19 December 1974, Launceston, Tasmania
Nickname: Punter
County debut: No first-team appearance
Test debut: 1995-96
Tests: 69
One-Day Internationals: 178
1st-Class 50s: 50
1st-Class 100s: 43
1st-Class 200s: 3
1st-Class catches: 159
One-Day 100s: 14
Strike rate: (career 97.15)
Parents: Graeme and Lorraine
Wife: Rianna

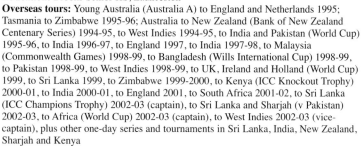

Family links with cricket: Father played for Mowbray CC in Tasmania; uncle Greg Campbell played for Tasmania and Australia
Education: Brooks Senior HS, Launceston
Overseas tours: Young Australia (Australia A) to England and Netherlands 1995; Tasmania to Zimbabwe 1995-96; Australia to New Zealand (Bank of New Zealand Centenary Series) 1994-95, to West Indies 1994-95, to India and Pakistan (World Cup) 1995-96, to India 1996-97, to England 1997, to India 1997-98, to Malaysia (Commonwealth Games) 1998-99, to Bangladesh (Wills International Cup) 1998-99, to Pakistan 1998-99, to West Indies 1998-99, to UK, Ireland and Holland (World Cup) 1999, to Sri Lanka 1999, to Zimbabwe 1999-2000, to Kenya (ICC Knockout Trophy) 2000-01, to India 2000-01, to England 2001, to South Africa 2001-02, to Sri Lanka (ICC Champions Trophy) 2002-03 (captain), to Sri Lanka and Sharjah (v Pakistan) 2002-03, to Africa (World Cup) 2002-03 (captain), to West Indies 2002-03 (vice-captain), plus other one-day series and tournaments in Sri Lanka, India, New Zealand, Sharjah and Kenya
Overseas teams played for: Tasmania 1992-93 –
Extras: Attended Commonwealth Bank [Australian] Cricket Academy 1992-93. Made first-class debut for Tasmania v South Australia at Adelaide 1992-93 aged 17, scoring 56. Played for Australia A in the Benson and Hedges World Series Cup 1994-95. Made Test debut in the first Test v Sri Lanka at Perth 1995-96, scoring 96. One of *Indian Cricket*'s five Cricketers of the Year 1998. *Wisden Australia*'s Cricketer of the Year 2002-03. Named One-Day International Player of the Year at the 2002 Allan Border Medal awards and Test Player of the Year at the 2003 awards; winner of the 2004

Allan Border Medal as well as being named Test Player of the Year for the second year running. Has won numerous Test awards, including Man of the Series in Sri Lanka 1999 (253 runs; av. 84.33), in West Indies 2002-03 (523 runs; av. 130.75; centuries in each of the first three Tests), and Man of the Match in the second Test v England at Adelaide 2002-03 (154). Has also won numerous ODI awards, including Man of the Series in South Africa 2001-02 (his first as captain), three match awards in the NatWest Series in England 2001, and Man of the Match v Sri Lanka at Centurion in the World Cup 2002-03 (114). Also won Man of the Match award in the final of the World Cup 2002-03, in which he scored 140* (a record for the final and including a World Cup record eight sixes) and shared with Damien Martyn (88*) in a new Australian record partnership for any wicket in ODIs and a new world record partnership for the third wicket in ODIs (234*). Captain of Tasmania since 2001-02. One-day captain of Australia since February 2002. ACB contract 2003-04. Has joined Somerset as an overseas player for 2004

Best batting: 233 Tasmania v Queensland, Brisbane 2000-01
Best bowling: 2-10 Australians v Mumbai, Mumbai 2000-01
Stop press: Scored 257 in the third Test v India at Melbourne 2003-04, winning Man of the Match award. Took over as Test captain of Australia (the first from Tasmania) on the retirement of Steve Waugh in January 2004

2003 Season (did not make any first-class or one-day appearances)

Career Performances

	M	Inns	NO	Runs	HS	Avge	100s	50s	Ct	St	Balls	Runs	Wkts	Avge	Best	5wI	10wM
Test	69	108	13	4856	206	51.11	17	18	85	-	401	171	4	42.75	1-0	-	-
All First	157	261	36	12576	233	55.89	46	50	159	-	1263	689	13	53.00	2-10	-	-
1-day Int	178	174	24	6324	145	42.16	14	33	70	-	144	104	3	34.66	1-12	-	
C & G																	
NCL																	
Twenty20																	

76. Which Worcestershire opener played for his country in 1973, 19 years after his father's final Test?

POPE, S. P. Gloucestershire

Name: <u>Stephen</u> Patrick Pope
Role: Right-hand bat, wicket-keeper
Born: 25 January 1983, Cheltenham
Height: 5ft 8in **Weight:** 12st
Nickame: Bod
County debut: 2003
1st-Class catches: 10
1st-Class stumpings: 1
Parents: John and Patricia
Marital status: Single
Education: Cheltenham Bournside
Comprehensive
Qualifications: 11 GCSEs, 2 A-levels
Overseas tours: ESCA South West U15 to
West Indies 1998; England U19 to Australia
and (U19 World Cup) New Zealand 2001-02;
Gloucestershire to South Africa 2002
Overseas teams played for: St Kilda,
Melbourne 2001-02

Career highlights to date: 'Playing for England U19 in the World Cup 2002'
Cricketers particularly admired: Jack Russell, David Partridge
Young players to look out for: Kadeer Ali, Mark Pettini, Nicky Peng
Other sports played: Rugby union (scrum half for England U16 v Portugal and
Wales; England U18 Development Squad)
Other sports followed: Football (Arsenal FC)
Relaxations: 'Going out with my friends'
Extras: Has represented England at U14, U15, U17 and U19 levels. Played for
Gloucestershire Board XI in the NatWest 1999 and 2000 and in the C&G 2001 and
2002. NBC Denis Compton Award for the most promising young Gloucestershire
player 2001. Represented England U19 v West Indies U19 2001 and v India U19
2002. Released by Gloucestershire at the end of the 2003 season
Opinions on cricket: 'Unless wicket-keepers are given regular specialist coaching, it
is impossible to develop your full potential at an early age.'
Best batting: 17* Gloucestershire v Worcestershire, Cheltenham 2003

2003 Season

	M	Inns	NO	Runs	HS	Avge	100s	50s	Ct	St	O	M	Runs	Wkts	Avge	Best	5wI	10wM
Test																		
All First	5	8	3	65	17 *	13.00	-	-	10	1								
1-day Int																		
C & G																		
NCL																		
Twenty20	3	1	1	4	4 *	-	-	-	1	2								

Career Performances

	M	Inns	NO	Runs	HS	Avge	100s	50s	Ct	St	Balls	Runs	Wkts	Avge	Best	5wI	10wM
Test																	
All First	5	8	3	65	17 *	13.00	-	-	10	1							
1-day Int																	
C & G	5	4	0	22	15	5.50	-	-	10	1							
NCL																	
Twenty20	3	1	1	4	4 *	-	-	-	1	2							

POTHAS, N. Hampshire

Name: Nicolas (Nic) Pothas
Role: Right-hand bat, wicket-keeper
Born: 18 November 1973, Johannesburg, South Africa
Height: 6ft 1in **Weight:** 13st 7lbs
Nickname: Skeg
County debut: 2002
County cap: 2003
One-Day Internationals: 3
1st-Class 50s: 26
1st-Class 100s: 9
1st-Class catches: 306
1st-Class stumpings: 28
Place in batting averages: 51st av. 44.94 (2002 195th av. 23.88)
Parents: Emmanuel and Penelope
Marital status: 'Very single'
Family links with cricket: 'Greek by nationality, therefore clearly none'
Education: King Edward VII High School; Rand Afrikaans University
Career outside cricket: 'Own two clothing businesses – 1) sport and corporate clothing; 2) fashion clothing. Own fabricare business in UK with my brother'

Off-season: 'Coaching the University Premier League team; running my businesses'
Overseas tours: South Africa A to England 1996, to Sri Lanka 1998-99, to West Indies 2000-01; Gauteng to Australia 1997; South Africa to Singapore (Singapore Challenge) 2000-01
Overseas teams played for: Transvaal/Gauteng 1993-94 – 2001-02
Career highlights to date: 'First tour for South Africa A. Playing for South Africa'
Cricket superstitions: 'Too many to mention'
Cricketers particularly admired: Ray Jennings, Jimmy Cook, Robin Smith
Young players to look out for: John Francis, Chris Tremlett
Other sports played: Hockey (South Africa U21, Transvaal)
Other sports followed: Football (Manchester United)
Injuries: Out for four weeks with a torn hamstring
Favourite band: Counting Crows, Gin Blossoms, Just Jinger
Relaxations: 'Shopping; designing clothes; sleeping; gym'
Extras: Scored maiden first-class century (147) for South African Students v England tourists at Pietermaritzburg 1995-96. Benson and Hedges Young Player of the Year 1996. Transvaal Player of the Year 1996, 1998. Was stand-by wicket-keeper for South Africa's tour to West Indies 2000-01. Awarded Hampshire cap 2003. Holds a Greek passport and is not considered an overseas player
Opinions on cricket: 'Need to make the game more spectator-friendly – looks like administrators are listening. Administrators should listen to player input far more.'
Best batting: 165 Gauteng v KwaZulu-Natal, Johannesburg 1998-99

2003 Season

	M	Inns	NO	Runs	HS	Avge	100s	50s	Ct	St	O	M	Runs	Wkts	Avge	Best	5wl	10wM
Test																		
All First	13	20	2	809	146 *	44.94	2	4	38	2								
1-day Int																		
C & G	1	1	0	40	40	40.00	-	-	1	-								
NCL	11	8	4	284	78	71.00	-	2	10	2								
Twenty20	5	3	1	32	22 *	16.00	-	-	-	-								

Career Performances

	M	Inns	NO	Runs	HS	Avge	100s	50s	Ct	St	Balls	Runs	Wkts	Avge	Best	5wl	10wM
Test																	
All First	115	179	28	5296	165	35.07	9	26	306	28	6	5	0	-	-	-	-
1-day Int	3	1	0	24	24	24.00	-	-	4	1							
C & G	3	2	1	50	40	50.00	-	-	3	-							
NCL	24	20	11	564	78	62.66	-	4	29	3							
Twenty20	5	3	1	32	22 *	16.00	-	-	-	-							

POWELL, M. J.   Northamptonshire

Name: <u>Mark</u> John Powell
Role: Right-hand bat, right-arm
medium bowler
Born: 4 November 1980, Northampton
Height: 5ft 11in **Weight:** 11st 5lbs
Nickname: Piggy, Perfect, Powelly
County debut: 2000
1st-Class 50s: 4
1st-Class 100s: 2
1st-Class catches: 38
Place in batting averages: 213th av. 21.47
Parents: David and Philippa
Marital status: 'Girlfriend'
Education: Campion School, Bugbrooke,
Northants; Loughborough University
Qualifications: 10 GCSEs, 3 A-levels,
BSc (Hons) Information Management and
Business Studies, Level 1 coach

Off-season: 'Playing for Sutherland in Sydney grade cricket'
Overseas tours: Northamptonshire U19 to South Africa 2000
Overseas teams played for: Rockingham-Mandurah, Western Australia 2002-03;
Sutherland, Sydney 2003-04
Career highlights to date: 'Scoring maiden first-class hundred against
Gloucestershire and breaking Northants opening partnership record at the same time.
Captaining Loughborough to the "clean sweep" of university trophies for the second
year running [2002]'
Cricket moments to forget: 'Bagging a pair on 2nd XI debut when 16'
Cricket superstitions: 'Always put right pad on first'
Cricketers particularly admired: Mike Hussey, Michael Vaughan, Rahul Dravid
Young players to look out for: Robert White, John Francis, Steve Selwood
Other sports played: Golf
Other sports followed: Football (Tottenham Hotspur), rugby union
(Northampton Saints)
Favourite band: Matchbox Twenty
Relaxations: 'Cinema, watching sport'
Extras: Played for England U15 in inaugural U15 World Cup 1996; knocked out in
semi-finals by Pakistan at Headingley. Played for Midlands U19 v Australia U19 1999.
2nd XI Player of the Month August/September 2000. Scored 50 in Loughborough
University's BUSA Championship final win at Fenner's 2000. Captained
Loughborough University to BUSA Championship and UCCE titles in 2001 and 2002;
scored 96* v Oxford in UCCE One-Day Challenge at Lord's 2002 and 44 v Durham in

the BUSA final at Fenner's 2002. Scored century (124*) for Loughborough UCCE v Hampshire at West End 2002. Scored maiden first-class century (107) v Gloucestershire at Northampton 2002 in his third Championship match, in the process sharing with Rob White (277; also a maiden first-class century) in a new record opening partnership for Northamptonshire (375); followed up with a second century (108*) in next Championship match v Glamorgan at Cardiff

Best batting: 108* Northamptonshire v Glamorgan, Cardiff 2002

2003 Season

	M	Inns	NO	Runs	HS	Avge	100s	50s	Ct	St	O	M	Runs	Wkts	Avge	Best	5wI	10wM
Test																		
All First	16	25	2	494	64	21.47	-	4	32	-	2	0	12	0	-	-	-	-
1-day Int																		
C & G																			
NCL	10	9	1	162	70	20.25	-	1	3	-								
Twenty20																			

Career Performances

	M	Inns	NO	Runs	HS	Avge	100s	50s	Ct	St	Balls	Runs	Wkts	Avge	Best	5wI	10wM
Test																	
All First	20	32	3	785	108 *	27.06	2	4	38	-	12	12	0	-	-	-	-
1-day Int																	
C & G																	
NCL	12	11	1	228	70	22.80	-	2	3	-							
Twenty20																		

POWELL, M. J.   Warwickshire

Name: <u>Michael</u> James Powell
Role: Right-hand opening bat, right-arm medium bowler
Born: 5 April 1975, Bolton
Height: 5ft 10in **Weight:** 12st 10lbs
Nickname: Powelly
County debut: 1996
County cap: 1999
1000 runs in a season: 1
1st-Class 50s: 31
1st-Class 100s: 8
1st-Class 200s: 1
1st-Class catches: 76
One-Day 100s: 1
One-Day 5 w. in innings: 1
Place in batting averages: 105th av. 34.27 (2002 139th av. 30.06)

Strike rate: (career 108.00)
Parents: Terry and Pat
Marital status: Single ('live with my girlfriend Michelle')
Family links with cricket: 'All love it'
Education: Rivington and Blackrod High School, Horwich; Lawrence Sheriff Boys Grammar School, Rugby
Qualifications: 6 GCSEs, 2 A-levels, Levels I-III coaching awards
Career outside cricket: PE teacher
Off-season: 'Club cricket in South Africa'
Overseas tours: England U18 to South Africa 1992-93 (captain), to Denmark 1993 (captain); England U19 to Sri Lanka 1993-94; England A to West Indies 2000-01
Overseas teams played for: Avendale CC, Cape Town 1994-95, 1996-97, 2000-01; Griqualand West, South Africa 2001-02

Career highlights to date: 'Lifting B&H trophy in the final final'
Cricket superstitions: 'None'
Cricketers particularly admired: Ian Botham, Dermot Reeve, Roger Twose
Young players to look out for: Moeen Ali, Naqaash Tahir, Jonathan Trott
Other sports played: Rugby (Warwickshire U16-U18), golf
Other sports followed: Football (Manchester United)
Injuries: Out for three months with a broken toe
Favourite band: Coldplay
Relaxations: 'Spending time with my girlfriend Michelle'
Extras: Captained Warwickshire age-group sides U14-U19. Captained England U17 and U18. Became first uncapped Warwickshire player for 49 years to carry his bat, for 70* out of 130 v Nottinghamshire at Edgbaston 1998. Scored 106 v Essex at Chelmsford 2000, in the process sharing with Mark Wagh (137) in a record first-wicket stand for Warwickshire in matches v Essex (230). Scored 96 v Barbados at Bridgetown 2000-01, in the process sharing with Ian Ward (135) in a record opening stand for England A (224). Captain of Warwickshire 2001-03
Opinions on cricket: 'Too many counties! Maximum two up/two down promotion/relegation.'
Best batting: 236 Warwickshire v OUCCE, The Parks 2001
Best bowling: 2-16 Warwickshire v Oxford University, The Parks 1998

2003 Season

	M	Inns	NO	Runs	HS	Avge	100s	50s	Ct	St	O	M	Runs	Wkts	Avge	Best	5wI	10wM
Test																		
All First	12	22	0	754	110	34.27	1	6	4	-	9	0	42	0	-	-	-	-
1-day Int																		
C & G																		
NCL	11	8	1	172	48	24.57	-	-	6	-	0.5	0	7	0	-	-	-	
Twenty20																		

Career Performances

	M	Inns	NO	Runs	HS	Avge	100s	50s	Ct	St	Balls	Runs	Wkts	Avge	Best	5wI	10wM
Test																	
All First	102	169	5	5246	236	31.98	9	31	76	-	1080	576	10	57.60	2-16	-	-
1-day Int																	
C & G	11	11	1	171	39	17.10	-	-	8	-	42	40	5	8.00	5-40	1	
NCL	58	46	6	977	78	24.42	-	2	25	-	467	415	14	29.64	3-44	-	
Twenty20																	

POWELL, M. J.   Glamorgan

Name: <u>Michael</u> John Powell
Role: Right-hand bat
Born: 3 February 1977, Abergavenny
Height: 6ft 1in   **Weight:** 14st 8lbs
Nickname: Powelly
County debut: 1997
County cap: 2000
1000 runs in a season: 3
1st-Class 50s: 28
1st-Class 100s: 14
1st-Class 200s: 1
1st-Class catches: 60
Place in batting averages: 64th av. 42.55
(2002 35th av. 50.08)
Strike rate: (career 82.00)
Parents: Linda and John
Marital status: Single
Family links with cricket: 'Dad John and
Uncle Mike both played for Abergavenny'
Education: Crickhowell Secondary School; Pontypool College
Qualifications: 5 GCSEs, BTEC National Diploma in Sports Science, Level 1
coaching award

Overseas tours: Glamorgan to Cape Town 1999, 2002
Overseas teams played for: Wests, Brisbane 1996-97; Cornwall CC, Auckland 1998-99, 2000-01
Career highlights to date: 'Glamorgan's 1997 season and Glamorgan's 2002 season'
Cricket moments to forget: 'You wouldn't want to forget any of it'
Cricket superstitions: 'None'
Cricketers particularly admired: Adam Hollioake
Other sports played: Rugby (Crickhowell RFC)
Other sports followed: Rugby (Cardiff)
Relaxations: Eating and sleeping
Extras: Scored 200* on his first-class debut v Oxford University at The Parks 1997. Scored 1210 runs at 75.63 in the 1997 2nd XI Championship, the second-highest ever total behind Alan Brazier's 1212 for Surrey 2nd XI in 1948. 2nd XI Championship Player of the Year 1997. NBC Denis Compton Award for the most promising young Glamorgan player 2000. Acted as 12th man in third Test v Sri Lanka at Old Trafford 2002, taking the catch that ended Sri Lanka's second innings and left England with a victory target of 50 runs in six overs. Scored century in each innings (125/142) v Worcestershire at Cardiff 2003
Opinions on cricket: 'Great game.'
Best batting: 200* Glamorgan v Oxford University, The Parks 1997
Best bowling: 2-39 Glamorgan v Oxford University, The Parks 1999

2003 Season

	M	Inns	NO	Runs	HS	Avge	100s	50s	Ct	St	O	M	Runs	Wkts	Avge	Best	5wI	10wM
Test																		
All First	17	30	1	1234	198	42.55	4	3	14	-								
1-day Int																		
C & G	2	2	0	32	22	16.00	-	-	1	-								
NCL	16	15	2	597	91 *	45.92	-	4	6	-								
Twenty20	4	4	1	96	66 *	32.00	-	1	2	-								

Career Performances

	M	Inns	NO	Runs	HS	Avge	100s	50s	Ct	St	Balls	Runs	Wkts	Avge	Best	5wI	10wM
Test																	
All First	103	170	16	6096	200 *	39.58	15	28	60	-	164	132	2	66.00	2-39	-	-
1-day Int																	
C & G	11	11	2	148	52	16.44	-	1	4	-							
NCL	94	87	14	2192	91 *	30.02	-	9	31	-							
Twenty20	4	4	1	96	66 *	32.00	-	1	2	-							

PRATT, A.   Durham

Name: Andrew Pratt
Role: Left-hand bat, wicket-keeper
Born: 4 March 1975, Bishop Auckland
Height: 5ft 11in **Weight:** 12st
Nickname: The Claw
County debut: 1997
County cap: 2001
50 dismissals in a season: 1
1st-Class 50s: 6
1st-Class catches: 117
1st-Class stumpings: 10
Place in batting averages: 248th av. 15.50
(2002 225th av. 20.59)
Parents: Gordon and Brenda
Wife: Laura
Family links with cricket: One brother was
with MCC Young Cricketers for four years.
Younger brother Gary also plays for Durham.
Father played for many years in Durham
Education: Willington Parkside Comprehensive School; Durham New College
Qualifications: 9 GCSEs, Advanced Diploma in Information Technology, qualified
cricket coach
Overseas tours: Durham Academy to Sri Lanka
Overseas teams played for: Hallam, Melbourne 1997-98
Career highlights to date: 'Making debut for Durham'
Cricketers particularly admired: Alan Knott, Jack Russell
Other sports followed: Football (Middlesbrough FC)
Relaxations: 'Music, drinking'
Extras: Played for Durham County Schools at all levels and for the North of England
U15. Played for MCC Young Cricketers for three years. He and brother Gary became
the first brothers to play in a Championship match for Durham, against Lancashire at
Old Trafford 2000. Durham Player of the Year 2001
Best batting: 93 Durham v Gloucestershire, Riverside 2002

2003 Season

	M	Inns	NO	Runs	HS	Avge	100s	50s	Ct	St	O	M	Runs	Wkts	Avge	Best	5wI	10wM
Test																		
All First	5	9	3	93	27	15.50	-	-	15	-								
1-day Int																		
C & G	1	0	0	0	0	-	-	-	5	-								
NCL	6	4	1	43	25 *	14.33	-	-	11	1								
Twenty20																		

Career Performances

	M	Inns	NO	Runs	HS	Avge	100s	50s	Ct	St	Balls	Runs	Wkts	Avge	Best	5wI	10wM
Test																	
All First	48	80	11	1356	93	19.65	-	6	117	10							
1-day Int																	
C & G	6	4	1	52	26 *	17.33	-	-	10	1							
NCL	45	37	9	573	86	20.46	-	3	49	16							
Twenty20																	

PRATT, G. J.   Durham

Name: <u>Gary</u> Joseph Pratt
Role: Left-hand bat, right-arm spin bowler, wicket-keeper ('if I need to')
Born: 22 December 1981, Bishop Auckland
Height: 5ft 10in **Weight:** 10st 7lbs
Nickname: Gonzo, Gazza, Gates
County debut: 2000
1000 runs in a season: 1
1st-Class 50s: 12
1st-Class 100s: 1
1st-Class catches: 25
One-Day 100s: 1
Place in batting averages: 119th av. 32.96 (2002 158th av. 27.62)
Parents: Gordon and Brenda
Marital status: Single
Family links with cricket: Father played for many years in Durham and one brother was on Lord's groundstaff (MCC Young Cricketers). Brother Andrew also plays for Durham

Education: Parkside Comprehensive
Qualifications: 9 GCSEs
Off-season: 'Playing golf and relaxing'
Overseas tours: England U19 to Malaysia and (U19 World Cup) Sri Lanka 1999-2000, to India 2000-01
Overseas teams played for: Melville, Perth 2001-02
Career highlights to date: 'Scoring first first-class 150 v Northants 2003 at Riverside'
Cricket moments to forget: 'Getting my first pair in my cricket career v Gloucestershire'
Cricket superstitions: 'Right pad first'

Cricketers particularly admired: Steve Waugh, Graham Thorpe, David Gower
Young players to look out for: Liam Plunkett, Mark Turner
Other sports played: Golf (14 handicap; 'can just play to it – should be higher')
Other sports followed: Football ('all northern teams')
Favourite band: Stereophonics
Relaxations: 'Golf, TV, singing, socialising'
Extras: Represented England U17 at the ECC Colts Festival in Northern Ireland 1999. NBC Denis Compton Award 1999. On his first-class debut, against Lancashire at Old Trafford 2000, he and brother Andrew became the first brothers to play in a Championship match for Durham. Scored century (114) for England U19 v India U19 in third 'Test' at Hyderabad 2000-01. Represented England U19 v Sri Lanka U19 2000 and v West Indies U19 2001, scoring century (100) in second 'One-Day International' at Chelmsford and another (188) in the second 'Test' at Trent Bridge 2001. Durham Player of the Year 2002. Durham Fielder of the Year 2002, 2003. Scored 79-ball hundred (101*; his maiden county century) v Somerset at Taunton 2003 to equal Dean Jones's record for the fastest one-day league century by a Durham player. Scored maiden first-class century (150) v Northamptonshire at Riverside 2003. Passed 1000 first-class runs in a season for the first time during his 59 v Glamorgan at Riverside 2003. Durham Young Player of the Year 2003
Opinions on cricket: 'Too many games; not enough prep. Two-hour sessions would be good, after all it's quality not quantity.'
Best batting: 150 Durham v Northamptonshire, Riverside 2003

2003 Season

	M	Inns	NO	Runs	HS	Avge	100s	50s	Ct	St	O	M	Runs	Wkts	Avge	Best	5wI	10wM
Test																		
All First	18	33	1	1055	150	32.96	1	8	11	-	1	0	5	0	-	-	-	-
1-day Int																		
C & G	2	2	1	9	8 *	9.00	-	-	-	-								
NCL	17	16	4	510	101*	42.50	1	2	11	-								
Twenty20	5	5	1	96	62*	24.00	-	1	1	-								

Career Performances

	M	Inns	NO	Runs	HS	Avge	100s	50s	Ct	St	Balls	Runs	Wkts	Avge	Best	5wI	10wM
Test																	
All First	38	67	1	1893	150	28.68	1	12	25	-	21	17	0	-	-	-	-
1-day Int																	
C & G	5	5	1	144	89	36.00	-	1	-	-							
NCL	33	32	8	816	101*	34.00	1	5	17	-							
Twenty20	5	5	1	96	62*	24.00	-	1	1	-							

PRETORIUS, D.   Warwickshire

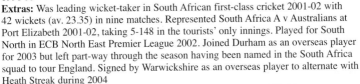

Name: Dewald Pretorius
Role: Right-hand bat, right-arm fast bowler
Born: 6 December 1977, Pretoria,
South Africa
County debut: 2003 (Durham)
Test debut: 2001-02
Tests: 4
1st-Class 5 w. in innings: 7
1st-Class catches: 12
Place in batting averages: 290th av. 7.00
Place in bowling averages: 77th av. 33.19
Strike rate: 47.53 (career 46.82)
Overseas tours: South African Academy to
Ireland and Scotland 1999; South Africa A to
Australia 2002-03; South Africa to England
2003
Overseas teams played for: Free State
1998-99 –
Extras: Was leading wicket-taker in South African first-class cricket 2001-02 with
42 wickets (av. 23.35) in nine matches. Represented South Africa A v Australians at
Port Elizabeth 2001-02, taking 5-148 in the tourists' only innings. Played for South
North in ECB North East Premier League 2002. Joined Durham as an overseas player
for 2003 but left part-way through the season having been named in the South Africa
squad to tour England. Signed by Warwickshire as an overseas player to alternate with
Heath Streak during 2004
Best batting: 43 Free State v Western Province, Bloemfontein 1998-99
Best bowling: 6-49 South Africa A v India A, Bloemfontein 2001-02

2003 Season

	M	Inns	NO	Runs	HS	Avge	100s	50s	Ct	St	O	M	Runs	Wkts	Avge	Best	5wI	10wM
Test	3	2	0	17	9	8.50	-	-	-	-	70	12	298	5	59.60	4-115	-	-
All First	10	10	3	49	16	7.00	-	-	4	-	206	31	863	26	33.19	4-15	-	-
1-day Int																		
C & G	1	1	0	2	2	2.00	-	-	-	-	10	1	32	3	10.66	3-32	-	
NCL	3	1	1	7	7 *	-	-	-	1	-	21.2	4	65	8	8.12	4-31	-	
Twenty20																		

Career Performances

	M	Inns	NO	Runs	HS	Avge	100s	50s	Ct	St	Balls	Runs	Wkts	Avge	Best	5wI	10wM
Test	4	4	1	22	9	7.33	-	-	-	-	570	430	6	71.66	4-115	-	-
All First	49	56	14	383	43	9.11	-	-	12	-	8710	4654	186	25.02	6-49	7	-
1-day Int																	
C & G	1	1	0	2	2	2.00	-	-	-	-	60	32	3	10.66	3-32	-	
NCL	3	1	1	7	7*	-	-	-	1	-	128	65	8	8.12	4-31	-	
Twenty20																	

PRIOR, M. J.   Sussex

Name: Matthew (Matt) James Prior
Role: Right-hand bat, wicket-keeper
Born: 26 February 1982, Johannesburg, South Africa
Height: 5ft 11in **Weight:** 13st
Nickname: MP, Cheese
County debut: 2001
County cap: 2003
1000 runs in a season: 1
1st-Class 50s: 9
1st-Class 100s: 5
1st-Class catches: 106
1st-Class stumpings: 4
Place in batting averages: 33rd av. 47.90 (2002 131st av. 30.87)
Parents: Michael and Teresa
Marital status: Single
Education: Brighton College, East Sussex
Qualifications: 9 GCSEs, 3 A-levels, Level 1 coaching certificate
Off-season: ECB National Academy
Overseas tours: Brighton College to India 1997-98; Sussex Academy to Cape Town 1999; Sussex to Grenada 2001, 2002; ECB National Academy (England A) to Malaysia and India 2003-04
Career highlights to date: 'Winning Championship 2003. Getting capped (2003)'
Cricket moments to forget: 'Falling on to stumps at the Rose Bowl on Sky TV!'
Cricket superstitions: 'Too many to name all of them'
Cricketers particularly admired: Steve Waugh, Alec Stewart, Mushtaq Ahmed, Murray Goodwin
Young players to look out for: Kevin Pietersen, Bilal Shafayat, Michael Lumb
Other sports played: Golf
Other sports followed: Football (Arsenal), golf, rugby

Favourite band: Red Hot Chili Peppers
Relaxations: 'Gym, listening to music, spending time with girlfriend (Emily)'
Extras: Has played for Sussex since U12. Represented England U14-U19, captaining England U17. Attended Sussex Academy. Represented England U19 v West Indies U19 2001, scoring 57 and 51 in the first 'Test' at Leicester. NBC Denis Compton Award for the most promising young Sussex player 2001, 2002. Scored century (148) v Middlesex at Hove 2003, sharing with Mark Davis (168) in a record seventh-wicket partnership for Sussex in matches against Middlesex (195). Scored 1000 first-class runs in a season for the first time 2003. Umer Rashid Award for Most Improved [Sussex] Player 2003. Awarded Sussex cap 2003
Opinions on cricket: 'The game is moving forward at a rapid rate – e.g. training techniques, work ethics etc. – and until everyone grasps hold of this idea then the game will stand still. There is so much scope for one and two per cent improvements in all areas, which makes it a very exciting game to be associated with.'
Best batting: 153* Sussex v Essex, Colchester 2003

2003 Season

	M	Inns	NO	Runs	HS	Avge	100s	50s	Ct	St	O	M	Runs	Wkts	Avge	Best	5wI	10wM
Test																		
All First	16	24	3	1006	153 *	47.90	4	3	28	-								
1-day Int																		
C & G	2	2	0	3	3	1.50	-	-	2	-								
NCL	16	13	2	168	60 *	15.27	-	1	6	1								
Twenty20	5	5	0	87	46	17.40	-	-	5	-								

Career Performances

	M	Inns	NO	Runs	HS	Avge	100s	50s	Ct	St	Balls	Runs	Wkts	Avge	Best	5wI	10wM
Test																	
All First	48	75	8	2180	153 *	32.53	5	9	106	4							
1-day Int																	
C & G	7	6	0	60	34	10.00	-	-	8	-							
NCL	37	29	3	359	73	13.80	-	2	16	3							
Twenty20	5	5	0	87	46	17.40	-	-	5	-							

77. Who was the Surrey spinner who achieved two pairs
in consecutive Test matches v West Indies in 1984?

PRITTIPAUL, L. R.   Hampshire

Name: <u>Lawrence</u> Roland Prittipaul
Role: Right-hand top-order bat, right-arm medium bowler
Born: 19 October 1979, Portsmouth
Height: 6ft **Weight:** 12st 7lbs
Nickname: Lawrie, Lol, Shep, Lozza, Throat
County debut: 1999 (one-day), 2000 (first-class)
1st-Class 50s: 4
1st-Class 100s: 1
1st-Class catches: 14
Place in batting averages: (2002 304th av. 7.50)
Strike rate: 50.40 (career 79.12)
Parents: Roland and Christine
Marital status: Engaged to Kim Marie Jervis ('also known as the Jervernator!')
Family links with cricket: 'Dad plays for Southsea. Cousin Shivnarine Chanderpaul plays for the West Indies'
Education: St John's College, Southsea; Portsmouth College
Qualifications: GCSEs, GNVQ, Level 2 coaching, lifeguard
Career outside cricket: 'Working for Fleet UK car sales/Exbury property developers/Scar Homes'
Off-season: 'Going to Perth, Australia'
Overseas tours: Hampshire to Cape Town 2001; MCC to Sierra Leone and Nigeria 2003
Overseas teams played for: Milnerton, Cape Town 1999-2001; Old Edwardian (Old Eds), Johannesburg 2002
Career highlights to date: '152 on home debut (broke county record). Any game my family comes to watch'
Cricket moments to forget: 'Too bad to remember – not worth thinking about'
Cricket superstitions: 'None'
Cricketers particularly admired: Carl Hooper, 'my father', Jon Ayling, Shane Warne
Young players to look out for: Deano Wilson, Tyler Philips, Tom May, Archie Ayling
Other sports played: Tennis, golf – 'any ball sports and boxing'
Other sports followed: Football (Pompey!!)
Favourite band: Lionel Richie 'and some of my own tunes'
Relaxations: 'Holidays; seeing friends; working with Pete Cohen, sports psychologist – brilliant guy!'
Extras: Scored first century at age 13 for St John's College. Played for Hants Colts

from age 11 to 18; took 29 wickets and broke bowling record aged 11. Represented England U17. Scored 185 for Hants U19 in 1998. Won Player of the Year award in Southern League 1998. Scored over 1000 runs for Hants 2nd XI in 1999. Played for Hampshire Board XI in the NatWest 1999. Scored 152 on home debut, v Derbyshire at Southampton 2000, breaking Dennis Baldry's Hampshire home Championship debut record of 151 set in 1959. Hampshire Young Player of the Year 2000

Opinions on cricket: 'Too many people remember failures rather than success! Enjoy good times.'

Best batting: 152 Hampshire v Derbyshire, Southampton 2000
Best bowling: 3-17 Hampshire v Worcestershire, West End 2003

2003 Season

	M	Inns	NO	Runs	HS	Avge	100s	50s	Ct	St	O	M	Runs	Wkts	Avge	Best	5wI	10wM
Test																		
All First	4	6	2	236	69 *	59.00	-	2	6	-	42	6	178	5	35.60	3-17	-	-
1-day Int																		
C & G																		
NCL	11	8	2	44	15	7.33	-	-	5	-	47.3	1	271	5	54.20	2-47	-	
Twenty20	3	2	0	17	15	8.50	-	-	2	-	9.5	0	67	2	33.50	2-17	-	

Career Performances

	M	Inns	NO	Runs	HS	Avge	100s	50s	Ct	St	Balls	Runs	Wkts	Avge	Best	5wI	10wM
Test																	
All First	18	27	2	744	152	29.76	1	4	14	-	633	372	8	46.50	3-17	-	-
1-day Int																	
C & G	4	4	0	75	30	18.75	-	-	3	-	156	125	4	31.25	2-53	-	
NCL	44	33	5	375	61	13.39	-	1	13	-	718	659	14	47.07	3-33	-	
Twenty20	3	2	0	17	15	8.50	-	-	2	-	59	67	2	33.50	2-17	-	

---

78. Viv Richards's 110* at Antigua in 1986 included
the fastest 100 in Test cricket in terms of balls faced.
How many balls?

PYRAH, R. M. Yorkshire

Name: Richard (<u>Rich</u>) Michael Pyrah
Role: Right-hand bat, right-arm
medium bowler
Born: 1 November 1982, Dewsbury
Height: 6ft **Weight:** 12st
Nickname: RP
County debut: No first-team appearance
One-Day 5 w. in innings: 1
Parents: Mick and Lesley
Marital status: Single
Family links with cricket: 'Dad and
Grandad both played for Ossett CC'
Education: Ossett High School;
Wakefield College
Qualifications: 10 GCSEs, Level 1 coaching
Off-season: District professional for
Taranaki, New Zealand

Overseas teams played for: Kaponga, New
Zealand 2000-2002; Taranaki, New Zealand 2003-04
Career highlights to date: 'Signing professional contract for YCCC. Twelfth man for
England at Headingley'
Cricket moments to forget: 'First ever pair!'
Cricket superstitions: 'Yellow grip'
Cricketers particularly admired: Jacques Kallis, Matthew Wood
Young players to look out for: Mark Lawson, John Sadler
Other sports played: Golf
Other sports followed: Football (Leeds United)
Favourite band: Oasis, Evanescence
Relaxations: XBox
Extras: Played for Yorkshire Board XI in the C&G 2001 and 2002, winning Man of
the Match award for his 5-50 (plus 26 runs) v Somerset at Scarborough in the third
round 2002; also played for Yorkshire Board XI in the second round of the C&G 2003,
which was played in September 2002
Opinions on cricket: 'Second XI cricket should be played on better playing surfaces.
No EU players allowed as it prevents young players coming through.'

Career Performances

	M	Inns	NO	Runs	HS	Avge	100s	50s	Ct	St	Balls	Runs	Wkts	Avge	Best	5wI	10wM
Test																	
All First																		
1-day Int																		
C & G	4	4	0	106	27	26.50	-	-	2	-	102	98	7	14.00	5-50	1	
NCL																		
Twenty20																		

RAMPRAKASH, M. R. Surrey

Name: <u>Mark</u> Ravindra Ramprakash
Role: Right-hand bat, right arm
off-spin bowler
Born: 5 September 1969, Bushey, Herts
Height: 5ft 10in **Weight:** 12st 4lbs
Nickname: Ramps, Bloodaxe
County debut: 1987 (Middlesex),
2001 (Surrey)
County cap: 1990 (Middlesex),
2002 (Surrey)
Benefit: 2000 (Middlesex)
Test debut: 1991
Tests: 52
One-Day Internationals: 18
1000 runs in a season: 13
1st-Class 50s: 110
1st-Class 100s: 57
1st-Class 200s: 9
1st-Class catches: 194
One-Day 100s: 11
One-Day 5 w. in innings: 1
Place in batting averages: 4th av. 76.00 (2002 18th av. 56.85)
Strike rate: (career 125.28)
Parents: Deonarine and Jennifer
Date of marriage: 24 September 1993
Children: Two
Family links with cricket: Father played club cricket in Guyana
Education: Gayton High School; Harrow Weald Sixth Form College
Qualifications: 6 O-levels, 2 A-levels, Level 3 cricket coach, Level 2 FA football
coach

Off-season: 'At home having a rest'

Overseas tours: England YC to Sri Lanka 1986-87, to Australia (U19 World Cup) 1987-88; England A to Pakistan 1990-91, to West Indies 1991-92, to India 1994-95 (vice-captain); Lion Cubs to Barbados 1993; England to New Zealand 1991-92, to West Indies 1993-94, to Australia 1994-95, to South Africa 1995-96, to West Indies 1997-98, to Australia 1998-99, to South Africa 1999-2000, to Zimbabwe (one-day series) 2001-02, to India and New Zealand 2001-02

Overseas teams played for: Nairobi Jafferys, Kenya 1988; North Melbourne 1989; University of Perth 1996-97

Career highlights to date: 'My two Test hundreds, v West Indies and Australia'

Cricket moments to forget: 'There are so many bad days!'

Cricket superstitions: 'Same piece of chewing gum in innings'

Cricketers particularly admired: 'All the great all-rounders'; Alec Stewart

Young players to look out for: Rikki Clarke, James Benning, Scott Newman

Other sports played: Football (Arsenal charity team)

Other sports followed: Football (Arsenal FC)

Injuries: Out for two four-day games and one NCL match after being hit on the shoulder while at short leg

Favourite band: 'Have lost touch!'

Relaxations: 'Taking up golf; my two children'

Extras: Played for Middlesex 2nd XI aged 16 and made first-team debut for Middlesex aged 17. Voted Best U15 Schoolboy of 1985 by Cricket Society (Sir John Hobbs Silver Jubilee Memorial Prize), Best Young Cricketer of 1986 and Cricket Society's Most Promising Young Cricketer of the Year in 1988. Man of the Match for his 56 in Middlesex's NatWest Trophy final win in 1988, on his debut in the competition. Played for England YC v New Zealand YC in 1989. Scored century in each innings (100*/125) v Kent at Canterbury 1990, becoming (at 20 years, 325 days) the youngest batsman to score twin centuries in the Championship. Won Cricket Writers' Young Cricketer of the Year award 1991. Finished top of the Whyte and Mackay batting ratings in 1995 and again in 1997. Appointed Middlesex captain during 1997 season after Mike Gatting stood down. Scored maiden Test 100 (154) v West Indies at Bridgetown 1997-98, sharing in a record sixth-wicket partnership for England in Tests v West Indies (205) with Graham Thorpe and receiving Man of the Match award. Achieved feat of scoring a century against all 17 other first-class counties with his 128* v Glamorgan at Lord's in 1998. Became the first player to score three 200s v Surrey with his 209* at Lord's 1999. Stood down as Middlesex captain at end of 1999 season. Leading run-scorer in the single-division four-day era of the County Championship with 8392 runs (av. 56.32) 1993-99. Scored two centuries (110*/112) in the match v Sussex at Southgate 2000 to become the first Middlesex player to record 100s in each innings of a game on four occasions; his 112 in the second innings was his 50th first-class century. Left Middlesex in the 2000-01 off-season and joined Surrey for 2001; his career average with Middlesex was 50.49, second only to that of Mike Gatting. Scored century (146) on Championship debut for Surrey v Kent at The Oval 2001. Scored 218 v Somerset at Taunton 2002, following up with 210* v Warwickshire at The Oval to become the first player to score a double hundred in successive Championship matches since Aravinda de Silva for Kent in 1995. Became first player to score a Championship century against all 18 first-class counties with his 110 v Middlesex at Lord's 2003. His 279* at Whitgift School 2003 is the highest individual score for matches between Surrey and Nottinghamshire

Opinions on cricket: 'What is wrong with the ball turning on the first day now and again to encourage English spinners?'

Best batting: 279* Surrey v Nottinghamshire, Croydon 2003
Best bowling: 3-32 Middlesex v Glamorgan, Lord's 1998

2003 Season

	M	Inns	NO	Runs	HS	Avge	100s	50s	Ct	St	O	M	Runs	Wkts	Avge	Best	5wI	10wM
Test																		
All First	15	23	4	1444	279 *	76.00	6	2	7	-	18	6	40	0	-	-	-	-
1-day Int																		
C & G	3	3	0	64	32	21.33	-	-	2	-	6	0	38	1	38.00	1-38	-	
NCL	13	12	3	686	107 *	76.22	2	6	4	-	4	0	23	0	-	-	-	
Twenty20	7	7	2	105	53	21.00	-	1	3	-								

Career Performances

	M	Inns	NO	Runs	HS	Avge	100s	50s	Ct	St	Balls	Runs	Wkts	Avge	Best	5wI	10wM
Test	52	92	6	2350	154	27.32	2	12	39	-	895	477	4	119.25	1-2	-	-
All First	340	560	70	23223	279 *	47.39	66	110	194	-	4009	2104	32	65.75	3-32	-	-
1-day Int	18	18	4	376	51	26.85	-	1	8	-	132	108	4	27.00	3-28	-	
C & G	39	38	3	1281	107 *	36.60	3	5	20	-	396	255	10	25.50	2-15	-	
NCL	195	186	34	6557	147 *	43.13	6	49	60	-	558	503	17	29.58	5-38	1	
Twenty20	7	7	2	105	53	21.00	-	1	3	-							

79. Name the left-arm half of the 1950 West Indies spin twins, who took 11-204 on Test debut at Old Trafford.

RANDALL, S. J.   Nottinghamshire

Name: <u>Stephen</u> John Randall
Role: Right-hand bat, right-arm
off-spin bowler
Born: 9 June 1980, Nottingham
Height: 5ft 10in **Weight:** 11st
Nickname: Rags, Rago
County debut: 1999
1st-Class catches: 5
Strike rate: (career 198.12)
Parents: Robert and Glenda
Marital status: Single
Family links with cricket: 'Dad played in
local bucket bangers league for 15 years'
Education: West Bridgford School
Qualifications: 9 GCSEs, Level 2 coach
Overseas tours: England U17 to Bermuda
1997; Nottinghamshire to South Africa 1998,
1999, 2000, 2001
Cricketers particularly admired: Tim Robinson, Robert Croft, Eddie Hemmings,
Paul Franks
Young players to look out for: Kev Pietersen, Richard Logan
Other sports played: Golf, tennis
Other sports followed: Football (Mansfield Town)
Extras: Played for Nottinghamshire Board XI in the NatWest 1999. Released by
Nottinghamshire at the end of the 2003 season
Best batting: 28 Nottinghamshire v Gloucestershire, Bristol 2001
Best bowling: 2-64 Nottinghamshire v Derbyshire, Trent Bridge 2001

2003 Season

	M	Inns	NO	Runs	HS	Avge	100s	50s	Ct	St	O	M	Runs	Wkts	Avge	Best	5wI	10wM
Test																		
All First																		
1-day Int																		
C & G	1	0	0	0	0	-	-	-	-	-	10	0	62	1	62.00	1-62	-	
NCL	6	4	1	26	17	8.66	-	-	3	-	36	1	191	3	63.66	1-33	-	
Twenty20																		

Career Performances

	M	Inns	NO	Runs	HS	Avge	100s	50s	Ct	St	Balls	Runs	Wkts	Avge	Best	5wI	10wM
Test																	
All First	10	15	2	116	28	8.92	-	-	5	-	1585	951	8	118.87	2-64	-	-
1-day Int																	
C & G	2	1	0	1	1	1.00	-	-	-	-	120	105	1	105.00	1-62	-	
NCL	19	13	6	121	25	17.28	-	-	7	-	822	676	14	48.28	3-44	-	
Twenty20																	

READ, C. M. W.   Nottinghamshire

Name: Christopher Mark Wells Read
Role: Right-hand bat, wicket-keeper
Born: 10 August 1978, Paignton
Height: 5ft 8in **Weight:** 10st 10lbs
Nickname: Readie, Reados
County debut: 1997 (one-day, Glos),
1998 (Notts)
County cap: 1999 (Notts)
Test debut: 1999
Tests: 3
One-Day Internationals: 19
50 dismissals in a season: 2
1st-Class 50s: 20
1st-Class 100s: 2
1st-Class catches: 320
1st-Class stumpings: 14
One-Day 100s: 1
Place in batting averages: 132nd av. 30.95
(2002 113th av. 34.65)
Parents: Geoffrey and Carolyn
Marital status: Engaged
Family links with cricket: 'Dad is now "chairman of selectors" at Paignton CC!'
Education: Torquay Boys' Grammar School; University of Bath; Loughborough University
Qualifications: 9 GCSEs, 4 A-levels, senior coaching award
Off-season: 'Touring with England'
Overseas tours: West of England U13 to Holland 1991; West of England U15 to West Indies 1992-93; England U17 to Holland (International Youth Tournament) 1995; England U19 to Pakistan 1996-97; England A to Kenya and Sri Lanka 1997-98, to Zimbabwe and South Africa 1998-99, to West Indies 2000-01; England to South Africa and Zimbabwe 1999-2000, to Australia 2002-03 (VB Series); to Bangladesh and Sri

Lanka 2003-04, to West Indies 2003-04; British Universities to South Africa 2002; ECB National Academy to Australia and Sri Lanka 2002-03

Career highlights to date: 'Winning NatWest Series 2003'

Cricket moments to forget: 'Ducking a slower ball from Chris Cairns in second Test v New Zealand at Lord's 1999'

Cricketers particularly admired: Adam Gilchrist, Bruce French, Alan Knott, Bob Taylor, Jack Russell, Ian Healy

Young players to look out for: Bilal Shafayat, Gary Pratt

Other sports played: Hockey (Devon U18, U21; West of England U17)

Other sports followed: Football (Torquay United)

Injuries: Out for three weeks with a broken thumb

Favourite band: Stereophonics

Relaxations: 'Reading, listening to music, keeping fit and going out with friends'

Extras: Represented Devon in Minor Counties Championship and NatWest in 1995, 1996 and 1997, the county winning the Minor Counties Championship three years running. Played for England U18 v New Zealand U19 in 1996 and for England U19 in the series v Zimbabwe U19 1997. Was selected for the England A tour to Kenya and Sri Lanka 1997-98 aged 18 and without having played a first-class game. Joined Nottinghamshire for 1998 season. Recorded eight dismissals on Test debut in the first Test v New Zealand at Edgbaston 1999. Leading wicket-keeper in English first-class cricket 2002 with 68 dismissals (also scored 797 runs at 34.65). Called up from ECB National Academy squad in Adelaide to England one-day squad in Australia 2002-03 and played v Prime Minister's XI in Canberra. Scored 79* v Sussex at Trent Bridge in the NCL 2003, sharing with Chris Cairns (91*) in a new record sixth-wicket partnership for the one-day league (167*)

Best batting: 160 Nottinghamshire v Warwickshire, Trent Bridge 1999

2003 Season

	M	Inns	NO	Runs	HS	Avge	100s	50s	Ct	St	O	M	Runs	Wkts	Avge	Best	5wI	10wM
Test																		
All First	13	23	3	619	94 *	30.95	-	4	32	3								
1-day Int	10	6	3	84	30 *	28.00	-	-	13	-								
C & G	1	1	0	13	13	13.00	-	-	1	1								
NCL	14	13	7	451	119 *	75.16	1	1	15	3								
Twenty20																		

Career Performances

	M	Inns	NO	Runs	HS	Avge	100s	50s	Ct	St	Balls	Runs	Wkts	Avge	Best	5wI	10wM
Test	3	4	0	38	37	9.50	-	-	10	1							
All First	115	179	27	4102	160	26.98	2	20	320	14	18	25	0	-	-	-	-
1-day Int	19	12	5	154	30 *	22.00	-	-	24	2							
C & G	14	11	3	195	51 *	24.37	-	1	13	6							
NCL	86	73	17	1493	119 *	26.66	1	3	97	18							
Twenty20																	

REES, T. M.   Lancashire

Name: Timothy (Tim) Martyn Rees
Role: Right-hand top-order bat, occasional off-spin bowler
Born: 4 September 1984
Height: 6ft 1in **Weight:** 11st
Nickname: Reesey, Chadders
County debut: 2002
1st-Class catches: 1
Parents: Simon and Rosey
Marital status: Girlfriend
Education: Canon Slade, Bolton
Qualifications: 9 GCSEs, 2 AS-levels, 2 A-levels
Off-season: 'Getting fit and going to the gym; also training with England U19 World Cup squad'
Overseas tours: England U17 to Australia 2000-01

Career highlights to date: 'Lancs 1st XI debut v Somerset in Championship'
Cricket moments to forget: 'Getting 0 on my 19th birthday v Yorkshire, and we lost by one run!'
Cricket superstitions: 'Too many to mention'
Cricketers particularly admired: Michael Vaughan, Sachin Tendulkar
Young players to look out for: Bilal Shafayat
Other sports followed: Football (Bolton Wanderers FC)
Favourite band: Oasis
Relaxations: 'Playing football; going to the cinema with friends; shopping'
Extras: Won the A.A. Thomson Fielding Prize 2000 (for the best schoolboy fieldsman) while playing for England U15 in the U15 World Cup. Played for Lancashire v India A in a 50-over match at Blackpool 2003
Opinions on cricket: 'Second-eleven cricket should be played at the same grounds as first-eleven cricket, and should also have the same standards in wickets prepared.'
Best batting: 16 Lancashire v Somerset, Taunton 2002

2003 Season (did not make any first-class or one-day appearances)

Career Performances

	M	Inns	NO	Runs	HS	Avge	100s	50s	Ct	St	Balls	Runs	Wkts	Avge	Best	5wI	10wM
Test																	
All First	1	1	0	16	16	16.00	-	-	1	-							
1-day Int																	
C & G																	
NCL	1	1	1	7	7*	-		-	-	1	-						
Twenty20																	

RHODES, J. N. Gloucestershire

Name: Jonathan (Jonty) Neil Rhodes
Role: Right-hand bat, right-arm
medium bowler
Born: 27 July 1969, Pietermaritzburg,
South Africa
Height: 5ft 8in
County debut: 2003
Test debut: 1992-93
Tests: 52
One-day Internationals: 245
1000 runs in a season: 1
1st-Class 50s: 52
1st-Class 100s: 22
1st-Class catches: 128
One-Day 100s: 2
Place in batting averages: 14th av. 58.77
Strike rate: (career 162.00)
Wife: Kate
Children: Daniella

Family links with cricket: Brother (C. B. Rhodes) played for Eastern Province B and
Natal B 1990-93
Education: Maritzburg College; Natal University (Pietermaritzburg)
Overseas tours: South Africa to Australia and New Zealand (World Cup) 1991-92, to
West Indies 1991-92, to Sri Lanka 1993-94, to India (Hero Cup) 1993-94, to Australia
1993-94, to England 1994, to New Zealand 1994-95, to India and Pakistan (World
Cup) 1995-96, to Sharjah (Pepsi Cup) 1995-96, to India 1996-97, to Pakistan 1997-98,
to Australia 1997-98, to England 1998, to Bangladesh (Wills International Cup)
1998-99, to New Zealand 1998-99, to UK, Ireland and Holland (World Cup) 1999, to
Zimbabwe 1999-2000, to Sri Lanka 2000, to Australia (Super Challenge) 2000,

to Kenya (ICC Knockout Trophy) 2000-01, to West Indies 2000-01 (one-day series), to Zimbabwe 2001-02 (one-day series), to Australia 2001-02 (VB Series), to Morocco (Morocco Cup) 2002, to Sri Lanka (ICC Champions Trophy) 2002-03

Overseas teams played for: Natal/KwaZulu-Natal 1988-89 – 2002-03

Career highlights to date: 1992 World Cup, including South Africa debut v Australia and running out Inzamam-ul-Haq v Pakistan; taking five catches v West Indies in ODI at Mumbai (Bombay) 1993-94; 117 v England at Lord's 1998

Cricketers particularly admired: Shane Warne (as bowler), Steve Waugh (as batsman), Mark Taylor (as fielder), Hansie Cronje (as captain and batsman to bat with)

Other sports played: Football, hockey

Other sports followed: Basketball (NBA)

Relaxations: Reading

Extras: Represented Natal Nuffield Schools and South Africa Schools 1986-87. One of *South African Cricket Annual*'s five Cricketers of the Year 1992, 1999. Scored 40 and took ODI world-record five catches v West Indies at Mumbai (Bombay) in Hero Cup 1993-94, winning Man of the Match award; has won numerous other ODI awards, including Man of the Series in Standard Bank International Series in South Africa 1997-98 and in Texaco Trophy in England 1998. His Test awards include Man of the Match in the second Test v England at Lord's 1998, in which he scored 117 and shared with Hansie Cronje (81) in a then record fifth-wicket partnership for South Africa in Tests (184). One of *Wisden*'s Five Cricketers of the Year 1999. Played for Ireland 1999. Scored 74 and 154 in the SuperSport Series final 2001-02 v Northerns at Durban, winning Man of the Match award. Voted best fielder in the world (75 per cent of vote) in a poll of international players held during the ICC Champions Trophy in Sri Lanka 2002-03. His image featured on a 50-cent South African coin released in October 2002 to commemorate the 2002-03 World Cup. Retired from international cricket (with a South African record 245 ODI caps) after breaking hand in pool match v Kenya in the 2002-03 World Cup. Joined Gloucestershire as an overseas player for 2003. Scored a century in each innings (103/102) v Durham at Bristol 2003 for the first time in his career on his last home appearance for Gloucestershire. Retired at the end of the 2003 season

Best batting: 172 KwaZulu-Natal v Griqualand West, Kimberley 2001-02

Best bowling: 1-13 Natal v Northern Transvaal, Durban 1990-91

2003 Season

	M	Inns	NO	Runs	HS	Avge	100s	50s	Ct	St	O	M	Runs	Wkts	Avge	Best	5wI	10wM
Test																		
All First	15	27	5	1293	151 *	58.77	5	7	7	-								
1-day Int																		
C & G	5	5	2	163	87	54.33	-	1	2	-								
NCL	12	11	1	197	45	19.70	-	-	3	-								
Twenty20	6	5	0	49	42	9.80	-	-	1	-								

Career Performances

	M	Inns	NO	Runs	HS	Avge	100s	50s	Ct	St	Balls	Runs	Wkts	Avge	Best	5wI	10wM
Test	52	80	9	2532	117	35.66	3	17	34	-	12	5	0	-	-	-	-
All First	164	263	31	9546	172	41.14	22	52	128	-	162	83	1	83.00	1-13	-	-
1-day Int	245	220	51	5935	121	35.11	2	33	105	-	14	4	0	-	-	-
C & G	5	5	2	163	87	54.33	-	1	2	-
NCL	12	11	1	197	45	19.70	-	-	3	-
Twenty20	6	5	0	49	42	9.80	-	-	1	-

RHODES, S. J. Worcestershire

Name: Steven (<u>Steve</u>) John Rhodes
Role: Right-hand bat, wicket-keeper,
county vice-captain
Born: 17 June 1964, Bradford
Height: 5ft 8in **Weight:** 12st 8lbs
Nickname: Bumpy
County debut: 1981 (Yorkshire),
1985 (Worcestershire)
County cap: 1986 (Worcestershire;
colours, 2002)
Benefit: 1996
Test debut: 1994
Tests: 11
One-Day Internationals: 9
1000 runs in a season: 2
50 dismissals in a season: 13
1st-Class 50s: 70
1st-Class 100s: 12
1st-Class catches: 1094
1st-Class stumpings: 120
Place in batting averages: 179th av. 25.75 (2002 83rd av. 39.75)
Parents: William Ernest and Norma Kathleen
Wife and date of marriage: Judy Ann, 6 March 1993
Children: Holly Jade, 20 August 1985; George Harry, 26 October 1993;
Lily Amber, 3 March 1995
Family links with cricket: Father played for Nottinghamshire 1959-64
Education: Carlton-Bolling Comprehensive, Bradford
Qualifications: 4 O-levels, Level III coach, 'attended Bradford Management Centre
for ECB – Coaching and Management Skills course'
Career outside cricket: Marketing department at Worcestershire CCC; cricket
coaching

Off-season: 'Coaching; participating in Level IV coaching course'
Overseas tours: England A to Sri Lanka 1986, to Zimbabwe and Kenya 1989-90, to Pakistan 1990-91, to West Indies 1991-92, to South Africa 1993-94; England to Australia 1994-95; MCC to Kenya 1999; Blade Group to Barbados 2000-01
Overseas teams played for: Past Bros, Bundaberg, Queensland; Avis Vogeltown, New Plymouth, New Zealand; Melville, Perth, Australia
Cricketers particularly admired: Richard Hadlee, Ian Healy, Glenn McGrath
Young players to look out for: Steve Davies
Other sports followed: Rugby league (Bradford Bulls), horse racing
Injuries: Out for three weeks with a torn hamstring; for three weeks with a torn intercostal
Favourite band: Robbie Williams
Relaxations: Horse racing
Extras: Played for England YC v Australia YC in 1983 and set record for most victims in an innings for England YC. Youngest wicket-keeper to play for Yorkshire. Released by Yorkshire to join Worcestershire at end of 1984 season. Set one-day record of four stumpings in an innings v Warwickshire in Sunday League at Edgbaston 1986. One of *Wisden*'s Five Cricketers of the Year 1995. Overtook David Bairstow (257) as the wicket-keeper with the most dismissals in the Sunday League, v Essex 1997. Made 1000th first-class dismissal of his career when he caught Graeme Swann off Alamgir Sheriyar v Northants at Northampton 1999. Equalled his own Worcestershire record for the most catches in a match with nine v Gloucestershire at Worcester 2000. Took 1000th first-class catch during the 2001 season. Coach of Zimbabwe U19 squad to U19 World Cup in New Zealand 2001-02. Scored 124 v Nottinghamshire at Trent Bridge 2002, in the process sharing with David Leatherdale (120) in a new record seventh-wicket partnership for Worcestershire (256). Vice-captain of Worcestershire since 2001
Opinions on cricket: 'Disappointed in those who jump on the bandwagon at county cricketers not being tough enough. We lose a Test to go 2-1 down to South Africa and the county system is all wrong, and win at The Oval to go to 2-2 and nothing is said and the future is bright and rosy!'
Best batting: 124 Worcestershire v Nottinghamshire, Trent Bridge 2002

2003 Season

	M	Inns	NO	Runs	HS	Avge	100s	50s	Ct	St	O	M	Runs	Wkts	Avge	Best	5wI	10wM
Test																		
All First	11	14	2	309	81 *	25.75	-	2	38	2								
1-day Int																		
C & G	5	3	1	61	29	30.50	-	-	3	-								
NCL	13	7	4	84	35 *	28.00	-	-	15	5								
Twenty20	3	2	0	12	9	6.00	-	-	-	5								

Career Performances

	M	Inns	NO	Runs	HS	Avge	100s	50s	Ct	St	Balls	Runs	Wkts	Avge	Best	5wl	10wM
Test	11	17	5	294	65 *	24.50	-	1	46	3							
All First	423	597	157	14406	124	32.74	12	70	1094	120	6	30	0	-		-	-
1-day Int	9	8	2	107	56	17.83	-	1	9	2							
C & G	54	41	15	598	61	23.00	-	3	64	10	6	1	0	-		-	-
NCL	284	180	59	2418	48 *	19.98	-	-	302	92							
Twenty20	3	2	0	12	9	6.00	-	-	-	5							

RICHARDS, M. A. Middlesex

Name: <u>Mali</u> Alexander Richards
Role: Left-hand bat
Born: 2 September 1983, Taunton
County debut: No first-team appearance
Parents: Vivian and Miriam
Family links with cricket: Father is West
Indies legend Viv Richards
Education: Cheltenham College
Overseas teams played for: Antigua and
Barbuda
Extras: Scored 958 runs for Cheltenham
College in 2001. Has played for
Gloucestershire 2nd XI. Played for Antigua
and Barbuda v Guyana in the Red Stripe
Bowl 2002-03. Scored triple century (319)
for Antigua and Barbuda v US and British
Virgin Islands 2003, a record for the Leeward
Islands tournament. Is not considered an
overseas player

> 80. Which opener, now retired from ODIs with 100 appearances,
> won two match awards in the 1997-98 ODI series in the West Indies?

RICHARDSON, A.   Warwickshire

Name: Alan Richardson
Role: Right-hand bat, right-arm
medium bowler
Born: 6 May 1975, Newcastle-under-Lyme,
Staffs
Height: 6ft 3in **Weight:** 13st
Nickname: Richo
County debut: 1995 (Derbyshire),
1999 (Warwickshire)
County cap: 2002 (Warwickshire)
1st-Class 50s: 1
1st-Class 5 w. in innings: 4
1st-Class 10 w. in match: 1
1st-Class catches: 16
One-Day 5 w. in innings: 1
Place in batting averages: 269th av. 11.28
(2002 252nd av. 16.50)
Place in bowling averages: 115th av. 39.81
(2002 23rd av. 25.02)

Strike rate: 82.36 (career 64.76)
Parents: Roy and Sandra
Marital status: Single
Family links with cricket: 'Dad played for and captained Little Stoke 3rd XI'
Education: Alleyne's High School, Stone; Stafford College of Further Education
Qualifications: 8 GCSEs, 2 A-levels, 2 AS-levels, senior cricket coach
Career outside cricket: 'Cutting grass and working for Boundary Sports'
Off-season: 'Watching Stoke City and thrashing Mark Wagh at squash and tennis.
Maybe the odd beer at the Station'
Overseas tours: Derbyshire to Malaga 1995; Warwickshire to Bloemfontein 2000,
to Cape Town 2001
Overseas teams played for: Northern Natal, South Africa 1994-96; Hawkesbury CC,
Sydney 1997-99; Northern Districts, Sydney 1999-2000, 2001-02
Career highlights to date: 'Getting capped by my native Staffordshire. Any attempted
catch by Charlie Dagnall. Oh, and 8-51'
Cricket moments to forget: 'Grasping a tie from the open jaws of victory for Little
Stoke in 1998. A true club pro at his best!'
Cricketers particularly admired: Angus Fraser, Jason Fellows, Dan Davis,
Will Speer
Young players to look out for: Ian Carr ('if he gets over the yips'), Alistair Natkiel
('if he ever turns up for his trial')
Other sports played: 'Part of sound defensive unit for the Bears football team.
Hoof!!!'

Other sports followed: 'One of the many passionate and knowledgeable Stoke City fans'

Favourite band: Powderfinger, Sterophonics, White Stripes, The Thrills, Feeder, 'and a bit of Stevie Wonder'

Relaxations: 'Music, football and "Champo Manager"'

Extras: *Cricket World* award for best bowling performance in Oxford U19 Festival (8-60 v Devon). Topped Minor Counties bowling averages with Staffordshire 1998 and won Minor Counties bowling award. Most Improved 2nd XI Player 1999. Outstanding Performance of the Year 1999 for his 8-51 v Gloucestershire on home debut; besides being the season's best analysis, it was the best return by a Warwickshire player on debut at Edgbaston. Scored 91 v Hampshire at Edgbaston 2002; it was the highest score by a Warwickshire No. 11 and in scoring it he shared with Nick Knight (255*) in a tenth-wicket stand of 214, which was a county best for the last wicket and the fifth highest tenth-wicket partnership in Championship history overall. Recorded maiden one-day five-wicket return (5-35) v Staffordshire (his native county) at Stone in the C&G 2002. His 8-46 in the second innings v Sussex at Edgbaston 2002 was the best return by a Warwickshire bowler since Bob Willis's 8-32 v Gloucestershire at Bristol in 1977

Opinions on cricket: 'Tea breaks have to be longer. Will someone in authority please listen to me?! No need for two overseas players – most counties already have three or four anyway!'

Best batting: 91 Warwickshire v Hampshire, Edgbaston 2002

Best bowling: 8-46 Warwickshire v Sussex, Edgbaston 2002

2003 Season

	M	Inns	NO	Runs	HS	Avge	100s	50s	Ct	St	O	M	Runs	Wkts	Avge	Best	5wI	10wM
Test																		
All First	14	19	5	158	47	11.28	-	-	1	-	453	104	1314	33	39.81	4-37	-	-
1-day Int																		
C & G																		
NCL	5	3	1	23	18	11.50	-	-	3	-	37	5	164	6	27.33	2-38	-	
Twenty20																		

Career Performances

	M	Inns	NO	Runs	HS	Avge	100s	50s	Ct	St	Balls	Runs	Wkts	Avge	Best	5wI	10wM
Test																	
All First	57	58	23	366	91	10.45	-	1	16	-	10362	4887	160	30.54	8-46	4	1
1-day Int																	
C & G	4	4	1	4	3	1.33	-	-	1	-	228	151	6	25.16	5-35	1	
NCL	21	9	5	51	18	12.75	-	-	5	-	883	703	23	30.56	3-17	-	
Twenty20																	

RICHARDSON, S. A. Yorkshire

Name: <u>Scott</u> Andrew Richardson
Role: Right-hand bat, right-arm
medium bowler
Born: 5 September 1977, Oldham
Height: 6ft 2in **Weight:** 13st 6lbs
Nickname: Richo, Tickle
County debut: 2000
1st-Class 50s: 3
1st-Class catches: 11
Place in batting averages: 237th av. 17.16
Parents: Mike and Anne
Marital status: Single
Family links with cricket: 'Dad is an ex-
professional in local leagues. He owns
Romida Sports (specialist cricket shop)'
Education: Hulme Grammar School,
Oldham; Manchester Grammar School
Qualifications: 11 GCSEs, 2 A-levels

Career outside cricket: 'Work for Romida Sports'
Overseas tours: Manchester GS to Barbados 1993, to Cape Town 1995; MCC to
Philadelphia 2000; Yorkshire to Grenada 2002
Overseas teams played for: Easts-Redlands, Brisbane 1996-98; Redbank Plains,
Queensland 1998-99
Career highlights to date: 'Making Championship debut'
Cricket moments to forget: 'Getting the "yips" when throwing the ball as 12th man
in an NUL game 2001'
Cricket superstitions: 'Too many to mention'
Cricketers particularly admired: Michael Atherton, Robin Smith
Young players to look out for: David Stiff
Other sports played: Golf, football
Other sports followed: Football (Manchester United), rugby league (Oldham)
Relaxations: 'Watching Man Utd and Oldham rugby league side; movies;
playing golf'
Extras: Lancashire Schools U19 Player of the Year 1995. Scored 69 v Kent at
Headingley 2001, in the process sharing with Matthew Wood in the highest first-
wicket partnership for Yorkshire in matches against Kent for 49 years (152). Released
by Yorkshire at the end of the 2003 season
Best batting: 69 Yorkshire v Kent, Headingley 2001

2003 Season

	M	Inns	NO	Runs	HS	Avge	100s	50s	Ct	St	O	M	Runs	Wkts	Avge	Best	5wI	10wM
Test																		
All First	3	6	0	103	50	17.16	-	1	3	-								
1-day Int																		
C & G																		
NCL																		
Twenty20																		

Career Performances

	M	Inns	NO	Runs	HS	Avge	100s	50s	Ct	St	Balls	Runs	Wkts	Avge	Best	5wI	10wM
Test																	
All First	13	23	2	377	69	17.95	-	3	11	-							
1-day Int																	
C & G																	
NCL																	
Twenty20																	

ROBERTS, T. W.   Northamptonshire

Name: Timothy (Tim) William Roberts
Role: Right-hand bat, right-arm
off-spin bowler
Born: 4 March 1978, Kettering
Height: 5ft 8in **Weight:** 11st
Nickname: Robbo
County debut: 2001 (Lancashire),
2003 (Northamptonshire)
1st-Class 50s: 2
1st-Class catches: 9
One-Day 100s: 1
Place in batting averages: 172nd av. 26.30
Parents: Dave and Shirley
Marital status: Single
Family links with cricket: 'Brother Andy
was a leg-spinner at Northants; Dad had trials
for Northants'
Education: Bishop Stopford School,
Kettering; Durham University
Qualifications: 2.1 degree in Geology, Level 3 cricket coach
Career outside cricket: Teaching/coaching
Off-season: 'Coaching cricket'

Overseas tours: England U17 to Holland (International Youth Tournament) 1995; Lancashire to South Africa 2000, 2001
Overseas teams played for: Eastern Suburbs, Wellington, New Zealand 1999-2000
Career highlights to date: 'Getting signed by Northants after having a good year in the league'
Cricketers particularly admired: Andy Roberts, Mike Hussey
Young players to look out for: 'A. Daniels, C. Goode, L. Cavill!'
Other sports played: Golf, football, squash, badminton
Other sports followed: Football (Rushden & Diamonds FC)
Favourite band: Oasis
Relaxations: 'Having a few Coronas with the lads at Finedon Dolben CC'
Extras: Played for British Universities v New Zealanders at The Parks 1999. Scored a 41-ball 50 (ending up with 55) in his second Norwich Union League match, v Derbyshire at Derby 2001. Released by Lancashire at the end of the 2002 season and joined Northamptonshire from club cricket during 2003. Scored 83 on Championship debut v Somerset at Northampton 2003, his first two scoring strokes being a four and a six. Scored maiden one-day century (131) v Nottinghamshire at Trent Bridge in the NCL 2003, reaching his hundred with a six. Played for Bedfordshire in the C&G 2003
Best batting: 83 Northamptonshire v Somerset, Northampton 2003

2003 Season

	M	Inns	NO	Runs	HS	Avge	100s	50s	Ct	St	O	M	Runs	Wkts	Avge	Best	5wI	10wM
Test																		
All First	7	10	0	263	83	26.30	-	2	7	-	4	0	4	0	-	-	-	-
1-day Int																		
C & G	1	1	0	48	48	48.00	-	-	-	-								
NCL	9	9	0	291	131	32.33	1	1	2	-	3	0	21	0	-		-	-
Twenty20																		

Career Performances

	M	Inns	NO	Runs	HS	Avge	100s	50s	Ct	St	Balls	Runs	Wkts	Avge	Best	5wI	10wM
Test																	
All First	12	17	0	373	83	21.94	-	2	9	-	36	10	0	-	-	-	-
1-day Int																	
C & G	1	1	0	48	48	48.00	-	-	-	-							
NCL	14	14	0	373	131	26.64	1	2	3	-	36	35	0	-	-	-	
Twenty20																	

ROBINSON, D. D. J.   Leicestershire

Name: <u>Darren</u> David John Robinson
Role: Right-hand bat, leg-spin bowler
Born: 2 March 1973, Braintree, Essex
Height: 5ft 11in **Weight:** 14st
Nickname: Pies, Pie Shop, Robbo
County debut: 1993 (Essex)
County cap: 1997 (Essex)
1000 runs in a season: 1
1st-Class 50s: 33
1st-Class 100s: 14
1st-Class 200s: 1
1st-Class catches: 111
One-Day 100s: 3
Place in batting averages: 120th av. 32.88
(2002 50th av. 46.06)
Strike rate: 53.00 (career 218.00)
Parents: Dorothy (deceased) and David
Wife and date of marriage: Alyssa,
2 December 2001
Children: Kalli, 20 July 1998; Cameron, 20 May 2000; Evie, 30 October 2002
Family links with cricket: Father plays club cricket for Halstead
Education: Tabor High School, Braintree; Chelmsford College of Further Education
Qualifications: 5 GCSEs, BTEC National Diploma in Building and Construction
Career outside cricket: Site investigation and surveying
Off-season: 'Drinking beer with my mates'
Overseas tours: England U18 to Canada (International Youth Tournament) 1991;
England U19 to Pakistan 1991-92
Overseas teams played for: Waverley, Sydney 1992-94; Eden Roskill CC,
Auckland 1995-96
Career highlights to date: 'Every trophy won'
Cricket moments to forget: 'Being bowled out for 57 against Lancashire in the
NatWest final [1996]'
Cricket superstitions: 'None'
Cricketers particularly admired: Steve Hale, David Denny
Young players to look out for: Alastair Cook, Ravinder Bopara
Other sports played: Football, golf, squash
Other sports followed: Golf, football, rugby, swimming
Injuries: Out for four weeks with a broken finger and with a dislocated shoulder
Relaxations: Reading, music
Extras: *Daily Telegraph* Batting Award 1988. International Youth Tournament in
Canada batting award 1991. Scored two centuries (102 and 118*) in match v

Leicestershire at Chelmsford 2001. Scored Championship career-best 175 v Gloucestershire at Gloucester 2002 while captaining Essex in the absence of Ronnie Irani on international duty. Essex Player of the Year 2002. Left Essex at the end of the 2003 season and has joined Leicestershire for 2004

Opinions on cricket: 'Two overseas players [are] too many, especially with so many EU players raping our game. Should be back to one overseas and send the rest back to Greece or Italy where they supposedly come from!'

Best batting: 200 Essex v New Zealanders, Chelmsford 1999

Best bowling: 1-7 Essex v Middlesex, Chelmsford 2003

2003 Season

	M	Inns	NO	Runs	HS	Avge	100s	50s	Ct	St	O	M	Runs	Wkts	Avge	Best	5wI	10wM
Test																		
All First	11	20	2	592	89	32.88	-	4	7	-	8.5	0	62	1	62.00	1-7	-	-
1-day Int																		
C & G	1	1	0	70	70	70.00	-	1	-	-								
NCL	7	6	0	173	78	28.83	-	1	2	-								
Twenty20	2	2	0	12	7	6.00	-	-	1	-								

Career Performances

	M	Inns	NO	Runs	HS	Avge	100s	50s	Ct	St	Balls	Runs	Wkts	Avge	Best	5wI	10wM
Test																	
All First	136	240	13	7149	200	31.49	15	33	111	-	218	215	1	215.00	1-7	-	-
1-day Int																	
C & G	20	18	1	475	70	27.94	-	5	6	-							
NCL	109	106	8	2531	129 *	25.82	1	13	33	-	17	26	1	26.00	1-7	-	
Twenty20	2	2	0	12	7	6.00	-	-	1	-							

81. Which Jamaican marked his Test debut at the age of 37 with five wickets in each innings against England at Kingston in 1948?

ROBINSON, M. A.   Sussex

Name: <u>Mark</u> Andrew Robinson
Role: Right-hand bat, right-arm
fast-medium bowler
Born: 23 November 1966, Hull
Height: 6ft 3in **Weight:** 13st
Nickname: Coddy, Smokie, Tiger,
Storm, Rodney
County debut: 1987 (Northamptonshire),
1991 (Yorkshire), 1996 (Sussex)
County cap: 1990 (Northamptonshire),
1992 (Yorkshire), 1997 (Sussex)
50 wickets in a season: 1
1st-Class 5 w. in innings: 13
1st-Class 10 w. in match: 2
1st-Class catches: 41
Strike rate: (career 64.53)
Parents: Malcolm and Joan
Wife and date of marriage: Julia, 8 October
1994
Children: Samuel Lewis, 11 January 1996; Eleanor Grace, 20 July 2000
Family links with cricket: Grandfather a prominent local cricketer and 'father was
hostile bowler in the back garden'
Education: Hull Grammar School
Qualifications: 6 O-levels, 2 A-levels, advanced cricket coach ('currently doing Level
4 ECB'), badminton coach, rugby union coach
Overseas tours: England U19 North to Bermuda; Yorkshire to Cape Town 1991-92,
1992-93, to West Indies 1993-94; Sussex to Grenada 2001
Overseas teams played for: East Shirley, Canterbury, New Zealand 1987-89;
Canterbury, New Zealand 1989-98
Career highlights to date: '9-37 v Northants'
Cricket moments to forget: 'Don't want to forget any moment of what is a
privileged existence'
Cricketers particularly admired: Peter Moores, Keith Greenfield, Tony Cottey 'and
any other player who lives for the game'
Young players to look out for: Steve Patterson, Joe Sayers, Matt Prior, Tim Ambrose,
Sam Robinson
Other sports played: Football
Other sports followed: Football (Hull City), 'all sports'
Extras: Took hat-trick with first three balls of innings in Yorkshire League playing for
Hull v Doncaster. First player to win Yorkshire U19 Bowler of the Season in two
successive years, 1984 and 1985. Northamptonshire Uncapped Player of the Year in

1989. Endured a world record 12 innings without scoring a run in 1990. Sussex Clubman of the Year 1997 and 1998. Scored 500th first-class run on the same day as he took 500th first-class wicket v Surrey at Hove 1999. Was not out in ten successive innings during 1999-2000, equalling the record for county cricket. His 5-59 v Durham at Hove 2001 included his 200th wicket for Sussex. Sussex club coach since 2003 but is still registered

Best batting: 27 Sussex v Lancashire, Old Trafford 1997
Best bowling: 9-37 Yorkshire v Northamptonshire, Harrogate 1993

2003 Season (did not make any first-class or one-day appearances)

Career Performances

	M	Inns	NO	Runs	HS	Avge	100s	50s	Ct	St	Balls	Runs	Wkts	Avge	Best	5wI	10wM
Test																	
All First	229	259	112	590	27	4.01	-	-	41	-	37689	17807	584	30.49	9-37	13	2
1-day Int																	
C & G	29	11	7	19	8 *	4.75	-	-	3	-	1908	1042	38	27.42	4-32	-	
NCL	176	69	31	127	15 *	3.34	-	-	16	-	7780	5488	171	32.09	4-23	-	
Twenty20																	

ROSE, F. A.   Surrey

Name: <u>Franklyn</u> Albert Rose
Role: Right-hand bat, right-arm fast bowler
Born: 1 February 1972, St Ann's Bay, Jamaica
Height: 6ft 5in **Weight:** 15st
Nickname: Bap-Bap
County debut: 1998 (Northamptonshire), 2003 (Surrey)
Test debut: 1996-97
Tests: 19
One-Day Internationals: 27
50 wickets in a season: 1
1st-Class 50s: 2
1st-Class 5 w. in innings: 14
1st-Class 10 w. in match: 2
1st-Class catches: 24
One-Day 5 w. in innings: 3
Strike rate: 56.00 (career 48.21)
Education: Ocho Rios Secondary; Holmwood Technical High School
Overseas tours: West Indies to Pakistan 1997-98, to Sharjah (Singer-Akai Champions Trophy) 1997-98, to South Africa 1998-99, to New Zealand 1999-2000, to England 2000

Overseas teams played for: Jamaica 1992-93 – 2002-03; Gauteng 2001-02
Cricketers particularly admired: Curtly Ambrose, Viv Richards
Other sports played: Basketball, football
Relaxations: Music, swimming
Extras: Represented West Indies U23 v Pakistanis 1992-93. Became first West Indies bowler to record a six-wicket innings return on Test debut when he took 6-100 in the first Test against India at Kingston 1996-97, winning the Man of the Match award. Was Northamptonshire's overseas player in 1998. Took 5-14, the best ever figures by a Northants bowler in the B&H Cup, on competition debut against Minor Counties at Luton 1998. Took 7-84 in South Africa's first innings in the third Test at Kingsmead, Durban, 1998-99, the then best Test innings figures at the ground by a visiting bowler (since bettered by Andrew Caddick's 7-46 in 1999-2000). Man of the [Test] Series v Zimbabwe 1999-2000. Took 5-23 v Pakistan at Kingstown, St Vincent, in the Cable and Wireless International Series 1999-2000, winning Man of the Match award. Took 5-19 for Herefordshire v Oxfordshire in the first round of the C&G 2004, which was played in August 2003, winning Man of the Match award. Has also won several domestic match awards in West Indies. Was an overseas player with Surrey towards the end of the 2003 season, deputising for Saqlain Mushtaq, absent on international duty
Best batting: 96 Jamaica v Leeward Islands, The Valley 1996-97
Best bowling: 7-39 Northamptonshire v Worcestershire, Worcester 1998

2003 Season

	M	Inns	NO	Runs	HS	Avge	100s	50s	Ct	St	O	M	Runs	Wkts	Avge	Best	5wI	10wM
Test																		
All First	1	2	0	37	36	18.50	-	-	-	-	28	8	101	3	33.66	3-101	-	-
1-day Int																		
C & G	1	1	0	2	2	2.00	-	-	-	-	7	2	19	5	3.80	5-19	1	
NCL	2	1	0	1	1	1.00	-	-	-	-	17	1	78	2	39.00	1-33	-	
Twenty20																		

Career Performances

	M	Inns	NO	Runs	HS	Avge	100s	50s	Ct	St	Balls	Runs	Wkts	Avge	Best	5wI	10wM
Test	19	28	2	344	69	13.23	-	1	4	-	3124	1637	53	30.88	7-84	2	-
All First	94	130	21	1426	96	13.08	-	2	24	-	14273	7849	296	26.51	7-39	14	2
1-day Int	27	23	5	217	30	12.05	-	-	6	-	1326	1046	29	36.06	5-23	1	
C & G	2	2	0	21	19	10.50	-	-	1	-	114	62	8	7.75	5-19	1	
NCL	15	5	1	14	9 *	3.50	-	-	2	-	625	458	17	26.94	2-19	-	
Twenty20																	

RUSSELL, R. C. Gloucestershire

Name: Robert Charles (<u>Jack</u>) Russell
Role: Left-hand bat, wicket-keeper
Born: 15 August 1963, Stroud
Height: 5ft 8¼in **Weight:** 9st 9lbs
County debut: 1981
County cap: 1985
Benefit: 1994
Test debut: 1988
Tests: 54
One-Day Internationals: 40
1000 runs in a season: 1
50 dismissals in a season: 15
1st-Class 50s: 89
1st-Class 100s: 11
1st-Class catches: 1192
1st-Class stumpings: 127
One-Day 100s: 2
Place in batting averages: 99th av. 36.33
(2002 53rd av. 45.04)
Strike rate: (career 56.00)
Parents: John (deceased) and Jennifer
Wife and date of marriage: Aileen Ann, 6 March 1985
Children: Stepson, Marcus Anthony, 1980; Elizabeth Ann, March 1988;
Victoria, 1989; Charles David, 1991; Katherine Jane, 1996
Family links with cricket: 'Late father and late brother played club cricket (plus
other sports)'
Education: Archway Comprehensive School; Bristol Polytechnic
Qualifications: 7 O-levels, 2 A-levels
Career outside cricket: Professional artist
Off-season: 'Painting'
Overseas tours: England A to Australia 1992-93 (vice-captain); England to Pakistan
1987-88, to India and West Indies 1989-90, to Australia 1990-91, to New Zealand
1991-92, to West Indies 1993-94, to Australia 1994-95, to South Africa 1995-96,
to Pakistan and India (World Cup) 1995-96, to Zimbabwe and New Zealand 1996-97,
to West Indies 1997-98, to Bangladesh (Wills International Cup) 1998-99
Career highlights to date: 'Running down the steps and on to the ground at Lord's to
make Test debut'
Cricket moments to forget: 'All ducks and missed chances!'
Cricket superstitions: 'None (if you believe that, you'll believe anything!). Too many
to mention'
Cricketers particularly admired: Alan Knott, Bob Taylor, Ian Botham,
Sir Don Bradman, Rodney Marsh, 'and other greats'

Others sports played: None – 'no time! Too busy painting'
Other sports followed: Football, rugby, snooker, 'anything competitive'
Relaxations: Playing cricket and painting pictures
Extras: Became youngest Gloucestershire wicket-keeper (17 years 307 days) and set record for most dismissals in a match on first-class debut: 8 (7 caught, 1 stumped) for Gloucestershire v Sri Lankans at Bristol 1981. Hat-trick of catches v Surrey at The Oval 1986 (one off Courtney Walsh; two off David Lawrence). Was chosen as England's Man of the Test Series, England v Australia 1989 and was one of *Wisden*'s Five Cricketers of the Year 1990. Captain of Gloucestershire and Player of the Year 1995. Whyte and Mackay wicket-keeper/batsman of the year 1995, 1996, 1997. Broke Bob Taylor's long-standing world record for the number of dismissals in a Test match with 11 (all caught) in the second Test v South Africa at Johannesburg 1995-96; his 27 Test dismissals in the series is a record for England. Awarded MBE in 1996 for services to cricket. Became seventh wicket-keeper to take 1000 first-class catches when he caught Tim Robinson v Notts at Bristol 1999. Set a new NatWest dismissals record by claiming his 67th victim (Adrian Rollins) v Derbyshire at Bristol 1999. Man of the Match in Gloucestershire's NatWest final victory over Somerset 1999. Conceded no byes in Northamptonshire's 746 v Gloucestershire at Bristol 2002, bettering the previous world record for a clean sheet in first-class cricket – 716 by Srinivasan Reuben Paul of Tamil Nadu v Karnataka in 1995-96. Took six catches in an innings for Gloucestershire for the first time, v Durham at Bristol 2002. During 2002 season passed Gloucestershire record for most first-class runs by a wicket-keeper and equalled club record for most first-class dismissals (1016 by Jack Board). Winner of Cricket Writers' Club Peter Smith Award (for presentation of cricket to the public) 2002. Made 100th NatWest/C&G dismissal (Geraint Jones) v Kent at Canterbury 2003. Made his 1311th dismissal (Jimmy Maher) v Glamorgan at Bristol 2003 to move into fifth place in the all-time wicket-keeping dismissals list. Opened Jack Russell Gallery (www.jackrussell.co.uk) in Chipping Sodbury, Gloucestershire, 1995; recent painting commissions include 'The Cenotaph' for Royal British Legion; 'Field Marshals of the British Army' for Army Benevolent Fund (hanging National Army Museum, London); Duke of Edinburgh; Duke of Kent. *Jack Russell – Unleashed*, an autobiography, made the top ten bestsellers in 1997. Granted a testimonial by Gloucestershire for 2004
Best batting: 129* England XI v Boland, Paarl 1995-96
Best bowling: 1-4 Gloucestershire v West Indians, Bristol 1991

2003 Season

	M	Inns	NO	Runs	HS	Avge	100s	50s	Ct	St	O	M	Runs	Wkts	Avge	Best	5wl	10wM
Test																		
All First	11	16	4	436	78 *	36.33	-	3	33	4								
1-day Int																		
C & G	5	4	1	62	30	20.66	-	-	9	2								
NCL	12	7	1	118	29 *	19.66	-	-	6	5								
Twenty20	2	1	1	11	11 *	-	-	-	1	1								

Career Performances

	M	Inns	NO	Runs	HS	Avge	100s	50s	Ct	St	Balls	Runs	Wkts	Avge	Best	5wl	10wM
Test	54	86	16	1897	128 *	27.10	2	6	153	12							
All First	463	688	144	16831	129 *	30.93	11	89	1192	127	56	68	1	68.00	1-4	-	-
1-day Int	40	31	7	423	50	17.62	-	1	41	6							
C & G	61	46	12	950	84	27.94	-	4	88	17							
NCL	278	216	47	3837	108	22.70	1	15	233	59							
Twenty20	2	1	1	11	11 *	-	-	-	1	1							

SADLER, J. L. Leicestershire

Name: <u>John</u> Leonard Sadler
Role: Left-hand top-order bat,
leg-spin bowler
Born: 19 November 1981, Dewsbury
Height: 5ft 11in **Weight:** 12st 7lbs
Nickname: Sads
County debut: 2003
1st-Class 50s: 1
1st-Class 100s: 2
1st-Class catches: 5
Place in batting averages: 58th av. 43.40
Parents: Michael and Sue
Marital status: Single
Family links with cricket: Father played for
25 years and now coaches. Brothers Dave and
Jamie play local league cricket; both played
for Yorkshire youth teams
Education: St Thomas à Becket RC School,
Wakefield
Qualifications: 9 GCSEs, Level 1 coaching award
Off-season: 'Six weeks in India, then two months in Perth, Western Australia'
Overseas tours: England U19 to Malaysia and (U19 World Cup) Sri Lanka
1999-2000, to India 2000-01; Yorkshire to Grenada 2002
Overseas teams played for: Tuart Hill, Perth 2001-04
Career highlights to date: 'First first-class 50 v Warwickshire; first first-class century
v Surrey'
Cricket moments to forget: 'Injury to knee in Sri Lanka January 2000, leading to
early return to England from U19 World Cup squad'
Cricket superstitions: 'None'
Cricketers particularly admired: Robin Smith, Sachin Tendulkar, Graham Thorpe,
Darren Lehmann, Brian Lara

Young players to look out for: John Maunders, David Brignull, Luke Wright, Tom New
Other sports played: Football ('loads to age 17, now play five-a-side in off-season'), rugby ('at school')
Other sports followed: Football (Leeds United), rugby league (Leeds Rhinos)
Favourite band: Oasis
Relaxations: 'Music, relaxing, socialising with friends, keeping fit, PlayStation 2'
Extras: Played for Yorkshire Schools at all levels and joined Yorkshire Academy 1998. Yorkshire Supporters' Club Young Player of the Year 1998. Represented England at U14, U15, U17, U18 and U19 levels; represented England U17 at the ECC Colts Festival in Northern Ireland 1999. Represented England U19 v Sri Lanka U19 2000 and v West Indies U19 2001. Played for Yorkshire Board XI in the NatWest 1999. Awarded Yorkshire 2nd XI cap 2002. Released by Yorkshire at the end of the 2002 season and joined Leicestershire for 2003. Scored maiden first-class century (145) v Surrey at Leicester 2003
Opinions on cricket: 'The best game and the hardest at times.'
Best batting: 145 Leicestershire v Surrey, Leicester 2003
145 Leicestershire v Sussex, Hove 2003

2003 Season

	M	Inns	NO	Runs	HS	Avge	100s	50s	Ct	St	O	M	Runs	Wkts	Avge	Best	5wl	10wM
Test																		
All First	7	11	1	434	145	43.40	2	1	5	-	7.5	1	40	0	-	-	-	-
1-day Int																		
C & G	1	1	0	8	8	8.00	-	-	-	-								
NCL	10	9	0	118	35	13.11	-	-	2	-								
Twenty20	5	4	2	7	4	3.50	-	-	2	-								

Career Performances

	M	Inns	NO	Runs	HS	Avge	100s	50s	Ct	St	Balls	Runs	Wkts	Avge	Best	5wl	10wM
Test																	
All First	7	11	1	434	145	43.40	2	1	5	-	47	40	0	-	-	-	-
1-day Int																	
C & G	2	2	0	17	9	8.50	-	-	-	-							
NCL	10	9	0	118	35	13.11	-	-	2	-							
Twenty20	5	4	2	7	4	3.50	-	-	2	-							

SAGGERS, M. J. Kent

Name: <u>Martin</u> John Saggers
Role: Right-hand bat, right-arm fast-medium bowler
Born: 23 May 1972, King's Lynn
Height: 6ft 2in **Weight:** 14st 2lbs
Nickname: Saggs, Saggy Bits, Bits of Aloo, Jurgen Burgen
County debut: 1996 (Durham), 1999 (Kent)
County cap: 2001 (Kent)
50 wickets in a season: 4
1st-Class 50s: 1
1st-Class 5 w. in innings: 15
1st-Class catches: 16
One-Day 5 w. in innings: 1
Place in batting averages: 245th av. 16.00 (2002 314th av. 5.61)
Place in bowling averages: 28th av. 24.84 (2002 9th av. 21.51)
Strike rate: 46.55 (career 44.69)
Parents: Brian and Edna
Marital status: Single
Family links with cricket: Grandfather played in the Essex League
Education: Springwood High School; University of Huddersfield
Qualifications: BA (Hons) Architectural Studies International
Overseas tours: England VI to Hong Kong 2002; England to Bangladesh 2003-04
Overseas teams played for: Randburg CC, Johannesburg 1996-98, 2000-01; Southern Suburbs CC, Johannesburg 1998-99
Career highlights to date: 'Winning the Norwich Union League [2001]'
Cricket superstitions: 'Getting a corner spot in the changing room'
Cricketers particularly admired: Neil Foster, Graham Dilley, Allan Donald, Richard Ellison, Willie Garbers
Young players to look out for: Amjad Khan, Duncan Bousted, John Payne
Other sports played: Golf (14 handicap), 'and any other sport where you can run around like a headless chicken'
Other sports followed: Football (Spurs), 'anything that is shown on Sky Sports channels'
Relaxations: 'Going on safari in the Kruger National Park in South Africa. Also spending many an hour in the jacuzzi'
Extras: Released by Durham at end of the 1998 season and joined Kent. Took career best 7-79 against his old county, Durham, at Riverside 2000. Won Most Promising Uncapped Player Award 2000. Joint Kent Player of the Year 2000 (with David Masters). Took two hat-tricks in two weeks for Randburg CC, Johannesburg 2000-01,

575

including one spell of five wickets in six balls. Took three wickets in four balls in last over of Norwich Union League match at Canterbury 2001, preventing Yorkshire from scoring the 13 needed to win. Underwood Award (Kent leading wicket-taker) 2001, 2002, 2003. Took 5-18 for The Brits v Rest of the World XI in the indoor Power Cricket tournament at the Millennium Stadium, Cardiff 2002. *Kent Messenger* Group Readers Player of the Season 2002. Shepherd Neame Award for Best Bowler 2002. Cowdrey Award (Kent Player of the Year) 2002. Joint leading wicket-taker in English first-class cricket 2002 (with Kevin Dean) with 83 wickets (av. 21.51). Included in provisional England squad of 30 for the 2002-03 World Cup

Opinions on cricket: 'It is great to have the two division system. However, there should only be two teams being promoted and relegated. Three is one too many.'

Best batting: 61* Kent v Lancashire, Canterbury 2001

Best bowling: 7-79 Kent v Durham, Riverside 2000

Stop press: Called up to the England Test tour of Bangladesh 2003-04 as replacement for the injured Andrew Flintoff, making Test debut in the second Test at Chittagong

2003 Season

	M	Inns	NO	Runs	HS	Avge	100s	50s	Ct	St	O	M	Runs	Wkts	Avge	Best	5wI	10wM
Test																		
All First	15	20	5	240	47	16.00	-	-	3	-	450	97	1441	58	24.84	5-42	2	-
1-day Int																		
C & G	2	1	1	2	2*	-	-	-	-	-	19.4	2	89	4	22.25	3-45	-	
NCL	13	6	2	20	17*	5.00	-	-	2	-	96	8	481	12	40.08	4-36	-	
Twenty20																		

Career Performances

	M	Inns	NO	Runs	HS	Avge	100s	50s	Ct	St	Balls	Runs	Wkts	Avge	Best	5wI	10wM
Test																	
All First	74	94	26	717	61*	10.54	-	1	16	-	13452	6887	301	22.88	7-79	15	-
1-day Int																	
C & G	11	5	3	3	2*	1.50	-	-	1	-	614	439	15	29.26	3-14	-	
NCL	58	29	15	124	21*	8.85	-	-	13	-	2571	1916	87	22.02	5-22	1	
Twenty20																	

82. Which Lancashire and Kent bowler took 5-37 and 6-59 v West Indies at The Oval in 1933 in his only Test Match?
(He ended his first-class career with 724 wickets but only 555 runs.)

SAKER, N. C.   Surrey

Name: Neil Clifford Saker
Role: Right-hand bat, right-arm fast-medium bowler
Born: 20 September 1984, Tooting, London
Height: 6ft 3in **Weight:** 12st 7lbs
Nickname: Sakes, For Goodness
County debut: 2003
Strike rate: 211.00 (career 211.00)
Parents: Pauline and Steve
Marital status: Girlfriend Kyra
Family links with cricket: 'Dad played at South Wimbledon, where I started'
Education: Raynes Park High; Nescot College
Qualifications: 2 GCSEs, City & Guilds Carpentry and Joinery
Off-season: 'Sydney after New Year'
Overseas tours: Surrey U19 to Sri Lanka 2002
Overseas teams played for: University of Port Elizabeth 2002-03
Career highlights to date: 'First-class debut v India A 2003; Championship debut v Essex 2003'
Cricket moments to forget: 'Once bowled a 13-ball over in a club game'
Cricket superstitions: 'Bowling marker cannot be pushed in ground; has to be resting on surface!'
Cricketers particularly admired: Ian Botham, Phil Sampson
Young players to look out for: Jade Dernbach, Chris Murtagh, Chris Salmons
Other sports played: Football, snooker
Other sports followed: Football (Tottenham)
Favourite band: Phil Collins
Relaxations: 'Socialising with friends and family'
Opinions on cricket: 'One overseas not two would give youngsters more opportunities.'
Best batting: 5 Surrey v India A, The Oval 2003
Best bowling: 1-71 Surrey v Essex, The Oval 2003

2003 Season

	M	Inns	NO	Runs	HS	Avge	100s	50s	Ct	St	O	M	Runs	Wkts	Avge	Best	5wI	10wM
Test																		
All First	2	3	0	6	5	2.00	-	-	-	-	35.1	2	179	1	179.00	1-71	-	-
1-day Int																		
C & G																			
NCL																			
Twenty20																			

Career Performances

	M	Inns	NO	Runs	HS	Avge	100s	50s	Ct	St	Balls	Runs	Wkts	Avge	Best	5wI	10wM
Test																	
All First	2	3	0	6	5	2.00	-	-	-	-	211	179	1	179.00	1-71	-	-
1-day Int																	
C & G																	
NCL																	
Twenty20																	

SALES, D. J. G.　　　　Northamptonshire

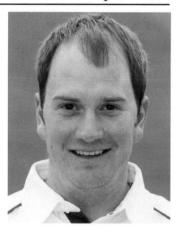

Name: <u>David</u> John Grimwood Sales
Role: Right-hand bat, right-arm medium bowler, county captain
Born: 3 December 1977, Carshalton, Surrey
Height: 6ft **Weight:** 14st 7lbs
Nickname: Jumble
County debut: 1994 (one-day), 1996 (first-class)
County cap: 1999
1000 runs in a season: 1
1st-Class 50s: 23
1st-Class 100s: 6
1st-Class 200s: 4
1st-Class 300s: 1
1st-Class catches: 79
One-Day 100s: 1
Place in batting averages: 53rd av. 44.85 (2002 180th av. 25.04)
Strike rate: (career 34.33)
Parents: Daphne and John
Wife and date of marriage: Abigail, 22 September 2001
Children: James, 11 February 2003

Family links with cricket: 'Father played club cricket, and father-in-law bowls a mean ball in the back garden'
Education: Caterham Boys' School
Qualifications: 7 GCSEs, cricket coach
Career outside cricket: 'Playing golf and working for "Friar Tuck"'
Off-season: Coaching
Overseas tours: England U15 to South Africa 1993; England U19 to West Indies 1994-95, to Zimbabwe 1995-96, to Pakistan 1996-97; England A to Kenya and Sri Lanka 1997-98, to Bangladesh and New Zealand 1999-2000, to West Indies 2000-01; Northants to Grenada 2000
Overseas teams played for: Wellington Firebirds, New Zealand 2001-02
Career highlights to date: '303 not out v Essex; 104 v Pakistan 2003'
Cricket moments to forget: 'Watching White and Powell for five hours, then getting 0' (*Rob White and Mark Powell shared in a new record Northamptonshire opening partnership of 375 v Gloucestershire at Northampton 2002*)
Cricket superstitions: 'None'
Cricketers particularly admired: Graham Gooch, Steve Waugh
Players to look out for: Jason Brown
Other sports followed: Rugby (Northampton Saints), football (Crystal Palace), golf
Favourite band: Coldplay
Relaxations: Fishing and golf
Extras: Sir John Hobbs Silver Jubilee Memorial Prize 1993. In 1994, became youngest batsman (16 years 289 days) to score a 50 in the Sunday League with his 56-ball 70* v Essex at Chelmsford. Scored 210* v Worcs at Kidderminster 1996 to become first player to score a double century on his Championship debut and the youngest ever (18 years 237 days) to score a Championship double century. Became the youngest Englishman to score a first-class 300 (303*) v Essex at Northampton 1999 aged 21 years 240 days (and became the first Englishman to 1000 runs for 1999 in the process). PCA/CGU Young Player of the Year 1999. Scored 276 off 375 balls v Nottinghamshire at Northampton 2000. Scored 62 for Wellington v Canterbury in the final of New Zealand's State Shield at Wellington 2001-02, winning the Man of the Match award. Appointed captain of Northamptonshire for 2004
Best batting: 303* Northamptonshire v Essex, Northampton 1999
Best bowling: 4-25 Northamptonshire v Sri Lanka A, Northampton 1999

2003 Season

	M	Inns	NO	Runs	HS	Avge	100s	50s	Ct	St	O	M	Runs	Wkts	Avge	Best	5wI	10wM
Test																		
All First	16	23	2	942	200 *	44.85	2	4	13	-	1	0	4	0	-	-	-	-
1-day Int																		
C & G	1	1	0	4	4	4.00	-	-	-	-								
NCL	18	17	4	638	133 *	49.07	1	4	6	-								
Twenty20	5	5	0	47	25	9.40	-	-	2	-								

Career Performances

	M	Inns	NO	Runs	HS	Avge	100s	50s	Ct	St	Balls	Runs	Wkts	Avge	Best	5wI	10wM
Test																	
All First	106	164	12	5316	303 *	34.97	11	23	79	-	309	167	9	18.55	4-25	-	-
1-day Int																	
C & G	12	12	1	345	65	31.36	-	3	5	-	12	13	0	-		-	-
NCL	99	93	14	2499	133 *	31.63	1	16	34	-	24	17	0	-		-	-
Twenty20	5	5	0	47	25	9.40	-	-	2	-							

SALISBURY, I. D. K. Surrey

Name: <u>Ian</u> David Kenneth Salisbury
Role: Right-hand bat, leg-break bowler
Born: 21 January 1970, Moulton,
Northampton
Height: 5ft 11in **Weight:** 12st 7lbs
Nickname: Solly, Dingle, Sals
County debut: 1989 (Sussex), 1997 (Surrey)
County cap: 1991 (Sussex), 1998 (Surrey)
Test debut: 1992
Tests: 15

One-Day Internationals: 4
50 wickets in a season: 6
1st-Class 50s: 19
1st-Class 100s: 2
1st-Class 5 w. in innings: 34
1st-Class 10 w. in match: 6
1st-Class catches: 177
One-Day 5 w. in innings: 1
Place in batting averages: 122nd av. 32.50 (2002 233rd av. 18.88)
Place in bowling averages: 101st av. 37.09 (2002 80th av. 32.10)
Strike rate: 67.48 (career 63.56)
Parents: Dave and Margaret
Wife and date of marriage: Emma Louise, 25 September 1993
Children: Anya-Rose, 10 August 2002
Family links with cricket: 'Dad is vice-president of my first club, Brixworth. He also re-lays cricket squares (e.g. Lord's, Northampton, Leicester)'
Education: Moulton Comprehensive, Northampton
Qualifications: 7 O-levels, NCA coaching certificate
Overseas tours: England A to Pakistan 1990-91, to Bermuda and West Indies 1991-92, to India 1994-95, to Pakistan 1995-96; England to India and Sri Lanka 1992-93, to West Indies 1993-94, to Pakistan 2000-01; World Masters XI v Indian Masters XI November 1996 ('Masters aged 26?')

Overseas teams played for: University of New South Wales, Sydney 1997-2000
Cricketers particularly admired: 'Any that keep performing day in, day out, for both country and county'
Young players to look out for: Jim Troughton, Kyle Hogg, Ricky Anderson, Scott Newman, Rikki Clarke, Akbar Ansari
Other sports played: 'Most sports'
Other sports followed: Football (Southampton FC, Northampton Town FC), rugby union (Northampton Saints), 'any England team'
Relaxations: 'Spending time with wife, Emma; meeting friends and relaxing with them and eating out with good wine'
Extras: In 1992 was named Young Player of the Year by both the Wombwell Cricket Lovers and the Cricket Writers. One of *Wisden*'s Five Cricketers of the Year 1993. Left Sussex during the 1996-97 off-season to join Surrey. Won the Bill O'Reilly Medal for Sydney first-grade player of the year 1999-2000, taking 36 wickets at 10.31 and averaging 40 with the bat playing for University of New South Wales
Opinions on cricket: 'Two up/two down in the Championship.'
Best batting: 101* Surrey v Leicestershire, The Oval 2003
Best bowling: 8-60 Surrey v Somerset, The Oval 2000

2003 Season

	M	Inns	NO	Runs	HS	Avge	100s	50s	Ct	St	O	M	Runs	Wkts	Avge	Best	5wI	10wM
Test																		
All First	14	18	4	455	101*	32.50	1	1	6	-	371.1	60	1224	33	37.09	4-116	-	-
1-day Int																		
C & G																		
NCL	7	4	0	62	33	15.50	-	-	3	-	44	2	210	6	35.00	3-40	-	
Twenty20	5	4	1	20	12*	6.66	-	-	2	-	14	0	93	3	31.00	2-20	-	

Career Performances

	M	Inns	NO	Runs	HS	Avge	100s	50s	Ct	St	Balls	Runs	Wkts	Avge	Best	5wI	10wM
Test	15	25	3	368	50	16.72	-	1	5	-	2492	1539	20	76.95	4-163	-	-
All First	275	354	72	5656	101*	20.05	2	19	177	-	48306	24500	760	32.23	8-60	34	6
1-day Int	4	2	1	7	5	7.00	-	-	1	-	186	177	5	35.40	3-41	-	
C & G	29	17	5	164	34*	13.66	-	-	5	-	1697	980	33	29.69	3-28	-	
NCL	147	98	24	947	48*	12.79	-	-	54	-	5431	4491	130	34.54	5-30	1	
Twenty20	5	4	1	20	12*	6.66	-	-	2	-	84	93	3	31.00	2-20	-	

SAMPSON, P. J. Surrey

Name: <u>Philip</u> James Sampson
Role: Right-hand bat, right-arm
fast-medium bowler
Born: 6 September 1980, Manchester
Height: 6ft 1in **Weight:** 14st
Nickname: Sammo, Boss Hogg
County debut: 2000 (one-day),
2002 (first-class)
Strike rate: 29.75 (career 34.81)
Parents: Les and Kay
Marital status: Single
Family links with cricket: Father played
league cricket and was chairman of the
Harlequins club in Pretoria. Brother was
captain of Northern Transvaal (Northerns) at
Youth level
Education: Pretoria Boys High School
Qualifications: Matriculation (A-level
equivalent)
Overseas teams played for: Harlequins, Pretoria 1999, 2000, 2001
Cricketers particularly admired: Allan Donald, Alec Stewart, Steve Waugh,
Sachin Tendulkar
Other sports played: Golf, social football
Other sports followed: Football (Manchester United), Formula One motor racing
Relaxations: Going to the theatre and movies, socialising with friends,
listening to music
Extras: Captain of school 1st XI 1998. Trophy for best all-round cricketer at school.
Represented Northerns at U15, U18, U19. Played for Buckinghamshire in the Minor
Counties 1999. Played for Surrey Board XI in the NatWest 2000. Is not considered an
overseas player
Best batting: 42 Surrey v CUCCE, Fenner's 2002
Best bowling: 3-52 Surrey v Leicestershire, The Oval 2002

2003 Season

	M	Inns	NO	Runs	HS	Avge	100s	50s	Ct	St	O	M	Runs	Wkts	Avge	Best	5wl	10wM
Test																		
All First	1	2	1	35	32 *	35.00	-	-	-	-	19.5	1	101	4	25.25	2-16	-	-
1-day Int																		
C & G	1	1	1	5	5 *	-	-	-	1	-	6	0	33	0	-		-	-
NCL	2	1	0	0	0	0.00	-	-	-	-	15	1	98	4	24.50	3-68	-	
Twenty20	4	2	2	7	4 *	-	-	-	2	-	15	0	123	4	30.75	2-29	-	

Career Performances

	M	Inns	NO	Runs	HS	Avge	100s	50s	Ct	St	Balls	Runs	Wkts	Avge	Best	5wl	10wM
Test																	
All First	3	5	2	78	42	26.00	-	-	-	-	383	261	11	23.72	3-52	-	-
1-day Int																	
C & G	2	2	2	9	5 *	-	-	-	2	-	96	59	0	-		-	-
NCL	8	4	0	21	16	5.25	-	-	1	-	318	290	8	36.25	3-68	-	
Twenty20	4	2	2	7	4 *	-	-	-	2	-	90	123	4	30.75	2-29	-	

SAQLAIN MUSHTAQ Surrey

Name: Saqlain Mushtaq
Role: Right-hand bat, off-spin bowler
Born: 29 December 1976, Lahore, Pakistan
Height: 5ft 9in **Weight:** 11st 4lbs
Nickname: Saqi, Baba
County debut: 1997
County cap: 1998
Test debut: 1995-96
Tests: 48
One-Day Internationals: 168
50 wickets in a season: 5
1st-Class 50s: 12
1st-Class 100s: 1
1st-Class 5 w. in innings: 54
1st-Class 10 w. in match: 14
1st-Class catches: 58
One-Day 5 w. in innings: 6
Place in batting averages: 123rd av. 32.38
(2002 176th av. 25.27)
Place in bowling averages: 78th av. 33.26 (2002 32nd av. 25.64)
Strike rate: 68.92 (career 53.26)
Parents: Nasim Akhtar and Mushtaq Ahmed
Wife and date of marriage: Sana ('Sunny') Saqlain, 11 April 2000
Education: Lahore MAO College
Overseas tours: Pakistan U19 to New Zealand 1994-95; Pakistan to Australia 1995-96, 1996-97, 1999-2000, to England 1996, 2001, to Sri Lanka 1996-97, 1997-98, to India 1996-97, 1998-99, to South Africa 1997-98, 2002-03, to Zimbabwe 1997-98, 2002-03, to Bangladesh (Wills International Cup) 1998-99, to UK, Ireland and Holland (World Cup) 1999, to West Indies 1999-2000, to Kenya (ICC Knockout Trophy) 2000-01, to New Zealand 2000-01, to Bangladesh 2001-02, to Sharjah (v West Indies) 2001-02, to Morocco (Morocco Cup) 2002, to Sri Lanka and Sharjah (v Australia) 2002-03,

to Africa (World Cup) 2002-03, plus other one-day tournaments in Toronto, Sharjah, Kenya, Bangladesh and Singapore

Overseas teams played for: PIA 1994-95 – ; Islamabad 1994-95, 1998
Cricketers particularly admired: Imran Khan, Wasim Akram, Waqar Younis
Other sports played: Squash
Other sports followed: Hockey (Pakistan), football (Manchester United and Arsenal)
Relaxations: 'I like listening to music when free or travelling'
Extras: Scored 79 v Zimbabwe in the first Test at Sheikhupura 1996-97, in the process sharing with Wasim Akram (257*) in a world record eighth-wicket partnership in Tests (313). Joined Surrey as overseas player in 1997. Won Man of the Series award in 1998-99 two-match Test series v India (20 wickets; av. 20.15). Took only the second hat-trick in World Cup cricket (Olonga, Huckle and Mbangwa), v Zimbabwe at The Oval 1999; it was his second hat-trick in ODIs v Zimbabwe. Topped the English first-class bowling averages in 1999, taking 58 wickets at 11.37 in the seven games he played for Surrey. One of *Wisden*'s Five Cricketers of the Year 2000. Took 7-11 from 9.3 overs v Derbyshire at The Oval 2000. Returned his best ODI figures (5-20) in the third ODI v England at Rawalpindi 2000-01, winning the Man of the Match award. Took 8-164 (all eight wickets to fall) from 74 overs in England's first innings in the first Test at Lahore 2000-01, winning the Man of the Match award. Scored maiden first-class century (101*) in the second Test v New Zealand at Christchurch 2000-01. Bowled unchanged for Surrey from 11 a.m. until 6 p.m. (47.2 overs) on the second day v Leicestershire at Leicester 2001, finishing with innings figures of 5-172 from a total of 52.2 overs. Man of the [two-match] Series v Zimbabwe 2002-03 (15 wickets; av. 21.53). Took 700th first-class wicket (Michael Carberry) v Kent at The Oval 2003, aged 26. Holds record for taking fewest matches to reach 100 (53 matches), 150 (78), 200 (104) and 250 (138) ODI wickets; also holds record for the most ODI wickets in a calendar year (69 in 1997)
Best batting: 101* Pakistan v New Zealand, Christchurch 2000-01
Best bowling: 8-65 Surrey v Derbyshire, The Oval 1998

2003 Season

	M	Inns	NO	Runs	HS	Avge	100s	50s	Ct	St	O	M	Runs	Wkts	Avge	Best	5wl	10wM
Test																		
All First	14	15	2	421	69	32.38	-	4	4	-	471	100	1364	41	33.26	5-46	3	-
1-day Int																		
C & G	3	2	0	7	5	3.50	-	-	-	-	25	1	120	3	40.00	2-58	-	
NCL	10	5	3	50	27 *	25.00	-	-	1	-	81	0	403	10	40.30	3-27	-	
Twenty20	3	2	0	5	5	2.50	-	-	1	-	11	0	87	4	21.75	2-35	-	

Career Performances

	M	Inns	NO	Runs	HS	Avge	100s	50s	Ct	St	Balls	Runs	Wkts	Avge	Best	5wl	10wM
Test	48	76	14	922	101 *	14.87	1	2	14	-	13812	6002	207	28.99	8-164	13	3
All First	160	223	53	2880	101 *	16.94	1	12	58	-	38301	16283	719	22.64	8-65	54	14
1-day Int	168	97	38	708	37 *	12.00	-	-	40	-	8722	6224	288	21.61	5-20	6	
C & G	20	7	2	51	24	10.20	-	-	1	-	1081	730	31	23.54	4-17	-	
NCL	56	34	12	267	38 *	12.13	-	-	12	-	2488	1775	61	29.09	3-12	-	
Twenty20	3	2	0	5	5	2.50	-	-	1	-	66	87	4	21.75	2-35	-	

SAYERS, J. J.   *Yorkshire*

Name: Joseph (<u>Joe</u>) John Sayers
Role: Left-hand bat, right-arm
off-spin bowler
Born: 5 November 1983, Leeds
Height: 6ft **Weight:** 12st 8lbs
Nickname: Leo, Ralph, Bradders
County debut: 2003 (one-day)
1st-Class 50s: 2
1st-Class 100s: 1
1st-Class catches: 2
Place in batting averages: (2002 232nd
av. 19.00)
Parents: Geraldine and Roger
Marital status: Single
Family links with cricket: 'Father played at
school, but otherwise none'
Education: St Mary's RC Comprehensive
School, Menston; Worcester College, Oxford
University
Qualifications: 12 GCSEs, 4 A-levels
Career outside cricket: 'Undecided at present'
Off-season: 'Completing final year of my three-year physics degree. Training with
OUCCE squad'
Overseas tours: Leeds Schools to South Africa 1998; Yorkshire U17 to South Africa
2001; England U17 to Australia 2001
Career highlights to date: 'Making one-day 1st XI debut for Yorkshire at Headingley
in 2003 and receiving man of the match award. Maiden first-class century v
Hampshire at The Parks 2003'
Cricket moments to forget: 'None'
Cricket superstitions: 'None'
Cricketers particularly admired: Matthew Wood, Stephen Fleming

Young players to look out for: Tim Bresnan
Other sports played: Football ('played as goalkeeper for Bradford City AFC for three years'), rowing (Worcester College)
Relaxations: 'Playing guitar; drawing/painting; reading autobiographies; listening to music'
Extras: Captained England U17 against Australia U17 in Adelaide 2001. Played for Oxford University CCE in 2002 and 2003 (captain 2003). Oxford Blue 2002 and 2003. Represented England U19 v India U19 2002 and v South Africa U19 2003 (captain in the third 'Test'). Scored maiden first-class century (122) for OUCCE v Hampshire at The Parks 2003. Scored 62 v Gloucestershire at Headingley on one-day debut in the NCL 2003
Opinions on cricket: 'The introduction of two overseas players per county will lead to an improved standard of first-class cricket, but admitting EU players will delay or prevent the emergence of promising young English cricketers.'
Best batting: 122 OUCCE v Hampshire, The Parks 2003

2003 Season

	M	Inns	NO	Runs	HS	Avge	100s	50s	Ct	St	O	M	Runs	Wkts	Avge	Best	5wI	10wM
Test																		
All First	4	6	1	243	122	48.60	1	1	1	-								
1-day Int																		
C & G																		
NCL	1	1	0	62	62	62.00	-	1	-	-								
Twenty20																		

Career Performances

	M	Inns	NO	Runs	HS	Avge	100s	50s	Ct	St	Balls	Runs	Wkts	Avge	Best	5wI	10wM
Test																	
All First	8	14	1	395	122	30.38	1	2	2	-	18	12	0	-	-	-	-
1-day Int																	
C & G																	
NCL	1	1	0	62	62	62.00	-	1	-	-							
Twenty20																	

83. Which of the 'Three Ws' kept wicket on Test debut in the first Test v England in Barbados in 1948?

SCHOFIELD, C. P.　　　　Lancashire

Name: Christopher (Chris) Paul Schofield
Role: Left-hand bat, leg-break bowler
Born: 6 October 1978, Rochdale
Height: 6ft 1in **Weight:** 11st 5lbs
Nickname: Scoey, Junior, Scoffer
County debut: 1998
County cap: 2002
Test debut: 2000
Tests: 2
1st-Class 50s: 17
1st-Class 5 w. in innings: 4
1st-Class catches: 40
One-Day 5 w. in innings: 1
Place in batting averages: 131st av. 31.00
(2002 121st av. 32.75)
Place in bowling averages: 125th av. 42.40
(2002 2nd av. 18.38)
Strike rate: 74.86 (career 61.51)
Parents: David and Judith
Marital status: Single
Family links with cricket: Father played with local club team Whittles and brother plays with local team Littleborough
Education: Wardle High School
Qualifications: 4 GCSEs, NVQ Levels 2 and 3 in Information Technology
Overseas tours: England U17 to Bermuda 1997; England U19 to South Africa (including U19 World Cup) 1997-98; England A to Bangladesh and New Zealand 1999-2000, to West Indies 2000-01; ECB National Academy to Australia 2001-02
Cricketers particularly admired: Shane Warne, Stuart Law
Other sports played: Football (Littleborough FC, Whittles FC), snooker (Wardle Con Club – handicap of four)
Other sports followed: Football ('like watching Liverpool FC')
Relaxations: Listening to music, playing snooker, socialising
Extras: Was part of England U19 World Cup winning squad 1997-98. Won double twice in two years with Littleborough CC (Wood Cup and Lancashire Cup 1997; League and Wood Cup 1998). Won Sir Ron Brierley/Crusaders Scholarship 1998. NBC Denis Compton Award for the most promising young Lancashire player 1998, 1999, 2000. Was the only uncapped player to be contracted to England in 2000. Leading first-class wicket-taker on England A tour to West Indies 2000-01 (22 wickets; av. 26.27)
Best batting: 91 Lancashire v Warwickshire, Old Trafford 2002
Best bowling: 6-120 England A v Bangladesh, Chittagong 1999-2000

2003 Season

	M	Inns	NO	Runs	HS	Avge	100s	50s	Ct	St	O	M	Runs	Wkts	Avge	Best	5wI	10wM
Test																		
All First	9	12	2	310	66	31.00	-	2	9	-	187.1	37	636	15	42.40	4-64	-	-
1-day Int																		
C & G	1	1	0	32	32	32.00	-	-	1	-								
NCL	14	9	2	140	38 *	20.00	-	-	4	-	38.2	0	249	5	49.80	2-21	-	
Twenty20	4	4	1	60	27	20.00	-	-	1	-	4	0	24	0	-	-	-	-

Career Performances

	M	Inns	NO	Runs	HS	Avge	100s	50s	Ct	St	Balls	Runs	Wkts	Avge	Best	5wI	10wM
Test	2	3	0	67	57	22.33	-	1	-	-	108	73	0	-	-	-	-
All First	65	89	14	2144	91	28.58	-	17	40	-	10457	5262	170	30.95	6-120	4	-
1-day Int																	
C & G	11	4	0	88	42	22.00	-	-	6	-	401	317	16	19.81	4-34	-	
NCL	52	40	10	582	52	19.40	-	1	11	-	1575	1368	47	29.10	5-31	1	
Twenty20	4	4	1	60	27	20.00	-	-	1	-	24	24	0	-	-	-	-

SCOTT, B. J. M. — Middlesex

Name: Benjamin (Ben) James Matthew Scott
Role: Right-hand bat, wicket-keeper
Born: 4 August 1981, Isleworth
Height: 5ft 9in **Weight:** 11st 7lbs
Nickname: Scotty, Head
County debut: 2002 (one-day, Surrey),
2003 (first-class, Surrey)
1st-Class 50s: 1
1st-Class catches: 6
Parents: Terry and Edna
Marital status: Single
Family links with cricket: 'Father and
brother played local cricket; nephews play for
Middlesex age groups'
Education: Whitton School, Richmond;
Richmond College
Qualifications: 9 GCSEs, 3 A-levels studied,
ECB Level 1 coach, YMCA Fitness
Instructor's Award
Career outside cricket: Fitness/gym instructor
Off-season: 'Australia'
Overseas tours: MCC YC to Cape Town 1999-2000

Overseas teams played for: Portland CC, Victoria 1999-2000; Mt Gambia, South Australia 2001-02
Career highlights to date: 'First-class debut v Essex at The Oval, scoring 58 not out'
Cricket superstitions: 'None'
Cricketers particularly admired: Alec Stewart, Graham Thorpe, Alan Butcher, Mark Butcher
Young players to look out for: 'Brandon Newman', Scott Newman, James Benning, Neil Saker
Other sports played: Football, golf, squash
Favourite band: Michael Jackson, The Jacksons, Usher
Relaxations: Music, golf, TV
Extras: Middlesex YC cap. Represented ESCA U14 and U15. Played for Development of Excellence XI v Australia U19 1999. Played for Middlesex Board XI in the NatWest 1999. Finchley CC Player of the Season 2000. Left Surrey at the end of the 2003 season and has joined Middlesex for 2004
Best batting: 58* Surrey v Essex, The Oval 2003

2003 Season

	M	Inns	NO	Runs	HS	Avge	100s	50s	Ct	St	O	M	Runs	Wkts	Avge	Best	5wI	10wM
Test																		
All First	2	3	1	79	58*	39.50	-	1	6	-								
1-day Int																		
C & G																		
NCL																		
Twenty20																		

Career Performances

	M	Inns	NO	Runs	HS	Avge	100s	50s	Ct	St	Balls	Runs	Wkts	Avge	Best	5wI	10wM
Test																	
All First	2	3	1	79	58*	39.50	-	1	6	-							
1-day Int																	
C & G	1	1	0	11	11	11.00	-	-	-	-							
NCL	1	1	0	4	4	4.00	-	-	-	-							
Twenty20																	

SCOTT, G. M.   Durham

Name: <u>Gary</u> Michael Scott
Role: Right-hand bat, right-arm
off-spin bowler
Born: 21 July 1984, Sunderland
Height: 6ft **Weight:** 13st
Nickname: Scotty, Dirk
County debut: 2001
1st-Class catches: 1
One-Day 100s: 1
Parents: Mary and Michael
Marital status: Single
Family links with cricket:
'Dad and uncle played but only at school;
brother (Martin) played club cricket with me
(Hetton Lyons CC)'
Education: Hetton Comprehensive
Qualifications: 8 GCSEs
Career outside cricket: 'Chill out'

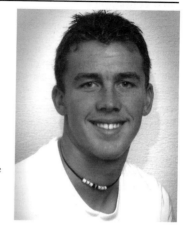

Off-season: 'Working at Northern Rock'
Overseas tours: England U17 to Australia 2000-01
Overseas teams played for: Northern Districts, Adelaide 2002-03
Career highlights to date: 'First-class debut against Derby. Scoring 100 off 64 balls
against Herefordshire at Darlington for Durham Board XI'
Cricket moments to forget: 'Getting my first pair against Warwickshire in the same
day for the 2nd XI'
Cricket superstitions: 'Not really'
Cricketers particularly admired: Steve Waugh, Jacques Kallis, Paul Collingwood
Young players to look out for: Liam Plunkett, Bilal Shafayat
Other sports played: Football (represented Sunderland Schoolboys), golf
Other sports followed: Football (Newcastle Utd)
Injuries: Out for eight weeks overall with a groin strain and a shoulder injury
Favourite band: U2
Relaxations: 'Golf, pool, eating out and watching TV'
Extras: Sir John Hobbs Silver Jubilee Memorial Prize 1999. Played for Durham
Board XI in the C&G 2001 and 2002; scored maiden one-day century (100) for
Durham Board XI v Herefordshire at Darlington in the second round of the C&G 2003
(which was played in September 2002), winning the Man of the Match award. Became
youngest to play first-class cricket for Durham when he made his debut v Derbyshire
at Riverside 2001 aged 17 years and 19 days. Is a Durham Academy player
Opinions on cricket: 'Too much cricket; not enough practice and rest time.'
Best batting: 25 Durham v Derbyshire, Riverside 2001

2003 Season (did not make any first-class or one-day appearances)

Career Performances

	M	Inns	NO	Runs	HS	Avge	100s	50s	Ct	St	Balls	Runs	Wkts	Avge	Best	5wl	10wM
Test																	
All First	1	2	0	33	25	16.50	-	-	1	-	18	11	0	-	-	-	-
1-day Int																	
C & G	3	3	0	130	100	43.33	1	-	2	-	174	107	4	26.75	2-32	-	
NCL																	
Twenty20																	

SEHWAG, V.   Leicestershire

Name: Virender Sehwag
Role: Right-hand bat, right-arm
off-spin bowler
Born: 20 October 1978, Delhi, India
County debut: 2003
Test debut: 2001-02
Tests: 14
One-Day Internationals: 73
1st-Class 50s: 20
1st-Class 100s: 15
1st-Class 200s: 1
1st-Class catches: 63
One-Day 100s: 5
Place in batting averages: 35th av. 47.80
Strike rate: (career 76.64)
Education: Jamia Millia Islamia University,
New Delhi
Overseas tours: India U19 to South Africa
(U19 World Cup) 1997-98; India to Zimbabwe 2001 (one-day series), to Sri Lanka
2001 (one-day series), to South Africa 2001-02, to West Indies 2001-02 (one-day
series), to England 2002, to Sri Lanka (ICC Champions Trophy) 2002-03, to New
Zealand 2002-03, to Africa (World Cup) 2002-03, to Bangladesh (TVS Cup) 2003, to
Australia 2003-04
Overseas teams played for: Delhi 1997-98 –
Extras: Scored 745 runs (av. 62.08) in eight Ranji Trophy appearances 1998-99 and
674 runs (av. 61.27) in eight appearances 1999-2000. One of *Indian Cricket*'s five
Cricketers of the Year 2000. Made Test debut in the first Test v South Africa at
Bloemfontein 2001-02, scoring century (105). Found himself at the centre of a
selection controversy ahead of the first Test v England at Mohali 2001-02 after having

been fined and banned for one Test by referee Mike Denness during previous series in South Africa and omitted from team for unofficial 'Test' at Centurion; in the end omitted from Mohali line-up. Scored century (147) in the first Test v West Indies at Mumbai (Bombay) 2002-03, in the process sharing with Sanjay Bangar (55) in a record first-wicket stand for India in Tests v West Indies (201) and winning Man of the Match award. Other international awards include Man of the Match for his 54-ball 58 plus 3-59 in the first ODI v Australia at Bangalore 2000-01, for his 104-ball 126 v England in the ICC Champions Trophy at Colombo 2002-03, and for his 82-ball 114* in the third ODI v West Indies at Rajkot 2002-03. Joined Leicestershire as an overseas player for 2003. Scored first century for Leicestershire between tea and close of play on the second day v Nottinghamshire at Leicester 2003. Left Leicestershire in late July 2003 after sustaining a back injury

Best batting: 274 North Zone v South Zone, Agartala 1999-2000
Best bowling: 4-32 North Zone v South Zone, Mumbai (Bombay) 1998-99

2003 Season

	M	Inns	NO	Runs	HS	Avge	100s	50s	Ct	St	O	M	Runs	Wkts	Avge	Best	5wI	10wM
Test																		
All First	6	10	0	478	137	47.80	2	1	4	-	34.2	4	153	0	-	-	-	-
1-day Int																		
C & G	3	3	0	74	56	24.66	-	1	-	-								
NCL	7	7	0	233	76	33.28	-	3	1	-	6	0	40	2	20.00	1-17	-	
Twenty20	6	6	0	86	26	14.33	-	-	1	-	14	0	70	7	10.00	3-14	-	

Career Performances

	M	Inns	NO	Runs	HS	Avge	100s	50s	Ct	St	Balls	Runs	Wkts	Avge	Best	5wI	10wM
Test	14	21	0	872	147	41.52	3	4	16	-	240	152	2	76.00	1-27	-	-
All First	60	92	3	4669	274	52.46	16	20	63	-	3832	2035	50	40.70	4-32	-	-
1-day Int	73	71	6	2255	126	34.69	5	11	27	-	1509	1323	33	40.09	3-25	-	
C & G	3	3	0	74	56	24.66	-	1	-	-							
NCL	7	7	0	233	76	33.28	-	3	1	-	36	40	2	20.00	1-17	-	
Twenty20	6	6	0	86	26	14.33	-	-	1	-	84	70	7	10.00	3-14	-	

84. Which West Indies and Kent all-rounder made his maiden first-class hundred in the Lord's Test in 1973?

SELWOOD, S. A.   Derbyshire

Name: Steven (<u>Steve</u>) Andrew Selwood
Role: Left-hand bat, left-arm spin bowler
Born: 24 November 1979, Barnet, London
Height: 5ft 11in **Weight:** 12st
Nickname: Sellers, Hollywood
County debut: 2001
1st-Class 50s: 4
1st-Class catches: 5
Place in batting averages: 221st av. 20.81
(2002 193rd av. 24.05)
Strike rate: (career 60.00)
Parents: Tim and Sarah
Marital status: 'Taken'

Family links with cricket: 'Father played for Middlesex 1969-74, Central Districts 1972-73 and is now youth coach at Finchley CC'
Education: Mill Hill School; Loughborough University
Qualifications: 9 GCSEs, 2 A-levels, BA (Hons) Politics, Level 1 coaching
Overseas tours: Middlesex Prep Schools to Australia 1990-91; British Universities to South Africa 2002
Overseas teams played for: Manly-Warringah, Sydney 1996-97; Claremont-Nedlands, Perth 1998-99
Career highlights to date: 'Every time we win'
Cricket moments to forget: 'Any time we lose and every time I fail'
Cricket superstitions: 'None'
Cricketers particularly admired: Darren Lehmann, Ian Botham
Young players to look out for: Rob White, Mark Powell, Jake Milton (Finchley), Geoff Cullen (Western Australia)
Other sports played: Football, rugby
Other sports followed: Football (Tottenham Hotspur)
Relaxations: 'Spending time with my girlfriend; travel; going out with friends'
Extras: Represented England U14 1994. Played for Finchley v Uxbridge in the *Evening Standard* final 2000, winning Man of the Match award. Played for Loughborough University CCE 2001 and 2002. Scored 93 v Gloucestershire at Bristol in the NUL 2002, in the process sharing with Mathew Dowman (45) in a new record sixth-wicket partnership for Derbyshire in the one-day league (123)
Opinions on cricket: 'There needs to be more aggressive marketing of the game worldwide. We must set our standards much higher in regard to wickets and practice facilities. There is too much four-day cricket. Club cricket must change to a two-day format.'

Best batting: 99 Derbyshire v Worcestershire, Derby 2002
Best bowling: 1-8 Derbyshire v Essex, Derby 2002

2003 Season

	M	Inns	NO	Runs	HS	Avge	100s	50s	Ct	St	O	M	Runs	Wkts	Avge	Best	5wI	10wM
Test																		
All First	9	17	1	333	88	20.81	-	2	3	-	7	0	28	0	-		-	-
1-day Int																		
C & G	3	3	1	30	19	15.00	-	-	-	-	2	0	7	1	7.00	1-7	-	
NCL	11	9	1	240	88 *	30.00	-	2	2	-								
Twenty20	5	3	0	17	12	5.66	-	-	-	-								

Career Performances

	M	Inns	NO	Runs	HS	Avge	100s	50s	Ct	St	Balls	Runs	Wkts	Avge	Best	5wI	10wM
Test																	
All First	21	40	1	833	99	21.35	-	4	5	-	120	95	2	47.50	1-8	-	-
1-day Int																	
C & G	4	4	1	31	19	10.33	-	-	-	-	12	7	1	7.00	1-7	-	
NCL	28	25	3	741	93	33.68	-	6	7	-	2	8	0	-		-	-
Twenty20	5	3	0	17	12	5.66	-	-	-	-							

SHAFAYAT, B. M.   Nottinghamshire

Name: <u>Bilal</u> Mustafa Shafayat
Role: Right-hand bat, right-arm medium-fast bowler, occasional wicket-keeper
Born: 10 July 1984, Nottingham
Height: 5ft 7in **Weight:** 10st 7lbs
Nickname: Billy, Muzzy, Our Kid
County debut: 2001
1st-Class 50s: 7
1st-Class 100s: 2
1st-Class catches: 8
Place in batting averages: 203rd av. 23.17 (2002 92nd av. 37.50)
Strike rate: 96.00 (career 180.00)
Parents: Mohammad Shafayat and Mahfooza Begum
Marital status: Single
Family links with cricket: 'Brother Rashid played for Notts up to 2nd XI and is now playing in Staffordshire Premier (took ten wickets in a game last year). Uncle Nadeem played for PCC. Father just loves it!'

Education: Greenwood Dale; Nottingham Bluecoat School and Sixth Form College
Qualifications: 9 GCSEs, 2 A-levels, Level 1 coaching
Career outside cricket: 'Just cricket, cricket and more cricket'
Off-season: 'At ECB National Academy and on England A tour to Malaysia and India'
Overseas tours: ZRK to Pakistan 2000; Sparkhill ('Kadeer Ali's dad's academy') to Pakistan; England U17 to Australia 2000-01; England U19 to Australia and (U19 World Cup) New Zealand 2001-02, to Australia 2002-03 (captain); Nottinghamshire to South Africa 2002, 2003; ECB National Academy (England A) to Malaysia and India 2003-04
Career highlights to date: 'Making my first-class debut for Notts v Middlesex (scoring 72). Scoring a hundred and double hundred v India in final U19 "Test" 2002. Scoring crucial hundred v Worcestershire for promotion in Championship. Beating Australia U19 in first "Test" 2002-03, scoring 66, 108 and taking six wickets'
Cricket moments to forget: 'Losing U19 "Test" series to Australia'
Cricketers particularly admired: Sachin Tendulkar, Carl Hooper, Andrew Jackman
Young players to look out for: Ravinder Bopara, Samit Patel, Liam Plunkett, Moeen and Kadeer Ali, Nadeem Malik, Aaqib Afzaal, Kamani, Sajid and Rakib Mahmood, Shaftab Khalid
Other sports played: Football, badminton, squash, pool
Other sports followed: Football (Liverpool), boxing (Prince Naseem Hamed), snooker (Ronnie O'Sullivan)
Favourite band: Sean Paul, 50 Cent, Tupac, Nusrat Fateh Ali Khan
Relaxations: 'Praying Namaz; chilling with loved ones'
Extras: Played for Nottinghamshire Board XI in the NatWest 2000 and for Nottinghamshire Board XI and Nottinghamshire in the C&G 2001. Represented England U19 v West Indies U19 2001. Scored 72 on Championship debut v Middlesex at Trent Bridge 2001; aged 16 years 360 days, he became the youngest player to represent Nottinghamshire in the competition. NBC Denis Compton Award for the most promising young Nottinghamshire player 2001, 2002. Represented England U19 v India U19 2002, scoring 118 and 201* in the third 'Test' at Northampton (only Mark Ramprakash had previously scored two centuries in a match for England U19, v Sri Lanka in 1987). Scored maiden first-class century (104) v Worcestershire at Trent Bridge 2002, becoming the youngest Nottinghamshire centurion. Scored 108 and 66 and had second innings figures of 6-54 in England U19's victory over Australia U19 in the first 'Test' at Adelaide 2002-03. Captained England U19 in the 'Test' series v South Africa U19 2003, scoring 121 in the second 'Test' at Worcester to equal the record number of 'Test' centuries scored by an England U19 batsman (four by Marcus Trescothick); missed third 'Test' after being recalled by Nottinghamshire. BBC East Midlands Junior Sportsman of the Year 2003
Opinions on cricket: 'Best [game] in the world.'
Best batting: 105 Nottinghamshire v DUCCE, Trent Bridge 2003
Best bowling: 1-22 Nottinghamshire v DUCCE, Trent Bridge 2003

2003 Season

	M	Inns	NO	Runs	HS	Avge	100s	50s	Ct	St	O	M	Runs	Wkts	Avge	Best	5wI	10wM
Test																		
All First	13	23	0	533	105	23.17	1	3	3	-	16	2	96	1	96.00	1-22	-	-
1-day Int																		
C & G	2	2	0	4	4	2.00	-	-	-	-	2	0	21	0	-		-	-
NCL	11	11	0	166	38	15.09	-	-	2	-	12	0	67	1	67.00	1-30	-	
Twenty20	5	5	1	65	28	16.25	-	-	2	1	3	0	37	0	-		-	-

Career Performances

	M	Inns	NO	Runs	HS	Avge	100s	50s	Ct	St	Balls	Runs	Wkts	Avge	Best	5wI	10wM
Test																	
All First	23	42	1	1214	105	29.60	2	7	8	-	180	148	1	148.00	1-22	-	-
1-day Int																	
C & G	6	6	1	76	36	15.20	-	-	-	-	12	21	0	-		-	-
NCL	25	25	0	461	66	18.44	-	1	9	-	292	261	9	29.00	4-35	-	
Twenty20	5	5	1	65	28	16.25	-	-	2	1	18	37	0	-		-	-

SHAH, O. A.   Middlesex

Name: <u>Owais</u> Alam Shah
Role: Right-hand bat, off-spin bowler,
county vice-captain
Born: 22 October 1978, Karachi, Pakistan
Height: 6ft 1in **Weight:** 12st
Nickname: Ace
County debut: 1995 (one-day),
1996 (first-class)
County cap: 1999
One-Day Internationals: 15
1000 runs in a season: 3
1st-Class 50s: 30
1st-Class 100s: 14
1st-Class 200s: 1
1st-Class catches: 72
One-Day 100s: 5
Place in batting averages: 59th av. 43.07
(2002 45th av. 47.13)
Strike rate: (career 62.47)
Parents: Jamshed and Mehjabeen
Marital status: Single
Family links with cricket: Father played for his college side

Education: Isleworth and Syon School; Lampton School; Westminster University, Harrow
Qualifications: 7 GCSEs, 2 A-levels
Off-season: 'Getting fit and working on batting'
Overseas tours: England U19 to Zimbabwe 1995-96, to South Africa (including U19 World Cup) 1997-98 (captain); England A to Australia 1996-97, to Kenya and Sri Lanka 1997-98; ECB National Academy to Australia 2001-02; England to Zimbabwe (one-day series) 2001-02, to India and New Zealand 2001-02 (one-day series), to Sri Lanka (ICC Champions Trophy) 2002-03, to Australia 2002-03 (VB Series)
Overseas teams played for: University of Western Australia, Perth
Career highlights to date: 'Playing for England in one-day game v Australia [2001]'
Cricket moments to forget: 'Getting a pair in first-class cricket'
Cricketers particularly admired: Viv Richards, Sachin Tendulkar, Mark Waugh
Young players to look out for: Chad Keegan, Bilal Shafayat, Kevin Pietersen
Other sports played: Snooker
Other sports followed: Football ('enjoy watching Manchester United play')
Favourite band: UB40, 'most R&B bands'
Relaxations: 'Movies, eating out'
Extras: Scored record 232 for England U15 against England U16. Man of the Series in U17 'Test' series against India 1994. Captained the England U19 side to success in the 1997-98 U19 World Cup in South Africa, scoring 54 not out in the final. Captain of England U19 in series against Pakistan U19 1998. Scored 62 v Pakistan at Lord's in the NatWest Series 2001, in the process sharing in a record fourth-wicket partnership for England in ODIs (170) with Marcus Trescothick. Cricket Writers' Young Player of the Year 2001. Middlesex Player of the Year 2002. Scored century (127) for England XI v Sir Donald Bradman XI in 50-over match at Bowral 2002-03. His 106 at Trent Bridge in the NCL 2003 was the first ever century by a Middlesex batsman against Nottinghamshire in the one-day league. Vice-captain of Middlesex since 2002
Opinions on cricket: 'Too much cricket played in this country. Need to cut down the amount of four-day cricket.'
Best batting: 203 Middlesex v Derbyshire, Southgate 2001
Best bowling: 3-33 Middlesex v Gloucestershire, Bristol 1999

2003 Season

	M	Inns	NO	Runs	HS	Avge	100s	50s	Ct	St	O	M	Runs	Wkts	Avge	Best	5wI	10wM
Test																		
All First	18	30	2	1206	147	43.07	3	6	11	-	11	0	55	0	-	-	-	-
1-day Int																		
C & G	3	3	0	38	29	12.66	-	-	1	-								
NCL	18	18	2	655	106	40.93	1	4	13	-								
Twenty20	5	5	2	71	40 *	23.66	-	-	3	-								

Career Performances

	M	Inns	NO	Runs	HS	Avge	100s	50s	Ct	St	Balls	Runs	Wkts	Avge	Best	5wI	10wM
Test																	
All First	113	186	13	6281	203	36.30	15	30	72	-	1062	682	17	40.11	3-33	-	-
1-day Int	15	15	2	283	62	21.76	-	2	6	-							
C & G	14	14	1	285	49	21.92	-	-	4	-	30	36	1	36.00	1-36	-	
NCL	104	98	11	2753	134	31.64	4	14	36	-	151	176	3	58.66	1-4	-	
Twenty20	5	5	2	71	40 *	23.66	-	-	3	-							

SHAHID AFRIDI Derbyshire

Name: Sahibzaha Mohammad Shahid Khan Afridi
Role: Right-hand bat, leg-break bowler
Born: 1 March 1980, Kohat, Pakistan
County debut: 2001 (Leicestershire), 2003 (Derbyshire)
Test debut: 1998-99
Tests: 14
One-Day Internationals: 176
1st-Class 50s: 17
1st-Class 100s: 7
1st-Class 5 w. in innings: 5
1st-Class catches: 46
One-Day 100s: 3
One-Day 5 w. in innings: 1
Place in batting averages: 249th av. 15.33
Strike rate: 82.00 (career 54.87)
Family links with cricket: Brother Tariq Afridi played first-class cricket in Pakistan
Overseas tours: Pakistan U19 to West Indies 1996-97; Pakistan to Kenya (one-day series) 1996-97, to Australia (one-day series) 1996-97, to India (one-day series) 1996-97, to Zimbabwe and South Africa 1997-98 (one-day series), to Bangladesh (Wills International Cup) 1998-99, to India 1998-99, to UK, Ireland and Holland (World Cup) 1999, to Australia 1999-2000 (one-day series), to West Indies 1999-2000 (one-day series), to New Zealand 2000-01 (one-day series), to England 2001 (one-day series), to Sharjah (v West Indies) 2001-02, to Australia (Super Challenge II) 2002, to Morocco (Morocco Cup) 2002, to Kenya (Nairobi Triangular) 2002, to Sri Lanka (ICC Champions Trophy) 2002-03, to Zimbabwe 2002-03, to South Africa 2002-03 (one-day series), to Africa (World Cup) 2002-03, plus other one-day tournaments in Toronto, Sharjah and India
Off-season: Playing for Griqualand West in South Africa

Overseas teams played for: Karachi Whites 1995-96 – 2001-02; Habib Bank 1997-98 – 2002-03; Karachi Blues 1996-97; Griqualand West 2003-04

Extras: Set record for fastest ODI century – 37 balls (out for 102) v Sri Lanka in Kenya 1996-97 in his first ODI innings, aged 16 years 217 days; innings included a record-equalling 11 sixes and won him Man of the Match award. Recorded his maiden Test five-wicket innings return (5-52) on debut v Australia at Karachi 1998-99, going on to score his maiden Test century (141) v India at Chennai (Madras) in his second match. Joined Leicestershire during the 2001 season as overseas player, replacing the injured Dan Marsh. Struck 32-ball 70 on NUL debut v Kent at Leicester 2001. C&G Man of the Match awards for his 44-ball 67 in the quarter-final v Worcestershire at Worcester and for his 58-ball 95 in the semi-final v Lancashire at Leicester 2001. Left Leicestershire at the end of the 2001 season. Has won numerous ODI awards, among them Man of the Finals in the CUB Series in Australia 1996-97 and Man of the Match v England at Lahore 2000-01 (5-40/61), v New Zealand at Sharjah 2000-01 (43-ball 70 plus 2-49), and v Bangladesh at Dhaka 2001-02 (44-ball 83). Struck 18-ball 55* v Holland at Colombo in the ICC Champions Trophy 2002-03, equalling his own record for the second-fastest fifty in ODIs (behind Sanath Jayasuriya's 17-ball fifty v Pakistan in Singapore 1995-96) set during his 37-ball century v Sri Lanka in Kenya 1996-97. His quicker ball was once timed at 86mph. Was an overseas player with Derbyshire April to May 2003

Best batting: 164 Leicestershire v Northamptonshire, Northampton 2001
Best bowling: 6-101 Habib Bank v KRL, Rawalpindi 1997-98

2003 Season

	M	Inns	NO	Runs	HS	Avge	100s	50s	Ct	St	O	M	Runs	Wkts	Avge	Best	5wI	10wM
Test																		
All First	3	6	0	92	67	15.33	-	1	-	-	54.4	15	147	4	36.75	2-29	-	-
1-day Int																		
C & G	1	1	0	23	23	23.00	-	-	-	-	10	0	45	2	22.50	2-45	-	
NCL	4	4	1	41	35	13.66	-	-	1	-	22	3	103	2	51.50	1-25	-	
Twenty20																		

Career Performances

	M	Inns	NO	Runs	HS	Avge	100s	50s	Ct	St	Balls	Runs	Wkts	Avge	Best	5wI	10wM
Test	14	25	1	780	141	32.50	2	4	8	-	1331	661	21	31.47	5-52	1	-
All First	69	116	3	3520	164	31.15	7	17	46	-	7900	4049	144	28.11	6-101	5	-
1-day Int	176	171	7	3887	109	23.70	3	22	65	-	6713	5154	131	39.34	5-40	1	
C & G	5	5	0	228	95	45.60	-	2	1	-	276	203	9	22.55	3-47	-	
NCL	12	12	1	317	70	28.81	-	3	1	-	468	369	13	28.38	3-45	-	
Twenty20																		

SHAHID, N.   Surrey

Name: Nadeem Shahid
Role: Right-hand bat, leg-spin bowler
Born: 23 April 1969, Karachi, Pakistan
Height: 6ft **Weight:** 12st
Nickname: Nad, Gonad,
'too many to mention'
County debut: 1989 (Essex), 1995 (Surrey)
County cap: 1998 (Surrey)
1000 runs in a season: 1
1st-Class 50s: 34
1st-Class 100s: 9
1st-Class catches: 151
One-Day 100s: 2
Place in batting averages: 266th av. 12.66
(2002 93rd av. 37.47)
Strike rate: 108.00 (career 72.35)
Parents: Ahmed and Salma
Marital status: Single
Family links with cricket: 'Brother plays in the leagues in Suffolk'
Education: Ipswich School; Plymouth Polytechnic
Qualifications: 6 O-levels, 1 A-level, coaching certificate
Overseas tours: Ipswich School to Barbados (Sir Garfield Sobers Trophy) 1987;
England (South) to Northern Ireland (Youth World Tournament) 1988
Overseas teams played for: Gosnells, Perth, Western Australia 1989-91;
Fairfield, Sydney 1992-93
Cricket moments to forget: 'Cannot remember … maybe a dropped catch against
Gloucestershire that cost us the game some years back'
Cricket superstitions: 'Not eating duck the night before I'm due to bat'
Cricketers particularly admired: 'All players at Surrey plus Ed Giddins and
Gavin Hamilton'
Young players to look out for: Rikki Clarke, Tim Murtagh
Other sports played: 'Golf, tennis, golf, football (centre forward), golf, snooker,
golf … most sports'
Other sports followed: Football (Ipswich Town), 'follow most sports'
Relaxations: 'Playing as much golf as possible; eating out; watching movies'
Extras: Youngest Suffolk player, aged 17. Played for HMC, MCC Schools, ESCA
U19, NCA Young Cricketers, England U25 and at every level for Suffolk. TSB Young
Player of the Year 1987, *Daily Telegraph* Bowling Award 1987 and 1988 and Cricket
Society's Leading All-rounder in English Schools Cricket 1988. Laidlaw Young Player
of the Year for Essex and Essex Society Player of the Year 1993. Released by Essex at
end of 1994 season and signed for Surrey. Member of the Surrey Sunday League

winning side of 1996. Member of Surrey County Championship winning squad of 1999, 2000 and 2002. Scored career best 150 v Sussex at The Oval 2002, in the process sharing with Alistair Brown (177) in a record fifth-wicket partnership for Surrey v Sussex (262). Surrey Team Man of the Year and Fielder of the Year 2002. Scored 266 v Derbyshire 2nd XI at The Oval 2003, sharing with Scott Newman (284) in an opening partnership of 552, just three runs short of the English all-cricket record first-wicket stand of 555 set by Percy Holmes and Herbert Sutcliffe for Yorkshire v Essex at Leyton 1932; scored 272 v Sussex 2nd XI at Hove in next match

Opinions on cricket: 'The two overseas players and the unlimited European passport holders playing county cricket cannot be good for the English game. You will have several counties fielding teams with half of the players not eligible to play for England. Cannot see how that can be good for English cricket. Cricket pitches have improved in general, which is good news as this will produce better quality cricketers.… We have competed with all other nations [besides Australia] and beaten some home and away.'

Best batting: 150 Surrey v Sussex, The Oval 2002
Best bowling: 3-91 Essex v Surrey, The Oval 1990

2003 Season

	M	Inns	NO	Runs	HS	Avge	100s	50s	Ct	St	O	M	Runs	Wkts	Avge	Best	5wI	10wM
Test																		
All First	4	6	0	76	67	12.66	-	1	2	-	18	3	75	1	75.00	1-33	-	-
1-day Int																		
C & G																		
NCL	2	2	0	19	19	9.50	-	-	2	-	2	0	13	0	-		-	-
Twenty20																		

Career Performances

	M	Inns	NO	Runs	HS	Avge	100s	50s	Ct	St	Balls	Runs	Wkts	Avge	Best	5wI	10wM
Test																	
All First	145	229	26	6344	150	31.25	9	34	151	-	3256	2146	45	47.68	3-91	-	-
1-day Int																	
C & G	12	9	2	249	85*	35.57	-	2	6	-	72	30	4	7.50	3-30	-	
NCL	127	113	18	2251	109*	23.69	2	7	40	-	78	85	0	-	-	-	
Twenty20																	

85. Who scored a record five consecutive Test centuries, the first of these being against England at Kingston in March 1948?

SHANTRY, A. J.   Northamptonshire

Name: <u>Adam</u> John Shantry
Role: Left-hand bat, left-arm
fast-medium bowler
Born: 13 November 1982, Bristol
Height: 6ft 3in **Weight:** 14st 6lbs
Nickname: Shants
County debut: 2003
1st-Class catches: 1
Strike rate: 40.00 (career 40.00)
Parents: Brian and Josephine
Marital status: Girlfriend Cat
Family links with cricket: 'Father Brian
played for Gloucestershire; cousin had trials
for Namibia'
Education: The Priory School, Shrewsbury;
Shrewsbury Sixth Form College
Qualifications: 11 GCSEs, 4 A-levels,
Level 2 coaching

Career outside cricket: 'Sign maker'
Off-season: 'Watching Bristol City get promoted (hopefully)'
Overseas teams played for: Balwyn, Melbourne 2001-02
Career highlights to date: 'County Championship debut v Somerset – after three
overs had figures of three for none'
Cricket moments to forget: 'Getting injured second ball of NCL career, v Scotland'
Cricket superstitions: 'Never attempt to follow Tom Huggins to any ground!'
Cricketers particularly admired: Brian Shantry, Andre Nel
Young players to look out for: Jack Shantry
Other sports played: Football (Shrewsbury Area)
Other sports followed: Football (Bristol City – 'Drink up ye cider!')
Injuries: Out for four weeks with an injured pelvic ligament
Favourite band: Feeder
Relaxations: 'Fishing; listening to music – Muse, InMe, Lostprophets'
Extras: England U17 squad. Represented ESCA U18 v West Indies U19 2001. Radio
Shropshire Young Player of the Year 2001. Played for Northamptonshire Board XI in
the first round of the C&G 2003, which was played in August 2002. Leading wicket-
taker for Northamptonshire Colts 2002; took 7-18 v Warwickshire U19 2002. Took 3-8
(including spell of three wickets in five balls before conceding a run) on
Championship debut v Somerset at Northampton 2003
Opinions on cricket: 'On the up. Bats should be made thinner. Left-armers should be
allowed to bowl from 18 yards. "Auto wickies" when bowling to overseas players.'
Best batting: 38* Northamptonshire v Somerset, Northampton 2003
Best bowling: 3-8 Northamptonshire v Somerset, Northampton 2003

2003 Season

	M	Inns	NO	Runs	HS	Avge	100s	50s	Ct	St	O	M	Runs	Wkts	Avge	Best	5wI	10wM
Test																		
All First	3	3	2	55	38 *	55.00	-	-	1	-	46.4	13	153	7	21.85	3-8	-	-
1-day Int																		
C & G																		
NCL	1	1	0	4	4	4.00	-	-	1	-	2	0	17	0	-		-	-
Twenty20																		

Career Performances

	M	Inns	NO	Runs	HS	Avge	100s	50s	Ct	St	Balls	Runs	Wkts	Avge	Best	5wI	10wM
Test																	
All First	3	3	2	55	38 *	55.00	-	-	1	-	280	153	7	21.85	3-8	-	-
1-day Int																	
C & G	1	1	0	15	15	15.00	-	-	-	-	42	21	2	10.50	2-21	-	
NCL	1	1	0	4	4	4.00	-	-	1	-	12	17	0	-		-	-
Twenty20																	

SHARIF, Z. K.   Essex

Name: <u>Zoheb</u> Khalid Sharif
Role: Left-hand bat, leg-spin bowler
Born: 22 February 1983, Leytonstone, London
Height: 5ft 10in **Weight:** 12st
Nickname: Bomber, Bundles, Muncher
County debut: 2001
1st-Class 50s: 2
1st-Class catches: 2
Place in batting averages: 118th av. 33.16
Strike rate: 82.80 (career 68.00)
Parents: Khalid and Robina
Marital status: Single
Family links with cricket: 'Dad played club cricket'
Education: Warwick School; Coopers Company and Coborn School; Loughborough University
Qualifications: 9 GCSEs, 3 A-levels
Career outside cricket: Student
Off-season: 'Reviewing bowling action'
Overseas tours: Essex U13 to Holland 1995

Overseas teams played for: PNT CC, Pakistan 1999-2000; Rawalpindi District 2001-02

Career highlights to date: 'Making my first-team debut'

Cricket moments to forget: 'None – you can learn from every game, especially as a leg-spinner'

Cricket superstitions: 'Pray to Allah'

Cricketers particularly admired: Abdul Qadir, Mushtaq Ahmed, Saeed Anwar, Saurav Ganguly

Young players to look out for: Bilal Shafayat, Ravi Bopara, Gurdeep Kandola

Favourite band: Tupac and the Outlawz, 'any underground hip-hop and R&B'

Interests/relaxations: 'Following Islam'

Extras: MCC Lord's Taverners' Player of the Year at U13, U15 and U19 level. Was on MCC groundstaff. Was in England U17 squad v Scotland 2000. Attended Abdul Qadir Cricket Academy, Lahore 2002. Took 4-98 v Northamptonshire at Northampton 2002 in his second first-class match. Played for Loughborough University CCE in 2003, scoring two fifties (64/67) v Leicestershire at Leicester

Opinions on cricket: 'Not enough players from the inner city are given opportunities to display their talents. More time needs to be spent there as this is where the natural talent lies. Youngsters should be encouraged to play shots, spin the ball hard and bowl fast. Natural talent should not be coached out of youngsters.'

Best batting: 67 LUCCE v Leicestershire, Leicester 2003

Best bowling: 4-98 Essex v Northamptonshire, Northampton 2002

2003 Season

	M	Inns	NO	Runs	HS	Avge	100s	50s	Ct	St	O	M	Runs	Wkts	Avge	Best	5wI	10wM
Test																		
All First	4	7	1	199	67	33.16	-	2	1	-	69	6	345	5	69.00	3-103	-	-
1-day Int																		
C & G																		
NCL																		
Twenty20																		

Career Performances

	M	Inns	NO	Runs	HS	Avge	100s	50s	Ct	St	Balls	Runs	Wkts	Avge	Best	5wI	10wM
Test																	
All First	7	10	1	258	67	28.66	-	2	2	-	612	532	9	59.11	4-98	-	-
1-day Int																	
C & G																	
NCL																	
Twenty20																	

SHAW, A. D. Glamorgan

Name: <u>Adrian</u> David Shaw
Role: Right-hand bat, wicket-keeper
Born: 17 February 1972, Neath
Height: 6ft **Weight:** 13st 6lbs
Nickname: Shawsy, AD, Hitler, Adolf,
ADS, Eddie
County debut: 1992 (one-day),
1994 (first-class)
County cap: 1999
50 dismissals in a season: 1
1st-Class 50s: 9
1st-Class 100s: 1
1st-Class catches: 180
1st-Class stumpings: 14
Parents: David Colin and Christina
Wife and date of marriage: Wendy,
December 2002
Children: Seren Georgia, 8 January 2002
Education: Llangatwg Comprehensive; Neath Tertiary College
Qualifications: 9 O-levels, 3 A-levels, various coaching badges
Overseas tours: Welsh Schools U17 to Barbados 1987; England YC to New Zealand
1990-91; Glamorgan pre-season tours, including to Cape Town 1999
Overseas teams played for: Welkom Police, Free State 1995-96
Cricketers particularly admired: 'Anyone who can laugh at themselves and not take
it all too seriously'
Young players to look out for: 'Those who can cope with the ups and downs. It's
ninety per cent temperament'
Other sports played: Rugby (formerly centre with Neath RFC – Back of the Year
1993-94; Welsh U19 and U21 squad member)
Other sports followed: Rugby (Neath)
Relaxations: 'As anyone with a baby will tell you, no time'
Extras: One of youngest players (18 years 7 days) to play first-class rugby for Neath.
Voted Glamorgan 2nd XI Player of the Year and Glamorgan Young Player of the Year
1995. 2nd XI Player of the Month, June 1996. Claimed eight catches in the second
innings and 12 for the match v Gloucestershire 2nd XI at Usk 1998, setting two
records for the 2nd XI Championship. Awarded county Young Player of the Month for
August 1999 'at the geriatric age of 27'. Glamorgan 2nd XI player/coach since 2002.
Scored eleventh century for Glamorgan 2nd XI (103) v Somerset 2nd XI at Cardiff
2003, surpassing Tony Cottey's record of ten centuries in 2nd XI cricket for
Glamorgan
Opinions on cricket: 'Perspective – get that right and if you work hard and luck's on

your side, you'll be OK. And if it's not, then so what? You tried. Over-inflated egos – we're only cricketers, and no one really notices a county player walking down the road, do they?'

Best batting: 140 Glamorgan v Oxford University, The Parks 1999

2003 Season

	M	Inns	NO	Runs	HS	Avge	100s	50s	Ct	St	O	M	Runs	Wkts	Avge	Best	5wI	10wM
Test																		
All First	1	1	0	33	33	33.00	-	-	-	-								
1-day Int																		
C & G																		
NCL																		
Twenty20																		

Career Performances

	M	Inns	NO	Runs	HS	Avge	100s	50s	Ct	St	Balls	Runs	Wkts	Avge	Best	5wI	10wM
Test																	
All First	77	103	16	1906	140	21.90	1	9	180	14	6	7	0	-		-	-
1-day Int																	
C & G	9	8	2	151	47	25.16	-	-	13	-							
NCL	56	38	9	436	48	15.03	-	-	29	10							
Twenty20																	

SHEIKH, M. A.   Warwickshire

Name: <u>Mohammed</u> Avez Sheikh
Role: Left-hand bat, right-arm medium bowler
Born: 2 July 1973, Birmingham
Height: 6ft
Nickname: Sheikhy
County debut: 1997
1st-Class 50s: 2
1st-Class catches: 3
Place in batting averages: (2002 143rd av. 29.66)
Place in bowling averages: 100th av. 36.86
Strike rate: 72.73 (career 82.72)
Education: Broadway School
Overseas teams played for: Western Province CC 1997-98
Extras: Played for Warwickshire U19 and played for both Worcestershire and Essex 2nd

XIs in 1995. Played for the Warwickshire Board side that won the last ECB 38-County competition 2002, taking 4-37 in the final. Released by Warwickshire at the end of the 2003 season
Best batting: 58* Warwickshire v Northamptonshire, Northampton 2000
Best bowling: 4-36 Warwickshire v Hampshire, Edgbaston 2001

2003 Season

	M	Inns	NO	Runs	HS	Avge	100s	50s	Ct	St	O	M	Runs	Wkts	Avge	Best	5wI	10wM
Test																		
All First	6	8	3	171	57 *	34.20	-	1	2	-	181.5	43	553	15	36.86	4-60	-	-
1-day Int																		
C & G	3	3	2	6	4 *	6.00	-	-	-	-	25	2	111	1	111.00	1-41	-	
NCL	7	6	2	58	25	14.50	-	-	1	-	53	3	285	5	57.00	2-20	-	
Twenty20																		

Career Performances

	M	Inns	NO	Runs	HS	Avge	100s	50s	Ct	St	Balls	Runs	Wkts	Avge	Best	5wI	10wM
Test																	
All First	20	27	7	572	58 *	28.60	-	2	3	-	2978	1391	36	38.63	4-36	-	-
1-day Int																	
C & G	11	7	3	50	14	12.50	-	-	2	-	606	420	10	42.00	2-18	-	
NCL	52	27	10	176	36	10.35	-	-	9	-	2313	1593	56	28.44	4-17	-	
Twenty20																	

86. Which former Sussex player and president of the MCC scored his maiden first-class 100 in his first Test innings in Trinidad in 1948?

SHERIYAR, A.   Kent

Name: Alamgir Sheriyar
Role: Right-hand bat, left-arm fast bowler
Born: 15 November 1973, Birmingham
Height: 6ft 1in **Weight:** 13st
Nickname: Sheri
County debut: 1993 (one-day, Leics),
1994 (first-class, Leics), 1996 (Worcs),
2003 (Kent)
County cap: 1997 (Worcs; colours, 2002)
50 wickets in a season: 4
1st-Class 5 w. in innings: 22
1st-Class 10 w. in match: 3
1st-Class catches: 22
Place in batting averages: 280th av. 8.81
(2002 294th av. 9.72)
Place in bowling averages: 76th av. 33.07
(2002 58th av. 28.86)
Strike rate: 59.13 (career 50.70)
Parents: Mohammed Zaman (deceased) and Safia Sultana
Marital status: Single
Family links with cricket: Brothers play a bit
Education: George Dixon Secondary School, Birmingham; Joseph Chamberlain Sixth
Form College, Birmingham; Oxford Brookes University
Qualifications: 6 O-levels
Overseas tours: Leicestershire to South Africa 1995; Worcestershire to Barbados
1996; England A to Bangladesh and New Zealand 1999-2000
Cricketers particularly admired: Wasim Akram
Other sports followed: Football, basketball
Relaxations: Time at home, music
Extras: Played for English Schools U17 and has also played in the Indoor National
League. Became only the second player to take a hat-trick on his Championship debut,
for Leics v Durham at Durham University 1994 (Vince Wells took a hat-trick for Leics
in the same match); the first player to achieve the feat was H. A. Sedgwick, for Yorks
v Worcs in 1906. Asked to be released by Leicestershire at the end of the 1995 season
and joined Worcestershire for 1996. First bowler to reach 50 first-class wickets in 1999
and ended season as leading wicket-taker with 92 wickets (av. 24.70). Took second
first-class hat-trick of his career v Kent at Worcester 1999. Left Worcestershire at the
end of the 2002 season and joined Kent for 2003
Best batting: 21 Worcestershire v Nottinghamshire, Trent Bridge 1997
            21 Worcestershire v Pakistan A, Worcester 1997
Best bowling: 7-130 Worcestershire v Hampshire, Southampton 1999

2003 Season

	M	Inns	NO	Runs	HS	Avge	100s	50s	Ct	St	O	M	Runs	Wkts	Avge	Best	5wI	10wM
Test																		
All First	15	20	9	97	18 *	8.81	-	-	3	-	374.3	76	1257	38	33.07	5-65	1	-
1-day Int																		
C & G																		
NCL	2	1	0	6	6	6.00	-	-	-	-	13	1	102	2	51.00	1-43	-	
Twenty20	3	2	2	13	9 *	-	-	-	-	-	10	0	64	2	32.00	1-18	-	

Career Performances

	M	Inns	NO	Runs	HS	Avge	100s	50s	Ct	St	Balls	Runs	Wkts	Avge	Best	5wI	10wM
Test																	
All First	142	154	59	780	21	8.21	-	-	22	-	24338	14132	480	29.44	7-130	22	3
1-day Int																	
C & G	9	4	1	14	10	4.66	-	-	1	-	389	299	9	33.22	2-47	-	
NCL	78	22	12	69	19	6.90	-	-	5	-	2740	2367	88	26.89	4-18	-	
Twenty20	3	2	2	13	9 *	-	-	-	-	-	60	64	2	32.00	1-18	-	

SHOAIB AKHTAR Durham

Name: Shoaib Akhtar
Role: Right-hand bat, right-arm fast bowler
Born: 13 August 1975, Rawalpindi, Pakistan
Height: 6ft
County debut: 2003 (*see Extras*)
Test debut: 1997-98
Tests: 27
One-Day Internationals: 87
1st-Class 50s: 1
1st-Class 5 w. in innings: 20
1st-Class 10 w. in match: 1
1st-Class catches: 30
One-Day 5 w. in innings: 4
Place in batting averages: 242nd av. 16.41
Place in bowling averages: 2nd av. 17.05
Strike rate: 32.29 (career 43.91)
Education: Elliott High School, Rawalpindi;
Asghar Mal Government College, Rawalpindi

Overseas tours: Pakistan A to England 1997; Pakistan to South Africa 1997-98,
to Zimbabwe 1997-98, to Malaysia (Commonwealth Games) 1998-99, to India 1998-
99, to UK, Ireland and Holland (World Cup) 1999, to Australia 1999-2000, to West
Indies 1999-2000, to England 2001, to Bangladesh 2001-02, to Sharjah (v West Indies)

2001-02, to Australia (Super Challenge II) 2002, to Sri Lanka (ICC Champions Trophy) 2002-03, to Sri Lanka and Sharjah (v Australia) 2002-03, to Zimbabwe 2002-03, to South Africa 2002-03, to Africa (World Cup) 2002-03, to England (NatWest Challenge) 2003, to New Zealand 2003-04, plus other one-day series and tournaments in Bangladesh, India, Sharjah, New Zealand, Kenya and Sri Lanka

Overseas teams played for: Rawalpindi 1993-94 – 1998-99; Pakistan International Airlines 1994-95 – 1995-96; Agriculture Development Bank of Pakistan 1996-97 – 1997-98; Khan Research Labs 2001-02 – 2002-03

Extras: Nicknamed the Rawalpindi Express. Represented Pakistan U19 in home series v New Zealand U19 1993-94. Played for Pakistan Cricket Board v England A 1995-96. Was to join Nottinghamshire as overseas player for 2000 but was prevented by injury. Played one first-class match for Somerset 2001, v Australians at Taunton. His ODI awards include Man of the Series in the Coca-Cola Sharjah Cup 1998-99 and in the Super Challenge II v Australia 2002, in which he took 5-25 at Brisbane; also Man of the Match v New Zealand at Old Trafford in the semi-finals of the World Cup 1999. Man of the Match in the first Test v West Indies in Sharjah 2001-02 (5-24). Took 6-11 from 8.2 overs as New Zealand were bowled out for 73 in their first innings of the first Test at Lahore 2001-02. Had match figures of 8-72 (3-51/5-21) in the first Test v Australia at Colombo 2002-03. Bowled the first official 100mph delivery (timed at 100.23mph) to Nick Knight v England at Cape Town in the World Cup 2002-03. Was an overseas player with Durham June to September 2003, replacing Dewald Pretorius, absent on international duty; has returned for 2004. Durham Bowler of the Year 2003

Best batting: 59* KRL v PIA, Lahore 2001-02

Best bowling: 6-11 Pakistan v New Zealand, Lahore 2001-02

Stop press: Had match figures of 10-80 (6-50/4-30) in the second Test v Bangladesh at Peshawar 2003-04 and 11-78 (5-48/6-30) in the second Test v New Zealand at Wellington 2003-04, winning the Man of the Match award in both cases

2003 Season

	M	Inns	NO	Runs	HS	Avge	100s	50s	Ct	St	O	M	Runs	Wkts	Avge	Best	5wI	10wM
Test																		
All First	7	14	2	197	37	16.41	-	-	-	-	183	40	580	34	17.05	4-9	-	-
1-day Int	2	2	1	0	0 *	0.00	-	-	1	-	19	1	109	2	54.50	2-69	-	
C & G																		
NCL	7	6	0	69	19	11.50	-	-	1	-	56	4	224	17	13.17	5-35	1	
Twenty20	1	1	0	0	0	0.00	-	-	-	-	4	0	31	1	31.00	1-31	-	

Career Performances

	M	Inns	NO	Runs	HS	Avge	100s	50s	Ct	St	Balls	Runs	Wkts	Avge	Best	5wI	10wM
Test	27	39	10	245	37	8.44	-	-	7	-	4737	2586	101	25.60	6-11	6	1
All First	97	131	43	992	59 *	11.27	-	1	30	-	14887	8943	339	26.38	6-11	20	1
1-day Int	87	42	24	225	43	12.50	-	-	14	-	4014	3052	142	21.49	6-16	3	
C & G																	
NCL	7	6	0	69	19	11.50	-	-	1	-	336	224	17	13.17	5-35	1	
Twenty20	1	1	0	0	0	0.00	-	-	-	-	24	31	1	31.00	1-31	-	

SHOAIB MALIK   Gloucestershire

Name: Shoaib Malik
Role: Right-hand bat, right-arm
off-spin bowler
Born: 1 February 1982, Sialkot, Punjab
County debut: 2003
Test debut: 2001-02
Tests: 3
One-Day Internationals: 48
1st-Class 50s: 4
1st-Class 100s: 4
1st-Class 5 w. in innings: 5
1st-Class 10 w. in match: 1
1st-Class catches: 23
One-Day 100s: 2
Strike rate: 79.20 (career 51.82)
Overseas tours: Pakistan U19 to South
Africa 1996-97, to Australia 1997-98, to
South Africa (U19 World Cup) 1997-98, to

England 1998; Pakistan A to England 1997; Pakistan to Sharjah (Coca-Cola
Champions Trophy) 1999-2000, to Australia 1999-2000 (CUB Series), to West Indies
1999-2000 (one-day series), to England 2001 (NatWest Series), to Sharjah (v West
Indies) 2001-02 (one-day series), to Australia (Super Challenge II) 2002, to Sri Lanka
(ICC Champions Trophy) 2002-03, to Sri Lanka (Bank Alfalah Cup) 2003, to England
(NatWest Challenge) 2003, to New Zealand 2003-04, plus other one-day series and
tournaments in Sharjah, Bangladesh, Sri Lanka, Morocco and Kenya
Overseas teams played for: Gujranwala 1997-98 – 1998-99; Pakistan International
Airlines 1998-99 – 2002-03; Pakistan Reserves (in domestic competition) 1999-2000;
Sialkot 2001-02
Extras: Represented Pakistan U19 in home series v England U19 1996-97, v Australia
U19 1996-97 and v South Africa U19 1998-99. Has won several domestic awards,
including Man of the Match for Pakistan International Airlines v Water and Power
Development Authority at Faisalabad 2000-01 (83/130* and 7-81/2-56). His ODI
awards include Man of the Series in the Bank Alfalah Cup in Sri Lanka 2003 and Man
of the Match v New Zealand at Lahore 2002 (115/3-37). Was an overseas player with
Gloucestershire in late July and early August 2003, deputising for Ian Harvey, absent
on international duty; has returned for 2004. Man of the Match for Gloucestershire v
Derbyshire at Bristol in the semi-final of the C&G 2003 (1-46/74)
Best batting: 130* PIA v WAPDA, Faisalabad 2000-01
Best bowling: 7-81 PIA v WAPDA, Faisalabad 2000-01
Stop press: ODI Man of the Match award for his 82* v South Africa at Lahore
2003-04

2003 Season

	M	Inns	NO	Runs	HS	Avge	100s	50s	Ct	St	O	M	Runs	Wkts	Avge	Best	5wI	10wM
Test																		
All First	2	4	0	80	60	20.00	-	1	-	-	66	19	146	5	29.20	3-76	-	-
1-day Int	3	3	0	49	24	16.33	-	-	-	-	17	2	52	4	13.00	3-26	-	
C & G	1	1	0	74	74	74.00	-	1	-	-	9	0	46	1	46.00	1-46	-	
NCL	3	2	1	24	21 *	24.00	-	-	-	-	25	0	130	1	130.00	1-45	-	
Twenty20																		

Career Performances

	M	Inns	NO	Runs	HS	Avge	100s	50s	Ct	St	Balls	Runs	Wkts	Avge	Best	5wI	10wM
Test	3	3	0	34	21	11.33	-	-	1	-	193	108	2	54.00	2-18	-	-
All First	43	61	7	1260	130 *	23.33	4	4	23	-	6634	3148	128	24.59	7-81	5	1
1-day Int	48	35	4	897	115	28.93	2	2	17	-	1898	1347	40	33.67	3-26	-	
C & G	1	1	0	74	74	74.00	-	1	-	-	54	46	1	46.00	1-46	-	
NCL	3	2	1	24	21 *	24.00	-	-	-	-	150	130	1	130.00	1-45	-	
Twenty20																	

~SHRECK, C. E.   Nottinghamshire

Name: Charles (Charlie) Edward Shreck
Role: Right-hand bat, right-arm
fast-medium bowler
Born: 6 January 1978, Truro
Height: 6ft 7in **Weight:** 15st 7lbs
Nickname: Shrecker, Ogre, Stoat, Chough
County debut: 2002 (one-day),
2003 (first-class)
1st-Class 5 w. in innings: 1
1st-Class catches: 1
One-Day 5 w. in innings: 2
Place in batting averages: 292nd av. 5.66
Place in bowling averages: 107th av. 38.17
Strike rate: 59.26 (career 59.26)
Parents: Peter and Sheila
Marital status: Single
Family links with cricket: 'Grandfather
watched Southampton'
Education: Truro School
Qualifications: Level 1 coaching
Career outside cricket: 'Sleeping'
Overseas tours: Cornwall U17 to South Africa 1997

Overseas teams played for: Merewether District CC, NSW 1997-98; Hutt District CC, New Zealand 2000-03
Cricket moments to forget: 'Being run out off the last ball of the game against Shropshire, walking off – we lost!'
Cricket superstitions: 'None'
Cricketers particularly admired: Viv Richards, Michael Holding, Ian Botham
Young players to look out for: Michael Munday, Carl Gazzard
Relaxations: 'Swimming, music'
Extras: Played for Cornwall in the NatWest 2000, in the C&G 2001 and 2002, and in the second round of the C&G 2003, which was played in September 2002; C&G Man of the Match award for his 5-19 (his maiden one-day five-wicket return) v Worcestershire at Truro in the third round 2002. Took wicket (Vikram Solanki) with his third ball in county cricket v Worcestershire at Trent Bridge in the NUL 2002, going on to record maiden one-day league five-wicket return (5-35). Recorded maiden first-class five-wicket return (5-100) v Leicestershire at Trent Bridge 2003
Opinions on cricket: 'The batters are trying to have it too easy. Put the boundaries back out.'
Best batting: 19 Nottinghamshire v Essex, Chelmsford 2003
Best bowling: 5-100 Nottinghamshire v Leicestershire, Trent Bridge 2003

2003 Season

	M	Inns	NO	Runs	HS	Avge	100s	50s	Ct	St	O	M	Runs	Wkts	Avge	Best	5wI	10wM
Test																		
All First	11	15	6	51	19	5.66	-	-	1	-	227.1	46	878	23	38.17	5-100	1	-
1-day Int																		
C & G																		
NCL	1	1	1	2	2*	-	-	-	-	-	7	0	62	1	62.00	1-62	-	
Twenty20	1	1	1	1	1*	-	-	-	-	-	4	0	25	1	25.00	1-25	-	

Career Performances

	M	Inns	NO	Runs	HS	Avge	100s	50s	Ct	St	Balls	Runs	Wkts	Avge	Best	5wI	10wM
Test																	
All First	11	15	6	51	19	5.66	-	-	1	-	1363	878	23	38.17	5-100	1	-
1-day Int																	
C & G	7	3	1	11	9	5.50	-	-	2	-	360	298	12	24.83	5-19	1	
NCL	2	2	2	3	2*	-	-	-	1	-	96	97	6	16.16	5-35	1	
Twenty20	1	1	1	1	1*	-	-	-	-	-	24	25	1	25.00	1-25	-	

SIDEBOTTOM, R. J.   Nottinghamshire

Name: <u>Ryan</u> Jay Sidebottom
Role: Left-hand bat, left-arm fast bowler
Born: 15 January 1978, Huddersfield
Height: 6ft 4in **Weight:** 14st 7lbs
Nickname: Siddy, Sexual, Jazz
County debut: 1997 (Yorkshire)
County cap: 2000 (Yorkshire)
Test debut: 2001
Tests: 1
One-Day Internationals: 2
1st-Class 50s: 1
1st-Class 5 w. in innings: 8
1st-Class 10 w. in match: 1
1st-Class catches: 23
One-Day 5 w. in innings: 2
Place in batting averages: 262nd av. 13.55
(2002 296th av. 9.64)
Place in bowling averages: 4th av. 20.28
(2002 60th av. 29.02)
Strike rate: 38.11 (career 51.51)
Parents: Arnie and Gillian
Marital status: Single

Family links with cricket: Father played cricket for Yorkshire and England and football for Manchester United and Huddersfield Town
Education: King James Grammar School, Almondbury
Qualifications: 5 GCSEs
Overseas tours: England U17 to Holland 1995; MCC to Bangladesh 1999-2000; England A to West Indies 2000-01; England to Zimbabwe (one-day series) 2001-02; ECB National Academy to Australia 2001-02
Overseas teams played for: Ringwood, Melbourne 1998
Cricketers particularly admired: Darren Gough, Chris Silverwood, Glenn McGrath
Young players to look out for: Joe Sayers
Other sports played: Football (once with Sheffield United), 'all sports'
Other sports followed: 'Love rugby league (any team)', football (Man Utd)
Relaxations: 'Music (R&B), films, clubbing, going out with my team-mates'
Extras: NBC Denis Compton Award for the most promising young Yorkshire player 1999, 2000. Recorded maiden first-class five-wicket return (5-27) v Kent at Headingley 2000, following up with 6-16 in second innings for maiden ten-wicket match. Top English bowler in first-class averages 2000 (second overall) with 24 wickets at 12.50. Took 5-31 (8-65 in match) in the Busta Cup for England A v Jamaica at Kingston 2000-01, winning the Man of the Match award; topped tour first-class

bowling averages (16 wickets; av.16.81). Made Test debut in first Test v Pakistan at Lord's 2001 (England's 100th Test at the ground), becoming the tenth player to follow his father into the England Test team. Left Yorkshire at the end of the 2003 season and has joined Nottinghamshire for 2004

Best batting: 54 Yorkshire v Glamorgan, Cardiff 1998
Best bowling: 7-97 Yorkshire v Derbyshire, Headingley 2003

2003 Season

	M	Inns	NO	Runs	HS	Avge	100s	50s	Ct	St	O	M	Runs	Wkts	Avge	Best	5wI	10wM
Test							-	-		-						-	-	-
All First	9	11	2	122	28	13.55	-	-	4	-	222.2	37	710	35	20.28	7-97	2	-
1-day Int																		
C & G	1	0	0	0	0	-	-	-	-	-	5	2	13	0	-	-	-	
NCL	9	6	2	65	17 *	16.25	-	-	1	-	69.5	4	333	15	22.20	5-42	1	
Twenty20	5	1	0	10	10	10.00	-	-	2	-	17.1	0	136	7	19.42	3-20	-	

Career Performances

	M	Inns	NO	Runs	HS	Avge	100s	50s	Ct	St	Balls	Runs	Wkts	Avge	Best	5wI	10wM
Test	1	1	0	4	4	4.00	-	-	-	-	120	64	0	-	-	-	-
All First	60	79	24	624	54	11.34	-	1	23	-	9221	4429	179	24.74	7-97	8	1
1-day Int	2	1	1	2	2 *	-	-	-	-	-	84	84	2	42.00	1-42	-	
C & G	14	2	1	13	7 *	13.00	-	-	4	-	654	432	20	21.60	4-39	-	
NCL	66	35	18	218	30 *	12.82	-	-	9	-	2729	2016	72	28.00	6-40	2	
Twenty20	5	1	0	10	10	10.00	-	-	2	-	103	136	7	19.42	3-20	-	

87. Which former Gloucestershire and Worcestershire batsman features in both the second- and eighth-wicket record stands for England against West Indies?

SILLENCE, R. J.   Gloucestershire

Name: <u>Roger</u> John Sillence
Role: Right-hand bat, right-arm
fast-medium bowler
Born: 29 June 1977, Salisbury, Wiltshire
Height: 6ft 3in **Weight:** 12st 10lbs
Nickname: Silly, Sillo
County debut: 2001
1st-Class 100s: 1
1st-Class 5 w. in innings: 2
1st-Class catches: 3
Place in batting averages: (2002 196th
av. 23.85)
Place in bowling averages: (2002 102nd
av. 34.53)
Strike rate: 67.22 (career 51.25)
Parents: Angela
Marital status: 'Living with girlfriend
Robin'
Family links with cricket: 'Dad played local cricket'
Education: Highbury, Salisbury; Salisbury Art College
Qualifications: 7 GCSEs, ND and HND Graphic Design, ECB Level II coach
Career outside cricket: Graphic design
Off-season: 'Working on fitness, batting and bowling. Catching up with old friends.
Having a holiday in the sun'
Overseas teams played for: Napier Old Boys, New Zealand 1997-98; St Augustine's,
Cape Town 1998-99; East Keilor, Melbourne 2000-01; Hamersley Carine, Perth
2001-02; South Melbourne 2002-03
Career highlights to date: 'First 100 v Derby on home debut'
Cricket moments to forget: 'Whenever I drop a catch'
Cricket superstitions: 'Always bowl in a short-sleeve shirt'
Cricketers particularly admired: Mike Smith ('good advice'), Jonty Rhodes
Young players to look out for: 'JP', Stephen Pope
Other sports played: Football ('social')
Other sports followed: Football
Relaxations: 'Design, music, eating out, coffee'
Extras: Played for Wiltshire in the NatWest 1999 and 2000. Wiltshire Player of the
Year 2000. Recorded maiden first-class five-wicket return (5-97) on debut v Sussex at
Hove 2001. Took 4-35 v West Indies A in a 50-over match at Cheltenham 2002.
Scored maiden first-class century (101) v Derbyshire at Bristol 2002 in only his third
Championship match and batting at No. 9
Opinions on cricket: 'Need more people (spectators) interested in the game. Give the
young guys a go.'

Best batting: 101 Gloucestershire v Derbyshire, Bristol 2002
Best bowling: 5-63 Gloucestershire v Durham, Bristol 2002

2003 Season

	M	Inns	NO	Runs	HS	Avge	100s	50s	Ct	St	O	M	Runs	Wkts	Avge	Best	5wI	10wM
Test																		
All First	4	5	0	98	42	19.60	-	-	1	-	100.5	15	408	9	45.33	3-55	-	-
1-day Int																		
C & G																			
NCL																			
Twenty20																			

Career Performances

	M	Inns	NO	Runs	HS	Avge	100s	50s	Ct	St	Balls	Runs	Wkts	Avge	Best	5wI	10wM
Test																	
All First	10	14	0	271	101	19.35	1	-	3	-	1384	957	27	35.44	5-63	2	-
1-day Int																	
C & G	4	3	0	89	82	29.66	-	1	-	-	96	75	4	18.75	3-47	-	
NCL	1	1	0	11	11	11.00	-	-	-	-							
Twenty20																		

SILVERWOOD, C. E. W.   Yorkshire

Name: Christopher (<u>Chris</u>) Eric
Wilfred Silverwood
Role: Right-hand bat, right-arm
fast bowler
Born: 5 March 1975, Pontefract
Height: 6ft 1in **Weight:** 12st 9lbs
Nickname: Spoons, Silvers, Chubby
County debut: 1993
County cap: 1996
Test debut: 1996-97
Tests: 6
One-Day Internationals: 7
50 wickets in a season: 1
1st-Class 50s: 6
1st-Class 5 w. in innings: 20
1st-Class 10 w. in match: 1
1st-Class catches: 31
One-Day 5 w. in innings: 1
Place in batting averages: 271st av. 10.85 (2002 250th av. 16.64)
Place in bowling averages: 26th av. 24.52 (2002 84th av. 32.83)

Strike rate: 43.95 (career 50.63)
Parents: Brenda
Marital status: Single
Family links with cricket: 'Dad played a bit'
Education: Garforth Comprehensive
Qualifications: 8 GCSEs, City and Guilds in Leisure and Recreation
Overseas tours: England A to Kenya and Sri Lanka 1997-98, to Bangladesh and New Zealand 1999-2000, to West Indies 2000-01; England to Zimbabwe and New Zealand 1996-97, to West Indies 1997-98, to Bangladesh (Wills International Cup) 1998-99, to South Africa 1999-2000, to Zimbabwe (one-day series) 2001-02, to Australia 2002-03; England VI to Hong Kong 2002, 2003
Overseas teams played for: Wellington, Cape Town 1993-94, 1995-96
Career highlights to date: 'Making Test debut. Winning the Championship [2001]'
Cricketers particularly admired: Ian Botham, Allan Donald
Other sports played: Karate (black belt), rugby league (Kippax Welfare), athletics (represented Yorkshire)
Other sports followed: Rugby league (Castleford)
Relaxations: 'Listening to music, watching videos, riding my motorbike'
Extras: Attended Yorkshire Academy. Represented England U19 v India U19 1994. Took 4-45 from 32 overs for England A in Trinidad and Tobago's first innings in the Busta Cup match at Port of Spain 2000-01. C&G Man of the Match award for his 61 and 2-35 v Northamptonshire at Northampton 2002. Called up to the England Test squad in Australia 2002-03 as a replacement for the injured Simon Jones; was himself injured (ankle) during the third Test at Perth and forced to return home. Granted a benefit for 2004
Best batting: 70 Yorkshire v Essex, Chelmsford 2001
Best bowling: 7-93 Yorkshire v Kent, Headingley 1997

2003 Season

	M	Inns	NO	Runs	HS	Avge	100s	50s	Ct	St	O	M	Runs	Wkts	Avge	Best	5wl	10wM
Test																		
All First	12	18	4	152	53	10.85	-	1	2	-	351.4	73	1177	48	24.52	5-63	2	-
1-day Int																		
C & G	2	2	0	17	17	8.50	-	-	-	-	17	2	70	1	70.00	1-49	-	
NCL	10	7	2	102	37	20.40	-	-	1	-	79	12	339	13	26.07	4-45	-	
Twenty20	5	2	1	16	13 *	16.00	-	-	3	-	19	0	137	4	34.25	2-22	-	

Career Performances

	M	Inns	NO	Runs	HS	Avge	100s	50s	Ct	St	Balls	Runs	Wkts	Avge	Best	5wl	10wM
Test	6	7	3	29	10	7.25	-	-	5	-	828	444	11	40.36	5-91	1	-
All First	135	180	36	2175	70	15.10	-	6	31	-	22228	11699	439	26.64	7-93	20	1
1-day Int	7	4	0	17	12	4.25	-	-	-	-	306	244	6	40.66	3-43	-	
C & G	23	11	3	159	61	19.87	-	1	7	-	1193	742	21	35.33	3-24	-	
NCL	99	60	26	527	58	15.50	-	2	10	-	4159	2949	136	21.68	4-11	-	
Twenty20	5	2	1	16	13 *	16.00	-	-	3	-	114	137	4	34.25	2-22	-	

SINGH, A. Nottinghamshire

Name: Anurag Singh
Role: Right-hand bat, right-arm 'all sorts'
Born: 9 September 1975, Kanpur, India
Height: 5ft 11½in **Weight:** 11st
Nickname: Ragi
County debut: 1995 (Warwickshire),
2001 (Worcestershire)
County colours: 2002 (Worcestershire)
1000 runs in a season: 2
1st-Class 50s: 21
1st-Class 100s: 9
1st-Class catches: 37
One-Day 100s: 1
Place in batting averages: 156th av. 29.00
(2002 103rd av. 36.46)
Parents: Vijay and Rajul
Marital status: Single
Family links with cricket: 'Brother (Rudi)
has played first-class cricket for Cambridge Uni and has a Cambridge Blue'
Education: King Edward's School, Birmingham; Gonville and Caius College,
Cambridge; College of Law, London
Qualifications: 12 GCSEs, 1 AO-level, 4 A-levels, passed Law School exams
Career outside cricket: Solicitor at Wragge & Co in Birmingham
Off-season: 'Working at Wragge & Co Solicitors'
Overseas tours: England U19 to West Indies 1994-95; Warwickshire U21 to
South Africa; Warwickshire CCC to South Africa; Quidnuncs to South Africa 2002;
Worcestershire to South Africa 2003
Overseas teams played for: Gordon CC, Sydney; Avendale CC, Cape Town
Career highlights to date: 'Scoring 62 v McGrath, Warne & Co at New Road 2001.
Reaching the 2000 NatWest final. Scoring 187 v Gloucestershire [2002]. Winning the
2003 C&G semi-final against Lancashire and getting to the final'
Cricket moments to forget: 'Losing two cup finals to Gloucestershire'
Cricket superstitions: 'None'
Cricketers particularly admired: Steve Waugh, Sachin Tendulkar, Michael Atherton,
Brian Lara
Young players to look out for: Bilal Shafayat, Samit Patel
Other sports played: Hockey ('college and school'), football ('college and firm')
Other sports followed: Football (Aston Villa FC)
Injuries: Out for four weeks with a torn hamstring
Favourite band: 'Too many to mention'
Relaxations: Reading, socialising with friends

Extras: Cambridge Blue 1996-98; captain of Cambridge University 1997-98. Scored 85 in NatWest semi-final v Hampshire at Edgbaston 2000, in the process sharing with Nick Knight (100) in a Warwickshire record first-wicket stand (185) for the competition. Left Warwickshire at the end of the 2000 season and joined Worcestershire for 2001. Scored maiden Championship century (168) v Middlesex at Worcester 2001, in the process sharing with Philip Weston (71) in a record opening partnership for Worcestershire in matches against Middlesex (180). Scored 1000 first-class runs in each of his first two full seasons of county cricket (2001 and 2002). Carried his bat for 83* v Gloucestershire at Worcester 2003. C&G Man of the Match award for his 74 v Leicestershire in the quarter-final at Leicester 2003. Scored 105 v Somerset at Bath 2003, sharing with Stephen Peters in a record opening partnership for Worcestershire in matches against Somerset (201). Left Worcestershire at the end of the 2003 season and has joined Nottinghamshire for 2004

Opinions on cricket: 'Given the influx of EU players, counties should only be allowed to sign one overseas player. Very few household names are available anyway, so the argument that having two overseas players will attract bigger crowds or more sponsors does not hold water, as they take more money out of the game than they bring in. In addition, the only way to learn is to play. It is one thing having an English player's place taken up by a Glenn McGrath or a Sachin Tendulkar; it is quite another to have a spot taken up by a run-of-the-mill state cricketer from another country who is admittedly maybe slightly better/more experienced than an English player but whose presence in the team serves only to prevent that English player improving. There is only so much you can learn from dominating second-team cricket.'

Best batting: 187 Worcestershire v Gloucestershire, Bristol 2002

2003 Season

	M	Inns	NO	Runs	HS	Avge	100s	50s	Ct	St	O	M	Runs	Wkts	Avge	Best	5wl	10wM
Test																		
All First	16	27	1	754	105	29.00	1	4	6	-								
1-day Int																		
C & G	3	3	0	165	74	55.00	-	2	-	-								
NCL	12	12	0	357	97	29.75	-	1	2	-								
Twenty20																		

Career Performances

	M	Inns	NO	Runs	HS	Avge	100s	50s	Ct	St	Balls	Runs	Wkts	Avge	Best	5wl	10wM
Test																		
All First	95	157	6	4804	187	31.81	9	21	37	-	95	111	0	-	-	-	-
1-day Int																		
C & G	12	12	0	447	85	37.25	-	4	3	-								
NCL	61	60	2	1462	97	25.20	-	10	15	-								
Twenty20																		

SMITH, A. M.   Gloucestershire

Name: Andrew <u>Michael</u> Smith
Role: Right-hand bat ('put bat to ball!'),
left-arm swing bowler
Born: 1 October 1967, Dewsbury
Height: 5ft 9in   **Weight:** 12st 3lbs
Nickname: Smudge, Cyril
County debut: 1991
County cap: 1995
Benefit: 2001
Test debut: 1997
Tests: 1
50 wickets in a season: 5
1st-Class 50s: 4
1st-Class 5 w. in innings: 22
1st-Class 10 w. in match: 5
1st-Class catches: 30
One-Day 5 w. in innings: 2
Place in batting averages: 283rd av. 8.28

(2002 273rd av. 13.14)
Place in bowling averages: 20th av. 23.63 (2002 64th av. 29.54)
Strike rate: 52.07 (career 49.79)
Parents: Hugh and Margaret
Wife and date of marriage: Sarah, 2 October 1993
Children: William James, 9 October 1994; Amelia Lucy, 14 June 1997
Family links with cricket: Father (Birstall club) and brother (East Ardsley club) local
league cricketers in Yorkshire
Education: Queen Elizabeth Grammar School, Wakefield; Exeter University;
University of the West of England, Bristol
Qualifications: 9 O-levels, 4 A-levels, BA (Hons) French and German, PGDip Law
Career outside cricket: 'I will start at law firm Osborne Clarke in September 2004'
Off-season: 'Trying to sort out my bad back!'
Overseas tours: Queen Elizabeth Grammar School to Holland 1985; Bradford Junior
Cricket League to Barbados 1986; Exeter University to Barbados 1987;
Gloucestershire to Kenya 1990, to Sri Lanka 1992-93, to Zimbabwe 1996, to Cape
Town 2000, to South Africa 2001; England A to Pakistan 1995-96; MCC to New
Zealand 1999
Overseas teams played for: Waimea, New Zealand 1990; WTTU, New Zealand 1991
Career highlights to date: 'My one Test match and the 1999 NatWest final
v Somerset'
Cricket moments to forget: 'My batting in my one Test match'
Cricket superstitions: 'I try not to rely on superstitions to bring me good luck'

Cricketers particularly admired: Wasim Akram, Malcolm Marshall, Richard Hadlee, Darren Gough, Jacques Kallis, Adam Gilchrist
Young players to look out for: Alex Gidman
Other sports played: Football, golf
Other sports followed: Football (Leeds United), horse racing
Injuries: Out for five games with a bad back
Relaxations: Looking after the kids ('hardly relaxing!'), crosswords, computers
Extras: Played for Yorkshire age groups. Played for English Schools U19, NAYC and represented Combined Universities in the B&H Cup in 1988 and 1990. Finished the 1997 English season as leading first-class wicket-taker with 83 wickets (av. 17.63). Gloucestershire Player of the Year 1997. Took 500th first-class wicket when Jack Russell caught David Hemp v Glamorgan at Cardiff 2003
Opinions on cricket: 'The game got a real boost through the introduction of Twenty20 cricket, although attendances at the four-day game and the disappearance of some sponsors is worrying. Maybe the green shoots of economic recovery will bring sponsors back to cricket. What's happened to the wicket at Lord's? It used to be a seamers' paradise – now it's a graveyard! If we make wickets too dry and abrasive, the swing sultans will become an endangered species. Let's not shoot ourselves in the foot!'
Best batting: 61 Gloucestershire v Yorkshire, Gloucester 1998
Best bowling: 8-73 Gloucestershire v Middlesex, Lord's 1996

2003 Season

	M	Inns	NO	Runs	HS	Avge	100s	50s	Ct	St	O	M	Runs	Wkts	Avge	Best	5wI	10wM
Test																		
All First	11	14	7	58	17 *	8.28	-	-	1	-	329.5	91	898	38	23.63	5-70	1	-
1-day Int																		
C & G	5	1	1	0	0 *	-	-	-	-	-	41	7	141	9	15.66	4-35	-	
NCL	11	3	2	12	11 *	12.00	-	-	3	-	87.4	8	325	12	27.08	2-22	-	
Twenty20	6	0	0	0	0	-	-	-	-	-	24	0	97	5	19.40	2-14	-	

Career Performances

	M	Inns	NO	Runs	HS	Avge	100s	50s	Ct	St	Balls	Runs	Wkts	Avge	Best	5wI	10wM
Test	1	2	1	4	4 *	4.00	-	-	-	-	138	89	0	-	-	-	-
All First	154	204	61	1744	61	12.19	-	4	30	-	26143	13031	525	24.82	8-73	22	5
1-day Int																	
C & G	33	11	7	53	13	13.25	-	-	8	-	1849	990	49	20.20	4-35	-	
NCL	163	81	49	354	26 *	11.06	-	-	27	-	6875	4747	182	26.08	5-30	1	
Twenty20	6	0	0	0	0	-	-	-	-	-	144	97	5	19.40	2-14	-	

SMITH, B. F. — Worcestershire

Name: Benjamin (<u>Ben</u>) Francis Smith
Role: Right-hand bat, right-arm medium bowler, county captain
Born: 3 April 1972, Corby
Height: 5ft 9in **Weight:** 11st
Nickname: Turnip, Sven
County debut: 1990 (Leicestershire), 2002 (Worcestershire)
County cap: 1995 (Leicestershire), 2002 (Worcestershire colours)
1000 runs in a season: 5
1st-Class 50s: 62
1st-Class 100s: 28
1st-Class 200s: 2
1st-Class catches: 113
One-Day 100s: 1
Place in batting averages: 36th av. 47.74 (2002 55th av. 44.51)
Strike rate: (career 179.66)
Parents: Keith and Janet
Wife and date of marriage: Lisa, 10 October 1998
Family links with cricket: Father, grandfather and uncles all played club and representative cricket
Education: Kibworth High School; Robert Smyth, Market Harborough
Qualifications: 5 O-levels, 8 GCSEs, NCA coaching certificate
Overseas tours: England YC to New Zealand 1990-91; MCC to Bangladesh 1999-2000; 'numerous pre-season tours to South Africa, Caribbean and Sri Lanka'
Overseas teams played for: Alexandria, Zimbabwe 1990; Bankstown-Canterbury, Sydney 1993-96; Central Hawke's Bay CC, New Zealand 1997-98; Central Districts, New Zealand 2000-01
Career highlights to date: 'Winning 1996 County Championship'
Cricket moments to forget: 'Lord's finals'
Cricketers particularly admired: Viv Richards, David Gower, Steve Waugh
Other sports played: Tennis (Leicestershire aged 12), golf, touch rugby, 'Vortex'
Other sports followed: Rugby union (Leicester Tigers)
Favourite band: Coldplay
Relaxations: 'Music, DIY, good wine'
Extras: Cricket Society Young Player of the Year 1991. Took part in Leicestershire record fifth-wicket partnership (322) with Phil Simmons v Notts at Worksop 1998. 'Two Championship medals so far!' Played in the Central Districts Shell Cup winning side in New Zealand 2000-01. Vice-captain of Leicestershire 2001. Scored 110 v Kent

at Canterbury 2001, in the process sharing with Iain Sutcliffe in a Leicestershire record second-wicket partnership for matches against Kent (190). Left Leicestershire at the end of the 2001 season and joined Worcestershire for 2002. Scored 200* for Central Districts v Canterbury at New Plymouth in the New Zealand State Championship 2001-02, following up with 78 in the second innings. Scored century (137) on first-class debut for Worcestershire v Oxford University CCE at The Parks and another (129) on Championship debut for the county v Gloucestershire at Worcester 2002 to become the first player to achieve this 'double' for Worcestershire. Scored 2024 runs for Worcestershire in all cricket 2002. Worcestershire Supporters' Player of the Year 2002. Worcestershire Player of the Year 2003. Captain of Worcestershire since 2003
Opinions on cricket: 'Twenty20 a huge success for spectators and also in helping develop other aspects of one-day cricket.'
Best batting: 204 Leicestershire v Surrey, The Oval 1998
Best bowling: 1-5 Leicestershire v Essex, Ilford 1991

2003 Season

	M	Inns	NO	Runs	HS	Avge	100s	50s	Ct	St	O	M	Runs	Wkts	Avge	Best	5wI	10wM
Test																		
All First	18	29	2	1289	110	47.74	2	12	4	-								
1-day Int																		
C & G	5	5	0	92	44	18.40	-	-	3	-	1	0	2	1	2.00	1-2	-	
NCL	16	15	4	496	93 *	45.09	-	3	8	-	0.1	0	6	0	-	-	-	
Twenty20	5	5	1	54	40 *	13.50	-	-	4	-								

Career Performances

	M	Inns	NO	Runs	HS	Avge	100s	50s	Ct	St	Balls	Runs	Wkts	Avge	Best	5wI	10wM
Test																	
All First	232	359	42	12737	204	40.17	30	62	113	-	539	350	3	116.66	1-5	-	-
1-day Int																	
C & G	30	29	5	701	85 *	29.20	-	4	15	-	24	17	1	17.00	1-2	-	
NCL	188	183	28	4988	115	32.18	1	30	51	-	31	36	0	-	-	-	
Twenty20	5	5	1	54	40 *	13.50	-	-	4	-							

88. The record opening partnership for England against West Indies (209) is shared by Dennis Amiss and which Yorkshireman?

SMITH, E. T.   Kent

Name: <u>Edward</u> Thomas Smith
Role: Right-hand bat, right-arm
medium bowler
Born: 19 July 1977, Pembury, Kent
Height: 6ft 2in **Weight:** 12st 8lbs
Nickname: Smudge
County debut: 1996
County cap: 2001
Test debut: 2003
Tests: 3
1000 runs in a season: 4
1st-Class 50s: 32
1st-Class 100s: 16
1st-Class 200s: 2
1st-Class catches: 42
One-Day 100s: 1
Place in batting averages: 21st av. 52.89
(2002 77th av. 41.30)
Parents: Jonathan and Gillie
Marital status: Single
Family links with cricket: Father wrote *Good Enough?* with Chris Cowdrey
Education: Tonbridge School; Peterhouse, Cambridge University
Qualifications: 11 GCSEs, 3 A-levels, degree in History
Career outside cricket: Writer
Overseas tours: ECB National Academy (England A) to Malaysia and India 2003-04
Overseas teams played for: 'Several Australian club sides'
Cricket superstitions: 'Too many to mention'
Cricketers particularly admired: Steve Waugh, Rahul Dravid
Young players to look out for: James Tredwell
Other sports played: Squash, rugby
Other sports followed: Football (Arsenal FC), baseball (New York Mets)
Relaxations: 'Travel, music, reading, socialising'
Extras: Scored century (101) on first-class debut v Glamorgan 1996, becoming the youngest player to score a century on debut for Cambridge University; was also the first person to score 50 or more in each of his first six first-class games. Cambridge Blue 1996. Represented England U19 v New Zealand U19 1996. Published book *Playing Hard Ball* (about baseball) in 2001. Scored century in each innings (149/113) v Nottinghamshire at Maidstone 2003. Scored maiden double century (203) v Lancashire at Blackpool 2003, in the process becoming the first batsman to pass 1000 first-class runs for the season. Scored 108 v Essex at Canterbury 2003, becoming only the third batsman after Wally Hardinge and Frank Woolley to record four consecutive

first-class centuries for Kent. Made Test debut in the third Test v South Africa at Trent Bridge 2003, scoring 64. *Kent Messenger* Readers Player of the Year 2003. Denness Award (Kent leading run-scorer) 2003. Cowdrey Award (Kent Player of the Season) 2003. Slazenger 'Sheer Instinct' award for 2003. A regular book reviewer for the *Sunday Telegraph*

Opinions on cricket: 'We should try to improve county cricket, but stop running it down. Is the standard really worse than other Test-playing nations? I doubt it.'
Best batting: 213 Kent v Warwickshire, Canterbury 2003

2003 Season

	M	Inns	NO	Runs	HS	Avge	100s	50s	Ct	St	O	M	Runs	Wkts	Avge	Best	5wI	10wM
Test	3	5	0	87	64	17.40	-	1	5	-								
All First	18	30	1	1534	213	52.89	7	3	15	-	3	1	14	0	-		-	-	-
1-day Int																		
C & G	2	2	0	39	25	19.50	-	-	-	-								
NCL	13	13	0	472	122	36.30	1	3	2	-								
Twenty20	2	2	0	65	56	32.50	-	1	1	-								

Career Performances

	M	Inns	NO	Runs	HS	Avge	100s	50s	Ct	St	Balls	Runs	Wkts	Avge	Best	5wI	10wM
Test	3	5	0	87	64	17.40	-	1	5	-							
All First	114	193	10	7334	213	40.07	18	32	42	-	72	59	0	-		-	-	-
1-day Int																	
C & G	5	5	0	72	25	14.40	-	-	-	-							
NCL	41	38	2	927	122	25.75	1	6	4	-							
Twenty20	2	2	0	65	56	32.50	-	1	1	-							

SMITH, G. J.   Nottinghamshire

Name: Gregory (Greg) James Smith
Role: Right-hand bat, left-arm fast bowler
Born: 30 October 1971, Pretoria, South Africa
Height: 6ft 4in **Weight:** 15st
Nickname: Claw, Smudge, G
County debut: 2001
County cap: 2001
50 wickets in a season: 2
1st-Class 50s: 2
1st-Class 5 w. in innings: 13
1st-Class 10 w. in match: 2
1st-Class catches: 23
One-Day 5 w. in innings: 1
Place in batting averages: 275th av. 9.55 (2002 236th av. 18.61)

Place in bowling averages: 24th av. 24.05 (2002 36th av. 26.56)
Strike rate: 41.90 (career 55.07)
Parents: Fred and Nellie
Wife and date of marriage: Thea, 5 September 1999
Children: Rob, 1989; Keeghan, 1999
Education: Pretoria BHS
Overseas tours: South Africa A to England 1996
Overseas teams played for: Northern Transvaal/Northerns Titans 1993-94 – 2001-02
Career highlights to date: 'Playing for South Africa A. Being capped by Notts'
Cricket moments to forget: 'Losing to Surrey in semi-final of B&H Cup [2001]. Losing to Natal in final of Standard Bank Cup [2000-01]'

Cricketers particularly admired: Wasim Akram, Fanie de Villiers, Kepler Wessels
Young players to look out for: Bilal Shafayat, Krier van Wyk
Other sports played: Golf
Other sports followed: Football (Arsenal), South African rugby
Relaxations: 'Spending time with my family and friends'
Extras: Attended National Academy in South Africa. Made first-class debut for Northern Transvaal B v Transvaal B at Johannesburg 1993-94. Took hat-trick (Mitchell, Drakes, Henderson) v Border at East London in semi-final (second leg) of Standard Bank Cup 2000-01; took 3-15 in deciding leg at East London, winning Man of the Match award. Nottinghamshire Player of the Year 2001. B&H Gold Award for his 5-39 (his maiden one-day five-wicket return for Nottinghamshire) v Yorkshire at Trent Bridge 2002. Scored 16* v Derbyshire at Derby 2002, in the process sharing with Jason Gallian (111*) in a Nottinghamshire record stand for the last wicket to win a Championship match (46*). Holds a British passport and is not considered an overseas player
Best batting: 68 Northerns v Western Province, Centurion 1995-96
Best bowling: 8-53 Nottinghamshire v Essex, Trent Bridge 2002

2003 Season

	M	Inns	NO	Runs	HS	Avge	100s	50s	Ct	St	O	M	Runs	Wkts	Avge	Best	5wI	10wM
Test																		
All First	13	21	3	172	42	9.55	-	-	4	-	356.1	78	1227	51	24.05	5-42	3	-
1-day Int																		
C & G	2	1	1	4	4 *	-	-	-	-	-	20	1	101	4	25.25	2-45	-	
NCL	12	4	1	9	5	3.00	-	-	1	-	96.5	6	421	15	28.06	3-16	-	
Twenty20	2	1	0	2	2	2.00	-	-	-	-	7	1	43	1	43.00	1-18	-	

Career Performances

	M	Inns	NO	Runs	HS	Avge	100s	50s	Ct	St	Balls	Runs	Wkts	Avge	Best	5wI	10wM
Test																	
All First	112	145	50	1259	68	13.25	-	2	23	-	19550	9758	355	27.48	8-53	13	2
1-day Int																	
C & G	6	2	1	5	4 *	5.00	-	-	-	-	336	227	13	17.46	4-25	-	
NCL	34	15	3	61	16 *	5.08	-	-	2	-	1606	1199	45	26.64	3-16	-	
Twenty20	2	1	0	2	2	2.00	-	-	-	-	42	43	1	43.00	1-18	-	

SMITH, N. M. K. Warwickshire

Name: <u>Neil</u> Michael Knight Smith
Role: Right-hand bat, off-spin bowler
Born: 27 July 1967, Solihull
Height: 6ft **Weight:** 14st 7lbs ('early season'); 15st 7lbs ('end of season')
Nickname: Gert
County debut: 1987
County cap: 1993
Benefit: 2002
One-Day Internationals: 7
1000 runs in a season: 1
1st-Class 50s: 35
1st-Class 100s: 4
1st-Class 5 w. in innings: 18
1st-Class catches: 73
One-Day 100s: 2
One-Day 5 w. in innings: 3
Place in batting averages: 235th av. 17.25 (2002 210th av. 22.46)
Place in bowling averages: (2002 101st av. 34.25)
Strike rate: 135.75 (career 75.13)
Parents: Mike (M.J.K.) and Diana
Wife and date of marriage: Rachel, 4 December 1993
Family links with cricket: Father (M.J.K.) captained Warwickshire and England
Education: Warwick School
Qualifications: 3 O-levels, cricket coach Grade 1
Career outside cricket: Sports coach
Overseas tours: England to South Africa 1995-96, to India and Pakistan (World Cup) 1995-96; England XI to New Zealand (Cricket Max) 1997-98
Overseas teams played for: Phoenix, Perth, Western Australia 1989-90
Career highlights to date: 'Playing for England'

Cricket moments to forget: 'Being known for spoiling people's breakfasts in the UK by throwing up in Pakistan during the World Cup'
Cricketers particularly admired: 'Anyone who has played for a long time'
Young players to look out for: Naqaash Tahir
Other sports played: Golf, squash, real tennis
Other sports followed: Rugby union (England, Leicester Tigers)
Relaxations: Sport, walking the dogs
Extras: Followed in his father's footsteps when he led the Warwickshire side out against Northamptonshire at Edgbaston in the Sunday League 1997 – the first time both father and son had captained Warwicks. His 147 v Somerset at Taunton 1998 is the highest score by a Warwickshire No. 9. Warwickshire captain 1999-2000
Best batting: 161 Warwickshire v Yorkshire, Headingley 1989
Best bowling: 7-42 Warwickshire v Lancashire, Edgbaston 1994

2003 Season

	M	Inns	NO	Runs	HS	Avge	100s	50s	Ct	St	O	M	Runs	Wkts	Avge	Best	5wl	10wM
Test																		
All First	6	8	0	138	57	17.25	-	1	2	-	90.3	9	408	4	102.00	2-111	-	-
1-day Int																		
C & G	2	1	0	0	0	0.00	-	-	3	-	16	1	67	1	67.00	1-28	-	
NCL	7	3	0	29	14	9.66	-	-	-	-	47	1	212	7	30.28	2-31	-	
Twenty20	7	4	1	24	12	8.00	-	-	1	-	14.3	0	127	6	21.16	2-20	-	

Career Performances

	M	Inns	NO	Runs	HS	Avge	100s	50s	Ct	St	Balls	Runs	Wkts	Avge	Best	5wl	10wM
Test																	
All First	205	289	34	6783	161	26.60	4	35	73	-	28100	13968	374	37.34	7-42	18	-
1-day Int	7	6	1	100	31	20.00	-	-	1	-	261	190	6	31.66	3-29	-	
C & G	47	41	9	671	72	20.96	-	4	17	-	1978	1268	51	24.86	5-17	1	
NCL	219	178	23	3315	111 *	21.38	1	18	74	-	7114	5479	206	26.59	6-33	2	
Twenty20	7	4	1	24	12	8.00	-	-	1	-	87	127	6	21.16	2-20	-	

89. Who became the youngest West Indian to score both a Test century (20 years 230 days) and a Test double century (20 years 315 days) in the 1929-30 series against England?

SMITH, R. A. Hampshire

Name: <u>Robin</u> Arnold Smith
Role: Right-hand bat, slip fielder
Born: 13 September 1963, Durban,
South Africa
Height: 6ft **Weight:** 15st
Nickname: Judge
County debut: 1982
County cap: 1985
Benefit: 1996; testimonial 2003
Test debut: 1988
Tests: 62
One-Day Internationals: 71
1000 runs in a season: 11
1st-Class 50s: 131
1st-Class 100s: 60
1st-Class 200s: 1
1st-Class catches: 233
One-Day 100s: 27

Place in batting averages: 92nd av. 37.28 (2002 112th av. 34.66)
Strike rate: (career 77.28)
Parents: John and Joy
Wife and date of marriage: Katherine, 21 September 1988
Children: Harrison Arnold, 4 December 1991; Margaux Elizabeth, 28 July 1994
Family links with cricket: Grandfather played for Natal in Currie Cup. Brother Chris played for Natal, Hampshire and England
Education: Northwood High School, Durban
Qualifications: Matriculation, '62 England caps'
Career outside cricket: 'Sports tours. Developing my manufacturing business (Chase Sport, Masuri Helmets)'
Overseas tours: England to India and West Indies 1989-90, to Australia 1990-91, to Australia and New Zealand (World Cup) 1991-92, to India and Sri Lanka 1992-93, to West Indies 1993-94, to South Africa 1995-96, to India and Pakistan (World Cup) 1995-96; England XI to New Zealand (Cricket Max) 1997-98
Overseas teams played for: Natal 1980-84; Perth, Australia 1984-85 (grade cricket)
Career highlights: '167* against Australia in an ODI at Edgbaston [1993] – currently still an England record for highest ODI score'
Cricket moments to forget: 'Too many to mention!'
Cricket superstitions: 'Four-leaf clover on the back of my bat'
Cricketers particularly admired: Malcolm Marshall, Brian Lara, Graeme Hick, Graham Gooch, Allan Lamb, Ian Botham
Young players to look out for: Ian Bell, Simon Jones

Other sports played: Golf
Other sports followed: Football (Southampton FC), golf
Relaxations: 'Reading (Leslie Thomas in particular), trout fishing, assembling a good wine cellar, keeping fit; enjoying the company of my wife and children (most of the time!); drinking in my local pub (the Lamb Inn) in the New Forest'
Extras: Played rugby for Natal Schools and for Romsey RFC as a full-back. Held 19 school athletics records and two South African schools records in shot putt and 100-metre hurdles. One of *Wisden*'s Five Cricketers of the Year 1990. Cornhill England Player of the Year 1991-92. Set record for the highest individual score for England in ODIs (167*) against Australia at Edgbaston 1993. Scored a century (113) in Hampshire's victory over the Australians in the Vodafone Challenge match at West End 2001. Awarded an honorary MA by Southampton Institute, November 2001, for services to the institute. Passed 25,000 first-class career runs during the match v Warwickshire at Edgbaston 2002. Hampshire captain 1998-2002. Testimonial 2003 (only the second Hampshire player after Peter Sainsbury to be thus rewarded). Retired at the end of the 2003 season
Opinions on cricket: 'I support the two-divisional system – it encourages more meaningful cricket throughout the season. Younger players should take the opportunity to speak more to experienced players in the bar after the game. This is where you learn your trade – I don't mean drinking five pints!'
Best batting: 209* Hampshire v Essex, Southend 1987
Best bowling: 2-11 Hampshire v Surrey, Southampton 1985

2003 Season

	M	Inns	NO	Runs	HS	Avge	100s	50s	Ct	St	O	M	Runs	Wkts	Avge	Best	5wI	10wM
Test																		
All First	10	15	1	522	92	37.28	-	5	9	-								
1-day Int																		
C & G	1	1	0	13	13	13.00	-	-	-	-								
NCL	7	7	2	257	92	51.40	-	2	1	-								
Twenty20																			

Career Performances

	M	Inns	NO	Runs	HS	Avge	100s	50s	Ct	St	Balls	Runs	Wkts	Avge	Best	5wI	10wM
Test	62	112	15	4236	175	43.67	9	28	39	-	24	6	0	-	-	-	-
All First	426	717	87	26155	209 *	41.51	61	131	233	-	1099	993	14	70.92	2-11	-	-
1-day Int	71	70	8	2419	167 *	39.01	4	15	26	-							
C & G	48	47	14	2377	158	72.03	8	10	22	-	19	14	2	7.00	2-13	-	
NCL	222	213	27	7050	131	37.90	10	42	79	-	2	0	1	0.00	1-0	-	
Twenty20																	

SMITH, W. R.   Nottinghamshire

Name: William (<u>Will</u>) Rew Smith
Role: Right-hand bat, right-arm off-spin
bowler, occasional wicket-keeper
Born: 28 September 1982, Luton
Height: 5ft 9in **Weight:** 11st 4lbs
Nickname: Jiggy, Jigs, Posh Kid, Smudger
County debut: 2002
1st-Class catches: 2
Place in batting averages: 255th av. 14.50
Parents: Jim and Barbara
Marital status: Single
Family links with cricket: 'Brother, Ben,
plays club cricket'
Education: Bedford School; Durham
University
Qualifications: 11 GCSEs, 3 A-levels
Career outside cricket: Student
Off-season: At Durham University

Overseas tours: Bedford School to Barbados (Sir Garfield Sobers International
Tournament) 1998
Overseas teams played for: Gordon CC, Sydney 2001-02
Career highlights to date: 'Scoring 120 for Gordon CC in their Sydney grade final
win [2001-02]. Scoring 38* on first-class debut v West Indies A. But hopefully better
moments will come along!'
Cricket moments to forget: 'Bagging my first ever pair for Notts 2nd XI v
Hampshire at the Rose Bowl'
Cricket superstitions: 'None'
Cricketers particularly admired: Ian Botham, Brian Lara, Sachin Tendulkar,
Paul Johnson
Young players to look out for: Bilal Shafayat, Samit Patel, Alastair Cook
Other sports played: Rugby (East Midlands age group), hockey (Eastern Counties
age group)
Other sports followed: Football (Rushden & Diamonds)
Injuries: Out for three/four weeks with torn ankle ligaments
Favourite band: U2
Relaxations: 'Going out with friends; music'
Extras: Captained Harrold CC U13 to Ken Barrington Trophy (national club
championship – 'a moment I'm very proud of!'). Played for Durham University
CCE 2003
Opinions on cricket: 'It seems to be that no sooner has the two-divisional system
been established than people feel the need to have to change it. Why not have faith in
our system and back what we have now?'

Best batting: 38* Nottinghamshire v West Indies A, Trent Bridge 2002

2003 Season

	M	Inns	NO	Runs	HS	Avge	100s	50s	Ct	St	O	M	Runs	Wkts	Avge	Best	5wI	10wM
Test																		
All First	3	6	0	87	31	14.50	-	-	2	-								
1-day Int																		
C & G																		
NCL	3	3	0	16	9	5.33	-	-	-	-								
Twenty20	1	1	0	1	1	1.00	-	-	1	-								

Career Performances

	M	Inns	NO	Runs	HS	Avge	100s	50s	Ct	St	Balls	Runs	Wkts	Avge	Best	5wI	10wM
Test																	
All First	4	7	1	125	38 *	20.83	-	-	2	-							
1-day Int																	
C & G																	
NCL	6	5	0	41	16	8.20	-	-	1	-							
Twenty20	1	1	0	1	1	1.00	-	-	1	-							

SNAPE, J. N.   Leicestershire

Name: <u>Jeremy</u> Nicholas Snape
Role: Right-hand bat, off-spin bowler; all-rounder
Born: 27 April 1973, Stoke-on-Trent
Height: 5ft 8in **Weight:** 12st
Nickname: Snapey, Coot, Jez, Snapper
County debut: 1992 (Northamptonshire), 1999 (Gloucestershire), 2003 (Leicestershire)
County cap: 1999 (Gloucestershire)
One-Day Internationals: 10
1st-Class 50s: 21
1st-Class 100s: 3
1st-Class 5 w. in innings: 1
1st-Class catches: 70
One-Day 100s: 1
One-Day 5 w. in innings: 1
Place in batting averages: 154th av. 29.05 (2002 266th av. 14.62)
Place in bowling averages: 151st av. 60.81
Strike rate: 96.81 (career 93.75)
Parents: Keith and Barbara

Wife and date of marriage: Joanne, 4 October 2003

Family links with cricket: 'Brother Jonathan plays league cricket for Rode Park CC in Cheshire. Dad loves cricket now, and Mum hates the sweep shot!'

Education: Denstone College, Staffordshire; Durham University

Qualifications: 8 GCSEs, 3 A-levels, BSc Natural Science

Career outside cricket: Director of Capetours – tailor-made holidays to Southern Africa (www.capetours.co.uk)

Off-season: 'Renovating old house and working in Leicester'

Overseas tours: England U18 to Canada (International Youth Tournament) 1991 (captain); England U19 to Pakistan 1991-92; Durham University to South Africa 1993, to Vienna (European Indoor Championships) 1994; Northamptonshire to Cape Town 1993; Christians in Sport to Zimbabwe 1994-95; Troubadours to South Africa 1997; Gloucestershire to Kimberley, South Africa 1999; England to Zimbabwe (one-day series) 2001-02, to India and New Zealand 2001-02 (one-day series), to Sri Lanka (ICC Champions Trophy) 2002-03, to Australia 2002-03 (VB Series)

Overseas teams played for: Petone, Wellington, New Zealand 1994-95; Wainuiamata, Wellington, New Zealand 1995-96; Techs CC, Cape Town 1996-99

Career highlights to date: 'Playing for England'

Cricket moments to forget: 'Breaking my thumb in Australia 2003 and being ruled out of World Cup'

Cricketers particularly admired: Allan Lamb, Jack Russell

Relaxations: Travelling, music, cooking, good food and wine

Extras: Sir John Hobbs Silver Jubilee Memorial Prize 1988. B&H Gold Award for his 3-34 for Combined Universities v Worcestershire at The Parks 1992. Player of the Tournament at European Indoor 6-a-side Championships in 1994. Left Northants at end of 1998 season and joined Gloucestershire for 1999. Scored maiden one-day century (104*) in the Norwich Union League v Nottinghamshire at Trent Bridge 2001, in the process sharing with Mark Hardinges (65) in a record seventh-wicket partnership for domestic one-day competitions (164). Made One-Day International debut in first ODI v Zimbabwe at Harare 2001-02, winning Man of the Match award for his 2-39 (the Flower brothers both stumped in the same over) and brilliant catch to dismiss Guy Whittall. BBC West Country Sports Cricketer of the Year for 2001. Left Gloucestershire at the end of the 2002 season and joined Leicestershire for 2003. Suffered fractured right thumb after being struck by a ball from Brett Lee v New South Wales in a warm-up match at Sydney ahead of the VB Series 2002-03

Best batting: 131 Gloucestershire v Sussex, Cheltenham 2001

Best bowling: 5-65 Northamptonshire v Durham, Northampton 1995

2003 Season

	M	Inns	NO	Runs	HS	Avge	100s	50s	Ct	St	O	M	Runs	Wkts	Avge	Best	5wI	10wM
Test																		
All First	16	23	6	494	54	29.05	-	2	8	-	177.3	25	669	11	60.81	3-108	-	-
1-day Int																		
C & G	3	3	0	56	30	18.66	-	-	4	-	7	0	39	0	-		-	-
NCL	16	15	3	262	39 *	21.83	-	-	1	-	92.2	1	370	14	26.42	3-14	-	
Twenty20	6	6	4	54	26 *	27.00	-	-	4	-	18	0	129	5	25.80	3-14	-	

Career Performances

	M	Inns	NO	Runs	HS	Avge	100s	50s	Ct	St	Balls	Runs	Wkts	Avge	Best	5wI	10wM
Test																	
All First	106	157	29	3734	131	29.17	3	21	70	-	10125	5228	108	48.40	5-65	1	-
1-day Int	10	7	3	118	38	29.50	-	-	5	-	529	403	13	31.00	3-43	-	
C & G	24	20	4	315	54	19.68	-	1	12	-	577	420	10	42.00	2-19	-	
NCL	123	100	27	1627	104 *	22.28	1	3	36	-	3506	2683	105	25.55	4-27	-	
Twenty20	6	6	4	54	26 *	27.00	-	-	4	-	108	129	5	25.80	3-14	-	

SOLANKI, V. S.　　　　Worcestershire

Name: <u>Vikram</u> Singh Solanki
Role: Right-hand bat, right-arm
off-spin bowler
Born: 1 April 1976, Udaipur, India
Height: 6ft **Weight:** 12st
Nickname: Vik
County debut: 1993 (one-day),
1995 (first-class)
County cap: 1998; colours, 2002
One-Day Internationals: 18
1000 runs in a season: 2
1st-Class 50s: 46
1st-Class 100s: 14
1st-Class 5 w. in innings: 3
1st-Class 10 w. in match: 1
1st-Class catches: 199
One-Day 100s: 5
Place in batting averages: 167th av. 26.54
(2002 65th av. 42.90)
Strike rate: (career 78.18)
Parents: Mr Vijay Singh and Mrs Florabel Solanki
Marital status: Single

Family links with cricket: 'Father played in India. Brother Vishal is a keen cricketer'

Education: Regis School, Wolverhampton; Open University

Qualifications: 9 GCSEs, 3 A-levels

Overseas tours: England U18 to South Africa 1992-93, to Denmark (ICC Youth Tournament) 1994; England U19 to West Indies 1994-95; Worcestershire CCC to Barbados 1996, to Zimbabwe 1997; England A to Zimbabwe and South Africa 1998-99, to Bangladesh and New Zealand 1999-2000, to West Indies 2000-01; England to South Africa and Zimbabwe 1999-2000 (one-day series), to Kenya (ICC Knockout Trophy) 2000-01, to Pakistan 2000-01 (one-day series), to Bangladesh and Sri Lanka 2003-04 (one-day series)

Overseas teams played for: Midland-Guildford, Perth, Western Australia

Career highlights to date: 'Playing for England'

Cricket moments to forget: 'Losing to Scotland (NatWest 1998)'

Cricketers particularly admired: Sachin Tendulkar, Graeme Hick

Young players to look out for: Kabir Ali, Kadeer Ali, Gareth Batty

Other sports played: 'Enjoy most sports'

Relaxations: 'Reading; spending time with family and friends'

Extras: Scored more first-class runs (1339) in 1999 season than any other English player. Topped batting averages with 597 first-class runs (av. 59.70) on England A tour of Bangladesh and New Zealand 1999-2000. Took 22 catches at slip in seven first-class matches on England A tour of West Indies 2000-01. C&G Man of the Match award for his 108 v Nottinghamshire at Trent Bridge 2002. Scored maiden ODI century (106) v South Africa at The Oval in the NatWest Series 2003, winning the Man of the Match award and sharing with Marcus Trescothick (114*) in a record England opening partnership in ODIs (200)

Best batting: 185 England A v Bangladesh, Chittagong 1999-2000

Best bowling: 5-69 Worcestershire v Middlesex, Lord's 1996

2003 Season

	M	Inns	NO	Runs	HS	Avge	100s	50s	Ct	St	O	M	Runs	Wkts	Avge	Best	5wI	10wM
Test																		
All First	15	23	1	584	79	26.54	-	4	24	-	2	1	9	0	-	-	-	-
1-day Int	10	10	1	266	106	29.55	1	1	4	-								
C & G	5	5	1	270	164 *	67.50	1	1	2	-								
NCL	12	12	0	246	70	20.50	-	1	6	-	4	0	24	1	24.00	1-24	-	
Twenty20																		

Career Performances

	M	Inns	NO	Runs	HS	Avge	100s	50s	Ct	St	Balls	Runs	Wkts	Avge	Best	5wI	10wM
Test																	
All First	157	258	19	8410	185	35.18	14	46	199	-	5635	3309	72	45.95	5-69	3	1
1-day Int	18	17	2	362	106	24.13	1	1	6	-							
C & G	20	19	1	634	164 *	35.22	2	3	5	-	225	174	3	58.00	1-25	-	
NCL	130	113	13	2776	120 *	27.76	2	16	44	-	234	247	5	49.40	1-9	-	
Twenty20																	

SPEARMAN, C. M.   Gloucestershire

Name: <u>Craig</u> Murray Spearman
Role: Right-hand opening bat
Born: 4 July 1972, Auckland, New Zealand
Height: 6ft **Weight:** 13st 5lbs
Nickname: Spears
County debut: 2002
County cap: 2002
Test debut: 1995-96
Tests: 19
One-Day Internationals: 51
1000 runs in a season: 1
1st-Class 50s: 42
1st-Class 100s: 16
1st-Class catches: 122
One-Day 100s: 4
Place in batting averages: 116th av. 33.44
(2002 39th av. 48.13)
Strike rate: (career 78.00)
Parents: Murray and Sandra
Wife and date of marriage: Maree, 4 March 2004
Education: Kelston Boys High School, Auckland; Massey University, Palmerston North, New Zealand
Qualifications: Bachelor of Business Studies (BBS; Finance major)
Career outside cricket: 'Will wait and see'
Off-season: 'Overseas pro in New Zealand'
Overseas tours: New Zealand to India and Pakistan (World Cup) 1995-96, to West Indies 1995-96, to Sri Lanka 1997-98, to India 1999-2000, to South Africa 2000-01
Overseas teams played for: Auckland 1993-96; Central Districts 1997-2001, 2002-03
Career highlights to date: 'Playing international cricket; Test century; winning ICC Knockout Trophy in Kenya [2000-01]'
Cricket moments to forget: 'Misfielding on the boundary at the SCG in the fifth over and hearing about it for the next 45 overs'

Cricketers particularly admired: Desmond Haynes and Gordon Greenidge
Young players to look out for: Alex Gidman
Other sports played: Golf
Other sports followed: 'Follow most sports except motor sport'
Relaxations: 'Travelling, seeing new places and cultures'
Extras: Scored maiden Test century (112) at Auckland 1995-96, in the process sharing with Roger Twose in a record first-wicket partnership for New Zealand in Tests against Zimbabwe (214). Played in the Central Districts Shell Cup winning side in New Zealand 2000-01. Scored century (111) on Championship debut for Gloucestershire v Worcestershire at Worcester 2002, reaching his hundred with a six. C&G Man of the Match award for his 77-ball 104* (his maiden one-day century for Gloucestershire) v Durham at Bristol 2002. Carried his bat for 180* (out of 293) v Glamorgan at Cheltenham 2002. Gloucestershire Players' Player of the Year 2002. Scored 123-ball 153 v Warwickshire at Gloucester in the NCL 2003 to set a new individual record score for Gloucestershire in the one-day league. Vice-captain of Gloucestershire 2003. 'Qualify to play for Gloucestershire because of my mother's Welsh background'
Opinions on cricket: 'Opponents seem to be getting younger – wonder why?!'
Best batting: 180* Gloucestershire v Glamorgan, Cheltenham 2002
Best bowling: 1-37 Central Districts v Wellington, New Plymouth 1999-2000
Stop press: Scored a 48-ball 85 for Central Districts v Canterbury in the final of the State Shield 2003-04 at Christchurch

2003 Season

	M	Inns	NO	Runs	HS	Avge	100s	50s	Ct	St	O	M	Runs	Wkts	Avge	Best	5wI	10wM
Test																		
All First	15	27	0	903	103	33.44	1	7	15	-								
1-day Int																		
C & G	5	5	0	189	76	37.80	-	2	-	-								
NCL	15	15	1	717	153	51.21	2	3	5	-								
Twenty20	6	6	1	180	88	36.00	-	1	1	-								

Career Performances

	M	Inns	NO	Runs	HS	Avge	100s	50s	Ct	St	Balls	Runs	Wkts	Avge	Best	5wI	10wM
Test	19	36	2	920	112	27.05	1	3	21	-							
All First	127	228	14	7837	180 *	36.62	16	42	122	-	78	55	1	55.00	1-37	-	-
1-day Int	51	50	0	936	86	18.72	-	5	15	-	3	6	0	-	-	-	-
C & G	8	8	1	303	104 *	43.28	1	2	-	-							
NCL	30	29	1	1259	153	44.96	3	7	8	-							
Twenty20	6	6	1	180	88	36.00	-	1	1	-							

SPIRES, J. A.   Warwickshire

Name: James (<u>Jamie</u>) Ashley Spires
Role: Right-hand bat, slow left-arm bowler
Born: 12 November 1979, Solihull
Height: 6ft **Weight:** 12st 10lbs
Nickname: Spiro, Highlights, Younis, Woolly, Basketball Sweed
County debut: 2001
1st-Class 5 w. in innings: 1
1st-Class catches: 3
Place in bowling averages: (2002 97th av. 34.05)
Strike rate: (career 66.50)
Parents: Carol and Stuart
Marital status: Single
Family links with cricket: 'Dad is "chief exec" at Knowle and Dorridge!'
Education: Solihull School; Leeds University ('for three months')
Qualifications: 11 GCSEs, 4 A-levels
Career outside cricket: 'Modelling'
Off-season: 'Bowling!!'
Overseas tours: Warwickshire U19 to Cape Town 1998; Warwickshire to Bloemfontein 2000, to Cape Town 2001, 2002
Overseas teams played for: SA Police, Bloemfontein 1999-2000; Tygerburg, Cape Town 2002
Career highlights to date: 'Five-fer v Yorkshire (nine in the game)'
Cricket moments to forget: 'Colliding with team-mate while fielding for club side. His knee went straight into my cheekbone – sidelined for two weeks!'
Cricket superstitions: 'Don't bowl full tosses and half-volleys'
Cricketers particularly admired: Trevor Penney
Young players to look out for: Ian Westwood, Moeen Ali
Other sports played: Football
Other sports followed: Football ('big Forest fan')
Injuries: Out for seven weeks with a spiral fracture of the little finger
Favourite band: Michael Jackson
Relaxations: 'Friends; Champo'
Extras: Warwickshire U19 Player of the Year 1999. Played for ECB U19 v Pakistan U19 1999. Played for Warwickshire Board XI in the C&G 2002. Recorded maiden first-class five-wicket return (5-165) v Yorkshire at Edgbaston 2002, taking 9-264 in the match
Opinions on cricket: 'Youth is the way forward!'

Best batting: 37* Warwickshire v Sussex, Hove 2002
Best bowling: 5-165 Warwickshire v Yorkshire, Edgbaston 2002

2003 Season (did not make any first-class or one-day appearances)

Career Performances

	M	Inns	NO	Runs	HS	Avge	100s	50s	Ct	St	Balls	Runs	Wkts	Avge	Best	5wI	10wM
Test																	
All First	7	7	3	70	37 *	17.50	-	-	3	-	1330	768	20	38.40	5-165	1	-
1-day Int																	
C & G	1	0	0	0	0	-	-	-	-	-	-	60	33	1	33.00	1-33	-
NCL																	
Twenty20																	

SRINATH, J. Durham

Name: Javagal Srinath
Role: Right-hand bat, right-arm
fast-medium bowler
Born: 31 August 1969, Mysore, India
Height: 6ft 3in
County debut: 1995 (Gloucestershire),
2002 (Leicestershire), 2003 (Durham)
County cap: 1995 (Gloucestershire)
Test debut: 1991-92
Tests: 67
One-Day Internationals: 229
50 wickets in a season: 1
1st-Class 50s: 7
1st-Class 5 w. in innings: 23
1st-Class 10 w. in match: 3
1st-Class catches: 62
One-Day 5 w. in innings: 3
Place in batting averages: (2002 270th
av. 14.00)
Place in bowling averages: (2002 3rd av. 18.70)
Strike rate: 84.00 (career 53.69)
Overseas tours: India to Australia and New Zealand (including World Cup) 1991-92,
to Zimbabwe and South Africa 1992-93, to Sri Lanka 1993-94, to New Zealand
1993-94, to New Zealand (NZ Centenary Tournament) 1994-95, to England 1996, to
South Africa 1996-97, to Zimbabwe 1998-99, to Bangladesh (Wills International Cup)
1998-99, to New Zealand 1998-99, to UK, Ireland and Holland (World Cup) 1999, to
Australia 1999-2000, to Bangladesh 2000-01, to Zimbabwe 2001, to South Africa

2001-02, to West Indies 2001-02, to Sri Lanka (ICC Champions Trophy) 2002-03, to
New Zealand 2002-03 (one-day series), to Africa (World Cup) 2002-03

Overseas teams played for: Karnataka 1989-90 – 2000-01

Extras: Took hat-trick on first-class debut for Karnataka v Hyderabad at
Secunderabad 1989-90. One of *Indian Cricket*'s five Cricketers of the Year 1992. Was
Gloucestershire's overseas player 1995. Represented India in 1995-96 World Cup. Had
match figures of 13-132 v Pakistan at Kolkata (Calcutta) 1998-99, a new best Test
match analysis for the ground. Took 5-140 in the first Test v South Africa at
Bloemfontein 2001-02, his return including his 200th Test wicket (Shaun Pollock).
Retired from Test cricket after India's tour of West Indies 2001-02 but later
reconsidered his decision. Has taken more Test wickets for India than any other pace
bowler except Kapil Dev. Was Leicestershire's overseas player for the latter part of the
2002 season, replacing Michael Bevan, absent on international duty. Took
Championship hat-trick (Ormond, Holliaoke, Sampson) v Surrey at The Oval 2002 and
ended up with 30 wickets (av. 18.70) from his five Championship appearances 2002.
Became the fifth bowler to take 300 ODI wickets when he dismissed Feiko
Kloppenburg v Holland at Paarl in the World Cup 2002-03. His international awards
include Man of the Match v Sri Lanka at Johannesburg in the World Cup 2002-03
(4-35). Was an overseas player with Durham in late April and May 2003, deputising
for Martin Love, absent on international duty

Best batting: 76 India v New Zealand, Hamilton 1998-99

Best bowling: 9-76 Gloucestershire v Glamorgan, Abergavenny 1995

Stop press: Has once more announced his retirement from international cricket

2003 Season

	M	Inns	NO	Runs	HS	Avge	100s	50s	Ct	St	O	M	Runs	Wkts	Avge	Best	5wI	10wM
Test																		
All First	3	5	3	24	13 *	12.00	-	-	1	-	84	24	226	6	37.66	3-70	-	-
1-day Int																		
C & G	1	0	0	0	0	-	-	-	-	-	8	2	26	1	26.00	1-26	-	
NCL	3	2	0	25	16	12.50	-	-	-	-	27	3	97	1	97.00	1-27	-	
Twenty20																		

Career Performances

	M	Inns	NO	Runs	HS	Avge	100s	50s	Ct	St	Balls	Runs	Wkts	Avge	Best	5wI	10wM
Test	67	92	21	1009	76	14.21	-	4	22	-	15104	7196	236	30.49	8-86	10	1
All First	147	191	34	2276	76	14.49	-	7	62	-	28618	14027	533	26.31	9-76	23	3
1-day Int	229	121	38	884	53	10.65	-	1	32	-	11935	8847	315	28.08	5-23	3	
C & G	4	2	1	11	11 *	11.00	-	-	1	-	200	89	8	11.12	4-38	-	
NCL	11	7	2	40	16	8.00	-	-	6	-	533	358	15	23.86	3-18	-	
Twenty20																	

STEPHENSON, J. P.   Essex

Name: <u>John</u> Patrick Stephenson
Role: Right-hand bat, right-arm
medium bowler
Born: 14 March 1965, Stebbing, Essex
Height: 6ft 1in **Weight:** 12st 7lbs
Nickname: Stan
County debut: 1985 (Essex), 1995 (Hants)
County cap: 1989 (Essex), 1995 (Hants)
Benefit: 2001 (Hants; £192,092)
Test debut: 1989
Tests: 1
1000 runs in a season: 5
1st-Class 50s: 76
1st-Class 100s: 24
1st-Class 200s: 1
1st-Class 5 w. in innings: 11
1st-Class 10 w. in match: 1
1st-Class catches: 181
One-Day 100s: 7
One-Day 5 w. in innings: 3
Place in batting averages: (2002 108th av. 35.12)
Place in bowling averages: (2002 14th av. 22.54)
Strike rate: 84.00 (career 58.55)
Parents: Pat and Eve
Wife and date of marriage: Fiona Maria, 24 September 1994
Children: Emma-Lydia, 19 May 1997; Camilla, 30 April 2000
Family links with cricket: 'Father was member of Rugby Meteors *Cricketer* Cup
winning side in 1973. Three brothers played in Felsted 1st XI; Guy played for Essex
2nd XI and now plays for Teddington'
Education: Felsted School; Durham University
Qualifications: 7 O-levels, 3 A-levels, BA General Arts, Level 3 coaching award,
SFA registered representative
Career outside cricket: Stockbroker at Durlachers
Off-season: 'ECB Level 4; part-time lecturer Southampton Institute'
Overseas tours: English Schools U19 to Zimbabwe 1982-83; England A to Kenya and
Zimbabwe 1989-90, to Bermuda and West Indies 1991-92; MCC to Kenya 1999
Overseas teams played for: Fitzroy, Melbourne 1982-83, 1987-88; Boland, South
Africa 1988-89; Gold Coast Dolphins and Bond University, Australia 1990-91;
St George's, Argentina 1994-95; Belgrano, Argentina 1994-95; Victoria CC, South
Africa 1995-96
Career highlights to date: 'Playing for England. Winning Championship in 1992 with

Essex. Captaining Hampshire. Rejoining Essex and winning second division Championship. B&H final'

Cricketers particularly admired: Brian Hardie

Young players to look out for: Alastair Cook

Injuries: Out for four months with ruptured ankle ligaments

Favourite band: The Smiths

Relaxations: 'Watching cricket, reading (*Sunday Telegraph*, *Wisden*), alternative music'

Extras: Essex Young Player of the Year 1985. Captained Durham University to victory in UAU Championship 1986 and was captain of Combined Universities team 1987 in the first year that it was drawn from all universities. Was leading wicket-taker on England A tour to Bermuda and West Indies 1991-92. Carried bat in first innings for 113* and scored 159* in the second v Somerset at Taunton in 1992 and was on the field for the whole game (the first Essex player to achieve this). First Essex player to achieve 500 runs and 20 wickets in a Sunday League season 1993. Joined Hampshire for 1995. Scored 107 v Norfolk in the NatWest at Southampton 1996, in the process sharing with Jason Laney (153) in a then competition record stand for the first wicket (269). Took over the captaincy of Hampshire in 1996, but relinquished it at the end of the 1997 season. Founded the One Test Wonder Club in 1996. Scored 83* v Durham 2000, becoming the first opening batsman to carry his bat five times in the Sunday/National League. Released by Hampshire at the end of the 2001 season; rejoined Essex for 2002 as 2nd XI captain/coach and ended up as the county's leading wicket-taker in the Championship with 48 wickets (av. 22.54) as well as scoring 562 runs (av. 35.12). Recorded maiden first-class ten-wicket match return (3-60 and a career-best 7-44) v Worcestershire at Worcester 2002, in his first Championship match after rejoining Essex

Opinions on cricket: 'Young players are given too much support and information. They will learn the game by standing on their own two feet.'

Best batting: 202* Essex v Somerset, Bath 1990

Best bowling: 7-44 Essex v Worcestershire, Worcester 2002

2003 Season

	M	Inns	NO	Runs	HS	Avge	100s	50s	Ct	St	O	M	Runs	Wkts	Avge	Best	5wI	10wM
Test																		
All First	3	5	1	137	75 *	34.25	-	2	-	-	42	8	162	3	54.00	2-55	-	-
1-day Int																		
C & G	1	0	0	0	0	-	-	-	-	-								
NCL	3	1	1	1	1 *	-	-	-	3	-	13.4	0	77	2	38.50	2-42	-	
Twenty20																		

Career Performances

	M	Inns	NO	Runs	HS	Avge	100s	50s	Ct	St	Balls	Runs	Wkts	Avge	Best	5wI	10wM
Test	1	2	0	36	25	18.00	-	-	-	-							
All First	297	503	54	14546	202 *	32.39	25	76	181	-	22427	12497	383	32.62	7-44	11	1
1-day Int																	
C & G	36	31	1	930	107	31.00	1	7	16	-	1225	965	29	33.27	5-34	1	
NCL	202	180	26	4339	110 *	28.17	4	19	85	-	5815	4605	180	25.58	6-33	2	
Twenty20																	

STEVENS, D. I. Leicestershire

Name: <u>Darren</u> Ian Stevens
Role: Right-hand bat, right-arm
medium bowler
Born: 30 April 1976, Leicester
Height: 5ft 11in **Weight:** 12st
Nickname: Stevo
County debut: 1997
County cap: 2002
1st-Class 50s: 18
1st-Class 100s: 4
1st-Class catches: 53
One-Day 100s: 2
Place in batting averages: 124th av. 32.36
(2002 123rd av. 32.69)
Strike rate: 138.00 (career 188.33)
Parents: Maddy and Bob
Marital status: Engaged to Sue
Family links with cricket: Father and
grandfather played league cricket in Leicestershire
Education: Mount Grace High School; John Cleveland College, Hinckley;
Hinckley Tech; Charles Klein College
Qualifications: 5 GCSEs, BTEC National in Sports Studies
Off-season: 'In Melbourne; resting, training, preparing for a big season next year'
Overseas tours: Leicestershire U19 to South Africa 1994-95; Leicestershire to
Barbados 1998, to Sri Lanka 1999, to Potchefstroom 2001; ECB National Academy to
Australia and Sri Lanka 2002-03
Overseas teams played for: Wanderers CC, Johannesburg, South Africa 1996-97;
Rhodes University, Grahamstown, South Africa 1997-98; Fairfield CC, Sydney
1998-99; Hawthorn-Waverley, Melbourne 1999-2000; Taita CC, Wellington,
New Zealand 2000-01; Ringwood CC, Melbourne 2001-02
Career highlights to date: 'The build-up to my first final at Lord's'

Cricket moments to forget: 'Losing in my first final in the C&G against Somerset 2001'
Cricketers particularly admired: Steve Waugh, Viv Richards, Ian Botham
Young players to look out for: John Maunders, John Sadler, Matt Prior
Other sports played: Golf, squash
Other sports followed: Football (Leicester City), rugby union (Leicester Tigers)
Injuries: Out for the last two months of the season with a broken collarbone
Favourite band: U2
Relaxations: 'Music, spending time with Sue and close friends'
Extras: Received painting from Sir Colin Cowdrey on day of maiden first-class 100 (130 in fourth Championship match), v Sussex at Arundel 1999. Won Sir Ron Brierley/Crusaders Scholarship 1999. Scored 83 v Sussex at Leicester in the C&G 2002, in the process sharing with Trevor Ward (112) in a competition record second-wicket partnership for Leicestershire (171). Scored a 114-ball 125 v Durham at Riverside in the NUL 2002; it was his maiden one-day league century and the highest individual one-day score recorded at Riverside. Included in provisional England squad of 30 for the 2002-03 World Cup
Opinions on cricket: 'A wonderful game. Not enough quality time to practise between games.'
Best batting: 149 Leicestershire v Essex, Southend 2003
Best bowling: 1-5 Leicestershire v Sussex, Eastbourne 1997
                 1-5 Leicestershire v Middlesex, Leicester 2003

2003 Season

	M	Inns	NO	Runs	HS	Avge	100s	50s	Ct	St	O	M	Runs	Wkts	Avge	Best	5wI	10wM
Test																		
All First	11	19	0	615	149	32.36	1	6	12	-	23	5	71	1	71.00	1-5	-	-
1-day Int																		
C & G	3	3	0	54	34	18.00	-	-	3	-	10	0	56	0	-		-	-
NCL	12	12	1	263	65	23.90	-	2	11	-	9	1	28	2	14.00	2-28	-	
Twenty20	6	6	0	83	32	13.83	-	-	5	-	2	0	16	1	16.00	1-16	-	

Career Performances

	M	Inns	NO	Runs	HS	Avge	100s	50s	Ct	St	Balls	Runs	Wkts	Avge	Best	5wI	10wM
Test																	
All First	68	113	5	2962	149	27.42	4	18	53	-	565	333	3	111.00	1-5	-	-
1-day Int																	
C & G	13	12	0	424	133	35.33	1	2	5	-	84	82	2	41.00	2-26	-	
NCL	70	66	6	1694	125	28.23	1	12	29	-	189	143	4	35.75	2-28	-	
Twenty20	6	6	0	83	32	13.83	-	-	5	-	12	16	1	16.00	1-16	-	

STEWART, A. J.   Surrey

Name: <u>Alec</u> James Stewart
Role: Right-hand bat, wicket-keeper
Born: 8 April 1963, Merton, London
Height: 5ft 11in **Weight:** 13st 2lbs
Nickname: Stewie, Ming, The Gaffer
County debut: 1981
County cap: 1985
Benefit: 1994 (£202,187); testimonial 2003
Test debut: 1989-90
Tests: 133
One-Day Internationals: 170
1000 runs in a season: 8
50 dismissals in a season: 1
1st-Class 50s: 148
1st-Class 100s: 46
1st-Class 200s: 2
1st-Class catches: 720
1st-Class stumpings: 32
One-Day 100s: 18
Place in batting averages: 61st av. 42.76 (2002 24th av. 53.64)
Strike rate: (career 167.33)
Parents: Michael and Sheila
Wife and date of marriage: Lynn, 28 September 1991
Children: Andrew James, 21 May 1993; Emily Elizabeth, 6 September 1996
Family links with cricket: Father (Micky) played for England (1962-64), Surrey (1954-72) and Malden Wanderers and was team manager of England (1987-1992). Brother Neil captained Malden Wanderers
Education: Tiffin Boys School
Qualifications: 'Streetwise'
Overseas tours: England to India (Nehru Cup) 1989-90, to West Indies 1989-90, 1993-94, 1997-98, to Australia 1990-91, 1994-95, 1998-99 (captain), 2002-03, to Australia and New Zealand (World Cup) 1991-92, to India and Sri Lanka 1992-93, to South Africa 1995-96, 1999-2000, to Pakistan and India (World Cup) 1995-96, to Zimbabwe and New Zealand 1996-97, to Sharjah (Champions Trophy) 1997-98, to Sharjah (Coca-Cola Cup) 1998-99, to Kenya (ICC Knockout Trophy) 2000-01, to Pakistan and Sri Lanka 2000-01, to Sri Lanka (ICC Champions Trophy) 2002-03, to Africa (World Cup) 2002-03
Overseas teams played for: Midland-Guildford, Perth, Western Australia 1981-89
Cricketers particularly admired: Graham Monkhouse, Graham Gooch, Alan Knott, Geoff Arnold, K. Gartrell
Young players to look out for: Tim Murtagh

Other sports followed: Football (Chelsea)

Relaxations: 'Spending as much time with my family as possible'

Extras: Cornhill England Player of the Year (jointly with Chris Lewis) 1992-93. One of *Wisden*'s Five Cricketers of the Year 1993. Shared in a record fifth-wicket partnership for England in Tests v West Indies (150) with Graham Thorpe at Bridgetown 1993-94, becoming in that match the first Englishman to score a century in each innings (118/143) against West Indies and winning Man of the Match award. Cornhill England Player of the Year (for the second time) 1996-97. Captain of England 1998-99 (though had captained England in a Test match for the first time v India at Madras 1992-93). Awarded MBE in HM The Queen's birthday honours list 1998. Leading run-scorer in world Test cricket in the 1990s with 6407 runs (av. 40.81); leading scorer in Test cricket in the 1996 calendar year (with 793 runs). Made 126th ODI appearance v Zimbabwe at The Oval 2000, breaking Graham Gooch's England record of 125 ODIs. Became the second wicket-keeper (after Adam Gilchrist) to record six dismissals in a ODI, v Zimbabwe at Old Trafford 2000. Scored century (105) on his 100th Test appearance in the third Test v West Indies 2000, winning Man of the Match award and taking part (with Marcus Trescothick) in a record England partnership for any wicket v West Indies at Old Trafford (179); his century, taking place as it did on The Queen Mother's 100th birthday, won him the Slazenger 'Sheer Instinct' award for 2000. Took 200th Test catch for England when he caught Rashid Latif off Darren Gough v Pakistan at Lord's 2001 in England's 100th Test match at the ground; it was Gough's 200th Test wicket. Scored 65 v Australia at Edgbaston 2001, in the process sharing with Andrew Caddick in the first century stand for the last wicket (103) since 1903-04 for England in Tests v Australia. Made ten dismissals in Championship match v Lancashire at The Oval 2002. Made 200th Test dismissal as a wicket-keeper (Kumar Sangakkara) in the second Test v Sri Lanka at Edgbaston 2002 and 200th Test catch as a wicket-keeper (Saurav Ganguly) in the fourth Test v India at The Oval 2002. Became first England player to win 150 ODI caps, v India at Riverside 2002. Won 119th Test cap, surpassing Graham Gooch's England record of 118, in the first Test v India at Lord's 2002. Retired from ODI cricket in April 2003 as England's leading run-scorer in ODIs (4677; av. 31.60). Scored 68 in the second Test v Zimbabwe at Riverside 2003, in the process passing David Gower's career total of 8231 Test runs to move into second place on the list of England's all-time Test run-scorers behind Graham Gooch (8900). Won numerous other Test and ODI awards, including England's Man of the [Test] Series v Pakistan 1996, and Man of the NatWest Series v Zimbabwe and West Indies 2000. Awarded OBE in HM The Queen's birthday honours list 2003. Published *Playing for Keeps: The Autobiography of Alec Stewart*, with Pat Murphy 2003. Captain of Surrey 1992-96, then honorary club captain. ECB Special Merit Award 2003. Retired at the end of the 2003 season and became Surrey's Director of New Business

Opinions on cricket: 'Too many "overseas" players in our domestic game.'

Best batting: 271* Surrey v Yorkshire, The Oval 1997

Best bowling: 1-7 Surrey v Lancashire, Old Trafford 1989

Stop press: Recipient of the inaugural C&G Man of the Year award 2003

2003 Season

	M	Inns	NO	Runs	HS	Avge	100s	50s	Ct	St	O	M	Runs	Wkts	Avge	Best	5wI	10wM
Test	7	10	0	276	72	27.60	-	2	16	1								
All First	13	18	1	727	98	42.76	-	7	36	1	2.3	0	23	0	-	-	-	-
1-day Int																		
C & G																		
NCL																		
Twenty20																		

Career Performances

	M	Inns	NO	Runs	HS	Avge	100s	50s	Ct	St	Balls	Runs	Wkts	Avge	Best	5wI	10wM
Test	133	235	21	8463	190	39.54	15	45	263	14	20	13	0	-	-	-	-
All First	447	734	81	26165	271 *	40.06	48	148	720	32	502	446	3	148.66	1-7	-	-
1-day Int	170	162	14	4677	116	31.60	4	28	159	15							
C & G	50	46	8	1842	125 *	48.47	3	13	57	5							
NCL	186	170	17	4652	125	30.40	7	26	148	14	4	8	0	-	-	-	
Twenty20																	

STIFF, D. A.   Kent

Name: <u>David</u> Alexander Stiff
Role: Right-hand bat, right-arm fast bowler
Born: 20 October 1984, Dewsbury
Height: 6ft 6in **Weight:** 15st
Nickname: Stiffy, Stiffler
County debut: No first-team appearance
Parents: Christine and Ian
Marital status: Single
Family links with cricket: 'Eldest brother, Peter, played club cricket in Yorkshire and is now trying to increase the profile of the game in Germany, where he now lives. Youngest brother, William, played for Yorkshire Schools and North of England Schools at U14 level last year'
Education: Batley Grammar School
Qualifications: 6 GCSEs
Off-season: 'Getting myself on the ECB National Academy'
Overseas tours: England U17 to Australia 2001; Yorkshire to Grenada 2002; England U19 to Australia 2002-03, to Bangladesh (U19 World Cup) 2003-04
Career highlights to date: 'Taking five wickets in the first innings of the third U19 "Test" match v Australia at Bankstown, Sydney [2002-03]'

Cricket moments to forget: 'Losing that same match [*see above*] and the series by 14 runs. My last two years at Yorkshire (2002-03)'
Cricketers particularly admired: Allan Donald, Brett Lee, Jason Gillespie, Courtney Walsh
Young players to look out for: Mark Lawson, Trent Kelly (Australian)
Injuries: Out for eight weeks with a side strain
Favourite band: Radiohead
Relaxations: Music
Extras: Yorkshire Cricket Academy 1999-2003. Played for Yorkshire Board XI in the C&G 2002. Took 5-35 for England U19 in the third 'Test' v Australia U19 at Bankstown Oval, Sydney 2002-03
Opinions on cricket: 'Less games, more competitive games. Less players who are happy just to play county cricket and not push themselves to play for England. More time to train during the season.'

2003 Season (did not make any first-class or one-day appearances)

Career Performances

	M	Inns	NO	Runs	HS	Avge	100s	50s	Ct	St	Balls	Runs	Wkts	Avge	Best	5wI	10wM
Test																	
All First																	
1-day Int																	
C & G	1	0	0	0	0	-	-	-	-	-	30	27	1	27.00	1-27	-	
NCL																	
Twenty20																	

90. Which former Kent captain was England's leading wicket-taker in the 1997-98 ODI series in the West Indies?

STRAUSS, A. J. Middlesex

Name: <u>Andrew</u> John Strauss
Role: Left-hand bat, left-arm medium bowler, county captain
Born: 2 March 1977, Johannesburg, South Africa
Height: 5ft 11in **Weight:** 13st
Nickname: Straussy, Johann, Levi, Mareman, Muppet
County debut: 1997 (one-day), 1998 (first-class)
County cap: 2001
1000 runs in a season: 3
1st-Class 50s: 27
1st-Class 100s: 11
1st-Class catches: 41
One-Day 100s: 1
Place in batting averages: 26th av. 50.96 (2002 40th av. 48.08)

Strike rate: 36.00 (career 48.00)
Parents: David and Dawn
Wife and date of marriage: Ruth, 18 October 2003
Education: Radley College; Durham University
Qualifications: 4 A-levels, BA (Hons) Economics
Off-season: England one-day tour to Bangladesh and Sri Lanka
Overseas tours: Durham University to Zimbabwe 1997-98; Middlesex to South Africa 2000; ECB National Academy to Australia 2001-02; England to Bangladesh and Sri Lanka 2003-04 (one-day series), to West Indies 2003-04 (one-day series)
Overseas teams played for: Sydney University 1998-99; Mosman, Sydney 1999-2001
Career highlights to date: 'Being selected for England one-day tour to Bangladesh and Sri Lanka'
Cricket moments to forget: 'Getting out second ball of the season 2001'
Cricket superstitions: 'Never call Yes to a David Nash call for a single!'
Cricketers particularly admired: Allan Donald, Brian Lara, Saqlain Mushtaq
Young players to look out for: David Nash – 'our middle order has been trying to find him for a while now!'
Other sports played: Golf (Durham University 1998), rugby (Durham University 1996-97)
Other sports followed: 'Anything with a ball'
Relaxations: 'Compiling statistical graphs on opposition teams!'
Extras: Scored 112* v Hampshire at West End 2001, in the process becoming the first Middlesex batsman to carry his bat since Mark Ramprakash did so against Kent at Lord's in 1997. Middlesex Player of the Year 2001. Scored century (113) in ECB

National Academy's innings victory over Commonwealth Bank [Australian] Cricket Academy in Adelaide 2001-02. Appointed Middlesex vice-captain for 2002, then took over as captain following the retirement of Angus Fraser early in the 2002 season. Put on standby for the third Test v South Africa at Trent Bridge 2003 as cover for Marcus Trescothick (fractured finger)

Opinions on cricket: 'The presence of two overseas players improved the standard, but at far too great a cost. I am sure the ECB will come to its senses and reduce the number back to one in 2005. It would be good if strategies were put into place at some stage to help the performance of the players, rather than vested interests.'

Best batting: 176 Middlesex v Durham, Lord's 2001
Best bowling: 1-27 Middlesex v Nottinghamshire, Lord's 2003
Stop press: Made One-Day International debut v Sri Lanka at Dambulla 2003-04

2003 Season

	M	Inns	NO	Runs	HS	Avge	100s	50s	Ct	St	O	M	Runs	Wkts	Avge	Best	5wI	10wM
Test																		
All First	18	33	3	1529	155	50.96	4	8	6	-	6	0	42	1	42.00	1-27	-	-
1-day Int																		
C & G	3	3	0	160	75	53.33	-	2	-	-								
NCL	18	18	0	563	127	31.27	1	3	2	-								
Twenty20	5	5	0	173	60	34.60	-	2	4	-								

Career Performances

	M	Inns	NO	Runs	HS	Avge	100s	50s	Ct	St	Balls	Runs	Wkts	Avge	Best	5wI	10wM
Test																	
All First	81	139	9	5437	176	41.82	11	27	41	-	48	58	1	58.00	1-27	-	-
1-day Int																	
C & G	8	8	0	284	75	35.50	-	3	-	-							
NCL	66	63	2	1572	127	25.77	1	11	10	-							
Twenty20	5	5	0	173	60	34.60	-	2	4	-							

91. This Kent wicket-keeper made his maiden Test century (104) against West Indies at Old Trafford in 1950. Who was he?

STUBBINGS, S. D. Derbyshire

Name: <u>Stephen</u> David Stubbings
Role: Left-hand bat, occasional right-arm
medium/spin bowler, 'very occasional
wicket-keeper'
Born: 31 March 1978, Huddersfield
Height: 6ft 3in **Weight:** 15st
Nickname: Stubbo
County debut: 1997
County cap: 2001
1000 runs in a season: 2
1st-Class 50s: 13
1st-Class 100s: 6
1st-Class catches: 19
Place in batting averages: 30th av. 50.00
(2002 208th av. 22.52)
Parents: Marie and David
Marital status: Single
Family links with cricket: 'My father used

to play in Cambridge, while my brother Jonathan (19) plays his cricket at my old club
Delacombe Park in Melbourne, Australia'
Education: Frankston High School; Swinburne University – both Melbourne,
Australia
Qualifications: Victorian Certificate of Education (VCE), ACB Level 1 coaching
Overseas tours: Derbyshire to Portugal 2000
Overseas teams played for: Delacombe Park CC, Melbourne 1990-94; Frankston
Peninsula CC, Victoria 1994-2000, 2002-03; Kingborough CC, Tasmania 2000-02
Career highlights to date: 'Being presented with my Derbyshire county cap at the
end of the 2001 season and receiving Player of the Year award'
Cricket moments to forget: 'Making a pair of noughts against Glamorgan at Derby
during the 2002 season'
Cricket superstitions: 'No sex during a cricket season!'
Cricketers particularly admired: Mark Taylor, Michael Atherton, Steve Waugh,
Ricky Ponting 'and a couple of Derbyshire players who shall remain anonymous!'
Young players to look out for: Sam Patel, Steve Selwood, Neil Gunter
Other sports followed: Australian Rules football (Essendon Bombers)
Relaxations: 'Chris Bassano fishing adventures; eating, drinking, sleeping'
Extras: Represented Victoria at all junior levels. Spent two years on the cricket
programme at the Victorian Institute of Sport. Scored maiden first-class century (135*)
v Kent at Canterbury 2000, taking part in an unbroken opening partnership of 293 with
Steve Titchard (141*); it was the first occasion on which Derbyshire had batted all day
without losing a wicket. Derbyshire Player of the Year 2001. Scored century (103) in

his first Championship innings of the season, v Gloucestershire at Bristol, September 2003, following up with 63 in the second innings and 93 in the next match v Somerset at Taunton
Best batting: 135* Derbyshire v Kent, Canterbury 2000

2003 Season

	M	Inns	NO	Runs	HS	Avge	100s	50s	Ct	St	O	M	Runs	Wkts	Avge	Best	5wl	10wM
Test																		
All First	4	7	0	350	103	50.00	1	2	1	-								
1-day Int																		
C & G																		
NCL	5	4	0	114	45	28.50	-	-	-	-								
Twenty20																		

Career Performances

	M	Inns	NO	Runs	HS	Avge	100s	50s	Ct	St	Balls	Runs	Wkts	Avge	Best	5wl	10wM
Test																	
All First	56	102	5	2954	135 *	30.45	6	13	19	-	54	77	0	-		-	-	-
1-day Int																	
C & G	3	2	0	63	47	31.50	-	-	-	-							
NCL	50	48	3	999	98 *	22.20	-	4	6	-							
Twenty20																	

SUPPIAH, A. V.   Somerset

Name: <u>Arul</u> Vivasvan Suppiah
Role: Right-hand bat, left-arm orthodox spin bowler
Born: 30 August 1983, Kuala Lumpur, Malaysia
Height: 6ft **Weight:** 12st 7lbs
Nickname: Ruley, Ja Rule
County debut: 2002
1st-Class catches: 1
Strike rate: 66.00 (career 39.00)
Parents: Suppiah and Baanumathi
Marital status: Single
Family links with cricket: 'Brother Rohan Vishnu plays cricket for Malaysia. Dad plays club cricket in Malaysia. Mum scores for Malaysia'
Education: Millfield School; Exeter University

Qualifications: 9 GCSEs, 4 A-levels, Level 1 coaching qualification
Career outside cricket: Studying for BA in Accounting and Finance at Exeter University
Overseas tours: Millfield School to South Africa 1997, to Sri Lanka 1999; West of England U15 to West Indies 1998; Malaysia to Sharjah (Asian Cricket Council Trophy) 2000-01
Career highlights to date: 'Making my first-class debut v West Indies A for Somerset 2002; making my debut in the NUL for Somerset v Durham 2002; being the youngest ever cricketer to play for Malaysia; playing for England through the age groups'
Cricket moments to forget: 'Being bowled out for a golden duck off the seventh ball of the over'
Cricketers particularly admired: Sachin Tendulkar, Wasim Akram, Marcus Trescothick
Young players to look out for: Richard Timms, Bilal Shafayat, Kadeer Ali, Matthew Wood
Other sports played: Hockey (Somerset U16), badminton (Millfield School 1st team)
Other sports followed: Football (Manchester United)
Relaxations: 'Web surfing, listening to music'
Extras: Youngest ever cricketer to play for Malaysia (aged 15 years). Has represented England at U14, U15, U17 and U18 levels. Somerset U15 Player of the Year 1998. West of England U15 Player of the Year 1998. Most Promising Sportsman for Malaysia 2000. NBC Denis Compton Award for the most promising young Somerset player 2002. Played for Somerset Board XI in the first round of the C&G 2003, which was played in August 2002, and for Devon in the third round of the C&G 2003
Opinions on cricket: 'Fast-moving game. There is always action. The game is moving forward.'
Best batting: 21 Somerset v Lancashire, Taunton 2002
Best bowling: 3-46 Somerset v West Indies A, Taunton 2002

2003 Season

	M	Inns	NO	Runs	HS	Avge	100s	50s	Ct	St	O	M	Runs	Wkts	Avge	Best	5wl	10wM
Test																		
All First	1	1	0	16	16	16.00	-	-	-		11	1	44	1	44.00	1-44	-	-
1-day Int																		
C & G	1	1	0	10	10	10.00	-	-	-	-	7	0	24	1	24.00	1-24	-	
NCL																		
Twenty20																		

Career Performances

	M	Inns	NO	Runs	HS	Avge	100s	50s	Ct	St	Balls	Runs	Wkts	Avge	Best	5wI	10wM
Test																	
All First	3	5	0	43	21	8.60	-	-	1	-	156	99	4	24.75	3-46	-	-
1-day Int																	
C & G	2	2	0	80	70	40.00	-	1	2	-	102	60	1	60.00	1-24	-	
NCL	4	4	0	45	22	11.25	-	-	1	-	66	62	2	31.00	2-36	-	
Twenty20																	

SUTCLIFFE, I. J. Lancashire

Name: <u>Iain</u> John Sutcliffe
Role: Left-hand bat, leg-spin bowler
Born: 20 December 1974, Leeds
Height: 6ft 2in **Weight:** 13st
Nickname: Sutty
County debut: 1995 (Leicestershire),
2003 (Lancashire)
County cap: 1997 (Leicestershire),
2003 (Lancashire)
1000 runs in a season: 2
1st-Class 50s: 33
1st-Class 100s: 9
1st-Class 200s: 1
1st-Class catches: 71
One-Day 100s: 3
Place in batting averages: 48th av. 45.40
(2002 70th av. 41.84)
Strike rate: 24.00 (career 49.00)
Parents: John and Valerie
Marital status: Single
Education: Leeds Grammar School; Oxford University
Qualifications: 10 GCSEs, 4 A-levels, 2.1 PPE degree
Overseas tours: Leeds GS to Kenya; Leicestershire to South Africa, to West Indies, to Sri Lanka
Career highlights to date: 'Championship winner's medal 1998'
Cricket moments to forget: 'Losing C&G final 2001 and B&H final 1998'
Cricketers particularly admired: Brian Lara, David Gower
Young players to look out for: S. Jones, T. Roberts
Other sports played: Boxing (Oxford Blue 1994, 1995; British Universities Light-middleweight Champion 1993)
Other sports followed: Football (Liverpool)

Relaxations: Socialising, cinema
Extras: Played NCA England U14 and NCA Development Team U18/U19. Scored 163* v Hampshire at The Parks 1995, in the process sharing with C. Gupte (119) in a record partnership for Oxford University against a first-class county (283). Scored 55 out of Leicestershire's first innings total of 96 v Pakistanis at Leicester 2001. Leicestershire vice-captain 2002. Leicestershire Player of the Year 2002. Left Leicestershire at the end of the 2002 season and joined Lancashire for 2003. Awarded Lancashire cap 2003
Opinions on cricket: 'Need to play less cricket in order to improve preparation and recovery.'
Best batting: 203 Leicestershire v Glamorgan, Cardiff 2001
Best bowling: 2-21 Oxford University v Cambridge University, Lord's 1996

2003 Season

	M	Inns	NO	Runs	HS	Avge	100s	50s	Ct	St	O	M	Runs	Wkts	Avge	Best	5wI	10wM
Test																		
All First	12	17	2	681	109	45.40	1	4	13	-	4	1	11	1	11.00	1-11	-	-
1-day Int																		
C & G	2	2	1	121	89 *	121.00	-	1	-	-								
NCL	9	9	1	219	71	27.37	-	2	2	-								
Twenty20	4	3	0	4	4	1.33	-	-	-	-								

Career Performances

	M	Inns	NO	Runs	HS	Avge	100s	50s	Ct	St	Balls	Runs	Wkts	Avge	Best	5wI	10wM
Test																	
All First	133	209	18	6416	203	33.59	10	33	71	-	441	329	9	36.55	2-21	-	-
1-day Int																	
C & G	12	12	3	522	103 *	58.00	1	3	2	-							
NCL	54	53	5	1311	104 *	27.31	1	8	14	-							
Twenty20	4	3	0	4	4	1.33	-	-	-	-							

SUTTON, L. D.   Derbyshire

Name: Luke David Sutton
Role: Right-hand bat, wicket-keeper, county vice-captain
Born: 4 October 1976, Keynsham
Height: 5ft 11in **Weight:** 12st 7lbs
Nickname: Sutts
County debut: 1997 (Somerset), 2000 (Derbyshire)
County cap: 2002 (Derbyshire)
1st-Class 50s: 8
1st-Class 100s: 4
1st-Class catches: 95

1st-Class stumpings: 4
Place in batting averages: 80th av. 39.28
(2002 214th av. 22.22)
Parents: David and Molly
Marital status: Single
Education: Millfield School, Street,
Somerset; Durham University
Qualifications: 9 GCSEs, 4 A-levels,
2.1 degree in Economics
Off-season: 'Mainly relaxing; some coaching
and lots of training'
Overseas tours: Various Somerset Schools
tours to Holland; West of England U15
to West Indies 1991; Millfield School to
Zimbabwe 1993, to Sri Lanka 1994; Durham
University to Zimbabwe 1997

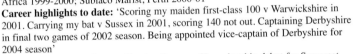

Overseas teams played for: UNSW, Sydney
1998-99; Northville, Port Elizabeth, South
Africa 1999-2000; Subiaco Marist, Perth 2000-01
Career highlights to date: 'Scoring my maiden first-class 100 v Warwickshire in
2001. Carrying my bat v Sussex in 2001, scoring 140 not out. Captaining Derbyshire
in final two games of 2002 season. Being appointed vice-captain of Derbyshire for
2004 season'
Cricket moments to forget: 'Scoring 0 on my Championship debut for Somerset
v Leicestershire in 1997. Losing C&G semi in 2003 by one wicket'
Cricket superstitions: 'Plenty, but it's a superstition to keep them a secret'
Cricketers particularly admired: Ian Healy, Jack Russell, Alec Stewart, Steve Waugh
Young players to look out for: 'All the crop of young Derbyshire players'
Other sports followed: Football (Newcastle United), rugby (Bath)
Injuries: Out for about 15 days overall with a pulled hamstring, a pulled groin and a
broken finger
Favourite band: 'Not sure – it varies'
Relaxations: 'Keeping fit; eating out; going out; and spending plenty of time with
my girlfriend'
Extras: Captain of the England U15 side that played against South Africa and also
played for England U18 and U19. Won Sir John Hobbs Silver Jubilee Memorial Prize
for the U16 Cricketer of the Year in 1992 and the Gray-Nicolls Award for the English
Schools Cricketer of the Year in 1995. Left Somerset at the end of the 1999 season and
joined Derbyshire for 2000. Voted Derbyshire 2nd XI Player of the Year 2000. NBC
Denis Compton Award for the most promising young Derbyshire player 2000, 2001,
2002. Scored 140* v Sussex at Derby 2001, in the process becoming the first
Derbyshire batsman for five years to carry his bat. Appointed vice-captain of
Derbyshire for 2004
Opinions on cricket: 'I actually think two overseas players is a good thing as it does
raise the standard. The issue over EU players drives me mad, but apparently there's

nothing we can do. I think the PLO [Pitch Liaison Officer] system is ridiculously inconsistent and I have no faith in it, but I'm sure the ECB will tell you I'm just another moaning Derby player.'

Best batting: 140* Derbyshire v Sussex, Derby 2001

2003 Season

	M	Inns	NO	Runs	HS	Avge	100s	50s	Ct	St	O	M	Runs	Wkts	Avge	Best	5wI	10wM
Test																		
All First	16	30	5	982	127	39.28	2	2	26	2								
1-day Int																		
C & G	4	2	1	14	13	14.00	-	-	9	-								
NCL	16	12	4	199	83	24.87	-	1	21	1								
Twenty20	4	3	1	42	22*	21.00	-	-	2	2								

Career Performances

	M	Inns	NO	Runs	HS	Avge	100s	50s	Ct	St	Balls	Runs	Wkts	Avge	Best	5wI	10wM
Test																	
All First	54	98	13	2518	140*	29.62	4	8	95	4							
1-day Int																	
C & G	8	6	1	96	45	19.20	-	-	10	-							
NCL	50	43	10	580	83	17.57	-	2	51	6							
Twenty20	4	3	1	42	22*	21.00	-	-	2	2							

SWANEPOEL, P. J.   Yorkshire

Name: <u>Pieter</u> Johannes Swanepoel
Role: Right-hand bat, right-arm medium bowler
Born: 30 March 1977, Paarl, South Africa
Height: 6ft 4in   **Weight:** 13st 9lbs
Nickname: Swanny
County debut: 2003
1st-Class catches: 1
Strike rate: 102.00 (career 102.00)
Parents: André and Johanita
Wife and date of marriage: Tara Jayne, 12 December 1999
Children: Jessica, 6 August 1992; Olivia, 24 December 2000
Education: Paarl Gymnasium High School
Qualifications: ECB Level 3 coach, UCBSA Level 3 coach

Career outside cricket: Cricket and football groundsman
Overseas teams played for: Boland 2nd XI 1994-96; Boland Academy 1995-98
Career highlights to date: 'Took hat-trick v Somerset in C&G Trophy 2002 for Yorkshire Cricket Board side'
Cricket superstitions: 'No – get on with it'
Cricketers particularly admired: Hansie Cronje, Justin Ontong
Young players to look out for: Justin Ontong 'and all young players at Yorkshire CCC'
Other sports played: Rugby union
Other sports followed: Rugby
Relaxations: '[Being] with family'
Extras: Played for South Africa Development XI 1998. Played for Yorkshire Board XI in the C&G 2001 and 2002, taking a hat-trick (K. Parsons, Dutch, Rose) v Somerset at Scarborough in the third round 2002; also played for Yorkshire Board XI in the second round of the C&G 2003, which was played in September 2002. Shared with Michael Lumb in a new record ninth-wicket partnership for Yorkshire in matches against Durham (79) at Headingley 2003. Awarded Yorkshire 2nd XI cap 2003. Plays for Sheffield United in the Yorkshire Premier League. Is not considered an overseas player. Released by Yorkshire at the end of the 2003 season
Opinions on cricket: 'Too much travelling.'
Best batting: 17 Yorkshire v Durham, Headingley 2003
Best bowling: 2-40 Yorkshire v Durham, Headingley 2003

2003 Season

	M	Inns	NO	Runs	HS	Avge	100s	50s	Ct	St	O	M	Runs	Wkts	Avge	Best	5wI	10wM
Test																		
All First	2	3	0	20	17	6.66	-	-	1	-	51	16	129	3	43.00	2-40	-	-
1-day Int																		
C & G																		
NCL	3	2	2	9	8 *	-	-	-	-	-	20	0	100	3	33.33	2-40	-	
Twenty20	2	1	1	2	2 *	-	-	-	1	-	7	0	60	3	20.00	2-33	-	

Career Performances

	M	Inns	NO	Runs	HS	Avge	100s	50s	Ct	St	Balls	Runs	Wkts	Avge	Best	5wI	10wM
Test																	
All First	2	3	0	20	17	6.66	-	-	1	-	306	129	3	43.00	2-40	-	-
1-day Int																	
C & G	4	4	2	59	28 *	29.50	-	-	1	-	216	139	8	17.37	3-9	-	
NCL	3	2	2	9	8 *	-	-	-	-	-	120	100	3	33.33	2-40	-	
Twenty20	2	1	1	2	2 *	-	-	-	1	-	42	60	3	20.00	2-33	-	

SWANN, A. J.   Lancashire

Name: <u>Alec</u> James Swann
Role: Right-hand opening bat, off-spin bowler, occasional wicket-keeper
Born: 26 October 1976, Northampton
Height: 6ft 2in **Weight:** 13st
Nickname: Ron, Swanny, 'recently Sheephead'
County debut: 1996 (Northamptonshire), 2002 (Lancashire)
County cap: 2002 (Lancashire)
1000 runs in a season: 1
1st-Class 50s: 14
1st-Class 100s: 8
1st-Class catches: 54
Place in batting averages: 197th av. 23.66 (2002 98th av. 37.00)
Strike rate: (career 106.20)
Parents: Ray and Mavis
Marital status: Single
Family links with cricket: Father played for Northumberland, Bedfordshire, Northants 2nd XI and England Amateurs. 'Brother Graeme [Northants] still refuses to play defensive shots'
Education: Sponne School, Towcester
Qualifications: 9 GCSEs, 4 A-levels, coaching badge
Off-season: 'Playing in Australia'
Overseas tours: Northants to Zimbabwe 1998, to Grenada 1999, 2000; Lancashire to Cape Town 2002, 2003
Overseas teams played for: Wallsend, NSW 1995-96, 1997-98, 2003-04; Montrose CC, Cape Town 1998-99
Career highlights to date: 'Maiden first-class 100 and first Lancs 100 at Headingley'
Cricket moments to forget: 'My two pairs and the 2000 cricket season as a whole'
Cricket superstitions: 'Bar towel in my front pad'
Cricketers particularly admired: Steve and Mark Waugh, Peter Martin
Young players to look out for: Saj Mahmood, Oliver Newby, Carl Gazzard
Other sports played: Golf, snooker
Other sports followed: Football (Newcastle United), rugby league (Warrington)
Favourite band: Linkin Park
Relaxations: 'Reading, bit of gambling, arguing'
Extras: Played for England Schools U15 and U19. Opened batting for Bedfordshire (with father in Minor Counties game). *Daily Telegraph* U15 Young Cricketer of the Year 1992. Midlands Club Cricket Conference Young Cricketer of the Year 1992.

Played for England U19 against New Zealand U19 in 1996. Released by
Northamptonshire at the end of the 2001 season and joined Lancashire for 2002.
Carried his bat for 84* v Hampshire at Old Trafford 2002, becoming the first
Lancashire batsman to achieve the feat since Gehan Mendis did so v Glamorgan at
Swansea 1988. Scored 112 v Yorkshire at Old Trafford 2002 to become the first
Lancashire batsman to score a century in each of his first two Roses matches, having
scored 128 at Headingley earlier in the season
Opinions on cricket: 'Why not play every game back to back with no rest days? For
half the season it feels like this anyway.'
Best batting: 154 Northamptonshire v Nottinghamshire, Northampton 1999
Best bowling: 2-30 Northamptonshire v Gloucestershire, Northampton 2000

2003 Season

	M	Inns	NO	Runs	HS	Avge	100s	50s	Ct	St	O	M	Runs	Wkts	Avge	Best	5wI	10wM
Test																		
All First	10	15	0	355	137	23.66	1	1	14	-	5	0	22	0	-	-	-	-
1-day Int																		
C & G	2	1	0	20	20	20.00	-	-	-	-								
NCL	9	8	2	116	73 *	19.33	-	1	4	-								
Twenty20	4	3	1	86	56	43.00	-	1	1	-								

Career Performances

	M	Inns	NO	Runs	HS	Avge	100s	50s	Ct	St	Balls	Runs	Wkts	Avge	Best	5wI	10wM
Test																	
All First	72	116	4	3193	154	28.50	8	14	54	-	531	308	5	61.60	2-30	-	-
1-day Int																	
C & G	7	5	0	173	74	34.60	-	1	1	-	18	16	0	-	-	-	-
NCL	36	34	6	685	73 *	24.46	-	4	7	-	18	32	0	-	-	-	-
Twenty20	4	3	1	86	56	43.00	-	1	1	-							

92. Which batsman was recalled to the wicket the following day
after being 'run out' by Tony Greig off the last ball of the previous day's
play in Trinidad in 1974?

SWANN, G. P.   Northamptonshire

Name: <u>Graeme</u> Peter Swann
Role: Right-hand bat, right-arm off-spin
bowler, 'benefit wicket-keeper'
Born: 24 March 1979, Northampton
Height: 6ft **Weight:** 12st 7lbs
Nickname: G-spot, Swanny, Cygnet
County debut: 1997 (one-day),
1998 (first-class)
County cap: 1999
One-Day Internationals: 1
50 wickets in a season: 1
1st-Class 50s: 15
1st-Class 100s: 4
1st-Class 5 w. in innings: 12
1st-Class 10 w. in match: 2
1st-Class catches: 62
One-Day 5 w. in innings: 1
Place in batting averages: 216th av. 21.33

(2002 117th av. 33.68)
Place in bowling averages: 14th av. 23.00 (2002 54th av. 28.51)
Strike rate: 43.33 (career 60.42)
Parents: Ray and Mave
Marital status: Single
Family links with cricket: Dad has played Minor Counties cricket for Bedfordshire
and Northumberland and also for England Amateurs. Brother was contracted to
Northants, now at Lancs. 'Cat is named after Gus Logie'
Education: Sponne School, Towcester
Qualifications: 10 GCSEs, 4 A-levels, Levels 1 and 2 coaching awards
Career outside cricket: Journalism
Off-season: 'Playing as much golf as the weather will permit'
Overseas tours: England U19 to South Africa (including U19 World Cup) 1997-98;
England A to Zimbabwe and South Africa 1998-99, to West Indies 2000-01; England
to South Africa 1999-2000; ECB National Academy to Australia 2001-02
Overseas teams played for: Old Colts, Christchurch 2002-03
Career highlights to date: 'Getting my own parking spot at the County Ground'
Cricket moments to forget: 'Being hit for an enormous six by Peter Such'
Cricket superstitions: 'Never wear a pair of socks that you get a duck in. I go
through far too many socks!'
Cricketers particularly admired: Neil Foster, Devon Malcolm
Young players to look out for: Tim Roberts
Other sports played: Golf, rugby (Northants U14, U15, U16), football

Other sports followed: Football (Newcastle United), rugby (Northampton Saints)
Injuries: Out for six weeks with a broken toe and ankle ligament damage; for six weeks with a broken left thumb
Favourite band: Oasis, Charlatans, Stone Roses
Relaxations: 'Golf, guitar, films, poker'
Extras: Played for England U14, U15, U17 and U19. *Daily Telegraph* Regional Bowling Award 1994. Gray-Nicolls Len Newbery Schools Cricketer of the Year in 1996. Took 8-118 for England U19 in second 'Test' v Pakistan U19 1998, the best ever figures in an U19 'Test'. Completed Championship double of 500 runs and 50 wickets 1999. Had match figures of 9-62 and scored 49 runs for England A v Windward Islands in St Lucia in the Busta Cup 2000-01, winning the Man of the Match award. Scored half-century (77) and had match figures of 3-91 in ECB National Academy's innings victory over Commonwealth Bank [Australian] Cricket Academy in Adelaide 2001-02. Scored 183 v Gloucestershire at Bristol 2002, in the process sharing with Mike Hussey (310*) in a stand of 318
Opinions on cricket: 'The game is great. Cricket committees at certain counties should make a more concerted effort to i) watch games of cricket; ii) know the names of their players. Twenty20 cricket is top drawer.'
Best batting: 183 Northamptonshire v Gloucestershire, Bristol 2002
Best bowling: 7-33 Northamptonshire v Derbyshire, Northampton 2003

2003 Season

	M	Inns	NO	Runs	HS	Avge	100s	50s	Ct	St	O	M	Runs	Wkts	Avge	Best	5wI	10wM
Test																		
All First	9	13	1	256	69	21.33	-	2	9	-	238.2	37	759	33	23.00	7-33	3	-
1-day Int																		
C & G	1	1	0	24	24	24.00	-	-	-	-	8	0	40	4	10.00	4-40	-	
NCL	7	5	0	67	26	13.40	-	-	4	-	49.1	1	224	13	17.23	4-57	-	
Twenty20	5	4	2	50	42 *	25.00	-	-	1	-	17	0	92	5	18.40	2-17	-	

Career Performances

	M	Inns	NO	Runs	HS	Avge	100s	50s	Ct	St	Balls	Runs	Wkts	Avge	Best	5wI	10wM
Test																	
All First	94	139	8	3494	183	26.67	4	15	62	-	15348	7791	254	30.67	7-33	12	2
1-day Int	1	0	0	0	0	-	-	-	-	-	30	24	0	-	-	-	
C & G	10	8	0	179	42	22.37	-	-	6	-	466	364	12	30.33	4-40	-	
NCL	71	56	4	993	83	19.09	-	6	18	-	2217	1799	69	26.07	5-35	1	
Twenty20	5	4	2	50	42 *	25.00	-	-	1	-	102	92	5	18.40	2-17	-	

SYMONDS, A.   Kent

Name: Andrew Symonds
Role: Right-hand bat, right-arm
medium or off-spin bowler
Born: 9 June 1975, Birmingham, England
Height: 6ft 1in   **Weight:** 13st 5lbs
Nickname: Roy
County debut: 1995 (Gloucestershire),
1999 (Kent)
County cap: 1999 (Kent)
One-Day Internationals: 73
1000 runs in a season: 2
1st-Class 50s: 44
1st-Class 100s: 27
1st-Class 200s: 1
1st-Class 5 w. in innings: 1
1st-Class catches: 111
One-Day 100s: 1
One-Day 5 w. in innings: 2
Place in batting averages: 39th av. 47.07 (2002 84th av. 39.00)
Place in bowling averages: 73rd av. 32.31 (2002 141st av. 46.30)
Strike rate: 57.00 (career 73.60)
Parents: Ken and Barbara
Marital status: Single
Family links with cricket: Father played Minor Counties cricket
Education: All Saints Anglican School, Gold Coast, Australia; Ballarat and Clarendon
College, Australia
Qualifications: Level 2 coaching, professional fisherman
Off-season: Playing cricket for Queensland and Australia
Overseas tours: Australia U19 to India 1993-94; Australia A to Los Angeles
(Moov America Challenge) 1999, to South Africa (one-day series) 2002-03; Australia
to Pakistan 1998-99 (one-day series), to Sri Lanka and Zimbabwe 1999-2000 (one-day
series), to New Zealand 1999-2000 (one-day series), to India 2000-01 (one-day series),
to England 2001 (one-day series), to Kenya (Nairobi Triangular) 2002, to Africa
(World Cup) 2002-03, to West Indies 2002-03 (one-day series), to India (TVS Cup)
2003-04
Overseas teams played for: Queensland Academy of Sport 1992-93 – 1997-98;
Australian Cricket Academy 1993-94; Queensland 1994-95 –
Cricketers particularly admired: Viv Richards, Shane Warne, Michael Holding
Other sports followed: Hockey, rugby, football
Relaxations: Fishing, camping and hunting
Extras: Nickname 'Roy' reportedly coined by his father after comic-book character

'Roy of the Rovers'. Born in England, he was brought up in Australia and has played for Queensland at various levels since 1991-92; attended the Commonwealth Bank [Australian] Cricket Academy 1994. In his first season of first-class cricket he scored a century (108*) for Queensland against England on their 1994-95 tour of Australia, sharing in an unbroken fifth-wicket partnership of 205 with Jimmy Maher (100*). Hit a world record number of sixes in a first-class innings (16) during his 254* for Gloucestershire v Glamorgan at Abergavenny 1995; struck four more sixes in the second innings to set a new world record for a first-class match. PCA Young Player of the Year 1995. Cricket Writers' Club Young Cricketer of the Year 1995. Turned down the invitation to tour with England A in 1995 so that he could remain eligible to play for Australia, for whom he made ODI debut v Pakistan at Lahore 1998. Scored 113 off 116 balls and took 4-83 for Queensland v Western Australia in the 1998-99 Sheffield Shield final at Brisbane. Joined Kent for 1999 as overseas player; released by Kent at the end of the 1999 season. Rejoined Kent as overseas player part-way through the 2001 season as replacement for the injured Daryll Cullinan. C&G Man of the Match award for his 5-21 and 40-ball 39* v Northamptonshire at Canterbury 2001. Took 5-18 in title-clinching Norwich Union League victory v Warwickshire at Edgbaston 2001. Man of the Match in the Pura Cup final 2001-02 for his first innings 91 and match figures of 6-65 v Tasmania at Brisbane. Scored maiden ODI century (143*) v Pakistan at Johannesburg in the World Cup 2002-03, winning Man of the Match award; it was the highest World Cup score by an Australian. Also Man of the Match in the semi-final v Sri Lanka at Port Elizabeth in the World Cup 2002-03 (91*). ACB contract 2003-04

Best batting: 254* Gloucestershire v Glamorgan, Abergavenny 1995
Best bowling: 6-105 Kent v Sussex, Tunbridge Wells 2002
Stop press: Selected for Australia's tour to Sri Lanka 2003-04

2003 Season

	M	Inns	NO	Runs	HS	Avge	100s	50s	Ct	St	O	M	Runs	Wkts	Avge	Best	5wI	10wM
Test																		
All First	10	16	2	659	121	47.07	2	4	6	-	152	26	517	16	32.31	3-38	-	-
1-day Int																		
C & G																		
NCL	9	9	2	375	93 *	53.57	-	3	4	-	71	4	286	11	26.00	2-33	-	
Twenty20	5	5	1	170	96 *	42.50	-	1	3	-	16.2	1	130	3	43.33	2-35	-	

Career Performances

	M	Inns	NO	Runs	HS	Avge	100s	50s	Ct	St	Balls	Runs	Wkts	Avge	Best	5wI	10wM
Test																	
All First	163	273	25	10295	254 *	41.51	28	44	111	-	11041	5650	150	37.66	6-105	1	-
1-day Int	73	52	10	1370	143 *	32.61	1	6	32	-	2096	1716	51	33.64	4-11	-	
C & G	15	14	1	486	87	37.38	-	3	4	-	437	308	16	19.25	5-21	1	
NCL	67	66	4	1795	95	28.95	-	10	33	-	1437	1091	43	25.37	5-18	1	
Twenty20	5	5	1	170	96 *	42.50	-	1	3	-	98	130	3	43.33	2-35	-	

TAHIR, N. Warwickshire

Name: Naqaash Tahir
Role: Right-hand bat, right-arm fast bowler
Born: 14 November 1983, Birmingham
Height: 5ft 10in **Weight:** 11st
Nickname: Naq, Naqy
County debut: No first-team appearance
Parents: Mohammed Amin and
Ishrat Nasreen
Marital status: Single
Family links with cricket: 'Dad played club
cricket and brother played for Worcestershire
and Warwickshire'
Education: Moseley School; Spring Hill
College

Qualifications: 3 GCSEs, Level 1 coaching
Off-season: 'Going to Australia to train
and play'
Overseas tours: Warwickshire U15 to South
Africa 1999
Overseas teams played for: Mirpur, Pakistan; Subiaco-Floreat, Perth
Career highlights to date: 'Taking six wickets for Warwickshire 2nd XI'
Cricket superstitions: 'Putting my pads on in a certain way'
Cricketers particularly admired: Waqar Younis, Wasim Akram, Darren Gough,
Brett Lee
Young players to look out for: Moeen Ali
Other sports played: Football
Other sports followed: Football (Man Utd)
Injuries: Stress fracture of the left shin
Relaxations: 'Watching TV; PlayStation 2'
Extras: Scored 103 in a 20-over match, setting a record for Moseley Ashfield U15.
Has been Moseley Ashfield U15 Player of the Year, Warwickshire U15 Youth Player of
the Year and top wicket-taker for Warwickshire U16. Warwickshire U19 Players'
Player of the Year. Warwickshire U19 Player of the Year (Coney Edmonds Trophy)
Opinions on cricket: 'The game is more competitive now.'

TAYLOR, B. V. Hampshire

Name: <u>Billy</u> Victor Taylor
Role: Left-hand bat, right-arm medium-fast bowler
Born: 11 January 1977, Southampton
Height: 6ft 3in **Weight:** 14st
Nickname: Crusty, BT, Howzat
County debut: 1999 (Sussex)
1st-Class 5 w. in innings: 1
1st-Class catches: 2
One-Day 5 w. in innings: 1
Place in batting averages: (2002 312th av. 5.83)
Place in bowling averages: 58th av. 29.60 (2002 81st av. 32.53)
Strike rate: 63.69 (career 65.80)
Parents: Jackie and Victor
Marital status: Single
Family links with cricket: Brother James plays for Wiltshire CCC
Education: Bitterne Park; Southampton Tech College; Sparsholt College, Hampshire
Qualifications: 5 GCSEs, NVQ Level 2 Carpentry and Joinery, NTPC Tree Surgery, Level 2 coaching
Career outside cricket: 'Probably tree surgery'
Off-season: 'Just recovering from season, and then in the gym to get ready for oncoming season'
Overseas tours: Sussex/Hampshire to Cyprus 1999; Sussex to Grenada 2002
Overseas teams played for: Central Hawke's Bay, New Zealand 1996-97; Manawatu Foxton CC and Horowhenua rep team, New Zealand 1998-99, 2000-01; Te Puke 2002
Career highlights to date: 'Winning the County Championship in 2003 with Sussex'
Cricket moments to forget: 'Probably holding the fastest pair in 2003. It took half an hour for me to bag them; 25 minutes of that was sitting in the changing room'
Cricket superstitions: 'Always kiss whalebone carving around neck'
Cricketers particularly admired: Malcolm Marshall, Robin Smith, Mushtaq Ahmed
Other sports played: Golf
Other sports followed: Football (Havant & Waterlooville)
Injuries: Out for five weeks with a bad strain in left thigh muscle
Favourite band: Dido
Relaxations: 'Golf, swimming, watching football'
Extras: Played for Wiltshire in Minor Counties cricket 1996-98 and in the NatWest 1999. Took 98 wickets in New Zealand club cricket in 1998-99. Sussex 2nd XI Player of the Year 1999, 2000. Took hat-trick (Ormond, Sampson, Giddins) v Surrey at Hove

in the B&H and another (G. Flower, Maddy, Malcolm) v Leicestershire at Leicester in the C&G 2002. Scored career best 35* v Middlesex at Hove 2003, sharing with Mark Davis (168) in a record tenth-wicket partnership for Sussex in matches against Middlesex (106). Left Sussex at the end of the 2003 season and has joined Hampshire for 2004

Opinions on cricket: 'Should shorten the Championship and play more Twenty20 matches – that's really what people want to come and watch. Championship should be 90 overs, two-hour sessions; start at ten o'clock, with new ball at 80 overs.'
Best batting: 35* Sussex v Middlesex, Hove 2003
Best bowling: 5-90 Sussex v Warwickshire, Hove 2002

2003 Season

	M	Inns	NO	Runs	HS	Avge	100s	50s	Ct	St	O	M	Runs	Wkts	Avge	Best	5wI	10wM
Test																		
All First	8	7	4	55	35 *	18.33	-	-	-	-	244.1	69	681	23	29.60	4-42	-	-
1-day Int																		
C & G	2	0	0	0	0	-	-	-	-	-	20	1	99	4	24.75	2-47	-	
NCL	14	9	5	33	13 *	8.25	-	-	2	-	109.1	6	578	17	34.00	3-25	-	
Twenty20																		

Career Performances

	M	Inns	NO	Runs	HS	Avge	100s	50s	Ct	St	Balls	Runs	Wkts	Avge	Best	5wI	10wM
Test																	
All First	28	32	11	183	35 *	8.71	-	-	2	-	4672	2493	71	35.11	5-90	1	-
1-day Int																	
C & G	9	1	0	1	1	1.00	-	-	1	-	498	344	17	20.23	4-26	-	
NCL	60	31	13	120	21 *	6.66	-	-	11	-	2553	1928	77	25.03	4-22	-	
Twenty20																	

TAYLOR, C. G.   Gloucestershire

Name: Christopher (<u>Chris</u>) Glyn Taylor
Role: Right-hand bat, right-arm off-spin bowler, county four-day captain
Born: 27 September 1976, Bristol
Height: 5ft 8in **Weight:** 10st
Nickname: Tales, Tootsie
County debut: 2000
County cap: 2001
1st-Class 50s: 6
1st-Class 100s: 5
1st-Class catches: 32
Place in batting averages: 215th av. 21.37 (2002 184th av. 24.59)
Strike rate: (career 97.00)

Parents: Chris and Maggie
Wife and date of marriage: Sarah,
8 December 2001
Family links with cricket: Father and
grandfather both played local club cricket
Education: Colston's Collegiate School
Qualifications: GCSEs and A-levels
Career outside cricket: Teaching
Overseas teams played for: Harbord CC,
Manly, Australia 2000
Cricket moments to forget: 'B&H loss to
Surrey at Lord's [2001]'
Cricketers particularly admired:
Jonty Rhodes, Mark Waugh
Other sports played: Rugby, hockey (both
county level); squash, tennis
Other sports followed: Rugby
Relaxations: Fishing

Extras: Represented England Schools U18. In 1995 won the Cricket Society's
A. A. Thomson Fielding Prize and Wetherell Award for Leading All-rounder in English
Schools Cricket. Set school record of 278* v Hutton Grammar School. Made his
highest score of 300* for Gloucestershire 2nd XI v Somerset 2nd XI at Taunton 1999.
Scored maiden first-class century (104) in the Championship match v Middlesex 2000,
becoming the first player from any county to score a century at Lord's on
Championship debut; also the first player to score a century for Gloucestershire in
match that was both first-class and Championship debut. NBC Denis Compton Award
for the most promising young Gloucestershire player 2000. His 196 v Nottinghamshire
at Trent Bridge 2001 included 100 runs scored between lunch and tea on the first day.
Appointed four-day captain of Gloucestershire for 2004
Best batting: 196 Gloucestershire v Nottinghamshire, Trent Bridge 2001
Best bowling: 3-126 Gloucestershire v Northamptonshire, Cheltenham 2000

2003 Season

	M	Inns	NO	Runs	HS	Avge	100s	50s	Ct	St	O	M	Runs	Wkts	Avge	Best	5wl	10wM
Test																		
All First	4	8	0	171	45	21.37	-	-	3	-	11	0	48	0	-	-	-	-
1-day Int																		
C & G																		
NCL	4	3	1	67	47	33.50	-	-	1	1								
Twenty20	5	4	1	74	36	24.66	-	-	2	-	1	0	11	0	-	-	-	

Career Performances

	M	Inns	NO	Runs	HS	Avge	100s	50s	Ct	St	Balls	Runs	Wkts	Avge	Best	5wI	10wM
Test																	
All First	43	79	5	2257	196	30.50	5	6	32	-	291	220	3	73.33	3-126	-	-
1-day Int																	
C & G	11	10	3	154	41	22.00	-	-	7	-							
NCL	36	29	4	350	63 *	14.00	-	1	8	1							
Twenty20	5	4	1	74	36	24.66	-	-	2	-	6	11	0	-		-	-

TAYLOR, C. R.   *Yorkshire*

Name: Christopher (<u>Chris</u>) Robert Taylor
Role: Right-hand opening bat, right-arm fast-medium bowler
Born: 21 February 1981, Leeds
Height: 6ft 4in **Weight:** 14st 6lbs
Nickname: CT
County debut: 2001
1st-Class 50s: 2
1st-Class catches: 6
Place in batting averages: (2002 235th av. 18.75)
Parents: Phil and Elaine
Marital status: Single
Family links with cricket: 'Brother Matthew plays in Bradford League for Drighlington. Dad slogged a few in Dales Council League. Mum gives good throw-downs in back garden!'
Education: Benton Park High School, Leeds
Qualifications: 9 GCSEs, 4 A-levels
Off-season: 'Uni and playing in Sydney'
Overseas tours: Yorkshire to Grenada 2002
Overseas teams played for: Western Suburbs Magpies, Sydney 1999-2003
Career highlights to date: 'To have played in County Championship winning team 2001. On a personal note, my maiden first-class half-century v Surrey at Headingley, April 2002' (*A 3¼-hour rearguard action of 52**)
Cricket moments to forget: 'To have bagged 'em in my first Roses match v Lancashire, which also just happened to be my first game live on Sky TV (I turned my phone off for a week after it!)'
Cricket superstitions: 'Always have two pieces of chewing gum and always wet my face before going out to bat'

Cricketers particularly admired: Geoffrey Boycott, Michael Vaughan, Damien Martyn

Young players to look out for: Michael Clarke (NSW), Steve Phillips (NSW), Mark Lawson

Other sports played: Rugby, football, tennis, basketball (all for Benton Park HS 1st teams)

Other sports followed: Football (Everton – 'since I was four years old'), 'enjoy watching all sports'

Injuries: Out for three weeks with a hernia

Favourite band: Matchbox Twenty

Relaxations: 'Going to beaches in Sydney; "Townhouse" and "Creation"; swilling; training at gym'

Extras: Represented Yorkshire U10-U17. Represented North of England at Bunbury Festival 1996 and was awarded Neil Lloyd Trophy for top run-scorer in festival. Selected for England U15 team for Lombard World Cup 1996. Has also represented England U17 and U19. Yorkshire CCC Supporters' Club Young Player of the Year 1999. Awarded Yorkshire 2nd XI cap 2001

Opinions on cricket: 'What about the ECB allowing two genuine English players per county instead of one! Laws have to be brought in to stop foreigners who qualify to be English by the fact they have a Greek great uncle. Pitches need to improve. Great game, though.'

Best batting: 52* Yorkshire v Surrey, Headingley 2002

2003 Season

	M	Inns	NO	Runs	HS	Avge	100s	50s	Ct	St	O	M	Runs	Wkts	Avge	Best	5wl	10wM
Test																		
All First	3	5	0	87	40	17.40	-	-	1	-								
1-day Int																		
C & G																		
NCL	1	1	0	28	28	28.00	-	-	-	-								
Twenty20																		

Career Performances

	M	Inns	NO	Runs	HS	Avge	100s	50s	Ct	St	Balls	Runs	Wkts	Avge	Best	5wl	10wM
Test																	
All First	11	20	1	297	52 *	15.63	-	2	6	-							
1-day Int																	
C & G																	
NCL	1	1	0	28	28	28.00	-	-	-	-							
Twenty20																	

TAYLOR, D. K. Worcestershire

Name: <u>David</u> Kenneth Taylor
Role: Left-hand opening bat, right-arm medium bowler
Born: 17 December 1974, Oxford
Height: 6ft 1in **Weight:** 16st
Nickname: The DT
County debut: 2003 (one-day)
One-Day 100s: 1
Parents: Mike and Pat
Marital status: Engaged
Children: Josh, 5 October 1991; Lochie, 2 November 1999
Education: Kent St High School, Perth, Western Australia (cricket scholarship)
Career outside cricket: Contracts manager for building company
Off-season: 'With my family'
Career highlights to date: 'Playing my debut for Worcester and getting man of the match'
Cricket moments to forget: 'Being run out while using a runner and going out to bat without my thigh pad in a 2nd XI game against Warwickshire 2nd XI'
Cricket superstitions: 'None'
Cricketers particularly admired: Viv Richards, Ian Botham
Other sports followed: Aussie Rules football (West Coast Eagles)
Favourite band: Bon Jovi
Extras: Played for Buckinghamshire in the first and second rounds of the C&G 2003, which were played in August/September 2002; Man of the Match award for his 140 v Suffolk at Dinton in the first round. Joined Worcestershire on short-term contract in 2003. Scored 20-ball 46 on county debut v Northamptonshire at Worcester in the Twenty20 2003, winning Man of the Match award. Broke batting record in Home Counties Premier League in 2003. Released by Worcestershire at the end of the 2003 season

2003 Season

	M	Inns	NO	Runs	HS	Avge	100s	50s	Ct	St	O	M	Runs	Wkts	Avge	Best	5wI	10wM
Test																		
All First																		
1-day Int																		
C & G																		
NCL	1	1	0	7	7	7.00	-	-	-	-								
Twenty20	4	4	0	53	46	13.25	-	-	2	-								

Career Performances

	M	Inns	NO	Runs	HS	Avge	100s	50s	Ct	St	Balls	Runs	Wkts	Avge	Best	5wI	10wM
Test																	
All First																	
1-day Int																	
C & G	2	2	0	154	140	77.00	1	-	1	-							
NCL	1	1	0	7	7	7.00	-	-	-	-							
Twenty20	4	4	0	53	46	13.25	-	-	2	-							

TAYLOR, S. A. Warwickshire

Name: Stephen (<u>Steve</u>) Andrew Taylor
Role: Right-hand bat, right-arm fast bowler
Born: 17 December 1985, Shrewsbury
Height: 6ft 3in **Weight:** 12st
Nickname: Tails
County debut: No first-team appearance
Parents: Paul and Sue
Marital status: Single
Education: Charlton School, Telford
Qualifications: 9 GCSEs, 2 AS-levels,
Level 1 coaching
Career highlights to date: 'Getting
professional contract'
Cricket moments to forget: 'Being relegated
from the Birmingham League after one
season'
Cricketers particularly admired:
Andrew Flintoff, Nick Knight
Young players to look out for: 'All Warwickshire youngsters'
Other sports played: Football (county)
Other sports followed: Football (Telford United FC)
Favourite band: Stereophonics
Relaxations: 'Socialising'
Opinions on cricket: 'Need to improve crowds/interest in game – make the game
appeal to more people.'

Name: <u>Ryan</u> Neil ten Doeschate
Role: Right-hand bat, right-arm medium-fast bowler
Born: 30 June 1980, Port Elizabeth, South Africa
Height: 5ft 11in **Weight:** 12st 8lbs
Nickname: Tendo
County debut: 2003
1st-Class catches: 1
Parents: Boudewyn and Ingrid
Marital status: Single
Education: Fairbairn College; University of Cape Town
Qualifications: Business science degree
Off-season: 'Playing cricket in South Africa'
Overseas teams played for: Western Province; Western Province B; Bloemendaal, Holland 2002-03
Cricket moments to forget: 'My county debut at Chelmsford'
Cricketers particularly admired: Jacques Kallis, Kepler Wessels
Young players to look out for: Jono Maclean
Other sports played: Rugby
Other sports followed: Football (Arsenal), rugby (Stormers)
Favourite band: Phil Collins
Relaxations: Golf, tennis, reading
Extras: Is not considered an overseas player
Best batting: 31 Essex v Sussex, Arundel 2003

2003 Season

	M	Inns	NO	Runs	HS	Avge	100s	50s	Ct	St	O	M	Runs	Wkts	Avge	Best	5wI	10wM
Test																		
All First	2	4	0	48	31	12.00	-	-	1	-	24	3	122	0	-		-	-	-
1-day Int																		
C & G																			
NCL	1	0	0	0	0	-	-	-	-	-	8	0	39	1	39.00	1-39	-
Twenty20	5	2	0	9	6	4.50	-	-	1	-	18.1	0	147	5	29.40	2-27	-

Career Performances

	M	Inns	NO	Runs	HS	Avge	100s	50s	Ct	St	Balls	Runs	Wkts	Avge	Best	5wI	10wM
Test																	
All First	2	4	0	48	31	12.00	-	-	1	-	144	122	0	-	-	-	-
1-day Int																	
C & G																	
NCL	1	0	0	0	0	-	-	-	-	-	48	39	1	39.00	1-39	-	
Twenty20	5	2	0	9	6	4.50	-	-	1	-	109	147	5	29.40	2-27	-	

THOMAS, A. C.   Nottinghamshire

Name: <u>Aaron</u> Courteney Thomas
Role: Right-hand bat, wicket-keeper
Born: 6 May 1985, Edmonton, London
Height: 5ft 11in **Weight:** 12st 4lbs
Nickname: Ridley
County debut: 2003
1st-Class catches: 1
Parents: Sharon and Patric
Marital status: Single
Family links with cricket: 'Dad plays local cricket for West Indian Cavaliers'
Education: Arnold Hill School and Sixth Form, Nottingham
Qualifications: 10 GCSEs, 3 A-levels
Career outside cricket: Student
Off-season: 'Improving all aspects of my game; going to Australia and Pakistan to play cricket'
Overseas tours: ACE to Pakistan 2003-04
Overseas teams played for: Macquarie University, Sydney 2003-04
Career highlights to date: 'Making my first-class debut and taking my first first-class catch (Shiv Das, India A)'
Cricket moments to forget: 'None really. I enjoy playing the great game and hope that I learn from any mistakes I may make (any dropped catch, missed stumping or any time I do not make runs)'
Cricket superstitions: 'None'
Cricketers particularly admired: Sachin Tendulkar, Adam Gilchrist, 'any cricket player who reaches the highest level, performs and stays there for an extended period of time'
Young players to look out for: Bilal Shafayat, Kimany Gregoire
Other sports played: 'All sports'

Other sports followed: Football (Tottenham), 'have an interest in most sports'
Favourite band: 'All R&B and Hip Hop'
Relaxations: 'Going out; spending time with family and friends; all sports; ACN (my business) and property'
Extras: U15 Wicket-keeper of the Tournament at Ampleforth Cricket Festival playing for Notts U15 2000. Made domestic one-day debut aged 15 in the C&G 2001 playing for Nottinghamshire Board XI; also played for Notts Board XI in the C&G 2002. Played for ECB U18 2003
Opinions on cricket: 'If young players are good enough they are old enough and should be given a chance to prove themselves. More should be done to encourage the sport in schools.'

2003 Season

	M	Inns	NO	Runs	HS	Avge	100s	50s	Ct	St	O	M	Runs	Wkts	Avge	Best	5wl	10wM
Test																		
All First	1	0	0	0	0	-	-	-	1	-								
1-day Int																		
C & G																		
NCL																		
Twenty20																		

Career Performances

	M	Inns	NO	Runs	HS	Avge	100s	50s	Ct	St	Balls	Runs	Wkts	Avge	Best	5wl	10wM
Test																	
All First	1	0	0	0	0	-	-	-	1	-							
1-day Int																	
C & G	2	1	1	7	7*	-	-	-	1	1							
NCL																	
Twenty20																	

THOMAS, I. J.   Glamorgan

Name: Ian James Thomas
Role: Left-hand bat, right-arm off-spin bowler
Born: 9 May 1979, Newport, Gwent
Height: 5ft 11in **Weight:** 14st
Nickname: Bolts, Homer
County debut: 1998
1st-Class 50s: 5
1st-Class catches: 17
Place in batting averages: 241st av. 16.54 (2002 230th av. 19.50)
Strike rate: (career 55.00)
Parents: Amanda and Alun

Marital status: Single
Family links with cricket: 'Father and brother play local league cricket for Machen; local legends for the Buzzards. Mother loves washing the whites'
Education: Bassaleg Comprehensive; University of Wales Institute Cardiff (UWIC)
Qualifications: 9 GCSEs, 2 A-levels, BSc (Hons) Sports Development
Career outside cricket: Management/marketing
Overseas tours: Wales U16 to Jersey and Isle of Wight; British Universities to Port Elizabeth 1999; Glamorgan to Cape Town 2002

Overseas teams played for: Mt Lawley Hawks, Perth 2001-02
Career highlights to date: 'Winning the NUL Division One 2002'
Cricket moments to forget: 'First first-class pair, v Derbys 2002'
Cricketers particularly admired: Steve James, David Hemp, Matt Maynard, Mike Powell
Young players to look out for: David Harrison and brother; Jon Hughes
Other sports played: Rugby (Machen RFC), golf (24 handicap), fishing
Other sports followed: Rugby (Newport RFC)
Relaxations: 'Golf, fishing, training'
Extras: Captained Welsh Schools at all age groups. Glamorgan Young Player of the Month June, July, August and September 2000. Scored 82 on Championship debut v Essex at Southend 2000
Best batting: 82 Glamorgan v Essex, Southend 2000
Best bowling: 1-26 Glamorgan v Nottinghamshire, Colwyn Bay 2002

2003 Season

	M	Inns	NO	Runs	HS	Avge	100s	50s	Ct	St	O	M	Runs	Wkts	Avge	Best	5wI	10wM
Test																		
All First	7	11	0	182	53	16.54	-	1	8	-								
1-day Int																		
C & G	2	2	0	127	93	63.50	-	1	-	-								
NCL	7	7	1	121	71 *	20.16	-	1	3	-								
Twenty20	3	3	0	18	12	6.00	-	-	-	-	1	0	5	1	5.00	1-5	-	

Career Performances

	M	Inns	NO	Runs	HS	Avge	100s	50s	Ct	St	Balls	Runs	Wkts	Avge	Best	5wI	10wM
Test																	
All First	26	43	4	835	82	21.41	-	5	17	-	55	32	1	32.00	1-26	-	-
1-day Int																	
C & G	4	4	0	161	93	40.25	-	1	2	-							
NCL	29	28	2	710	72	27.30	-	5	10	-							
Twenty20	3	3	0	18	12	6.00	-	-	-	-	6	5	1	5.00	1-5	-	

THOMAS, S. D. Glamorgan

Name: Stuart <u>Darren</u> Thomas
Role: Left-hand bat, right-arm fast-medium bowler
Born: 25 January 1975, Morriston, Swansea
Height: 6ft **Weight:** 13st
Nickname: Teddy
County debut: 1992
County cap: 1997
50 wickets in a season: 5
1st-Class 50s: 14
1st-Class 100s: 1
1st-Class 5 w. in innings: 18
1st-Class 10 w. in match: 1
1st-Class catches: 48
One-Day 5 w. in innings: 3
Place in batting averages: 191st av. 24.16 (2002 274th av. 13.04)
Place in bowling averages: 11th av. 22.53 (2002 74th av. 31.48)
Strike rate: 37.92 (career 51.75)
Parents: Stu and Ann
Wife and date of marriage: Claire, 30 September 2000
Children: Ellie Sofia, 20 August 2002
Family links with cricket: 'Dad used to play local club cricket for Llanelli'
Education: Graig Comprehensive, Llanelli; Neath Tertiary College
Qualifications: 5 GCSEs, BTEC National Diploma in Sports Studies, Level 2 coaching award, 'and all the DIY knowledge in the world'
Career outside cricket: Sales rep
Overseas tours: Glamorgan to Cape Town 1993, 1999, 2002, to Zimbabwe 1994, to Pretoria 1995, to Portugal 1996, to Jersey 1998; England U18 to South Africa 1992-93; England U19 to Sri Lanka 1993-94; England A to Zimbabwe and South Africa 1998-99, to Bangladesh and New Zealand 1999-2000

Overseas teams played for: Rovers CC, Welkom, Free State 1994
Career highlights to date: 'Winning the County Championship 1997 and NUL 2002. Also my two England A tours'
Cricket moments to forget: 'Being left out of B&H final 2000'
Cricket superstitions: 'None'
Cricketers particularly admired: 'Anyone who plays or has played for Glamorgan'
Young players to look out for: 'Any young Glamorgan players'
Injuries: Out for much of the 2003 season with a cartilage problem
Relaxations: 'Enjoy seeing the globe, eating out'
Extras: Became youngest player (17 years 217 days) to take five wickets (5-80) on debut, v Derbyshire 1992, and finished eighth in national bowling averages. BBC Welsh Young Sports Personality 1992. Played in third U19 'Test' against India U19 at Edgbaston 1994. Bettered Alan Wilkins's Glamorgan best B&H bowling figures on his debut in the competition with 6-20 v Combined Universities at Cardiff 1995. Took 7-16 v Surrey at Swansea in the Sunday League 1998, the best analysis by a Glamorgan bowler in the competition. Glamorgan Player of the Year 1998. Took 8-50 for England A v Zimbabwe A at Harare on 1998-99 tour – the first eight-wicket haul by an England A tourist. Scored maiden first-class century v Essex at Chelmsford 2001, his 138 being a record Championship score by a Glamorgan No. 8. Scored a 41-ball 71* v Surrey at The Oval in the C&G 2002 as Glamorgan made 429 in reply to Surrey's 438-5
Best batting: 138 Glamorgan v Essex, Chelmsford 2001
Best bowling: 8-50 England A v Zimbabwe A, Harare 1998-99

2003 Season

	M	Inns	NO	Runs	HS	Avge	100s	50s	Ct	St	O	M	Runs	Wkts	Avge	Best	5wI	10wM
Test																		
All First	5	8	2	145	69 *	24.16	-	1	1	-	82.1	8	293	13	22.53	4-47	-	-
1-day Int																		
C & G																		
NCL																		
Twenty20	3	3	0	45	25	15.00	-	-	1	-	5	0	66	1	66.00	1-26	-	

Career Performances

	M	Inns	NO	Runs	HS	Avge	100s	50s	Ct	St	Balls	Runs	Wkts	Avge	Best	5wI	10wM
Test																	
All First	148	201	38	3203	138	19.65	1	14	48	-	23860	14160	461	30.71	8-50	18	1
1-day Int																	
C & G	16	13	3	238	71 *	23.80	-	1	3	-	909	770	29	26.55	5-74	1	
NCL	84	64	13	708	38 *	13.88	-	-	13	-	3006	2545	101	25.19	7-16	1	
Twenty20	3	3	0	45	25	15.00	-	-	1	-	30	66	1	66.00	1-26	-	

THORBURN, M.

Hampshire

Name: Mark Thorburn
Role: Right-hand 'No. 11' bat, right-arm fast-medium bowler
Born: 11 August 1978, Bath
Height: 6ft 4in **Weight:** 13st 7lbs
Nickname: Thorbs, Cliffy, Thorpedo, The Chef
County debut: 2003
1st-Class catches: 1
Strike rate: 62.00 (career 59.00)
Parents: Ann and Graham
Marital status: Girlfriend Helen
Education: Beechen Cliff School, Bath; Durham University
Qualifications: 9 GCSEs, 3 A-levels, BA (Hons), ECB Level 2 coach, Financial Planning Certificate
Career outside cricket: 'Working for Chase de Vere Financial Solutions'
Off-season: 'Working'
Overseas tours: Durham University to South Africa 2000
Overseas teams played for: Belmont District CC, Newcastle, NSW; Melville CC, Perth
Career highlights to date: 'Asking Robin Smith to come on as 12th man against Oxford UCCE at The Parks whilst I answered a call of nature'
Cricket moments to forget: 'It's probably one of my funniest cricketing moments – leaving my first ball against AJ Harris at Trent Bridge for Durham UCCE; it flattened my leg stump. The funny thing about it was the attempts of my team-mates not to wet themselves laughing (probably had to be there)'
Cricket superstitions: 'None'
Cricketers particularly admired: Charles Van Der Gucht, Glenn McGrath
Young players to look out for: Tom Stayt, Robert Ferley, Kadeer Ali, Gareth Andrew, Tim Phillips
Other sports played: Golf ('very badly'), football ('even worse'), swimming
Other sports followed: Rugby (England and Bath RFC), football (England and Spurs)
Favourite band: 'Currently Feeder *Comfort in Sound*'
Relaxations: 'Reading, especially autobiographies; watching TV and films; playing on Chris Walley's PS2'
Opinions on cricket: 'I'm not sure that I've played enough to have an informed opinion.'
Best batting: 12 DUCCE v Nottinghamshire, Trent Bridge 2002
Best bowling: 2-53 Hampshire v OUCCE, The Parks 2003

2003 Season

	M	Inns	NO	Runs	HS	Avge	100s	50s	Ct	St	O	M	Runs	Wkts	Avge	Best	5wI	10wM
Test																		
All First	1	0	0	0	0	-	-	-	-	-	31	6	120	3	40.00	2-53	-	-
1-day Int																		
C & G																		
NCL																		
Twenty20																		

Career Performances

	M	Inns	NO	Runs	HS	Avge	100s	50s	Ct	St	Balls	Runs	Wkts	Avge	Best	5wI	10wM
Test																	
All First	6	5	1	35	12	8.75	-	-	1	-	708	523	12	43.58	2-53	-	-
1-day Int																	
C & G																	
NCL																	
Twenty20																	

THORNICROFT, N. D.   *Yorkshire*

Name: Nicholas (Nick) David Thornicroft
Role: Left-hand bat, right-arm fast bowler
Born: 23 January 1985, York
Height: 5ft 11in **Weight:** 12st 8lbs
Nickname: Thorny, Mad Dog, Harry Potter
County debut: 2002
One-Day 5 w. in innings: 1
Strike rate: (career 112.75)
Parents: Lyn and David
Marital status: Single
Education: Easingwold
Qualifications: 'Common sense'
Career outside cricket: Groundworker
Overseas tours: Yorkshire U16 to Cape Town, to Jersey; England U19 to Australia 2002-03
Career highlights to date: 'Getting Neil Fairbrother as my first first-class wicket'
Cricket moments to forget: 'Haven't got one yet'
Cricketers particularly admired: Darren Gough, Brett Lee, Ian Botham, Craig White, Andrew Flintoff
Young players to look out for: Charlie Thornicroft, Haroon Rashid, Andrew Gale, Liam Plunkett

Other sports played: Athletics, football, basketball
Other sports followed: Football (York City FC), horse racing
Relaxations: 'Spending time with family; music; fox hunting; shooting'
Extras: Played for Yorkshire Board XI in the C&G 2002. Became youngest ever Roses match debutant, v Lancashire at Old Trafford 2002, aged 17. Represented England U19 v India U19 2002 and v South Africa U19 2003, striking an 11-ball 42* in the second 'Test' at Worcester 2003. Shared new ball with fellow 17-year-old Tim Bresnan v Warwickshire at Edgbaston in the NUL 2002. Recorded maiden one-day five-wicket return (5-42) v Gloucestershire at Headingley in the NCL 2003
Opinions on cricket: 'I think the game is becoming more entertaining, especially with the introduction of the new 20-over competition. This may also give more youngsters a chance, which is also very positive for the future.'
Best batting: 4* Yorkshire v Lancashire, Old Trafford 2002
Best bowling: 2-51 Yorkshire v Lancashire, Old Trafford 2002

2003 Season

	M	Inns	NO	Runs	HS	Avge	100s	50s	Ct	St	O	M	Runs	Wkts	Avge	Best	5wI	10wM
Test																		
All First	1	1	1	1	1*	-	-	-	-	-	14	2	57	0	-	-	-	-
1-day Int																		
C & G																			
NCL	1	0	0	0	0	-	-	-	-	-	9	1	42	5	8.40	5-42	1	
Twenty20																		

Career Performances

	M	Inns	NO	Runs	HS	Avge	100s	50s	Ct	St	Balls	Runs	Wkts	Avge	Best	5wI	10wM
Test																	
All First	4	7	4	10	4*	3.33	-	-	-	-	451	305	4	76.25	2-51	-	-
1-day Int																	
C & G	1	0	0	0	0	-	-	-	-	-	30	19	0	-	-	-	
NCL	4	1	1	0	0*	-	-	-	1	-	144	131	8	16.37	5-42	1	
Twenty20																	

THORPE, A. M.   Durham

Name: <u>Ashley</u> Michael Thorpe
Role: Left-hand bat, right-arm medium bowler
Born: 2 April 1975, Kiama, New South Wales, Australia
Height: 5ft 11in **Weight:** 14st
Nickname: Thorpedo
County debut: 2002
1st-Class 50s: 2
1st-Class catches: 5

Place in batting averages: (2002 223rd av. 20.84)
Parents: Michael and Helen
Wife and date of marriage: Kathleen, 18 April 1998
Children: Michael, 11 December 1998
Family links with cricket: 'Father played for Albion Park and now plays for Scarborough CC veterans in Western Australia'
Education: Kent St Senior High School, WA
Career outside cricket: Qualified trainer with London Electricity
Off-season: 'Working'
Overseas tours: Qantas to Malaysia 1995; Durham to Cape Town 2002
Overseas teams played for: Scarborough CC, Western Australia 1996-97
Career highlights to date: 'First appearance at Lord's'

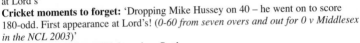

Cricket moments to forget: 'Dropping Mike Hussey on 40 – he went on to score 180-odd. First appearance at Lord's! (*0-60 from seven overs and out for 0 v Middlesex in the NCL 2003*)'
Cricket superstitions: 'Right pad on first'
Cricketers particularly admired: Paul Collingwood, Justin Langer
Young players to look out for: Gary Pratt, Liam Plunkett ('pace')
Other sports followed: Football (Newcastle United FC), rugby union (ACT Brumbies), rugby league (Canberra Raiders)
Injuries: Out for four weeks with a twisted knee
Favourite band: Red Hot Chili Peppers
Relaxations: 'Watching TV, sleeping; family time'
Extras: Played for Western Australia U17 and U19. Has played for Chester-le-Street in the North East Premier League. Scored 138 and 85 on 2nd XI debut v Yorkshire 2nd XI. Is not considered an overseas player. Released by Durham at the end of the 2003 season
Opinions on cricket: 'Reduce to 90 overs per day.'
Best batting: 95 Durham v Essex, Riverside 2002

2003 Season

	M	Inns	NO	Runs	HS	Avge	100s	50s	Ct	St	O	M	Runs	Wkts	Avge	Best	5wl	10wM
Test																		
All First	2	3	0	50	35	16.66	-	-	-	-								
1-day Int																		
C & G																		
NCL	7	7	0	160	76	22.85	-	1	5	-	11	0	82	0	-		-	-
Twenty20	5	5	2	79	35 *	26.33	-	-	1	-	5	0	33	4	8.25	3-20	-

Career Performances

	M	Inns	NO	Runs	HS	Avge	100s	50s	Ct	St	Balls	Runs	Wkts	Avge	Best	5wl	10wM
Test																	
All First	9	16	0	321	95	20.06	-	2	5	-	48	32	0	-	-	-	-
1-day Int																	
C & G																	
NCL	11	11	0	243	76	22.09	-	2	5	-	132	149	2	74.50	2-49	-	
Twenty20	5	5	2	79	35 *	26.33	-	-	1	-	30	33	4	8.25	3-20	-	

THORPE, G. P. Surrey

Name: <u>Graham</u> Paul Thorpe
Role: Left-hand bat, occasional right-arm medium bowler
Born: 1 August 1969, Farnham
Height: 5ft 10in **Weight:** 12st 9lbs
Nickname: Chalky
County debut: 1988
County cap: 1991
Benefit: 2000
Test debut: 1993
Tests: 78
One-Day Internationals: 82
1000 runs in a season: 9
1st-Class 50s: 107
1st-Class 100s: 41
1st-Class 200s: 4
1st-Class catches: 265
One-Day 100s: 9
Place in batting averages: 19th av. 56.61 (2002 91st av. 37.57)
Strike rate: 66.00 (career 91.80)
Parents: 'Mr and Mrs Thorpe'
Children: Henry and Amelia
Education: Weydon Comprehensive; Farnham College
Qualifications: 7 O-levels, PE Diploma
Overseas tours: England A to Zimbabwe and Kenya 1989-90, to Pakistan 1990-91, to Bermuda and West Indies 1991-92, to Australia 1992-93; England to West Indies 1993-94, to Australia 1994-95, to South Africa 1995-96, to India and Pakistan (World Cup) 1995-96, to Zimbabwe and New Zealand 1996-97, to Sharjah (Champions Trophy) 1997-98, to West Indies 1997-98, to Australia 1998-99, to Sharjah (Coca-Cola Cup) 1998-99, to Kenya (ICC Knockout Trophy) 2000-01, to Pakistan and Sri Lanka 2000-01, to India and New Zealand 2001-02, to Bangladesh and Sri Lanka 2003-04, to West Indies 2003-04

Cricketers particularly admired: Grahame Clinton, Waqar Younis, Ian Botham, Viv Richards
Other sports followed: Football (Chelsea FC), golf
Relaxations: Sleeping
Extras: Played for English Schools cricket U15 and U19 and England Schools football U18. Scored a century (114*) v Australia on his Test debut at Trent Bridge 1993, winning Man of the Match award. Scored 84 v West Indies at Bridgetown 1993-94, in the process sharing with Alec Stewart (143) in a record fifth-wicket partnership for England in Tests v West Indies (150). Scored 138 v Australia at Edgbaston 1997, in the process sharing with Nasser Hussain (207) in a record fourth-wicket partnership for England in Tests v Australia (288). Scored 103 v West Indies at Bridgetown 1997-98, in the process sharing with Mark Ramprakash (154) in a record sixth-wicket partnership for England in Tests v West Indies (205). Cornhill England Player of the Year 1997-98. One of *Wisden*'s Five Cricketers of the Year 1998. Represented England in the 1999 World Cup. With Craig White (93), shared in a new record sixth-wicket partnership for England in Tests v Pakistan (166) in the first Test at Lahore 2000-01; his century was the first in Test history to contain only one boundary (he added a second four before being out for 118). Scored match-winning 64* in the third Test at Karachi 2000-01 to steer England to a series victory v Pakistan. Captained England in one-day series v Sri Lanka 2000-01. Scored 138 v Pakistan at Old Trafford 2001, in the process sharing with Michael Vaughan (120) in a record partnership for any wicket for England in Tests v Pakistan (267). Scored maiden Test double century (200*) v New Zealand in the first Test at Christchurch 2001-02, sharing with Andrew Flintoff in a stand of 281 that set several new records, including that for the highest sixth-wicket partnership for England in Tests, and winning Man of the Match award; his 200 took 231 balls and was the second fastest for England in terms of balls received (after Ian Botham's 220-ball double hundred v India at The Oval in 1982). Scored century (123) in the second Test v Sri Lanka at Edgbaston 2002, in the process passing 5000 runs in Test cricket and sharing with Matthew Hoggard (17*) in a record tenth-wicket stand for England in Tests v Sri Lanka (91). Retired from ODI cricket after the NatWest Series 2002. Recalled to the England Test side for the fifth Test v South Africa 2003 at his home ground of The Oval, scoring century (124) and sharing with Marcus Trescothick (219) in a ground record partnership for the third wicket in Tests (268). His other international awards include England's Player of the Series in the 1997 Ashes campaign, England Man of the Series v Pakistan 2001, and Man of the Match in the third Test v Sri Lanka at Colombo 2000-01 (113*/32*)
Best batting: 223* England XI v South Australia, Adelaide 1998-99
Best bowling: 4-40 Surrey v Australians, The Oval 1993

2003 Season

	M	Inns	NO	Runs	HS	Avge	100s	50s	Ct	St	O	M	Runs	Wkts	Avge	Best	5wI	10wM
Test	1	1	0	124	124	124.00	1	-	1	-								
All First	13	20	2	1019	156	56.61	2	7	9	-	11	1	73	1	73.00	1-73	-	-
1-day Int																		
C & G	3	3	1	144	102 *	72.00	1	-	1	-								
NCL	13	12	4	378	79 *	47.25	-	3	8	-								
Twenty20	5	4	0	95	50	23.75	-	1	1	-								

Career Performances

	M	Inns	NO	Runs	HS	Avge	100s	50s	Ct	St	Balls	Runs	Wkts	Avge	Best	5wl	10wM
Test	78	141	18	5233	200 *	42.54	12	30	87	-	138	37	0	-	-	-	-
All First	303	505	68	19644	223 *	44.95	45	107	265	-	2387	1378	26	53.00	4-40	-	-
1-day Int	82	77	13	2380	89	37.18	-	21	43	-	120	97	2	48.50	2-15	-	
C & G	33	32	9	1303	145 *	56.65	2	9	19	-	13	12	0	-	-	-	
NCL	143	132	21	4323	126 *	38.94	6	29	59	-	318	307	8	38.37	3-21	-	
Twenty20	5	4	0	95	50	23.75	-	1	1	-							

TODD, M. J.   Surrey

Name: <u>Matthew</u> Julian Todd
Role: Right-hand bat, right-arm
off-spin bowler
Born: 25 May 1983, Chertsey
Height: 6ft 2in **Weight:** 14st 7lbs
Nickname: Toddy, Gears, Traction,
Toadfish, Treadmill
County debut: 2003
Strike rate: 84.00 (career 84.00)
Parents: Deborah and Julian
Marital status: Single
Family links with cricket: 'Grandad's
cousin was Peter May; grandad was good
player, now great analyst! Sister works at
Surrey Cricket Centre'
Education: Halliford School and Sixth Form
Qualifications: 10 GCSEs, A-levels,
ECB coaching Levels 1 and 2
Career outside cricket: 'Now looking for one!'
Off-season: 'Earning money to save for the future'
Overseas tours: Surrey U19 to Barbados 1999
Overseas teams played for: Upper Hutt United, Wellington, New Zealand

Career highlights to date: 'First-class debut v India A 2003'
Cricket moments to forget: 'I'd like to remember it all, good or bad'
Cricket superstitions: 'Take a bat with me when batting'
Cricketers particularly admired: Alec Stewart, Ian Ward, Dave Boothman
Young players to look out for: Rikki Clarke, James Benning, Dan Miller, Neil Saker, Andy Poynter
Other sports played: Golf ('badly'), football ('even worse')
Other sports followed: Football (Spurs), rugby, 'most sports'
Favourite band: Led Zeppelin, Jimi Hendrix
Relaxations: 'Spending time with family and friends; nights out with Messrs Sampson, Saker, Miller!'
Extras: Represented England U19 A v West Indies U19 and India U19. Apprentice contract with Surrey 2003; released by Surrey at the end of the 2003 season
Opinions on cricket: 'It's a great game, and to be a professional you're getting paid for what you love doing. But the powers that be must keep their finger on the pulse in order for the county game to provide the best players for England to be more successful. It's too easy to stay in the county game being average.'
Best batting: 6* Surrey v India A, The Oval 2003
Best bowling: 1-92 Surrey v India A, The Oval 2003

2003 Season

	M	Inns	NO	Runs	HS	Avge	100s	50s	Ct	St	O	M	Runs	Wkts	Avge	Best	5wI	10wM
Test																		
All First	1	1	1	6	6*	-	-	-	-	-	14	0	92	1	92.00	1-92	-	-
1-day Int																		
C & G																		
NCL																		
Twenty20																		

Career Performances

	M	Inns	NO	Runs	HS	Avge	100s	50s	Ct	St	Balls	Runs	Wkts	Avge	Best	5wI	10wM
Test																		
All First	1	1	1	6	6*	-	-	-	-	-	84	92	1	92.00	1-92	-	-
1-day Int																		
C & G																		
NCL																		
Twenty20																		

TOMLINSON, J. A.   Hampshire

Name: <u>James</u> Andrew Tomlinson
Role: Left-hand lower-order bat, left-arm
fast-medium bowler
Born: 12 June 1982, Appleshaw, Hants
Height: 6ft 1½in **Weight:** 12st 8lbs
Nickname: Tommo, Mr T, Dangerous Dave
County debut: 2002
1st-Class 5 w. in innings: 1
1st-Class catches: 4
Place in batting averages: 295th av. 3.37
Place in bowling averages: 135th av. 46.70
(2002 156th av. 62.33)
Strike rate: 60.64 (career 70.41)
Parents: Ian and Janet
Marital status: Single
Family links with cricket: Grandfathers
played cricket in Yorkshire
Education: Harrow Way Secondary School,
Andover; Cricklade College, Andover; Cardiff University
Qualifications: 9 GCSEs, 3 A-levels
Career outside cricket: 'Trying to get a degree (student at Cardiff Uni)'
Overseas tours: BUSA to South Africa ('hopefully')
Career highlights to date: 'Playing against India, Sri Lanka and Zimbabwe. Playing
with "the Judge". Playing for Hampshire'
Cricketers particularly admired: Robin Smith, Dimitri Mascarenhas, Shaun Udal,
John Crawley, Chaminda Vaas, Will Kendall
Young players to look out for: Kevin Latouf, Mark Pettini
Other sports played: Darts
Favourite band: 'Any '80s band!'
Relaxations: 'Walking dog; eating good food'
Extras: Played for Hampshire Board XI in the NatWest 2000 and for Wiltshire in the
C&G 2001. Played for Development of Excellence XI (South) v West Indies U19 at
Arundel 2001. Part of Hampshire's 2nd XI Championship winning side 2001. Played
for Cardiff University CCE 2002, taking 5-104 (7-134 the match) v Somerset at
Millfield School; also played for Cardiff UCCE 2003. Represented British Universities
2002 and v India A 2003. Recorded maiden first-class five-wicket
return (6-63) v Derbyshire at Derby 2003
Opinions on cricket: 'Do not agree with two overseas players. Two division cricket is
excellent. Needs to be more of a break between games.'
Best batting: 23 Hampshire v Indians, West End 2002
Best bowling: 6-63 Hampshire v Derbyshire, Derby 2003

2003 Season

	M	Inns	NO	Runs	HS	Avge	100s	50s	Ct	St	O	M	Runs	Wkts	Avge	Best	5wI	10wM
Test																		
All First	8	13	5	27	10	3.37	-	-	2	-	171.5	22	794	17	46.70	6-63	1	-
1-day Int																		
C & G																		
NCL	2	2	1	3	2	3.00	-	-	-	-	9	0	49	1	49.00	1-23	-	
Twenty20																		

Career Performances

	M	Inns	NO	Runs	HS	Avge	100s	50s	Ct	St	Balls	Runs	Wkts	Avge	Best	5wI	10wM
Test																	
All First	14	23	10	61	23	4.69	-	-	4	-	2042	1542	29	53.17	6-63	1	-
1-day Int																	
C & G	2	2	0	4	4	2.00	-	-	-	-	102	46	1	46.00	1-29	-	
NCL	11	6	3	10	6	3.33	-	-	1	-	446	368	11	33.45	2-15	-	
Twenty20																	

TREDWELL, J. C.   Kent

Name: James Cullum Tredwell
Role: Left-hand bat, right-arm
off-spin bowler
Born: 27 February 1982, Ashford, Kent
Height: 5ft 11in   **Weight:** 14st 2lbs
Nickname: Tredders, Pingu, Chad
County debut: 2001
1st-Class 50s: 2
1st-Class catches: 23
Place in batting averages: 240th av. 16.68
(2002 165th av. 26.83)
Place in bowling averages: 117th av. 40.17
(2002 107th av. 35.80)
Strike rate: 70.64 (career 72.00)
Parents: John and Rosemary
Marital status: Single
Family links with cricket: 'Father played for
Ashford and Folkestone in Kent League'
Education: Southlands Community Comprehensive
Qualifications: 10 GCSEs, 2 A-levels, ECB Level 1 coach
Off-season: ECB National Academy
Overseas tours: Kent U17 to Sri Lanka 1998-99; Kent to Port Elizabeth 2002; ECB
National Academy (England A) to Malaysia and India 2003-04

Overseas teams played for: Redlands Tigers, Brisbane 2000-02

Career highlights to date: 'Captaining England U19. Fifty against Somerset first time opening the innings in first-class cricket'

Cricket moments to forget: 'Being hit for six in a crucial B&H Cup match v Essex, which probably cost Kent's qualification to next stage'

Cricketers particularly admired: 'All the great spinners'

Young players to look out for: Rob Ferley, Joe Denly

Extras: Played for Kent Board XI in the NatWest 2000 and in the C&G 2001. Called up from England U19 for first-class debut for Kent v Leicestershire 2001, entailing a dash from Hove to Leicester on the day of the game. Represented England U19 v West Indies U19 2001 (captain in second 'Test'). Captained Kent to victory in the 2nd XI Trophy final at West End 2002, scoring 111. Kent Most Improved Player Award 2003

Best batting: 61 Kent v Yorkshire, Headingley 2002

Best bowling: 4-48 Kent v Sussex, Hove 2003

Stop press: Took over captaincy of ECB National Academy (England A) in India after Alex Gidman was forced to return home with a hand injury. Had match figures of 9-231 (5-101/4-130) for England A v East Zone at Amritsar in the Duleep Trophy 2003-04

2003 Season

	M	Inns	NO	Runs	HS	Avge	100s	50s	Ct	St	O	M	Runs	Wkts	Avge	Best	5wI	10wM
Test																		
All First	13	19	3	267	36	16.68	-	-	15	-	329.4	73	1125	28	40.17	4-48	-	-
1-day Int																		
C & G	2	2	0	9	9	4.50	-	-	1	-	12	3	36	0	-		-	-
NCL	15	11	3	121	29	15.12	-	-	4	-	90.2	0	406	14	29.00	3-38	-	
Twenty20	5	5	0	90	34	18.00	-	-	2	-	14	0	129	3	43.00	1-33	-	

Career Performances

	M	Inns	NO	Runs	HS	Avge	100s	50s	Ct	St	Balls	Runs	Wkts	Avge	Best	5wI	10wM
Test																	
All First	18	26	3	438	61	19.04	-	2	23	-	2880	1606	40	40.15	4-48	-	-
1-day Int																	
C & G	11	8	1	190	71	27.14	-	2	4	-	444	273	8	34.12	3-7	-	
NCL	26	20	7	131	29	10.07	-	-	8	-	865	671	25	26.84	3-28	-	
Twenty20	5	5	0	90	34	18.00	-	-	2	-	84	129	3	43.00	1-33	-	

93. Which current Lancashire bowler was Man of the Match on ODI debut v West Indies at The Oval in 1995 with figures of 4-44?

TREGO, P. D.   Kent

Name: <u>Peter</u> David Trego
Role: Right-hand bat, right-arm
'quickish' bowler
Born: 12 June 1981, Weston-super-Mare
Height: 6ft **Weight:** 12st 7lbs
Nickname: Tregs 'and many more'
County debut: 2000 (Somerset), 2003 (Kent)
1st-Class 50s: 1
1st-Class 100s: 1
1st-Class catches: 6
Place in batting averages: (2002 85th
av. 38.57)
Strike rate: 39.00 (career 61.89)
Parents: Carol and Paul
Marital status: Single
Family links with cricket: 'Brother Sam
played for Somerset; Dad plays for Uphill
Castle – both strong batsmen'

Education: Wyvern Comprehensive
Cricketers particularly admired: Ian Botham and Graham Rose – 'they have both
been huge inspirations to me'
Other sports played: Football
Other sports followed: Football (Man Utd), darts, golf
Relaxations: Golf, snooker, music, socialising with friends, shopping
Extras: Won Best Batsman award at U16 – averaged 137 in nine games. Attended
Lilleshall with England U17. Represented England U19 v Sri Lanka U19 2000,
scoring 53* and taking 3-41 in the second 'ODI' at Cardiff. NBC Denis Compton
Award for the most promising young Somerset player 2000. Played for Somerset
Board XI in the C&G 2001 and 2002. Scored maiden first-class century (140) at
Taunton 2002 as Somerset, chasing 454 to win, tied with West Indies A. Left Somerset
at the end of the 2002 season and joined Kent for 2003. Struck a 23-ball 31* and took
4-39 v Leicestershire at Canterbury in the NCL 2003. Released by Kent at the end of
the 2003 season
Best batting: 140 Somerset v West Indies A, Taunton 2002
Best bowling: 4-84 Somerset v Yorkshire, Scarborough 2000

2003 Season

	M	Inns	NO	Runs	HS	Avge	100s	50s	Ct	St	O	M	Runs	Wkts	Avge	Best	5wI	10wM
Test																		
All First	1	1	0	13	13	13.00	-	-	1	-	13	0	69	2	34.50	1-26	-	-
1-day Int																		
C & G	1	1	0	2	2	2.00	-	-	-	-	5.1	0	22	2	11.00	2-22	-	
NCL	7	7	2	109	31 *	21.80	-	-	1	-	39.2	1	244	10	24.40	4-39		
Twenty20	4	4	0	15	11	3.75	-	-	-	-	3	0	34	4	8.50	2-17		

Career Performances

	M	Inns	NO	Runs	HS	Avge	100s	50s	Ct	St	Balls	Runs	Wkts	Avge	Best	5wI	10wM
Test																	
All First	15	22	3	534	140	28.10	1	1	6	-	1795	1272	29	43.86	4-84	-	-
1-day Int																	
C & G	4	3	0	13	11	4.33	-	-	-	-	163	115	8	14.37	2-21	-	
NCL	21	18	4	203	31 *	14.50	-	-	3	-	602	560	19	29.47	4-39	-	
Twenty20	4	4	0	15	11	3.75	-	-	-	-	18	34	4	8.50	2-17	-	

TREMLETT, C. T.   Hampshire

Name: <u>Christopher</u> Timothy Tremlett
Role: Right-hand bat, right-arm
fast-medium bowler
Born: 2 September 1981, Southampton
Height: 6ft 7in **Weight:** 16st 1lb
Nickname: Twiggy, Goober
County debut: 2000
1st-Class 5 w. in innings: 3
1st-Class catches: 11
Place in batting averages: 231st av. 18.09
(2002 209th av. 22.50)
Place in bowling averages: 84th av. 34.40
(2002 62nd av. 29.47)
Strike rate: 55.25 (career 50.70)
Parents: Timothy and Carolyn
Marital status: Single
Family links with cricket: Grandfather
[Maurice] played for Somerset and in three
Tests for England. Father played for Hampshire and is now director of cricket at
the county
Education: Thornden School, Chandlers Ford; Taunton's College, Southampton
Qualifications: 5 GCSEs, BTEC National Diploma in Sports Science, Level 2 coach

Overseas tours: West of England U15 to West Indies 1997; Hampshire U16 to Jersey; England U17 to Northern Ireland (ECC Colts Festival) 1999; England U19 to India 2000-01; ECB National Academy to Australia 2001-02, to Australia and Sri Lanka 2002-03

Career highlights to date: 'Taking first five-wicket haul against Lancashire at the Rose Bowl'

Cricket moments to forget: 'Getting injured against Essex in an NUL game and being put out for the rest of the 2002 season'

Cricketers particularly admired: Glenn McGrath, Mark Waugh, Shane Warne

Young players to look out for: John Francis

Other sports played: Basketball, volleyball

Other sports followed: Football (Arsenal)

Relaxations: 'Socialising with friends; cinema'

Extras: Played for Hampshire Board XI in the NatWest 2000. Took wicket (Mark Richardson) with first ball in first-class cricket v New Zealand A at Portsmouth 2000; finished with debut match figures of 6-91. Represented England U19 v Sri Lanka U19 2000 and v West Indies U19 2001. NBC Denis Compton Award for the most promising young Hampshire player 2000, 2001. Hampshire Young Player of the Year 2001. Took career best 6-51 as Hampshire defeated Glamorgan at West End 2003 after following on

Opinions on cricket: 'The game is a lot more exciting with the introduction of two leagues. However, there is far too much cricket played in this country and it puts a strain on players, especially fast bowlers. The Australian system seems to be a better way of doing things. They play less games and the injury rate doesn't seem to be as high. The intensity of the game would rise as well.'

Best batting: 43 Hampshire v Somerset, West End 2003

Best bowling: 6-51 Hampshire v Glamorgan, West End 2003

2003 Season

	M	Inns	NO	Runs	HS	Avge	100s	50s	Ct	St	O	M	Runs	Wkts	Avge	Best	5wI	10wM
Test																		
All First	10	13	2	199	43	18.09	-	-	5	-	248.4	48	929	27	34.40	6-51	1	-
1-day Int																		
C & G	1	0	0	0	0	-	-	-	-	-	9.3	1	47	0	-	-	-	-
NCL	11	4	1	11	9	3.66	-	-	2	-	79	8	342	17	20.11	4-26	-	
Twenty20																		

Career Performances

	M	Inns	NO	Runs	HS	Avge	100s	50s	Ct	St	Balls	Runs	Wkts	Avge	Best	5wI	10wM
Test																	
All First	32	43	13	510	43	17.00	-	-	11	-	5020	2722	99	27.49	6-51	3	-
1-day Int																	
C & G	5	1	0	10	10	10.00	-	-	-	-	242	189	6	31.50	3-20	-	
NCL	37	22	7	144	30 *	9.60	-	-	9	-	1666	1131	56	20.19	4-25	-	
Twenty20																	

TRESCOTHICK, M. E. Somerset

Name: <u>Marcus</u> Edward Trescothick
Role: Left-hand bat, right-arm swing bowler, reserve wicket-keeper
Born: 25 December 1975, Keynsham, Bristol
Height: 6ft 3in **Weight:** 14st 7lbs
Nickname: Banger
County debut: 1993
County cap: 1999
Test debut: 2000
Tests: 38
One-Day Internationals: 71
1st-Class 50s: 52
1st-Class 100s: 12
1st-Class 200s: 1
1st-Class catches: 166
One-Day 100s: 15
Place in batting averages: 24th av. 51.62 (2002 7th av. 69.11)
Strike rate: (career 69.27)
Parents: Martyn and Lin
Wife and date of marriage: Hayley, 24 January 2004
Family links with cricket: Father played for Somerset 2nd XI; uncle played club cricket
Education: Sir Bernard Lovell School
Qualifications: 7 GCSEs
Off-season: Touring with England
Overseas tours: England U18 to South Africa 1992-93; England U19 to Sri Lanka 1993-94, to West Indies 1994-95 (captain); England A to Bangladesh and New Zealand 1999-2000; England to Kenya (ICC Knockout Trophy) 2000-01, to Pakistan and Sri Lanka 2000-01, to Zimbabwe (one-day series) 2001-02, to India and New Zealand 2001-02, to Sri Lanka (ICC Champions Trophy) 2002-03, to Australia 2002-03, to Africa (World Cup) 2002-03, to Bangladesh and Sri Lanka 2003-04, to West Indies 2003-04
Overseas teams played for: Melville CC, Perth 1997-99
Career highlights to date: 'Scoring my first Test hundred in Galle, Sri Lanka [2001]'
Cricketers particularly admired: Adam Gilchrist, Andy Caddick
Young players to look out for: Matthew Wood
Other sports followed: Golf, football (Bristol City FC)
Relaxations: 'Spending time at home (it's such a rare thing), playing golf'
Extras: Scored more than 1000 runs for England U19. Took a hat-trick for Somerset v Young Australia at Taunton 1995. Scored 322 v Warwickshire 2nd XI 1997, being the

last man out with the score on 605 as Somerset 2nd XI chased 612. Made ODI debut v Zimbabwe at The Oval in the NatWest Series 2000, scoring 79. Made Test debut in the third Test v West Indies 2000, scoring 66 and sharing with Alec Stewart (105) in record England partnership for any wicket in Tests v West Indies at Old Trafford (179). Scored 78 in the fifth Test v West Indies 2000, sharing with Michael Atherton (83) in a new record first-wicket stand for England in Tests v West Indies at The Oval (159). PCA Player of the Year 2000. Scored three B&H centuries in eight days 2001, winning three Gold Awards. Man of the Match for his 142-ball 137 (his maiden ODI century) v Pakistan at Lord's in the NatWest Series 2001, in the process of scoring which he shared in a record fourth-wicket partnership for England in ODIs (170) with Owais Shah (62). C&G Man of the Match award for his 83-ball 121 v Glamorgan at Taunton 2001. Sports.com Cricketer of the Year 2001. Captained England v Zimbabwe in the fourth ODI at Bulawayo 2001-02, deputising for Nasser Hussain. BBC West Country Sports Sportsman of the Year 2001. Man of the Match award v India at Kolkata (Calcutta) 2001-02 for his 109-ball 121, which included the fastest century for England in ODIs (80 balls). Scored 76 as England followed on in the first Test v Sri Lanka at Lord's 2002, in the process sharing with Michael Vaughan (115) in a record first-wicket partnership for England in Tests v Sri Lanka (168). Took part in first-wicket stand of 50 in five overs with Michael Vaughan to bring England victory with an over to spare in the third Test v Sri Lanka at Old Trafford 2002. C&G Man of the Match award for his 133 v Hampshire at Taunton 2002. Vice-captain of Somerset 1999-2002; captained the county on his appearances in 2002. Scored 114* v South Africa at The Oval in the NatWest Series 2003, sharing with Vikram Solanki (106) in a record England opening partnership in ODIs (200). Scored maiden first-class double century (219) in the fifth Test v South Africa at The Oval 2003, sharing with Graham Thorpe (124) in a ground record partnership for the third wicket in Tests (268); also scored 69* in second innings and was Man of the Match. His other international awards include Man of the NatWest Series v Sri Lanka and India 2002, Man of the Series in the NatWest Challenge v Pakistan 2003, and Man of the Match v Zimbabwe at Colombo in the ICC Champions Trophy 2002-03 (102-ball 119). ECB central contract 2003-04
Best batting: 219 England v South Africa, The Oval 2003
Best bowling: 4-36 Somerset v Young Australia, Taunton 1995

2003 Season

	M	Inns	NO	Runs	HS	Avge	100s	50s	Ct	St	O	M	Runs	Wkts	Avge	Best	5wI	10wM
Test	7	12	2	589	219	58.90	1	4	9	-								
All First	11	18	2	826	219	51.62	1	7	17	-								
1-day Int	10	10	2	443	114 *	55.37	2	2	6	-								
C & G	2	2	1	120	103 *	120.00	1	-	1	-								
NCL	3	3	1	154	80 *	77.00	-	2	2	-								
Twenty20																		

Career Performances

	M	Inns	NO	Runs	HS	Avge	100s	50s	Ct	St	Balls	Runs	Wkts	Avge	Best	5wI	10wM
Test	38	71	6	2802	219	43.10	4	19	35	-	120	52	1	52.00	1-34	-	-
All First	157	267	13	8803	219	34.65	13	52	166	-	2494	1438	36	39.94	4-36	-	-
1-day Int	71	71	3	2604	137	38.29	6	14	28	-	46	45	2	22.50	2-7	-	
C & G	20	18	1	835	133	49.11	4	1	5	-	174	141	4	35.25	2-23	-	
NCL	88	79	11	1975	110	29.04	1	11	30	-	978	823	31	26.54	4-50	-	
Twenty20																	

TROTT, B. J.   Kent

Name: Benjamin (<u>Ben</u>) James Trott
Role: Right-hand bat, right-arm
fast-medium bowler
Born: 14 March 1975, Wellington, Somerset
Height: 6ft 5in **Weight:** 14st
Nickname: Tony Rott, Trotsky, Trotty
County debut: 1997 (Somerset), 2000 (Kent)
1st-Class 5 w. in innings: 4
1st-Class 10 w. in match: 1
1st-Class catches: 7
One-Day 5 w. in innings: 1
Place in batting averages: 291st av. 6.16
Place in bowling averages: 142nd av. 49.92
Strike rate: 69.46 (career 51.33)
Parents: Alan Robert and Jane Elizabeth
Marital status: Single
Family links with cricket: Younger brother
Thom and father both play
Education: Court Fields Community School, Taunton; Richard Huish College,
Taunton; College of St Mark and St John, Plymouth
Qualifications: 8 GCSEs, 3 A-levels, BEd (Hons) Physical Education and Information
Technology; sports coaching – cricket, rugby, football, hockey
Career outside cricket: Teacher (primary)
Overseas teams played for: Claremont-Nedlands, Perth 1998-99
Career highlights to date: 'Winning the Norwich Union League 2001 with the last
game of the season'
Cricketers particularly admired: Glenn McGrath, Darren Gough, Andrew Caddick
Young players to look out for: Alex Loudon, James Tredwell, Robert Ferley
Other sports played: Golf, football
Other sports followed: Football (Manchester United)
Relaxations: 'Spending time with my girlfriend, music, golf'

Extras: Wellington Young Player of the Year 1993. Wellington Players' Player of the Year 1996. Played for Somerset 1997-99; has also played for Devon. Joined Kent in 2000. Recorded maiden first-class five-wicket return (5-65) v Essex at Tunbridge Wells 2001, going on to take 6-13 in the second innings for a maiden first-class ten-wicket match. Also recorded maiden one-day five-wicket return in 2001, 5-18 v Cumberland at Barrow on C&G debut, winning Man of the Match award. Scored 26 v Sussex at Tunbridge Wells 2002, in the process sharing with Mark Ealham (83*) in a ground record tenth-wicket partnership for Kent (77)

Best batting: 26 Kent v Sussex, Tunbridge Wells 2002
Best bowling: 6-13 Kent v Essex, Tunbridge Wells 2001

2003 Season

	M	Inns	NO	Runs	HS	Avge	100s	50s	Ct	St	O	M	Runs	Wkts	Avge	Best	5wI	10wM
Test																		
All First	7	10	4	37	12*	6.16	-	-	2	-	150.3	27	649	13	49.92	4-73	-	-
1-day Int																		
C & G	2	1	0	3	3	3.00	-	-	-	-	20	3	51	4	12.75	3-16	-	
NCL	9	5	4	3	1*	3.00	-	-	3	-	70.2	4	354	13	27.23	3-19	-	
Twenty20	2	0	0	0	0	-	-	-	-	-	7	0	49	2	24.50	2-17	-	

Career Performances

	M	Inns	NO	Runs	HS	Avge	100s	50s	Ct	St	Balls	Runs	Wkts	Avge	Best	5wI	10wM
Test																	
All First	29	30	10	122	26	6.10	-	-	7	-	4004	2461	78	31.55	6-13	4	1
1-day Int																	
C & G	5	2	0	3	3	1.50	-	-	1	-	295	168	12	14.00	5-18	1	
NCL	27	14	9	9	2*	1.80	-	-	5	-	1232	997	32	31.15	3-19	-	
Twenty20	2	0	0	0	0	-	-	-	-	-	42	49	2	24.50	2-17	-	

94. Which Gloucestershire off-spinner was batting with the broken-armed Colin Cowdrey when the second Test at Lord's ended in an exciting draw in 1963?

TROTT, I. J. L.   Warwickshire

Name: Ian <u>Jonathan</u> Leonard Trott
Role: Right-hand bat, right-arm medium bowler; all-rounder
Born: 22 April 1981, Cape Town, South Africa
Height: 6ft **Weight:** 13st 5lbs
Nickname: Booger
County debut: 2003
1st-Class 50s: 12
1st-Class 100s: 2
1st-Class 5 w. in innings: 1
1st-Class catches: 17
Place in batting averages: 66th av. 42.38
Strike rate: 42.14 (career 57.45)
Parents: Ian and Donna
Marital status: Single
Family links with cricket: Father is a professional cricket coach. Brother (Kenny Jackson) played for Western Province and Boland. Is related to the late-19th-century Test cricketers Albert (Australia and England) and Harry Trott (Australia)
Education: Rondebosch Boys' High School; Stellenbosch University
Qualifications: Level 2 coaching
Off-season: 'Playing club cricket in Cape Town'
Overseas tours: South Africa U15 to England (U15 World Cup) 1996; South Africa U19 to Pakistan 1998-99, to Sri Lanka (U19 World Cup) 1999-2000
Overseas teams played for: Boland 1999-2000 – 2000-01; Western Province 2001-02
Career highlights to date: 'Winning the Standard Bank Cup 2000 and hundred on debut for Warwickshire'
Cricket moments to forget: 'Losing in the final of the Standard Bank Cup 2002'
Cricket superstitions: 'Personal'
Cricketers particularly admired: Sachin Tendulkar, Adam Hollioake, Steve Waugh
Young players to look out for: John McInroy
Other sports played: Hockey (Western Province U16, U18, U21), golf
Other sports followed: Football (Tottenham Hotspur)
Favourite band: Roxette, Robbie Williams
Relaxations: 'Music, watching sport'
Extras: Represented South Africa A. Struck a record debut score of 245 for Warwickshire 2nd XI v Somerset 2nd XI at Knowle & Dorridge 2002, sharing in a third-wicket stand of 397 with Trevor Penney. Scored 248 v Worcestershire 2nd XI at Barnt Green 2003, in the process sharing with Ian Westwood (250*) in a record opening partnership for Warwickshire 2nd XI (429). Scored century (134) on

Championship debut for Warwickshire v Sussex at Edgbaston 2003. Became the first player to bat for the full 20 overs in the Twenty20, for a 54-ball 65* v Gloucestershire at Edgbaston 2003. Scored century (126) v Lancashire 2003, sharing with Dougie Brown (112) in a new record sixth-wicket partnership for Warwickshire at Edgbaston (216). Recorded maiden first-class five-wicket return (7-39) v Kent at Canterbury 2003. Is a British passport holder and is not considered an overseas player

Opinions on cricket: 'Should be less cricket, which would make the cricket we play more competitive.'

Best batting: 134 Warwickshire v Sussex, Edgbaston 2003
Best bowling: 7-39 Warwickshire v Kent, Canterbury 2003

2003 Season

	M	Inns	NO	Runs	HS	Avge	100s	50s	Ct	St	O	M	Runs	Wkts	Avge	Best	5wI	10wM
Test																		
All First	10	18	0	763	134	42.38	2	5	4	-	49.1	4	215	7	30.71	7-39	1	-
1-day Int																		
C & G																		
NCL	8	8	2	284	59	47.33	-	4	4	-	3	0	19	0	-		-	-
Twenty20	5	4	1	86	65 *	28.66	-	1	-	-	1	0	10	0	-		-	-

Career Performances

	M	Inns	NO	Runs	HS	Avge	100s	50s	Ct	St	Balls	Runs	Wkts	Avge	Best	5wI	10wM
Test																	
All First	27	50	3	1563	134	33.25	2	12	17	-	632	435	11	39.54	7-39	1	-
1-day Int																	
C & G																	
NCL	8	8	2	284	59	47.33	-	4	4	-	18	19	0	-		-	-
Twenty20	5	4	1	86	65 *	28.66	-	1	-	-	6	10	0	-		-	-

95. Which Jamaican barrister and former chairman of the West Indies Cricket Board toured England in 1950, scoring two Test centuries?

TROUGHTON, J. O.   Warwickshire

Name: Jamie (Jim) Oliver Troughton
Role: Left-hand bat, slow left-arm bowler
Born: 2 March 1979, London
Height: 5ft 11in   **Weight:** 12st 12lbs
Nickname: Troughts
County debut: 2001
County cap: 2002
One-Day Internationals: 6
1000 runs in a season: 1
1st-Class 50s: 8
1st-Class 100s: 7
1st-Class catches: 17
One-Day 100s: 1
Place in batting averages: 68th av. 41.55
(2002 32nd av. 50.80)
Parents: Ali and David
Wife and date of marriage: Naomi,
28 September 2002
Family links with cricket: Father was a Middlesex Colt. Great-grandfather Henry Crichton played for Warwickshire
Education: Trinity School, Leamington Spa; Birmingham University
Qualifications: 8 GCSEs, 3 A-levels, BSc Sport & Exercise Psychology
Career outside cricket: Coaching/acting
Overseas tours: Warwickshire Development of Excellence squad to Cape Town 1998; MCC to Australia and Singapore 2001; ECB National Academy to Australia and Sri Lanka 2002-03
Overseas teams played for: Harvinia CC, Free State, South Africa 2000; Avendale CC, Cape Town 2001-02
Career highlights to date: 'Being selected for ODI squad and enjoying the double series win'
Cricket moments to forget: 'Getting shin splints last year [2002]'
Cricket superstitions: 'None'
Cricketers particularly admired: Graham Thorpe, Steve Waugh, Allan Donald, Ashley Giles
Young players to look out for: Jonathan Trott, Ian Westwood, Naqaash Tahir
Other sports played: Football (Stoke City youth player; 'I enjoy skinning Alan Richardson for a pastime')
Other sports followed: 'Hooked on Manchester United since going to their soccer school aged five'
Injuries: Out for two weeks with a torn hip flexor
Favourite band: Red Hot Chili Peppers, Coldplay, Stone Roses

Relaxations: 'Music, films, playing my guitar, spending time with Naomi, going abroad'

Extras: Is grandson of *Dr Who* actor Patrick Troughton; father also an actor. County colours U12-U19. Has represented England U15, U16 and U17. Represented ECB Midlands U19 v Pakistan U19 1998. Has won the Alec Hastilow Trophy and the Coney Edmonds Trophy (Warwickshire awards). Warwickshire 2nd XI Player of the Year 2001. Scored maiden first-class century (131*) v Hampshire at West End 2002, following up with another century (130) in his next innings, v Leicestershire at Edgbaston 2002. Scored 1067 first-class runs in his first full season 2002. NBC Denis Compton Award for the most promising young Warwickshire player 2002. Warwickshire Young Player and Most Improved Player of the Year 2002. Nominated for PCA Young Player of the Year award 2002. Made ODI debut v Pakistan at Old Trafford in the NatWest Challenge 2003

Opinions on cricket: 'Twenty20 was a great success. Hope they don't try to expand the amount of games, though; keep it as it is. One overseas, please.'

Best batting: 131* Warwickshire v Hampshire, West End 2002

2003 Season

	M	Inns	NO	Runs	HS	Avge	100s	50s	Ct	St	O	M	Runs	Wkts	Avge	Best	5wI	10wM
Test																		
All First	12	20	2	748	129 *	41.55	3	2	5	-	13	0	85	0	-		-	-	-
1-day Int	6	5	1	36	20	9.00	-	-	1	-								
C & G	3	3	0	107	52	35.66	-	1	-	-								
NCL	12	10	0	209	77	20.90	-	2	4	-	6	0	32	1	32.00	1-19	-	
Twenty20	2	2	1	34	33 *	34.00	-	-	-	-								

Career Performances

	M	Inns	NO	Runs	HS	Avge	100s	50s	Ct	St	Balls	Runs	Wkts	Avge	Best	5wI	10wM
Test																	
All First	30	52	6	2053	131 *	44.63	7	8	17	-	210	199	0	-	-	-	-
1-day Int	6	5	1	36	20	9.00	-	-	1	-							
C & G	8	8	1	361	115 *	51.57	1	2	3	-	130	83	7	11.85	4-23	-	
NCL	22	20	3	424	77	24.94	-	3	5	-	36	32	1	32.00	1-19	-	
Twenty20	2	2	1	34	33 *	34.00	-	-	-	-							

TUDOR, A. J. Surrey

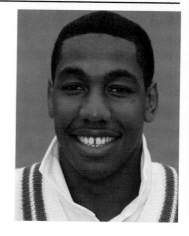

Name: Alexander (<u>Alex</u>) Jeremy Tudor
Role: Right-hand bat, right-arm fast bowler
Born: 23 October 1977, West Brompton, London
Height: 6ft 4in **Weight:** 13st 7lbs
Nickname: Big Al, Bambi, Tudes
County debut: 1995
County cap: 1999
Test debut: 1998-99
Tests: 10
One-Day Internationals: 3
1st-Class 50s: 6
1st-Class 100s: 1
1st-Class 5 w. in innings: 13
1st-Class catches: 24
Place in batting averages: 150th av. 29.50 (2002 260th av. 15.85)
Place in bowling averages: 147th av. 53.20 (2002 38th av. 26.76)
Strike rate: 86.40 (career 47.60)
Parents: Daryll and Jennifer
Marital status: Single
Family links with cricket: Brother was on the staff at The Oval
Education: St Mark's C of E, Fulham; City of Westminster College
Overseas tours: England U15 to South Africa 1992-93; England U19 to Zimbabwe 1995-96, to Pakistan 1996-97; England to Australia 1998-99, to South Africa 1999-2000, to Pakistan 2000-01, to Australia 2002-03; England A to West Indies 2000-01; ECB National Academy to Australia 2001-02, to Australia 2002-03
Cricketers particularly admired: Curtly Ambrose, Brian Lara
Other sports followed: Basketball, football (QPR)
Relaxations: Listening to music
Extras: Played for London Schools at all ages from U8. Played for England U17 v India U19 1994. MCC Young Cricketer. Took 4-89 in Australia's first innings on Test debut at Perth 1998-99; his victims included both Waugh twins. Scored 99* in second innings of the first Test v New Zealand at Edgbaston 1999, bettering the highest score by a nightwatchman for England (Harold Larwood's 98 v Australia at Sydney 1932-33) and winning Man of the Match award; in total he scored 131 unbeaten runs in the match. Cricket Writers' Club Young Cricketer of the Year 1999. Scored maiden first-class century (116) at The Oval 2001, in the process sharing with Alec Stewart (106) in a new record seventh-wicket partnership for Surrey in matches v Essex (206). Recorded match figures of 7-109 in the third Test v Sri Lanka at Old Trafford 2002, winning Man of the Match award

Best batting: 116 Surrey v Essex, The Oval 2001
Best bowling: 7-48 Surrey v Lancashire, The Oval 2000

2003 Season

	M	Inns	NO	Runs	HS	Avge	100s	50s	Ct	St	O	M	Runs	Wkts	Avge	Best	5wI	10wM
Test																		
All First	6	7	1	177	55	29.50	-	1	-	-	144	24	532	10	53.20	3-56	-	-
1-day Int																		
C & G																			
NCL	2	2	2	13	11 *	-	-	-	1	-	18	0	102	7	14.57	4-45	-	
Twenty20																			

Career Performances

	M	Inns	NO	Runs	HS	Avge	100s	50s	Ct	St	Balls	Runs	Wkts	Avge	Best	5wI	10wM
Test	10	16	4	229	99 *	19.08	-	1	3	-	1512	963	28	34.39	5-44	1	-
All First	90	118	26	2023	116	21.98	1	6	24	-	13043	7751	274	28.28	7-48	13	-
1-day Int	3	2	1	9	6	9.00	-	-	1	-	127	136	4	34.00	2-30	-	
C & G	7	3	2	28	17 *	28.00	-	-	2	-	399	269	10	26.90	4-39	-	
NCL	35	25	7	186	29 *	10.33	-	-	8	-	1388	1119	47	23.80	4-26	-	
Twenty20																		

TURK, N. R. K.   Sussex

Name: <u>Neil</u> Richard Keith Turk
Role: Left-hand bat, right-arm medium bowler
Born: 28 April 1983, Cuckfield
Height: 6ft **Weight:** 11st 8lbs
Nickname: Turkish, Neilo
County debut: 2002 (one-day)
Parents: Keith and Lorraine
Marital status: Single
Family links with cricket: 'Father PE teacher and grade coach. Brother county junior. Mother junior cricket coach/manager'
Education: Sackville Community College, East Grinstead; Exeter University (Sports Science degree)
Qualifications: 9 GCSEs, 1 AS-level, 3 A-levels, FIFA-approved referee
Career highlights to date: 'County debut 2002 v Essex Eagles. Maiden 2nd XI Championship century (123) v Hampshire'

Cricket moments to forget: 'Being dismissed by Hampshire's wicket-keeper in a match for Sussex 2nd XI, having scored a century in the first innings; his only wicket to date'

Cricket superstitions: 'I don't believe you need superstitions to help you'

Cricketers particularly admired: Brian Lara, Jacques Kallis

Young players to look out for: Arul Suppiah

Other sports played: Hockey (West of England U21, Exeter University, ISCA HC), golf, football

Other sports followed: Football (Liverpool FC), rugby league (Wigan Warriors), hockey (East Grinstead HC)

Favourite band: Usher

Relaxations: 'I enjoy most sports; I also like to spend time on the golf course when I'm not playing cricket'

Extras: Youngest player ever to score a Sussex League century. Sussex U17 Player of the Year. Played for Sussex Board XI in the second round of the C&G 2003, which was played in September 2002. Is a Sussex Academy player

Opinions on cricket: 'The quality of cricket at present hopefully will attract a greater audience and help to promote the game to those people who do not already enjoy it. It is also good to see a number of young players given a chance at the top level.'

2003 Season

	M	Inns	NO	Runs	HS	Avge	100s	50s	Ct	St	O	M	Runs	Wkts	Avge	Best	5wI	10wM
Test																		
All First																		
1-day Int																		
C & G																		
NCL	1	1	0	8	8	8.00	-	-	-	-								
Twenty20																		

Career Performances

	M	Inns	NO	Runs	HS	Avge	100s	50s	Ct	St	Balls	Runs	Wkts	Avge	Best	5wI	10wM
Test																	
All First																	
1-day Int																	
C & G	1	1	0	20	20	20.00	-	-	-	-	12	21	0	-		-	-
NCL	2	2	0	44	36	22.00	-	-	-	-							
Twenty20																	

TURNER, R. J.   Somerset

Name: Robert (<u>Rob</u>) Julian Turner
Role: Right-hand middle-order bat,
wicket-keeper
Born: 25 November 1967, Malvern
Height: 6ft 2in **Weight:** 14st
Nickname: Noddy, Turns
County debut: 1991
County cap: 1994
Benefit: 2002
1000 runs in a season: 2
50 dismissals in a season: 8
1st-Class 50s: 45
1st-Class 100s: 10
1st-Class catches: 620
1st-Class stumpings: 45
Place in batting averages: 89th av. 37.70
(2002 140th av. 30.04)
Parents: Derek and Doris
Wife and date of marriage: Lucy, 25 September 1999
Children: Jamie Jonathan Paul, 4 April 2001
Family links with cricket: 'Father and both brothers (Richard and Simon) are closely associated with Weston-super-Mare CC. Simon played for Somerset in 1984, also as a wicket-keeper. My wife, Lucy, plays for MCC Ladies and Somerset Ladies (also as a wicket-keeper!)'
Education: Broadoak Comprehensive, Weston-super-Mare; Millfield School, Street; Magdalene College, Cambridge University
Qualifications: BEng (Hons) Engineering, Diploma in Computer Science, NCA coaching award, approved person under the Financial Services Authority
Career outside cricket: Rowan Dartington stockbrokers
Off-season: 'Working at the Taunton branch office of stockbrokers Rowan Dartington'
Overseas tours: Millfield School to Barbados 1985; Combined Universities to Barbados 1989; Qantas Airlines Tournament, Kuala Lumpur, Malaysia 1992-93; English Lions to New Zealand (Cricket Max) 1997; MCC to New Zealand 1999, to Canada 2000; England A to Bangladesh and New Zealand 1999-2000 (vice-captain)
Overseas teams played for: Claremont-Nedlands, Perth, Western Australia 1991-93
Career highlights to date: 'Winning the C&G Trophy 2001 at Lord's – especially catching a skyer to remove Afridi'
Cricket moments to forget: 'Any dropped catch!'
Cricket superstitions: 'Being last out on to the pitch (but that is just an excuse for being late, really!)'
Cricketers particularly admired: Jack Russell

Young players to look out for: Lachlan Cox, Adam Burns, Jamie Turner, Robert Bowler, Fraser Caddick, Felix Rose, Jack and Thomas Shine

Other sports played: Golf ('badly, but holed in one at the par three fourth at Oake Manor GC!')

Other sports followed: Football ('The Villa'), hockey (Taunton Vale Ladies)

Injuries: Out for three weeks with a ruptured tendon in a foot

Relaxations: 'Being entertained by my son'

Extras: Captain of Cambridge University (Blue 1988-91) and Combined Universities 1991. Wombwell Cricket Lovers' Society Wicket-keeper of the Year 1999. Highest-placed Englishman in the 1999 batting averages (6th with 1217 runs at 52.91). Sheffield Cricket Lovers' Society Allrounder of the Year 1999. Was on stand-by for England tours of West Indies 1997-98 and South Africa and Zimbabwe 1999-2000. Made nine dismissals (all caught) in the match v Surrey at Taunton 2001, breaking his own (shared) Somerset record. Took seven catches in an innings v Northamptonshire at Taunton 2001, breaking his own (shared) Somerset record. Wombwell Cricket Lovers' Society Highlight of the Year 2001 (for catching Shahid Afridi in the C&G final)

Opinions on cricket: 'Twenty20 proved to be a great success. I think this will lead to bigger scores in other one-day cricket and more excitement for both players and spectators.'

Best batting: 144 Somerset v Kent, Taunton 1997

2003 Season

	M	Inns	NO	Runs	HS	Avge	100s	50s	Ct	St	O	M	Runs	Wkts	Avge	Best	5wI	10wM
Test																		
All First	16	26	9	641	139 *	37.70	1	3	65	5								
1-day Int																		
C & G	2	1	1	13	13 *	-	-	-	4	-								
NCL	9	7	3	114	27 *	28.50	-	-	4	3								
Twenty20	5	4	0	24	11	6.00	-	-	3	-								

Career Performances

	M	Inns	NO	Runs	HS	Avge	100s	50s	Ct	St	Balls		Runs	Wkts	Avge	Best	5wI	10wM
Test																		
All First	225	349	64	8896	144	31.21	10	45	620	45	79		58	0	-	-	-	-
1-day Int																		
C & G	29	23	9	504	52	36.00	-	2	43	3								
NCL	144	125	39	2018	67	23.46	-	6	132	26								
Twenty20	5	4	0	24	11	6.00	-	-	3	-								

UDAL, S. D.

Name: <u>Shaun</u> David Udal
Role: Right-hand bat, off-spin bowler
Born: 18 March 1969, Farnborough, Hants
Height: 6ft 3in **Weight:** 14st
Nickname: Shaggy
County debut: 1989
County cap: 1992
Benefit: 2002
One-Day Internationals: 10
50 wickets in a season: 7
1st-Class 50s: 25
1st-Class 100s: 1
1st-Class 5 w. in innings: 29
1st-Class 10 w. in match: 4
1st-Class catches: 97
One-Day 5 w. in innings: 1
Place in batting averages: 162nd av. 27.11
(2002 174th av. 25.80)
Place in bowling averages: 71st av. 32.14 (2002 87th av. 33.17)
Strike rate: 62.38 (career 69.29)
Parents: Robin and Mary
Wife and date of marriage: Emma Jane, 5 October 1991
Children: Katherine Mary, 26 August 1992; Rebecca Jane, 17 November 1995
Family links with cricket: Grandfather (G. F. Udal) played for Leicestershire and Middlesex. Father played for Camberley CC for over 40 years and also for Surrey Colts; brother Gary is captain of Camberley 1st XI
Education: Cove Comprehensive
Qualifications: 8 CSEs, print finisher, company director
Career outside cricket: Sales and marketing for Quality Forum
Off-season: 'Shoulder op, work, Barbados training'
Overseas tours: England to Australia 1994-95; England A to Pakistan 1995-96; England XI to New Zealand (Cricket Max) 1997; Hampshire to Anguilla 1998, to Cape Town 2001
Overseas teams played for: Hamilton Wickham, Newcastle, NSW 1989-90
Career highlights to date: 'Winning B&H, NatWest and promotion with Hants. Playing for England'
Cricket moments to forget: 'Getting out twice as nightwatchman hooking'
Cricket superstitions: 'Left side on first'
Cricketers particularly admired: Ian Botham, Shane Warne, Robin Smith
Young players to look out for: James Anderson, Chris Tremlett
Other sports played: Football, golf (12 handicap)

Other sports followed: Football (West Ham Utd, Aldershot Town)
Injuries: Two torn tendons in right shoulder requiring surgery in late September 2003
Favourite band: Blue
Relaxations: 'Going out for a beer and meal; living life to the full; my children'
Extras: Has taken two hat-tricks in club cricket. Has scored a double hundred (202) in a 40-over club game. Man of the Match on NatWest debut against Berkshire 1991. Took 8-50 v Sussex in the first game of the 1992 season, his seventh Championship match. Named Hampshire Cricket Association Player of the Year 1993. Vice-captain of Hampshire 1998-2000. Passed 550 first-class wickets and 5000 first-class runs during the 2002 season. Hampshire Players' Player of the Year 2001, 2002. Recorded Hampshire record benefit 2002. Passed 900 career wickets in all cricket for Hampshire during the 2003 season
Opinions on cricket: 'Pitches have to improve – majority are awful. Finger spin is slowly dying as batters see it as their chance for quick runs and try to smash you! Keep supporting county cricket – it is where we all started, even the England contracted players!'
Best batting: 117* Hampshire v Warwickshire, Southampton 1997
Best bowling: 8-50 Hampshire v Sussex, Southampton 1992

2003 Season

	M	Inns	NO	Runs	HS	Avge	100s	50s	Ct	St	O	M	Runs	Wkts	Avge	Best	5wI	10wM
Test																		
All First	16	24	6	488	60 *	27.11	-	3	5	-	436.4	87	1350	42	32.14	4-50	-	-
1-day Int																		
C & G	1	1	1	3	3 *	-	-	-	-	-	10	0	34	1	34.00	1-34	-	
NCL	17	9	4	68	18 *	13.60	-	-	8	-	125.3	4	604	23	26.26	4-40	-	
Twenty20	4	3	2	12	9 *	12.00	-	-	1	-	12	0	106	3	35.33	2-31	-	

Career Performances

	M	Inns	NO	Runs	HS	Avge	100s	50s	Ct	St	Balls	Runs	Wkts	Avge	Best	5wI	10wM
Test																	
All First	216	310	58	5781	117 *	22.94	1	25	97	-	41852	20455	604	33.86	8-50	29	4
1-day Int	10	6	4	35	11 *	17.50	-	-	1	-	570	371	8	46.37	2-37	-	
C & G	31	13	6	139	39 *	19.85	-	-	12	-	1755	1037	40	25.92	4-20	-	
NCL	206	138	40	1489	78	15.19	-	8	71	-	8784	6927	232	29.85	5-43	1	
Twenty20	4	3	2	12	9 *	12.00	-	-	1	-	72	106	3	35.33	2-31	-	

VAAS, W. P. U. J. C.   Hampshire

Name: Warnakulasuriya Patabendige
Ushantha Joseph <u>Chaminda</u> Vaas
Role: Left-hand bat, left-arm
fast-medium bowler
Born: 27 January 1974, Mattumagala,
Sri Lanka
County debut: 2003
Test debut: 1994-95
Tests: 68
One-Day Internationals: 227
1st-Class 50s: 10
1st-Class 5 w. in innings: 16
1st-Class 10 w. in match: 2
1st-Class catches: 31
One-Day 5 w. in innings: 3
Strike rate: 70.50 (career 55.86)
Overseas tours: Sri Lanka U19 to England
1992; Sri Lanka to India 1993-94, to

Zimbabwe 1994-95, to South Africa 1994-95, to New Zealand 1994-95, to Pakistan
1995-96, to Australia 1995-96, to India and Pakistan (World Cup) 1995-96, to New
Zealand 1996-97, to India 1997-98, to South Africa 1997-98, to Bangladesh (Wills
International Cup) 1998-99, to UK, Ireland and Holland (World Cup) 1999, to
Zimbabwe 1999-2000, to Pakistan 1999-2000, to Kenya (ICC Knockout Trophy)
2000-01, to South Africa 2000-01, to England 2002, to South Africa 2002-03, to Africa
(World Cup) 2002-03, to West Indies 2003, plus numerous other one-day series and
tournaments in Sharjah, Singapore, West Indies, Kenya, India, Pakistan, Australia,
Bangladesh, New Zealand and Morocco
Overseas teams played for: Colts CC, Sri Lanka 1990-91 –
Extras: Had match figures of 10-90 (5-47/5-43) in the first Test v New Zealand at
Napier 1994-95, winning Man of the Match award; Man of the Match in the following
Test at Dunedin for his innings of 51 and first innings figures of 6-87. Had match
figures of 14-191 (7-120/7-71) in the third Test v West Indies at Colombo 2001-02,
sharing the Man of the Match award with Brian Lara and becoming only the second
pace bowler to take 14 wickets in a Test on the subcontinent (the first being Imran
Khan – 14-116 v Sri Lanka at Lahore 1981-82). Five days later won Man of the Match
award for his 8-19 v Zimbabwe in the LG Abans Triangular Series at Colombo 2001-02,
a new world's best analysis for ODIs (superseding Muttiah Muralitharan's 7-30 v India
in Sharjah 2000-01); his figures included a hat-trick (Carlisle, Wishart, Taibu) as
Zimbabwe were bowled out for 38. Took a hat-trick (Hannan Sarkar, Mohammad
Ashraful, Ehsanul Haque) with the first three balls of the match v Bangladesh at
Pietermaritzburg in the World Cup 2002-03; took a further wicket in the same over and

finished with 6-25 and the Man of the Match award. Was an overseas player with Hampshire in the latter part of the 2003 season, replacing Wasim Akram
Best batting: 74* Sri Lanka v Zimbabwe, Colombo 2001-02
Best bowling: 7-71 Sri Lanka v West Indies, Colombo 2001-02
Stop press: Man of the Match in ODI v England at Dambulla 2003-04 (3-15)

2003 Season

	M	Inns	NO	Runs	HS	Avge	100s	50s	Ct	St	O	M	Runs	Wkts	Avge	Best	5wI	10wM
Test																		
All First	3	6	2	64	35	16.00	-	-	2	-	94	18	310	8	38.75	4-82	-	-
1-day Int																		
C & G																		
NCL	8	4	2	35	28 *	17.50	-	-	2	-	66.3	8	284	9	31.55	2-24	-	
Twenty20																		

Career Performances

	M	Inns	NO	Runs	HS	Avge	100s	50s	Ct	St	Balls	Runs	Wkts	Avge	Best	5wI	10wM
Test	68	95	15	1557	74 *	19.46	-	6	19	-	15017	6626	216	30.67	7-71	7	2
All First	114	144	30	2249	74 *	19.72	-	10	31	-	22403	10144	403	25.17	7-71	16	2
1-day Int	227	157	53	1481	50 *	14.24	-	1	44	-	11079	7701	282	27.30	8-19	3	
C & G																	
NCL	8	4	2	35	28 *	17.50	-	-	2	-	399	284	9	31.55	2-24	-	
Twenty20																	

VAN JAARSVELD, M.   Northamptonshire

Name: Martin van Jaarsveld
Role: Right-hand top-order bat
Born: 18 June 1974, Klerksdorp, South Africa
Height: 6ft 2in **Weight:** 12st 12lbs
Nickname: Jarre
County debut: No first-team appearance
Test debut: 2002-03
Tests: 3
One-Day Internationals: 9
1st-Class 50s: 22
1st-Class 100s: 15
1st-Class 200s: 1
1st-Class catches: 97
Strike rate: (career 86.17)
Parents: Leon and Isobel
Marital status: Single
Education: Warmbads High School; University of Pretoria

Qualifications: BComm (Financial Management)

Off-season: 'Playing cricket for Northerns Titans in South Africa'

Overseas tours: South Africa A to Sri Lanka 1998, to Zimbabwe (one-day series) 2002-03, to Australia 2002-03; South African Academy to Zimbabwe 1998-99; South Africa to England 2003

Overseas teams played for: Northern Transvaal/Northerns Titans 1994-95 –

Career highlights to date: 'Playing for South Africa. Being chosen as one of the five Cricketers of the Year in South Africa 2002'

Cricket moments to forget: 'Losing the NatWest Series final at Lord's, July 2003'

Cricket superstitions: 'Left pad first when padding up'

Cricketers particularly admired: Michael Atherton, Kepler Wessels

Other sports played: Golf, tennis

Other sports followed: Rugby, 'and most other sports'

Favourite band: Live

Relaxations: 'Having throw-downs; going to the cinema'

Extras: Made first-class debut for Northern Transvaal B v Natal B at Durban 1994-95. Player of the SuperSport Series 2001-02 for his 934 runs at 84.90; also topped South African first-class averages for the season with 1268 runs at 74.58. Scored 182* and 158* v Griqualand West at Centurion 2001-02, becoming only the second batsman to record two 150s in the same match in South Africa and setting a new record individual aggregate score for South African first-class cricket (340). Scored 155 (out of 286) in Northerns' first innings in the 2001-02 SuperSport Series final v KwaZulu-Natal at Durban. One of *South African Cricket Annual*'s five Cricketers of the Year 2002. Played for Suffolk in the first round of the C&G 2004, which was played in August 2003. Has joined Northamptonshire as an overseas player for 2004

Best batting: 238* Northerns v Griqualand West, Kimberley 1999-2000

Best bowling: 1-1 Northerns v Boland, Centurion 1998-99

2003 Season

	M	Inns	NO	Runs	HS	Avge	100s	50s	Ct	St	O	M	Runs	Wkts	Avge	Best	5wI	10wM
Test																		
All First																		
1-day Int	7	5	1	82	45	20.50	-	-	2	-	5	1	18	1	18.00	1-18	-	
C & G	1	1	0	21	21	21.00	-	-	3	-	10	0	50	0	-	-	-	-
NCL																		
Twenty20																		

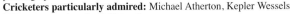

Career Performances

	M	Inns	NO	Runs	HS	Avge	100s	50s	Ct	St	Balls	Runs	Wkts	Avge	Best	5wI	10wM
Test	3	3	1	53	39 *	26.50	-	-	4	-							
All First	81	133	13	5386	238 *	44.88	16	22	97	-	517	298	6	49.66	1-1	-	-
1-day Int	9	6	1	124	45	24.80	-	-	3	-	31	18	2	9.00	1-0	-	
C & G	1	1	0	21	21	21.00	-	-	3	-	60	50	0	-		-	-
NCL																	
Twenty20																	

VAUGHAN, M. P.   Yorkshire

Name: <u>Michael</u> Paul Vaughan
Role: Right-hand bat, off-spin bowler
Born: 29 October 1974, Eccles, Manchester
Height: 6ft 2in **Weight:** 11st 7lbs
Nickname: Frankie, Virgil
County debut: 1993
County cap: 1995
Test debut: 1999-2000
Tests: 35
One-Day Internationals: 35
1000 runs in a season: 4
1st-Class 50s: 48
1st-Class 100s: 32
1st-Class catches: 88
One-Day 100s: 1
Place in batting averages: 86th av. 38.06
(2002 5th av. 75.07)
Strike rate: 120.00 (career 79.00)
Parents: Graham John and Dee
Wife and date of marriage: Nichola, September 2003
Family links with cricket: Father played league cricket for Worsley CC. Brother plays for Sheffield Collegiate. Mother is related to the famous Tyldesley family (Lancashire and England)
Education: Silverdale Comprehensive, Sheffield
Qualifications: 7 GCSEs
Off-season: Touring with England
Overseas tours: Yorkshire to West Indies 1994, to South Africa 1995, to Zimbabwe 1996; England U19 to India 1992-93, to Sri Lanka 1993-94 (captain); England A to India 1994-95, to Australia 1996-97, to Zimbabwe and South Africa 1998-99 (captain); England to South Africa 1999-2000, to Pakistan and Sri Lanka 2000-01, to India and New Zealand 2001-02, to Australia 2002-03, to Africa (World Cup) 2002-03, to Bangladesh and Sri Lanka 2003-04 (captain), to West Indies 2003-04 (captain)

Cricket moments to forget: 'My one-day series in 2001'
Cricketers particularly admired: Darren Lehmann, 'all the Yorkshire and England squads'
Other sports played: Football (Baslow FC), golf (10 handicap)
Other sports followed: Football (Sheffield Wednesday), all golf
Relaxations: Most sports. 'Enjoy a good meal with friends'
Extras: *Daily Telegraph* U15 Batsman of the Year 1990; Maurice Leyland Batting Award 1990; Cricket Society's Most Promising Young Cricketer 1993; A. A. Thompson Memorial Trophy – The Roses Cricketer of the Year 1993. Scored 1066 runs in first full season of first-class cricket 1994. Captained England U19 v India U19 1994. Scored two centuries (100/151) v Essex at Chelmsford 1999. Scored maiden Test century (120) at Old Trafford 2001, in the process sharing in a record partnership for any wicket for England in Tests v Pakistan (267) with Graham Thorpe (138). Scored 115 as England followed on in the first Test v Sri Lanka at Lord's 2002, in the process sharing with Marcus Trescothick (76) in a record first-wicket partnership for England in Tests v Sri Lanka (168). Took part in first-wicket stand of 50 in five overs with Marcus Trescothick to bring England victory with an over to spare in the third Test v Sri Lanka at Old Trafford 2002. Scored 195 in the fourth Test v India at The Oval 2002, in the process becoming only the sixth batsman to score four Test centuries in an English summer; England's Man of the Series v India. PCA Player of the Year 2002. Scored century (145) in the fourth Test v Australia at Melbourne 2002-03, becoming the highest-scoring batsman in Test cricket for the calendar year 2002 with 1481 runs; it was the third highest total by any Test batsman in a calendar year after Viv Richards's 1710 in 1976 and Sunil Gavaskar's 1555 in 1979. Scored century (183) in the fifth Test v Australia at Sydney 2002-03, becoming only the fifth England batsman to score three Test centuries (or more) in a series in Australia; was Man of the Series. His other international awards include Man of the Match in the fifth Test v South Africa at Centurion 1999-2000, in the fourth Test v West Indies at his home ground of Headingley 2000, and in the second Test v India at Trent Bridge 2002. One of *Wisden*'s Five Cricketers of the Year 2003. Topped PricewaterhouseCoopers rankings for Test batsmen in early summer 2003. Vodafone Cricketer of the Year 2002-03. Appointed England one-day captain in May 2003. Appointed England Test captain on the resignation of Nasser Hussain after the first Test v South Africa at Edgbaston 2003. Book *A Year in the Sun* published 2003. ECB central contract 2003-04
Best batting: 197 England v India, Trent Bridge 2002
Best bowling: 4-39 Yorkshire v Oxford University, The Parks 1994
Stop press: Man of the Match in the second Test v Sri Lanka at Kandy 2003-04 (52/105)

2003 Season

	M	Inns	NO	Runs	HS	Avge	100s	50s	Ct	St	O	M	Runs	Wkts	Avge	Best	5wI	10wM
Test	7	12	0	346	156	28.83	1	-	2	-	19	2	63	1	63.00	1-26		
All First	10	18	2	609	156	38.06	2	1	3	-	20	2	68	1	68.00	1-26	-	
1-day Int	9	9	2	241	83	34.42	-	1	3	-	7	0	36	0	-		-	-
C & G	2	2	0	57	47	28.50	-	-	1	-	8	0	41	1	41.00	1-18	-	
NCL	3	3	0	117	90	39.00	-	1	-	-	5	0	32	0	-		-	-
Twenty20																		

Career Performances

	M	Inns	NO	Runs	HS	Avge	100s	50s	Ct	St	Balls	Runs	Wkts	Avge	Best	5wI	10wM
Test	35	61	3	2689	197	46.36	9	5	19	-	654	373	5	74.60	2-71	-	-
All First	193	339	19	12182	197	38.06	32	48	88	-	8928	4978	113	44.05	4-39	-	-
1-day Int	35	34	3	805	83	25.96	-	6	9	-	334	278	8	34.75	4-22	-	
C & G	25	24	2	676	85	30.72	-	5	7	-	342	217	6	36.16	1-4	-	
NCL	95	93	6	2003	90	23.02	-	9	29	-	1028	845	31	27.25	4-27	-	
Twenty20																	

VETTORI, D. L.   Nottinghamshire

Name: <u>Daniel</u> Luca Vettori
Role: Left-hand bat, slow left-arm bowler
Born: 27 January 1979, Auckland, New Zealand
County debut: 2003
County cap: 2003
Test debut: 1996-97
Tests: 46
One-Day Internationals: 111
1st-Class 50s: 9
1st-Class 100s: 1
1st-Class 5 w. in innings: 16
1st-Class 10 w. in match: 1
1st-Class catches: 37
Strike rate: 48.50 (career 70.30)
Family links with cricket: Cousin (J. V. Hill) and uncle (A. J. Hill) played for Central Districts in New Zealand
Overseas tours: New Zealand U19 to England 1996; New Zealand Academy to South Africa 1997; New Zealand to Zimbabwe 1997-98, to Australia 1997-98, to Sri Lanka 1998, to Malaysia (Commonwealth Games) 1998-99, to Bangladesh (Wills International Cup) 1998-99, to UK, Ireland and Holland (World Cup) 1999, to England

1999, to India 1999-2000, to Zimbabwe 2000-01, to Australia 2001-02, to Pakistan 2002, to West Indies 2002, to Sri Lanka (ICC Champions Trophy) 2002-03, to Africa (World Cup) 2002-03, to Sri Lanka 2003, to India 2003-04, plus other one-day series and tournaments in Singapore, Sri Lanka, India and Pakistan

Overseas teams played for: Northern Districts 1996-97 – 2002-03

Extras: Became youngest player to play Test cricket for New Zealand when he made his debut in the second Test v England at Wellington 1996-97 aged 18. One of *New Zealand Cricket Almanack*'s two Cricketers of the Year 2000. Test Man of the Match awards in the second Test v Sri Lanka at Hamilton 1996-97 (4-46/5-84), in the first Test v Australia at Auckland 1999-2000 (5-62/7-87) and in the third Test v Australia at Perth 2001-02 (6-87/2-142). ODI Man of the Match awards v Zimbabwe at Auckland 1997-98 (21/3-29), v West Indies at Taupo 1999-2000 (4-24) and v Sri Lanka in the Bank Alfalah Cup at Dambulla 2003 (4-14 from ten overs). Was an overseas player with Nottinghamshire during July 2003, deputising for Stuart MacGill, absent on international duty; awarded Nottinghamshire cap 2003

Best batting: 112 New Zealanders v Leicestershire, Leicester 1999

Best bowling: 7-87 New Zealand v Australia, Auckland 1999-2000

Stop press: Scored maiden Test century (137*) in the first Test v Pakistan at Hamilton 2003-04

2003 Season

	M	Inns	NO	Runs	HS	Avge	100s	50s	Ct	St	O	M	Runs	Wkts	Avge	Best	5wI	10wM
Test																		
All First	2	3	0	10	10	3.33	-	-	1	-	48.3	2	302	6	50.33	4-74	-	-
1-day Int																		
C & G																		
NCL	1	0	0	0	0	-	-	-	-	-	9	0	36	1	36.00	1-36	-	
Twenty20																		

Career Performances

	M	Inns	NO	Runs	HS	Avge	100s	50s	Ct	St	Balls	Runs	Wkts	Avge	Best	5wI	10wM
Test	46	67	10	940	90	16.49	-	5	22	-	10896	4812	141	34.12	7-87	7	1
All First	80	111	16	1827	112	19.23	1	9	37	-	18489	8157	263	31.01	7-87	16	1
1-day Int	111	71	11	542	30	9.03	-	-	28	-	5018	3599	94	38.28	4-14	-	
C & G																		
NCL	1	0	0	0	0	-	-	-	-	-	54	36	1	36.00	1-36	-	
Twenty20																		

VOROS, J. A. Sussex

Name: <u>Jason</u> Alexander Voros
Role: Left-hand lower-middle-order bat,
left-arm fast-medium bowler
Born: 31 December 1976, Canberra,
Australia
Height: 6ft 2in **Weight:** 14st 6lbs
Nickname: JV, Oz
County debut: No first-team appearance
Parents: Peter and Debbie
Marital status: Single
Family links with cricket: 'Dad coached me
for five years'
Education: Daramalan College, Canberra
Qualifications: Year 10 and Year 12, Levels
1 and 2 cricket coaching
Career outside cricket: Coaching
Off-season: 'Coaching and playing golf;
travelling home to Australia'

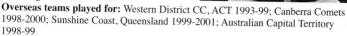

Overseas teams played for: Western District CC, ACT 1993-99; Canberra Comets
1998-2000; Sunshine Coast, Queensland 1999-2001; Australian Capital Territory
1998-99
Career highlights to date: 'Man of the Match v Tasmania – took 3-28 and a classic
catch in a televised match' (*ACT v Tasmania at Canberra in the Mercantile Mutual
Cup 1998-99*)
Cricket moments to forget: 'Going for 85 runs off nine overs at the hands of Adam
Gilchrist and Damien Martyn'
Cricket superstitions: 'None'
Cricketers particularly admired: Dennis Lillee, Merv Hughes, Wasim Akram
Young players to look out for: Michael Clarke, Sam Latus, Jack Latus,
Tim Appleyard, Chris Gray
Other sports played: Golf, tennis, rugby union (Australian Schoolboys 1996)
Other sports followed: Football (Arsenal)
Injuries: Out for 'a few games' with an ankle injury
Favourite band: Hunters and Collectors, Crowded House
Relaxations: 'Golf; spending time with my girlfriend Helen'
Extras: 'Life-saving back in Oz.' Played for Commonwealth Bank [Australian]
Cricket Academy 1999-2001. Was in Queensland Bulls training squad 2000-01. Played
for Sussex 2nd XI 2003. Has Hungarian parents and is not considered an overseas
player
Opinions on cricket: 'I think there should be more focus on bringing our juniors
through. There is not enough four-day and five-day cricket played for younger
cricketers.'

WAGG, G. G. Warwickshire

Name: <u>Graham</u> Grant Wagg
Role: Right-hand bat, left-arm
fast-medium bowler
Born: 28 April 1983, Rugby
Height: 6ft **Weight:** 12st 10lbs
Nickname: Stiggy, Waggy, Captain
Caveman, Wild Card, Ug
County debut: 2002
1st-Class 50s: 2
1st-Class catches: 1
Place in batting averages: (2002 166th
av. 26.83)
Place in bowling averages: (2002 55th
av. 28.58)
Strike rate: 48.00 (career 43.35)
Parents: John and Dawn
Marital status: Single
Family links with cricket: Father is
qualified coach

Education: Ashlawn School, Rugby
Qualifications: Level 1 cricket coach
Off-season: ECB National Academy
Overseas tours: Warwickshire Development tour to South Africa 1998, to West Indies
2000; ECB National Academy (England A) to Malaysia and India 2003-04
Overseas teams played for: Hams Tech, East London, South Africa 1999
Career highlights to date: 'Four wickets and 50 on first-class debut'
Cricket moments to forget: 'Being hit for 10 off the last two balls against India U19
when they needed eight to win'
Cricketers particularly admired: Stuart MacGill, John Wagg
Other sports played: Golf, carp fishing
Other sports followed: Football (Man United), cricket (Leamington CC)
Relaxations: 'Fishing, music, clubbing'
Extras: Represented England U16, U17 and U18. Played for Warwickshire Board XI
in the NatWest 2000 and C&G 2002. Member of Warwickshire's ECB U19 County
Championship winning squad 2001. Took 5-57 and scored 40* for Development of
Excellence (Midlands) XI v West Indies U19 at Oakham School 2001. Represented
England U19 v India U19 2002. Scored 42* from 50 balls, 51 from 57 balls and took
4-43 on first-class debut v Somerset at Edgbaston 2002. Took 4-50 on NUL debut v
Kent at Edgbaston 2002. Selected for the ECB National Academy squad to Australia
and Sri Lanka 2002-03 but was forced to withdraw with a back injury. Struck 52-ball
74 (having taken 14 balls to get off the mark) v India A at Edgbaston 2003

Best batting: 74 Warwickshire v India A, Edgbaston 2003
Best bowling: 4-43 Warwickshire v Somerset, Edgbaston 2002

2003 Season

	M	Inns	NO	Runs	HS	Avge	100s	50s	Ct	St	O	M	Runs	Wkts	Avge	Best	5wI	10wM
Test																		
All First	2	3	0	89	74	29.66	-	1	-	-	40	4	250	5	50.00	2-61	-	-
1-day Int																		
C & G	2	2	0	20	19	10.00	-	-	1	-	9	1	59	0	-		-	-
NCL	4	3	1	74	32	37.00	-	-	3	-	26	1	170	5	34.00	2-38	-	
Twenty20	7	6	0	52	15	8.66	-	-	1	-	17	0	134	8	16.75	3-33	-	

Career Performances

	M	Inns	NO	Runs	HS	Avge	100s	50s	Ct	St	Balls	Runs	Wkts	Avge	Best	5wI	10wM
Test																	
All First	7	11	2	250	74	27.77	-	2	1	-	737	593	17	34.88	4-43	-	-
1-day Int																	
C & G	4	4	0	41	21	10.25	-	-	1	-	144	111	3	37.00	3-35	-	
NCL	7	4	1	76	32	25.33	-	-	5	-	288	276	11	25.09	4-50	-	
Twenty20	7	6	0	52	15	8.66	-	-	1	-	102	134	8	16.75	3-33	-	

WAGH, M. A.   Warwickshire

Name: <u>Mark</u> Anant Wagh
Role: Right-hand bat, off-spin bowler
Born: 20 October 1976, Birmingham
Height: 6ft 2in **Weight:** 13st
Nickname: Waggy
County debut: 1997
County cap: 2000
1000 runs in a season: 2
1st-Class 50s: 27
1st-Class 100s: 14
1st-Class 200s: 1
1st-Class 300s: 1
1st-Class 5 w. in innings: 2
1st-Class catches: 53
Place in batting averages: 47th av. 45.48
(2002 157th av. 27.94)
Place in bowling averages: 99th av. 36.50
(2002 124th av. 40.26)
Strike rate: 58.05 (career 86.08)
Parents: Mohan and Rita

Marital status: Single
Education: King Edward's School, Birmingham; Keble College, Oxford
Qualifications: BA degree, Level 2 coaching award
Off-season: 'Mumbai/Perth'
Overseas tours: Warwickshire U19 to South Africa 1992; ECB National Academy to Australia 2001-02
Career highlights to date: '315 at Lord's 2001'
Cricket moments to forget: 'Too many to mention'
Cricketers particularly admired: Andy Flower
Young players to look out for: Moeen Ali
Injuries: Out for ten days with a shoulder injury
Favourite band: Dido
Extras: Oxford Blue 1996-98; Oxford University captain 1997. Scored maiden first-class century (116) v Glamorgan at The Parks 1997, following up with another 100 (101) in the second innings to become the first batsman to score a century in each innings of a match for Oxford University since Imran Khan did so v Nottinghamshire in 1974 and the fourth youngest batsman (at 20 years 230 days) to score twin centuries in English first-class cricket. Attended Zimbabwe Cricket Academy 1999. With Michael Powell, shared in record first-wicket stand for Warwickshire in matches v Essex (230) at Chelmsford 2000. His 315 v Middlesex at Lord's 2001 is the second highest score by a batsman for Warwickshire (behind Brian Lara's 501* in 1994) and the equal second highest individual Championship score made at Lord's (behind Jack Hobbs's 316 in 1926)
Best batting: 315 Warwickshire v Middlesex, Lord's 2001
Best bowling: 7-222 Warwickshire v Lancashire, Edgbaston 2003

2003 Season

	M	Inns	NO	Runs	HS	Avge	100s	50s	Ct	St	O	M	Runs	Wkts	Avge	Best	5wI	10wM
Test																		
All First	16	30	3	1228	138	45.48	3	7	15	-	193.3	28	730	20	36.50	7-222	1	-
1-day Int																		
C & G	3	3	0	23	17	7.66	-	-	1	-	19	1	81	3	27.00	3-35	-	
NCL	9	9	1	204	66	25.50	-	1	4	-	45	0	237	4	59.25	2-19	-	
Twenty20	1	0	0	0	0	-	-	-	-	-								

Career Performances

	M	Inns	NO	Runs	HS	Avge	100s	50s	Ct	St	Balls	Runs	Wkts	Avge	Best	5wI	10wM
Test																	
All First	108	178	16	6302	315	38.90	16	27	53	-	6715	3533	78	45.29	7-222	2	-
1-day Int																	
C & G	6	6	0	91	46	15.16	-	-	1	-	114	81	3	27.00	3-35	-	
NCL	33	31	2	682	84	23.51	-	5	5	-	402	349	4	87.25	2-19	-	
Twenty20	1	0	0	0	0	-	-	-	-	-							

WALKER, G. W.   Leicestershire

Name: <u>George</u> William Walker
Role: Left-hand bat, slow left-arm bowler
Born: 12 May 1984, Norwich
Height: 5ft 10in **Weight:** 12st 8lbs
Nickname: Walks, Walksy
County debut: 2002
1st-Class catches: 2
Strike rate: 174.00 (career 252.00)
Parents: John and Sarah
Marital status: Single
Family links with cricket: 'Just a family
interest'
Education: Norwich School; Loughborough
University ('studying Geography')
Qualifications: 9 GCSEs, 1 AS-level,
3 A-levels, ECB Level II coaching award
Off-season: University at Loughborough
Career highlights to date: 'First-class debut
v Kent 2002. First first-class wicket – Chris Adams – v Sussex 2003'
Cricket moments to forget: 'Any dropped catch'
Cricketers particularly admired: Brian Lara, Jacques Kallis
Young players to look out for: David Thomas, Rod Bunting (both Norfolk)
Other sports played: Football ('only socially for fun')
Other sports followed: Football ('Mighty Norwich City FC. Premiership Champions
2004-05??')
Injuries: Out for two weeks with removal of index fingernail
Favourite band: 50 Cent, Eminem, Groove Amada, JT
Relaxations: 'Socialising, films, chilling with friends'
Extras: Played for Norfolk from U12 to 1st XI. Represented Midlands U13 and U14
and England U14, U15 and U17
Opinions on cricket: 'Enjoy the Twenty20 game – was a good way to increase
spectators and fans, as without these, cricket as a business would fail.'
Best batting: 37* Leicestershire v Kent, Canterbury 2002
Best bowling: 1-92 Leicestershire v Sussex, Hove 2003

2003 Season

	M	Inns	NO	Runs	HS	Avge	100s	50s	Ct	St	O	M	Runs	Wkts	Avge	Best	5wI	10wM
Test																		
All First	2	2	1	25	21	25.00	-	-	1	-	29	3	111	1	111.00	1-92	-	-
1-day Int																		
C & G																		
NCL																		
Twenty20																		

Career Performances

	M	Inns	NO	Runs	HS	Avge	100s	50s	Ct	St	Balls	Runs	Wkts	Avge	Best	5wI	10wM
Test																	
All First	3	4	2	69	37 *	34.50	-	-	2	-	252	161	1	161.00	1-92	-	-
1-day Int																	
C & G																	
NCL																	
Twenty20																	

WALKER, M. J.   Kent

Name: Matthew (Matt) Jonathan Walker
Role: Left-hand bat, right-arm medium bowler
Born: 2 January 1974, Gravesend
Height: 5ft 6in **Weight:** 13st
Nickname: Walks, Pumba
County debut: 1992-93
County cap: 2000
1000 runs in a season: 1
1st-Class 50s: 18
1st-Class 100s: 9
1st-Class 200s: 1
1st-Class catches: 81
One-Day 100s: 3
Place in batting averages: 57th av. 43.79 (2002 231st av. 19.10)
Strike rate: 102.00 (career 111.77)
Parents: Richard and June
Wife and date of marriage: Claudia, 25 September 1999
Children: Charlie Jack, 20 November 2002
Family links with cricket: Grandfather Jack played one game for Kent as a wicket-keeper. Father played for Kent and Middlesex 2nd XIs and was on Lord's groundstaff. Mother coached ex-England Ladies captain Megan Lear

Education: King's School, Rochester
Qualifications: 9 GCSEs, 2 A-levels, advanced coaching award
Career outside cricket: Teacher
Off-season: 'Teaching sport at St Edmund's School'
Overseas tours: Kent U17 to New Zealand 1990-91; England U19 to Pakistan 1991-92, to India 1992-93 (captain); Kent to Zimbabwe 1992-93, to Port Elizabeth 2001
Career highlights to date: 'Captaining England U19. Winning Norwich Union League 2001'
Cricket moments to forget: 'Losing Lord's [B&H] final against Surrey 1997'
Cricket superstitions: 'Try to change as far away from Amjad Khan as possible'
Cricketers particularly admired: Sachin Tendulkar, Darren Lehmann, Damien Martyn
Young players to look out for: Bob Ferley, Joe Denly, Charlie Hemphrey
Other sports played: Hockey (England U14-U21 [captain U15-U17], Kent U14-U21, South East U16-U18), rugby (Kent U18), football (trials for Chelsea and Gillingham), athletics (Kent U15 javelin champion)
Other sports followed: Football (Charlton Athletic), hockey (Gore Court HC)
Favourite band: Matchbox Twenty, Counting Crows, Red Hot Chili Peppers, Stereophonics
Relaxations: Music and films ('avid collector of both')
Extras: Captained England U16 cricket team and England U16 hockey team in same year. Captained England U19 v West Indies U19 in 1993 home series. Sir John Hobbs Silver Jubilee Memorial Prize for outstanding U16 cricketer 1989; *Daily Telegraph* U15 batting award 1989. Woolwich Kent League's Young Cricketer of the Year 1994. Scored 275* against Somerset in 1996 – the highest ever individual score by a Kent batsman at Canterbury – and was on the pitch for the whole game. Scored 94 v Worcestershire at Canterbury in the NUL 2002, in the process sharing with Paul Nixon (60) in a record sixth-wicket partnership for Kent in the one-day league (116). Passed 1000 first-class runs in a season for the first time during his 121 v Warwickshire at Canterbury 2003. Ealham Award for Fielding Excellence 2003. Became an Eminent Roffensian in 1995
Opinions on cricket: 'Should be two up/two down; only one overseas player. Apart from that it's a great game and the sport is in better shape than the press always make it out to be.'
Best batting: 275* Kent v Somerset, Canterbury 1996
Best bowling: 1-3 First-Class Counties XI v New Zealand A, Milton Keynes 2000

2003 Season

	M	Inns	NO	Runs	HS	Avge	100s	50s	Ct	St	O	M	Runs	Wkts	Avge	Best	5wI	10wM
Test																		
All First	17	27	3	1051	150	43.79	3	4	22	-	17	2	75	1	75.00	1-24	-	-
1-day Int																		
C & G	2	2	1	45	23 *	45.00	-	-	2	-								
NCL	16	15	4	573	101	52.09	1	3	1	-	2	0	14	0	-		-	-
Twenty20	5	5	0	84	35	16.80	-	-	1	-								

Career Performances

	M	Inns	NO	Runs	HS	Avge	100s	50s	Ct	St	Balls	Runs	Wkts	Avge	Best	5wI	10wM
Test																	
All First	116	192	21	5263	275*	30.77	10	18	81	-	1006	563	9	62.55	1-3	-	-
1-day Int																	
C & G	16	15	4	358	73	32.54	-	2	5	-	132	92	2	46.00	1-33	-	
NCL	128	121	15	2643	101	24.93	1	13	27	-	363	295	15	19.66	4-24	-	
Twenty20	5	5	0	84	35	16.80	-	-	1	-							

WALLACE, M. A. Glamorgan

Name: Mark Alex Wallace
Role: Left-hand bat, wicket-keeper
Born: 19 November 1981, Abergavenny
Height: 5ft 10in **Weight:** 12st
Nickname: Wally, Gromit, Marcellus
County debut: 1999
County cap: 2003
50 dismissals in a season: 2
1st-Class 50s: 9
1st-Class 100s: 3
1st-Class catches: 162
1st-Class stumpings: 6
Place in batting averages: 149th av. 29.51
(2002 171st av. 26.33)
Parents: Ryland and Alvine
Marital status: Single
Family links with cricket: 'Father plays for
Abergavenny Beavers and Wales Over 50s'
Education: Crickhowell High School
Qualifications: 10 GCSEs, 2 A-levels
Overseas tours: Gwent U15 to South Africa 1996; Wales U16 to Jersey 1996, 1997;
England U19 to New Zealand 1998-99, to Malaysia and (U19 World Cup) Sri Lanka
1999-2000, to India 2000-01; ECB National Academy to Australia 2001-02, to
Australia and Sri Lanka 2002-03
Career highlights to date: 'Winning NUL 2002. Academy selection'
Cricketers particularly admired: Ian Healy, Steve Rhodes, Keith Piper, Alec
Stewart, Adam Gilchrist
Young players to look out for: David Harrison, Jamie Pipe, Jon Hughes, Matthew
Wood ('both'), Kyle Hogg
Other sports played: Football, golf, touch rugby, pool
Other sports followed: Football ('the mighty Merthyr Tydfil FC')

Relaxations: 'Golf, sleep, a few racks with Long, PR work'
Extras: Represented England U17 at the ECC Colts Festival in Northern Ireland 1999. Represented England U19 v Pakistan U19 1998, Australia U19 1999 and Sri Lanka U19 (captain for second 'Test') 2000. Made first-class debut v Somerset at Taunton 1999 aged 17 years 287 days – youngest ever Glamorgan wicket-keeper. NBC Denis Compton Award 1999. Took eight catches in match v Kent at Maidstone 2001, one short of Colin Metson's Glamorgan record. Captained ECB National Academy to innings victory over Commonwealth Bank [Australian] Cricket Academy at Adelaide 2001-02. Made 51 first-class dismissals and scored 856 first-class runs 2003. Byron Denning [Glamorgan] Clubman of the Year Award 2003
Opinions on cricket: 'EU passport situation needs to be sorted. Tea break too short.'
Best batting: 121 Glamorgan v Durham, Riverside 2003

2003 Season

	M	Inns	NO	Runs	HS	Avge	100s	50s	Ct	St	O	M	Runs	Wkts	Avge	Best	5wl	10wM
Test																		
All First	17	29	0	856	121	29.51	2	3	49	2								
1-day Int																		
C & G	2	2	0	15	11	7.50	-	-	2	-								
NCL	16	12	2	111	21 *	11.10	-	-	21	3								
Twenty20	5	4	2	45	19 *	22.50	-	-	1	1								

Career Performances

	M	Inns	NO	Runs	HS	Avge	100s	50s	Ct	St	Balls	Runs	Wkts	Avge	Best	5wl	10wM
Test																	
All First	53	85	10	2045	121	27.26	3	9	162	6							
1-day Int																	
C & G	4	3	0	20	11	6.66	-	-	4	-							
NCL	38	29	6	286	37 *	12.31	-	-	45	12							
Twenty20	5	4	2	45	19 *	22.50	-	-	1	1							

96. Which former Lancashire and Tasmania bowler took 19 wickets in his debut series against England in 1986?

WAQAR YOUNIS Warwickshire

Name: Waqar Younis Maitla
Role: Right-hand bat, right-arm fast bowler
Born: 16 November 1971, Vehari, Pakistan
Height: 5ft 11in **Weight:** 12st
County debut: 1990 (Surrey),
1997 (Glamorgan), 2003 (Warwickshire)
County cap: 1990 (Surrey),
1997 (Glamorgan)
Test debut: 1989-90
Tests: 87
One-Day Internationals: 262
50 wickets in a season: 3
100 wickets in a season: 1
1st-Class 50s: 6
1st-Class 5 w. in innings: 63
1st-Class 10 w. in match: 14
1st-Class catches: 58
One-Day 5 w. in innings: 17
Place in batting averages: 115th av. 33.50
Place in bowling averages: 18th av. 23.51
Strike rate: 37.58 (career 40.78)
Family links with cricket: Younger brother Faisal played for Lahore City 1995-96
Education: Pakistani College, Sharjah; Government College, Vehari
Overseas tours: Pakistan to Sharjah (Champions Trophy) 1989-90, to Australia 1989-90,
to England 1992, to New Zealand 1992-93, to West Indies 1992-93, to New Zealand
1993-94, to Sri Lanka 1994, to South Africa 1994-95, to Australia 1995-96,
to New Zealand 1995-96, to England 1996, to South Africa 1997-98, to Zimbabwe
1997-98, to India 1998-99, to UK, Ireland and Holland (World Cup) 1999, to Australia
1999-2000, to West Indies 1999-2000, to Sri Lanka 2000, to Kenya (ICC Knockout
Trophy) 2000-01, to New Zealand 2000-01, to England 2001 (captain), to Bangladesh
2001-02 (captain), to Sharjah (v West Indies) 2001-02 (captain), to Sri Lanka (ICC
Champions Trophy) 2002-03 (captain), to Sri Lanka and Sharjah (v Australia) 2002-03
(captain), to Zimbabwe 2002-03 (captain), to South Africa 2002-03 (captain), to Africa
(World Cup) 2002-03 (captain), plus numerous other one-day series and tournaments
in India, Sharjah, Australia, South Africa, Zimbabwe, Sri Lanka, Singapore, Toronto,
Kenya and Morocco
Overseas teams played for: Multan 1987-88 – 1997-98; United Bank 1988-89 –
1995-96; Rawalpindi 1998-99; REDCO 1999-2000; Lahore Blues 2000-01; National
Bank of Pakistan 2001-02 – 2002-03; Allied Bank 2003-04
Other sports followed: Football, badminton, squash
Extras: Represented Pakistan U19 in home series v India U19 1988-89. Made Test

debut for Pakistan in the first Test v India at Karachi 1989-90, aged 17, taking 4-80 in India's first innings. Played for Surrey as an overseas player 1990-91 and 1993, taking 113 County Championship wickets (av. 14.36) in 1991 and being named PCA Player of the Year. One of *Wisden*'s Five Cricketers of the Year 1992 and one of *South African Cricket Annual*'s five Cricketers of the Year 1993. Played in World Cup 1995-96. Was Glamorgan's overseas player 1997-98. Took 7-25 (including hat-trick) as Lancashire were bowled out for 51 in 14 overs at Liverpool 1997; took career best 8-17 in next Championship innings as Sussex were bowled out for 54 inside 23 overs at Swansea 1997. Took his 300th Test wicket (Muttiah Muralitharan) in the first Test v Sri Lanka at Colombo 2000 and his 350th (Ryan Hinds) in the second Test v West Indies in Sharjah 2001-02. Became the second bowler (after Wasim Akram) to take 400 ODI wickets when he dismissed Jonty Rhodes v South Africa at Durban 2002-03. Man of the [Test] Series v New Zealand 1990-91 (29 wickets; av. 10.86), performances including 3-20/7-86 in the second Test and 7-76/5-54 in the third. Man of the [Test] Series (jointly with Wasim Akram) v England 1992 (22 wickets; av. 25.31). Man of the NatWest Series 2001, performances including 7-36 v England at Headingley (the then second best analysis in ODI history) and 6-59 v Australia at Trent Bridge in the following match. Has won numerous other Test and ODI awards. Captain of Pakistan 2001 to 2002-03. Was an overseas player with Warwickshire in 2003, replacing the injured Shane Bond.

Best batting: 64 National Bank of Pakistan v Customs, Gujranwala 2001-02
Best bowling: 8-17 Glamorgan v Sussex, Swansea 1997

2003 Season

	M	Inns	NO	Runs	HS	Avge	100s	50s	Ct	St	O	M	Runs	Wkts	Avge	Best	5wI	10wM
Test																		
All First	8	13	5	268	61	33.50	-	2	1	-	244.2	39	917	39	23.51	5-40	3	-
1-day Int																		
C & G	2	1	1	1	1 *	-	-	-	-	-	18.5	2	102	3	34.00	2-41	-	
NCL	11	3	1	25	9	12.50	-	-	2	-	83.3	4	404	20	20.20	4-20	-	
Twenty20	7	3	2	6	6	6.00	-	-	1	-	26	0	181	5	36.20	3-21	-	

Career Performances

	M	Inns	NO	Runs	HS	Avge	100s	50s	Ct	St	Balls	Runs	Wkts	Avge	Best	5wI	10wM
Test	87	120	21	1010	45	10.20	-	-	18	-	16224	8788	373	23.56	7-76	22	5
All First	225	279	62	2907	64	13.39	-	6	58	-	38791	21143	951	22.23	8-17	63	14
1-day Int	262	139	45	969	37	10.30	-	-	35	-	12698	9920	416	23.84	7-36	13	
C & G	16	6	3	76	34 *	25.33	-	-	2	-	1044	705	36	19.58	5-40	1	
NCL	63	26	7	154	39	8.10	-	-	9	-	2814	2097	114	18.39	5-26	1	
Twenty20	7	3	2	6	6	6.00	-	-	1	-	156	181	5	36.20	3-21	-	

WARD, I. J. Sussex

Name: <u>Ian</u> James Ward
Role: Left-hand bat
Born: 30 September 1973, Plymouth
Height: 5ft 9in **Weight:** 13st
Nickname: Wardy, Cocker, Son of Baboon, Dwarf, Stumpy, Pig in a Passage
County debut: 1996 (Surrey)
County cap: 2000 (Surrey)
Test debut: 2001
Tests: 5
1000 runs in a season: 2
1st-Class 50s: 38
1st-Class 100s: 17
1st-Class catches: 63
One-Day 100s: 1
Place in batting averages: 93rd av. 37.21
(2002 13th av. 62.82)
Strike rate: (career 104.33)
Parents: Tony and Mary

Wife and date of marriage: Joanne, 15 February 1998
Children: Robert, 21 September; Lennox, 10 April
Family links with cricket: Grandfather and father played for Devon
Education: Millfield School
Qualifications: 8 GCSEs, 3 A-levels, NCA coaching award
Career outside cricket: 'Sky television/media'
Off-season: 'Working for Sky Sports'
Overseas tours: Surrey U19 to Barbados 1990; Millfield to Jamaica 1991, to Australia; Malden Wanderers to Jersey 1994; England A to Bangladesh and New Zealand 1999-2000, to West Indies 2000-01
Overseas teams played for: North Perth CC, Western Australia 1996-97; Perth CC, Western Australia; Marist Newman Old Boys CC, Perth
Career highlights to date: 'Test debut'
Cricket moments to forget: 'Surrendering County Championship 2003 to Sussex!!'
Cricket superstitions: 'None'
Cricketers particularly admired: Alec Stewart, Saqlain Mushtaq, Graham Thorpe
Young players to look out for: Rory Hamilton-Brown, 'Darren Gough'
Other sports played: Golf
Other sports followed: Football (Liverpool), Formula One, skiing
Injuries: Out for one one-day game with a hip/groin injury
Favourite band: 'The Mark Butcher Band!'
Relaxations: Running, walking dog

Extras: Released by Surrey at 18 and missed four years of cricket, returning to the county in 1996. Scored centuries in three successive Busta Cup matches for England A in West Indies 2000-01 and was leading first-class run-scorer on tour (769 av. 64.08); during his 135 v Barbados at Bridgetown, he shared in record opening stand for England A (224) with Michael Powell. Made Test debut v Pakistan at Lord's 2001 in England's 100th Test at the ground. Scored 95-ball 97 v Glamorgan at The Oval in the C&G 2002 as Surrey posted 438-5 from 50 overs. Scored 168* opening the innings as Surrey scored 410-8 to beat Kent in the Championship at Canterbury 2002 (at one point Surrey were 208-7). Scored four centuries in consecutive Championship innings 2002 – including two centuries in match (112/156) v Hampshire at West End – to equal a Surrey record last achieved by Jack Hobbs in 1925. Leading run-scorer in English first-class cricket 2002 with 1759 runs (av. 62.82). Surrey Player of the Year 2002. Left Surrey at the end of the 2003 season and has joined Sussex for 2004

Opinions on cricket: 'No idea who is English and who is not! Clarification! Cricket needs to evolve as in any business. Must make better use of money filtering down from international revenue. More time for practice needed but with better net facilities. At the moment they are hopeless.'

Best batting: 168* Surrey v Kent, Canterbury 2002
Best bowling: 1-1 Surrey v Hampshire, West End 2002

2003 Season

	M	Inns	NO	Runs	HS	Avge	100s	50s	Ct	St	O	M	Runs	Wkts	Avge	Best	5wI	10wM
Test																		
All First	15	24	1	856	158	37.21	3	2	8	-	16.3	0	76	0	-		-	-
1-day Int																		
C & G	2	2	0	114	108	57.00	1	-	-	-	10	0	49	0	-		-	-
NCL	11	11	1	257	70 *	25.70	-	1	1	-								
Twenty20	6	6	0	186	50	31.00	-	1	3	-								

Career Performances

	M	Inns	NO	Runs	HS	Avge	100s	50s	Ct	St	Balls	Runs	Wkts	Avge	Best	5wI	10wM
Test	5	9	1	129	39	16.12	-	-	1	-							
All First	112	189	16	6923	168 *	40.01	17	38	63	-	313	197	3	65.66	1-1	-	-
1-day Int																	
C & G	19	17	2	611	108	40.73	1	4	1	-	60	49	0	-		-	-
NCL	89	86	9	1940	91	25.19	-	11	17	-	59	92	0	-		-	-
Twenty20	6	6	0	186	50	31.00	-	1	3	-							

---

97. Which former Middlesex batsman, born in St Vincent, made his ODI debut in Trinidad when flown in as a replacement for Mike Gatting in 1986?

WARD, T. R.   Leicestershire

Name: <u>Trevor</u> Robert Ward
Role: Right-hand bat, occasional
off-spin bowler
Born: 18 January 1968, Farningham, Kent
Height: 5ft 11in **Weight:** 13st
Nickname: Wardy, Chikka
County debut: 1986 (Kent),
2000 (Leicestershire)
County cap: 1989 (Kent),
2001 (Leicestershire)
Benefit: 1999 (Kent)
1000 runs in a season: 6
1st-Class 50s: 77
1st-Class 100s: 28
1st-Class 200s: 1
1st-Class catches: 226
One-Day 100s: 10
Place in batting averages: 148th av. 29.53
(2002 202nd av. 23.08)

Strike rate: (career 127.66)
Parents: Robert Henry and Hazel Ann
Wife and date of marriage: Sarah Ann, 29 September 1990
Children: Holly Ann, 23 October 1995; Samuel Joseph, 25 April 1998
Family links with cricket: Father played club cricket
Education: Hextable Comprehensive
Qualifications: 7 O-levels, NCA coaching award
Overseas tours: NCA to Bermuda 1985; England YC to Sri Lanka 1986-87,
to Australia (U19 World Cup) 1987-88
Overseas teams played for: Scarborough, Perth, Western Australia 1985;
Gosnells, Perth 1993
Cricketers particularly admired: Ian Botham, Graham Gooch, Robin Smith
Other sports followed: 'Most sports'
Relaxations: Fishing, watching television, golf
Extras: Was awarded £1000 for becoming the first player to score 400 runs in the
Benson and Hedges Cup in 1995. Released by Kent at the end of the 1999 season and
joined Leicestershire for 2000. Awarded Leicestershire cap on the same day as he
scored a century (110) against his old county Kent at Leicester 2001. Scored 112 v
Sussex at Leicester in the C&G 2002, in the process sharing with Darren Stevens (83)
in a competition record second-wicket partnership for Leicestershire (171). Released
by Leicestershire at the end of the 2003 season
Best batting: 235* Kent v Middlesex, Canterbury 1991
Best bowling: 2-10 Kent v Yorkshire, Canterbury 1996

2003 Season

	M	Inns	NO	Runs	HS	Avge	100s	50s	Ct	St	O	M	Runs	Wkts	Avge	Best	5wI	10wM
Test																		
All First	9	15	0	443	168	29.53	1	1	7	-								
1-day Int																		
C & G	1	1	0	13	13	13.00	-	-	1	-								
NCL	11	11	1	338	104	33.80	1	1	2	-								
Twenty20	2	2	0	8	5	4.00	-	-	-	-								

Career Performances

	M	Inns	NO	Runs	HS	Avge	100s	50s	Ct	St	Balls	Runs	Wkts	Avge	Best	5wI	10wM
Test																	
All First	248	425	22	13876	235 *	34.43	29	77	226	-	1149	694	9	77.11	2-10	-	-
1-day Int																	
C & G	30	30	1	1177	120	40.58	2	9	6	-	174	154	4	38.50	2-25	-	
NCL	223	217	8	5860	131	28.03	5	36	57	-	228	187	6	31.16	3-20	-	
Twenty20	2	2	0	8	5	4.00	-	-	-	-							

WARNE, S. K. Hampshire

Name: <u>Shane</u> Keith Warne
Role: Right-hand bat, leg-spin bowler, county captain
Born: 13 September 1969, Upper Ferntree Gully, Victoria, Australia
Height: 6ft
Nickname: Warney, Hollywood
County debut: 2000
County cap: 2000
Test debut: 1991-92
Tests: 107
One-Day Internationals: 193
50 wickets in a season: 1
1st-Class 50s: 15
1st-Class 5 w. in innings: 40
1st-Class 10 w. in match: 6
1st-Class catches: 156
One-Day 5 w. in innings: 1
Strike rate: (career 59.32)
Parents: Keith and Brigitte
Wife and date of marriage: Simone, 1 September 1995
Children: Brooke, Jackson and Summer

Education: Mentone Grammar School
Overseas tours: Australia YC to West Indies 1990; Australia B to Zimbabwe 1991-92; Australia to Sri Lanka 1992, to New Zealand 1992-93, to England 1993, to South Africa 1993-94, to Pakistan 1994-95, to West Indies 1994-95, to India, Pakistan and Sri Lanka (World Cup) 1995-96, to South Africa 1996-97, to England 1997, to India 1997-98, to West Indies 1998-99, to UK, Ireland and Holland (World Cup) 1999, to Sri Lanka 1999, to Zimbabwe 1999-2000, to New Zealand 1999-2000, to India 2000-01, to England 2001, to South Africa 2001-02, to Sri Lanka (ICC Champions Trophy) 2002-03, to Sri Lanka and Sharjah (v Pakistan) 2002-03, plus other one-day series and tournaments in Sharjah, Sri Lanka, Pakistan, New Zealand, India, South Africa and Kenya
Overseas teams played for: St Kilda, Victoria; Victoria 1990-91 –
Cricketers particularly admired: Ian Chappell, Allan Border, Peter Hartley
Other sports played: Golf (14 handicap)
Other sports followed: Football (Chelsea), Australian Rules (St Kilda)
Extras: Attended Australian Cricket Academy 1990. One of *Wisden*'s Five Cricketers of the Year 1994, one of *South African Cricket Annual*'s five Cricketers of the Year 1994, and one of *Indian Cricket*'s five Cricketers of the Year 1996. Took hat-trick (DeFreitas, Gough, Malcolm) in the second Test v England at Melbourne 1994-95. Was leading wicket-taker in world Test cricket in the 1990s with 351 wickets (av. 25.67). Voted one of *Wisden*'s Five Cricketers of the Century 2000. Voted Carlton and United One-Day International Player of the Year at the inaugural Allan Border Medal awards January 2000. Tops the list of Australian Test wicket-takers, having passed Dennis Lillee's record of 355 by dismissing Paul Wiseman of New Zealand in the first Test at Auckland 2000. Featured on a limited-edition Australian stamp issued in 2000. Took 400th Test wicket (Alec Stewart) in the fifth Test v England at The Oval 2001. Returned match figures of 6-70 in the first Test v South Africa at Johannesburg 2001-02, in the process moving into second place in the all-time list of Test wicket-takers behind Courtney Walsh. Bowled 98 overs for his 8-231 (2-70/6-161) in the second Test v South Africa at Cape Town 2001-02, winning the Man of the Match award in his 100th Test; also scored 63 in the first innings to become the fourth cricketer to pass 2000 runs and 400 wickets in Tests. Has won numerous other Test match and series awards, among them Man of the Series in the 1993 Ashes in England (34 wickets; av. 25.79) and v South Africa in Australia 1997-98 (20; 20.85). Also Man of the Series v Pakistan in Colombo and Sharjah 2002-03 for his 27 wickets (av. 12.66), an Australian three-match-series record; his figures included 8-24 (4-11/4-13) as Pakistan were bowled out for 59 and 53 in the second Test in Sharjah. Has also won numerous ODI awards, including Man of the Match in the 1999 World Cup semi-final v South Africa at Edgbaston (4-29) and final v Pakistan at Lord's (4-33). Has captained Australia in ODIs. Was Hampshire's overseas player in 2000; he was due to return in 2003 but was suspended from all cricket for 12 months from February of that year by the ACB anti-doping committee after testing positive for a banned diuretic; has rejoined Hampshire as an overseas player and as captain for 2004. ACB contract 2003-04
Opinions on cricket: 'Play to win. Never give up!'

Best batting: 99 Australia v New Zealand, Perth 2001-02
Best bowling: 8-71 Australia v England, Brisbane 1994-95
Stop press: Selected for Australia's tour to Sri Lanka 2003-04

2003 Season (did not make any first-class or one-day appearances)

Career Performances

	M	Inns	NO	Runs	HS	Avge	100s	50s	Ct	St	Balls	Runs	Wkts	Avge	Best	5wl	10wM
Test	107	146	13	2238	99	16.82	-	8	86	-	29876	12624	491	25.71	8-71	23	6
All First	200	267	34	4103	99	17.60	-	15	156	-	50427	22220	850	26.14	8-71	40	6
1-day Int	193	106	28	1016	55	13.02	-	1	79	-	10600	7513	291	25.81	5-33	1	
C & G	3	2	1	20	20	20.00	-	-	-	-	162	84	8	10.50	4-34	-	
NCL	13	13	1	151	34	12.58	-	-	5	-	678	438	25	17.52	4-23	-	
Twenty20																	

WARREN, N. A.   Warwickshire

Name: <u>Nick</u> Alexander Warren
Role: Right-hand bat, right-arm
medium-fast bowler
Born: 26 June 1982, Moseley
Height: 5ft 11in **Weight:** 12st 7lbs
Nickname: Wazza
County debut: 2002
Strike rate: (career 60.00)
Parents: Lesley
Marital status: Single
Education: Wheelers Lane Boys School;
Solihull Sixth Form College
Qualifications: 9 GCSEs, BTEC Sports
Science
Overseas tours: Warwickshire U19 to Cape
Town 1998-99; England U17 to Ireland 1999;
England U19 to Malaysia and (U19 World
Cup) Sri Lanka 1999-2000
Cricketers particularly admired: Allan Donald, Graeme Welch
Other sports played: Football
Other sports followed: Football (Birmingham City)
Relaxations: Watching films; planes, music
Extras: Played for Warwickshire Board XI in the C&G 2002. Played for the
Warwickshire Board XI side that won the final ECB 38-County competition 2002
Best batting: 11 Warwickshire v West Indies A, Edgbaston 2002
Best bowling: 2-48 Warwickshire v West Indies A, Edgbaston 2002

2003 Season

	M	Inns	NO	Runs	HS	Avge	100s	50s	Ct	St	O	M	Runs	Wkts	Avge	Best	5wI	10wM
Test																		
All First																		
1-day Int																		
C & G																		
NCL	1	1	1	0	0*	-	-	-	-	-	6	1	42	0	-	-	-	
Twenty20																		

Career Performances

	M	Inns	NO	Runs	HS	Avge	100s	50s	Ct	St	Balls	Runs	Wkts	Avge	Best	5wI	10wM
Test																	
All First	1	2	1	13	11	13.00	-	-	-	-	120	90	2	45.00	2-48	-	-
1-day Int																	
C & G	1	1	0	0	0	0.00	-	-	2	-	36	29	0	-	-	-	
NCL	2	2	1	2	2	2.00	-	-	-	-	66	76	3	25.33	3-34	-	
Twenty20																	

WARREN, R. J.   Nottinghamshire

Name: Russell John Warren
Role: Right-hand bat, wicket-keeper
Born: 10 September 1971, Northampton
Height: 6ft 2in **Weight:** 13st 4lbs
Nickname: Rab C, Rabbit
County debut: 1992 (Northamptonshire),
2003 (Nottinghamshire)
County cap: 1995 (Northamptonshire)
1000 runs in a season: 1
1st-Class 50s: 33
1st-Class 100s: 12
1st-Class 200s: 1
1st-Class catches: 115
1st-Class stumpings: 5
One-Day 100s: 1
Place in batting averages: 45th av. 45.87
(2002 99th av. 36.90)
Parents: John and Sally
Marital status: Engaged
Family links with cricket: 'Dad likes a bet. Mum follows scores on Teletext'
Education: Kingsthorpe Middle and Upper Schools
Qualifications: 8 O-levels, 2 A-levels

Overseas tours: England YC to New Zealand 1990-91; Northamptonshire to Cape Town 1993, to Zimbabwe 1995, to Johannesburg 1996, to Grenada 2000; Nottinghamshire to Pretoria 2003

Overseas teams played for: Lancaster Park, Christchurch, and Canterbury B, New Zealand 1991-93; Riverside CC, Lower Hutt, New Zealand 1994-95; Petone CC, Wellington, New Zealand 1995-96; Alma Marist CC, Cape Town, South Africa 1997-98

Career highlights to date: 'Scoring a century in both innings at Lord's v Middlesex 2003'

Cricketers particularly admired: Allan Lamb, Wayne Larkins

Young players to look out for: Samit Patel

Other sports played: Golf, snooker

Other sports followed: Football (Manchester United, Northampton Town, Nottingham Forest), rugby (Northampton Saints), golf, snooker and horse racing

Injuries: Out for five weeks with two broken fingers; for six weeks with a torn disc in the lower back

Favourite band: The Thrills

Relaxations: 'Music, watching golf'

Extras: Scored 175 v Glamorgan at Northampton 2001, in the process sharing with Tony Penberthy (132*) in a record sixth-wicket partnership for Northants in matches against Glamorgan (250). Scored 144 v Somerset at Taunton 2001, in the process sharing with Mike Hussey (208) in a record third-wicket partnership for Northants in matches against Somerset (287). Released by Northamptonshire at the end of the 2002 season and joined Nottinghamshire for 2003. Scored century in each innings (123/113*) v Middlesex at Lord's 2003

Best batting: 201* Northamptonshire v Glamorgan, Northampton 1996

2003 Season

	M	Inns	NO	Runs	HS	Avge	100s	50s	Ct	St	O	M	Runs	Wkts	Avge	Best	5wI	10wM
Test																		
All First	9	18	2	734	123	45.87	3	2	9	2								
1-day Int																		
C & G																		
NCL	10	10	1	197	91	21.88	-	1	7	1								
Twenty20																		

Career Performances

	M	Inns	NO	Runs	HS	Avge	100s	50s	Ct	St	Balls	Runs	Wkts	Avge	Best	5wI	10wM
Test																	
All First	119	197	22	6501	201 *	37.14	13	33	115	5	6	0	0	-	-	-	-
1-day Int																	
C & G	21	19	3	459	100 *	28.68	1	2	21	1							
NCL	106	95	14	1957	93	24.16	-	9	82	10							
Twenty20																	

WASIM AKRAM　　　　　　　Hampshire

Name: Wasim Akram
Role: Left-hand bat, left-arm
fast bowler
Born: 3 June 1966, Lahore, Pakistan
Height: 6ft 3in　**Weight:** 12st 7lbs
County debut: 1988 (Lancashire),
2003 (Hampshire)
County cap: 1989 (Lancashire)
Benefit: 1998 (Lancashire; £100,000)
Test debut: 1984-85
Tests: 104

One-Day Internationals: 356
50 wickets in a season: 5
1st-Class 50s: 24
1st-Class 100s: 6
1st-Class 200s: 1
1st-Class 5 w. in innings: 70
1st-Class 10 w. in match: 16
1st-Class catches: 97
One-Day 5 w. in innings: 9
Place in batting averages: 278th av. 9.16
Place in bowling averages: 29th av. 25.15
Strike rate: 50.25 (career 48.25)
Parents: Choudhary Mohd. Akram and Irshad Begum
Wife: Huma Akram
Children: Tahmoor Akram (son), 21 August 1997
Education: Cathedral School, Lahore; Islamia College, Civil Lines, Lahore
Overseas tours: Pakistan U23 to Sri Lanka 1984-85; Pakistan to New Zealand 1984-85, to Sri Lanka 1985-86, to India 1986-87, to England 1987, to West Indies 1987-88, to Australia 1989-90, to Australia and New Zealand (World Cup) 1991-92, to England 1992, to New Zealand 1992-93, to West Indies 1992-93 (captain), to New Zealand 1993-94, to Sri Lanka 1994, to South Africa 1994-95, to Zimbabwe 1994-95, to Australia 1995-96 (captain), to New Zealand 1995-96 (captain), to England 1996 (captain), to South Africa 1997-98, to Zimbabwe 1997-98, to Bangladesh (Wills International Cup) 1998-99, to India 1998-99 (captain), to UK, Ireland and Holland (World Cup) 1999 (captain), to Australia 1999-2000, to West Indies 1999-2000, to Sri Lanka 2000, to Kenya (ICC Knockout Trophy) 2000-01, to New Zealand 2000-01, to England 2001, to Bangladesh 2001-02, to Sharjah (v West Indies) 2001-02, to Sri Lanka (ICC Champions Trophy) 2002-03, to South Africa 2002-03, to Africa (World Cup) 2002-03, plus other one-day series and tournaments in Australia, Sharjah, Bangladesh, India, South Africa, Zimbabwe, Sri Lanka, Toronto, Kenya and Morocco

Overseas teams played for: Pakistan Automobile Corporation 1984-85 – 1985-86; Pakistan International Airlines 1987-88 – 2001-02; has also played for Lahore City Whites, Lahore City and Lahore Blues
Cricketers particularly admired: Viv Richards, Imran Khan
Other sports played: Golf, hunting, fishing, squash
Other sports followed: Golf, football (Manchester United)
Relaxations: TV, reading, golf
Extras: Made Test debut in only his fourth first-class match in the second Test v New Zealand at Auckland 1984-85 and was Man of the Match in the third Test at Dunedin (5-56/5-72). One of *Indian Cricket*'s five Cricketers of the Year 1987. Played in the 1987-88 and 1995-96 World Cups. Overseas player with Lancashire 1988-91, 1993-95 and 1997-98 (captain 1998). One of *Wisden*'s five Cricketers of the Year 1993. Captain of Pakistan in several spells from 1992-93 to 2000, including 1995-96 and 1999 World Cups. Took 300th Test victim (Alan Mullally) v England in the third Test at The Oval 1996. Scored 257* in the first Test v Zimbabwe at Sheikhupura 1996-97 (the highest score by No. 8 in Test history), in the process sharing with Saqlain Mushtaq (79) in a world record eighth-wicket partnership in Tests (313) and winning Man of the Match award. Became the first bowler to take 300 wickets in ODIs when he dismissed David Houghton v Zimbabwe at Quetta 1996-97. Took 363rd Test wicket (N. Mongia) in the second Test v India at New Delhi 1998-99, taking him past Imran Khan's 362 and making him Pakistan's highest Test wicket-taker. Took 400th ODI wicket (Damien Martyn) v Australia at Sydney 1999-2000 and 400th Test wicket (Russel Arnold) in the first Test v Sri Lanka at Colombo 2000. Was first Pakistan cricketer to take a Test hat-trick, v Sri Lanka at Lahore in the Asian Test Championship 1998-99, following up with another, also v Sri Lanka, at Dhaka in the next match (the final). Has taken two ODI hat-tricks, v West Indies in Sharjah 1989-90 and v Australia, also in Sharjah 1989-90. Has won numerous Test series and match awards, including Man of the Series v Australia 1989-90 (in which he took 17 wickets at 18.70; also scored his maiden Test 100 – 123 – in the second Test at Adelaide) and (jointly with Waqar Younis) v England 1992 (21 wickets; av. 22.00). Has also won numerous ODI awards, including Man of the Match in the 1991-92 World Cup final v England for his 19-ball 33 and figures of 3-49. Became the first bowler to take 500 ODI wickets when he dismissed Nick Statham v Holland at Paarl in the World Cup 2002-03. Made a record 38 World Cup appearances. Retired from international cricket in May 2003. Joined Hampshire as an overseas player for 2003 but left part-way through the season due to ill health and has retired. Lifetime Achievement Award and Pride of Performance from President of Pakistan
Best batting: 257* Pakistan v Zimbabwe, Sheikhupura 1996-97
Best bowling: 8-30 Lancashire v Somerset, Southport 1994

2003 Season

	M	Inns	NO	Runs	HS	Avge	100s	50s	Ct	St	O	M	Runs	Wkts	Avge	Best	5wI	10wM
Test																		
All First	5	7	1	55	23	9.16	-	-	-	-	167.3	44	503	20	25.15	3-31	-	-
1-day Int																		
C & G	1	1	0	38	38	38.00	-	-	-	-	10	1	47	0	-		-	-
NCL	8	4	2	11	10 *	5.50	-	-	-	-	63.4	9	231	10	23.10	3-17	-	
Twenty20	5	5	1	55	24	13.75	-	-	-	-	19	1	121	8	15.12	2-19	-	

Career Performances

	M	Inns	NO	Runs	HS	Avge	100s	50s	Ct	St	Balls	Runs	Wkts	Avge	Best	5wI	10wM
Test	104	147	19	2898	257 *	22.64	3	7	44	-	22627	9780	414	23.62	7-119	25	5
All First	257	355	40	7161	257 *	22.73	7	24	97	-	50277	22549	1042	21.64	8-30	70	16
1-day Int	356	280	55	3717	86	16.52	-	6	88	-	18186	11811	502	23.52	5-15	6	
C & G	21	17	4	267	50	20.53	-	1	6	-	1340	860	29	29.65	4-27	-	
NCL	114	90	24	1414	75 *	21.42	-	3	23	-	4862	3406	173	19.68	5-41	1	
Twenty20	5	5	1	55	24	13.75	-	-	-	-	114	121	8	15.12	2-19	-	

WATKINS, R. E.　　　　　Glamorgan

Name: Ryan Edward Watkins
Role: Left-hand bat, right-arm
medium bowler
Born: 9 June 1983, Abergavenny,
Monmouthshire
Height: 6ft **Weight:** 13st 7lbs
Nickname: Tetanus
County debut: 2003 (one-day)
Parents: Huw and Gaynor
Marital status: Single
Family links with cricket: 'Father and
brother keen club cricketers'
Education: Pontllanfraith CS;
Cross Keys College
Qualifications: Level 2 coach
Career outside cricket: Motor trade
Off-season: 'Playing in Australia'
Overseas teams played for: North Balwyn

CC, Victoria, Australia 2003
Career highlights to date: 'First-team debut in Twenty20 Cup'
Cricket superstitions: 'Always put right pad on before the left'
Cricketers particularly admired: 'Too many to single one out'

Young players to look out for: Adam Harrison, Mike O'Shea
Other sports played: Football (Ynysddu Crusaders – 'George Ford Gwent County Third Division!')
Other sports followed: Football (Tottenham Hotspur)
Favourite band: 'No one favourite'
Relaxations: Golf, pool

2003 Season

	M	Inns	NO	Runs	HS	Avge	100s	50s	Ct	St	O	M	Runs	Wkts	Avge	Best	5wI	10wM
Test																		
All First																		
1-day Int																		
C & G																		
NCL																		
Twenty20	2	1	1	6	6 *	-	-	-	2	-	4	0	38	2	19.00	2-8	-	

Career Performances

	M	Inns	NO	Runs	HS	Avge	100s	50s	Ct	St	Balls	Runs	Wkts	Avge	Best	5wI	10wM
Test																	
All First																	
1-day Int																	
C & G																	
NCL																	
Twenty20	2	1	1	6	6 *	-	-	-	2	-	24	38	2	19.00	2-8	-	

WATKINSON, M.   Lancashire

Name: Michael Watkinson
Role: Right-hand bat, right-arm medium or off-spin bowler
Born: 1 August 1961, Westhoughton, Greater Manchester
Height: 6ft 1½in **Weight:** 13st
Nickname: Winker
County debut: 1982
County cap: 1987
Benefit: 1996 (£209,000)
Test debut: 1995
Tests: 4
One-Day Internationals: 1
1000 runs in a season: 1
50 wickets in a season: 7
1st-Class 50s: 50
1st-Class 100s: 11
1st-Class 5 w. in innings: 27

1st-Class 10 w. in match: 3
1st-Class catches: 156
One-Day 100s: 2
One-Day 5 w. in innings: 3
Strike rate: (career 64.69)
Parents: Albert and Marian
Wife and date of marriage: Susan,
12 April 1986
Children: Charlotte, 24 February 1989;
Liam, 27 July 1991
Education: Rivington and Blackrod High
School, Horwich
Qualifications: 8 O-levels, HTC Civil
Engineering
Career outside cricket: Draughtsman
Overseas tours: England to South Africa
1995-96
Cricketers particularly admired:
Clive Lloyd, Imran Khan
Other sports followed: Football
Relaxations: Watching Bolton Wanderers
Extras: Played for Cheshire in Minor Counties Championship and in NatWest Trophy
(v Middlesex) 1982. Man of the Match in the first Refuge Assurance Cup final 1988
and for his 50 plus 2-37 in B&H Cup final 1990. Lancashire captain 1994-97, leading
the county to one NatWest and two B&H titles. Lancashire Player of the Year 1995.
2nd XI captain and coach 2000-01. Cricket manager since 2002; retired but
registration retained
Best batting: 161 Lancashire v Essex, Old Trafford 1995
Best bowling: 8-30 Lancashire v Hampshire, Old Trafford 1994

2003 Season (did not make any first-class or one-day appearances)

Career Performances

	M	Inns	NO	Runs	HS	Avge	100s	50s	Ct	St	Balls	Runs	Wkts	Avge	Best	5wl	10wM
Test	4	6	1	167	82 *	33.40	-	1	1	-	672	348	10	34.80	3-64	-	-
All First	308	459	49	10939	161	26.68	11	50	156	-	47806	24960	739	33.77	8-30	27	3
1-day Int	1	0	0	0	0	-	-	-	-	-	54	43	0	-	-	-	-
C & G	46	40	7	1064	130	32.24	1	7	12	-	2681	1751	46	38.06	3-14	-	
NCL	236	189	38	3262	121	21.60	1	9	59	-	8730	7113	225	31.61	5-46	1	
Twenty20																	

WEBLEY, T.   Somerset

Name: Thomas (Tom) Webley
Role: Left-hand bat, left-arm spin bowler
Born: 2 March 1983, Bristol
Height: 6ft 1in **Weight:** 12st 5lbs
Nickname: Webbers, Trev, Mincer
County debut: 2003
1st-Class 50s: 2
1st-Class 100s: 1
1st-Class catches: 3
Place in batting averages: 137th av. 30.57
Strike rate: 82.00 (career 82.00)
Parents: Bob and Christine
Marital status: Single
Education: Kings College, Taunton; Anglia
Polytechnic University, Cambridge
Qualifications: Level 2 coach
Off-season: 'Uni and tour to Grenada with
Uni'

Overseas tours: West of England to West Indies 1998; Somerset Academy to South
Africa 2000; APU to Grenada 2003-04
Overseas teams played for: South Perth CC, Western Australia 2001-02
Career highlights to date: '104 v Northants for Cambridge UCCE and winning
the game'
Cricket moments to forget: 'Getting a golden duck at Chester-le-Street on debut,
bowled by Shoaib Akhtar'
Cricket superstitions: 'Always wear a box'
Cricketers particularly admired: Jamie Cox, Steffan Jones, Ian Blackwell
Young players to look out for: Matthew Kay, Nick Lee, Tobias Hembry
Other sports followed: Rugby (Bath), football (Bristol Rovers)
Injuries: Out for a month with spasms in the lower back
Favourite band: Red Hot Chili Peppers
Relaxations: 'Walking, gym'
Extras: Played for Somerset Board XI in the C&G 2001 and in the first round of the
C&G 2003, which was played in August 2002. Played for Cambridge University CCE
in 2003, scoring maiden first-class century (104) v Northamptonshire at Fenner's
Opinions on cricket: 'Two overseas players is good – brings standard up in first-class
game. Any more than two overseas would prevent opportunities for young talent to
develop in the county game. Lunch should be five minutes shorter, and tea five
minutes longer. Twenty20 good for the game – entertaining.'
Best batting: 104 CUCCE v Northamptonshire, Fenner's 2003
Best bowling: 2-57 CUCCE v Kent, Fenner's 2003

2003 Season

	M	Inns	NO	Runs	HS	Avge	100s	50s	Ct	St	O	M	Runs	Wkts	Avge	Best	5wI	10wM
Test																		
All First	9	16	2	428	104	30.57	1	2	3	-	82	8	344	6	57.33	2-57	-	-
1-day Int																		
C & G																			
NCL																			
Twenty20																			

Career Performances

	M	Inns	NO	Runs	HS	Avge	100s	50s	Ct	St	Balls	Runs	Wkts	Avge	Best	5wI	10wM
Test																	
All First	9	16	2	428	104	30.57	1	2	3	-	492	344	6	57.33	2-57	-	-
1-day Int																	
C & G	2	2	0	12	8	6.00	-	-	1	-							
NCL																	
Twenty20																	

WEEKES, P. N.   Middlesex

Name: <u>Paul</u> Nicholas Weekes
Role: Left-hand bat, right-arm
off-spin bowler; all-rounder
Born: 8 July 1969, Hackney, London
Height: 5ft 10½in **Weight:** 12st 4lbs
Nickname: Twidds, Weekesy
County debut: 1990
County cap: 1993
Benefit: 2002
1000 runs in a season: 1
1st-Class 50s: 41
1st-Class 100s: 16
1st-Class 5 w. in innings: 4
1st-Class catches: 189
One-Day 100s: 4
Place in batting averages: 127th av. 31.66
(2002 30th av. 52.10)
Place in bowling averages: 108th av. 38.71
(2002 155th av. 57.04)
Strike rate: 77.34 (career 84.47)
Parents: Robert and Carol
Marital status: Single
Children: Cherie, 4 September 1993; Shyann, 3 May 1998

Family links with cricket: Father played club cricket
Education: Homerton House, Hackney; Hackney Technical College
Qualifications: Level 2 coaching award
Career outside cricket: Cricket coach, Hackney Cricket Academy
Overseas tours: England A to India and Bangladesh 1994-95; Middlesex to Johannesburg; 'various tours to the West Indies with BWIA'
Overseas teams played for: Newcastle University, NSW 1988-89; Sunrise CC, Harare 1990-91
Career highlights to date: 'Scoring 171* and 160 in the same match, v Somerset at Uxbridge 1996'
Cricket moments to forget: 'Getting a pair against Essex in 1996'
Cricketers particularly admired: Viv Richards, Courtney Walsh, Brian Lara
Young players to look out for: Owais Shah
Other sports followed: Boxing
Favourite band: Jay-Z, Notorious BIG
Relaxations: DIY
Extras: Scored 50 in debut innings for both 2nd and 1st teams. Took two catches whilst appearing as 12th man for England in the second Test against West Indies at Lord's in 1995. Middlesex Player of the Year 1999. Only Englishman to have scored more than 150 in both innings of a first-class game. Has won six one-day Man of the Match awards (two NatWest; four B&H). Captained Middlesex to their one-day victory over the Australians at Lord's 2001
Opinions on cricket: '[Would] still like to see more coverage on TV as youngsters prefer to do what they see or visualise top players doing.'
Best batting: 171* Middlesex v Somerset, Uxbridge 1996
Best bowling: 8-39 Middlesex v Glamorgan, Lord's 1996

2003 Season

	M	Inns	NO	Runs	HS	Avge	100s	50s	Ct	St	O	M	Runs	Wkts	Avge	Best	5wI	10wM
Test																		
All First	18	29	5	760	102*	31.66	1	4	20	-	451.1	85	1355	35	38.71	4-55	-	-
1-day Int																		
C & G	3	3	0	91	73	30.33	-	1	-	-	27	0	137	3	45.66	2-55	-	
NCL	18	18	0	746	104	41.44	1	7	8	-	113.1	0	666	18	37.00	4-45	-	
Twenty20	5	5	0	163	56	32.60	-	1	1	-	18	0	123	2	61.50	1-20	-	

Career Performances

	M	Inns	NO	Runs	HS	Avge	100s	50s	Ct	St	Balls	Runs	Wkts	Avge	Best	5wI	10wM
Test																	
All First	196	305	41	8869	171*	33.59	16	41	189	-	21880	10490	259	40.50	8-39	4	-
1-day Int																	
C & G	24	24	5	687	143*	36.15	2	4	6	-	1203	889	23	38.65	3-35	-	
NCL	198	171	22	3884	119*	26.06	2	20	88	-	6987	5892	210	28.05	4-26	-	
Twenty20	5	5	0	163	56	32.60	-	1	1	-	108	123	2	61.50	1-20	-	

WELCH, G.   Derbyshire

Name: Graeme Welch
Role: Right-hand bat, right-arm
medium-fast bowler
Born: 21 March 1972, Durham
Height: 6ft **Weight:** 13st
Nickname: Pop
County debut: 1992 (one-day,
Warwickshire), 1994 (first-class,
Warwickshire), 2001 (Derbyshire)
County cap: 1997 (Warwickshire),
2001 (Derbyshire)

50 wickets in a season: 3
1st-Class 50s: 14
1st-Class 5 w. in innings: 11
1st-Class 10 w. in match: 1
1st-Class catches: 44
One-Day 5 w. in innings: 3
Place in batting averages: 223rd av. 20.42
(2002 175th av. 25.55)
Place in bowling averages: 49th av. 27.84 (2002 31st av. 25.61)
Strike rate: 54.73 (career 59.44)
Parents: Jean and Robert
Wife and date of marriage: Emma, 4 October 1997
Children: Ethan, 4 April 2000
Family links with cricket: Brother and father play club cricket in Leeds and
Durham respectively
Education: Hetton Comprehensive
Qualifications: 9 GCSEs, City and Guilds in Sports and Leisure, senior
coaching award
Career outside cricket: Coaching
Overseas tours: Warwickshire to Cape Town 1992-97; England XI to New Zealand
(Cricket Max) 1997
Overseas teams played for: Avendale, Cape Town 1992-94; Wellington Collegians
and Wellington 1996
Career highlights to date: 'Winning the treble with Warwickshire in 1994'
Cricket moments to forget: 'Benson and Hedges game against Lancashire in 1995'
(*Became first bowler to concede 100 runs in B&H match*)
Cricketers particularly admired: Brian Lara, Allan Donald, Sachin Tendulkar
Young players to look out for: Ian Bell, Nicky Peng
Other sports played: Football
Other sports followed: Football (Newcastle United)

Relaxations: 'A beer at The Brook; spending time with Emma and Ethan'
Extras: Played for England YC v Australia YC 1991. Took two hat-tricks in the 2nd XI, against Durham in 1992 and against Worcestershire. Warwickshire's Most Improved Player 1994. Won seven trophies with Warwickshire 1994-97. Left Warwickshire at the end of the 2000 season and joined Derbyshire for 2001. Recorded five-wicket innings return (5-53) and scored a fifty (64) against his old county Warwickshire at Edgbaston 2001
Best batting: 84* Warwickshire v Nottinghamshire, Edgbaston 1994
Best bowling: 6-30 Derbyshire v Durham, Riverside 2001

2003 Season

	M	Inns	NO	Runs	HS	Avge	100s	50s	Ct	St	O	M	Runs	Wkts	Avge	Best	5wI	10wM
Test																		
All First	15	27	6	429	54	20.42	-	2	3	-	483.3	121	1476	53	27.84	6-102	2	-
1-day Int																		
C & G	4	3	1	50	22	25.00	-	-	1	-	29.5	1	134	9	14.88	4-26	-	
NCL	15	11	3	159	26	19.87	-	-	3	-	117.1	12	567	20	28.35	3-44	-	
Twenty20	5	3	0	29	13	9.66	-	-	2	-	19	0	177	2	88.50	1-15	-	

Career Performances

	M	Inns	NO	Runs	HS	Avge	100s	50s	Ct	St	Balls	Runs	Wkts	Avge	Best	5wI	10wM
Test																	
All First	123	188	31	3295	84 *	20.98	-	14	44	-	19973	10752	336	32.00	6-30	11	1
1-day Int																	
C & G	22	16	5	226	41	20.54	-	-	1	-	1132	743	18	41.27	4-26	-	
NCL	117	94	26	1197	71	17.60	-	3	19	-	4797	3597	110	32.70	6-31	3	
Twenty20	5	3	0	29	13	9.66	-	-	2	-	114	177	2	88.50	1-15	-	

WELLS, V. J.   Durham

Name: Vincent (Vince) John Wells
Role: Right-hand bat, right-arm medium bowler, occasional wicket-keeper
Born: 6 August 1965, Dartford
Height: 6ft **Weight:** 14st 4lbs
Nickname: Vinny, Wellsy, Wily One, Gazza's Dad
County debut: 1987 (one-day, Kent), 1988 (first-class, Kent), 1992 (Leicestershire), 2003 (Durham)
County cap: 1994 (Leicestershire)
Benefit: 2001 (Leicestershire)
One-Day Internationals: 9
1000 runs in a season: 2
1st-Class 50s: 46
1st-Class 100s: 15

1st-Class 200s: 3
1st-Class 5 w. in innings: 5
1st-Class catches: 134
One-Day 100s: 3
One-Day 200s: 1
One-Day 5 w. in innings: 3
Place in batting averages: 218th av. 21.00
(2002 97th av. 37.20)
Place in bowling averages: 17th av. 23.40
(2002 11th av. 22.15)
Strike rate: 44.90 (career 53.48)
Parents: Pat and Jack
Wife and date of marriage: Debbie,
14 October 1989
Children: Harrison John, 25 January 1995;
Molly Louise, 2 June 1996
Family links with cricket: Brother plays
club cricket in Kent
Education: Downs School, Dartford; Sir William Nottidge School, Whitstable
Qualifications: 1 O-level, 8 CSEs, junior and senior coaching certificates ('up to old
advanced')
Career outside cricket: Coaching
Off-season: Coaching and training
Overseas tours: Leicestershire to Jamaica 1993, to Bloemfontein 1994, 1995,
to Western Transvaal 1996, to Durban 1997, to Barbados 1998, to Anguilla 2000;
England to Australia 1998-99 (CUB Series), to Sharjah (Coca-Cola Cup) 1998-99
Overseas teams played for: Parnell, Auckland 1986; Avendale, Cape Town 1986-89,
1990-91; Potchefstroom University, North West Transvaal 1996-97; Cornwall CC,
Auckland 1998-99
Career highlights to date: 'Winning trophies for Leicestershire. Captaining
Leicestershire. Playing for England. First 100 for Durham CCC'
Cricket moments to forget: 'Losing a match'
Cricket superstitions: 'Don't put second glove on until on field of play'
Cricketers particularly admired: Phil Simmons, Mike Kasprowicz, Anil Kumble,
Javagal Srinath
Young players to look out for: 'A lot of very good youngsters at Durham; two to
mention – Nicky Peng, Gary Pratt'
Other sports played: Golf ('badly')
Other sports followed: Football (Chelsea and Leicester)
Injuries: Out for two weeks with a back injury; for four weeks with a wrist damaged
while batting
Favourite band: 'I like all sorts'
Relaxations: 'Good food, pint of Guinness, walking Jasper the dog, spending time
with my family'
Extras: Was a schoolboy footballer with Leyton Orient. Scored 100* on NatWest

debut v Oxfordshire at Oxford 1990. Left Kent at the end of 1991 season to join Leicestershire. Hat-trick for Leicestershire v Durham at Durham 1994; Alamgir Sheriyar also took hat-trick for Leicestershire in same match. Scored 201 v Berkshire at Leicester in the NatWest 1996. Member of England's 1999 World Cup squad and was reserve wicket-keeper. Captain of Leicestershire from retirement of James Whitaker during 1999 season to end of 2002 season. Scored century (138) and recorded five-wicket innings return (5-36) against his old county Kent at Canterbury 2001. Left Leicestershire at the end of the 2002 season and joined Durham for 2003. Scored first first-class century for Durham in 2003, 106 v Derbyshire at Derby, in the process sharing with Nicky Peng (99) in a new record fifth-wicket partnership for Durham (197). Has won one-day man of the match awards with Kent, Leicestershire and Durham. Retired during the 2003-04 off-season but is still registered

Opinions on cricket: 'Two up/two down promotion and relegation. Only one overseas player. I don't know how we stop it but too many EU players.'

Best batting: 224 Leicestershire v Middlesex, Lord's 1997

Best bowling: 5-18 Leicestershire v Nottinghamshire, Worksop 1998

2003 Season

	M	Inns	NO	Runs	HS	Avge	100s	50s	Ct	St	O	M	Runs	Wkts	Avge	Best	5wI	10wM
Test																		
All First	12	21	1	420	106	21.00	1	2	11	-	164.4	36	515	22	23.40	4-16	-	-
1-day Int																		
C & G	1	1	1	63	63 *	-	-	1	1	-	9	3	20	6	3.33	6-20	1	
NCL	10	10	1	148	47	16.44	-	-	4	-	60.5	3	278	7	39.71	2-24	-	
Twenty20	4	4	0	63	23	15.75	-	-	2	-	16	0	137	6	22.83	3-39	-	

Career Performances

	M	Inns	NO	Runs	HS	Avge	100s	50s	Ct	St	Balls	Runs	Wkts	Avge	Best	5wI	10wM
Test																	
All First	196	306	22	9314	224	32.79	18	46	134	-	16153	7920	302	26.22	5-18	5	-
1-day Int	9	7	0	141	39	20.14	-	-	7	-	220	189	8	23.62	3-30	-	
C & G	29	28	8	948	201	47.40	2	6	6	-	1203	728	37	19.67	6-20	1	
NCL	172	165	14	3507	101	23.22	2	14	44	-	5694	4381	152	28.82	5-10	1	
Twenty20	4	4	0	63	23	15.75	-	-	2	-	96	137	6	22.83	3-39	-	

98. Which current Lancashire player has scored 693 runs and taken 24 wickets in ODI matches between England and the West Indies?

WELTON, G. E.   Nottinghamshire

Name: <u>Guy</u> Edward Welton
Role: Right-hand opening bat
Born: 4 May 1978, Grimsby
Height: 6ft 1in **Weight:** 13st 7lbs
Nickname: Trigger, Giggs, Welts
County debut: 1997
1st-Class 50s: 19
1st-Class 100s: 1
1st-Class 200s: 1
1st-Class catches: 43
One-Day 100s: 1
Place in batting averages: 185th av. 24.86
(2002 100th av. 36.69)
Parents: Robert and Diana
Marital status: Single
Family links with cricket: Father is a
qualified cricket coach and keen club
cricketer

Education: Healing Comprehensive; Grimsby College of Technology;
Nottingham Trent University
Qualifications: 9 GCSEs, BTEC in Business and Finance, senior level cricket coach
Overseas tours: England U17 to Holland (International Youth Tournament) 1995;
Nottinghamshire to South Africa 1998
Overseas teams played for: Randfontein CC, Johannesburg, South Africa 1996-97;
Willetton CC, Perth, Western Australia 1997-98; Coolbinia CC, Perth 1998-99
Cricketers particularly admired: David Gower, Viv Richards, Steve Waugh,
Sachin Tendulkar, Mark Lavender
Other sports played: Football ('youth trainee at Grimsby Town Football Club 1994-96')
Relaxations: Music and going to the gym
Extras: Completed a two-year YTS with Grimsby Town Football Club where he made
one first-team appearance as a substitute. Played cricket for England U14, U15 and
U17. Won the Lord's Taverners' Young Player Award in 1993 and was MCC Young
Cricketer 1994-95. Was 12th man for England at Lord's and The Oval against West
Indies 1995. Scored maiden first-class century v Warwickshire at Edgbaston 2000,
going on to score 200* and become Nottinghamshire's then youngest double
centurion; in the process he shared in a first-wicket stand of 406* with Darren Bicknell
(180*) that broke several records, including that for the highest Nottinghamshire
partnership for any wicket, formerly 398 by Arthur Shrewsbury and William Gunn v
Sussex at Trent Bridge 1890, and that for the highest unbeaten first-wicket partnership
in Championship history. Released by Nottinghamshire at the end of the 2003 season
Best batting: 200* Nottinghamshire v Warwickshire, Edgbaston 2000

2003 Season

	M	Inns	NO	Runs	HS	Avge	100s	50s	Ct	St	O	M	Runs	Wkts	Avge	Best	5wI	10wM
Test																		
All First	12	23	0	572	99	24.86	-	5	6	-								
1-day Int																		
C & G	1	1	0	23	23	23.00	-	-	-	-								
NCL	6	6	0	142	50	23.66	-	1	-	-								
Twenty20	5	5	1	89	39	22.25	-	-	1	-								

Career Performances

	M	Inns	NO	Runs	HS	Avge	100s	50s	Ct	St	Balls	Runs	Wkts	Avge	Best	5wI	10wM
Test																	
All First	73	133	5	3299	200 *	25.77	2	19	43	-	12	5	0	-	-	-	-
1-day Int																	
C & G	4	4	0	78	26	19.50	-	-	2	-							
NCL	44	43	2	778	104 *	18.97	1	2	12	-							
Twenty20	5	5	1	89	39	22.25	-	-	1	-							

WESTON, R. M. S. Middlesex

Name: <u>Robin</u> Michael Swann Weston
Role: Right-hand bat, leg-break bowler
Born: 7 June 1975, Durham
Height: 6ft **Weight:** 12st 6lbs
County debut: 1995 (Durham),
1998 (Derbyshire), 2000 (Middlesex)
County cap: 2001 (Middlesex)
1st-Class 50s: 9
1st-Class 100s: 7
1st-Class catches: 37
Place in batting averages: (2002 169th
av. 26.33)
Strike rate: (career 93.50)
Parents: Kathleen Mary (deceased)
and Michael Philip
Marital status: Single
Family links with cricket: Father played for
Durham (and played rugby union for
England); brother Philip plays for Gloucestershire
Education: Durham School; Loughborough University
Qualifications: 10 GCSEs, 4 A-levels, degree in Economics with Accountancy,
basic cricket coaching certificate

Career outside cricket: Working in marketing
Overseas tours: England U18 to South Africa 1992-93, to Denmark (International Youth Tournament) 1993; England U19 to Sri Lanka 1993-94
Overseas teams played for: Fremantle, Western Australia 1996-98; Parnell CC, Auckland 1999-2000
Cricketers particularly admired: 'Anyone at the highest level'
Young players to look out for: Ed Joyce
Other sports played: Golf, rugby union (Loughborough Students 1994-96, England U18 1993)
Other sports followed: Football (Sunderland AFC)
Relaxations: Most sports, listening to music and socialising with friends
Extras: Sir John Hobbs Silver Jubilee Memorial Prize 1990. Became youngest to play for Durham 1st XI, in Minor Counties competition, aged 15 in 1991. Released by Durham at the end of the 1997 season and joined Derbyshire. Scored maiden first-class century (129*) v Essex at Chelmsford 1999 and followed up with centuries in the next two Championship matches (124 v Middlesex at Lord's; 156 v Somerset at Derby) to become the fourth Derbyshire batsman to score centuries in three successive Championship games. NBC Denis Compton Award 1999. Left Derbyshire at the end of 1999 season and joined Middlesex for 2000. 2nd XI Championship Player of the Year 2000. Scored century (129) v Zimbabweans at Shenley 2003. Released by Middlesex at the end of the 2003 season
Best batting: 156 Derbyshire v Somerset, Derby 1999
Best bowling: 1-15 Derbyshire v Hampshire, Derby 1999

2003 Season

	M	Inns	NO	Runs	HS	Avge	100s	50s	Ct	St	O	M	Runs	Wkts	Avge	Best	5wI	10wM
Test																		
All First	2	4	0	207	129	51.75	1	-	-	-								
1-day Int																		
C & G																		
NCL	4	4	0	72	34	18.00	-	-	1	-								
Twenty20	5	3	1	74	34 *	37.00	-	-	3	-								

Career Performances

	M	Inns	NO	Runs	HS	Avge	100s	50s	Ct	St	Balls	Runs	Wkts	Avge	Best	5wI	10wM
Test																	
All First	62	104	6	2842	156	29.00	7	9	37	-	187	104	2	52.00	1-15	-	-
1-day Int																	
C & G	7	7	1	150	56	25.00	-	1	1	-							
NCL	43	42	3	693	80 *	17.76	-	3	10	-							
Twenty20	5	3	1	74	34 *	37.00	-	-	3	-							

WESTON, W. P. C. Gloucestershire

Name: William <u>Philip</u> Christopher Weston
Role: Left-hand opening bat, left-arm
seam bowler
Born: 16 June 1973, Durham
Height: 6ft 4in **Weight:** 13st 9lbs
Nickname: Tickle
County debut: 1991 (Worcestershire),
2003 (Gloucestershire)
County cap: 1995; colours, 2002
(Worcestershire)
1000 runs in a season: 4
1st-Class 50s: 49
1st-Class 100s: 18
1st-Class 200s: 1
1st-Class catches: 100
One-Day 100s: 2
Place in batting averages: 111th av. 33.73
(2002 188th av. 24.23)

Strike rate: (career 244.25)
Parents: Michael and Kate (deceased)
Wife and date of marriage: Sarah, 30 September 2000
Family links with cricket: Brother Robin played for Middlesex, Derbyshire and
Durham. Father played Minor Counties cricket for Durham (and rugby union for
England)
Education: Durham School
Qualifications: 9 GCSEs, 4 A-levels, coaching and computer qualifications
Career outside cricket: 'Looking to pursue a career in property'
Off-season: 'Taking a diploma in business and management and gaining work
experience'
Overseas tours: England U18 to Canada (International Youth Tournament) 1991
(vice-captain); England YC to New Zealand 1990-91; England U19 to Pakistan 1991-
92 (captain); Worcestershire to Zimbabwe 1996
Overseas teams played for: Melville, Perth 1992-94, 1996-97; Swanbourne,
Perth 1995-96
Career highlights to date: '2003 C&G final. The 2003 season – a new lease of life to
my career at Gloucester'
Cricket moments to forget: 'The 2002 season and the way my career at Worcester
ended'
Cricket superstitions: 'Not really'
Cricketers particularly admired: 'Anyone who has played at the peak of their
powers over a long period'

750

Young players to look out for: Alex Gidman, Kadeer Ali
Other sports followed: Rugby union, football (Sunderland AFC)
Injuries: 'Niggles'; out for two weeks with a damaged wrist
Favourite band: U2
Relaxations: 'Spending time with Sarah; travelling, films'
Extras: Scored century (146) for England YC v Australia YC 1991. Scored century (107) for England U19 v Sri Lanka U19 1992 and was Man of the Series. Cricket Society's Most Promising Young Cricketer 1992. Worcestershire Uncapped Player of the Year 1992. Member of Whittingdale Fringe Squad 1993. Scored 71 v Middlesex at Worcester 2001, in the process sharing with Anurag Singh in a record opening partnership for Worcestershire in matches against Middlesex (180). Left Worcestershire by mutual agreement before the beginning of the 2003 season with a year left on contract and joined Gloucestershire
Opinions on cricket: 'Players are not over the hill at 30. The obsession for youth at domestic and international level should not ignore the fact that opportunities have to be earned by achievements in the middle as well as potential. Wickets at county level must replicate Test wickets.'
Best batting: 205 Worcestershire v Northamptonshire, Northampton 1997
Best bowling: 2-39 Worcestershire v Pakistanis, Worcester 1992

2003 Season

	M	Inns	NO	Runs	HS	Avge	100s	50s	Ct	St	O	M	Runs	Wkts	Avge	Best	5wI	10wM
Test																		
All First	15	27	1	877	179	33.73	2	2	10	-	2	0	10	0	-	-	-	-
1-day Int																		
C & G	5	5	1	180	88 *	45.00	-	1	2	-								
NCL	14	14	0	395	92	28.21	-	3	5	-								
Twenty20																		

Career Performances

	M	Inns	NO	Runs	HS	Avge	100s	50s	Ct	St	Balls	Runs	Wkts	Avge	Best	5wI	10wM
Test																	
All First	185	326	32	10009	205	34.04	19	49	100	-	977	650	4	162.50	2-39	-	-
1-day Int																	
C & G	16	16	1	330	88 *	22.00	-	1	3	-							
NCL	104	90	8	2050	134	25.00	2	8	22	-	6	2	1	2.00	1-2	-	
Twenty20																	

99. Which Sussex player took his 100th Test catch as a wicket-keeper in his final Test, at Bridgetown, Barbados, in 1967-68?

WESTWOOD, I. J.   Warwickshire

Name: <u>Ian</u> James Westwood
Role: Left-hand opening bat, right-arm off-spinner
Born: 13 July 1982, Birmingham
Height: 5ft 7½in **Weight:** 11st
Nickname: Westy, Tomato Head, Wezzo, Sammy Lee, Tot
County debut: 2003
Parents: Ann and David
Marital status: Single
Family links with cricket: 'Brother represented Warwickshire Schools from 11 to 16'
Education: Wheelers Lane; Solihull Sixth Form College
Qualifications: 8 GCSEs, BTEC Sports Science
Off-season: 'Perth for two months after Christmas'

Overseas tours: Warwickshire Development squad to Cape Town 1998
Overseas teams played for: Hawkesbury CC, Sydney 2001-02; Subiaco Marist CC, Perth 2002-03
Career highlights to date: 'Took 6-104 and scored 250* in the same game v Worcestershire 2nd XI [2003]'
Cricket moments to forget: 'Being relegated from the Birmingham Premier League after losing the last game of season, for Moseley CC'
Cricket superstitions: 'Put right pad on first'
Cricketers particularly admired: Brian Lara, Nick Knight
Young players to look out for: Nick Chase, Vanraj Padhaal
Other sports played: Football (Coleshill Town FC 2001; Moseley Mariners FC)
Other sports followed: Football (Birmingham City)
Injuries: Out for two and a half weeks with a broken finger
Favourite band: Fleetwood Mac
Relaxations: 'Music, films, fruit machines, socialising'
Extras: Played for Warwicks Board XI in the C&G 2001, 2002, and in the first round of the C&G 2003, which was played in August 2002. Scored 250* v Worcs 2nd XI at Barnt Green 2003, sharing with Jonathan Trott (248) in a record opening partnership for Warwicks 2nd XI (429); also took 6-104 in Worcs 2nd XI's only innings
Opinions on cricket: 'Play on too many poor pitches in England, resulting in bowlers not needing to be as good as Australian, South African etc. We don't know how to bowl on flat pitches against quality opposition.'
Best batting: 19 Warwickshire v India A, Edgbaston 2003

2003 Season

	M	Inns	NO	Runs	HS	Avge	100s	50s	Ct	St	O	M	Runs	Wkts	Avge	Best	5wI	10wM
Test																		
All First	1	1	0	19	19	19.00	-	-	-	-	8	0	57	0	-	-	-	-
1-day Int																		
C & G																		
NCL																		
Twenty20																		

Career Performances

	M	Inns	NO	Runs	HS	Avge	100s	50s	Ct	St	Balls	Runs	Wkts	Avge	Best	5wI	10wM
Test																	
All First	1	1	0	19	19	19.00	-	-	-	-	48	57	0	-	-	-	-
1-day Int																	
C & G	4	4	0	78	55	19.50	-	1	1	-	180	139	2	69.50	1-28	-	
NCL																	
Twenty20																	

WHARF, A. G. B.   Glamorgan

Name: Alexander (<u>Alex</u>) George
Busfield Wharf
Role: Right-hand bat, right-arm fast-medium
bowler; all-rounder
Born: 4 June 1975, Bradford
Height: 6ft 4in **Weight:** 15st
Nickname: Gangster
County debut: 1994 (Yorks), 1998 (Notts),
2000 (Glamorgan)
County cap: 2000 (Glamorgan)
50 wickets in a season: 1
1st-Class 50s: 5
1st-Class 100s: 2
1st-Class 5 w. in innings: 2
1st-Class catches: 29
Place in batting averages: 170th av. 26.38
Place in bowling averages: 79th av. 33.34
Strike rate: 49.90 (career 53.92)
Parents: Jane and Derek
Wife and date of marriage: Shelley Jane, 1 December 2001
Children: Tristan Jack Busfield Wharf, 15 November 1997; Alf Alexander Busfield
Wharf, 30 June 2001

Family links with cricket: Father played local cricket and brother Simon plays local cricket

Education: Buttershaw Upper School; Thomas Danby College

Qualifications: 6 GCSEs, City and Guilds in Sports Management, NCA coaching award, junior football coaching award

Career outside cricket: 'House husband'

Overseas tours: Various pre-season tours with Yorks, Notts and Glamorgan

Overseas teams played for: Somerset West, Cape Town 1993-95; Johnsonville CC, Wellington, New Zealand 1996-97; Universities, Wellington 1998-99

Career highlights to date: 'Playing alongside some great players!'

Cricket moments to forget: 'Too many to mention'

Cricket superstitions: 'None'

Cricketers particularly admired: Ian Botham

Young players to look out for: 'Plenty of youngsters out there, but only if they get the chance!'

Other sports played: Football ('goalkeeper – watch this space')

Other sports followed: 'Follow most sports but my passion is Manchester United; also very proud of Bradford City'

Relaxations: 'Spending time with family and friends, movies, PlayStation 2, eating (too much), TV, gym, football'

Extras: Attended Dennis Lillee coaching school, Chennai (Madras), during winter 1997-98. Scored 78 for Notts v Glamorgan at Colwyn Bay 1999, having arrived at the wicket with his side on 9 for 6. Left Nottinghamshire at end of the 1999 season and joined Glamorgan for 2000. Took 50 first-class wickets in a season for the first time 2003

Best batting: 101* Glamorgan v Northamptonshire, Northampton 2000

Best bowling: 5-63 Glamorgan v Yorkshire, Swansea 2001

2003 Season

	M	Inns	NO	Runs	HS	Avge	100s	50s	Ct	St	O	M	Runs	Wkts	Avge	Best	5wI	10wM
Test																		
All First	16	27	9	475	79	26.38	-	2	7	-	432.3	72	1734	52	33.34	4-53	-	-
1-day Int																		
C & G	2	2	0	19	18	9.50	-	-	-	-	16.4	1	77	2	38.50	2-22	-	
NCL	15	9	1	35	14	4.37	-	-	6	-	88.5	2	510	20	25.50	4-18	-	
Twenty20																		

Career Performances

	M	Inns	NO	Runs	HS	Avge	100s	50s	Ct	St	Balls	Runs	Wkts	Avge	Best	5wI	10wM
Test																	
All First	62	89	17	1389	101 *	19.29	2	5	29	-	8682	5391	161	33.48	5-63	2	-
1-day Int																	
C & G	8	6	1	61	24 *	12.20	-	-	-	-	436	249	9	27.66	3-18	-	
NCL	53	32	11	286	38 *	13.61	-	-	13	-	2037	1755	53	33.11	4-18	-	
Twenty20																	

WHARTON, L. J.   Derbyshire

Name: <u>Lian</u> James Wharton
Role: Left-hand bat, slow left-arm bowler
Born: 21 February 1977, Derby
Height: 5ft 9in **Weight:** 10st 4lbs
Nickname: Tetley, King, Two Thumbs, Weasel
County debut: 2000
1st-Class 5 w. in innings: 3
1st-Class catches: 14
Place in batting averages: (2002 303rd av. 7.54)
Place in bowling averages: (2002 49th av. 27.80)
Strike rate: 76.66 (career 78.37)
Parents: Pete and Di
Marital status: Single
Education: Ecclesbourne; Mackworth College

Qualifications: 9 GCSEs, BTEC National Computer Studies, Level 2 coach
Career outside cricket: Sports manager
Overseas tours: MCC to Kenya 2002
Overseas teams played for: Merewether CC, Newcastle, NSW 2000-01
Career highlights to date: 'Taking nine wickets against the West Indians'
Cricket moments to forget: 'Had complete nightmare fielding at Durham – running wrong way for balls, balls going through my legs etc.'
Cricket superstitions: 'None'
Cricketers particularly admired: Phil Tufnell, Ian Botham, Shane Warne, Stewart Edge, Ian Fraser, Daniel Vettori, Rory Williams, Andrew Williams, Ewan Craig, Alec Stubbs
Young players to look out for: Luke Sutton, Steve Stubbings, Tom Lungley, Sam Patel, Steve Selwood
Other sports played: Indoor cricket, golf, football, tennis
Other sports followed: Football (Derby County), basketball (Derby Storm)
Relaxations: 'Reading, going to the cinema, socialising, sleeping'
Extras: Had match figures of 10-58 from 37 overs on debut for Derbyshire 2nd XI. Had match figures of 9-179 (5-96/4-83) v West Indians at Derby 2000. Released by Derbyshire at the end of the 2003 season
Best batting: 30 Derbyshire v Worcestershire, Worcester 2003
Best bowling: 6-62 Derbyshire v Middlesex, Lord's 2002

2003 Season

	M	Inns	NO	Runs	HS	Avge	100s	50s	Ct	St	O	M	Runs	Wkts	Avge	Best	5wI	10wM
Test																		
All First	6	9	5	46	30	11.50	-	-	4	-	115	24	364	9	40.44	4-50	-	-
1-day Int																		
C & G	2	1	1	0	0 *	-	-	-	-	-	12	1	50	3	16.66	2-31	-	
NCL	7	1	1	5	5 *	-	-	-	-	-	40	3	202	4	50.50	2-37	-	
Twenty20																		

Career Performances

	M	Inns	NO	Runs	HS	Avge	100s	50s	Ct	St	Balls	Runs	Wkts	Avge	Best	5wI	10wM
Test																	
All First	38	59	30	173	30	5.96	-	-	14	-	4232	2167	54	40.12	6-62	3	-
1-day Int																	
C & G	3	2	2	0	0 *	-	-	-	-	-	132	91	4	22.75	2-31	-	
NCL	33	13	11	46	11 *	23.00	-	-	2	-	1343	974	28	34.78	3-23	-	
Twenty20																	

WHILEY, M. J. A. Leicestershire

Name: Matthew (<u>Matt</u>) Jeffrey Allen Whiley
Role: Right-hand bat, left-arm fast bowler
Born: 6 May 1980, Nottingham
Height: 6ft 3½in **Weight:** 14st
Nickname: Oggy
County debut: 1998 (Nottinghamshire), 2001 (Leicestershire)
1st-Class catches: 3
Place in batting averages: (2002 311th av. 5.85)
Place in bowling averages: (2002 146th av. 50.18)
Strike rate: 100.71 (career 89.07)
Parents: Paul and Barbara
Marital status: Single
Family links with cricket: 'Dad played indoor cricket and local league cricket'
Education: Harry Carlton Comprehensive School, East Leake; 'membership of Jeremy Snape's corner'
Qualifications: 10 GCSEs, Level 1 coaching certificate, 'good judge of character'
Career outside cricket: 'Being a great lad'
Off-season: 'Playing in New Zealand (Christchurch)'

Overseas tours: England U19 to New Zealand 1998-99; Nottinghamshire to Johannesburg 1999; Leicestershire to Potchefstroom 2001; MCC to Kenya 2002

Overseas teams played for: Manawatu-Foxton CC and Horowhenua District Cricket Association, both New Zealand 1997-98; Melville CC, Perth 2000-01; Sydenham, New Zealand 2003-04

Career highlights to date: 'Watching some of my friend Kevin Pietersen's knocks'

Cricket moments to forget: 'The 2003 season'

Cricket superstitions: 'Always listen to the Rocky CD in my car on the way to the ground'

Cricketers particularly admired: Kevin Pietersen, Trevor Ward, Devon Malcolm, Paul Nixon, Jeremy Snape, Darren Stevens, Paul Franks, Graham Dilley

Young players to look out for: John Maunders, Richard Logan

Other sports followed: Football (Man Utd), hockey (Cannock; 'come on the Knockers')

Injuries: Out for seven weeks with a fractured metatarsal

Favourite band: Usher, Jagged Edge, P. Diddy, 'all Hip Hop, R&B and urban music'

Relaxations: 'Shopping, cars, women'

Extras: Represented England U19. Attended the Dennis Lillee MRF Pace Foundation, February 2000. Awarded Nottinghamshire 2nd XI cap September 2000. Came second in the Freeserve Speedster Challenge; bowled the fastest delivery (86.6 mph) but was adjudged to have bowled a no-ball. Left Nottinghamshire in the 2000-01 off-season and joined Leicestershire for 2001. NBC Denis Compton Award for the most promising young Leicestershire player 2001. Released by Leicestershire at the end of the 2003 season

Opinions on cricket: 'Having read the Lance Armstrong autobiography, it showed me that no matter what obstacles people put in your way or no matter how you are treated in the game, if you believe in yourself, just hang in there. It taught me to be strong, train hard and have fun. Thanks for the chats. Magic. Great lads.'

Best batting: 16 Leicestershire v Warwickshire, Edgbaston 2003

Best bowling: 3-60 Leicestershire v Kent, Leicester 2002

2003 Season

	M	Inns	NO	Runs	HS	Avge	100s	50s	Ct	St	O	M	Runs	Wkts	Avge	Best	5wI	10wM
Test																		
All First	5	6	2	29	16	7.25	-	-	1	-	117.3	14	562	7	80.28	2-76	-	-
1-day Int																		
C & G																		
NCL																		
Twenty20																		

Career Performances

	M	Inns	NO	Runs	HS	Avge	100s	50s	Ct	St	Balls	Runs	Wkts	Avge	Best	5wI	10wM
Test																	
All First	18	24	6	72	16	4.00	-	-	3	-	2405	1797	27	66.55	3-60	-	-
1-day Int																	
C & G	1	1	1	0	0 *	-	-	-	-	-	24	27	0	-	-	-	-
NCL	12	5	4	25	14 *	25.00	-	-	4	-	362	321	6	53.50	2-37	-	
Twenty20																	

WHITE, C.   Yorkshire

Name: Craig White
Role: Right-hand bat, right-arm
fast-medium bowler, county captain
Born: 16 December 1969, Morley, Yorkshire
Height: 6ft 1in **Weight:** 11st 11lbs
Nickname: Chalky, Bassey
County debut: 1990
County cap: 1993
Benefit: 2002
Test debut: 1994
Tests: 30
One-Day Internationals: 51
1st-Class 50s: 52
1st-Class 100s: 17
1st-Class 5 w. in innings: 11
1st-Class catches: 144
One-Day 100s: 3
One-Day 5 w. in innings: 3

Place in batting averages: 31st av. 49.53 (2002 64th av. 43.04)
Place in bowling averages: (2002 131st av. 42.26)
Strike rate: (career 53.88)
Parents: Fred Emsley and Cynthia Anne
Wife and date of marriage: Elizabeth Anne, 19 September 1992
Family links with cricket: Father played for Pudsey St Lawrence
Education: Flora Hill High School; Bendigo Senior High School (both Victoria,
Australia)
Overseas tours: Australia YC to West Indies 1989-90; England A to Pakistan
1995-96, to Australia 1996-97; England to Australia 1994-95, to India and Pakistan
(World Cup) 1995-96, to Zimbabwe and New Zealand 1996-97, to South Africa and
Zimbabwe 1999-2000 (one-day series), to Kenya (ICC Knockout Trophy) 2000-01,
to Pakistan and Sri Lanka 2000-01, to India and New Zealand 2001-02, to Australia
2002-03, to Africa (World Cup) 2002-03

Overseas teams played for: Victoria, Australia 1990-91; Central Districts, New Zealand 1999-2000
Cricketers particularly admired: Graeme Hick, Mark Waugh, Brian Lara
Other sports followed: Leeds RFC, motocross, golf, tennis
Relaxations: Playing guitar, reading, gardening and socialising
Extras: Recommended to Yorkshire by Victorian Cricket Academy, being eligible to play for Yorkshire as he was born in the county. Formerly bowled off-spin. Took 5-21 and scored 26 in the second ODI v Zimbabwe at Bulawayo 1999-2000, winning Man of the Match award. Took National League hat-trick (Fleming, Patel, Masters) v Kent at Headingley 2000. Recorded maiden Test five-wicket return (5-57) in the fourth Test v West Indies on his home ground of Headingley 2000, following up with 5-32 in the fifth Test at The Oval. Scored 93 in England's first innings in the first Test at Lahore 2000-01, in the process sharing with Graham Thorpe (118) in a new record sixth-wicket partnership for England in Tests v Pakistan (166); also took 4-54 in Pakistan's only innings of the match. Scored maiden Test century (121) in the second Test v India at Ahmedabad 2001-02, winning Man of the Match award and sharing with James Foster in a record seventh-wicket partnership for England in Tests in India (105). C&G Man of the Match award for his 4-35 and 78-ball 100* in the semi-final v Surrey at Headingley 2002. Scored 64 and then took a career one-day best 5-19 v Somerset at Scarborough in the NUL 2002. Scored 85* in England's first innings of the fourth Test v Australia at Melbourne (once his home ground) 2002-03, in the process passing 1000 runs in Test cricket. Appointed captain of Yorkshire for 2004
Best batting: 186 Yorkshire v Lancashire, Old Trafford 2001
Best bowling: 8-55 Yorkshire v Gloucestershire, Gloucester 1998

2003 Season

	M	Inns	NO	Runs	HS	Avge	100s	50s	Ct	St	O	M	Runs	Wkts	Avge	Best	5wl	10wM
Test																		
All First	10	16	3	644	173 *	49.53	2	3	4	-	21	3	64	0	-	-	-	-
1-day Int																		
C & G																		
NCL	9	8	0	176	47	22.00	-	-	3	-	7.4	0	51	0	-	-	-	
Twenty20	5	5	0	67	24	13.40	-	-	-	-								

Career Performances

	M	Inns	NO	Runs	HS	Avge	100s	50s	Ct	St	Balls	Runs	Wkts	Avge	Best	5wl	10wM
Test	30	50	7	1052	121	24.46	2	9	14	-	3959	2220	59	37.62	5-32	3	-
All First	227	359	47	9952	186	31.89	17	52	144	-	20424	10821	379	28.55	8-55	11	-
1-day Int	51	41	5	568	57 *	15.77	-	1	12	-	2364	1727	65	26.56	5-21	1	
C & G	31	28	7	1043	113	49.66	2	7	11	-	1368	880	32	27.50	4-35	-	
NCL	152	136	15	2946	148	24.34	1	9	45	-	4502	3251	143	22.73	5-19	1	
Twenty20	5	5	0	67	24	13.40	-	-	-	-							

WHITE, R. A.   Northamptonshire

Name: Robert (<u>Rob</u>) Allan White
Role: Right-hand bat, leg-spin bowler
Born: 15 October 1979, Chelmsford, Essex
Height: 5ft 11in **Weight:** 11st 7lbs
Nickname: Chalky, Toff, Zorro,
Whitey, Lamb
County debut: 2000
1st-Class 50s: 5
1st-Class 200s: 1
1st-Class catches: 7
Place in batting averages: 229th av. 18.64
(2002 3rd av. 92.66)
Strike rate: 108.00 (career 47.66)
Parents: Dennis and Ann
Marital status: Single
Family links with cricket: 'Grandfather on
Essex committee for many years. Dad flailed
the willow and brother travels the local
leagues high and low'
Education: Stowe School; St John's College, Durham University;
Loughborough University
Qualifications: 9 GCSEs, 3 A-levels
Cricket moments to forget: 'Franklyn Rose telling me my mates had bet £10 that he
couldn't injure me, as I walked out to play Lashings'
Cricketers particularly admired: Ian Botham, Viv Richards, Steve Waugh
Young players to look out for: Monty Panesar, Mark Powell
Other sports played: Badminton, squash, golf, kabaddi
Other sports followed: Football (West Ham), rugby (Northampton Saints)
Extras: Northamptonshire League Young Player of the Year and Youth Cricketer of
the Year 1999. Scored the first ever double century (206) in the history of the
Cricketer Cup, for Stowe Templars v Old Whitgiftians at Stowe 2001.
Northamptonshire Young Player of the Year (Frank Rudd Trophy) 2001. Played for
Loughborough University CCE 2001, 2002 and 2003; scored 99 v Nottinghamshire at
Trent Bridge 2001 and received Man of the Match award for his 58 in the first One-
Day UCCE Challenge Match at Lord's 2001. Recorded the highest maiden century in
the history of English first-class cricket (277, including a hundred before lunch on the
first day), v Gloucestershire at Northampton 2002 in his fifth first-class match; in the
process he shared with Mark Powell (107; also a maiden first-class century) in a new
record opening partnership for Northamptonshire (375). NBC Denis Compton Award
for the most promising young Northamptonshire player 2002. Represented British
Universities v Zimbabweans and India A 2003

Best batting: 277 Northamptonshire v Gloucestershire, Northampton 2002
Best bowling: 2-30 Northamptonshire v Gloucestershire, Northampton 2002

2003 Season

	M	Inns	NO	Runs	HS	Avge	100s	50s	Ct	St	O	M	Runs	Wkts	Avge	Best	5wl	10wM
Test																		
All First	7	14	0	261	76	18.64	-	2	4	-	18	0	123	1	123.00	1-35	-	-
1-day Int																		
C & G																		
NCL	5	5	0	46	22	9.20	-	-	2	-								
Twenty20	5	5	0	80	28	16.00	-	-	1	-								

Career Performances

	M	Inns	NO	Runs	HS	Avge	100s	50s	Ct	St	Balls	Runs	Wkts	Avge	Best	5wl	10wM
Test																	
All First	13	25	1	854	277	35.58	1	5	7	-	286	221	6	36.83	2-30	-	-
1-day Int																	
C & G																	
NCL	10	10	0	116	22	11.60	-	-	2	-	36	37	2	18.50	2-18	-	
Twenty20	5	5	0	80	28	16.00	-	-	1	-							

WIGLEY, D. H.   Worcestershire

Name: <u>David</u> Harry Wigley
Role: Right-hand bat, right-arm fast-medium bowler
Born: 26 October 1981, Bradford, Yorkshire
Height: 6ft 4in **Weight:** 13st 6lbs
Nickname: Wiggers, Reverend
County debut: 2002 (Yorkshire), 2003 (Worcestershire)
County colours: 2003 (Worcestershire)
Strike rate: 91.75 (career 98.20)
Parents: Max and Judith
Marital status: Girlfriend Sarah
Family links with cricket: 'Dad played league cricket in Liverpool Competition, Bradford League and Durham Senior League'
Education: St Mary's Roman Catholic Comprehensive, Menston; Loughborough University
Qualifications: 9 GCSEs, 3 A-levels, ECB Level I coaching

Off-season: 'Studying at Loughborough University while training with ECB Centre of Excellence there'

Overseas teams played for: Gormandale CC, Victoria, Australia 2001

Career highlights to date: 'Making Yorkshire first-team debut v Surrey at Guildford. Taking "five-for" at Lord's in University final. Worcestershire debut in NCL v Warwickshire at Edgbaston'

Cricket moments to forget: 'Going for sevens in first innings of [Yorkshire] first-team debut against Surrey!'

Cricket superstitions: 'Prefer to receive ball from right and must turn left to run in when bowling'

Cricketers particularly admired: Darren Gough, Allan Donald, Jason Gillespie

Young players to look out for: Joe Sayers, Monty Panesar, Tim Bresnan

Other sports played: Rugby union ('played until 17 for district; had county trials')

Other sports followed: Football (Leeds United), rugby (Wales)

Injuries: Out for four weeks at the start of the season with a hamstring injury

Relaxations: 'Watching films; listening to music'

Extras: Played for ECB Schools v Sri Lanka U19 2000. Yorkshire U19 Bowling Award 2000. Played for Loughborough University CCE 2002, taking 5-71 v Hampshire at West End and 5-52 v Oxford in the UCCE One-Day Challenge at Lord's; also played for LUCCE 2003. Left Yorkshire at the end of the 2002 season and joined Worcestershire for 2003. Represented British Universities v India A 2003

Opinions on cricket: 'Too many teams playing too much cricket. Far cry from the Australians, who play ten one-dayers a season and ten first-class games a season. This would allow more rest and preparation time.'

Best batting: 15 Yorkshire v Surrey, Guildford 2002
15 Worcestershire v Yorkshire, Worcester 2003

Best bowling: 2-56 Worcestershire v Yorkshire, Worcester 2003

2003 Season

	M	Inns	NO	Runs	HS	Avge	100s	50s	Ct	St	O	M	Runs	Wkts	Avge	Best	5wI	10wM
Test																		
All First	2	4	0	38	15	9.50	-	-	-	-	61.1	12	280	4	70.00	2-56	-	-
1-day Int																		
C & G																			
NCL	2	1	0	1	1	1.00	-	-	-	-	18	0	99	1	99.00	1-58	-	
Twenty20																		

Career Performances

	M	Inns	NO	Runs	HS	Avge	100s	50s	Ct	St	Balls	Runs	Wkts	Avge	Best	5wI	10wM
Test																	
All First	3	6	1	57	15	11.40	-	-	-	-	491	396	5	79.20	2-56	-	-
1-day Int																	
C & G																	
NCL	2	1	0	1	1	1.00	-	-	-	-	108	99	1	99.00	1-58	-	
Twenty20																	

Name: <u>Matthew</u> Guy Newman Windows
Role: Right-hand bat, left-arm
medium bowler
Born: 5 April 1973, Bristol
Height: 5ft 7in **Weight:** 11st 7lbs
Nickname: Steamy, Bedos, Boat
County debut: 1992
County cap: 1998
1000 runs in a season: 3
1st-Class 50s: 44
1st-Class 100s: 16
1st-Class catches: 84
One-Day 100s: 3
Place in batting averages: 134th av. 30.68
(2002 101st av. 36.62)
Strike rate: (career 68.50)
Parents: Tony and Carolyn
Wife and date of marriage: Emma,
12 October 2002

Family links with cricket: 'Father (A.R.) played for Gloucestershire (1960-69) and
was Cambridge cricket Blue'
Education: Clifton College; Durham University
Qualifications: 9 GCSEs, 3 A-levels, BA (Hons) Sociology (Dunelm), SFA securities
representative of the London Stock Exchange
Career outside cricket: Working with Rowan Dartington stockbrokers
Overseas tours: Clifton College to Barbados 1991; England U19 to Pakistan 1991-92;
Durham University to South Africa 1992-93; England A to Zimbabwe and South
Africa 1998-99; Gloucestershire's annual pre-season tour to South Africa
Overseas teams played for: Gold Coast Dolphins, Queensland 1996-97
Career highlights to date: 'Winning all the Lord's finals, but [especially] being not
out against Glamorgan in the 2000 [B&H] final'
Cricketers particularly admired: David Boon, Courtney Walsh
Young players to look out for: Monty Panesar, Alex Gidman
Other sports played: Rackets (British Open runner-up 1997)
Relaxations: 'Travelling and understanding financial jargon'
Extras: Played for Lincolnshire. Represented England U19 v Sri Lanka U19 1992.
Scored 71 on county debut v Essex at Bristol 1992. Gloucestershire Young Player of
the Year 1994. Set record for highest individual score for Durham University (218*), v
Hull University in the BUSA Championships 1995. Gloucestershire Player of the Year
1998. Scored three consecutive one-day centuries against Northants 2001-02 – 108* in
the B&H 2001, his maiden one-day hundred and for which he won the Gold Award;

117 off 94 balls in the NUL at Cheltenham 2001, his maiden one-day league century; 112* in the NUL 2002, in which innings he equalled the most sixes hit in an innings at Bristol
Best batting: 184 Gloucestershire v Warwickshire, Cheltenham 1996
Best bowling: 1-6 Combined Universities v West Indians, The Parks 1995

2003 Season

	M	Inns	NO	Runs	HS	Avge	100s	50s	Ct	St	O	M	Runs	Wkts	Avge	Best	5wI	10wM
Test																		
All First	16	29	0	890	150	30.68	1	5	11	-								
1-day Int																		
C & G	5	4	0	62	29	15.50	-	-	5	-								
NCL	15	15	7	510	91 *	63.75	-	5	8	-								
Twenty20	5	3	0	36	27	12.00	-	-	3	-								

Career Performances

	M	Inns	NO	Runs	HS	Avge	100s	50s	Ct	St	Balls	Runs	Wkts	Avge	Best	5wI	10wM
Test																	
All First	145	258	17	8248	184	34.22	16	44	84	-	137	131	2	65.50	1-6	-	-
1-day Int																	
C & G	24	21	4	446	82	26.23	-	2	11	-							
NCL	123	116	14	2616	117	25.64	2	12	41	-	48	49	0	-		-	-
Twenty20	5	3	0	36	27	12.00	-	-	3	-							

WOOD, J.   Lancashire

Name: John Wood
Role: Right-hand bat, right-arm fast-medium bowler
Born: 22 July 1970, Crofton, Wakefield
Height: 6ft 3in **Weight:** 16st 7lbs
Nickname: Woody
County debut: 1992 (Durham), 2001 (Lancashire)
County cap: 1998 (Durham), 2003 (Lancashire)
50 wickets in a season: 1
1st-Class 50s: 3
1st-Class 5 w. in innings: 11
1st-Class catches: 27
One-Day 5 w. in innings: 1
Place in batting averages: 270th av. 11.16 (2002 246th av. 16.81)
Place in bowling averages: 69th av. 31.62 (2002 106th av. 35.05)
Strike rate: 49.48 (career 54.56)
Parents: Brian and Anne
Wife and date of marriage: Emma Louise, 30 October 1994

Children: Alexandra Mae, 7 April 1996; Joseph Samuel, 3 July 1998; Kate Amelia, 22 January 2004

Family links with cricket: 'Brother Ian plays for Spen Victoria in Bradford League; Dad played local league cricket for Crofton'

Education: Crofton High School; Wakefield District College; Leeds Polytechnic

Qualifications: 6 O-levels, BTEC Diploma Electronic Engineering, HND Electrical and Electronic Engineering, Level III cricket coach

Overseas tours: Durham CCC to South Africa 1994-95

Overseas teams played for: Griqualand West Cricket Union, South Africa 1990-91; TAWA, Wellington and Wellington B, New Zealand 1993-95

Career highlights to date: 'Reaching C&G semi-final'

Cricket moments to forget: 'C&G semi-final' (*Lancashire lost to Leicestershire as Shahid Afridi struck a 58-ball 95*)

Cricketers particularly admired: Wasim Akram, David Boon, Wayne Larkins

Young players to look out for: Andrew Pratt, Steve Harmison, Paul Collingwood, Jimmy Anderson

Other sports played: Golf

Other sports followed: Football (Leeds United), rugby (England)

Injuries: Out for three weeks with shin splints

Relaxations: 'Spending time with my family; playing golf'

Extras: Played in the Bradford League. Made his debut for Durham (Minor Counties) in 1991. Durham Players' Player of the Year 1998. Left Durham at the end of the 2000 season and joined Lancashire for 2001. Awarded Lancashire cap 2003

Opinions on cricket: 'Time to get rid of EU players and give English youth a chance.'

Best batting: 64 Lancashire v Yorkshire, Headingley 2002

Best bowling: 7-58 Durham v Yorkshire, Headingley 1999

2003 Season

	M	Inns	NO	Runs	HS	Avge	100s	50s	Ct	St	O	M	Runs	Wkts	Avge	Best	5wI	10wM
Test																		
All First	9	8	2	67	30	11.16	-	-	2	-	222.4	32	854	27	31.62	3-17	-	-
1-day Int																		
C & G	2	1	0	0	0	0.00	-	-	-	-	14.1	2	64	4	16.00	4-33	-	
NCL	16	3	1	12	7 *	6.00	-	-	2	-	111.5	8	520	16	32.50	4-22	-	
Twenty20	4	2	1	15	15 *	15.00	-	-	1	-	13.5	0	81	3	27.00	1-15	-	

Career Performances

	M	Inns	NO	Runs	HS	Avge	100s	50s	Ct	St	Balls	Runs	Wkts	Avge	Best	5wI	10wM
Test																	
All First	113	161	23	1714	64	12.42	-	3	27	-	17140	10544	314	33.57	7-58	11	-
1-day Int																	
C & G	16	8	2	50	25	8.33	-	-	-	-	691	483	16	30.18	4-33	-	
NCL	110	65	24	424	28 *	10.34	-	-	20	-	4766	3774	112	33.69	5-49	1	
Twenty20	4	2	1	15	15 *	15.00	-	-	1	-	83	81	3	27.00	1-15	-	

WOOD, M. J.   Somerset

Name: <u>Matthew</u> James Wood
Role: Right-hand bat, occasional right-arm off-spin bowler
Born: 30 September 1980, Exeter
Height: 5ft 11in **Weight:** 12st 3lbs
Nickname: Woody, Grandma
County debut: 2001
1st-Class 50s: 12
1st-Class 100s: 5
1st-Class catches: 8
Place in batting averages: 187th av. 24.36
(2002 111th av. 34.67)
Parents: James and Trina
Marital status: Single
Family links with cricket: Father is chairman of Exmouth CC
Education: Exmouth Community College; Exeter University (first year)
Qualifications: 8 GCSEs, 2 A-levels, ECB Level II coach
Overseas tours: West of England U15 to West Indies 1995
Overseas teams played for: Doubleview CC, Perth 2000, 2001
Career highlights to date: 'Two hundreds in the match v Surrey 2002'
Cricketers particularly admired: Marcus Trescothick
Young players to look out for: Arul Suppiah
Other sports played: Football, golf
Other sports followed: Football (Liverpool FC)
Relaxations: 'Music, spending time with friends, golf'
Extras: Scored 71 on debut v Yorkshire at Bath 2001. NBC Denis Compton Award for the most promising young Somerset player 2001. Scored century in each innings (106/131) v Surrey at Taunton 2002, becoming (at 21 years, 279 days) the fourth youngest batsman to score twin centuries in the Championship. Somerset Player of the Year 2002. Has played for Devon

2003 Season

	M	Inns	NO	Runs	HS	Avge	100s	50s	Ct	St	O	M	Runs	Wkts	Avge	Best	5wI	10wM
Test																		
All First	12	23	1	536	100	24.36	1	3	1	-	5.1	0	32	0	-	-	-	-
1-day Int																		
C & G	1	1	0	13	13	13.00	-	-	-	-								
NCL	2	2	0	72	58	36.00	-	1	1	-								
Twenty20																		

Career Performances

	M	Inns	NO	Runs	HS	Avge	100s	50s	Ct	St	Balls	Runs	Wkts	Avge	Best	5wI	10wM
Test																	
All First	34	63	1	2036	196	32.83	5	12	8	-	73	62	0	-	-	-	-
1-day Int																	
C & G	4	3	0	38	19	12.66	-	-	1	-							
NCL	21	19	1	482	88 *	26.77	-	4	5	-							
Twenty20																	

WOOD, M. J.   Yorkshire

Name: <u>Matthew</u> James Wood
Role: Right-hand bat, off-spin bowler, county vice-captain
Born: 6 April 1977, Huddersfield
Height: 5ft 9in **Weight:** 12st
Nickname: Ronnie, Chuddy
County debut: 1997
County cap: 2001
1000 runs in a season: 3
1st-Class 50s: 16
1st-Class 100s: 12
1st-Class 200s: 2
1st-Class catches: 62
One-Day 100s: 3
Place in batting averages: 20th av. 53.03 (2002 280th av. 11.82)
Strike rate: 24.00 (career 33.00)
Parents: Roger and Kathryn
Marital status: Single
Family links with cricket: 'Father played for local team Emley. Mum made the teas and sister Caroline scored'

Education: Shelley High School and Sixth Form Centre
Qualifications: 9 GCSEs, 2 A-levels, NCA coaching award
Off-season: 'Club cricket in Australia'
Overseas tours: England U19 to Zimbabwe 1995-96; Yorkshire CCC to West Indies 1996-97, to Cape Town 1997, 1998; MCC to Kenya 1999, to Bangladesh 1999-2000; ECB National Academy to Australia 2001-02
Overseas teams played for: Somerset West CC, Cape Town 1994-95; Upper Hutt United CC, New Zealand 1997-98; Mosman Park, Western Australia 2000-01
Career highlights to date: 'Being on the pitch as fielding 12th man for England series win v South Africa at Headingley [1998]. Winning the Championship in 2001 and winning the C&G 2002 at Lord's'
Cricket moments to forget: 'Most of the 2002 season'
Cricket superstitions: 'Not any more!'
Cricketers particularly admired: Darren Lehmann, Matthew Maynard, Stephen Fleming, Michael Vaughan
Young players to look out for: Ben Heritage, Nick Thornicroft
Other sports played: Football (Kirkburton FC)
Other sports followed: Football (Liverpool FC)
Favourite band: Atomic Kitten
Relaxations: 'Music, dining out, socialising, watching sport'
Extras: Played for England U17 against India 1994. Attended Yorkshire Academy. Scored 81 on first-class debut v Lancashire at Headingley 1997. Scored 1000 runs in first full season 1998. Scored 85* v Surrey at Headingley 2001, in the process sharing with Darren Lehmann in a record third-wicket partnership for Yorkshire in matches against Surrey (190*). Scored century (116) v Gloucestershire at Headingley 2003, sharing with Damien Martyn (238) in the highest Championship stand for any wicket at Headingley (330). Yorkshire Coach's Player of the Year, Yorkshire Club Player of the Year and Yorkshire Players' Player of the Year 2003. Vice-captain of Yorkshire since 2003
Opinions on cricket: 'Twenty20 was a huge success. Whatever brings the crowds in should be promoted and encouraged.'
Best batting: 207 Yorkshire v Somerset, Taunton 2003
Best bowling: 1-4 Yorkshire v Somerset, Headingley 2003

2003 Season

	M	Inns	NO	Runs	HS	Avge	100s	50s	Ct	St		O	M	Runs	Wkts	Avge	Best	5wl	10wM
Test																			
All First	17	33	6	1432	207	53.03	5	3	8	-		8	0	22	2	11.00	1-4	-	-
1-day Int																			
C & G	2	2	1	147	118 *	147.00	1	-	-	-		6	0	45	3	15.00	3-45	-	
NCL	16	16	0	390	91	24.37	-	3	7	-									
Twenty20	4	4	1	114	57	38.00	-	1	4	-									

Career Performances

	M	Inns	NO	Runs	HS	Avge	100s	50s	Ct	St	Balls	Runs	Wkts	Avge	Best	5wI	10wM
Test																	
All First	89	156	16	4660	207	33.28	14	16	62	-	66	38	2	19.00	1-4	-	-
1-day Int																	
C & G	12	12	3	452	118 *	50.22	1	2	4	-	36	45	3	15.00	3-45	-	
NCL	66	57	3	1211	105 *	22.42	1	6	27	-							
Twenty20	4	4	1	114	57	38.00	-	1	4	-							

WRIGHT, D. G.   Northamptonshire

Name: <u>Damien</u> Geoffrey Wright
Role: Right-hand bat, right-arm fast-medium
bowler, gully fielder
Born: 25 July 1975, Casino, NSW, Australia
County debut: 2003
1st-Class 50s: 4
1st-Class 5 w. in innings: 1
1st-Class catches: 20
Strike rate: 63.28 (career 72.18)
Overseas tours: Australia A to South Africa
(one-day series) 2002-03
Overseas teams played for: Tasmania
1997-98 –
Extras: Was professional at Grange CC in
Edinburgh 2000-01 and played for Scotland
in the first and second rounds of the C&G
2002 (played late summer 2001), winning the
Man of the Match award on both occasions.
Has also won several domestic awards in Australia, including Man of the Match v
Victoria in the ING Cup at Melbourne 2001-02 (4-23/40). Represented Australia A in
home matches against South Africa A 2002-03. Tasmania's leading wicket-taker in the
Pura Cup 2002-03 (31 wickets; av. 27.25). Tasmanian Player of the Year 2002-03.
Named in Australia's initial squad of 30 for the 2002-03 World Cup. Was an overseas
player with Northamptonshire in June and July 2003, deputising for Andre Nel, absent
on international duty. Was due to join Derbyshire as an overseas player for 2004 but
was forced to withdraw with a knee injury
Best batting: 63 Tasmania v Western Australia, Hobart 2001-02
Best bowling: 6-39 Tasmania v New South Wales, Hobart 2002-03

2003 Season

	M	Inns	NO	Runs	HS	Avge	100s	50s	Ct	St	O	M	Runs	Wkts	Avge	Best	5wI	10wM
Test																		
All First	2	2	0	73	46	36.50	-	-	1	-	73.5	19	194	7	27.71	3-38	-	-
1-day Int																		
C & G																		
NCL	2	2	0	15	9	7.50	-	-	1	-	15.3	1	85	1	85.00	1-52	-	
Twenty20																		

Career Performances

	M	Inns	NO	Runs	HS	Avge	100s	50s	Ct	St	Balls	Runs	Wkts	Avge	Best	5wI	10wM
Test																	
All First	42	61	13	1002	63	20.87	-	4	20	-	8301	4021	115	34.96	6-39	1	-
1-day Int																	
C & G	2	2	1	108	55	108.00	-	2	2	-	102	51	3	17.00	2-37	-	
NCL	2	2	0	15	9	7.50	-	-	1	-	93	85	1	85.00	1-52	-	
Twenty20																	

WRIGHT, L. J.   Sussex

Name: <u>Luke</u> James Wright
Role: Right-hand bat, right-arm medium-fast bowler; all-rounder
Born: 7 March 1985, Grantham
Height: 5ft 11in **Weight:** 12st 3lbs
Nickname: Wrighty
County debut: 2003 (Leicestershire)
Parents: Keith and Anna
Marital status: Single
Family links with cricket: 'Father very keen cricketer (Level 2 coach).' Brother Ashley played for Leicestershire
Education: Belvoir High School, Bottesford; Ratcliffe College; Loughborough University
Qualifications: 8 GCSEs, National Diploma in Sports Science and Sports Massage, ECB Level 1 coaching
Off-season: England U19 World Cup tour to Bangladesh
Overseas tours: Leicestershire U13 to South Africa; Leicestershire U15 to South Africa; England U19 to Australia 2002-03, to Bangladesh (U19 World Cup) 2003-04
Career highlights to date: 'Getting a hat-trick for England U19 v South Africa U19 in a one-day game on Sky TV'

Cricket superstitions: 'Too many to name'
Cricketers particularly admired: Andrew Flintoff, Jacques Kallis
Young players to look out for: Ashley Wright, Richard Robinson, Andrew Hodd, Tom New
Other sports played: Football, hockey, squash, tennis
Other sports followed: Football (Newcastle United)
Relaxations: Music, cinema, going out
Extras: Set record for best debut for Ratcliffe College with 130. Scored 86 v MCC, the highest score by a Ratcliffe player against the club. Played for Leicestershire Board XI in the second round of the C&G 2002, which was played in September 2001. NBC Denis Compton Award for the most promising young Leicestershire player 2002. Represented England U19 v South Africa U19 2003, taking the first ever hat-trick for England U19 in one-day cricket, at Hove, finishing with 5-46. Left Leicestershire in the 2003-04 off-season and has joined Sussex for 2004
Opinions on cricket: 'Too many EU players coming into the game, which is stopping English cricket developing.'
Best batting: 11* Leicestershire v Sussex, Hove 2003

2003 Season

	M	Inns	NO	Runs	HS	Avge	100s	50s	Ct	St	O	M	Runs	Wkts	Avge	Best	5wI	10wM
Test																		
All First	1	2	1	11	11*	11.00	-	-	-	-	19	0	95	0	-	-	-	-
1-day Int																		
C & G																		
NCL	2	1	0	7	7	7.00	-	-	-	-	1	0	8	0	-	-	-	
Twenty20																		

Career Performances

	M	Inns	NO	Runs	HS	Avge	100s	50s	Ct	St	Balls	Runs	Wkts	Avge	Best	5wI	10wM
Test																	
All First	1	2	1	11	11*	11.00	-	-	-	-	114	95	0	-	-	-	-
1-day Int																	
C & G	1	1	0	16	16	16.00	-	-	-	-							
NCL	2	1	0	7	7	7.00	-	-	-	-	6	8	0	-	-	-	
Twenty20																	

100. Which Gloucestershire pace bowler recorded his maiden Test five-wicket return (5-106) in England's win at The Oval in 1991?

YARDY, M. H.

Name: Michael (<u>Mike</u>) Howard Yardy
Role: Left-hand bat, left-arm medium-fast bowler
Born: 27 November 1980, Pembury, Kent
Height: 6ft **Weight:** 14st 2lbs
Nickname: Yards, Paolo
County debut: 1999 (one-day), 2000 (first-class)
1st-Class 50s: 8
1st-Class catches: 24
Place in batting averages: (2002 149th av. 28.94)
Strike rate: (career 284.00)
Parents: Beverly and Howard
Marital status: Engaged to Karin Mason
Family links with cricket: 'Brother plays for local team'
Education: William Parker School, Hastings
Qualifications: 5 GCSEs, 2 A-levels, ECB Level 1 coach, Sports Psychology diploma
Career outside cricket: Sales assistant
Overseas tours: Sussex Academy to Barbados 1997; Sussex to Grenada 2001, 2002
Overseas teams played for: Cape Town CC 1999
Career highlights to date: 'Winning County Championship'
Cricket superstitions: 'Loads – all secrets'
Cricketers particularly admired: 'All those who have reached the pinnacle of their careers'
Young players to look out for: Greg Hobbs, Russ Jones, Fraser Key, Martin Smith, Jon McSweeney, Richard Chynoweth
Other sports followed: Football (West Ham)
Favourite band: Bluetones
Relaxations: 'Watching West Ham; relaxing with my girlfriend'
Extras: Played in the Sussex U15 side that won the U15 County Championship 1996, the U16 side that won the U16 County Championship 1997 and the U19 side that were runners-up in the NAYC Two-Day Cup 1997. Represented England U17 1998. Attended Sussex Academy. Played for Sussex Board XI in the NatWest 1999 and 2000. Sussex Most Improved Player 2001
Opinions on cricket: 'It's a great game. Twenty20 cricket was a huge success. People must make sure this stays as popular.'
Best batting: 93 Sussex v Surrey, The Oval 2002
Best bowling: 1-13 Sussex v Derbyshire, Arundel 2001

2003 Season

	M	Inns	NO	Runs	HS	Avge	100s	50s	Ct	St	O	M	Runs	Wkts	Avge	Best	5wI	10wM
Test																		
All First	3	4	0	134	69	33.50	-	1	4	-	32	3	99	0	-	-	-	-
1-day Int																		
C & G	1	1	0	12	12	12.00	-	-	-	-	2	0	16	0	-	-	-	
NCL	10	8	1	108	36	15.42	-	-	3	-	10.4	0	100	1	100.00	1-39	-	
Twenty20																		

Career Performances

	M	Inns	NO	Runs	HS	Avge	100s	50s	Ct	St	Balls	Runs	Wkts	Avge	Best	5wI	10wM
Test																	
All First	34	58	7	1486	93	29.13	-	8	24	-	852	475	3	158.33	1-13	-	-
1-day Int																	
C & G	9	8	0	102	52	12.75	-	1	4	-	266	251	6	41.83	3-39	-	
NCL	22	19	2	246	36	14.47	-	-	5	-	334	300	7	42.85	3-36	-	
Twenty20																	

YATES, G.   Lancashire

Name: Gary Yates
Role: Right-hand bat, right-arm off-spin bowler
Born: 20 September 1967, Ashton-under-Lyne
Height: 6ft 1in **Weight:** 13st 1lb
Nickname: Sweaty, Yugo, Pearly, Backyard, Zippy
County debut: 1990
County cap: 1994
1st-Class 50s: 5
1st-Class 100s: 3
1st-Class 5 w. in innings: 5
1st-Class catches: 38
Strike rate: (career 74.73)
Parents: Alan and Patricia
Marital status: Single – 'girlfriend Christine B. Haigh'
Children: Francis Leonard George, 1 May 1999
Family links with cricket: 'Father played for Denton St Lawrence and other teams in the Lancashire League'
Education: Manchester Grammar School

Qualifications: 6 O-levels, Level 3 coach, Australian Cricket Coaching Council coach
Career outside cricket: 'Sales rep with family business (Digical Ltd), selling diaries, calendars and business gifts'
Off-season: 'Taking Level 4 [coaching award]; Lancs to Grenada'
Overseas tours: Lancashire to Tasmania and Western Australia 1990, to Western Australia 1991, to Johannesburg 1992, to Barbados and St Lucia 1992, to Calcutta 1997, to Cape Town 1997-98, to Grenada 2003; MCC to Bangladesh 1999-2000
Overseas teams played for: South Barwon, Geelong, Australia 1987-88; Johnsonville, Wellington, New Zealand 1989-90; Western Suburbs, Brisbane 1991-92; Old Selbornian, East London, South Africa 1992-93; Hermanus CC, South Africa 1995-96
Career highlights to date: 'All trophies won while playing with Lancashire'
Cricket moments to forget: 'Not being selected for a 2nd XI Bain Hogg final after playing all ten round matches and semi-final'
Cricket superstitions: 'They vary – at the moment my car outside the house has to be parked facing the same way'
Cricketers particularly admired: Michael Atherton, Ian Botham, John Emburey
Young players to look out for: Chris Schofield, James Anderson
Other sports played: Golf ('represented Lancashire CCC at National *Times* Corporate Golf Challenge, La Manga, Spain, December 2001')
Other sports followed: 'All sports, especially football (Manchester City season-ticket holder), golf, motor rallying'
Relaxations: 'Playing golf, watching football and good films, eating; spending time with my son'
Extras: Scored century (106) on Championship debut v Nottinghamshire at Trent Bridge 1990. Rapid Cricketline Player of the Month April/May 1992. 2nd XI captain/coach since 2002. Won the double with Bowdon CC (Cheshire County League) 2002 and 2003; took 77 wickets and scored 930 runs (av. 103.00) in league 2003. Leading wicket-taker for Lancashire 2nd XI (354)
Opinions on cricket: 'Congratulations to Twenty20 – a success. Relegation and promotion in county cricket should be for two teams only.'
Best batting: 134* Lancashire v Northamptonshire, Old Trafford 1993
Best bowling: 6-64 Lancashire v Kent, Old Trafford 1999

2003 Season

	M	Inns	NO	Runs	HS	Avge	100s	50s	Ct	St	O	M	Runs	Wkts	Avge	Best	5wI	10wM
Test																		
All First																		
1-day Int																		
C & G	1	0	0	0	0	-	-	-	-	-	10	1	20	1	20.00	1-20	-	
NCL	1	0	0	0	0	-	-	-	-	-	9	0	29	1	29.00	1-29	-	
Twenty20																		

Career Performances

	M	Inns	NO	Runs	HS	Avge	100s	50s	Ct	St	Balls	Runs	Wkts	Avge	Best	5wI	10wM
Test																	
All First	82	107	36	1789	134 *	25.19	3	5	38	-	13751	7025	184	38.17	6-64	5	-
1-day Int																	
C & G	22	10	5	91	34 *	18.20	-	-	5	-	1266	712	19	37.47	2-15	-	
NCL	115	53	25	435	38	15.53	-	-	28	-	4122	3309	105	31.51	4-34	-	
Twenty20																	

YUVRAJ SINGH   *Yorkshire*

Name: Yuvraj Singh
Role: Left-hand bat, left-arm medium or orthodox spin bowler
Born: 12 December 1981, Chandigarh, India
County debut: 2003
One-Day Internationals: 73
1st-Class 50s: 11
1st-Class 100s: 6
1st-Class 200s: 1
1st-Class catches: 41
One-Day 100s: 1
Place in batting averages: 256th av. 14.50
Strike rate: 69.00 (career 73.66)
Family links with cricket: Father Yograj Singh played for Haryana, Punjab and India
Overseas tours: India U19 to Sri Lanka (U19 World Cup) 1999-2000; India A to South Africa 2001-02; India to Kenya (ICC Knockout Trophy) 2000-01, to Sharjah (Coca-Cola Champions Trophy) 2000-01, to Sri Lanka (Coca-Cola Cup) 2001, to South Africa 2001-02 (Standard Bank Triangular Tournament), to West Indies 2001-02 (one-day series), to England 2002 (NatWest Series), to Sri Lanka (ICC Champions Trophy) 2002-03, to New Zealand 2002-03 (one-day series), to Africa (World Cup) 2002-03, to Bangladesh (TVS Cup) 2003, to Australia 2003-04 (VB Series)
Overseas teams played for: Punjab 1996-97 –
Extras: Represented India U19 in home series v Sri Lanka U19 1998-99 and was Man of the Series in the U19 World Cup in Sri Lanka 1999-2000. Has won several ODI awards, including Man of the Match v Australia in the quarter-final of the ICC Knockout Trophy in Kenya 2000-01 (84), v Sri Lanka at Colombo in the Coca-Cola Cup 2001 (98*) and v England at Lord's in the NatWest Series 2002 (3-39/64*). Also scored 69 in India's victory in the NatWest Series final v England at Lord's 2002,

sharing in a stand of 121 from 106 balls with Mohammad Kaif. Joined Yorkshire as an overseas player for 2003; left Yorkshire at the end of the 2003 season

Best batting: 209 North Zone v South Zone, Faridabad 2001-02
Best bowling: 3-25 Punjab v Jammu & Kashmir, Jammu 2001-02
Stop press: Man of the Series in the Challenger Trophy (India Seniors v India A v India B) 2003-04. Made Test debut in the second Test v New Zealand at Mohali 2003-04. Man of the Match v Zimbabwe at Brisbane in the VB Series 2003-04 (69) and again in the following match v Australia at Sydney, scoring 139 and sharing in a new record ODI fourth-wicket partnership for India (213) with V.V.S. Laxman (106*)

2003 Season

	M	Inns	NO	Runs	HS	Avge	100s	50s	Ct	St	O	M	Runs	Wkts	Avge	Best	5wI	10wM
Test																		
All First	7	12	2	145	56	14.50	-	1	12	-	34.3	5	130	3	43.33	1-8	-	-
1-day Int																		
C & G	1	1	0	27	27	27.00	-	-	-	-	6	0	27	0	-		-	-
NCL	8	8	0	169	50	21.12	-	1	1	-	29.1	0	170	3	56.66	2-48	-	
Twenty20	5	5	0	154	71	30.80	-	1	-	-	7	0	51	5	10.20	3-20	-	

Career Performances

	M	Inns	NO	Runs	HS	Avge	100s	50s	Ct	St	Balls	Runs	Wkts	Avge	Best	5wI	10wM
Test																	
All First	35	57	4	2204	209	41.58	7	11	41	-	711	359	9	39.88	3-25	-	-
1-day Int	73	63	10	1644	102 *	31.01	1	12	23	-	975	787	23	34.21	4-6	-	
C & G	1	1	0	27	27	27.00	-	-	-	-	36	27	0	-		-	-
NCL	8	8	0	169	50	21.12	-	1	1	-	175	170	3	56.66	2-48	-	
Twenty20	5	5	0	154	71	30.80	-	1	-	-	42	51	5	10.20	3-20	-	

ZUIDERENT, B. Sussex

Name: Bastiaan (Bas) Zuiderent
Role: Right-hand top-order bat, right-arm off-spin bowler
Born: 3 March 1977, Utrecht, Holland
Height: 6ft 3in **Weight:** 14st 2lbs
Nickname: Bazy, Bastil
County debut: 1999 (one-day), 2001 (first-class)
One-Day Internationals: 13
1st-Class 50s: 4
1st-Class 100s: 1
1st-Class catches: 19
One-Day 100s: 1
Parents: Eduard and Jacqueline
Marital status: Single

Family links with cricket: Cousins J. J. Esmeijer and Ben Goedegebuur have represented Holland
Education: Erasmiaans Gymnasium, Rotterdam; University of Amsterdam ('two years; Economics')
Qualifications: Level 2 coaching
Overseas tours: Various Holland sides to Denmark, Kenya, South Africa and Scotland; Holland to India and Pakistan (World Cup) 1995-96, to Malaysia (ICC Trophy) 1998, to Sri Lanka (ICC Champions Trophy) 2002-03, to Africa (World Cup) 2002-03
Overseas teams played for: VOC Rotterdam 1989-97; Wits Technikon, Johannesburg 1997; VRA Amsterdam 1998
Cricketers particularly admired:
Tim de Leede, Steven Lubbers, P. J. Bakker
Other sports played: Football (VOC Rotterdam), golf (Broekpolder), skiing, squash, tennis
Other sports followed: Football (PSV Eindhoven)
Relaxations: 'Cooking, DIY'
Extras: Has represented Holland at various levels since the age of 12. Player of the Tournament, International Youth Tournament, Denmark 1993. Scored 54 v England in 1995-96 World Cup, becoming the second youngest player (after Sachin Tendulkar) to score a fifty in a World Cup. Played for Holland in the NatWest 1996-98; scored 99 (run out) v Worcestershire in the 1997 competition, winning the Man of the Match award. B&H Gold Award for his 102* v Hampshire at West End 2001 (his maiden one-day century); two days later scored maiden first-class century (122) v Nottinghamshire at Hove in only his second first-class match. Is not considered an overseas player. Released by Sussex at the end of the 2003 season
Best batting: 122 Sussex v Nottinghamshire, Hove 2001

2003 Season

	M	Inns	NO	Runs	HS	Avge	100s	50s	Ct	St	O	M	Runs	Wkts	Avge	Best	5wI	10wM
Test																		
All First	1	1	0	50	50	50.00	-	1	1	-								
1-day Int																		
C & G																		
NCL	4	4	0	93	47	23.25	-	-	-	-								
Twenty20	5	5	0	110	42	22.00	-	-	2	-								

Career Performances

	M	Inns	NO	Runs	HS	Avge	100s	50s	Ct	St	Balls	Runs	Wkts	Avge	Best	5wl	10wM
Test																	
All First	19	30	1	679	122	23.41	1	4	19	-							
1-day Int	13	13	1	133	54	11.08	-	1	11	-							
C & G	7	7	0	199	99	28.42	-	2	3	-	12	15	0	-		-	-
NCL	28	25	0	499	68	19.96	-	3	6	-							
Twenty20	5	5	0	110	42	22.00	-	-	2	-							

GUEST PLAYER

McMILLAN, C. D.   Gloucestershire

Name: <u>Craig</u> Douglas McMillan
Role: Right-hand bat, right-arm medium bowler
Born: 13 September 1976, Christchurch, New Zealand
Extras: Has played 48 Tests and 145 ODIs for New Zealand. Played one 50-over match for Gloucestershire v India A at Cheltenham 2003

STOP PRESS

ELLIOTT, M. T. G.   Glamorgan

Name: <u>Matthew</u> Thomas Gray Elliott
Role: Left-hand bat, left-arm medium bowler
Born: 28 September 1971, Chelsea, Victoria, Australia
Extras: Has played 20 Tests and 1 ODI for Australia. Was Yorkshire's overseas player for part of 2002. Was Glamorgan's overseas player in 2000 and has returned for 2004

SHABBIR AHMED   Gloucestershire

Name: Shabbir Ahmed Khan
Role: Right-hand bat, right-arm fast-medium bowler
Born: 21 April 1976, Khanewal, Punjab
Extras: Has played 6 Tests and 19 ODIs for Pakistan. Has joined Gloucestershire as an overseas player for 2004

NOTE: <u>Heath</u> Hilton Streak, Zimbabwe Test cricketer, has been signed by Warwickshire as an overseas player to alternate with Dewald Pretorius during 2004

SCOTTISH SALTIRES 2004

WRIGHT, C. M.

Name: <u>Craig</u> McIntyre Wright
Role: Right-hand bat, right-arm medium-fast bowler, captain
Born: 28 April 1974, Paisley
Extras: Scotland debut 1997; captain since 2002. Represented Scotland in the Commonwealth Games in Malaysia 1998-99 and in the ICC Trophy in Canada 2001. Has played grade cricket in Australia. Marketing manager with Cricket Scotland

BRINKLEY, J. E.

Name: <u>James</u> Edward Brinkley
Role: Right-hand bat, right-arm fast-medium bowler
Born: 13 March 1974, Helensburgh
Extras: Scotland debut 1998. Formerly with Worcestershire (for whom he took 6-98 on County Championship debut v Surrey at The Oval 1994), Essex and Durham. Represented Scotland in the 1999 World Cup

COETZER, K. J.

Name: <u>Kyle</u> James Coetzer
Role: Right-hand bat, right-arm medium-fast bowler
Born: 14 April 1984, Aberdeen
Extras: Scotland debut 2003. Represented Scotland in the U19 World Cup in New Zealand 2001-02 and in Bangladesh 2003-04 (captain). Has attended Western Province Academy, South Africa; is at the Durham CCC Academy and has played for the county 2nd XI

ENGLISH, C. V.

Name: <u>Cedric</u> Vaughan English
Role: Right-hand bat, right-arm fast-medium bowler
Born: 13 September 1973, Kimberley, South Africa
Extras: Scotland debut 2002. Has played first-class cricket for Griqualand West, Western Province and Boland

HAQ, R. M.

Name: Rana <u>Majid</u> Haq Khan
Role: Left-hand bat, right-arm off-spin bowler
Born: 11 February 1983, Paisley
Extras: Scotland debut 2002. Took 4-36 v Durham at Riverside in Scotland's victory in their debut NCL match 2003 and scored 55* v Durham in the return at Edinburgh

HOFFMANN, P. J. C.

Name: <u>Paul</u> Jacob Christopher Hoffmann
Role: Right-hand bat, right-arm fast-medium bowler
Born: 14 January 1970, Rockhampton, Queensland, Australia
Extras: Scotland debut 2001. Leading wicket-taker in Scottish National Cricket League history with 218 at 13.07

IQBAL, M. M.

Name: <u>Moneeb</u> Mohammed Iqbal
Role: Right-hand bat, right-arm leg-spin bowler
Born: 28 February 1986, Glasgow
Extras: Scotland debut 2002. Represented Scotland in the U19 World Cup in New Zealand 2001-02 (aged 15) and in Bangladesh 2003-04. Became youngest player to win full Scotland cap, aged 16 v Surrey at Edinburgh in the C&G 2002. Attends Durham CCC Academy

KERR, J. A. M.

Name: James (<u>Jamie</u>) Alexander MacKenzie Kerr
Role: Right-hand bat, wicket-keeper
Born: 12 June 1975, Edinburgh
Extras: Has played for Scotland A but has yet to make full Scotland debut

KNOX, S. T.

Name: <u>Steven</u> Thomas Knox
Role: Right-hand bat, right-arm medium bowler
Born: 16 February 1974, Barrow-in-Furness, Lancashire
Extras: Scotland debut 2003. Has played for Cumberland, including appearances in the NatWest and C&G competitions

LOCKHART, D. R.

Name: <u>Douglas</u> Ross Lockhart
Role: Right-hand bat, wicket-keeper, occasional right-arm fast-medium bowler
Born: 19 January 1976, Glasgow
Extras: Scotland debut 1995. Player of the Tournament at International Youth Tournament, Holland 1995. Oxford Blue 1998

MAIDEN, G. I.

(*See main A-Z entry*)

McLAREN, K. A.

Name: <u>Kevin</u> Alexander McLaren
Role: Left-hand bat, right-arm off-spin bowler
Born: 23 February 1981, Edinburgh
Extras: Has played for Scotland U23 and Scotland A but has yet to make full Scotland debut

MORE, R. E.

Name: <u>Robert</u> Edwards More
Role: Left-hand bat, occasional off-spin bowler
Born: 1 June 1982, Edinburgh
Extras: Scotland debut 2002. Captained Scotland at the U19 World Cup in New Zealand 2001-02. Nephew of former Scotland batsman-wicket-keeper Hamish More

PARSONS, R. A.

Name: Robert Andrew (<u>Drew</u>) Parsons
Role: Left-hand bat, left-arm medium bowler
Born: 26 February 1975, Irvine, Ayrshire
Extras: Scotland debut 1997. Captained Scotland U16 and U19. Represented Scotland at the Commonwealth Games in Malaysia 1998-99 and at the ICC Trophy in Canada 2001

SMITH, C. J. O.

Name: <u>Colin</u> John Ogilvie Smith
Role: Right-hand bat, wicket-keeper
Born: 27 September 1972, Aberdeen
Extras: Scotland debut 1999. Represented Scotland U16, Scotland U19 and Scotland A. Represented Scotland at the ICC Trophy in Canada 2001

STANGER, I. M.

Name: <u>Ian</u> Michael Stanger
Role: Right-hand bat, right-arm medium-fast bowler
Born: 5 October 1971, Glasgow
Extras: Scotland debut 1992. Scotland Young Cricketer of the Year 1992, 1993. Played for Leicestershire 1994. Represented Scotland in the 1999 World Cup

WATSON, R. R.

Name: <u>Ryan</u> Robert Watson
Role: Right-hand bat, right-arm medium/off-spin bowler
Born: 12 November 1976, Harare, Zimbabwe
Extras: Scotland debut 2002. Represented South Africa Schools B 1995 and captained Transvaal U24 1996. Struck a 43-ball century (103*) v Somerset at Edinburgh in the NCL 2003; also scored two half-centuries in the 2003 competition

WATTS, D. F.

Name: David <u>Fraser</u> Watts
Role: Right-hand bat, right-arm medium bowler
Born: 5 June 1979, King's Lynn, Norfolk
Extras: Scotland debut 1998. Represented Scotland in the U19 World Cup in South Africa 1997-98. Represented Scotland in the ICC Trophy in Canada 2001

WILLIAMSON, J. G.

Name: John <u>Greig</u> Williamson
Role: Right-hand bat, right-arm fast-medium bowler
Born: 28 December 1968, Glasgow
Extras: Scotland debut 1989. Represented Scotland in the World Cup 1999. Became fourth player to win 100 Scotland caps 2001

THE UMPIRES

BENSON, M. R.

Name: <u>Mark</u> Richard Benson
Born: 6 July 1958, Shoreham, Sussex
Height: 5ft 10in
Nickname: Benny
Wife and date of marriage: Sarah Patricia,
20 September 1986
Children: Laurence, 16 October 1987;
Edward, 23 June 1990
Education: Sutton Valence School
Off-season: 'Improving my golf and bridge.
At the U19 World Cup in Bangladesh
(umpiring)'
Other sports played: Bridge, golf,
swimming, cycling
Relaxations: Bridge, golf
Appointed to 1st-Class list: 2000
International panel: 2004 –
One-Day Internationals umpired: 1 as
TV umpire

Other umpiring honours: Stood in the C&G Trophy final 2003
County as player: Kent
Role: Left-hand bat
County debut: 1980
County cap: 1981
Benefit: 1991 (£174,619)
Test debut: 1986
Tests: 1
One-Day Internationals: 1
1000 runs in a season: 11
1st-Class 50s: 99
1st-Class 100s: 47
1st-Class 200s: 1
1st-Class catches: 140
One-Day 100s: 5
Overseas tours: None
Highlights of playing career: '257 v Hampshire. Winning Sunday League as captain of Kent. Two 90s to win a game against Hampshire with Malcolm Marshall bowling.

One of only four cricketers in the history of Kent to have scored more than 10,000 runs and have an average in excess of 40'

Extras: Scored 1000 runs in first full season. Kent captain 1991-95. Captained England in two one-day matches against Holland in 1993

Opinions on cricket: 'Wish the game was played in an honest fashion (à la golf). Why fellow pros cheat fellow pros is beyond me. If it happened in golf, the guilty player would probably be ostracised for the rest of his career.'

Best batting: 257 Kent v Hampshire, Southampton 1991

Best bowling: 2-55 Kent v Surrey, Dartford 1986

First-Class Career Performances

	M	Inns	NO	Runs	HS	Avge	100s	Ct	St	Runs	Wkts	Avge	Best	5wI	10wM
Test	1	2	0	51	30	25.50	-	-	-						
All First	292	491		34	18387	257	40.23	48	140	-	493	5	98.60	2-55	-	-

BURGESS, G. I.

Name: <u>Graham</u> Iefvion Burgess
Born: 5 May 1943, Glastonbury, Somerset
Education: Millfield School
Appointed to 1st-Class list: 1991
One-Day Internationals umpired:
2 as TV umpire
County as player: Somerset
Role: Right-hand bat, right-arm
medium bowler
County debut: 1966
County cap: 1968
Testimonial: 1977
1st-Class 100s: 2
1st-Class 5 w. in innings: 18
1st-Class 10 w. in match: 2
1st-Class catches: 120
One-Day 5 w. in innings: 2
Extras: Played Minor Counties cricket for

Wiltshire 1981-82 and Cambridgeshire 1983-84

Best batting: 129 Somerset v Gloucestershire, Taunton 1973

Best bowling: 7-43 Somerset v Oxford University, The Parks 1975

First-Class Career Performances

	M	Inns	NO	Runs	HS	Avge	100s	Ct	St	Runs	Wkts	Avge	Best	5wI	10wM
Test															
All First	252	414	37	7129	129	18.90	2	120	-	13543	474	28.57	7-43	18	2

CLARKSON, A.

Name: Anthony (<u>Tony</u>) Clarkson
Born: 5 September 1939, Killinghall,
North Yorkshire
Height: 6ft
Wife's name: Cheryl
Children: André, 5 September 1964;
Chantal, 27 May 1967; Pierre, 1 May 1969
Family links with cricket: Father was a
league professional
Education: Harrogate Grammar School;
Leeds College of Building; Bradford
Polytechnic; Brunel College, Bristol
Career outside cricket: Architectural, civil
engineering and surveying consultant
Other sports followed: Golf and rugby
Relaxations: Golf, DIY, and gardening
Appointed to 1st-Class list: 1996
Counties as player: Yorkshire, Somerset
Role: Right-hand bat, right-arm off-spin bowler
County debut: 1963 (Yorkshire), 1965 (Somerset)
County cap: 1969 (Somerset)
1000 runs in a season: 2
1st-Class 50s: 23
1st-Class 100s: 2
1st-Class catches: 52
One-Day 100s: 1
Extras: First English player to score a century in the Sunday League. Was league
professional 1973-89
Best batting: 131 Somerset v Northamptonshire, Northampton 1969
Best bowling: 3-51 Somerset v Essex, Yeovil 1967

First-Class Career Performances

	M	Inns	NO	Runs	HS	Avge	100s	Ct	St	Runs	Wkts	Avge	Best	5wI	10wM
Test															
All First	110	189	12	4458	131	25.18	2	52	-	367	13	28.23	3-51	-	-

CONSTANT, D. J.

Name: <u>David</u> John Constant
Born: 9 November 1941,
Bradford-on-Avon, Wiltshire
Height: 5ft 7in
Nickname: Connie
Wife's name: Rosalyn
Children: Lisa, 6 July 1966;
Julie, 21 February 1969
Family links with cricket: Father-in-law,
G.E.E. Lambert, played for Gloucestershire
Education: Grove Park Secondary Modern
Off-season: Bowls
Other sports followed: Football (Millwall)
Interests/relaxations: 'Six grandchildren
and bowls'
Appointed to 1st-Class list: 1969
First appointed to Test panel: 1971
Tests umpired: 36 (plus 5 as TV umpire)
One-Day Internationals umpired: 33 (plus 5 as TV umpire)
Other umpiring honours: Stood in 1975, 1979 and 1983 World Cups
Counties as player: Kent, Leicestershire
Role: Left-hand bat, slow left-arm bowler
County debut: 1961 (Kent), 1965 (Leicestershire)
1st-Class 50s: 6
1st-Class catches: 33
Extras: County bowls player for Gloucestershire 1984-86 (outdoor). Also represented
Somerset at indoor version of the game in the Liberty Trophy
Best batting: 80 Leicestershire v Gloucestershire, Bristol 1966
Best bowling: 1-28 Leicestershire v Surrey, The Oval 1968

First-Class Career Performances

	M	Inns	NO	Runs	HS	Avge	100s	Ct	St	Runs	Wkts	Avge	Best	5wI	10wM
Test															
All First	61	93	14	1517	80	19.20	-	33	-	36	1	36.00	1-28	-	-

COWLEY, N. G.

Name: <u>Nigel</u> Geoffrey Cowley
Born: 1 March 1953, Shaftesbury, Dorset
Height: 5ft 6½in
Marital status: Divorced
Children: Mark Antony, 14 June 1973;
Darren James, 30 October 1976
Family links with cricket: Darren played
Hampshire Schools U11, U12, U13; Natal
Schools 1993, 1994, 1995; and toured India
with South Africa U19 1996
Education: Duchy Manor, Mere, Wiltshire
Other sports played: Golf (8 handicap)
Other sports followed: Football
(Liverpool FC)
Appointed to 1st-Class list: 2000
Counties as player: Hampshire, Glamorgan
Role: Right-hand bat, off-spin bowler
County debut: 1974 (Hampshire),
1990 (Glamorgan)

County cap: 1978 (Hampshire)
Benefit: 1988 (Hampshire; £88,274)
1000 runs in a season: 1
50 wickets in a season: 2
1st-Class 50s: 36
1st-Class 100s: 2
1st-Class 5 w. in innings: 5
1st-Class catches: 105
One-Day 5 w. in innings: 1
Overseas tours: Hampshire to Barbados 1985, 1986, 1987, to Dubai 1989
Overseas teams played for: Paarl CC, 1982-83; Amanzimtoti, 1984-96
(both South Africa)
Extras: Played for Dorset 1972. NatWest Man of the Match award
Best batting: 109* Hampshire v Somerset, Taunton 1977
Best bowling: 6-48 Hampshire v Leicestershire, Southampton 1982

First-Class Career Performances

	M	Inns	NO	Runs	HS	Avge	100s	Ct	St	Runs	Wkts	Avge	Best	5wI	10wM
Test															
All First	271	375	62	7309	109*	23.35	2	105	-	14879	437	34.04	6-48	5	-

DUDLESTON, B.

Name: Barry Dudleston
Born: 16 July 1945, Bebington, Cheshire
Height: 5ft 9in
Nickname: Danny
Wife and date of marriage: Louise Wendy,
19 October 1994
Children: Sharon Louise, 29 October 1968;
Matthew Barry, 12 September 1988;
Jack Nicholas, 29 April 1998
Family links with cricket: 'Dad was a
league cricketer'
Education: Stockport School
Career outside cricket: Managing director
of Sunsport Tours & Travel
Other sports played: Golf
Other sports followed: All sports
Relaxations: Bridge, red wine
Appointed to 1st-Class list: 1984
First appointed to Test panel: 1991
Tests umpired: 2 (plus 14 as TV umpire)
One-Day Internationals umpired: 4 (plus 10 as TV umpire)
Other umpiring honours: Stood in C&G final 2001 and B&H final 2002; also
officiated at the inaugural Twenty20 finals day at Trent Bridge 2003, including
standing in the final
Players to watch for the future: James Anderson
Counties as player: Leicestershire, Gloucestershire
Role: Right-hand opening bat, slow left-arm bowler, occasional wicket-keeper
County debut: 1966 (Leicestershire), 1981 (Gloucestershire)
County cap: 1969 (Leicestershire)
Benefit: 1980 (Leicestershire; £25,000)
1000 runs in a season: 8
1st-Class 50s: 64
1st-Class 100s: 31
1st-Class 200s: 1
1st-Class catches: 234
One-Day 100s: 4
Overseas tours: Kent (as guest player) to West Indies 1972; D.H. Robins' XI
to West Indies 1973; Wisden XI to West Indies 1984; MCC to Kenya 1993
Overseas teams played for: Rhodesia 1976-80
Highlights of playing career: 'Winning County Championship [with Leicestershire]'

Extras: Played for England U25. Holder with John Steele of the highest first-wicket partnership for Leics, 390 v Derbys at Leicester in 1979. Fastest player in Rhodesian cricket history to 1000 first-class runs in Currie Cup; second fastest ever in Currie Cup
Opinions on cricket: 'My team-mate Duncan Fletcher is doing a great job.'
Best batting: 202 Leicestershire v Derbyshire, Leicester 1979
Best bowling: 4-6 Leicestershire v Surrey, Leicester 1972

First-Class Career Performances

	M	Inns	NO	Runs	HS	Avge	100s	Ct	St	Runs	Wkts	Avge	Best	5wI	10wM
Test															
All First	295	501	47	14747	202	32.48	32	234	7	1365	47	29.04	4-6	-	-

EVANS, J. H.

Name: Jeffrey (<u>Jeff</u>) Howard Evans
Born: 7 August 1954, Llanelli
Height: 5ft 8in
Wife and date of marriage: Christine, 29 December 1983
Children: Rhian, 9 February 1986; Siân, 3 September 1987; Seren (golden retriever)
Education: Llanelli Boys Grammar School; Dudley College of Education
Career outside cricket: Supply teacher
Off-season: Teaching; coaching
Other sports followed: 'Most sports, rugby in particular'
Relaxations: Keeping fit, walking, cycling, skiing
Appointed to 1st-Class list: 2001
Highlights of umpiring career: 'First Championship match – Yorkshire v Somerset at Headingley 2001'
Cricket moments to forget: 'Any error of judgement!'
Players to watch for the future: James Anderson, Ian Bell
County as player: Did not play first-class cricket. Played league cricket in South Wales as a right-hand bat
Extras: Coach to Welsh Schools Cricket Association team on tour to Australia 1993. Taught in the Gwendraeth Grammar School – 'the old "outside half factory"'
Opinions on cricket: 'Would like to see more honesty throughout the game!'

Did not play first-class cricket

GOULD, I. J.

Name: Ian James Gould
Born: 19 August 1957, Taplow, Bucks
Height: 5ft 7in
Nickname: Gunner
Wife and date of marriage: Joanne,
27 September 1986
Children: Gemma; Michael; George
Education: Westgate Secondary Modern,
Slough
Career outside cricket: 'Learning to be a
groundsman'
Other sports played: Golf
Other sports followed: Football (Arsenal),
racing
Relaxations: 'Spending many hours
listening to Richard Edmondson (Racing
Correspondent of *The Independent*) telling
me what might win tomorrow'

Appointed to 1st-Class list: 2002
Players to watch for the future: John Maunders
Counties as player: Middlesex, Sussex
Role: Left-hand bat, wicket-keeper
County debut: 1975 (Middlesex), 1981 (Sussex)
County cap: 1977 (Middlesex), 1981 (Sussex)
Benefit: 1990 (Sussex; £87,097)
One-Day Internationals: 18
1st-Class 50s: 47
1st-Class 100s: 4
1st-Class catches: 536
1st-Class stumpings: 67
Overseas tours: England YC to West Indies 1976; D.H. Robins' XI to Canada
1978-79; International XI to Pakistan 1980-81; England to Australia and New Zealand
1982-83; MCC to Namibia
Overseas teams played for: Auckland 1979-80
Highlights of playing career: 'Playing in the World Cup'
Extras: Represented England in the 1983 World Cup. Retired from county cricket in
1991
Opinions on cricket: 'Cricket seems to be going the right way. People seem more
positive about the game and I feel that they are enjoying playing.'
Best batting: 128 Middlesex v Worcestershire, Worcester 1978
Best bowling: 3-10 Sussex v Surrey, The Oval 1989

First-Class Career Performances

	M	Inns	NO	Runs	HS	Avge	100s	Ct	St	Runs	Wkts	Avge	Best	5wl	10wM
Test															
All First	297	399	63	8756	128	26.06	4	536	67	365	7	52.14	3-10	-	-

HAMPSHIRE, J. H.

Name: <u>John</u> Harry Hampshire
Born: 10 February 1941, Thurnscoe, Yorks
Height: 6ft
Nickname: Hamps
Marital status: Widowed
Wife and date of marriage: Judith Ann,
5 September 1964 (deceased 20 April 2002)
Children: Ian Christopher, 6 January 1969;
Paul Wesley, 12 February 1972
Family links with cricket: Father (J.) and
brother (A.W.) both played for Yorkshire
Education: Oakwood Technical High School,
Rotherham; Sheffield College of Art
Other sports followed: Most sports
Relaxations: Golf, gardening, cooking
Appointed to 1st-Class list: 1985
First appointed to Test panel: 1989
International panel: 1999-2002
Tests umpired: 21 (plus 4 as TV umpire)
One-Day Internationals umpired: 20 (plus 8 as TV umpire)
Other umpiring honours: Umpired four Tests in Pakistan 1989-90. Toured
Bangladesh 1999-2000 with MCC (as umpire). Stood in Coca-Cola Cup, Sharjah
2000. Umpired NatWest final 2000, B&H final 2001, 2002, and C&G final 2003
Counties as player: Yorkshire, Derbyshire
Role: Right-hand bat, leg-spin bowler
County debut: 1961 (Yorkshire), 1982 (Derbyshire)
County cap: 1963 (Yorkshire), 1982 (Derbyshire)
Benefit: 1976 (Yorkshire)
Test debut: 1969
Tests: 8
One-Day Internationals: 3
1000 runs in a season: 15
1st-Class 50s: 142
1st-Class 100s: 43
1st-Class 5 w. in innings: 2

1st-Class catches: 445
One-Day 100s: 7
Overseas tours: MCC (England) to Australia and New Zealand 1970-71
Overseas teams played for: Tasmania 1966-69, 1977-79
Extras: Captained Yorkshire 1979-80. Scored a century (107) at Lord's on Test debut (v West Indies 1969); the only England player to have done so. Retired from county cricket in 1984. Manager/coach of the Zimbabwe squad for their first Test matches against India and New Zealand 1992-93
Best batting: 183* Yorkshire v Surrey, Hove 1971
Best bowling: 7-52 Yorkshire v Glamorgan, Cardiff 1963

First-Class Career Performances

	M	Inns	NO	Runs	HS	Avge	100s	Ct	St	Runs	Wkts	Avge	Best	5wl	10wM
Test	8	16	1	405	107	26.86	1	9	-						
All First	577	924	112	28059	183*	34.55	43	445	-	1637	30	54.56	7-52	2	-

HARRIS, M. J.

Name: <u>Michael</u> John Harris
Born: 25 May 1944, St Just-in-Roseland, Cornwall
Height: 6ft 1in
Nickname: Pasty
Wife and date of marriage: Danielle Ruth, 10 September 1969
Children: Jodie, Richard
Education: Gerrans Comprehensive
Career outside cricket: Sports teacher
Other sports followed: Squash, golf
Appointed to 1st-Class list: 1998
Counties as player: Middlesex, Nottinghamshire
Role: Right-hand bat, leg-break bowler, wicket-keeper
County debut: 1964 (Middlesex), 1969 (Nottinghamshire)

County cap: 1967 (Middlesex), 1970 (Nottinghamshire)
1000 runs in a season: 11
1st-Class 50s: 98
1st-Class 100s: 40
1st-Class 200s: 1
1st-Class catches: 288
1st-Class stumpings: 14

One-Day 100s: 3
Overseas teams played for: Eastern Province 1971-72; Wellington 1975-76
Extras: Shared Middlesex then record first-wicket partnership of 312 with Eric Russell v Pakistanis at Lord's 1967. Scored nine centuries in 1971 to equal Nottinghamshire county record for a season, scoring two centuries in a match twice and totalling 2238 runs at an average of 50.86
Best batting: 201* Nottinghamshire v Glamorgan, Trent Bridge 1973
Best bowling: 4-16 Nottinghamshire v Warwickshire, Trent Bridge 1969

First-Class Career Performances

	M	Inns	NO	Runs	HS	Avge	100s	Ct	St	Runs	Wkts	Avge	Best	5wI	10wM
Test															
All First	344	581	58	19196	201*	36.70	41	288	14	3459	79	43.78	4-16	-	-

HARTLEY, P. J.

Name: <u>Peter</u> John Hartley
Born: 18 April 1960, Keighley, Yorkshire
Height: 6ft
Nickname: Jack
Wife and date of marriage: Sharon, 12 March 1988
Children: Megan, 25 April 1992; Courtney, 25 July 1995
Family links with cricket: Father played local league cricket
Education: Greenhead Grammar School, Keighley; Bradford College
Career outside cricket: Sports footwear agent
Off-season: Development and sales of footwear within cricket
Other sports played: Golf
Other sports followed: Football (Chelsea)
Relaxations: 'Gardening, walking the hound'
Appointed to 1st-Class list: 2003
Counties as player: Warwickshire, Yorkshire, Hampshire
Role: Right-hand bat, right-arm fast-medium bowler
County debut: 1982 (Warwickshire), 1985 (Yorkshire), 1998 (Hampshire)
County cap: 1987 (Yorkshire), 1998 (Hampshire)
Benefit: 1996 (Yorkshire)
50 wickets in a season: 7
1st-Class 50s: 14

1st-Class 100s: 2
1st-Class 5 w. in innings: 23
1st-Class 10 w. in match: 3
1st-Class catches: 68
One-Day 5 w. in innings: 5
Overseas tours: Yorkshire pre-season tours to Barbados 1986-87, to South Africa 1991-92, 1992-93, to Zimbabwe
Overseas teams played for: Melville, New Zealand 1983-84; Adelaide, Australia 1985-86; Harmony and Orange Free State, South Africa 1988-89
Extras: Returned 8-65, his best figures for Hampshire, against Yorkshire, his former county, at Basingstoke 1999. Recorded his highest B&H score (32*) and best one-day analysis (5-20) v Sussex at Hove 2000. Retired at the end of the 2000 season
Best batting: 127* Yorkshire v Lancashire, Old Trafford 1988
Best bowling: 9-41 Yorkshire v Derbyshire, Chesterfield 1995

First-Class Career Performances

	M	Inns	NO	Runs	HS	Avge	100s	Ct	St	Runs	Wkts	Avge	Best	5wI	10wM
Test															
All First	232	283	66	4321	127*	19.91	2	68	-	20635	683	30.21	9-41	23	3

HOLDER, J. W.

Name: <u>John</u> Wakefield Holder
Born: 19 March 1945, Barbados
Height: 5ft 11in
Nickname: Benson
Wife's name: Glenda
Children: Christopher, 1968; Nigel, 1970
Education: Combermere High School, Barbados; Rochdale College
Off-season: 'Relaxing initially, then working part-time for the European Cricket Council'
Other sports followed: Football (Manchester United)
Relaxations: 'Regular visits to the gym trying to keep fit. Love watching wildlife programmes on TV and travel'
Appointed to 1st-Class list: 1983
First appointed to Test panel: 1988
Tests umpired: 11 (plus 5 as TV umpire)

One-Day Internationals umpired: 19 (plus 3 as TV umpire)
Other umpiring honours: Umpired in Nehru Cup in India and in Pakistan v India Test series 1989-90. Umpired in Pepsi Champions Trophy, Sharjah 1993-94 and

Masters Cup, Sharjah 1995-96. MCC tours to Kenya 1999, 2002 and to Greece 2003 (as umpire). Has stood in Refuge Assurance Cup, B&H Cup and NatWest Trophy finals and in C&G Trophy final 2002. Officiated at the inaugural Twenty20 finals day at Trent Bridge 2003, including standing in the final

Highlights of umpiring career: 'Umpiring Lord's Ashes Test in 2001, when I met the Queen'

County as player: Hampshire
Role: Right-hand bat, right-arm fast bowler
County debut: 1968
50 wickets in a season: 1
1st-Class 5 w. in innings: 5
1st-Class 10 w. in match: 1
1st-Class catches: 12
Highlights of playing career: 'Taking 6-7 against International Cavaliers in 1968'
Extras: Championship hat-trick v Kent at Southampton 1972. Retired from county cricket in 1972
Opinions on cricket: 'In view of the amount of fitness training today's players do, I am amazed that there are so many injuries.'
Best batting: 33 Hampshire v Sussex, Hove 1971
Best bowling: 7-79 Hampshire v Gloucestershire, Gloucester 1972

First-Class Career Performances

	M	Inns	NO	Runs	HS	Avge	100s	Ct	St	Runs	Wkts	Avge	Best	5wl	10wM
Test															
All First	47	49	14	374	33	10.68	-	12	-	3415	139	24.56	7-79	5	1

HOLDER, V. A.

Name: <u>Vanburn</u> Alonza Holder
Born: 8 October 1945, St Michael, Barbados
Height: 6ft 3in
Nickname: Van
Wife's name: Christine
Children: James Vanburn, 2 September 1981
Education: St Leonard's Secondary Modern; Community High
Other sports followed: Football (Liverpool)
Relaxations: Music, doing crosswords
Appointed to 1st-Class list: 1992
One-Day Internationals umpired: 2 as TV umpire
County as player: Worcestershire
Role: Right-hand bat, right-arm fast-medium bowler
County debut: 1968
County cap: 1970

Benefit: 1979
Test debut: 1969
Tests: 40
One-Day Internationals: 12
1st-Class 50s: 4
1st-Class 100s: 1
1st-Class 5 w. in innings: 38
1st-Class 10 w. in match: 3
1st-Class catches: 98
One-Day 5 w. in innings: 3
Overseas tours: West Indies to England
1969, 1973, 1975 (World Cup), 1976,
to India, Sri Lanka and Pakistan 1974-75,
to Australia 1975-76, to India and Sri Lanka
1978-79 (vice-captain); Rest of the World to
Pakistan 1973-74
Overseas teams played for: Barbados
1966-78
Extras: Made his debut for Barbados in the Shell Shield competition in 1966-67. Won
John Player League 1973 and County Championship 1974 with Worcestershire. Played
in West Indies 1975 World Cup winning side
Best batting: 122 Barbados v Trinidad, Bridgetown 1973-74
Best bowling: 7-40 Worcestershire v Glamorgan, Cardiff 1974

First-Class Career Performances

	M	Inns	NO	Runs	HS	Avge	100s	Ct	St	Runs	Wkts	Avge	Best	5wl	10wM
Test	40	59	11	682	42	14.20	-	16	-	3627	109	33.27	6-28	3	-
All First	311	354	81	3559	122	13.03	1	98	-	23183	948	24.45	7-40	38	3

JESTY, T. E.

Name: <u>Trevor</u> Edward Jesty
Born: 2 June 1948, Gosport, Hampshire
Height: 5ft 9in
Nickname: Jets
Wife and date of marriage: Jacqueline,
12 September 1970
Children: Graeme Barry, 27 September
1972; Lorna Samantha, 7 November 1976
Family links with cricket: Daughter played
for England XI 2000
Education: Privett County Secondary
Modern, Gosport
Off-season: Cricket coaching
Other sports followed: Football (Arsenal)
Relaxations: Gardening, reading
Appointed to 1st-Class list: 1994
One-Day Internationals umpired: 3 as
TV umpire

Counties as player: Hampshire, Surrey, Lancashire
Role: Right-hand bat, right-arm medium bowler
County debut: 1966 (Hampshire), 1985 (Surrey), 1988 (Lancashire)
County cap: 1971 (Hampshire), 1985 (Surrey), 1990 (Lancashire)
Benefit: 1982 (Hampshire)
One-Day Internationals: 10
1000 runs in a season: 10
50 wickets in a season: 2
1st-Class 50s: 110
1st-Class 100s: 33
1st-Class 200s: 2
1st-Class 5 w. in innings: 19
1st-Class catches: 265
1st-Class stumpings: 1
One-Day 100s: 7
Overseas tours: International XI to West Indies 1982; joined England tour to
Australia 1982-83; Lancashire to Zimbabwe 1989
Overseas teams played for: Border, South Africa 1973-74; Griqualand West 1974-76,
1980-81; Canterbury, New Zealand 1979-80
Highlights of playing career: 'Winning Championship with Hampshire in 1973.
Playing against Australia for England in one-day match on 1982-83 tour'
Extras: One of *Wisden*'s Five Cricketers of the Year 1983
Best batting: 248 Hampshire v Cambridge University, Fenner's 1984
Best bowling: 7-75 Hampshire v Worcestershire, Southampton 1976

	M	Inns	NO	Runs	HS	Avge	100s	Ct	St	Runs	Wkts	Avge	Best	5wI	10wM
Test															
All First	490	777	107	21916	248	32.71	35	265	1	16075	585	27.47	7-75	19	-

JONES, A. A.

Name: <u>Allan</u> Arthur Jones
Born: 9 December 1947, Horley, Surrey
Height: 6ft 4in
Nickname: Jonah
Marital status: Single
Education: St John's College, Horsham
Career outside cricket: Sports tours
Off-season: 'Enjoying life'
Other sports played: Golf
Other sports followed: Football (Arsenal)
Relaxations: English history, reading,
cooking
Appointed to 1st-Class list: 1985
First appointed to Test panel: 1996
Tests umpired: 3 as TV umpire
One-Day Internationals umpired: 1
(plus 4 as TV umpire)
Other umpiring honours: Has umpired at
Hong Kong Sixes. Chairman of the First-Class Umpires' Association
Players to watch for the future: Ed Joyce
Counties as player: Sussex, Somerset, Middlesex, Glamorgan
Role: Right-hand bat, right-arm fast bowler
County debut: 1964 (Sussex), 1970 (Somerset), 1976 (Middlesex), 1980 (Glamorgan)
County cap: 1972 (Somerset), 1976 (Middlesex)
50 wickets in a season: 4
1st-Class 5 w. in innings: 23
1st-Class 10 w. in match: 3
1st-Class catches: 50
One-Day 5 w. in innings: 5
Overseas teams played for: Northern Transvaal 1971-72; Orange Free State 1976-77;
Auckland (Birkenhead)
Highlights of playing career: '9-51 v Sussex 1972'
Extras: Won two Championship medals with Middlesex (1976 and 1977). Was on
stand-by for England tour of India 1976-77. Represented MCC v Australians 1977.
Was the first person to play for four counties

Best batting: 33 Middlesex v Kent, Canterbury 1978
Best bowling: 9-51 Somerset v Sussex, Hove 1972

First-Class Career Performances

	M	Inns	NO	Runs	HS	Avge	100s	Ct	St	Runs	Wkts	Avge	Best	5wl	10wM
Test															
All First	214	216	68	799	33	5-39	-	50	-	15414	549	28.07	9-51	23	3

KITCHEN, M. J.

Name: Mervyn (Merv) John Kitchen
Born: 1 August 1940, Nailsea, Somerset
Height: 5ft 11in
Nickname: MJ
Wife and date of marriage: Anne,
March 1972
Children: Faye, 30 September 1975;
Jody, 5 March 1977
Family links with cricket: Father played
local cricket for the village of Nailsea
Education: Backwell Secondary Modern,
Backwell
Career outside cricket: 'Many varied winter
jobs – driver, labourer, decorator, printing;
worked on the racetracks, horses and
greyhounds, for a bookmaker for ten years'
Other sports played: Golf, bowls, skittles
Other sports followed: 'Love TV football
now the coverage is so good; no allegiance to any teams'
Relaxations: 'Like crosswords but very rarely complete one; DIY'
Appointed to 1st-Class list: 1982
First appointed to Test panel: 1990
International panel: 1995-99
Tests umpired: 20 (plus 3 as TV umpire)
One-Day Internationals umpired: 28 (plus 8 as TV umpire)
Other umpiring honours: Stood in 1983 World Cup. Has umpired finals of the
domestic one-day competitions. Umpired in a one-day series in Kenya between the
hosts, Bangladesh and Zimbabwe, including the final, 1997-98
Highlights of umpiring career: 'My first Test match, England v New Zealand at
Lord's with D. Shepherd'
Players to watch for the future: James Troughton
County as player: Somerset
Role: Left-hand bat, occasional right-arm medium bowler

County debut: 1960
County cap: 1966
Testimonial: 1973
1000 runs in a season: 7
1st-Class 50s: 68
1st-Class 100s: 17
1st-Class catches: 157
One-Day 100s: 1
Overseas tours: Whitbread Wanderers to Rhodesia
Highlights of playing career: 'Many happy memories but perhaps playing with such talent as Viv Richards, Ian Botham and Joel Garner all in the same side ranks [at] the top of my list'
Cricket moments to forget: 'I once scored three ducks in three days – one on Saturday in the Championship, one on the Sunday in the John Player League and another, second, Championship innings on the Monday'
Extras: Won two Gillette Cup Man of the Match awards and two B&H Gold Awards. Retired in September 1979 and played local cricket for Mendip Acorns
Opinions on cricket: 'Microscopic examination of umpires and players by TV replays. Tremendous coverage of cricket all over the world by TV, which I think has increased the knowledge of the armchair watcher.'
Best batting: 189 Somerset v Pakistanis, Taunton 1967
Best bowling: 1-4 Somerset v Sussex, Taunton 1969

First-Class Career Performances

	M	Inns	NO	Runs	HS	Avge	100s	Ct	St	Runs	Wkts	Avge	Best	5wI	10wM
Test															
All First	354	612	32	15230	189	26.25	17	157	-	109	2	54.50	1-4	-	-

LEADBEATER, B.

Name: Barrie Leadbeater
Born: 14 August 1943, Leeds
Height: 6ft
Nickname: Leady
Marital status: Widowed
Wife and date of marriage: Jacqueline,
18 September 1971 (deceased 1997)
Children: Richard Barrie, 23 November
1972; Michael Spencer, 21 March 1976;
Daniel Mark Ronnie, 19 June 1981
Education: Harehills County Secondary,
Leeds
Career outside cricket: LGV Class 1 driver
Other sports played: Golf, snooker,
table tennis

Other sports followed: All sport – football
(Leeds United), rugby league (Leeds Rhinos)
Relaxations: 'Reading, going to the pub,
running'
Appointed to 1st-Class list: 1981
Tests umpired: 2 as TV umpire
One-Day Internationals umpired: 5 (plus 2 as TV umpire)
Other umpiring honours: Stood in 1983 World Cup. MCC tours to New Zealand
1999 and to Argentina and Chile 2001. Former chairman of the First-Class Umpires'
Association
County as player: Yorkshire
Role: Right-hand opening bat, right-arm medium bowler, slip fielder
County debut: 1966
County cap: 1969
Benefit: 1980 (joint benefit with G.A. Cope)
1st-Class 50s: 27
1st-Class 100s: 1
1st-Class catches: 82
Overseas tours: Duke of Norfolk's XI to West Indies 1970
Overseas teams played for: Johannesburg Municipals 1978-79
Highlights of playing career: 'Man of the Match in Gillette Cup final 1969'
Cricket moments to forget: 'I've forgotten'
Extras: Took part in London Marathon 1997, 1998, 2000. Retired from county cricket
in 1979 and played social cricket
Best batting: 140* Yorkshire v Hampshire, Portsmouth 1976
Best bowling: 1-1 Yorkshire v Middlesex, Headingley 1971

First-Class Career Performances

	M	Inns	NO	Runs	HS	Avge	100s	Ct	St	Runs	Wkts	Avge	Best	5wI	10wM
Test															
All First	147	241	29	5373	140*	25.34	1	82	-	5	1	5.00	1-1	-	-

LLONG, N. J.

Name: <u>Nigel</u> James Llong
Born: 11 February 1969, Ashford, Kent
Height: 6ft
Nickname: Nidge
Wife and date of marriage: Melissa,
20 February 1999
Children: Andrew Stuart, 30 August 2002
Family links with cricket: Father and
brother played local club cricket
Education: North School for Boys, Ashford
Off-season: Coaching – Kent Cricket Board;
Duke of York School, Dover
Other sports followed: Football (Arsenal),
'generally most sports'
Relaxations: Fishing, clay-pigeon shooting
Appointed to 1st-Class list: 2002
Players to watch for the future:
Ben Phillips

County as player: Kent
Role: Left-hand bat, right-arm off-spin bowler
County debut: 1991
County cap: 1993
1st-Class 50s: 16
1st-Class 100s: 6
1st-Class 5 w. in innings: 2
1st-Class catches: 59
One-Day 100s: 2
Overseas tours: Kent to Zimbabwe 1993
Overseas teams played for: Ashburton, Melbourne 1988-90, 1996-97; Greenpoint,
Cape Town, 1990-95
Highlights of playing career: 'B&H final 1997. Sunday League winners 1995. First
Championship hundred, Lord's 1993'
Cricket moments to forget: 'Sunday League [1993], last match against Glamorgan
at Canterbury – lost the match and were runners-up. Plus not making the most of
my ability'

Extras: Kent Young Player of the Year 1992. Man of the Match in 2nd XI Trophy semi-final and final 1999. Retired from county cricket in September 1999 and played for Norfolk in 2000

Opinions on cricket: 'Good pitches produce good players. With central contracts, we now need two overseas players per club (especially bowlers).'

Best batting: 130 Kent v Hampshire, Canterbury 1996

Best bowling: 5-21 Kent v Middlesex, Canterbury 1996

First-Class Career Performances

	M	Inns	NO	Runs	HS	Avge	100s	Ct	St	Runs	Wkts	Avge	Best	5wl	10wM
Test															
All First	68	108	11	3024	130	31.17	6	59	-	1259	35	35.97	5-21	2	-

LLOYDS, J. W.

Name: <u>Jeremy</u> William Lloyds

Born: 17 November 1954, Penang, Malaya

Height: 5ft 11in

Nickname: Jerry

Wife and date of marriage: Janine, 16 September 1997

Children: Kaeli, 16 November 1991

Family links with cricket: Father played cricket in Malaya. Brother Chris played for Somerset 2nd XI

Education: Blundell's School, Tiverton

Career outside cricket: Coaching and setting up Western Province Youth Programme 1992-95 in South Africa. Works for National Car Rental

Off-season: Umpiring in U19 World Cup, Bangladesh

Other sports played: Golf (6 handicap)

Other sports followed: Golf, football (Tottenham Hotspur), American football (San Francisco 49ers), Formula One and saloon car racing, rugby (Gloucester)

Relaxations: 'Reading, music and spending time at home with my family'

Appointed to 1st-Class list: 1998

International panel: 2004 – (from 2002 as TV umpire)

Tests umpired: 6 as TV umpire

One-Day Internationals umpired: 2 (plus 12 as TV umpire)

Counties as player: Somerset, Gloucestershire

Role: Left-hand bat, off-spin bowler

County debut: 1979 (Somerset), 1985 (Gloucestershire)

County cap: 1982 (Somerset), 1985 (Gloucestershire)
1000 runs in a season: 3
1st-Class 50s: 62
1st-Class 100s: 10
1st-Class 5 w. in innings: 13
1st-Class 10 w. in match: 1
1st-Class catches: 229
Overseas tours: Somerset to Antigua 1982; Gloucestershire to Barbados 1985, to Sri Lanka 1987
Overseas teams played for: St Stithian's Old Boys, Johannesburg 1978-79; Toombull DCC, Brisbane 1980-82; North Sydney District 1982-83; Alberton, Johannesburg 1984; Preston CC, Melbourne 1986; Orange Free State 1987; Fish Hoek CC, Cape Town 1988-92
Highlights of playing career: 'Winning 1983 NatWest final'
Extras: Highest score in Brisbane Premier League 1980-81 (165). Britannic Player of the Month July 1987. Gloucestershire Player of the Year 1987. Leading run-scorer in Western Province Cricket League 1988, 1989
Opinions on cricket: 'Too much overseas influence on how to play the game in England. We have more variations in wickets and weather conditions than in most other countries. Yes, take the best of what they have and work it into our game. Also, too much emphasis on all the various levels of coaching certificates. We have been dragged too far away from the *basics* – batting, bowling and fielding. The game hasn't really changed – people's perception of it has! We show people how to play but not the thinking side of it. At times, some players are too robotic. Whatever happened to natural flair?'
Best batting: 132* Somerset v Northamptonshire, Northampton 1982
Best bowling: 7-88 Somerset v Essex, Chelmsford 1982

First-Class Career Performances

	M	Inns	NO	Runs	HS	Avge	100s	Ct	St	Runs	Wkts	Avge	Best	5wI	10wM
Test															
All First	267	408	64	10679	132*	31.04	10	229	-	12943	333	38.86	7-88	13	1

MALLENDER, N. A.

Name: <u>Neil</u> Alan Mallender
Born: 13 August 1961, Kirk Sandall, Doncaster
Height: 6ft
Nickname: Ghostie
Marital status: Divorced
Children: Kirstie, 15; Dominic, 12; Jacob, 7
Education: Beverley Grammar School
Off-season: 'ICC appointments [including] Pakistan v South Africa, first Test at Lahore, October 2003 (*his debut Test match as an umpire*)'
Other sports played: Golf (3 handicap)
Other sports followed: 'Most sports'
Relaxations: 'Most sports; music'
Appointed to 1st-Class list: 1999
International panel: 2002-2004
Tests umpired: 1 (plus 5 as TV umpire)

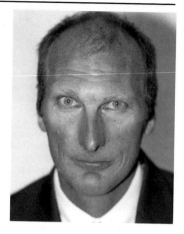

One-Day Internationals umpired: 22 (plus 9 as TV umpire)
Other umpiring honours: Went with MCC to umpire in Namibia March/April 2001. PCA Umpire of the Year 2001, 2002, 2003. Stood in the 2002-03 World Cup
Highlights of umpiring career: 'First ODI at Lord's, England v Pakistan – and game went to the last ball'
Players to watch for the future: Michael Lumb, James Troughton, Ian Hunter
Counties as player: Northamptonshire, Somerset
Role: Right-hand bat, right-arm fast-medium bowler
County debut: 1980 (Northamptonshire), 1987 (Somerset)
County cap: 1984 (Northamptonshire), 1987 (Somerset)
Benefit: 1994 (Somerset)
Test debut: 1992
Tests: 2
50 wickets in a season: 6
1st-Class 50s: 10
1st-Class 100s: 1
1st-Class 5 w. in innings: 36
1st-Class 10 w. in match: 5
1st-Class catches: 111
One-Day 5 w. in innings: 3
Overseas tours: England YC to West Indies 1979-80
Overseas teams played for: Kaikorai, Dunedin, New Zealand; University, Wellington, New Zealand; Otago, New Zealand 1983-84 – 1992-93

Highlights of playing career: 'Test debut at Headingley'
Extras: Represented England YC 1980-81. Took 5-50 on Test debut v Pakistan at Headingley in 1992. Retired from county cricket in 1996
Best batting: 100* Otago v Central Districts, Palmerston North 1991-92
Best bowling: 7-27 Otago v Auckland, Auckland 1984-85

First-Class Career Performances

	M	Inns	NO	Runs	HS	Avge	100s	Ct	St	Runs	Wkts	Avge	Best	5wI	10wM
Test	2	3	0	8	4	2.66	-	-	-	215	10	21.50	5-50	1	-
All First	345	396	122	4709	100*	17.18	1	111	-	24654	937	26.31	7-27	36	5

PALMER, R.

Name: Roy Palmer
Born: 12 July 1942, Hampshire
Height: 6ft 3in
Nickname: Arp
Wife and date of marriage: Alyne, 5 November 1983
Children: Nick, 7 October 1968
Family links with cricket: Brother of Ken Palmer, former Test umpire and Somerset player; nephew Gary also played for Somerset
Education: Southbroom Secondary Modern, Devizes
Off-season: Golf, DIY
Relaxations: Golf
Appointed to 1st-Class list: 1980
First appointed to Test panel: 1992
Tests umpired: 2 (plus 1 as TV umpire)
One-Day Internationals umpired: 8 (plus 2 as TV umpire)
Other umpiring honours: Stood in 1983 World Cup
Players to watch for the future: Ian Bell
County as player: Somerset
Role: Right-hand bat, right-arm fast-medium bowler
County debut: 1965
50 wickets in a season: 1
1st-Class 50s: 1
1st-Class 5 w. in innings: 4
1st-Class catches: 25
One-Day 5 w. in innings: 1
Extras: Won two Man of the Match Awards in the Gillette Cup

Best batting: 84 Somerset v Leicestershire, Taunton 1967
Best bowling: 6-45 Somerset v Middlesex, Lord's 1967

First-Class Career Performances

	M	Inns	NO	Runs	HS	Avge	100s	Ct	St	Runs	Wkts	Avge	Best	5wI	10wM
Test															
All First	74	110	32	1037	84	13.29	-	25	-	5439	172	31.62	6-45	4	-

SHARP, G.

Name: George Sharp
Born: 12 March 1950, West Hartlepool,
County Durham
Height: 5ft 11in
Nickname: Sharpy, Blunt, Razor, Toffee
Wife and date of marriage: Audrey,
14 September 1974
Children: Gareth James, 27 June 1984
Education: Elwick Road Secondary Modern,
Hartlepool
Career outside cricket: Watching all sports
Off-season: Working as joint director of GSB
Loams Ltd for soils and top dressing
Other sports played: Golf (8 handicap)
Other sports followed: Football (Newcastle
Utd and Middlesbrough), rugby
(Northampton Saints)
Relaxations: Golf; 'spend a lot of time in the
gym during the off-season'
Appointed to 1st-Class list: 1992
International panel: 1996-2002
Tests umpired: 15 (plus 1 as TV umpire)
One-Day Internationals umpired: 31 (plus 13 as TV umpire)
Other umpiring honours: Has umpired three B&H finals and one NatWest final and
stood in the inaugural C&G final 2001 and the 2002 final; also officiated at the
inaugural Twenty20 finals day at Trent Bridge 2003. Has stood in four overseas
tournaments, including the Singer Cup (India, Sri Lanka, Pakistan) in Singapore
1995-96 and the Singer Champions Trophy (Pakistan, Sri Lanka, New Zealand) in
Sharjah 1996-97
County as player: Northamptonshire
Role: Right-hand bat, wicket-keeper
County debut: 1967
County cap: 1973

Benefit: 1982
1st-Class 50s: 21
1st-Class catches: 565
1st-Class stumpings: 90
Overseas tours: England Counties XI to Barbados and Trinidad 1975
Best batting: 98 Northamptonshire v Yorkshire, Northampton 1983
Best bowling: 1-47 Northamptonshire v Yorkshire, Northampton 1980

First-Class Career Performances

	M	Inns	NO	Runs	HS	Avge	100s	Ct	St	Runs	Wkts	Avge	Best	5wI	10wM
Test															
All First	306	396	81	6254	98	19.85	-	565	90	70	1	70.00	1-47	-	-

SHEPHERD, D. R.

Name: <u>David</u> Robert Shepherd
Born: 27 December 1940, Bideford, Devon
Height: 5ft 10in
Nickname: Shep
Marital status: Single
Family links with cricket: Father: club
cricketer and local umpire. Brother Bill:
MCC Young Professional, Devon CCC and
North Devon CC; local umpire
Education: Barnstaple Grammar School;
St Luke's College, Exeter
Career outside cricket: Schoolteacher
Off-season: 'With international umpiring
now, there is no close season'
Other sports played: 'Used to play rugby
(school, Devon Public & Grammar Schools
XV, South Molton RFC)'
Other sports followed: 'All sports'
Relaxations: Stamp collecting
Appointed to 1st-Class list: 1981
First appointed to Test panel: 1985
International panel: 1994-2002
Elite panel: 2002 –
Tests umpired: 78
One-Day Internationals umpired: 145 (plus 13 as TV umpire)
Other umpiring honours: Has stood in each World Cup since 1983, including the
1995-96 final at Lahore, the 1999 final at Lord's and the 2002-03 final between
Australia and India at Johannesburg. Umpired the MCC Bicentenary Test, England

v Rest of the World, at Lord's in 1987. Has umpired numerous domestic finals. Received National Grid/ICC 'bronze award' in March 1998 for long service as a Test umpire. Umpired 50th Test, India v South Africa, Mumbai (Bombay) February 2000, receiving ICC 'silver award' to acknowledge this achievement. Known for his superstition regarding 'Nelson' score 111, and multiples – 222, 333 etc.

Highlights of umpiring career: 'Standing in first Test match. Three World Cup finals.'

County as player: Gloucestershire

Role: Right-hand bat, right-arm ('occasional!') medium bowler

County debut: 1965

County cap: 1969

Benefit: 1978 (joint benefit with J. Davey)

1000 runs in a season: 2

1st-Class 50s: 55

1st-Class 100s: 12

1st-Class catches: 95

One-Day 100s: 2

Highlights of playing career: 'Winning two domestic finals with Gloucestershire at Lord's – the Gillette Cup in 1973 and the B&H Cup in 1977'

Extras: Played Minor Counties cricket for Devon 1959-64. First player to score a century for Gloucestershire on his first-class debut, v Oxford University 1965. Retired from county cricket in 1979 and played a little cricket for his original club, North Devon CC. Was awarded the MBE in 1997 for services to cricket. Wrote autobiography (*Shep*) 2001

Opinions on cricket: 'Players at the highest level must realise that they have a tremendous responsibility to the game as a whole. Their behaviour on the field is of the utmost importance, as they set an example to the rest of the sport. We must get some trust back in the game between players and officials and administrators, as well as between players themselves. How I hate the cheats!! Any batsman who stands at the crease knowing he is out is in my book a cheat! Any player who appeals knowing the batsman is not out is also a cheat!'

Best batting: 153 Gloucestershire v Middlesex, Bristol 1968

Best bowling: 1-1 Gloucestershire v Northamptonshire, Gloucester 1968

First-Class Career Performances

	M	Inns	NO	Runs	HS	Avge	100s	Ct	St	Runs	Wkts	Avge	Best	5wI	10wM
Test															
All First	282	476	40	10672	153	24.47	12	95	-	106	2	53.00	1-1	-	-

STEELE, J. F.

Name: <u>John</u> Frederick Steele
Born: 23 July 1946, Stafford
Height: 5ft 10in
Nickname: Steely
Wife and date of marriage: Susan,
17 April 1977
Children: Sarah Jane, 2 April 1982;
Robert Alfred, 10 April 1985
Family links with cricket: Uncle Stan
played for Staffordshire. Brother David
played for Northamptonshire, Derbyshire and
England. Cousin Brian Crump played for
Northamptonshire and Staffordshire
Education: Endon School, Stoke-on-Trent;
Stafford College
Other sports followed: Soccer (Stoke City,
Port Vale), golf
Relaxations: Music and walking
Appointed to 1st-Class list: 1997
Counties as player: Leicestershire, Glamorgan
Role: Right-hand bat, slow left-arm bowler
County debut: 1970 (Leicestershire), 1984 (Glamorgan)
County cap: 1971 (Leicestershire), 1984 (Glamorgan)
Benefit: 1983 (Leicestershire)
1000 runs in a season: 6
1st-Class 50s: 69
1st-Class 100s: 21
1st-Class 5 w. in innings: 16
1st-Class catches: 414
One-Day 100s: 1
One-Day 5 w. in innings: 4
Overseas teams played for: Springs HSOB, Northern Transvaal 1971-73;
Pine Town CC, Natal 1973-74, 1982-83; Natal 1975-76, 1978-79
Extras: Played for England U25. Was voted Natal's Best Bowler in 1975-76. First-wicket record partnership for Leicestershire of 390 with Barry Dudleston v Derbyshire at Leicester 1979. Won two Man of the Match Awards in the Gillette Cup and four in the Benson and Hedges Cup. Won the award for the most catches in a season in 1984
Best batting: 195 Leicestershire v Derbyshire, Leicester 1971
Best bowling: 7-29 Natal B v Griqualand West, Umzinto 1973-74
7-29 Leicestershire v Gloucestershire, Leicester 1980

	M	Inns	NO	Runs	HS	Avge	100s	Ct	St	Runs	Wkts	Avge	Best	5wI	10wM
Test															
All First	379	605	85	15053	195	28.94	21	414	-	15793	584	27.04	7-29	16	-

WHITEHEAD, A. G. T.

Name: <u>Alan</u> Geoffrey Thomas Whitehead
Born: 28 October 1940, Butleigh, Somerset
Appointed to 1st-Class list: 1970
First appointed to Test panel: 1982
Tests umpired: 5 (plus 5 as TV umpire)
One-Day Internationals umpired: 14
(plus 2 as TV umpire)
Other umpiring honours: Stood in the 1979
and 1983 World Cups
County as player: Somerset
Role: Left-hand bat, slow left-arm bowler
County debut: 1957
1st-Class 5 w. in innings: 3
1st-Class catches: 20
Best batting: 15 Somerset v Hampshire,
Southampton 1959
Best bowling: 6-74 Somerset v Sussex,
Eastbourne 1959

First-Class Career Performances

	M	Inns	NO	Runs	HS	Avge	100s	Ct	St	Runs	Wkts	Avge	Best	5wI	10wM
Test															
All First	38	49	25	137	15	5.70	-	20	-	2306	67	34.41	6-74	3	

WILLEY, P.

Name: Peter Willey
Born: 6 December 1949, Sedgefield,
County Durham
Height: 6ft 1in
Nickname: Will, 'many unprintable'
Wife and date of marriage: Charmaine,
23 September 1971
Children: Heather Jane, 11 September 1985;
David, 28 February 1990
Family links with cricket: Father played
local club cricket in County Durham
Education: Seaham Secondary School,
County Durham
Off-season: 'Fishing and helping in the
home. Watching son play sport'
Other sports followed: All sports
Relaxations: 'Dog-walking, keeping fit (??),
fishing'
Appointed to 1st-Class list: 1993
International panel: 1996 – 2004
Tests umpired: 25 (plus 7 as TV umpire)
One-Day Internationals umpired: 34 (plus 16 as TV umpire)
Other umpiring honours: Stood in the 1999 and 2002-03 World Cups and in the
1999 Benson and Hedges Super Cup final
Counties as player: Northamptonshire, Leicestershire
Role: Right-hand bat, off-break bowler
County debut: 1966 (Northamptonshire), 1984 (Leicestershire)
County cap: 1971 (Northamptonshire), 1984 (Leicestershire)
Benefit: 1981 (Northamptonshire; £31,400)
Test debut: 1976
Tests: 26
One-Day Internationals: 26
1000 runs in a season: 10
50 wickets in a season: 2
1st-Class 50s: 101
1st-Class 100s: 43
1st-Class 200s: 1
1st-Class 5 w. in innings: 26
1st-Class 10 w. in match: 3
1st-Class catches: 235
One-Day 100s: 9

Overseas tours: England to Australia and India 1979-80, to West Indies 1980-81, 1985-86; unofficial England XI to South Africa 1981-82
Overseas teams played for: Eastern Province, South Africa 1982-85
Extras: Became youngest player ever to play for Northamptonshire, at 16 years 180 days, v Cambridge University in 1966. Leicestershire captain 1987. Played for Northumberland in 1992. Offered membership of the ICC Elite Panel of umpires in 2002 but declined because of the amount of time the appointment would require away from his family
Opinions on cricket: 'Game is being made too complicated from U9 to first-class at county level. Kids can't enjoy the game. They have too many different coaches giving different opinions so they get confused. Some of the coaches may have passed all the exams, but they frighten me to death with the things they come out with. Keep it simple. Concentrate more on cricket and less on fitness. [Have] no technique and it doesn't matter how fit you are.'
Best batting: 227 Northamptonshire v Somerset, Northampton 1976
Best bowling: 7-37 Northamptonshire v Oxford University, The Parks 1975

First-Class Career Performances

	M	Inns	NO	Runs	HS	Avge	100s	Ct	St	Runs	Wkts	Avge	Best	5wI	10wM
Test	26	50	6	1184	102*	26.90	2	3	-	456	7	65.14	2-73	-	-
All First	559	918	121	24361	227	30.56	44	235	-	23400	756	30.95	7-37	26	3

THE PRIMARY CLUB

PO Box 12121, Saffron Walden,
Essex, CB10 2ZF
Telephone: 01799 586507
e-mail: primaryclub @aol.com
website: www.primaryclub.org

erek Underwood, the patron of the Primary Club, qualified for
embership in some style in 1965. Playing for Kent against the
uth Africans he was out first ball twice in the same match.

However, members do not have to be playing Test or county
icket when the ultimate disaster strikes in order to qualify for
e club. As long as you are out first ball at ANY level of cricket
u are eligible to join The Primary Club.

Why join? The Primary Club is a charity (Registered Charity
o. 285285) and all profits from subscriptions, donations and the
nge of items for sale (ties, sweaters, shirts, mugs, umbrellas,
c.) go to pay for sporting and recreational facilities for the
ind and partially sighted. All the club's workers are
olunteers.

For many of us sport is an important part of our every day
ves; for the blind and partially sighted, sport can mean so
uch more. The confidence and sense of achievement they get
om mastering a physical skill helps them a great deal in
ckling the problems of their lives.

MEMBERSHIP APPLICATION

ame _____

ddress _____

_____

_____

ining subscription:

To include City tie – £20	
To include Club tie – £20	
To include City & Club tie – £30	
To include 100% silk tie (City) – £30	
To include 100% silk tie (Country) – £30	
To include Bow tie – £20	
ady, to include brooch – £15	
ONATION	
MITTANCE TO 'THE PRIMARY CLUB' £	

gistered Charity No. 285285

The value of your remittance to The Primary
Club can be increased by 28p for every £1
you give under Gift Aid tax reclaim
arrangements, *at no extra cost to you.*
To enable the Club to benefit from this
scheme, please sign and date the declaration
below, provided that you pay income tax, or
capital gains tax, of an amount equal to the
tax to be reclaimed.

**I wish The Primary Club to reclaim tax on all
donations I make on or after the date of this
declaration.**

Signed   **Date**

It would be of great benefit to the Club if you
pay future donations by banker's standing
order. Please tick the box and
a form will be sent to you.

ROLL OF HONOUR 2003

FRIZZELL COUNTY CHAMPIONSHIP

Division One

		P	W	L	D	T	Bt	Bl	Pts
1	Sussex (I/6)	16	10	4	2	0	62	47	257
2	Lancashire (I/4)	16	6	2	8	0	64	43	223
3	Surrey (I/1)	16	6	3	7	0	63	44	219
4	Kent (I/3)	16	6	5	5	0	47	47	198
5	Warwickshire (I/2)	16	4	5	6	1	50	37	171.50
6	Middlesex (II/2)	16	3	3	10	0	46	41	169
7	Essex (II/1)	16	3	5	7	1	34	45	156
8	Nottinghamshire (II/3)	16	2	8	6	0	36	45	132
9	Leicestershire (I/5)	16	1	6	9	0	36	40	125.50

The bottom three counties were relegated to Division Two for the 2004 season

Division Two

		P	W	L	D	T	Bt	Bl	Pts
1	Worcestershire (II/4)	16	10	1	5	0	42	44	245.75
2	Northamptonshire (II/7)	16	10	2	4	0	45	44	237
3	Gloucestershire (II/8)	16	5	2	9	0	38	46	190
4	Yorkshire (I/9)	16	4	5	7	0	54	47	183.50
5	Glamorgan (II/5)	16	5	5	6	0	45	45	183
6	Durham (II/9)	16	5	7	4	0	31	43	159.25
7	Somerset (I/8)	16	4	8	4	0	41	44	157
8	Hampshire (I/7)	16	2	6	8	0	36	44	140
9	Derbyshire (II/6)	16	2	11	3	0	30	44	114

The top three counties were promoted to Division One for the 2004 season

Teams are docked 0.25 points for each over they fail to bowl of the target figure of 16 per hour. Northamptonshire were deducted eight points for a poor pitch.

NATIONAL CRICKET LEAGUE

Division One

		P	W	L	T	NR	Pts
1	Surrey (II/2)	16	12	3	0	1	50
2	Gloucestershire (II/1)	16	11	4	0	1	46
3	Essex (II/3)	16	8	7	1	0	34
4	Warwickshire (I/3)	16	8	8	0	0	32
5	Glamorgan (I/1)	16	8	8	0	0	32
6	Kent (I/5)	16	7	8	1	0	30
7	Leicestershire (I/6)	16	7	9	0	0	28
8	Yorkshire (I/4)	16	5	11	0	0	20
9	Worcestershire (I/2)	16	4	12	0	0	16

The bottom three counties were relegated to Division Two for the 2004 season

Division Two

		P	W	L	T	NR	Pts
1	Lancashire (II/5)	18	14	3	0	1	58
2	Northamptonshire (II/6)	18	12	5	0	1	50
3	Hampshire (II/7)	18	11	7	0	0	44
4	Middlesex (II/9)	18	10	7	0	1	42
5	Nottinghamshire (I/9)	18	9	9	0	0	36
6	Derbyshire (II/4)	18	8	8	0	2	36
7	Durham (I/8)	18	7	10	0	1	30
8	Sussex (II/8)	18	6	12	0	0	24
9	Somerset (I/7)	18	5	12	0	1	22
10	Scotland (N/A)	18	4	13	0	1	18

The top three counties were promoted to Division One for the 2004 season

CHELTENHAM & GLOUCESTER TROPHY

Winners: Gloucestershire   **Runners-up:** Worcestershire

TWENTY20 CUP

Winners: Surrey

Runners-up: Warwickshire   **Semi-finalists:** Gloucestershire, Leicestershire

2003 AVERAGES (all first-class matches)

BATTING AVERAGES – including fielding
Qualifying requirements: 6 completed innings

Name	Matches	Inns	NO	Runs	HS	Avge	100s	50s	Ct	St
S.G.Law	16	24	4	1820	236*	91.00	7	6	17	-
M.E.K.Hussey	14	21	2	1697	331*	89.31	6	5	17	-
G.C.Smith	8	13	1	980	277	81.66	3	2	6	-
M.R.Ramprakash	15	23	4	1444	279*	76.00	6	2	7	-
A.Flintoff	10	14	1	942	154	72.46	3	5	7	-
G.Kirsten	7	12	2	713	130	71.30	2	4	5	-
C.L.Hooper	14	20	2	1219	201	67.72	6	3	15	-
B.J.Hodge	16	26	2	1495	302*	62.29	5	3	12	-
G.L.Brophy	7	12	5	436	152*	62.28	2	1	14	-
M.A.Butcher	14	20	1	1162	144	61.15	4	5	17	-
S.M.Katich	13	22	3	1143	143*	60.15	4	6	15	-
M.L.Love	7	13	0	778	273	59.84	1	4	8	-
M.W.Goodwin	17	29	3	1545	335*	59.42	4	5	12	-
J.N.Rhodes	15	27	5	1293	151*	58.77	5	7	7	-
N.D.McKenzie	6	11	3	470	105*	58.75	1	3	2	-
P.A.Jaques	16	25	1	1409	222	58.70	5	6	9	-
W.Jaffer	6	9	0	522	218	58.00	1	3	2	-
J.N.Batty	12	22	5	968	168*	56.94	3	4	32	2
G.P.Thorpe	13	20	2	1019	156	56.61	2	7	9	-
M.J.Wood	17	33	6	1432	207	53.03	5	3	8	-
E.T.Smith	18	30	1	1534	213	52.89	7	3	15	-
J.H.Kallis	5	9	0	471	200	52.33	1	2	6	-
S.V.Carlisle	6	9	0	469	157	52.11	2	1	2	-
M.E.Trescothick	11	18	2	826	219	51.62	1	7	17	-
K.P.Pietersen	16	30	0	1546	221	51.53	4	11	17	-
A.J.Strauss	18	33	3	1529	155	50.96	4	8	6	-
M.B.Loye	15	22	1	1062	144	50.57	5	2	4	-
I.D.Blackwell	15	26	3	1160	247*	50.43	3	2	7	-
M.J.Chilton	17	25	2	1154	125	50.17	6	3	15	-
S.D.Stubbings	4	7	0	350	103	50.00	1	2	1	-
C.White	10	16	3	644	173*	49.53	2	3	4	-
M.J.DiVenuto	16	31	0	1520	150	49.03	5	8	25	-
M.J.Prior	16	24	3	1006	153*	47.90	4	3	28	-
A.Flower	17	29	3	1244	201*	47.84	2	7	17	-
V.Sehwag	6	10	0	478	137	47.80	2	1	4	-
B.F.Smith	18	29	2	1289	110	47.74	2	12	4	-
J.E.R.Gallian	13	24	3	1002	126*	47.71	4	5	16	-
S.G.Koenig	16	27	3	1140	166*	47.50	1	7	3	-
A.Symonds	10	16	2	659	121	47.07	2	4	6	-
D.R.Brown	16	26	4	1028	140*	46.72	3	7	10	-
M.P.Maynard	16	28	0	1297	142	46.32	5	4	11	-
N.Hussain	11	19	2	783	206	46.05	2	3	3	-
P.A.Cottey	15	25	0	1149	188	45.96	3	7	8	-
A.W.Laraman	13	18	5	597	148*	45.92	1	3	5	-

Name	Matches	Inns	NO	Runs	HS	Avge	100s	50s	Ct	St
R.J.Warren	9	18	2	734	123	45.87	3	2	9	2
J.R.C.Hamblin	5	8	2	273	96	45.50	-	2	1	-
M.A.Wagh	16	30	3	1228	138	45.48	3	7	15	-
I.J.Sutcliffe	12	17	2	681	109	45.40	1	4	13	-
J.Cox	15	27	3	1087	160	45.29	3	5	10	-
M.A.Vermeulen	6	11	1	451	198	45.10	1	3	4	-
N.Pothas	13	20	2	809	146*	44.94	2	4	38	2
I.J.Harvey	6	12	3	404	128*	44.88	1	1	4	-
D.J.G.Sales	16	23	2	942	200*	44.85	2	4	13	-
G.O.Jones	18	27	5	985	108*	44.77	2	7	54	5
G.W.Flower	6	10	1	399	130	44.33	1	2	7	-
N.V.Knight	14	26	3	1012	146	44.00	3	5	11	-
M.J.Walker	17	27	3	1051	150	43.79	3	4	22	-
J.L.Sadler	7	11	1	434	145	43.40	2	1	5	-
O.A.Shah	18	30	2	1206	147	43.07	3	6	11	-
S.S.Das	7	10	0	428	125	42.80	1	3	8	-
A.J.Stewart	13	18	1	727	98	42.76	-	7	36	1
A.G.R.Loudon	6	11	1	427	172	42.70	1	1	4	-
D.L.Maddy	17	29	3	1110	229*	42.69	1	6	15	-
M.J.Powell	17	30	1	1234	198	42.55	4	3	14	-
A.McGrath	14	23	3	850	127*	42.50	1	7	8	-
I.J.L.Trott	10	18	0	763	134	42.38	2	5	4	-
H.H.Gibbs	8	14	0	590	183	42.14	2	1	6	-
J.O.Troughton	12	20	2	748	129*	41.55	3	2	5	-
M.J.Lumb	17	27	2	1038	115*	41.52	2	7	7	-
S.D.Peters	18	30	1	1177	165	40.58	2	9	15	-
P.J.Franks	16	26	8	729	123*	40.50	2	1	9	-
T.R.Ambrose	15	26	3	931	93*	40.47	-	9	29	7
B.L.Hutton	18	30	6	961	107	40.04	4	1	17	-
M.P.Bicknell	14	15	4	440	141	40.00	2	-	4	-
N.J.Edwards	5	9	0	360	160	40.00	1	1	1	-
J.W.M.Dalrymple	7	11	2	357	236*	39.66	1	-	6	-
D.C.Nash	17	26	7	752	113	39.57	2	2	42	3
R.Clarke	11	16	2	551	139	39.35	2	1	10	-
E.C.Joyce	18	30	4	1023	117	39.34	3	4	7	-
L.D.Sutton	16	30	5	982	127	39.28	2	2	26	2
S.P.Fleming	7	14	2	469	98	39.08	-	3	13	-
M.Burns	18	32	3	1133	118*	39.06	2	8	15	-
J.K.Maunders	12	22	2	777	171	38.85	2	3	3	-
A.J.Hollioake	14	19	1	688	122	38.22	2	3	11	-
C.D.Nash	3	6	0	229	60	38.16	-	2	1	-
M.P.Vaughan	10	18	2	609	156	38.06	2	1	3	-
A.K.D.Gray	9	13	2	415	104	37.72	1	1	12	-
G.Chapple	16	21	3	679	132*	37.72	2	3	8	-
R.J.Turner	16	26	9	641	139*	37.70	1	3	65	5
R.W.T.Key	14	22	2	754	140	37.70	2	1	13	-
D.P.Fulton	11	19	1	674	94*	37.44	-	5	4	-
R.A.Smith	10	15	1	522	92	37.28	-	5	9	-
I.J.Ward	15	24	1	856	158	37.21	3	2	8	-
D.O.Brown	3	6	0	223	59	37.16	-	2	1	-
J.J.B.Lewis	18	34	2	1188	124	37.12	1	11	5	-

Name	Matches	Inns	NO	Runs	HS	Avge	100s	50s	Ct	St
Azhar Mahmood	11	14	2	445	98	37.08	-	4	17	-
R.S.C.Martin-Jenkins	16	25	3	811	121*	36.86	1	5	7	-
M.A.Ealham	17	25	0	911	101	36.44	1	7	18	-
R.C.Russell	11	16	4	436	78*	36.33	-	3	33	4
M.V.Boucher	8	11	1	360	89	36.00	-	3	21	1
M.A.Carberry	14	24	1	824	137	35.82	1	6	2	-
C.J.Adams	16	27	0	966	190	35.77	4	2	18	-
A.Habib	13	22	1	738	151	35.14	2	4	9	-
T.H.C.Hancock	12	21	0	720	97	34.28	-	5	13	-
M.J.Powell	12	22	0	754	110	34.27	1	6	4	-
P.D.Bowler	9	15	1	477	92	34.07	-	5	11	-
U.Afzaal	9	15	1	477	161*	34.07	1	2	3	-
W.I.Jefferson	14	27	4	781	125*	33.95	1	5	12	-
H.H.Dippenaar	7	11	1	339	92	33.90	-	3	4	-
J.P.Crawley	16	27	1	878	93	33.76	-	8	5	-
W.P.C.Weston	15	27	1	877	179	33.73	2	2	10	-
D.L.Hemp	12	21	3	607	85*	33.72	-	5	5	-
R.R.Montgomerie	17	29	2	908	105	33.62	1	7	24	-
G.A.Hick	13	23	3	670	155	33.50	1	3	19	-
Waqar Younis	8	13	5	268	61	33.50	-	2	1	-
C.M.Spearman	15	27	0	903	103	33.44	1	7	15	-
D.J.Bicknell	16	29	1	936	81	33.42	-	9	4	-
Z.K.Sharif	4	7	1	199	67	33.16	-	2	1	-
G.J.Pratt	18	33	1	1055	150	32.96	1	8	11	-
D.D.J.Robinson	11	20	2	592	89	32.88	-	4	7	-
A.F.Giles	12	18	1	556	96	32.70	-	4	2	-
I.D.K.Salisbury	14	18	4	455	101*	32.50	1	1	6	-
Saqlain Mushtaq	14	15	2	421	69	32.38	-	4	4	-
D.I.Stevens	11	19	0	615	149	32.36	1	6	12	-
A.J.Hall	11	16	2	445	104	31.78	1	3	11	-
T.Taibu	6	10	2	254	57	31.75	-	1	17	2
P.N.Weekes	18	29	5	760	102*	31.66	1	4	20	-
R.C.Irani	13	20	1	597	102*	31.42	1	4	4	-
G.S.Blewett	7	12	0	377	71	31.41	-	3	7	-
W.K.Hegg	16	20	7	404	61*	31.07	-	1	46	3
C.P.Schofield	9	12	2	310	66	31.00	-	2	9	-
C.M.W.Read	13	23	3	619	94*	30.95	-	4	32	3
C.L.Cairns	13	23	2	645	104	30.71	1	4	7	-
M.G.N.Windows	16	29	0	890	150	30.68	1	5	11	-
J.P.Maher	8	16	0	491	95	30.68	-	4	7	-
D.J.Pipe	5	9	3	184	104*	30.66	1	-	20	2
T.Webley	9	16	2	428	104	30.57	1	2	3	-
I.R.Bell	17	30	2	854	107	30.50	1	5	5	-
Kadeer Ali	8	14	0	426	99	30.42	-	3	2	-
W.S.Kendall	9	13	0	391	114	30.07	1	1	6	-
G.R.Napier	15	24	8	480	89*	30.00	-	2	3	-
V.Atri	5	10	2	240	82*	30.00	-	2	3	-
J.A.Rudolph	8	13	0	389	92	29.92	-	4	6	-
J.D.C.Bryant	14	24	2	658	109*	29.90	1	2	8	-
Abdul Razzaq	8	11	0	328	81	29.81	-	3	2	-
N.Peng	15	25	0	743	158	29.72	2	2	12	-

Name	Matches	Inns	NO	Runs	HS	Avge	100s	50s	Ct	St
R.D.B.Croft	17	29	4	739	122	29.56	1	4	9	-
T.R.Ward	9	15	0	443	168	29.53	1	1	7	-
M.A.Wallace	17	29	0	856	121	29.51	2	3	49	2
A.J.Tudor	6	7	1	177	55	29.50	-	1	-	-
P.A.Nixon	17	27	4	676	113*	29.39	1	3	50	2
R.K.J.Dawson	12	18	2	467	77	29.18	-	2	11	-
A.P.R.Gidman	8	16	2	407	68	29.07	-	2	7	-
J.N.Snape	16	23	6	494	54	29.05	-	2	8	-
M.M.Betts	10	14	2	348	73	29.00	-	2	2	-
A.Singh	16	27	1	754	105	29.00	1	4	6	-
P.D.Collingwood	4	7	1	169	68	28.16	-	2	4	-
D.A.Kenway	16	28	1	760	115	28.14	2	3	14	-
V.J.Craven	6	11	1	281	47	28.10	-	-	-	-
R.J.Blakey	13	19	2	468	223*	27.52	1	-	32	1
P.S.Jones	8	12	2	273	63	27.30	-	2	2	-
S.D.Udal	16	24	6	488	60*	27.11	-	3	5	-
D.D.Ebrahim	6	11	1	271	68	27.10	-	3	4	-
S.M.Ervine	5	8	2	161	57*	26.83	-	1	5	-
Mushtaq Ahmed	16	19	2	456	60	26.82	-	3	3	-
A.I.Gait	13	25	0	664	110	26.56	1	4	10	-
V.S.Solanki	15	23	1	584	79	26.54	-	4	24	-
J.S.Foster	17	26	0	689	85	26.50	-	4	49	2
J.H.K.Adams	13	26	1	661	107	26.44	1	3	6	-
A.G.Wharf	16	27	9	475	79	26.38	-	2	7	-
J.M.Kemp	6	11	0	290	90	26.36	-	1	9	-
T.W.Roberts	7	10	0	263	83	26.30	-	2	7	-
R.S.Ferley	10	14	4	262	78*	26.20	-	2	5	-
R.L.Johnson	11	15	3	314	118	26.16	1	-	5	-
M.J.G.Davis	11	12	2	259	168	25.90	1	-	4	-
J.W.Cook	14	22	2	517	85	25.85	-	3	3	-
G.J.Muchall	13	25	1	620	121	25.83	2	3	5	-
A.Nel	13	13	3	258	42	25.80	-	-	4	-
S.J.Rhodes	11	14	2	309	81*	25.75	-	2	38	2
A.D.Brown	14	21	2	484	74	25.47	-	5	12	-
M.C.J.Ball	10	15	3	304	75	25.33	-	2	12	-
M.S.Kasprowicz	15	26	4	556	78	25.27	-	2	7	-
A.Dale	15	27	1	657	123	25.26	1	2	12	-
A.D.Mascarenhas	17	26	2	600	100*	25.00	1	2	7	-
G.E.Welton	12	23	0	572	99	24.86	-	5	6	-
N.R.C.Dumelow	10	17	3	347	75	24.78	-	3	2	-
M.J.Wood	12	23	1	536	100	24.36	1	3	1	-
I.D.Fisher	10	12	3	219	71	24.33	-	1	4	-
A.P.Grayson	10	18	2	388	90	24.25	-	3	5	-
J.M.Dakin	11	19	2	411	59	24.17	-	2	2	-
S.D.Thomas	5	8	2	145	69*	24.16	-	1	1	-
T.M.B.Bailey	14	19	3	384	101*	24.00	1	-	29	6
G.D.Bridge	8	13	3	240	50	24.00	-	1	7	-
A.J.Maiden	3	6	0	144	53	24.00	-	2	2	-
T.Frost	13	21	1	477	84	23.85	-	4	33	2
Kabir Ali	14	20	4	381	84*	23.81	-	2	2	-
A.J.Swann	10	15	0	355	137	23.66	1	1	14	-

Name	Matches	Inns	NO	Runs	HS	Avge	100s	50s	Ct	St
A.Khan	8	10	0	236	78	23.60	-	1	1	-
K.J.Innes	8	12	4	188	103*	23.50	1	-	1	-
D.A.Leatherdale	4	7	0	164	61	23.42	-	2	2	-
L.E.Plunkett	7	12	5	164	40*	23.42	-	-	2	-
M.A.Gough	13	25	0	584	73	23.36	-	4	8	-
B.M.Shafayat	13	23	0	533	105	23.17	1	3	3	-
D.G.Cork	16	29	3	593	92	22.80	-	3	11	-
J.Ormond	13	15	5	226	47	22.60	-	-	2	-
S.Elworthy	5	8	0	179	52	22.37	-	1	3	-
A.A.Noffke	7	7	1	134	40	22.33	-	-	2	-
R.J.Kirtley	13	17	7	223	40*	22.30	-	-	5	-
M.Kaif	8	15	0	332	87	22.13	-	1	5	-
P.Mustard	13	23	1	486	70*	22.09	-	1	42	3
G.J.Batty	18	28	4	529	60	22.04	-	3	14	-
J.Hughes	10	17	0	372	73	21.88	-	2	10	-
M.J.Powell	16	25	2	494	64	21.47	-	4	32	-
P.A.J.DeFreitas	16	25	2	493	103	21.43	1	2	6	-
C.G.Taylor	4	8	0	171	45	21.37	-	-	3	-
G.P.Swann	9	13	1	256	69	21.33	-	2	9	-
D.G.Brandy	6	9	2	148	52	21.14	-	1	2	-
V.J.Wells	12	21	1	420	106	21.00	1	2	11	-
R.M.Khan	9	16	0	336	76	21.00	-	2	3	-
J.E.Bishop	5	6	0	125	50	20.83	-	2	1	-
S.A.Selwood	9	17	1	333	88	20.81	-	2	3	-
D.Gough	9	13	1	248	83	20.66	-	2	3	-
G.Welch	15	27	6	429	54	20.42	-	2	3	-
J.D.Middlebrook	16	25	1	484	82*	20.16	-	2	7	-
B.J.Phillips	7	8	2	119	48*	19.83	-	-	1	-
K.J.Piper	4	7	0	137	42	19.57	-	-	12	1
J.D.Francis	10	19	0	369	65	19.42	-	2	6	-
M.W.Alleyne	8	13	3	193	32*	19.30	-	-	9	-
R.A.White	7	14	0	261	76	18.64	-	2	4	-
H.H.Streak	5	7	0	127	51	18.14	-	1	1	-
C.T.Tremlett	10	13	2	199	43	18.09	-	-	5	-
J.D.Lewry	12	15	3	215	70	17.91	-	1	4	-
G.M.Fellows	6	8	0	142	53	17.75	-	1	1	-
J.Lewis	14	18	4	248	47	17.71	-	-	3	-
N.M.K.Smith	6	8	0	138	57	17.25	-	1	2	-
C.E.Dagnall	10	11	5	103	23*	17.16	-	-	-	-
S.A.Richardson	3	6	0	103	50	17.16	-	1	3	-
N.M.Carter	5	7	0	118	38	16.85	-	-	1	-
N.A.M.McLean	17	23	4	318	76	16.73	-	1	2	-
J.C.Tredwell	13	19	3	267	36	16.68	-	-	15	-
I.J.Thomas	7	11	0	182	53	16.54	-	1	8	-
Shoaib Akhtar	7	14	2	197	37	16.41	-	-	-	-
A.M.Blignaut	5	8	1	114	42	16.28	-	-	2	-
K.P.Dutch	7	10	0	161	61	16.10	-	1	9	-
M.J.Saggers	15	20	5	240	47	16.00	-	-	3	-
C.B.Keegan	17	20	3	270	36*	15.88	-	-	5	-
M.S.Mason	15	20	4	250	52	15.62	-	1	2	-

Name	Matches	Inns	NO	Runs	HS	Avge	100s	50s	Ct	St
A.Pratt	5	9	3	93	27	15.50	-	-	15	-
Shahid Afridi	3	6	0	92	67	15.33	-	1	-	-
J.F.Brown	14	12	6	91	38	15.16	-	-	2	-
S.J.Cook	12	17	3	211	65	15.07	-	1	5	-
D.P.Ostler	5	8	0	119	58	14.87	-	1	3	-
D.R.Heath	4	7	0	104	32	14.85	-	-	4	-
C.W.G.Bassano	12	22	3	277	53*	14.57	-	2	7	-
W.R.Smith	3	6	0	87	31	14.50	-	-	2	-
Yuvraj Singh	7	12	2	145	56	14.50	-	1	12	-
D.R.Law	6	10	1	127	74	14.11	-	1	1	-
N.C.Phillips	13	22	5	239	39	14.05	-	-	9	-
D.R.Hewson	9	16	0	222	57	13.87	-	1	4	-
J.H.Dawes	10	12	5	97	32*	13.85	-	-	3	-
T.J.Murtagh	7	11	4	95	21	13.57	-	-	-	-
R.J.Sidebottom	9	11	2	122	28	13.55	-	-	4	-
D.S.Harrison	16	25	5	271	66	13.55	-	1	3	-
D.D.Masters	17	23	3	269	119	13.45	1	-	4	-
D.A.Cosker	9	12	6	80	42	13.33	-	-	7	-
N.Shahid	4	6	0	76	67	12.66	-	1	2	-
S.R.G.Francis	10	13	2	133	44	12.09	-	-	2	-
T.Lungley	5	8	1	80	29	11.42	-	-	2	-
A.Richardson	14	19	5	158	47	11.28	-	-	1	-
J.Wood	9	8	2	67	30	11.16	-	-	2	-
C.E.W.Silverwood	12	18	4	152	53	10.85	-	1	2	-
M.J.Cawdron	6	6	0	63	24	10.50	-	-	1	-
P.J.McMahon	6	9	0	93	30	10.33	-	-	3	-
P.J.Martin	14	12	0	120	23	10.00	-	-	8	-
G.J.Smith	13	21	3	172	42	9.55	-	-	4	-
V.C.Drakes	5	7	1	57	18	9.50	-	-	1	-
S.C.G.MacGill	11	18	6	112	27	9.33	-	-	2	-
Wasim Akram	5	7	1	55	23	9.16	-	-	-	-
S.M.Guy	6	8	0	73	26	9.12	-	-	16	2
A.Sheriyar	15	20	9	97	18*	8.81	-	-	3	-
S.J.Harmison	11	14	5	78	14*	8.66	-	-	2	-
J.T.A.Bruce	8	11	3	68	21*	8.50	-	-	3	-
A.M.Smith	11	14	7	58	17*	8.28	-	-	1	-
S.P.Kirby	14	18	4	113	33	8.07	-	-	5	-
N.Killeen	11	18	4	110	26	7.85	-	-	2	-
M.Hayward	16	21	5	123	28	7.68	-	-	5	-
Mohammad Ali	10	17	3	101	31	7.21	-	-	1	-
K.J.Dean	16	24	3	148	30*	7.04	-	-	4	-
M.Muralitharan	5	7	0	49	15	7.00	-	-	1	-
D.Pretorius	10	10	3	49	16	7.00	-	-	4	-
B.J.Trott	7	10	4	37	12*	6.16	-	-	2	-
C.E.Shreck	11	15	6	51	19	5.66	-	-	1	-
A.D.Mullally	8	10	3	38	14	5.42	-	-	2	-
S.A.Brant	11	14	6	37	23	4.62	-	-	3	-
J.A.Tomlinson	8	13	5	27	10	3.37	-	-	2	-
A.J.Harris	10	12	1	37	16*	3.36	-	-	2	-

BOWLING AVERAGES

Qualifying requirements: 10 wickets taken, having bowled in a minimum of 6 innings

Name	Overs	Mdns	Runs	Wkts	Avge	Best	5wI	10wM
M.Muralitharan	178	41	447	33	13.54	6-36	4	-
Shoaib Akhtar	183	40	580	34	17.05	4-9	-	-
B.J.Phillips	149	47	400	21	19.04	4-45	-	-
R.J.Sidebottom	222.2	37	710	35	20.28	7-97	2	-
D.T.Hondo	94	23	312	15	20.80	5-26	1	-
M.S.Kasprowicz	572.3	140	1629	77	21.15	9-36	4	2
M.S.Mason	439.3	128	1144	53	21.58	6-68	2	-
M.K.Munday	80	8	305	14	21.78	5-83	1	-
S.M.Pollock	198	61	480	22	21.81	6-39	1	-
H.H.Streak	123.3	38	263	12	21.91	4-64	-	-
S.D.Thomas	82.1	8	293	13	22.53	4-47	-	-
J.M.Kemp	102.1	17	319	14	22.78	5-48	1	-
M.Hayward	427.3	83	1533	67	22.88	5-46	2	-
G.P.Swann	238.2	37	759	33	23.00	7-33	3	-
I.J.Harvey	195.2	54	625	27	23.14	4-43	-	-
Kabir Ali	415.2	72	1552	67	23.16	8-53	3	-
V.J.Wells	164.4	36	515	22	23.40	4-16	-	-
Waqar Younis	244.2	39	917	39	23.51	5-40	3	-
A.J.Hall	293.4	70	823	35	23.51	3-10	-	-
A.M.Smith	329.5	91	898	38	23.63	5-70	1	-
A.McGrath	134.1	21	403	17	23.70	3-16	-	-
J.F.Brown	647	188	1565	66	23.71	7-69	4	-
P.A.J.DeFreitas	540.3	154	1443	60	24.05	7-51	4	1
G.J.Smith	356.1	78	1227	51	24.05	5-42	3	-
J.Lewis	551.2	142	1800	74	24.32	7-117	5	1
C.E.W.Silverwood	351.4	73	1177	48	24.52	5-63	2	-
Mushtaq Ahmed	836.3	163	2539	103	24.65	7-85	10	5
M.J.Saggers	450	97	1441	58	24.84	5-42	2	-
Wasim Akram	167.3	44	503	20	25.15	3-31	-	-
M.J.Cawdron	142.3	31	504	20	25.20	6-87	1	-
J.W.Cook	162.3	46	479	19	25.21	5-31	1	-
D.E.Malcolm	94	22	358	14	25.57	5-40	1	-
R.L.Johnson	364.1	85	1077	42	25.64	6-33	2	-
E.S.H.Giddins	98.5	18	336	13	25.84	4-88	-	-
G.J.Batty	574.4	142	1575	60	26.25	6-88	1	-
S.P.Kirby	463	80	1769	67	26.40	8-80	5	2
A.Bhandari	119.2	23	424	16	26.50	6-38	2	-
G.Keedy	555.5	126	1593	60	26.55	6-68	5	1
J.D.Lewry	337.2	73	1118	42	26.61	8-106	3	1
M.A.Ealham	357.5	106	1013	38	26.65	6-35	3	-
R.J.Kirtley	529.1	127	1662	62	26.80	6-26	3	-
S.J.Harmison	349.2	97	1002	37	27.08	4-33	-	-
D.G.Cork	445.1	100	1363	50	27.26	6-28	3	2
I.D.Fisher	225.1	50	767	28	27.39	5-30	3	1
J.H.Kallis	131.3	29	412	15	27.46	6-54	1	-
J.M.Dakin	352.3	79	1099	40	27.47	5-86	1	-
M.P.Bicknell	444.4	110	1391	50	27.82	5-42	3	-
D.L.Maddy	297.1	59	1002	36	27.83	5-49	1	-
G.Welch	483.3	121	1476	53	27.84	6-102	2	-

Name	Overs	Mdns	Runs	Wkts	Avge	Best	5wI	10wM
J.Ormond	392.1	74	1428	51	28.00	6-34	3	-
Mohammad Akram	145	31	560	20	28.00	8-49	2	1
I.G.Butler	124	24	478	17	28.11	4-74	-	-
P.R.Adams	130.3	21	425	15	28.33	9-79	1	1
N.A.M.McLean	551.3	115	1872	65	28.80	5-43	3	-
M.J.Hoggard	225.3	57	606	21	28.85	7-49	1	-
D.R.Law	103.3	15	353	12	29.41	4-30	-	-
S.I.Mahmood	109	16	444	15	29.60	5-37	1	-
B.V.Taylor	244.1	69	681	23	29.60	4-42	-	-
R.D.B.Croft	731.5	192	1928	65	29.66	6-71	5	1
J.M.Anderson	332.5	72	1232	41	30.04	5-61	3	-
S.A.Brant	344.5	77	1117	37	30.18	6-45	1	-
C.L.Hooper	366.2	86	912	30	30.40	6-51	2	-
C.B.Keegan	585.4	121	1925	63	30.55	6-114	3	-
G.M.Andrew	78	13	310	10	31.00	3-14	-	-
Azhar Mahmood	283.5	52	1097	35	31.34	5-78	1	-
S.Elworthy	160.1	22	627	20	31.35	5-71	1	-
J.H.Dawes	331.4	58	1071	34	31.50	5-46	1	-
P.J.Martin	432.1	99	1295	41	31.58	5-54	1	-
J.Wood	222.4	32	854	27	31.62	3-17	-	-
D.S.Harrison	366	84	1284	40	32.10	5-80	1	-
S.D.Udal	436.4	87	1350	42	32.14	4-50	-	-
A.D.Mascarenhas	489.1	150	1287	40	32.17	6-55	1	-
A.Symonds	152	26	517	16	32.31	3-38	-	-
A.M.Blignaut	130.5	21	487	15	32.46	4-89	-	-
P.J.McMahon	203.4	51	595	18	33.05	4-59	-	-
A.Sheriyar	374.3	76	1257	38	33.07	5-65	1	-
D.Pretorius	206	31	863	26	33.19	4-15	-	-
Saqlain Mushtaq	471	100	1364	41	33.26	5-46	3	-
A.G.Wharf	432.3	72	1734	52	33.34	4-53	-	-
S.A.Khalid	90.5	14	334	10	33.40	4-131	-	-
S.C.G.MacGill	412.2	73	1408	42	33.52	6-117	2	-
J.E.Bishop	87.1	10	369	11	33.54	4-111	-	-
S.R.G.Francis	328.1	72	1179	35	33.68	4-47	-	-
C.T.Tremlett	248.4	48	929	27	34.40	6-51	1	-
J.A.R.Blain	87.1	7	449	13	34.53	5-84	1	-
S.M.Katich	160.4	29	591	17	34.76	4-21	-	-
J.D.Middlebrook	593	87	1979	56	35.33	6-123	3	-
L.E.Plunkett	164	34	672	19	35.36	5-53	1	-
D.R.Brown	377.5	81	1274	36	35.38	5-72	2	-
P.M.Havell	106.4	18	498	14	35.57	4-129	-	-
G.Chapple	494.2	90	1744	49	35.59	6-98	2	-
L.Balaji	137	32	430	12	35.83	3-58	-	-
A.Nel	422.3	99	1292	36	35.88	5-47	1	-
C.E.Dagnall	295.5	70	1005	28	35.89	5-66	1	-
A.A.Noffke	245.4	52	754	21	35.90	5-52	1	-
M.C.J.Ball	378.3	99	1008	28	36.00	5-104	1	-
A.Mishra	134	22	468	13	36.00	5-183	1	-
N.Killeen	290	70	946	26	36.38	7-70	1	-
M.A.Wagh	193.3	28	730	20	36.50	7-222	1	-
M.A.Sheikh	181.5	43	553	15	36.86	4-60	-	-
I.D.K.Salisbury	371.1	60	1224	33	37.09	4-116	-	-
I.D.Blackwell	466.4	111	1336	36	37.11	5-65	2	-

Name	Overs	Mdns	Runs	Wkts	Avge	Best	5wI	10wM
N.G.Hatch	149.4	28	484	13	37.23	3-66	-	-
M.M.Betts	240.2	30	970	26	37.30	5-43	1	-
Mohammad Ali	221	36	1060	28	37.85	4-79	-	-
M.Ntini	222.2	40	910	24	37.91	5-75	2	1
C.E.Shreck	227.1	46	878	23	38.17	5-100	1	-
P.N.Weekes	451.1	85	1355	35	38.71	4-55	-	-
S.J.Cook	332.2	78	1048	27	38.81	4-42	-	-
K.J.Dean	444.3	107	1593	41	38.85	4-39	-	-
K.P.Pietersen	108.4	18	428	11	38.90	4-31	-	-
A.D.Mullally	229.1	55	664	17	39.05	3-31	-	-
M.Burns	153.5	29	514	13	39.53	3-35	-	-
N.C.Phillips	408.4	63	1513	38	39.81	5-144	1	-
A.Richardson	453	104	1314	33	39.81	4-37	-	-
G.D.Bridge	289	59	996	25	39.84	4-47	-	-
J.C.Tredwell	329.4	73	1125	28	40.17	4-48	-	-
R.S.C.Martin-Jenkins	364	82	1258	31	40.58	3-9	-	-
A.W.Laraman	279.5	58	979	24	40.79	3-20	-	-
D.A.Cosker	264.5	67	695	17	40.88	3-49	-	-
R.Clarke	164.1	22	709	17	41.70	4-21	-	-
P.J.Franks	296	49	1177	28	42.03	4-62	-	-
V.C.Drakes	143.1	33	463	11	42.09	3-58	-	-
P.S.Jones	204.3	27	930	22	42.27	5-42	1	-
C.P.Schofield	187.1	37	636	15	42.40	4-64	-	-
D.D.Masters	425.3	85	1581	37	42.72	5-53	1	-
M.S.Panesar	161.2	30	557	13	42.84	3-92	-	-
R.S.Ferley	259	44	1032	24	43.00	4-76	-	-
N.R.C.Dumelow	214.5	43	776	18	43.11	5-78	2	1
D.Gough	271.1	55	866	20	43.30	3-40	-	-
J.T.A.Bruce	196	39	829	19	43.63	3-42	-	-
J.W.M.Dalrymple	172.1	27	529	12	44.08	5-49	1	-
G.R.Napier	379.3	60	1506	33	45.63	5-66	1	-
A.M.Davies	149	35	509	11	46.27	2-34	-	-
J.A.Tomlinson	171.5	22	794	17	46.70	6-63	1	-
A.Khan	165	16	797	17	46.88	4-65	-	-
C.G.Greenidge	230.4	25	1039	22	47.22	3-33	-	-
Abdul Razzaq	202.4	28	761	16	47.56	3-69	-	-
A.Flintoff	232	57	727	15	48.46	2-47	-	-
R.K.J.Dawson	241.5	47	840	17	49.41	3-119	-	-
M.A.Harrity	166.5	37	549	11	49.90	4-39	-	-
B.J.Trott	150.3	27	649	13	49.92	4-73	-	-
C.L.Cairns	184	31	755	15	50.33	3-59	-	-
M.J.G.Davis	237	46	761	15	50.73	3-44	-	-
T.J.Murtagh	146.5	17	615	12	51.25	4-130	-	-
A.F.Giles	374.5	62	1146	22	52.09	5-115	1	-
A.J.Tudor	144	24	532	10	53.20	3-56	-	-
A.K.D.Gray	233.2	51	692	13	53.23	3-43	-	-
A.P.Palladino	162	31	594	11	54.00	6-41	1	-
A.J.Harris	208.5	31	850	15	56.66	4-23	-	-
J.N.Snape	177.3	25	669	11	60.81	3-108	-	-

INDEX OF PLAYERS BY COUNTY

*denotes not registered for the 2004 season. Where a player is known to have moved in the off-season he is listed under his new county.

DERBYSHIRE

BASSANO, C.W.G.
BOTHA, A.G.
BRYANT, J.D.C.
DEAN, K.J.
DIVENUTO, M.J.
DUMELOW, N.R.C.
GAIT, A.I.
GUNTER, N.E.L.
HARRIS, C.Z.*
HASAN ADNAN
HAVELL, P.M.R.
HEWSON, D.R.
KAIF, M.*
KHAN, R.M.
KRIKKEN, K.M.*
LUNGLEY, T.
MOHAMMAD ALI
SELWOOD, S.A.
SHAHID AFRIDI*
STUBBINGS, S.D.
SUTTON, L.D.
WELCH, G.
WHARTON, L.J.*

DURHAM

BREESE, G.R.
BRIDGE, G.D.
COLLINGWOOD, P.D.
DAVIES, M.A.
GIBBS, H.H.
GOUGH, M.A.
HAMILTON, G.M.
HARMISON, S.J.
HATCH, N.G.*

HUNTER, I.D.*
KILLEEN, N.
LAW, D.R.*
LEWIS, J.J.B.
LOVE, M.L.*
LOWE, J.A.
MUCHALL, G.J.
MUSTARD, P.
ONIONS, G.
PATTISON, I.
PENG, N.
PHILLIPS, N.C.*
PLUNKETT, L.E.
PRATT, A.
PRATT, G.J.
SCOTT, G.M.
SHOAIB AKHTAR
SRINATH, J.*
THORPE, A.M.*
WELLS, V.J.

ESSEX

BISHOP, J.E.
BOPARA, R.S.
BRANT, S.A.
CLARKE, A.J.
COOK, A.N.
COWAN, A.P.
DANISH KANERIA
DENNING, N.A.*
FLOWER, A.
FOSTER, J.S.
GOUGH, D.
GRANT, J.B.*
GRAYSON, A.P.
HABIB, A.
HUSSAIN, N.

IRANI, R.C.
JEFFERSON, W.I.
MCCOUBREY, A.G.A.M.
MCGARRY, A.C.*
MIDDLEBROOK, J.D.
NAPIER, G.R.
PALLADINO, A.P.
PETTINI, M.L.
PHILLIPS, T.J.
SHARIF, Z.K.
STEPHENSON, J.P.
TEN DOESCHATE, R.N.

GLAMORGAN

CHERRY, D.D.
COSKER, D.A.
CROFT, R.D.B.
DALE, A.
DAVIES, A.P.
ELLIOTT, M.T.G.
HARRISON, D.S.
HEMP, D.L.
HUGHES, J.
JAMES, S.P.*
JONES, S.P.
KASPROWICZ, M.S.
MAHER, J.P.*
MAYNARD, M.P.
PARKIN, O.T.*
POWELL, M.J.
SHAW, A.D.
THOMAS, I.J.
THOMAS, S.D.
WALLACE, M.A.
WATKINS, R.E.
WHARF, A.G.B.

INDEX OF PLAYERS BY COUNTY

GLOUCESTERSHIRE

ADSHEAD, S.J.
ALLEYNE, M.W.
AVERIS, J.M.M.
BALL, M.C.J.
BRESSINGTON, A.N.
BUTLER, I.G.*
FISHER, I.D.
GIDMAN, A.P.R.
HANCOCK, T.H.C.
HARDINGES, M.A.
LEWIS, J.
PEARSON, J.A.
POPE, S.P.*
RHODES, J.N.*
RUSSELL, R.C.
SHABBIR AHMED
SHOAIB MALIK
SILLENCE, R.J.
SMITH, A.M.
SPEARMAN, C.M.
TAYLOR, C.G.
WESTON, W.P.C.
WINDOWS, M.G.N.

HAMPSHIRE

ADAMS, J.H.K.
BENHAM, C.C.
BROWN, M.J.
BRUCE, J.T.A.
BRUNNSCHWEILER, I.*
BURROWS, T.G.
CLAPP, D.A.
CLARKE, M.J.
CRAWLEY, J.P.
GIDDINS, E.S.H.*
HAMBLIN, J.R.C.

HINDLEY, R.J.E.
KATICH, S.M.*
KENDALL, W.S.
KENWAY, D.A.
LAMB, G.A.
LATOUF, K.J.
MASCARENHAS, A.D.
MORRIS, A.C.*
MULLALLY, A.D.
POTHAS, N.
PRITTIPAUL, L.R.
SMITH, R.A.*
TAYLOR, B.V.
THORBURN, M.
TOMLINSON, J.A.
TREMLETT, C.T.
UDAL, S.D.
VAAS, W.P.U.J.C.*
WARNE, S.K.
WASIM AKRAM*

KENT

BANES, M.J.*
BLEWETT, G.S.*
CARBERRY, M.A.
CUSDEN, S.M.J.
DENLY, J.L.
DENNINGTON, M.J.
FERLEY, R.S.
FULTON, D.P.
HEWITT, J.P.*
JONES, G.O.
KEY, R.W.T.
KHAN, A.
LOUDON, A.G.R.
MOHAMMAD SAMI
MURALITHARAN, M.*
O'BRIEN, N.J.

PATEL, M.M.
SAGGERS, M.J.
SHERIYAR, A.
SMITH, E.T.
STIFF, D.A.
SYMONDS, A.
TREDWELL, J.C.
TREGO, P.D.*
TROTT, B.J.
WALKER, M.J.

LANCASHIRE

ANDERSON, J.M.
CHAPPLE, G.
CHILTON, M.J.
CORK, D.G.
CROOK, S.P.
CURRIE, M.R.
FLINTOFF, A.
HAYNES, J.J.
HEGG, W.K.
HOGG, K.W.
HOOPER, C.L.
HORTON, P.J.
KEEDY, G.
LAW, S.G.
LOYE, M.B.
MAHMOOD, S.I.
MAIDEN, G.I.
MARTIN, P.J.
NEWBY, O.J.
REES, T.M.
SCHOFIELD, C.P.
SUTCLIFFE, I.J.
SWANN, A.J.
WATKINSON, M.
WOOD, J.
YATES, G.

INDEX OF PLAYERS BY COUNTY

LEICESTERSHIRE

AMIN, R.M.*
BRANDY, D.G.
BRIGNULL, D.S.
CUNLIFFE, R.J.*
DAGNALL, C.E.
DAKIN, J.M.
DEFREITAS, P.A.J.
DRAKES, V.C.*
FERRABY, N.J.
GROVE, J.O.*
HODGE, B.J.
KRUGER, G. J-P.
LIDDLE, C.J.
MADDY, D.L.
MALCOLM, D.E.*
MASTERS, D.D.
MAUNDERS, J.K.
NEW, T.J.
NIXON, P.A.
ROBINSON, D.D.J.
SADLER, J.L.
SEHWAG, V.*
SNAPE, J.N.
STEVENS, D.I.
WALKER, G.W.
WARD, T.R.*
WHILEY, M.J.A.*

MIDDLESEX

ABDUL RAZZAQ*
BETTS, M.M.
BLOOMFIELD, T.F.
COMPTON, N.R.D.
COOK, S.J.
DALRYMPLE, J.W.M.

DAWES, J.H.*
GANNON, B.W.*
HAYWARD, M.
HUNT, T.A.*
HUTCHISON, P.M.
HUTTON, B.L.
IMRAN TAHIR*
JOYCE, E.C.
KEEGAN, C.B.
KLUSENER, L.
KOENIG, S.G.
NASH, D.C.
NOFFKE, A.A.*
PEPLOE, C.T.
RICHARDS, M.A.
SCOTT, B.J.M.
SHAH, O.A.
STRAUSS, A.J.
WEEKES, P.N.
WESTON, R.M.S.*

NORTHAMPTONSHIRE

AFZAAL, U.
ANDERSON, R.S.G.
BAILEY, T.M.B.
BLAIN, J.A.R.*
BROPHY, G.L.
BROWN, J.F.
CAWDRON, M.J.
COOK, J.W.
COVERDALE, P.S.
GOODE, C.M.
GREENIDGE, C.G.
HUGGINS, T.B.
HUSSEY, M.E.*
JAQUES, P.A.
JONES, P.S.
KING, R.E.

LOUW, J.
NEL, A.*
PANESAR, M.S.
PAYNTER, D.E.*
PENBERTHY, A.L.*
PHILLIPS, B.J.
POWELL, M.J.
ROBERTS, T.W.
SALES, D.J.G.
SHANTRY, A.J.
SWANN, G.P.
VAN JAARSVELD, M.
WHITE, R.A.
WRIGHT, D.G.*

NOTTINGHAMSHIRE

ALLEYNE, D.
ATRI, V.
BICKNELL, D.J.
CAIRNS, C.L.*
CLOUGH, G.D.
EALHAM, M.A.
ELWORTHY, S.*
FRANKS, P.J.
GALLIAN, J.E.R.
HARRIS, A.J.
HUSSEY, D.J.
LOGAN, R.J.
LUCAS, D.S.
MACGILL, S.C.G.
MARTYN, D.R.
MCMAHON, P.J.
NOON, W.M.
PATEL, S.R.
PIETERSEN, K.P.
RANDALL, S.J.*
READ, C.M.W.
SHAFAYAT, B.M.

INDEX OF PLAYERS BY COUNTY

SHRECK, C.E.
SIDEBOTTOM, R.J.
SINGH, A.
SMITH, G.J.
SMITH, W.R.
THOMAS, A.C.
VETTORI, D.L.*
WARREN, R.J.
WELTON, G.E.*

SOMERSET

ANDREW, G.M.
BLACKWELL, I.D.
BOWLER, P.D.
BURNS, M.
CADDICK, A.R.
COX, J.
DURSTON, W.J.
DUTCH, K.P.
EDWARDS, N.J.
FRANCIS, J.D.
FRANCIS, S.R.G.
GAZZARD, C.M.
GILDER, G.M.*
HILDRETH, J.C.
HOLLOWAY, P.C.L.*
JOHNSON, R.L.
LARAMAN, A.W.
MCLEAN, N.A.M.
MUNDAY, M.K.
PARSONS, K.A.
PARSONS, M.
PONTING, R.T.
SUPPIAH, A.V.
TRESCOTHICK, M.E.
TURNER, R.J.
WEBLEY, T.
WOOD, M.J.

SURREY

AZHAR MAHMOOD
BATTY, J.N.
BENNING, J.G.E.
BICKNELL, M.P.
BROWN, A.D.
BUTCHER, M.A.
CLARKE, R.
DERNBACH, J.
HODD, A.J.
HOLLIOAKE, A.J.
MILLER, D.J.
MURTAGH, T.J.
NEWMAN, S.A.
ORMOND, J.
RAMPRAKASH, M.R.
ROSE, F.A.*
SAKER, N.C.
SALISBURY, I.D.K.
SAMPSON, P.J.
SAQLAIN MUSHTAQ
SHAHID, N.
STEWART, A.J.*
THORPE, G.P.
TODD, M.J.*
TUDOR, A.J.

SUSSEX

ADAMS, C.J.
AMBROSE, T.R.
COTTEY, P.A.
DAVIS, M.J.G.
GOODWIN, M.W.
HOPKINSON, C.D.
INNES, K.J.
KIRTLEY, R.J.
LEWRY, J.D.

MARTIN-JENKINS, R.S.C.
MOHAMMAD AKRAM
MONTGOMERIE, R.R.
MUSHTAQ AHMED
PRIOR, M.J.
ROBINSON, M.A.
TURK, N.R.K.
VOROS, J.A.
WARD, I.J.
WRIGHT, L.J.
YARDY, M.H.
ZUIDERENT, B.

WARWICKSHIRE

ALI, M.M.
ALLEN, A.P.W.
BELL, I.R.
BROWN, D.R.
CARTER, N.M.
CLARK, M.W.*
CLIFFORD, I.J.
COLLYMORE, C.D.*
FROST, T.
GILES, A.F.
HOGG, G.B.
JONES, H.R.
KNIGHT, N.V.
MEES, T.
OBUYA, C.O.*
OSTLER, D.P.
PENNEY, T.L.
PIPER, K.J.
POWELL, M.J.
PRETORIUS, D.
RICHARDSON, A.
SHEIKH, M.A.*
SMITH, N.M.K.
SPIRES, J.A.
STREAK, H.H.

QUIZ ANSWERS

1. The Wisden Trophy
2. Joel Garner
3. Dominic Cork
4. Robin Hobbs
5. 375
6. Andy Lloyd
7. Graham Gooch
8. For the first time in West Indies Test history there was no player from Barbados in the team
9. Dean Headley
10. Adam Hollioake
11. Mark Ramprakash
12. M.J.K. Smith
13. Trevor Bailey
14. Garfield Sobers
15. John Emburey
16. Paul Franks
17. Alec Stewart
18. Sir Frank Worrell
19. It was abandoned – pitch unfit – after 10.1 overs, with England 17 for 3
20. Marcus Trescothick
21. Brian Close
22. Alan Wells
23. Jack Russell
24. Jimmy Adams
25. Darren Gough, Andrew Caddick and Dominic Cork
26. John Edrich
27. Ted Dexter
28. Fred Trueman
29. Sonny Ramadhin
30. Mike Watkinson
31. Shivnarine Chanderpaul
32. Phil Tufnell
33. Chris Lewis
34. Robin Smith
35. Clive Lloyd
36. Peter Willey
37. John Snow
38. Hugh Morris
39. A pair in first-class cricket
40. Courtney Walsh
41. Jim Laker and Tony Lock
42. Phil Simmons
43. Michael Atherton
44. Darren Gough
45. Lance Gibbs
46. Wilfred Rhodes
47. Michael Holding
48. Lawrence Rowe
49. John Childs
50. Peter May
51. Jason Gallian
52. Angus Fraser
53. Gordon Greenidge
54. Richard Illingworth
55. Allan Lamb
56. Sir Len Hutton
57. Curtly Ambrose
58. Matthew Maynard
59. Colin and Chris Cowdrey
60. Alan Knott
61. Chris Tavare
62. Lancashire
63. Derek Pringle
64. Wayne Larkins
65. Malcolm Marshall
66. Peter Loader
67. John Hampshire
68. Colin Milburn
69. Rohan Kanhai
70. David Holford
71. Roland Butcher
72. Ian Botham
73. Tony Greig
74. Dennis Amiss
75. Frank Hayes
76. Ron Headley
77. Pat Pocock
78. 56 (58 in his whole innings)
79. Alf Valentine
80. Nick Knight
81. H.H.H. Johnson
82. C.S. Marriott
83. Clyde Walcott
84. Bernard Julien
85. Everton Weekes
86. S.C. Griffith
87. Tom Graveney
88. Geoffrey Boycott
89. George Headley
90. Matthew Fleming
91. Godfrey Evans
92. Alvin Kallicharran
93. Peter Martin
94. David Allen
95. Allan Rae
96. Patrick Patterson
97. Wilf Slack
98. Carl Hooper
99. Jim Parks
100. David Lawrence